psychology

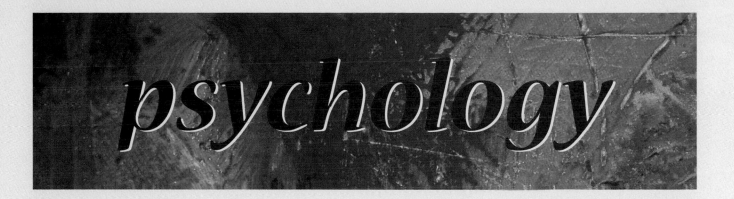

psychology

second edition

Philip G. Zimbardo
STANFORD UNIVERSITY

Ann L. Weber
UNIVERSITY OF NORTH CAROLINA AT ASHEVILLE

 LONGMAN

An imprint of Addison Wesley Longman, Inc.

New York • Reading, Massachusetts • Menlo Park, California • Harlow, England
Don Mills, Ontario • Sydney • Mexico City • Madrid • Amsterdam

Acquisitions Editor: Catherine Woods
Developmental Editor: Nancy Crochiere
Supplements Editor: Diane Wansing
Project Coordination, Text Design, and Electronic Page Makeup: Thompson Steele Production Services
Cover Designer: Mary McDonnell
Cover Painting: by Joan Miro, "Woman and Bird in the Moonlight," 1949. Tate Gallery, London, Great Britain.
Art Studio: Thompson Steele Production Services
Artists: Kevin Somerville and Nadine Sokol
Photo Researcher: Diane Kraut
Electronic Production Manager: Eric Jorgensen
Manufacturing Manager: Hilda Koparanian
Printer and Binder: RR Donnelley & Sons Company
Cover Printer: Phoenix Color Corp.

For permission to use copyrighted material, grateful acknowledgment is made to the copyright holders on p. C-1, which are hereby made part of this copyright page.

Library of Congress Cataloging-in-Publication Data

Zimbardo, Philip G.
    Psychology / Philip G. Zimbardo, Ann L. Weber. — 2nd ed.
        p.   cm.
    Includes bibliographical references and indexes.
    ISBN 0-673-99968-8
        1. Psychology.   I. Weber, Ann L.   II. Title.
BF121.Z53   1997
150—dc20   96-33118
                                                             CIP

ISBN 0-673-99968-8

2345678910—DOW—999897

Dedicated to our little sisters:
The memory of Vera Zimbardo Massimino,
and the daily love and support of Julie Weber Wehrle.
We are better oldests, and better people, because of you.

Brief Contents

Detailed Contents

CHAPTER 1   *Mind, Behavior, and Science 2*

CHAPTER 4   *Psychological Development   108*

CHAPTER 7   *Cognitive Processes*   248

CHAPTER 8   *Motivation and Emotion   284*

CHAPTER 9   *Stress, Health, and Well-Being   330*

CHAPTER 10   *Personality   378*

CHAPTER 11   *Individual Differences*   418

CHAPTER 12   *Social Psychology*   458

CHAPTER 13   *Psychopathology   502*

Preface

TO THE INSTRUCTOR

Our text is based on the solid research foundation provided by the scholarship in *Psychology and Life,* Fourteenth Edition, by Philip Zimbardo and Richard Gerrig. Our book represents a marriage of that scientific tradition with the immediacy and vitality of teaching what we know about the human condition. Our goal is to present an enriched view of psychological knowledge that combines the basic, accumulated wisdom from scientific psychology with the contemporary views of human nature that emerge from the study of human diversity.

History

Three years ago, we coauthors began our collaboration on our first edition with the intention to create an "essential" version of the popular text, *Psychology and Life,* Thirteenth Edition, by Philip G. Zimbardo. *Psych and Life,* as its authors and users know it, is the oldest continuously selling textbook in the discipline of psychology. The excellence of the "big book" by Zimbardo (now in its fourteenth edition, with coauthor Richard Gerrig) is based on a research focus and a comprehensiveness that is challenging, and sometimes not practical, for many instructors and students to fit into the constraints of an academic semester. For *Psychology,* therefore, we hoped to capture the "essence" of the big book, retain the solid information and research base, and build into this a strong, supportive pedagogy and an engaging, inviting voice.

As we undertook that first edition, therefore, we imagined a brief text that would be distinct from its progenitor in two dimensions: it would be comprehensive but shorter than *Psychology and Life;* and it would be more accessible to a broader range of students through its reader-friendly language, special "teacherly" features, and rich examples and explanations. As we worked, however, something more happened. We found our book was surpassing our original ideas and taking on a life of its own. We became inspired and creative in our congenial collaboration, and explored some new ideas and presentations that were not part of our original blueprint. We kept the essential content, but reduced the *level* of detail. We maintained its wisdom, but added new perspectives. We also retained its "voice" in speaking directly to student-readers, yet we tried to speak with both authority and friendship to a diverse audience of readers—students who might be beginning a major in psychology as well as those who might not ever have another opportunity to study psychology formally.

As we wrote, rewrote, and revised, we continually asked, "What does an introductory psychology student need to know about our field? How can we present that information in ways that are irresistibly inviting and readily accessible?" Our colleagues and students gave us suggestions and answers when we were stumped. Terrific outside reviewers—instructors like yourself, representing a wide range of teaching goals and responsibilities—offered us detailed feedback at each stage in the development of our manuscript. We provided each other encouragement and criticism in honing what to say and how to say it most effectively. We relied on our common values to help us shape the text. We both love teaching and especially enjoy teaching the introductory psychology course. We share a love of our work, a delight in psychology's diversity, a commitment to the scientific perspective, and an appreciation of exchanging ideas. It is our fervent hope that our enthusiasm for psychology was communicated constructively in the first edition of *Psychology.*

To our delight, *Psychology* has outgrown its first edition and now qualifies for the updating and massive revision necessary for a second edition. In addition to including critical new research findings and reworking familiar topics into more logical presentation, we had the paradoxical twofold mission of making the text more *complete* while also somehow making it more *compact.* To put it simply, we had to make the book bigger, and then make it smaller!

Feedback from reviewers, from instructors who used the text, and from a surprising number of students who took us up on our invitation to tell us what they thought gave us clear direction for developing this new second edition. We have done our best to incorporate their creative and constructive comments in revising our book, and we hope they will be happy to see their contributions well represented in the outcome.

Organization

We have retained the basic organization of the first edition and made some important changes in organization and key features. Scan the Brief Contents on p. vii and you will see that we begin with history and the perspective of scientific research, and examine first basic processes, then individual and social processes, and finally abnormal psychology and treatment. But you will find some important changes:

- In the second edition, we have adjusted Chapter 4, Psychological Development, to present a more modern topical approach to this subject rather than the traditional chronological approach of infancy-childhood-adulthood, by examining topics within broad ranges of life span development.
- We took the discussion of memory from the end of Chapter 7, Cognitive Processes, and incorporated it—more soundly, we believe—into the integrated material in Chapter 6, now retitled Learning and Remembering.
- You can't tell from the title, but Chapter 8, Motivation and Emotion, now begins with a thorough review and update of emotion research and theory, before making a transition to examining the principles of motivation, from basics like hunger to aspirations for work and self-actualization. Emotions are at the root of many students' questions about psychology, yet the topic has often been given short shrift—or a "tacked-on" status—in textbook treatments. We hoped to address this concern by shifting the order of presentation (though the old title seems a bit easier to say than "Emotion and Motivation"), and also by including new material on animal emotions.
- We changed the title of Chapter 9, formerly "Stress, Coping, and Health," to the more positive and comprehensive title Stress, Health, and Well-being. We devote as much discussion as ever to the important business of stress management, but we extend our exploration into health psychology and also explore the psychology of happiness.
- In Chapter 10, Personality, we introduce this vast and complex subject with the discussion of personality assessment, instead of postponing this material till the end of the chapter. This makes possible in-class reviews of what students think and know about personality testing *before* instructors and students move on to consider the intricacies of personality theories.
- Late-breaking news stories and recent research findings have left their mark especially in Chapter 11, Individual Differences, where we now consider the debate sparked by a recent book alleging racial heredity in IQ; and in Chapter 12, Social Psychology, where we consider both classical research and ever-new examples of the power of social forces in people's behavior—and the implications this has for societal policy and human relations.

Key Features

Instructors and students told us what they liked about the first edition, so we have retained and tried to enhance these features in the second edition of *Psychology:*

- **Current Research and Applications.** Every chapter opens with a vignette drawn from real life, whether from history or recent news. We also tried to jump on reports of research findings that seemed both relevant to psychology and of promising significance or lasting value. Some examples of such reports include the discussion of "the meaning of mind" (Chapter 3); controversy over so-called false-memory recovery (Chapter 6); the use of psychological profiling to identify criminals such as the Unabomber (Chapter 7); explorations of how people cope with massive disasters such as the Oklahoma City bombing (Chapter 9); identification of a genetic link with a specific personality trait (Chapter 10); and new findings about sources of congenital risk for schizophrenia (Chapter 13).
- **Cultural Context Boxes.** Students and teachers alike appreciated knowing how we might be influenced by the cultural environment in which we are immersed. As with the goldfish in the fishbowl, we have a hard time *seeing* our cultural environment from the inside. Throughout the text we have offered glimpses of the power of culture "from the outside," whether the focus is on subcultural influences within a larger society, or on how things might be done differently in various parts of the globe. We offer two forms of this occasional focus on cultural context: Cultural Context boxes, brief discussions of how topics in some chapters are explained or applied in cultural considerations; and in-text cultural-context "reminders"—flagged with the symbol of a small globe, 🌐—to alert the reader to the implications of certain examples or research findings.
- **Focus on Science Boxes.** In the previous edition we distinguished between boxed discussions with a "Focus on Research" and those with a "Focus on Theory." But the distinction between research and theory is artificial in a scientific discipline such as ours: research is based on theory, and theories are revised as new research findings are reported. We retain our focus on both classic and cutting-edge research and the usefulness of good theories in

boxed discussions with a Focus on Science throughout the text.

- **Focus on Application Boxes.** Some research and theories are so immediately or recognizably useful that they are best presented in the context of how they are specifically applied in meeting the goals of psychology. We highlight these ideas in Focus on Application boxes throughout the text.

The first edition featured in-text, highlighted discussions of "Critical Thinking," posing questions and suggesting ways the reader might review topics for personal relevance in her or his own life. For the second edition we use both distinctive in-text treatments and boxed presentations for our three new types of *critical thinking exercises:*

- **Ask Yourself:** In most chapters we digress from discussing a topic briefly to invite the reader to relate personally to the material, perhaps by asking some values-clarification questions or by speculating on how he or she might address a dilemma or solve a problem.
- **Assess Yourself:** One way to relate to abstract material is to "see how you score" on some constellation of attitudes or traits. Where appropriate, we have provided brief self-assessments to help students feel more connected with the ideas presented. We also try to emphasize that individual worth or reality is not dictated by any single test score.
- **Weigh the Evidence:** For some controversies, the jury is still out. In a few chapters we present intriguing debates that are far from settled, and ask students to hone their skills at becoming wiser "research consumers" by evaluating what they know—and don't know—before making any judgment.

Pedagogical Support

No textbook "teaches itself." Students always learn better with the encouragement and instruction of an accessible, interested person—you. However, that interaction can be enhanced by effective pedagogical supports. Here's a summary of the teacher's aids we have built into *Psychology:*

- **Opening Case.** Each chapter opens with a real-life vignette designed to grab student attention and vividly depict the relevance of the chapter's topic.
- **In-Text Glossary.** Whenever a key term is introduced, it is defined in the text in a complete sentence, in the context of immediate discussion and examples. To guide the students in their review of key terms, these are (1) boldfaced at their introductory definition in the text; (2) listed in the Chapter Review; and (3) defined in the end-of-text Glossary.

- **Check Your Recall.** Each major section within a chapter concludes with a brief summary to recap the main points and to show how they are interrelated, as well as how they lead to the material that follows.
- **Cultural Context "Globe" Icons.** Whenever we introduce a comment or finding relevant to how culture and subculture influence behavior, we flag the key text with a small globe icon to alert students to these ideas.
- **Chapter Review.** Each chapter concludes with a multi-part review, including these highlights:
  1. The whole-chapter *Summary* reviews the main themes and meanings of material presented in the chapter.
  2. The *Section Review* lists the *Key Terms* and the *Names to Know* for each major chapter section. At the beginning of each listing, we urge the reader to turn back to the appropriate page to reread the *Check Your Recall* summary of that section.
  3. The *Review Test* presents ten multiple-choice items testing basic information and applications of chapter material.
  4. *If You're Interested . . .* invites students who are especially curious and intrigued to go the extra distance and look up some original sources. We have selected both accessible, solidly written works for this list and original feature films released on videotape, which should be available from video rental outlets or libraries. Many of the books and videos listed in If You're Interested . . . were originally suggested to us by our students, so we are confident these sources are good ones for inspiration and information. Brief comments note the strengths or special relevance of each source listed.
- **Statistical Appendix.** While we briefly review the "brass tacks" of conducting psychological research in Chapter 1, we realize that many courses require a more thorough review of methodology and data analysis than this. To this end we have included, as Appendix A, a brief but complete review, Understanding Statistics: Analyzing Data and Forming Conclusions. Using original examples and clear graphics, this "crash course" in research methodology should help students gain a better grasp of the origins and meaning of the research findings on which *Psychology* is based.
- **Answer Key for Chapter Review Tests.** Appendix B presents an annotated answer key for the chapter's multiple-choice Review Tests. Each entry explains not only why the correct answer *is* correct (along with a page reference for quick review), but also why the other choices are *incorrect*.
- **End-of-Text Glossary.** The key terms introduced in each chapter are listed here with their definitions, along with page references for original key terms.

- **References.** Complete source material is provided for every reference cited in the text. Students are encouraged to consult the Reference section to find out where and how to learn more about topics of special interest to them.

- **Name Index and Subject Index.** All authors whose works are cited and all major topics and subjects are catalogued in these indexes, along with page references.

- **Mastery Tests.** A special, perforated section at the very end of the text provides of a 25-item test for each chapter. After careful rereading and study, the student can use each test to master the material prior to a formal in-class evaluation or examination. Each Mastery Test is composed of 20 multiple-choice items and 5 short-answer items. Unlike the Chapter Review Tests, the Mastery Tests *do not have* an answer key included in this text. The answer key is included in your Instructor's Manual, so each student can obtain the correct answers or confirm his or her test performance only by consulting with *you*. Our rationale in giving the answer key to the instructors and not to the students was that this arrangement would allow each instructor to decide whether to require students to take the Mastery Tests or leave them as options, and in any event would encourage students to make contact with their instructors at some point in their course work.

- **Art Program.** The tables, graphs, figures, and photographs that illustrate the text have been collected, developed, and revised to ensure that the art is clear, vivid, and contemporary. Captions and labels complement and support the text.

Support Materials

The introductory psychology course is one of the most difficult courses to teach because it surveys an enormous range of topics, from many different levels of analysis, and must overcome students' initial misconceptions about psychology learned from mass media "pop psych." A good textbook is only one part of the package of educational materials that makes an introductory psychology course more engaging to students and more gratifying for instructors. To make it easier for you and more worthwhile for your students, Longman has worked with us to prepare a valuable collection of ancillary materials:

- **Instructor's Resource Kit** (ISBN #0-673-97540-1) by Rose McDermott and text coauthor Phil Zimbardo. This comprehensive, up-to-date teacher's resource features chapter outlines, lecture notes referenced to chapter preview questions, discussion questions, in-class experiments and demonstrations, biographical profiles, student handouts, and tips for effective teaching. Original time lines put key figures and important developments in psychology in historical perspective. The manual includes a section on how to teach concept mapping, to support that topic in the Study Guide and Workbook; a detailed bibliography; and references to media that can be used in the classroom.

- **Test Bank** (ISBN #0-673-97541-X) by Thomas G. Land. This file contains approximately 2000 multiple-choice, true-false, statement-completion, and essay items. Questions are balanced for a range of difficulty and content: 25 percent are applied; 25 percent are factual, and 50 percent are conceptual in nature. Items also reflect sensitivity to nonnative English speakers. Items in the Bank are represented by comparable items in the self-tests provided in the Study Guide, so that students are likely to be rewarded for using study aids when they recognize and respond correctly to relevant questions on tests they take in your course.

- **The Study Guide and Workbook** (ISBN #0-673-98231-9) by Peter Gram was developed with the assistance of text coauthor Ann Weber. Each chapter begins with a concept map of major topics, followed by an exploded chapter outline featuring lots of room for note-taking and personal mnemonics. Key Terms from those presented in boldface in the text are presented in a flash-card format for student review. All exercises and features lead the student back to the text. Two sets of multiple-choice Practice Quizzes with answers (and, for the first set, explanations) and page references are included. Special material is provided on *concept mapping*, making visual connections among key concepts and theories in each chapter. Each chapter concludes with a student-generated lexicon of Words Worth Review, an extended glossary of words other than key terms worth readers' review. The Study Guide and Workbook also contains worksheets and procedural materials that are coordinated with a set of original experiments and demonstrations (developed and class tested by Phil Zimbardo) found in the Instructor's Manual.

- **SuperShell** (ISBN #0-673-97544-4, DOS; ISBN #0-673-97542-8, Mac) Prepared by Pam Griesler, this computerized, interactive study guide helps students learn the major facts and concepts through drill and practice exercises. The SuperShell features multiple-choice, true-false, and short-answer questions, as well as chapter outlines and a complete text glossary. Available for IBM and Macintosh computers.

- **TestMaster** (ISBN #0-673-97546-0, DOS; ISBN #0-673-97545-2, Mac) TestMaster is a powerful test generation system that allows professors to customize their own tests on a built-in processor—from adding and deleting items to revising questions as necessary. Available for IBM and Macintosh computers.

■ **How to Write Psychology Papers** (ISBN #0-06-501798-6) by Les Parrott III guides students step-by-step through the process of writing psychology papers. The book gives students directions, confidence, and the ability to maintain a sense of the big picture as they are writing.

■ **Thinking Critically About Research on Sex and Gender** (ISBN #0-06-501621-1) by Paula J. Caplan and Jeremy B. Caplan offers students the right level of support to learn about—and make sense of—the varied research in the field. The text unveils a revolutionary approach to understanding sex and gender research—one that puts students in touch with the practical meaning behind research and its vital effects on daily life.

■ **Industrial and Organizational Psychology Supplement for Introductory Psychology** (ISBN #0-673-99317-5) by Sherri Lind Hughes. This stand-alone supplement provides students with a thorough look at industrial and organizational (I/O) psychology. This "mini-text" includes discussions of recruitment and selection, training, motivation, and job satisfaction. Detailed references and cases are also included.

Personal Acknowledgments

Many experts and teachers of introductory psychology shared their constructive criticism with us on every chapter and feature of our text. We acknowledge here, in alphabetical order, reviewers for both our first edition and this second edition, and hope they will recognize their valued input in all that is good in *Psychology.*

Larry M. Anderson, Kwantlen College
Doug Bonesteel, Sheridan College
Michael Britt, Marist College
Thomas and Corinne Crandell, Broome
    Community College
Beverly Fridley, Los Angeles Harbor College
Helen J. Gilbart, St. Petersburg Junior College
Peter Gram, Pensacola Junior College
Richard A. Griggs, University of Florida
Charles Halcomb, Wichita State University
Stephen Hamilton, Mount San Antonio
    Community College
Christine Hollmann, Ohio University
James A. Johnson, Sam Houston State University
Mary-Louise Kean, University of California, Irvine
Edward E. Kennedy, Finger Lakes Community
    College

Richard A. King, University of North Carolina,
    Chapel Hill
Gail Knapp, C. S. Mott Community College
Connie Lanier, Central Piedmont Community
    College
Harold L. Mansfield, Fort Lewis College
Robert F. Massey, Seton Hall University
Lillie McCain, C. S. Mott Community College
J. D. McDonald, University of North Dakota
Edward R. Mosley, Passaic County Community
    College
Elliot Palefsky, Armstrong State College
David Perkins, College of St. Elizabeth
Bobby J. Poe, Belleville Area College
Cornelius P. Rea, Douglas College
Steven Richman, Nassau Community College
Marc Riess, Middlebury College
Manly N. Spigelman, University of Winnipeg
Kendell C. Thornton, South Dakota State
    University
Frank J. Vaccaro, Hofstra University
Anthony A. Walsh, Salve Regina University
David A. Wittrock, North Dakota State University

We received substantial contributions to our text from several colleagues, but four who are especially notable are Richard Brislin, professor at East-West Center at the University of Hawaii, who developed our original Cultural Context boxes; Roger A. Drake, professor at Western State College of Colorado, who created the material for our box on "Hemispheric Differences and 'Risky Business'" in Chapter 2; and Rex Robison of Stanford University, who provided a superb review of Chapter 5.

We adapted, built on, and borrowed ideas and illustrations from virtually every poor soul we came in contact with in the course of revising this book. The following individuals deserve special mention for creative suggestions and original research: Christina Harrington of BookPeople in Austin, TX; Anita Rose of UNC-Greensboro Department of English; and Christa Jane Ruiz and her family of Asheville, NC.

Composing and revising this book has been an ongoing life-lesson in social support: We relied on our friends and colleagues for help and understanding that was well beyond the call of duty—and we cultivated new friends among helpful colleagues and students. Our first officer and primary contact with the publisher (and sometimes reality!) was Acquisitions Editor Catherine Woods, who has mastered the art of disguising a friendly nudge as a social call. Many thanks are also due to Erica Smith, editorial assistant, for her help with all the phases of this project. We simply could not have survived the production of a manuscript—much less a book—without the humor, patience, creativity, and efficiency of our outstanding Developmental

Editor, Nancy Crochiere. Lisa Pinto, Director of Development with Longman College Publishing, and Andrea Fincke and her staff at Thompson Steele Production Services, collaborated to see our words take final, elegant form and go into production within our imaginable lifetimes. Supplements Editor Diane Wansing has assembled and shepherded our favorite supporting cast for the Study Guide and Workbook, the Test Bank, and the Instructor's Manual. To all of them we express thanks and sincere appreciation.

Ann Weber owes her sanity, her sense of humor, and her two remaining brain cells to the following friends, colleagues, and support staff *sine qua non:* John Boyd of Stanford, CA, who was our West Coast correspondent for news, science, and literary research; Angela Marshburn of Hickory, NC, who provided stolid and top-quality research assistance and Reference checking; Louise Maret of Asheville, NC, who did a superb job as Glossary editor; Drs. Lisa Friedenberg, Allan Combs, Pam Laughon, and William Bruce, all of UNC-Asheville, who heard about this book every day (but never complained); Mike Honeycutt of the UNC-Asheville Computer Center, who walks on water in cyberspace; Leigh Faulconer and Dr. Beverley Fehr, who saved her from severe e-mail withdrawal symptoms; Jay, Melinda, Whitney, and Alex Seifert and family of Dripping Springs, TX, who provided much-needed mental health breaks; and Dr. John Harvey of the University of Iowa, who always gives friendship and life perspective. Most of all, she thanks her husband, John Quigley, their cats, Minerva, Lucinda, Wilhelmina, Philip, and Mink and their new puppy Bear, for providing love, fluffiness, and laughter.

Finally, it hardly seems possible for two people now to have written *two* books together, yet feel ever greater affection and respect for each other—but Phil Zimbardo and Ann Weber are here to tell you it not only *can* be done, but *we have done it,* and we are grateful for the collaboration and friendship we have enjoyed because of (and sometimes in spite of!) this book, *Psychology,* a genuine labor of love.

TO THE STUDENT

The course you are beginning and the text you are reading together represent a *journey* of sorts. Your teacher will act as tour director, this text can be your travel guide book, and we authors have done our best to describe the terrain that lies ahead. But only *you* make the journey, and decide why and how to undertake the challenge of making this journey in the first place.

Why make this effort—why invest yourself in what we consider to be the most challenging of disciplines, the science of behavior and mental processes? One answer is that your destination is to *change your life and your world view* by seeking to understand the most fascinating wonders of the universe: the human brain, the human mind, and the behavior of all living creatures (especially your own). Psychology is devoted to exploring the mysterious processes that give rise to our innermost thoughts, complex feelings, and pivotal actions.

Get the most out of this experience—whether this will be your first of many psychology courses, or possibly your only formal psychology course for some time. Following are some general guidelines and specific tips on how to use this book to get the benefit (and the grade) you deserve for your performance and effort in appreciating *Psychology.*

General Study Strategies

1. *Set aside sufficient time* to do assigned reading and review your class notes. This text contains much new technical information, many principles to learn, and a challenging glossary of terms you will have to memorize and use. To master this material, you will need at least *three hours' reading time per chapter!* Skimming is not "reading," and cramming is not understanding. Don't limit your options; plan now to invest the time you need to do well.

2. *Keep a record of your study time* for this course. Plot the number of hours (in half-hour intervals) you study at each reading session. Chart your time investment on a cumulative graph, adding each new study time to your previous total on the y-axis and each study session to the x-axis (baseline). The graph will provide visual feedback of your progress and show you when you have not been hitting the books as you should.

3. *Study actively.* Optimal learning occurs when the learner is actively involved with the material. Read attentively, listen mindfully to lectures, ask questions, create examples, and paraphrase the words you read or hear as you take notes. In the text, *underline* brief key sections, *write notes* to yourself in the margins (making notes in pen or pencil is much more memorable and helpful than "highlighting" text passages with brightly colored markers). In your own words, *summarize* points you expect will be covered on class tests. Ally yourself with a *study partner* from among your classmates, and take turns explaining each chapter's concepts to each other. (The Study Guide and Workbook can facilitate this partnership, but the text alone will

provide all you need to get started.) Don't underestimate the value of a friend and study partner: We authors long ago discovered that teaching is the best way to learn!

4. *Distribute your study periods over time.* Research in psychology tells us that it is best to space out your studying efforts, scheduling brief but regular sessions to read and review, rather than cramming just before tests. If you let yourself fall behind, it is difficult to catch up on the information in introductory psychology during that last-minute panic.

5. *Get "study-centered."* Find a place with minimal distractions where you can study. Reserve that location for reading, writing, and course review—and nothing else (no food, television, or socializing). Soon you will find that this place is so completely associated with course work that you already "feel" like studying when you arrive at your study center.

6. *Encode what you learn so you can retrieve it for testing.* To benefit from a text like *Psychology*, you must feel alert and focus your attention. What you remember from reading the text depends on your deliberate efforts to remember, especially as you prepare for tests. Such efforts begin with *encoding*—putting the information you read into a form that is suitable for retrieving it for later use or tests. To encode what you read, you must *summarize* key points, *rehearse* sections of material (sometimes aloud), and ask *questions* about content you expect to be tested on.

How will you be tested in this course? Take the teacher's perspective: Imagine the kinds of questions you would ask if you were the instructor, and then try to answer those questions yourself. Essay items, multiple-choice questions, and short-answer items require different kinds of answers, so you will need to encode information differently for each kind of test item.

Decide whether you should focus on big ideas or on small details. Essays and fill-ins require an ability to *recall*—to produce information from memory; multiple choice and true-false tests rely on your *recognition* skills—your ability to match test materials with previously learned information. Your instructor is your best guide (and your ally) in determining how best to study for examinations in your course. Work with your instructor in preparing to study effectively and to maximize your potential on tests. Your grade can be a matter not of "luck," but of the real work and planning you put into preparing for your course assignments.

After carefully reading each chapter, take the Review Test at the end of each chapter, and review both the correct answers *and their explanations* at the back of the text. Do all self-testing far in advance of in-class examinations, so that you can begin to think like a test-taker.

After reading a chapter, taking the Review Test, and reviewing any items you missed, complete the Mastery Tests for each chapter, in the section at the very back of the book. These tests are similar in content, form, and difficulty to the tests in the test bank from which your teacher may select items to compose his or her course examinations. The answers to the Mastery Tests *cannot be found* in your text; they are provided only in your teacher's Instructor's Manual that accompanies this text. We put the answer keys there so that, to review your progress, you will have an incentive to *make contact with your instructor* prior to course examinations. Use this opportunity both to check your learning and to show your extra effort and interest to your instructor, who is your most invaluable resource and guide in your journey into *Psychology*.

Mastering the Chapter Material

1. Before reading the chapter, *review the chapter outline* as it appears in the detailed table of contents. The chapter outline shows you the main topics covered, their sequence, and their relationship, giving you an overview of what is to come. Next, skim through the pages of the chapter before you begin reading seriously, to get an idea of what you will read and how it will be presented. Think about what you expect the chapter to cover, and jot down any questions or topics you find particularly interesting.

2. *Flip through the chapter.* Don't even try to "read" it at this point; just get an overview, in the same way a savvy traveler will glance over a large map before zooming in on detailed maps of the specific locales she plans to visit. Instead, turn the pages at a rate of about one every 2 to 5 seconds, as if you were flipping through a magazine in search of an interesting article. Glance at photos, headings, tables, figures, and get an impression of the colors, layout, and length of the chapter ahead of you.

This brief flip-through exercise will accomplish two important goals right away: first, it will *reassure you* that the chapter is of a manageable size, and that most of the terms and images are either familiar or interesting; second, it will give you a *feel* for how "busy" the chapter is, how many topics are covered, and what kind of relevance they might have in your life. Both these accomplishments will help you get into the mood for effective studying.

3. Not so fast! Don't start reading the chapter just yet. *Jump to the end of the chapter for the Chapter Review.* The Chapter Review includes a summary of the themes and key content of the entire chapter, followed by sectional summaries of key terms and names to know. Glance at—but don't read—the Review Test, to see the kinds of things you *will know* after carefully studying the chapter. Finally, look over the books and videos

recommended in *If You're Interested . . .* to see if any appear familiar or appealing. This can help you to feel motivated to learn what you are about to read.

4. *Skim through the chapter,* reading lightly—as if you were reading an entertaining magazine article or short story, for pleasure. Turn the pages at an even pace: you only need to get the *gist* of the chapter's contents at this point, not memorize details. Don't stop or take notes, and read as quickly as you can (one hour maximum time allowed).

When you are finished, close the book. Think for a few minutes about your *impressions* of what you have read. You will not retain much new information, but you will have made a beginning at connecting the knowledge and experience you already have with the new ideas introduced in the chapter.

5. *Finally, dig in and master the material,* by actively reading, underlining, taking notes in a separate notebook, making marginal notes to yourself, questioning, rehearsing, and paraphrasing as you go. *Two hours' minimum time should be invested* in this deep-reading phase. Be sure to read the opening case, as well as the boxed discussions and special sections: Focus on Science, Focus on Application, Cultural Context, Ask Yourself, Assess Yourself, and Weigh the Evidence.

Special Features to Use

1. The Opening Case that begins each chapter was written to grab and focus your attention. Taken together, these cases present a wide range of vivid, personalized material about people in different types of behavior settings. Each opener illustrates a central theme of the chapter, and the cases are often referenced later in the chapter.

2. At the end of each major section within a chapter is an interim summary, called Check Your Recall. These summaries review the key points presented in the section and explain the relationships between concepts. Be sure that you understand the ideas in this summing-up unit of the current section before you move ahead.

3. **Key Terms** are printed in boldface type and defined in the text in *italic*. **Names to Know** identify major contributors to psychological research and theory; these names appear in boldface type to help you keep track of the people whose ideas are central to the continuing story of psychology. Both Key Terms and Names to Know are listed again, with page number references, in each sectional summary of the **Chapter Review,** in the order of their original appearance.

4. At the end of the text (as with most scholarly works) comes the References section, which provides essential bibliographic information on every book, journal article, or other source that documents some point made in the text. This is a valuable resource in case you wish to know more, or look up specific information for your own research and interest. In the text, when a name and date are set off in parentheses—for example, (Zimbardo, 1990)—this *citation* is your clue to finding the rest of the information in the References section.

Citations of references that have more than two authors typically list the senior author's last name only, followed by the abbreviation *et al.,* the Latin abbreviation for *et alias,* "and the others."

5. The Name Index and Subject Index, appearing at the end of the text, provide you with an alphabetized listing of people cited in the text, all terms, and subject matter, along with page references.

6. Finally, your studying and test performance are likely to be enhanced by using the Study Guide and Workbook to accompany *Psychology, Second Edition.* The Study Guide was prepared to give students a boost in studying more efficiently and taking tests more effectively. The Study Guide contains *concept maps* to guide you through the many concepts and connections each chapter introduces. It also provides helpful tips—from senior author Dr. Peter Gram—as well as practice tests, flash cards, outlines, and suggestions for creatively using and reviewing the material.

We sincerely appreciate the opportunity your teacher has given us by choosing *Psychology* for your course, and we appreciate your willingness to let this book be your written guide in your journey into this fascinating and challenging discipline. We urge you to *use this book:* Carry it with you; scribble in it; flip through it whenever you are waiting in line somewhere; bend down the corners of any pages you want to reread; refer to it for ideas, information, or examples. Get your money's worth—and your study's worth—out of this book *now.*

Enough packing for the trip! It's time to get started. Please begin reading your first assignment in what we trust will become one of your favorite courses and most enjoyable intellectual journeys.

About the Authors...

After almost 40 years of teaching, Phil Zimbardo still gets excited about teaching Introductory Psychology to large lecture classes at Stanford University. Numerous awards for distinguished teaching attest to the impact he has had on his students and colleagues. His influence as a mentor goes beyond direct contact in the classroom by virtue of his authorship of one of the most widely read texts in psychology, *Psychology and Life,* as well as through the prize-winning television series, *Discovering Psychology,* which he created, wrote, and hosted. Although writing texts and teaching about psychology are Phil's main priorities, he has managed to find time to do some provocative and influential research on shyness, violence, prisons, time perspective, and madness. His wife, Christina Maslach, is also a professor of psychology at the University of California, Berkeley. They live in San Francisco with their two daughters, Zara and Tanya, both students. Son Adam is a psychotherapist.

Like Phil Zimbardo, Ann Weber is a social psychologist who is enthusiastic about introducing psychology to her students. Her college work in psychology at the Catholic University of America inspired her to become a teacher and writer in the field. After completing graduate work at The Johns Hopkins University in 1978, she joined the faculty at the University of North Carolina at Asheville. In addition to teaching, she does extensive consulting and writing in the area of personal relationships, with a special focus on loss and grief. Originally from Maryland, Ann lives in the mountains of western North Carolina with her husband, John Quigley, their five "perfect" cats (Nervie, Lucy, Mina, Philip, and Mink) and their "adorable" puppy, Bear.

psychology

CHAPTER 1

Mind, Behavior, and Science

As the runners lined up to start the 1986 NCAA 10,000-meter championship race, Kathy O. was the odds-on favorite. She had broken high school track records in three distances and recently set a new American collegiate record for the 10,000-meter race. Her parents, always supportive fans, watched from the sidelines. Kathy got off to a slow start, but she was only a few paces behind the leaders. Her fans knew she could soon catch up. But this time Kathy didn't bolt to the lead. Instead, she veered away from the other runners. Without breaking her stride, she ran off the track, scaled a 7-foot fence, raced down a side street, and jumped off a 50-foot bridge. Ten minutes later, her coach found her on the concrete floodplain of the White River. She had two broken ribs and a punctured lung, and she was paralyzed from the waist down. Not only would she never run again, she might never walk again.

What happened to Kathy? Why did she quit the race and nearly self-destruct? As a star athlete and premed student on the dean's list, Kathy had everything going for her. She had been valedictorian of her high school class. Teachers and coaches described her as sweet, sensible, diligent, courteous, and religious.

Nobody understood her behavior. It didn't make sense.

Kathy's father thought the tragedy "had something to do with the pressure that is put on young people to succeed." Teammates felt the pressure may have come from within Kathy herself. "She was a perfectionist," said one of them. Determined to excel at everything, Kathy had studied relentlessly, even during team workouts.

How did Kathy explain her actions? She told an interviewer that she was overcome by the terrifying fear of failure as she began falling behind in the race. "All of a sudden . . . I just felt like something snapped inside of me." She felt angry and persecuted. These negative reactions were new to Kathy, and they made her feel as if she were someone else. "I just wanted to run away," she recalled. "I don't see how I climbed that fence . . . I just don't feel like that person was me. I know that sounds strange, but I was just out of control. . . . I was watching everything that was happening and I couldn't stop" (UPI, 12/22/86).

Different fields of psychology would focus on different aspects of Kathy's baffling experience. Personality, social, and developmental psychologists might ask how athletic ability, intelligence, parental *support, competition, motivation to achieve, and personality traits combined to make Kathy a superstar in the first place. Clinical psychologists would want to know why something "snapped" inside Kathy at this race, why feelings of anger were so foreign to her, and why she felt persecuted. Those who study the nature of consciousness would try to understand Kathy's perception that she was outside herself, unable to stop her flight toward self-destruction. Health psychologists and sports psychologists might try to identify signs of stress and clues in earlier behaviors that could have signaled an impending breakdown. Biopsychologists might consider the role*

of brain and hormonal factors in her sudden, abnormal reaction.

We may never completely understand what motivated Kathy's behavior, but psychology provides the tools (research methods) and the instructions (theories about the causes of behavior) for exploring basic questions about who we are and why we think, feel, and act as we do. Psychologists are challenged to make sense of cases that, like Kathy's, violate people's usual expectations about human nature. Psychologists are motivated not only by intellectual curiosity, but also by a desire to discover how to help people prevent such tragedies in the future.

Introduction

All persons are puzzles until at last we find in some word or act the key to the man, to the woman: straightway all their past words and actions lie in light before us.

—Emerson, *Journals* (1842)

Thus comments Ralph Waldo Emerson (1803–1882), one of America's great writers, on the subject of human complexity. Motivated to find such a "key" to understanding the puzzles that are persons, we now undertake a fascinating journey into the realms of the human mind. Foremost in our journey will be a scientific quest for understanding. We want to know why people think, feel, and behave as they do. What makes each person different from all other people? Yet why do they often behave so alike in some situations? We must travel many paths to understand "the nature of human nature." We will explore the inner spaces of the brain and mind and the outer dimensions of human behavior. Between those extremes, we shall investigate events and experiences that one takes for granted, such as how we perceive our world, communicate, learn, think, remember, and even sleep. We will also try to understand how and why people dream, fall in love, feel shy, act aggressively, and become mentally ill.

Psychology seeks a general understanding of how human beings function. As you discover what psychologists know about people in general, you can apply that knowledge to change your own behavior, and the behavior of other people, for the better. Ideally, you will also perceive ways to change society, since efforts to resolve many of the urgent problems of our time benefit from a psychological perspective.

Our first goal in *Psychology* is to survey what psychologists have discovered about the workings of the brain, mind, and behavior. Our second goal is to apply that knowledge in our everyday lives, and to enhance many aspects of the human condition. By the end of this journey, if you have put in the time and effort necessary to qualify as a novice psychologist, you will know the fascination of "people watching," and perhaps you will also know better how to understand, inform, and comfort others.

The Discipline of Psychology

In this section we formally define psychology and establish what this discipline is all about. We compare psychology to other disciplines that analyze behavior, the brain, and the mind. Finally we preview five general goals that guide the work of professional psychologists.

Psychology as a Science

Psychology *is the scientific study of the behavior of individuals and their mental processes.* A basic question that psychology asks is this: What is the nature of human nature? Psychologists answer this question by looking at *processes* that occur within individuals as well as within the physical and social environment. Let's examine each aspect of the definition of psychology—scientific, behavioral, individual, and mental.

Science is a unique approach to knowledge. The *scientific* aspect of psychology requires that psychological conclusions be based on evidence collected following the principles of the scientific method. Instead of relying on a conclusion that "makes sense," seems logical, or is personally satisfying, the scientist is trained to use a particular method in answering questions. The **scientific method** *consists of a set of orderly steps using empirical evidence to analyze and solve problems.* Empirical evidence is information (data) gathered directly by the observer. Unbiased methods are used to make observations, collect data, and formulate conclusions.

For example, proponents of the antidrug education program DARE (Drug Abuse Resistance Education), used in schools to teach children to say "no" to drugs, claim that it works because teachers, parents, and students all report that they like the program. However, when recent scientific investigations evaluated whether this treatment actually had any effect on later drug-taking *behavior,* not just the attitudes of the students compared to those not exposed to it, the outcome was quite different. The scientific conclusion was that DARE had *no* measurable impact on ability to resist drug use (Harmon, 1993).

In psychology, the scientific method usually focuses on *behavior*. **Behavior** *is the observable action an organism uses to adjust to the environment.* The subject matter of psychology is largely the observable behavior of humans and other species of animals. Psychologists observe how an individual functions, what the individual does, and how the individual goes about doing it within a given behavioral setting and social context. The subject of psychological analysis is usually an *individual* (rather than groups or institutions), and usually human, although much basic research in psychology focuses on nonhumans. The research setting might be the individual's natural habitat or the more controlled environment of a research laboratory.

Observable behaviors such as speaking, running, or taking a test can be directly observed, but an individual's mental processes cannot. Many human activities are really private, internal events: reasoning, creating, and dreaming. Many psychologists believe that such mental processes, though not directly observable, represent the most important subject of psychology inquiry. The challenge of studying mental events has led to the development of innovative research techniques which we will discuss later.

Ties to Other Disciplines

Psychology is unique because it has ties to so many different areas of knowledge. As one of the *social sciences,* psychology draws on some of the same observations as economics, political science, sociology, and cultural anthropology—all sciences of social behavior. Some psychologists are especially

Colleagues in cultural anthropology, such as this researcher in Kenya, furnish important data for cross-cultural psychologists.

interested in comparing the behaviors of people who are from different cultures or live in different parts of the world. These cross-cultural psychologists draw heavily from the work of colleagues in cultural anthropology. Throughout this text we will highlight the influence of culture in various psychological investigations. (If you like, you may turn now to page 21 and consider the discussion in Cultural Context: The Importance of Diversity before going on to psychology's other disciplinary links.)

Because it systematically analyzes behavior, psychology is also a *behavioral science,* like education and environmental design. Behavioral sciences seek to identify and apply psychological principles in training people or shaping their surroundings. Psychologists also share interests with researchers in *biological sciences,* especially those who study brain processes and the biochemical bases of behavior. As part of the emerging area of *cognitive science,* psychologists' questions about how the human mind works are related to research and theory in computer science, artificial intelligence, and applied mathematics. Finally, as a *health science,* psychology seeks to improve the quality of our individual and collective well-being.

While the remarkable breadth and depth of modern psychology delights psychologists, it can make the field a challenge to the student exploring it for the first time. There is much more to the study of psychology than you probably expect. We now examine the specific goals of the discipline of psychology—goals that yield valuable insights and useful lessons about life.

The Goals of Psychology

The goals of the psychologist conducting basic research are to describe, explain, predict, and control behavior. The applied psychologist has a fifth goal—to improve the quality of human life. The issue here is the distinction between *basic* and *applied research.* Some research, for example, starts with a practical problem to be solved, such as how to reduce social violence or how to conserve energy. Such research by its very nature is applied. What gets applied, however, is basic research, work conducted to answer basic questions—such as whether violence is "instinctive"—which may or may not ultimately have any application to real-world problem solving. The process of accomplishing one goal and moving on to the next is ideally a natural, flowing experience, energized by the psychologist's interest in the question being studied.

Describing What Happens   The first task in psychology is to observe behavior carefully and to describe it objectively. *Data* are reports of observations (*data* is the plural form and *datum* is the singular). For example, the prices of specific items in different grocery stores are data that can help you decide where to shop.

Behavioral data *are reports of observations about the behavior of organisms and the conditions under which the behavior occurs or changes.* The specific behavior that is being observed and measured is the individual's *response.* A response is triggered by an environmental condition known as a *stimulus* (the plural of *stimulus* is *stimuli*). When you are startled by the sudden, loud ringing of a telephone in a quiet room, the ringing is the stimulus that causes your startled response.

Psychologists look for consistent, reliable relationships between stimuli and responses. They also look for relationships between two or more particular responses, such as the response of usually letting someone else answer the ringing telephone and the response of avoiding eye contact with a person of the other gender. Such a pattern might lead a psychologist to infer that shyness is at work, influencing this person's responses.

Psychologists identify and study these relationships to understand something about the individual making the responses or about the underlying process that causes or relates responses and stimuli.

Describing one's observations may sound like a straightforward task, but it is very challenging for people to be *objective* or free from biases when describing what they observe. Because of our prior experiences, both personal and cultural, we often see in data what we *expect* to see. Consider how expectations about gender can alter the way American parents perceive their children. When parents of newborn infants (less than 24 hours old) were asked to describe their babies, they gave very different descriptions depending on the baby's sex. Compared to sons, daughters were rated as seeming softer, smaller, weaker, more delicate, and more awkward. However, when objective measures were then made (of the infants' weight, length, state of health, and other attributes), no actual differences were found between the boys and girls (Rubin et al., 1974). Within 24 hours of an infant's birth, the parents have already begun to "see" what they expect rather than what is true. Without realizing it, people often distort information to make the data fit their preexisting beliefs. Even professional observers can fall prey to this tendency to let their own perspectives interfere with objective observation. We will discuss this problem further—and offer some safeguards used to solve it—when we discuss psychological research later in this chapter.

Try for a moment to describe a specific scene objectively. Examine the photograph of two people interacting. How would you describe them? To be objective, you must restrict yourself to describing their gestures, facial expressions, postures, and other observable characteristics. But if you are tempted to comment on their emotions or intentions—such as whether they seem happy, excited, or affectionate—then you are inferring inner states, not describing behavior. As hard as it is to do so, scientific observers must resist making subjective judgments about the meaning of what they observe.

Explaining What Happens   While *descriptions* must come from perceivable information, *explanations* deliberately go beyond what can be observed impartially. We began this chapter by asking for an explanation of why Kathy O. quit the race and nearly destroyed her life. Fans of mystery stories, after figuring out *who* committed the crime, want to understand the reason why. In many areas of psychology, the central goal is to find regular patterns in behavioral and mental processes. Psychologists want to discover "how behavior works." Understanding behavior involves finding out how certain stimuli cause observed responses and discovering relationships between sets of responses. For example, to understand workers' behavior, a manager needs to

An objective description of what you observe includes only external features; it stops short of making inferences about motives and emotions.

understand how either punishment or reward can affect their productivity, or how employee morale is influenced by either teamwork or job-related stress.

Correct explanations may also come from research that systematically evaluates alternative views about a psychological event. There is no better path to understanding than that of informed imagination. Successful researchers rely on creativity and insight developed through their experience with collecting and interpreting information. Sometimes they make an *inference*—a logical or reasonable judgment not based on direct observation—about a process that is happening inside an animal or human being. This inference helps make the observed behavior more understandable. For example, if your cat meows and paws at your ankles, and you notice her food dish is empty, you may make an inference: "She must be hungry. No wonder she was trying to get my attention!"

The inner states that psychologists make inferences about are often summarized as *intervening variables*. **Intervening variables** *are inner, unseen conditions that are assumed to function as the links between the observable stimulus and the individual's response*. Examples of intervening variables include emotions such as anger, and motives such as hunger. You cannot directly see anger or hunger, but you can often observe the likely triggers or causes, and you can measure the behavioral results.

Psychological explanations often center on sources of motivation that might account for observed behavior. For example, one psychological explanation for Kathy O.'s behavior may be that a buildup of pressures to achieve and succeed led her to believe that anything less than perfection was failure. For Kathy, winning was everything. When she thought she was losing the race, she felt frustrated and ashamed, and her self-image suffered. Running away from the scene of her "failure" and attempting to end her life might have been impulsive reactions to these overpowering feelings and motivations. In contrast, a purely biological explanation would propose a very different cause for Kathy's tragedy, such as a brain tumor or chemical imbalance distorting her judgment in a stressful situation.

The explanation one proposes depends on both one's perspective and the evidence collected. But any such proposition must be checked against carefully collected data that either support it or rule out alternative explanations. A psychologist proposing that Kathy O.'s actions were influenced by conflicting emotions would have to demonstrate that eyewitnesses' accounts and other evidence supported such an explanation, and that there was no evidence for a medical condition that might cause Kathy to behave as she did.

Predicting What Will Happen   Predictions in psychology are statements about the likelihood that a certain behavior will occur or that a given relationship will be found. When differing explanations are offered to account for some behavior or relationship, they are judged by how well they predict the circumstances or events being studied.

Everyday life requires a certain amount of predictive ability. For example, before you pay a tutor to help you study some subject, you would expect to be shown evidence of the tutor's competence and experience. People need to predict what will happen in the future because our well-being and even our survival depend on making accurate judgments about situations that could be either dangerous or favorable. Making a scientific prediction is a more rigorous process, seeking to identify relationships between events, links between events and predictors, and signs of future occurrences. Scientific predictions must be worded precisely, communicated to other scientists, tested—and perhaps disconfirmed if the evidence fails to support them.

A common form of prediction starts with the assumption that people's past actions are a good indicator of their future behavior. If you are not familiar with someone's past record, you might consider the past behavior of similar people who were in the same situation. This is a *base rate* prediction. A **base rate** is *a statistic that identifies the normal frequency, or probability, of a given event*. Insurance companies use base rate data of accidents by drivers of different ages to compute their premiums. These are really predictions of the greater likelihood of accidents by those in some groups than in others—such as males more than females, and adolescents more than middle-aged drivers.

When making predictions, psychologists usually recognize that most behavior is influenced by a combination of factors rather than a single obvious cause. Some influences are common to most people while others are unique to the individual in question. Still others are external factors, such as the distinctive environment or circumstances. What made Kathy O. suddenly "snap" and take drastic action? Perhaps it was no single problem or threat, but a combination of factors, including her past training, recent pressures, and a momentary fear of failure in this particular race.

To make a *causal prediction*, a psychologist must be able to specify that a given stimulus will influence an individual to make a specific response. To find out, the investigator asks this question in terms of *variables*. A **variable** is *any condition, process, or event that changes or varies*. For example, your mood is a variable because it changes from time to time; the weather is a variable because it varies from day to day. Any relationship between the weather and your mood—for example, feeling depressed on rainy days, but happy on sunny days—can be considered a relationship between two variables.

In trying to predict what will happen, psychologists try to identify a sequence of events in which a stimulus leads to a psychological response. Suppose a researcher wanted to determine if a certain drug would reduce the disruptive reactions of schoolchildren whose behavior was labeled as "hyperkinetic." She would first administer the drug in different dosages to those children as well as to others not in the hyperkinetic group. Then the investigator would record any changes in *all* the children's behavior from before to after the drug treatment. Her prediction would be that the drug would lower the intensity of those negative classroom behaviors of children in the hyperkinetic group. In addition, measures of learning and school performance would also be taken to see if there were positive consequences of the children's more attentive behavior.

In this experiment, the drug treatment is called the *independent variable* and its measurable effects on the children's behavior make up the *dependent variable*. The **independent variable** is *the stimulus condition that is systematically varied by the investigator in order to predict a given effect on subjects' behavior*. An experimenter may manipulate the independent variable by presenting certain amounts (dosages, durations, varieties) to the subjects being observed. The **dependent variable** is *any behavioral variable whose values result from or depend on changes in the independent variables*. The dependent variable "depends on" the effects of the independent variable. In psychological research, the dependent variable is always some type of measurable behavioral reaction—a reported mood, a test score, or an overt action.

In the experimental scenario, the independent variable is the predictor, and the dependent variable is the predicted response. The goal of prediction is "built into" the design of the experiment—as we shall explain further when we review research methods in a later section.

Controlling What Happens Controlling behavior—making it happen or not happen, starting it or stopping it, and influencing its quality and strength—is an important goal for psychologists. This ability to control is crucial to validating scientific explanations for behavior. But in a practical sense, control enables psychologists to help people improve their lives. It is at the heart of all programs of psychological treatment or therapy. Whether a client wishes to quit smoking or cope with serious trauma, a psychotherapist will seek to empower the client with the ability to control his or her own behavior in the direction desired.

Ethical problems can arise when one person seeks to control another's behavior, because the controller's values may violate those of the recipient. For example, not too long ago psychotherapists sought to "cure" homosexual men of their alleged "sickness" by applying aversive treatments—pain or discomfort—to discourage their nonheterosexual feelings and actions. However, once the scientifically accepted conception of homosexuality changed from one of sexual *deviance* to one of sexual *preference,* that "treatment" stopped. As times change, so do values—and well-intentioned efforts to control may later be seen as unethical, if not illegal, practices.

 Control is not a universal goal among psychologists. In many Asian and African countries, psychologists seek *understanding* rather than control (Nobles, 1972). Psychological research and practice in Western societies may be biased by the value placed on control in those cultures. Gender may also influence whether control is valued: many notions of masculinity prize being in control, and most of the early shapers of psychological scholarship were men. Had women been able to play a more prominent role in developing modern psychology, it is possible that values other than control might have prevailed in psychology's defining goals (Bornstein & Quinna, 1988; Riger, 1992).

Improving the Quality of Life   Many psychological findings are applied to solve human problems. Psychology enriches life in profound ways and also shapes and clarifies much of what people come to consider "common sense." In Focus on Application: Professional Psychology on page 11, we describe the diverse tasks, settings, and roles involved in the work of professional psychologists. After reviewing that discussion, ASK YOURSELF how you can use psychology in your life, beginning with these questions:

- If you were to choose one field of psychology from those reviewed in the "Professional Psychology" box, which would you choose? Why?
- If what you learn in this course could help you to solve one real problem in your life, which problem would that be?
- Of the five goals of psychology reviewed above, which one appeals to you the most? Identify a recent experience when being able to meet this goal was (or would have been) helpful to you.

Check Your Recall

Psychology studies individuals' behavior and mental processes. Psychology employs the scientific method to study observed behavior and to make inferences about mental processes and inner states. Psychology is distinct from other disciplines, but overlaps in interests and perspectives with other social, behavioral, biological, cognitive, and health sciences. Research psychologists pursue four goals: description, explanation, prediction, and control. Applied psychologists also pursue a fifth goal—improving the quality of individual lives and society. Psychology is a broad and diverse discipline. Most professional psychologists work in either academic, business, or clinical settings. Different fields of psychology reflect specializations in certain tasks, problems, and methods.

FOCUS on Application

Professional Psychology

Most professional psychologists work in academia: settings such as universities, colleges, and medical schools. But for many other psychologists, the principal employment setting is in business, government, hospitals, or clinics. Those in private practice may treat clients in their offices or conduct personal consulting services for private firms. Psychologists are "unified by diversity"—linked worldwide by a diversity of professional concerns and environments all devoted to the study of behavior and mental processes.

The largest single category of psychologists concentrates on the diagnosis and treatment of severe emotional and behavioral problems. *Clinical psychologists* tackle problems of mental illness, juvenile delinquency, drug addiction, criminal behavior, mental disability, and marital and family conflict. The work of *counseling psychologists* is similar to that of clinical psychologists, but often the problems they treat are of a less severe nature, and the treatment they provide is usually shorter in duration. *Community psychologists* work in community settings delivering social and psychological services to the poor, minorities, immigrants, and the growing number of homeless people in American cities.

Researchers in *biological psychology* study the biological bases of behavior, feelings, and mental processes. Specialists in *neuroscience* study mechanisms that link the brain to behavior. *Psychopharmacologists* investigate the effects of drugs on behavior and thought.

Experimental psychology primarily uses experimental methods to work with both human and animal subjects in the quest for general laws of psychology that apply to all species.

Cognitive psychologists focus their research on consciousness and mental processes such as thinking and communicating, remembering and forgetting, and making decisions and solving problems. *Psycholinguistics* involves a particular study of the psychology of language.

Developmental psychology focuses on how human functioning changes over time, identifying the factors that shape behavior from birth to death. *Personality psychology* concentrates on the ways individuals differ from each other, despite the fact that human beings obviously share common goals, challenges, and experiences. *Social psychology* reverses this orientation, focusing on the common situations and social contexts that influence human behavior despite individual differences.

Industrial psychology and *organizational behavior* examine the relationships between people and jobs. A field allied with industrial psychology is *human factors psychology*, which studies the interaction between worker, machines, and work environment.

Further specialization can be found among many areas of applied psychology. *Educational* and *school psychologists* study ways to improve the learning process, both by applying learning theory and working with students in the school environment. *Environmental psychologists* work with architects, city planners, and environmental designers to meet the needs of users and residents. *Health psychologists* collaborate with medical researchers to understand how different lifestyles and behavior patterns affect health and stress. *Forensic psychologists* apply psychological knowledge to human problems in the field of law enforcement. Finally, *sports psychologists* analyze the performance of athletes and use psychological principles in training them to achieve peak performance.

The Foundations of Psychology

"Psychology has a long past, but only a short history," wrote one of the first experimental psychologists, Hermann Ebbinghaus (1908). While the formal start of modern psychology as a science can be traced to only a century ago (relatively recently in terms of human history), scholars and thinkers have long asked important questions about how people perceive reality, the nature of consciousness, and the origins of madness. In the fifth and fourth centuries B.C., the classical Greek philosophers Socrates, Plato, and Aristotle began rational dialogues about how the mind works, the nature of free will, and the relationship of individual citizens to their community state. Later, as early Christian doctrines spread throughout Europe, theologians taught that the mind and soul had free will (God's gift to humans) and were not subject to the natural laws and principles that determined the actions of physical bodies and nonhuman creatures. No scientific psychology was possible until this assumption was challenged.

The formal beginning of psychology as a modern science came in 1879, when **Wilhelm Wundt** (probably the first person to refer to himself as a *psychologist*) founded, in Leipzig, Germany, the first laboratory devoted to experimental psychology. In the late 1880s German physicists, physiologists, and philosophers began to challenge the notion that the human organism is special in the great chain of being, and demonstrated that natural laws determine human actions. Hermann von Helmholtz, trained as a physicist, conducted simple but revealing experiments on perception and the nervous system. At about the same time, another German, Gustav Fechner, studied how physical stimuli were translated psychologically as they were sensed and perceived.

As Wundt had done, Helmholtz and Fechner advocated a *deterministic* perspective in these studies of psychological experience. **Determinism** *is the doctrine that physical, behavioral, and mental events are determined by specific causal factors.* Determinism is essential to science because it assumes that complex realities can be understood—answers to questions can be found—if they are investigated and their causes identified. In its simplest sense, determinism holds that events and behaviors *have* causes that can be investigated. In its most stringent interpretation, however, determinism argues that the causes of behavior are somewhat beyond the control of the individual—a challenge to the notion of *free will*, the power each person has to direct his or her own behavior. Institutions such as law are based more on notions of free will and *rationalism* (reasoned choice) than on determinism. In contrast, modern sciences ranging from psychology to medicine rely on determinism in their investigations.

Ideas and traditions from both philosophy and natural science converged to give rise to the development of the new field of psychology in the late nineteenth century. A young Harvard philosophy professor who had studied medicine and had strong interests in literature and religion developed a uniquely American psychological perspective. **William James,** brother of the great novelist Henry James, wrote a two-volume work, *The Principles of Psychology* (1890), which many experts consider to be the most important psychology text ever written.

Today the rapid pace of technology has led to an explosion of new psychological ideas and applications, but if we look closely we see it has been an "orderly" explosion. Modern concepts of thought and behavior have descended from earlier ideas, some of which were organized into influential

In 1879, Wilhelm Wundt (1832–1920) founded the first formal laboratory devoted to experimental psychology. He's shown here (center) in his laboratory in Leipzig in 1912.

"schools" of psychology. Each school influenced the training and thinking of generations of scholars whose work shaped what psychology is today. Two of the most historically significant schools of psychology are *structuralism* and *functionalism*. To appreciate the richness and usefulness of modern psychology, we must first understand the development of these two seminal approaches.

Structuralism

The structuralist school of psychology focused on understanding the "contents" of the mind. When psychology became a laboratory science organized around experiments, its unique contribution to knowledge was established and recognized. In Wundt's laboratory, the data were collected through systematic, objective procedures, so that independent observers could repeat the results of these experiments. Wundt's psychological tradition was characterized by an emphasis on experimental methods (controlling conditions and observing psychological responses), precise measurement, and statistical analysis of data. In Wilhelm Wundt's laboratory, students took the role of subjects, making simple, measurable responses (saying yes or no, pressing a button) to stimuli presented under varying conditions.

William James (1842–1910)

The American psychologist **Edward Titchener** had studied with Wundt in Germany. When Titchener returned to the United States, he brought with him Wundt's conviction that psychology should focus on consciousness and the elements of mental life. The research method of choice at that time was *introspection,* a subject's systematic examination of his or her own thoughts and feelings about specific sensory experiences. Titchener emphasized the "what" of mental contents rather than the "why" or "how." Consequently this approach, **structuralism,** *refers to the study of the structure of mind and behavior, including their elements and components.*

Structuralism presumed that all human mental experience could be understood as the combination of simpler events or elements. You make structuralist assumptions when you evaluate an experience by analyzing its parts, such as judging how good a movie is by its cast and director, or deciding whether you want to try a dish by asking first what the ingredients are. Structuralist ideas in psychology include the assumption that some experiences are "made up of" combinations of separate thoughts, emotions, or motives. As appealing as this model may seem, structuralism was criticized as too simplistic, reducing complex experiences to basic sensations. It was also considered too "mentalistic," relying excessively on unobservable inner processes and unverifiable verbal reports. Although its influence was limited and not enduring in modern psychology, structuralism represented the early development of psychology from its roots in physical sciences and methods.

Functionalism

Whereas structuralists focused on content, *functionalists* believed mental processes could best be understood in terms of purpose and function. As a school of psychology, **functionalism** *gave primary importance to learned habits which enabled organisms to adapt to their environments and function effectively.* Functionalism had been developed by the American philosopher **John Dewey,** who originally applied this perspective to improving educational practices. Dewey's functionalism emphasized that every organism's practical goal is to adapt to its environment. It is therefore reasonable to ask what adaptive purpose is served by a particular behavior or psychological experience.

William James advanced this functionalist view in developing early scientific psychology. James agreed with the structuralist Titchener that the study of consciousness must be central to psychology. But James disagreed with the structuralist search for elements and contents. Instead, he argued that consciousness was an ongoing stream, a process of mind continually interacting with the environment. Human consciousness helped one to adjust to the environment; thus, the *functions* of mental processes—not the contents of the mind—were significant. In order to understand a given thought or behavior, one should ask what function or purpose it served, not what its structure contained. James believed that psychology should focus on explaining rather than controlling behavior and mental processes.

Check Your Recall

Two historically important approaches to the study of psychology are structuralism and functionalism. Structuralism, developed first by Wilhelm Wundt and extended by Edward Titchener, originated in early laboratory research on the elements or contents of the human mind. Structuralist research employed the technique of introspection to identify how subjects mentally organize sensory experiences. Structuralism reflects early influences by physical science, but was criticized as simplistic and mentalistic. Functionalism, developed by John Dewey and William James, proposed that an understanding of consciousness depended on appreciating the purpose or function of behavior. Functionalists argued that organisms seek to adapt to their environments, so their behavior is best understood in terms of its adaptive purpose. ✔

Current Perspectives in Psychology

Because psychology deals with such a broad range of material and ideas about how individuals behave, think, and feel, psychologists have taken different approaches to what is most significant to study and how it should be studied. These approaches represent alternative perspectives on the nature of psychological knowledge. For example, they vary in their focus on whether to study the smallest (*micro*) units of behavior, such as nerve cell reactions; or big (*macro*) ones, such as trends toward violence in society. They also differ in assumptions about influences on behavior that come from the past, present, or future. There are seven such conceptual perspectives underlying modern psychology:

- the biological approach;
- the psychodynamic approach;
- the behavioristic approach;
- the cognitive approach;
- the humanistic approach;
- the evolutionary approach; and,
- the sociocultural approach.

Together these seven approaches make up the major ways that psychologists try to understand "the nature of human nature" and the structure and purpose of all animal behavior.

The Biological Approach

We mentioned above that psychology shares many interests with biological sciences such as genetics and medicine. In fact, this overlap has led to the development of a *biological approach* to psychology. The **biological approach** *in psychology searches for the causes of behavior in the functioning of genes,*

Early psychologists used the analogy of a telephone switchboard as an approach to understanding how the brain communicates information.

the brain and nervous system, and the endocrine (internal gland) system. This approach makes four assumptions:

1. Psychological and social phenomena can be understood in terms of biochemical processes.
2. Complex behaviors can be understood by analyzing them into smaller, more specific units.
3. All behavior—or behavior potential—is determined by physical structures and hereditary processes.
4. Experience can modify behavior by altering these underlying biological structures and processes.

The biological approach to Kathy O.'s behavior would assume that biochemical processes account for her experience. Perhaps the stress of running aggravated an undetected physical disease (such as a thyroid disorder) and interfered with Kathy's ability to control her behavior. The biological approach is also concerned with hereditary factors. Could Kathy have inherited a brain chemistry or a biologically based temperament that prevented her from controlling her self-destructive impulse to flee? While heredity cannot be changed, once these influences are understood, people like Kathy can be helped with medication and other forms of therapy.

The Psychodynamic Approach

Related to a biological approach is a perspective that assumes behavior to be internally driven and energized—not directly by genes and brain function but indirectly by intervening psychological states. Such a perspective is termed *psychodynamic* because it proposes that the mind (*psyche*) is the source of behavioral energy (*dynamics*). The **psychodynamic approach** *views behavior as driven or motivated by powerful mental forces and conflicts.* In this view, human actions stem from inherited instincts, biological drives, and attempts to resolve conflicts between personal needs and societal demands to act appropriately. Motivation is the key concept in the psychodynamic model. Deprivation, bodily arousal, conflict, and frustration provide the power for behavior just as fuel drives an engine. The organism stops reacting only when its needs are satisfied and its drives reduced.

Sigmund Freud (1856–1939), shown here in the office of his Vienna home, developed the psychodynamic approach to behavior.

Psychodynamic principles of motivation were most fully developed by Viennese physician **Sigmund Freud** in the late nineteenth and early twentieth centuries. According to Freud's theory, each person is fully determined by a combination of heredity and early childhood experiences. Personality develops as a child learns to resolve the conflict between personal desires ("I want to eat dessert now," "I want to play in the mud") and social restrictions ("Eat your dinner first," "Come inside and wash your hands"). Unresolved conflicts ("My parents don't love me," "No one lets me do what I want to do") may lead to long-lasting emotional conflicts. Freud's model was the first to recognize that human behavior is not always rational or easy to explain. Despite criticisms and the rise of alternative viewpoints, Freud's psychodynamic ideas have probably influenced more areas of psychology than those of any other person, and they continue to inspire new research and practice today.

Applying the psychodynamic perspective to the case of Kathy O., we wonder what forces and desires could have driven her so hard that she "snapped" and lost control. Perhaps as a child she tried to please her parents or overcome feelings of inadequacy by excelling and becoming a "winner." When she doubted her ability to keep this up, perhaps she panicked and tried, irrationally, to "escape" painful failure by ending her life. Therapy based on the psychodynamic approach might be undertaken for individuals who feel pressures and self-expectations building up, in order to intervene *before* the person "snaps."

The Behavioristic Approach

Recall that early structuralism was criticized as being too mentalistic because it attempted to deal with mental processes that were actually hidden from direct observation. In the early twentieth century, a few scholars pioneered an approach that excluded all mental events as inappropriate for psychological inquiry because they could not be investigated scientifically. Instead, they championed the study of *behavior* alone. **Behaviorism** *asserts that only the overt behavior of organisms is the proper subject of scientific study.* Early behaviorists sought to persuade all psychologists to adopt this view. The **behavioristic approach** *in psychology focuses on overt behaviors that can be objectively recorded and manipulated.* Much behavioristic research concentrates on specific, measurable responses for its data, such as blinking an eye, pressing a lever, or saying yes when the subject recognizes an identifiable stimulus (such as a light or bell). In contrast with the biological and psychodynamic approaches, behaviorists do not try to infer biochemical processes or unconscious motives to explain these responses.

The behaviorists reduce psychological understanding to a simple ABC formula: First, identify the *antecedent* (triggering) stimulus conditions that elicit behavior. Next, measure changes in observable *behavior*. Finally, record the *consequences* that the behavior has on the environment or the *changes* it leads to. Note that all three of these ABC elements—antecedent conditions, behaviors, and consequences/changes—must be objectively observable, not hidden mental events or interpretations.

The first American behaviorist was **John B. Watson**, a professor and researcher whose ideas had been influenced by work that identified biological processes basic to *learning*. (We will look more closely at this research on *conditioning* in Chapter 6). Watson concluded that mental events could not be studied scientifically and that psychology must look not within the individual for the causes of behavior, but outside the individual, at the environment and the observable stimuli that led to behavioral responses.

Through basic research conducted with animal subjects, B. F. Skinner (1904–1990) and his disciples developed the principles of behaviorism that have been so widely applied to human problems.

Watson's early groundwork was expanded upon by the late Harvard psychologist **B. F. Skinner**, who further restricted the proper domain of psychology to the study of how behavior and the environment operate on and affect each other. Skinner and his disciples conducted their basic research with animal subjects (such as pigeons and rats), but the principles of behaviorism have been widely applied to human problems. For example, individual and institutional efforts to change people's behavior draw heavily on behavioristic research about how to encourage certain responses and discourage others. Parent-child relationships, schools, prison policies, diplomatic missions are all centrally concerned with how best to eliminate unwanted responses (disobedience, violence) and encourage productive alternatives (cooperation, peaceful conflict resolution).

We would expect a behaviorist to examine the mystery of Kathy O. in a very different way from the biological or psychodynamic search for inner causes. More likely, a behaviorist would rule out any speculation about Kathy's "inner states" as impossible to confirm—no one can know what Kathy was thinking or feeling. Instead, we should focus on Kathy's observable behavior and the factors that might have influenced it. Just before Kathy "snapped," she was falling behind in the race. In past races, how did she react when she fell behind? Did falling behind usually mean she would lose the race? Were past losses followed by aversive experiences like disapproval or derision—consequences she would want to avoid experiencing yet again? By analyzing Kathy's reinforcement history and her most recent behavior and its consequences, the behaviorist would seek to explain her sudden, tragic flight.

The Cognitive Approach

Right now you might be thinking that, for all its logic, the behavioristic approach seems somewhat limited if it excludes any consideration of mental processes. In fact, many psychologists have argued that the behavioristic approach is unnecessarily restrictive. They argue that psychology could and should develop methods to study subtle, unobvious human activity including paying attention, thinking, remembering, problem-solving, fantasizing, and experiencing consciousness. The resulting **cognitive approach** *emphasizes human thought and all the processes of knowing as central to the study of psychology.* From the cognitive perspective, people act because they *think*, and they think because the design and function of the human brain naturally equips them to engage in thinking processes.

Cognitive psychologists believe that how we process information about a stimulus is at least as important in determining behavior as is the stimulus itself. Humans are not simply reactive creatures; they also actively choose and create individual stimulus environments. For example, if your television set malfunctions, you can *react* by adjusting the controls to alter the sound or picture. But even if there is no malfunction, you can *act* spontaneously, changing channels and seeking more interesting programming—or turning off the power completely.

In the cognitive model, some of the most significant behavior emerges from totally new ways of thinking, not necessarily from predictable ways used in the past. The ability to imagine options and alternatives enables people to work toward new futures that transcend limited realities. For example, a threatened animal has only limited options for defending itself, and it may behave wildly if it is unsuccessful in meeting this need. In contrast, a threatened human can think of many ways to escape, fight back, or seek protection. The ability to think of options makes everyone responsible for the choices he or she eventually makes.

The cognitive perspective on the case of Kathy O. invites us to look "inside Kathy's head." As behaviorists note, we cannot directly observe inner processes or know *what* Kathy was thinking—but we are fairly certain that Kathy *was* thinking and that her thoughts had some impact on her behavior. During the race, what was Kathy paying attention to? Did she notice who was watching her? Could she have felt distracted? Did running prevent her from thinking clearly, so that her fear of losing the race overwhelmed her? The cognitive approach assumes there are connections between what people perceive, think, decide, and do. To understand human action, we must first understand human cognition.

The Humanistic Approach

Just as cognitive psychology developed in part as a reaction against the rigidity of behaviorism, the *humanistic* approach developed in part as a reaction against the limits of the psychodynamic approach. Psychodynamic views are sometimes criticized as pessimistic about human nature, characterizing behavior as determined by ancient and unconscious conflicts. In contrast, the humanistic view characterizes human beings as active, not reactive, as well as innately good and capable of choice. The **humanistic approach** *to psychology views the main task for human beings as striving for growth and developing their potential.* For example, you have a sense not only of the person you actually are, but also of the person you could be if you succeeded in living up to your potential. The gap between your actual and possible selves can be a source of motivation in your life, and inspire you to overcome obstacles and meet challenges.

The humanistic psychologist takes a *holistic* view of the individual, dealing with the interplay among mental, bodily, behavioral, social, and cultural forces in the whole person. The humanistic psychologist also examines the individual's life history for patterns and themes. For example, suppose you felt unloved as a child, and undertook some risky and self-defeating behaviors to make up for the love you missed. A humanistic psychologist would focus on whether and why *you felt* you were unloved—not on whether or not you really were unloved. It is only your view of your life that provides understanding of your behavior; your subjective view of yourself and your world is the only view that has any *psychological reality*.

From a humanistic perspective, Kathy O.'s actions would be seen as the outcome of Kathy's own view of herself and her world. Was Kathy's self-image tied to feeling loved and respected only when she competed successfully? Was she testing her friends and family to see how they would deal with her failure? Was she trying to dramatically change the basis of her sense of self-worth? Only Kathy can answer these questions, and only her answers would satisfy a humanistic psychologist's questions about why she ended her race—and almost her life—so tragically.

The humanistic perspective diverges not only from the psychodynamic view of motivation, but also from the behaviorist prohibition against investigating inner states. Since the humanistic approach first emerged in the 1950s, it has expanded psychology beyond the confines of science to include valuable lessons from other human endeavors, such as literature, history, and the arts. By growing in this way, psychology becomes a more complete discipline, balancing scientific empiricism (which relies on sensory evidence) with the nonempirical, imaginative riches of the humanities.

The Evolutionary Approach

Where did human beings come from? Why are we built as we are, and why do we behave as we do? For most of human history, no *scientific* account was developed to answer these questions. Other, nonscientific approaches to knowledge offered biblical, revelatory, or other explanations for human nature. But in 1859, British scholar **Charles Darwin** published *On the Origin of Species*, which first proposed that environmental forces "naturally selected" certain biological organisms for survival and procreation. Darwin theorized that those organisms that inherited advantageous features survived and succeeded in passing these features on to their offspring. Eventually, species *evolved* because their inherited adaptive characteristics made them fittest in the competition to survive in particular environments.

The concept of behavioral and mental *adaptiveness* is the basis for an *evolutionary* perspective in psychology. The **evolutionary approach** *assumes that human mental abilities, like physical abilities, evolved over millions of years to serve particular adaptive purposes.* "Adaptive" behavior, however, is not necessarily the same as promoting the good of the species or even of the individual. Adaptiveness means only that the genes carried in the individual will be replicated and further carried by the adapting individual's offspring and relatives. Since gene survival is the goal of adaptation, it may even be adaptive to sacrifice one's own life to save the lives—and protect the genes—of one's children or kin.

Archaeological evidence indicates that, for most of humans' evolutionary history, people lived in small groups as hunter-gatherers. Evolutionary psychologists have considered the unique threats and challenges these evolving protohumans faced, and then generated inferences about the psychological features and strategies that might have evolved to solve those problems. The ways we cope with life today may be a legacy inherited from ancestors who survived in a very harsh world very different from our own. It is possible that some of our natural reactions to difficulty in modern life are better suited to the simple but lethal dangers our ancestors faced many thousands of years ago. In the evolutionary view, human behavior is still evolving.

Was Kathy O.'s tragedy a case of adaptive behavior gone awry? Running away makes sense if a predator is threatening to harm you. But what if the

By giving humans a common ancestry with other animals, Darwin's theory of evolution changed the way people think of themselves—a change not entirely pleasing to some.

threat were *inside* you, as were Kathy's fears and frustrations? One might have an impulse to flee, but you cannot escape yourself. A runner as swift as Kathy might easily have escaped an attacker, but giving in to her inherited impulse to run would not be adaptive to modern psychological threats such as disappointment and humiliation.

The Sociocultural Approach

Each of the above perspectives helps us to understand some aspects of behavior and mental processes by focusing on one general model or approach to examining the causes of human functioning. Curiously, psychologists have long ignored one of the most important determinants of people's perception, thought, emotion, and action: *culture*. Only recently have some psychological scholars begun to argue that a *sociocultural perspective* must be central to modern psychology. **Culture** *is a set of concepts, values, and assumptions about life developed to increase survival and satisfaction, and communicated or shared with others in the same environment.* Culture imposes a special set of lenses for seeing the world in certain ways, and these differ across different societies. Guidelines for behaviors set by culture are transmitted in child-rearing and shape personalities. Your society (*socio-*) and your culture (*cultural*) influence you, throughout your life, to cultivate certain habits and reject other practices.

Surrounded by your own sociocultural influences, you may take them for granted, or not even be able to recognize how what seems "natural" to you is alien to others. Wearing shorts and a tank top and drinking beer in public on a hot day might seem perfectly acceptable behavior for an American college woman, for example, but would be prohibited among Moslem women. Crossing the street against a red traffic light is common for many New Yorkers, but it is alien behavior among Japanese pedestrians in Tokyo. The groups, traditions, and institutions that maintain sociocultural influences are so broad, so much larger than the individual's daily level of interaction, that they may seem invisible (Georgas, 1989). The **sociocultural approach** *to psychology argues that, to predict individual behavior, it is necessary to take into account very broad influences, including the individual's environment, social organization, community, cultural values, and family.*

An individual's culture includes his or her way of categorizing people and events, naming and interpreting experiences, and distinguishing between what we share and do not share in common with others. Sociocultural influences also determine the roles we play and the informal rules or *norms* society uses to govern our behavior. Since sociocultural influences pervade psychology, this text devotes special discussions (Cultural Context boxes) to sociocultural considerations in most chapters. You will also notice specific research and examples highlighted with the 🌎 logo, indicating other instances of sociocultural influence. (After reading this section, please turn to the box on Cultural Context: The Importance of Diversity on page 21.)

A streamlined way to outline the interplay between the broad factors of the sociocultural approach is suggested in the following framework (Triandis, 1994):

Ecology → Culture → Socialization → Personality → Individual Behavior

Ecology represents the physical environment: the climate, geography, and natural resources that underlie a community's ability to maintain its survival. These resources make possible behaviors such as hunting, fishing, farming, mining, and relating to the land and the natural world. Practiced over time,

CULTURAL CONTEXT

The Importance of Diversity

Assume that a Caucasian male from the American middle class is attending Protestant church services with an acquaintance who is an African American from a similar economic background. Are there cultural differences that, if poorly understood, might influence whether or not this acquaintanceship becomes a friendship? The answer is "yes" (Kochman, 1981).

One cultural difference centers on the amount of emotional expressiveness considered appropriate for churchgoers. At church services where most members are white, the culture dictates that highly emotional displays of religious fervor are rare. People pray and sing aloud, but rarely with intense emotions. They listen to the pastor's sermon but rarely make comments about its content while the pastor is speaking. The cultural guidance is different, however, at church services where most members are African American. At many such churches, it is considered appropriate for people to have very intense emotional experiences during church services. People sing with great fervor. While the pastor speaks, congregation members shout their comments about various parts of the message. During some services, one or more people faint. This rarely causes a problem, however, since the cultural guidance includes provision of a nurse at church services.

In investigating the influence of culture, we study the reasons for observed behaviors. For an investigation of different cultural behaviors at church, psychologists could look to history. When slavery was an accepted part of American culture, African Americans were not allowed to express strong emotions in the presence of Caucasians. Attendance at church provided one of the few opportunities for African Americans to express themselves freely.

Whenever culture and cultural differences are discussed, psychologists should be careful to keep in mind that there will be individual differences. Not all people will accept the guidance that their culture offers. Some African Americans will prefer to attend services at churches where emotional expressiveness is low. Some Caucasians join churches where emotional displays are prominent, such as some Fundamental Baptist groups in the American South. Without paying attention to individual differences, people also run the risk of holding unhelpful and demeaning stereotypes. For example, this discussion of one cultural difference should not be expanded to a broader statement about the amount of control people have over their emotions.

Students of psychology face the challenge of not only keeping in mind that cultural differences exist, but also of knowing that there will always be exceptions, due to the complexities of individuals.

these responses become automatic ways of acting, developing into habits and customs—that is, they cultivate a *culture*. Individuals within that culture draw on their experiences and knowledge in deciding how to rear their children and teach them to fit into that social setting, a set of practices known as *socialization*. Children raised to be adventurous or risk-taking in order to become good hunters, for example, will incorporate these lessons into their own *personalities*, their individual patterns of responding and interacting with the environment and other people. Ultimately, therefore, the chain of sociocultural influence translates a group's response to an ecological setting into each group member's *individual behavior*.

The sociocultural perspective provides an important reminder that most of the psychology you will study in this text and in your course is based on the distinctive *individualistic* cultural tradition of Western, Anglo-European values. In these societies—of which we authors and most of you, our readers, are a part—what is most prized is individual achievement, with special value awarded to independence, dominance, and competition. In contrast, in the *collectivist* societies that make up the majority of the world's documented cultures, different basic values apply. Collectivist cultures emphasize community over self, cooperation over competition, humility over "winning," politeness at the expense of self-promotion, and devoting one's efforts to service rather than to individual achievement. These values lead not only to different social structures but also to alternative ways of relating to people, the environment, and one's very sense of self.

Incorporating such a sociocultural perspective into "mainstream" psychology, born of extremely individualistic traditions, will be difficult but also enriching, because of the greater diversity it will bring to our discipline, and broadening, because of the wider range of people addressed by—and involved in—the work of psychology thus defined(see Markus & Kitayama, 1991; Triandis, 1989, 1990).

For a final perspective on Kathy O.'s experience, consider what Kathy's society and culture have taught her about competition, winning—and the price of failure. Even if her parents and friends did not care whether Kathy won this particular race, Kathy would surely have learned that in American culture, as one coach has been quoted as saying, "Winning isn't everything—it's the *only* thing." For a dedicated, trained athlete like Kathy O., what would the prospects be for life after defeat? How would Kathy expect to be treated by others, and how would she treat herself? A cliché in our language involves protesting that, rather than going through some dreaded experience, we "would rather die." If Kathy felt, in a stressful moment during the race, that she "would rather die" than fall behind and possibly lose, she may have felt she no longer had anything else to lose. Fortunately, with greater global awareness and communication, psychologists are addressing the messages culture transmits to us. Eventually people may be able to question cultural assumptions carefully enough to make choices that are informed and healthy, rather than desperate.

Table 1.1 depicts a summary of the key distinctions among the seven current perspectives in modern psychology. Take a moment to review it now, and then check your recall of this section before moving on to learn about how psychologists ask and answer psychological questions.

TABLE 1.1	COMPARISON OF SEVEN APPROACHES TO MODERN PSYCHOLOGY			
Approach	View of Human Nature	What Determines Behavior	Focus of Study	Primary Focus of Research
Biological	Passive; mechanistic	Heredity; biochemistry	Brain, nervous system; endocrine system	Biochemical basis of behavior and mental processes
Psychodynamic	Instinct-driven	Heredity; early experience	Mental forces; conflicts	Behavior as overt expression of inner motives
Behavioristic	Reactive to stimulation; modifiable	Environment; stimulus conditions	Specific overt responses	Behavior and its stimulus causes and consequences
Cognitive	Creatively active; stimulus reactive	Stimulus conditions; mental processes	Mental processes; language	Mental processes inferred from behavioral responses
Humanistic	Active ; unlimited in potential	Potentially self-directed	Human experience and potentials	Life patterns; values; goals
Evolutionary	Adapted to solving problems of early human societies	Adaptations and environmental cues for survival	Evolved psychological adaptations	Mental mechanisms in terms of evolved adaptive functions
Sociocultural	Responsive to social and traditional influences	Environmental demands on culture; socialization	Value systems; mechanisms for transmitting culture	Cross-cultural differences; norms; social roles

Check Your Recall

Psychologists have developed seven major approaches to studying behavior and the mental processes underlying behavior. Each of these perspectives offers a unique view of what is considered most important, what should be investigated, and how.

The biological approach explains mental and behavioral events in terms of biological processes such as brain function and genetic influences. The psychodynamic approach originated by Sigmund Freud explains behavior in terms of psychological drives and conflicts within an individual's past and personality. The behavioristic approach rejects mentalistic concerns as unscientific and advocates the study of only the causes and consequences of observable behavior. The cognitive perspective calls for a legitimate focus on the thoughts that cause and shape behavior. The humanistic approach adopts a more positive view of human nature than psychodynamic theories do, arguing that people are motivated to grow productively and meet their potential as human beings. The evolutionary approach emphasizes that behavior must be adaptive, either now or in humans' evolutionary past. Finally, the sociocultural approach reminds us that individual behavior is developed and expressed in a cultural context, which has influenced it according to the values of a particular time, place, and people. No one of these seven approaches is better than the others, but together they form an array of angles that reflect the diversity and richness of modern psychology.

Psychological Research

After a consideration of the subject matter and perspectives of psychology, we turn now to an examination of how psychologists *do* psychology. Given the definition of psychology and its distinction as a science, psychologists must gather data about behavior and mental processes. Exactly how is this accomplished?

You are already a daily consumer of mass media reports on research findings, some surprising and others seemingly "commonsensical." But some of the "research" you may learn about in news or entertainment broadcasts may be confusing, misleading, or downright false. Given that most people are fascinated with the substance of psychology—their own and others' thoughts, feelings, and actions—it has become necessary to be a careful, choosy consumer of research-based conclusions. For example, when a news broadcaster cites the results of a recent preelection poll, you will only be able to use—or discard—the "information" presented if you know how to interpret the conclusions offered. You can do this by learning *how* psychological research is conducted and *why* the scientific view of knowledge dictates such methods. We turn now to *how* psychologists know *what* they know.

Recall that scientific investigation requires collecting information first-hand, a process known as *empirical investigation*. **Empirical investigation** *is research that relies on sensory experience and observation as research data.* In contrast, some people may rely on "a personal hunch," feeling lucky, or clues in their daily horoscope to collect information and make decisions. To investigate a question empirically is to ask the questions directly and collect information, rather than consult a second-hand reference or a source that no one else can hear or see. "Empirical" means "experience-based" rather than based on faith, armchair speculation, or "common sense." Empirical investigation is a useful strategy for learning about every aspect of life in the natural world. Even if you never do psychological research, you will find that asking and answering empirical questions will improve your critical thinking skills and life choices.

The Context of Discovery

All scientific researchers begin with the assumption of determinism, the idea that natural events result from specific causes that can be *determined* through careful study. Psychologists further assume that behavior and mental activities follow set patterns—relationships that can be discovered through research. The research process itself proceeds in two stages: getting an idea (*discovery*) and then testing it (*justification*). The **context of discovery** *is the initial phase of research during which an investigator comes up with a new idea or a different way of thinking about phenomena.* (Note: We will often refer to "phenomena" in this text, meaning events and processes that can be described but are not yet fully explained. The word is borrowed from ancient Greek, so the singular form is *phenomenon* while the plural is *phenomena*).

Asking Research Questions   Research often begins with a question: Why or how does a particular psychological event or process occur? For example, most people belong to various groups, including friendship networks, families, clubs, business organizations, and religious congregations. Some of these group ties are taken very seriously and become part of one's identity, while others are more casual and easily lost or severed. *What causes a person to be more loyal to one group than to another?* In pursuing this and other research questions, the psychological researcher focuses on four sets of concerns:

1. The *stimulus events* that cause a particular response to begin, end, or change;
2. The *structure* of behavior that links certain actions to other actions in a predictable, orderly way;
3. The *relationships* between internal psychological processes and external, observable patterns of behavior; and,
4. The *consequences* the responsive behavior has on the individual's social and physical environment.

To show how these concerns guide research, we will first summarize a classic experimental study in social psychology, and then identify each of these four focal concerns in our example.

Beginning with a question about why some groups foster greater loyalty among their members than others, two social psychologists, Elliot Aronson and Judson Mills, in 1959 conducted a now-classic study of the effects of *group initiation*. In response to their own research question, Aronson and Mills guessed that a member's loyalty to a group might actually be strengthened by a difficult initiation. They reasoned that surviving a painful or embarrassing initiation might cause a new member to work harder to rationalize the less enjoyable aspects of membership, whereas a member who gained easy access to a group would be less motivated to value and enjoy the benefits of belonging. To test their idea, Aronson and Mills invited college women (their subjects) to join group discussions about sex, a daring topic in the late 1950s. Before being permitted to join the group, each woman was required to prove her ability to discuss the subject freely by reading a word list aloud to a male organizer. Some women were given a word list that included common terms that were easy to read; others were given a list containing embarrassing obscenities and slang. All "passed" the initiation and were asked to "listen in" on a group discussion in progress. Although the discussion the women heard was scripted to be a disappointing bore, only the women who had read the easy list rated it as uninteresting. The women who had survived the embar-

Most people belong to several different groups, but not all groups evoke the same level of involvement or loyalty from their members.

rassment of reading the difficult list aloud insisted they enjoyed listening to the discussion and looked forward to joining it. This elegant experiment confirmed the researchers' suspicion: the more severe their initiation, the greater the loyalty members will feel to the group.

In this example of the principle that "people come to love what they have suffered for," the stimulus event is the nature of the initiation, whether it was severe or easy. The dependent variable was the subjects' rating of how enjoyable and interesting they found the group discussion to be. Intervening between the initiation ritual and the misperception of the boring discussion (judging it to be really interesting) was the subjects' need to justify having endured an embarrassing task only to be disappointed in the "prize," an uninteresting group discussion. This motivation to rationalize one's behavior when it does not fit with its consequences is known as *cognitive dissonance,* about which we will say more in Chapter 12.

Proposing Explanations   While much research begins with a good question, the investigative process can also be inspired by a good *theory.* A **theory** *is a set of related principles used to explain or predict some phenomenon.* Psychological theories attempt to understand how brain, mind, behavior, and the environment function and how they may be interrelated. For example, in the study by Aronson and Mills (1959) summarized above, the researchers relied on a theory that humans seek consistency and meaning. When individuals' experiences seem conflicting or unexplainable, they will try to figure out what to do by first restoring a sense of consistency and "rightness." The women whose initiation into the "sex discussion group" had been fairly easy rightly judged the subsequent discussion to be as boring as it was scripted to be. But those who had undergone humiliation and embarrassment in order to join the same discussion group needed to *rationalize* having suffered to participate in this same discussion—so they formed positive, loyal attitudes about the group and its talk in order to feel their initiation was "worth it."

The value of a theory can be measured in terms of the new ideas and potential explanations it generates. A **hypothesis** *is a tentative and testable explanation of the relationship between two or more events or variables being studied.* In the Aronson and Mills study, the variables were the *difficulty level* of the lists the women were asked to read aloud (easy versus difficult) and the *ratings* the women gave the brief group discussion they listened in on. The researchers' hypothesis was that list difficulty would determine ratings—specifically, that women who read the difficult list would justify the experience by giving the group discussion more positive ratings than those who read the easy list. To be useful in research, a hypothesis must be *testable*—that is, the researchers must be able to formulate ways to find out whether the hypothesis is or is not borne out by the actual data collected. If Aronson and Mills had found no difference in the ratings of the women who read the easy versus the difficult lists, their hypothesis would not have been supported, and they might have questioned the validity of the original theory that people need consistency in their experiences.

Overcoming Research Biases   The hardest part of doing research is remaining objective, as we noted earlier in this chapter. Most of your ideas and beliefs are probably somewhat biased because they are influenced by your opinions or values. Five specific sources of bias regularly challenge researchers:

1. *External influences* such as culture or media can persuade people to accept a particular world view. (A college student may be influenced by classmates' conservative politics to adopt views very different from the more liberal ones she was raised to accept.)

2. *Personal bias* distorts one's ability to estimate or evaluate what is observed because of one's personal beliefs, characteristics, or past experiences. (An interviewer who is racially prejudiced may find it hard to believe that a job applicant of his own race is less qualified than an applicant who happens to be a member of the disliked race.)

3. *Observer bias* occurs when one's prejudices or opinions act as "filters" to determine whether some events are noticed or seen as meaningful while others are not. (Some sports announcers seem to believe that white athletes must work hard to be successful, while African-American athletes are naturally gifted so their achievements do not represent the same degree of motivated effort. Observing failure, such a biased observer might advise a white athlete to practice more, but conclude that a failing African-American athlete just "doesn't have it" any more.)

4. *Expectancy bias* affects observations when the observer expects—and looks for—certain outcomes to follow observed events. (A teacher who believes a particular student will do outstanding work may award her an A without really noticing that her performance was not deserving of such a high grade.)

5. Finally, *placebo biases* occur when people strongly believe that a treatment is working when in fact there is no objective basis for its alleged success. Believing in the power of a drug can lead to marked pain reduction, even though the "medication" is chemically inert, a sugar pill (see Roberts et al., 1993). The same placebo effect can occur in those who are positive placebo responders when they believe a certain person has the power to heal their pain or sickness. (A chronic pain patient may claim he has been cured by a healer whom he strongly believes in.)

In the context of discovery, researchers formulate questions, consider the predictions of theories, and formulate hypotheses. They also decide what processes and which individuals to study. Research "subjects" are really living people or animals, cooperating with researchers to provide clues to important psychological processes. All subjects deserve care, respect, and ethical treatment. Consider Focus on Science: The Ethical Treatment of Subjects (page 28) before reading on about the details of the second phase of scientific investigation, the context of justification.

HIRAM S. DUDSON
1930 - 1993

Member,
Placebo Group

D. Reilly

The Context of Justification

After discovering an idea that might answer one's research question, the researcher must *justify* this idea. The **context of justification** *is the second phase of research, in which results are prepared for useful communication with other scientists.* Data must be collected, based on the ideas generated in the context of discovery. These data must be analyzed in order to ascertain their meaning—that is, whether the few measurements a researcher has taken can really prove something about the hypothesis one way or the other. Two components in justification are a commitment to *scientific values* and the employment of *objectivity safeguards.*

Scientific Values   Before a new theory or hypothesis makes a difference in science, it must undergo an "ordeal of proof." Most often this happens when researchers publish (make public) their findings and other scholars investigate whether they find the same patterns in their own data. This process of publication and communication moves scientific research into the public eye, where ideas are tested and proven. After Aronson and Mills concluded their study of the effects of initiation on group liking, they submitted their research report for publication in the *Journal of Abnormal and Social Psychology* so their findings might be considered—and they hoped, verified—by other researchers.

Turn now to the alphabetized References section near the end of this book to find the complete listing for Aronson and Mills's published report. Throughout this text you will find we have listed one or more *citations*—authors' names and publication dates—to indicate the published source of ideas and arguments we are presenting here. Make it a habit to look up the complete reference for any citation whose point seems especially interesting to you. A good library will enable you to complete the search process and locate a copy of the original article, chapter, or book. References are what you must track down in conducting a literature review, the first step in pursuing your own first-hand investigation into a topic or process that interests you. By doing a "reference check" from time to time, you will make the material your own, and will benefit from it more than if you simply take our word for it.

Scientists approach their work with a combination of curiosity, skepticism, and discipline. Being curious leads most scientists to be fairly open-minded while retaining high standards for data collection and analysis. Skepticism makes researchers cautious about abandoning useful theories before good alternative explanations have been verified. Discipline guarantees that scientific research will be reviewed by other scholars in order to determine what it means and how it can be utilized. These are the values of the *scientific community,* a collection of individuals sharing the commitment to seek verifiable knowledge. Science is not a set of rules but a *process* of asking, observing, explaining, testing, retesting, and communicating discoveries about reality. Science is a way of knowing, not a political game or a hierarchy of authorities. You do not need a special degree or uniform to act like a scientist, but you *do* need to make a commitment to safeguarding objectivity.

Objectivity Safeguards   In the context of justification, the researcher is challenged to overcome the various sources of bias anticipated in the discovery phase. Preventive measures or safeguards begin with keeping complete *records* of observations and data analyses in a form that other researchers can understand and evaluate. This is why, within a discipline, most scientific reports are written in a similar form and published by organizations of scientists.

A second safeguard is *standardization.* **Standardization** *refers to the use of uniform, consistent procedures in all phases of data collection.* When all

The Ethical Treatment of Subjects

Respect for the basic rights of humans and animals who participate in psychological research is a fundamental obligation of all researchers. To guarantee that these rights are honored, special committees oversee every research proposal, imposing strict guidelines issued by the U.S. Department of Health and Human Services. Psychology departments at universities and colleges, hospitals, and research institutes each have review panels that approve and reject proposals for human and animal research. The American Psychological Association (1982) has established clear ethical standards for researchers. Here we briefly review several ethical concerns and their guidelines: risk/gain assessment; informed consent; deception and debriefing; and humane treatment of animals.

Risk/Gain Assessment In most psychological experiments, the risk to subjects is minimal (for example, brief eye strain from focusing on visual stimuli). Some procedures, however, can be upsetting or disturbing because they involve emotional reactions or social pressures. Subjects' physical and psychological well-being is a priority of all research, so these risks must be minimized, explained, and safeguarded by precautions. The same procedures apply to animal research, where humane and considerate treatment is essential.

Informed Consent Typically all research with human subjects begins with a description of the procedures, risks, and benefits each subject might experience. After receiving this information, subjects voluntarily sign statements indicating that they have given their *informed consent* to participate, and are reminded they may cease their participation at any time. Subjects are also invited to contact the researchers for further information.

Deception and Debriefing For some kinds of research, advance explanations make unbiased study impossible. Informed subjects may be too self-conscious to behave in a natural or genuine way. In such cases subjects are usually deceived with a cover story that distorts the true nature or purpose of the experiment. For example, if a subject were told that the study in which she will participate involves the effects of frustration on performance, she might become more nervous than usual because she anticipates being frustrated, or she might perform better than usual because she has prepared herself after being forewarned. To avoid either extreme, the researcher may tell her only that the experiment focuses on problem solving; this half-truth omits any mention of frustration, and it avoids either alarming or warning the subject in advance.

After the experiment, all subjects are *debriefed*. **Debriefing** *involves giving each subject a full and honest account of the true purposes and assumptions of the research at the conclusion of the subject's participation.* During postexperimental debriefing, the researcher provides as much information as possible about the study, making certain that no subject departs with any remaining confusion, discomfort, or embarrassment. Any deception and its purpose are completely explained, and all questions are answered. Ultimately, subjects have the right to withdraw their data if they feel abused or misused in any way.

Advocates of the use of limited deception argue that most subjects enjoy participation and, when debriefed, accept having been deceived. Critics argue that this does not excuse deception, which violates every subject's basic right of informed consent. Most researchers seek compromise by (1) avoiding designs that would require deception, (2) minimizing deception when it is used, and (3) debriefing all subjects thoroughly after their participation.

Humane Treatment of Animals In recent years, concern over the care and treatment of animals used in psychological and biomedical research has led to the development of strict guidelines that researchers must follow to obtain funding and approval. Laboratory facilities must be maintained properly, use qualified staff, and monitor animals' health and well-being. Pain and discomfort must be minimized, and the least stressful treatments must be applied whenever possible.

The debate over animal testing and research goes beyond issues of ethics. It centers on society's recognition of the contributions that animal and human research make every day to the health and well-being of all species, notably in drug treatment for humans and veterinary medicine for domestic animals. Animal researchers today subscribe to higher standards of care and concern than most keepers of companion animals (pets) and farm animals. Attitudes about animal research may also be complicated by cultural prejudices that favor "cute" creatures (such as dogs, cats, and mice) and regard others (such as slugs, worms, and rats) with less sympathy.

Ultimately, all citizens must keep themselves informed about the overall costs and benefits of animal research to humans and to animals. Taking uninformed actions to end such research would be both unnecessary and self-defeating. In a democracy, as in scientific endeavors, rational information should guide decisions. Research is not developed in a vacuum, but is produced in a cultural context of attitudes about values, priorities, and human and animal rights. As attitudes change across the cultures, so do research practices and ethics.

subjects are treated in the same way, researchers ensure they will have the same basic experiences.

A third safeguard involves setting clear, specific meanings for the concepts being studied. An **operational definition** *of a concept defines that concept in terms of how it is being measured or what operations produce it.* For example, an operational definition of an A in one class may be "earning at least 90 percent of all possible test points." This definition tells you that the instructor adds the points each student earns and then calculates the percentage that represents of all points possible—that is, the definition tells you the operation used to determine a particular grade. Operational definitions are important in psychological research because many psychological terms are also words used in everyday language, but in a different way than psychologists use them. For example, if a new drug promises to reduce "anxiety," what does that mean for you? You need to know whether the drug manufacturer's definition of anxiety is the same as yours. For you, anxiety could mean feeling occasionally nervous before being evaluated, such as before a test. But for the pharmaceutical company's researchers, anxiety could refer to a set of symptoms observed among patients in psychiatric hospitals. A drug developed to reduce that kind of anxiety might not be appropriate for treating what you call anxiety. You and the drug company have different operational definitions.

As reviewed earlier, bias from external sources, personal beliefs, observers' prejudices, and human expectations can all distort data. A fourth way researchers attempt to safeguard objectivity is to use various *control* procedures to keep hypothesis-testing fair and unbiased. One such control strategy is to keep research subjects experimentally *blind*. **Blind** *subjects are uninformed about the purpose of the research study or some key part of it.* An even stronger strategy is for the researcher to have assistants conduct the study, and to keep both them and the subjects uninformed about the purpose and conditions of the research. *A control procedure in which both researchers and subjects are uninformed about the nature of the independent variable being administered to the subjects is a* **double-blind** *control.* For example, in a double-blind drug study, neither those administering the drug nor the volunteers taking the pills will know who is getting the real drug and who is receiving the placebo. The experimenters will not inadvertently treat the "real drug" subjects differently or scrutinize them more closely, and the subjects will not be able to detect any clue about how they are "supposed" to be responding to the pills.

Finally, researchers must be careful to consider all possible influences on the behavior being studied. Recall that the independent variable is the stimulus condition assumed to influence the psychological process or event being studied, and the dependent variable is the influenced action or experience. **Confounding variables** *are changeable factors that could be confused with the independent variable and thus distort the results.* For example, in the study we presented earlier of administering a drug (such as Ritalin) to control hyperkinetic behavior among schoolchildren, what might be some confounding variables at work to distort the results or confuse their interpretation? The drug's effect might differ because of: different body weights; when the subjects had last eaten; administration at different times of day; whether the drug was administered orally or by injection; and whether the drug was given in a group setting or individually. Unless the researcher arranges to have all such possible confounding variables controlled—that is, similar among all the subjects, or statistically adjusted for individual differences among the subjects—the results could be due to any or all of these variables and not limited to the kind and amount of the independent variable.

Research Methods

All research is designed to answer some question of interest to the investigator. Some questions are generated by a theory or basic research issues, such as Aronson and Mills's test of a prediction made by *dissonance theory* that people will come to love what they suffer for (Festinger, 1957). Other questions come from curiosity based on personal experience, such as whether and how men

"WE PLAN TO DETERMINE, ONCE AND FOR ALL, IF THERE REALLY <u>ARE</u> ANY CULTURAL DIFFERENCES BETWEEN THEM."

dominate conversations they have with women. And still others emerge from practical problems that psychologists wish to help solve, such as whether and how high-risk individuals can be taught behavior that reduces their chances for contracting AIDS.

The first step in research is to formulate the question to be investigated in as precise a way as possible, defining the relevant variables' objective, and then deciding how to *measure* them. After we outline the three major ways that psychologists measure behaviors of interest to them, we will consider the two most basic types of research design: those that try to correlate different sets of responses (*correlational methods*) and those that try to establish causal links between stimuli and responses (*experimentation*).

Psychological Measurement   Because psychological processes are so varied and complex, measuring them poses major challenges to researchers. The first challenge is to access the psychological phenomenon one wants to understand. A second challenge is to find the right measure, or the best *outcome variable*, to assess the psychological phenomenon described in the theory or hypothesis. In our study of hyperkinetic behavior reduction, the outcome variable might be time spent sitting at one's desk or reading assigned work, or it might be calories burned within a given time period, or even teachers' ratings of the subjects' mobility or calm.

All attempts at measurement use some procedure to assign numbers to, or *quantify,* different levels, sizes, intensities, or amounts of a variable. Assigning numbers to variables increases the precision of scientific communication procedures and results. Psychologists use three important methods of descriptive measurement: self-reports, behavior analysis, and physiological measures.

Self-report measures *are verbal answers, either written or spoken, to questions posed by researchers.* When you tell a poll-taker your age, occupation, and political preferences, you are providing a self-report. Although self-reports cannot be obtained in many research circumstances (for example, from nonhuman subjects or preverbal children), such self-report measures as questionnaires, surveys, and interviews are popular because they are often convenient and easy to obtain.

Behavioral measures *are techniques used to study overt, observable, and recordable actions.* It is often most useful, especially early in an investigation, to directly observe subjects being studied or tested in their normal environments. For example, to study how college students form close relationships, you should begin by going where *they* go and watching them meet, make contact, and interact.

Physiological measures *collect data based on subjects' biological responses to stimuli.* Such measures would be undertaken to access information about less observable processes like brain activity. For example, the *electroencephalogram (EEG)* is one apparatus for recording the electrical activity of the brain. The patterns of waveforms it records provide clues about which parts of the brain are involved in various activities. Physiological measures are difficult to obtain since they are *invasive* (they intrude on subjects' sensory awareness and can change their behavior) and require sophisticated equipment and operation. Such problems, however, might be compensated for if the questions are important, the subjects are cooperative, and alternative measures (such as self-reports) could not be relied on for the information needed.

Research Design   When first asking a research question, a psychologist often looks for evidence of any kind of relationship between the variables of interest. Is intelligence related to creativity? Are optimists healthier than

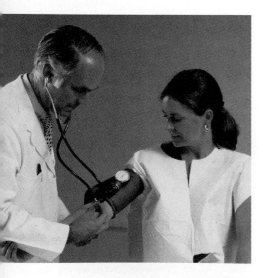

Physiological measures, such as blood pressure, can indicate subtle behavioral changes that reveal psychological states such as anxiety or arousal.

pessimists? For such a search, a *correlational design* is the most sensible approach to research. Once the existence of a relationship has been discovered and confirmed, however, the next question will likely focus on which variable is influencing which—that is, defining the exact *causal relationship* between the variables. To specify causality, only an *experimental design* will serve the researcher's purposes.

Correlation **Correlational methods** *are used to determine the extent to which two variables, traits, or attributes are related.* General questions like those above—concerning the relationship of intelligence to creativity, or optimism and health—are correlational questions.

To determine the precise extent of a correlational relationship between two variables, a psychologist will collect two sets of scores, one for each of the two variables, and use these numbers to calculate a single statistic, known as a *correlation coefficient.* A **correlation coefficient,** *symbolized by the letter* r, *summarizes the size (ranging from 0 to 1) and the direction (positive or negative) of the relationship between two variables.* If two variables are completely related, each accounts for 100 percent of what happens to the other, and their correlation coefficient is 1.00; if they have no relationship at all, their coefficient is 0. If they are related in the same direction—as one variable's scores increase, so do the other's—they are *positively* correlated (for example, $+1.00$). In contrast, if one variable decreases as the other increases, they are *negatively* correlated, and their coefficient would have a minus sign (for example, -1.00).

Consider variables in your own life that might be correlated. When you were a growing child, your age was probably positively correlated with your physical height. As you got older, you also grew taller: records of your age and height at regular intervals would both steadily increase. On the other hand, some of your behaviors might be negatively correlated with other experiences. How is study time correlated with the amount of anxiety you feel just prior to taking a test? For most people, the *less* time spent studying for a test, the *more* anxiety they probably experience before and during the test session. If this is true for you, then the variable "study time" is negatively correlated with the variable "test anxiety."

Experimentation These examples are purposely simple to help clarify the meaning of correlational power and direction (positive or negative). But for most psychological research, the relationship among variables may not be so obvious. Further, researchers often want to know not only whether two variables are related, but which one is causing the other to change. To find out if one variable is causally related to another, a researcher must rely on *experimental methods.*

Every experiment is designed to answer the question: Does the independent variable cause a predicted change in the dependent variable? Scientists often use the notation X to represent the independent variable and the symbol Y for the dependent variable. Thus the relationship being tested by the experiment is $X \rightarrow Y$. (The arrow indicates the direction of causality.) In a **controlled experiment,** *observations of specific behavior are made under systematically varied conditions, in which subjects have been randomly assigned to experimental and control (nontreatment) conditions.* Let's examine this process one concept at a time: experimental conditions, control conditions, random assignment, and behavioral observation.

An experimenter first selects subjects who will participate in the research and whose behavior will be recorded. Next, the experimenter designs two or more different ways of treating these subjects. For example, in a study of a

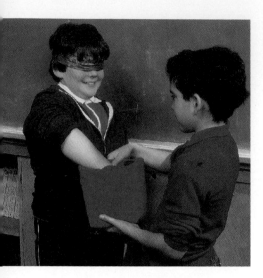

In random assignment, experimental subjects are chosen to be in a particular condition (either experimental or control) totally at random. Thus each subject has an equal chance of being in any of the conditions. We use random procedures, such as drawing names out of a hat, in order to ensure fairness of opportunity for all participants.

drug's effectiveness, some subjects will receive the experimental drug and others will receive a placebo. The treatment or treatments that apply the independent variable make up the *experimental condition* of the experiment. Subjects who receive the placebo or no treatment at all—so they can be compared to the experimental subjects—are in the *control condition*.

Essential to any experiment is *randomization*. Once subjects volunteer and are selected for participation, their assignment to either the experimental or control conditions must not be confounded with any characteristics of the subjects themselves. **Randomization** *is a process of assigning subjects in such a way that each subject has an equal chance of ending up in any of the conditions, experimental or control.* In this way, there should be no differences between groups of subjects *before* the independent variable is administered. For example, suppose you wanted to study the effects of hunger on behavior, and you ask some friends to skip one, two, three, or no meals during a 24-hour period just prior to your measuring the behavior that interests you. If you assign only willing friends, such as experienced dieters, to the skip-three-meals condition, the effects of hunger (skipping meals) will be confounded with their preferences, and you will not know what your experimental results really mean. Did your subjects act as they did because they were hungry or not hungry, or because they were more or less experienced in skipping meals already? To guard against such errors, you must assign subjects to each of the four meal conditions entirely at random, so that each one might end up in any of the four situations.

While experimentation can answer questions about causality that correlation alone cannot address, there are limits and disadvantages to the experimental method. First, in order to create the treatments that make up the experimental and control conditions, the experimenter must bring subjects into the *laboratory*, an artificial environment where conditions are so heavily controlled that behavior may be a distortion of what would occur naturally. Second, research subjects typically know they are being studied, and this

Become a Wiser Research Consumer

I mprove your life with this miraculous treatment program! Call now and have your credit card handy!

How can you tell the difference between a deceptive claim and a genuine breakthrough? Our society is rich in information, and we are surrounded by claims of truth, false myths, and biased conclusions that serve special interests. To be a responsible citizen, you must hone your critical thinking skills and assess the believability of claims made about what research shows. You must become an informed consumer of psychological research.

Psychology is often misrepresented in media such as talk shows and self-help books. Consequently, professional psychologists need to keep the public accurately informed about what the discipline has to offer. National surveys of public opinion reveal that for many of the 25 million American adults without high school diplomas, the world is a confusing and threatening place that operates in incomprehensible ways. They feel that they are controlled by fate and can do little to direct their lives. It follows that such people are inclined to believe in lucky numbers, cosmic signs, omens, horoscopes, and mystical forces. Frighteningly, such beliefs are sometimes shared by more educated people. You may recall, for instance, the furor created when, in the mid-1980s, then–First Lady Nancy Reagan admitted she regularly consulted a "psychic" in planning her husband's presidential itinerary. Clearly, our schools are failing in their goal to provide the conceptual framework for separating superstition and science fiction from scientific understanding and fact.

The multimillion-dollar pseudoscience industry sells diverse products to the legions of "true believers" who are prepared to accept the unexplained, the unevaluated, and the unproven— often merely at the urging of a charismatic or famous spokesperson. Because unfounded authorities can mislead and betray our trust, we must cultivate an open-minded skepticism about those who would totally restructure our view of reality.

Psychology is inevitably a part of your real world. Every day you address the same issues psychologists do: You ask questions about your own behavior and that of other people; you seek answers in your theories or observations of what "authorities" say; and you check out the answers against the evidence available to you. As part of your formal education, psychology will help you make wiser decisions based on the evidence collected. Some of these decisions are the everyday ones about which products to buy or services to use. Others are more substantial and affect your entire lifestyle and perhaps even the life of this planet. Here are some suggestions for skills and habits worth cultivating in order to become a wiser consumer of information about psychological research:

■ Ask empirical questions—questions that can be answered with information gathered by documented observations.

■ Be wary of personal testimonials and case studies that do not offer objective data or comparative base rates.

■ Search for alternative explanations to those that are being proposed.

■ Consider the possibility that your own biases can distort your perceptions of reality.

■ Be suspicious of simple answers to complex problems.

■ Be cognitively flexible: instead of ruling out every new idea, try to consider new possibilities while maintaining high standards for what you accept as true.

■ Develop the courage to challenge authority that is unjust, that uses personal opinion in place of evidence, and that is not open to constructive criticism.

awareness can lead them to feel self-conscious or to try to do what the experimenter "expects" of them. Such motives can seriously bias and contaminate the data and nullify the value of the experiment. In sum, an experiment is a simplified version of reality. This simplification can be helpful in answering some questions, but at times it may be too simplified to reveal much about real life and behavior.

This brief introduction to psychological measurement and research design is no substitute for a more careful study of research methods. For a more detailed review of how data are analyzed and interpreted, turn to the Statistical Appendix (Appendix B) near the end of this book. There you will find a summary of key points and examples of how psychological concepts are *quantified* (measured and expressed as numbers) and how those quantities can provide meaning and understanding. Meanwhile, review the preceding section—research methods are often the most challenging new concept for the beginning psychology student!—and then go on to consider Weigh the Evidence: Become a Wiser Research Consumer.

Check Your Recall

Psychological research depends on empirical investigation of observable events and behaviors. The research process involves two phases: the context of discovery and the context of justification. During discovery, research questions are asked, theories are developed, and hypotheses are proposed to answer those questions. Research studies examine how stimuli affect behavior, how behaviors are structured and interrelated, how inner processes explain observable actions, and what the consequences of behavior are. Scientists seek to explain the relationships among variables and must overcome a variety of biases in order to do so objectively. During justification, scientists are motivated by curiosity, skepticism, and discipline. They must employ standard procedures, safeguard their objectivity, and communicate their findings. Research methods may involve self-report, behavioral, and physiological measures. Correlational methods can identify the existence and strength of relationships between variables, but only experimental methods can specify a causal relationship between variables. Experimentation requires selection and ethical treatment of subjects, control of treatment conditions, and random assignment to those conditions. The experimental method is limited because it simplifies reality, but it can yield helpful answers to questions of causality.

CHAPTER REVIEW

Summary

Psychology is the scientific study of behavior and mental processes. Despite having distinctive concerns, psychology also shares interests with other social, behavioral, biological, cognitive, and health sciences. Psychology's five goals include describing, explaining, predicting, controlling, and enhancing behavior. Professional psychologists specialize in various fields depending on the populations and problems of interest.

Scientific psychology is based on determinism, an assumption that the causes of psychological events and processes can be determined through careful study. Two schools of thought significantly contributed to psychology's historical foundations. Structuralism, developed by Wilhelm Wundt and Edward Titchener, advocated understanding mental processes such as consciousness by investigating their contents and structure. Functionalism, developed by John Dewey and William James, argued that mental processes are best understood in terms of their adaptive purposes and functions.

Seven perspectives or points of view characterize modern psychology. The biological approach looks for the causes of behavior in biological processes such as brain function and genetics. In the psychodynamic approach, behavior and thought are influenced by inner psychological forces and conflicts. The behavioristic approach rejects mentalistic explanations and explains behavior in terms of observable stimuli and responses. Cognitive approaches to psychology argue that behavior is based on thinking, a process for which the brain is naturally designed. The humanistic approach characterizes human functioning as motivated by a desire to grow, be productive, and fulfill human potential. The evolutionary approach sees human mental and behavioral abilities as the result of a process of adapting for survival in the environment. Finally, the sociocultural approach recognizes the power of society and cultural context on individual thought, feeling, and action.

In the discovery phase of scientific research, investigators ask research questions, propose explanations, and consider how to overcome biases that may distort their observations. Subjects selected for research participation must be treated according to ethical guidelines dictated by organizations of professional scientists. In the justification phase, researchers approach their work with a combination of curiosity and skepticism, safeguard their objectivity in data collection, and produce disciplined reports to be communicated to other scientists. Research begins with determining how to measure the behavior or psychological processes of interest. Data are collected and analyzed according to either correlational or experimental designs. Correlational methods identify the existence and strength of a relationship between variables. Experimental methods demonstrate whether an independent variable has a hypothesized effect on a dependent variable. Familiarity with these processes can help to make you a wiser consumer of information yielded by psychological research.

Section Reviews

The Discipline of Psychology

Be sure to *Check Your Recall* by reviewing the summary of this section on page 10.

Key Terms
psychology (p. 5)
scientific method (p. 5)
behavior (p. 5)
behavioral data (p. 7)
intervening variable (p. 8)

base rate (p. 9)
variable (p. 9)
independent variable (p. 9)
dependent variable (p. 9)

The Foundations of Psychology

Be sure to *Check Your Recall* by reviewing the summary of this section on page 14.

Key Terms
determinism (p. 12)
structuralism (p. 13)
functionalism (p. 13)

Names to Know
Wilhelm Wundt (p. 11)
William James (p. 12)
Edward Titchener (p. 13)
John Dewey (p. 13)

Current Perspectives in Psychology

Be sure to *Check Your Recall* by reviewing the summary of this section on page 23.

Key Terms
biological approach (p. 14)
psychodynamic approach (p. 15)
behaviorism (p. 16)
behavioristic approach (p. 16)
cognitive approach (p. 18)
humanistic approach (p. 18)
evolutionary approach (p. 19)

culture (p. 20)
sociocultural approach (p. 20)

Names to Know
Sigmund Freud (p. 16)
John B. Watson (p. 16)
B. F. Skinner (p. 17)
Charles Darwin (p. 19)

Psychological Research

Be sure to *Check Your Recall* by reviewing the summary of this section on page 34.

Key Terms
empirical investigation (p. 23)
context of discovery (p. 24)
theory (p. 25)
hypothesis (p. 25)
context of justification methods (p. 27)
standardization (p. 27)
debriefing (p. 28)
operational definition (p. 28)
blind (p. 29)
double blind (p. 29)
confounding variable (p. 29)

self-report measures (p. 30)
behavioral measures (p. 30)
physiological measures (p. 30)
correlational measures (p. 31)
correlation coefficient (p. 31)
controlled experiment (p. 31)
randomization (p. 32)

Chapter 1: Mind, Behavior, and Science

For each of the following items, choose the single correct or best answer. The correct answers, explanations, and page references appear in Appendix B.

1. Scientific psychology employs empirical investigation methods. This means that the data collected must be based on _____.
   a. first-hand sensory evidence
   b. reasoned speculation
   c. the observer's subjective interpretation of events
   d. established traditions of philosophical inquiry

2. A college admissions officer examines an applicant's secondary school records in order to estimate the student's likelihood of performing well in college. The goal of psychology represented in this task is that of _____ behavior.
   a. controlling
   b. improving
   c. explaining
   d. predicting

3. Which of the following fields of psychology is *not* concerned with delivering services and treatment in solving personal or social problems?
   a. social psychology
   b. counseling psychology
   c. clinical psychology
   d. community psychology

4. Although psychology has a "long past," it has a short history. Its origins are usually traced to the late nineteenth century, when _____ established the first psychological laboratory.
   a. William James
   b. Wilhelm Wundt
   c. Sigmund Freud
   d. John B. Watson

5. "To understand consciousness or behavior, you must focus on the probable purpose of an action or process." This statement reflects the arguments of _____.
   a. humanism
   b. functionalism
   c. structuralism
   d. behaviorism

6. According to the _____ perspective in psychology, one's behavior and personality develop as a result of inner tensions and conflicts, created when selfish urges are restricted by societal controls.
   a. biological
   b. cognitive
   c. psychodynamic
   d. socio-cultural

7. According to the evolutionary approach in modern psychology, human behavior has evolved in the direction of ever greater _____.
   a. cultural conformity
   b. ability to process information

c. adaptation and genetic survival

d. conflict between individual goals and societal limits

8. Which of the following research studies would *not* require the use of debriefing?

a. Student volunteers are paired to collaborate on tasks of varying levels of difficulty.

b. Candidates are asked to complete job applications in either quiet or noisy rooms in order to ascertain how stress affects their self-presentations.

c. As part of a study of learning techniques, some participants are asked to administer painful punishment to others whenever they make mistakes.

d. Pigeons are rewarded with food pellets when they peck at red keys on a keyboard.

9. In psychological research, a _____ is a tentative and testable explanation of the relationship between the events or variables being studied.

a. model

b. theory

c. hypothesis

d. correlation

10. A researcher wonders how to stimulate young school-children to be more creative. She randomly divides a class of first graders in half, reading stories to one group, and having members of the other group take turns making up stories to go with the same set of titles. After two weeks, she finds that those who made up stories are producing more work in their reading, writing, and art classes than those who merely listened as she read stories to them. Which of the following statements is *not* true about this study?

a. The experimental group was the group that made up their own stories.

b. Making up stories is part of the dependent variable.

c. There are two levels or conditions in the independent variable.

d. This is an example of a correlational investigation.

IF YOU'RE INTERESTED . . .

Career Encounters in Psychology. (Video: 1991, color, 30 min.)

Several psychologists with diverse careers describe their work in this American Psychological Association documentary.

Colman, A. M. (1987). *Facts, fallacies, and frauds in psychology.* London: Hutchinson.

Short, readable, and fascinating review of myths and realities in psychological theory and research.

Eysenck, H. J. (1988). *Fact and fiction in psychology.* Baltimore: Penguin Books.

Engaging review of what is and is not known in the realm of scientific psychology, written by one of its most articulate ambassadors to popular culture.

Falcon, C. T. (1992). *Happiness and personal problems: Psychology made easy.* Lafayette, LA: Sensible Psychology Press.

An interesting and accessible presentation of psychology applied to everyday life. Divided into three sections: general information and advice; how to solve personal problems; and conclusions (about self-understanding and seeking professional help). Offers some refreshing directness as well as some questionable suggestions. Exercise open-minded skepticism and consult other resources for validation.

Fancher, R. E. (1990). *Pioneers of psychology* (2nd ed.). New York: W. W. Norton & Co.

Collected brief biographies of the men and women who established and developed psychology as a scientific discipline.

Gay, P. (1988). *Freud: A life for our time.* New York: W. W. Norton & Co.

The definitive biography by the foremost Freud historian of our day, told sympathetically and yet realistically.

Gonick, L., & Smith, W. (1993). *The cartoon guide to statistics.* New York: HarperPerennial.

A rich, helpful, and entertaining "comic book" explaining and illustrating descriptive statistics, sampling techniques, hypothesis testing, and experimental design.

Hilgard, E. R. (1987). *Psychology in America: A historical survey.* New York: Harcourt Brace Jovanovich.

An interesting reference work that describes the historical context, lives, and personal endeavors that have distinguished psychology in research, academia, and professional practice in the United States.

Hunt, M. (1993). *The story of psychology.* New York: Doubleday.

A fascinating history of the lives and times of the "Magellans of the mind," from ancient philosophy to modern research.

Inherit the Wind. (Video: 1960, B&W, 127 min.) Directed by Stanley Kramer; starring Spencer Tracy, Fredric March, Gene Kelly, Dick York.

Wonderful adaptation of Broadway play fictionalizing the 1925 "Scopes Monkey Trial," challenging a Tennessee biology teacher's right to teach his students about the bases for the theory of evolution. The original trial was dramatic in its own right as it pitted defense attorney Clarence Darrow against prosecutor and frequent presidential hopeful William Jennings Bryan. The film captures the drama underlying fears, misunderstandings, and prejudices about the coexistence of scientific theory with religious faith.

King's Row. (Video: 1942, B&W, 127 min.) Directed by Sam Wood; starring Robert Cummings, Ann Sheridan, Ronald Reagan, Claude Rains.

In a small Midwestern town at the beginning of the twentieth century, a young man turns his life's lessons and losses into a determination to study psychiatry and heal broken minds. Soap-opera story features an outstanding score and a fine performance by Ronald Reagan—including his "Where's the rest of me?" speech—in his role as the hero's best friend.

Stanovich, K. E. (1996). *How to think straight about psychology* (4th ed.). Glenview, IL: Scott, Foresman.

Very practical handbook for surviving and thriving by using what you know about psychological research and applications.

Woods, P. (1987). *Is psychology the major for you?* Washington, DC: American Psychological Association.

Everything you ever wanted to know about how and why to major in psychology—and what kind of life and career you might expect after college.

CHAPTER 2

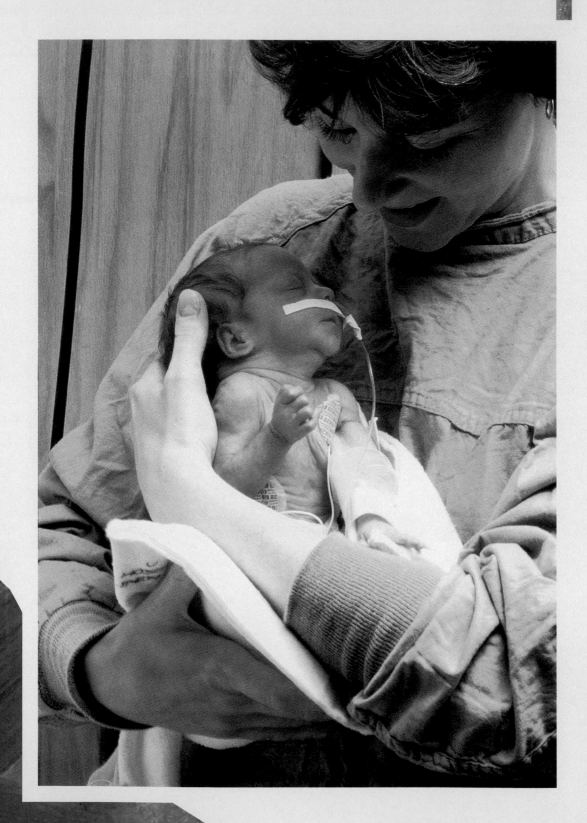

Biopsychology

Five-and-a-half weeks before her twins were due, Christine felt the first sharp pains of labor. Her husband drove her to the hospital where, for 16 hours, the two of them followed the breathing instructions they had learned in their natural-childbirth class. Then a fetal monitor showed that the heartbeat of one of the babies was weakening. Doctors quickly performed a cesarean section. Within minutes, Nicole (4 pounds) and Alexis (3 pounds 14 ounces) had entered the world.

Immediately after birth, Nicole and Alexis joined half a dozen other babies in the neonatal intensive care unit. For two-and-a-half weeks, electronic devices monitored their vital signs. Experienced nurses tended to their physical needs and held them frequently. Christine spent a good part of each day with her babies, holding and rocking them and feeding them her breast milk from bottles, awaiting the day when she could actually breastfeed them. Wearing diapers barely the size of cocktail napkins, the twins looked fragile and unfinished. With no layers of baby fat, every little rib in their bodies showed.

Had Nicole and Alexis been born 20 years earlier, their first few weeks of life would have been quite different. Until the late 1970s, prematurely born infants were touched as little as possible. Parents and medical personnel feared that any unnecessary contact with the outside world might harm the babies. Fortunately for Nicole and Alexis, we now know better.

Research with infant rats and humans has led scientists to conclude that brain functioning can be altered by touch, and that touch is essential for the normal growth and development of newborns. Biologist **Saul Schanberg** found that when rat pups were separated from their mothers, the levels of an enzyme important for growth decreased dramatically (Schanberg et al., 1990). The longer they were deprived of maternal contact, the less responsive the pups became. These effects of maternal deprivation could be reversed in only two ways: by returning them to the mother, who immediately started licking them, or by having a researcher vigorously stroke them with a small paintbrush to mimic the mother's massaging. Schanberg (1990) concluded that: "the need for a mother's touch is really brain based. It isn't just nice to have it. It's a requirement for the normal development and growth of the baby."

Complementing this research with animals are studies by psychologist **Tiffany Field**, who collaborated with Schanberg (Field & Schanberg, 1990) to conduct studies of prematurely born human infants. Her research team randomly selected 20 preemies to receive periodic massages throughout the day, while 20 others received the normal hospital treatment in the *intensive care unit, which did not include massages. According to Field, "The premature babies who were massaged for 45 minutes a day for ten days before they were discharged gained 47 percent more weight than the babies who did not get massaged. They were more active. They were more alert." Eight months later, the massaged babies had maintained their weight advantage and were also more advanced in motor, cognitive, and emotional development (Field, 1990). This research is being extended and replicated in larger samples of preemies in order to establish the effects of human touch on biological and psychological health.*

In the United States, more than a quarter of a million infants are born prematurely each year. Those who are touched and cuddled leave the hospital several days sooner than they would have otherwise, reducing health-care costs by about $3,000 per child.

Unfortunately, not all hospitals apply what scientists have learned about the positive effects of early touch on development. If they did, the lives of thousands of children would be improved, and billions of dollars would be saved each year—two very practical benefits of this basic research.

When Nicole and Alexis left the hospital, they were still rather small, but they were developing so well that the doctors felt confident they would be all right. At home, the babies shared a crib in the living room, where relatives and friends who remarked on their tiny size were encouraged to gently pick them up and cuddle them. Christine and her husband were acutely aware that such physical stimulation is apparently critical for optimal development of the brain and, in turn, the mental and physical processes that the brain controls.

Introduction

When fully matured, the adult brain weighs only 3 pounds, less than either Nicole or Alexis did at birth. Even though it weighs little and is made up of the basic chemical molecules found throughout the universe, the brain is the most complex structure in the known universe. This biocomputer contains more cells than there are stars in our entire galaxy—over 100 billion nerve cells designed to communicate and store information. The brain holds the basis for communicating all the information that is possible for the brightest of us to know or the most sensitive of us to experience.

The evolution of the human brain has taken place over millions of years. The brain is the subject of study for a new breed of researchers who rely on research in *biopsychology,* a rapidly growing area of psychology that studies the relationship among biology, behavior, and environment. Biopsychologists seek to identify the biochemical processes that underlie the actions of all living creatures, and they want to explain how these components cooperate to produce all the complex forms of human action.

Ironically, you must *use* your brain in order to *understand* your brain. This conscious aspect of one's mind—the sense of self that looks out at the world and in at its own thoughts and mortality—seems to exist independently of its biology. We may even think of the body as mere flesh, "inferior" to the sophisticated realm of the higher mind. But when brain cells are destroyed by disease, drugs, and accidents, we are dramatically reminded of the biological basis of the human mind. In such cases, we are forced to recognize the physical matter, our biology, from which sensation and language, learning and memory, passion and pain, and human reason and madness spring.

In this chapter, we first examine how evolution and heredity determine the biology of behavior. Next we review research on the workings of the brain, the nervous system as a whole, and the related functions of the endocrine system. Finally we consider how external stimulation can actually modify the brain, changing both its structure and functions. This material may be more challenging than the rest of *Psychology* because it involves much new terminology. But we urge you to keep in mind the image of a "journey" into the discipline of psychology. When you travel someplace new, you may at first find it daunting to read the local maps and learn your way around. With patience and time, though, you become more familiar with the geography, landmarks, and place names. Eventually, you feel quite comfortable, even though you may be far from home. In the case of this chapter, too, consider that we are not really taking you far from home! We are asking you to look closely at yourself and at some of the processes that contribute to the person you have become. By understanding your biological nature, you will better appreciate how brain, mind, behavior, and the environment interact to create the uniqueness of every human being.

The Evolution of Behavior

How did this marvelous piece of biology called the brain come to be? This question requires us first to consider **evolution,** *the theory that, over time, organisms originate within, and adapt to, their unique environments.* The environmental challenges every organism faces and the resources it possesses combine to determine which organisms survive and which of the survivors' characteristics are most likely to be passed on to their offspring and descendants. We will consider how these *inherited* characteristics influence behavior; but first, we must briefly review the key concepts in the theory of evolution.

Human Evolution

About 50 years before Wilhelm Wundt established psychology's first experimental laboratory, **Charles Darwin,** a new college graduate, set sail on a five-year cruise that would have an enormous impact on his life and on the history of science. In 1831, the HMS *Beagle,* an ocean research vessel, left England to survey the coast of South America. During the trip, Darwin studied every life-form and fossil he encountered. He drew on this data to write his most famous book, *On the Origin of Species* (1859), in which he set forth science's grandest theory, that of the *evolution* of life on this planet.

Darwin's observations convinced him that some natural mechanism influenced the breeding of organisms from one generation to the next, so that species ultimately either adapted to their environments, or failed to adapt and became extinct. Specifically, plants' and animals' characteristics (such as physical size, coloring, and abilities) are either favored by environmental conditions and preserved, or they are not favored and end up being "selected out." For those organisms that survive, the result of this process of adaptation over time, claimed Darwin, "would be the formation of a new species" (Darwin, 1859).

Natural Selection   According to Darwin's theory of **natural selection,** *some members of a species tend to produce more offspring than others because natural environmental conditions have selected for those organisms and their inheritable features.* These fortunate, or "favored," individuals survive, reproduce, and pass their advantageous traits on to the next generation. Organisms

Charles Darwin (1809–1882)

that have adapted well to a given environment will produce more offspring (because more of them will survive and live longer) than those less well adapted. These offspring will pass along the survival-promoting traits they possess, and their descendants will eventually outnumber those who have not inherited the helpful features. In evolutionary terms, an individual's success is measured only by the number of offspring he or she produces.

Today, natural selection suggests that some observable human behaviors or differences may have been inherited from ancestors whose circumstances made those qualities advantageous. For example, some seemingly "natural differences" between the abilities of men and women may be partially rooted in inherited features—body structure, strength, and abilities—that supported human survival and procreation in an ancient, very different environment (Daly & Wilson, 1983). In early human communities, labor was probably divided so that men did most of the distant gathering and hunting while women focused on local foraging and child care. Given the different priorities and demands of those two roles, environmental and cultural conditions may have selected for women to be better at fine motor tasks (for example, preparing food and attending to infants) and for men to be more adept at orienting to new locations, tracking, and hunting (Kimura, 1987). Today such "left-over" selections are less obviously advantageous. In modern industrialized cultures, a wide range of human abilities is more adaptive than narrow role assignments, and most tasks can be performed as necessary by members of either sex.

Evolution is best thought of as a *process,* still unfolding as people's environments and the demands of living continue to change. Although the environment is the driving force behind natural selection, is it not the only process influencing evolution. Two others, *variation* and *competition*, also play key roles.

Variation   Variation *refers to differences in biological and psychological traits among individuals within a given population.* Some people are big and strong; some are intelligent; and some are big, strong, *and* intelligent. Features by which individuals are recognized make up their **phenotype,** *the observable or measurable expression of an individual's genetic make-up. The genetic structure inherited from one's parents is referred to as one's* **genotype.** An individual's genotype permits a particular range of biological possibilities; environmental forces such as nutrition determine where, within that range the phenotype will be expressed.

Darwin's original theories of the process of natural selection were inspired by his observations of 13 species of finches living in the Galápagos Islands off the west coast of South America. In this environment, isolated from the continental mainland, the originally small finch population had apparently adapted to different food sources and environmental niches with different genetic variations. Birds with thin, pointed beaks were unable to crush and eat seeds, but fed well when they migrated to locales rich in insects. In those places, birds with thick, seed-crushing beaks died out, having insufficient seed resources and being unable to take advantage of the abundance of insect life.

In the example of Darwin's finches, the genotype of a particular bird is the genetic structure—the biological potential—it inherits from its parents. Within a particular environment, the genotype determines the finch's outward appearance and behavior; this expressed pattern is its phenotype. Suppose our finch's genotype has interacted with its habitat to produce the phenotype of *small beak* and *able to peck smaller seeds.* If all types of seeds are plentiful, this phenotype gives no particular survival advantage to our bird. But if only small seeds happen to be available in this environment, our finch has a *selective advantage* over finches with, say, large beaks that cannot pry into small-seed-bearing crevices. On the other hand, if only large seeds are available, our finch is disadvantaged and may not survive or produce offspring.

Competition   The particular environmental conditions an organism faces contribute to *competition* in natural selection. Unless a habitat offers a wide range of all sorts of edible resources, the inhabitants will compete with each other for limited food and other necessities such as shelter. Resource scarcity and environmental change guarantee that only certain phenotypes (and the genotypes that give rise to them) will promote successful survival. Only those organisms that survive can reproduce and pass on the "winning" genotypes. Over several generations, therefore, specific successful genotypes (such as those for small-beaked finches) can come to outnumber the competition and emerge as stable species with characteristics shaped by both genetic variation and environmentally enhanced competition. Where once a variety of beak shapes and sizes abounded, for example, a change in habitat to only one type of reliable food source will result in an abundance of primarily the type of finch that is genetically best suited to survive there.

The first stage of this process can already be seen in the changing food habits of grizzly bears in the forests of the American Northwest. Faced with shortages of traditional food supplies, some bears have turned to a new diet of moths. Moths are high in nutritional value and are plentiful at certain times of the year. The adventurous eaters, as well as their offspring, are more likely to survive than those bears who restrict their diet to familiar but scarce foods.

Environmental competition sharpens the *selective advantage* of particular genetically based variations among organisms. Trace this sequence through Figure 2.1, which depicts a simplified model of natural selection through the processes of variation and competition.

The Human Advantage   The marvelous piece of biology that is the human brain exists because it was favored by natural selection in our ancestors' quest for survival. Our brains differ from those of other species for much the same reason (Harvey & Krebs, 1990). The earliest humans lived and survived in an environment different from that of other species, so their brains evolved differently to meet the needs of that environment.

Consider how our modern lifestyle, with its conveniences and comforts, has resulted from the natural selection of certain genotypes passed on to us by our ancestors. Social and biological scientists now know that natural selection favored two particular adaptations in the evolution of our species: *bipedalism* and *encephalization*. **Bipedalism** *refers to the ability to walk upright, and* **encephalization** *refers to increases in brain size and in the proportion of specialized brain tissue.* The ability to walk upright made humans better able to explore and relocate than other species. Increases in brain size, especially in certain kinds of brain tissue, led to increased capacity for complex thinking, reasoning, remembering, and planning. Ultimately, only intelligent bipedal humans survived to reproduce and roam the earth's varied habitats. Together these two adaptations made possible the rise of human civilization. They are responsible for most, if not all, of the other major advances in human evolution, including cultural development (see Figure 2.2).

After bipedalism and encephalization, perhaps the other most important evolutionary milestone for our species was the advent of *language* (see Diamond, 1990). Language, a product of highly sophisticated brain processes, makes it possible for individuals to have interactions ranging from simple instructions for tool use to complex historical documentation. Language is the basis for *cultural evolution,* the tendency of cultures to learn to respond adaptively to environmental change and to transmit this knowledge across generations.

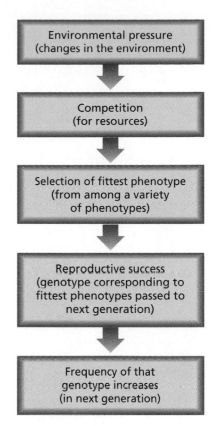

FIGURE 2.1   How Natural Selection Works ■ Environmental changes create competition for resources among species members. Individuals that inherit characteristics which promote survival will probably survive and reproduce. The next generation will then have a greater number of individuals possessing these advantageous genes.

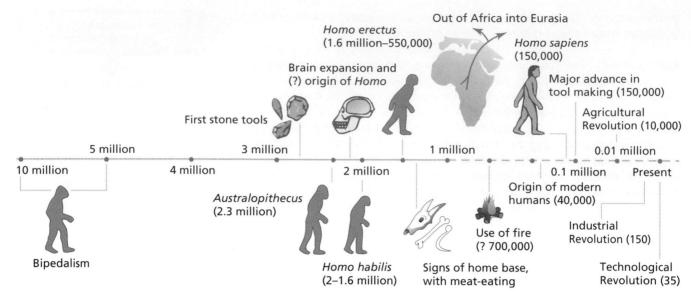

FIGURE 2.2   Approximate Time Line for Major Events in Human Evolution ■
Bipedalism freed the hands for grasping and tool use. Encephalization provided the
capacity for higher cognitive processes such as abstract thinking and reasoning.
These two adaptations facilitated other major advances in human evolution.

Genes and Behavior

Despite a similar heritage, children are different from their parents. One
reason is that children grow up and live in different environments from those
of their parents. Another reason is that children possess a unique combination
of genes, unlike that of either parent. A mother and father pass on to their
offspring a part of what past generations of their family lines have given them.
This inheritance results in a distinct biological blueprint and timetable for individual development. *The study of the inheritance of physical and psychological traits from ancestors is called* genetics.

Genetic Potential   In the nucleus of each cell in an organism's body is
genetic material called DNA (deoxyribonucleic acid). DNA contains the
instructions for the production of proteins. These proteins regulate the body's
physiological processes and the expression of phenotypic traits: body build,
physical strength, intelligence, and many behavior patterns. *DNA is organized
into tiny molecular units called* genes *that are assembled into strings along
structures known as* chromosomes. (Most chromosomes are roughly X-
shaped; the single exception is the Y-shaped chromosome containing material
that determines an individual as genetically male, not female.) The chromosomes of an individual's cells are copied and stored in *germ cells*, forming eggs
or sperm cells in reproductive organs.

At the moment you were conceived, you inherited 46 chromosomes from
your parents: 23 from your mother and 23 from your father. Each of these
chromosomes contains thousands of genes. The *sex chromosomes* contain
genes for development of male or female anatomy. An XX combination in this
pair (both chromosomes resembling X shapes) codes for femaleness. An XY
combination (one X-shaped and one Y-shaped chromosome) codes for male-
ness. You inherited an X chromosome from your biological mother, and *either*
an X (if you are female) *or* a Y (if you are male) from your biological father.
Your genotype (XX for female or XY for male) determines your biological

gender and its development, including changes in body structure and chemistry, throughout your lifetime.

Your genetic heritage can set the stage for important life experiences. Whatever the genetic influence of *being* male or female, how much more have you been influenced by the *meaning* of being male or female in your social world? Obviously, people have treated you differently because of your gender. Your self-concept, aspirations, and relationships would all be different had you been born the other sex. Thus you see that your psychology—how you get along in the world—is rooted in your biology.

Nevertheless, your biology does not define your destiny, because your genotypes only set your *potential*. Being tall doesn't mean you must play basketball. Being female may give you the option of bearing children, but doing so is a matter of choice. Physical strength clearly can be determined by exercise—or the lack of it. Intellectual growth depends both on genetic potential and educational experiences. Thus the person you are results from the *interaction* of your genetic potential with the environment in which you live.

Behavior Genetics   The task for psychologists is to determine which environments help people develop their full potential. Consider, for example, people with Down syndrome. *Down syndrome* is caused by an extra chromosome in what geneticists have labeled the 21st pair in each cell. It is characterized by impaired psychomotor and physical development as well as mental retardation. Without intervention from mental health professionals, people with Down syndrome depend almost wholly on others to fulfill their basic needs. However, with special educational programs, persons with this disorder can learn to care for themselves, work, and establish some personal independence. The behavior of persons with Down syndrome can be modified through education and experience.

As this example shows, the disciplines of psychology and genetics have an important relationship. Together they seek to understand how genes influence behavior and to determine how environmental variables (such as training programs, diet, and social interactions) can modify genetically influenced behavior (Fuller, 1982; Plomin & Rende, 1991). **Behavior genetics** *is a*

relatively new field uniting geneticists and psychologists interested in deter-mining the genetic basis of behavioral traits and functioning. Traits might include an individual's intelligence or predisposition to experience certain mental disorders; examples of behavioral functioning include altruistic behavior or aggressiveness.

The behavior genetics of disorders has yielded two distinct approaches to understanding the inherited elements of psychological problems (Plomin et al., 1994). The traditional approach assumes that a single gene is necessary and sufficient to lead an individual to develop a disorder. This approach is termed "one gene, one disorder" (OGOD). The OGOD approach seems to explain one example in which a particular biochemical mutation appeared to cause impulsive violence in several members of a Dutch family (Brunner et al., 1993). The alternative approach involves searching for multiple genes (at mappable "loci," or locations, on chromosomes) which combine to create disordering effects, but none of which is necessary or sufficient to cause the trait by itself. This view is termed the "quantitative trait loci" (QTL) approach because it assumes that a quantity of different gene locations determine a disordering trait. The QTL approach seems to account for a particular form of Alzheimer's disease whose frequency increases as individuals with a particular gene age from their sixties to their nineties. The "culprit" is not this gene alone, however, as many individuals who possess the gene never develop this form of Alzheimer's disease, and many with the disease have been found not to have the gene at all (Skoog et al., 1993). The "culprit," therefore, may really be several different genes that interact to cause the disorder.

The more we learn about behavior genetics, the better we understand the forces that determine human potential and life experience. The American Psychological Association has identified genetics as one of the disciplines with the greatest promise for psychology's future (Plomin & McClearn, 1993). However, knowledge alone is not sufficient for improving our quality of life—one of the goals of psychology reviewed in the last chapter. Psychologists are increasingly called on to provide guidance about how genetic knowledge can best be applied (Wingerson, 1990). Before we turn our attention to the structure and function of the brain, nervous system, and related bodily processes, consider how the ethics of genetic science and technology might affect your own life. ASK YOURSELF the following questions:

■ How important is it to you to someday have children? Is there an important difference to you between having biological children and raising children you have adopted or fostered but whom you have not biologically parented?

■ If you knew a biological child of yours might be born disabled or fatally ill because of your own genetic heritage, would it be a responsible act for you to have children anyway? What circumstances or conditions would affect your decision?

■ If you knew you might carry a gene responsible for a serious medical or behavioral disorder, would you want to be tested before having children? Would you consider it fair for a prospective spouse to require you to be tested before conceiving children? Would it be fair for the state to make such a requirement?

Check Your Recall

According to Charles Darwin's theory of evolution, organisms originate and change over time because of natural selection. In all organisms' competition for survival and procreation, environmental forces favor certain variations. In human evolution, adaptations such as bipedalism and encephalization have supported the development of language and culture. Both normal and disordered behavior result from an interaction of genetic potential with influential experiences and environmental conditions. Behavior genetics has developed approaches to understanding behavior disorders, but genetic knowledge can only be applied if we consider individual and societal ethics. ✔

Brain Structures and Functions

Humans have probably always recognized the existence of a link between body and mind. Even today one might speak of "giving one's heart" to another when falling in love, or of "not having the stomach" for something when describing fear. Now we know that love does not reside in the heart, nor courage in the digestive system. However, not long ago in human history, people believed that specific bodily processes controlled and determined their emotions and actions. Prevailing beliefs about how the body influences the mind also determined whether and how people studied this connection.

Brain Research

Archaeological evidence has shown that some early human cultures practiced *trephination*, in which a small, sawlike instrument (a trephine) was used to cut holes in the skulls of living patients to release disruptive demons or parasites presumed to be causing the problem. Many trephined skulls show signs of renewed bone growth around the cut, indicating that some patients, at least, survived this crude if well-intentioned medical procedure. Later, the ancient Hindus and Greeks developed systems of medical thought in which individuals' moods, health, and behavior were influenced by physical substances and bodily fluids (*humors*). Since about the third century B.C., the Chinese practice of acupuncture to relieve pain and promote well-being has assumed that human functioning is governed by five elements (wood, earth, fire, metal, and water) and the two cosmic principles of *yin* and *yang* (a bodily and spiritual balance between female and male, dark and light, passivity and activity). Human curiosity about the origins of thought, feeling, and action has long fueled thoughtful speculation. However, empirical research was impossible for hundreds of years due to the primitive state of research technology as well as religious proscriptions against the study of human bodies.

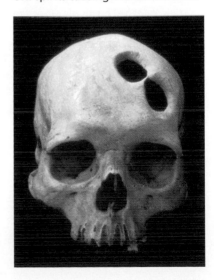

Trephination—perforating the skull with a sharp instrument—was long thought to be a means of treating mental disorder. The process was originally believed to drive out the evil spirits causing the disturbance.

The Mind-Body Problem   One of the most important figures to address the question of how to study the mind-body link was French philosopher **René Descartes** (1596–1650). Descartes (pronounced *DAY-kart*) proposed that the human body was an "animal machine" that could be understood scientifically and studied through empirical observation. Human action, Descartes maintained, was a mechanical reflex to environmental stimulation—no different from the behavior of nonhuman animals. In deference to prevailing religious doctrine, which insisted that human minds were divinely endowed, Descartes moderated his arguments by adding the idea of a rational soul that guides human decisions and action.

Descartes's ideas that human behavior can be scientifically studied as a physical system, in which the body affects the mind, eventually led to the development of modern brain research. Modern scientific psychology recognizes that it is the brain, not the heart or soul, that guides human behavior. In the nineteenth century, medical researchers began to identify the components of the nervous system and some of their basic functions. More recently,

FOCUS on Science

Eavesdropping on the Brain

In September 1848, a 25-year-old railroad worker named **Phineas Gage** sustained a horrible head injury when a construction explosion blasted an iron rod through his face and head. Astoundingly, he recovered from this injury and lived another 12 years—but as a *psychologically* changed man. Those who knew him remarked that he had gone from being an efficient and capable manager to behaving in irresponsible, fitful, and even profane ways. In essence, he was no longer himself (Damasio et al., 1994). Had the site of his injury—the front and top of his brain—been the "residence" of his "old self"?

At about the same time that Gage was recovering from his injury, the French neurosurgeon **Paul Broca** was studying the brain's role in language. His first laboratory research in this area involved an autopsy of a man whose name was derived from the only word he had been able to speak, "Tan." Broca found that the left front portion of Tan's brain had been severely damaged. When he studied the brains of similarly injured patients, Broca discovered that damage to the same region of the brain resulted in similar language impairments. He concluded that language ability depended on the functioning of structures in a specific region of the brain.

Thus the study of functions associated with different regions of the brain began with examinations of accidentally damaged brains. However, this hit-and-miss technique soon frustrated researchers, who had no control over the location, extent, or context of the damage they would have the opportunity to study. Consequently, some re-

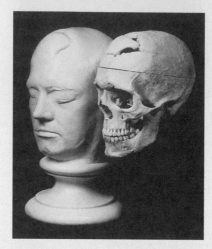

Phineas Gage

searchers began, with deliberation and skill, to destroy sections of the brains of otherwise intact animals (typically rats) and then to systematically measure the outcomes. A **lesion** *is a carefully inflicted injury or alteration of tissue applied to specific brain areas.* Early neuroscientists believed lesions were a superior strategy for some brain research, despite the ethical concerns that seem obvious to us today.

Researchers create three methods for producing of lesions: They either surgically *remove* specific brain areas, *cut the neural connections* to those areas, or *destroy* those areas by applying intense heat, cold, electricity, or lasers. Comparisons between the behavior of lesioned and nonlesioned animals has dramatically affected the development of brain science. For example, suppose that a rat were unable to run a recently learned maze after a specific part of its

hippocampus had been lesioned. This would be evidence that learning and memory are processed in the lesioned structure.

In the middle of the twentieth century, Canadian neurosurgeon **Wilder Penfield** "mapped" cortical tissue (the outermost layers of the brain) as part of his surgical procedures on epileptic patients before making any lesions. His purpose was to localize the origin of the seizures and leave unharmed other areas vital to the patient's functioning. Using an electrode (a thin wire conducting mild electrical current), Penfield tested the results of stimulating different specific sites. He discovered that probing a certain area might stimulate a particular body movement, sensory experience, emotion, or memory (Penfield & Baldwin, 1952). Later, in the mid-1950s, **Walter Hess** pioneered the use of electrical stimulation to probe structures deeper in the brain. Hess found that deeply placed electrodes stimulated elaborate sequences of behavior and emotional activity.

Other neuroresearchers discovered they could record the electrical activity of the brain as it responded to environmental stimulation. Electrodes positioned over the surface of the head can transmit signals about the brain's electrical activity to a machine called an electroencephalograph. This machine produces an electroencephalogram (EEG), an amplified tracing of the brain's electrical activity—from electro- (electrical) encephalo- (brain) gram (writing). An EEG is used to study the brain during states of arousal. It has been particularly useful in helping psychologists to study sleeping and dreaming processes and to diagnose abnormalities in brain activity.

technological innovations such as the electron microscope and brain scanning systems have led to an explosion in the number of new theories and tests of how the brain works. What we know today about the brain and nervous system is a result of the quest begun by Descartes in the seventeenth century. Read Focus on Science: Eavesdropping on the Brain for a brief history of the methods applied to study the brain and nervous system.

Brain Scanning Modern advances in brain science really began when researchers developed ways to study brain *activity* without needing to expose or physically invade the brain tissue. **Brain scans** *are mechanical and electronic measurements of biochemical and electrical activity at specific brain sites.* Originally, these exciting technological innovations for brain study were developed to help neurosurgeons detect brain abnormalities such as tumors or stroke-related damage. Brain scanning machines produce images of different regions of the living brain. Comparable to x-ray techniques, brain scans do not surgically alter or damage brain tissue. Most of the new scanning procedures employ *brain imaging* technique and are based on two assumptions: first, increased activity by cells in specific parts of the brain will lead to increased blood flow and other biochemical processes in those locations; second, these physiological changes can be *detected* and "imaged" using devices sensitive to the aftereffects of the processes (Posner, 1993). When sophisticated computer techniques are used to enhance the images, brain scans can show how specific regions of the brain seem to "light up" and different structures collaborate when an individual performs certain activities (Raichle, 1994).

The five brain scanning devices currently used by researchers and clinicians are referred to as *CT scanning, PET scanning, MRI, SPECT,* and *SQUID:*

- Computerized tomography or *CT scanning* creates a computerized image of X rays passed through the brain at various angles, detecting soft-tissue structures that normal X rays do not reveal. "Tomography" records different views and cross-sections (from the Greek *tomos,* "section").
- Positron emission tomography, or *PET scanning,* measures neural (brain cell) functioning by tracking the movement of radioactive substances in active regions of the brain. (PET scans rely on detection of material particles called *positrons* that are *emitted* by the radioactive dye).
- The process of magnetic resonance imaging, or *MRI,* uses radio waves to glimpse the effects of magnetic pulses of energy to reveal whether brain cells are functioning normally. ("Resonance" refers to a physical condition that allows body tissue to absorb the energy transmitted by the radio wave.) An even newer technique is *echo-planar MRI,* which produces high-resolution MRI images swiftly enough to view brain and body functions (Alper, 1993).
- *SPECT* refers to single-photon emission computerized tomography, another computer-enhanced system for tracking cerebral blood flow. (A "photon" is a particle of light, as opposed to an energy wave.)
- *SQUID* refers to superconducting quantum interference device, which senses tiny changes in the brain's magnetic fields and depicts the pattern of neural activity in a three-dimensional portrait.

Figure 2.3 displays the quality and detail possible with these five brain scanning techniques. As you can see from the figure, each one provides a different "window" onto brain-mind connections.

Each scanning device also has its particular strengths and weaknesses. For example, PET is good at tracking the brain's functioning, but not as good as MRI for distinguishing between closely related brain structures. In addition, both PET and MRI techniques have difficulty scanning processes that occur at rates faster than hundreds of milliseconds. To track the very fast "conversations" brain cells are capable of conducting, electrical recording techniques are required. One such technique is, of course, the *EEG* (refer to Focus on Science conclusion on page 48). Another electrical scanning process is *magnetoencephalography (MEG),* which measures the magnetic fields generated by

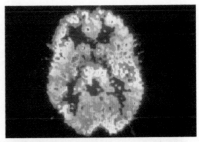

PET

MRI

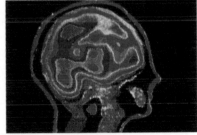

SPECT

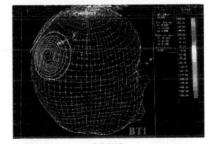

SQUID

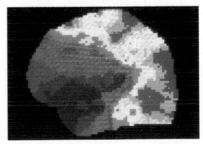

EEG

FIGURE 2.3 Windows on the Mind
■ Reports from five brain scanning devices. From top: PET, MRI, SPECT, SQUID, and EEG. Each scanning and recording device has strengths and weaknesses.

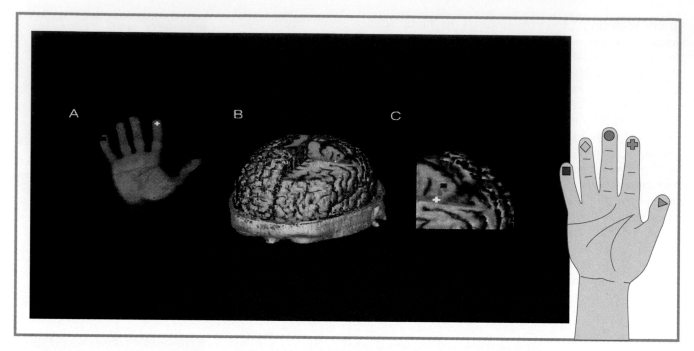

FIGURE 2.4   MEG Image of Sensory Sites in the Brain ■ Magnetoencephalography (MEG) records neural activity that is too brief to be detected by PET or MRI scans. This photo shows how MEG has identified the areas in the somatosensory cortex associated with the fingers of the right hand (see colored symbols).

electrical activity in the brain (Mogilner et al., 1993). Figure 2.4 shows that MEG is able to detect the brain sites where very brief sensations of touch are processed and can map these locations onto a larger picture provided by MRI. While EEG and MEG are superior in their ability to scan brain activity of very brief duration, they are limited in their spatial detail and accuracy (Raichle, 1994). At present no single scanning technique gives psychologists the perfect "window," but ongoing developments continue to improve our view of the living, functioning brain at work.

The Organization of the Brain   Brain scanning confirms that while some cognitive (mental) functions are widely distributed among different brain areas, many activities are highly *localized* or specific to a particular location of brain tissue (Posner, 1993). Nonetheless, the brain is a single organ whose many components collaborate to activate human thought and behavior. To study the parts of the brain, it helps first to visualize the whole. Examine Figure 2.5 and you will see that the brain is composed of different but interconnected layers of tissue and structures. Most psychologists distinguish among three levels of structures, from the earliest to the most recently developed in the evolution of the human brain: first, the *brain stem and cerebellum,* primarily involved in processes such as heart rate, breathing, digestion, and motor coordination; next, the *limbic system,* involved in emotional, motivated, and sexual behavior; and last, the "crowning" achievement of brain evolution, the *cerebrum,* particularly the outermost layer of cells known as the *cerebral cortex,* the site of reasoning, planning, creating, and problem solving. Within the cerebral cortex, sensory information is integrated, precise bodily movements of the mouth and hands are controlled, and abstract thinking and reasoning are facilitated. Let us examine more closely the structure and function of each of these layers of the brain.

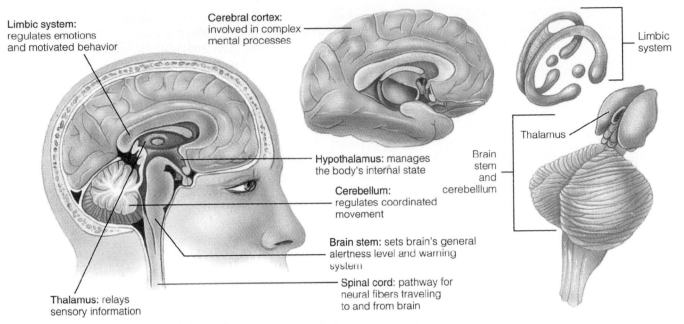

Limbic system: regulates emotions and motivated behavior

Cerebral cortex: involved in complex mental processes

Limbic system

Thalamus

Brain stem and cerebelllum

Hypothalamus: manages the body's internal state

Cerebellum: regulates coordinated movement

Brain stem: sets brain's general alertness level and warning system

Spinal cord: pathway for neural fibers traveling to and from brain

Thalamus: relays sensory information

FIGURE 2.5   Major Structures of the Brain ■ From an evolutionary perspective, the brain stem and cerebellum represent the oldest part of the brain; the limbic system evolved next; and the cerebral cortex is the most recent achievement in brain evolution.

The Brain Stem and Cerebellum

The **brain stem,** *found in all vertebrate species, contains five structures that collectively regulate the internal state of the body* (see Figure 2.6). At the very top of the spinal cord is a slight bulge in neural tissue, the **medulla,** *the center for regulating breathing, and the beating of the heart.* Nerve fibers connecting the brain and the body cross over at the medulla, so that the left side of the body is linked to the right side of the brain and the right side of the body is connected to the left side of the brain.

FIGURE 2.6   Brain Stem and Cerebellum ■ These structures in the central core of the brain are primarily involved with basic life processes: breathing, pulse, arousal, movement, balance, and early processing of sensory information.

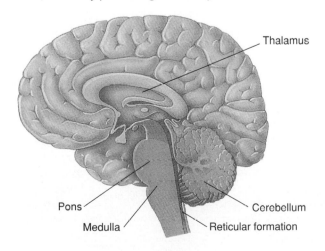

Thalamus

Pons

Medulla

Cerebellum

Reticular formation

Directly above the medulla is the **pons,** *which is involved in brain activity during sleep.* Situated between the medulla and the pons is a dense network of nerve cells, the *reticular formation.* The **reticular formation** *serves as the brain's sentinel, arousing the cerebral cortex to attend to new stimulation and keeping the brain alert even during sleep.*

Nerve fibers run from the reticular formation to the spinal cord, the limbic system, and a brain stem structure called the *thalamus.* The **thalamus** *is a relay station that receives sensory information and channels it to appropriate areas of the cerebral cortex.* For example, the thalamus relays visual information from the eyes to the visual cortex at the back of the brain. The thalamus is also considered essential to learning and to the coordination of sensation into the experience of consciousness.

The last major structure within this "central core" of brain tissue is the *cerebellum.* A distinctive bundle of tissue attached to the brain at the base of the skull, the **cerebellum** *organizes bodily motion, controls posture, and maintains equilibrium.* Your ability to walk, run, and dance reflects the functioning of the cerebellum. Consider the common functions and properties of these core structures: the medulla, pons, reticular formation, thalamus, and cerebellum are all involved in the *coordination* of arousal, information, and physical movement.

The Limbic System

The brain stem and cerebellum are found in all vertebrates, but only mammals and reptiles are equipped with the more recently evolved limbic system. The **limbic system** *processes motivated behaviors, emotional states, and certain kinds of memory.* It also regulates body temperature, blood pressure, and blood-sugar level. The limbic system is comprised of three structures: the hippocampus, amygdala, and hypothalamus (see Figure 2.7).

The largest of the limbic system's structures, the **hippocampus** *plays an important role in memory, especially in long-term storage of information* (Galluscio, 1990). The hippocampus gets its name from the ancient Greek word for "seahorse," referring to its distinctively curved ridges. Damage to the hippocampus impairs the ability to remember newly-learned information.

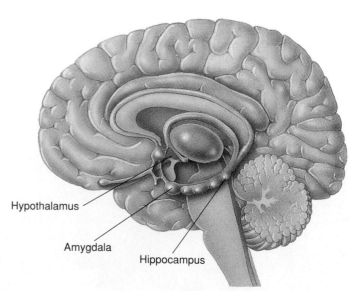

FIGURE 2.7 Limbic System ■
The structures of the limbic system are involved with motivation, emotion, and certain memory processes.

Evidence for the hippocampus's role in memory is derived mostly from clinical research, notably from studies of a patient referred to only as "H. M.," perhaps psychology's most famous subject. When he was 27, H. M. underwent surgery in an attempt to reduce the frequency and severity of his epileptic seizures. During the operation, parts of his hippocampus were removed. As a result, H. M. could recall only the very distant past; his ability to put new information into long-term memory was seriously impaired. Long after his surgery, he continued to believe he was living in 1953, the year the operation had been performed. It appears that hippocampal damage has similar effects on memory in humans, monkeys, and rats, although exactly *how* similar cannot be determined because the species are studied via different methods (Squire, 1992).

The **amygdala** *is known best for its role in aggression; it is also involved in memory, emotion, and certain basic motivations.* Studies with several animal species, including humans, have shown that cutting parts of the amygdala has a calming effect on otherwise mean-spirited individuals, while electrically stimulating the amygdala triggers aggressive behavior.

The *hypothalamus* is one of the smallest structures in the brain, yet it plays a vital role in many of our most important daily actions. Composed of several bundles of neurons, the **hypothalamus** *regulates physiological processes involved in emotional and motivated behavior, including eating, drinking, temperature regulation, and sexual arousal.* For example, when your body is "running low" on nutrients, it is the hypothalamus that sends signals to prompt hunger and eating behavior. The hypothalamus also regulates the activities of the endocrine system and influences the hormones it secretes. The hypothalamus basically maintains **homeostasis,** *the body's internal balance or equilibrium.*

The limbic system structures (the hippocampus, amygdala, and hypothalamus) all function to maintain *balance,* both within the body and between the individual and the environment.

The Cerebrum

Evolution has designed the **cerebrum** to be *the part of the brain that regulates higher levels of cognitive and emotional functioning.* It makes up two-thirds of the total mass of the human brain and is the major reason why our brains are so much larger than those of other species (see Figure 2.8). Cerebral tissue covers and enfolds the limbic system and brain stem. *The outermost layer of the cerebrum is composed of billions of cells called the* **cerebral** cortex (from the Latin for "bark" or "shell"). What is unique about this brain structure is its wrinkled or convoluted formation, folding in on itself to enable so much of new human "thinking tissue" to be squeezed into a relatively small space inside the skull.

The two nearly symmetrical halves of the cerebrum are the **cerebral hemispheres,** each mediating different cognitive and emotional functions. *The two hemispheres are connected by a thick mass of nerve fibers, collectively referred to as the* **corpus callosum.** This connecting pathway sends messages back and forth between the hemispheres. (See the right-hand illustration in Figure 2.8 for a top view of the two hemispheres and the corpus callosum connecting them.)

The Cortical Lobes   Neuroscientists have mapped each hemisphere using two important landmarks as their guides. The *central sulcus* divides each hemisphere vertically, while the *lateral fissure* divides each one horizontally (consult the side view in Figure 2.8). These vertical and horizontal divisions roughly define four anatomical regions, or lobes, in each hemisphere. Each of these lobes contains structures that serve specific functions. The *frontal lobe,*

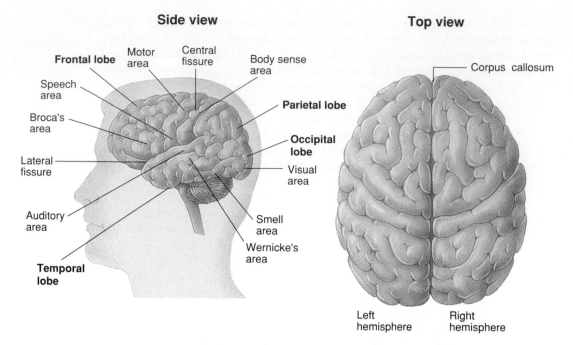

Side view

Frontal lobe
Motor area
Central fissure
Body sense area
Speech area
Parietal lobe
Broca's area
Occipital lobe
Lateral fissure
Visual area
Auditory area
Smell area
Wernicke's area
Temporal lobe

Top view

Corpus callosum

Left hemisphere   Right hemisphere

FIGURE 2.8   Cerebral Cortex ■ Each of the two hemispheres of the cerebral cortex has four lobes. Different sensory and motor functions have been associated with specific parts of each lobe. The two hemispheres are connected by a thick bundle of fibers called the corpus callosum.

above the lateral fissure and in front of the central fissure, is involved with motor control and cognitive activities such as planning, deciding, and pursuing goals. Accidents that damage the frontal lobes can have devastating effects on human behavior and personality, as in the famous case of Phineas Gage (review the introduction to the Focus on Science: Eavesdropping on the Brain, page 48). The *parietal lobe,* located directly behind the central sulcus toward the top of the head, controls incoming sensory information. The *occipital lobe,* at the back of the head, is the major destination for visual information. The *temporal lobe,* at the side of each cerebral hemisphere, is where auditory information is processed.

No one brain lobe controls any specific behavior alone. For example, when you do something as simple as answering a ringing telephone, you hear it in your temporal lobes, visually locate it in your occipital lobes, grasp and handle the receiver with the help of your parietal lobes, and engage in thoughtful conversation through processes in your frontal lobes. The brain's structures always work in concert to perform all complex functions, although specific structures appear to be necessary for specific activities, such as vision, hearing, language, and memory.

The Cortical Functions *The actions of the body's more than 600 voluntary muscles, are controlled by the* **motor cortex,** located just in front of the central fissure in the frontal lobes. As you can see in Figure 2.9, the upper parts of the body receive far more detailed motor instructions than the lower parts. In fact, the two largest areas of the motor cortex are devoted to the fingers (especially the thumb) and to the muscles involved in speech; this reflects the importance of manipulating objects and talking in human activity. Remember that commands from one side of the brain are directed to muscles on the opposite side of the body. Thus, the motor cortex in the right hemisphere of your brain controls the muscles in your left foot.

Located in the left and right parietal lobes, just behind the central fissure, is the **somatosensory cortex,** *which processes information about temperature, touch, body position, and pain.* Similar to the motor cortex, the upper region of the somatosensory cortex relates to the lower parts of the body, and the lower part relates to the upper parts of the body. Most of the somatosensory cortex area is devoted to the lips, tongue, thumb, and index fingers—the parts of the body that provide the most important sensory input (see Figure 2.9; also, review Figure 2.4 on page 50 showing brain scan identification of finger-tip sensory sites in the parietal lobe). Similar to the motor cortex, the right half of the somatosensory cortex communicates with the left side of the body and the left half with the right side of the body.

Auditory information is processed in the **auditory cortex,** *which is in the temporal lobes.* The auditory cortex in *each* hemisphere receives information from *both* ears. One area of the auditory cortex is involved in the production of language and a different area is involved in language comprehension. *Visual input is processed at the back of the brain in the* **visual cortex,** *located in the two occipital lobes.* Input from the center part of the retina at the back of the eye, the area that transmits the most focused, detailed visual information, claims the greatest proportion of space in the visual cortex

FIGURE 2.9 Motor Cortex and the Somatosensory Cortex ■ Actions of the body's voluntary muscles are controlled by the motor cortex in the frontal lobe. The somatosensory cortex in the parietal lobe processes information about temperature, touch, body position, and pain. The diagram below shows the proportion of tissue devoted to various activities or sensitivities in each cortex.

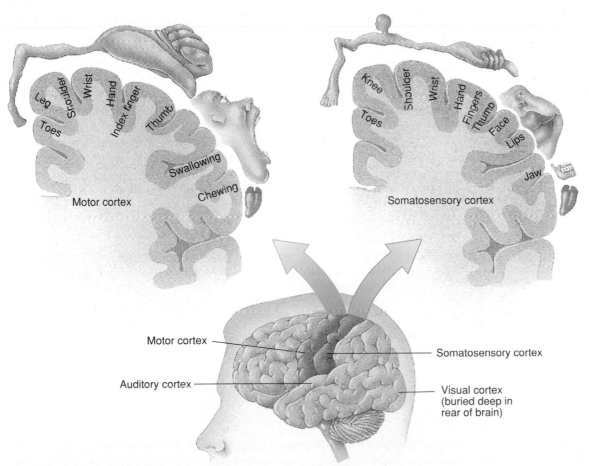

Not all of the cerebral cortex is devoted to processing sensory information and commanding the muscles to action. In fact, the majority of the cortex is involved in *integrating information* from various brain centers (those many areas of the cortex that are *not* specifically labeled in Figure 2.8 on page 54). Collectively, these distributed brain centers, known as the **association cortex,** *process such mental activities as planning and decision making.* Humans have more of their cerebral cortex area devoted to the association cortex than do non-human species, and show much greater flexibility in their behavior. Human associative ability underlies much of our species' adaptive ability to learn, think, anticipate, and creatively solve problems.

Check Your Recall

Humans have long recognized a link between body and mind, although scientific study of the brain was not undertaken until modern times. Beginning with René Descartes's assertion that the body could be studied through observation, research has continued to develop technologies and theories to explain the body's role in behavior. Research methods include early studies of brain injuries and lesions, and recent brain scanning techniques for imaging brain tissue during mental activity.

The brain consists of three layers of connected structures: the brain stem and cerebellum, the limbic system, and the cerebral cortex. The brain stem and cerebellum control processes involved in survival and movement. The limbic system's structures control balance, motivation, and emotion. The cerebral cortex surrounds most other brain structures and controls the most complex mental processes. Different lobes of the two cerebral hemispheres contain cortices that process sensation, movement, and association. The different structures of the brain function as an integrated whole, with no one brain region operating independently of the others.

The Biology of Behavior

Our bodies actually have two distinct and highly complex communication systems. One system, the **nervous system,** *is a massive network of nerve cells that rapidly relays messages to and from the brain.* The nervous system's messages rely on the production and release of **neurotransmitters,** *chemicals that carry information between nerve cells.* The other system, the **endocrine system,** *is a network of glands that manufacture and secrete chemical messengers directly into the bloodstream.* These chemical messengers, called **hormones,** *affect the operation of other glands and organs.* (See Figure 2.10 for the location of the body's endocrine glands.)

The nervous system and endocrine system work together to trigger various types of individual human action. We will look first at the structures and physiology of the nervous system and next at the components and effects of the endocrine system.

The Nervous System

The body's fastest communication network, the nervous system, is composed of billions of highly specialized *nerve cells,* or **neurons,** that are organized either into densely packed clusters (nuclei) or pathways (nerve fibers). The nuclei make up the brain, and they process information; the nerve fibers and the brain together make up the nervous system.

Organization of the Nervous System   The nervous system is subdivided into two major subsystems: the **central nervous system** (CNS) and the **periph-**

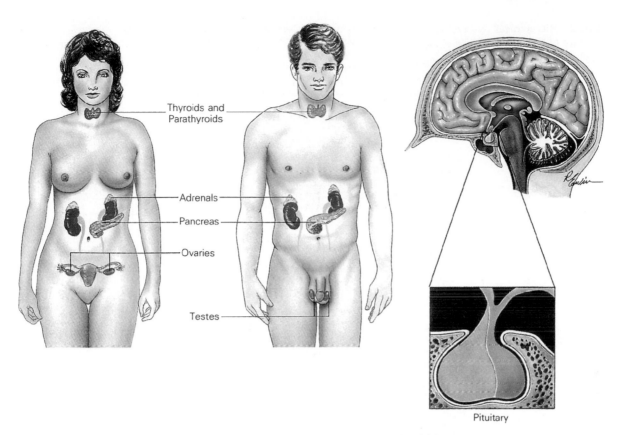

Thyroids and Parathyroids

Adrenals

Pancreas

Ovaries

Testes

Pituitary

FIGURE 2.10   Endocrine Glands in Females and Males ■ The pituitary gland (shown at right) is the "master gland," regulating the endocrine glands whose locations are illustrated at left. The pituitary gland is under the control of the hypothalamus, an important structure in the limbic system.

eral nervous system (PNS). *The CNS is composed of all the neurons in the brain and spinal cord, while the PNS is made up of all the neurons forming the nerve fibers that connect the CNS to the rest of the body.* In Figures 2.11 and 2.12 you can better see the distribution and relationship of the central and peripheral nervous systems.

The CNS integrates and coordinates all bodily functions, processes incoming neural messages, and sends out commands to different parts of the body, depending upon the environmental situation. For example, if a vicious-looking dog approaches you, your CNS signals your legs to run; if a friend greets you, your CNS signals your arms to reach out, and signals your voice to speak. The CNS sends and receives neural messages through the *spinal cord,* a trunk line of neurons that connects the brain to the PNS. The trunk line is housed in the spinal column, the hollow central tube running through your vertebrae.

The spinal cord also coordinates the activity of the left and right sides of the body and is responsible for simple, swift reflexes that do not involve the brain. For example, an organism whose spinal cord has been severed from its brain can still withdraw its limb from a painful stimulus. Though normally the brain is notified of such action, the organism can complete the action without directions from the brain. Damage to the nerves of the spinal cord can result in paralysis of the legs or trunk, as seen in paraplegic individuals. The extent of paralysis depends on how high up on the spinal cord the damage occurred: the higher up the site of damage, the greater the extent of the paralysis. In late spring of 1995, American actor Christopher Reeve was paralyzed from the neck down by an injury sustained during a horseback riding accident.

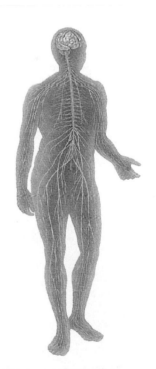

FIGURE 2.11   Physical Organization of the Nervous System ■ The sensory and motor nerves that make up the peripheral nervous system are linked to the brain by the spinal cord.

FIGURE 2.12 Hierarchical Organization of the Nervous System ■

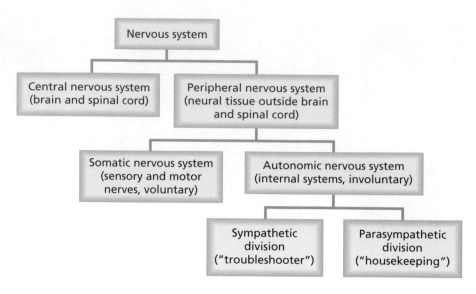

Nervous system

Central nervous system (brain and spinal cord)

Peripheral nervous system (neural tissue outside brain and spinal cord)

Somatic nervous system (sensory and motor nerves, voluntary)

Autonomic nervous system (internal systems, involuntary)

Sympathetic division ("troubleshooter")

Parasympathetic division ("housekeeping")

When actor Christopher Reeve ("Superman") broke his neck in a horseback riding accident in the spring of 1995, physicians could only assess the extent of his subsequent paralysis by first identifying where in his spinal cord the damage had been done.

Physicians caring for Reeve emphasized that his prognosis (likely future condition) depended on the extent and location of damage to his spinal cord.

Despite its commanding position, the CNS is isolated from any direct contact with the outside world. The PNS provides the CNS with information from sensory receptors, such as those found in the eyes and ears, and relays commands from the brain to the body's organs and muscles. The PNS is actually composed of two subdivisions of nerve fibers (see Figure 2.12). The **somatic nervous system** *regulates the actions of the body's skeletal muscles.* For example, when you type a message on a keyboard, the movement of your fingers is regulated by the somatic nervous system. As you plan what to say, your brain sends signals about which fingers to use on which keys, and your fingers return feedback about their position and movement. If you strike the wrong ke*e*, the somatic nervous system informs the brain, which issues a correction so you can quickly delete the error and hit the right key.

The other subdivision of the PNS is the **autonomic nervous system** (ANS), *which sustains basic life processes.* *Autonomic* means self-regulating or independent. The ANS operates constantly, regulating bodily processes we don't usually control consciously, such as respiration, digestion, and arousal. It works during sleep, and sustains life processes during anesthesia and coma. The autonomic nervous system is subdivided into the *sympathetic* and *parasympathetic* nervous systems. These two systems work together "in opposition" to deal with survival matters by maintaining bodily function and preparing the body to respond to threat. The **sympathetic division** *governs responses to stress in emergencies,* when action must be quick and powerfully energized. This is the "fight or flight" response system. It energizes you to respond to a stressor quickly by either fighting what threatens you or taking flight from what you cannot fight. In contrast, the **parasympathetic division** *monitors the routine operation of the body's internal functions;* this division returns the body to calmer functioning after sympathetic arousal. The separate duties of the sympathetic and parasympathetic nervous systems are illustrated in Figure 2.13.

The Neuron   To interact with the world, we depend on the nervous system more than the endocrine system. Exactly how does the nervous system permit us to sense and respond to the world outside our bodies? To answer this question, we will begin by discussing the structure and function of the neuron, the basic unit of the nervous system. The **neuron** *is a cell specialized to receive, process, and/or transmit information to other cells within the body.* Neurons vary in shape, size, chemical composition, and function. Over 200 different types have been identified in mammal brains, but all neurons have the same basic structure (see Figure 2.14).

The number of neurons in the brain does not increase significantly in one's lifetime, and this stability may be essential for the *continuity* of learning and memory over a long lifetime (Rakic, 1985). However, human neurons die in astonishing numbers—about 200,000 will die *every day* of your life (see Dowling, 1992)! Fortunately, because we start out with so many neurons, we will lose less than 2 percent of our original supply in 70 years.

The Structure of a Neuron Neurons typically take in information at one end and send out messages from the other. *The part of the cell that receives incoming signals consists of branched fibers called* **dendrites,** which extend outward from the cell body. The dendrites receive stimulation from other neurons or sense receptors.

The *cell body, or* **soma,** *contains the nucleus of the cell and the cytoplasm* that sustains its life. The soma integrates information about the stimulation received from the dendrites (or in some cases received directly from another neuron) and passes it on to a *single, extended fiber, the* **axon.**

FIGURE 2.13　Divisions of the Autonomic Nervous System ■ The parasympathetic nervous system (diagrammed at left) regulates day-to-day internal processes and behavior. The sympathetic nervous system (at right) regulates internal processes and behavior in stressful situations. On their way to and from the spinal cord, sympathetic nerve fibers make connections with specialized clusters of neurons called ganglia.

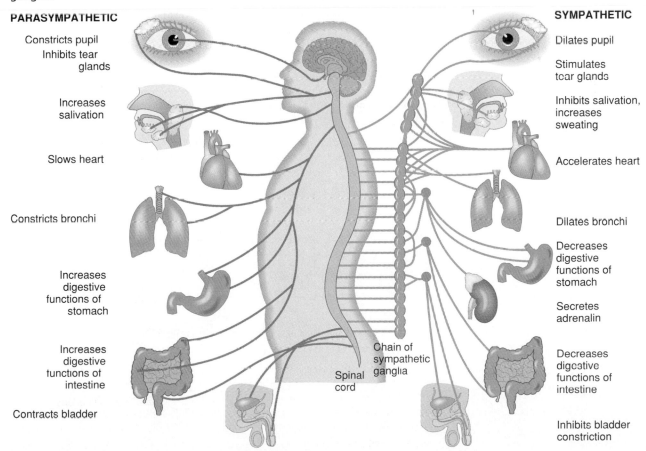

PARASYMPATHETIC

Constricts pupil
Inhibits tear glands
Increases salivation
Slows heart
Constricts bronchi
Increases digestive functions of stomach
Increases digestive functions of intestine
Contracts bladder

SYMPATHETIC

Dilates pupil
Stimulates tear glands
Inhibits salivation, increases sweating
Accelerates heart
Dilates bronchi
Decreases digestive functions of stomach
Secretes adrenalin
Decreases digestive functions of intestine
Inhibits bladder constriction

Chain of sympathetic ganglia
Spinal cord

The axon conducts this information along its length, which can be several feet in the spinal cord and less than a millimeter in the brain. *At the far end of an axon are swollen, bulblike structures called* **terminal buttons,** *through which stimulation passes* to nearby glands, muscles, or other neurons.

Neurons generally transmit information in only one direction: from the dendrites through the soma to the axon to the terminal buttons, as illustrated by the arrows depicted in Figure 2.14.

Types of Neurons   In general, there are three major classes of neurons: *sensory neurons, motor neurons,* and *interneurons.* **Sensory neurons,** *a category of afferent neurons (from a Latin term meaning "carrying toward"), carry messages from sense receptor cells toward the central nervous system.* Receptor cells are highly specialized sensory neurons that are sensitive to light, sound, or other stimuli.

Motor neurons, *a kind of efferent neurons (meaning "carrying from"), carry messages away from the central nervous system toward the muscles and glands.*

Sensory neurons rarely communicate directly with motor neurons. Instead, they rely on the *interneurons* that make up most of the brain's billions of cells. **Interneurons** *relay messages from sensory neurons to other interneurons or to motor neurons.* For every motor neuron in the body there are as many as 5,000 interneurons in the great intermediate network that forms the computational system of the brain (Nauta & Feirtag, 1979).

Interspersed among the brain's vast web of neurons are about five to ten times as many *glial* cells, from the Greek word for "glue," hinting at one of their major functions. The **glia** *bind neurons to each other* (without actually touching). Glial cells also form a **myelin sheath,** *a fatty insulation around some types of axons, which biochemically speeds the conduction of internal impulses.* Neural impulses are sped between the **nodes of Ranvier,** *indentations that punctuate the myelin sheath.*

FIGURE 2.14   Major Structures of the Neuron ■ The neuron receives nerve impulses through its dendrites. These impulses are then transmitted through the cell body to the axon and to the terminal buttons, where neurotransmitters are released to stimulate other neurons.

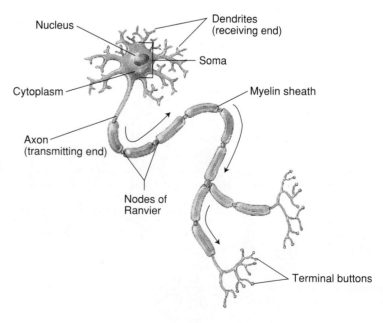

Neurotransmission   You may wonder why you need to understand the nervous system function in such great detail. After all, this is psychology, not an advanced physiology course. Neural activity, however, is the biological medium in which behavior, thinking, and emotion all occur. Changes in nervous system activity lead to changes in how people behave, think, and feel. This text includes this information to help you understand the basic terms and operations of the biology of psychology.

The Neural Impulse   The nervous system uses electrochemical signals to process and transmit information. A single neuron's electrical activity changes when electrically charged particles called *ions* flow through the membrane that separates the cell's inside from the outside environment.

The neuron and its environment both contain ions (atoms of sodium, chloride, calcium, and potassium) that are either positively or negatively charged. The membrane separating the inner cell from the outer environment determines the cell's *polarity*, which is its electrical charge relative to the outside. An inactive, *polarized* nerve cell has a slightly more negative voltage inside relative to outside.

The cell membrane is not a perfect seal, so ions "leak" in and out of the neuron. The polarized balance is maintained with powerful transport mechanisms that pump certain ions in and others out, keeping neurons inactive but "ready" (Kalat, 1984).

When a neuron is stimulated by another neuron's impulse or by sensory stimulation, it becomes less negatively charged, or *depolarized,* and begins to produce its own electrical signals. In this depolarized state, the cell membrane is more easily permeated by ions flowing into and out of the cell body. In the jargon of neuroscience, the neuron is said to be "firing."

As a neuron fires, the inner cell's charge becomes relatively more *positive* relative to the outside environment: it becomes fully depolarized. The depolarizing impulse, once begun, moves throughout the soma, from the reception site through the length of the axon. After firing, the transport mechanisms in the membrane restore the ionic balance that returns the neuron to a state of readiness once more.

Synaptic Transmission   The neural impulse travels the length of the neuron along the axon, finally arriving at the terminal buttons—where there is no direct physical connection to the next destination. No two neurons ever touch; they are always separated by *a gap at the near-junction of the two nerve cells, termed the* **synapse.** Firing sets off activity at the synapse. This begins a remarkable sequence of events called **synaptic transmission,** *in which information is relayed from one neuron to another across the synaptic gap* (see Figure 2.15).

As the neural impulse proceeds, small packets called *synaptic vesicles* move from within the cell to the inner membrane of the terminal buttons. Each vesicle contains **neurotransmitters,** *biochemical substances that stimulate other neurons.* The vesicles rupture, spilling their contents into the synaptic gap, and the neurotransmitters attach themselves to the receiving neuron.

If the neurotransmitter inputs are sufficiently stimulating, the receiving neuron will experience a change (either being excited into firing or inhibited from firing). Thus the impulse "message" will be relayed, cell to cell, as far as the strength of the relayed impulse can carry it.

Neurotransmitters   All nervous system activity depends on synaptic transmission, making neurotransmitters worth a closer look. More than 60 different

FIGURE 2.15 Synaptic Transmission ■ Firing in the presynaptic ("sending") neuron causes neurotransmitters to be released into the synaptic gap. After crossing the gap, these substances stimulate receptor molecules in the postsynaptic ("receiving") neuron. A single neuron may contain many different neurotransmitters.

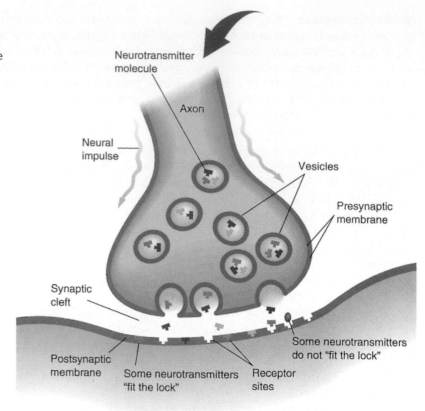

chemical substances are known or suspected to function as neurotransmitters in the brain. In addition to neurotransmitters, exciting recent research has focused on transmitter substances that are gases (Barinaga, 1993). We will distinguish particularly among six neurotransmitters that researchers have identified as important in daily brain functioning: *acetylcholine, GABA, dopamine, norepinephrine, serotonin,* and the *endorphins.*

- *Acetylcholine* is found in both the central and peripheral nervous systems. In the brain, it appears to be associated with memory processes.
- The chemical *GABA* (gamma-amino butyric acid) is affected by a variety of depressants, chemical compounds that reduce central nervous system activity. These depressants may cause sedation or reduction of anxiety by increasing levels of GABA active at synapses (Paul et al., 1986).
- Both *dopamine* and *norepinephrine* have been found to play important roles in psychological disorders such as schizophrenia and mood disturbances. Norepinephrine is also apparently involved in some forms of depression. Levels of dopamine that are higher than normal have been found in persons with schizophrenia, leading researchers to develop treatments that might decrease brain levels of dopamine.
- All neurons producing *serotonin* are located in the brain stem, which is involved with arousal and many autonomic processes. Hallucinogenic drugs such as LSD (lysergic acid diethylamide) have profound effects on these serotonin neurons by influencing their receptivity to neural impulses (Jacobs, 1987). Hallucinogens produce vivid, bizarre, and sometimes long-lasting sensory experiences.

■ The *endorphins* are chemical substances that change or modify a neuron's receptivity to a transmitted impulse. Endorphins were discovered during experiments on morphine, a powerful sedative drug (Pert & Snyder, 1973). The brain was found to produce its own morphinelike substances, including the endorphins, which play an important role in the experience of emotion, pain, and pleasure. Research indicates that the pain relief provided by acupuncture or placebo effects may be caused by the release of endorphins (Fields & Levine, 1984; Hopson, 1988; Watkins & Mayer, 1982).

Volume Transmission   Is it possible for information to leave the structured circuits of neurons and closely linked synapses to travel to receptors in distant parts of the brain? If you think of neuronal circuits as railroad networks whose information "trains" need to stay on track, then it would seem impossible. Instead of the railroad model, however, think of communication in the brain as being like a radio broadcast in which signals are picked up by any properly tuned receptor. A new theory of how the brain transmits information proposes two types of cerebral communication: (1) the traditional, swift relaying of messages across synapses (railroad example) and (2) a slower diffusion of messages in the fluid-filled space between the cells of the brain (radio example). In the second process, called **volume transmission,** *remote cells are influenced by neurons that release chemical signals into the brain's extracellular space* (Agnati et al., 1992).

Volume transmission is a complement, not an alternative, to synaptic transmission. For fast, precise signaling, as in reading and understanding these words, you rely on efficient neurotransmission across the synapses of intimately related neurons. However, new research reveals that neurons also release chemical signals that are not necessarily detected by neighboring cells but are picked up by distant cells (see Figure 2.16 for a diagram of how these signals are thought to travel in the cerebrospinal fluid). This medium of communication works similarly to the way glands release hormones into the

FIGURE 2.16 Volume Transmission in the Brain ■ In volume transmission, cells communicate when chemical signals travel various distances through the space outside and between brain cells. In this diagram, activating substances can affect the neuron (blue) that releases the signal, a neighboring neuron (orange), or a distant neuron (green). Chemical signals can also travel great distances in the cerebrospinal fluid.

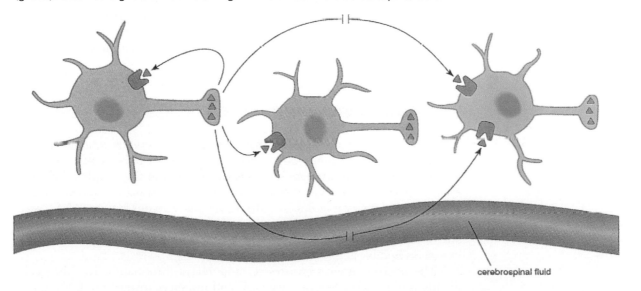

cerebrospinal fluid

bloodstream; the process is slower than neuronal communication but has longer-lasting effects.

Volume transmission distributes information to a general region of sensitive brain cells, rather than only to a specific set of neurons in a circuit. Because of this distribution, volume transmission influences the general activity level of these neural connections instead of determining their specific activity. In this way, the release of chemical signals into the extracellular spaces of the brain may serve to regulate an individual's alertness and mood. Ongoing research on volume transmission has two areas of focus: (1) studying the interaction with synaptic transmission and (2) identifying the properties of the spaces between neurons that provide the medium for the slow, general messages.

The Endocrine System

As described earlier, chemicals called hormones are secreted into the bloodstream by the endocrine glands (the glands take their name from the Greek *endo* for "within" and *krinein* for "secrete"). Hormones are involved in a wide array of bodily functions and behaviors. They influence body growth, sexual development, arousal, mood, and metabolism (the body's rate of energy use). Endocrine glands are stimulated in three ways: by chemical levels in the bloodstream, other hormones, or nerve impulses from the brain. Once secreted into the blood, hormones are pumped to their bodily targets.

Endocrine communication not only sustains our slow and continuous bodily processes, but also helps us to respond in crises. When you encounter a stressor or an emergency (such as the sound of an alarm or a cry for help), the hormone adrenaline is released into the bloodstream, energizing your body for quick defensive action—for "fight or flight." Your heart pounds, your muscles tense, and you feel impelled to take whatever action your brain tells you makes sense.

Hormones have been called "the messengers of life" because their influence is diverse but specific (Crapo, 1985). The body's different hormone "factory" sites produce chemicals that influence a variety of bodily processes. Table 2.1 outlines the major glands and their hormonal targets.

A small structure in the limbic system, the hypothalamus, is the brain center in charge of the endocrine system. The hypothalamus is an important relay station among other parts of the brain, the endocrine system, and the central nervous system. Specialized cells in the hypothalamus receive messages from other brain cells commanding it to release a number of different chemicals. These chemicals then influence the adjacent **pituitary gland,** *the so-called master gland which can either stimulate or inhibit the release of other glands' hormones.* The pituitary gland also releases a hormone that directly influences bodily growth and development.

Check Your Recall

The body's two communication systems are the nervous system and the endocrine system. The nervous system, composed of billions of neurons, is subdivided into the central nervous system (CNS) and the peripheral nervous system (PNS). The PNS is further divided into the somatic nervous system, regulating voluntary muscles, and the autonomic nervous system (ANS), regulating basic living functions. The sympathetic division of the ANS acts during stress and crises, while the parasympathetic division restores calm and conserves bodily energy.

The neuron receives, processes, and relays information to other cells, glands, and muscles. Sensory neurons send messages toward the CNS; motor

TABLE 2.1	**HORMONAL FUNCTIONS OF MAJOR ENDOCRINE GLANDS**
These Glands	**Produce Hormones That Regulate**
Hypothalamus	Release of pituitary hormones
Anterior pituitary	Ovaries and testes Breast milk production Metabolism Reactions to stress
Posterior pituitary	Conservation of water in the body Breast milk excretion Uterus contraction
Thyroid	Metabolism Physical growth and development
Parathyroid	Calcium levels in the body
Gut	Digestion
Pancreas	Glucose metabolism
Adrenal glands	Fight-or-flight response Metabolism Sexual desire (in women)
Ovaries	Development of female sexual characteristics Production of ova (eggs)
Testes	Development of male sexual characteristics Sperm production Sexual desire (in men)

neurons channel messages from the CNS; and interneurons relay information between neurons. Glia bind neurons together. When a neuron fires, information is relayed from the dendrites, through the soma, and through the axon to the terminal buttons. Neurotransmitters are released into the synaptic gap, where they may be taken up by the receiving neuron. The receiving neuron's activity can be either excited or inhibited by a transmitted impulse.

In volume transmission, which affects general neural activity and individual mood, neural impulses release both fast-acting synaptic transmissions and slower-acting chemical messages sent to more distant cells.

The endocrine system, controlled by the hypothalamus, consists of ductless glands that produce and secrete hormones into the bloodstream. These chemicals influence body growth, sexual development, metabolism, digestion, and arousal.

The Biology of Consciousness

The nervous system is the basis for all of our conscious experience. Anything that changes how the nervous system operates also changes normal consciousness. In the next chapter, we will focus our attention on the realm of consciousness and the mind, but first we will take a closer look at the links between the biological processes of the nervous system and the human experience of consciousness.

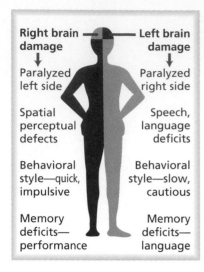

Right brain damage → Paralyzed left side

Spatial perceptual defects

Behavioral style—quick, impulsive

Memory deficits—performance

Left brain damage → Paralyzed right side

Speech, language deficits

Behavioral style—slow, cautious

Memory deficits—language

FIGURE 2.17   Effects of Damage to the Cerebral Hemispheres ■

Cerebral Dominance

The cerebral cortex is the part of the brain responsible for consciousness. Each hemisphere appears to be involved in regulating different aspects of conscious experience, as suggested by some provocative research findings:

■ Patients suffering strokes that paralyze the right side of their bodies often develop speech disturbances, suggesting that speech production is "localized" in the left hemisphere.

■ Patients suffering strokes that damage the left hemisphere often develop problems using and understanding language. (Recall Paul Broca's early findings, mentioned in the Focus on Science: Eavesdropping on the Brain on page 48, that language comprehension is situated in the left hemisphere.)

■ The left hemisphere is usually slightly larger than the right one.

Though the two hemispheres appear to be physically similar, both clinical and experimental evidence clearly indicate dissimilarity in their styles of processing. *The tendency for each hemisphere to dominate the control of different functions is called* **cerebral dominance**. Although the brain typically functions in an integrated and harmonious, or holistic, fashion, some actions and processes are more under the control of the right hemisphere, while others are left-hemisphere dominant.

Much of our knowledge about cerebral dominance comes from observing people who have suffered brain damage on one side or whose cerebral hemispheres could not communicate with each other (see Figure 2.17). Patients with right-hemisphere damage are more likely to have perceptual and attentional problems, which can include serious difficulties in spatial orientation. For example, they may feel lost in a previously familiar place or be unable to perform tasks that require assembling geometric shapes.

In general, studies of healthy individuals have shown that the left side of the brain is more involved in controlling verbal activities, and the right side is more important in directing visual-spatial activities (see Bradshaw, 1989; Bryden, 1982; Davidson, 1992; Lempert & Kinsbourne, 1982; Springer & Deutsch, 1993). However, the two hemispheres often make different contributions to the same function. The two hemispheres seem to researchers to have different "styles" for processing information. For example, on matching tasks, the left hemisphere matched objects analytically and verbally—by similarity in function. The right hemisphere matched things that looked alike or fit together to form a whole pattern (Gazzaniga, 1970; Sperry, 1968, 1982).

On the other hand, differences between the two hemispheres do not clearly outweigh similarities. Both hemispheres contribute to language and memory functions, to perceptual-cognitive functions, and to emotional functions (see Figure 2.18). The differences between the hemispheres are hard to detect except in the cases of rare surgical patients. Generally, each hemisphere seems to *complement* rather than oppose the other. Both hemispheres appear to be capable of either analytic (piece-by-piece) or holistic (as-a-whole) processing, and use one mode or the other depending on the nature of the task (Trope et al., 1992).

Hemispheric asymmetries—differences in the two sides—have captured popular interest in recent years, and many nonpsychologists feel free to discuss whether someone is a "right-brain" or "left-brain" person. Clearly such a distinction is simplistic: research findings to date do not warrant categorizing people in one way or the other. However, a better understanding of cerebral dominance may suggest practical applications in real life. See Focus on Application: Hemispheric Differences and "Risky Business," and consider how to test the effects of cerebral dominance in your own life.

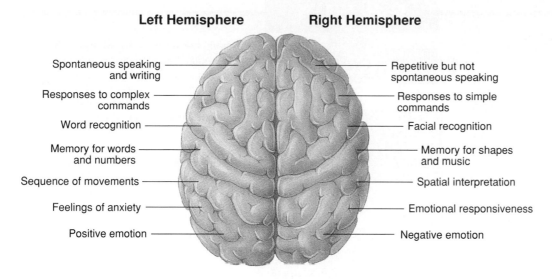

Left Hemisphere   **Right Hemisphere**

Spontaneous speaking and writing

Responses to complex commands

Word recognition

Memory for words and numbers

Sequence of movements

Feelings of anxiety

Positive emotion

Repetitive but not spontaneous speaking

Responses to simple commands

Facial recognition

Memory for shapes and music

Spatial interpretation

Emotional responsiveness

Negative emotion

FIGURE 2.18   Specialization of the Cerebral Hemispheres ■

One Brain or Two?

The fact that the two cerebral hemispheres have apparently different process-ing styles raises an intriguing question: Would each half of the brain be able to act as an independent conscious mind if it were somehow separated from the other? One treatment to relieve the symptoms of severe epilepsy has provided the clinical opportunity to investigate this possibility. In this procedure, surgeons sever the corpus callosum, the bundle of nerve fibers that transfers information between the two hemispheres (review Figure 2.8, top view, on page 54). The goal of the surgery (called a *callosotomy*) is to prevent the violent electrical rhythms that accompany epileptic seizures from crossing between the hemispheres (Trope et al., 1992; Wilson et al., 1977). The opera-tion is usually successful, and a patient's subsequent behavior appears normal. Patients who undergo this type of surgery are often referred to as *split-brain patients*.

Why would researchers think that either hemisphere might be able to function independently? Early studies of hemispheric differences focused on the way the brain combines information from two-sided sources. For example, when sensory input from the eyes is registered by the receptors, it automati-cally goes to the opposite side of the brain (right visual field to left hemisphere; left field to right hemisphere). However, the information is shared by both hemispheres through the corpus callosum. So when split-brain patients can coordinate input from both visual fields, they can function without problems. But when they perform special tasks that present separate information to each visual field or each hand, the behavior of the split-brain patients differs from that of patients with brains whose hemispheres communicate with each other.

The first split-brain operations on human patients were performed by neurosurgeon William Van Wagener in the early 1940s (Van Wagener & Herren, 1940). To test the capabilities of the separated hemispheres of epilep-tic patients, **Roger Sperry** (1968) and **Michael Gazzaniga** (1970) devised situa-tions that allowed visual information to be presented separately to each hemisphere (see Figure 2.19). The left hemisphere was found to be superior to the right in problems involving language or logic and sequential or analytic processing of concepts. The left hemisphere could also "talk back" to the researchers while the right hemisphere could not. Communication with the right hemisphere was achieved by confronting it with manual tasks involving

Hemispheric Differences and "Risky Business"

Risk-taking behavior is the major cause of hospitalization among teenagers and young adults (Quadrel & Fischoff, 1993). Persons in this age group are most susceptible to unwanted pregnancies, addictions, automobile accidents, and sexually transmitted diseases as a result of the risky choices they make. Often "the young and the reckless" waver between danger and safety before deciding what to do. Think for a moment of friends you wish you could have talked to before they made choices that eventually hurt them. Perhaps you too would like a second chance in your own life, an opportunity to go back and reassess the possible costs of something you once said or did.

Research has uncovered an interesting link between risk-taking behavior and cerebral hemispherical "specialization." Canadian researchers Laurie Miller and Brenda Milner demonstrated that, after frontal lobe surgery for brain tumors, patients who became more dependent on their left cerebral hemisphere (LH) were more risk-oriented than normal. Those who had to rely on their right hemisphere (RH) became more cautious (Miller & Milner, 1985). Might this interesting insight be useful to anyone other than neurosurgeons and psychologists? It might, especially when paired with the following finding: when a normal individual pays attention to one side of the environment or the other—such as when you scan the view to your right, or listen to a conversation being carried on to your left— activity increases in the *opposite* cerebral hemisphere. This *selective activation* can be measured by the EEG (De Toffol et al., 1992) or blood flow (Malamed & Larsen, 1977). Researchers have also found that the activation of the opposite cerebral hemisphere by such sideways or *lateral attention* improves performance in activities associated with that hemisphere. For example, rightward attention (paying attention to stimuli on your right) improves verbal task performance, a skill associated with the LH. Likewise, left-

Because alcohol acts as a depressant on the brain, it affects our judgment and ability to gauge risk. Research has uncovered an interesting link between risk-taking behavior and our cerebral hemispheres. Why might these students (if they're right-handed) want to put down their beers and turn to the left for a while?

ward orientation improves spatial task performance, part of the repertoire of the RH (Lempert & Kinsbourne, 1982; Walker et al., 1982).

Based on these two sets of findings, would it be possible to manipulate risky decision making in normal individuals? This was done in an experiment where right-handed students heard choice dilemmas in either their right or left ear. For example, in one dilemma, a man with a limp is offered an operation that would either improve or worsen his ability to walk. Students had to decide whether to advise surgery, basing their decisions on different probabilities that the surgery would succeed. As expected, the students gave significantly *more risky recommendations* (accepting a lower probability of success) when the message about the dilemma had been played into their *right ear*, and subsequently processed in the

more risk-oriented LH (Drake, 1985). Attentional orientation toward the direction of the message's source (such as whether the speaker stood to one's right or left) had a significant effect on whether the listener recommended a more or less risky choice.

What psychological processes might underlie this connection between lateral attention and risk-taking? Consider a body of hemispheric research evidence: LH activity in right-handers has been linked with positive emotions (Davidson, 1992; Leventhal & Tomarken, 1986); furthermore, positive emotions can lower people's estimate of the likelihood of unpleasant events (Johnson & Tversky, 1983). Attention toward one's right side has been linked with making more positive evaluations of music (McFarland & Kennison, 1986) and of pictures seen while looking to one's right (Merckelbach & van Oppen, 1989). So a choice may appear less dangerous and more attractive when we are in a positive mood, and our mood can become more positive by orienting attention to the right—thus activating the LH. Such attentional orientation can increase risky choices by increasing one's sense of optimism and personal control, and reducing feelings of helplessness (Drake & Seligman, 1989).

Life is full of decision-making conflicts, and many options have both potential gains and losses associated with them. Your attention can be manipulated to activate the more risk-oriented tendencies of the LH when it is drawn to the right, or to arouse the RH's greater sense of caution when attention is drawn to the left. To persuade a friend to be more careful, get him or her to turn to the left while listening to you. To alter your own behavior in more adventurous directions, such as overcoming shyness in social situations or applying for a job, try to sit, stand, and walk so your attention is turned to your right. Don't wait for the environment to fuel the risky or cautious tendencies of you and those you care about—take charge of those cues to move in a healthier direction, by applying research on hemispheric differences.

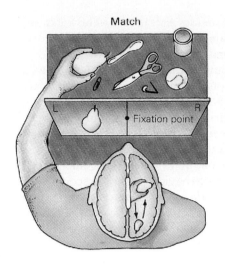 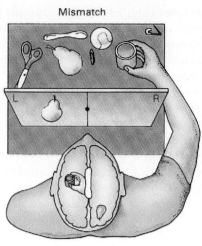

Match   Mismatch

FIGURE 2.19 Eye-Hand Coordination in Split-Brain Subjects ■ When a split-brain patient uses the left hand to find a match to an object appearing in the left visual field, eye-hand coordination is normal, because both are registered in the right hemisphere (left figure). But when asked to use the right hand to match an object seen in the left visual field, the patient cannot perform the task and mismatches a pear with a cup (right figure). This is because sensations from the right hand go to the left hemisphere, and there is no longer a connection between the two hemispheres.

identification, matching, or assembly of objects—tasks that did not require the use of words. Once this communication mode was discovered by researchers, the right hemisphere turned out to be better than the left at solving problems involving spatial relationships and at pattern recognition.

Because the brain is designed to function as a whole, the result of disconnecting the cerebral hemispheres is a *duality of consciousness*. Each hemisphere can respond independently and simultaneously when stimuli are presented separately to each side. When stimuli are presented to only one side, responses are either emotional or analytic, depending on which hemisphere has the task of *interpreting* the message. Because it lacks language competence, the disconnected right hemisphere has limited and vastly inferior visual-spatial communication skills, as compared to the cognitive skills of the left hemisphere.

We must be cautious about generalizing such findings from split-brain patients into a basic view of the way that normal brains function. Does the brain function holistically as a uniform central command system, or is it organized according to specialized functions for each hemisphere? A number of investigators propose that the human mind is neither a single entity nor a dual entity but rather a confederation of multiple mind-modules, each one specialized to process a specific kind of information. The input from these many separate "mini-minds" is synthesized and coordinated for action by central, executive processors (Fodor, 1983; Hinton & Anderson, 1981; Ornstein, 1986a).

The Responsive Brain

It is one thing to recognize that the brain controls behavior and our mental processes, but it is quite another to understand *how* it serves all those functions that we take for granted. It is also important to understand what happens when the brain doesn't work properly.

We began our study of the biology of behavior with the example of how touch can have a biological effect in transforming the growth of premature infants. This positive effect of physical stimulation on bodily growth is mediated by changes in brain functioning. Despite similar formula and calorie intake, the massaged babies gained more weight than the unstimulated control infants, became more physically active, and their sleep patterns changed. Stimulated babies apparently release more of several neurotransmitters. Deprivation of contact with the mother shuts down the growth hormone, but in turn, massaging the infants can maintain the brain's release of the hormone

(Field & Schanberg, 1990). This example provides a clear case of how external stimulation can profoundly modify the brain's functioning. Therapeutic touch also profoundly improves the mental and physical health of the elderly (Fanslow, 1984). Psychologists have concluded that physical touch between people who care about each other not only symbolizes affection but also achieves real biological benefits (Brown, 1984; Gunzenhauser, 1990).

Research demonstrates that the brain is a *dynamic* system capable of changing both its functions and its physical structure in response to various kinds of stimulation and environmental challenges (Sapolsky, 1990). Because of such research, a new perspective on the nature of the brain is emerging. In addition to the *behaving brain* that controls behavior, we now recognize the *responsive brain* that is changed by the behavior it generates and by environmental stimulation. The capacity for its own internal modification makes the complex human brain the most dynamic, responsive system on the planet (Rosenzweig, 1984b).

Check Your Recall

The cerebral cortex is the basis of consciousness. The cortex is divided into two hemispheres connected by the corpus callosum. While the hemispheres are physically symmetrical, their processing styles are not. Language, anxiety, and positive emotions are regulated by the left hemisphere, while the right hemisphere controls spatial interpretation, facial recognition, and negative emotions.

The cortical hemispheres can be physically disconnected by severing the corpus callosum. When one split-brain hemisphere receives information, the other hemisphere is not aware of either the stimulation or the cognitive activity it causes. Although severing the corpus callosum can create dual consciousness, the brain is designed to function as an integrated whole.

Research confirms that the brain not only controls and guides behavior but is also responsive. It continually reacts to environmental stimulation, changing and adapting in ways that reveal its "plasticity."

CHAPTER REVIEW

Summary

Charles Darwin's theory of evolution explains behavior as the result of naturally selected biological features. Variation among individuals and competition for resources and goals lead to survival of the fittest behavior as well as the fittest features. Bipedalism, encephalization, and language gave humans a distinct evolutionary advantage and promoted the development of human cultures.

Early medicine gave way to the study of brain injuries, and lesioning studies assisted in more precise brain localization. Electrical stimulation and recording of brain activity have led to brain scanning techniques that can produce images of mental activity.

The brain is organized in three integrated layers: the brain stem and cerebellum, the limbic system, and the cerebral cortex. The brain stem and cerebellum control survival functions and locomotion, the limbic system maintains balance in motivation and emotion, and the cortex controls complex mental activity. The cerebral cortex is divided into two hemispheres, each with four lobes containing specialized structures for sensation, perception, association, and the initiation of movement.

The body's two communication systems are the nervous system and the endocrine system. The nervous system is composed of neurons, organized into a central and peripheral nervous system, each of these further subdivided for different behavioral and bodily functions. The basic unit of the nervous system is the neuron, which fires when it is stimulated, causing neurotransmitters to be released which can relay the impulse to other nerve cells throughout the system. The slower communication system is that of the endocrine glands, which secrete hormones into the bloodstream, influencing the activity of other glands or bodily structures.

The cerebral cortex is responsible for consciousness. Language, analytical thinking, and positive emotions are regulated by the left hemisphere, while the right hemisphere controls spatial interpretation, visual and musical memory, and negative emotions. If the hemispheres are surgically severed, each functions independently of the other and is not aware of stimulation or cognitive activities that affect the other.

The behaving brain initiates and controls behavior. The responsive brain's functions and structure are changed by stimulation from the environment and from its own behavior. Research indicates that the brain's functioning is modified in profound ways by external stimulation, showing that the brain is a dynamic system, responsive to environmental stimulation and capable of self-modification.

Section Reviews

The Evolution of Behavior

Be sure to *Check Your Recall* by reviewing the summary of this section on page 46.

Key Terms
evolution (p. 41)
natural selection (p. 41)
variation (p. 42)
phenotype (p. 42)
genotype (p. 42)
bipedalism (p. 43)
encephalization (p. 43)
genetics (p. 44)

genes (p. 44)
chromosomes (p. 44)
behavior genetics (p. 45)

Names to Know
Saul Schanberg (p. 39)
Tiffany Field (p. 39)
Charles Darwin (p. 41)

Brain Structures and Functions

Be sure to *Check Your Recall* by reviewing the summary of this section on page 56.

Key Terms
lesions (p. 48)
brain scans (p. 49)
brain stem (p. 51)
medulla (p. 51)
pons (p. 52)
reticular formation (p. 52)
thalamus (p. 52)
cerebellum (p. 52)
limbic system (p. 52)
hippocampus (p. 52)
amygdala (p. 53)
hypothalamus (p. 53)
homeostasis (p. 53)
cerebrum (p. 53)
cerebral cortex (p. 53)

cerebral hemispheres (p. 53)
corpus callosum (p. 53)
motor cortex (p. 54)
somatosensory cortex (p. 54)
auditory cortex (p. 55)
visual cortex (p. 55)
association cortex (p. 56)

Names to Know
René Descartes (p. 47)
Phineas Gage (p. 48)
Paul Broca (p. 48)
Wilder Penfield (p. 48)
Walter Hess (p. 48)

The Biology of Behavior

Be sure to *Check Your Recall* by reviewing the summary of this section on page 64.

Key Terms
nervous system (p. 56)
neurotransmitters (p. 56)
endocrine system (p. 56)
hormones (p. 56)
neurons (p. 56)
central nervous system (p. 56)
peripheral nervous system (p. 56)
somatic nervous system (p. 58)
autonomic nervous system (p. 58)
sympathetic division (p. 58)
parasympathetic division (p. 58)

dendrite (p. 59)
soma (p. 59)
axon (p. 60)
terminal buttons (p. 60)
sensory neurons (p. 60)
motor neurons (p. 60)
interneurons (p. 60)
glia (p. 60)
myelin sheath (p. 60)
nodes of Ranvier (p. 60)
synapse (p. 61)
synaptic transmission (p. 61)
neurotransmitters (p. 61)
volume transmission (p. 63)
pituitary gland (p. 64)

The Biology of Consciousness

Be sure to *Check Your Recall* by reviewing the summary of this section on page 70.

Key Terms
cerebral dominance (p. 66)

Names to Know
Roger Sperry (p. 67)
Michael Gazzaniga (p. 67)

REVIEW TEST

Chapter 2: Biopsychology

For each of the following items, choose the single correct or best answer. The correct answers, explanations, and page references appear in Appendix B.

1. Studies conducted by Tiffany Field and Saul Schanberg show that when premature infants are _____ on a regular basis, they gain more weight and are more active and alert than those who are not.
   a. kept in a quiet, unstimulating environment
   b. physically restrained
   c. gently massaged
   d. allowed to cry
2. In natural selection, an example of _____ is the many different genotypes and phenotypes that are represented in a population.
   a. variation
   b. environment
   c. competition
   d. cerebral dominance
3. Human beings' capacity for _____ stemmed from the development of _____ in the course of our evolution.
   a. bipedalism; encephalization
   b. language; bipedalism
   c. language; encephalization
   d. culture; bipedalism
4. The idea that the mind-body relationship could be scientifically studied like any other natural phenomenon was first advanced by _____.
   a. René Descartes
   b. Wilder Penfield

c. Paul Broca

d. Charles Darwin

5. A researcher surgically destroys a minute section of brain tissue in a living animal and later observes the animal's ability to learn and retain new information. This demonstrates the use of _____ in conducting brain research.

a. lesioning

b. CT scanning

c. the EEG

d. MRI

6. Which of the following statements identifying the locations of important brain structures is true?

a. The hypothalamus is part of the brain stem.

b. The medulla is part of the limbic system.

c. The occipital lobe is part of the cerebral cortex.

d. All of the above.

7. _____ is an example of behavior controlled primarily by the autonomic nervous system.

a. Typing a sentence accurately on a keyboard

b. Solving a mathematical problem

c. Breathing and swallowing while asleep

d. None of the above

8. During a neural impulse, a neuron "fires" when _____.

a. it is physically contacted by another cell that is transmitting the signal

b. it undergoes a change in its electrical charge relative to the outside environment

c. it contracts and releases powerful chemicals directly into the bloodstream

d. signals entering at the axon travel the length of the cell and exit through the dendrites

9. The left hemisphere of the cerebral cortex is more involved than the right hemisphere in experiences such as _____.

a. recognizing and appreciating visual stimuli

b. enjoying and appreciating music

c. using spoken and written language

d. understanding spatial relationships

10. The brain is characterized as "responsive" because we recognize that _____.

a. it dictates every action and experience with specialized control centers

b. it is a closed system, communicating with other biological processes but not with the outside environment

c. every brain cell has a single, unvarying function

d. its functioning is modified in profound ways by external stimulation

IF YOU'RE INTERESTED . . .

Awakenings. (Video: 1990, color, 121 min.). Directed by Penny Marshall; starring Robin Williams, Robert DeNiro, Julie Kavner.

The film is based on the research and experiences of Oliver Sacks, a clinical neurologist studying the relationship between brain and behavior.

Edelman, G. M. (1992). *Bright air, brilliant fire: On the matter of the mind*. New York: Basic Books.

Nobel Prize–winning immunologist's account—intended for the lay reader—of how the brain is designed not to mirror the world but to produce a mind that constructs consciousness.

Edwards, B. (1989). *Drawing on the right side of the brain* (revised edition). New York: Putnam.

Popular and engaging manual suggesting how to use a different way of thinking, and a different way of seeing, to tap artistic abilities you might not realize you have.

Gazzaniga, M. (1985). *The social brain: Discovering the networks of the mind*. New York: Basic Books.

An invitation to the layperson to review the findings of modern brain research and their implications, by one of the pioneers of split-brain research.

Leakey, R., & Lewin, R. (1992). *Origins reconsidered: In search of what makes us human*. New York: Doubleday.

Anthropologist and archaeologist Richard Leakey reviews research into and theory on the origins and evolutionary development of the human race, considering possible answers to the mysteries of language, consciousness, and violent social behavior.

Posner, M. I., & Raichle, M. E. (1994). *Images of mind*. New York: W. H. Freeman.

    Interesting and helpful guide to the development and use of the new brain scanning and imaging techniques.

Restak, R. (1984). *The brain*. Toronto: Bantam.

    A highly readable introduction to the brain by a noted researcher and science writer.

Sacks, O. (1985). *The man who mistook his wife for a hat, and other clinical tales*. New York: Summit Books.

    A fascinating series of clinical stories about patients with neurological disorders that have had extraordinary effects on their lives.

Sacks, O. (1995). *An anthropologist on Mars*. New York: Random House.

    In his most recent collection of essays, neurologist Oliver Sacks explores how several individuals have sought to meet the challenges of unusual neurological disorders, including autism and Tourette's syndrome, by constructing extraordinarily "ordinary," adaptive lives.

Weiner, J. (1994). *The beak of the finch*. New York: Random House.

    Weiner tells "the story of evolution in our time" with examples of classic and contemporary observations of species' adaptation to changing environmental challenges.

CHAPTER 3

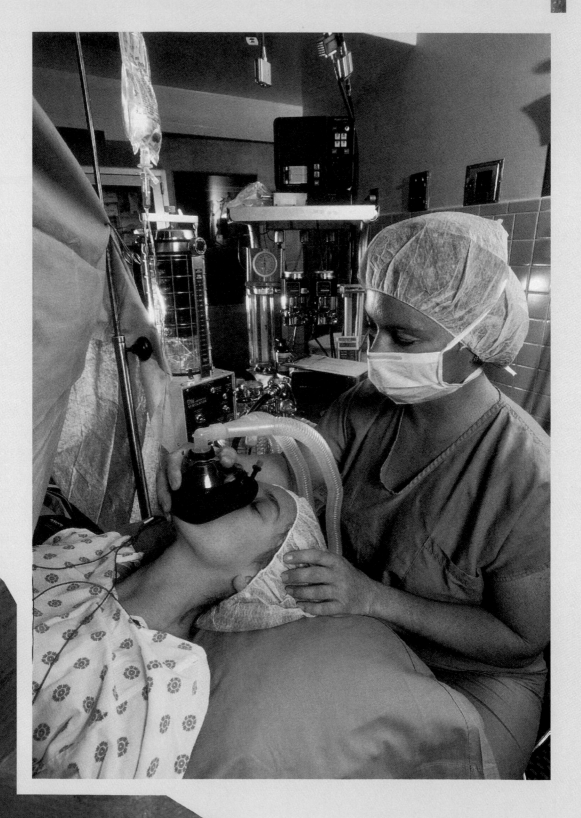

States of Mind

One hundred, 99, 98, 97 . . ." Karen counted as the anesthetic flowed from the needle into her vein. Geometric patterns oscillated wildly before her. "Ninety-two, 91, 9. . . ." Darkness descended. Sensation and awareness shut down. Karen's surgery began.

Karen hadn't worried about this operation—it was only minor surgery to remove a cyst in her mouth. Minutes into the operation, however, the surgeon exclaimed, "Why, this may not be a cyst at all. It may be cancer!" Fortunately, the biopsy proved him wrong. In the recovery room the surgeon told Karen, who was still groggy and slightly nauseous, that everything was fine; the operation was a complete success.

That night, Karen felt anxious and had trouble falling asleep. She started crying for no apparent reason. Finally, when she did fall asleep, she dreamed about a puppy she couldn't get because of her allergy to dogs. Karen awoke feeling sad and was depressed all day. At first, she attributed her bad mood to her dream. But when all attempts to restore her usual good spirits failed and her depression worsened, Karen sought professional help. A therapist hypnotized Karen and asked her to lift her hand if something was disturbing her. Karen's hand rose, and the therapist suggested that she report what was disturbing her. Karen exclaimed, "The cyst may be cancerous!"

Karen's depression lifted after she received assurances that the cyst was benign. Consciously, Karen had not understood the source of her anxiety. But even in an unconscious, anesthetized state, some part of her mind had understood the surgeon's words. The dire meaning of that information became psychologically traumatic to Karen.

Karen's case is not unusual. Increasing evidence indicates that patients who are fully anesthetized and have no conscious recall of their operations may still hear what is going on during their surgery. Our hearing sensitivity appears to remain on alert even under adequate anesthesia. The reasons for this auditory alertness may be deeply rooted in our evolutionary history: animals in the open had to respond swiftly to sounds of possible danger even when asleep. Whatever the reason, highly specialized cells in the auditory nerve make the signals passing along it exceptionally clear and hard to block out with anesthetics. Because of this sensitivity, even casual remarks in the operating room can be dangerous. Anesthetized patients may not be awake, but they are not entirely unaware: at some level they may perceive others' comments and react with shock or fear if those comments are frightening.

Physicians and psychologists are intrigued by research findings on the capacity of anesthetized patients to learn and remember auditory information *experienced during an operation. Such recall seems to occur despite patients' insistence of amnesia when they are conscious. Although not all research supports the operation of memory under general anesthesia, most recent, controlled experiments support several important conclusions (Ghoneim & Block, 1992). Patients under general anesthesia may not be oblivious to their operative experiences, partly because there is no adequate way to measure the depth of anesthesia while a patient is unconscious. Patients also perform well on experimental tasks that measure memory of informa-*

tion they were exposed to during anesthesia (Block et al., 1991; Kihlstrom et al., 1990). More important for patients' health are findings that unfavorable comments voiced about them during anesthesia may harm them, as in Karen's case (Blacher, 1987; Eich et al., 1985; Levinson, 1967). On the positive side, therapeutic suggestions during anesthesia may improve patients' postoperative recovery, as shown by reduced use of morphine and earlier discharge (Evans & Richardson, 1988; McLintock et al., 1990).

Introduction

Karen's case introduces us to the complexities of human consciousness. Her ordinary state of conscious awareness was altered in many ways: by drugs, by sleeping and dreaming, and by hypnosis. Her waking thoughts and moods were influenced by memories and subtle impulses, such as her frustrated desire for a puppy and her fear of cancer. Even when Karen's body was immobilized by a general anesthetic, her brain was still subconsciously processing environmental stimuli.

What is "ordinary" conscious awareness? Can unconscious mental events influence our thoughts, emotions, and actions? Why does consciousness change? How can people intentionally change their states of mind?

Our search for answers to these questions puts the human mind in the spotlight. In the previous chapter we began to explore the relationship between brain and behavior. In this chapter we continue that exploration by considering how the brain produces mind and consciousness and how behaviors interact with states of mind. We will first consider some of the mental changes people experience every day, and then examine how special techniques and experiences can dramatically and deliberately alter consciousness.

Consciousness

Our early ancestors traced the causes of human actions to their *anima,* or inner life force, and the operation of outer spiritual forces (divine and demonic) that they believed existed in nature. They assumed that an individual's spirit, or soul, was separate from the body; they also assumed that the soul controlled the person. If evil spirits entered a person's body, they could cause disease or bizarre behavior. When the person's spirit left the body, the person ceased to exist, and the body died. Over the centuries, philosophers and theologians have debated the nature of the mind, its relation to a soul, and the importance of a body-mind connection. In the last century, the distinctive view of science has focused particularly on the mind and what it does that contributes to the uniqueness of human nature.

The Meaning of the Mind

When psychology first emerged as distinct from philosophy and from other sciences in the late 1800s, it became the "science of the mind." What exactly does the mind *do?* For the earliest psychologists, the mind's major work consisted of producing *consciousness.*

Consciousness *refers to one's awareness of one's mind, of its particular mental contents, or of oneself.* Consciousness brings to the fore certain contents of an individual's thoughts and feelings by keeping one aware of them. But *awareness* is not as focused or deliberate as *attention.* You can think of consciousness as the front page of your mental newspaper, and attention as the lead story, the one you can't resist reading. Awareness is your knowledge that the story is in the newspaper in the first place. Attention involves greater effort than conscious awareness, and also yields precise results, as we shall review in Chapter 5 when we examine attention's role in sensation and perception.

Early Approaches to Consciousness   Wilhelm Wundt and E. B. Titchener advocated using introspection in their structuralist analysis of the mind. They asked their subjects to undergo various tasks and sensations, reflect, and report on the events and ideas in their "stream of consciousness." From his functionalist perspective, William James asserted on the first page of his classic 1890 text *The Principles of Psychology* that "psychology [is] the description and explanation of 'consciousness' as such."

Despite the early enthusiasm of structuralists and functionalists in studying consciousness scientifically, it proved elusive and easier to describe than to define. John B. Watson's objective behaviorism dismissed introspection as too subjective to be scientifically useful. Instead he urged only direct observations of behavior. In the three decades that behaviorism dominated American psychology (from the 1930s to the 1960s), the discipline focused solely on external behavior.

In the 1960s, cognitive psychologists and psycholinguists studying thought and communication examined the workings of the mind and its products. Humanistic psychologists, who focus on the processes of self-knowledge and self-actualization, made their entire discipline the study of the human mind.

Neuroscientific Approaches   With the emergence of *neuroscience,* a multidisciplinary effort to understand the nervous system, biologically oriented psychologists supported the position that the mind and the brain were identical. After all, the brain has vast resources we cannot begin to comprehend—approximately 100 billion neurons, each with thousands of individual and collective interconnections and degrees of firing strength. Surely the human brain is capable of much more than we imagined, including the universe of imagination we think of as the mind (Churchland, 1995). In this *materialistic view,* the brain is a sort of super machine—far more complex than a television or a computer, perhaps, but still a machine composed of physical material—and its primary product is the mind. From this perspective, the mind *is* what the brain *does,* and only biological-materialistic explanations are required to understand their equivalence. In this view, any creature with a brain, therefore, also has a mind, whether it is a human being, a leopard, a computer, or a robot.

In the television and movie series *Star Trek: The Next Generation,* Commander Data of the Starship *Enterprise* is an officer who happens to be an android, a computerized robot. Does a machine, even an incredibly sophisticated machine, have consciousness?

The Nobel Prize–winning biochemist **Francis Crick** anticipates that most of us find it difficult to believe that neurochemistry is "all there is" to the mind, despite the great complexity and sophistication of that neurochemistry. In the introduction to his book *The Astonishing Hypothesis: The Scientific Search for the Soul* (1994), Crick phrases the neuroscientific view of the mind this way:

> The Astonishing Hypothesis is that "You," your joys and your sorrows, your memories and your ambitions, your sense of personal identity and free will, are in fact no more than the behavior of a vast assembly of nerve cells and their associated molecules. As Lewis Carroll's Alice might have phrased it: "You're nothing but a pack of neurons." This hypothesis is so alien to the ideas of most people alive today that it can truly be called astonishing. (p. 3)

But critics point out that the materialistic model remains incapable of explaining consciousness (Wright, 1995b). ASK YOURSELF: Is consciousness the same thing as the brain activity that produces it? For example:

- When you enjoy a good joke and laugh out loud, is "enjoyment" the sum of the physical processes involved in your hearing, understanding, and responding to the joke?
- Or is there something more to your experience, something about how you experienced your enjoyment that an observer would not "get" just by recording data about your responses?

The differences between the processes involved in your enjoyment and the experience of enjoyment itself is the elusive mental function of consciousness. Some materialistic theorists have argued that although consciousness is "there," it is not essential to mental functioning, just as the smoke produced by an engine is not what makes the engine work. Consciousness, like smoke, may be merely a by-product of the brain's work. Such by-products of a process are known as *epiphenomena,* phenomena (observable processes that are not yet fully understood) that occur "on the surface" but are not part of the cause (from the Greek *epi,* "upon"). For example, some theorists argue that mental images are epiphenomena: they are produced by the same mental processes that yield verbal information and ideas, but they are not essential to producing those verbal concepts.

Emergent-Interaction Theory   The narrow neuroscientific view of human mental activity has been challenged by the research of **Roger Sperry** and **Michael Gazzaniga** (see Gazzaniga, 1970; Sperry, 1976, 1987). In independent, as well as collaborative investigations, Sperry and Gazzaniga found that surgically disconnecting the cerebral hemispheres created a duality of conscious experience in patients, as described in Chapter 2. Out of their research came a new perspective, called the *emergent-interaction theory* of mind-brain relationships.

The **emergent-interaction theory** *asserts that brain activities give rise to different mental states, and that brain and mind interact with and influence each other.* Thus according to emergent-interaction theory, mental states are not "merely" biological brain processes. Unique experiences *emerge* as a result of the brain's biological responses to the human environment. Further, mental states do not operate totally independently of the brain. On the contrary, brain and mind *interact,* so just as the brain acts on the mind, the mind also influences the brain in governing its neural and chemical events.

In explaining the example above, emergent-interaction theory would argue that when you enjoy a good joke, your awareness of your enjoyment is more than the elements of the joke that made it funny plus the total of your mental and physical responses to the joke. In experiencing enjoyment, you had to be conscious of your own responses to the joke. This conscious enjoyment emerges from the brain activity that led you to "get" the joke, judge its humor, and laugh. Further, your awareness of your enjoyment now influences the processes involved in your general brain activity. Another person who hears the same joke and carefully observes your response still cannot measure or know your "enjoyment." That experience remains a part of your private consciousness, something that cannot be reduced to biochemical processes alone.

It is not possible (either scientifically or logically) to prove or disprove the existence of the mind. The mind is by definition something each person experiences subjectively. While you are aware of the *products* of mind (such as thoughts and ideas), you cannot perceive the *processes* that give rise to your attention, awareness, and personal experience of consciousness. Ultimately, then, accepting the existence of one's own mind remains a matter of faith.

Studying Conscious Activity

Because mental activities are, by definition, private and unobservable, psychological researchers use techniques that rely on subjects' self-reports and on inferences about the processes that produce certain measurable behaviors. One research technique employs a modern variation of *introspection* as an exploratory procedure to map the workings of the mind. Subjects are asked to speak aloud as they work through puzzles, operate unfamiliar machines, or carry out other complex tasks. They report in as much detail as possible the sequence of thoughts they experience as they work (Ericsson & Simon, 1993; Newell & Simon, 1972). *Subjects' reports which document their mental strategies or analyze their awareness of using them are called* **think-aloud protocols.**

In another ingenious application of modern technology, subjects volunteer to wear electronic pagers as they otherwise go about their normal activities. Researchers arrange for them to be paged or signaled at prearranged or random moments in order to collect "samples" of their thoughts and feelings (Emmons, 1986; Hurlburt, 1979). In this **experience-sampling method,** *subjects write down or tape-record what they are thinking and feeling whenever the pager signals.* Subjects may also be asked to respond to questions such as "How well were you concentrating?" Researchers thus keep a running record of people's thoughts, awareness, and attention as they go about their everyday lives (Csikszentmihalyi, 1990). (Note to readers: Because we will see more of the work of Mihalyi Csikszentmihalyi, you may find it helpful to know that his name is pronounced *me-HIGH chick-SENT-me-high.*)

Both think-aloud protocols and experience-sampling methods rely on subjects' awareness of conscious experience, and on their ability to articulate or report it. However, not all levels or aspects of consciousness may be accessible to self-report. It can be argued that our minds are constantly filling with, and "working on," more unconscious than conscious information. Therefore researchers have devised other methods to provide clues to processes not completely available to subjects' introspections. One of these takes advantage of *selective attention,* the tendency to pay more attention to certain stimuli in the environment while remaining aware of nonattended stimulation. An example of a selective attention method is the *dichotic listening task.*

In the **dichotic listening task,** *a subject listens through stereo earphones to two different channels of input while being instructed to attend to just one channel* (Broadbent, 1954). The subject is required to repeat the input aloud as it enters the attended ear—that is, to "shadow" or echo it while ignoring the

In one type of experience-sampling study, subjects are signaled by electronic pagers. As soon as they can pause amid their activities, they record what they were thinking and feeling when they were signaled.

input to the other ear. Not surprisingly, subjects do not remember information presented to the unattended ear. They don't even notice major changes in that input, such as when the tape is played backwards or the language changes. They *do* notice changes in pitch, as when a speaker's voice switches from male to female (Cherry, 1953), and special signals, such as their own names. Obvious physical features of the unattended message are apparently perceived at another level of awareness, but the meaning does not get processed into consciousness at a level where subjects are able to recall or report it (Lackner & Garrett, 1973).

These techniques allow psychological researchers to explore and illuminate the secret world of other people's consciousness. Now that you know *how* private thoughts can be studied, the next question is *why* consciousness is worth investigating in the first place. We now turn to this question.

The Nature of Consciousness

Ordinary waking consciousness includes the immediate mental experiences that make up your perceptions, thoughts, feelings, and desires at a given moment. You are conscious of what you are doing and why you are doing it. If you were unconscious, you would be behaving and experiencing the world very differently—a difference that is unmistakable but still hard to define. Since the early days of the discipline, psychologists have explored the many faces and forms of consciousness. We will first consider what can be concluded about the *functions* of consciousness—that is, answers to the question, "*Why* be conscious?" We next review what research and theory tell us about *how* consciousness is layered, its forms, structures, and dynamics.

Functions of Consciousness   The evolutionary perspective on psychology (introduced in Chapter 1) reminds us that consciousness must be highly *adaptive* to have become part of human behavior today. In general, consciousness aids human survival and enables people to construct both personal realities and culturally shared realities. For example, imagine waking up to find yourself in a strange bed, being examined by white-coated strangers who tell you, "You've been in an accident, but you're in a hospital, and you're going to be all right." Your conscious abilities will enable you to organize your thoughts ("What happened? Was anyone else hurt?") and to recognize culturally meaningful information ("A hospital is a place where I will get medical care").

From a biological perspective, consciousness probably evolved because it helped individuals to make sense of environmental information and to use that information in planning the most appropriate and effective actions. How does this work?

- First, consciousness *restricts attention,* controlling what we notice and think about. It allows us to attend to only what is "relevant" and to rule out anything unessential or trivial for a given time and context.
- Second, consciousness helps us *select and store* in memory personally meaningful stimuli from the flow of all this relevant input.
- Third, consciousness makes us stop, think, and use past lessons in order to *consider alternative responses and imagine the effectiveness of their consequences in the future.*

For example, you rely on these three dimensions of consciousness in order to begin your day. As part of your morning routine, you must restrict attention to certain immediate tasks, such as showering, dressing, and eating. You probably rule out other, less pressing tasks, such as shopping for new clothes or rereading your high school yearbook. You also notice and remember weather

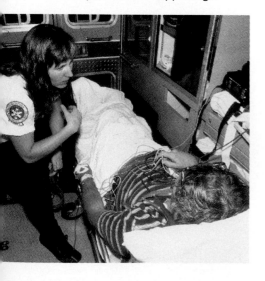

Consciousness helps us to adapt to changing environments. If you waken in an ambulance and are told you've had a heart attack, your consciousness enables you to organize your memories and interpret what is happening.

announcements on the radio, consider how to dress for the circumstances, and imagine the consequences of certain choices such as carrying an umbrella or bringing books and other supplies along with you. Consciousness is obviously handy—it is helpful and adaptive in everyday life. It offers humans great potential for flexible, appropriate responses to life's changing demands (Baars, 1988; Baars & McGovern, 1994; Ornstein, 1986b; Rozin, 1976).

Levels of Consciousness   Psychologists have identified three different levels of consciousness: awareness of the world, reflection on awareness, and awareness of ourselves (Hilgard, 1980; Natsoulas, 1981; Tulving, 1985). Consider the subtle but important differences in these three levels:

1. A basic level of *awareness of the world:* At this basic level, consciousness is being aware that we are perceiving and reacting to available perceptual information.
2. A second level of *reflection* on what we are aware of: Here, consciousness relies on symbolic knowledge to free us from the constraints of real objects and present events; it gives us *imagination.* At this second level, you can think about what you perceive.
3. A top level of *awareness of ourselves* as conscious, reflective individuals: This top level of consciousness is called **self-awareness,** *knowing that personally experienced events have an autobiographical character.* Thus you know that *you* are perceiving the world first-hand, not receiving input from someone else. Self-awareness gives us our sense of personal history and identity. When you reflect on events and tell others about them, your memories of what you have experienced become a part of your personality.

Structures of Consciousness   Just now, were you aware of your heartbeat? Probably not; controlling your heartbeat is one of your *nonconscious processes.* **Nonconscious processes** *involve information that is not represented in consciousness or memory but still influences fundamental bodily and mental activities.* The regulation of blood pressure is an example of a nonconscious process. Physiological information is detected and changes are acted on continually without requiring or involving your awareness.

Preconsciousness   As you began to read this paragraph, were you thinking about your last vacation, or perhaps about the play *Hamlet?* Again, probably not either of those things; control of such thoughts is part of *preconscious memories. Memories accessible to consciousness only after something calls one's attention to them are* **preconscious memories.** They function in the background of your mind until they are needed or stimulated, until something interferes with your usual performance, or until you try to teach or explain tasks that you usually do automatically, like tying shoelaces. Here is another example of a preconscious memory: what did you have for breakfast this morning? If you can answer this question, some representation of your meal must have been stored in your mind. That is, although you did not expect to be quizzed about your morning meal, you not only ate your breakfast, you thought about it and stored those thoughts at the preconscious level of awareness—until just now, when you pulled the memory out to answer the question (Baars & McGovern, 1994). Recalling something consciously is an attention-demanding act, requiring one to seek and shift information from preconsciousness to conscious memory (Jacoby et al., 1989).

Subconscious Processing   Just as you began reading this line in the text, were you thinking about background noises, like a clock ticking or traffic on nearby streets? Probably not—you couldn't pay attention to such peripheral stimuli and still pay attention to reading. Awareness of nonrelevant stimuli is part of "subconscious awareness," the processing of *unattended information.* Much of the stimulation around you must be put out of your mind so that you can focus attention on the small part of it that is relevant. Still, a great deal of nonattended stimulation gets registered and evaluated at some level below that of conscious awareness. **Subconscious awareness** *involves information that is not currently in consciousness but is retrievable from memory by special recall or attention-getting procedures.* Psychologist use the term "subconscious" to refer to processing of material one has been aware of but has *not attended* to. Research indicates that we are influenced by stimuli not perceived consciously (Kihlstrom, 1987). In addition, much cognitive processing seems to occur automatically, without awareness or effort, as when we correctly navigate a familiar route to work or school without apparent thought (Uleman & Bargh, 1989). In the case that opened this chapter, Karen's depression was the result of a subconscious process; once it was brought into her consciousness by hypnotic therapy, she could recognize it and deal with it appropriately.

The Unconscious Finally, are you aware of how some of your unpleasant early life experiences, as well as present desires and impulses, can affect what you say and do? According to psychodynamic analysis, powerful *unconscious* forces block awareness of emotions. In common speech, we use the term "unconscious" to refer to someone who has fainted, is comatose, or is under anesthesia. In psychology, however, the term has a special meaning. The founder of psychoanalytic theory, Sigmund Freud, argued that unconscious associations can powerfully shape human behavior even though we may have no awareness or understanding of the feelings they support (Freud, 1925). According to Freud, within psychoanalytic theory, the **unconscious** *refers to a mental process that retains memories, ideas, and emotions which, at a conscious level, would cause one extreme anxiety.* Such processes are assumed to stem from the need to *repress* traumatic memories and taboo desires. The function of the unconscious is to protect the self from threatening mental experiences and memories.

For example, a young child who is sexually molested by a family member may repress her awareness of being attacked. Buried in her unconscious for years, these memories might surface only when she is older and emotionally equipped to face the reality of having been such a victim. During the intervening years, the secrets stored in the unconscious nonetheless remain alive and even influential. They may slip out in dreams, adult emotions, and motivations. The grown woman might not yet "remember" the repressed memories, but still finds herself avoiding the abuser or anyone who resembles him, and feeling discomfort about her own sexuality. In these ways, Freud argued, unconscious associations and reminders of repressed trauma can shape our behavior even if we have no awareness or recognition of these thoughts.

A New Look at the Unconscious Outside the psychodynamic perspective, there has been little support for the notion of the unconscious. Recently, however, advances in research methods have made it possible to study *unconscious cognition* (thought processes) in an empirical way (Rozin, 1976; Kihlstrom, 1990). This "new look" at unconscious processes supports a much simpler structure than the sophisticated censoring and repressing system early Freudian theory proposed (Greenwald, 1992). The general meaning of "unconscious" has usually implied that one is "unaware of" something.

One can be unaware in two ways: by not *attending* to events, or by failing to *introspect.* In the first sense, one is unaware of stimuli that are outside one's attention. For example, if a classmate enters the room late while you are very focused on the professor's lecture, you will be unconscious of the student's lateness because you were not attending to it. In the second sense of being unaware, one is unable to reflect and report on events even when one did pay attention. For example, that latecomer who sat down in front of you during the lecture may have distracted your attention momentarily, but you may still be unable to report how she was dressed, the color of her hair, or other "irrelevant" details you no doubt observed, if only for a moment. The key to determining whether an experience is conscious or unconscious, in this view, is the use and focus of one's *attention*.

The "new look" at the unconscious suggests that it is not necessarily as dramatic or mysterious as the popularized Freudian imagery had been painted. The unconscious may use more of its storage space for license numbers and background music, and less for fearsome, repressed memories of childhood pain. On the other hand, the unconscious may have an even larger capacity than Freud originally suggested—more "work" to do for the adapting individual, and a greater set of abilities for doing that work. A person has to deal with so much stimulation every moment, the working unconscious may have to act as a clearinghouse in sorting and storing the enormity of data that are encountered but not attended to. Further study may show that the unconscious itself has many levels and many analytic abilities of its own for dealing with a wide range of input, from trivia to trauma (Kihlstrom et al., 1992).

Organizing the Structures of Consciousness   How can you tie together these five structures of the conscious mind: consciousness, nonconscious processes, preconscious memories, subconscious processes, and the unconscious? A popular metaphor for explaining their theorized coexistence is the image of an iceberg, most of which is submerged (not conscious). See Figure 3.1 for such a depiction of the relationships among these structures of consciousness.

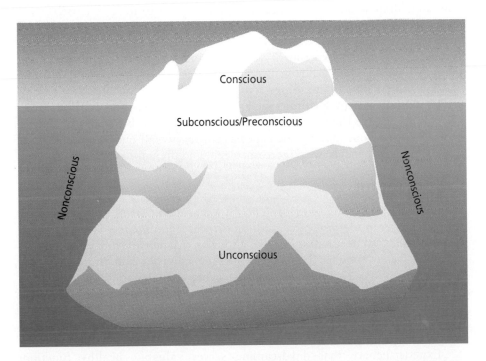

FIGURE 3.1   Structures of Consciousness ■ If consciousness were represented as an iceberg, conscious processes would be those located above the water's surface, while the unconscious would be submerged. Subconscious and preconscious processes both lie beneath the surface but are accessible through special attention and recall. Nonconscious processes influence bodily processes but never become accessible to consciousness.

Check Your Recall

The way psychology conceptualizes consciousness has been influenced by an ongoing debate about how mind and brain are related. Materialistic theories argue that brain and mind are the same, but such models are unable to explain the distinctive qualities of consciousness. The emergent-interaction theory proposes that while brain activities create mental states, they are not the same thing, and brain and mind interact and influence each other.

Consciousness evolved in human beings because it aids survival in many ways. By restricting input, selectively storing information, and using knowledge to plan future action, consciousness permits intentional, adaptive responses to the environment. Because consciousness is a private experience, research designs to study it employ different forms of introspection, such as think-aloud protocols and experience-sampling methods. With the dichotic listening task, researchers are also able to distinguish between levels of attention and consciousness.

There are at least three levels of consciousness: a basic awareness of the world; a level of reflection about what one is aware of; and a top level of self-consciousness. The structures of consciousness include nonconscious processes that regulate bodily functions, preconscious memories, subconscious processes involving unattended information, and the unconscious, which is both a process of repressing anxiety-arousing memories and the mental storehouse for those repressed elements. Research supports a "new look" at the unconscious, viewing it as unawareness caused by either not attending to events or failing to introspect.

Everyday Changes in Consciousness

Watch children stand on their heads or spin around to make themselves feel dizzy. Why do they do it? It seems that "human beings are born with a drive to experience modes of awareness other than the normal waking one; from very young ages, children experiment with techniques to change consciousness" (Weil, 1977, p. 37). As they grow older, some people continue these mind-altering practices by taking drugs that change ordinary awareness, including legal, culturally acceptable drugs such as alcohol, tobacco, and caffeine. Other individuals change their consciousness through specific behaviors or experiences. Even without making such special efforts, we all undergo a change of consciousness whenever we daydream, sleep, and dream.

Daydreaming

Daydreaming *is a mild form of consciousness alteration in which attention shifts away from the immediate situation to other thoughts.* These thoughts may be elicited almost automatically, either by deliberate effort or when triggered by some stimulus. Daydreams include fantasies and thoughts about current concerns. Daydreaming occurs when people are alone, relaxed, engaged in a boring or routine task, or just about to fall asleep (Singer, 1966, 1975). Research suggests that most people daydream daily. Young adults report the most daydreaming, and daydreaming declines significantly with age (Singer & McCraven, 1961).

Experts believe that daydreaming serves valuable, healthy functions (Klinger, 1987). Current research using the experience-sampling method suggests that most daydreams dwell on practical and current concerns, everyday tasks, future goals (trivial or significant), and interpersonal relationships. Daydreaming reminds us to make plans, helps us solve problems, and gives us creative opportunities for a time-out.

Fantasy is one aspect of daydreaming. When you *fantasize*—imagine unrealistic, unlikely, or impossible experiences—you are not necessarily escaping from life. Instead, you may be confronting the mysteries of life and working through difficulties with wonder and respect. Fantasy may be the only way you can experience feelings or motives you feel you could never act on in real life. For example, you may feel too shy to approach an attractive classmate about going out sometime, but fantasizing about the kind of interaction you might have is easy, and may even give you courage to find a way to act out your wishful thinking.

On the other hand, perhaps destructive wishes are the ones people are least likely to admit harboring—fantasies about breaking rules, acting out aggression, or taking revenge on a wrongdoer. Have you ever vividly imagined telling someone off in a dramatic and effective way? Such fantasized conversations might reduce the impulse to act too hastily, or they might become "dress rehearsals" for the real thing.

Suppose your fantasies were suppressed, or someone encouraged you to stop having a particular wish or fantasy. A surprising research finding is that efforts to *suppress* unwanted thoughts are likely to backfire. In a study by Wegner et al. (1987), subjects spoke into a tape recorder about anything that came to mind, but they had been instructed *not* to think about "a white bear." Consequently, subjects mentioned a *white bear* about once per minute, despite their instructions! Ironically, trying to suppress a thought or put something out of your mind may result in an obsession with the very images you seek to escape. At the heart of this frustrating cycle is the process of mental control. In a tug-of-war between your feelings and your will, you may only "win" peace of mind if you stop tugging and let go. Allow your mind to roam freely, as daydreaming and fantasy naturally do, and the unwanted or upsetting thoughts will become less intrusive and finally cease (Wegner, 1989).

Regardless of how realistic or pertinent to our lives our fantasies may be, daydreams are rarely as vivid and compelling as night dreams. The dreams our minds present while we sleep seem to mean more because we are not consciously fabricating them—and we don't always even understand them! To understand dreams, we must first examine the terrain in which they reside, the mysterious realm of sleep.

Sleep

About one-third of your life is spent sleeping, with your body resting and your brain humming with varied activity. We take this daily dramatic alteration of consciousness for granted because it generally happens spontaneously. We slip in and out of different states of consciousness as a natural consequence of daylight cycles and patterns of wakefulness and sleep. These ordinary fluctuations in consciousness are part of the rhythm of nature.

Circadian Rhythms All creatures are influenced by nature's rhythms; humans are attuned to a time cycle known as **circadian rhythms,** *bodily patterns that repeat approximately every 24 hours* (*circadian* comes from the Latin *circa* for "around" + *dies* for "a day"). An individual's circadian rhythm corresponds to daily changes in the physiological activities of his or her nervous system. Arousal levels, metabolism, heart rate, body temperature, and hormonal activity ebb and flow according to the ticking of this internal clock. The "clock" itself is not a single mechanism but a coordinated set of physiological operations whose exact cycle may be dictated by an individual's genetic makeup (Page, 1994).

The clock the body uses to pace its activity is not the same clock we use to track our appointments and schedules. Biochemical processes in your brain

Daydreaming is common among people of all ages. It provides a means of transcending time and space.

and endocrine system influence the settings and tempo of your biological clock. ASK YOURSELF: What would your ideal 24-hour schedule be?

- If you could rise at any time you chose, follow your own tendencies to be either alert or sleepy, and retire any time you like at night, how would your day differ from your present routine?
- Now, return to earth with this thought: How much of your life depends on other people, and how necessary is it to develop a routine that *agrees* with others' schedules? For example, if you showed up for your psychology class only when it was convenient for you, you would have only a slim chance of finding class in session. In order to meet objectives such as attending class or arriving at work on time, you compromise somewhat on your personal time preferences.

Thus the circadian rhythms you have developed are not dictated solely by your biological clock, but have been influenced by social goals and cultural expectations. As an example of the social construction of time and concepts of "lateness," consider the recent experience of your first author when he gave a lecture at a conference in Mexico. At the time of the scheduled beginning of the talk, there were only two psychologists in the audience, both from the United States. But over the next hour, more than fifty additional professional psychologists, all from various Latin cultures, gradually drifted in. The value of being someplace "on time" and the meaning of "time" itself clearly depend on one's cultural background.

Air travel, mixed-shift work (work schedules that vary over different periods in a 24-hour cycle), and other interruptions in one's sleep-wake habits all take their toll (Moore-Ede, 1993). This is because circadian rhythms are sensitive to environmental change. Anything that throws off your biological clock affects how you feel and behave. Flying across several time zones causes *jet lag*, because the internal circadian rhythm is disrupted by your new temporal environment. If it is 1:00 A.M. in your body but only 10:00 P.M. to the people around you, you must use energy and resources to adapt to your surroundings. The symptoms of jet lag include fatigue, irresistible sleepiness, and subsequent unusual sleep-wake schedules. Traveling eastbound (losing hours in your day) creates greater jet lag than traveling westbound (gaining hours), because our biological clocks can actually adjust and lengthen more readily than shorten. It is easier to stay awake a bit longer than it is to fall asleep sooner than usual (Klein & Wegmann, 1974).

The Activity of Sleep   About one-third of circadian rhythm is devoted to the period of energy-restoring rest called *sleep*. Since the development of the electroencephalogram (EEG), researchers have been able to record brain activity during this quiescence without disturbing the sleeper. They found that brain waves change in form, first at the onset of sleep, and then in further systematic, predictable changes during the entire period of sleep (Loomis et al., 1937).

After EEG technology, the most significant discovery in sleep research was that of **rapid eye-movement (REM)**, *bursts of quick eye movements under closed eyelids, occurring at periodic intervals during sleep* (Aserinsky & Kleitman, 1953). *The time when a sleeper is not showing REM is known as* **non-REM** or **NREM sleep (NREM)**. During one study, sleepers were awakened and asked to describe their mental activity during REM sleep and NREM sleep (Dement & Kleitman, 1957). The NREM reports were filled with brief descriptions of ordinary daily activities, similar to waking thoughts. But most of the REM reports were qualitatively different; they were vivid, fanciful, bizarre scenes from incomplete plots—in essence, *dreams*. Rapid eye-movements (REM) are reliable behavioral signs that a sleeper's mental activity is centered around dreaming, as if the sleeper's eyes were darting about to keep track of sensory images on some private internal screen.

The Sleep Cycle Imagine that you are a subject in a laboratory specializing in sleep research. Already connected to EEG recording equipment, you have adapted somewhat to the wires between your body and the machinery and are preparing to sleep. As you undress, an EEG records that your brain waves are moving along at a rate of about 14 cycles per second (cps). Once you are comfortably in bed, you relax and your brain waves slow down to a rate of about 8 to 12 cps. Soon you are asleep, and the EEG shows further changes. In fact, over the course of the night, your sleep cycle crosses several stages, each of which shows a distinct EEG pattern:

■ In stage 1 sleep, the EEG shows brain waves similar to the waking state, if a bit slower.

■ During stage 2, the EEG is characterized by *sleep spindles*—minute bursts of electrical activity, faster than stage 1 brain waves.

■ In the next two stages (3 and 4), you enter a very deep state of relaxed sleep. Your brain waves slow dramatically, and your breathing and heart rate decrease.

■ After stage 4, the electrical activity of your brain increases; your EEG looks very similar to those recorded during stages 1 and 2. You experience REM sleep during this period, when your eyes move rapidly back and forth and you begin to dream (see Figure 3.2).

It takes about 90 minutes to progress through the first four stages of sleep (NREM sleep). The first period of REM sleep lasts for about 10 minutes. Over the course of an average night's sleep, an individual passes through this 100-minute cycle four to six times. With each cycle, the amount of time spent in deep sleep (stages 3 and 4) decreases, and the amount of time spent in REM sleep increases. During the last cycle, you may spend an hour in REM sleep. See Figure 3.3 for the pattern of sleep through the average night.

If you were deprived of REM sleep for a night, you would have more REM sleep than usual the next night. (Perhaps we need sleep only to get REM rather than to rest.) REM sleep can also play a role in the maintenance of mood and emotion, and it may be required for storing memories and fitting recent experiences into networks of previous beliefs or memories (Cartwright, 1978; Dement, 1976).

The Work of Sleep Apparently there is an evolutionary basis as well as a biological need for sleep. Sleep has two general functions: to *conserve* and to *restore*. Researchers suggest that sleep evolved because it enabled animals to *conserve* energy at times when there was no need to forage for food, search for mates, or work (Allison & Cicchetti, 1976; Cartwright, 1982; Webb, 1974). Sleep also enables the body to *restore* itself in several ways. During sleep, neurotransmitters build up to compensate for the quantities used in daily activities, and neurons return to their optimal level of sensitivity (Stern & Morgane, 1974).

Consciousness researcher **Francis Crick** and mathematician Graeme Mitchison propose a different function for sleep. They believe that sleep and dreams help the brain to flush out the day's accumulation of unwanted and useless information. Dreams may also serve to reduce fantasy and obsession, thereby minimizing bizarre connections among our many memories (Crick & Mitchison, 1983).

William Shakespeare proposed a somewhat more elegantly stated hypothesis about the restorative function of sleep: "Sleep knits up the ravelled sleeve

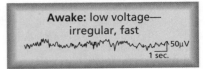

Awake: low voltage—irregular, fast

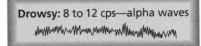

Drowsy: 8 to 12 cps—alpha waves

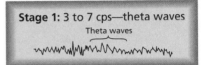

Stage 1: 3 to 7 cps—theta waves

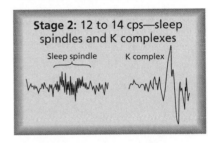

Stage 2: 12 to 14 cps—sleep spindles and K complexes

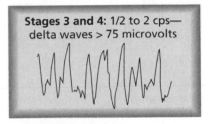

Stages 3 and 4: 1/2 to 2 cps—delta waves > 75 microvolts

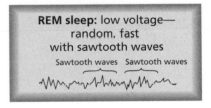

REM sleep: low voltage—random, fast with sawtooth waves

FIGURE 3.2   EEG Patterns in Stages of Sleep ■

FIGURE 3.3   Stages of Sleep ■ During a typical night's sleep, one spends more time in the deepest stages of the early cycles. In later cycles, one spends more time in REM.

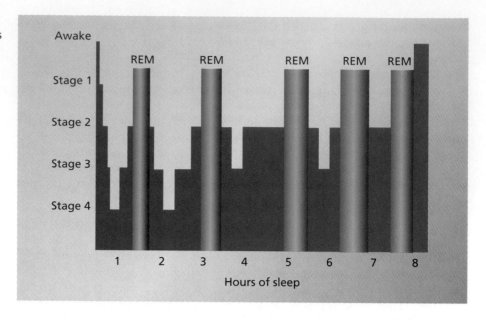

of care." During sleep, unravelled material—loose ends of information—may be either integrated or eliminated. According to sleep researcher Ernest Hartmann, "In the morning, sleep has done its thing. If you're in good shape your sleeve has been restored for the next day's wear" *(Discovering Psychology,* 1990, program 13).

So sleep accomplishes important physical and psychological work. This implies a minimum investment of time: how long must you sleep? This is an intriguing question, since sleep may be as much a *habit* as it is a *need.* The length of nocturnal sleep depends on many factors. There is a *genetic need* for sleep which is different for each species. But more important for humans are *volitional* determinants—that is, *wanting* to sleep. Depending on what they want to do, people may actively control sleep length in a number of ways, such as staying up late or using alarm clocks. Sleep duration is also controlled by circadian rhythms, so that how long you sleep may depend on your personal peak times for REM.

People vary in the amount of sleep they need. Individuals who sleep longer than average are found to be more nervous, worrisome, artistic, creative, and nonconforming. Short sleepers tend to be more energetic and extroverted (Hartmann, 1973). Strenuous physical activity during the day increases the amount of time spent in the slow-wave sleep of stage 4, but it doesn't affect REM time (Horne, 1988).

Finally, sleep duration varies over one's lifetime. As Figure 3.4 shows, we begin life by sleeping about 16 hours per day, with half that time devoted to REM. Young adults typically sleep 7 to 8 hours, with 20 percent REM. By old age, we sleep very little, with only 15 percent of sleep in REM.

Because sleep has definite functions and is not merely a state of being "not awake," people become concerned when their sleep is disrupted or inadequate. In Focus on Application: Sleep Disorders on page 90, we discuss several distinct types of sleep disorders, each traceable to different factors and treatable in different ways.

Dreaming

During every ordinary night of your life, you experience the most fascinating event staged by the human mind—the dream. Vivid, colorful, completely nonsensical hallucinations characterized by complex miniplots that transform time, sequence, and place occupy the theater of your sleep. Dreamers may feel as if they are behaving in unusual—or impossible—ways. They may talk, hear, and feel sexually excited, but they cannot consciously process or sense smell, taste, or pain. Dreams are probably best characterized as theater of the absurd—chaotic dramas that appear illogical when analyzed in the rational mindset of our waking hours.

Freud called dreams "the royal road to the Unconscious," rich with clues to an individual's mental life. Once only the province of prophets, psychics, and psychoanalysts, dreams have become a vital area of study for scientific researchers. Dream research got its impetus from sleep laboratory findings that correlated rapid eye-movements, unique EEG patterns, and the sleeper's report of having dreamed.

Although dreams are primarily REM phenomena, some dreaming (of a different quality) also takes place during NREM periods. Dreaming associated with NREM states has less of a story-like quality and has little sensory imagery. Subjects also recall a much higher percentage of REM dreams than NREM dreams (Freeman, 1972).

Theories about the causes and meaning of dreams abound in human history and culture (Moffitt et al., 1993). Here we consider two broad views of dreaming: the general theory that dreaming is *adaptive* because it serves valuable functions; and the idea that dreaming is merely an *outcome* of biological processes on which we impose our own interpretations.

Dreaming as Adaptation   **Sigmund Freud** made the analysis of dreams the cornerstone of psychoanalysis with his classic book *The Interpretation of Dreams* (1900). In the Freudian perspective, dreams have two main functions: to *guard sleep* (by disguising disruptive thoughts with symbols) and to serve as sources of *wish fulfillment*. Dreams guard sleep by relieving psychic tensions created during the day, and by allowing the dreamer to work through unconscious desires. Interpreting dreams can help people to understand themselves better, but it also runs the risk of revealing unsettling thoughts and feelings. Before trying to interpret your dreams, therefore, you should consider both the possible costs and the benefits of such an exercise.

Decoding Dreams   In Freud's psychoanalytic interpretation, he theorized that dreams have two levels of meaning: *manifest content* and *latent content*.

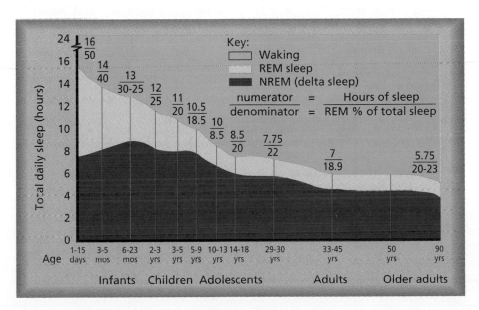

FIGURE 3.4   Patterns of Human Sleep over a Lifetime ■ The graph shows changes with age in the total amounts of REM and NREM sleep and in the percentage of time spent in REM sleep. Note that, over the years, the amount of REM sleep decreases considerably, while NREM diminishes less sharply.

Sleep Disorders

For millions of Americans, sleep disorders pose a persistent, serious burden that can disrupt marriages, interfere with careers, and even result in death. It is estimated that more than 100 million Americans get insufficient sleep. Of those working night shifts, more than half nod off at least once a week on the job. Some of the world's most serious accidents—Three Mile Island, Chernobyl, Bhopal, and the Exxon Valdez disaster—have occurred during late evening hours. People have speculated that such accidents occur because key personnel fail to function optimally as a result of insufficient sleep (Dement, 1976). Some types of sleep disorders are biological, while others are more psychological. Here we review three different sleep problems: insomnia, sleep apnea, and daytime sleepiness.

When people are dissatisfied with the amount or quality of their sleep, they are suffering from *insomnia*. **Insomnia** *is defined as a chronic failure to get adequate sleep, characterized by an inability to fall asleep quickly, frequent arousals during sleep, and/or early morning awakening* (Bootzin & Nicasio, 1978). Insomnia is a complex disorder caused by a variety of psychological, environmental, and biological factors (Borkovec, 1982). When insomniacs are studied in sleep laboratories, the objective quantity and quality of their actual sleep varies considerably, and ranges from disturbed sleep to normal sleep. Many people complaining of insomnia actually show completely normal patterns of sleep. This condition is described as *subjective insomnia.* Equally curious is the finding that some people who show detectable sleep disturbances report no complaints of insomnia (Trinder, 1988). The discrepancies may result from differences in the way people recall and interpret a state of light sleep.

Sleep apnea *is an upper respiratory sleep disorder in which the person stops breathing while asleep.* When this happens, the blood's oxygen level drops and emergency hormones are secreted, causing the sleeper to awaken,

Insomnia is a complex disorder caused by a variety of psychological, environmental, and biological factors. This college student anxiously contemplates her inability to get enough rest for the next day's classes.

to begin breathing again, and then to fall back to sleep. While most of us have a few apnea episodes a night, someone with sleep apnea disorder can have hundreds of such cycles every night. Sleep apnea is frequent in premature infants, who sometimes need physical stimulation to start breathing again. Because of their underdeveloped respiratory system, these infants must remain attached to monitors in intensive care nurseries as long as the problem continues.

Sometimes apnea episodes frighten the sleeper, but often they are so brief that the sleeper fails to attribute accumulating sleepiness to them (Guilleminault, 1989). Delay in recognizing the nature of the problem can cause sufferers—and their families and coworkers—to mistakenly interpret unusual daytime behavior as laziness or neglect, when the behavior is traceable to a nighttime disorder.

Sleepiness is a common problem, an inevitable consequence of not getting enough nocturnal sleep. However, excessive **daytime sleepiness** *is a persistent problem that qualifies as a sleep disorder because it is a physiological state not remedied by simply getting more sleep.* About 4 to 5 percent of the general population surveyed reports excessive daytime sleepiness (Roth et al., 1989). This sleepiness causes diminished alertness, delayed reaction times, and impaired performance of motor and cognitive tasks. Nearly half the patients with excessive sleepiness report automobile accidents, and more than half have had job accidents—some serious.

You may wonder if it is an exaggeration to call sleepiness a disorder. Can't boring lectures, overheated rooms, heavy meals, or monotonous tasks cause daytime sleepiness? No, say the experts. These conditions only obscure the presence of physiological sleepiness; they do not cause it (Roth et al., 1989). Although the cause of daytime sleepiness is not simply insufficient sleep—tension, worry, depression, and agitation are often responsible—learning how to get longer, more restful sleep can reduce its undesirable symptoms.

If you show the signs of sleep deprivation—dozing off rather than getting fidgety when bored, or falling instantly asleep when you finally do go to bed, for example—experts recommend several steps you can take to get the sleep you need (see Brody, 1994):

■ Figure out how much sleep you need and schedule your night to allow for it.

■ Sleep in a continuous block rather than several interrupted naps or sessions.

■ Try a short, 20-minute "power nap" rather than longer, deeper sleep.

■ Stick to a routine, going to bed and getting up at the same times every day.

■ Get daily physical exercise—but not within three hours of bedtime.

Remember that sleep deprivation is a real problem to be taken seriously. Pretending to be awake or relying on stimulants like caffeine to get you through the day will only mask the problem and allow it to worsen. The first step to solving the problem is admitting it exists—and understanding that you can solve it.

The manifest content of a dream is what the dream seems to be about, the story the dream tells to the dreamer. But the manifest content is really a "code" or disguise for the latent content. The latent content is the true meaning of the dream, hidden behind the symbols of the manifest story. For example, a child who is very jealous of her new little sister might dream about squashing a bug. The manifest content, bug squashing, disguises the latent meaning of the dream, which is the child's wish to destroy the tiny invader in her home.

To the therapist who uses dream analysis to understand and treat a patient's problems, dreams reveal the patient's unconscious wishes, the fears attached to those wishes, and the characteristic defenses the patient employs to handle the resulting psychic conflict between the wishes and the fears. Dreams offer the therapist an opportunity to understand the patient better, and offer the dreamer clues to the true motives and conflicts normally hidden in the unconscious. In the traditional system of psychoanalytic practice, interpretation is not easy, however, and dream analysis requires extensive training and careful detective work to avoid drawing the wrong conclusions about the meaning of dreams.

Content Analysis Are your dreams necessarily so hard to interpret that only a trained psychoanalyst could undertake the task? Your own experience probably says no. If you waken from a frightening dream, you can probably identify the life stressors that found their way into your sleeping thoughts. Mental problems seem to have the effect of extending REM sleep. Some of our dreams have fairly obvious meaning and relevance to our waking lives and personal experiences, so they are not difficult to decode. One study of individuals depressed about divorce found their sleep was often disrupted with REM periods starting too early or lasting too long, and their dreams were often "stuck in the past" (Cartwright, 1984). By analyzing the patterns and content of your own dreams, you may find it is not difficult to assign meaning to the images and actions you recall (Hall, 1953/1966; Van de Castle, 1994). Keep in mind that such "amateur dream detection" is not encouraged as part of the psychoanalytic tradition, so your conclusions might differ from those of a professional therapist trained in the Freudian system described above.

In a *content analysis* of dreams, researchers collect subjects' detailed, written descriptions of recent dreams (Hall & Van de Castle, 1966). Specific settings, characters, objects, and actions are identified and categorized among the many dream stories collected. Sometimes patterns are identified by subjects' gender, age group, or other classification. For example, dream researcher Calvin Hall found that, in a sample of over 1800 dreams, women dreamed about both men and women, while men dreamed about men twice as often as about women. In another sample of over 1300 dreams, Hall found that hostile interactions between characters outnumbered friendly exchanges, and that 64 percent of dreamed emotions were negative, such as anger and sadness (Hall, 1951).

To conduct a content analysis of your dreams, you must be willing to accept obvious or superficial explanations as well as more exotic interpretations. A dream about swimming may really be about swimming and not necessarily about some life conflict or issue that the dream has symbolically transformed into water. Dreams may also use images that have similar meaning for many people, not just the dreamer. For example, Van de Castle (1994) reports that children are more likely to dream about animals than adults are, and that in children's dreams animals are more likely to be large, threatening, and wild. In contrast, college students dream more usually of small animals, pets, and tame creatures. A general interpretation might be that dream animals represent the "animal side" of human nature and experience. Children feel less

Perhaps because children lack a sense of control over their environment, they often dream about large or frightening animals.

in control of their world than adults do and so may find that world depicted in scarier imagery while they sleep (Van de Castle, 1983)

If dreams reflect the dreamer's world during sleep, it is possible that dreams can offer solutions to life problems and creative ideas that defy waking expression. If dreams are truly adaptive, it is in people's interest to pay attention to their dreams, remember them, and try to understand them, in order to use the ideas and lessons they offer.

Dreaming as an Outcome   The adaptive view of dreams described above argues that they are produced intentionally, if not consciously, to serve important functions. By interpreting or analyzing dreams for content, psychologists might learn what those functions are. However, an alternative view sees dreams as accidental events, the *unintentional* outcomes of biological processes involved in sleep. This model, the **activation-synthesis theory,** *states that dreams result when biological activation throughout the sleeping brain is organized into a meaningful pattern.* During sleep, the brain stem emits random electrical discharges. As this energy activates higher areas of the cerebral cortex, the sleeper experiences impressions of sensation and movement. Although the activation is purely biological and the events are not logically connected, the brain tries to make sense of the flood of input it receives. To impose order on random events, the sleeper's brain *synthesizes* or pulls together the separate bursts of electrical *activation* by creating a coherent story—a dream.

The proponents of this theory, **J. Allan Hobson** and **Robert McCarley** (1977), argue that REM sleep furnishes the brain with an internal source of activation when external stimulation is turned down to promote the growth and development of the brain. Dream content results from random stimulation, not unconscious wishes. Hobson (1988) claims that meaning is added as a "brainstorm afterthought." When meaningless activations are synthesized, dreams seem familiar and meaningful.

The activation-synthesis approach helps explain many of the mysteries of sleep we posed earlier. The "stuff" of dreams may be a brain chemical, *acetylcholine*, which is turned on by one set of neurons in the brain stem during

REM. Those neurons are "on" only when the others, which trigger the release of *serotonin* and *norepinephrine,* are "off." Serotonin and norepinephrine are brain chemicals necessary for storing memories. We forget some 95 percent of our dreams because they are only stored temporarily in our short-term memory. They cannot be "printed" to more permanent memory because serotonin and norepinephrine are shut off during the dream. We dream with such rich, vivid images because the brain uses its storehouse of preexisting symbols and metaphors to create meaning out of the madness of chaotic brain discharges.

What proof is there that the "stuff of dreams" is a neurotransmitter? Hobson's research team injected Carbachol, a drug that mimics the action of acetylcholine, into the brain stems of cats. Not only did this drug trigger the flow of special brain waves from the brain stem to the occipital cortex (where the dreams are visualized), but the cats' REM sleep increased by 300 percent! This technique of generating REM sleep allows researchers to study how REM sleep is related to various forms of behavioral and mental functioning. Hobson believes that his findings "have opened the door to the molecular biology of sleep," and closed it on the psychoanalytic theory of dreams (see Bianchi, 1992; Hobson, 1992).

It appears, then, that humans are so good at making sense out of things, we even do it in our sleep. By better understanding the mechanisms of dreaming, we can enhance our knowledge of waking aspects of imagery and conscious thought processes (Antrobus, 1991).

Check Your Recall

Everyday changes in consciousness include daydreaming, sleeping, and night dreaming. Daydreaming is a mild altered state in which attention is shifted away from a current situation to personal concerns, future goals, or fantasies. A certain amount of free-roaming thought may be necessary to keep suppressed thoughts from creating intrusions or distractions.

Many changes in consciousness correspond to the body's circadian rhythm and to physiological and neural activities. Daily stresses, physical exertion, and traveling across time zones are examples of the kinds of activities that can disrupt circadian rhythms.

Sleep represents an important change in consciousness, characterized by a series of changes in the brain's electrical activities. Humans cycle through five stages of sleep several times each night. REM sleep is significant because of its heightened brain activity and because dreams occur primarily in this stage. In the standard sleep cycle, REM and NREM follow a predictable, alternating pattern throughout the night. Sleep serves two functions: to conserve energy and to restore resources used by the nervous system. Sleep duration is determined by both genetic need and volitional factors. Sleep disorders such as insomnia, sleep apnea, and daytime sleepiness are surprisingly common and are costly to individuals and society.

Dreams are the most common variations of consciousness. Dreams have been explained as either intentional, adaptive mental activity, or unintentional byproducts of brain activity during sleep. In Freudian interpretation, dreams are disguised manifestations of unconscious wishes. A content-analysis approach to dream interpretation invites individuals to relate the images in their dreams to the events and concerns of real life. A competing activation-synthesis theory argues that dreams are biologically based, caused by random activation of the brain stem's nerve discharges. The mind then tries to make sense of and synthesize the associated sensations and memories into a coherent story.

Extended States of Consciousness

Sleep and dreams can be such satisfying alternatives to consciousness that they sometimes make it difficult for one to rise in the morning and start the waking day. But fantasies and dreams may not be "enough." In every society, people have been dissatisfied with such ordinary transformations of their waking consciousness. They have developed practices that enable them to experience extended states of consciousness.

Some people turn to meditation, while others rely on drugs to alter their state of consciousness. Psychological researchers and therapists have also developed procedures for deliberately altering states of consciousness. Such procedures include using hypnosis or relaxation training to modify ordinary mental and emotional processes. We now consider how these procedures create alternate states of consciousness.

Hypnosis

Picture an individual being put into a trance by a hypnotist. What is the hypnotist doing or saying? When hypnotized, how does the subject behave? A hypnotized person may seem to be "asleep," but can obviously hear suggestions and carry out requests. Because hypnosis seems exotic, even contradictory, most people find the subject fascinating. Here we will explore some of the realities behind popular images: the nature of hypnosis as a state of mind, its important features, and some of its valid psychological uses.

The term "hypnosis" is derived from *Hypnos,* the name of the Greek god of sleep. Sleep plays no part in hypnosis, except that the subject often appears to be in a deeply relaxed, sleeplike state. If a subject were actually asleep, he or she would not respond to hypnosis. There are many different theories about what hypnosis is and how it works. In a general sense, **hypnosis** *is an induced alternate state of awareness, characterized by deep relaxation and heightened suggestibility.* When hypnotized, some people have the special ability to respond to suggestion with changes in perception, memory, motivation, and sense of self-control (Orne, 1980). In the hypnotic state, the subject experiences heightened responsiveness to the hypnotist's suggestions and often feels that his or her behavior is performed without intention or any conscious effort.

As a form of popular entertainment, stage hypnotists frequently amaze their audiences with the feats of memory and concentration their voluntary subjects perform; although these are not laboratory conditions, there is no scientific control, and thus audiences cannot be sure about the nature of the hypnotic effects they are seeing with "their own eyes" (Barber, 1986). More practically, the same qualities that make hypnosis entertaining may also be employed with qualified, professional guidance in self-help and therapy. Individuals who are able to reach deep levels of hypnosis may find it easier to concentrate their attention, focus their imagination, or change their own behavior in a desired direction. However, not everyone can achieve the same levels of hypnosis.

Hypnotizability   The most dramatic stage performances of hypnosis give the impression that the power of hypnosis lies with the hypnotist. However, the real star is the person who is hypnotized; the hypnotist is more like an experienced guide showing the way. Some individuals can even practice self-hypnosis, or *autohypnosis,* without a hypnotic operator, by inducing the hypnotic state through self-administered suggestions.

The single most important factor in hypnosis is a participant's ability or "talent" to become hypnotized. **Hypnotizability** *is the degree to which an indi-*

vidual is responsive to standardized suggestions to experience hypnotic reactions. There are *individual differences* in this susceptibility, varying from no responsiveness to any suggestion to total responsiveness to virtually every suggestion. A highly hypnotizable person may respond to suggestions to change motor reactions, experience hallucinations, have amnesia for important memories, and become insensitive to powerful, painful stimuli.

Figure 3.5 shows the percentage of college-age subjects at various levels of hypnotizability the first time they were given a hypnotic induction test. High scorers are more likely than low scorers to experience pain relief (analgesia) as a result of hypnosis (*hypnotic analgesia*) and to respond to hypnotic suggestions for experiencing perceptual distortions of various kinds. For example a hypnotist may test a new subject's acceptance of suggestion by saying, "Your right hand is lighter than air," and observing whether the subject allows his or her arm to float upward.

Hypnotizability is a unique cognitive ability—a special expression of human imagination. It develops early in life along with the sense of being able to become completely absorbed in an experience. A hypnotizable person is one who is capable of deep involvement in the imaginative-feeling areas of experience, such as reading fiction or listening to music. Such an individual can be hypnotized by anyone he or she is willing to respond to, while an *un*hypnotizable person will *not* respond to the tactics of even the most skilled hypnotist. However, we should note that hypnosis is not the result of gullibility or conformity. Hypnosis is real, and a hypnotized individual experiences a genuinely altered state of consciousness.

Altered Reality   It is necessary to maintain a scientific skepticism about the claims made about hypnosis, especially when such claims are based on individual case reports or research that lacks proper control conditions (Barber, 1976). Researchers disagree about the psychological mechanisms involved in hypnosis (Fromm & Shor, 1979). Some argue that hypnosis is simply heightened motivation (Barber, 1979). That is, perhaps subjects are not entranced but merely aroused to channel more energy to suggested attention and activities. They are hypnotized because they want to be, so they focus on expressing and achieving the responses the hypnotist tries to evoke. Others believe that hypnosis is only social role playing, a kind of *placebo response* of trying to please the hypnotist (Sarbin & Coe, 1972). Still other researchers present evidence that suggests hypnosis is more than merely an attempt at role playing or a reaction to the social demands of the situation (Fromm & Shor, 1979). Perhaps even when "faking" hypnosis, subjects experience reality as sufficiently altered to achieve tasks or feelings that are harder to achieve by themselves.

Empirical evidence and expert opinion strongly suggest that hypnosis can exert a powerful influence on many psychological and bodily functions (Bowers, 1983; Burrows & Dennerstein, 1980; E. Hilgard, 1968, 1973; Miller & Bowers, 1993). Hypnosis is a useful tool for researchers who wish to study the effects of certain emotional and mental experiences. Instead of being limited to soliciting subjects who already have certain conditions or disorders, researchers can recruit normal volunteers and hypnotically create the conditions they wish to study. For example, in one revealing study, subjects given the hypnotic suggestion to become deaf on cue admitted feeling paranoid and excluded because they "could not hear" what other subjects were saying and assumed they were being deliberately whispered about and excluded (Zimbardo et al., 1981).

Pain Control   One of the most common and undisputed values of hypnosis is its effect on pain (Miller & Bowers, 1993; Orne, 1980). Our minds can amplify painful stimuli through anticipation and fear; we can also diminish the

FIGURE 3.5   Level of Hypnosis Reached at First Induction ■ This graph shows the results achieved by 533 subjects hypnotized for the first time. (Hypnotizability was measured by the 12-item Stanford Hypnotic Susceptibility Scale.)

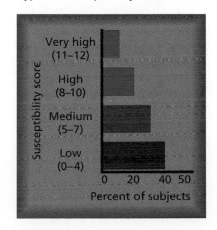

An individual who is able to reach a deep level of hypnosis may find it easier to concentrate his or her attention and change behavior in a desired direction. Here, a pregnant woman learns hypnosis in preparation for childbirth.

psychological component of pain with hypnosis. Pain control is accomplished through a variety of hypnotic suggestions:

1. *Distracting* the subject from the painful stimulus;
2. Imagining the part of the body in pain as *nonorganic* (for example, made of wood or plastic) or as *separate* from the rest of the body;
3. Taking one's mind on a *vacation* from the body; and,
4. *Distorting time* in various ways.

Hypnosis has proven especially valuable to surgery patients who cannot tolerate anesthesia, to patients with extreme burns, to mothers in natural childbirth, and to cancer patients learning to endure the pain associated with their disease and its treatment. Moreover, self-hypnosis enables patients to use these techniques to control their pain as it arises.

Meditation

Many religions and traditional psychologies of the Eastern world (Asian and Pacific cultures) purposely direct consciousness away from immediate worldly concerns and external stimulation. They seek to achieve an inner focus on the mental and spiritual self. **Meditation** *is a change in consciousness designed to enhance self-knowledge and well-being by reducing self-awareness.* During meditation, a person focuses on and regulates breathing, assumes certain bodily positions (yogic poses), minimizes external stimulation, and either generates specific mental images or frees the mind of all thought.

To view meditation as an altered state of consciousness may reflect a particularly Western worldview. For example, Asian cultures' beliefs about the mind are very different from those of Western cultures. Buddhism teaches that the visible universe is an illusion of the senses; the world is nothing but what the mind creates; and the individual's mind is part of the collective, universal mind. Excessive mental activity distracts one from focusing on inner experience and allowing mind to rise above sensory experience. Meditation is a lifelong exercise in discovering how to remove the mind from distractions and illusions, thus allowing it to roam freely and discover wisdom. To become an enlightened being, a Buddhist tries to control bodily yearnings, stop the ordinary experiences of the senses and mind, and discover how to see things in their truest (most real) light. In contrast, the Western scientist views meditation as an *altered* (changed) form of experience and behavior.

What exactly are the effects of meditation? One consequence of meditation is mental and bodily relaxation. Meditation reduces anxiety, especially in those who function in stress-filled environments (Benson, 1975; Shapiro, 1985). Meditating is like resting in some ways, since it has been found to reduce some measures of bodily arousal, although results depend on the particular meditation technique applied and the type of arousal being studied (Dillbeck & Orme-Johnson, 1987; Holmes, 1984; Morrell, 1986)

Meditative practices can function as more than valuable time-outs from tension. When practiced regularly, some forms of meditation can heighten consciousness, achieve enlightenment by enabling the individual to see familiar things in new ways, and free perception and thought from the restrictions of automatic, well-learned patterns. When practiced regularly, meditation is said to lead to *mindful awareness* in one's daily life. Awareness of the routine activity of breathing, especially, creates a sense of peace. A prominent Buddhist teacher of meditation recommends awareness of breathing and simple appreciation of our surroundings and brief daily actions as paths to psychological equilibrium (Nhat Hanh, 1991).

The practice of using meditation to achieve peace of mind, a sense of connectedness with the world, and spiritual awakening requires neither group participation nor a group leader. Any individual who is sufficiently motivated to modify the standard operating procedures of his or her consciousness can effectively practice meditation. While researchers dispute whether its effects are measurable, advocates claim wide-ranging benefits and little or no risk (Holmes, 1984).

Hallucinations

Under unusual circumstances, a distortion in consciousness occurs during which the individual sees or hears things that are not really present. **Hallucinations** *are vivid perceptions that occur in the absence of objective stimulation; they are mental constructions of an individual's altered reality.* Hallucinations differ from *illusions,* which are perceptual distortions of real stimuli and are experienced by most people. For example, for most people, the flashing lightbulbs on a theater marquee look like a single light zooming around the edge of the sign. Perceiving stationary lights to be moving is a common illusion, the *phi phenomenon.* But if you "see" lights around people where there are no such lights, you are experiencing a hallucination. Not all hallucinations are bizarre or even vivid, but they are all "false" in the sense that they do not accurately reflect an external reality.

The complex functioning of the brain requires constant external stimulation. When it lacks such stimulation, the brain manufactures its own. Some subjects, when kept in a special environment that minimizes all sensory stimulation, show a tendency to hallucinate. *Sensory isolation* "destructures" the environment and may force subjects to try to restore meaning and stable orientation to a situation. Hallucinations may be a way of reconstructing a reality in accordance with one's personality, past experiences, and the demands of the present experimental setting (Zubeck et al., 1961; Suedfeld, 1980).

A more common form of hallucination in response to a social need is the insistence by young children that they have imaginary friends. Though rarer, similar adult experiences can occur in the wake of grief, as when one experiences a "visit" from a recently deceased loved one. In both children's and adults' experiences, such hallucinations may be the mind's response to a loss or lack of stimulation, to loneliness or isolation (Siegel, 1992).

Just as insufficient stimulation might prompt hallucination, too much of the wrong type of stimulation can also create hallucinations. Hallucinations can occur during high fever, epilepsy, and migraine headaches. They also occur in cases of severe mental disorders, especially *schizophrenia* (see Chapter 13), when patients respond to private mental events as if they were external sensory stimuli. Many episodes of altered states of consciousness have been reported following overstimulating experiences, such as mob riots, religious revival meetings, prolonged dancing (such as that done by the religious sect of dervishes), extreme fright or panic, trance states, and moments of extreme emotion. Hallucinations have been associated with heightened states of arousal and religious ecstasies as well. (See Weigh the Evidence: Can Religious Experience Alter Consciousness?) In some cultures and circumstances, hallucinations are interpreted as mystical insights that confer special status on the visionary. Thus, in two different settings, the same vivid perception of direct contact with spiritual forces might be either devalued as a sign of mental illness or respected as a sign of special gifts.

Finally, hallucinations may be induced by psychoactive drugs, such as peyote and LSD (lysergic acid diethylamide), as well as by withdrawal from alcohol in severe cases of alcoholism. Anthropologists and ethnologists note that some cultures advocate the use of *hallucinogenic* drugs as a way of experiencing hallucinations, either as an end in themselves, or as a means to self-discovery or spiritual awakening (Castaneda, 1968). In the next section we will focus on how various chemicals are sought for their ability to quickly produce alterations in perception, consciousness, and mood.

Psychoactive Drugs

Since ancient times, people have taken drugs to alter their perception of reality. Individuals throughout the world take drugs to relax, cope with stress, avoid the unpleasantness of current realities, feel comfortable in social situations, or experience an alternate state of consciousness. In 1954, the publication of Aldous Huxley's *The Doors of Perception* popularized the use of drugs to alter consciousness. Huxley took mescaline as a personal experiment to explore his own consciousness. He wanted to test the validity of poet William Blake's assertion in *The Marriage of Heaven and Hell* (1793): "If the doors of perception were cleansed every thing would appear to man as it is, infinite. For man has closed himself up, till he sees all thro' narrow chinks of his concern."

The 1960s and 1970s ushered in a unique period in the United States, a time when many people "played" with recreational drugs and admitted to experimenting with mind-altering substances such as LSD. By 1989, nearly 55 percent of American high school seniors (in annual surveys of over 16,000 students) had reported using one or more illegal drugs in their senior year (Johnston et al., 1989). Although this figure has declined somewhat since 1982, it has recently stabilized and, for some drugs, even gone up. More frighteningly, the number of adolescents *addicted* to drugs has reached epidemic proportions. Despite government-sponsored campaigns against drug use, most young Americans continue to see at least some drug use as acceptable. Starting in the late 1970s, a longitudinal study of junior high school students showed that, over time, fewer than 10 percent of the subjects were regular or chronic users, but fewer that 10 percent of the sample reported not using *any* drugs (Newcomb & Bentler, 1988; Stacy et al., 1991).

Dependence and Addiction   Psychoactive drugs *are chemicals that affect mental processes and behavior by temporarily changing conscious awareness.* Once in the brain, they may attach themselves to synaptic receptors, blocking

Can Religious Experience Alter Consciousness?

The beliefs and practices of the Holy Ghost People of Appalachia enable them to do some remarkable things. At church services they handle deadly poisonous snakes, drink deadly poison, handle fire, and speak in imaginary languages (see also Covington, 1995). In many religions this last behavior, "speaking in tongues" or word-like utterances others cannot interpret, is valued as a sign the speaker has received important spiritual gifts. The scientific term for this is **glossolalia,** *fabricated speech occurring chiefly in states of religious ecstasy and altered states* (English & English, 1958; Malony & Lovekin, 1985). Glossolalia has appeared in various religious traditions, but is most often associated with Christianity, specifically with references in New Testament scripture to the power of the Holy Spirit to endow believers with the ability to speak in tongues (see Acts 2:2–5; 1 Cor. 12:27–31, *Revised Standard Version*). Groups that define themselves as Pentecostal, or otherwise identify with the centrality of the Holy Spirit in their theology, may encourage their members to seek and experience some altered state as "proof" of their status or sincerity.

Is speaking in tongues an example of achieving a religiously altered state of mind? One perspective on glossolalia, the *extraordinary approach,* assumes that speaking in tongues reflects an altered state of consciousness. The goal for glossolalics is to experience and demonstrate being "possessed" by the spirit they believe in, entering an apparent trance and having their actions "taken over" by another power or pattern. The glossolalia is thus an outcome of the trance (Goodman, 1969, 1971).

Critics argue that glossolalia is influenced by both the setting and subculture (for example, the particular congregation in which it occurs) and by learning—that is, glossolalics get "better" at speaking in tongues over time, and their utterances come more and more to resemble fellow church members' utterances, using the same rhythms and symbols (Samarin, 1969, 1971, 1973). In this view, speaking in tongues is produced not by an altered state but by group

The Holy Ghost People of Appalachia and other religious sects engage in such practices as snake handling to prove faith and achieve changes in consciousness. Rayford Dunn was bitten on the hand by a cottonmouth moments after this picture was taken in Kingston, Georgia. Although he survived—going out to eat, and returning to church the next day to handle snakes again—some believers have died from poisonous snake bites.

membership, socialization, and role playing—learning to speak the "special language" of the church. Compare this discussion to the debate between contrasting explanations for hypnosis (see page 95). One group of researchers proposes that the behavior observed is caused by an altered state of consciousness, while another argues that it is the result of adopting the social role of entranced subject.

Even mainstream religious groups may value special behaviors such as trances, emotional outbursts, and unusual language as esteemed demonstrations of faith. Religious historian Martin E. Marty (1984) explains that, beginning in the early 1960s, increasing numbers of American congregations sought "charismatic" experiences, proof that they had achieved a high level of spirituality:

. . . .In the middle-class churches, the [charismatic] movement often turned out to be abrasive, as its members tended to stand apart from others who had not yet had "the experience." To insiders it meant a new sense of belonging to a group, a new awareness of God, and a new step on the inward journey. (p. 470)

Episcopal priest Leo Booth (1991) warns that, for some religious adherents, "God becomes a drug" because religious involvement is based on a deep need to escape personal pain or to maintain a trancelike euphoria when joy is not forthcoming from other life experiences. According to Booth, "religion addicts" adopt rigid, black-and-white belief systems and reject healthy relationships as their habits become more demanding. Booth recommends a twelve-step program, similar to those of support groups for overcoming substance abuse, as a strategy for accepting that one can be empowered—and even happy—without relying solely on a particular group, lifestyle, or substance.

Do you find it perplexing or even uncomfortable to link the scientific perspective of psychology to issues of religious faith? People today continue to wrestle with the distinctions between brain, mind, and soul, just as past generations of scholars have done. As our research techniques advance, we still struggle to find words for experiences that are ultimately personal, private, and impossible to prove.

The line between substance use and abuse is easy to cross for those who become addicted.

or stimulating certain reactions. Drugs profoundly alter the brain's communication system, affecting perception, memory, mood, and behavior. Continued use of certain drugs lessens their effect on the nervous system, so that greater dosages are required to achieve the same effect. *Such reduced effectiveness with repeated use of a drug is called* **tolerance.**

Hand-in-hand with tolerance goes **physiological dependence**—*a process in which the body adjusts to and becomes dependent on the substance, in part because neurotransmitters are depleted by the frequent presence of the drug.* *Addiction* is the tragic outcome of tolerance and dependence. A person with an **addiction** *requires the drug in his or her body and suffers painful withdrawal symptoms if the drug is not present.* **Withdrawal** *symptoms can include physical trembling, perspiring, nausea, and in the case of alcohol withdrawal, even death.*

With or without being addicted, an individual may find himself or herself craving or hungering for the drug and its effects. This is a result of **psychological dependence,** *a pervasive desire to obtain or use a drug, irrespective of any physiological addiction.* Psychological dependence can occur with any drug, including caffeine and nicotine, prescription medication, and over-the-counter drugs. In extreme cases, a person's lifestyle comes to revolve around drug use so that his or her capacity to function is limited or impaired. In addition, the expense of maintaining an illegal drug habit often drives an addict to robbery, assault, prostitution, or drug peddling. One of the gravest dangers currently facing addicts is the threat of infection with HIV (the virus that causes AIDS). By sharing hypodermic needles (a practice addicts rely on because syringes cannot be obtained legally), intravenous drug users can unknowingly inject themselves with drops of bodily fluid from others with HIV.

Varieties of Psychoactive Drugs   Table 3.1 summarizes common psychoactive drugs. We will discuss some of the effects and characteristics common to each category of substances.

Hallucinogens   Drugs known as **hallucinogens** or **psychedelics** *produce the most dramatic changes in consciousness.* These drugs alter perceptions of the external environment and inner awareness. They often create hallucinations and blur the boundary between self and the external world. For example, an individual experiencing hallucinogenic effects might listen to music and suddenly feel she is producing the music or that the music is coming from within herself. Hallucinogenic drugs, such as LSD, act in the brain at specific receptor sites for the chemical neurotransmitter serotonin (Jacobs, 1987).

The four most commonly known hallucinogens are *mescaline* (from a type of cactus); *psilocybin* (a mushroom); and *LSD* and *PCP* (phencyclidine), both of which are synthesized in chemical laboratories. Young people are most likely to abuse PCP, or *angel dust.* PCP produces a strange dissociative reaction in which the user becomes insensitive to pain, becomes confused, and feels apart from her surroundings.

Cannabis   Often classified as a hallucinogen but different in many ways from LSD and PCP, **cannabis** *is a drug (derived from the hemp plant) whose psychoactive effects include altered perception, sedation, pain relief, and mild euphoria.* The active ingredient in the cannabis plant is THC (tetrahydrocannabinol), found in both the plant's dried leaves and flowers *(marijuana)* and in the solidified resin of the plant *(hashish).* The experience derived from inhaling THC depends on its dose: small doses create mild, pleasurable highs, and larger doses result in long hallucinogenic reactions. The positive effects reported by regular users include changes at a sensory and perceptual level, notably euphoria, well-being, and distortions of space and time. However, depending on the social context and other factors, the effects may also be negative: fear, anxiety, and confusion. Motor coordination is impaired with marijuana use, so those who work or drive under its influence suffer a higher risk of accidents (Moskowitz, 1985).

Opiates The class of drugs known as *opiates*—derivatives of the unripened seed pods of the opium poppy—includes *morphine, heroin*, and *codeine*. **Opiates** *are highly addictive drugs that suppress physical sensation and response to stimulation.* Morphine and codeine have analgesic (pain-relieving) properties; morphine has long been used in postsurgical medicine, and codeine is employed as a cough suppressant. Heroin is a derivative of morphine, originally developed in the nineteenth century in Germany by the Bayer Company (of aspirin fame), but abandoned because of its undesirable side effects. The initial effect of an intravenous injection of heroin is a rush of pleasure. Feelings of euphoria supplant all worries and awareness of bodily needs, although there are no major changes in consciousness. Serious addiction is likely once a person begins to inject heroin. To avoid withdrawal, a heroin user takes the drug very frequently—once daily or more often—making it a very expensive habit to maintain. Because addicts often steal to support their expensive, illegal habit, the use of heroin has been blamed for a high proportion of property crime in cities and cultures worldwide.

Depressants *Drugs that slow down the mental and physical activity of the body by inhibiting central nervous system activity are known as* **depressants.**

TABLE 3.1	PSYCHOACTIVE DRUGS: MEDICAL USES, EFFECTS, LIKELIHOOD OF DEPENDENCE			
Category	**Medical Uses**	**Duration (Hours)**	**Dependence**	
			Psychological	**Physiological**
Opiates				
Morphine	Painkiller, cough suppressant	3–6	High	High
Heroin	Under investigation	3–6	High	High
Codeine	Painkiller, cough suppressant	3–6	Moderate	Moderate
Hallucinogens				
LSD	None	8–12	None	Unknown
PCP	Veterinary anesthetic	Varies	Unknown	High
Mescaline	None	8–12	None	Unknown
Psilocybin	None	4–6	Unknown	Unknown
Cannabis	Reduce nausea from chemotherapy	2–4	Unknown	Moderate
Depressants				
Barbiturates	Sedative, sleep, anticonvulsant, anesthetic	1–16	Moderate–High	Moderate–High
Benzodiazepines	Antianxiety, sleep, anticonvulsant, sedative	4–8	Low–Moderate	Low–Moderate
Alcohol	Antiseptic	1–5	Moderate	Moderate
Stimulants				
Amphetamines	Weight control, counteract anesthesia	2–4	High	High
Cocaine	Local anesthetic	1–2	High	High
Nicotine	Gum, patch for cessation of smoking	Varies	Low–High	Low–High
Caffeine	Weight control, stimulant in acute respiratory failure, analgesia	4–6	Unknown	Unknown

Depressants include *barbiturates* (usually prescribed for sedation), *benzodiazepines* (tranquilizers), and *alcohol*. By decreasing the transmission of nerve impulses in the central nervous system, depressants tend to depress (slow down) the mental and physical activity of the body. At low levels or appropriate dosages, depressants relieve symptoms of pain or anxiety, but overuse or abuse of depressants is extremely dangerous.

High dosages of *barbiturates* induce sleep but reduce the time spent in REM sleep. Overdoses of barbiturates lead to loss of all sensations, and coma. More deaths are caused by overdoses of barbiturates, taken either accidentally or with suicidal intent, than by any other poison (Kolb, 1973).

The *benzodiazepines* (or minor tranquilizers) are much safer to use than barbiturates, and are most commonly prescribed to treat anxiety. Probably the best known and most widely prescribed benzodiazepine is Valium. Benzodiazepines (pronounced *BEN-zo-dye-AZ-a-peens*) calm a patient without causing sleepiness or sedation. Because benzodiazepines are so widely prescribed, they may be overused and abused. Overdoses of benzodiazepines may cause muscle incoordination, slurred speech, weakness, and irritability, while withdrawal symptoms include increased anxiety, muscle twitching, and sensitivity to sound and light.

Alcohol was one of the first psychoactive substances used extensively by our ancestors. Under its influence, people become silly and talkative, abusive, or quietly depressed. In small dosages, alcohol can induce relaxation and slightly improve an adult's reaction speed. However, the body breaks down alcohol at the rate of only one ounce per hour, and greater amounts consumed in short periods overtax the central nervous system. When the level of alcohol in the blood reaches 0.15 percent, an individual experiences gross negative effects on thinking, memory, and judgment along with emotional instability and motor incoordination.

When psychologists talk about drugs, they include legal substances such as tobacco and caffeine, two extremely popular stimulants in most cultures.

Advertisers in the United States spend millions of dollars annually depicting the social and personal benefits of drinking alcoholic beverages. Alcohol-related automobile accidents are the leading cause of death among people between the ages of 15 and 25. Physical dependence, tolerance, and addiction all develop with prolonged heavy drinking. When the amount and frequency of drinking alcohol interferes with job performance, impairs social and family relationships, and creates serious health problems, the diagnosis of *alcoholism* is appropriate.

Stimulants Stimulants *are drugs that increase central nervous system activity, speeding up both mental and physical rates of activity.* Users of stimulants such as *amphetamines* and *cocaine* seek three major effects: increased self-confidence, greater energy and alertness, and euphoria. Heavy users experience frightening hallucinations and develop beliefs that others are out to harm them, a thought pattern known as a *paranoid delusion.* Special dangers of cocaine use include both euphoric highs and very depressive lows, which lead users to increase the frequency and dosage of use beyond their own control.

Crack is a highly purified form of cocaine that produces a swift high that wears off quickly. Because crack is sold in small, inexpensive quantities, this drug is readily available to the young and the poor, and is destroying social communities. Despite the well-publicized deaths of prominent people from crack overdoses, there is little evidence that its use is declining.

Two stimulants that you may not even think of as psychoactive drugs are *caffeine* and *nicotine*. Within ten minutes, two cups of strong coffee or tea administer enough caffeine to profoundly affect the heart, blood, and circulatory functions. They can also disturb sleep. Is it accurate or fair to think of commonplace, legal substances like coffee or tobacco as drugs? For example, is nicotine really addictive? Definitely. Like all addictive drugs, nicotine mimics natural chemicals released by the brain. These chemicals stimulate receptors that make us feel good whenever we have done something right—a phenomenon that aids our survival. Unfortunately, nicotine teases those same brain receptors into responding as if it were good for us to be smoking, chewing tobacco, or using snuff.

By short-circuiting our brains, nicotine shortens our lives as well. The total negative impact of nicotine on health is greater than that of all other psychoactive drugs combined, including heroin, cocaine, and alcohol. The U.S. Public Health Service attributes 350,000 deaths annually to cigarettes. While smoking is the leading cause of preventable sickness and death, it is both legal and actively promoted—$2.7 billion are spent annually on its advertising and promotion. Although antismoking campaigns have been somewhat effective in reducing the overall level of smoking in the United States, some 54 million Americans still smoke. Of the million people who start smoking each year, the majority are under 14, female, or adult members of a racial minority (Goodkind, 1989). (African-American adolescents appear to be an anomaly: they are *not* smoking more.)

In the summer of 1995, the American Medical Association formally recommended that the U.S. Food and Drug Administration regard nicotine as a drug to be regulated. The line between legal and illegal drugs has always been arbitrary; clinicians often find that for patients with serious substance abuse disorders, the "starter drugs" were not illegal drugs such as marijuana but rather tobacco and alcohol—both legal, affordable, and extremely accessible. Before our society can reduce the damage done by illegal drugs, we must take a harder look at our individual and cultural attitudes toward the use of legal drugs.

The Adaptability of Consciousness

Why do humans experience consciousness—and then seek to alter it? The evolution of the human brain permitted survival of those of our forebears who could cope with a hostile environment even when their sensory and physical abilities were not adequate. Humans became capable of *symbolic representation* of the outer world and of their own actions, enabling them to remember, anticipate, and plan (Craik, 1943). *Homo sapiens'* complex brain was able to model its world, to imagine how present realities could be transformed into alternative scenarios. A brain that can deal with both objective and subjective realities needs a mechanism to keep track of the focus of attention. That part of the brain is the conscious mind.

Human intelligence and consciousness evolved as a result of competition with the most hostile force in the evolutionary environment—*other humans.* Thus the human mind may have evolved as a consequence of the extreme sociability of our ancestors. Living together in close groups required new skills in co-operation as well as competition with other humans. Natural selection favored those who could think, plan, and imagine *alternative realities* that could promote both bonding with kin and victory over adversaries (Lewin, 1987).

Consciousness makes possible the active mental construction of incoming information into a meaningful, organized pattern of symbols. This construction makes sense of a confusing world, imposes order on chaos, and finds meaning in the events people experience (Johnson-Laird, 1983). Consciousness is also complex, composed of several levels and many structures, just beginning to be scientifically understood. Recall the Opening Case, in which Karen overheard comments made in the operating room, although she was supposedly anesthetized for surgery. Such experiences are rare but not impossible, and their occurrence tells anesthetists and psychologists alike that there are not only many levels of consciousness, but also many pathways to *unconsciousness* based on different brain processes (Blakeslee, 1994). "Consciousness" may be a misnomer: it might be more accurate to say that an individual who is aware of the world, and aware of that awareness, is really drawing on several "consciousnesses."

As complex as it already is, why then would people seek to *alter* consciousness? Perhaps, at times, we all long to reach beyond the confines of ordinary reality (Targ & Harary, 1984). The human need to expand consciousness seeks the uncertainty of freedom instead of settling for the security of the status quo. Exploring and extending consciousness can broaden the universal experience of what it means to be a thoughtful human being.

Check Your Recall

Extended states of consciousness include hypnosis, meditation, and drug-induced states of mind. Hypnosis is induced by suggestions that affect perceptions, thoughts, motives, and self-control. Hypnosis is a useful tool for psychologists studying physical or emotional conditions. Hypnosis can also be applied for relieving pain.

Meditation is an alteration in self-awareness with an enhancing effect on self-knowledge and well-being. While meditation is viewed by some cultures as a natural extension of personal experience, it is viewed by Western culture as an altered state of consciousness. Although there is dispute about its effectiveness, some argue that meditation offers a completely self-controlled route to peace of mind and spiritual awakening.

A hallucination is a vivid perception that does not accurately reflect physical stimulation. Hallucinations may be brought on by some psychoactive drugs, psychological disorders such as schizophrenia, or excessive sensory isolation.

Religious experiences may induce altered states as a result of individuals' beliefs or actions. Such alterations in awareness may include resistance to pain or injury, changes in perception, and speaking in imaginary languages.

Psychoactive drugs are substances that temporarily affect thoughts and behaviors. Hallucinogens such as LSD and cannabis distort perception and performance. Opiates suppress physical sensation and responsiveness. Depressants slow down the body's rate of activity. Stimulants speed physical and psychological activity and improve mood. Psychoactive drugs offer their effects at a high price, which may include health risk, damage to performance and relationships, psychological dependence, and physiological addiction.

Consciousness evolved as humans' ability to represent their experiences symbolically improved their chances for survival. Memory, foresight, planning, and imagination all provided a selective advantage for our ancestors in competition with the environment and each other.

CHAPTER REVIEW

Summary

Theorists continue to debate the nature of the relationship between brain and mind. However, the mental function of greatest interest to psychologists is consciousness. In addition to the waking awareness that defines consciousness, other structures contribute to human thought and be-

havior: nonconscious, preconscious, subconscious, and unconscious processes. Consciousness shifts and changes in everyday life, in the form of daydreaming, sleep, and dreams. Altered experience can result in extended states of consciousness, including hypnosis, meditation, hallucinations, and the effects of psychoactive drugs. Just as consciousness has been highly adaptive for human survival, the achievement of altered states may represent the human quest for greater achievement and self-understanding.

Section Reviews

Consciousness

Be sure to *Check Your Recall* by reviewing the summary of this section on page 84.

Key Terms
consciousness (p. 77)
emergent-interaction
 theory (p. 78)
think-aloud protocols
 (p. 79)
experience-sampling
 method (p. 79)
dichotic listening task
 (p. 79)
self-awareness
 (p. 81)

nonconscious processes
 (p. 81)
preconscious memories
 (p. 81)
subconscious awareness
 (p. 82)
unconscious (p. 82)

Names to Know
Francis Crick (p. 78)
Roger Sperry (p. 78)
Michael Gazzaniga (p. 78)

Everyday Changes in Consciousness

Be sure to *Check Your Recall* by reviewing the summary of this section on page 93.

Key Terms
daydreaming (p. 84)
circadian rhythm
 (p. 85)
rapid eye-movement
 (REM) sleep (p. 86)
non-REM (NREM) sleep
 (p. 86)
insomnia (p. 90)
sleep apnea (p. 90)

daytime sleepiness
 (p. 90)
activation-synthesis theory
 (p. 92)

Names to Know
Francis Crick (p. 87)
Sigmund Freud (p. 89)
J. Allan Hobson (p. 92)
Robert McCarley (p. 92)

Extended States of Consciousness

Be sure to *Check Your Recall* by reviewing the summary of this section on page 104.

Key Terms
hypnosis (p. 94)
hypnotizability (p. 94)
meditation (p. 96)
hallucinations (p. 97)
psychoactive drugs
 (p. 98)
glossolalia (p. 99)
tolerance (p. 100)
physiological dependence
 (p. 100)

addiction (p. 100)
withdrawal (p. 100)
psychological dependence
 (p. 100)
hallucinogens (p. 100)
psychedelics (p. 100)
cannabis (p. 100)
opiates (p. 101)
depressants (p. 101)
stimulants (p. 102)

REVIEW TEST

Chapter 3: States of Mind

For each of the following items, choose the single correct or best answer. The correct answers, explanations, and page references appear in Appendix B.

1. According to _____, the activities of the brain give rise to mental states that are not the same as brain activities and cannot be reduced to biochemical events. Instead, mind and brain interact and influence each other.
   a. activation-synthesis theory
   b. emergent-interaction theory
   c. the content analysis method
   d. psychoanalytic theory

2. A research subject wears headphones that channel a spoken monologue into her right ear while her left ear receives a familiar popular song. This demonstrates use of the _____ method of consciousness research.
   a. introspection
   b. think-aloud protocol
   c. dichotic listening
   d. experience-sampling

3. Which of the following is *not* one of the basic functions of consciousness cited by your text?
   a. restricting attention to what is relevant
   b. selective attention and memory
   c. imagining and considering alternatives
   d. relinquishing control to enhance self-awareness

4. Which of the following choices correctly pairs an example of an experience or process with its appropriate level of consciousness?
   a. unconscious: repressing sexual attraction to someone
   b. subconscious: regulation of blood pressure
   c. nonconscious: remembering how to tell time
   d. preconscious: preventing awareness of traumatic memories

5. Rapid eye-movements are reliable behavioral signs that _____.
   a. an individual has reached the deepest level of sleep
   b. a sleeper's mental activity is centered on dreaming
   c. one has achieved a genuine meditative state
   d. a subject is very low in hypnotizability

6. _____ is a sleep disorder characterized by brief interruptions when the sleeper stops breathing, wakens, resumes breathing, and falls back asleep.
   a. Apnea
   b. Daytime sleepiness
   c. Insomnia
   d. Analgesia

7. Which of the following statements about hypnosis is true?
   a. Hypnosis is actually a form of NREM sleep.
   b. Hypnotizability relies on a subject's ability to respond to suggestion.
   c. Anyone can be hypnotized if the hypnotist knows the most effective techniques to use.
   d. The less intelligent or educated a person is, the more hypnotizable he or she will be.

8. One of the most common explanations for the popularity of meditation is that with regular practice its users _____.
   a. experience increased levels of energy and alertness
   b. experience hallucinations and delusions
   c. have less self-awareness and self-consciousness
   d. feel more physically and mentally relaxed

9. Which of the following is a condition that would lead one to experience hallucinations?
   a. sensory isolation
   b. use of the drug mescaline
   c. withdrawal from alcohol in severe alcoholism
   d. all of the above
10. Three major effects sought by users of _____ are increased alertness, greater self-confidence, and euphoria.

a. stimulants
b. depressants
c. opiates
d. hallucinogens

IF YOU'RE INTERESTED . . .

Altered States. (Video: 1980, color, 102 min.). Directed by Ken Russell; starring William Hurt, Blair Brown, Bob Balaban, Charles Haid.

Loosely based on Paddy Chayefsky's novel. A scientist experiments with sensory deprivation, primal consciousness, and mind expansion. Good for imagery and dialogue—not a valid source of scientific information.

Borbely, A. (1986). *Secrets of sleep.* New York: Basic Books.

An intriguing review of sleep research and its applications.

Bowers, K. S. (1983). *Hypnosis for the seriously curious* (2nd ed.). New York: W. W. Norton & Co.

A volume written to inform the reader who is more than a layperson but less than a scholar. A good update on what is known and not yet known about hypnosis.

Bright Lights, Big City. (Video: 1988, color, 110 min.). Directed by James Bridges; starring Michael J. Fox, Kiefer Sutherland, Phoebe Cates, Tracy Pollan.

Good cinematic translation of Jay McInerney's novel about a young Midwesterner transplanted to New York yuppiedom and overwhelmed by nightlife and cocaine—and the need to maintain the addictive cycle.

Castaneda, C. (1968). *The teachings of don Juan: A Yaqui way of knowledge.* New York: Washington Square Press.

While studying anthropology at UCLA, Carlos Castaneda met don Juan, an elderly Yaqui Indian from Mexico who was learned in the use of medicinal plants. Under don Juan's tutelage, Castaneda experimented with hallucinogenic drugs, documenting his experiences and the lessons the "beneficent sorcerer" taught about their proper use and meaning. The first in several works by Castaneda

on these themes, others including *A Separate Reality* and *Journey to Ixtlan.*

Churchland, P. M. (1995). *The engine of reason, the seat of the soul: A philosophical journey into the brain.* Cambridge, MA: MIT Press.

A neuroscientist's argument that the brain represents a "quart-size universe" whose uncountable connections and processes more than account for the mysteries of the mind.

Crick, F. (1994). *The astonishing hypothesis: The scientific search for the soul.* New York: Charles Scribner's Sons.

Challenging but absorbing and interesting, Crick's work argues for the "astonishing hypothesis" that consciousness is ultimately an outcome of the brain's biochemistry.

Days of Wine and Roses, The. (Video: 1962, B&W, 117 min.). Directed by Blake Edwards; starring Jack Lemmon, Lee Remick, Jack Klugman.

Realistic depiction of how a man and woman fall in love, marry, fall into alcoholism, and ultimately must decide separately whether and how to stop drinking. Excellent writing, action, and music.

DuMaurier, G. (1894/1995). *Trilby.* New York: Oxford University Press.

George duMaurier's curious tale of a young woman transformed from Parisian artist's model to great singer by the malevolent hypnotist Svengali. Not even remotely accurate about hypnosis, the novel nevertheless produced lasting images and prejudices about hypnotists' motives and methods.

Freud. (Video: 1962, B&W, 120 min.). Directed by John Huston; starring Montgomery Clift, Susannah York.

Popularized film biography of the founder of psychoanalysis. Features fascinating dream sequences with classic psychoanalytic symbolism and interpretation.

Greenfield, S. A. (1995). *Journey to the centers of the mind.* New York: W. H. Freeman.

A neuroscientist offers "an accessible theory of consciousness" that seeks to link the our comprehension of the brain as a physical and biological entity with philosophers' concepts of mental function and experience.

Hobson, J. A. (1988). *The dreaming brain.* New York: Basic Books.

Hobson's presentation of his own research and theory about the nature and meaning of dreams.

I'm Dancing as Fast as I Can. (Video: 1982, color, 107 min.). Directed by Jack Hofsiss; starring Jill Clayburgh, Nicol Williamson, Dianne Wiest, Joe Pesci.

Excellent cast in okay story, based on personal memoir about the horror a woman experiences when she tries to quit her Valium addiction.

Lost Weekend, The. (Video: 1945, B&W, 101 min.). Directed by Billy Wilder; starring Ray Milland, Jane Wyman, Howard da Silva, Frank Faylen.

This classic Oscar-winning film (Best Director, Film, Actor, Screenplay) pioneered dramatic screen portrayals of alcoholism, its consequences, and efforts at treatment.

Siegel, R. K. (1992). *Fire in the brain.* New York: Dutton.

Lyrically written and technically precise, up-to-date collection of case studies of hallucinations and the individuals who experienced them.

Svengali. (Video: 1931, B&W, 82 min.). Directed by Archie Mayo; starring John Barrymore, Marian Mash, Donald Crisp.

Based on duMaurier's novel *Trilby* (above), this early film version created the dominant popular image of hypnosis as a form of mind control and hypnotists as obsessed victimizers. (Not to be confused with the lesser 1955 remake or the awful 1983 rock 'n' roll retelling.)

CHAPTER 4

Psychological Development

1984. *The two tiny figures in buntings are not quite three weeks old. They lie in their crib on their stomachs in mirror-image positions—a small fist inches from each mouth, one head turned to the right, the other to the left. Nicole wakes up first. She lies there, quite content, listening to her mother in the kitchen. Ten minutes later, Alexis awakens. Almost immediately, she begins to howl. The babies' mother runs in from the kitchen, picks up Alexis, and reaches for a clean diaper.*

Nicole and Alexis are genetically identical twins, the products of a fertilized ovum that split sometime in the first two weeks of prenatal life. Because of their positions on the placenta, Nicole was always first to get the nutrients that support prenatal growth. Thus, at birth she weighed 4 pounds; Alexis weighed a little less. Although no one can tell the girls apart when they are dressed identically, there are important differences between the babies.

1985. Much to her mother's dismay, Alexis starts climbing on chairs as soon as she learns to crawl. Nicole follows in a couple of days. Alexis takes her first step on her first birthday. Friends and relatives clap and cheer. Nicole watches. In less than a week, she is walking too. After her morning Cheerios, Alexis sits in her daddy's lap and opens her mouth wide for bites of his scrambled eggs. She never seems to get enough. When anyone offers eggs to Nicole, she turns away and grimaces. She sticks to Cheerios.

1986. When Alexis and Nicole are 19 months old, their mother goes away for four days. This is the first time she has left her daughters for more than a day. The girls accompany their father to the hospital where their mother and a newborn baby, Mikey, are waiting. Nicole greets her mom with a big smile and a hug, as though nothing has happened. Alexis looks away, fidgets, and shows little emotion.

1987. When the girls work at their little table, Alexis scribbles intently on sheets of paper, "writing" letters and stories that she later dictates to her mother. Nicole is more interested in three-dimensional art projects. She sculpts Play-Doh™ into intricate shapes and makes collages out of miscellaneous objects she finds. Nicole still sucks her thumb and likes to stay close to her mom. She also loves to climb on the tire swing in the backyard, and she begs to be pushed "higher, higher." Alexis prefers to watch.

Nicole likes sleeping alone, while Alexis often gets anxious if she feels she has lost track of her sister, even in her sleep. Sometimes Alexis wakes up in the night. "I had a bad dream," she cries. "I lost 'Cole and I couldn't find her anywhere." Together or apart, they sleep in identical, sometimes mirror-image, positions.

1990. *Although Alexis sometimes eats up to three times as much as Nicole, the girls' weight never differs by more than 4 ounces (Nicole is the heavier one.) Nicole loves fruits and vegetables. Alexis prefers eggs and meat. Nicole takes violin lessons and practices every day. Alexis would like to take lessons too, but she doesn't want to practice. While Nicole practices, Alexis reads. She can read anything, even the instructions for the family's new laptop computer. When Nicole picks up a book, she looks first at the pictures and then reads each word carefully.*

On vacation, Alexis likes to sleep with her aunt and grandma. Nicole prefers to stay with her mother. When Nicole is nearby, Alexis is theatrical and out-going, but on her own, Alexis seems more withdrawn. Nicole is more self-contained than Alexis and seems less dependent on social approval. Alexis reacts immediately and intensely to everything that happens, with her emotions seemingly just beneath her skin. Nicole is more likely to watch and wait passively, not revealing what she is feeling.

At the end of each day, after listening to a bedtime story, Alexis and Nicole climb into their beds and curl up in identical mirror-image positions. Their parents wonder which aspects of their future development will be identical and which will be shaped by the unique experiences they will have in school and outside the home.

Introduction

Although Alexis and Nicole developed from the same egg and sperm, the preceding excerpts from their baby book illustrate how very different they were three weeks after birth. The book also describes the unique personality traits and behaviors each was exhibiting six years later. How is it possible that two people with identical origins could be developing into such different people?

To answer that question we turn to **developmental psychology,** *the branch of psychology that is concerned with the changes in physical and psychological functioning that occur from conception through an entire life span.* The task of developmental psychologists is to find out how organisms change over time. They study the ages and stages of development at which different abilities and functions first appear and observe how those functions are modified. This chapter presents a vast amount of information, spanning both the individual lifetime and the complexity of human experience. We begin by considering *how* to think about psychological development, starting with the study of infant behavior. We next review the major developmental processes in two major periods in the life span: first childhood, then adolescence and adulthood.

Perspectives on Development

Try to describe your life in 25 words or less. If you then compare your description to those of others, you will find that in some ways you are much like other people: you were born, have matured, and will someday die. In other ways you are distinctive: perhaps you matured socially earlier than your friends and are more self-confident than others. Or maybe you are not quite the scholar or athlete that your friends are. Your unique story is about both similarities and differences; it is the result of importance influences in your life.

Continuity and Discontinuity

Some psychologists believe that development is essentially continuous. According to this view, we become more skillful in thinking, talking, or using our muscles in much the same way that we become taller—through the cumulative action of the same continuing processes.

In contrast, other psychologists see development as a succession of reorganizations: behavior is different in different *age-specific life periods,* such as infancy, childhood, and adolescence. Thus, while development itself is continuous, particular aspects of it are discontinuous. In this view, for example, newborns are not perceived as less dependent on the mother than they were before birth; they are *as* dependent but in different ways.

Psychologists who believe development is discontinuous theorize about **developmental stages,** *periods during which physical or psychological functioning differs qualitatively from that of either earlier or later periods.* They believe different behaviors appear at different ages or life periods because different underlying processes are operating then. A *stage* is a period of time when psychological functions are observably changed. You may have heard parents dismissing a child's misbehavior or moodiness as "just going through a stage." In developmental theories, stages are assumed to be temporary and focused on specific tasks or experiences. A stage progresses toward an assumed goal—a state or ability that the individual must achieve in the same order as other individuals, although perhaps at a different rate (Cairns & Valsinger, 1984). In a stage theory, every individual progresses by engaging in one central task or challenge at a time before progressing to the next stage in the sequence.

The concept of *critical periods* is related to stages of development. A **critical period** *is a sensitive time in an organism's development when the organism may acquire a particular behavior conditional on the occurrence of certain stimuli and events.* If stimulus conditions are not met, however, the individual will not develop the behavior and will have difficulty doing so later. Experiments have confirmed that critical periods for certain behaviors occur in both animals and humans. For example, when dogs and monkeys are raised in isolation for a few months after birth, they lack contact with their species during a critical period of social development. Even if they are then reared with other normal animals, they behave in abnormal ways throughout the rest of their lives (Scott, 1963). Moreover, a female adult rhesus monkey who was initially reared in isolation will not react appropriately to signals for mating, and if she gives birth, she will not give her baby normal maternal care (Harlow & Harlow, 1966).

Nature and Nurture

Return for a moment to your description of yourself. Where did "you" come from? Are you more a product of your chance inheritance, the character and physical features of your ancestors, or of your unique life experiences and opportunities? Developmental psychologists apply this question to human development in general: to what extent is human behavior determined by heredity (nature), and to what extent is it a product of learned experiences (nurture)? The **nature-nurture controversy** *is a long-standing debate among philosophers, psychologists, and educators over the relative importance of heredity and learning in many aspects of functioning.* To appreciate the importance of this controversy for modern developmental psychology we must go back to a curious discovery that began in the year 1800.

At the end of the eighteenth century, scholars in "mental medicine," an early version of modern psychology, debated the true nature of the human species. On one side of the debate, championed by British philosopher **John Locke,** was the belief that the human infant is born without knowledge or skills. Experience, in the form of human learning, etches messages on the blank tablet, or *tabula rasa*, of the infant's unformed mind. What directs human development, Locke claimed, is the stimulation people receive as they are *nurtured* by experience and education.

Opposing the nurture argument were scholars led by French philosopher **Jean-Jacques Rousseau.** He argued the view that *nature*, the totality of predispositions and abilities we are born with, shapes development (from the Latin *natus*, "born"). At birth, people are "noble savages," unsophisticated but innocent, and more likely to be spoiled or corrupted by contact with society than improved by it (Cranston, 1991).

The nature-nurture debate was intensified by the discovery in 1801 of a wild boy who had apparently been raised by animals in the forests around the village of Aveyron, France. This 12-year-old, uncivilized, *feral* (wild) child, who became known as the Wild Boy of Aveyron, was thought to hold the key to these profound questions about human nature (Candland, 1993). A young doctor, **Jean Marie Itard,** tried to civilize and educate the Wild Boy, whom he named Victor. At first Itard's intensive training program seemed to work. Victor became affectionate and well-mannered and learned to follow instructions and utter a few words. After five years, however, his progress stopped, and the teacher reluctantly ended the "experiment" (Itard, reprinted, 1962; Shattuck, 1981). Victor continued to live with a caretaker until he died at about age 40.

Was it nature or nurture that failed in this case? Perhaps Victor had been abandoned as an infant because he was developmentally disabled (nature). If that were so, training would have only limited success. Alternatively, if Victor was capable of learning, then it was his special education that failed (nurture). A third, compromise explanation is possible: Victor may have been able to learn the lessons of civilization at one time, but may have outgrown his receptivity to education by the time he was discovered, well past his early childhood and the critical period for language acquisition.

Contemporary developmental research confirms that the extreme positions of Locke and Rousseau do injustice to the richness of human behavior. Almost any complex action is shaped both by an individual's biological inheritance and by personal experience, including learning. Heredity and environment have a continuing influence on each other: *nature and nurture* interact. Your heredity establishes your potential, but it is your experiences that determine how, and how much of, that potential will be realized. Although the debate continues, investigators today are more interested in how heredity and environment interact to contribute to development than in the relative importance of each (Bronfenbrenner & Ceci, 1994; Dannefer & Perlmutter, 1990).

Developmental Research

An obvious challenge in the study of feral children is researchers' inability to identify the contributions of either nature or nurture in their development. Their origins and past experiences are unknown, and the possibilities of subsequent training cannot be estimated. How do psychologists know what children feel and think? Developmental psychologists are primarily interested in *age* as an independent variable, so they observe, compare, and test children's performance and responses at various ages. Researchers rely on specific research designs to study development, and also develop strategies for observing behaviors that reveal less obvious influences on individuals' behavior.

A scene from François Truffaut's film *The Wild Child*. The young doctor, Itard, attempts to civilize and educate a wild boy who, apparently for twelve years, had been raised by animals in the forest until he was discovered in 1801.

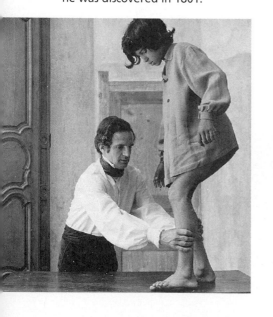

Research Designs   Developmental researchers rely on four research designs distinctly useful in the study of the effects of age: *normative investigations, longitudinal designs, cross-sectional designs,* and *sequential designs.* **Normative investigations** *describe a characteristic of a specific age or stage of development.* Researchers test individuals of different ages to determine developmental "landmarks" such as those listed in Table 4.1. These data provide *norms:* standards or average ages for certain patterns or achievements. An individual child's behavior can be compared to the norm for her age group to evaluate her development. "Abnormal" development—faster or slower than the norm—can then be given special attention, support, or training.

In a **longitudinal design,** *researchers repeatedly observe and test the same individuals over a long period.* By following a particular, well-known sample of individuals as they grow older, developmental researchers can identify the changes and pathways associated with age. If different individuals show similar changes at similar times, the researcher assumes that such developments are caused by their ages rather than by coincidental environmental influences. Memory skills, moral development, and shyness have all been tested and tracked over time in careful programs of longitudinal research (see

TABLE 4.1	**NORMS FOR INFANT MENTAL AND MOTOR DEVELOPMENT (BASED ON THE BAYLEY SCALES)**

One month
Responds to sound
Becomes quiet when picked up
Retains a large easily grasped object placed in hand
Vocalizes occasionally

Two months
Smiles socially
Engages in anticipatory excitement (to feeding, being held)
Recognizes mother
Inspects surroundings
Blinks at object or shadow (flinches)
Lifts head and holds it erect and steady

Three months
Vocalizes to the smiles and talk of an adult
Searches for sound
Makes anticipatory adjustments to lifting
Reacts to disappearance of adult's face
Sits with support, head steady

Four months
Head follows dangling ring, vanishing spoon, and ball moved across table
Inspects and fingers own hands
Shows awareness of strange situations
Picks up cube with palm grasp
Sits with slight support

Five months
Discriminates strange from familiar persons
Makes distinctive vocalizations (e.g., pleasure, eagerness, satisfaction)
Turns from back to side
Has partial use of thumb in grasp

Six months
Reaches persistently, picks up cube deftly
Lifts cup and bangs it
Smiles at mirror image and likes frolicking
Reaches unilaterally for small object

Seven months
Makes playful responses to mirror
Retains two or three cubes offered
Sits alone steadily and well
Show clear thumb opposition in grasp
Scoops up pellet from table

Eight months
Vocalizes four different syllables (such as da-da, me, no)
Listens selectively to familiar words
Rings bell purposively
Attempts to obtain three presented cubes
Shows early stepping movements (prewalking progression)

NOTE: This table shows the average age at which each behavior is performed up to 8 months. Individual differences in rate of development are considerable, but most infants follow this sequence.

Bullock, 1995). Ideal as longitudinal designs are, they are very expensive to carry out. They require a long-term commitment from researchers, in spite of which it remains difficult to keep track of subjects who move away or cease to participate.

Because longitudinal designs are not always practical, most developmental research uses **cross-sectional designs,** *in which subject groups of different ages are observed and immediately compared to each other.* For example, suppose a researcher gives the same task to a group of 5-year-olds and a group of 7-year-olds. If the older children can perform the task with few errors, but the younger children are largely unable to complete the task, the researcher attributes the performance difference to their age difference. The disadvantage of cross-sectional designs lies in the lack of control over other differences between the age groups. For example, the 7-year-olds may have been exposed to a cultural influence—such as a popular television show, a competitive game, or a specific classroom lesson—that was not available to the 5-year-olds. This influence might have given them an advantage in task performance that is not directly caused by the children's ages. Cross-sectional studies alone may not distinguish between age effects and those of one's environment—the events and people that shape one's life.

In *sequential designs,* researchers seek to combine the best features of cross-sectional and longitudinal designs. In a **sequential design,** *subjects who span a specific, short age range are repeatedly observed over time.* In the course of study, the younger children will reach the ages of older ones and beyond. This built-in "overlap" of subjects' ages helps researchers to separate the effects of age from those of environmental influence. The sequential design thus avoids the confounding effects of cross-sectional designs and the difficulty and expense of purely longitudinal work.

Data Collection   But how can we know what a baby is thinking, or what babies already know about the world when they can't tell us? One of the behavior patterns most useful to developmental psychologists who study infants is *habituation.* If an infant looks at one stimulus more than another, this is an indication that the infant can perceive the difference between them. Babies soon stop responding if they get too much of the same stimulus. A decrease in response to any repeatedly presented event is known as **habituation,** *a basic response process found in most species. In a sense, the old familiar sight or sound or flavor has become a "habit" that no longer demands the child's attention.* **Dishabituation** *occurs when the infant responds to a new stimulus, revealing that the baby perceives it to be different and novel.* Long before children have the language skills to express what they find interesting or boring, therefore, researchers can find clues to their reactions in their habituated or dishabituated behavior.

Patterns of facial expressions are also useful as data. A baby's pattern of facial expressions and gazing can reveal much about the baby's mind when the testing situation is arranged so that those reactions indicate mental processes. For example, when a baby expects a certain event to occur, it will look less long and smile less at the event than it will at an unexpected, surprising event. By comparing the length of time that a baby stares at an expected event with the length of time the baby stares at an unexpected event, we can begin to understand what the baby must know in order to produce that difference.

For example, in one research strategy, a baby sees one object added to a second, and then a screen is dropped to block the objects from view. When the screen is quickly raised, revealing three objects, the baby stares longer at them than at the first two objects. This is taken to mean that the baby has developed a basic sense of numbers or addition long before having any formal arithmetic

FOCUS on Application

Conceptions of Childhood

Prior to the sixteenth century, children above 6 years of age were considered small adults and were expected to perform accordingly if possible. Parents and employers had virtually unlimited power over children, who might be abused, abandoned, sold as slaves, or sometimes even mutilated (McCoy, 1988; Pappas, 1983).

From the sixteenth through the eighteenth centuries, children were considered *chattel*, family property useful for getting work done and contributing to household income. Infant and child mortality was high, and adults generally considered young children to be interchangeable and replaceable. Children's individual identities were not acknowledged; all that mattered was their ability to contribute to family livelihood.

When nineteenth century industrialization reduced the need for children as cheap labor, the concept of childhood was extended to include *adolescence,* a period when a child might be regarded as having more responsibilities than a child, but not quite the rights of an adult. Eventually, children began to be treated as *valuable* and also as *vulnerable* property by parents, schools, and society. During the 1800s, people began to realize that many conditions were threatening to children. These concerns led to child labor laws, compulsory education, and juvenile court systems.

During the first half of the twentieth century, children became valued as "potential persons." Child-oriented family life emerged, as did institutions like the field

In August 1993, 2½-year-old Jessica was carried from her adoptive parents' Michigan home to be turned over to her biological parents in Iowa because the courts ultimately ruled in favor of her biological father's right to custody. Are the wishes of biological parents necessarily harmonious with the "best interests of the child"?

of developmental psychology and juvenile courts. But not until the second half of this century did the emerging status of *child as person* afford children legal rights, including protection from abuse and neglect, due process in juvenile courts, and self-determination. Children are today recognized as competent persons worthy of considerable freedom (Horowitz, 1984).

However, in many ways the law still regards children less as persons than as property—sometimes with newsmaking consequences. In August 1993, 2½-year-old Jessica DeBoer was ordered to be removed from the custody of her adoptive parents in Michigan and turned over to her biological parents in Iowa, who had never raised her, because the courts ultimately ruled in favor of her biological father's right to custody (DeBoer, 1994; Gibbs, 1993). In the spring of 1995, the adoptive parents of 4-year-old "Richard" were ordered to relinquish custody to the boy's biological father in Chicago. These cases (and others) evoked a flood of protest from psychologists and developmental experts, who warned of the inevitable consequences of treating a child as an object in a property dispute. Are the wishes of biological parents necessarily harmonious with the "best interests of the child"?

Judges, attorneys, social workers, and parents must regularly make decisions based on what is "known" about children's needs, rights, and best interests. Psychologists can obviously contribute to a better understanding of what children can do, how children see the world, what they need from us—and who, as persons, they are and will become. As scientists, psychologists can provide empirical evidence of children's readiness or capacities for acting independently or choosing with whom to live. However, it is only when parents and society value such input that the legal and political systems are likely to reconsider their notions of the status of the child.

training. A similar research approach is being used to show that babies of only 3 or 4 months have already developed some sense of basic laws of physics, such as recognizing that solids cannot pass through solids. In demonstrating this perceptual ability, infants stare longer at "impossible" events than at "possible" ones, showing surprise when they view toy cars that seem to pass through obstacles on a hidden track (Baillargeon, 1986).

Developmental research is motivated not only by scientific curiosity but also by the need to know how best to care for children and help people of all ages to achieve their potential in life. Research findings can be applied in parenting, teaching, and protecting the rights of children. Such applications are only possible in a world that values children and respects their unique needs. As you will read in Focus on Application: Conceptions of Childhood,

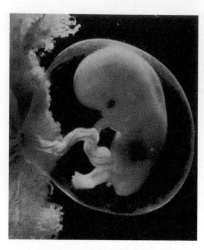

As the brain grows in the developing embryo, it generates 250,000 new neurons per minute.

respect for the well-being and rights of children is only a recent historical development, and is still not universal, even in affluent industrial societies.

Developmental Processes

Your body build, behavior, and development were all determined, to some extent, at the moment the genetic material in the sperm and egg cells of your parents united. The blueprint provided by your genes directs your physical development in a predictable sequence. The blueprint is also responsible for the appearance of certain behaviors at roughly the same time for all normal members of a species, although there are some cultural variations.

Psychological development is assumed to progress in parallel to an individual's lifetime biological development. Here we will consider four sets of processes that underlie and explain later psychological development: physical growth, maturation, sensory development, and newborn behavior.

Physical Growth   The heartbeat is the earliest behavior of any kind. It begins in the *prenatal period*, before birth, when the embryo is about three weeks old and a sixth of an inch long. Responses to stimulation have been observed as early as the sixth week, when the embryo is not yet an inch long. Spontaneous movements are observed by the eighth week (Carmichael, 1970; Humphrey, 1970).

After the eighth week the developing embryo is called a *fetus*. The mother feels fetal movements in about the sixteenth week after conception. In the sixteenth week, the fetus is about 7 inches long (the average length at birth is 20 inches). As the brain grows prenatally, it generates new neurons at the rate of 250,000 per minute, reaching a full complement of over 100 billion neurons by birth (Cowan, 1979). This cell proliferation and migration of neurons to their correct locations takes place prenatally, while the development of the branching processes of axons and dendrites largely occurs after birth (Kolb, 1989). The sequence of brain development, from 25 days to nine months, is shown in Figure 4.1. The neural tissue of the brain (the total mass of brain cells) grows at an astonishing rate, increasing by 50 percent in the first two years, 80 percent above birth size in the next two years, and leveling off by about 11 years of age.

Human growth has traditionally been viewed as a continuous process whose rate changes with age, slowing over time after a very rapid start in the early years. However, research now indicates that at least one aspect of growth—the increase in length of infants' bodies—occurs in discontinuous "bursts," a pattern known as *saltation* (from the Latin *saltare*, "to leap"). These new data suggest that human physical growth is based not on a single continuous process but on two processes: an inactive phase and a growth phase (Lampl et al., 1992).

Maturation   Most of what you do—your voluntary movement and action—requires coordination and strength from many different parts of your body. Your ability to exhibit many behaviors depends on such basic physical support. For example, most children sit without support by 7 months of age, pull themselves up to a standing position a month or two later, and walk soon after their first birthday. Once the underlying physical structures are sufficiently developed, proficiency in these behaviors requires only a minimally adequate environment and a little practice. However, you can't rush Mother Nature; special efforts to accelerate these behaviors will not work until the infant is maturationally ready. These processes seem to "unfold from within,"

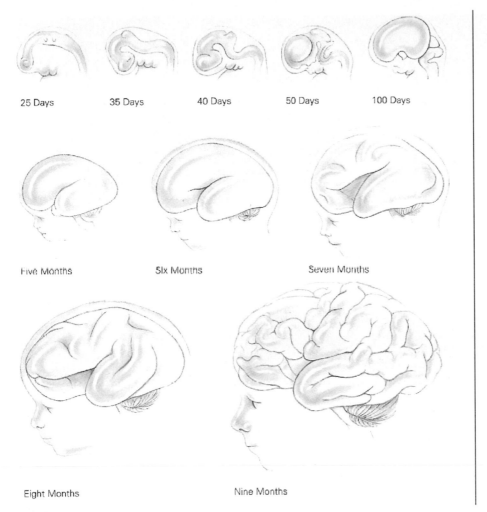

25 Days   35 Days   40 Days   50 Days   100 Days

Five Months   Six Months   Seven Months

Eight Months   Nine Months

FIGURE 4.1
Prenatal Development of the Human Brain ■

following an inner, genetically determined timetable that is characteristic for the species.

Maturation *refers to the process of growth typical of all members of a species who are reared in the usual environment of the species.* Maturation includes the systematic changes in bodily functioning and behavior that are influenced by genetic factors, chemical factors (e.g., nutrition), and sensory factors (e.g., gravity) that are the same for all members of a species.

The characteristic maturational sequences of physical and mental growth are determined by the interaction of biology and environment that is normal for a given species. For example, in the sequence for locomotion, as shown in Figure 4.2, a child learns to walk without special training. Development of walking follows a fixed, time-ordered sequence that is typical of all physically capable members of our species. In cultures where there is more physical stimulation, children begin to walk sooner because they have the practice at the time they are maturationally ready.

Sensory Development Long before babies achieve motor coordination and locomotion, they take in information about their surroundings that attracts, interests, or upsets them. This is *sensation,* an awareness of environmental stimulation the organism might respond to. Because infants' experiences are

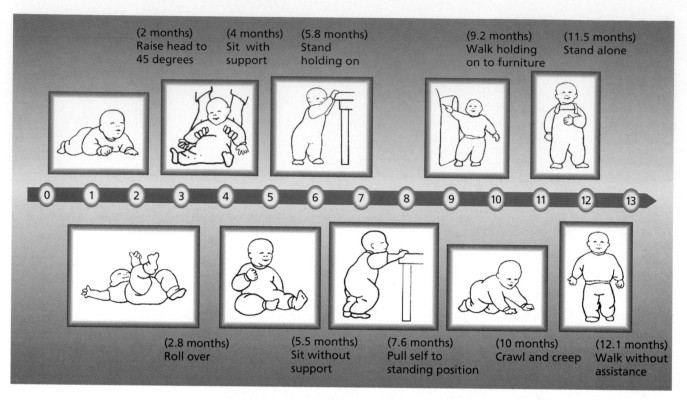

(2 months)
Raise head to
45 degrees

(4 months)
Sit with
support

(5.8 months)
Stand
holding on

(9.2 months)
Walk holding
on to furniture

(11.5 months)
Stand alone

(2.8 months)
Roll over

(5.5 months)
Sit without
support

(7.6 months)
Pull self to
standing position

(10 months)
Crawl and creep

(12.1 months)
Walk without
assistance

FIGURE 4.2   Maturational Timetable for Locomotion ■ The development of walking requires no specific training, but follows a fixed sequence typical of all physically capable human children. In cultures where there is more stimulation, children begin to walk sooner.

difficult to study, there has long been confusion, even among psychologists, about sensory development. The father of American psychology, William James, believed that, to the newborn infant, the world was an overwhelming and disorganized set of stimuli—"one great blooming, buzzing confusion" (James, 1890). In 1928, behaviorist John Watson described the human infant as "a lively, squirming bit of flesh, capable of making a few simple responses." Eminent as they were, these scholars could not have been more wrong about infants' sensory capabilities.

Research accumulated in the past two decades confirms that babies come into the world with all sorts of mental and perceptual abilities. Minutes after birth, for example, a newborn's eyes are alert. She turns in the direction of a voice and searches inquisitively for the source of preferred sounds, or stretches out an exploratory hand. And babies *do* have preferences. As early as 12 hours after birth, they show distinct signs of pleasure at the taste of sugar water or vanilla. Infants smile when they smell banana essence and prefer salted to unsalted cereal (Bernstein, 1990; Harris et al., 1990). However, they recoil from the taste of lemon or shrimp or the smell of rotten eggs. Their hearing functions even before birth, so they are prepared to respond to certain sounds when they are born. They prefer female voices, are attentive to familiar sound patterns, and recognize their mothers' speech a few weeks after birth (Carpenter, 1973; DeCasper & Fifer, 1980; DeCasper & Spence, 1986; Spelke & Owsley, 1979).

Vision is less well developed than the other senses at birth; indeed, babies are born "legally blind," with a visual acuity of about 20/500. Good vision requires that a great many receptor cells function in the eye's retina. At birth, not enough of these connections are laid down. But these immature systems develop very rapidly and the baby's visual abilities soon become evident (Banks & Bennett, 1988). Early on, infants can perceive large objects that display a great deal of contrast. A 1-month-old child can detect contours of a head at close distances; at 7 weeks the baby can scan the interior features of his caregiver's face, and as the caregiver talks, the baby can scan his or her eyes. Just as infants prefer human voices to other sounds, they prefer human faces to most other visual patterns (Fantz, 1963). As early as 2 months, the baby begins to see color, differentiating patterns of white, red, orange, and blue. At 3 months, the baby can perceive depth and is well on the way to enjoying the visual abilities of adults.

Babies apparently start life already equipped with remarkable know-how, and they can use many of their senses to take in and react to information. They might be thought of as prewired "friendly computers," well suited to respond to adult caregivers and to influence their social environments. What do newborns' abilities tell researchers about the direction of later development?

The Neonatal Blueprint   The *infancy period* lasts the first 18 months of life, while the child is incapable of speech. (The Latin root *infans* means "incapable of speech.") Much research on infancy focuses on the *neonate*, the newborn infant from birth to one month of age. Neonates are hardly passive recipients of a "blooming, buzzing confusion." Even within the first hours of life, a newborn infant, given an appropriate stimulus, is capable of a variety of responses. If placed on the mother's abdomen, the baby will usually make crawling motions. The baby will also turn its head toward anything that strokes its cheek—a nipple or a finger—and begin to suck it. *Sucking* is the only behavior that is common to all mammals (Blass & Teicher, 1980). It is an exceedingly complex, but already highly developed, behavior pattern. Most babies know how to do it from the start. Sucking is an adaptable behavior that can be changed by its *consequences*. For example, the sweeter the fluid, the more continuously and forcefully an infant will suck (Lipsitt et al., 1976).

Infants apparently come into the world preprogrammed to like and seek pleasurable sensations, such as sweetness, and to avoid or seek to escape unpleasant stimulation, such as loud noises, bright lights, strong odors, and painful stimuli.

Elliott Blass (1990) and his research team at Johns Hopkins University started studying human newborns after having conducted studies with rats. They taught newborns, only days old, to *anticipate* the pleasurable sensation of the sweet taste of sucrose. When they stroked the babies' foreheads and gave them sugar water, most extended their tongues and became calm. Soon, the stroking alone would cause the baby to turn its head in the direction from which the sweet fluid had been delivered—in anticipation of more of the same. What do you predict happened when the stroking was *not* followed by sucrose? The babies got upset. Almost all (7 of 8) newborns cried when the sweets failed to show up, while few cried (1 of 16) in the control group not conditioned to expect sucrose after stroking. It is as if the babies were responding emotionally to a violation of a reliable relationship that had been established (Blass, 1990).

It seems that babies start to build up their knowledge of the world by observing relations between connected sensory events. Through the interaction of inherited tendencies and learned experiences, babies can become competent survivors able to learn vast amounts of information.

Babies are designed to be sociable. Babies not only respond to, but also interact with, their caregivers. High-speed film studies of this interaction reveal a remarkable degree of *synchronicity:* close coordination between the gazing, vocalizing, touching, and smiling of mothers and infants (Martin, 1981; Trevarthen, 1977). Babies respond and learn, but they also send out

Babies are equipped at birth with a number of instinctive reflexes and behavior patterns that cause them to spend their first several years trying to kill themselves. If your home contains a sharp, toxic object, your baby will locate it; if your home contains no such object, your baby will try to obtain one via mail order.

—Dave Barry

Babies are "designed" to be sociable.

messages to those willing to listen to and love them. The feelings of mothers and infants are also matched in a socially dynamic fashion (Fogel, 1991). A 3-month-old infant may laugh when its mother laughs and frown or cry in response to her display of negative emotion (Tronick et al., 1980).

Babies seem to come equipped to accomplish three basic tasks of survival: sustenance (feeding), maintenance of contact with people (for protection and care), and defense against harmful stimuli (withdrawing from pain or threat). These tasks require perceptual skills, the ability to understand experiences, and basic thinking skills (von Hofsten & Lindhagen, 1979).

✓ Check Your Recall ✓✓✓✓✓✓✓✓✓✓✓✓✓✓

Developmental psychologists study the processes and changes that proceed from aging through the life span. The traditional debate about whether nature or nurture has greater influence on development is now viewed as simplistic. Both inherited characteristics and life experiences interact in individual development. Early studies of development were influenced by cultural attitudes about the nature of childhood. Modern scientific research uses normative investigations, and longitudinal, cross-sectional, and sequential designs to identify the effects of age on behavior. Researchers also rely on a variety of responses and behaviors as data on which to base inferences about developmental processes.

Physical growth and abilities follow a genetically based timetable. Prenatal growth of brain tissue is very rapid. After birth, early physical growth may proceed from as a result of bursts of bodily development rather than continuous activity. Whole-body physical abilities, such as locomotion, depend on maturation, a sequence similar for all members of a species. Sensory activity is evident from birth, with rapid development in hearing, smell, and taste, and slower initial development in vision. Neonates demonstrate a variety of abilities and reflexes, which ready them for seeking nourishment, maintaining social contact, and defending themselves against harm. ✓

Beginning with Childhood

Developmental psychology requires both a view of the child as a person and a research strategy appropriate for studying young people. Researchers interested in early development have been especially interested in how infants and young children develop three sets of abilities: understanding and producing language; thinking and reasoning; and relating to other people.

Acquiring Language

Infants know no language at all, yet in only a few years virtually all young children become fluent speakers of any language they hear spoken and have the opportunity to speak. What makes infants such adept language learners? Human infants appear to be born with important, innate (inborn) language-learning abilities (Locke, 1994). Research has shown that infants are "super-equipped" to deal with any sound that a given language contains. In addition, interest in social interaction strongly motivates children to learn language so they can communicate with others.

Speech Production   In addition to their ability to perceive speech sounds, infants have a biological predisposition to produce the sounds that they will later use in speaking. The basic apparatus for speech production (the vocal tract) is inborn. Moreover, well before they begin to use true words, infants *babble,* repeating speech-like sounds and syllables such as "mamama" or "beebee." The age of onset of babbling seems to be biologically determined. Some linguists have argued that babblings are the direct precursors of speech sounds. They suggest that a baby babbles all sounds in all languages, and the repertoire is eventually narrowed down to those sounds found in the language he or she learns (Mowrer, 1960). This view is not entirely accurate, because infants do not babble certain speech sounds (consonant clusters such as *str* in *strong* and *xth* in *sixth*). In addition, some sounds (*r* and *l*, for example) are present in babbling but not in a child's first words. Babbling allows children to practice making sounds, grouping the sounds into sequences and adding intonation (Clark & Clark, 1977).

Many theorists agree that an innate, biologically based mental structure plays a major role in children's language learning. These **innateness theories of language** argue *that children acquire language not merely by imitating but by following an innate program of steps to acquire vocabulary and grammar.* An early innateness theorist, psycholinguist **Noam Chomsky** (1965, 1975), has proposed that children are born with mental structures that make it possible to comprehend and produce speech. Chomsky refers to *these biological speech-enabling structures as a* **language acquisition device** or **LAD.** In Chomsky's theory, the LAD helps children to overcome the immense complexity of language, to understand the grammar of language, and to make it easier for them to discover patterns and rules in messages.

Innateness theorists were originally reacting to observations that, despite wide variations among cultures and languages, children worldwide seem to proceed through very similar stages of learning language. A logical hypothesis for this pattern would be that children possessed inborn "blueprints" for language development that unfolded with time and experience. However, more recent research has emphasized that, despite similarities in the sequence, the language-learning process also varies across cultures. Such variations argue against an LAD as Chomsky describes it, since a built-in program for learning language would be the same for all children, regardless of the culture and language in which they were raised. Instead, later innateness theories suggest that children's built-in capacity for language is not a rigid device but a set of lessons and "listening rules" or guidelines for perceived language (Bee, 1994; Slobin, 1985a, 1985b). That is, babies pay attention to the sounds and rhythms of the sound strings they *hear* others speak (or in sign language, *see*), especially the beginnings, endings, and stressed syllables. Relying on their built-in "listening guides," young children deduce the patterns and rules for producing their own speech.

Language researchers have been impressed with the fact that children are both attentive and ready to acquire language, and flexible about its final form and context. Children are prepared to learn gestural communication systems, such as American Sign Language, as well as any of the world's 4,000 different spoken languages. Such adaptability suggests that children are creative, not rigidly imitative, in their language acquisition (Goldin-Meadow & Mylander, 1990; Meier, 1991).

Learning to Communicate   Recall that, in Chapter 2, we discussed how language abilities, supported by our species' greater brain power (encephalization), promoted the survival of human life and culture. In essence, language is an extremely useful tool, a means to an end: *communication* with others. Communication is not only useful for a species or a group, it is immediately useful and necessary for individual survival. Long before they can use speech to communicate abstract concepts, young children can use sounds and gestures to indicate that they are hungry, unhappy, or tired. As new parents will readily

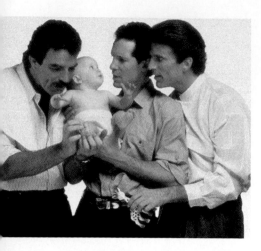

Men, as well as women, understand that rising intonations get babies' attention and falling intonations comfort them. In the film *Three Men and a Baby*, the three bachelors readily adopt "motherese" when talking to the infant girl.

testify, an infant's crying is almost impossible to ignore—it very effectively wins the attention of the baby's caregivers! Infants also smile when they are pleased, and reach for attractive objects. Initially, caregivers have the burden of interpreting these signs, but eventually children take on more of the responsibility for communicating clearly.

Caregivers—adults who are motivated to attend to and care for children—act in ways that stimulate infants' interest in and education about language. Adults speaking to babies and young children tend to use *an exaggerated, high-pitched intonation of speech known as* **motherese**. This "cute talk" pattern accomplishes several goals: getting and holding the infant's attention; communicating emotion; and signaling turn-taking in parent-infant dialogues. Motherese consists more of intonation—pitch and inflection—than words: rising intonation gets babies' attention, falling intonation comforts them, and short staccato bursts ("Ah! Uh-oh!") signal prohibitions.

Research by **Anne Fernald** and her colleagues shows that parents in many different cultures use motherese patterns, and babies understand them even if they are not in their native tongue (Fernald et al., 1989). Even adults who are not full-time caregivers may learn the "rules" of motherese and be able to produce it when they must communicate with a child. For example, in the 1987 film *Three Men and a Baby,* one of three bachelors entertains the baby girl who has been left on their doorstep by reading a description of a boxing match to her from the newspaper's sports page—but he does so in a gentle, lilting, high-pitched voice, to soothe and entertain her, rather than in the more matter-of-fact, flat style he might use to read to an adult.

Caregivers engage infants in simple "training dialogues," initially doing all the talking, but pausing and accepting almost anything the baby does—even a burp or a sneeze—as a valid response before continuing. Later, when babies are older, caregivers become more demanding conversational partners. First children are required to verbalize (not merely burp), then to use actual words, and finally to use words relevant to the topic at hand. This pattern, gradually increasing the demands made on the speaking child, is called *scaffolding*. It provides a scaffold, or support, on which children build their own communication skills, relying less and less on their caregivers to be interpreters. Eventually, children use their first words to communicate messages to others, usually making assertions and requests (Greenfield & Smith, 1976). That is, a child who knows the word "cookie" will not usually say it when she is alone, but will utter it only when others are present, using the word not just to practice speaking but specifically to ask for a cookie or to point to a cookie.

Vocabulary and Grammar   Acquiring a basic vocabulary is an important project for children in their first few years of life. Despite the challenges of understanding others and acquiring language, young children are excellent word learners. By the age of 6, the average child is estimated to understand 14,000 words (Templin, 1957). Assuming that most of these words are learned between the ages of 18 months and 6 years, this works out to about nine new words a day, or almost one word per waking hour (Carey, 1978). The cumulative growth of a child's vocabulary is shown in Figure 4.3.

Children develop vocabulary and grammar through three initial stages: the *one-word stage,* the *two-word stage,* and *telegraphic speech*. During the one-word phase, children use only one word at a time, usually concrete nouns or verbs. Children use them to *name* objects that move, make noise, or can be handled, such as "mama," "ball," and "dog." Children sometimes *overextend* words, using them incorrectly to cover a wide range of objects, such as using the word *dog* to refer to all animals. Overextension may simply result from having a still-limited vocabulary: a child who sees a goat for the first time may say "Kitty!" because she does not know the word "goat," but recognizes some common features (fuzzy, four-legged, smaller than a person). Her desire to communicate exceeds her short vocabulary, so instead of remaining silent she uses a word she *does* know, although it is not the correct word (Clark, 1983, 1987).

Names and Abstractions At around 18 months, children's word learning often takes off at an amazing rate. At this age, children might point to every object in a room and ask, "What's that?" Researchers have called this phase the *naming explosion* because children begin to acquire new words, especially names for objects, at a rapidly increasing rate. Children also discern that some words are not names but actions (verbs) which describe how named objects and persons affect each other. As children experiment with verbs, they develop the beginnings of *syntax,* rules about combining words to indicate specific meanings (Naigles, 1990; Naigles & Kako, 1993).

As children grow older, they begin to express more abstract meanings, going beyond their physical world to talk about their psychological world. For example, around the age of 2, children begin to use words such as *dream, forget, pretend, believe, guess,* and *hope,* as they talk about internal states (Shatz et al., 1983). They also use words such as *happy, sad,* and *angry* to refer to emotional states. Finally, after cognitive advances that occur later in childhood, they understand and use abstract words such as *truth, justice,* and *idea.*

As their vocabularies grow, children combine their new words in utterances of two or more words. It is in these two-word and telegraphic stages that they first develop *grammar.*

The Rules of Grammar Even if you have a limited vocabulary, you can combine the same words in different sequences to convey a rich variety of meanings. For example, "I saw him chasing a big dog" and "I saw a big dog chasing him" both use exactly the same words, but switching the order of the words "him" and "dog" yields completely different meanings. **Grammar** *is a language's set of rules about combining and ordering words to make understandable sentences.* Different languages use considerably different rules about grammatical combinations.

After the naming explosion occurs between 18 months and 2 years of age, children begin to use one-word utterances in different sequences to convey more complex meanings. In the early *two-word stage,* children can already increase the range of meanings they can convey. Studies of different languages

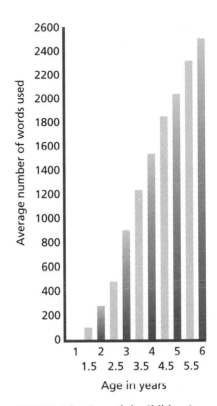

FIGURE 4.3 Growth in Children's Vocabulary ■ The number of words a child is able to use increases rapidly between 18 months and 6 years of age. This study shows children's average vocabularies at six-month intervals. (SOURCE: B. A. Moskovitz, "The Acquisition of Language," *Scientific American,* Inc. All rights reserved; reprinted by permission.)

While grownups encourage and try to understand, babies develop vocabulary and start to communicate in three stages: one-word, two-word, and telegraphic speech.

show that children's two-word utterances divide the world into different categories of ideas. For example, ten children speaking different languages (English, Samoan, Finnish, Hebrew, and Swedish) were found to talk mostly about three categories of ideas: movers, movable objects, and locations (Braine, 1976). When Tanya kicks a ball, for example, the mover is Tanya and the movable object is the ball. Tanya can express this relationship in the two-word sequence, "Tanya ball."

In their early two- and three-word sentences, children's speech is *telegraphic:* short, simple sequences of nouns and verbs without plurals, tenses, or function words like "the" and "of." For example, "Ball hit Evie cry" is telegraphic speech. To develop full sentences, children must not only learn to use other forms of speech, such as modifiers (adjectives and adverbs) and articles (the, those), they must learn how to put words together. In English, this means recognizing and producing the familiar subject-verb-object order, as in "The lamb followed Mary." It becomes complicated when the same meaning is conveyed by alternative orders, such as "Mary was followed by the lamb."

Finally, children need to acquire skill in using **morphemes,** *the meaningful units that make up words.* Morphemes mark verbs to show tense (walk*ed,* walk*ing*) and mark nouns to show possession (Maria*'s,* the people*'s*) and plurality (fox*es,* child*ren*). Children use trial-and-error in applying morphemes to words, so their hypotheses are not always correct. One common error is **overregularization,** *applying a rule too widely and creating incorrect forms.* For example, after learning to make past tense verb forms by adding *-d* or *-ed,* children may apply this "rule" even to its exceptions, the irregular verbs, creating such nonwords as "hitted" and "breaked." Learning to add *-s* or *-es* to make plurals, children may apply the rule to irregular nouns, as in "foots" or "mouses."

Children are not alone in their confusion about the rules of grammar. An adult may find it amusing or curious when young children have not yet mastered the irregular plurals of such common words as "women," "men," and "children." But adults also struggle with irregular words, mistakenly using terms like "data," "criteria," "stimuli," or "phenomena," as if they were singular forms, when in fact they are all plural. The grammar of one's own language can be a matter of lifelong learning.

Most language-learners succeed well enough to be able to communicate for all practical purposes. Researchers often focus on errors rather than successes, however, because mistakes provide a glimpse into the workings of language acquisition. By studying errors, researchers conclude that children's language learning depends on acquiring the general rules of grammar (and learning the exceptions) rather than merely imitating what adults say (Slobin, 1979). The errors people make in thinking and communicating can reveal patterns in how well these abilities normally develop.

To communicate well, children need not only the ingredients of dialogue and the grammatical rules, they also need to learn the rules of conversation: how to join a discussion, take turns talking and listening, and make contributions that are relevant. Adult speakers use body language, intonation, and facial expressions to enhance their communication. They also use feedback they get from listeners, and are able to take the perspective of the listener. Children must master these skills in order to become successful communicators—to become part of a human language community.

Cognitive Development

In reading about language acquisition, you may have the impression that children's minds are bursting with thoughts and ideas long before they have the words to express them. For example, if you have ever had contact with a toddler going through the naming explosion, you have seen that children have an insatiable appetite for the labels of things they know. Clearly, long before they have the vocabulary, babies and young children see and think about the world.

Cognitive development *is the study of the processes and products of the mind as they emerge and change over time.* Do children know objects still exist even when they can't see them? Do they know that it is possible to believe in ideas that aren't true? Can they understand that people have desires and dreams, but objects do not? Developmental psychologists investigate both *what* children think and *how* they think it.

There are two dominant views on the nature of human thought processes: the cognitive development approach and the information-processing approach. We will first examine the key concepts of the cognitive development approach. We then consider the information-processing approach, one of several alternative explanations more recent research has proposed for the way people's thinking processes change with age.

The *cognitive development view* originates from the pioneering work of the late Swiss psychologist **Jean Piaget.** For nearly 50 years, he observed children's intellectual development. Piaget's training in biological methods of observation helped him investigate human cognition as a form of biological adaptation. Piaget saw the human mind as an active biological system that seeks, selects, interprets, and reorganizes environmental information to fit with or adjust to its own existing mental structures. Piaget began his quest to understand the nature of the child's mind by carefully observing the behavior of his own three children. He would pose problems to them, observe their responses, slightly alter the situations, and once again observe their responses. Piaget used simple demonstrations and sensitive interviews to generate complex theories about early mental development.

In early life, children learn to transform specific information about concrete events into general, abstract concepts. Piaget's focus on the transitions in a child's thinking, reasoning, and problem solving emphasized a discontinuous, *stage model* of development. There are three key components of Piaget's approach to cognitive development: *schemes; assimilation and accommodation;* and the four *stages of cognitive growth.*

Schemes   Think of a four-legged animal. Now think of one that is friendly. Now think of one that barks. You might have started by imagining elephants and tigers (both four-legged), then narrowed your choices down to cats and dogs (four-legged and friendly), and finally to just dogs (which bark). You have developed mental *structures* that enable you to interpret events and experiences in your world in systematic ways. Piaget terms such mental structures **schemes**—*mental structures or programs that guide developing sequences of thinking.* Schemes are the building blocks of developmental change. They organize past experiences into knowledge structures that help children to understand the present and predict future events. (Piaget's *schemes* are sometimes incorrectly called "schemas," more complex cognitive structures that we will discuss in Chapter 12).

The first schemes an infant develops are those which involve its senses and actions, abilities jointly known as *sensorimotor intelligence.* The infant looks at things, grasps at them, suckles at the breast or on the nipple of a bottle. All these responses are sensorimotor sequences that aid the infant's adaptation to the environment. Initially simple schemes are combined with others, becoming more complex and differentiated with practice and maturation. Eventually, a child's schemes go beyond reliance on the physical presence of objects so that a symbolic representation suffices. As this occurs, the child performs more complex mental operations (Gallagher & Reid, 1981; Piaget, 1977). For

Although an infant will begin to suck a bottle just the way he or she sucked a breast (assimilation), the infant will soon discover that some changes are necessary (accommodation). The child will make an even greater accommodation in the transitions from bottle to cup.

example, a toddler sees the string attached to a favorite pull-toy but cannot see the toy itself, so she pulls the string to "bring" the toy out of hiding and close enough to touch. She must be able to imagine the toy and remember that the string is attached to it before she can use a pulling scheme to gain access to it.

Assimilation and Accommodation   According to Piaget, there are two basic processes at work in cognitive growth: *assimilation* and *accommodation.* In assimilation, the new is changed to fit the known; in accommodation, the known is changed to fit the new.

Assimilation *modifies new environmental information to fit into what is already known.* A baby reflexively knows how to suck from a nipple, for example, and will try to use the same technique on new objects, sucking on a sugary finger, for example, or messily slurping at the rim of a cup.

In contrast, in **accommodation,** *new information restructures or modifies the child's existing schemes so that the new data fit in better.* Consider the transitions a baby must make from sucking at mother's breast, to sucking from a bottle, sipping through a straw, and drinking from a cup. The initial sucking response is a reflex action present at birth, but it must be modified to *accommodate* new vessels.

For Piaget, cognitive development results from the constant interweaving of assimilation and accommodation. Through these two processes, children's behavior and knowledge become less dependent on concrete external reality and more reliant on abstract thought.

Stages of Cognitive Development   There are four qualitatively different Piagetian stages of cognitive growth: the *sensorimotor stage* (infancy), the *preoperational stage* (early childhood), the *concrete operational stage* (middle childhood), and the *formal operational stage* (adolescence). Distinct styles of thinking emerge at each stage as the child progresses from sensory reaction to logical thought. All children progress through these stages in the same sequence, although one child may take longer to pass through a given stage than another.

Object permanence, the perception that objects exist independently of one's own actions or awareness, develops gradually during the first stage of cognitive development and is solidly formed before age 1. The baby in these pictures clearly believes that the toy no longer exists once it is obscured by the screen.

Sensorimotor Stage (Birth to age 2) Many new cognitive achievements appear during the first two years of a child's life. In this section we will examine only two main trends: changes in how the infant interacts with its environment, and the infant's understanding of object permanence.

During the first year of life, the sensorimotor sequences are improved, combined, coordinated, and integrated. They become more varied as the infant tests different aspects of the environment and discovers that actions can have an effect on external events. But in the sensorimotor period, the child is tied to the immediate environment and motor-action schemes, lacking the cognitive ability to represent objects symbolically.

The most important lesson acquired in the second year is the ability to form mental representations of absent objects. There is a vast mental difference, for example, between *pointing* to the toy one wants and *knowing* it must be somewhere so that it can be sought or asked for. By the end of the second year, the child has developed this understanding. **Object permanence** *refers to the perception that objects exist independently of one's own actions or awareness.* I may not be able to *see* the doll, but I know that there *is* a doll that I can find and play with. Object permanence develops gradually during this first stage of cognitive development. The basics are in place by one year of age, but the concept of object permanence continues to develop through the second year (Flavell, 1985). This and other forms of representational thought become fully functioning in the preoperational stage.

Preoperational Stage (From 2 to 7 years of age) The major cognitive advance in the next developmental stage is the ability to represent objects mentally that are not physically present. Except for this development, Piaget characterizes the preoperational stage according to what the child can't do, such as solve problems requiring logical thought *(operations)*. Three of the most interesting features of the child's mind in this period are *egocentrism*, *animistic thinking*, and *centration*.

- Because of **egocentrism,** *a self-centered focus,* children see the world only in terms of themselves and their own position. They are not yet able to sympathize with others or take others' points of view. For this reason children may act in ways that have destructive or hurtful consequences, even though they don't intend to upset or harm others.
- Young children also confuse physical events with mental intentions. They engage in **animistic thinking,** *imagining that inanimate objects have life and mental processes.* For example, if a child slips and bangs her head on the table, she might complain about the "bad table," blaming it for hurting her.
- Finally, **centration** *involves being too focused on a single perceptual quality to be able to notice or understand an event.* For example, a thirsty child may insist on drinking a "big glass" of juice, preferring a tall container to a short one, mistakenly assuming that the height of the glass ensures that it will hold more juice.

Concrete Operational Stage (From 7 to 11 years of age) At this stage, the child is capable of *mental operations* but still cannot reason abstractly. He or she depends heavily on concrete sensory impressions to make choices and judgments—for example, needing to see ice cream colors before identifying a favorite flavor. In this stage children begin to break through their centration, looking past a single compelling feature to take other features into account.

For example, most 7-year-olds have acquired the concept of **conservation,** *the idea that physical properties do not change when nothing is added or taken away, even though their appearance changes.* A string of red beads is *not* longer than an identical string of blue beads, even though the red beads are stretched out in a line while the blue beads lie in a small pile. They may *look* different, but this does not mean that they *are* different, in length or number of beads.

This 5-year-old girl is aware that the two containers have the same amount of colored liquid. However, when the liquid from one is poured into a taller container, she indicates that there is more liquid in the taller one. She has not yet grasped the concept of conservation, which she will understand by age 6 or 7.

Although children learn to use logic and inference to solve concrete problems, the symbols they use in reasoning are still symbols for concrete objects and events and not abstractions. The limitations of their thinking are shown in the familiar game of "20 Questions," the goal of which is to determine the identity of an object by asking the fewest possible yes/no questions of the person who thinks up the object. A child of 7 or 8 usually sticks to very specific questions ("Is it a bird?" "Is it a cat?"), but does not ask abstract questions that more efficiently narrow down the possibilities for the correct answer ("Does it fly?" "Does it have hair?").

Formal Operational Stage (From about age 11 on) In this final stage of cognitive growth, thinking becomes abstract. Adolescents can see that their particular reality is only one of several imaginable realities. They begin to ponder deep questions of truth, justice, and existence. Most young adolescents have acquired all the mental structures needed to go from being naive thinkers to experts. Adolescents and adults approach the "20 Questions" game in a way that demonstrates their ability to use abstractions and to adopt an information-processing strategy that is not merely random guesswork. They impose their own structures on the task, starting with broad categories and then formulating and testing hypotheses in light of their knowledge of categories and relationships. Their questioning moves from general categories ("Is it an animal?") to subcategories ("Does it fly?") and then to specific guesses ("Is it a bird?") (Bruner et al., 1966).

Contemporary Perspectives Piaget's theory of the dynamic interplay of assimilation and accommodation is generally accepted as a valid account of the way a child's mind develops. Piaget's *stage* approach to cognitive development is the model used by many developmental psychologists to understand how other mental and behavioral processes develop. However, ongoing research has suggested alternatives to the stage approach.

Contemporary researchers have come up with ways to study cognitive development that differ from Piaget's methods. Their research has shown that children are much more intellectually sophisticated at each stage than Piaget had found. Investigators also challenge Piaget's theory of the sensorimotor foundations of thought and turn more to *continuous* models of cognitive development not characterized by distinct, separate stages (Siegler, 1986). This research benefits from the use of innovations in technology (e.g., computer modeling) and research designs involving many children, not just single case studies.

Some recent work in the field of cognitive development has refined concepts originally introduced by Piaget. For example, preoperational children may actually *understand* some of the same concepts as children at the concrete operational stage, but they may still lack the memory or language skills to *perform* accordingly. For example, a 5-year-old child who has watched her father prepare breakfast in the past can watch him and understand what he is cooking, but may not be able to describe it to her visiting grandmother, or express why she likes her pancakes "the way Daddy fixes them." Researchers have found, in contrast with Piaget's notion of centration, that young children (ages 3 and 4) understand that the "insides" of objects, although they are invisible, are not necessarily identical to their external appearances (Gelman & Wellman, 1991). And in contrast with Piaget's claims about animistic thinking, 3- to 5-year-old children are consistently able to distinguish between real and purely mental (imaginary) entities (Wellman & Estes, 1986).

Many contemporary researchers have rejected Piaget's stage approach altogether, in favor of the **information-processing approach,** *which likens the child's mind to a computer.* In this view children are, like adults, constantly taking in information about the world. But unlike adults, children are restricted by limited memory capacity; as they overcome these limitations, their cognitive functioning visibly improves. Developmental research is not a closed book; researchers today continue to force the field to rethink long-cherished ideas about the child's mind and how it grows and continually changes.

Moral Development

One of the hallmarks of adult thinking is the development of higher levels of moral reasoning. **Morality** *is a system of beliefs, values, and underlying judgments about the rightness or wrongness of human acts.* Parents and society want children to become adults who accept their elders' moral value system and whose behavior is guided by these shared moral principles. As we shall consider, however, there is an important difference between moral understanding and moral behavior.

Moral Reasoning　How does one's sense of right and wrong develop? The best-known psychological approach to moral development was created by **Lawrence Kohlberg** (1964, 1981), who based his theory on Piaget's theory of cognitive development. Each stage in Kohlberg's theory of *moral reasoning* is based on a different standard of moral judgment. Table 4.2 summarizes the seven stages proposed by Kohlberg.

Kohlberg theorizes that an individual attains the same stages in the same order in all cultures. The acquisition of these stages parallels the stages of Piaget's theory of cognitive development in its movement from concrete, egocentric targets to more other-oriented, abstract ideas of right and wrong. The lowest level of moral reasoning is based on self-interest, while higher levels center on social good, regardless of personal gain. Not all people attain stages 4 to 7; many adults never even reach stage 5, and few go beyond it. The cosmic orientation of stage 7 is very rare; Kohlberg presents it as an ideal

According to Kohlberg's theory, an individual's sense of what is morally right develops from a very self-centered focus in childhood, to a greater appreciation for the rules of society and the feelings of others, including strangers and even nonhumans.

TABLE 4.2	KOHLBERG'S STAGES OF MORAL REASONING
Levels and Stages	**Reasons for Moral Behavior**
I. Preconventional Morality	
Stage 1: Pleasure/pain orientation	Avoid pain or avoid getting caught
Stage 2: Cost/benefit orientation; reciprocity ("an eye for an eye")	Achieve/receive rewards
II. Conventional Morality	
Stage 3: "Good child" orientation	Gain acceptance, avoid disapproval
Stage 4: Law and order orientation	Follow rules, avoid penalties
III. Postconventional (Principled) Morality	
Stage 5: Social contract orientation	Promote the welfare of one's society
Stage 6: Ethical principle orientation	Achieve justice, avoid self-condemnation
Stage 7: Cosmic orientation	Be true to universal principles; feel oneself part of a cosmic direction that transcends social norms

upper limit. Research suggests real-world limits to Kohlberg's theory. The higher stages have not been found in all cultures. In our own culture they appear to be associated with education and verbal ability—experiences that should not necessarily be prerequisites for moral judgment (Rest & Thoma, 1976).

Kohlberg's stages of moral reasoning have generated considerable controversy. Especially controversial is Kohlberg's early claim that women generally lag behind men in moral development and stop at a less advanced level than men do. **Carol Gilligan** (1982) proposes that this finding—that women's morality is less fully developed than that of men's—can be explained by the fact that Kohlberg's original work was based on observations of boys only. Gilligan believes that women develop *differently,* but not *less* morally. She proposes that women's moral development is based on a standard of *caring for others* and progresses to a stage of self-realization, whereas men base their reasoning on a standard of *justice.*

Since Gilligan posed these questions about gender differences in moral development, other researchers have had difficulty establishing consistent, observable differences in the moral reasoning "scores" of men and women. One group of researchers has suggested that men and women may arrive at similar moral judgments, but through a very different process of educational, occupational, and relational choices (Boldizar et al., 1989). A related view emphasizes that women come to prefer "care reasoning" and men come to prefer "justice reasoning" because they encounter different kinds of dilemmas in their lives. When both men and women were presented with the same domain of moral problems (focusing on parenthood), they did not differ in their use of care or justice reasoning (Clopton & Sorell, 1993). Thus there may indeed be gender-related differences in moral reasoning, but these differences may have more to do with men's and women's normal experiences and expertise, not with inborn, sex-linked reasoning skills.

Moral Action   Other questions concern Kohlberg's decision to study moral *reasoning* instead of moral *action.* Critics believe that what people *say* and what they *do* when faced with moral choices often differ (Kurtines & Greif,

According to researcher Carol Gilligan, women value a connectedness to others and use items, like makeup, which emphasize how they will relate to others. Men, on the other hand, learn to value independence and "power!" (as Tim Allen of the television show *Home Improvement* would say).

1974). If we want to understand moral development more completely, we must consider what it is that motivates people to behave honestly, cooperatively, or altruistically. Researchers investigating the roots of morality suggest that inner emotions, especially *empathy,* motivate the child to behave morally (Hoffman, 1987). Children may experience empathy at very young ages, and some researchers believe that empathy may be an innate response like sucking or crying.

Empathy *is the condition of feeling someone else's emotion.* For example, feeling another's distress may trigger a sympathetic response. Many psychologists now believe such helpful and positive behaviors signal the beginning of moral development. When a 4-year-old gently hands her favorite toy to her unhappy little brother because she feels sorry for him and wishes to cheer him up, this simple gesture indicates a significant leap in her social and cognitive functioning. Empathy may well represent part of the foundation for future moral behavior.

We seem to need a new theory of moral development, one that integrates patterns of moral reasoning with the motives and social conditions that can prompt helpful and altruistic acts (Zahn-Waxler & Radke-Yarrow, 1982). We might begin by considering the social environment in which every person develops ideas about what is right and wrong. Consider the power of one's family and society by reviewing Cultural Context: The Individual and the Community on page 132.

Social and Emotional Development

A child who is competent in language and cognitive skills would still be deficient without appropriate social and emotional reactions and capabilities. Children's basic survival depends on forming meaningful, effective relationships with other people. Children need to learn the rules that their society uses for governing its members' social and political interactions. They must be in touch with their own feelings and respond to the feelings of others. But children are not sophisticated communicators; even adults can experience difficulty talking about their feelings and intentions. How do children even begin to learn how to interact with others?

Smiling is one way to begin simple interactions. The delight parents take in a baby's first smile represents the beginning of lifelong social lessons. People smile not only as a sign of positive feelings, but also because their audience expects such a facial expression (Fridlund, 1990).

Temperament **Temperament** *refers to an individual's inherited, enduring pattern of reacting to environmental stimuli and situations.* Harvard researcher **Jerome Kagan** has shown that about 10 to 15 percent of infants are "born shy" or "born bold" (Kagan et al., 1994; Kagan & Snidman, 1991; Kagan et al., 1986). The infants differ in sensitivity to physical and social stimulation—the shy baby is more easily frightened and less socially responsive. People are less likely to interact and be playful with the shy baby, accentuating the child's initial disposition.

Kagan began his initial work on temperament with the assumption that reaction styles were best explained by social influences. For example, a shy child must have learned timidity as a result of unpleasant social experiences. Today, however, Kagan has adopted a position that gives much greater credit to biological predisposition (Gallagher, 1994; Kagan, 1994). Kagan and other temperament researchers suggest that there are three basic temperament styles expressed in all people's behavior: fear, aggression, and sociability. Fearful children may have been born with a tendency

CULTURAL CONTEXT

The Individual and the Community

It's a universal human dilemma: how to reconcile our personal goals with our responsibility to others. For example, suppose you were offered a challenging and high-paying job in a city 2000 miles away. Should you accept the job even if it means leaving the care for your elderly parent to professionals in a nursing home? Accepting the job would fulfill your personal goals of prestige and advancement, but it would interfere with your parent's desire to be close to you and see you frequently.

You may be surprised to learn that the culture you have been raised in will influence such a "personal" decision. Cross-cultural psychologists argue that one's culture provides a great deal of guidance when personal goals conflict with group goals (Triandis, 1989; Schwartz, 1990; Hofstede, 1991). In *individualistic* countries such as the United States, Canada, and Australia, people are socialized to place a high value on their own goals. This does not mean that they will always ignore the wishes of others, but it does mean that cultural norms encourage them to think carefully about their own desires when making decisions. In *collectivist* countries such as Japan, Hong Kong, and Colombia, people are socialized to think carefully about the wishes of others and to be attentive to others' needs. At times, this will require setting aside one's own goals because a higher priority is placed on the conflicting goals of others in one's family or community.

For example, many graduate students in the United States come from collectivist countries in Asia. Some of these students could have begun their graduate studies years ago, but first had to take care of obligations to others at home. When they finally found themselves able to leave home and come to the United States, they first had to obtain approval from extended family members. In a process that seems quite reasonable to Asians but might seem extreme to Americans, the prospective students consulted with uncles, aunts, grandparents, and sometimes

One's culture, be it individualistic or collectivist, greatly influences the decisions we make when weighing our personal goals against our responsibilities to others.

cousins, before being permitted to continue their studies.

A collectivist morality requires the students to consider other group members even in the course of pursuing their own life goals. Indeed, students from Asia, as well as Asian Americans, study a great deal and place great emphasis on good grades because when one person does well, the entire group is honored. Similarly, when one person fails, the entire group may feel a shared sense of shame.

Psychologists interested in moral development have asked whether or not the concept of "obligation to others" has been given enough attention in the development of Kohlberg's seven stages (Snarey, 1985; Miller et al., 1990). In developing his original scoring system, Kohlberg had emphasized the reasoning of people with an individualistic orientation toward moral dilemmas. Has this emphasis on individualism downplayed the cultural guidance people receive in collectivist cultures?

Consider this moral dilemma: A man's wife is dying. To save her life, he needs a very expensive drug, but he does not have the money to buy the drug. So he breaks

into a drug store and steals it. Was his action morally right or wrong? Carefully consider your answer and the reasoning behind it. Perhaps you think he had no choice but to put human life above monetary gain. Or perhaps his actions were rash, and he should have at least tried to talk to the store owner and negotiate an affordable price.

Now consider the moral conclusion of a Maisan village leader in Papua New Guinea (an island north of Australia): "If nobody helped him [to save his dying wife] and so he [stole to save her], I would say *we* had caused that problem" (Snarey, 1985, p. 225). Does this man's conclusion differ from yours? Would you agree that the community had failed an individual who was driven to commit a crime in order to save a life? Based on his response, would you guess that the Maisan leader lived in an individualist or a collectivist culture?

Clearly, future work on moral development must consider the reasoning of people from different cultures, collectivist and individualist alike, before any general conclusions can be drawn about the roots of moral action.

to exaggerate the danger in the situations they encounter, and they grow to become avoidant, uncomfortable adults. Aggressive individuals approach problems by trying to fight them, becoming irritated, blaming others, and striking out at them. Sociable, outgoing children approach the world boldly and handle difficulties with equanimity. They are able to adapt to both surprise and disappointment without becoming either depressed or offensive.

While these temperaments are in place from birth, they are not written in stone. Experience and special training can modify the way a constitutional factor such as temperament is expressed. For example, a bold child reared by bold parents will certainly experience and respond to the world differently from a bold child reared by timid or fearful parents. Likewise, if a shy baby's parents recognize the child's withdrawal and gently play with her and encourage her to interact, the child may become more outgoing than her temperament would otherwise have predicted. Thus family members and friends can teach every individual a variety of responses to the world, all within his or her temperamental range. Finally, no one temperament is ideal for all situations. We should "remember that in a complex society like ours, each temperamental type can find its adaptive niche" (Kagan, quoted in Gallagher, 1994, p. 47).

Socialization and Attachment   In order to help their children find the most adaptive niche for their abilities and temperament, parents *socialize* their offspring. **Socialization** *is the lifelong process of shaping an individual's behavior patterns, values, standards, skills, attitudes, and motives to conform to those regarded as desirable in a particular society* (Hetherington & Parke, 1975). Besides parents, many individuals and institutions exert pressure on the individual to adopt socially approved values. The family is certainly the most influential regulator of socialization, however. The family helps the individual form basic patterns of responsiveness to others; these patterns, in turn, form the basis of the individual's habitual style of relating to other people. The most basic, primal lesson for later-life relationships is learned in the infant's experience of *attachment*.

Infant Attachment Social development begins with the establishment of a close emotional relationship between a child and parent figure. This *intense, enduring, social-emotional relationship an infant forms with a parent or caregiver is called* **attachment.** (Attachment does not refer to the parent's feelings toward the child; the relationship in that direction is sometimes informally referred to as "bonding").

Attachment behaviors appear to occur instinctively in many species, but are not necessarily restricted to the infant's biological parents. One example of instinctive attachment is **imprinting,** *the powerful attraction of infants of some species to the first moving object or individual they see.* A baby chick hatched by a mother duck will form an attachment to this surrogate parent, staying close to her and following her right up to the water's edge when she and her ducklings go for a swim. The imprinting tendency is an innate predisposition, but the organism's environment and experience determine what form it will take. Human infants and human caregivers may have similar instinctive attachment patterns.

Biological research indicates that, while imprinting increases the desire of offspring to make contact with caregivers, there is no guarantee that parents will respond to these needs. Hormonal influences do not dictate *parental* feelings or actions toward their children. What, then, can babies do to increase the chances of getting the contact they want? Human babies are not yet mobile enough to use their own locomotion to get closeness or attention from a caregiver: when they want to get close to the attachment figure (e.g., their mother),

Children become attached to their caregivers, and parents bond to their children. These bonds of love and responsibility help offset the daily struggles for survival faced by poor families the world over.

Konrad Lorenz (1903–1989), the researcher who pioneered the study of imprinting, graphically demonstrated what can happen when young animals become imprinted on someone other than their mother.

they cannot simply crawl or move toward her. However, babies *can* emit signals—such as smiling, crying, and vocalizing—to promote responsive behavior (Campos et al., 1983). Who can resist a baby's smile? According to John Bowlby (1973), an influential theorist on human attachment, infants will form attachments to individuals who consistently and appropriately respond to their signals.

Developmental psychologist **Mary Ainsworth** studied attachment by putting young children in a variety of situations, such as separating them by a barrier from their mothers, or introducing a stranger in the room when their mothers were nearby (Ainsworth, 1989; Ainsworth et al., 1978; Ainsworth & Wittig, 1969). Ainsworth found that the children's responses indicated they were either *securely* or *insecurely* attached. Securely attached children felt close to their mothers, safe, and more willing to explore or tolerate a novel experience—confident that they could cry out for help or to be reunited with the missing parent. Insecurely attached children reacted in one of two ways: with *anxiety and ambivalence* or with *avoidance*. The anxious-ambivalent children wanted contact but cried with fear and anger when separated, and proved difficult to console even when reunited with their mothers. The avoidant children initially acted as though they were unconcerned about being separated from their mothers, not crying when she left and not seeking contact when she returned. Avoidant children may be showing the effects of repeated rejection, no longer seeking attachment because their efforts have failed in the past (Shaver & Hazan, 1994).

Attachment fascinates researchers because patterns established in infancy seem to persist in a variety of childhood and even adult behaviors, influencing later-life job satisfaction, relationship choices, and intimacy experiences (Collins & Read, 1990; Hazan & Shaver, 1990; Shaver & Hazan, 1994). Phillip Shaver and Cindy Hazan have explored the manifestations and consequences in adult life of early childhood attachment patterns (1993; 1994; Hazan & Shaver, 1990; 1992). Before going on to examine how the secure and insecure attachment patterns have been linked to adult behaviors, take the quiz on your own attachment style in Assess Yourself: What's Your Attachment Style?

Assess Yourself

What's Your Attachment Style?

Identify which *one* of the following three self-descriptions you most agree with (adapted from Shaver & Hazan, 1994):

1. I am somewhat uncomfortable being close to others; I find it difficult to trust them completely, difficult to allow myself to depend on them. I am nervous when anyone gets too close, and often, love partners want me to be more intimate than I feel comfortable being.

2. I find that others are reluctant to get as close as I would like. I often worry that my partner doesn't really love me or won't want to stay with me. I want to get very close to my partner, and this sometimes scares people away.

3. I find it relatively easy to get close to others and am comfortable depending on them. I don't often worry about being abandoned or about someone getting to close to me.

If you selected the first statement, you agreed with the attitude that reflects an avoidant, insecure attachment; this style was chosen by 25 percent of Shaver and Hazan's respondent sample. The second statement reflects an anxious-ambivalent, insecure attachment style, selected by 20 percent of Shaver and Hazan's sample. The third statement reflects a secure attachment style, the most common pattern identified, accounting for 55 percent of Shaver and Hazan's sample (Shaver & Hazan, 1994).

What do these styles portend for later life? Through interviews, observations, and questionnaires, researchers have identified several consequences of attachment style, secure or insecure, in adulthood (see Ainsworth, 1989; Collins & Read, 1990; Hazan & Shaver, 1990; Kirkpatrick & Shaver, 1992; Shaver & Hazan, 1993, 1994; Simpson, 1990):

- Secure individuals have more positive self-concepts and believe that most other people are good-natured and well-intentioned. They see their personal relationships as trustworthy and satisfying.
- Secure respondents are satisfied with their job security, coworkers, income, and work activity. They put a higher value on relationships than on work, and derive their greatest pleasure from connections to others.
- Insecure, anxious-ambivalent persons report emotional extremes and jealousy. They feel unappreciated, insecure, and unlikely to win professional advancement. They make less money than those with other attachment styles, working more for approval and recognition than financial gain. They fantasize about succeeding, but often slack off after receiving praise.
- Avoidant people fear intimacy and expect their relationships to fail. They place a higher value on work than on relationships, and generally like their work and job security. They follow a workaholic pattern, but (not surprisingly) they are dissatisfied with their coworkers.
- Secure individuals tend to choose as partners others who are secure. After breakups, avoidants claim to be less bothered by the loss of the relationship, although this may be a defensive claim, with distress showing up in other ways (e.g., physical symptoms).

The major threat to attachment is *separation*, and everyone who loses an attachment figure experiences some degree of **separation distress**, *a pattern of negative emotions, mental disruption, and anxiety when an attachment figure is not available* (Weiss, 1975). Babies cry when their parents leave them in the care of a babysitter. Adult survivors of breakup or divorce suffer from depression, insomnia, and distraction until they eventually "get over" the loss. Just as our earliest attachment experiences set the pattern for lifelong attitudes toward intimacy, likewise our earliest fears and abandonments may sensitize us to the impact of loss in later life.

Contact Comfort Why and how do infants become attached to caregivers in the first place? An evolutionary explanation assumes that close attachment to parents safeguards an infant's survival by assuring the support and protection it requires. Individuals with genetic tendencies to "attach" will survive, thrive, and pass those tendencies along to their own offspring. Bowlby (1969; 1973) and Ainsworth (1973; Ainsworth et al. 1978) theorized that the earliest attachment processes develop in the first two years of life, but intriguing research suggests that attachments are formed and experienced much earlier. Mizukami et al. (1990) found that 2- 4-month-old babies' skin temperature dropped—a sign of stress—when their mothers left the room. It dropped more when a stranger replaced the mother. But skin temperature did not drop if the mother remained in the room, even if the stranger were present. Children only a few months old seem to rely on their caretakers as a "safe base" long before they can indicate attachment with crying or locomotion (Bee, 1994).

One of Harlow's monkeys and its artificial terry cloth mother. Harlow found that the contact comfort mothers provide is essential for normal social development.

Other theorists have argued that attachment is simply a child's response to the fact that the parents provide food, an infant's most basic physical need. This has been dubbed the "cupboard theory" of attachment: individuals become attached to those who provide the cupboard containing the food supply. **Harry Harlow,** believing the cupboard did not completely explain attachment motivation, guessed that infants might also become attached to those who provided *contact comfort* (Harlow 1965; Harlow & Harlow, 1966). To test this idea, Harlow studied the behavior of infant macaque monkeys who had been separated from their mothers at birth. The baby monkeys were placed in cages where they had access to two artificial "mother" dummies: one a wire construction that provided milk through a nipple, and the other a soft cloth-covered model that did not provide any milk. Harlow found that, confirming his expectation, the monkeys nestled close to the cloth mother but spent little time with the wire model, despite the "cupboard" of nourishment the latter provided. The baby monkeys also sought comfort by clinging to the cloth dummy when they were frightened, and used it as a base of operations when exploring new situations. Thus, as Harlow predicted, the infant monkeys became attached to and preferred the "mother" figure that provided **contact comfort,** *reassurance derived from physical touch and access to the caregiver.*

Human infants also need contact comfort. The lack of a close, loving relationship in infancy affects an individual's physical growth and survival. In some hospitals, premature infants and those born at risk (such as those born to crack-addicted mothers) are scheduled to receive regular holding and cuddling by staff members and even by unrelated volunteers, who visit regularly and hold the babies to help support their recovery and survival. Children who lack contact comfort in infancy do not thrive and may not even survive. In emotionally detached or hostile family environments, children have been found to have slowed bone development. They may grow again if removed from the poor environment, but their growth is stunted again if they are returned to it, a phenomenon known as *psychosocial dwarfism.* Clearly, a close, interactive relationship with loving adults is a child's first step toward healthy physical growth and normal socialization.

Erikson's Theory of Psychosocial Crises   As a middle-aged immigrant to America, **Erik Erikson** (1963) became aware of conflicts he faced because of his new status. Erikson's reflections on the many such conflicts all individuals face in the continuing process of development inspired a new way of thinking about human development. Erikson saw human development as a sequence of conflicts and challenges that emerge at many stages in the life course, from infancy to old age. **Psychosocial crises** *are successive turning points or choices about self and others that influence personality growth across the entire life span.* Each crisis requires a new level of social interaction; success or failure in achieving such interaction can change the course of subsequent development in a positive or negative direction.

Erikson identified eight psychosocial crises characterizing development throughout life. At each choice point, a particular conflict comes into focus, as shown in Table 4.3. Although the conflict continues in different forms, it must be sufficiently resolved at a given stage if an individual is to cope successfully with the conflicts of later stages. Here we will review the psychosocial crises of childhood; in the next section we will review the crises experienced in adolescence and adulthood.

Trust versus Mistrust   In this first crisis, an infant needs to develop a basic sense of trust in the environment through interaction with her caregivers. Trust is a natural accompaniment to a strong attachment relationship with a caregiver who provides food, warmth, and the comfort of physical closeness. A child whose basic needs are not met, who experiences inconsistent handling, lack of physical closeness and warmth, and the frequent absence of a caring adult, may develop a pervasive sense of mistrust, insecurity, and anxiety. This child will not be prepared for the second stage, which requires the individual to be adventurous.

Autonomy versus Self-doubt With the development of walking and the beginning of language, a child's exploration and manipulation of objects (and sometimes of people) expands. With these activities should come a comfortable sense of autonomy and of being a capable and worthy person. Excessive restriction or criticism at this stage may lead to self-doubts. Demands made beyond the child's ability—such as attempting toilet training too early—can discourage efforts to persevere in mastering new tasks. Such demands also can lead to stormy scenes of confrontation, disrupting the supportive parent-child relationship. The 2-year-old who demands the right to do something without help is acting out of a need to affirm his or her autonomy and adequacy.

Initiative versus Guilt Toward the end of the preschool period, a child who has developed a basic sense of trust is now a person who can initiate

TABLE 4.3	ERIKSON'S PSYCHOSOCIAL CRISES		
Age/Period (approximate)	**Crisis**	**Adequate Resolution**	**Inadequate Resolution**
0 to 1½ years	Trust vs. mistrust	Basic sense of safety, security; ability to rely on forces outside oneself	Insecurity, anxiety
1½ to 3 years	Autonomy vs. self-doubt	Perception of self as agent; capable of controlling one's own body and making things happen	Feelings of inadequacy about self-control, control of events
3 to 6 years	Initiative vs. guilt	Confidence in oneself as being able to initiate, create	Feeling of lack of self-worth
6 years to puberty	Competence vs. inferiority	Adequacy in basic social and intellectual skills; acceptance by peers	Lack of self-confidence; feelings of failure
Adolescence	Identity vs. role confusion	Comfortable sense of self as a person, both unique and socially accepted	Sense of self as fragmented, shifting, unclear sense of self
Early adulthood	Intimacy vs. isolation	Capacity for closeness and commitment to another	Feeling of aloneness, loneliness, separation; denial of intimacy needs
Middle adulthood	Generativity vs. stagnation	Focus of concern beyond oneself, to family, society, future generations	Self-indulgent concerns; lack of future orientation
Late adulthood	Ego-integrity vs. despair	Sense of wholeness; basic satisfaction with life	Feelings of futility, disappointment

intellectual and motor tasks. For example, a child in this stage wants to do things for himself, such as pour a glass of juice, choose what to wear, or get dressed. Caregivers' responses to these self-initiated activities either encourage the freedom and self-confidence needed for the next stage or produce guilt and feelings of incompetence.

Competence versus Inferiority During the elementary school years, the child who has successfully resolved the crises of the earlier stages is ready to go beyond random exploration to systematically develop competencies. School and sports offer arenas for learning intellectual and motor skills, and peer interaction offers the chance to develop social skills. Successful efforts in these pursuits lead to feelings of competence. Some youngsters, however, become spectators rather than performers, or they experience discouraging failure that leaves them with a sense of inferiority. Such children will find it more difficult to face continuing challenges and crises of psychosocial development.

Erikson's formulation has been widely accepted, although it does have some shortcomings. Some critics point out that the crises do not describe the experiences of girls and women as well as those of boys and men, especially in later life. However, Erikson's theory looks at the life cycle as a whole, putting into perspective both the unfolding changes and the continuity of life experience.

Check Your Recall

Children are master language learners, coming into the world prepared to use language and supported by social systems that encourage and motivate them to communicate. They may also have innate mental structures that help them to listen well to speech, and through experience, to expand their vocabularies and learn the rules of grammar. Language development begins with preverbal babbling, and continues through the one-word and two-word stages, telegraphic speech, and better sentence construction.

Theories of cognitive development address how children think and what they think about. Jean Piaget's stage theory of cognitive development proposes that children's behavior is guided by schemes, assimilation, and accommodation. These processes form four stages, each characterized by a distinct theme or set of tasks: the sensorimotor, preoperational, concrete operational, and formal operational stages.

Developing a sense of right and wrong depends on both moral reasoning and moral action. Lawrence Kohlberg's theory proposes that moral reasoning develops in three stages: preconventional, conventional, and postconventional (principled). Moral action may be less motivated by thoughts than by feelings, such as empathizing with others and wishing to relieve their pain.

Relations with others are influenced by one's temperament, or early emotional reactions to stimulation. Researchers have identified three fairly stable patterns in infants' temperament that are observable throughout life: fearful, aggressive, and bold. Personality is influenced by both temperament and experience, especially the guidance offered by parents and family. Socialization by one's family and culture begins with infant attachment to the caregiver. Researchers have observed three attachment styles—secure, insecure anxious-ambivalent, and insecure avoidant—which can influence later life experiences in love and work. An important view of lifelong social development is Erik Erikson's theory of psychosocial crises. The four crises of childhood deal with lessons about trust, autonomy, initiative, and competence. Erikson's theory addresses personal and social choices made throughout the life span.

The Maturing Individual

Psychological development spans the entire course of life. Though the childhood years are formative, we have a remarkable capacity for change throughout our life span (Brim & Kagan, 1980). The long-term effects of early infant and childhood experiences are highly variable and continue to be influenced by later experiences (Henderson, 1980; Simmel, 1980).

Most early theorists who influenced the study of individual development focused only on early life periods. They assumed that the burden of development is carried on only through adolescence; after that, the psyche was set for life and would experience few important changes. Contemporary research is challenging such notions. Out of this research has emerged an approach to development that does not categorize growth in specific periods of childhood, adolescence, and adulthood. The basic premise of **life-span developmental psychology** *is that personality, mental functioning, and other vital aspects of human nature continue to change throughout the entire life cycle.*

The Transitions of Adolescence

Adolescence *is commonly defined as the stage of life that begins at the onset of puberty, when sexual maturity, or the ability to reproduce, is attained.* However, it is not very clear where adolescence ends and adulthood begins. Variations among cultures account for much of the difficulty in defining the span of adolescence. Although the physical changes that take place at this stage are universal, the social and psychological dimensions of the adolescent experience depend on the cultural context. For example, if you enter your teen years in a culture that celebrates puberty as the start of adult status and rewards you with the power to make responsible choices, you will have a very different experience from someone whose culture condemns teenagers as confused and potentially dangerous troublemakers.

Most nonindustrial societies do not identify an actual adolescent stage as we know it. Instead, many such societies have *rites of passage* or **initiation rites.** *These rituals usually take place around puberty and serve as a public acknowledgment of the transition from childhood to adulthood.* The rites vary widely from extremely painful rituals, to periods of instruction in sexual and cultural practices, or periods of seclusion involving survival ordeals. For example, in tribal cultures, the young person may be asked to take a meditative journey alone, or to submit to symbolic scarring or circumcision surrounded by friends and family. Once individuals have passed through that period, there is no ambiguity about their status—they are adults, and the ties to their childhood have been severed

In our society, there are few transition rituals to help children clearly mark their new adolescent status or for adolescents to know when they have become young adults. One subtle rite of passage for many teenagers in our society is qualifying for a driver's license. Both symbolically and practically, legally being able to drive a car provides a young person with some freedom, independence, and mobility that is not available to children.

Although many issues are important in adolescence, we will focus on three developmental tasks that commonly confront adolescents in Western society: coming to terms with physical *maturity* and adult *sexuality;* redefining *social roles,* including achieving autonomy from parents; and deciding upon *occupational goals.* Each of these issues is a component of the central task of establishing an *integrated identity.*

Maturation The first concrete indicator of the end of childhood is the *pubescent growth spurt.* Two to three years after the onset of the growth

Many cultures have initiation rites that signal a child's passage into adulthood. Shown at the top is a bar mitzvah, a Jewish ceremony marking a boy's thirteenth birthday. The middle photo records the puberty rites of the White Mountain Apaches of Arizona, and the photo at the bottom shows the initiation ceremony of a young Lamaist monk.

spurt, **puberty**, or *sexual maturity,* is reached. Puberty for males begins with the production of live sperm (usually about age 14 in the United States), while for girls it begins at **menarche,** *the onset of menstruation* (between ages 11 and 15).

Part of achieving a personal identity involves coming to terms with one's physical self by developing a realistic, yet accepting image of physical appearance. Attractiveness influences the way we view each other at all ages (Hatfield & Sprecher, 1986), and during adolescence one becomes increasingly focused on appearance. The term **body image** *refers to the way one subjectively views one's own appearance.* This image is dependent not only on measurable features, such as height and weight, but also on other people's assessments and on cultural standards of physical beauty. During adolescence, dramatic physical changes and heightened emphasis on peer acceptance (especially peers of the opposite sex) can intensify concern with one's body image.

Approximately 44 percent of American adolescent girls and 23 percent of boys claimed that they "frequently felt ugly and unattractive" (Offer et al., 1981). In another study, physical appearance was the biggest source of concern for a group of 240 high school students (Eme et al., 1979). Girls' self-concepts are particularly tied to perceptions of their physical attractiveness, while boys seem more concerned with their physical prowess, athletic ability, and effectiveness in achieving goals (Lerner et al., 1976). Girls and women are more dissatisfied with their weight and shape than are males, and experience more conflict about food and eating (Rolls et al., 1991). These differences probably mirror a cultural preoccupation with female beauty and male strength—an inevitable source of concern since not all adolescents can embody the cultural ideals of attractiveness. There are also subcultural influences on self-concept; some research indicates that the self-esteem of white adolescents of both sexes is more tied to physical attractiveness than is that of black adolescents (Wade, 1991). Over time, adolescents seem to become more accepting of their appearances. Nonetheless, the attainment of acceptable body images can be a difficult task.

Sexuality   A new awareness of sexual feelings and impulses accompanies physical maturity. In one large study of American adolescents, the majority of adolescent males and females said that they often think about sex (Offer et al., 1981). Yet many adolescents still lack adequate knowledge or have misconceptions about sex and sexuality. Sex is a topic parents find difficult to discuss with children, so adolescents tend to be secretive about sexual concerns, making exchange of information and communication even more difficult. The development of a sexual identity that defines sexual orientation and guides sexual behavior thus becomes an important task of adolescence.

In early adolescence, masturbation is the most common expression of sexual impulses (Bell et al., 1981; Hass, 1979; Sorensen, 1973). Homosexual experiences are also common in adolescence; 14 to 17 percent of teenage boys and half that many girls report some homosexual experiences (Hass, 1979; Sorensen, 1973; Wyatt et al., 1988), though most of these individuals ultimately identify with a heterosexual orientation. Exclusively homosexual feelings are much more difficult to resolve during adolescence, when individuals are intensely concerned with the conventions and norms of their society. While most gays and lesbians first become aware of their sexual orientation in early adolescence, many may not attain self-acceptance of their sexual identities until their middle or late twenties (Riddle & Morin, 1977). The time lag undoubtedly reflects the relative lack of social support for homosexual orientation and exemplifies the importance of society's role in all aspects of identity development.

The proportion of adolescents engaging in sexual intercourse has risen substantially in the last 20 years. At least half of all young people have engaged in intercourse before age 18, and about 75 percent have done so by the age of 20 (Chilman, 1983; London et al., 1989). There is evidence that the initial sexual experiences of males and females differ substantially. The vast majority of females become sexually involved with individuals whom they love. In contrast, for most adolescent males, personal relationships appear to be less important than the sex act itself; the average male reports no emotional involvement with his first sexual partner (Miller & Simon, 1980).

Developing a sexual identity is a central challenge of adolescence. It involves more than recognizing and accepting one's own sexual orientation and gaining sexual experience. Those who choose to become sexually active are challenged to conduct their sexual relationships in a responsible fashion. This means considering the consequences of one's actions as well as being sensitive to the needs of one's partner and oneself. This balance is difficult to achieve if the adults in a young person's life cannot themselves talk comfortably about sex, and if the images of sex displayed in the media—such as perfect bodies having sex without consequences, sexist rap lyrics—tend to be extreme and unrealistic. Most adolescents, however, do face and meet the challenge of making their sexuality a part of a healthy, functioning adult sense of self.

Social Identity   Erik Erikson believed that the essential crisis of *adolescence* is discovering one's true *identity* amid the confusion of playing many different roles for different audiences in an expanding social world. Resolving this crisis helps the individual develop a sense of a coherent self. Failure to resolve the crisis adequately may result in a self-image that lacks a stable core. Resolution of the identity crisis is both a personal process and a social experience (Erikson, 1968). (Review Table 4.3 on page 137 for Erikson's concept of the adolescent identity crisis.)

Several factors influence the move toward self-identity. Family ties become stretched as the adolescent spends more time outside the home. In American society, the adolescent experiences less structure and adult guidance, is exposed to new values, and develops a strong need for peer support and acceptance. Adolescents report spending more than four times as much time talking to peers as to adults (Csikszentmihalyi et al., 1977). With their peers, adolescents refine their social skills and try out different social behaviors, gradually defining their social identities, the kind of people they choose to be, and the sorts of relationships they will pursue.

As the need for close friendships and peer acceptance becomes greater, anxiety about the possibility of rejection increases. As a result, young adolescents may choose the "safe" route of conformity and go along with their friends to avoid weakening those relationships. Females may be especially concerned with personal relationships, but less likely than males to give in to group pressure to behave antisocially (Berndt, 1979). Many parents worry that their teenagers might endanger themselves in proving their loyalty to unreasonable friends or norms. Fortunately, research suggests that most adolescents are able to "look before they leap" by considering the wisdom of committing risky acts (Berndt, 1992).

Loneliness becomes significant during adolescence. Between 15 and 25 percent of adolescents report feeling very lonely (Offer et al., 1981). Similarly, shyness reaches its highest level in early teenage years as the desire for social acceptance markedly increases (Zimbardo, 1990). Studies of adolescent suicide show that the triggering experience for such a tragedy is often a shaming or humiliating event, such as failure in some achievement or romantic rejection (Garland & Zigler, 1993). The intensity of a young person's social

According to Erikson's social identity stage, adolescents must define their identities as individuals even as they seek the comfort and feeling of belonging that comes from being with friends and family. One compromise might be to experiment with different norms—such as clothing or hair styles—within the security of supportive relationships with companions, cliques, or romantic partners.

and personal motives can make it hard to keep perspective and recognize that even difficult times will pass, and that everyone makes mistakes.

The dual forces of parents and peers at times exhibit conflicting influences on adolescents, fueling the separation from parents and increasing identification with peers. But generally parents and peers serve complementary functions and fulfill different needs in adolescents' lives (Davis, 1985). For example, adolescents look to their families for structure and support, while they look to their friends for acceptance and approval. Ultimately, identity development involves establishing independent commitments that are sensitive to both parents *and* peers.

Occupational Choices   According to Erikson, deciding on a vocational commitment is the hallmark of adolescent identity formation. The question, "What are you going to be when you grow up?" reflects the common assumption that what you *do* determines what you *are*. It also requires the ability to think about the future, and to set realistic goals that are both achievable and likely to be satisfying. Anticipating one's future—mentally imagining its possibilities—strongly influences adolescents' motivation and abilities to plan and evaluate life choices (Nurmi, 1991).

While many factors affect vocational interests and achievement, the clearest factor is socioeconomic background. Adolescents from families of higher socioeconomic status are more likely to pursue and complete education beyond high school and to aspire toward and achieve higher levels of personal and social success. Middle-class and upper middle-class parents encourage higher achievement motivation in their children, model greater career success, and supply the economic resources unavailable to poorer children (Achenbach, 1982; Featherman, 1980; Gustafson & Magnusson, 1991).

Educational and occupational choices made in later adolescence can profoundly affect future options. But perhaps occupational identity is best understood within the context of the entire life cycle. Success in adulthood can be measured by flexibility and a willingness to explore new directions, which extend from the self-confidence developed by successfully negotiating the demands of adolescence.

The Challenges of Adulthood

The transition from adolescence to young adulthood is marked by decisions about advanced education, vocation, intimate relationships, and marriage. What are the tasks of adulthood and what form does psychological development take over the course of adulthood? How might one's experiences in childhood and adolescence affect the choices made in adulthood?

Love and Work   Several developmental theories deal with the tasks of adulthood. According to Freud, adult development is driven by two basic needs: *love* and *work*. Abraham Maslow (1970) described these needs as *love* and *belonging*, which, when satisfied, develop into the needs for *success* and *esteem*. Other theorists describe these basic needs as *affiliation* or *social acceptance* needs and *achievement* or *competence* needs. In Erikson's theory, the last three of the eight lifelong stages are crises of adulthood. The first of these concerns intimacy, and the second focuses on one's sense of productivity, including work. The third crisis will be examined later, in our discussion of late adulthood.

Intimacy   The psychosocial crisis of young adulthood is *intimacy versus isolation* (see Table 4.3 on page 137). Erikson described **intimacy** *as the capac-*

ity to make a full commitment—sexual, emotional, and moral—to another person. The individual must resolve the conflict between wanting to establish closeness to another and fearing the risks and losses such closeness can entail. Making intimate commitments requires compromising personal preferences, accepting responsibilities, and yielding some privacy and independence. Failure to resolve this crisis leads to isolation and the inability to connect to others in meaningful ways. Much research supports one of the most important conclusions that you should take with you from this text: *Anything that isolates us from sources of social support—from a reliable network of friends and family—puts us at risk for a host of physical ills, mental problems, and even social pathologies. We are social creatures, and we need each other's help and support to be effective and healthy.*

For Erikson, a young adult must consolidate a clear and comfortable sense of identity (the crisis of adolescence) *before* being able to cope successfully with the risks and benefits of intimacy. In essence, you must know who and what you are before you can begin to love someone else and share your life with that person. However, the sequence from identity to intimacy that Erikson described may not accurately reflect present-day realities. The trend in recent years has been for young adults to live together before marrying, to delay making contractual commitments to lifelong intimacy with one person. Many individuals today must struggle with identity issues (for example, career choices) at the same time they are trying to deal with intimacy issues.

Today, marriage, as the prototype of the successful resolution of the search for intimacy, often occurs more than once in an individual's life. In fact, married adults are now divorcing at a rate four times greater than adults did 50 years ago. Divorce and separation lead many adults to reexamine their ideas and hopes for intimacy at later points in the life cycle. Spouses have had high—unrealistically high—expectations of each other and about what constitutes an ideal marriage and family structure (Cleek & Pearson, 1985). However, there is evidence that communication and affection between spouses today is substantially better than it was in earlier times (Caplow, 1982).

Married people in the late twentieth century are more likely to see each other as partners and friends, and to feel less constrained by what society expects of a "husband" or "wife." Partners in "peer marriages" talk with and help each other in ways that work best for their relationship, irrespective of traditional ideas about the man being "boss" or the wife being responsible for "women's work" (Schwartz, 1994). The key to such a fair and satisfying relationship is communication, in which both partners feel able to openly express their hopes and fears (Klagsbrun, 1985). A mushrooming of research on how good communication can maintain relationships has helped our culture to view marriage as a worthwhile investment, and therapy as a valuable option for supporting such efforts (Gottman, 1994; Notarius, 1996). In essence, relating is no longer viewed as a set of skills that "comes naturally" with the establishment of intimacy. Instead, close relationships are seen as lifelong works-in-progress, worthwhile investments of time and energy whose quality can be improved with clearer self-understanding, effective conflict resolution, and good communication.

Generativity The next major opportunity for growth, Erikson's second adult stage, is the *generativity* crisis of adult midlife. People in their thirties and forties move beyond a focus on self and partner toward broader commitments to family, work, society, and the world. Research confirms that adults who express a strong sense of being generative and productive also report high life satisfaction (McAdams et al., 1993). Those who haven't resolved earlier crises of identity and intimacy may experience a midlife crisis. Such people

In recent years, a growing tolerance for divorce has led many adults to change their ideas about traditional marriage. Communication and affection between modern spouses has also changed, improving over earlier times. Shown here on their wedding day are Ril and Sayoko Bandy with Ril's children from a previous marriage.

you judge it would be worse to miss your date's call than to track water through the house while hurrying to the telephone, your payoff matrix favors guessing "yes"—even if it risks a false alarm—rather than more conservatively guessing "no."

Sensory Adaptation

In addition to being determined by the meaning and relationships of stimuli, sensation is also critically determined by *change*. The main role of our stimulus detectors is to announce changes in the external world. Thus our senses are ultimately novelty detectors. Our receptors bring each new event into the total pool of information we use to interpret the momentary status of our sensory field. If not for a specially evolved function of all sensory systems—*adaptation*—this great quantity of new incoming stimuli would overwhelm our ability to deal with old sensations. **Sensory adaptation** *is the diminishing responsiveness of sensory systems to prolonged stimulus input.* More simply, we cease to notice stimulation that does not change in intensity or some other quality. For example, you do not realize—until you read these words and consider their meaning—that you have already adapted to the press of furniture against your body at this moment; until you focus attention there, you do not "feel" the chair against your posterior, the upholstery at your back, or the pillow under your neck. In a similar way, you do not notice the tension of socks or hose on your legs and feet, the concentration of cologne near your own nose, or the unvarying drone of an air conditioner. As long as these streams of stimulation remain relatively constant, your attention is diverted to other sensations. However, any shift in the signals you are receiving—for example, if the air conditioner suddenly becomes louder or higher-pitched—will rivet your sensory attention once more because the signals have changed.

The process of adaptation reveals the dynamic and vital nature of sensation. As our response to old stimuli fades quickly over time, we are continually refreshed by the vibrant world of sensory impressions around us. Sensory adaptation is another application of sensory *comparisons* that adjust to stimulation over time. Some of our sensory systems are so efficient at adapting to extreme conditions that we may not realize how extreme those conditions are. When you're at a noisy party, you may not realize that you and your companions are shouting; in the morning your sore throat will remind you how screaming strains your voice. Similarly, after watching a film in a dark theater in the afternoon, you may emerge feeling blinded by an overcast day and momentarily paralyzed by discomfort that, under normal conditions, would not even warrant sunglasses.

Check Your Recall

Sensation consists of processes that put us in direct contact with the physical energies of the world. Translating the physical energy of stimuli into neural impulses via transduction is the process that produces sensation. Psychophysicists examine the measurable relationships between psychological responses and physical stimuli.

Early psychophysicists sought to identify absolute thresholds, the minimum stimulation necessary to activate the senses. Difference thresholds are minimally detectable changes in stimuli. According to Weber's law, the just noticeable difference (JND) between two stimuli is a constant fraction of the intensity of background stimulation. Signal detection theory (SDT) explains sensation as involving both physical stimulation and decision making. Sensory adaptation enables receptors to fade out responsiveness to prolonged stimulation in preparation for processing new signals.

Vision

Now that we have considered the purposes of sensation, we will explore its processes in several bodily sensory systems, especially vision and hearing. Vision is the most complex, highly developed, and important sense for humans and most other mobile creatures. Animals with good vision have an enormous evolutionary advantage. Good vision helps us detect desired targets, threats, and changes in our physical environment and adapt our behavior accordingly. With specialized instruments we can even enhance our visual detection to see distant galaxies or microscopic life forms. Not surprisingly, vision is the most studied of all the sense modalities.

The Neuroanatomy of Vision

Here we will review the anatomical structures and neural pathways that conduct visual processing and create the qualities of visual sensation.

The Structures of the Eye   The eye is the camera for the brain's motion pictures of the world (see Figure 5.2). Like a camera, the eye gathers and focuses light. Light first enters through the *cornea,* the transparent layer covering the front of the eye that does most of the focusing. Next it passes through the *pupil,* an opening in the opaque, ringed muscle that is the *iris.* The iris controls the amount of light that enters the eye, by either relaxing to constrict the pupil (and shut out light) or contracting to dilate the pupil (and let more light in). To focus a camera, we move its lens closer to or further from the object viewed. To adjust the focus of the eye, neural signals change the shape of the eye's rubbery, bean-shaped crystalline *lens,* thinning it to focus on distant objects and thickening it to focus on near ones.

FIGURE 5.2   Structures of the Human Eye ■

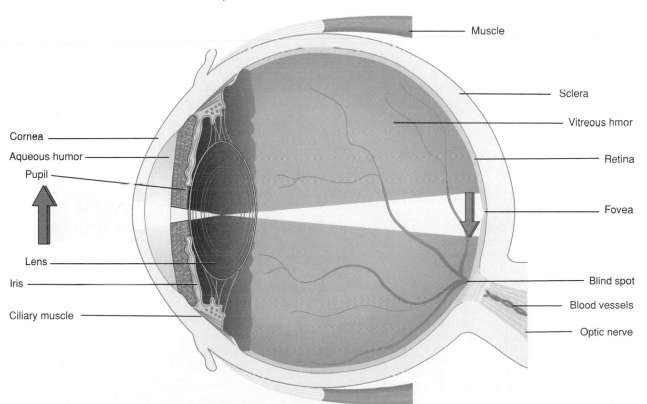

At the back of a camera body, photosensitive film records the variations in light that have passed through the lens. Similarly, in the eye, light travels through the thick, translucent vitreous humor, finally striking the *retina,* a thin sheet of neurons that lines the rear wall of the eyeball.

How exactly does the camera of the eye "snap" pictures of our dynamic, living world? We look with our eyes but we *see* with our brains. The eye gathers light, focuses it, and sends a neural signal on its way for subsequent processing into a visual image. The eye's critical function is this last task: to convert the information about the world from light waves into neural signals the brain can process. This transduction happens in the **retina,** *the light-sensitive layer of cells at the back of the eye.* The eye's retina, functioning somewhat like the film in a camera, is a layered structure interweaving five types of neurons: (1) the photoreceptors ("light receptors"), specialized neurons called the *rods* and *cones,* (2) the *bipolar neurons,* (3) the *ganglion cells,* (4) the *horizontal* cells, and (5) the *amacrine* cells.

Photoreceptors *are neurons that absorb light energy and convert it into neural responses.* Intriguingly, the rods and cones are positioned at the rearmost layer of the retina. Light rays must make it through the maze of preceding neurons to the very back of the retina to trigger photoreception. The transformed (now neural) impulse is then relayed *forward* to the other neurons of the retina before being channeled via nerve fibers to the brain (see Figure 5.3).

Why *two* kinds of photoreceptors? Because we sometimes function in darkness and sometimes in bright light, nature has provided two different ways of processing light stimuli, with two distinct types of receptor cells (named roughly for their shape). The 125 million thin rods "see in the dark"— that is, they detect low intensities of light at night, though they cannot discriminate colors. The 7 million fat cones "view" the bright, color-filled day, each specialized to detect either blue, red, or green hues. In the very center of the

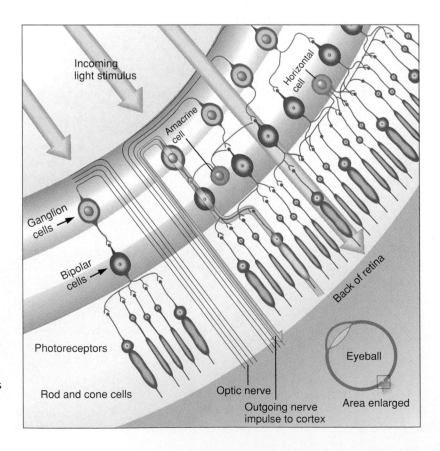

FIGURE 5.3 Transduction of Light in the Retina ■ This simplified diagram shows the pathways that connect three layers of nerve cells in the retina. Incoming light passes through the ganglion cells and bipolar cells first before striking the photoreceptors at the back of the eyeball. Once stimulated, the rods and cones then transmit information to the bipolar cells (note that one bipolar cell combines information from several receptor cells). The bipolar cells then transmit neural impulses to the ganglion cells. Impulses travel from the ganglia to the brain via axons that make up the optic nerve.

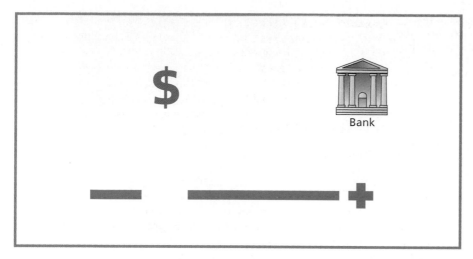

FIGURE 5.4 Find Your Blind Spot ■ *Demonstration 1:* Hold the book at arm's length, close your right eye, and fix your left eye on the bank figure. Bring the book slowly closer to your eyes. When the dollar sign is in your blind spot, it will disappear—but you will not see a "hole" in your visual field. Instead, your visual system "fills in" the missing area with information from the white background. You have "lost" your money, which you should have put into the bank in the first place!

Demonstration 2: To convince yourself that brain processes "fill in" the missing part of the visual field with appropriate background, close your right eye again and focus on the cross in the lower part of Figure 5.4. Once again, bring the book closer to you as you focus your left eye on the cross. This time, the gap in the line will disappear and will be filled in with a continuation of the line on either side. At least in your blind spot, what you see may be a false version of reality.

retina is a small region called the *fovea* that contains nothing but densely packed cones—it's rod-free. The fovea is the area of our sharpest vision; both color and spatial detail are most accurately detected there.

The retina's bipolar and ganglion cells gather the responses of many nearby receptors. Each *bipolar cell* has a single branching dendrite and a single axon, creating two "poles." These cells combine impulses from many receptors and send the results to ganglion cells. Each *ganglion cell* combines the impulses from many bipolar cells into a single impulse to be transmitted further along the visual pathway. *The axons of the ganglion cells contain nerve fibers that, bundled together, make up the* **optic nerve,** *which carries visual information from the eye to the brain.*

At the point where the optic nerve exits each eye, there is a small area of the retina that is not "coated" with a layer of photoreceptors, so there are no cells there to detect light. This creates a gap in the visual field called the *blind spot.* You do not normally experience blindness there because what one eye misses is registered by the other eye, and the brain "fills in" the spot with information that matches the background. To find your own blind spot, examine Figure 5.4, and follow the caption's instructions for two revealing exercises.

Pathways to the Brain   At the back of the brain is a special area for processing the neural coded information coming from the eyes. *This area in the occipital cortex is known as the primary* **visual cortex.** Here the brain "sees" the messages that the eyes have "collected." Research has revealed how visual information is routed and analyzed, cell by cell, from eye to brain.

Nerve impulses leaving the retina project to several different parts of the brain. The bundled axons of the ganglion cells forming the optic nerve first travel to the base of the brain, where they come together in the *optic chiasma,* an X-shaped intersection named for the Greek letter *chi,* resembling our

FIGURE 5.5   Neural Pathways in the Human Visual System ■ Light from the visual field projects onto the two retinas; neural messages from the retinas are sent to the two visual centers of each hemisphere.

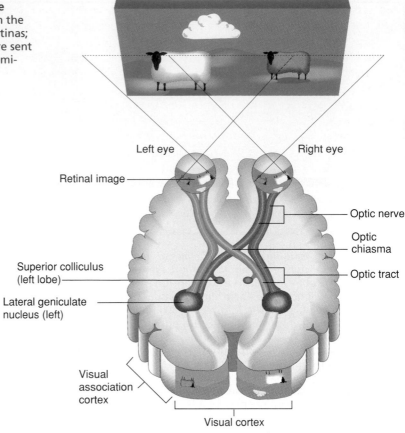

Left eye   Right eye

Retinal image

Optic nerve

Optic chiasma

Optic tract

Superior colliculus (left lobe)

Lateral geniculate nucleus (left)

Visual association cortex

Visual cortex

Isaac Newton (1642–1726) showed that white light passing through a prism yields a rainbow of all colors of the spectrum.

alphabet's X (see Figure 5.5.) At the chiasma (pronounced *KYE-azma*), half of each eye's bundled fibers cross to the other side toward the back of the brain. Most of the visual information, now divided between halves of the visual field rather than the two eyes, is relayed to the primary visual cortex via the *lateral geniculate nucleus* (LGN).

Color Vision

A remarkable feature of the human visual system is that our experiences of form, color, position, and depth are based on processing the same sensory information in different ways. Physical objects and beams of light seem to have the marvelous property of being painted with color, but the red valentines, green fir trees, blue oceans, and rainbows that you see are themselves actually colorless. Despite appearances, color does not exist in the objects you see; it only exists in the mind of the viewer.

Color is a psychological property of your sensory experience, created when your brain processes the information coded in the light source. Although the processes involved are fairly complex, color vision is one of the best understood aspects of our visual experience.

Dimensions of Color   Sir Isaac Newton, who in the seventeenth century discovered the laws of motion and of gravity, also discovered that when white light passes through a prism it separates into a rainbow of colors: the *visible spectrum.*

Visible light is a kind of energy that our sensory receptors can detect. The light we see is a small portion of a physical dimension called the *electromagnetic spectrum,* which also includes X rays, microwaves, radio waves, and television waves. Because we have no receptors sensitive to these energies, we need special detection instruments to help us convert them into the signals we use.

All electromagnetic energy travels across distance—even through a vacuumlike, airless space—and can be described in terms of its *wavelength*, determined by its speed or frequency. Wavelengths of visible light are measured in *nanometers* (*nm*—billionths of a meter). Visible light ranges from short, high-frequency waves (400 nm at the violet end of the spectrum) to long, low-frequency waves (700 nm at the red end). White sunlight combines all these wavelengths in equal amounts, but a prism can separate them into their distinctive wavelengths. Light is described physically by particular wavelengths; colors exist only in your visual experience.

All experiences of color can be described in terms of three basic dimensions of our perception of light: hue, saturation, and brightness. *Hue* refers to the essential color of a light. *Saturation* is the purity and vividness of color sensations. Undiluted colors have the highest saturation; muted, muddy, and pastel colors have intermediate amounts of saturation; and grays have zero saturation. Finally, *brightness* is the intensity of light. White has the greatest brightness, while black has the least. When colors are analyzed along these three dimensions, a remarkable finding emerges: Humans are capable of visually discriminating among about 5 million different colors! However, most people can identify only 150 to 200 colors.

Afterimages   After you stare at a brightly colored object for a while and then turn away to look at a blank surface, you will see the object's complementary color as a *visual afterimage*. Since seeing is sometimes believing, try the Patriotism Test in Figure 5.6 before continuing.

Afterimages may be negative or positive. *Positive afterimages* are caused by a continuation of the receptor and neural processes following stimulation; they are rare and brief. An example of positive afterimages occurs when you blink after you look at a flashbulb light. *Negative afterimages* are the opposite or the reverse of the original experience, as in the flag example; they are more common and last longer.

Color Blindness   Not everyone sees colors in the same way; some people are born with a color deficiency. *Color blindness* is the partial or total inability to distinguish colors. (The negative afterimage effect of viewing the green, yellow, and black flag in Figure 5.6 will not work if you are color-blind.)

The combination of any two unique hues yields the complement of a third color. The combination of all three wavelengths produces white light, as does the combination of two complementary colors.

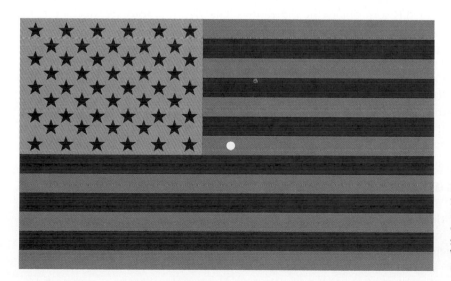

FIGURE 5.6   The Patriotism Test: A Demonstration of Color Afterimages. ■ Stare at the dot in the center of the green, black, and yellow flag for at least 30 seconds. Then fix your gaze on the center of a sheet of white paper or on a blank wall. What do you see? Do others see the same image when you have them take the test?

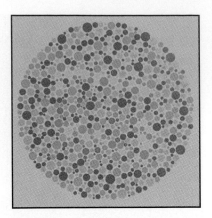

FIGURE 5.7   The Ishihani Color Blindness Test ■ Someone who cannot discriminate between red and green hues will not be able to identify the number hidden in the figure. What do you see? If you see the number 26 in the dot pattern, your color vision is probably normal.

There are different forms of color blindness. People with one form called *color weakness* can't distinguish pale colors, such as pink or tan. Most color blindness involves trouble distinguishing red from green, especially at weak saturations. Those who confuse yellows and blues are rare, about one or two people per thousand. Rarest of all are those who see no color at all and see only variations in brightness. Only about 500 cases of this total color blindness have ever been reported. To see whether you have a major color deficiency, look at Figure 5.7 and note what you see. If you see the number 26 in the dot pattern, your color vision is probably normal. If you see something else, you are probably at least partially color blind.

What Happened to Jonathan I?   After his accident, it seemed to Jonathan I. that the color had gone out of his world. In reality, however, the wavelength reflections that produce color were intact in the objects around him. The "color"—the ability to meaningfully sense different hues—had gone out of Mr. I.'s visual system. Discussing Mr. I.'s achromatopsia, Oliver Sacks (1995) notes that most early researchers into color blindness doubted the existence of a single "color center" in the brain. Later research, however, confirmed that color is not a quality of objects, but is an experience constructed in the brain of the viewer (Land, 1977; Sharpe & Nordby, 1990; Zeki, 1993). Further, color and color vision have powerful personal and social meaning. A world without color is "colorless," lifeless, gray, and even "dirty." Sacks observes that Mr. I.'s greatest challenge was to overcome the psychological depression caused by his loss. As an artist, Mr. I. might have given in to complete despair; but ironically he learned to use his artistic skill to reinterpret his view of the world:

> Although Mr. I. does not deny his loss, and at some level still mourns it, he has come to feel that his vision has become "highly refined," "privileged," that he sees a world of pure form, uncluttered by color. . . . He feels he has been given "a whole new world," which the rest of us, distracted by color, are insensitive to. (Sacks, 1995, pp. 38–39).

Check Your Recall

Vision is the most complex and important sense for humans and other mobile vertebrates. Light is focused by the cornea and lens of the eyes onto photoreceptors (rods and cones) in the retina. The photoreceptors transduce light energy into neural energy, which travels to the bipolar and ganglion cells, and is transmitted via the optic nerve to the visual cortex of the brain. The two optic nerves meet in the brain at the optic chiasma, where half the nerve fibers from each eye cross to the opposite side of the brain.

Rods provide information about illumination, while cones provide color information. The stimulus for color is the wavelength of light in the visible spectrum. Color sensations differ in hue, saturation, and brightness. Color blindness involves a deficiency in distinguishing or detecting colors.

Hearing

Although vision is the most investigated of our senses, the study of hearing is also of great psychological importance. Stop for a moment and reflect on a difficult question: Would you rather be blind or deaf? Which deficit might be a more difficult adjustment for you to make? Your choice might indicate some of the sensations you rely on—and take for granted—in everyday life.

Like vision, hearing provides us with reliable spatial information over extended distances. However, hearing may be even more important than vision in orienting us toward distant events. We often hear stimuli before we see them, and we often have readier access to sound than to vision. For example, you can remain seated in your room, studying for tomorrow's test and seeing only the words on the page, and your sense of hearing will still inform you about traffic outside your window, footsteps in the hall, and voices at the door. You may take for granted your ability to use these cues to determine what time it is, who is nearby, and what you should do.

Besides orienting us, hearing plays a crucial role in our understanding of spoken language; it is the principal sensory modality for human communication. The importance of hearing and the tragedy of its loss is captured in the following eloquent description by poet Diane Ackerman (1990):

> The world will still make sense to someone who is blind or armless or minus a nose. But if you lose your sense of hearing, a crucial thread dissolves and you lose track of life's logic. You become cut off from the daily commerce of the world, as if you were a root buried beneath the soil (p. 175).

You may better understand the details of the process of sensing sound if you first appreciate its value in human experience. Take a moment to reflect on the power of hearing in your life and the lives of those around you. Then move on to the next section, where we review how sound is first sensed and then understood.

The Physics of Sound

Sounds are created when actions cause objects to vibrate. The vibrational energy is transmitted to the surrounding medium—usually air—as the vibrating objects push the molecules of the medium back and forth. Resulting changes in pressure spread outward in the form of sound waves traveling at a rate of about 1100 feet per second. Sound cannot travel in a true vacuum (such as outer space) because there is no medium there to move or vibrate.

Changes in air pressure travel in *sine waves*, energy changes that unfold in time and space. A *pure tone* such as that made by a tuning fork is the sound produced by a single sine wave (see Figure 5.8.) Frequency and amplitude are the physical properties of a sine wave that determine how it sounds to us. A pure tone has only one frequency and one amplitude. *Frequency measures the number of cycles the wave completes in a given amount of time; it is usually expressed in* **cycles per second (cps)** *or* **hertz (Hz)**. *Amplitude* measures the physical strength of the sound wave (shown in its peak-to-valley height); it is defined in units of sound pressure or energy.

Most sounds are produced not by pure tones but by complex waves containing a combination of frequencies and amplitudes. We hear different qualities of sounds (clarinet versus piano, for example) because most sounds contain different combinations of frequencies and amplitudes.

The Psychology of Hearing

The three dimensions of sound that we experience psychologically are pitch, loudness, and quality.

FIGURE 5.8 Sound Waves ■
Sound waves produced by the vibration of a tuning fork create waves of compressed and expanded air.

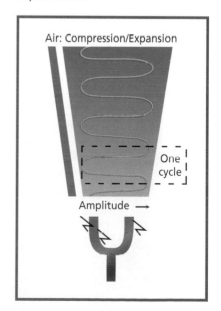

Air: Compression/Expansion

One cycle

Amplitude →

Pitch Perception   Pitch *is the highness or lowness of a sound determined by the sound's frequency;* high frequencies produce high pitch, and low frequencies produce low pitch. The full range of human sensitivity to pure tones extends from frequencies as low as 20 cps to frequencies as high as 20,000 cps.

We "read" a rich amount of information in the pitches of the sounds we hear. Can you imagine music without the high-pitched delicacy of strings, or the low-pitched soul of bass? The pitch of a voice gives us clues about the age, gender, and mood of the speaker. A change to a higher-pitched voice warns us of alarm, while a lowering of pitch might mean calm—or a signal that one is about to stop speaking. Just as the visual system "specializes" in sensing color, the auditory system is particularly adept at detecting and distinguishing pitch. How does it do so? A complex sensory task, pitch perception is divided between two systems that, together, offer greater sensory precision than either system alone could provide.

- When sound waves are conducted through the inner ear, the basilar membrane moves. Different frequencies produce maximum movement at different specific *places* on the membrane. The pitch one hears depends on the basilar membrane site of the greatest stimulation. Different places are coded for different pitches when auditory information is processed in the brain—an explanation of pitch perception known as *place theory*.

- However, it is also true that neurons on the basilar membrane fire only at a particular point in each sound wave. Their firing rate is determined by the tone's *frequency*; this rate of firing is the code for pitch perception in the brain. In this explanation, pitch is a matter of *time* as well as place—a view known as *frequency theory*.

- Place theory accounts well for perception of pitch at frequencies above 1000 Hz; frequency theory accounts well for coding frequencies below about 5000 Hz. Between 1000 and 5000 Hz, both mechanisms can operate.

Why does our auditory system seem designed for greatest precision for sounds within the range of 1000 to 5000 Hz? Not coincidentally, the frequency of human speech has a considerable overlap with this range. The shape of the auditory canal magnifies sounds within the range of human speech. Thus the auditory system may well have evolved especially for hearing the human voice.

Loudness   The **loudness** *or physical intensity of a sound is determined by its amplitude.* Sound waves with large amplitudes are experienced as loud and those with small amplitudes as soft. People can hear sounds across a wide range of loudness. The auditory system is sensitive enough to hear the tick of a wristwatch at 20 feet; this is the system's absolute threshold. If our hearing were more sensitive, we would hear the blood flowing in our ears. At the other extreme, a jet airliner taking off 100 yards away is so loud that it is painful. When we compare the two sounds in terms of physical units of sound pressure, the jet produces a sound wave with more than a billion times the energy of the ticking watch.

Because our range of hearing is so great, physical intensities of sound are usually expressed in ratios rather than absolute amounts; loudness is measured in units called *decibels* (dB). Figure 5.9 shows the loudness of some representative natural sounds in decibel units. It also shows the corresponding sound pressures for comparison. Notice that sounds louder than about 90 dB can produce hearing loss, depending on how long one is exposed to them.

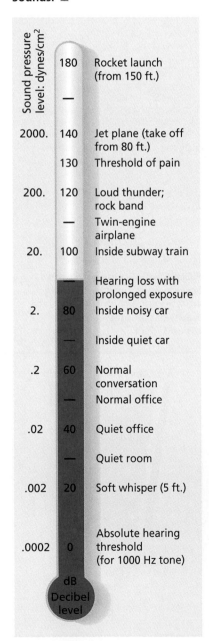

FIGURE 5.9   Loudness of Familiar Sounds. ■

Sound pressure level: dynes/cm²	dB Decibel level	
	180	Rocket launch (from 150 ft.)
	—	
2000.	140	Jet plane (take off from 80 ft.)
	130	Threshold of pain
200.	120	Loud thunder; rock band
	—	Twin-engine airplane
20.	100	Inside subway train
	—	Hearing loss with prolonged exposure
2.	80	Inside noisy car
	—	Inside quiet car
.2	60	Normal conversation
	—	Normal office
.02	40	Quiet office
	—	Quiet room
.002	20	Soft whisper (5 ft.)
.0002	0	Absolute hearing threshold (for 1000 Hz tone)

Timbre *The quality of a sound wave's complexity is its* **timbre** (pronounced *TAM-b'r*). A complex sound can be analyzed as a sum of many different pure tones, each with a different amplitude and frequency. Figure 5.10 shows the complex waveforms that correspond to several familiar sounds. The graph in the figure shows the sound spectrum for middle C on a piano—the range of all the frequencies actually present in that note and their amplitudes. The human ear analyzes complex waves by breaking them down into their simpler component waves.

The sounds that we call *noise* contain many frequencies that are not systematically related to each other. For instance, the static noise you hear between radio stations contains energy at all audible frequencies; you perceive it as having no pitch because it has no frequency common to all components.

The Physiology of Hearing

How does the physiological activity of the auditory system give rise to the psychological experience of sound? For people to hear, four basic *energy transformations* must take place.

1. *Airborne sound waves must be translated into fluid waves within the cochlea of the ear.* In this first transformation, vibrating air molecules enter the ears (see Figure 5.11). Sound enters the ear either directly or after being bounced off the pinna. At the end of the auditory canal, sound waves strike the eardrum or *tympanic membrane*. The eardrum transmits these vibrations to three tiny bones: the hammer, anvil, and stirrup. The vibrations of these bones transmit concentrated energy to the primary organ of hearing, the *cochlea*, located in the inner ear.

2. *The fluid waves must then stimulate mechanical vibrations of the basilar membrane.* This second transformation occurs in the cochlea, where the airborne sound wave becomes "seaborne." The cochlea is a fluid-filled, coiled tube made of cartilage. *A thin tissue known as the* **basilar membrane** *runs through the core of the cochlea.* The stirrup vibrates against the oval window at the base of the cochlea and sets the inner fluid into wave motion. The fluid wave causes the basilar membrane to move similarly, bending the membrane's tiny hair cells.

3. *Vibrations on the basilar membrane must be converted into electrical impulses.* The bending of the hair cells stimulates sensory nerve endings. These transform the mechanical vibrations of the basilar membrane into neural activity.

4. *Finally, the neural impulses must travel to the auditory cortex. Nerve impulses leave the cochlea in a bundle of fibers called the* **auditory nerve**. These fibers meet in the brain stem, with stimulation from each ear traveling to both sides of the brain. *Auditory signals ultimately proceed to the* **auditory cortex** *in the temporal lobes of the cerebral hemispheres, for higher-order processing.*

If the auditory system seems complicated, you might think of it as a sensory "relay race." Sound waves are first funneled in by the outer ear, then transferred from tissue to bone in the middle ear. Mechanical vibrations become waves in the inner ear, and finally these waveforms trigger neural impulses to the brain. This series of steps ingeniously transforms commonplace vibrations and shifts in air pressure into experiences as exquisite and varied as music, doorbells, whispers, shouts—and psychology lectures. An understanding of this sequence is also essential to developing technology to aid those with hearing impairments, as reviewed in Focus on Application: A Bionic Hearing Aid.

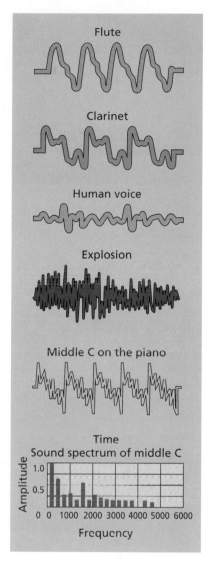

FIGURE 5.10 Waveforms of Familiar Sounds ■ Below the complex waveforms of five familiar sounds is the *sound spectrum* for middle C produced on the piano.

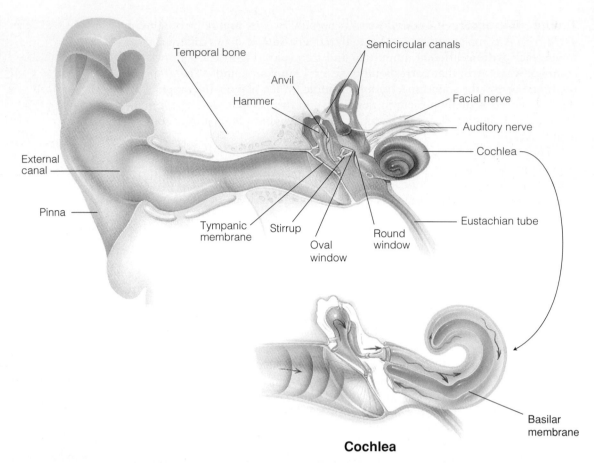

Cochlea

FIGURE 5.11   Structures of the Human Ear ■ Sound waves are channeled by the external ear (pinna) through the external canal, causing the tympanic membrane to vibrate. The vibration activates the tiny bones in the middle ear (hammer, anvil, and stirrup). These mechanical vibrations pass from the oval window to the cochlea, when they set internal fluid in motion. The fluid movement stimulates tiny hair cells along the basilar membrane, inside the cochlea, to transmit neural impulses from the ear to the brain along the auditory nerve.

Check Your Recall

Hearing is produced by sound waves that vary in frequency, amplitude, and complexity. Our sensations of sound vary in pitch, loudness, and timbre. Place theory and frequency theory have both been proposed to account for precise pitch perception.

Hearing is made possible when the ear and the brain convert physical vibrations into the experience of sound. Sound waves travel into the ear, transfer from tissues to bones in the middle ear, and finally are transformed into fluid waves in the inner ear. Vibrations stimulate tiny hair cells in the cochlea to generate nerve impulses, which then travel to the auditory cortex of the brain.

The Other Senses

Of all our senses, vision and hearing have been studied the most because they are the most important; however, our survival depends on many other senses as well. To conclude our discussion of sensation, we will briefly review (1) the

A Bionic Hearing Aid

In the summer of 1995, when he was 4 years old, Trenton Crabtree first heard the world clearly. Profoundly deaf since shortly after he was born, Trenton was finally able to hear his parents' voices with the aid of a *cochlear implant*. Most hearing aids are inserted like plugs into the outer ear and magnify sound vibrations as they enter the auditory canal. In contrast, Trenton's implant, called the Clarion, bypasses his outer and middle ears, and sends signals directly to the inner ear.

The device consists of four components: a tiny microphone and transmitter worn just above Trenton's outer ear; a speech processor that "hears" sounds and converts them into radio signals; a receiver and antenna implanted just inside the head above the ear; and a set of electrodes implanted in the cochlea. The ear implant works by collecting and processing sounds, transmitting these as signals to the implanted receiver, and further transmitting these signals via antenna to the inner-ear electrodes (Pimentel, 1995).

Trenton passed every test to show that his new implant worked once it was

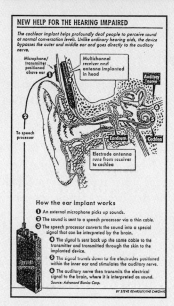

switched on. He was able to repeat sounds and words spoken by an instructor at the California Ear Institute at Stanford University. He showed interest in the sounds plunked out on a toy piano, and

tried to play it himself. His father predicted that Trenton would soon be listening avidly to the soundtrack of his favorite video, *The Lion King*.

The Clarion implant represents an improvement on other cochlear devices that have already been implanted in over 1000 American children. It may also represent new hope for the estimated 300,000 profoundly deaf people in the United States. But celebrations of technological improvements cannot settle debate about the wisdom and ethics of such treatments. For example, the National Association of the Deaf has condemned cochlear implant technology as "invasive and severe" (Pimentel, 1995). Not every hearing-impaired person is necessarily eager to experience the world in the same way as the hearing majority.

Whatever its significance to deaf culture, however, an implant such as the Clarion can make it possible for a child like Trenton to have and to make choices he would not otherwise have. "I'm excited about his future," his father said. "This will allow him to talk on the telephone, to hear music, to do things he would normally not do" (Pimentel, 1995, p. A19).

processes that enable us to sense position and movement, (2) smell, (3) taste, (4) the skin senses, and (5) pain.

Position and Movement

To act purposefully in our environment and literally keep on balance, we need constant information about where our limbs and other body parts are in relation to each other and to objects in the environment. Without this knowledge, even our simplest actions would be hopelessly uncoordinated. The **vestibular sense** *is the sense of bodily orientation with respect to gravity*. It tells us how our bodies—especially our heads—are postured, whether straight, leaning, reclining, or upside down. The vestibular sense also tells us when we are moving or how our motion is changing. The receptors for this information are tiny hairs in the inner ear, which are triggered when the pull of gravity on surrounding fluid signals information about body position and orientation.

The **kinesthetic sense** *is the sense of body position and the movement of body parts relative to each other*. Your kinesthetic sense, also called *kinesthesis*, keeps you aware of whether you are crossing your legs, for example, and of which hand is closer to the telephone when it rings. It provides constant sensory feedback about what the body is doing during motor activities, such as whether to continue reaching for your cup of coffee, or to stop before you knock it over. Without the kinesthetic sense, people could not coordinate most of the voluntary movements they make so effortlessly.

Receptors for kinesthetic information can be found in the joints and in the muscles and tendons. We most often take kinesthetic information for granted and make automatic adjustments in our movements. But we do not necessarily know our own limits! If you have ever injured yourself while exercising or physically working, you know that healthy action depends both on understanding how your body works and on paying attention to the signals it may be sending to you.

Smell

The sense of smell or **olfaction** involves a sequence of biochemical activities that trigger neural impulses. Odors, in the form of chemical molecules, interact with receptor proteins on the membrane of tiny hairs in the nose (Buck & Axel, 1991). Once initiated, these nerve impulses convey odor information to the **olfactory bulb,** *the brain site of olfactory processing,* located just below the frontal lobes of the cerebral cortex. The brain center that specializes in processing information about smell is the *rhinencephalon,* one of the primitive parts of the brain. Smell may be our most primitive sense, having evolved before other senses were differentiated. Smell signals go directly to the brain's smell center, rather than being relayed indirectly through the thalamus like other sensory information.

Smell presumably evolved as a system for detecting and locating food (Moncrieff, 1951). It is also used for detecting potential sources of danger. In addition, smell can be a powerful form of active communication. Members of some species (for example, insects such as ants and termites, and vertebrates such as dogs and cats) communicate with each other by secreting and detecting chemical signals called *pheromones.* **Pheromones** *are chemical substances used as communication within a given species to signal relevant stimuli,* such as others' sexual receptivity, danger, territorial boundaries, and food sources. Humans primarily seem to use the sense of smell in conjunction with taste to seek and sample food, but there is some evidence that humans may also secrete and sense sexual pheromones.

Taste

When you eat, the senses of taste and smell work together closely. When you have a cold, food seems tasteless because your nasal passages are blocked and you can't smell the food. The subtle distinctions you detect in flavors are really signaled by smell; your *sense of taste or* **gustation** is far less precise in its sensitivity. There are only four true, or primary, taste qualities: sweet, sour, bitter, and salty (saline).

The taste receptor cells are gathered in the **taste buds,** *receptors for taste that are located primarily on the upper side of the tongue.* Taste buds are clustered in very small mucous-membrane projections called *papillae,* which are distributed throughout the mouth cavity, particularly on the upper side of the tongue, as shown in Figure 5.12. Sensitivity to sweetness is greatest at the tip of the tongue; sensitivity to sourness is greatest on the sides; and sensitivity to bitterness is greatest at the back. Sensitivity to saltiness is particularly acute at the edges of the tongue. Individuals vary in their sensitivity to taste sensations, a function of the density of taste buds on the tongue (Bartoshuk et al., 1992). Those with more taste buds are "supertasters," more sensitive than regular tasters or extreme "nontasters" to bitter flavors—a survival advantage, since most poisons are bitter (Bartoshuk, 1993).

Taste is important to survival. Even when you are too young to know what's good for you, you know what you like and what you don't like. Taste sensitivity is exaggerated in infants and decreases with age. Many elderly people who complain that food has lost its taste really mean that they have lost

Taste is influenced by age and experience. Adults can appreciate flavors that young children dislike, and some cultures disdain foods that Americans consider delicious.

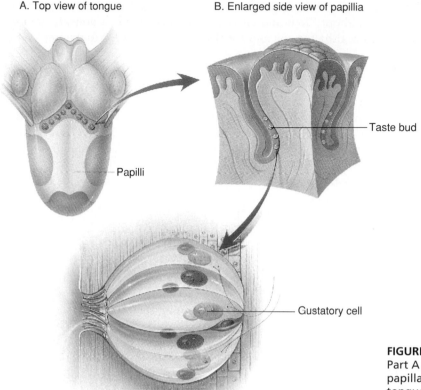

A. Top view of tongue

B. Enlarged side view of papillia

Taste bud

Papilli

Gustatory cell

C. Enlarged view of taste bud

FIGURE 5.12   Receptors for Taste ■
Part A shows the distribution of the papillae on the upper side of the tongue. Part B shows a single papilla enlarged so that the individual taste buds are visible. Part C shows one of the taste buds enlarged.

much of their sensory ability to detect differences in the taste and smell of food. Despite the fact that taste receptors can be damaged (by alcohol, smoke, acids, or hot foods), they are replaced every few days—even more frequently than the smell receptors. The taste system is the most resistant to damage of all your senses, and a total, permanent loss of taste is extremely rare (Bartoshuk, 1990).

The Skin Senses

The skin is a remarkably versatile organ. It protects us against surface injury, holds in body fluids, and helps regulate body temperature. The skin also contains nerve endings that, when they are stimulated by contact with external objects, produce *sensations of pressure, warmth, and cold. These sensations are the* **skin senses,** and we could not survive without them.

The skin's sensitivity to pressure varies tremendously over the body. For example, we are ten times more accurate in sensing the position of stimulation on our fingertips than the position of stimulation on our backs. Our sensitivity is greatest where we need it most—on our faces, tongues, and hands. Precise sensory feedback from these parts of the body permits effective eating, speaking, and grasping.

One aspect of skin sensitivity plays a central role in human relationships, emotions, and sexuality: *touch*. Through touch we communicate our desire to give or receive comfort, support, love, and passion (Fisher, 1992; Givens, 1983; Harlow, 1965; Henley, 1977; Masters & Johnson, 1966; Morris, 1967). Touch is the primary stimulus for sexual arousal in humans. It is also essential for healthy development (Field & Schanberg, 1990). In Chapter 2, we saw from Tiffany Field's research that massaging helps premature babies to survive and develop. Deprivation of touch stimulation has been shown to stunt the growth of rat babies and human children. The practical message is clear: touch those you care about often and encourage others to touch you—it not only feels good, it's healthy for you and for them (Lynch, 1979; Montague, 1986).

Pain

The final sense we will examine is the most puzzling of all—our sense of pain. Pain is the universal complaint of the human condition. About one-third of Americans are estimated to suffer from persistent or recurring pain (Wallis, 1984). Depression and even suicide can result from the seemingly endless nagging of chronic pain. **Pain** *is the body's response to stimulation from noxious stimuli*—those stimuli which are intense enough to cause tissue damage or threaten to do so.

The pain response is complex, involving a remarkable interplay between biochemistry, nerve impulses, and psychological and cultural factors. Pain is itself unpleasant, so it is more than a mere signal of danger; pain acts as a window into our experience of being hurt or damaged. "It is always more than a distressing sensation. It is useful to think of pain as a person's emotional experience of a distressing sensation; thus, morale and mood can be as important as the intensity of the feeling itself in determining the degree of pain" (Brody, 1986, p. 1).

Acute pain is sharp or sudden stimulation. It is studied experimentally in laboratories with paid volunteers who experience varying degrees of a precisely regulated stimulus, such as heat applied briefly to a small area of the skin. This procedure can test a subject's tolerance for pain and measure responses to it without causing any tissue damage. *Chronic pain* (prolonged or enduring sensation) is typically studied in hospital research clinics as part of treatment programs designed to find new ways to alleviate such pain.

Pain is affected by experience and circumstance. A person who is unhappy may find the pain of a headache unbearable, while another individual, in a more satisfactory job, considers a headache merely annoying.

Would it be nice never to experience pain? Actually, such a condition would be deadly. People born with congenital insensitivity to pain do not feel what is hurting them, but their bodies often become scarred and their limbs often become deformed from injuries that they could have avoided if their brains were able to warn them of danger. In fact, because of their failure to notice and respond to tissue-damaging stimuli, they tend to die young (Manfredi et al., 1981). Pain serves as an essential defense signal; it warns us of potential harm. It helps us to survive in hostile environments and to cope with sickness and injury.

Much research points to the conclusion that the pain one feels is affected by several social and psychological factors: (1) the meaning one attaches to the experience, (2) culturally learned habits, (3) social support and attention, and (4) learned gender roles (Weisenberg, 1977). Because of its psychological qualities, pain can be modified by treatments that use mental processes, such as hypnosis, deep relaxation, and thought-distraction procedures. The way you perceive your pain, how you communicate it to others, and even the way you respond to pain-relieving treatments may reveal more about your psychological state—about the kind of inferences you are making—than about the intensity of the pain stimulus. For example, what pain "means" to an individual can depend on one's goals, developmental stage, and past experience. Pain may be more likely to cause distress and depression among patients who interpret its causes and consequences pessimistically than among those who are more hopeful about its meaning (e.g., Turk, 1995). For example, a patient who believes that her pain signals a deteriorating or inoperable condition will experience more distress, and more extreme pain, than one who feel confident that the condition can be treated and the pain can be managed. As we will see in the following section on perceptual processes, what you perceive may be different from—even independent of—what you sense.

Check Your Recall

Besides vision and hearing, other senses are also important to human experience and survival. The vestibular sense processes information about bodily orientation. The kinesthetic sense provides continuous feedback about bodily movement and position. Smell (olfaction) may be the most primitive sense, processing chemical information directly to the brain and powerfully influencing behaviors involved in motivation and emotion. Taste (gustation) works with smell for subtler sensations, because receptors in the taste buds alone sense only the primary tastes of sweet, sour, bitter, and salty. The skin senses, concentrated in the most sensitive bodily regions, are responsible for sensitivity to touch, and are important to sexuality, health, and basic survival. The sense of pain is also essential for survival, warning of acute threats and chronic conditions that endanger one's well-being. Like all the senses, pain interacts with other information and experience, and is influenced by individual concerns and expectations.

Perception

So sensory signals have been transduced and transmitted to specific regions of your brain for further processing: now what? Once your sensory processes have enabled you to detect and collect information about your environment, you must employ perceptual processes to understand what that information *means* to you. The role of perception is to make *sense* of sensation—to create a personal understanding of the experienced physical world. Perception involves many different mental processes: synthesizing elements into combinations; judging sizes, distances, intensities, and proportions; distinguishing known from unknown features; remembering past experiences; comparing different stimuli; and associating perceived qualities with appropriate ways of responding to them. Every action of perception then becomes a series of very complex *computational* problems to be solved by the perceiving person's brain. Most of these problems are solved without one's awareness—a time-saving and life-saving legacy of evolution inherited from our early human ancestors.

The task of perception is to extract sensory input from the environment and organize it into stable, meaningful *percepts*. A **percept** *is what is perceived—the experienced outcome of the process of perception* (the psychological product of perceptual activity). Perception must discover what features of the world are *invariant* (fixed and unchanging) by sorting through an influx of varying information collected by a perceiver in motion. For example, as you move about the room, the sights in the environment create a rapidly changing, blurred sequence of images—yet you remain sure that it is you who are moving, while the objects around you remain stationary. Consider how challenging it is to sort through overwhelming or confusing sensations in search of clear, reliable information about the real world. We will first discuss how perception discerns what is real, and then we will consider the perceptual tasks of attention, organization, and identification.

Interpreting Reality

We can understand the process of perception best if we divide it into three stages: sensation, perception, and identification/recognition of objects. Keep in mind that these stages are not clearly separated—one flows into the next, and elements may even interact between stages, as we will soon discuss.

Sensation is the first stage in this continuum; physical energy is transduced into neural activity that codes information about the nature of the stimulation.

Perception refers to the next stage, in which an internal representation of an object is formed and a *percept* of the external stimulus is developed. The representation provides a working description of the perceiver's external environment. For example, a visual pattern made up of three straight lines could be recognized as the percepts 1–1, H, Δ, or III, depending on the context. Perception involves *synthesis* (integration and combination) of simple sensory features, such as colors, edges, and lines, into the percept of an object that can be recognized later.

The third stage, **identification and recognition,** *assigns meaning to the percepts.* Circular objects may "become" baseballs, coins, clocks, oranges, and moons. People may be identified as friend or foe, pretty or ugly, movie star or rock star. At this stage, the perceptual question ("What does the object look like?") changes to a question of identification ("What is this object?") and to a question of recognition ("What is the object's function?").

Perception and the combined processes of identification and recognition work so swiftly that they seem to act as one process in our everyday lives. However, they are conceptually different from one another. Throughout the rest of this chapter we will use perception in its narrow sense—that of going beyond sensory information to provide a meaningful awareness and knowledge of the world of objects, actors, and episodes. Thus, we will focus on the second and third steps in the overall perceptual process.

Stages of Perception

Imagine that you are the person in section A of Figure 5.13. You are seated in a furnished room; light reflected by objects in the room enters your eye, forming an image on your retina. In section B of Figure 5.13 you can see what would appear to your left eye as you sat in the room. How does this retinal image compare with the environment that produced it?

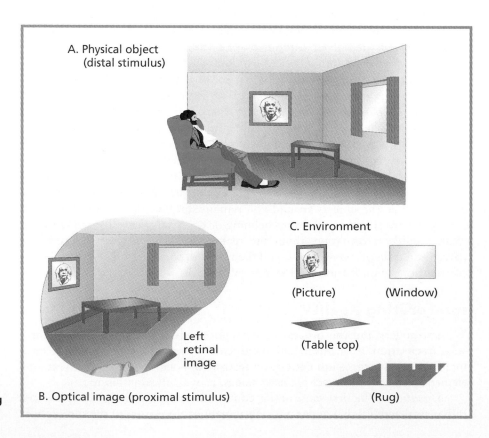

FIGURE 5.13   Interpreting Retinal Images. ■

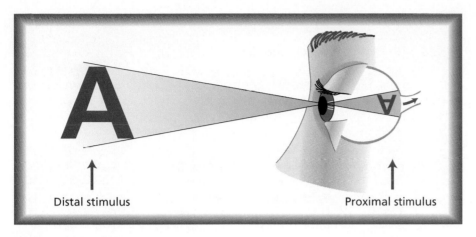

FIGURE 5.14   Distal and Proximal Stimuli ■ The distal stimulus is the external pattern or condition that one senses and perceives. The proximal stimulus is the pattern of sensory activity caused by the distal stimulus. As illustrated here, the proximal stimulus may resemble the distal stimulus, but they are separate events.

One important difference is that the retinal image is *two-dimensional,* whereas the environment it represents is *three-dimensional.* Compare the shapes of the physical objects out there in the world with the shapes of their corresponding retinal images. The shapes in Figure 5.13 that you "know" are really rectangular do not necessarily *appear* rectangular to your eyes. As you see in section C of Figure 5.13, only the window, viewed straight on, is perceived as an intact rectangle. The other shapes are distorted into trapezoids or are partially blocked by other objects. On reflection, it is amazing that you are able to see and recognize these shapes when their retinal images are so distorted and different from each other.

The differences between a physical object in the world and its optical image on your retina are so profound and important that psychologists distinguish between them as two different stimuli for perception. *The physical object in the world is called the* **distal stimulus** (distant from the observer) and *the optical image on the retina is called the* **proximal stimulus** (proximate or near to the observer), as shown in Figure 5.14. What you *perceive* corresponds to the *distal stimulus*—the "real" object in the environment. The stimulus that generated your sensory information is the *proximal stimulus*—the image on the retina. The major task of perception is to determine the distal stimulus based on information contained in the proximal stimulus—to ascertain what the world out there is "really like" using only the imagery inside one's mind.

There is more to perceiving a scene, however, than determining the *physical properties* of the distal stimulus. Besides accurately perceiving the shapes and colors of the objects, you *interpret* them in terms of your past experience with similar objects. You see objects as familiar and meaningful: a window, a picture, a table, and a rug. This process of identification and recognition is part of what you do automatically and almost constantly as you go about perceiving your environment.

To illustrate the distinction among the three stages in perceiving, let's examine one of the objects in the scene from Figure 5.13: the picture hanging on the wall. In the *sensory stage,* this picture corresponds to a two-dimensional trapezoid in your retinal image. In the *perceptual stage,* you see this trapezoid as a rectangle turned away from you in three-dimensional space. In the *recognition stage,* you recognize this rectangular object as a *picture.*

Figure 5.15 depicts a flow chart of this sequence of events. The processes that take information from one stage to the next are shown as arrows between

FIGURE 5.15 Stages of Sensory and Perceptual Processing ■ In bottom-up processing, perception depends on the data originally provided in environmental stimulation. In top-down processing, perception is affected by an individual's knowledge, motivation, and expectations.

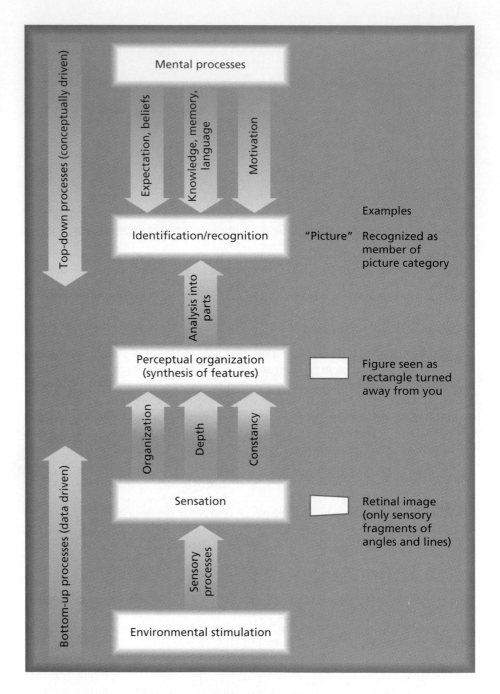

the boxes. *Taking sensory data into the system through receptors and sending it upward for extraction and analysis of relevant information is called* **bottom-up processing**. This "outside → in" process is also known as *stimulus-driven* or *data-driven* because perceptual processes are powered or "driven" only as input is fed into the system.

At the same time, however, the opposite process is also occurring: **top-down processing** *involves a perceiver's past experience, knowledge, expectations, memory, motivations, cultural background, and language in the interpretation of the object of perception.* This "insider only" process is also known as *conceptually driven* processing, because the system is fed by concepts and other products of the perceiver's own thinking. The two types of processes—bottom-up and top-down—usually interact to enable us to perceive our environment in meaningful, action-oriented ways.

Ambiguity and Distortion

A primary goal of perception is to get an accurate "fix" on the world—to recognize predators, prey, possible danger, and pleasure, and to behave appropriately. Survival depends on accurately perceiving the environment, but the environment is not always easy to "read." Take a look at the photo of black and white splotches in Figure 5.16. What is it? Try to extract the stimulus figure from the background: a Dalmatian sniffing at the ground. The dog is hard to find because it blends with the background.

When your senses deceive you into experiencing a stimulus pattern in a manner that is demonstrably incorrect, you are experiencing an **illusion.** Typically, illusions become more common when the stimulus is *ambiguous,* information is missing, elements are combined in unusual ways, or familiar patterns are not apparent. Research on perceptual illusions is used to illuminate some fundamental properties of ordinary perception.

Learning the Lessons of Illusions   Psychologists who study perception have often appreciated ambiguities and the illusions they generate. Since the first scientific analysis of illusions was published by **J. J. Oppel** in 1854, thousands of articles have been written about illusions in nature, sensation, perception, and art. Oppel called his work the study of *geometrical optical illusions.* Illusions point out the discrepancy between percept and reality, and can help us understand some fundamental properties of perception (Cohen & Girgus, 1978).

First examine an illusion that works at the level of sensation: the black-and-white *Hermann grid* (Figure 5.17). As you stare at the center of the grid, dark, fuzzy spots appear at the intersections of the white bars. Focus closely on one intersection: the spot vanishes. As you shift focus, the spots you focus on disappear, while new spots appear at the other intersections. How do you do that? The answer lies in the way receptor cells in your eyes interact with each other. The firing of certain ganglion cells in the retina prevents or *inhibits* the

FIGURE 5.16   An Ambiguous Picture ■ What is depicted here? How do you know?

FIGURE 5.17   The Hermann Grid ■ The Hermann grid is an example of an illusion that occurs at the sensory level (at the level of receptor cells).

firing of adjacent cells. Because of this inhibiting process, you see dark spots—the *nonwhite* areas—at white intersections just outside your focus. Even though you know the squares in the Hermann grid are black and the lines are white, this knowledge cannot overcome the illusion, which operates at the more basic, sensory level. Illusions at the sensory level generally occur because a pattern stimulates receptor processes in an unusual way that generates a distorted image.

To study illusions at the level of *perception*, psychologists rely on ambiguous figures—stimulus patterns that can be seen in two or more distinct ways. Ambiguity is an important concept in understanding perception because it shows that a *single image* at the level of sensation can result in *multiple interpretations* at the perceptual and identification levels.

In Figure 5.18, A, B, and C all show examples of ambiguous figures. In A and B, the illusions affect your *interpretation*. Each figure is accompanied by two unambiguous but conflicting interpretations. Look at each image until you can see its two interpretations. Once you have seen both interpretations, your perception will flip back and forth between them as you look at the ambiguous figure. This perceptual instability of ambiguous figures is one of the most important characteristics of such figures. The vase/faces and the Necker cube are examples of ambiguity in the perception stage. The alternatives are different physical arrangements of objects in three-dimensional space, both resulting from the same stimulus image. Your perceptual system cannot recognize both alternatives simultaneously, so it has focused on certain features to decide how to synthesize the elements.

The duck/rabbit figure in C is an example of ambiguity in the *recognition* stage. You perceive the figure as one physical shape but ambiguity arises when you try to determine what it represents and how to classify the figure with the mixed information available. Transforming ambiguity and uncertainty about the environment into a clear interpretation is a fundamental property of normal human perception.

Perceptual illusions make us aware of two considerations: the active role the mind plays in structuring our view of the world, and the effects of *context* on the way we perceive stimuli within it. Examine the classic illusions in the third figure. These illusions occur because the central nervous system does not simply record events. Instead, your brain utilizes complex processes for detecting, integrating, and interpreting information about the world in terms of what we already know and expect. Thus, what we "see" goes beyond present physical stimulus properties. These processes usually occur effortlessly and they help us decode the world around us, but this does not mean that they are simple or error-free. When cues or context mislead us, for example, we may easily "fall for" even a familiar illusion.

Applying the Lessons of Illusions   Several prominent modern artists fascinated with the visual experiences created by ambiguity have used perceptual illusion as a central artistic device in their work. Consider the three examples of art shown here. *Gestalt Bleue* by Victor Vasarely produces depth reversals like those in the Necker cube, with corners that alternately project and recede. In *Sky and Water* by M. C. Escher, you can see birds and fishes only through the process of figure-ground reversal, as in the vase/faces illusion. Finally, surrealist Salvador Dali's *Slave Market with the Disappearing Bust of Voltaire* reveals a more complex ambiguity in which the viewer must reorganize a whole section of the scene in order to perceive the "hidden" bust of the French philosopher and writer Voltaire. Although it might be difficult at first for some to "find" the picture-in-the-picture, once you have seen Voltaire you will find him obvious every time you look. This discovery underscores the determina-

FIGURE 5.18   Perceptual Illusions
■ A and B are illusions of perceptual interpretation. C is an illusion of recognition.

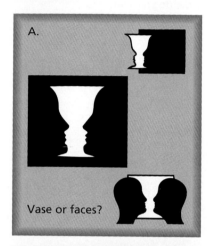

A.

Vase or faces?

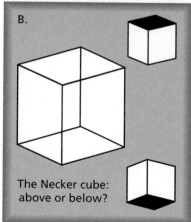

B.

The Necker cube: above or below?

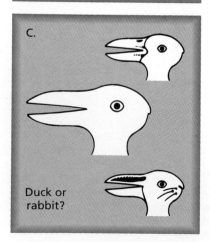

C.

Duck or rabbit?

tion of human perception to make sense of the world and to stick with the best interpretation we can make.

Illusions are an inescapable aspect of the subjective reality we each construct with our personal experiences, learning, and motivation. People can even control illusions to achieve desired effects. Architects and interior designers use principles of perception to make spaces seem larger or smaller than they really are. A small apartment appears more spacious when it is painted in light colors and sparsely furnished. Set and lighting designers in movies and theatrical productions purposely create illusions on film and on stage. Many of us make everyday use of illusion in our choices of cosmetics and clothing (Dackman, 1986). Light-colored clothing and horizontal stripes can make our bodies seem larger, while dark-colored clothing and vertical stripes can make our bodies seem slimmer. In continually trying to resolve the discrepancy between the distal (real) stimulus and the proximal (sensed) stimulus, we establish personal perceptions that guide our decisions and behavior—for better or for worse.

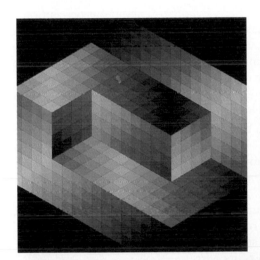

Three paintings using perceptual illusion as the central artistic device: Victor Vasarely's *Gestalt Bleue* (top left); M. C. Escher's *Sky and Water* (top right); and Salvador Dali's *Slave Market with the Disappearing Bust of Voltaire* (bottom).

Although one of these photos clearly has been altered, they look similar when viewed this way. However, turn the book upside down and look again.

Explaining Perception

How does perception "work"? This question has long fascinated psychologists and philosophers, who have generated many theories to explain the key functions and operating principles of perception. Let's examine two prominent explanations: *experience-based inference* and *Gestalt principles* of perception.

Inferring from Experience   For almost a century the dominant model among perception theorists was the approach established by **Hermann von Helmholtz.** In 1866 Helmholtz argued for the importance of *experience* in perception. According to his theory, an observer uses prior knowledge of the environment to make sense of the proximal stimulus. Based on this experience, the observer makes inferences—reasonable guesses or hunches—about what these sensations mean. Ordinarily these inferences are fairly accurate, but as we have seen, confusing sensations and ambiguous arrangements can create perceptual illusions and erroneous conclusions. Helmholtz's theory proposes that we learn how to interpret sensations on the basis of our experience with the world; our interpretations are, in effect, *hypotheses* about our perceptions. For example, a baby learns that faces always possess certain features in fixed arrangements (pair of eyes above nose, mouth below nose), and that the right-side-up arrangement is better for communicating. We learn to see faces in their usual orientation to such an extent that we fail to "see" facial patterns that violate our expectations. For example, when you scan the two upside-down portraits of Russian leader Boris Yeltsin, do you detect any important differences between them?

The Gestalt Approach   Founded in Germany in the 1920s, **Gestalt psychology** *maintained that psychological phenomena could be understood only when viewed as organized, structured wholes,* and not when broken down into primitive perceptual elements (by introspective analysis). The German word *Gestalt* (pronounced *gush-TAWLT*) roughly means *form, whole,* or *configuration.* It challenged the views of the structuralists and behaviorists by arguing that the whole is more than the sum of its parts.

For example, a particular melody is perceived as a whole tune even though it is composed of separate notes. Gestalt psychologists argued further that we perceive the world of objects as whole units because our brain is organized to function that way—to coordinate incoming stimuli into meaningful arrays. That is, when you hear a familiar song, you do not remember the exact duration and pitch of each of its hundreds of notes; rather, you perceive the *melody,* which is your perception of the entire pattern of notes. The connected pattern has a meaning that the individual notes by themselves do not provide. We organize sensory information according to meaningfulness because this method is the simplest, most economical way to package sensory input within our nervous systems. In a later section, we will see Gestalt theory in action as we examine the organizational powers of perception.

Perceptual processes reveal the influence of both nature and nurture. For example, Gestalt theory emphasizes that the brain is predisposed—possibly even *designed*—to influence perception in specific ways. But we can also say with confidence that perception is influenced by experience and learning. Helmholtz's theory of experience-based inference is one example of how "nurture" shapes perception. Further, as reviewed in Cultural Context: Influence on Perception, one's culture also powerfully influences how she or he sees the world.

CULTURAL CONTEXT

Cultural Influences on Perception

Cross-cultural psychologists have argued that, since people in various cultures have very different everyday experiences, there should be differences in people's perception of some objects and events. Strong arguments support a theoretical relationship between culture and perception (Segall, et al., 1966). People's responses to visual illusions have played an important part in many cross-cultural investigations (Deregowski, 1980).

Consider the following two figures, both versions of the Ponzo illusion:

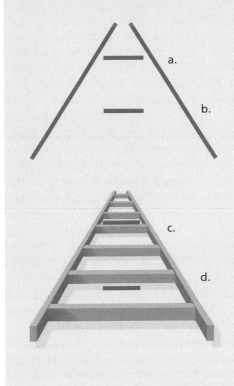

The question for respondents looking at the top figure is: "Which line is longer, the one on top (marked 'a') or the one on the bottom (marked 'b')?" The same question is asked about the bottom figure, where the top line is marked "c" and the bottom line is marked "d."

In actuality, all four lines are the same length. Many readers of this book, however, will report that the top lines are longer than the bottom lines. People make a perspective correction about the size of objects by considering cues for apparent distance when making these judgments. In their everyday experiences, most readers of this book have learned that objects far away from themselves look smaller than they actually are. How have we learned to perceive the world this way?

People use a variety of cues in making judgments about objects that are far away. One cue is converging lines. When you look down a long corridor, the hallway seems to converge in the distance. Yet you have learned from your everyday experience that the walls of a hallway do not actually converge or meet each other. The fact that hallways seem to converge is a cue to distance.

Another opportunity to see objects "converge" in the distance occurs when people look down a long, flat highway or peer down railroad tracks (as pictured in the figure on the bottom). In the Ponzo illusion illustrated, the top line is judged to be longer because its higher position implies it is farther away along the converging edges or tracks. Intellectually, you know that far off objects are bigger than they appear. Consequently, you apply this knowledge to judgments about the figures; however, in this instance, such a judgment is incorrect.

The world you have grown up in probably includes many structures with parallel lines, roadsides, edges, and borders, so your experience leaves you vulnerable to the Ponzo illusion. But what about people from cultures where individuals have had far less experience with this distance cue? Will they be as susceptible to the Ponzo illusion? The answer is "no." Research has been carried out on the Pacific island of Guam, where there are no railroad tracks (Brislin, 1974; 1993). The roads there are winding, and so there are few opportunities to see roadsides "converge" in the distance. There are several long runways for jet airplanes, but safety considerations prevent most people from standing at one end and looking into the distance. There are buildings with corridors, but these are fewer than in most medium-sized cities, given the high costs of air conditioning for buildings large enough to have long hallways. People who have spent their entire lives on Guam, then, have fewer opportunities to learn the strong perceptual cue that converging lines indicate distance.

As researchers predicted, adult respondents on Guam were less susceptible to the Ponzo illusion than were respondents from the mainland United States. Respondents from Guam were less likely to report that the top lines in the figures were longer. In addition, children 12 years of age and younger were less susceptible to the illusion in both Guam and the mainland United States. These data support the argument that people's experiences affect their perception. Children have had less time than adults to learn strong perceptual cues such as converging lines. Consequently, they will be less likely to use this cue when presented with stimuli that illustrate the Ponzo illusion.

Attentional Processes

When your teacher encourages you to pay *attention*, exactly what does this mean? You are aware that *attention* is something you can control voluntarily—that you can *choose* to pay attention, or not. **Attention** *is a complex process, combining a state of focused awareness with a readiness to respond.* Attention influences both the stimuli an individual processes and the responses one is likely to make.

You have probably discovered that sometimes, even when you try, you *cannot* pay attention; you have become distracted. **Distraction** *occurs when interfering demands prevent perception from being focused on relevant stimuli.* Attention appears to be critical for effective perception and thought, yet it is a vulnerable process.

Some researchers now believe that we have several kinds of attention, each with its own mechanisms and functions (Posner, 1990). New approaches to attention may lead to different conclusions about how it works. We'll briefly review what research has already suggested about attentional processes, and consider what this reveals about the nature of perception.

Preattentive Processing Even though conscious memory and recognition of objects require attention, complex processing of information does go on without our awareness and without attention. For example, even if you are attentive in reading this passage and ignoring background stimuli, you are still able to notice certain qualities and changes in those background stimuli. If a radio were playing in the background and your favorite song came on, you would easily recognize that "ignored" experience, even before deciding to pay attention to it. *This earlier stage of processing is called* **preattentive processing** *because it operates on sensory inputs before we attend to them,* as they first come into the brain from the sensory receptors.

Attention is important for integrating features into composites that we recognize as whole units (based on experiments by Beck, 1982; Julesz, 1982; and Treisman, 1988, 1990, 1992). When asked to locate boundaries between regions of a scene, subjects report that the boundaries "pop out" when they are defined by a difference in a single simple feature, such as color, curved versus straight line shape, or orientation of lines (vertical versus horizontal), as shown in panel A of Figure 5.19. The boundaries of red and blue and of V's and O's in panel B are distinct. In contrast, the boundaries between red V's or blue O's and red O's or blue V's in panel C must be sought out with more mental effort. While boundaries based on a single feature emerge *preattentively,* boundaries defined by a combination of features do not, since combining features requires attention.

The Functions of Attention Psychologists have proposed several important functions for attention within the complex interrelated processes of perceiving, responding, and consciously remembering sensory and perceptual information. Research has identified three possible functions of attention: (1) as a *sensory filter;* (2) as *response selection;* and (3) as a *gateway to consciousness.*

Attention as Sensory Filter Attention may act as a sensory filter by selecting some part of sensory input for further processing. British psychologist **Donald Broadbent** introduced the modern version of this view in his 1958 book, *Perception and Communication.* Broadbent was the first to compare the mind to a *communications channel* similar to a telephone line or computer link that actively processes and transmits information. The amount of information the channel can handle accurately at any one time is severely limited. Therefore, people must focus on one source of information at a time.

Imagine listening to a lecture while people on both sides of you are engaged in conversations. What do you hear, understand, and remember? You will probably be able to stay tuned to the lecturer if the material is interesting or important. But if the lecture is boring and irrelevant to your goals, and if either of the conversations is particularly intriguing, you'll most likely tune out the lecture and tune in to the alternative stimuli. You cannot listen carefully to all three sources of input simultaneously, or even to two of them at once. You

FIGURE 5.19 Locating Boundaries ■ How readily can you distinguish between regions of different stimuli?

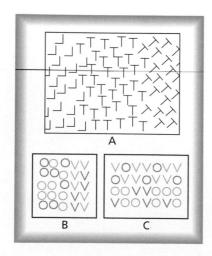

must *selectively attend* to only one at a time if you are to fully understand and remember anything.

Broadbent conceived of attention as a *selective filter* that deals with the overwhelming flow of incoming sensory information by blocking out the unwanted sensory input and passing on specific desired input. Since the mind has a *limited capacity* for carrying out complete processing, attention filters out some information and allows other information to continue. The filter theory of attention asserts that the selection occurs early in the process, before the input's meaning is processed.

Selection theory was challenged by research that showed how some subjects perceived things they would have been unable to have noticed if attention totally filtered out all ignored material. For example, subjects sometimes noticed their own names or other personally relevant information in the message they had been ignoring (Cherry, 1953). Personal interest or special meaning can apparently "pull" attention over to the nonattended channel. These findings forced researchers to conclude that attention is more flexible than filter theory postulated. **Anne Treisman** subsequently proposed that ignored information may get some partial higher-level, meaningful analysis, although this analysis may not reach consciousness (Treisman, 1964, 1990; Norman, 1968). Attention is still necessary to guarantee that sensory fragments will be meaningfully organized. This modified view of feature selection is now more widely accepted.

Attention as Response Selection Another function of attention is to select responses. Look at Figure 5.20. As the caption instructs, try to read the red letters in each column while disregarding the overlapping green letters. Is one column harder to read than the other? Why should there be a difference?

In the first column, there is no relationship between the green letters and the red letters. But in the second list, starting with the second letter, each red letter is the same as the green letter *above* it—the one you just *ignored*. Several experiments show that subjects take longer to read the second list because the ignored letters are first processed and then suppressed. The second encounter with each such letter requires the reader to "undo" the suppression, and this slows one's reading of the list overall (Tipper & Driver, 1988; Driver & Tipper, 1989). Of course, you were not conscious of processing, suppressing, and then "unsuppressing" your attention to the letters in the second list. Just because something did not enter consciousness does not mean it was not processed completely. The *late selection* view hypothesizes that all sensory inputs may be processed completely without attention (Deutsch & Deutsch, 1963; Driver & Tipper, 1989). According to this view, attention is limited not in handling input but in producing output or responses. That is, limited attention results not in processing less *incoming* information but in producing fewer *outgoing* responses. Put simply, you can only parcel out so much attention in responding to stimuli. When you are overloaded with alternative responses, you become "selective" about which ones you might make. Such *late selection* occurs particularly when the stimuli are few and familiar and have been processed many times before in the past (Posner, 1988).

Attention as Gateway to Consciousness Finally, a third function of attention may be to control what is allowed into consciousness. When we select something to attend to, either because of its striking characteristics or its relevance to a goal, we inevitably ignore many other possibilities. Attention is the bridge that carries pieces of the external world—the pieces selectively focused on—to the subjective world of consciousness (Carver & Scheier, 1981; Posner, 1982, 1988).

FIGURE 5.20 Test Your Attentional Mechanisms ■ First read aloud the red letters in column one as quickly as you can. Next, quickly read the red letters in column two, also disregarding the green letters. Which task took longer? See the text for the explanation.

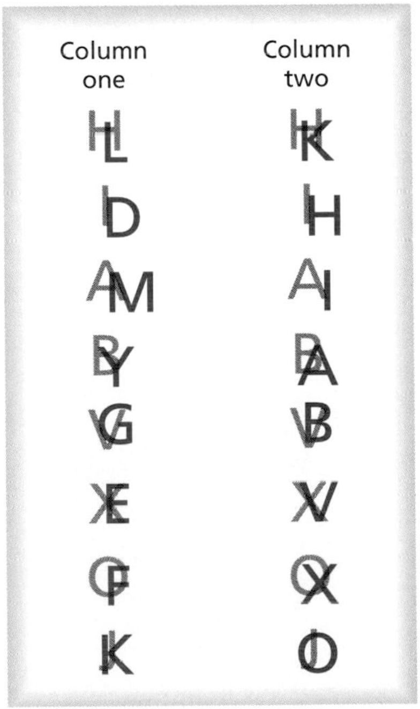

As you pay attention to these words, you lose the meaning of background voices and other stimuli in your surroundings—until you momentarily refocus your attention on them to make sure you are not missing anything important. Information that does not reach consciousness can be stored—and may influence later behavior—but people have difficulty explicitly remembering such material (Jacoby et al., 1989; Richardson-Klavehn & Bjork, 1988; Schacter, 1989). Only conscious processing allows new ideas to be developed about the "attended to" material (Baddeley, 1986; Mullin & Egeth, 1989; Nissen & Bullemer, 1987). For example, in Chapter 3 we suggested the example of being distracted momentarily by a latecomer to your psychology lecture. While you notice and adapt to the presence of the latecomer, you "lose" input from the lecture that is already in progress. However, at the beginning of a lecture class, many people are arriving noisily and taking seats in the classroom. At such a time, it is unlikely that you will notice or pay attention to a specific individual's movements; this person is more *salient* (attention-getting) and memorable—and consciously distracting—when she is the only person taking a seat. The power of your attention and the accuracy of your memory are thus influenced by the context of your surroundings.

Organizational Processes

Imagine how confusing the world would be if we could not put together and organize the information available from the output of our millions of retinal receptors. **Perceptual organization** *puts sensory information together to give us the perception of coherence.* For example, your percept of the two-dimensional geometric design in section A of Figure 5.21 is probably three diagonal *rows* of figures: one of squares, one of arrowheads, and one of diamonds. This perception may not seem remarkable to you, but consider all the organizational processing that you must perform to see the design in this way. Many of the organizational processes we will discuss in this section were first described by Gestalt theorists who argued that perception depends on laws of organization, or simple rules by which we perceive shapes and forms.

Region Segregation   Now consider your initial *sensory* response to section A of Figure 5.21. Your retina is composed of many separate receptors; your eye responds to this stimulus pattern with a mosaic of millions of neural responses coding the light falling on your retina. (This mosaic pattern is represented in section B of Figure 5.21). The first task of perceptual organization is to segregate the pattern into meaningful regions. The primary information for this region segregation process comes from color and texture. An abrupt change in color or texture signifies a boundary between two regions. Finding these boundaries is the first step in organizational processing. Notice that a sort of "sensory decision" must be made about where to draw boundary lines, as in sketching a topographical map of hills, valleys, and plateaus. The lines drawn by a map-maker—or by one's perceptual system—will be somewhat smoother and simpler than the fuzzy, bumpy terrain of reality. In the very early stages of perception, therefore, regions of stimulus patterns are segregated according to their features, adding to the information that assists later perceptual processing.

Figure and Ground   As a result of region segregation, the stimulus in section A of Figure 5.21 has already been divided into ten regions: nine small dark ones and a single large light one. Another organizational process now divides the regions into figures and background. A **figure** *is an object-like region in the forefront,* and **ground** *is the backdrop against which the figures stand out.*

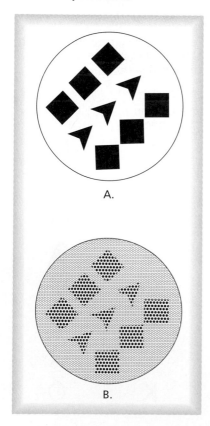

FIGURE 5.21   Percept of a Two-Dimensional Design ■ What is your percept of the geometric design in A? Figure B represents the mosaic pattern that stimulus A creates on your retina.

A.

B.

In section A of Figure 5.22, you probably see the dark regions (squares, arrowheads, and diamonds) as figures, and the light region as ground. (You could also reverse this interpretation, like the vase/faces illusion, by imagining the circle as a sheet of white paper with dark cutouts.) When you perceive a region as a figure, boundaries between light and dark are interpreted as edges or contours belonging to the figure, and the ground seems to extend and continue behind these edges.

The tendency to perceive a figure as being in *front* of a ground is very strong. In fact, you can even get this effect from a stimulus when the perceived figure doesn't actually exist! In Figure 5.22, section A, you probably perceive a fir tree shape against a ground of red circles on a white surface. But of course there is no fir tree shape; the figure consists only of three solid red shapes and a black-line base. You see the illusory white triangle in front because the wedge-cuts in the red circles seem to be the corners of a solid white triangle. To see an illusory six-pointed star, look at Figure 5.22, section B. Here, the nonexistent "top" triangle appears to blot out parts of red circles and a black-lined triangle, when in fact none of these is depicted as such complete figures.

Contours and Closure In Figures 5.22 A and B, there seem to be three levels of organization: the pure white triangle—superimposed on red circles and black lines—*and* a larger white surface behind everything else. Perceptually you have divided the white area into two regions: the illusory triangle and the background. Where this division occurs you perceive **subjective contours:** *boundaries that exist not in the distal stimulus, but only in your subjective experience.*

Your perception of the white triangles demonstrates a powerful organizing process known as closure. **Closure** *makes you see incomplete figures as complete and supplies the missing edges beyond gaps and barriers.* Humans have a natural tendency to perceive stimuli as complete and balanced even when pieces are missing. Besides subjective contours and closure, other perceptual tendencies appear to influence the way humans experience the world, as we explore in the next section.

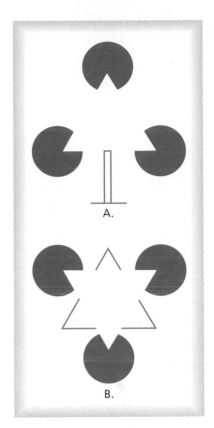

FIGURE 5.22 Subjective Contours ■
A. A subjective fir tree.
B. A subjective 6-pointed star.

Principles of Perceptual Grouping In Figure 5.23 on page 190, an array of 36 tiny circles in six rows and six columns (section A) is presented in six variations (sections). Section B seems to be made up of horizontal rows, while C looks more like vertical columns. In section D, the color varies to show alternating rows of light and dark, while in E the size of the circles is varied to show columns of large and small circles. In section F the circles become tiny quadrangles, oriented so you "read" them either across or down. Finally in section G, some columns of circles seem as though they could be moving (underlined with tiny "wobble" lines), while the alternate columns seem stationary.

How does your visual system accomplish this **perceptual grouping,** *the perception that sets of stimuli belong together?* The perception of stimuli as "grouped" was first studied extensively by Gestalt psychologist **Max Wertheimer** (1923). Wertheimer presented subjects with arrays of simple geometric figures. By varying a single factor and observing how it affected the way people perceived the structure of the array, he was able to formulate a set of laws of grouping. Figure 5.23 illustrates several of these laws.

For example, in sections B and C, the circles are spaced somewhat closer to each other, vertically and horizontally, so that the closer circles seem to "belong" together. These groupings illustrate Wertheimer's *law of proximity:* All else being equal, the nearest (most proximal) elements are grouped together.

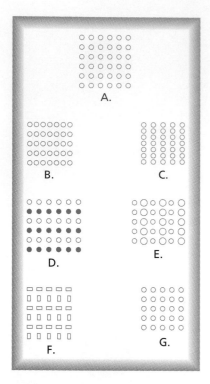

FIGURE 5.23 Grouping Phenomena ■ Arrangements B through G are all modifications of the basic figure in A. We perceive B through G as being organized in different ways, according to different Gestalt principles of grouping.

Once you learn in-line skating, you don't need to think about how to do it. This routinizing of a task makes your supply of mental energy go further when you must attend to other events and stimuli—like staying alert to people, vehicles, and signals while negotiating city streets on tiny wheels.

The rows in section D are either dark or light; the columns in E are either large or small circles. The shapes in section F are all tiny oblongs, but some belong in horizontal rows and others in vertical columns. Our tendency to perceive things as belonging together because they share common features reflects the *law of similarity.*

When elements in the visual field are moving, similarity of motion also produces a powerful grouping. The *law of common fate* states that, all else being equal, elements moving in the same direction and at the same rate are grouped together. If the dots in alternate columns of section G were moving upward, as indicated by the blurring, you would group the image into columns because of their similarity in motion. You get this effect at a ballet when several dancers move in a pattern different from the others.

The Gestalt grouping laws operate only when two or more elements are simultaneously present in a visual field. According to the Gestaltists, the whole stimulus pattern somehow determines the organization of its own parts; in other words, the whole percept is different from the mere collection of its parts. Gestalt psychologists believe that all of these grouping laws are particular examples of a single general principle—the **law of Prägnanz** (*"meaningfulness"), which argues that the simplest organization requiring the least cognitive effort will always emerge.* The most general Gestalt principle, Prägnanz (pronounced *PRAYG-nonce*) proposes that we perceive the simplest organization that fits the stimulus pattern. Thus Prägnanz has also been called the *minimum principle of perception.*

Identification and Recognition

The perceptual processes described so far provide reasonably accurate knowledge about physical properties of the distal stimulus—the position, size, shape, texture, and color of three-dimensional things in a three-dimensional world. With just this knowledge and some basic motor skills, you would be able to walk around without bumping into objects, manipulate objects that are small and light enough to move, and make accurate models of the objects that you perceive. However, you would not know what these objects were and whether you had seen them before. Your experience would resemble a visit to an alien planet where all the objects were new to you; you would not know what to eat, what to put on your head, what to run away from, or what to approach.

To get information about the objects you perceive, you must be able to identify or recognize them as something you have seen before and as members of the meaningful categories that you know from experience. Identification and recognition attach meaning to percepts.

Bottom-Up Versus Top-Down Processing Identifying objects implies matching what you see against your stored knowledge. Recall from our earlier discussion that the processes of bringing in and organizing information from the environment are called data-driven or *bottom-up processes,* because they are guided by sensory information—the raw data of direct experience. For example, if you see something up in a tree as you walk by, but cannot make out what it is, your inspection of the tree is a data-driven effort, determined by the information you collect. Sensations of visual features and perceptions of organized objects are largely the result of such bottom-up processes.

In contrast, processes that originate in the brain and influence the selection, organization, or interpretation of sensory data are called conceptually driven (or hypothesis-driven) or *top-down processes.* For example, your experience teaches you that the mysterious object in the tree is more likely to be a bird or squirrel than a doll or catcher's mitt. Abstract thoughts, prior knowledge, beliefs, values, and other mental processes control the way incoming stimulation is managed and even what qualifies as relevant (review Figure 5.15 on page 180). When you first perceive a new, somewhat abstract stimulus, you may not be able to make sense of it; once given its title, label, or explanation, however, its meaning seems to "snap" into place and you never again have difficulty "seeing" or remembering it.

Identification and recognition give our experiences continuity over time and across situations. The third stage of perception is a process in which memory, analysis, expectation, motivation, personality, and social experience all interact to help us understand what is being perceived. This stage adds *conception* (mental activity) to perception, and *meaning* to facts.

Contexts and Expectations   Have you ever had the experience of seeing people you knew in places where you didn't expect to see them, such as in a different city or an unusual social group? It takes much longer to recognize them in such situations, and sometimes you aren't even sure that you really know them. The problem is not that they look different but that the context is unfamiliar: you didn't expect them to be there. Once you have identified the *context,* you form *expectations* about what objects you are likely and unlikely to see nearby (Biederman, 1989).

Quickly scan this photo. Then look away and describe as much as you recall. Turn to the next page to learn what you, or other perceivers, might not have seen.

Did you see a woman committing suicide in the photo, entitled "The Moment Before Death," on the previous page? Most people have difficulty identifying the falling woman in the center of the photo because they have no perceptual schema for seeing a person positioned horizontally in midair.

Perceptual identification depends on your expectations as well as on objects' physical properties. Object identification is a constructive, interpretive process. Depending on what you already know, where you are, what else you see around you, and your expectations from context, the identification you make will vary. Read the following:

It says *THE CAT*, right? Now look again at the middle letter of each word. Physically, these two letters are exactly the same, yet you perceived the first as an *H* and the second as an *A*. Why? Clearly, your perception was affected by what you know about words in English. The context provided by *T__E* makes an *H* highly likely and an A unlikely, whereas the reverse is true of the context of *C__T* (Selfridge, 1955). Context can fool you into misperceiving some stimuli, as in this demonstration. But context is an enormously useful cue to deciphering difficult stimuli, such as hard-to-read handwriting. If you receive a scenic postcard from a friend whose scrawled note describes "having a wonderful time on v____," you rely on context cues to guess that the V-word is probably "vacation," and probably *not* a series of alternatives such as "vacuum," "viaduct," or "Venus"!

Perceptual Set   Another aspect of the influence of context and expectation on your perception (and response) is set. In general, **set** *is a temporary readiness to perceive or to react to a stimulus in a particular way;* and **perceptual set** *is a readiness to detect a particular stimulus in a given context.* For example, a new mother is perceptually set to hear the cries of her child. Often, a perceptual set leads you to see an ambiguous stimulus as the one you are expecting.

Read quickly through the series of words that follow in row 1. Then do the same with row 2. Do the words in row 1 lead you to read D?CK differently than at the end of row 2?

1. FOX; OWL; SNAKE; TURKEY; SWAN; D?CK
2. BOB; RAY; DAVE; BILL; TOM; D?CK

Perceptual set is created by the *meanings* of the words read prior to the ambiguous stimulus. Words that refer to animals create a perceptual set that influences you to read D?CK as "DUCK." Names create a perceptual set leading you to see D?CK as DICK.

Labels are another context that can create a perceptual set for an ambiguous figure. Look carefully at the picture of the woman in Figure 5.24; have a friend examine Figure 5.25 on page 194. Next, together look at Figure 5.26 on the page 194. Each of you will probably *see* something different, though you are *looking at* the same stimulus pattern. Prior exposure to the picture with a specific label will normally affect perception of the ambiguous figure.

People develop different views of the same target after prior conditions create different sets. Sets can also influence social attitudes and bias how we interpret some part of our world.

Constructive Perception   The top-down effects of contexts, expectations, and set all highlight the same important fact: perceptual experience in response to a stimulus event is a response of the whole person. In addition to the information provided when your sensory receptors are stimulated, your final perception depends on who you are, whom you are with, and what you expect, want, and value.

The interaction of top-down and bottom-up processes also means that perception is an act of *constructing reality* to fit one's assumptions about how reality probably is or should be. If perceiving were a completely *data-driven* process, everyone would be bound to the same concrete reality of the here-and-now. We would register experience but not learn or profit from it. For example, without the lessons of experience to help you interpret the world, you could not make assumptions about new perceptions.

But if processing in perception were completely conceptually driven (or hypothesis driven), each of us would be lost in our individual fantasy worlds of what we expect and hope to perceive. Your perceptions of someone you love, for example, might never be grounded in reality, since you would see only what you wished to see. A proper balance between the two extremes of data-driven and hypothesis-driven construction achieves the basic goal of perception: to experience what is out there in a way that best serves our needs as biological and social beings living in and adapting to our physical and social environment.

FIGURE 5.24   A Young Beauty ■

Creative Perception   Because of our ability to go beyond the sensory gifts that evolution has bestowed on our species, we can become more creative in the way we perceive the world. Our role model for creative perception ought to be someone like the late, great, modern artist Pablo Picasso (1881–1973). Picasso's genius was in part attributed to his talent for "playful perception." He could free himself from the bonds of perceptual sets, and see not the old in the new but the new in the old, the novel in the familiar, and the unusual figure concealed within the ground.

Perceptual creativity involves experiencing the world in ways that are imaginative, personally enriching, and fun. You can achieve perceptual creativity by consciously directing your attention and full awareness to the objects and activities around you. Become more flexible in what you allow yourself to perceive and think; remain open to alternative responses to situations in your life.

We conclude this rather formal presentation of the psychology of perception by proposing several suggestions, adapted from the work of Herbert Leff (1984), for playfully enhancing your powers of perception:

1. Imagine everyone you meet is really a machine designed to look humanoid. Are some more convincing than others?

2. Imagine that your mental clock is hooked up to a video recorder that can rewind, fast forward, and freeze time. Which buttons would you press, and why?

3. View the world from the point of view of an animal or a home appliance. How would *you* look from such a perspective?

4. Consider one new use for each object you view (for example, a tennis racket could be used to drain cooked spaghetti). Why didn't you think of these before?

5. Surprise yourself (and others): Violate some assumption about what you "normally" would or wouldn't do (without engaging in dangerous or threatening behavior). Could this be the "real you"?

Check Your Recall

In perception, sensory input from external energy sources is organized into stable, meaningful percepts. The distal stimulus is the real source of the stimulation. The proximal stimulus is the pattern of neural activity triggered in a

FIGURE 5.25   An Old Woman ■

receptor. The process of perception consists of three stages: sensation; the organization and combination of sensory information; and identification/recognition. While perception is usually accurate, it can fail when sensory data are confusing or ambiguous. Cultural experiences can determine how individuals perceive and interpret stimuli and illusions. Two theories attempt to explain perceptual processes: Helmholtz's view that human experience educates perceptual inference, and the Gestalt view that brain processes organize stimulus details into meaningful units.

Attention divides stimulation into that which is processed and that which is not. Preattentive processing registers simple sensory features. Attention serves several functions: filtering early sensations; selecting appropriate responses; and processing stimuli into consciousness.

In perceptual organization, sensory data are assembled into coherent scenes. Detection of different stimulus features results in region segregation. Figure-ground separation distinguishes objects from backgrounds. Illusory contours illustrate the principle of closure, the tendency to perceive images as whole and balanced. Separate figures may be perceived as grouped if they are proximal (close together); similar; or moving toward a common direction. Underlying these grouping laws is the principle of Prägnanz (meaningfulness): the simplest configuration is the one that will emerge.

During identification and recognition, meaning is attached to percepts. These processes involve both bottom-up and top-down interpretations. Identification is also based on context and expectations surrounding a stimulus. Expectations can create a perceptual set or readiness to make specific inferences. Bottom-up and top-down processes interact to produce the most meaningful perceptions. By challenging assumptions and adopting a playful perspective, people can apply creative perception to make perception more flexible and open. ✔

FIGURE 5.26   What Do You Now See? ■

CHAPTER REVIEW

Summary

Sensory processes transduce external stimuli into neural events. Psychophysics examines thresholds for sensations and differences. Signal detection theory explains sensation as a process involving both sensitivity and judgment. Senses adapt when unchanging stimuli are no longer processed. Vision and hearing have been thoroughly investigated by sensory psychologists. In vision, the presence and qualities of light are transduced by photoreceptors into color sensations and neural codes transmitted to the brain. In the ear, vibrations are transduced into neural energy and transmitted to the brain where qualities of pitch and loudness are experienced. An understanding of how sound is sensed helps to develop technologies and educational programs for the deaf. Other senses include position and movement (the vestibular and kinesthetic senses); smell; taste; the skin senses (touch, pressure, and temperature); and pain.

Stimuli are organized and interpreted in three stages: sensation; perceptual organization; and identification/recognition. By studying illusions, researchers can learn how normal perception succeeds. Perception has been explained by several theories, which differ in their accounts of the role of brain processes versus experience in human functioning. Learning and culture influence the quality of individual perception. Attentional processes select part of the sensory input and disregard the rest. Organization processes in perception include segregating the perceptual field into distinct regions; distinguishing figure from ground; identifying contours and applying closure; and grouping stimuli that are near each other, similar, or share a common fate—all indications of meaningfulness. During identification and recognition, percepts are given meaning through processes involving context, expectation, perceptual set, and cultural and personal factors. Ultimately, perception depends on who you are and what you know and expect, as well as the nature of the sensory stimulus.

Section Reviews

Sensory Processes

Be sure to *Check Your Recall* by reviewing the summary of this section on page 162.

Key Terms

sensuality (p. 156)
sensation (p. 157)
perception (p. 157)
transduction (p. 157)
afferent systems (p. 157)
efferent systems (p. 157)
psychophysics (p. 158)
absolute threshold (p. 158)
difference threshold
  (p. 159)

just noticeable difference
  (JND) (p. 159)
Weber's law (p. 159)
signal detection theory
  (SDT) (p. 160)
sensory adaptation
  (p. 162)

Names to Know

Gustav Fechner (p. 158)
Ernst Weber (p. 159)

Vision

Be sure to *Check Your Recall* by reviewing the summary of this section on page 168.

Key Terms

retina (p. 164)
photoreceptors (p. 164)
optic nerve (p. 165)
visual cortex (p. 165)

Names to Know

Sir Isaac Newton (p. 166)

Hearing

Be sure to *Check Your Recall* by reviewing the summary of this section on page 172.

Key Terms

cycles per second (cps)
  (p. 169)
hertz (Hz) (p. 169)
pitch (p. 170)
loudness (p. 170)

timbre (p. 171)
basilar membrane
  (p. 171)
auditory nerve (p. 171)
auditory cortex (p. 171)

The Other Senses

Be sure to *Check Your Recall* by reviewing the summary of this section on page 177.

Key Terms

vestibular sense (p. 173)
kinesthetic sense
  (p. 173)
olfaction (p. 174)
olfactory bulb (p. 174)
pheromones (p. 174)

gustation (p. 174)
taste buds (p. 174)
skin senses (p. 175)
pain (p. 176)

Perception

Be sure to *Check Your Recall* by reviewing the summary of this section on page 193.

Key Terms

percept (p. 177)
identification and recognition (p. 178)
distal stimulus (p. 179)
proximal stimulus
  (p. 179)
bottom-up processing
  (p. 180)
top-down processing
  (p. 180)
illusion (p. 181)
Gestalt psychology
  (p. 184)
attention (p. 185)
distraction (p. 186)
preattentive processing
  (p. 186)
perceptual organization
  (p. 188)
figure (p. 188)
ground (p. 188)

subjective contours
  (p. 189)
closure (p. 189)
perceptual grouping
  (p. 189)
law of Prägnanz
  (p. 190)
set (p. 192)
perceptual set (p. 192)

Names to Know

J. J. Oppel (p. 181)
Hermann von Helmholtz
  (p. 184)
Donald Broadbent
  (p. 186)
Anne Treisman (p. 187)
Max Wertheimer
  (p. 189)

REVIEW TEST

Chapter 5: Sensation and Perception

For each of the following items, choose the single correct or best answer. The correct answers, explanations, and page references appear in Appendix B.

1. _____ is the process that converts one form of physical energy, such as sound waves, to another form, such as neural impulses.
   a. Sensory adaptation
   b. Psychophysics
   c. Transduction
   d. Kinesthesis

2. Luisa agrees to look after her friends' new baby while they run an errand. Luisa tries to read with the stereo on, but keeps listening for signs that the baby might be crying in the bedroom. Several times, Luisa thinks she can hear whimpering—but when she checks the baby, she finds her still sound asleep. Which of the following explains why Luisa is hearing imaginary cries?
   a. classical absolute threshold theory
   b. signal detection theory
   c. the law of Prägnanz
   d. Weber's law

3. Which of these sensory structures does *not* belong with the others?
   a. lens
   b. ganglion cells
   c. basilar membrane
   d. visual cortex

4. Place theory and frequency theory are explanations for processes involved in the sensation of _____.
   a. the hue created by a light's wavelength
   b. the timbre of sound
   c. different olfactory stimuli
   d. the pitch of sound

5. _____ may be our most primitive sense, since it is processed in the oldest part of the brain and has basic connections to survival and interaction with other creatures.
   a. Olfaction
   b. Kinesthesis
   c. The vestibular sense
   d. Vision

6. _____ is most commonly experienced when a stimulus is ambiguous, information is missing, elements are combined in unusual ways, or familiar patterns are not apparent.
   a. An illusion
   b. Closure
   c. A false alarm
   d. A correct rejection

7. According to Gestalt explanations of how perceptual processes work, when a person encounters an unfamiliar collection of stimuli, he or she will try to _____.
   a. judge whether each stimulus matches a familiar signal
   b. assemble the parts into a meaningful whole or pattern that makes sense
   c. analyze each stimulus component separately to ascertain its meaning
   d. make guesses about its symbolism until finding a matching concept

8. While attending a crowded party, Natalie tries to overhear a conversation between two strangers who are talking about her. She pretends to smile at other people and watch the party while she strains to eavesdrop. She will most likely lose track of the conversation and be forced to pay attention to a new stimulus if the new stimulus is _____.
   a. visual rather than auditory
   b. a voice louder than the conversation she is listening to
   c. a whispered request she is not expecting to hear
   d. a familiar one, such as a song played in the background

9. Although the markings in the ceiling tiles are of all different shapes and sizes, you notice that the larger, darker spots seem to be floating against a background made up of the smaller, lighter ones. Which principle of perceptual grouping explains this distinction?
   a. the law of similarity
   b. the law of proximity
   c. the law of common fate
   d. the principle of closure

10. At a crime scene, a detective finds a slip of paper with three symbols printed on it in ink. She cannot identify the source of the figures or which orientation is up. Thus she cannot determine if the figures are the numbers 771 or the letters ILL. Because she has no context to help explain the meaning of the figures, her perception of them now must be _____.
    a. hypothesis-driven
    b. conceptually driven
    c. data-driven
    d. top-down

IF YOU'RE INTERESTED . . .

Ackerman, D. (1990). *A natural history of the senses.* New York: Vintage.

Poet Diane Ackerman's collection of provocative and evocative essays on smell, touch, taste, hearing, vision, and synesthesia (experiencing a sensation in the "wrong" sense, such as seeing a sound or feeling a fragrance).

Babette's Feast. (Video: 1987, Danish, color, 102 min.). Directed by Gabriel Axel; starring Stéphane Audran, Jean-Philippe Lafont, Gudmar Wivesson, Jarl Kulle.

A story of taste—the pleasures of eating, the limits of propriety. Set in a small seaside town in nineteenth century Denmark, this beautiful tale contrasts the lives of two women, provincial minister's daughters, who use religion to hide from life, with that of their Parisian housekeeper, Babette. A refugee from the old regime in France, Babette unexpectedly wins a lottery back home—and decides to spend her fortune preparing a great feast for her employers and their friends. (This film may make you hungry!)

Cytowic, R. E. (1993). *The man who tasted shapes: A bizarre medical mystery offers revolutionary insights into emotions, reasoning, and consciousness.* New York: Jeremy P. Tarcher.

Inspired by a personal encounter with synesthesia (multiple sensations from a single stimulus), a neurologist documents instances and explanations of sensory experiences that appear to be hooked together. A fascinating story of how a researcher transforms an idea into a question and a research program with widespread effect.

Immortal Beloved. (Video: 1995, color, 121 min.). Directed by Bernard Rose; starring Gary Oldman, Jeroen Krabbé, Isabella Rossellini, Johanna Ter Steege, Valeria Golino.

After the death of composer Ludwig van Beethoven in 1827, his manager seeks to identify the love of Beethoven's life, whom he intended to be his true heir. A dramatic and beautiful film, which blends fiction and speculation with the facts of Beethoven's life. Note especially the filmmaker's theory of why Beethoven became deaf, Oldman's portrayal of how Beethoven coped with and sought to cover up his hearing loss, and the ultimate triumph of the composer's musical genius over his disability and early life trauma. (The soundtrack, conducted by Sir Georg Solti, is breathtaking, especially the Ninth Symphony, the "Ode to Joy," composed when Beethoven was completely deaf.)

Like Water for Chocolate. (Video: 1992, Mexican, color; 113 min.). Directed by Alfonso Arau; starring Lumi Cavazos, Marco Leonardi, Regina Torne, Mario Ivan Martinez, Ada Carrasco.

Evocative and provocative story of a young woman who, deprived of love and freedom by her domineering mother, expresses her passions and longings in the dramatic, sometimes magical effects of her cooking. Vivid, memorable, and funny.

Lumet, S. (1995). *Making movies.* New York: Alfred A. Knopf.

Award-winning film director Sidney Lumet *(Twelve Angry Men, Serpico, Murder on the Orient Express, Dog Day Afternoon, Network—* and many others) explains the art and science of cinema. Enjoyable presentation of filmmaking as a wonderful metaphor for perception, with separate contributions creating memory and meaning.

Miracle Worker, The. (Video: 1962, B&W, 107 min.). Directed by Arthur Penn; starring Patty Duke, Anne Bancroft, Victory Jory, Inga Swenson.

Powerful film adaptation of William Gibson's play about Helen Keller (1880–1968), blind and deaf since infancy, and her relationship with Anne Sullivan, the young woman who taught her to perceive and communicate about the world through signing (and feeling the manual alphabet on her hands). Both Duke's and Bancroft's performances won Oscars.

Rashomon. (Video: 1950, Japanese, B&W, 88 min.). Directed by Akira Kurosawa; starring Toshiro Mifune, Machiko Kyo, Masayuki Mori, Takashi Shimura.

After a rape and murder, four witnesses provide vastly different accounts of the crime. A classic film and a wonderful illustration of how perception and memory are biased by individual motives and perspectives.

Süskind, P. (1991). *Perfume: The story of a murderer.* (Translated from the German *Das Parfum* by John E. Woods). New York: Pocket Books.

A man with an exquisite sense of smell, devastated by the fact that he has no scent of his own, becomes a murderous "vampire of scent" in order to "acquire" it. Passionate, evocative, scary novel about the possible power of fragrance for self and in relationships.

CHAPTER 6

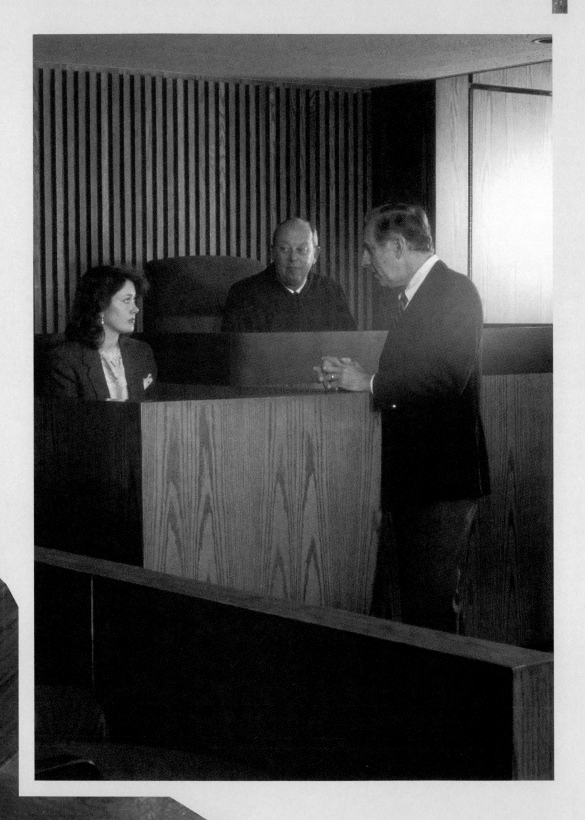

Learning and Remembering

In the mid-1980s, 12-year-old Donna Smith began to suffer from severe migraine headaches, which left her sleepless and depressed. Her parents, Judee and Dan, agreed to seek therapy for her. During a psychiatric evaluation recommended by her therapist, Donna disclosed—for the first time—that she had been sexually molested at the age of three by a neighbor when the family lived in the Philippines. Memories of the assault, repressed and kept secret for so long, were probably responsible for some of Donna's current problems, and she continued with therapy.

In 1990 Donna, now a teenager, began work with a new therapist, Cathy M., a private social worker specializing in child abuse. In their first session, Donna was asked if she had been sexually abused by her own father. Donna denied this but did mention the neighbor's assault. The therapist, however, believed there must be more behind Donna's current problems. For many months, she repeatedly asked Donna whether her father hadn't actually abused her. Eventually Donna told her a lie, claiming her father had once "touched" her, hoping this false claim would enable her therapy to move on. The therapist immediately reported Donna's father to the local sheriff, and to the Maryland Department of Social Services (ABC News, 1995).

When Donna realized the drastic consequences of her false claim, she tried to set the record straight, but Cathy M. dismissed Donna's confession, replying that all abuse victims recant their accusations once they learn their therapists are required to report such claims. Donna began to believe that it was her father, not the neighbor, who had assaulted her as a toddler, and that he had continued the abuse. She related this to county authorities, who removed Donna from her home and placed her in foster care.

To Donna's parents, these sudden accusations were "like a bomb [had] hit"—and it got worse. Still in therapy, Donna became convinced her father had been a chronic abuser, and she began to hate him "wholeheartedly." Committed to another psychiatric hospital, Donna was diagnosed as having several different personalities, one of which claimed that her parents practiced ritual satanic abuse of Donna's younger brothers. The courts forbade Donna's parents to have contact with her. Judee Smith lost her license to run a day care center. Dan Smith, a retired naval officer, was arrested *at his home and handcuffed in front of their two young sons. Financially ruined, Dan Smith was tried on charges of abuse, based solely on his daughter's testimony. His two-week trial ended in a hung jury and Dan Smith went free, but Donna moved to Michigan with her foster family.*

In her new surroundings, far away from the system that had supported her fabricated story, Donna regained perspective and found the courage to tell the truth. She admitted the charges had all been lies, and her doctor recommended she be sent back to her family. The Smiths had a tearful reunion and began the slow process of rebuilding lost relationships and trust. "She's been a victim of this system, as much as we've been a victim," says Dan Smith. "You know, there's a lot of healing to be done." Now in her early twenties, Donna is no longer a minor and cannot be separated from her family by the courts. But how could she have "remembered" something she says never happened? How does a single unfounded claim turn into a destructive witch hunt?

Johns Hopkins psychiatrist Paul McHugh criticizes the practice of "recovering" long-repressed memories

to use as evidence. He argues that such recollections are constructed from suggestions therapists offer in order to blame psychological problems on long-hidden trauma (ABC News, 1995). An expert on reconstructed memories, Elizabeth Loftus notes that most clinicians are prepared to believe in their clients' memories, even fantastic tales of ritualistic abuse (Loftus, 1993). In his book Making Monsters, *social psychologist Richard Ofshe argues that clients tailor their recollections to fit their therapists' expectations, explaining that "therapists often encourage patients to redefine their life histories based on the new pseudo-memories and, by doing so, redefine their most basic understanding of their families and themselves" (Ofshe & Watters, 1994, p. 6).*

Today Donna and her family are "in wonderful shape, back together" (ABC News, 1995). But the painful memories of the Smith family's ordeal will remain with them at some level for the rest of their lives. Fortunately, the same flexibility in human learning and remembering that created these problems can also provide the key to forgiving and healing.

Introduction

You may think of "learning" as something that normally occurs in a classroom or other educational circumstances. But Donna Smith clearly *learned* what to say in order to satisfy her therapist and the other authorities she turned to when she left her family. Further, you may think of "memory" as a mental recording system, a more reliable intellectual capacity than it seems to have been for Donna Smith. But if people sometimes "remember" events that never took place, and forget things they once knew, then how reliable is memory, after all?

In fact, human learning and memory are especially valuable to our species exactly because they *are* flexible, adaptive processes. Human behavior is not controlled or preprogrammed by inborn instincts. Instead, humans rely on learning lessons through *experience*, and refining recollection of those lessons as new knowledge is acquired.

Flexibility in learning and memory accounts for some of life's problems. For example, human memory does not accurately "record" events like a videotape machine, so eyewitness testimony is not a reliable source of information. But such flexibility can also provide solutions to dilemmas. For example, bad habits can be "unlearned" and replaced with healthy ones. Learning is the first stage in acquiring new information or ways of behaving. To affect future behavior, however, the lessons we learn must be remembered.

Learning About Learning

We begin this chapter by considering how psychologists study learning and what processes account for changes in human behavior and thought. We then examine the workings and limits of human memory, and some recommendations for enhancing our ability to remember important people, events, or ideas.

The Capacity for Learning

Consider the significance of learning from an *evolutionary perspective*. Learning is influenced by experience; that is, nature does not bequeath us a fixed tendency to learn only certain things. Instead, we inherit a *capacity* for learning. Whether and how much that capacity is realized depends on the individual. We all have similar capacities for learning, but we learn different things to different degrees, and at different rates, because our life experiences are ultimately unique. Our capacity for learning separates us from many of our fellow creatures. Some species, such as reptiles and amphibians, do not benefit as much from interactions with the environment. For them, life is a series of rigid stimulus-response patterns. Their survival depends on living in a relatively *constant habitat,* where their responses to specific environmental events get them what they need or protect them from harm. The behavior of primates such as monkeys and humans is less influenced by genetic factors. Such behavior is based on greater *plasticity,* or variability, in learning.

The learning process reflects the democratic ideal that people can shape their lives by their actions and that they are not limited by biology or family history. People can aspire to better lives, regardless of their origins. The psychology of learning is at the heart of much that is human nature—some for better and some for worse.

Defining the Learning Process

Learning *is a process by which experience produces a consistent or enduring change in behavior or behavior potential.* Let's consider each of these learning criteria in turn: *behavior* or behavior potential; *consistent or enduring* change; a process based on *experience.*

A Change in Behavior or Behavior Potential   Learning cannot be observed directly but is inferred from changes in observable behavior. Learning is apparent from improvements in your *performance,* but performance may not show everything that has been learned. For example, if test questions seem unfair or you feel anxious, you may perform poorly despite having learned the material. Further, learning may affect your *potential for behavior* more than your immediate behavior. An inspiring course or a powerful lecture can increase your appreciation or understanding of a subject, but these changes may not be immediately measurable on a test or examination. Although learning may not be visible at the time it occurs, it can still affect your attitudes and choices for years to come.

A Consistent, Enduring Change   To qualify as learned, a change in behavior or behavior potential must be consistent over time and under different conditions. If a behavior is exhibited on some occasions but does not recur, this inconsistency suggests that the lesson has not endured. Much learned knowledge is forgotten or changed by later experiences, so specific lessons may not last forever. However, learning always involves *memory* for what has been learned, so that on subsequent occasions you can recall or do again what you learned before.

THE FAR SIDE   By GARY LARSON

THE FAR SIDE, by Gary Larson. © 1986.
Universal Press Syndicate.

"Stimulus, response. Stimulus, response! Don't you ever think?*"*

A Process Based on Experience Learning can take place only through experience. Experience includes taking in information and making responses that affect the environment. Some lasting changes in behavior require a combination of experience and maturational readiness. For example, a child is ready to crawl, stand, walk, and run according to a specific developmental timetable. No amount of training or practice will produce those behaviors before the child has matured sufficiently. But once it has, then practice in locomotion will refine it into a learned skill.

Not all behavior change results from learned experiences. A tap on your knee results in a knee-jerk reflex that will recur with each stimulus tap. This stimulus-response sequence is an inborn *reflex* unaffected by experience, so it does not qualify as an example of learning.

The Behaviorist Perspective

To study learning as it happens, psychologists must choose subjects whose behavior does not reflect other influences—past learning, for example. Human subjects are disqualified from much basic research on learning because, whatever their age, they have already learned most of their behavior. However, animal subjects can be raised in controlled environments and their behavior can be protected from contamination by unwanted prior lessons. Research with nonhuman subjects has contributed greatly to psychologists' ability to study learning and analyze behavior as it happens, "on-line."

Much of modern psychology's view of learning finds its roots in the work of **John B. Watson** (1878–1958). As you might recall from Chapter 1, Watson founded the behaviorist school of psychology. For nearly fifty years the behaviorist tradition dominated American psychology. In perhaps his most influential work, *Psychology from the Standpoint of a Behaviorist,* Watson (1919) argued that introspection—verbal reports of sensations, images, and feelings— was *not* an acceptable means of studying behavior because it was too subjective. The subject matter of psychology should be *observable behavior.*

B. F. Skinner (1904–1990) began his graduate study in psychology at Harvard after reading Watson's 1924 book *Behaviorism.* During his career, Skinner pioneered *radical behaviorism,* challenging earlier theories that accepted internal states and mental events as legitimate causes of behavior (Skinner, 1990). In Skinner's view, mental events such as thinking and imagining do not cause behavior, but are themselves reactions caused by environmental stimuli.

Although the behavioristic position has yielded many valuable explanations of human nature, we will see that it has been challenged by other psychologists who insist on keeping a thinking brain and a rational mind in control of the behaving body. Behaviorism has also been slow to be accepted by the public, largely due to misunderstandings about its premises, and misrepresentations of behaviorism as controlling, absolutist, and intolerant (Todd & Morris, 1992, 1993). As a student of psychology, you will learn most about learning if you keep an open mind and try to appreciate the rigor of the behaviorist perspective as well as the contributions of alternative approaches. (See Delprato & Midgley, 1992, for a synopsis of themes throughout Skinner's written work).

Check Your Recall

Learning is a relatively consistent, enduring change in behavior or behavior potential based on experience. Our capacity for learning depends on both genetic heritage and environmental conditions. Early learning research focused on animal behavior, but it has many applications in comparable human experiences. The study of learning has traditionally been dominated by the behavioristic approach of John Watson and B. F. Skinner. An understanding of learning is critical in modifying the behavior of individuals, groups, and societies.

Classical Conditioning

How do people and animals learn to make *associations* between events and experiences? For example, the sound of a plaintive song may cause you to feel sad—but when and how did you learn to associate a sad emotion with a certain melodic pattern? This is an association between two *stimuli*—a condition that makes you feel sad, and the sound of a particular piece of music. This type of association is the result of *classical conditioning,* a basic type of learning in which stimulus pairings are programmed into learning creatures.

A second type of association is involved when one's response is connected with specific outcomes. For example, after receiving good service in a restaurant, you might leave a large tip, hoping the waitress will connect the gratuity to her performance, feel rewarded, and learn to provide the same good service in the future. This type of association occurs as a result of *operant conditioning,* a learned connection between a response and its consequences. We will discuss both these types of conditioning in some detail because of their important role in the psychology of learning. But first let's return to our opening case, Donna Smith's false memories, and consider some vivid examples of these processes.

Donna initially sought therapy because some personal problems caused her to feel moderate discomfort in her life. In the therapist's office, she came to feel accepted, appreciated, and respected—and even to see herself as an "interesting person" because of how attentively the therapist regarded her stories of abuse. The therapeutic environment—the therapist's office, the therapist's body language and voice—became a set of *stimuli* that Donna learned to associate with feeling good, even though the content of her stories was basically unpleasant. The formation of an association of one set of stimuli (environmental conditions) with another (attention that makes you feel good about yourself) is *classical conditioning.*

Then Donna succumbed to the therapist's pressure and told a lie about her father having sexually abused her. That response was reinforced by even greater attention and comfort from the therapist. Thus Donna's lying and fabricating were *responses* that were reinforced, strengthened, by the *consequences* they evoked: greater attention and support from the therapist and other authorities. When responses are influenced by the nature of their consequences, the underlying learning process is *operant conditioning.* Both classical and operant conditioning worked to generate the false memory scenario that had such destructive effects on Donna Smith and her family. With this example in mind, we now examine the structure and effects of each basic form of learning.

Principles of Classical Conditioning

To pick up an example we introduced above, can you think of a song that makes you feel sad? Have you ever found that the sound of a certain person's voice immediately cheers you up—perhaps a good friend, or a favorite comedian? Have you ever felt suddenly nauseated merely by the aroma of a food that once made you ill? In these experiences, your responses to powerful stimuli seem to be involuntarily pulled out—*elicited*—and to resist any conscious control. Where do such reactions originate?

To study classical conditioning, Pavlov placed his dogs in a restraining apparatus. The dogs were then presented with a neutral stimulus, such as a tone. Through its association with food, the neutral stimulus became a conditional stimulus eliciting salivation.

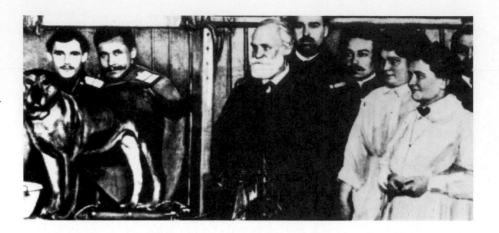

Experience accounts for these nonconscious and emotional responses to specific stimuli. If you were exposed to a particular song during an emotional event, you might associate the song with the original cause of your emotions. Or, if you associate a past illness with a particular food, anything associated with that food, such as a similar aroma, may arouse the old feelings of nausea and distaste. All these experiences have in common the association of a new stimulus (e.g., an aroma) with an old one (e.g., a food that made you sick). Because of this stimulus-stimulus (S-S) association, the new stimulus acquires the power to evoke the same response the old one did, so you might have a *classically conditioned* negative response (nausea) to an aroma that itself is not negative.

This is **classical conditioning:** *a basic form of learning in which two stimuli become associated so that one acquires the power to elicit the same behavioral response as the other one.* This seemingly simple association process is in fact a powerful form of learning, with profound implications in both everyday life and psychological theory. The Russian physiologist **Ivan Pavlov** (1849–1936) is credited with first developing the basic principles of classical conditioning. He began to formulate the tenets of classical conditioning while conducting research on digestion, research for which he won a Nobel Prize in 1904.

Pavlov had devised a technique to study digestive processes in dogs. He implanted tubes in their glands and digestive organs to divert bodily secretions to containers outside their bodies; he then measured and analyzed those secretions. Pavlov's assistants put meat powder into the dogs' mouths to trigger these processes. After repeating this procedure a number of times, Pavlov observed an unexpected behavior in his dogs: they salivated *before* the powder was put in their mouths! They would start salivating when they saw the food or the assistant who brought it. Any stimulus that regularly preceded the presentation of food came to elicit salivation. Quite by accident, Pavlov had discovered that learning may result when two stimuli became associated with each other.

To Pavlov, this finding did not make sense physiologically. What is the survival value, for example, in getting ready to eat at the sound of footsteps? Why should a new stimulus be added to an already effective, existing stimulus-response sequence? Pavlov turned his attention to understanding these "psychic secretions"—automatic responses triggered by mental ("psychic") events rather than environmental stimuli. He abandoned his work on digestion and, in so doing, changed the course of psychology forever (Pavlov, 1928).

Originally, the behavior Pavlov studied was the **reflex,** *an unlearned response, such as salivation, pupil contraction, knee jerks, or eye blinking, that is naturally elicited by specific stimuli that have biological relevance for the organism.* Simply put, a reflex is an elicited behavior that promotes biological adaptation to a changing environment. For example, salivation helps digestion; blinking protects the eyes. After conditioning, however, organisms make reflexive responses to new stimuli that have no original biological relevance.

To discover what was causing his dogs to salivate, Pavlov knew that he would have to manipulate various aspects of his experimental setting and observe what effects, if any, would follow. His strategy was elegant and simple. He first placed a dog in a restraining harness. At regular intervals, a tone was sounded and the dog was given a bit of food. The dog's first reaction to the tone was only an *orienting response:* the dog pricked its ears and turned its head (oriented) to locate the source of the sound. But with *repeated pairings* of the tone and the food, the orienting response stopped, and salivation began. This pattern could be replicated under controlled conditions. A neutral stimulus (one without any eliciting power, such as the tone), when paired with a more relevant stimulus (such as food), will eventually elicit a response (salivation) very similar to the original reflex. The same kind of conditioning occurs in kitchens everywhere when a pet owner uses an electric can opener before dispensing dog or cat food: the pet, hearing the sound and associating it with food, salivates in preparation for a meal. The animal may also exhibit more obvious, voluntary learning, such as running to the food dish, but this is not *classically conditioned* behavior, because running is not involuntary or "built-in" like salivation. Rather, the pet has been *operantly conditioned* to run or beg for food because such actions have been rewarded in the past. In the pet–can opener example, as in Donna Smith's story, you can see that both classical and operant conditioning are interwoven to affect a broad range of behaviors.

The Stimulus-Response Sequence The main features of Pavlov's classical conditioning procedure are illustrated in Figure 6.1. Because learning is *not* a necessary *condition* for the original stimulus to control the behavior, *any*

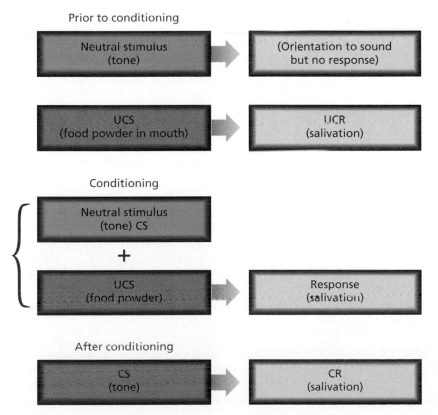

FIGURE 6.1 **Basic Features of Classical Conditioning** ■ Before conditioning, the UCS naturally elicits the UCR. A neutral stimulus (such as tone) has no eliciting effect. During conditioning, the neutral stimulus is paired with the UCS. Through its association with the UCS, the neutral stimulus becomes a CS and elicits a CR similar to the UCR.

stimulus that naturally elicits a reflexive behavior is called an **unconditional stimulus (UCS).** In this case, the food powder is the UCS because it elicits the reflexive behavior of salivating. *The behavior elicited by the unconditional stimulus is called the* **unconditional response (UCR).** During conditioning trials, a neutral stimulus (the tone) is repeatedly paired with the UCS so that it predictably follows the neutral stimulus.

After several trials, the neutral stimulus is presented alone and elicits the same response as the UCS does—salivation. The formerly neutral stimulus has now become a **conditional stimulus (CS),** *a stimulus that has acquired the power to elicit the same response as the unconditional stimulus.* The response elicited is the same reflexive behavior—such as salivation—but *when it occurs in response to the CS, the elicited response is referred to as the* **conditional response (CR).** The UCS-UCR sequence is the naturally occurring stimulus-response connection. When learning creates a new association between the UCS and another stimulus, the result of this classical conditioning process is a new CS-CR sequence.

Pavlov's careful laboratory experiments showed how once-neutral stimuli could come to exert powerful control over reflexive behavior. His research uncovered a number of important processes involved in classical conditioning, most of which are still being studied by modern psychologists. Classical conditioning is also called *Pavlovian conditioning,* due to Pavlov's discovery of the phenomenon and his dedication to tracking down the variables that influence it. In the next section, we will examine the processes and conditions essential to classical conditioning.

Basic Processes

What conditions are optimal for classical conditioning? The answers provide clues to the fundamental processes underlying learning. We will first identify how the conditioned association is acquired, then how it is extinguished and sometimes spontaneously recovered. After distinguishing between the processes of stimulus generalization and discrimination, we analyze the conditions essential to effective classical conditioning.

Acquisition   Under most conditions, the two stimuli—the CS and UCS—must be paired at least several times before the CS reliably elicits a CR. **Acquisition** *refers to the process at the beginning of a classical conditioning experiment by which the CR is first elicited and gradually increases in strength over repeated trials.* The first panel in Figure 6.2 shows the acquisition phase of a hypothetical experiment. At first, only weak CRs are elicited by the CS. With continued CS-UCS pairings, however, the CR is elicited with increasing strength, and the organism acquires the conditional response (CR).

In conditioning (as in telling a good joke) *timing* is critical. The CS and UCS must be presented close together in time (contiguously) so that the organism perceives them as being related. The range of time intervals between the CS and UCS that will produce the best conditioning depends on the response being conditioned. For motor and skeletal responses, such as eye blinks, a short interval of a second or less is best. For visceral responses, such as heart rate and salivation, longer intervals of 5 to 15 seconds work best. Conditional fear, as we explore next, usually requires longer intervals of many seconds or even minutes to develop.

Aversive Conditioning   Pavlov's conditioning with meat powder is an example of *appetitive conditioning*—conditioning in which the UCS is of positive value to an organism. However, classical conditioning may also involve an aversive, painful UCS. **Aversive conditioning** *occurs when the CS predicts the*

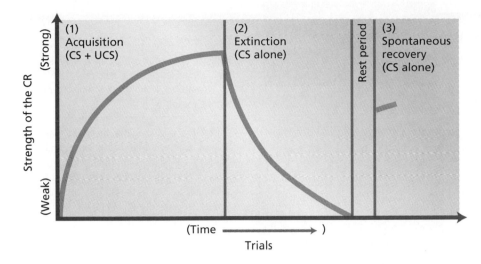

FIGURE 6.2 Acquisition, Extinction, and Spontaneous Recovery ■ During acquisition (CS + UCS), the strength of the CR increases rapidly. During extinction, when the UCS no longer follows the CS, the strength of the CR drops to zero. The CR may reappear after a brief rest period, even when the UCS is still not presented; only the CS alone appears. The reappearance of the CR is called "spontaneous recovery."

presentation of an aversive UCS, such as an electrical shock. An organism's natural response to such stimuli is reflexive behavior that reduces the intensity of the UCS or removes it entirely. If you touch something painfully hot, for example, you jerk your hand away reflexively, preventing any further pain or damage. Through its association with the UCS, the CS also comes to elicit such responses of avoidance when it is presented later independently of the UCS.

Aversive conditioning studies have shown that the organism learns not only a specific conditional muscle response but also a *generalized fear reaction*. The subject learns a specific response to a stimulus and reevaluates the previously neutral stimulus as affectively negative. Withdrawal from the negative stimulus is accompanied by reactions of the autonomic nervous system, such as changes in heart rate and respiration. These changes become part of an overall conditional fear response.

Interestingly, when strong fear is involved, conditioning may take place after only *one* pairing of a neutral stimulus with the UCS. Traumatic events in our lives that may occur only once can condition us to respond with strong physical, emotional, and cognitive reactions that are highly resistant to extinction. Conditional fear is often easy to acquire and difficult to extinguish. Aversive conditioning explains how an emotion as basic as fear can be modified by experience. In Focus on Science: Learning to Fear, we review classic and applied research on how aversive associations influence human emotions.

Extinction and Spontaneous Recovery Once a conditional response is acquired, does it last forever? When the UCS no longer follows the CS, the CR becomes weaker over time and eventually stops occurring. *When the CR no longer occurs in the presence of the CS (and absence of UCS)*, **extinction** *is said to have occurred* (see Figure 6.2, second panel). Conditional responses, then, are not necessarily a permanent aspect of the organism's behavioral repertoire. However, the CR will reappear in a weak form when the CS is again presented alone (Figure 6.2, third panel). Pavlov referred to this *sudden reappearance of the CR after a rest period (or time-out) without further exposure to the UCS* as **spontaneous recovery.**

For example, a little girl develops an aversion to seafood after associating the taste with the results of a childhood illness (acquisition). As a young adult she manages to overcome the learned aversion with the help of friends who like seafood and encourage her to try it (extinction). But after moving away and going without seafood for some time, she experiences the childhood nausea again the first time she orders seafood in a restaurant. She has spontaneously recovered the conditioned response (feeling sick) after a period during which the CS's power seemed to be extinguished.

FOCUS on Science

Learning to Fear

In 1920, psychologists John B. Watson and Rosalie Rayner conducted a classic study of conditional fear with an infant named Albert. Watson and Rayner sought to discover whether fears could be learned through simple conditioning, and their experiment with "Little Albert," as he came to be known, confirmed they could. Using techniques that would be unlikely to receive approval from modern research review committees, Watson and Rayner trained Albert to fear a white rat he had initially liked by pairing the appearance of the rat with an aversive UCS—the sound of a loud gong struck just behind Albert. The unconditional startle response and the emotional distress to the noxious noise was the basis of Albert's learning to react with fear to the appearance of the white rat. His fear was developed in just seven conditioning trials. The emotional conditioning was then extended to behavioral conditioning when Albert learned to escape from the feared stimulus. The infant's learned fear then generalized to other furry objects, such as a rabbit, a dog, and even a Santa Claus mask (Harris, 1979)!

We now know that conditioned fear is highly resistant to extinction. Even if it

John Watson and Rosalie Rayner conditioned Little Albert to fear furry objects like this Santa Claus mask (*Discovering Psychology*, 1990).

has been a long time since you encountered the conditioned stimuli for a fear response, your nervous system will retain reflexive patterns that leave you vulnerable to stimuli you thought you had forgotten. Thus you may find yourself feeling nervous "for no reason" or suspecting that a strange food will "make you sick"

because of associations in your past experience. And some people have lifelong fears of snakes or other, generally harmless, creatures without even remembering the reason.

Conditioned fear reactions may persist for years, as shown in the study that follows. During World War II, the signal used to call sailors to battle stations aboard U.S. Navy ships was a gong sounding at the rate of 100 rings a minute. To personnel on board, the sound was associated with danger; thus, it became a CS for strong emotional arousal. Fifteen years after the war, a study was conducted on the emotional reactions of hospitalized navy and army veterans to a series of 20 different auditory stimuli. Although none of the sounds were current signals for danger, the sound of the old "call to battle stations" still produced strong emotional arousal in the navy veterans who had previously experienced that association (Edwards & Acker, 1962).

All of us retain learned readiness to respond with fear, joy, or other emotions to old signals. When we are unaware of their origins, fear reactions that were once reasonable may be interpreted as anxiety, and we become more upset because we seem to be reacting irrationally (Dollard & Miller, 1950).

Stimulus Generalization and Discrimination   Once a CR has been conditioned to a particular CS, similar stimuli may also elicit the response. For example, if conditioning was to a high-frequency tone, a lower tone may also elicit the response. A child bitten by a big dog is likely to respond with fear even to smaller dogs, or to all furry animals. This *automatic extension of responding to stimuli that have never been paired with the original UCS is called* **stimulus generalization.** The more similar the new stimulus is to the original CS, the stronger the response will be.

Important stimuli rarely occur in exactly the same form every time in nature. Thus, stimulus generalization operates as a similarity safety factor by extending the range of learning beyond the original specific experience. With this feature, new but comparable events can be recognized as having the same meaning or behavioral significance despite apparent differences. For example, a predator can make a different sound or be seen from a different angle and still be recognized and responded to quickly.

Though stimuli similar to the original CS may elicit a similar response, it is possible for an organism to respond only to one particular CS and not to other stimuli, regardless of how similar they are. **Stimulus discrimination** *is the process by which an organism learns to respond differently to stimuli that are distinct from the CS in some dimension* (for example, differences in hue or in pitch). Early in conditioning, stimuli similar to the CS will elicit a similar response, though it will not be quite as strong. As discrimination training proceeds, the responses to the other, dissimilar stimuli weaken. The organism gradually learns which signal predicts the onset of the UCS and which signals do not.

In everyday life, you must frequently discriminate among many stimuli that are at least superficially similar. You learn to respond to the lights and sirens of a fire engine by moving your vehicle out of the way, but respond with anxiety to the lights and sirens of a police car behind you in traffic. You learn to answer the ring of a phone in your home but do not act on the sound of a phone ringing on a television program.

For optimum adaptation, an organism's initial tendency to generalize all somewhat similar stimuli must give way to discrimination among them—to responding only to those that are followed by the UCS. Conditioning is a process in which *discrimination* ultimately wins over *generalization;* but it is a balancing act between these two counteracting tendencies of being overselective (too picky) and overresponsive (reacting the same way to too many stimuli).

Conditions for Conditioning

Many of the emotions we experience and many of our attitudes can be explained by classical conditioning. Not surprisingly, real-life conditioning must occur in circumstances that are quite different from the neat system that makes up the laboratory environment. Modern research on classical conditioning has refined the earlier understanding of how it occurs. Research on classical conditioning shows that stimulus-response (S-R) connections are more effectively learned when the CS has three qualities: contrast, contingency, and information.

Contrast Conditioning occurs most rapidly when the CS stands out against the many other stimuli that are also present. Thus, a stimulus will be more readily noticed the more *intense* it is and the more it *contrasts* with other stimuli. A fragrance that has special associations for you, for example, will be more likely to evoke those remembered emotions if it stands out as different from other aromas and odors in the environment.

Contingency In his original conceptualization, Pavlov argued that for a CR to be learned, the CS and the UCS must occur close together in time. Work by **Robert Rescorla** (1966) further indicates that the learner must see the CS as a dependable signal for the occurrence of the UCS. In other words, the occurrence of the powerful UCS must seem *contingent* on the presentation of the once neutral CS. This contingency makes the CS more meaningful to the learner (Hearst, 1988).

Learning creatures are always scanning their environments to detect useful signals. If certain sights, smells, or sounds (CSs) reliably signal danger (the UCS), they will be identified and responded to (the CR) more readily than signals that are only randomly synchronized with the meaningful stimuli. For example, in Focus on Science: Learning to Fear, war veterans were found to associate fear arousal (the CR) with the sound of a gong (the CS) that had reliably signaled danger (the UCS). This lesson took hold, seemingly for a lifetime.

Information In general, the feature of the CS that most facilitates conditioning is its *informativeness*—its reliability in predicting the onset of the UCS (Rescorla, 1972; Rescorla & Wagner, 1972). Work by **Leon Kamin** (1969) has revealed that a learner will form a CS-CR connection only if the CS seems to provide unique information about the UCS. Some experiences are signaled not by a single stimulus but by a series of stimuli. Do you pay attention to *all* of them? According to Kamin, no: You learn to respond particularly to the stimuli that provide important *information* about the environment. For example, before something catches fire, you may see smoke as well as smell the acrid odor of something burning. You have learned from experience that smoke is not always visible during a fire, but the *smell* of something burning is a telltale sign of fire. The smell provides better *information* about whether there is a fire, so you pay closer attention to the smell than to the sight of smoke.

The Survival Value of Conditioning

From an evolutionary perspective, the capacity to learn is inherited because it aids survival. To fit a given ecological niche, each species must develop certain behaviors that aid survival and the production of successful offspring. By associating new stimuli with old ones and producing conditioned responses, organisms can learn from experience and modify their behavior. A clear example of such survival-oriented conditioning is the readiness of humans and nonhumans alike to learned conditioned responses to food.

When we were children, both of your authors had bad experiences with specific foods. One of us got sick after eating pork and beans in the grade school lunchroom. The other had been ill and experienced worsening nausea after eating homemade apple fritters. In both cases, we attributed our sickness to the distinctive smell and taste of the food, not to any other possible environmental cause or preexisting condition. And for both of us, the very smell or appearance of the "culprit" food subsequently triggered reactions of nausea and avoidance.

Our experience with these biases is not strange. Humans and many other animals readily form an association between illness and a small class of likely causes—food. Did we learn this bias or is it a part of the genetic endowment? **Taste-aversion learning,** *the tendency to associate a substance's taste with illness caused by eating that substance,* represents a genetic bias in learning. Indeed, studies of taste aversion seem to violate the usual principles of conditioning but make sense when viewed as part of a species' adaptiveness to its natural environment.

Bait Shyness   Suppose that a rat eats poisoned bait, and many hours later becomes ill but survives. After this single pairing, and despite the long interval (up to 12 hours) between tasting the food (CS) and experiencing poisoned-based illness (UCS), the rat learns to *avoid* other, similar-tasting foods (CR). No principle in classical conditioning can adequately explain such *one-trial learning* and why such a long CS-UCS interval is effective in eliciting a CR.

Interestingly enough, other stimuli present at the same time are not avoided later, only those associated with *taste,* as shown in a study by **John Garcia,** the psychologist who first discovered the phenomenon of taste-aversion learning. According to Garcia's work with his colleague Robert Koelling (1966), in particular species of animals there are some CS-UCS combinations that can be classically conditioned—and some that cannot be learned. For example, the experimental rats learned an association between the flavor of the bait and a later illness; they did not learn to associate the flavor with a simultaneous pain. Similarly, they learned to associate sound and light cues with a shock-produced pain, but did not connect these sensory cues with illness (see Figure 6.3). This probably makes "sense" to the rat's brain, since experience has taught it that illness can follow drinking and pain can follow an event involving light and noise. Garcia and Koelling's results suggest that rats have an inborn bias to associate particular stimuli with particular consequences.

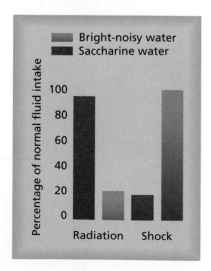

FIGURE 6.3   Associating Cues with Outcomes ■ Rats possess an inborn bias to associate certain cues with certain outcomes. Rats avoided saccharine-flavored water when it predicted illness, but not when it predicted shock. They avoided the "bright-noisy" water when it predicted shock, but not when it predicted illness (Garcia & Koelling, 1966).

Even without conditioning, most animals show **bait shyness,** *an unlearned reluctance to sample new foods or even familiar food in a strange environment.* Of all the stimuli available to them, animals seem to use the sensory cues—of taste, smell, or appearance—that are most adaptive in their natural environments to respond to potential edible or dangerous foods. Evolution has provided organisms with a survival mechanism for avoiding foods that are toxic and thus illness-producing, and perhaps all unfamiliar foods are responded to as potentially toxic until proven otherwise. In a sense, only "fools rush in" where wise animals fear to eat.

Applications of Taste Aversion   The principles of conditioned food aversion have been applied to treating a diverse range of subjects, from coyotes to cancer patients. To stop coyotes from killing sheep (and sheep ranchers from shooting coyotes), John Garcia and his colleagues put toxic lamb burgers wrapped in sheep fur on the outskirts of fenced-in areas of sheep ranches. The coyotes who ate these lamb burgers got sick, vomited, and developed an instant distaste for lamb meat. Their subsequent disgust at the mere sight of sheep made them back away instead of attack them (Garcia, 1990).

Cancer patients often develop aversions to normal foods in their diets to such an extent that they become anorexic and malnourished. In part their aversions are a serious consequence of their chemotherapy treatments, which produce nausea and are often administered following meals. Researchers are working to prevent the development of aversions to nutritive foods, which are necessary in the diets of children with cancer, by arranging for meals not to be given just before the chemotherapy and by presenting the children with a "scapegoat" aversion. They are given candies or unusually flavored ice cream before the treatments so that the taste aversion becomes conditioned only to those special flavors. Extension of this practical solution to problems with chemotherapy may be a lifesaver for some cancer patients (Bernstein, 1988, 1991).

Some instances of conditioning, then, depend on the way an organism is genetically predisposed toward stimuli in its environment (Barker et al., 1978). What any organism can—and cannot—learn in a given setting is to some extent a product of its evolutionary history (Garcia, 1993).

Check Your Recall

In classical conditioning, a biologically significant stimulus, the unconditional stimulus (UCS) elicits a reflex called the unconditional response (UCR). During acquisition, a neutral stimulus is repeatedly paired with the UCS until it becomes a conditional stimulus (CS), eliciting a similar conditional response (CR). If the CS is presented without the UCS, extinction or disappearance of the CR occurs. After a rest period, presentation of the CS alone may elicit the CR in spontaneous recovery.

Stimulus generalization involves making a similar CR to stimuli which, though different, resemble the CS. Stimulus discrimination occurs if similar stimuli are not followed by the UCS; the organism ceases responding to irrelevant stimuli, and makes the CR only to the original CS. Classical conditioning is most effective if the CS contrasts with other stimuli, if the UCS appears contingent on the CS, and if the CS is uniquely informative about the UCS. Classical conditioning occurs because it enables the organism to learn behaviors that promote survival. An example is learned taste aversion, in which an organism avoids food it has learned to associate with illness. Taste aversions are quickly learned, long lasting, and can be difficult to extinguish.

Operant Conditioning

Pavlov's pioneering work in classical conditioning demonstrated the power of stimulus associations between stimuli (S-S connections) to create new stimulus-response (S-R) sequences. These principles are at work in many everyday situations—such as in the visibility of vivid advertising designed to evoke feelings and promise need gratification. However, we have been designed by evolution not merely to *feel,* but to take *action.* We are behaving organisms, and we survive by acting right, not only by feeling good. Further, most of our actions are more complex than reflexes like salivation. When we face complex situations, how do we learn which path to choose? Simple—the choices we make depend on the *consequences* we face.

Connections and Consequences

At about the same time that Pavlov was using classical conditioning to induce Russian dogs to salivate to the sound of a bell, **Edward L. Thorndike** (1898) was watching American cats trying to escape from puzzle boxes (see Figure 6.4). He reported his observations and his inferences about the kind of learning taking place in his subjects: "When put into the box, the cat shows evident signs of discomfort and develops an impulse to escape from confinement. . . . The cat that is clawing all over the box in [its] impulsive struggle will probably claw the string or loop or button so as to open the door. And gradually . . . the particular impulse leading to the successful act will be *stamped in* by the resulting pleasure, until, after many trials, the cat will, when put in the box, immediately claw the button or loop in a definite way" (Thorndike, 1898, p. 13).

For Thorndike's cats, learning was an association not between two stimuli but between situational stimuli and a response that a subject learned to make—a *stimulus-response connection (S-R).* Thorndike believed that responses repeatedly followed by rewards brought satisfaction and were strengthened or "stamped in"; nonrewarded responses were weakened or "stamped out." Thorndike's conditioning procedure allowed an animal to respond freely, but only one of its responses would have a satisfying consequence.

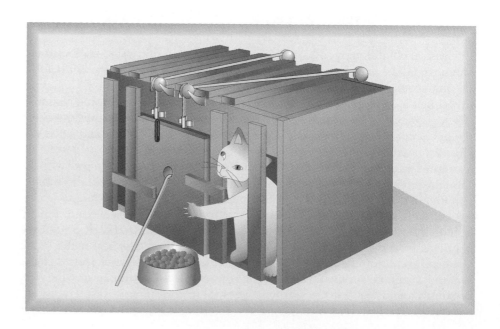

FIGURE 6.4   A Thorndike Puzzle Box ■ To escape the puzzle box and obtain food, Thorndike's cat had to operate a mechanism to release a weight that would pull the door open.

The Law of Effect The strengthening of S-R connections, according to Thorndike's theory, occurs gradually and mechanically as the animal experiences the consequences of its actions through blind trial-and-error. Gradually, the behaviors that have satisfying consequences increase in frequency; they eventually become the dominant response when the animal is placed in the puzzle box. According to Thorndike's **law of effect,** *the power of a stimulus to evoke a response is strengthened when the response is followed by a reward, and weakened when the response is not followed by a reward.*

The law of effect has an important conceptual parallel to *natural selection* in evolution (Skinner, 1981). In natural selection, the environment determines which genes become more frequent in future populations. Similarly, the law of effect describes how environmental consequences produced by behavior increase the frequency of that behavior in the future. Behaviors that lead to satisfying or rewarding consequences are "selected": they become more likely to occur than behaviors leading to unsatisfying or punishing consequences. For example, if you find that, as you go to bed, punching up your pillow makes you sleep more comfortably, you are likely to repeat the pillow-punching behavior more frequently, even when you sleep in a different bed with a different pillow.

Thorndike based his theories on animal learning, but he believed that the law of effect also applied to human learning. His ideas had a major impact on the field of educational psychology in his time. In his own work, however, Thorndike found that animal learning was easier to study scientifically than human learning was. In most cases, his ultimate hope was that basic research with nonhumans would shed more light on the mysteries of human learning—on how we have learned the many *habits* that form our behavioral repertoires.

Behavior Analysis **B. F. Skinner** embraced Thorndike's view that environmental consequences influenced the responses that preceded them. However, Skinner rejected any inferences about an organism's intentions, purposes, or goals. What an animal "wanted" was not important. Skinner refused to hypothesize about what happens inside an organism. For example, while approaching and eating can be observed and recorded, desire for food or pleasure at eating cannot be measured or confirmed. In contrast with classical conditioning, Skinner's research did not focus on reflexive behaviors elicited by environmental stimuli. Instead, Skinner concentrated on *operant responses.* An **operant** *is an observable, voluntary behavior that an organism emits to "operate" or have an effect on the environment.*

Classical conditioning involves building up the strength of respondent behavior (salivation) that is an automatic, involuntary response to a powerful stimulus (food) with a neutral stimulus signaling food is on the way. In contrast, Skinner's operant conditioning starts with the organism making a voluntary response (seeking food) that operates on the environment to produce either rewarding (gets food) or punishing consequences (getting lost or hurt by seeking the wrong food in the wrong places). For Pavlov, the food stimulus precedes the conditional response; for Skinner, the food stimulus *follows* the operant response, thereby making that reinforced action more likely to be repeated.

The basic data of operant conditioning research are the frequency and strength of responding (for rats, pressing a bar; for pigeons, pecking a key) that is followed by various consequences. Some consequences increase the probability of the operant response, while others decrease that likelihood. For example, among human beings, smoking cigarettes is an operant behavior, which is reinforced by the nicotine-addictive properties of inhaled tobacco. However, in recent years many people have cut down or stopped smoking

B. F. Skinner is shown at work building a scale model of a Skinner box, a small cage for housing an animal. The experimenter is in control of the subject's physical environment.

altogether, because their behavior is now followed by social rejection from peers—a more powerful consequence to them than the sensory pleasure they associate with inhaling smoke into their lungs.

Reinforcement

Significant events that strengthen an organism's responses—if they are delivered only in connection with those responses—are called **reinforcers.** If an attractive classmate seems to smile at you only when you offer help, and you volunteer your help more and more often as a result, this winsome smile is your reinforcer. Reinforcers are always defined empirically—in terms of their observable effects on changing the probability of a response.

A **reinforcement contingency** *is a consistent relationship between a response and the changes in the environment that it produces.* Using Skinner's work as a foundation, modern behavior analysts seek to understand how behavior is shaped and maintained by reinforcement contingencies. For example, if you were to attend a dinner meeting designed to get new college student recruits for Reverend Sun Myung Moon's Unification Church, you would be "love-bombed" for agreeing with members and lecturers: members would reward you with attentive glances, smiles, praise, hugs, and warm gestures of approval. But if you showed any doubt or dissatisfaction, those reinforcers would be withheld. If you valued the approval you got, it is likely your behavior, like that of others we have known in these circumstances, would come to be controlled by the rewards *contingent on* (following from) your behavior. Note that such "power" would be possible only if you were someone who needed strokes from strangers. Recruiters for the Unification Church and similar groups are amateur behavior analysts, who count on strong social motivation among potential new members as they design strategies to influence the likelihood of their joining and becoming loyal members.

By varying *schedules of reinforcement*—the timing and frequency of reinforcements—behavior analysts can affect the rate at which any response is learned and how well it endures over time. Curiously, if you want to develop a hardy response that persists over time, it is better to reinforce it only partially—that is, on some occasions, rather than all the time. Why would this be so? If reinforcement is continuous, as when a friend smiles every time you tell her a joke, then the first time it doesn't occur—the first time you relate a joke but get no smile—you know that something is wrong. Perhaps your joking was in poor taste, or you told it badly. After continuous reinforcement, the first withholding of reinforcement weakens the response; next time you see your friend, you feel hesitant to tell another joke.

In contrast, if the response was reinforced only intermittently, you have not developed an expectation that reward will follow every response. The first time reinforcement is withheld "for good" may seem like just one more of the familiar delays in getting rewarded, so the response continues to be emitted for a longer period. You consider that perhaps your friend didn't smile at your joke because she had something on her mind—it may have had nothing to do with your response or how you made it. So you try again and again before eventually giving up. This pattern of greater resistance to weakening of a learned response by training under partial reward conditions is known as the *partial reinforcement effect.* Because most of our social behaviors are "trained" with only occasional rewards—smiles, formal thanks, salary increases—we may persist in habits that no longer work well past the time when others have ceased reinforcing them simply because we have gotten used to such partial reinforcement in the past.

By understanding the key properties of reinforcement, behavior analysts can apply their understanding of reinforcement contingencies to a wide variety of situations—from helping people to stop smoking to training porpoises to jump through hoops.

Increasing Responses   The term *reinforcement* includes all contingencies that *increase* a behavior. Behavior analysts have identified both positive reinforcers (which work when they are *presented*) and negative reinforcers (which work when they are *removed or prevented*).

Positive Reinforcers *Any stimulus that is contingent upon a behavior and increases the probability of that behavior over time is a* **positive reinforcer.** A food pellet positively reinforces a rat's lever-pressing behavior. Getting a laugh positively reinforces joke-telling in humans. Your obvious attention to your instructor's lecture positively reinforces that lecturing behavior.

Behavior that produces desirable consequences is reinforced and repeated. We can use this principle to identify exactly *what* is desirable to organisms that cannot communicate their desires. For example, newborn infants cannot directly tell researchers whether they recognize or prefer their own mothers' voices. Research has shown, however, that newborns will learn a response (sucking on an artificial nipple) that gives them the opportunity to hear their mothers' voices instead of the voice of another female (DeCasper & Fifer, 1980).

Negative Reinforcers *If removing, reducing, or preventing a particular stimulus increases the probability of a given behavior over time, the stimulus is a* **negative reinforcer.** The process of removing or withholding such a stimulus following a response is called *negative reinforcement*. Using an umbrella to prevent getting wet during a downpour is a common example of a behavior that is maintained by negative reinforcement. You avoid the negative reinforcer (getting wet) by using an umbrella. An automobile seat-belt buzzer also serves as a negative reinforcer; its annoying sound stops only when the driver makes the desired response by buckling up.

To distinguish between positive and negative reinforcement, try to remember the following: Both positive and negative *reinforcement* will *reinforce or increase* the probability of the response they follow. The gratitude of a friend is a positive stimulus that positively reinforces you to share your umbrella with that friend; getting wet is a negative stimulus that negatively reinforces you to use the umbrella in the first place.

Social Reinforcers In the opening case we saw that young Donna Smith deliberately lied to her therapist—claiming that her father had once molested her—and then repeated similar stories to other authorities. Donna later explained that she hoped her first lie would satisfy (and put an end to) her therapist's repeated demands that Donna "admit" such abuse had happened. The pressure her therapist put on Donna may have created negative reinforcement: Donna told one lie to lessen this pressure, then fabricated additional stories (increased her lying response) to produce the same result with other social workers and clinicians. Later, the attention and approval Donna received once she took her case to the authorities provided positive reinforcement for maintaining her new pattern of relating stories of parental abuse.

Whether Donna was seeking to *reduce* her therapist's nagging or to *keep* the rewarding approval she got from foster parents or other authorities, both consequences had the same reinforcing effect of increasing her tendency to make up, tell, and even believe false accusations against her parents. Before condemning Donna for acting as she did, it is important to consider how much of people's behavior is socially reinforced, fed and strengthened by the attention, praise, and support of significant others and of those considered influential in one's culture. Different cultures reinforce behaviors.

Kicking a vending machine would be reinforced if candy or soda came out as a result.

Decreasing Responses   Positive and negative reinforcement explain how new behaviors are acquired and old ones maintained. Suppose, however, that you wanted to *eliminate* an existing operant. How would you do it? You have two options: you can *extinguish* the response, or you can *punish* it.

Extinction   If a learned response ceases to produce the reinforcing consequences it once led to, the response will be extinguished. **Operant extinction** *is a procedure in which reinforcement is withheld in order to weaken the response to its original level.*

For example, smiling and nodding are behaviors you can use to reinforce your professor's tendency to make eye contact with you. Withholding these social reinforcers will decrease the probability of the professor looking at you as often. But extinction does not require human manipulation; situations can change so that circumstances no longer reinforce learned behaviors. For example, if the light switch to your classroom stops working, students and instructors will eventually stop flicking the switch as they enter the room. And have you ever had the experience of dropping money into a vending machine only to get nothing in return? If you kicked the machine and your soda or candy came out, kicking would be reinforced. However, if your kicking produced no soda, candy, or satisfaction, this useless response would soon be extinguished.

To deliberately extinguish an unwanted response, one must somehow withhold all possible reinforcers. This is harder than you might think outside the control of the laboratory. In real life, many stimuli may strengthen or maintain a particular behavior. A parent, teacher, or work supervisor will not be able to identify easily—much less control—the many reinforcers that maintain another person's unwanted response pattern. For this reason, extinction outside the laboratory is more likely to take effect when withholding of reinforcement is combined with positive reinforcement of the *desired* response. A child who throws public tantrums to get his parents' attention is more likely to stop such misbehavior if (1) the rewarding attention is withheld (operant extinction) and (2) alternative behaviors are rewarded with attention and social approval (positive reinforcement of desired behavior). If a tantrum-pitching child learns that tantrums never work but requests made in a polite voice do result in rewarding outcomes, the tantrums will be extinguished and replaced.

Punishment   Punishment is another technique for decreasing the probability of a response. *Punishment* is the delivery of a punisher following a response. *Any stimulus that is made contingent upon a response and decreases the probability of that response over time is called a* **punisher.** If you touch a hot stove, for example, the pain will punish you and reduce the likelihood of repeating that mistake. Responses that are punished immediately tend to decrease in frequency; however, responses that produce delayed aversive consequences are only suppressed temporarily. If a misbehaving child is immediately punished, she is less likely to repeat the misbehavior; but if her distracted babysitter delays punishment with a threat of "Wait till your parents get home!," the child may repeat her offense. Punishment must also be administered consistently or it loses effectiveness. When a formerly punished response no longer produces aversive consequences, it tends to increase in frequency to prepunishment levels.

Just as reinforcement comes in both positive and negative forms, punishment can also be either positive (by *presenting* a stimulus) or negative (by *removing* one). *Positive punishment* involves delivering a painful or unpleasant consequence to a response. Examples of positive punishment are abundant in life and media, and easy to imagine: inflicting pain, criticism, humiliation,

Calvin and Hobbes
by Bill Watterson

The probability of someone making a response can be decreased if that response is followed by an aversive consequence, such as a loud noise or angry complaint.

disapproval, rejection, and fines. Positive punishment is clearly popular in most societies and institutions, but it is costly in the sense that it is destructive and creates hostility. Positive punishment can also inadvertently *teach* some of the very responses it is meant to eliminate. If a child who hits others is punished with a spanking, he is being given a mixed message: hitting others is wrong—unless you are powerful enough to get away with it.

In contrast, *negative punishment* does not inflict pain or shame, but deprives the learner of a valued goal or activity. For example, a misbehaving child can be given an immediate "time out," a brief confinement in a room without toys, television, or companionship. Other types of negative punishment involve withholding privileges, such as dessert, opportunities for leisure activity, transportation, or freedom. Negative punishment is less impulsive and harder to devise than positive punishment, but negative punishment does not send the same mixed messages, model aggression, or foster hostility and despair in learners to the same degree that positive punishment does.

Punishment is *not* the same as negative reinforcement. Although punishment and negative reinforcement are closely related, they differ in important ways. By definition, punishment always *decreases* a behavior, or reduces its probability of recurring. In contrast, negative reinforcement—like all reinforcement—always *increases* a response's probability of occurring again. Despite some surface similarities (they both involve unpleasant stimuli or experiences), punishment and negative reinforcement are completely opposite in their *effects on behavior* (Baum, 1994). Remember that reinforcement—even negative reinforcement—always reinforces or strengthens a response. Punishment always decreases or eliminates a response. In discussing operant conditioning, the descriptors "positive" and "negative" are not synonyms for "pleasant" and "unpleasant," but rather for "present" and "absent." Positive reinforcement and positive punishment both involve administering or presenting a stimulus. Negative reinforcement and punishment always involve withholding or removing a stimulus. Whether the consequences are pleasant or unpleasant depends on the nature of the stimulus. See Table 6.1 for a summary of the distinctions between positive and negative reinforcement and punishment.

The Uses and Abuses of Punishment   To eliminate undesired behaviors, it is more effective and lasting to reinforce alternative, desired behavior. If you want a child to stop reaching for food without asking permission first, you will get better results if you reinforce a desired behavior—teaching the child to say, "Please pass the French fries"—than by scolding the child, smacking the reaching hand, or depriving the child of dinner for the offense. However, people and institutions may decide that such reinforcement is not practical or cannot be delivered expediently. If punishment is the only alternative and the unwanted

TABLE 6.1	REINFORCEMENT AND PUNISHMENT	
	Effect of Consequence on Response	
Nature of Stimulus That Follows Response	**Increases Response (Reinforcer)**	**Decreases Response (Punisher)**
Presented or added (positive)	*Positive reinforcer:* reward, food, prize, award, praise, thanks	*Positive punisher:* inflicting pain, discomfort, criticism, disapproval
Removed or withheld (negative)	*Negative reinforcer:* removing/preventing pain, discomfort, penalty	*Negative punisher:* removing/withholding privileges, nonvital resources, freedom

response must be decreased, research shows that punishment will be most effective if it meets the conditions outlined below (Walters & Grusec, 1977):

- Punishment should be swift and brief.
- It should be administered immediately after the unwanted response.
- It should be limited in intensity.
- It should target the behavior, not the character of the behaver.
- It should be limited to the situation where the response occurs.
- The punishment should not give mixed messages to the punished person (e.g., "You are not permitted to hit others" but "I am allowed to hit you").
- The most effective punishment consists of penalties (such as loss of privileges) rather than physical pain.

As you examine this extensive checklist, it may occur to you that most old-fashioned disciplinarians would fail to meet these requirements. It is widely accepted in this and other cultures that punishment is not only necessary, but actually "beneficial" to character—"Spare the rod and spoil the child" (not a quote from the Bible, incidentally, but certainly a sentiment in the Book of Proverbs). Are the consequences of punishment, such as physically and verbally assaulting wrongdoers, serious enough that we should question such sacred assumptions? Research consistently argues that they are. When those in authority resort to using punishment to control people's behavior, they show that they have failed to find ways to motivate or reward those they have power over. Those who deliver punishment can lose control too easily and abuse their victims, especially children. Punishment causes physical harm, emotional scars, and hatred of the punisher. Worst of all, the punished person learns that aggression is an acceptable means of controlling others (Bongiovanni, 1977; Hyman, in Schmidt, 1987). Finally, as we review in Focus on Application: To Become Helpless—Or Hopeful?, it is clear that when responses are punished or merely seem to be ineffective, individuals may become helpless, defeated, and depressed. In light of these findings, punishment may be impossible to administer effectively, responsibly, and without costly side effects.

Controlling Reinforcement Contingencies

Reinforcers and punishers are the power brokers of operant conditioning; they change or maintain behavior. Contingent reinforcement (reinforcement that consistently follows behavior) strengthens responding; contingent punishment

FOCUS on Application

To Become Helpless— or Hopeful?

If reinforcement increases desirable responses while punishment suppresses undesirable responses, what happens when the individual gets punished arbitrarily regardless of the response? Suppose that, after standing in long, slow lines to register for your college courses, you find that a class you wanted is closed. You choose a substitute and join another line to register for it. After a boring, uncomfortable wait, you finally reach the registration desk— only to find that this course, too, is closed. What do you do? Eventually, you probably give up—you stop trying to register for any desirable class. Because environmental consequences seem unrelated to your responses—obediently waiting until it is your turn—you stop making any effort to register. This *passive resignation following prolonged, noncontingent, inescapable punishment is termed* **learned helplessness.**

Learned helplessness was discovered by **Martin Seligman** and his colleagues (Maier & Seligman, 1976; Seligman, 1975; Seligman & Maier, 1967). As a graduate student, Seligman conducted research in which he conditioned dogs to associate a high-pitched auditory tone (the CS) with a mild shock (the UCS)—about as strong as a jolt of static electricity you would feel when you touch a doorknob or car door on a cold day. Some dogs had no control over receiving shocks while others could turn the shocks off by pressing a panel with their noses; a control group received no shocks at all. After exposure to this shock/control experience, the dogs were transferred to a shuttlebox, with a low wall separating the shocking side from the nonshocking side. Dogs were placed in the shocking compartment, and the researchers watched for their escape responses—except that the dogs who had received uncontrollable shocks *never made an effort to escape the shocks.* Seligman concluded these animals had already learned that nothing they did mattered or altered the consequences, so they "gave up and lay down" (Seligman, 1991, p. 23), and passively accepted the occasional shocks delivered by the compartment (Seligman & Maier, 1967).

There are some obvious parallels between learned helplessness in animals and depression in humans (Seligman, 1975). An experiment by Donald Hiroto (1974) employed human subjects in a variation of Seligman's dog research. Subjects were first placed in a room where they were bombarded by loud noise. Some quickly learned to turn off the noise by pressing various buttons on a control panel, but other subjects could not find any pattern of button-pressing to stop the noise. When all subjects were placed in a new situation, in which a different annoying "whooshing" noise could be easily stopped by a simple hand movement, only those who had learned to stop the loud noise *attempted* to stop the whooshing sound. The veterans of inescapable noise just sat in the new room, making no effort to stop the latest stressor. They had already learned to be helpless.

Seligman (1991) wonders whether human loss in general—rejection, failure, death of a loved one—sometimes "teaches" people to be helpless, depressed, and pessimistic. If helplessness is learned, then the antidote to helplessness—an optimistic pattern in thinking and action—might also be learnable. "Life inflicts the same setbacks and tragedies on the optimist as on the pessimist," writes Seligman in *Learned Optimism* (1991), "but the optimist weathers them better." He advises those who feel depressed or helpless to learn to be more optimistic, mainly by acquiring new skills in *talking to themselves* about the meaning and causes of personal setbacks. For example, if a dieter splurges on a piece of dessert, instead of thinking, "Since I've ruined my whole diet—I might as well eat the whole cake!", she should try to tell herself, "Well, I enjoyed that, but I'll stop with that piece, and I know I am strong enough to stick to this diet most of the time." In essence, Seligman argues that optimism is learned by adopting a *constructive* style of thinking, self-assessment, and behavioral planning.

---

suppresses responding. Noncontingent stimuli have little effect on behavior; if your behavior does not seem to be a condition for the good or bad things that befall you, you are unlikely to change it. In applied settings, researchers have identified a wide array of strategies for applying reinforcement contingencies to modify humans' and nonhumans' behavior. Here we will briefly discuss three approaches to applied reinforcement: conditioned reinforcers, preferred activities, and shaping.

Conditioned Reinforcers   In operant conditioning, *neutral stimuli paired with primary reinforcers, such as food and water, acquire a reinforcing effect, becoming* **conditioned reinforcers** for operant responses. Conditioned reinforcers serve as ends in themselves, substituting for the *primary reinforcers* that directly meet an organism's needs. Human behavior is influenced by a wide variety of conditioned reinforcers. Money, grades, praise, smiles of approval, gold stars, and various kinds of status symbols are among the many potent conditioned reinforcers that can influence our learning and behavior.

Virtually any stimulus can become a conditioned reinforcer by being paired with a primary reinforcer.

In one early study, simple tokens were used as conditioned reinforcers with animal learners. Chimps were trained to learn how to solve problems with edible raisins as primary reinforcers. Then tokens were delivered along with the raisins. When only the tokens were presented, the chimps continued working for their "money" because they could later deposit their hard-earned tokens in a "chimp-o-mat" designed to exchange tokens for the raisins (Cowles, 1937).

In some mental institutions, *token economies* have been set up to influence patients' behavior. Desired behaviors (grooming or taking medication, for example) are explicitly defined, and token payoffs are given by the staff when these behaviors are performed. Tokens can later be exchanged by the patients for a wide array of rewards and privileges (Ayllon & Azrin, 1965; Holden, 1978). These systems of reinforcement are especially effective in promoting patients' self-care, maintenance of their environment, and positive interactions with others. Systems of behavior modification that rely on token reinforcement have been criticized by humanistic psychologists as promoting materialistic values. True, it is easier to establish conditioned reinforcement when the units of exchange have a familiar, concrete value. Token economies fall short of the higher goal of having individuals cultivate their own, more abstract value systems. But they provide useful strategies for teaching people how to act effectively in the world beyond the artificial control of the laboratory or institution (Kazdin, 1994).

Preferred Activities   In the laboratory positive reinforcers are usually substances, such as food or water. However, outside the laboratory, activities are just as likely to operate as behavior reinforcers. People who exercise regularly might use a daily run or fitness class as a "reward" for getting other tasks done. Grade school teachers have even found that children will learn to sit still if such behavior is reinforced with occasional permission to run around and make noise (Homme et al., 1963).

The principle that a more probable activity can be used to reinforce a less preferred one is called the **Premack principle**—so named after its discoverer **David Premack** (1965). He found that water-deprived rats learned to increase their running in an exercise wheel when the running was followed by an opportunity to drink. Other rats that were not thirsty but exercise-deprived would learn to increase their drinking when that response was followed by a chance to run. According to the Premack principle, a reinforcer may be any event or activity that is valued by the organism.

The Premack principle is often used by parents and teachers to get children to engage in low-probability activities. For a shy child, the opportunity to read a new book could be used to reinforce the less preferred activity of playing with other children. The preferred activity, used as a reinforcer, increases the probability that the individual will engage in an activity that is less preferred. Over time, there is the possibility that less-favored activities will become more valued as exposure to them leads individuals to discover their intrinsic worth. The once-shy child might eventually enjoy playing with others and no longer require the promise of a preferred activity to reinforce social interaction.

Shaping   A problem encountered by many behavior analysts is the difficulty of getting the organism to perform the desired behavior so that it can be reinforced. Suppose you want to train your dog to roll over on command. Must you wait and watch until the moment finally arrives when the dog spontaneously rolls over, so you can immediately reward this behavior? Chances are you will wait a long time for the animal to display such a specific sequence of action purely by chance. A more efficient option is to *shape* the dog's behavior, administering reinforcement in steps that get closer and closer to what you want—a complete sequence of rolling over on command.

Shaping *is a procedure for changing behavior in small steps that successively approximate the desired end performance.* When shaping begins, any element of the target response is reinforced. Once this element occurs regularly, only responses more like the final goal response are reinforced. By reinforcing more and more specific versions of the target behavior, an experimenter can shape this higher-level action.

Suppose a psychologist wishes to train a rat to press a lever in an operant chamber. The rat uses its paws in many ways but has probably never pressed a lever before. First, the experimenter deprives the rat of food for a day, to make food a valuable reinforcer. Next, she teaches it to eat food pellets from the food tray in an operant chamber. When the rat is properly motivated and trained in finding food, the psychologist begins the shaping process. First she delivers food only when the rat behaves in specific ways, such as when it leans toward the lever. Next, food is delivered only as the rat moves closer to the lever. Soon the requirement for reinforcement is for the rat actually to touch the lever. Finally, the rat must depress the lever to trigger food delivery. Now the chamber can be rigged to deliver food pellets automatically when the lever is pressed, and the rat can be left on its own; it has learned—one step at a time—that it can produce food by pressing the lever.

Shaping is of interest to those who would influence human behavior as well. We often wish to get other people to make responses that seldom appear spontaneously. For example, suppose a teacher wants to encourage class participation, especially among those students who don't usually offer answers or opinions. Could you devise a shaping procedure for an instructor to use to teach the quieter students first to volunteer answers, then to offer more assertive and thoughtful statements on a regular basis?

Animals can learn to do some surprising things (like water skiing!), with a little help from their human friends and the application of operant conditioning techniques.

The Limits of Operant Conditioning

You may have seen animals in public aquariums or water shows trained to engage in very "human" behavior, such as riding small bicycles or playing musical instruments. Clearly their behavior has been carefully shaped by their trainers. What is the prognosis for such behavior? Once learned, do such intricate lessons last a lifetime? The answer is no: the less relevant a learned behavior is to a species' survival, the more artificial and temporary that behavior will be. For example, all cats normally cover their urine and feces by scratching local dirt and brush. House cats therefore can readily learn to use litter boxes and to maintain that behavior. However, a cat trained to use and flush a toilet is responding in ways that are not part of the species' inherited behavior patterns. The cat's owner may value the novelty or convenience of the trained behavior, but will probably find that, without constant maintenance training, the cat will revert to a more natural place and pattern.

Biological constraints on learning *are limitations on learning imposed by a species' genetic endowment.* These constraints can apply to the animal's sensory, behavioral, and cognitive capacities. The fact that there are such constraints suggests that the principles of conditioning cannot be universally applied to all species across all situations and that not all reinforcement contingencies work equally well to produce learning in any given species. Research on *species-specific behavior*—behavior patterns that are unique to a particular species—shows that behavior-environment relations can be *biased* by an organism's genotype.

In the 1950s and 1960s, animal trainers **Keller** and **Marian Breland** used operant conditioning techniques to train thousands of animals from many

Researchers Keller and Marian Breland used operant conditioning techniques to train thousands of animals like this basketball-playing raccoon. Although initially the animals may behave perfectly, they eventually "misbehave" and conform with inborn action patterns, a trend known as instinctual drift.

different species to perform a remarkable array of behaviors. The Brelands believed that they could apply general principles derived from laboratory research using virtually any type of response or reward to control animal behavior outside the laboratory. At some point after their training, however, some of their animals began to "misbehave." For example, a raccoon was trained (after great difficulty) to pick up a coin, put it into a toy bank, and collect an edible reinforcer. Eventually, however, the raccoon would not immediately deposit the coin. Later, when there were two coins to be deposited, conditioning broke down completely—the raccoon would not give up the coins at all. Instead, it would rub the coins together, dip them into the bank, and then pull them back out. Such behavior seems strange until you consider that raccoons often engage in rubbing and washing behaviors as they remove the outer shells of a favorite food, crayfish.

Such experiences convinced the Brelands that, even when animals have learned to make operant responses perfectly, the newly "learned behavior drifts toward instinctual behavior" over time. The Brelands coined the term **instinctual drift** *for this tendency over time for learned behavior to relapse and resemble instinctual behavior* (Breland & Breland, 1951, 1961). The animals' behavior is understandable if we consider the species-specific tendencies imposed by an inherited genotype—for example, that raccoons naturally rub objects together before eating them. These tendencies override the temporary changes in behavior brought about by operant conditioning. In fact, the inherited behavioral pattern is incompatible with the operant conditioning task. The animals' misbehaviors were a manifestation of natural, biologically significant relationships interfering with learning a new sequence of behaviors.

We have seen that the two forms of basic learning, classical and operant conditioning, account for a dramatic range of human and nonhuman behavior change. There are limits or constraints, however, on their applicability and effectiveness. In addition to biological constraints, we next consider the implications—both limits and possibilities—offered by a cognitive perspective on learning, one that contrasts with a purely behavioristic one. Finally, for any learning to be effective over time, the lessons we learn must be stored in memory for later use. We conclude this chapter with an exploration of the mental processes involved in remembering lessons and experiences.

✓ Check Your Recall

According to Edward L. Thorndike's law of effect, behavior that produces satisfying outcomes tends to be repeated. B. F. Skinner incorporated the principles of Thorndike's law into his study of operant conditioning. In behavior analysis, reinforcement contingencies are manipulated and the effects on behavior are observed. Responses increase when they are positively or negatively reinforced; they decrease when they are extinguished or punished. Punishment can have unwanted consequences for individuals and society. When responses are punished or ineffective, individuals can learn to become helpless or depressed.

Neutral stimuli—such as money, status, or praise—can become conditioned reinforcers through their association with primary reinforcers. Activities can function as reinforcers if they are preferred or more probable for the learner. Complex sequences of behavior can be taught through shaping, a step-by-step process of reinforcing responses that come close to the desired response pattern. Operant conditioning is limited by biological constraints. Animals taught unnatural responses may revert eventually to preconditioning patterns, a process known as instinctual drift. ✓

Cognitive Views of Learning

Skinner insisted on building a psychology of learning based solely on observable events. However, psychologists have found that cognitive processes are significant in many kinds of learning. **Cognition** *is any mental activity involved in the representation and processing of knowledge.* Cognitive activities include

"Well, you don't look like an experimental psychologist to me."

The New Yorker by S. Gross, November 12, 1994

Recognition is also the method employed when police ask an eyewitness to identify a perpetrator among a lineup of suspects. In both multiple choice examinations and criminal investigations, the tested individual must determine whether—and which—immediate stimuli match those previously encountered.

On examinations, recall questions usually give fewer and less specific cues than recognition questions, and thus seem "harder" to those taking the test. There is another important difference between recognition and recall. For recognition, you need simply to match a remembered stimulus against a present perception; both the stimulus and the perception are in your consciousness. For recall, however, you must reconstruct from memory something that is not in the present environment and then describe it well enough so that an observer can be sure about what is really in your mind.

Encoding, storage, and retrieval processes take place in each of three basic memory systems. Before we turn to examine what these memory systems do, take a moment to answer the questions that follow:

1. What is your social security number? What is your best friend's?
2. Name the title and authors of this textbook.
3. When did you *last* experience the emotion of guilt?
4. How is classical conditioning different from operant conditioning?
5. What is the significance of "Rosebud" in the movie *Citizen Kane?*

Your recall was probably quick and certain on some items, incomplete and vague on others. You cannot recall what you have never learned (e.g., your friend's social security number).

Is your memory for negative emotional experiences like guilt similar to your ability to recall numbers or names? Are there answers you are sure you do *not* know? Familiarizing yourself with your own memory and retrieval mechanisms will help clarify some of the abstract discussions of the memory types and processes that follow.

Three Memory Systems

Psychologists are fairly confident that, within the overall system of remembering and recalling information, there are three memory systems: sensory memory, working memory, and long-term memory. *Sensory memory* preserves fleeting impressions of sensory stimuli—sights, sounds, smells, and textures—for only a second or two, as when the sound of a television commercial seems to ring in your ears after you turn off the set. *Working memory* includes recollections of what you have recently perceived, such as a phone number you have just looked up; such limited information lasts only up to 20 seconds unless it receives special attention. *Long-term memory* preserves information for retrieval at any later time—up to an entire lifetime. Information in long-term memory constitutes our knowledge about the world, and includes such varied material as the lyrics to your favorite song, and the year that Wilhelm Wundt founded the first experimental laboratory in psychology. (*Quiz:* What year was that? 18__.)

The three memory systems are also thought of as *stages* in the sequence of processing information. The three systems or stages of remembering are conceptual models of the way psychologists believe we process incoming information, retain it, and then later use it. By learning how information is processed in each subsystem, psychologists hope to understand why some conditions help us remember experiences, even trivial ones, while other conditions allow us forget even important experiences. Figure 6.7 shows one hypothesized flow of information into and among these subsystems.

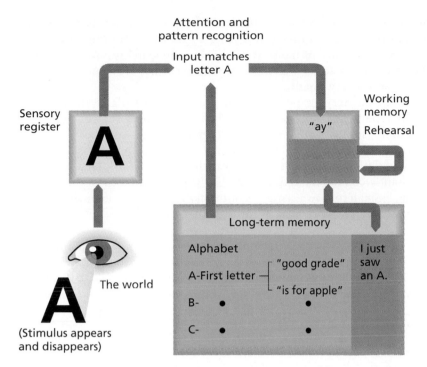

FIGURE 6.7 **A Model of the Three Systems of Human Memory** ■ As a stimulus is briefly presented to the eye, it is first processed by the sensory register, then attended to and recognized. Once it is recognized as the letter A, the pronunciation "ay" is rehearsed in short-term (working) memory. Finally, the episode of seeing the A and its meaning are stored in long-term memory.

Sensory Memory   A **sensory memory** *is an impression formed from input from any of the senses.* Sensory memory represents a primitive kind of memory and a register for each sense; it also holds appropriate incoming stimulus information for a brief interval. A visual memory, or *icon*, lasts about one-half second. An auditory memory, or *echo*, lasts several seconds (Neisser, 1967). You can easily demonstrate the difference between the sensory registers for yourself. When you turn off a radio, the sounds of the music literally echo in your head for a while after the sound is gone, but if you pull down a window shade, the scene outside is gone almost at once. Without icons and echoes, we could see and hear stimuli only at the moment they were physically present, which would not be long enough for recognition to occur. These sensory memories are essential to hold input until it is recognized and passed on for further processing.

Storage of Sensory Memories Though fleeting, your sensory storage capacity is large—more than your senses can process at one time. Early researchers underestimated the amount of stimuli that sensory memory could store because they asked subjects to report entire arrays. Subjects shown an array like the following for only a fraction of a second could report only about four items:

$$\begin{array}{ccc} D & J & B \\ X & H & G \\ C & L & Y \end{array}$$

Researcher **George Sperling** guessed that subjects had a limited ability to *report* all viewed items, but not necessarily to *recall* them. Immediately after flashing stimulus arrays, Sperling gave subjects an auditory signal about which row of letters to report. Asked to give this smaller "partial report," subjects achieved perfect accuracy—no matter *which* row was signaled. Further research confirmed that, although reporting might be limited to about four items, the span of sensory memory was as great as nine items (Sperling, 1960, 1963). However, while sensory memory is quite accurate, the image or *trace* of the stimulus decays very rapidly.

In auditory memory as well, more information is available than people can typically report (Darwin et al., 1972). Echoic memories may be necessary to process many subtle, simultaneously presented aspects of speech, such as intonation and emphasis. Would it be better if sensory memories lasted longer so that we would have more time to process them? Not really. New information is constantly coming in, and it must also be processed. Sensory memories last just long enough to give a sense of continuity but not long enough to interfere with new sensory impressions (Loftus et al., 1992).

Working Memory Working memory, *also called* **short-term memory (STM)**, *includes processes that preserve recently perceived events or experiences.* Working memory occurs between the fleeting moments of sensory memory and the more permanent storage of long-term memory. A number of interesting characteristics distinguish this memory-processing phase:

- Working memory has very *limited capacity,* retaining less information than either sensory memory or long-term memory.
- Working memory retains material for a very *short duration* of time; what is stored is lost after 18 to 20 seconds unless it is held in consciousness.
- Working memory is the only memory system in which material is *consciously processed,* and retention lasts as long as it is held in attention.

This system is called "working" memory because the material transferred in from either sensory memory or long-term memory must be worked on, thought about, and mentally organized. Working memory provides a mental "working space" to help in sorting and processing new information (Shiffrin, 1993). Working memory is an essential preliminary stage for explicit (attended) long-term memory (Cowan, 1993). For example, after looking up an unfamiliar phone number, you may repeat it to yourself or recite it aloud until you dial it, in order to keep the digit sequence in working memory. After using the number, you may "discard" it and no longer find it in memory. But if the number proves to be useful or memorable, you can use rehearsal and associations to "upgrade" it to long-term memory.

Encoding Information enters working memory as organized images and patterns that are recognized as familiar and meaningful. Verbal patterns entering working memory seem to be held there in *acoustic* form—according to the way they sound—even when they come through an individual's eyes rather than ears. When subjects are asked to recall lists of letters they have just seen, their errors tend to be confusions of letters that *sound* similar—such as D and T—rather than letters that look similar—such as D and O (Conrad, 1964). Acoustic coding may reflect our preference for verbal rehearsal of information.

Storage When the items to be remembered are *unrelated,* the capacity of working memory seems to be between five and nine bits of information—about seven (plus or minus two) familiar items, such as letters, words, numbers, or almost any kind of meaningful item. When you try to force more than seven items into working memory, earlier items are lost to accommodate more recent ones. This displacement process is similar to laying out seven 1-foot bricks on a 7-foot table. When an eighth brick is pushed on at one end, the brick at the opposite end is pushed off the table. Early work by George Miller (1956) suggested that human memory was bound by this "magic number" 7, but more recent work suggests that the limits of working memory are probably even smaller—perhaps between only two and four items (Crowder, 1976).

Processing in Working Memory There are two important ways to increase the limited capacity of short-term storage so that more of the information there can be transferred into long-term memory. These two methods—*chunking* and *rehearsal*—should be familiar to you since you already use them regularly.

A **chunk** *is a meaningful unit of information.* A chunk can be a single letter or number, a group of letters or other items, or even a group of words or an entire sentence. For example, the sequence 1–9–8–4 consists of four digits that could constitute four chunks, about the size of what your working memory can hold. However, if you see the four digits as a single meaningful sequence, they constitute only one chunk. For example, *1984* is the title of George Orwell's frightening futuristic novel (written in 1948, the last two digits transposed to suggest a distant future). **Chunking** *is the process of recoding single separate bits of information into a single meaningful unit.* When you memorize a seven-digit phone number (e.g., 5551212) as two shorter sequences of digits (555–1212, "five-five-five, one-two-one-two"), you have reduced seven bits to two chunks and have immediately increased the capacity of your remaining working memory.

Between looking up a needed telephone number and successfully dialing it, you probably repeat or recite the digits to yourself to keep them in mind. This technique is called *maintenance rehearsal.* Undistracted rehearsal appears to be essential to retaining information in working memory. Rehearsal keeps information in working memory and prevents competing inputs from pushing it out; but maintenance rehearsal is not an efficient way to transfer information to long-term memory.

To make sure that information is transferred, you need to engage in *elaborative rehearsal*, a process in which the information is not just repeated but actively analyzed and related to already stored knowledge. Suppose you must memorize the phone number 358–9211. By examining it, you realize that the two sequences are also sums: 3 + 5 = 8, and 9 + 2 = 11. The ability to develop such elaborations requires knowledge of addition rules and summations. If these rules and summations are in long-term memory, you can find patterns and meanings in otherwise unrelated and meaningless items. The same principle—using meaning to organize information—is used by services whose telephone numbers are memorable words, such as 1–800–FLOWERS for a florist delivery service.

Retrieval from Working Memory. You now know something about how to get variously sized chunks of information into your working memory, but how do you get them out? Getting them out is the task of *retrieval.* Research by Saul Sternberg (1966, 1969) has indicated that, when subjects review a list of digits in STM to discover whether it contains a specific digit, they review the entire series before answering yes or no. Thus longer lists take longer to review, although both short and long series are exhausted before a subject is sure of the answer.

Long-Term Memory (LTM)   Long-term memory (LTM) *preserves information for retrieval at any later time, and is theorized to have unlimited capacity.* LTM is the storehouse of all the experiences, events, information, emotions, skills, words, categories, rules, and judgments that have been transferred from sensory and short-term memories. LTM constitutes each person's total knowledge of the world and of the self. Material in long-term memory enables you to solve new problems, reason, keep future appointments, and use a variety of rules to manipulate abstract symbols—so that you can think about situations you have never experienced, or create new words.

Given the amount of information stored in long-term memory, it is a marvel that it is so accessible. You can often get the exact information you want in a split second:

- Who first developed classical conditioning?
- Name a play by Shakespeare.

Your responses to these requests probably came effortlessly because of several special features of long-term memory: words and concepts have been encoded by their *meanings,* linking them to many other stored items; the knowledge in your long-term memory is stored in an organized order; and many alternative cues can help you retrieve exactly what you want from all that is there.

Types of Long-Term Memory There are actually two main varieties of long-term memory—*procedural* and *declarative.* Each is distinguished by the kind of information it holds. **Procedural memory** *is the LTM subsystem that stores memory for how things are done.* It is used to acquire, retain, and employ perceptual, cognitive, and motor skills (Anderson, 1982; Tulving, 1983). Skill memories are memories of *action sequences,* such as riding a bicycle or tying shoelaces. You can consciously recall skill memories only during the early phases of performance (right after you first learn the skill). Experts perform tasks requiring advanced skills without conscious recall of the appropriate skill memories. In fact, experts are often unable to consciously think through their tasks without hindering their performance. It's easier to perform the task than to describe how to do it.

Declarative memory *is the LTM subsystem for remembering explicit information.* Declarative memory is also known as "fact memory." Unlike procedural memory, which can involve easy or automatic retrieval, declarative memory involves at least some conscious effort. When people try to produce material from declarative memory, they may roll their eyes or make facial gestures to indicate such effort. Remembering how to drive is a procedural process; recalling the directions for driving to a specific location requires declarative memory. There are two different types of declarative memory, depending on the type of material being stored: *episodic* and *semantic.*

Episodic memory stores autobiographical information—an individual's own perceptual experiences—along with some *temporal coding* (or time tags) to identify when the event occurred and some *context* coding for where it took place. For example, memories of a happiest birthday or of a first love affair are stored in episodic memory.

Semantic memory stores the basic *meanings* of words and concepts, without reference to their time and place in the rememberer's experience. Semantic memory more closely resembles an encyclopedia than an autobiography. Your semantic memory stores a vast array of generic facts about grammar, history, musical composition, manners, scientific principles, and religious beliefs. The things you know and ideas you learn are stored in semantic memory. Semantic memory can be either *explicit* (learned through deliberate effort such as in memorizing material for a test) or *implicit* (learned incidentally without your awareness). Implicit memory can come in handy when you realize you know something you never set out to learn "on purpose," but this nondeliberate quality can also cause implicit memories to be biased and inaccurate (Seger, 1994). The central distinction between accurate explicit memories and less reliable implicit memories is *attention,* the effort one makes to consciously process material.

Alex Trebek, host of the television game show *Jeopardy,* challenges contestants to identify facts by drawing on their semantic, declarative, long-term memories.

Semantic and episodic memories are not necessarily stored or retrieved separately. To successfully recall factual (semantic) information, you have to rely somewhat on episodic memory, because you often store information according to its context—the event or personal symbolism it triggers. For example, in answering a test question, you may remember not only the lecture material that provides the correct answer, but also where you were sitting when you took the notes, and where on the chalkboard the lecturer inscribed the key terms.

Remembering Meaning and Context

Sensory memory encodes brief sensations, and working memory records items in their order of arrival. In contrast, LTM stores items according to their meanings, and cross-references them with other stored information. Every item in LTM is connected by its meaning to many other indexes for retrieval. When people refer to "memory" in everyday, nonpsychological language, they usually mean the contents and processes of LTM. Because LTM is central to so much of psychology, we now take a closer look at how material in LTM is encoded, stored, and retrieved.

Meaningful Organization   The role that *meaningful organization* plays in long-term storage is demonstrated when you remember the gist or sense of an idea rather than the actual sentence you heard. For example, you may hear the sentence, "The book was returned to the library by Mary." Later, you are asked if you heard the sentence, "Mary returned the book to the library." You may indeed mistakenly remember having "heard" the second sentence, because even though the two sentences are completely different utterances, they mean the same thing. Human LTM more accurately stores meaning than form (Bransford & Franks, 1971).

Meaning is the key to organizing knowledge. If you fail to understand the meaning of a paragraph you read or a lecture you hear, you will be unable to organize the material into a memorable unit of information. Once meaning is clear, however, it can be organized in a number of different ways in LTM. Sometimes you encode by noticing the *structure* already imposed on the material, such as the different levels of headings in this chapter. At other times you may impose your own organization by outlining the main points and subpoints or by fitting new items into a structure of knowledge you already have. You may also organize material on the basis of relevant *personal* experiences or physical reminders. For example, you might remember the names of people you met over a year ago by recalling that you all attended a friend's birthday party, and the celebration included games and jokes involving all the guests' names.

The difficulties of storing new information in LTM have challenged people to develop strategies for simplifying organization and memorization. See Focus on Applications: Using Mnemonics on page 236 for a review of the most effective techniques—short-cuts you might try to use right away in learning the material in this chapter!

The Context of Encoding   Your method of organizing material in the encoding stage directly affects not only how the material is stored but, equally important, what cues will work when you want to retrieve it. Researchers assume there is a close relationship among encoding, storage, and retrieval in long-term memory. In particular, it is easier to retrieve material if certain environmental cues—the *context* of the material—are present which were also present at time of encoding. This *assumption, that information retrieval is enhanced if cues received at time of recall are consistent with those present at*

FOCUS on Application

Using Mnemonics

To help yourself remember, you can use special mental strategies called mnemonics (pronounced *nee-MON-ix,* from the Greek word meaning "remember"). **Mnemonics** *are short, verbal devices that encode a long series of facts by associating them with familiar and previously encoded information.* Three types of mnemonic strategies have been studied: natural language mediators, the method of loci, and visual imagery.

Natural language mediators are meanings or spelling patterns of words that are already stored in LTM. These can easily be associated with new information. For instance, to remember a grocery list you can concoct a story linking the items: "The cat discovers I'm out of *tuna* so she interrupts me while I'm using the *shampoo* and meows to *egg* me on," for example, to remember to buy tuna, shampoo, and eggs. The use of rhyming slogans and rhythmic musical jingles can make it easier to remember material as diverse as brand names (Kleenex), grammar rules ("I before E except after C"), and calendars ("Thirty days hath September/April, June, and November/All the rest have thirty-

one . . . "). Acronyms—words made up of initials—use natural language mediators to chunk unwieldy strings of words into pronounceable abbreviations, such as "Roy G. Biv" for the colors of visible spectrum light (red, orange, yellow, green, blue, indigo, violet) or RADAR for Radio Detecting and Ranging.

You can make places for specific memories with the *method of loci* (pronounced *LOW-sigh,* from the Latin *locus,* "place"). To use the method of loci, imagine a familiar sequence of places, such as shelves, pillows, and desktops in your room. When memorizing a series of words or names, you mentally put one in each of those places; to retrieve the series, you take a mental tour, examining those places to "see" what you have put in each one. To recall the grocery list, you might picture a can of *tuna* on your bed, *shampoo* spilled on your desktop, and a box of *eggs* open on top of your desk. More bizarre or unconventional image combinations are easier to remember; a can of tuna in your bedroom will make a more memorable

image than tuna in your kitchen (Bower, 1972).

The method of loci relies on the mnemonic power of *visual imagery,* one of the most effective forms of encoding. Mental images may work well because they use both verbal and visual memories simultaneously (Paivio, 1986). With visual imagery, you remember words by associating them with vivid, distinctive mental pictures. In the case of the infamous grocery list, for example, you might simply combine mental images of tuna, shampoo, and eggs in a bizarre but memorable way: Picture a *tuna* floating on an enormous fried *egg* in a sea of foamy *shampoo,* for example. Or imagine a politician you dislike eating *tuna* from the can, his hair covered with *shampoo* suds, while you throw *eggs* at him.

The use of mnemonics teaches us that memory is flexible, personal, and creative. You can devise techniques for encoding and retrieval that work well for you regardless of what works for others. Ultimately a mnemonic technique is judged not by how silly it is or how popular with others, but by how well it works for the person utilizing it.

---

time of encoding, is called the **encoding specificity principle** (Tulving & Thomson, 1973). The better the match between your encoding and later cues, the better your recall will be.

For example, if you memorize the word "jam" in the context of *strawberry jam,* you will have trouble recognizing it when the context is changed to *traffic jam.* Expectations can also determine context. If you expect to be given an essay test, for example, you should try to encode the material you are studying by remembering general information about abstract relationships, concepts, and analysis, because that is probably what you will be asked to retrieve. But if you expect multiple-choice questions, you should pay more attention to specific, concrete facts, definitions, and distinctions—the kind of information most easily translated into multiple-choice items.

The Contents of Memory   Psychologists know that information in LTM is stored in organized patterns, with networks of meaning connecting chunks of knowledge. Psychologists have proposed three hypotheses about the ways that people represent ideas and experiences in LTM. These three are eidetic imagery, propositional storage, and dual-code memory.

Actual images—records of sensory impressions—may be stored in LTM. Some individuals even claim to have "photographic memory," known technically as *eidetic imagery.* Such individuals, called "eidetikers," report being able to envision a previously viewed scene in their minds, with their eyes closed, as if they were experiencing the scene directly rather than scanning memory for traces or details. While most people can retain some imaging ability, very few—only about 5 percent of subjects studied—can pass tests of detailed eidetic memory (Gray & Gummerman, 1975; Gummerman et al., 1972; Leask et al., 1969).

Most information is not experienced as a visual image, so it must be encoded and stored in a nonimaginal form. The smallest unit of meaning that people store is called a proposition. A **proposition** *is an idea that expresses a relationship between concepts, objects, or events.* The proposition expresses a relationship by combining a subject with a predicate, such as the statements "People drink water" and "Children are spoiled by their grandparents." According to some theorists, networks of propositions form the structural building blocks of LTM. These semantic networks (networks of meanings) enable us to locate stored information, alter it, or add to it (Anderson, 1976).

Still other investigators believe that people use both images and propositions in LTM. *The theory that both visual and verbal codes are used to store information in memory is known as the* **dual-code model** *of memory* (Begg & Paivio, 1969; Kounios & Holcomb, 1994; Paivio, 1983). According to this view, sensory information and concrete sentences are more likely to be stored as images, while abstract sentences are coded verbally. Verbal codes cannot act as indexes or reference pegs for visual codes. Memory may use different types of codes to represent different types of information. For example, propositional networks are used to encode test information (Anderson & Bower, 1973), and mental images are used for maps (Tversky, 1981). The answer to the debate seems to be that both propositions and images represent information, but at different times and for different processing demands.

Deciphering the Code   Some researchers argue that all information encoded in LTM is stored there permanently. However, retrieval failures occur when the appropriate retrieval location or pathway for a given memory is forgotten (Linton, 1975). *The internal or external stimuli available to help in recovering information from memory are known as* **retrieval cues.** External cues might include the wording and references in questions on a quiz ("What memory principles do you associate with the research of *George Sperling*?"). You can also generate retrieval cues internally to prompt your own memory search ("Where have I met her before? She knows that instructor, maybe she is a classmate in my psychology class").

Because information in LTM storage is organized according to meaning, cues based on *organization* can also help you retrieve what you know. You may rely on this principle when you review different categories of experience and knowledge in mentally searching for the answer to a question (Mandler, 1972; Tulving & Pearlstone, 1966). For example, to answer the question "Where did I leave my keys?" you might first think about what activities you engaged in, when you did so, and where each activity took place. Because organization is such an effective *retrieval* cue, it makes sense to organize new material as you first *encode* it in memory. For example, as you read the material in this chapter, create an outline and add your own notes to explain the concepts you want to remember. Later, when taking a test on this material, you can recreate the structure of that outline in your mind, and use it to recall ideas and meanings according to their order in that arrangement.

Even with good cues, not all stored content is equally accessible, as you know only too well. In the case of familiar, well-learned information, more aspects of it have been stored and more connections between it and the many different parts of the memory network have been established, so a number of cues can give you access to it. On the other hand, when trying to find the one key that will unlock a less familiar memory, you may have to use special search strategies. For example, to remember the name of someone you met only once, you must recall your impressions of that one meeting. In contrast, to retrieve the name of a more familiar individual, you may be able to imagine several mutual friends all speaking the elusive name.

Constructive Memory

Sometimes what people remember is either more than or different from what they actually experienced. Based on laboratory studies about the way people process and remember meaningful material, psychologists view remembering as a continuation of the active, constructive process of perception. According to this new view, as we organize material to make it meaningful, we frequently add details to make it more complete or change it to make it fit better with other, already existing information in our personal memory store.

Psychologist Jerome Bruner first noted that when we construct memories we "go beyond the information given" (1973). The study of such constructive processes is guided by the general principle that *how and what you remember is determined by who you are and what you already know*. In other words, what is perceived and remembered is a function of the individual's past history, current values, and future expectations, as well as the nature of the stimulus being committed to memory.

Schemas   Many studies have demonstrated the importance of schemas in helping us organize and remember details. A **schema** *is a mental collection of knowledge and expectations about a topic or concept*. People have schemas about familiar categories of objects, events, and people, and these schemas influence how we perceive new information. For example, if a friend recommends a book to you and says it is a "romance novel," your expectation and opinion about it (based on your schema for "romance novels") will probably not be the same as if she had recommended a "suspense thriller."

Schemas can also shape our memories of past experiences. For example, if you hear that a couple you know has divorced, your schema for "divorce"—including the likelihood that the partners were incompatible or experienced conflict—will affect how you remember past interactions with the pair. You may recall a time when they were quiet in a social gathering, and reinterpret that memory as an early sign that they were "angry" or "not speaking." Our people-related schemas can influence how we perceive and remember those we meet or hear about (Cantor & Mischel, 1979). For example, most of us have schemas about particular professions. How honest and trustworthy are members of the following professions: clergy, law, police, real estate sales, car sales? If you meet someone new who is described as a member of one of these categories, your schema for that profession will probably affect your willingness to interact with the individual.

When trying to recall information that is not consistent with a schema, your memory may distort the input to make it more schema-consistent. For example, suppose you hear that a couple you know, who always seemed very happy together, is getting a divorce. Once you learn of their impending divorce, it may be difficult for you to recall episodes when they seemed compatible. In contrast, you will more easily remember times when they acted unhappy, because those memories match the divorce schema that describes their current status.

The study of constructive processes in memory actually began over 50 years ago with British psychologist **Sir Frederic Bartlett,** who described his work in his classic book, *Remembering* (1932). Bartlett focused on the kinds of constructions that take place when people try to remember material that is unfamiliar to them. He observed the way British undergraduates transmitted and remembered simple stories whose themes and wording were taken from another culture. When a story was unclear to a student because he lacked an understanding of the story's original culture, he misremembered the details in a way that fit his own cultural schemas and thus "made more sense."

Eyewitness Recall   If memory is reconstructed to fit our schemas, how far should the memory of eyewitnesses be trusted in revealing the truth about criminal events? The ease with which we can be misled into "remembering" false information has been amply demonstrated in the laboratory research of **Elizabeth Loftus** (1979, 1984) and her colleagues. During the research, bright college students with good memories were misled into "recalling" that a yield sign at the scene was actually a stop sign, a nonexistent barn was visible, and a green traffic light was shining red. They might have heard another "witness" report something about a man's mustache when, in fact, the man had no mustache. Although many subjects resisted being misled, a significant proportion integrated the new information into their memory representations and confidently reported the nonexistent mustache, barn, and stop sign as part of what they actually saw "with their own eyes."

Because so much of our criminal justice system relies on eyewitness identifications and descriptions, the vulnerability of such memories to error and distortion has important implications for social policy. Research by Loftus and her colleagues (Lindsay, 1990, 1993; Loftus, 1992, 1993; Loftus & Ketcham, 1991, 1994; Weingardt et al., 1995) has identified several factors influencing the accuracy of eyewitness recall:

- When the passage of time allows the original memory to fade, people are more likely to misremember information.
- People's recollections are more influenced by leading questions if they are not forewarned that interrogations can create bias.
- Age matters: Younger children and adults over 65 may be most susceptible to influence by misinformation in their efforts to recall.
- Misinformation may not only distort reported recollections but also impair storage or retrieval of the original memory.
- Confidence does not predict accuracy: Misinformed subjects can actually come to believe the misinformation they claim to remember.

A bulletin board in Boston Police Headquarters highlights the extent to which our criminal justice system relies on eyewitness identifications and descriptions.

The process by which a person perceives an event, encodes that information, and recalls it at a later time is at the heart of psychological interest in learning and memory. Our human capacity for constructive memory not only increases the difficulty of getting accurate eyewitness testimony, but also shields people from some truths they do not want to accept. We distort incoming information to fit our prejudices and remember what we expected rather than what really happened.

Recovered Memories   In our opening case, the Smith family's ordeal began with Donna Smith's claim that she had been sexually abused by her father. Subsequently, Donna came to believe her own claims, although she now insists they were all lies—and at one time she herself knew they were lies. Research on eyewitness recall confirms that, as a result of misinformation or distortion, people not only report false memories, they come to believe them completely. At one point, Donna Smith believed her "newfound" memories so completely that she "wholeheartedly hated" her father. Donna and her family got a second chance when she was able to face and admit the truth, away from the influences that had supported her false memories and accusations. But other stories of "recovered memories" have very different endings.

The Case of Eileen Franklin   In 1989, 28-year-old Eileen Franklin contacted county investigators with information about a case they had been unable to solve for 20 years in the northern California neighborhood where she had grown up. In 1969, Eileen's friend, 8-year-old Susan Nason, had disappeared; after weeks of searching, Susan's remains were finally found, but her killer was never identified or apprehended. Eileen's new information emerged from a long-buried memory of witnessing Susan's rape and murder and recognizing her killer: Eileen's father. After two decades, the horrible events that Eileen had forgotten came flooding back in a brief moment, when she made eye contact with her own daughter and was suddenly reminded of the look in Susan's eyes before she was killed—or so she alleged.

At a preliminary hearing to a charge of murder, Eileen Franklin demonstrates her image of her father killing Susan Nason—an image Ms. Franklin claims she recovered 20 years after the event.

According to Eileen her father had threatened to kill her if she reported Susan's rape and murder. Knowing that this was no idle threat (Eileen later testified her father had molested and beaten her when she was a child), she "forgot" the horror and trauma of what she had seen. When the memory returned 20 years later, the investigation was reopened, and Eileen's father was charged on the basis of her testimony. Newspapers reported that "the testimony of memory experts played a key role in the trial, which some believe may give more credence to other victims of violence who have repressed memories . . . " (Workman, 1990). Elizabeth Loftus testified as an expert witness about the susceptibility of memories to suggestion and distortion, but prosecutor Elaine Tipton argued that Loftus' expertise was not relevant to Eileen's testimony. After less than eight hours of deliberation, the jury found Eileen's father guilty. He was sentenced to life imprisonment by a judge who called him "a depraved and wicked man" (Workman, 1990).

Was George Franklin guilty? Was Eileen's recovered memory of her father's crime a valid mental record of a real event? An alternative explanation of Eileen's experience shows eerie parallels with those of Donna Smith: Shortly before making her accusations, Eileen was a trapped, unhappy person in therapy—and a sudden recollection that her own father had molested her seemed to explain so much about her current misery (MacLean, 1993). Factors other than the truth, therefore, may have been involved in the timing and nature of Eileen's actions. Questions about the validity of recovered memories led an appeals judge to overturn Franklin's conviction, but early in 1996 the district attorney announced that he would retry the case, relying once again on Eileen Franklin's eyewitness testimony. This time, however, the validity of Eileen Franklin's "recovered memory" was in doubt, and her father was freed—but ruined financially and socially.

False Memory Syndrome By now it has become a familiar story: An adult enters therapy to resolve persistent conflict or unhappiness and, with the therapist's support, revives a long-buried memory of traumatic abuse, incest, or molestation. No longer repressed, the horrible memories are unleashed and may prompt the individual to take long-delayed action—just as Eileen Franklin charged her father with sexually assaulting her and murdering her girlfriend. In theory, the shock and terror of such childhood experiences causes decades, possibly a lifetime, of amnesia. After recall, the painful memories can be turned into legal evidence for criminal and civil prosecution. *But what if the memories are false?*

This is the question raised by the more than 3000 families who have registered their stories with the False Memory Syndrome Foundation based in Philadelphia. The **false memory syndrome** *is a pattern of thoughts, feelings, and actions based on mistaken or distorted recollection of experiences the rememberer claims to have previously repressed.* Three common elements appear in the stories of family members who say they have been unjustly accused of harming children (Salter, 1993):

- The daughter or son makes the accusations after a period of remoteness during which he or she only vaguely reports being in therapy.
- After confronting the parents by letter or telephone, the accusing child severs further contact.
- The parents are condemned by the child's therapist, who typically refuses to meet them or hear their protests that the charges are false.

When an individual accuses a once trusted family member of rape or assault, whether recent or long ago, subsequent suspicion and concern that it *might* be true can forever alter and even destroy relationships and reputations.

Naturally, if the charges are true, the truth must be told to meet the goals of justice and therapy. But how can any outsider know the facts?

Pamela Freyd is an accused parent and the director of the False Memory Syndrome Foundation; her daughter is a reputable cognitive psychologist. Freyd notes that when most people hear that someone has accused family members of incest or abuse, their "knee-jerk reaction" is to assume the accused are guilty. After all, why would anyone willingly disrupt her own life and others' lives by falsely claiming to be a victim and making up such lies? Freyd speculates that at least some of the therapists who help their patients recover memories of childhood traumas actually implant false memories—whether intentionally or not—through hypnotic suggestion, asking leading questions, and broadly defining "incest" and "abuse."

Taking the false memory syndrome seriously means doubting the testimony of at least some self-described victims of horrible crimes. As we have already reviewed, however, experts on the nature of constructive memory argue that there now exists sufficient research evidence to support such doubt (Lindsay, 1993; Loftus & Ketchum, 1994). This does not mean that a traumatic experience cannot be repressed, of course, nor that there are not many victims of actual abuse. The concern remains that there is no scientific evidence for repression of multiple traumatic events over an extended time. Citizens, attorneys, judges, and therapists should exercise greater caution and skepticism, and less readily accept claims of repressed and recovered memories in the absence of any independent verification.

The Value of Constructive Memory Despite its faults, constructive memory is an enormously positive feature of creative minds. More often than not, it helps us make sense of our uncertain world by providing the right context in which to understand, interpret, remember, and act on minimal or fragmentary evidence. Without it, our memories would be little more than second-rate transcription services that could not assign any special significance to our many unique and personal experiences. With this constructive ability, of course, we are at risk for distorted, changing, and false memories. Research on constructive memory continues to teach us about both its possibilities and limits, and how such knowledge might be considered in applications in therapy and the law.

Forgetting

We all remember an enormous amount of material over long periods of time. College students can accurately recall details about the births of younger siblings even when those events occurred 16 years earlier (Sheingold & Tenney, 1982). Knowledge in semantic memory (for example, knowing what historic event happened in the year 1066) is retrieved even better than knowledge in episodic memory (recalling where and when you first learned about 1066), regardless of the time that has elapsed since the actual gaining of the knowledge. In semantic memory, you will retain generalizations longer than details. However, even well-learned material may be irretrievable over time. We forget much of what we have learned. Why?

Early psychologists theorized that we forget because we suffer a gradual loss of the "memory traces" in our minds. Such *decay* seems to be a factor in sensory memory loss and working memory loss when maintenance rehearsal is prevented. But simple decay cannot explain why some memories, unretrieved for years, can still emerge clear and accurate decades after the fact. Motor skills are also retained for many years, even without practice—"just like riding a bicycle." Trivia, commercial jingles, and odors from one's childhood all persist in memory despite years of disuse. Other theories seem to explain forgetting better than the notion of mere physical decay does. Here we briefly examine three perspectives on forgetting: *interference*; *retrieval failure*; and *motivated forgetting*.

Interference   Interference from other experiences affects both learning and retaining new material. **Proactive interference** *occurs when previously stored information prevents the learning of similar, new information. Pro-* means "forward," and in this case old lessons move forward and block your ability to remember new ones. An example of proactive interference in procedural memory is shown when, after moving to a new home, you still look for items in "the old places" where you used to store them, although no such locations exist in your new environment. The old habit has proactively interfered with your efforts to retrieve the more recent memory of the new storage places.

Retroactive interference *occurs when newly learned information prevents the retrieval of previously stored, similar material. Retro-* means "backward"; the newer material seems to reach back into your memory to block access to old material. Retroactive interference describes what happens when studying for your Spanish test tomorrow makes it difficult for you to remember the French you learned in high school. Recent material retroactively interferes with your ability to retrieve an older memory.

Three general principles govern interference. First, the greater the *similarity* between two sets of material, the greater the interference between them. Second, *meaningless* material is more vulnerable to interference than meaningful material. (It would be more difficult for you to memorize the nonsense syllables ZAX, QOG, and KIV than the more meaningful TAX, FOG, and KIT.) Third, the more difficult the *intervening task* between learning and recall the more it will interfere with memory of material learned earlier. (Between studying for a test and taking it, you will forget more if you study for another course than if you do your laundry, a simpler and less relevant distraction.)

The most obvious prediction that emerges from interference theory is that information undisturbed by new material will be recalled best. A classic study by Jenkins and Dallenbach (1924) provided support for this hypothesis. Subjects who went to sleep immediately after learning new material recalled it better the next morning than those who spent the same amount of time performing their usual activities after learning.

Retrieval Failure   An apparent memory loss often turns out to be only a failure of retrieval. A question worded a little differently will guide us to the information, or a question requiring only recognition will reveal knowledge that we could not access and reproduce by recall. It seems clear that many failures to remember reflect poor encoding or inadequate retrieval cues rather than loss of memories. Failure to call up a memory is never positive proof that the memory is not there.

Why do we forget the names of many of our high school classmates or even college teachers when we meet them away from school? When the social context is different from that in which we met those people originally, we have lost the *social context* we once used to form memories for those acquaintances, so we lack the necessary retrieval cues (Reiser et al., 1985). Memories of people are formed around the social contexts in which they were encountered, and only later, with more interaction, do we add secondary retrieval cues based on the personality traits and personal attributes of those people (Bond & Brockett, 1987). Such cues are a part of encoding specificity, and remind us that forgetting is influenced by the way material was first encoded into memory.

Motivated Forgetting   If Eileen Franklin is telling the truth and remembering real experiences of childhood trauma, why did those important memories lie buried for so many years? In cases of psychologically caused amnesia, the forgotten material is retained but blocked from retrieval. Not until an effective retrieval cue is experienced does the traumatic memory come flooding back. According to theories that forgetting can be psychologically motivated, only the frightening or traumatic elements are "forgotten," while other elements— an individual's identity, skills, and friends—are retained intact. People may forget because they do not want to remember experiences that were frightening, painful, or personally degrading.

Sigmund Freud (1923) was the first to perceive memory and forgetting as dynamic processes that enable us to maintain a sense of self-integrity. Research on childhood memories recalled by adults found that, in general, unpleasant events were more often forgotten than pleasant events (Waldvogel, 1948). We all forget some experiences we do not want to recognize as part of us, appointments we do not want to keep, names of people we do not like, and past events that threaten our basic sense of self or security. Freud gave the label **repression** to *the mental process by which we protect ourselves from unacceptable or painful memories, pushing them out of consciousness.*

Our motivational needs not only prevent retrieval of certain memories but even change the tone and content of memories that we do retrieve. A study of early recollections revealed that many memories judged as traumatic by the researchers were selectively recoded as neutral or even pleasant by the subjects during recall. Evidently, we can reconstruct our early childhood so that we remember the "good old days" not the way they were, but the way they should have been (Kihlstrom & Harackiewicz, 1982).

Check Your Recall

Memory is the process whereby we retain and reproduce information we have learned. Hermann Ebbinghaus originally studied the savings and relearning of meaningless verbal material, finding that most material is forgotten soon after it is first learned. The study of memory for meaningful material shows several processes and systems at work. New material is first encoded, then stored, and finally retrieved when needed. Three separate systems process sensory memories, working (or short-term) memory, and long-term memory. Sensory memory is very brief, prolonging visual or auditory information long enough to make processing possible. Working memory can be maintained with attentive rehearsal, but its capacity is limited to seven or fewer chunks of information. Long-term memory includes memory for procedures and information, including meaning as well as personal experiences.

Long-term memory is organized according to meaning, context, and content of information. Mnemonic strategies can be employed to improve memorization and retrieval. Long-term memory is constructive in the sense that one's experiences and knowledge will influence how new information is remembered. Schemas influence the way we remember and form expectations about people, events, and objects. Research shows that eyewitness memories are susceptible to distortion and inaccuracy as a result of suggestion or misinformation. Victims of the false memory syndrome allege that recovered memories may be examples of such distortions. Research attributes forgetting to three processes: either proactive or retroactive interference; retrieval failure; and motivation to repress.

CHAPTER REVIEW

Summary

Most human behavior reflects the influence of learning and remembering. Research on learning has long been influenced by the behaviorist emphasis on observable stimuli and responses. However, studies of both human and nonhuman subjects have contributed to cognitive views of learning. The earliest learning research focused on classical conditioning, beginning with Ivan Pavlov's discovery of how conditional stimuli can elicit reflexive responses. Classical conditioning affects basic, survival-oriented responses, including emotions and taste aversions. In contrast, operant conditioning explains how more complex, voluntary responses are influenced by their environmental consequences. Reinforcement contingencies determine whether a particular response will be increased or decreased. Operant conditioning can be applied in training both humans and nonhumans. Work on instinctual drift indicates there are biological constraints on what various species can learn. Learned material is only usable if it is remembered. Memory involves processes for encoding new material, storing it, and allowing it to be retrieved. Researchers have identified three different human memory systems: sensory memory, working memory, and long-term memory. Information in long-term memory is coded, stored, and retrieved according to the meaning and context of the material. Long-term memory is considered constructive because schemas and experiences can influence the accuracy of memory. Eyewitness accounts are subject to distortion, and even false memories may seem believable to the rememberer. Forgetting can be attributed to interference, failure in retrieval, or motivation to repress.

Section Reviews

Learning About Learning

Be sure to *Check Your Recall* by reviewing the summary of this section on page 202.

Key Terms
learning (p. 201)

Names to Know
John B. Watson (p. 202)
B. F. Skinner (p. 202)

Classical Conditioning

Be sure to *Check Your Recall* by reviewing the summary of this section on page 211.

Key Terms
classical conditioning (p. 204)
reflex (p. 204)
unconditional stimulus (UCS) (p. 205)
unconditional response (UCR) (p. 206)
conditional stimulus (CS) (p. 206)
conditional response (CR) (p. 206)
acquisition (p. 206)
aversive conditioning (p. 206)
extinction (p. 207)
spontaneous recovery (p. 207)
stimulus generalization (p. 208)
stimulus discrimination (p. 208)
taste-aversion learning (p. 210)
bait shyness (p. 211)

Names to Know
Ivan Pavlov (p. 204)
Robert Rescorla (p. 209)
Leon Kamin (p. 209)
John Garcia (p. 210)

Operant Conditioning

Be sure to *Check Your Recall* by reviewing the summary of this section on page 223.

Key Terms
law of effect (p. 213)
operant (p. 213)
reinforcers (p. 214)
reinforcement contingency (p. 214)
positive reinforcer (p. 215)
negative reinforcer (p. 215)
operant extinction (p. 216)
punisher (p. 216)
learned helplessness (p. 219)
conditioned reinforcer (p. 219)
Premack principle (p. 220)
shaping (p. 221)
biological constraints on learning (p. 221)
instinctual drift (p. 222)

Names to Know
Edward L. Thorndike (p. 212)
B. F. Skinner (p. 213)
Martin Seligman (p. 219)
David Premack (p. 220)
Keller Breland (p. 221)
Marian Breland (p. 221)

Cognitive Views of Learning

Be sure to *Check Your Recall* by reviewing the summary of this section on page 227.

Key Terms
cognition (p. 223)
comparative psychology (p. 224)
cognitive map (p. 225)
observational learning (p. 226)

Names to Know
Edward C. Tolman (p. 225)
Albert Bandura (p. 226)

Remembering

Be sure to *Check Your Recall* by reviewing the summary of this section on page 244.

Key Terms
encoding (p. 229)
storage (p. 229)
retrieval (p. 229)
elaboration (p. 229)
recall (p. 229)
recognition (p. 229)
sensory memory
  (p. 231)
working memory or short-
  term memory (STM)
  (p. 232)
chunk (p. 233)
chunking (p. 233)
long-term memory (LTM)
  (p. 233)
procedural memory
  (p. 234)
declarative memory
  (p. 234)
mnemonics (p. 236)
encoding specificity principle (p. 236)
proposition (p. 237)
dual-code model
  (p. 237)
retrieval cues (p. 237)

schema (p. 238)
false memory syndrome
  (p. 241)
proactive interference
  (p. 243)
retroactive interference
  (p. 243)
repression (p. 244)

Names to Know
Hermann Ebbinghaus
  (p. 228)
George Sperling
  (p. 231)
Sir Frederic Bartlett
  (p. 239)
Elizabeth Loftus (p. 239)

REVIEW TEST

Chapter 6: Learning and Remembering

For each of the following items, choose the single correct or best answer. The correct answers, explanations, and page references appear in Appendix B.

1. Much of modern psychology's view of learning finds its roots in the work of _____, emphasizing the analysis of behavior.
   a. Wilhelm Wundt
   b. William James
   c. Sigmund Freud
   d. John B. Watson

2. During classical conditioning, for an organism to learn a conditioned association between two stimuli, the UCS must seem to _____.
   a. predict the CS
   b. be predicted by the CS
   c. be independent of the CS
   d. follow the UCR

3. According to Thorndike's law of effect, behavior is strengthened or not strengthened as a result of its _____.
   a. consequences in the organism's environment
   b. association with stimuli similar to those that have triggered it
   c. purpose in the organism's efforts to survive
   d. level of complexity in the organism's repertoire

4. A _____ is a consistent relationship between a response and the changes in the environment that it produces.
   a. behavior potential
   b. behavior analysis
   c. reinforcement contingency
   d. conditioned reinforcer

5. "The best part of going to the beach," your friend exclaims as you start your vacation, "is getting away from all the stress of work and school." If this is true, then your friend's vacation-taking behavior has been influenced by _____.
   a. positive reinforcement
   b. negative reinforcement
   c. extinction
   d. punishment

6. Which of the following is *not* a recommendation for making punishment most effective?
   a. It should be swift and brief.
   b. It should be intense.
   c. It should be delivered immediately.
   d. It should be focused on the response.

7. According to the Premack principle, a reinforcer can be anything that _____.
   a. changes behavior from its past norms
   b. rewards rather than penalizes behavior
   c. becomes associated with an unconditional stimulus
   d. is valued by the organism, such as an activity

8. In his research with rats running mazes, Edward C. Tolman concluded that place learning required each subject to rely on _____.
   a. a CS-UCS connection
   b. conditioned reinforcers
   c. a cognitive map
   d. spontaneous recovery

9. Your knowledge of how to use a can opener, boot up your computer, address an envelope, and program a VCR are all examples of _____ memory.
   a. procedural
   b. semantic
   c. sensory
   d. constructive

10. Elise used to live in a house with a large kitchen, where all the silverware was stored in a drawer to the right of the sink. Since she moved to her new apartment, she finds that she habitually looks for the silverware in a drawer to the right of the sink, although no such drawer exists. Her behavior reflects forgetting due to _____.
    a. absence of appropriate retrieval cues
    b. retroactive interference
    c. proactive interference
    d. repression

IF YOU'RE INTERESTED . . .

Baum, W. M. (1994). *Understanding behaviorism: Science, behavior, and culture.* New York: HarperCollins.

This short, readable text explains the specific goals and methods of behaviorism, with discussions of stimuli and reinforcement, and complex issues such as freedom, responsibility, and culture.

Benne, B. (1988). *WASPLEG and other mnemonics.* Dallas, TX: Taylor Publishing.

Handy strategies for remembering the seven deadly sins (Wrath, Anger, Sloth, Pride, Lust, Envy, Greed) and other lists that might otherwise exceed the initial limits of memory.

Clockwork Orange, A. (Video: 1971, color, 137 min.). Directed by Stanley Kubrick; starring Malcolm McDowell, Patrick Magee, Adrienne Corri, Aubrey Morris, James Marcus.

Fascinating, disturbing film based on Anthony Burgess's novel about a futuristic society's efforts to reform a violent criminal by applying conditioning techniques.

Groundhog Day. (Video: 1993, color, 103 min.). Directed by Harold Ramis; starring Bill Murray, Andie MacDowell, Chris Elliott.

What if you were the only one around who seemed to remember the recent past? That's the dramatic conflict in this funny fantasy about a cynical TV weatherman who must change his ways when he finds he mysteriously relives the same day over and over—but only he remembers "this day has happened before."

Hilts, P. J. (1995). *Memory's ghost: The strange tale of Mr. M. and the nature of memory.* New York: Simon & Schuster.

The true story of Henry M., a young man who underwent experimental surgery for a severe epileptic condition in 1953 only to completely lose all ability to form new memories or learn new information. Based on numerous interviews with the subject, Hilts's book relates several stories: the abused ethics of medicine, the fragility of psychological reality, the complexity of mental life, and the centrality of memory to one's very sense of self.

MacLean, H. N. (1993). *Once upon a time: A true story of memory, murder, and the law.* New York: HarperCollins.

The true story of the case of Eileen Franklin, whose "recovered memories" led to the conviction of her father for the murder of her childhood friend. The book documents the trial of George Franklin, with the prosecution's case based totally on recollected testimony, and also explores whether Eileen's memories were not repressed but totally fabricated.

Ofshe, R., & Watters, E. (1994). *Making monsters: False memories, psychotherapy, and sexual hysteria.* New York: Charles Scribner's Sons.

Since the Eileen Franklin case (previous listing), the media have exploded with stories of long-repressed memories—of childhood molestation, satanic abuse, or murder—suddenly surfacing when victims enter therapy as adults. The authors examine how such memories may be constructed and shaped not by truth but by the suggestions of therapists and the victims' own prejudices.

Phillips, D., & Judd, R. (1978). *How to fall out of love.* New York: Fawcett Popular Library.

Short, extremely useful and practical application of behavioral modification techniques to getting over a painful romantic loss. Some techniques (e.g., thought-stopping, positive image building) can also be applied to various other intentional behavior changes. Good examples and suggestions.

Seligman, M. E. P. (1991). *Learned optimism.* New York: Alfred A. Knopf.

A well-written guide to developing a healthy, positive lifestyle and overcoming learned helplessness, mild depression, and pessimism. Includes self-assessment techniques and programs for acquiring optimistic, constructive life skills.

Total Recall. (Video: 1990, color, 109 min.). Directed by Paul Verhoeven; starring Arnold Schwarzenegger, Rachel Ticotin, Sharon Stone, Ronny Cox.

In the twenty-first century, a man discovers that false memories—and a false identity—have been planted in his mind, so he travels to Mars to confront the perpetrators of the crime. Oscar-winning special effects highlight the film, based on science-fiction writer Phillip K. Dick's tale, "We Can Remember It For You Wholesale."

Wright, J. C., with Lashnits, J. W. (1994). *Is your cat crazy?* New York: Macmillan.

All right, it *is* a cat book, but John C. Wright is an animal behaviorist who documents interesting (and fun) case histories of "problem felines," some behavioral principles applied to modify their habits, and insights into the repertoires and instincts that influence what cats learn and do. Many of the principles could be applied to other companion animals—and companion humans!

CHAPTER 7

Cognitive Processes

In May 1978 a deadly mystery was set in motion when a package sent to Northwestern University exploded and injured a security guard. In 1979 another mail bomb injured a student in Northwestern's Technological Institute; and onboard an American Airlines plane en route from Chicago to Washington, D.C., a third bomb partially detonated. After the plane's emergency landing, enough bomb fragments remained for a lab examiner from the Federal Bureau of Investigation (FBI) to recognize critical similarities between the American Airlines bomb and the Northwestern devices. He concluded that the three attacks were the work of a serial terrorist targeting universities and airlines. The FBI assigned the terrorist the acronym UNABOM—the University-Airlines-Bomber. Thus began a 17-year series of 16 packaged bombs placed or sent by the terrorist "Unabomber"—bombs that have been sent all over the country, injuring 23 people and killing three. The Unabomber blames industrialization and technology for creating social alienation and unhappiness in our society. By sending specially prepared packages that explode when they are opened, he attacks those he believes enable this technology to advance.

In April 1995, his bombing murder of a timber industry lobbyist was eclipsed in the news by the explosion days earlier at the Alfred P. Murrah Federal Building in Oklahoma City. Perhaps jealous that other terrorists were getting all the attention, the Unabomber made a bizarre offer: if major newspapers such as the New York Times *and the* Washington Post *would publish a 35,000-word manifesto from the Unabomber's "organization," FC, he would vow not to kill again. Although reluctant to acquiesce to the terrorist tactics of the Unabomber, the editors agreed, hoping that publication of his viewpoint would provide additional clues (Alter, 1995)*

To find the Unabomber and solve the mystery, the FBI had to look at all the elements: a chronology of events, a connecting pattern, leads from possible witnesses, physical evidence, and the Unabomber's written introspections. Although the Unabomber referred to himself as "we" and used the signature "FC" for the antitechnology terrorist group he called the Freedom Club, FBI agents believed that he acted alone. They concluded that the Unabomber was well educated and highly skilled in carpentry and metalwork, an unmarried white male in his thirties or forties who moved from the Midwest to California in the 1980s. In 1987, just before a computer store owner became the Unabomber's victim, a witness saw a man in sunglasses and a white hooded sweatshirt leave the explosive device in a parking lot and calmly walk away. Her description provided the basis for the now-famous composite sketch (Beck et al., 1995), duplicated in our chapter opening graphic.

In late 1995 the Unabomber went public again, to challenge comments made in a San Francisco newspaper interview with Tom Tyler, a social psychologist at the University of California at Berkeley. Tyler compared the Unabomber to Timothy McVeigh, the *man accused of the Oklahoma City bombing. Tyler noted that while the Unabomber, a left-wing anarchist, is the political opposite of McVeigh, who is drawn to right-wing militia movements, they share the same mindset. Both express an exaggerated fear of "a kind of secret, all-powerful group that's controlling people's lives"* (San Francisco Chronicle, *May 1, 1995, p. A1).*

The Unabomber responded: "The trouble with psychologists is that in commenting on what people say or do they often concentrate exclusively on the non-rational motivations behind the speech or behavior. But human behavior has a rational as well as an irrational component, and psychologists should not neglect the rational component" (The Daily Californian, *July 7, 1995, p. 6). Tyler agreed that "we should allow the possibility that some social problems, not personal problems, are responsible for at least some of the unhappiness in our society"* (Tyler, personal communication, November 11, 1995). *Tyler does not believe the Unabomber, FC, is "crazy," nor that his manifesto consists of "rantings," but rather that he gives a coherent, organized presentation of his beliefs about the causes of social malaise. But Tyler challenges FC's tactics, arguing that violence is a poor persuasive technique. Violence creates fear, insecurity, and a resistance to considering the terrorist's alternate ideology.*

As of this writing, a break in the case has led FBI investigators to a prime suspect in the Unabomber mystery. In April 1996, federal agents detained 53-year-old Theodore John ("Ted") Kaczynski, a recluse who had lived alone for 25 years in a shack in the woods outside Lincoln, Montana. Searches of Kaczynski's crude home and his background have

While a television series such as *The X Files* suggests that FBI agents can solve paranormal mysteries, most detective work requires an ability to collect and interpret data in a systematic and objective way—using the same skills as any good scientist.

revealed an eerie number of "hits" in the FBI's profile of the Unabomber: Kaczynski was born and raised outside Chicago, educated at Harvard, and worked as a mathematics professor at the University of California, Berkeley—when he suddenly dropped out of mainstream society. Always brilliant yet aloof, Kaczynski matches the profile of a terrorist who was a perfectionist about making bombs but remained socially isolated. In other ways the crime solvers' profile misses Kaczynski: the suspect is older than investigators theorized the Unabomber to be, and he did not live near the urban centers or have transportation that would enable him to attack victims in such a widespread geographic range, and remain undetected for so long.

If Ted Kaczynski turns out to be the Unabomber, the solution to this mystery will reflect both efficient investigation and good luck. Investigators had hoped that the Unabomber's 1995 manifesto would be recognizable to someone from clues in the writer's words and arguments. The person who finally identified Kaczynski to the FBI was his younger brother David Kaczynski, who became convinced of his brother's guilt only after he read the Unabomber's words in the newspapers—and recognized in them his brother's own opinions and writing style.

Good detectives must attend to disconfirming evidence and new hypotheses. The painstaking collection and analysis of clues may eventually lead to an identification, a solution to the mystery, and an end to the crimes. The human mind is uniquely suited to solving mysteries, to going beyond the givens of evidence to a reasoned solution that seizes new opportunities, insights, and interpretations.

Introduction

Solving a crime is really solving a mystery, a form of problem solving. In this sense, every detective story or news account of crime investigation is about applying the mind's abilities to collect, analyze, and apply information. Perhaps Sherlock Holmes would have seemed less interesting if he were a "systems analyst" rather than a consulting detective, but his faculties and strategies were really applications of basic human abilities to collect and interpret data. Our abilities to go beyond the surface of the data—to make sense of clues and solve mysteries—are the gifts of our cognitive processes. In particular we derive spectacular benefits from *the processes of knowing—including attending, thinking, remembering, and reasoning—collectively referred to as* **cognition.** Philosopher René Descartes said, "*Cogito ergo sum*"—"I think, therefore I am." Contemporary research has enabled us to recognize how this can be true, how our *cognitions*—our thoughts, ideas, and realizations—make up our sense of awareness and our very identities.

Only humans have the capacity to go beyond the perception of what is here and now to think about what was, will be, might be, and should be. Thinking provides the context for perception, the purposes for learning, and the meaning for memories. Thoughts developed in the inner universe of our minds enable us to form abstract working models of our physical and social worlds. We then use these personal mental representations of reality to reshape and sometimes improve aspects of those worlds (Hunt, 1982). The contents of cognitive processes are concepts ("apples"), facts ("Apples grow on trees"), propositions ("You can make applesauce from fresh apples"), rules ("Add liquid to the apples so the applesauce doesn't burn"), and memories ("Grandma's house smelled like cinnamon when she made fresh applesauce"). Some *cognitive processes* mentally represent the world around us, such as those that classify information and interpret experiences; others are internally focused, such as those in our dreams and fantasies. Knowledge-based processes of the mind make sense of the neurally coded signals coming from the eye and other sensory systems. In Figure 7.1, you can see that the domain of cognitive psychology includes a dramatic variety of processes and abilities.

We will begin by analyzing the ways in which researchers try to measure the inner, private processes involved in cognitive functioning. We will then outline some of the models and basic ideas of information processing that are used to account for the ways we think and reason—in short, the way we come to understand ourselves. Finally, we will examine basic topics in cognitive psychology that are generating much excitement among researchers and those who are applying this knowledge to education and other areas: including reasoning, problem solving, decision making, and judging.

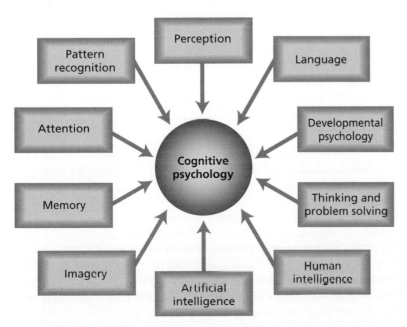

FIGURE 7.1   The Domain of Cognitive Psychology ∎

Investigating Cognition

Cognitive psychology *is the scientific study of mental processes and mental structures.* Cognitive psychologists investigate the ways people take in, transform, manipulate, and transmit information. If ours has become "The Information Age," then cognitive psychology is a central player in the era of cyberspace.

Although it seems obvious that thinking and using knowledge should occupy a central position in psychology, it was not always so. During the decades when psychology was entrenched in behaviorism, the discipline focused on examining the organism's behavioral reactions to the external world. A "science of the mind" developed in the 1950s when researchers and scholars from different fields began to seek an understanding of the ways the mind processes information and gives observed behavior its direction, meaning, and coherence. The shift in focus from behaviorism to cognition began with the convergence of three significant approaches to human thought involving computers, children, and communications (see Figure 7.1).

Historical Development

The modern conception of a computer as a general-purpose logic machine with built-in intelligence that is able to operate flexibly on internal instructions came from the vision of a brilliant young mathematician, **John von Neumann.** In 1945, he compared the electronic circuits of a new digital computer to the brain's neurons and the computer program to the brain's memory. Psychological researchers **Herbert Simon** and **Allen Newell** were the first to develop computer programs to simulate human problem solving, thereby also providing new ways of studying mental processes (Newell, Shaw, & Simon, 1958).

Around the same time, developmental psychologist **Jean Piaget** was pioneering a successful way to infer the mental processes children go through to understand physical realities (Piaget, 1954). As we saw in Chapter 4, Piaget's notion of stages of cognitive development was based on observations of the mental tasks that children of different ages could perform.

Finally, and also at about the same time, linguistic researcher **Noam Chomsky** studied language as part of a unique cognitive system for comprehending and producing symbols (Chomsky, 1957). Chomsky postulated that an innate *language acquisition device (LAD)* made it possible for young children to understand the basic rules of grammar in the absence of any formal education or systematic reinforcement.

These three new approaches to human thought involving computers, children, and communication boosted the scientific legitimacy of research on all forms of higher mental processes. Since then, cognitive theory has developed into the foundation of the psychology of the 1990s (Mayer, 1981; Solso, 1991).

Cognitive Science

Cognitive science *is an interdisciplinary field that studies the variety of systems and processes that manipulate information.* Figure 7.2 shows that cognitive science draws on the three overlapping disciplines of cognitive psychology, computer science, and neuroscience (Farah, 1984). Cognitive science also receives input from economics and cultural anthropology. Cognitive science seeks to explore the classic questions of Western thought (Gardner, 1985): What is knowledge, and how is it represented in the mind ?

Researchers who study how information is represented and processed build conceptual models to help them understand cognitive processes. A **cognitive model** *is an explanatory metaphor that describes how information is detected, stored, and used by people and machines.* Cognitive models are

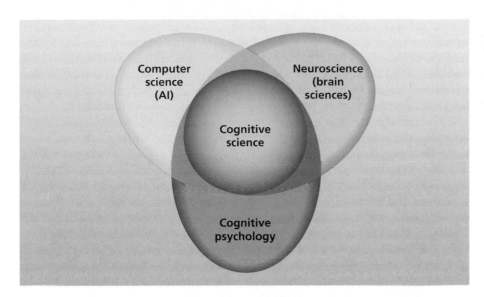

FIGURE 7.2 The Domain of Cognitive Science ■ The domain of cognitive science occupies the intersection of cognitive psychology, computer science (artificial intelligence), and neuroscience. It also includes study of the philosophy of the mind.

useful ways of thinking about specific phenomena because they can guide new research and make sense of existing knowledge. Although a model might seem correct, it must still withstand the "data test," which allows for new empirical research to modify or discard the model.

The basic approach or cognitive model favored by most cognitive psychologists is the **information-processing model.** *This model proposes that thinking and all other forms of cognition can be understood by organizing them into the component parts and processes of information flow.* Incoming information goes through a series of stages from complex input to simpler throughput to complex output. As the information passes through all of the brain systems, different subsystems break down the complex input to be decoded, simplified, and understood on its own terms. Then these subsystems respond appropriately—with thoughts, memories, feelings, and often actions.

You might think of cognition as an assembly line process, building from primitive stages, such as basic sensations and perception, to more complex stages, such as naming, classifying, reasoning, and problem solving. However, the human mind works on parallel paths simultaneously. The mind can also make remote associations between thought units, and come up with novel concepts and links between them that have never before been processed.

Measuring the Mind

Cognitive researchers study what is going on in the secret world of private experiences by discovering ways to externalize the internal and to measure and map the territory of the mind. If thinking is an internal, subjective process that only you can experience, how can it be studied scientifically? Cognitive psychologists have developed several methods to assess that which is not directly observable. Some of the techniques currently used include introspection, think-aloud protocols, behavioral observation, measuring reaction time, error analysis, and brain scanning.

Introspection and Thinking Aloud *Introspection*, a research method developed by Wilhelm Wundt in the late 1800s, involved training people to analyze the contents of their own consciousness into component parts, such as sensations, images, and feelings. However, the introspective approach provided no clues about the actual sequence of mental processes in life situations. When the introspections of two people differed in the same situation, there was no empirical way to resolve the discrepancy between them. Moreover, many mental processes are not even available for conscious inspection. For example, in the five seconds or so that it took you to read that last sentence, you identified the letters and words, retrieved the stored meaning of each of them, and comprehended the meaning of the sentence. You even began to store that unit of information under different retrieval labels for ready access should it appear on a test. Do you know *how* you did *what* you just did so efficiently?

Recently, however, researchers have found a way to use introspection as an *exploratory procedure* to help map out more precise research. As they work on tasks, experimental subjects describe what they are doing and why. *Subjects' reports of what they are doing and why are called* **think-aloud protocols.** Researchers use these reports to infer the mental strategies the subjects employed to do the task and the ways the subjects represented knowledge.

Think-aloud protocols show how people *actually* proceed instead of how a purely logical approach assumes they *ought* to behave. Such protocols have been collected in a wide variety of studies; they have proven especially useful in studying the cognitive processes involved in problem solving. For example, one study that investigated how people plan shopping trips found that shoppers were not logical and organized but rather opportunistic, switching among several simultaneous trains of thought to discover relevant information (Hayes-Roth & Hayes-Roth, 1979). By having subjects describe aloud their mental plans, it was possible to detect how the mind shifted from using logical, time-saving strategies to less rational actions guided by mental associations.

Behavioral Observation   A basic task of much psychological research is to infer internal states and processes from observations of external behavior. If we know the context in which behavior occurred, we can theorize about the affective, motivational, or cognitive determinants of that behavior. Crying at a funeral is evidence of grief, while crying at a prize ceremony is evidence of joy.

In a direct test of the acquisition of an early kind of symbolic understanding, researchers observed the behavior of children as they searched a room for a hidden object. They wanted to determine at what age a child comes to understand that a model represents or symbolizes something else. Researcher Judy DeLoache (1987) devised an ingenious hide-and-seek problem for toddlers to solve. First a child had to retrieve a hidden miniature object from a scale model of a room. Next the child had to find the full-size object in its corresponding hiding place in the real environment. Children aged 2½ did the first task as well as 3-year-olds, but not the second task. Apparently the children who were six months older had developed the ability to represent their environment symbolically, and use this representation to learn from experience and conduct a systematic search.

Measuring Reaction Time   *The elapsed time between the presentation of a stimulus or signal and a subject's response to it is known as* **reaction time.** Cognitive psychologists use reaction time to assess mental responses on different tasks. They then infer underlying differences in the thought processes involved in generating those responses, with slower reaction times indicating more complex mental processing. Adopting the principle that complex mental processes take more time, researchers today use reaction time to infer the occurrence of various cognitive processes. Reaction time also reflects experience and familiarity. We learn to respond faster to stimuli that are anticipated and known. Thus, runners decrease their reaction time when they practice fast starts at the sound of a starting pistol. This motor set can save a fraction of a second that may win the dash. More serious is the use of reaction times to detect the dangerous effects of alcohol on driving skills: one reacts more slowly in braking one's car to an emergency signal as the alcohol blood level rises above a certain point.

What is this student thinking? Some students may be frustrated when taking tests; others may be reviewing their knowledge and finding answers to the test questions. An observer of a test-taker's behavior must use context to make an inference about internal states.

Analyzing Errors   Cognitive psychologists assume that errors, such as reaching an incorrect conclusion or remembering something incorrectly, are probably not random but reflect systematic properties of the thought processes involved. Analysis of thought errors can give us clues about these properties. Sigmund Freud (1904) pioneered the analysis of speech errors—slips of the tongue—to detect latent sexual or hostile impulses. For example, a competitor pretending to like you might say, "I'm pleased to *beat* you" instead of "I'm pleased to *meet* you." In such cases the true intention slips past the conscious censor we all use to suppress socially inappropriate thoughts.

Current researchers believe that some slips arise merely from lapses of attention to the specifics of what is being said; others reveal a mental competition between similar verbal choices. People often say, "I'd be *interesting* in . . ." instead of the correct "I'd be *interested* in . . ." The sentence structure allows the two suffixes to be exchanged if the speaker fails to focus attention on the task. Although many tasks such as making small talk have "automatic" aspects, they still require some effort to be efficient and error-free.

Brain Scanning   Recall from Chapter 2 that sophisticated imaging techniques have now been developed to provide windows on the mind—records of various kinds of brain activity. In particular, the electroencephalogram (EEG) produces a graphic record of brain wave patterns. One such pattern is an *event-related potential (ERP)*, a change in potential related to a particular mental event (as opposed to the spontaneous electrical activity that brain cells continually produce). Researchers who use ERP can isolate and compare the level of brain activity devoted to specific tasks (Garnsey, 1993). The findings of ERP research indicate that a single general task, such as reading, involves several subtasks addressed by different mental processes. For example, when a reader encounters an unexpected grammatical construction in a sentence, a different ERP pattern is produced than if the reader encounters an unexpected word (Osterhout & Holcomb, 1992).

Brain scanning provides glimpses of cognitive processes through new windows. To understand what these glimpses mean, however, researchers still depend on each other to share information collected by various methods. The "big picture" of human cognitive processes is thus still emerging, piece by piece, just as detectives collect and assemble one clue at a time to arrive at a suspect profile or solution to a crime.

Check Your Recall

The study of cognitive psychology includes looking at the mental processes and mental structures that enable us to think, reason, make inferences and decisions, solve problems, and use language. Cognition is the general term for all forms of knowing. Cognitive psychologists generally use an information-processing approach to analyze information in components that are processed in stages or sequences. Cognitive psychology began to emerge in the 1950s with the triple developments of digital computers; the study of knowledge development in children; and the analysis of language acquisition as an innate system for manipulating symbols.

Cognitive science utilizes cognitive psychology, philosophy and neuroscience, and computer science to study the way knowledge guides thought and action. Cognitive researchers employ a variety of techniques to test their models and hypotheses, including introspection and think-aloud protocols, behavioral observation, reaction time, error analysis, and brain scanning techniques.

The Structure of Thinking

Human thought processes are at the upper end of the information-processing sequence, building on the more fundamental components of lower-order cognitions, such as pattern recognition and perceptual analysis. What happens when we reach that ultimate stage of information processing called *thinking*?

Thinking *is a complex mental process of forming a new representation by transforming available information.* That transformation involves the interaction of many mental activities, such as inferring, abstracting, reasoning, imagining, judging, problem solving, and, at times, creativity. From the perspective of cognitive psychology, thinking has three general features:

1. Thinking occurs in the mind but is *inferred from observable behavior.*
2. Thinking is a process that *manipulates knowledge* in a person's cognitive system.
3. Thinking is *directed toward finding solutions* to problems facing the individual (Mayer, 1981).

As we store information from our encounters with people and things, we build mental representations—models in our minds—of their features. We also develop generalizations based on specific experiences, such as "It is safer to approach a stranger who is smiling than one whose expression is angry." Thinking relies on a variety of mental structures. These structures include concepts, schemas, scripts, and visual imagery. Let's examine how we utilize each of them to form thoughts.

Concepts

You have probably had the experience known as *déjà vu* (from the French for "already seen"), the sensation that something you are perceiving now is also part of a memory of the past—that "this has happened before." Perhaps you visit a new place that seems oddly familiar, or have a social conversation that seems repetitive. But what would it be like to experience the opposite sensation, what comedian George Carlin calls "vujà dé"—the feeling that "none of this has ever happened before"? Imagine that every object or event looked truly new to you and seemed unrelated to anything you had ever experienced before. This tragedy actually befell a patient famous in psychiatric literature as "Henry M.," a young man who underwent experimental brain surgery to treat his severe epilepsy in 1953. The surgery destroyed or removed the tissue of his hippocampus, and when Henry awoke he was no longer able to form or retain

new memories. He recalled—and for the rest of his life has congenially retold—episodes and information he knew prior to the operation. But Henry M.'s life since 1953 has not been categorized or recorded in his own mind (Hilts, 1995).

Fortunately, normal individuals do have the brain-based capacity to treat new stimuli as instances of familiar, remembered categories. This ability to *categorize individual experiences*—to take the same action toward them or give them the same label—is regarded as one of the most basic abilities of thinking organisms (Mervis & Rosch, 1981).

Categorizing into Concepts   *The categories we form, which are mental representations of related items that are grouped in some way, are called* **concepts.** Concepts are the building blocks of thinking, enabling us to organize knowledge in systematic ways. Concepts may represent *objects, activities,* or *living organisms.* They may also represent *properties,* (such as "red" or "large"), *abstractions* (such as "truth" or "love") and *relations* (such as "smarter than") (Smith & Medin, 1981). Because concepts are mental structures, researchers cannot observe them directly but must infer their influence in people's thinking by studying their observable effects on people's behavior. For example, you cannot be sure that someone you care about shares your concept of "trust" or its importance in your relationships, but you can observe whether he or she behaves in ways that are trustworthy—and trusting.

A basic task of thinking is concept learning or concept formation: identifying the stimuli properties that are common to a class of objects or ideas. The mind lives by the principle of **cognitive economy,** *minimizing the amount of time and effort required to process information.* We learn not only features that form concepts, such as the colors of traffic lights, but also conceptual rules by which these features are related. For example, consider basic traffic light rules: If the light is red, stop; if yellow, slow down and prepare to stop; if green, go. It is amazing how many conceptual rules we learn, store, retrieve on demand, and use to direct our interactions with people and the environment (Haygood & Bourne, 1965).

Critical Features Versus Prototypes   What is the unit of information that is stored in memory when we form a concept? Psychologists have not yet agreed on the unit. Currently, two competing theories attempt to account for the form in which information is stored.

According to the *critical feature approach,* we store and consult mental lists of critical features that define concepts. These **critical features** *are stimuli that are necessary and sufficient conditions for a concept to be included in a category.* A concept is a member of the category if (and only if) it has every feature on the list. For example, a fax (facsimile) machine has a telephone connection, receiver, number keypad, and paper dispenser. Suppose you encounter an elaborate machine that looks like a fax machine but has no way of dispensing paper for messages. It may be some kind of telephone, but you cannot confidently categorize it as a fax machine because it lacks a critical feature.

The *prototype approach* suggests that categories are structured around *an ideal or most representative instance, called a* **prototype** (Rosch, 1973). A concept is classified as a member of a category if it is more similar to the prototype of that category than it is to the prototype of any other category. If a stimulus did not fit precisely within the limits of a stored category, but its variance from the prototype was within an acceptable range, it would still be classified as belonging to the category. For example, although the fonts illustrated on this page are very different, we still recognize them as belonging to the same category—the letter Z. All the variations depicted lie within an acceptable range of "Z-ness."

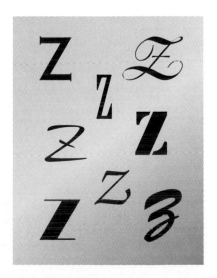

Fuzzy Concepts and Pseudomemories   Which approach—critical feature or prototype—best explains typical human thinking? In fact, we seem to use them both, each for different kinds of concepts. For example, the concept *mammals* is defined as "vertebrates that nurse their young." Organisms possessing these critical features qualify as mammals, while those that lack them do not. But the critical features approach does not work as well with the concept of *birds*. The dictionary defines a *bird* as "a warm-blooded vertebrate with feathers and wings." But when you think of a bird, what example comes to mind? If you are like most people, you will answer with birds like robins, blue jays, and sparrows—birds that seem *typical*. You won't think of examples that technically fit into the dictionary category but don't fit our usual way of thinking about the "concept" of a bird as an animal that flies, is small, and has feathers. Ostriches, eagles, and penguins fit the dictionary definition but not our basic conceptual view of birds. They are *atypical*. Atypical examples qualify for categorical membership but do not seem to "belong" to our psychological concept as well as the typical examples. Thus *bird* is a fuzzy concept; it has no well-defined boundaries between members of its class that fly and do not fly, are small or large (Zadeh, 1965). To correct this fuzziness, you probably define the concept not only by critical features (such as feathers) but in relation to your ideas about typical members of the category.

Many of our concepts in everyday life are like this. We can identify clusters of properties that are shared by different instances of a concept, but there may be no one property that is present in all instances. We consider some instances as more representative of a concept—more typical of our mental prototype—than others. Research studies show that people respond more quickly to typical members of a category than to more unusual ones (their reaction times are faster). For example, the reaction time to determine whether a robin is a bird is shorter than the reaction time to determine whether an ostrich is a bird, because robins resemble the prototype of a bird more closely than ostriches do (Kintsch, 1981; Rosch et al., 1976). A prototype is formed on the basis of frequently experienced features. These features are stored in memory, and the more often they are perceived, the stronger their overall memory strength is. Thus, the prototype can be rapidly accessed and recalled.

The police use the general principle of the prototype when they help witnesses identify criminal suspects. They prepare a prototype face made of plastic overlays of different facial features (from a commercially prepared "Identi-Kit"). The witness then is asked to modify the prototype model until it

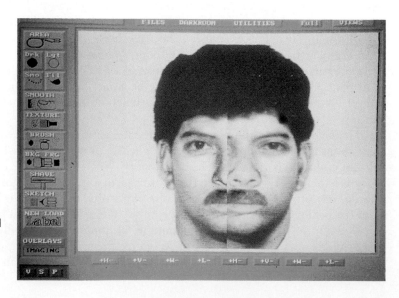

Witnesses' descriptions of criminal suspects can be transformed into composite sketches by assembling prototypical facial features and patterns.

is most similar to the suspect's face. Psychological researchers have used the overlay technique to study memory for prototypes. In a typical exercise, subjects study a series of "exemplar faces" that vary from a prototype. In one study (Solso & McCarthy, 1980), subjects were shown a set of 12 exemplar faces made from three prototype faces. Then they saw a second group of faces: some of the original exemplar faces, some new ones that were made to differ from the prototype, and the original prototype face, which they had never seen. The subjects' task was to rate their confidence in having seen each face before, during the first presentation. Three results clearly emerge, as seen in the chart in Figure 7.3.

Recall confidence was equally high for all the old items. The new items were accurately identified as unfamiliar, but false confidence—a feeling of having seen them before—became greater as the items more closely resembled the prototype. Finally, the highest level of confidence was for the prototype face itself, although the subjects had never seen it before. The subjects' reaction here is known as **pseudomemory** (pronounced *SUE-doe-memory*), *recall of a new stimulus because its attributes were stored in memory* (Solso & McCarthy, 1981).

Hierarchies and Basic Levels   Concepts are often organized in *hierarchies*, from general to specific, as seen in Figure 7.4. The broad category of *animal* has several subcategories, such as *bird* and *fish*, which in turn are subdivided into their specific forms, such as *canary, ostrich, shark,* and *salmon.* The animal category is itself a subcategory of the still larger category of *living*

FIGURE 7.3   Prototype and Exemplar Faces ■ One hundred percent of the prototype face's features have been seen previously by subjects. The 75-percent face has all the features of the prototype except the mouth; the 50-percent face has different hair and eyes; the 25-percent face has only the eyes in common; and the 0-percent face has no features in common. Subjects had least confidence in recalling faces with unfamiliar features, but ironically were most confident about the prototype face—which they had never actually seen.

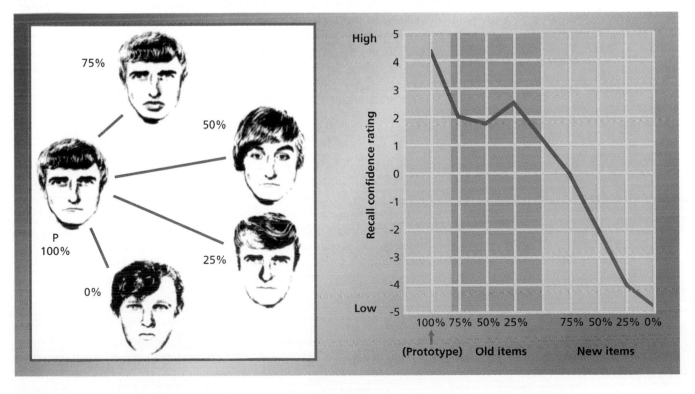

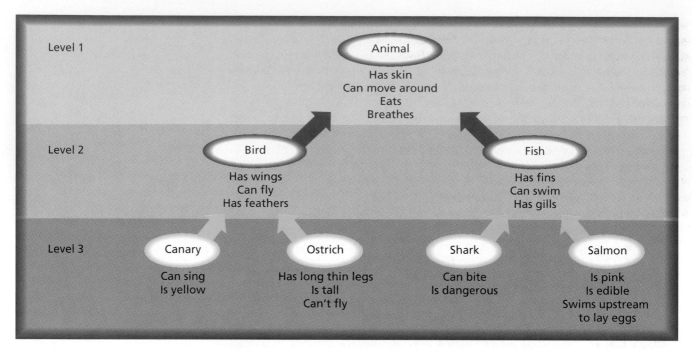

Level 1

Animal
Has skin
Can move around
Eats
Breathes

Level 2

Bird
Has wings
Can fly
Has feathers

Fish
Has fins
Can swim
Has gills

Level 3

Canary
Can sing
Is yellow

Ostrich
Has long thin legs
Is tall
Can't fly

Shark
Can bite
Is dangerous

Salmon
Is pink
Is edible
Swims upstream
to lay eggs

FIGURE 7.4   Hierarchically Organized Structure of Concepts ■

beings. These concepts and categories are arranged in a hierarchy of levels, with the most general and abstract at the top and the most specific and concrete at the bottom. They are also linked to many other concepts: some birds are *edible,* some are *endangered,* some are *national symbols.*

Psychologists have identified *a level in concept hierarchies at which people best categorize and think about objects. That level—the* **basic level**—can be retrieved from memory most quickly and used most efficiently. For example, the chair at your desk belongs to three obvious levels in a conceptual hierarchy: *furniture, chair,* and *desk chair.* The lower level category, *desk chair,* would provide more detail than you generally need, whereas the higher level category, *furniture,* would not be precise enough. When spontaneously identifying it, you would be more likely to call it a *chair* than a *piece of furniture* or a *desk chair.* It is now believed that our dependence on basic levels of concepts is another fundamental aspect of thought.

Schemas and Scripts

Much of what we know is stored in our brains as *schemas.* **Schemas** *are knowledge clusters, information packets, and general conceptual frameworks regarding certain objects, people, and situations in one's life.* These knowledge modules provide expectations about the features likely to be found when you encounter that concept or category, that person or situation. For example, to a student, the term *registration day* probably conjures up a schema that includes scenes of hassle, long lines, delay, and frustration. For a political candidate, however, the schema for *registration day* might include feelings of nervousness and excitement and scenes of photographers, large crowds, and campaign posters.

Making Inferences   Schemas include expectations about the features and effects that are typical of particular concepts or categories. New information, which is often incomplete or ambiguous, makes more sense when we can

Having a "picnic" schema enables one to make inferences about what is likely to be in a picnic basket as opposed to other sorts of baskets.

relate it to existing knowledge in our stored schemas. So we may say that schemas enable us to make inferences about missing information. What can you infer about the statement, "Tanya was upset to discover, upon opening the basket, that she'd forgotten the salt"? With no further information, you can infer a great deal about this event that is not explicit in the description. Salt implies that the basket is a picnic basket. The fact that Tanya is upset that the salt is missing suggests that the food in the basket is food that is usually salted, such as hardboiled eggs or vegetables. You automatically know what other foods might be included and, equally important, what definitely is not—everything in the world that is larger than a picnic basket and anything that would be inappropriate to take on a picnic—from a boa constrictor to bronze-plated baby shoes. The body of information you now have has been organized around a "picnic-basket" schema. By relating the statement about Tanya to your preestablished picnic-basket schema, you understand the statement better.

How important are schemas to us? According to researchers **David Rumelhart** and **Donald Norman**, schemas are the primary units of meaning in the human information-processing system (1975). We comprehend new information by integrating consistent new input with what we already know. If we find a discrepancy between new input and already stored schemas, we overcome it by changing what we know or ignoring the new input.

Do the following sentences make sense to you?

- The notes were sour because the seam was split.
- The haystack was important because the cloth ripped.

Taken alone, these sentences make little sense. What notes are being referred to, what is the seam, and how does a split seam cause sour notes? Why should ripped cloth make a haystack important?

Now, how does your thinking change with the addition of two words: *bagpipes* and *parachute?* Presto! The sentences suddenly become understandable. The notes were sour because the seam in the bag of the bagpipe was split. If you were falling from a plane in a torn parachute, the haystack could save your life. The sentences became comprehensible when you could integrate them into what you already knew—into appropriate schemas. They would remain confusing to anyone who did not know what a bagpipe or a parachute was. Thinking is a *constructive process* in which we draw on our existing mental structures to make as much sense as possible out of new information. We construct our subjective reality and personal world views of all the information we process. Once we interpret information as belonging to a particular schema, we may unwittingly change the information in our internal representation of it. To see how this transformation can occur, read the following passage:

> Chief Resident Jones adjusted his face mask while anxiously surveying a pale figure secured to the long gleaming table before him. One swift stroke of his small, sharp instrument and a thin red line appeared. Then the eager young assistant carefully extended the opening as another aide pushed aside glistening surface fat so that the vital parts were laid bare. Everyone stared in horror at the ugly growth too large for removal. He now knew it was pointless to continue.

Stop! Without looking back, please complete the following exercise: Circle below the words that appeared in the passage:

patient	scalpel	blood	tumor
cancer	nurse	disease	surgery

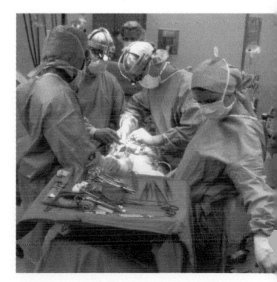

In an experiment on the influence of schema-based expectations, subjects were asked to read a medical story. Because they had connected the story to their personal schemas for hospital surgery, the subjects "remembered" reading terms that were not in the story.

In the original study, most of the subjects who read this passage circled the words *patient, scalpel,* and *tumor.* Did you? However, none of the words were there! Interpreting the story as a medical story made it more understandable, but also resulted in inaccurate recall (Lachman et al., 1979). Once the subjects had related the story to their schema for hospital surgery, they "remembered" labels from their schema that were not present in what they had read. Drawing on a schema not only gave the subjects an existing mental structure to tie the new material to but also led them to change the information to make it more consistent with their *schema-based expectations.*

Scripts as Event Schemas   We have schemas not only about objects and environmental events but also about persons, roles, and ourselves. These schemas help us to decide what to expect or how people should behave under specific circumstances. An event schema or **script** *is a cluster of knowledge about sequences of interrelated, specific events and actions expected to occur in a certain way in particular settings.* We have scripts for going to a restaurant, using the library, listening to a lecture, going on a first date, and even making love.

Some scripts in other cultures differ from ours, such as the scripts that govern exchanging gifts, attending funerals, and ways to treat women. In Japan, for example, giving money is almost always an appropriate wedding present. Choosing a wedding gift is thus an extremely easy task. This contrasts sharply with custom in the United States, where many types of wedding gifts are appropriate and people often spend a great deal of time selecting a "good" gift. Cultural distinctions in scripts emerge in everyday life as well as on special occasions. For example, during the Persian Gulf War, American women stationed in Arab locales discovered that many behaviors they might take for granted at home—such as walking unescorted in public, wearing clothing that showed their faces and legs, or driving a car, were considered scandalously inappropriate by citizens of their host country. To maintain good relations, these servicewomen had to change their habits and plans to accommodate local customs. The rules that govern different cultures may have developed from distinct ways of viewing the world.

When all people in a given setting follow similar scripts, they feel comfortable because they have comprehended the "meaning" of that situation in the same way and have the same expectations of each other (Abelson, 1981; Schank & Abelson, 1977). When people do not all follow similar scripts, however, they are made uncomfortable by the script "violation" and may have difficulty understanding why the scene was "misplayed." The discomfort we experience when scripts "clash" may signal trauma or danger. For example, in a case of date rape, the rapist's script tells him that when she says "no" she means "yes," and that she wants to be physically overpowered so she won't feel responsible for agreeing to sex. In contrast, the victim's script tells her that "no" means "no," that the rapist's assault is his wish, not hers, that he wants not intimacy but power, and that the experience is violent, not passionate.

We have trouble comprehending situations that do not fit scripted patterns. When we encounter new information that challenges or contradicts existing expectations, we feel discomfort and tension. One reason why relatively unprejudiced people do not interact with members of other ethnic groups (for example, Caucasian Americans with African Americans) is that people do not understand each others' scripts. When scripts clash, people can say, "I tried to interact, but it was so awkward that I don't want to try again" (Brislin, 1993). One way to reduce such discrepancies is to keep learning—to enlarge and change our schemas to *accommodate* new ideas. The reward for such mental flexibility is an easier understanding and acceptance of diversity and novelty.

The penalty for mental rigidity, by contrast, is continual frustration in trying to fit new experiences into narrow, old molds, and making "special exceptions" for events that break the rules. We do so by maintaining the status quo, without ever changing the schemas or scripts themselves that might no longer be relevant or appropriate. Isn't that a problem you've faced as you've matured but relatives and old friends keep treating you on the basis of their earlier schema of the adolescent version—or even the childhood version—of you? Schemas are at work in maintaining the thinking of prejudiced individuals, who resist contrary information and persist in discriminating against entire groups, instead of understanding the actual traits and abilities of any given individual.

Imagery and Cognitive Maps

Do you think only in words, or do you sometimes think in pictures and spatial relationships? Although you may not actually store visual memories in visual codes, you clearly are able to use imagery in your thinking. *Visual mental imagery* is a review of information previously perceived and stored in memory. It takes place in the absence of appropriate immediate sensory input and relies on internal representations of events and concepts in visual forms. For example, answer the following question:

What shape are a German shepherd's ears?

Assuming you answered correctly, how did you know that information? You probably have not memorized the shapes of dog ears, or ever expected to be quizzed about such knowledge. To answer that a German shepherd has pointed ears, you probably consulted a visual image of a German shepherd stored in your memory. Many psychologists believe that visual thought differs from verbal thought in the ways information is processed and stored (Kosslyn, 1983; Paivio, 1983).

Visual thought adds complexity and richness to our thinking, as do forms of thought that involve the other senses (sound, taste, smell, and touch). Visual thinking can be useful in solving problems in which relationships can be grasped more clearly in diagram form than in word form. Visual thought, for example, is useful in spatial or geographical relationships.

A cognitive representation of physical space is called a **cognitive map.** Learning theorist **Edward C. Tolman** was the first to hypothesize that people form mental maps of their environment as they learn their way through life's mazes, and these internal maps guide their future actions toward desired goals (see Chapter 6, page 225). Cognitive maps help people get where they want to go, and they enable them to give directions to others. By using cognitive maps, people can move through their homes with their eyes closed or go to familiar destinations even when their usual routes are blocked (Hart & Moore, 1973; Thorndyke & Hayes-Roth, 1978). If you found the main door to the psychology classroom building locked, your cognitive map would tell you where to look for the back door or side entrance.

Cultural Influences on Cognitive Maps   Mental maps seem to reflect our subjective impressions of physical reality. The maps often mirror the distorted view we have developed about the world from our personal or culturally egocentric perspective. For example, if you were asked to draw a world map, where would you begin and how would you represent the size, shape, and relations between various countries? This task was given to nearly 4000 students

FIGURE 7.5
Chicagocentric View of the World ■ How does this sketch compare with your view of the world?

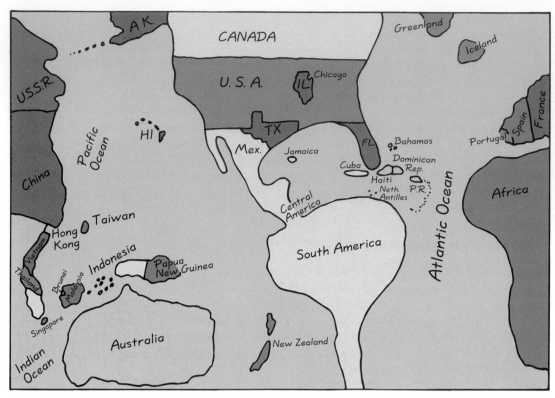

FIGURE 7.6
Australiocentric View of the World ■ Now who's "down under"?

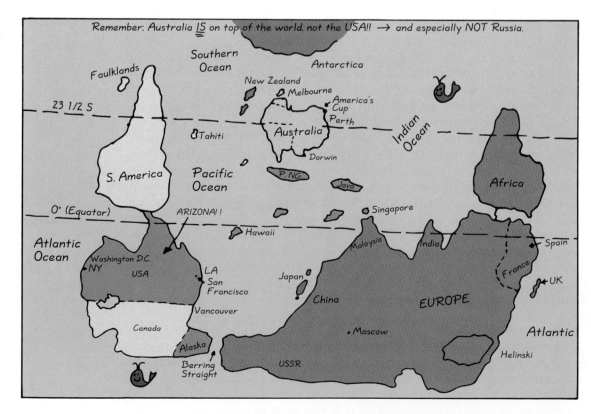

from 71 cities in 49 countries as part of an international study of the way people of different nationalities visualize the world. The goal of the study was to broaden understanding of cultural differences and to promote world peace. The study found that the majority of maps had a Eurocentric world view—Europe was placed in the center of the map and the other countries were arranged around it (probably due to the dominance for many centuries of Eurocentric maps in geography books). The study also yielded many instances of culture-biased maps, such as the ones by a Chicago student (Figure 7.5) and an Australian student (Figure 7.6).

American students did poorly on this task, misrepresenting the placement of countries, while students from the former Soviet Union and Hungary made the most accurately detailed maps (Saarinen, 1987). This suggests that cultural differences—perhaps in education or world view—have an impact on geographical thinking.

Check Your Recall

Thinking is a higher-order mental process that goes beyond the information given by sensory processing. Thinking transforms available information into new abstract representations. Human thought relies on many types of mental structures. One of the most basic abilities of thinking organisms is categorizing individual experiences. Concepts, the building blocks of thinking, are mental representations that group related items in particular ways. We form concepts by identifying those properties that are common to a class of objects or ideas. We store the critical features of well-defined concepts in order to identify their members. For concepts with ill-defined boundaries, we seem to store the prototypical or the most average instance of the concept. We respond to prototypes more quickly and recall them with more confidence than nonprototypical instances. Concepts are often arranged in hierarchies, from general to specific, and there is an optimal level of describing a complex concept—called the basic level—to which we respond most effectively.

Other mental structures that guide thinking are the knowledge packages of schemas and scripts. Schemas are collections of information about objects; scripts are schemas for experiences and actions. These mental structures help to encode and store information in memory and also to form expectations about appropriate attributes and effects of concepts. Scripts are event schemas: organized knowledge about expected sequences of action in given settings. In addition to these verbal thinking structures, we rely on visual imagery that adds further richness to thinking. Cognitive maps are mental representations of physical space that help us learn our way around and represent our personal and cultural worldviews. Taken together, these mental structures form the basis of how we think so efficiently.

The Functions of Thinking

Our thoughts range between two extremes: the autistic and the realistic. **Autistic thinking** *is a personal, idiosyncratic process involving fantasy, daydreaming, unconscious reactions, and ideas that cannot be tested against reality.* This type of individualized thought is part of most creative acts. However, when it generates delusions and hallucinations, autistic thinking can be evidence that the individual has lost touch with reality and suffers from some type of mental illness.

In contrast, **realistic thinking** *requires that ideas fit into the reality of situational demands, time constraints, operational rules, and personal resources.* Thinking realistically involves frequent checks on reality and tests that measure the appropriateness and correctness of one's ideas against some acceptable standard.

Reasoning

Reasoning *is a process of realistic, goal-directed thinking in which conclusions are drawn from a set of facts.* In reasoning, information from the environment and stored information are used in accordance with a set of rules (either formal or informal) for transforming information. There are two types of reasoning: deductive and inductive.

Deductive Reasoning   Deductive reasoning *involves drawing a conclusion that follows logically according to established rules from two or more statements, or premises.* More than 2000 years ago, Aristotle introduced the form of deductive reasoning known as the **syllogism,** which has three components: a major premise, a minor premise, and a conclusion. He also developed rules for syllogistic reasoning. If these rules are adhered to, the conclusion will be drawn *validly* from the premises. Consider the following example:

Major premise:	All people are thinking creatures.
Minor premise:	Descartes was a person.
Valid conclusion:	Therefore, Descartes was a thinking creature.
Invalid conclusion:	Therefore, all thinking creatures are Descartes.

If the conclusion is not derived by the rules of logic, it is *invalid,* as shown in the second conclusion of the example. You immediately knew the second conclusion was invalid—evidence that deductive reasoning is a fundamental part of reasoning ability (Rips, 1983).

Cognitive psychologists study the errors people make in logic and in syllogistic reasoning to understand their mental representations of premises and conclusions (Johnson-Laird & Byrne, 1989). Some errors occur because the individual's personal beliefs about the premises and conclusions get in the way of logic. People tend to judge as valid those conclusions with which they agree and as invalid those with which they do not agree (Janis & Frick, 1943).

Inductive Reasoning   Inductive reasoning *uses available evidence to generate a conclusion about the likelihood of something.* When you reason inductively, you construct a hypothesis based on limited evidence and then test it against other evidence. The hypothesis is not drawn from the logical structure of the argument, as in deductive reasoning. Rather, inductive reasoning requires leaping from data to decisions. These inferential leaps are accomplished by integrating past experience, perceptual sensitivity, weighted value of the importance of each element of evidence, and a dash of creativity.

Most scientific reasoning is inductive. After solving a difficult mystery, fictional detective Sherlock Holmes frequently explains to his companion Dr. Watson that his conclusions were based on observation and "deduction." Wrong! In fact, Holmes's solutions involve shrewd *induction:* piecing together bits of data—clues in the case, and his own vast general knowledge—into a compelling web of evidence that eventually explains the manner and perpetrator of the crime. In our lives, inductive reasoning plays a key role in helping all of us solve many of the problems we face. If you misplace your keys, for example, you use inductive reasoning to search your memory and review the evidence—"I set my umbrella down there," "I remember the phone was ring-

All cats have four legs. I have four legs. Therefore, I am a cat.

ing as I opened the door"—to retrace your steps and find your missing keys (still in the lock, right where you left them).

Problem Solving

Problem solving is a basic part of our everyday existence. We continually encounter problems that require solutions: how to manage work and tasks within a limited time frame, how to succeed at a job interview, how to break off an intimate relationship, how to conserve energy, or how to avoid sexually transmitted diseases. For psychologists, **problem solving** *is thinking that is directed toward solving specific problems*. Such thinking moves from an initial state to a goal state by means of a set of mental operations.

Many problems arise from discrepancies between what you know and what you need to know. When you solve a problem, you reduce that discrepancy by finding a way to get the missing information. To get into the spirit of problem solving yourself, try the problems in Figure 7.7 (the answers are on page 268, as depicted in Figure 7.8).

FIGURE 7.7   Can You Solve It? ■
A. Can you connect all the dots in the pattern by drawing four straight, connected lines without lifting your pen from the paper?
B. A prankster has put 3 Ping-Pong balls into a 6-foot-long pipe that is standing vertically in the corner of the physics lab, fastened to the floor. How would you get the Ping-Pong balls out?
C. The checkerboard shown has 2 corner pieces cut out, leaving 62 squares. You have 31 dominoes, each of which covers exactly 2 checkerboard squares. Can you use them to cover the whole checkerboard?
D. You are in the situation depicted and given the task of tying 2 strings together. If you hold one, the other is out of reach. You have a stapler and a scissors handy. Can you do it?
E. You are given the objects shown (a candle, tacks, matches, and a matchbox). The task is to mount a lighted candle on a door. Can you do it?
F. You are given 3 "water-jar" problems. Using only the 3 containers (water supply is unlimited), can you obtain the exact amount specified in each case?

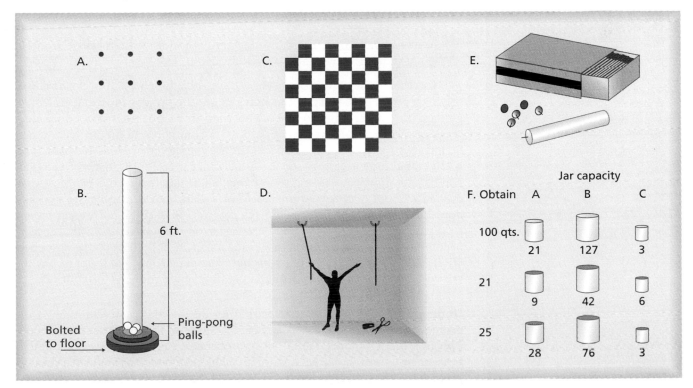

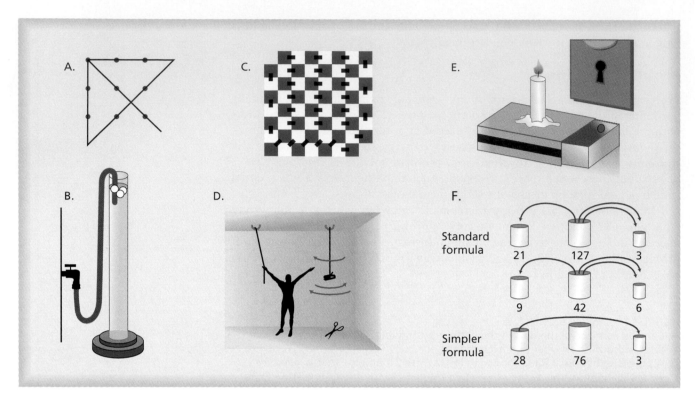

FIGURE 7.8   Solutions to the Problems ■

The Problem Space   In information-processing terms, a problem has the following three parts:

1. *An initial state.* The initial state of the problem includes the incomplete information with which you start. Perhaps that information corresponds to some unsatisfactory set of conditions in the world.
2. *A goal state.* Your goal is the set of information or state of the world you hope to achieve.
3. *A set of operations.* These are the steps you must take to move from an initial state to a goal state (Newell & Simon, 1972).

Together these three parts define the problem space. You can think of solving a problem as walking through a maze (the problem space) from where you are (the initial state) to where you want to be (the goal state), making a series of turns (the allowable operations). A common real-life problem might be having to pay an unexpected bill. In the *initial state* of this problem, you receive a bill for a necessary service—such as a car repair or doctor's visit—but you did not anticipate having to pay this bill at this time. Your *goal* is to pay the bill without upsetting your budget or sacrificing other expenses you had hoped to cover. Some problem-solving *operations* (such as borrowing money from your own savings account) are easier or more acceptable than others (asking your parents for a loan or writing a bad check). By using the best operations, you hope to move from your initial state to your goal state: to pay the bill without doing anything wrong or creating new problems for yourself.

Understanding the Problem   Setting up an internal representation of the problem space—specifying all the elements in it—is not an automatic process. This task often requires finding the appropriate schema from previous similar tasks or situations. However, existing schemas can be restricting when the new problem calls for a new solution.

If you solved the problems in Figure 7.7, you recognized the importance of an accurate internal representation of the problem space. To connect the nine dots, you had to realize that nothing in the instructions limited you to the area of the dots themselves. To get the Ping-Pong balls out of the pipe, you had to realize that the solution did not involve reaching into the pipe. In the checkerboard problem, you had to realize that you could use the domino at any angle to cover any two squares, regardless of their color. To connect the two strings, you had to see one of the tools on the floor as a weight. To mount the candle on the door, you had to alter your usual perspective and perceive the matchbox as a platform instead of as a container, and you had to perceive the candle as a tool as well as the object to be mounted on the door.

Mental Blocks   In the last two problems, one has to overcome a phenomenon called *functional fixedness* (Duncker, 1945; Maier, 1931). **Functional fixedness** *is a mental block that hinders problem solving and creativity by making it hard to perceive a new function for an object that was previously associated with some other purpose.* Functional fixedness would prevent you, for example, from seeing that a knife blade can be used as a screwdriver, and that metal pliers can be used as a hammer. When your thinking is functionally fixed, you put your conceptual "blinders" on and use only your familiar schemas; this shows again the power of schemas to guide or misguide perception of reality. For example, seeing the matchbox as a platform and the candle as a tool are examples of overcoming functional fixedness.

Another kind of mental rigidity may have hampered your solving the water-jar problem. If you had discovered in the first two problems the conceptual rule that $B - A - 2(C)$ = the answer, you probably tried the same formula for the third problem and found it didn't work. Actually, simply filling jar A and pouring off enough to fill jar C would have left you with the right amount. If you were using the other formula, you probably did not notice this simpler possibility—your previous success with the other rule would have led you to rely on a habitual strategy, a problem-solving *set,* similar to *perceptual set* (discussed in Chapter 5), which is a readiness to perceive stimuli in a particular way. A **mental set** *is a tendency to respond to a new problem in the same manner used to solve a previous problem.* A mental set can enhance the quality and speed of perceiving and of problem solving under some conditions, but it can also inhibit or distort the quality of our mental activities at times when old ways of thinking and acting are nonproductive. In fact, much real-life problem solving involves "breaking set"—temporarily giving up your reliance on past learning and mental habits in order to fully explore the present stimulus array so that you can see all your options from a new perspective. For example, when a serious 1993 snowstorm blocked roads and downed power lines in the mountain city where your second author lives, power-less citizens had to think of using their fireplaces as stoves and their icy porches as temporary refrigerators until electricity was restored.

Avoiding Pitfalls in Reasoning   Another approach to problem solving contrasts *descriptive thinking*—the way computers and people solve problems—with *prescriptive thinking*—the way people *ought* to solve problems (Levine, 1987). People need to be taught ways to avoid pitfalls in reasoning and to be sensitive to perceptual sets and biases. They also need to adhere to the following prescriptive principles for solving problems:

- *Formulate a plan.* Make it sufficiently concrete to be action oriented and sufficiently abstract to generalize beyond specific, limited applications.
- Work in an *organized* way.
- Work, at first, with *simpler versions* of complex problems.

- *Mentally rehearse* taking the right action. Visual imaging can be especially helpful for learning motor habits.
- *Engage yourself* in the problem. Inform yourself, and work up enthusiasm for solving it. Give it time and energy.
- *Set yourself up for success.* Anticipate challenges as part of your situation, not as part of yourself. Don't assume you are disadvantaged or inadequate because of prejudices like "I'm not good at numbers," "Men aren't good listeners," or "Women don't know how to operate power tools."

You will recognize that most of the above advice seems like common sense. This is good! It will help you to make better problem-solving strategies a more natural extension of your customary approach to challenges and difficulties. Table 7.1 offers additional tips for improving your cognitive skill functioning.

Search Strategies: Algorithms Versus Heuristics   Once you know the problem space, you have defined the problem but you haven't yet solved it. Solving the problem requires using the operations that get you from the initial state to the goal state. If a problem is like a maze, you must still decide on a strategy for selecting the right path.

One search strategy is an **algorithm,** *a methodical, step-by-step problem-solving procedure that guarantees reaching a correct outcome by reviewing every possible strategy.* The drawback to relying on algorithms is that they can be tedious, and using these fail-safe strategies requires both time and patience. For example, there are 120 possible combinations of the letters *otrhs,* but only one combination produces an actual English word. You could try each combination to find that word: *short.* But for an eight-letter group such as *teralbay,*

TABLE 7.1	TIPS FOR IMPROVING COGNITIVE SKILLS
Applications of basic principles for developing your cognitive skills can be summarized as follows (Anderson, 1981, 1982):	
1. Space your practice.	In learning a new skill, practice a short time each day, trying to complete a unit of study or one action pattern in one session.
2. Master the subskills.	Many skills have component parts. Develop these to the point where they are automatic so you don't have to attend to them. Then start focusing on the next, higher level and, finally, on the overall skill.
3. Internalize an ideal model.	Observe the correct performance of an expert role model so you can get a good picture of what you are trying to achieve. Then monitor your own performance, noting explicitly how it compares with that of your model.
4. Seek immediate feedback and use it immediately.	Get knowledge as quickly as you can about the quality of your performance—if possible while the feeling of your action is still in your working memory. Then try to use the feedback while it is still in your working memory.
5. Anticipate initial frustrations, setbacks, and plateaus in performance.	Overcoming difficulties requires persistence, practice, renewed effort, and a sense of one's self-efficacy in achieving preset goals.

there would be 40,320 possible combinations: $8 \times 7 \times 6 \times 5 \times 4 \times 3 \times 2 \times 1 = 40,320$. A search of all the combinations would eventually reveal the solution, but the search would be long and tedious. The price of a guaranteed solution is sometimes intense, careful labor.

Luckily, there is an alternate approach that you can use to solve a great many problems every day. You can use a **heuristic,** *a cognitive strategy or "rule of thumb" used as a shortcut to solve more complex mental tasks.* Heuristics are general strategies or reliable operations that have been found to work in similar situations in the past and may also work in the present case. Some heuristics have become familiar aphorisms, such as reminding yourself to "Consider the source" or evaluate the credibility of a message's origins in deciding whether to believe the message. Other heuristics are habits or guidelines that some people find personally effective. For instance, where should you put a note to remind yourself to run early morning errands? If one of the first things you look at every morning is your reflection in the bathroom mirror, the mirror is a good place to post a note to yourself. When you have a problem to solve or a decision to make, a heuristic offers a handy strategy in place of a guaranteed solution.

A heuristic that can help you solve the word jumble of *teralbay* is "Make short words or familiar syllables from some of the letters, and then see if the remaining letters fit around them." Using such a strategy, you might generate *ably* (tear*ably?*), *able* (ray*table?*), and *tray* (la*tray*be?). By using this search strategy, you would probably not need to try more than a few of the possibilities before you came up with the solution: *betrayal* (Glass et al., 1979).

Using a heuristic does not guarantee that a solution will be found; using an algorithm, tedious though it might be, does. One way experience helps us become better problem solvers is by teaching us which heuristics have served us well, and when and how to use them. When the "guaranteed solution" route will not be too time consuming, rely on the algorithm; when this demands time or resources you do not have, go for the heuristic. The previous sentence is itself one kind of heuristic that can guide rational problem-solving strategies.

Created as a strategy to help in solving the problem of forgetfulness, the written reminder operates as a heuristic.

Judging and Deciding

We live in a world of *uncertainty.* We can never be completely confident in our predictions about how people will behave or how events will unfold. Despite this uncertainty, we are constantly called upon to make personal, economic, and political decisions that have enormous impacts on our lives. Are there accepted guidelines or models for making good decisions? In this section, we will see that decision making is always subjective, often error-prone, and sometimes irrational. In addition, we will see that human intuition can be fallible—at times it leads us to make mistakes. By recognizing the underlying cognitive mechanisms that guide our choices, however, we have an opportunity to improve our decision making skills.

Psychologists often distinguish between judgment and decision making. **Judgment** *is the process by which we form opinions, reach conclusions, and make critical evaluations of events and people on the basis of available information.* We often make judgments—the product of the judging process—spontaneously, without prompting. In many situations we carry with us attitudes and previously developed evaluations of the stimuli and options we perceive. Some judgmental choices are basic and habitual, such as having eggs and coffee for breakfast if you are American, but noodles and smoked fish for breakfast if you are Japanese. Other judgments involve less clear or familiar criteria, and may involve some on-the-spot evaluation, as when you meet a brand new instructor and must decide within minutes whether to register for her class.

When you register for new classes, you must make judgments about the topics and instructors, as well as decisions about your own priorities and needs.

If judgment often feels automatic or spontaneous, making choices or decisions usually involves more effort and prioritizing. **Decision making** *is the process of choosing between alternatives, selecting and rejecting available options.* Some choices, like many judgments, are so easy they seem habitual and automatic, such as always preferring cream but no sugar in your coffee. Other decisions require some review of priorities, such as when you must choose between two college classes, one by a favorite instructor but at a difficult day and time for you, the other more conveniently scheduled but taught by an unknown instructor. Some mental effort is involved in deciding whether, for this course and this time in your life, you prefer to keep a familiar schedule or stick with a favorite teacher.

Judgment and decision making are interrelated processes. For example, you might meet a new instructor at a campus function, and after a brief discussion of shared interests, you might *judge* the person to be intelligent, interesting, honest, and sincere—all qualities you value in a teacher. You might then *decide* to take a new course offered by that person even if it means changing your previous plans or altering your schedule to accommodate this choice.

Judging: Making Sense of the World   Our everyday world is complicated, and we often must rely on relevant knowledge we have accumulated previously to guide our behavior. Most of the situations in which we find ourselves share basic properties with previous situations we have encountered. The theories we have developed through a wide variety of experiences can help us understand novel events and new information. For example, as a student you have attended a great number of classes, and your memory of these experiences will determine how you behave on the first day of a new class. Using previous knowledge simplifies matters; you do not need to relearn the guidelines for class behavior every time you begin a new course.

Our judgments are based on **inference**, *the reasoning process of drawing a conclusion on the basis of evidence or prior beliefs and theories.* We use a variety of *inferential strategies* to simplify the inferences we make. Ordinarily these strategies serve us well. In some circumstances, however, we misapply these strategies to new data. When faced with new information that is inconsistent with previous knowledge, we are often too ready to try to fit such information into an established theory rather than consider the possibility that the theory itself requires revision. Thus, it took centuries of astronomers collecting hard empirical data before people would give up the theory that the earth was the center of the universe and accept that it is a planet that revolves around the sun as do all the others. Currently many psychologists are waging their own intellectual battle: between those who theorize that intelligence is primarily inherited and not modifiable in any major way by education or special intervention and those who believe intelligence can be affected by experience. We will visit the protagonists of this argument in Chapter 11, but for now the point is that in the past each side has failed to accommodate the evidence that might modify its theory into one that proposed an *interaction* between heredity and environmental influences.

In an ongoing quest for efficiency and economy, we do not always choose strategies that are exhaustive and thorough. People habitually use mental shortcuts to make up their minds quickly, easily, and with maximum confidence (Kahneman et al., 1982). Unfortunately, overuse of shortcuts can lead to systematic errors. In fact, people can be misled by the same cognitive processes that work effectively in most situations. However, it might make more sense to use a mental shortcut that *usually* works than to employ a more ideal approach that *always* yields the correct answer but takes a great deal of time and mental effort.

CULTURAL ⊕ CONTEXT

Comprehending Social Diversity

Assume that you have a good friend named Carla, someone with whom you went to high school. You took many classes together and shared learning experiences. Your high school teachers introduced a variety of activities, alternating formal lectures with group discussions and real-life problem solving. They even encouraged students to disagree with them or with the textbooks and to defend their positions with sound arguments. Carla went on to attend a college with a study-abroad program. Her Spanish is good, so this year she is taking courses at a university in Spain. Now you get a letter from Carla asking for your advice:

I can't figure out what's going on in my classes. I thought I knew what professors did from my experiences in America, but here they just lecture all the time—there is no opportunity for class discussions. Forget about having your own opinion on anything! The professors seem to think that they know it all and that students have nothing to contribute! They even assign topics for our term papers—we can't even suggest our own ideas. And students better not ask about an extension on handing in a paper for any reason, because deadlines here are really strict! I know you are taking psychology now; I sure wish I had taken it at my school before I came here. Can you help me to understand what is going on,

maybe pass along something you learned in psychology? I know you can't change things for me here, but maybe you can at least help me understand the professors' behavior. If I can understand them, maybe I'll be more sympathetic. I sure am frustrated now!

Does cross-cultural research in psychology allow you to make some suggestions in your return letter to Carla? The answer is yes: culture provides guidance for behavior. A concept that is very helpful when analyzing cultural differences is *uncertainty avoidance*. The Dutch psychologist Geert Hofstede (1986, p 308) argues that uncertainty avoidance "defines the extent to which people within a culture are made nervous by situations that they perceive as unstructured, unclear, or unpredictable—situations which they try to avoid by maintaining strict codes of behavior and a belief in absolute truths."

Different cultures have developed ways of dealing with uncertainty. Some cultures, called "high uncertainty avoidant," have many rules that guide behavior. Such cultures also avoid uncertainty by having widely accepted views of truth. If many people accept a certain set of "facts" as true, they can turn to these facts when challenged by any of life's problems. Other cultures, called "low uncertainty avoidant," have fewer strict rules and less rigidity concerning views of absolute truths. They prefer to believe that flexible rules and multiple approaches to discovering truth will provide better preparation for the future.

How can you apply these insights, developed by Hofstede (1986, 1991), to your friend Carla's concerns? Spain is a *high-uncertainty-avoidant* country. Other high-uncertainty-avoidant countries to which many students travel for study-abroad opportunities include Greece, Belgium, France, Israel, and Italy. High uncertainty avoidance leads to strict rules in the classroom, precise objectives for courses, and norms that enforce the expectation that the professor is the source of knowledge. Students are not expected to have their own opinions or to make suggestions about course content. In *low-uncertainty-avoidant* countries (such as the United States, Canada, and Sweden) professors are allowed to say "I don't know" and to accept suggestions from students. Professors are also far more tolerant of students who take opposing views, and often view disagreements as intellectually stimulating.

A knowledge of culture and cultural differences won't always solve problems immediately. Carla will face the same issues in her classes whether or not she understands concepts such as uncertainty avoidance. But if the stress indicated in her letter becomes severe, an understanding of the reasons for her problems can help her make general adjustments to her life in another culture. Different cultures present different "knowledge packages" concerning topics such as classroom structure, lectures, and disagreements with students. Concepts such as uncertainty avoidance help us understand differences in the knowledge packages people encounter in different cultures.

In social situations, it undoubtedly is cognitively efficient to identify a few significant, stable characteristics around which to organize our initial reactions to others. Unfortunately, however, we may form overgeneralized *stereotypes* based on minimal, faulty, or false information. These stereotypes can influence the way we behave toward other people and, in turn, the way they behave toward us. For example, if you are told that someone you are about to meet is schizophrenic, you are likely to form an emotional impression that differs from the impression you would have formed had you not been given the label, regardless of the person's behavior (Fiske & Pavelchak, 1986).

Why are initial impressions so persistent over time and so resistant to new information and contradictory data? What are the forces that distort the way we interpret the evidence of our senses, the memories we retrieve, and the decisions we make? One way to learn about judging and decision making is to examine the errors and biases that beset us as we try to make evaluations and choices (Kahneman, 1991). We might begin by asking about the assumptions we learn to make from our own cultures. As explored in Cultural Context: Comprehending Social Diversity, we make assumptions about our world based on our experiences with the culture and people we live with. Cultures differ from each other in the degree to which they value certainty and structure in life. In a world made ever smaller by mass marketing and instant telecommunication, we must examine our cultural biases before we can confidently make sense of our world.

The Perseverance of False Beliefs   A child interprets the new by *assimilating* it into known categories and *accommodating* old mental structures to fit this new information. For instance, a toddler used to sucking on bottles' nipples might, when given a new clown doll, suck on its protruding plastic nose. Her early efforts to assimilate the doll's nose into the "suckable" category will cease when the child accommodates "sucking" (adjusts it) to exclude things (like dolls' noses) that "don't give milk." In a similar way, the adult mind must decide again and again whether new data support or fit old theories, and when old theories must be changed because new data just doesn't fit. By balancing our efforts to assimilate and accommodate, we make the best use of new knowledge while also benefiting from past lessons. For example, after surviving a painful breakup, you may approach new relationships with mistrust, assimilating new people into your old system of fears. But if you meet someone who seems trustworthy, you must drop your guard and accommodate your attitude to give another relationship a chance.

We often continue to persevere in beliefs, theories, and ways of doing things because we assimilate data or new experiences in a *biased* fashion (Ross & Lepper, 1980). Data consistent with our beliefs are given only brief attention and quickly filed away mentally since they meet our expectations. But we pay closer attention to data that are incongruent and challenging, and we devote our efforts to reinterpreting and explaining this information within the context of our theories. *The process of collecting data without careful attention because the information supports one's preexisting beliefs is known as* **biased assimilation.** This tendency creates a familiar, error-prone "rut" in thinking. We inadvertently set high standards for attention-getting information, requiring experiences or information to "surprise" us somehow—to violate expectations or prior beliefs—before we will take a second look. For example, a detective trying to solve a crime forms hypotheses about which suspects are likely to be guilty, and fails to question someone who doesn't "seem" like the "criminal type." If the real criminal offers an alibi that fits the detective's prejudices, the detective may fail to check on the alibi, allowing the criminal to go unsuspected while other leads are pursued.

It is natural to relax and rely on tried-and-true ideas much of the time, but what if those earlier beliefs are wrong? In such a case, critical new information could help us correct such mistaken thinking. Instead of assuming that new data "fit" our old ideas, we should scrutinize incoming information for its meaning. Where we find a mismatch between old ideas and new information, instead of rejecting the new data as false, we might consider them as *evidence* that a shift in our way of thinking is required.

Avoiding biased assimilation is a trickier business than simply paying attention and keeping an open mind. Complicating the bias is the fact that we may choose to ask questions in ways that they are bound to yield the answers we want (Snyder & Swann, 1978a). For example, which of the following two questions should you ask if you want useful information from an applicant for a job?

"Just one more thing. . . ." The television detective Lt. Columbo (actor Peter Falk) resists biased thinking by keeping an open mind about the meaning of clues and the possible guilt of suspects.

Question 1: Are you the kind of honest, hard worker we need on this job?

Question 2: Please give me some examples of what you consider your commitment to honesty and effort on a job.

Obviously the first question will get the affirmative answer—"Yes, of course!"—from anyone who wants the job. This is the question to ask if you are willing to hire anyone. Answers to the second question allow you to estimate the work traits in comparison to the standard he or she offers in the examples. Your motives—desperation to hire *someone* versus need to hire just the *right* person—will determine which questions you ask. Thus the way we collect information may be biased by our expectations. In addition, we tend to surround ourselves with people who share our biases (Festinger, 1957; Olson & Zanna, 1981). It appears we are quite good at shoring up our opinions once they are in place.

What's wrong with occasionally relying on personal biases as a form of cognitive "self-protection"? One problem is that our tendency to cling to initial theories can lead to *overconfidence* in the truth of our beliefs, because it causes us to underestimate the probability that these beliefs could be wrong. For example, a prejudiced employer refuses to hire members of a specific ethnic group because she believes "those people" make unreliable workers. Since she doesn't hire them, she never sees them on the job *or* witnesses the high quality of their performance, so she maintains her belief that "those people" are not qualified. Ironically, the consequences of prejudice may keep such biased thinking in place by preventing it from being challenged.

Humans have a tendency to overestimate their accuracy in making predictions and social judgments. Is this overconfidence necessarily costly? Researchers still debate whether such overconfidence does more harm than good (Taylor & Brown, 1988). On one hand, an inflated sense of confidence may encourage persistence and help you accomplish feats you might not otherwise take on. On the other hand, overconfidence in your impressions could lead you to trust someone who does not deserve it, to put yourself in jeopardy, or to expose yourself to danger. Unrealistic optimism can get you into trouble by preventing you from seeing the potential error—and danger—in your situation, and from taking preventive action or coping effectively (Weinstein, 1980).

Despite our ability to think scientifically—that is, to base conclusions on factual verifiable evidence—we are often swayed by incomplete information, by rumors, and by unfounded beliefs. We ask you to take a moment to "Weigh the Evidence" (page 276) and to draw your own conclusions about why so many people put faith in ideas that are not only unproven, but are downright frightening.

Cognitive Biases We make decisions based on judgments, and we make judgments based on inferences about the evidence we have. Our use of mental shortcuts can result in **cognitive bias,** *systematic error in this sequence of inference, judgment, and decision.* At times, these biases are not "errors" but differences in emphasis or perspective that we bring to a situation we are trying to understand. They are similar to perceptual biases that can misdirect our perceptions because of learned expectations and other factors, as discussed in Chapter 1, but cognitive biases are biases not in the way we perceive the world, but in how we think about it.

Researchers have identified a number of different types of biases in judgment. For example, we tend to perceive random events as nonrandom (as when we superstitiously whisper to dice before rolling them) and correlated

Strange Beliefs

An old proverb advises that "truth is the daughter of time"—in other words, sooner or later, as time passes, the truth about a historical event becomes apparent, even if it was not so initially. In seventeenth-century New England, people (mostly women) were executed for witchcraft. Three hundred years later, their "crimes" seem to have been nothing more than gossiping, offending authority figures, nonconformist practices, or the symptoms of mental illness (Karlsen, 1987). Why were the victims' neighbors so ready to believe the enemy was Satan, and the only "solution" was to kill the witches?

Perhaps we feel reassured by science and modern technology that such persecutions "can't happen here." Yet before we become too smug about our invulnerability to such witch-hunting hysteria today, we must ask why so many communities in the 1990s in America believe their children have been victimized by sexually abusive day care workers or secret "satanic rituals"—especially when not only the accused but many of the alleged victims themselves deny such acts ever occurred (Ofshe & Watters, 1994). Why are people often willing to believe the worst, when there may be other, noncriminal explanations for the "evidence"?

Consider the bizarre case of alien abduction. By one estimate, approximately 2 percent of the U.S. population may have "experienced" contact, abduction, and molestation by alien beings. The symptoms reported by "experiencers" include diffuse anxiety, disturbed sleep, and images of having been contacted and taken by extraterrestrials (Hopkins et al., 1992). Although the symptoms themselves might be explained by posttraumatic stress disorder, (see Chapter 9), the number of affected individuals is alarmingly high—so high, in fact, that we might expect to find *some* physical evidence, or anything more validating than mere eyewitness memory and dream fragments, to confirm that such abductions have really occurred.

A 1991 national poll calculated that 31 percent of adult respondents made at least one positive response when asked whether they had ever experienced any of the following key "indicators" of alien abduction (Hopkins et al., 1992; The Roper Organization, 1992):

■ Waking up paralyzed with the sense of a strange figure or presence in the room;

■ Apparently being lost for an hour or more without remembering why;

■ Flying through the air without knowing why or how;

■ Seeing unusual lights or balls of light in a room without understanding what caused them;

■ Discovering puzzling scars on one's body without remembering what caused them.

Any of these "indicators" might inspire emotion or confusion in the one who has experienced them. Maybe it isn't surprising that the victims grasp at bizarre hypotheses to explain such disturbing sensations and memories. But *weigh the evidence:* Are there *alternative*, non-alien-abduction explanations possible for any of them? And aren't some alternative explanations—such as different levels of consciousness, individual differences in brain function, misperceiving or misremembering natural events—more appealing than the alien abduction hypothesis? Could UFO sightings, like witch hunts, be a product not of reality but of fear, prejudice, and ignorance?

In 1992, award-winning journalist and author C. D. B. Bryan attended a five-day conference held at the Massachusetts Institute of Technology for the "experiencers" of alien abduction and professionals seeking to understand them (Bryan, 1995). Skeptical but open-minded, Bryan was struck by the similarity of details among the abductees' reports of their experiences, which led one conferee to remark, "If what these abductees are saying isn't happening to them, then what is?" Even if their symptoms suggested a common source of trauma, then what was the trauma that had so afflicted such a large and diverse group of people? Bryan notes that the "abductees" were not enjoying their celebrity, but were generally distressed at having been victimized and unhappy at being the targets of scrutiny and doubt (Wolcott, 1995). Why then would they make up such preposterous fictions?

Psychology is a science, relying on facts and empirical evidence to support or weaken hypotheses. Beliefs are not the same as facts, and faith is not the same kind of "knowing" as science. People have always relied simultaneously on several systems for knowing the world, juxtaposing scientific thought with superstition and religious doctrine. And there remains much to study and understand. Human history is rife with tales of unexplained phenomena, from religious apparitions and demonic possession to miraculous healings and psychic abilities. Science does not require its practitioners to dismiss incredible stories as lies or fabrications. But science does demand *verifiable, empirical evidence* before any explanation can be accepted. To remain open-minded yet skeptical, we face a challenge: to listen carefully to children's stories and adults' accounts—but to resist the temptation to react emotionally by blaming either earthly or otherworldly entities for events we cannot prove and do not understand—yet!

events as causally related (like believing that a full moon makes people crazy). We also tend to perceive people as causing rather than being victimized by their experiences (as when we accuse a rape victim of "asking for it"). Psychologists study these biases to understand the cognitive strategies people use to make complex judgments.

We have noted that heuristics are mental shortcuts used to solve problems by reducing the range of possible solutions. However, overreliance on heuristics can backfire by making mistakes more likely. For example, perhaps you use a heuristic such as "select the longest answer" when taking one professor's multiple-choice tests. But another professor may write test items in which the longest answer is usually the wrong choice—so your trusty heuristic can hurt you if you apply it in the wrong context.

Two heuristics in particular have been found to cause mistakes when they are overused or relied on to excess. These are the *availability heuristic* and the *representativeness heuristic,* first studied by **Amos Tversky** and **Daniel Kahneman.**

The Availability Heuristic   You probably try to make intelligent choices about your own health and safety, and seek to avoid unnecessary risks. Consider what you have learned about various threats to well-being. In the United States, which kills more people annually: tornadoes or asthma? And how do accidental deaths compare with fatal diseases? When research subjects were asked such questions about the frequency of different causes of death, they overestimated those that were rare but dramatic (such as tornadoes, accidents) and underestimated those that were more frequent but private and "quieter" (such as asthma, diseases) (Slovic, 1984). In fact, the death rate from asthma is 20 times greater than from tornadoes, and diseases kill 16 times as many people as accidents do. How can people's estimates be so far off, especially in matters of life and death?

The **availability heuristic** *is a cognitive strategy that estimates probabilities based on personal experience.* When you rely on the availability heuristic, you estimate the likelihood of an outcome based on how easily you can imagine similar or identical outcomes. This heuristic causes you to judge as *more frequent or probable* those events that are *more readily imagined* or retrieved from memory—those that are cognitively more "available." For example, tornadoes are rare natural disasters that merit news coverage in headlines and television. The very rarity of such vivid threats makes them newsworthy—just as bad news has more shock value than good news. Therefore, an event may be mentally available not because it is frequent, but because it is vivid or recent. Don't make the mistake of equating mental availability (how easily certain things "come to mind") with their actual frequency of occurrence in the world.

The Representativeness Heuristic   Another judgmental heuristic that simplifies the complex task of social judgment under uncertain conditions is based on the presumption that, once a person or event is "categorized," it shares all the features of other members in that category. *The cognitive strategy that assigns items to such categories based on whether they possess some representative characteristics of the category is the* **representativeness heuristic.** The danger in this strategy is oversimplified thinking: People, events, and objects do not "belong" to categories simply because we find it mentally convenient to assign them to certain groups and labels. By relying on category memberships to organize our experiences, we risk ignoring or underestimating the tremendous diversity of individual cases and complexity of people.

When estimating the likelihood that a specific case belongs to a given category, we look to see whether it has the features found in a typical category member. For example, is your new acquaintance, Holly, a vegetarian? You've invited her to dinner but have not discussed her dietary restrictions. If she is a vegetarian, you do not want to offend her by serving her a cooked animal on a plate. Perhaps you could simply *ask* Holly her preference, but if that is not an option, you might guess based on what you *do* know about her. Does Holly resemble a "typical" vegetarian? Perhaps you believe that most vegetarians wear (nonleather) sandals, ride bicycles, and support liberal social causes. If Holly fits this description, you might feel safest guessing she must also be a

Does this woman represent enough of the characteristics of your concept of "vegetarians" to belong to that group? And is it fair to rely on the representativeness heuristic to categorize her?

Your ability to make good decisions and choices depends on being aware of your values and being able to make predictions and commitments.

vegetarian. In other words, you might judge Holly *represents* enough of the characteristics of your concept of "vegetarians" to belong to the same group.

But is such an analysis reasonable? Perhaps Holly wears sandals because when the weather is warm, sandals are the best footwear. She rides a bicycle as many other students do—although most are not vegetarians. And it's likely that, since most people are not vegetarians, then likewise most people who support liberal social causes are not vegetarians. By ignoring the *base rate information*—the real probabilities that features of a given category occur or co-occur in the larger population—you have drawn erroneous conclusions. Holly may in fact be an omnivore like most of your acquaintances, although she will probably accept the cheese pizza and salad you offer her without complaint. The penalty for relying on the representativeness heuristic—judging people or events by what seems to be their "type"—may not be great in all instances, but small "acceptable" mistakes can accumulate over time into larger, painful misjudgments, such as in the numerous misjudgments people make regarding characteristics of minorities.

Availability and representativeness are just two of many heuristics that we use in making judgments about the world every day. The biased judgments that result from these and other rules of thumb can distort our views of reality, and remain compelling even when we know the true state of affairs.

Decision Making   Judgments involve evaluating information about the world, while decisions require making choices. How do people make choices? Classic economic theory starts with the assumption that people act to maximize gain, minimize loss, and allocate their resources efficiently. It assumes that people do the best they can with available information and that most people have the same set of information and act as if they understand and can apply the laws of probability properly. However, people do not always understand and correctly apply the laws of probability, and they are often required to make decisions under *conditions of uncertainty* in which the relevant probabilities are not known. Research shows that different descriptions of the same decision can result in different choices. In addition, decision makers may be more influenced by risks than by reason.

Decision Frames   In decision making, a **frame** *is the structure or context of a problem's presentation.* While preferences between options should be consistent—the same regardless of how a problem is worded, for example—this is often not the case. Decisions *are* influenced by the decision frame, even when the alternatives are formally equivalent or technically the same. Consider, for example, the choice between surgery and radiation for treatment of lung cancer. Statistical information about the results of each treatment for previous patients can be presented either in terms of survival rates or mortality rates.

First read the survival frame for the problem and choose your preferred treatment; then read the mortality frame and see if you feel like changing your preference.

Survival Frame

Surgery: Of 100 people having surgery, 90 live through the postoperative period, 68 are alive at the end of the first year, and 34 are alive at the end of five years.

Radiation Therapy: Of 100 people having radiation therapy, all live through the treatment, 77 are alive at the end of one year, and 22 are alive at the end of five years.

Question: Which do you choose: surgery or radiation?

Mortality Frame

Surgery: Of 100 people having surgery, 10 die during surgery or the postoperative period, 32 die by the end of one year, and 66 die by the end of five years.

Radiation Therapy: Of 100 people having radiation therapy, none die during treatment, 23 die by the end of one year, and 78 die by the end of five years.

Question: *Which do you choose: surgery or radiation?*

You can see that, objectively, the data are identical in both frames. But research subjects faced with both presentations were more likely to choose radiation therapy when given the mortality frame (44 percent of them) than when given the survival frame (only 18 percent). This framing effect held equally for a group of clinic patients, statistically sophisticated business students, and experienced physicians (McNeil et al., 1982). One conclusion? Presentation matters! By providing specific reference points, presentational frames influence the way one evaluates the available options (Kahneman, 1992).

Values and Evaluations When you make a decision, you consider the likelihood of various outcomes and how much you value each one. Most of the research on decision making has focused mainly on people's probability estimates and related concepts. Recently, psychologists have turned their attention to the value component and have raised some fascinating questions. People with materialistic values—a desire for better and more expensive possessions—will make different choices than those with altruistic or spiritual values.

In studying values, one area of particular interest is our ability to predict how much we will like something at a later time or after repeated exposure. Tastes change—later we might not enjoy something that we do now—and so do values. But recent evidence suggests that people are not always accurate predictors of changes in their tastes (Kahneman & Snell, 1990), and that their theories of how tastes change lead them to decisions they later regret. We can avoid many common pitfalls in decision making by becoming better information processors. Awareness of the power of biases, base rates, heuristics, and decision frames can help you improve your own decision making. Assess your own decision-making "conscience" with the following questions.

ASSESS YOURSELF

Values Clarification

How would you rank the importance of the following goals in your life right now: health, happiness, love, status, self-respect, freedom, salvation, equality, world peace? Are the issues that are important to you now likely to endure? Or is it possible that changing circumstances will lead to new priorities?

Each of the following questions involves a choice, a sacrifice, or trade-off. Try to imagine each scenario vividly before deciding how you would answer.

■ What kind of relationship would you need to have with someone to be willing to die for that person?

■ If you could make the world a better place by doing so, would you be willing to make yourself uncomfortable? to experience pain? to move away and leave your friends and family behind forever?

■ If you and your best friend were the final contestants in competition for a vast sum of money, would you be willing to let your friend win? In the same situation, do you think your friend would let *you* win?

■ Would you be willing to donate hard labor to an important cause if your contribution would always remain anonymous?

■ What processes do you use to make important decisions in your life? Have these strategies worked well so far, or could you improve on them by adding new ideas from this chapter?

The process of asking yourself such questions—whether forced to by life lessons, or as an exercise in a textbook—can help you to clarify your values. By understanding more clearly how you think and what you value in life, you can make better decisions and move more consistently in a direction that achieves your goals. Socrates said that the unexamined life is not worth living, so take a moment to examine yours—and make it more worthwhile.

Check Your Recall

The extremes of human reasoning are autistic and realistic. Autistic reasoning is personal, individually distinctive, and not validated by external reality. Realistic reasoning is governed by reality constraints. Deductive reasoning involves drawing conclusions from premises on the basis of rules of logic. Inductive reasoning involves inferring a conclusion from evidence on the basis of its likelihood or probability. Scientific hypotheses and testing are typically based on inductive reasoning.

When solving problems, we must define the initial state, the goal state, and the operations that can get us from the first to the second—a difficult task on ill-defined problems. Mental sets such as functional fixedness can hamper creative problem solving until the set is broken. Algorithms ensure an eventual solution if there is one, but are impractical in many cases. Heuristics are mental shortcuts that often help us reach a solution quickly, although they do not guarantee success.

To make sense of uncertainty in our world, we draw inferences on which to base judgments or critical evaluations. By relying on mental shortcuts that usually serve us well, we may become prone to error and bias. Prior beliefs can bias our assimilation of new data. Relying on the availability heuristic involves judging examples to be common simply because they are cognitively available. The representativeness heuristic involves judging individual cases by whether they possess features representative of familiar categories. Decision making is influenced by the way choices are framed, the risks people are willing to take, and the values that guide their choices.

CHAPTER REVIEW

Summary

The study of cognitive psychology includes theories and research on the mental processes and structures that enable us to think, reason, solve problems, and make inferences and decisions. Cognitive psychologists generally use an information-processing approach to analyze information into components that are then processed in stages or sequences. Cognitive psychology has replaced behaviorism as the core area of research in American psychology. Cognitive science pools the efforts of psychologists, researchers in the brain sciences, and computer scientists to study how the brain and mind represent and use knowledge.

Thinking is a higher-order mental process that forms new abstract representations by transforming available information. Concepts are the building blocks of thinking; they are formed by identifying properties that are common to a class of objects or ideas. We store well-defined concepts as definitions and fuzzy concepts as prototypes. Concepts are often arranged in hierarchies, ranging from general to specific. Other mental structures that guide thinking include schemas and scripts. We also rely on visual imagery such as mental maps.

Deductive reasoning involves drawing conclusions from premises on the basis of rules of logic. Inductive reasoning involves inferring a conclusion from evidence on the basis of its likelihood or probability. Forming and testing scientific hypotheses typically involves inductive reasoning. In solving problems, we must define the initial state, goal state, and the operations that get us from the initial to the goal state. Heuristics are mental shortcuts that can help us reach solutions quickly.

Decision making is always subjective and prone to error. Becoming aware of mental traps is the first step in avoiding them. Inferential strategies normally serve us well, but occasionally we misapply these strategies to new data; we may not consider that new data inconsistent with prior knowledge can indicate a need to revise a particular theory. We continue to hold certain beliefs and theories or to persist in certain ways of doing things because we assimilate data or new experiences in a biased way. Cognitive biases are now assumed to generate most apparently irrational decisions. The availability heuristic leads us to estimate an outcome according to how easily similar or identical outcomes can be imagined. The representativeness heuristic is based on the presumption that belonging to a category implies having the characteristics considered typical of all members of that category. People often do not follow normative behavioral rules. Decisions are influenced by the way a problem is framed, even when alternatives are technically the same. People's values and their attitudes about taking risks can also influence decision making. Finally, an optimistic bias can affect the choices people make.

Section Reviews

Investigating Cognition

Be sure to *Check Your Recall* by reviewing the summary of this section on page 255.

Key Terms
cognition (p. 251)
cognitive psychology
  p. 252)
cognitive science
  (p. 252)
cognitive model
  (p. 252)
information-processing
  model (p. 253)
think-aloud protocols
  (p. 254)
reaction time (p. 254)

Names to Know
John von Neumann
  (p. 252)
Herbert Simon (p. 252)
Allen Newell (p. 252)
Jean Piaget (p. 252)
Noam Chomsky (p. 252)

The Structure of Thinking

Be sure to *Check Your Recall* by reviewing the summary of this section on page 265.

Key Terms
thinking (p. 256)
concepts (p. 257)
cognitive economy
  (p. 257)
critical feature (p. 257)
prototype (p. 257)
pseudomemory (p. 259)
basic level (p. 260)
schema (p. 260)

script (p. 262)
cognitive map (p. 263)

Names to Know
David Rumelhart (p. 261)
Donald Norman (p. 261)
Edward C. Tolman
  (p. 263)

The Functions of Thinking

Be sure to *Check Your Recall* by reviewing the summary of this section on page 280.

Key Terms
autistic thinking (p. 265)
realistic thinking (p. 266)
reasoning (p. 266)
deductive reasoning
  (p. 266)
syllogism (p. 266)
inductive reasoning
  (p. 266)
problem solving (p. 267)
functional fixedness
  (p. 269)
mental set (p. 269)
algorithm (p. 270)
heuristic (p. 271)
judgment (p. 271)
decision making (p. 272)
inference (p. 272)

biased assimilation
  (p. 274)
cognitive bias (p. 275)
availability heuristic
  (p. 277)
representativeness heuristic
  (p. 277)
frame (p. 278)

Names to Know
Amos Tversky (p. 277)
Daniel Kahneman (p. 277)

REVIEW TEST

Chapter 7: Cognitive Processes

For each of the following items, choose the single correct or best answer. The correct answers, explanations, and page references appear in Appendix B.

1. According to the _____ model of cognition, cognitive processes can best be understood as separate but connected components in a sequence of operations from simpler to more complex.
   a. information-processing
   b. organic continuum
   c. procedural
   d. logical

2. As a participant in a cognitive psychology experiment, a student solving a math problem thinks out loud as

she tries first one then another approach to finding the answer. This is a modern version of the approach known as _____.

a. behavioral observation
b. reaction time
c. error analysis
d. introspection

3. Which of the following statements about thinking is true?

a. It transforms available information to form new mental representations.
b. It cannot be inferred from observable behavior.
c. It stores but does not manipulate one's knowledge.
d. All of the above.

4. An alien being from another galaxy has landed on the earth and is overwhelmed by the sensory input it must process. Eventually the alien simplifies its thinking by categorizing sets of experiences and objects according to common features. In other words, the alien learns to form _____.

a. schemas
b. concepts
c. heuristics
d. hypotheses

5. A mental _____ outlines the proper sequence in which actions and reactions might be expected to happen in given settings, as when you visit a new grocery store but are still able to shop and complete your purchases although you have never visited this particular location before.

a. prototype
b. script
c. algorithm
d. map

6. A syllogism is a form of _____ reasoning, in which a conclusion is drawn by applying rules relating a minor premise to a major premise.

a. inductive
b. deductive
c. heuristic
d. algorithmic

7. In information-processing terms, a(n) _____ has an initial state, goal state, and operations.

a. prototype
b. concept
c. assimilation
d. problem

8. Mack wants to estimate the total number of miles he will be driving during his vacation, so he carefully and tediously records every point-to-point mileage index in the road atlas between his hometown and his destination city. This slow but sure process is an example of a(n) _____.

a. prototype
b. algorithm
c. mnemonic
d. syllogism

9. Judgments are based on _____, the reasoning process of drawing a conclusion based on evidence or prior beliefs.

a. inference
b. biased assimilation
c. functional fixedness
d. autistic thinking

10. Susanne wants to borrow money from her mother to join several classmates on a trip out of town. Instead of presenting the loan in terms of what it will cost her mother, Susanne instead emphasizes that this trip will make her more employable after graduation, thus saving them both money in the long run. By focusing on presentation, Susanne has applied her knowledge of how _____ affect decision making.

a. cognitive biases
b. prototypes
c. scripts
d. frames

If You're Interested . . .

Apollo 13. (Video: 1995, color, 140 min.). Directed by Ron Howard; starring Tom Hanks, Kevin Bacon, Bill Paxton, Gary Sinise, Kathleen Quinlan, Ed Harris.

"Houston, we have a problem . . ." Gripping docudrama of the real-life crisis of the Apollo 13 astronauts whose 1970 moon-bound flight was crippled—and nearly doomed—by a mysterious explosion and fuel loss. Suspenseful portrayals of character, creativity, problem solving, and decision making by both crew and ground control staff under conditions of unimaginable stress and pressure. Based on the book *Lost Moon* by crew commander Jim Lovell and coauthor Jeffrey Kluger (New York: Pocket Books, 1994). The film includes a brilliant scene in which flight control experts on earth must solve a critical air-filtering problem using only the same materials the astronauts have available to them 200,000 miles away in space.

Bryan, C. D. B. (1995). *Close encounters of the fourth kind: Alien abduction, UFOs, and the conference at MIT.* New York: Alfred A. Knopf.

The author, a distinguished journalist, examines the claims of otherwise ordinary citizens who insist they have been contacted and abducted by extraterrestrials. At first skeptical, Bryan becomes sympathetic, noting the sincerity of the "abductees'" accounts at a recent conference. Basic questions are left unaddressed—such as the aliens' possible motives, and alternate, nonalien explanations for so many people's "memories." Bryan regards these stories as harmless, even imaginative, speculations on the nature of earth and earthlings.

Coles, R. (1989). *The call of stories: Teaching and the moral imagination*. Boston: Houghton Mifflin.

Social scientist Robert Coles relates powerful stories and examines the storytelling process. Why do we pay better attention and enjoy a lesson more when it begins with a personal account or a fable? Are we basically narrative thinkers, arranging our thoughts and plans in plot lines? Coles identifies some common threads linking writers and readers, our human quest for order and comprehension.

Frankl, V. E. (1984). *Man's search for meaning*. New York: Washington Square Books.

The latest edition of psychologist Viktor Frankl's classic and moving memoir of surviving the Nazi concentration camps. Originally published in 1946 to introduce Frankl's system of "logotherapy," based on the human need to find and construct meaning in life.

Hall, D., with Wecker, D. (1994). *Jump start your brain*. New York: Little, Brown & Co.

With quotes, exercises, and advice, Doug Hall reviews several successful techniques for making yourself more creative. Contents include "Ten Commandments" for making dreams into reality; how humor can make your thinking more productive; ways to get out of a rut; and criteria for evaluating whether your ideas have "magic."

Kerr, P. (1992). *A philosophical investigation*. New York: Penguin Books USA.

A mystery that blends cognitive challenge with old-fashioned detective thrills, Philip Kerr's absorbing novel depicts a stunning scenario for the early twenty-first century. Governments routinely test young men for the sex-linked genetic clues that predict they will become serial killers. But one such man has used his knowledge of computer science and psychology to track and serially murder others who have also tested positive for this criminal trait. His nemesis is a woman named Jake, the detective who must identify the killer and prevent him from killing everyone on the list. A challenging, grim, suspenseful murder mystery.

Lewis, D. (1983). *Thinking better*. New York: Holt, Rinehart & Winston.

A "how-to" manual for using your head. Helpful and encouraging for those who would like to reason better and rely less on simple heuristics—especially when it's not always easy to remember what a "heuristic" is!

Plous, S. (1993). *The psychology of judgment and decision making*. Philadelphia: Temple University Press.

Making the simple but elegant point that common sense is an unreliable guide to intelligent living, Scott Plous reviews the surprising and silly findings in the literature on how people "normally" make evaluations and choices. Focus is on applications in making decisions affecting war and international politics. Fun to read, with recommended antidotes for irrational thinking and illogical logic.

Randi, J. (1995). *An encyclopedia of claims, frauds, and hoaxes of the occult and supernatural: James Randi's decidedly skeptical definitions of alternate realities*. New York: St. Martin's Press.

The Amazing Randi, a professional illusionist and debunker of phony faith healers, psychics, and charlatans, reviews some of his more noteworthy exposés and explains "how people are deceived, and . . . how people deceive themselves" (Yam, 1995). The success of Randi and the group he founded, the Committee for the Scientific Investigation of Claims of the Paranormal (CSICOP), has earned him both acclaim and trouble—the latter from litigation brought by angry self-proclaimed healers and psychics and some of their committed flock. The ultimate guide to skeptical consumerism, Randi's book is a gold mine of stories, revelations, warnings, and advice.

Rothstein, E. (1995). *Emblems of mind: The inner life of music and mathematics*. New York: Random House.

A "speculative rumination" (jacket) by the *New York Times* chief music critic about the interwoven human experiences of science and art in their respective forms of mathematics and music. Both begin in sensory experience and create abstraction, balancing proportion and size, analysis and synthesis. Fascinating insights into how cultural mindset determines both the discovery of symbol and the appreciation of rhythm, tone, and harmony.

CHAPTER 8

Motivation and Emotion

Tuesday, April 14, 1970. Marilyn Lovell chatted with visitors in her home as her family struggled to cope with a crisis of otherworldly proportions. Marilyn's husband, Jim Lovell, was away—200,000 miles away, orbiting the moon, with crew members Fred Haise and Jack Swigert. Their mission, dubbed Apollo 13, was planned to be NASA's third lunar landing. But two days away from Earth—and far short of their lunar goal—the astronauts were shaken by the explosion of an oxygen tank in the service module of their spacecraft. The loss of fuel and energy meant their moon landing would be impossible. But the horrifying reality facing the astronauts, their families, and mission control was that it might also now be impossible for the crew to return safely to Earth.

Shutting down nonvital systems in the spacecraft, Lovell and his crew huddled in the chill and struggled to maintain radio contact with the experts at Flight Control in Houston. Back at home, in the early moments of the crisis, Apollo 13 was not even news. Bored by talky, jargon-ridden news broadcasts, jaded by the seemingly easy success of two previous moon landings, Americans were barely aware that the mission had launched on April 11—until regular television programming was interrupted with the grim news that Apollo 13 had been mysteriously and dangerously crippled.

Marilyn Lovell went through the motions of receiving visitors and keeping a vigil with her children, wondering if they would ever see their father again. This day was the nightmare, the feared lot of the wives and children of fliers and astronauts. In his 1979 book The Right Stuff, writer Tom Wolfe chronicles how, in the 1950s, the wife of every test pilot would brace herself for the dreadful, breathtaking news that "something has happened," dully awaiting the moment when "the front doorbell would ring and some competent long-faced figure would appear, some Friend of Widows and Orphans, who would inform her, officially," that her husband had died in a fiery crash (Wolfe, 1979, p. 7).

In the early 1950s, as new jets were breaking the sound barrier and families were losing husbands and fathers to experimental flight technology, high schooler Jim Lovell had dreamed of rockets. "Did you know Jim liked rockets as a kid?" Marilyn asked a visiting colleague of her husband's, gathered with other friends in a tense vigil in their home in the Houston suburbs.

These wistful, nostalgic moments were rare breaks in Marilyn Lovell's reserve. Since the early days of the Mercury program, through Gemini and now the Apollo missions, astronauts' wives had developed a culture of conserved emotions, each woman measuring her feelings and learning to "ration her reactions." Each moment now was a crisis, and she could not afford to spend and waste her energy early in the vigil (Lovell & Kluger, 1994).

How does a rocket-inspired boy become a strong and quick-thinking astronaut, when so many others abandon youthful dreams as mere fantasies? What enables a person like Jim Lovell to cope with the freezing temperature in his disabled spacecraft, the claustrophobia, and the anxiety suffered by his desperate crew? As Marilyn Lovell waited for word of her husband's fate, where did she put her fear and worst anxieties? What resources prevented her from breaking down, and enabled her to reassure her children and others that everything would be all right, even when

she knew the odds were against a happy ending? How did both Marilyn and Jim Lovell deal with the roller coaster of their own mood swings as they sought to balance hope with fear?

In fact, Apollo 13 did have a happy ending: through a complex strategy of ingenious problem solving, good timing, and good fortune, the crew piloted their disabled spacecraft around the moon and back to Earth, entering but not burning up in the atmosphere, and safely splashing down in the Pacific Ocean on Friday, April 17. In the aftermath, grateful to be alive and reunited with those they loved, the astronauts reflected on their "lost moon," and resigned themselves to the knowledge that they would never set foot on the lunar surface. Before their safe return, in the desperate days and nights while the astronauts, their families, and ground control worked to bring them home, most Americans paid little or no attention to the news story, and had no idea this mission nearly ended in tragedy.

Introduction

What is it that moves some people to take aim almost literally at the stars—to "boldly go where no one has gone before," the mission of the long-running fictional television series *Star Trek*? Whatever it is, Jim Lovell had it, and it carried him through a harrowing adventure most people would find impossible to endure. Clearly, our life experiences and even our dreams can shape the goals that carry us through life.

Inextricably entwined with people's *motives* are their *emotions*. Jim Lovell wasn't drafted to be an astronaut—he had sought the challenge and the accomplishment, felt proud and thrilled. Stranded in space, Lovell and his colleagues needed to put their conflicts and terror on hold in order to solve the problems that would demand all their wits. Back on Earth, the astronauts' wives and families had to carefully conserve their energy and channel their expressions of emotion appropriately.

Contemporary psychologists recognize that human actions are *motivated* by a variety of needs—from fundamental physiological needs to psychological needs for love, achievement, and spirituality. Even a simple biological drive such as hunger can become distorted into an eating disorder through its connection to one's need for personal control and social acceptance. Somewhat more difficult to study are *emotions*, the touchstones of human experience. Our feelings enrich our interactions with others and our contacts with nature; they add joy to our existence, significance to our memories, and hope to our expectations. Emotions help to motivate our adaptation to our circumstances.

In this chapter we first examine what is known about emotion: how emotion can be studied, what functions emotions serve, and how people express emotions. The rest of the chapter is devoted to motivation: understanding motivational concepts and theories, and closely examining specific motivated behaviors, including eating, sexual behavior, and the drive to achieve. Although there are no simple answers to what drives people or how they cope with both everyday and emergency emotions, by the end of this chapter we will have a better appreciation of the complexity of motivation and emotion, and the relationships between them in our own lives.

Understanding Emotion

Emotions are complex experiences composed of several processes: physiological and neurological activity, subjectively experienced feelings, and behavioral expressions and responses. The concept of emotion is similar to that of motivation. You can see that both words share a common root, "mot-," from the Latin *motus* meaning "moved"; emotions move you to experience and express feeling, while motivations move you to action. What is the difference between an emotion and a motivation? In many ways, emotions are both more obvious and recognizable (even affecting people's facial expressions) and yet also harder to define and study than motivation. Motivation can often be tied to— or its effects measured by—overt actions, such as test performance or perseverance in trying to overcome barriers. We focus first on exactly how psychologists address the challenge of studying emotion and then move on to examine some major theories psychologists have proposed to explain emotion.

Studying Emotion

Emotions are elicited by experiences that are important for our survival and general well-being. Emotional reactions focus attention on these experiences by marking them as special in some way, by recording them more indelibly in memory, and by rousing us to take action. Because emotions involve so many aspects of human functioning, the study of emotions has emerged recently as a central issue in research and theory for a host of psychologists from different backgrounds. (For a sense of recent research and theory, see Bower, 1981; Frijda et al., 1989; Lang, 1995; Lazarus, 1991a, 1991b; Plutchik, 1980, 1984; Van Goozen et al., 1994; Zajonc, 1982.)

Emotion *is a complex pattern of bodily and mental changes including physiological arousal, feelings, cognitive processes, and behavioral responses to a personally significant situation.* The physiological *arousal* includes neural, hormonal, visceral, and muscular changes (some of which were described in Chapter 2). The *feelings* include both a general affective state (good-bad, positive-negative) and a specific tone, such as joy or disgust. The *cognitive processes* include interpretations, memories, and expectations. The overt *behavioral responses* include expressive reactions (crying, smiling) and action-oriented responses (screaming for help). Finally, we may perceive the situation as *significant* either consciously or nonconsciously. See Table 8.1 for a summary of the components of emotion.

Humans are unique in that such a broad range of stimuli and personal experiences can trigger our emotions (Hebb, 1980). However, emotions are surprisingly similar among people throughout the world, and some emotions can even be expressed in similar ways among other animals. As we ascend the evolutionary scale from simpler organisms to humans, we observe increasing differentiation of the facial muscles used to express emotion and an increasing

TABLE 8.1	PHYSICAL AND PSYCHOLOGICAL CHANGES ASSOCIATED WITH EMOTION	
Type of Change	**Description**	**Example**
Physiological Arousal	Neural, hormonal, visceral, and muscular changes	Increased heart rate, blushing
Feelings	Subjective interpretation of affective state	Anger, sadness, happiness
Cognitive Processes	Interpretations, memories, beliefs, expectations	Blaming someone, looking forward to something, believing oneself to be threatened
Behavioral Reactions	Expressing emotion, taking action	Smiling, crying, screaming for help
Significance	Conscious or unconscious perception	Judgment that one is in love; realizing that this is an emergency

diversity of emotional behavior. Humans have not evolved *away* from nonrational, primitive emotions but *toward* a combination of intellect and emotion (Scherer, 1984).

In some cases it is easy to infer a connection between motivations and emotions. For example, when you are unable to relate to others (an important social *motive*) you will probably experience unpleasant *emotions* such as sadness, loneliness, or anger. But in other cases the motive-emotion connection is not as direct or obvious. For example, a food-deprived infant will experience hunger *motivation*. But what is the child's most likely *emotion*: Will she cry out of anger, sadness, or fear? These feelings are not typically associated with hunger, although they are considered basic human emotions.

The ability to *explain* emotion is complicated by individual assessments of *experiencing* emotion. Emotions are subjective experiences that are distinctive and personal for every individual. As such, they defy attempts to describe them in purely objective terms. A brief examination of emotional experience may reveal the possible connections between motivation and emotion—and the challenges researchers face in being scientific about human feelings.

The Physiology of Emotion   Bodily reactions provide the machinery of emotional experience. The body reacts to internal and external stimuli by sending signals that activate or inhibit emotional responses. Research has identified the important roles played by the divisions of the nervous system, hormones, hemispheric differences (between the two sides of the cerebral cortex), and brain biochemistry.

The Reticular Activating System   Physiological reactions begin with the arousal of the brain as a whole by the *reticular activating system* (RAS). Incoming sensory messages pass through it on their way to the brain (Lindsley, 1951; Zanchetti, 1967). This system functions as a general alarm system for the rest of the brain. Strong emotional arousal stimulates physical arousal just as sexual arousal stimulates genital arousal. Your heart races, your respiration goes up, your mouth dries, your muscles tense, and maybe you feel shaky. All of these reactions are designed to mobilize the body for action.

The Autonomic Nervous System The *autonomic nervous system* (ANS) prepares the body for emotional responses through the action of both its divisions, which act in balance and in response to the nature of arousal. With mild, *unpleasant* stimulation, the sympathetic division is more active; with mild, *pleasant* stimulation, the parasympathetic division is more active. Physiologically, strong emotions such as fear or anger activate the body's *emergency reaction system,* which swiftly and silently prepares the body for potential danger. The sympathetic nervous system directs the release of hormones from the adrenal glands, which in turn lead the internal organs to release blood sugar, raise blood pressure, and increase sweating and salivation. Finally the emergency has passed: now what? The parasympathetic nervous system takes over, calming us by inhibiting the release of those hormones. We may remain aroused for some time after experiencing a strong emotional activation because some hormones continue to circulate in the bloodstream.

Brain Structures The hormonal and neural aspects of emotional arousal are integrated by two regions of the brain: the *hypothalamus* and the *limbic system*. These structures are old-brain control systems for emotions and patterns of attack, defense, and flight. Lesioning (cutting) or electrically stimulating parts of the limbic system produces dramatic changes in emotional responding. Tame animals may become killers; prey and predators may become peaceful companions (Delgado, 1969).

In all complex emotions, the cerebral *cortex*—the outermost layers of brain tissue, our "thinking cap"—is involved. The cortex provides the associations, memories, and meanings that integrate psychological and biological experiences. Research suggests there are different emotional centers in the cortex for processing positive and negative emotions. The left hemisphere seems to be more involved in positive emotions, such as happiness, while the right hemisphere influences negative emotions, such as anger (Davidson, 1984). *This discovery—that the two cerebral hemispheres "specialize" in different valences of emotion—has been dubbed* **lateralization of emotion.** That is, it appears that certain emotions are processed in different sides of the cerebral cortex. Lateralization of emotion has been found through EEG recordings that allow analysis of normal subjects' emotional reactions, as well as in other research relating emotional facial expression to right or left hemisphere brain damage (Ahern & Schwartz, 1985; Borod et al., 1988).

Interesting research with PET scanning techniques has revealed the complex role played by important structures in the cerebrum in experiencing and even controlling emotional impulses. The brains of volunteers suffering from schizophrenia (pronounced *SKITS-oh-FREN-ya*), a serious thought disorder often accompanied by hallucinations, were imaged while the patients were hearing voices. The hallucinations were audible only to the patients themselves, but their activity seemed to "light up"—for all to see—PET scans of brain structures involved in motivation and emotion. In the normal brain, these regions work to keep mental activity in touch with reality. In the schizophrenic brain, however, the voices engaged in exaggerated commentary—"How horrible!" and "Don't act stupid"—about the patients' private mental experiences (Begley, 1995; Silbersweig, 1995). In addition, in the patients' brains there was *no* activity in the part of the frontal lobe that engages in reality checking. Thus they had no way of knowing whether their sensations were real or their emotional responses were reasonable. "The brain . . . is creating its own reality," commented one researcher (Begley, 1995, p. 77). Thus it becomes difficult for the thought-disordered patient to judge the source of an arousing voice: Is it the voice of God, the CIA—or her own conscience? Because PET scanning permits imaging of very brief "moments" of brain activity, the new research suggests how the brain may associate sensations

("Someone is coming toward me") with memories ("This is not a safe neighborhood") and feelings ("Uh-oh, I'm in danger!").

Hormones   Several kinds of studies have shown the influence of *hormones* on emotion. When hormones are administered medicinally or when diseases affect the endocrine glands, changes occur in one's emotional responses. Hormone levels in the blood and urine rise during emotional states because hormones are released when one perceives emotional stimuli. *Steroid hormones* act on many different kinds of body tissue, including nerve cells, by causing them to change their excitability rapidly and directly. They can produce euphoria in short-term low doses but depression in long-term high doses (Majewska et al., 1986). Many of the mood changes associated with stress, pregnancy, and the menstrual cycle may be related to the effects that steroid hormones have on brain cells.

Biochemistry   The biochemical responses involved in emotional reactions may differ according to the *meaning* we attach to the situations in which the reactions are experienced. Tears are usually associated with sorrow, but we cry in response to many types of emotional arousal—for example, when we're angry or when we're filled with joy and ecstasy. Of course, tears also flow in response to eye-irritating stimuli. But when researchers compared the biochemistry of emotional tears and irritant tears, they found that emotional tears (generated when subjects watched a sad movie) differ significantly from irritant tears (generated when subjects inhaled the vapor of freshly grated onions). Under emotional conditions, the lacrimal glands which stimulate the tear ducts secrete a greater volume of tears and also produce tears with a higher concentration of protein (Frey & Langseth, 1986). There are no differences between the sexes on either of these measures, but an analysis of *reported* emotional crying over a one-month period shows that women reported crying for emotional reasons more frequently than did men (Frey et al., 1983). See Figure 8.1 for a summary of this analysis.

The Psychology of Emotion   Because we attach meaning to emotional experiences, we can sometimes become confused or be mistaken about what we and others are feeling. Consider the following example, a true story. A man

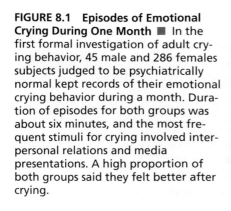

FIGURE 8.1   Episodes of Emotional Crying During One Month ■ In the first formal investigation of adult crying behavior, 45 male and 286 females subjects judged to be psychiatrically normal kept records of their emotional crying behavior during a month. Duration of episodes for both groups was about six minutes, and the most frequent stimuli for crying involved interpersonal relations and media presentations. A high proportion of both groups said they felt better after crying.

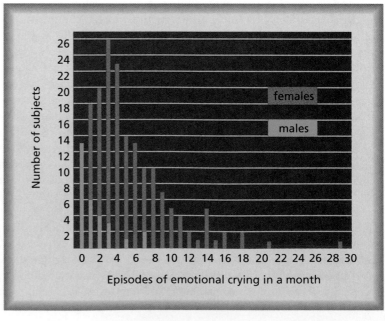

had confided to friends that he felt attracted to a new coworker, and could tell that the feeling was mutual. "Whenever I go into her office to ask her or her boss something, she acts very nervous. She stumbles over her words and drops pencils and things. I'm pretty sure she likes me!" Months later, the twosome—a committed couple now—chatted about their early attraction with friends. "Remember how nervous you were whenever I was around?" he teased her. "Oh, it wasn't *you* that was making me nervous," she corrected, "but since it was my first real job ever, I was always pretty self-conscious whenever my *boss* was around. Remember that, when I first met you, you only saw me when I was at work, so you only saw me when I was kind of jumpy! You may have jumped to the wrong conclusion about *why* I was nervous—but I'm glad you did!"

As in many joint stories of relationship history, each partner's version of their early days depicts the other's behavior differently. He attributes her nervousness to his attractiveness, whereas she insists it was her boss, not her boyfriend-to-be, who made her jumpy. In fact, they may both be correct. Emotions—our own or others'—can be difficult to interpret accurately. Because arousal symptoms and internal states for different emotions are similar, it is possible to confuse them when they are experienced in ambiguous or novel situations.

Interpreting Emotions As the story above illustrates, the cognitive processes involved go beyond physiological arousal to *interpret* what we are feeling. We *appraise* our physiological arousal in an effort to discover what we are feeling, what emotional label fits best, and what our reaction means in the particular context in which it is being experienced. For example, if you think you are nervous because you are anxious to do well in your new job, you will make job-relevant changes in your behavior. But if instead you think it is an attractive co-worker who is making you nervous, you might focus on improving your appearance and exploring the possibility of getting to know this person better—all based on how you explain your feelings.

Misattributing Emotional Arousal Typically, the external situation determines your definition of the emotional arousal being experienced, without much need for elaborate interpretation. We can also experience physical arousal from nonemotional sources, such as caffeine, exercise, arousing drugs, or intense heat. When we are aware that these sources are the causal stimuli, we make no emotional interpretation. However, what happens when we do not recognize their direct physiological impact?

We sometimes *misattribute* physically based arousal as emotion-based arousal, mislabeling our physical symptoms as part of a psychological state. Being overheated can become feeling anxious; being physically aroused from exercise can be misinterpreted as being sexually aroused. Psychological researchers have contrived several experiments to illustrate this emotional misattribution. In one study, a female researcher interviewed male subjects who had just crossed one of two bridges in Vancouver, Canada. One bridge was a safe, sturdy structure; the other was a wobbly, precarious bridge. The researcher pretended to be interested in the effects of scenery on creativity and asked the men to write brief stories about an ambiguous picture depicting a woman. She also invited them to call her if they wanted more information about the research. Those men who had just crossed the dangerous bridge wrote stories with more sexual imagery, and four times as many of them called the female researcher as did those who had crossed the safe bridge. To show that arousal was the independent variable influencing the emotional misinterpretation, the researchers also arranged for another group of men to be interviewed 10 minutes or more *after* crossing the dangerous bridge, enough time

After crossing a scary bridge, your level of physiological arousal may be heightened. You might then be vulnerable to misattributing your arousal as due to some other emotion.

for their physical arousal symptoms to be reduced. These nonaroused men did not show the signs of sexual interest that the aroused men showed (Dutton & Aron, 1974).

Basic Human Emotions

Despite the complexity of emotional experience, some researchers believe there is a set of basic emotions that is biologically and experientially distinct. Two models explaining this basic set of emotions are those proposed by Robert Plutchik and by Carroll Izard.

Plutchik's Emotion Wheel   The **emotion wheel,** developed by **Robert Plutchik** (1980, 1984) *proposes an innate continuum of human emotions.* As Figure 8.2 shows, the model depicts eight basic emotions, made up of four pairs of opposites: joy-sadness, fear-anger, surprise-anticipation, and acceptance-disgust. All other emotions are assumed to be variations, or *blends,* of these basic eight. Complex emotions, shown on the outside of the emotion wheel, result from combinations of two adjacent primary emotions. For example, love is a combination of joy and acceptance, while remorse combines sadness and disgust.

Plutchik proposes that emotions are best separated from each other when they are at high intensities, such as loathing and grief, and least different when they are low in intensity, such as disgust and sadness. He also believes that each primary emotion is associated with an adaptive evolutionary response. Disgust is considered an evolutionary result of rejecting distasteful foods from the mouth, while joy is associated with reproductive capacities.

Izard's Developmental Model   Carroll Izard (1977) proposes a slightly different set of basic emotions. His model specifies ten emotions: joy, surprise, anger, disgust, contempt, fear, shame, guilt, interest, and excitement—with combinations of them resulting in other emotional blends (joy + interest or excitement = love).

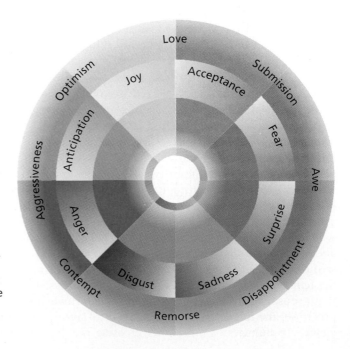

FIGURE 8.2   The Emotion Wheel ■
Plutchik's model arranges eight basic emotions within a circle of opposites. Pairs of these adjacent primary emotions combine to form more complex emotions noted on the outside of the circle. Secondary emotions emerge from basic emotions more remotely associated on the wheel.

As we saw earlier, a child's ability to think and to use language follows a built-in timetable of development. The same is generally true of emotional development, if appropriate stimulation is available. Some developments in emotional response may be linked to specific anatomical changes in the brain (Konner, 1977). For example, smiling emerges in infants of all cultures as soon as the necessary nerve pathways mature, one or two months after birth.

Izard contends that a newborn is capable of feeling only a generalized positive state, a generalized negative state, and the emotions of interest and sadness (Izard, 1982). A few months later, joy and anger develop. By the age of nine months, shame and fear appear, emotions that require a self-awareness that younger infants do not yet have. Emotional responses may continue to change throughout life, reflecting both physiological and cognitive changes (Mandler, 1984).

Check Your Recall

The concepts of emotion and motivation are related psychologically and experientially. Emotion is a complex pattern of physical changes, feelings, cognitive appraisal, and behavioral responses. These changes occur in response to situations seen as personally significant, and evolved as part of human survival. When emotions are ambiguous or novel, arousal may be misattributed to unrelated current or past situations. Some theorists maintain that we possess a set of basic, innate emotions. Robert Plutchik's wheel of emotions includes eight primary emotions that are blended to produce secondary states. According to Carroll Izard's theory, emotions develop from early infantile response patterns that have evolved from human survival skills.

Exploring Emotion

From an evolutionary perspective, we experience emotions because they have survival value. Psychologists also explain the existence and nature of emotions by examining what purpose or function they serve for us beyond survival. A third approach to understanding emotion involves considering *how* emotions meet their unique goals. In this section we will briefly examine the evolutionary origins of emotions; the functions of emotions in both humans and nonhumans; and several major theories that have been proposed to account for their operation.

The Evolution of Emotion

In order to develop a better way of categorizing emotions and investigating how they work, an evolutionary perspective encourages us to look at the situations emotions are designed to handle. Following in Charles Darwin's path, evolutionary psychologists consider the *adaptive* functions of emotions, not as vague, unpredictable, personal states that color how we see the world, but as highly specific, coordinated modes of operation of the human brain. In evolutionary terms, emotions are viewed as inherited, specialized mental states designed to deal with a certain class of *recurring situations* in the world.

Many of the situations that affect an individual's survival—and thus his or her chances for reproduction—are not isolated flukes but are part of a repeating pattern or series. Over the history of our species, humans have been attacked by predators, fallen in love, given birth to children, fought each other, confronted their mates' sexual infidelity, and witnessed the death of loved ones—all innumerable times. Any special mode of behavior that could be turned on specifically to help humans deal better with these recurring life situations would tend to be passed on to offspring and proliferate through the species. It would become part of the human emotional repertoire. For example, *sexual jealousy* can be seen as a special mode that is "turned on" to deal with the situation of mate infidelity. Physical arousal increases in preparation for possible violent conflict; motivations to deter or injure the rival and to punish or desert the mate emerge; memories are selectively activated to reanalyze the past relationship, and other reactions emerge to cope with the distressing situation. Evolving humans who had different, less adaptive emotional responses to important life situations did not leave as many offspring, so their nonadaptive responses were not passed on.

Emotions evolve to control whatever biological or psychological processes are relevant to dealing with their target situation. This way of thinking can help us understand some aspects of emotion that have puzzled researchers. Rather than asking if every emotion has an opposite (for example, happy versus sad), we can ask if the *situation* corresponding to an emotion has an opposite. Perhaps happiness and sadness are opposites because they are moods designed to regulate energy expenditure in opposite directions, depending on whether the *environment* is favorable or not (Neese, 1990). Happiness results when we sense that the environment is rewarding our efforts in situations indicating increased survival or reproductive success. When happy, we generally show more optimism, exuberance, energy, and activity, which is appropriate when these qualities are rewarded with increased species fitness. However, in situations when the environment is not favorable—when it does not reward us—we conserve energy by becoming more passive, and our mood is one of sadness. We wait for the situation to change, but we do not take direct action to change it because those actions will not be reinforced. The moods of happiness and sadness may be complementary regulatory processes that match our level of activity to the accommodation of the environment.

Animal Emotions

Do elephants weep? Naturally their eyes will water when their eyes are irritated, but could this great beast also cry emotional tears? The provocative and yet commonsense assertion of former psychoanalyst Jeffrey Moussaieff Masson is that animals do experience and express emotions, generally for the same reasons people do: they have feelings, and they respond to their world (Masson & McCarthy, 1995). In their book *When Elephants Weep*, the authors note that many scientists as well as laypersons have great difficulty accepting that nonhuman animals have consciousness, much less feelings—although they agree that there is danger in reading *human* emotions and assumptions *into* animal behavior. Caution about such "anthropomorphizing"—describing nonhuman actions in human terms—is a leftover from the period in early twentieth century psychology when behaviorism forbid any inferences into the reasons or invisible motives behind action. Yet anyone who has lived with and especially loved an animal—whether a cat, dog, horse, cockatiel, or iguana—*knows* that this creature has a rich emotional life and a distinct personality. As a result of such dogmatic denial of animals' inner lives, ". . . most modern scientists—especially those who study the behavior of animals—have succeeded in becoming almost blind to these matters" (Masson & McCarthy, 1995, p. xiii).

Perhaps it is easier to accept that animals experience very primitive or "base" emotions such as anger and fear, but it has been harder for scholars to attribute to animals "nobler" emotions like love, sorrow, and joy. But if you have had a beloved pet become ill or lethargic, you may have concluded your companion was obviously depressed. When you grab your dog's leash and prepare to take him for a walk, he is clearly, happily excited. When you ignore your cat's ankle-rubbing enticements to feed her or toss a favorite toy, she seems to slump in disappointment or crawl away dejectedly. When your healthy animal companion seeks petting and brushing, and sleeps contentedly in the home you have made, is this creature merely "content" with the food and shelter you have provided—or are you glimpsing real love and happiness? In her best-selling books on dogs and cats, the ethologist Elizabeth Marshall Thomas has documented a wealth of observations that both domesticated species and their wild cousins show a rich range of emotions, from primitive self-preservation to sensitive attachment, guilt, and sorrow (Thomas, 1993, 1994).

Humans may feel "possessive" about the power to experience emotions such as shame, enjoyment of beauty, and grief because these seem essentially *civilized,* and thus necessarily the products of human society. But this begrudging attitude—a refusal to grant animals some of the same virtues with which we so readily credit ourselves—may also be a sort of human arrogance, a "species-ism" similar to between-human prejudices such as racism and sexism. Old habits die hard and people still refer to heinous criminals as "beasts," to sloppy humans as "pigs" (which are in fact both clean and intelligent), and to nonhuman creatures as "dumb animals"—when evidence abounds that species ranging from dolphins and seagulls to chimpanzees use sounds and/or gestures to communicate with other members of their own species. We clearly operate on a double standard: we believe that humans are capable of greatness but nonhumans possess neither feelings nor equal status with human life.

An abundance of examples can be found that seem to question the notion that animals do not experience emotions. In Chapter 6, we reviewed the landmark research of Martin Seligman, who found that after they had suffered uncontrollable electric shocks, dogs acquired "learned helplessness," with symptoms that correspond to aspects of human depression. Ethologist Jane Goodall relates a story of how an elderly, paralyzed chimpanzee was snubbed by companions, who refused to groom or touch him (Goodall, 1972). Animals can take revenge, as did a young killer whale in captivity, pushing and briefly holding to the floor of a tank an oceanarium worker (who continued to breathe safely in his diving apparatus). When aquarium managers investigated, they learned this particular worker had a history of surreptitiously teasing the killer whale (Masson & McCarthy, 1995; Pryor, 1975).

Most affecting are accounts of animals' terror and grief. A biologist studying peregrine falcons in the Rocky Mountains observed what seemed to be distraction and bereavement in a male falcon whose mate did not return one day to their nest and five offspring. (The biologist later surmised the female falcon had been shot.) As the hours and days passed, the male parent emitted unfamiliar cries, waited by the aerie, finally screeched as if in mortal pain, and sat motionless on a rock for an entire day. Afterward, the father suddenly began hunting energetically and incessantly, and although three of the nestlings died from the hunger of this "mourning period," the other two did survive, grow, and leave the nest (Houle, 1991). Animals not only exhibit what appears to be grief, but there is evidence that they remember loss and horror, as in the example of baby African elephants who exhibited signs of delayed trauma, wailing, and disrupted sleep after having seen their families killed by poachers (Masson & McCarthy, 1995).

If the subjects being observed were human, observers would feel more comfortable inferring emotional states and describing their actions in terms of "snubbing," "taking revenge," expressing "love" or "gratitude," and suffering from "traumatic memories." Why are both scientists and laypersons seemingly

Animals undoubtedly experience emotions such as fear and aggression. In addition, ample evidence suggests that animals have and express feelings such as love and gratitude.

reluctant to admit that animals experience emotions? Masson warns that such an admission would lead to certain moral choices that humans are afraid or unwilling to make: if animals have *feelings like humans*, then it becomes difficult for us to treat them so differently that it is acceptable to hurt, hunt, use, or eat them. Consider how hard it is to wish ill on a person whom you identify with—someone with whom you have something in common. Empathy with other creatures provides great insights and discoveries, but also carries with it great obligations. "Animals are, like us, endangered species on an endangered planet" (Masson & McCarthy, 1995, p. 236). Before we can understand human feelings, we must recognize the reality of emotions in nonhuman creatures.

The Functions of Emotions

Whether for people or animals, what good are emotions? What functions do emotions serve for us? Different theorists point to different functions as central to the role of emotions in human life (Frijda, 1986; Frijda et al., 1986). Consider the role of emotions in these nine psychological experiences:

1. Emotions serve a motivational function by *arousing* us to move and to take action with regard to some experienced or imagined event.

2. Emotions then *direct* and *sustain* our actions toward specific goals that benefit us, such as energizing behavior toward helpful stimulation and away from the harmful. For example, to obtain the love of another person, you may do all in your power to attract, be near, or possess that person.

3. Emotions *amplify* or intensify certain life experiences. We feel frustrated when we are unable to act in ways that get us what we want—for example, when a slow-moving vehicle pulls in front of us and prevents us from traveling faster. We feel angry when we are forced to confront a punishing situation—for example, when our boss insists we must work on a traditional holiday (Roseman, 1984).

4. Emotions help to *organize* our experiences by influencing what we attend to, how we perceive ourselves and others, and the way we interpret and remember various features of life situations (Bower, 1981).

5. Emotions signal that a response is especially significant or that an event has *self-relevance* (Tompkins, 1981). A song you hear or a certain cologne you smell can evoke an important emotional memory, causing you to pause and pay closer attention to its source.

6. Emotions can give us an *awareness of inner conflicts* when we observe how they can make us react irrationally or inappropriately to a given situation (Jung, 1923/1971). When your actions leave you feeling guilty or regretful, you become less likely to repeat such behavior in the future.

7. On a social level, emotions regulate relationships with others, promote prosocial behaviors, and are part of our nonverbal communication system. Emotions serve the broad function of *regulating social interactions*: as a positive social glue, they bind us to some people; as a negative social repellent, they distance us from others. Some psychologists further argue that most emotions emerge from and are central to fully experiencing human relationships (DeRivera, 1984).

8. An ample amount of research points to the impact of emotion on stimulating *prosocial behavior* (Hoffman, 1986; Isen, 1984). When individuals are made to feel good, they are more likely to engage in a variety of helping behaviors. Similarly, when research subjects were made to feel guilty about a misdeed in a current situation, they were more likely to volunteer aid in a future situation, presumably to reduce their guilt (Carlsmith & Gross, 1969).

9. Finally, the *communication* function of emotion reveals our attempts to conceal from others what we are feeling and intending. We back off when someone is bristling with anger; we approach when someone signals receptivity with a smile, dilated pupils, and a "come hither" glance. Strong, negatively felt emotions are often suppressed out of respect for another person's status or out of concern that they will reveal information being concealed. Much human communication is carried on in the silent language of nonverbal bodily messages (Buck, 1984; Mehrabian, 1971).

A Biocultural Model of Emotion   Robert Levenson has summarized the many functions of emotions as being *intrapersonal* (coordinating and organizing one's internal and behavioral responses to stimuli); *interpersonal* (communicating with others and clarifying moral choices); and *biocultural* (linking innate influences with the lessons learned in one's culture). In Levenson's **biocultural model of emotion,** *personal and social stimuli are appraised, responses to them are channeled, and expressions of feeling are guided by the rules and traditions held by one's culture.*

As you can see in Figure 8.3, antecedent conditions are appraised to create an initial prototype or early sense of one's emotional state. This prototype can be channeled into feelings, facial expressions, tone of voice, movement, and bodily arousal—with each of these channels translated into measurable responses according to the learned rules of one's culture. Thus, part of the work of growing up in a particular society is learning how to identify what you are feeling, what causes it, and what your culture permits you to do and say about it.

An example of a complex emotional experience that fits Levenson's biocultural analysis is *guilt.* Roy Baumeister and his colleagues define guilt as "an individual's unpleasant emotional state associated with possible objections to his or her actions, inaction, circumstances, or intentions" (Baumeister et al.,

FIGURE 8.3   Levenson's Biocultural Model of Emotion ■

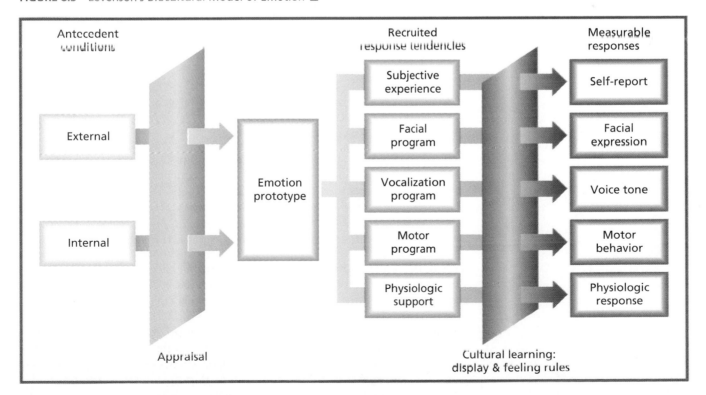

1994, p. 245). By reviewing numerous studies and episodes of guilt, the researchers were able to identify three functions of guilt:

- Guilt motivates people to act in ways that *enhance relationships* with others;
- Guilt can be manipulated as a form of *social influence,* so that a relatively powerless person (such as a child or shy person) can get his or her way (from a parent or a superior); and,
- Guilt is a way for partners in a relationship to *restore justice or resources* in the relationship. For example, if you cheat a friend, you may benefit in the short run but feel somewhat bad about the consequences to your relation ship. By feeling guilty you, the transgressor, are less benefited—and in a way, at least emotionally, this restores some fairness. More importantly, you may feel bad enough to regret the transgression, to feel for your wronged friend, and to work to restore genuine respect and closeness.

Far from being a patently negative emotional experience, guilt seems to be a complex set of feelings and ideas with both good and bad correlates. People who experience guilt are more likely to be able to empathize with others, to be sensitive to their feelings and needs (Eisenberg & Miller, 1987; Hoffman, 1982). On the other hand, not surprisingly, people who experience guilt suffer from relatively low self-esteem (Tennen & Herzberger, 1987; Vangelisti et al., 1991) and from dissatisfaction with their personal relationships (Baumeister et al., 1994).

Examine Figure 8.3 and consider how the experience of guilt is explained by Levenson's biocultural model: Antecedent conditions might include some personal or social circumstances that prompt you to feel that your actions would be considered objectionable by someone who matters to you. These second thoughts lead you to feel the first twinges of guilt, which, in turn, lead you to make excuses, avoid contact with the person you have wronged, and simply to feel bad. Your culture has taught you that guilt is a function of your conscience, a self-realization that you have done something wrong. Your options now include not only continuing to hide your crime or avoid contact with the person you have betrayed, but also perhaps to seek out that person, confess, ask for forgiveness—and expect to pay some penalty.

Emotions are clearly not only adaptive in an evolutionary sense, but they serve valuable functions on many levels of our lives. Given their importance to our well-being, how exactly do emotions "work"—physically and psychologically? That question has long been of interest to psychological theorists.

Theories of Emotion

Theories of emotion attempt to explain what causes emotions, what are the necessary conditions for emotion, and what sequence best captures the way emotions are built up from the complex interaction of the factors we have discussed. Here we will review three key theories of emotional processing: a theory of *bodily reaction*; a theory of *central neural processes,* and a theory of *cognitive interpretation.* Figure 8.4 compares these three theories of emotion.

The James-Lange Theory of Bodily Reactions   It is reasonable to assume that when we perceive an emotional stimulus that induces an emotional feeling, it in turn creates a chain of bodily reactions—physiological, expressive, and behavioral. The sight of a beautiful person induces feelings of desire. This physically arouses us, which in turn motivates approach reactions and appropriate displays of passion. This explanation of emotion seems reasonable, but is it the true sequence? A hundred years ago, American psychologist **William James** argued, as Aristotle had much earlier, that the sequence was reversed—we feel *after* our body reacts. As James put it, "We feel sorry because we cry,

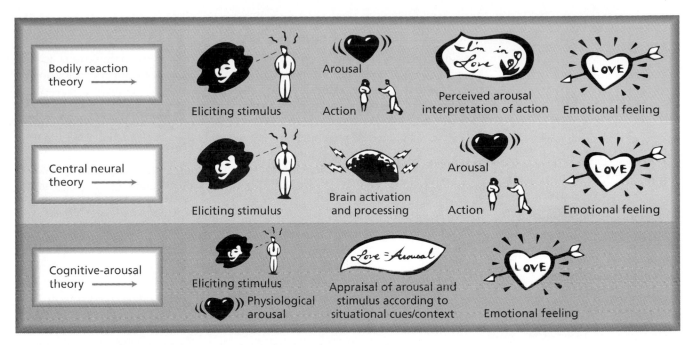

FIGURE 8.4 Comparing Three Theories of Emotion ■ These classic theories of emotion propose different components of emotion. They also propose different process sequences by which a stimulus event results in the experience of emotion. In bodily reaction theory (James-Lange), events trigger both autonomic arousal and behavioral action, which are perceived and then result in a specific emotional experience. In central neural theory (Cannon-Bard), events are first processed at various centers in the brain, which then direct three simultaneous reactions of arousal, behavioral action, and emotional experience. In cognitive arousal theory (Lazarus-Schachter), both stimulus events and physiological arousal are cognitively appraised at the same time according to situational cues and context factors, with the emotional experience resulting from the interaction of arousal and appraisal.

angry because we strike, afraid because we tremble" (James, 1950, p. 450). Although contrary to common sense, many psychologists took seriously *this view that emotion stems from bodily feedback, which became known as the* **James-Lange theory of emotion.** Danish scientist Carl Lange (pronounced *LONG-uh*) had presented similar ideas in the same year that James did. According to this theory, perceiving a stimulus causes autonomic arousal and other bodily actions that lead to the experience of a specific emotion (see the James-Lange theory in Figure 8.4). According to the James-Lange theory, for example, when the object of your affections walks into the room, your perception of this intensely emotional stimulus causes your body to respond: your heartbeat speeds, you blush, your palms feel sweaty. Then, recognizing your own bodily response, you interpret your emotion: "I'm in love!"

The James-Lange theory assigns the most prominent role in the emotion chain to visceral gut reactions, from actions of the autonomic nervous system that are peripheral to the central nervous system. In this model, then, if you experience no physical reaction to a stimulus, you neither have nor identify an emotional response.

The Cannon-Bard Theory of Central Neural Processes Physiologist **Walter Cannon** (1927, 1929) rejected the James-Lange theory in favor of a focus on the action of the central nervous system (CNS). With experimental evidence and logical analysis (Leventhal, 1980), Cannon fired criticisms against the James-Lange theory. He (and other critics) raised four major objections. First, visceral activity was irrelevant for emotional experience;

Facial expressions convey universal messages. Although their culture is very different, it is probably not hard for you to tell how these people from New Guinea are feeling.

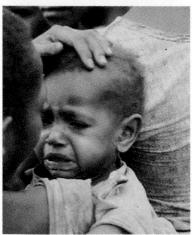

animals in experiments continued to respond emotionally even after their viscera were separated surgically from the CNS. Second, visceral reactions are similar across different arousal situations: the same heart palpitations accompany aerobic exercise, lovemaking, and fleeing danger—but the reactions do not lead to the same emotion from perceiving feedback on how one is responding. Third, many emotions cannot be distinguished from each other simply by their physiological components; they "look the same" under the skin. Finally, autonomic nervous system responses are typically too slow to be the source of split-second elicited emotions.

According to Cannon, emotion requires that the brain intercede between the input and output of stimulation and response. Signals from the thalamus get routed to one area of the cortex to produce emotional feeling and to another for emotional expressiveness. Another physiologist, Philip Bard, also concluded that visceral reactions were not primary in the emotion sequence. Instead, an emotion-arousing stimulus has two simultaneous effects, causing both bodily arousal via the sympathetic nervous system and the subjective experience of emotion via the cortex. The views of these physiologists were combined in the theory given both their names. *According to the* **Cannon-Bard theory of emotion,** *an emotional stimulus produces two concurrent reactions, arousal and experience of emotion, which do not cause each other.* As you can see in the Cannon-Bard theory in Figure 8.4 on page 299, the sudden sight of the one you love prompts two parallel reactions: you experience a bodily response (heart rate increase, perspiration) and *at the same time* your brain interprets what you feel as "love."

Strong evidence *against* the Cannon-Bard theory comes from a recent study of people with spinal cord injuries (Chwalisz et al., 1988). Although their injuries prevented them from perceiving any autonomic arousal, they still reported strong emotions, some even stronger than before their injuries. Clearly, autonomic arousal cannot be a necessary condition for emotion.

The Lazarus-Schachter Theory of Cognitive Arousal Many contemporary theories of emotion suggest that cognitive processes direct most adaptive emotional responses (Lazarus, 1991a, 1991b; Leventhal, 1980; Roseman, 1984; Smith & Ellsworth, 1985). Sensory experiences lead to emotion only when the stimuli are cognitively appraised as having personal significance. As we noted earlier, the particular emotion that is felt depends on the way a situation is interpreted and the meaning attributed to it by the individual.

Richard Lazarus, a leading proponent of the cognitive appraisal view, maintains that emotional experience "grows out of ongoing transactions with the environment that are evaluated" (1984a, p. 124). According to **Stanley Schachter** (1971), the experience of emotion is the joint effect of physiological arousal and cognitive appraisal, with both parts necessary for an emotion to occur. All arousal is assumed to be general and undifferentiated, and it comes first in the emotion sequence. Cognition serves to determine how this ambiguous inner state will be labeled (Mandler, 1984; Schachter & Singer, 1962). *This position—that emotion involves the cognitive interpretation of physiological arousal—has become known as the* **two-factor theory of emotion** *or the* **Lazarus-Schachter theory of emotion.** Organic, visceral factors *interact* with mental factors to produce an emotion. Thus, when there is sympathetic arousal *without* a known, specified source, a person will search the environment for relevant, salient cognitions that can be used to label the arousal and give it emotional meaning.

As you see in the Lazarus-Schachter theory in Figure 8.4, as the person you adore approaches your table, your heart palpitates, your mouth becomes dry, and your palms become damp. Noticing these changes, and searching for an explanation, you focus on that special person. If he or she is the cause of your reaction, you conclude, then "it must be love." This view of emotion and the ingenious research used to demonstrate it (Schachter & Singer, 1962) drew attention to the role of cognitive interpretations in emotional experience. Also, it showed that independent components of emotion—arousal states and situational cues—could be manipulated experimentally and studied in a laboratory setting.

However, some of the specific aspects of the two-factor theory have been challenged. Awareness of one's physiological arousal is *not* a necessary condition for emotional experience. When experimental subjects are exposed to emotion-inducing stimuli after receiving beta-blockers that reduce heart rate, they still experience anxiety or anger even though they have minimal physical feelings (Reisenzein, 1983). In addition, experiencing strong arousal without any obvious cause does *not* lead to a neutral, undifferentiated state, as the two-factor theory assumes. Unexplained physical arousal is generally interpreted as *negative*, an indication that something is wrong. However, the search for an explanation tends to be *biased* toward finding stimuli that will explain or justify this negative interpretation (Marshall & Zimbardo, 1979; Maslach, 1979).

Expressing Emotions

If one function of emotion is to prepare and motivate a person to respond adaptively to the demands of living, then two specific abilities are essential to coordinate our social behavior: We must be able to *communicate* our emotional feelings effectively, and we need to be able to *decode* the way others are feeling. If, for instance, we can signal that we are angry at someone and are likely to become aggressive, we can often get the person to stop doing whatever is angering us without resorting to overt aggression. Similarly, if we can communicate to others that we feel sad and helpless, we increase our chances of soliciting their aid. By reading the emotional displays of others, we can predict more accurately when to approach and when to avoid them, how to respond, and what to believe.

Facial Expressions   According to **Paul Ekman**, the leading researcher on the nature of facial expressions, all people speak and understand the same "facial language" (Ekman, 1984; Ekman, 1982; Ekman & Friesen, 1975). Ekman and his associates have demonstrated what Darwin first proposed—that the same set of emotional expressions is *universal* to the human species, presumably because they are innate components of our evolutionary heritage. What about the influence of culture on emotion? Culture does play a role in *emotional displays* by establishing social rules for *when* to show certain emotions and for the social *appropriateness* of certain types of emotional displays by given types of people in particular settings. However, people all over the world, regardless of cultural differences, race, sex, or education, express basic emotions in the same way and are able to identify the emotions others are experiencing by reading their facial expression (Ekman & Friesen, 1986). Refer now to the exercise in Assess Yourself: Facial Expressions of Emotion to test your own ability to identify emotions by facial expression alone

Assess Yourself

Facial Expressions of Emotion

Take the facial emotion identification test in Figure 8.5 to see how well you can identify each of the seven emotional expressions displayed. Do not go on to the next paragraph until you have taken a moment to assess your emotion-recognition ability.

FIGURE 8.5   What Emotion is Being Expressed in Each Face? ■

Answers: The facial expressions in Figure 8.5 are (top row, from left) *surprise, disgust,* and *happiness;* and (bottom row, from left) *sadness, anger,* and *fear.* How well did you do on this self-assessment? How confident were you in labeling each face? Do you think you might have done better if the faces depicted were those of people you knew? Cross-cultural researchers have asked people from different cultures to identify the emotions associated with a variety of expressions in standardized photographs. They are generally able to identify the expressions associated with the seven listed emotions. Children above age 5 can detect the emotions depicted in stimulus displays about as accurately as college students can.

How Experiences Become Expressions Emotion researchers generally agree about which specific *facial muscle movements* are associated with each of the basic emotions (Smith, 1989). Studies that record facial muscle movements while subjects imagine various mood settings show specific patterns of muscle group movements that are different for happy, sad, and angry thoughts (Schwartz, 1975)

For example, the expression of happiness consists of raised mouth corners (a smile) and tightened lower eyelids. The expression of surprise consists of raised eyebrows, raised upper eyelids that widen the eyes, and an open mouth. The expression of fear is very similar to the expression of surprise, except that, in addition to being raised, the eyebrows are pulled together and lowered back down slightly into an "eyebrow frown." (The similarity between the two expressions might explain why subjects have such trouble discriminating between them.)

Managing Emotional Expression The experience of emotion is spontaneous, triggered by emotional stimuli in your environment. But your expression of emotion may be something you can control. There are many situations in everyday life when it may be desirable to mask what you are really feeling. If you dislike someone who has power over you, such as a boss or professor, you may be wise to disguise your contempt. If you like someone more than he or she realizes, it might be safest to keep the other person from realizing this and taking advantage of your vulnerability. Even in leisure activities like playing poker or planning your next move in chess, you will be most successful if you keep your own judgments and intentions a secret. How good are people at deceiving others about their real feelings? Can we train ourselves to detect deception in some circumstances?

Deception Detection It must have been critical to our ancestors' survival to determine whether others meant them harm. Even today, it would be adaptive if you could tell whether a salesperson were lying to you, or a physician were concealing something about your medical condition. You might think you could spot a liar by whether or not she "looked you in the eye" or fidgeted nervously. It is true that, whatever a speaker's words might be, he or she will still "leak" uncontrolled nonverbal clues about any conscious deception. Unfortunately, most of us are very poor lie detectors—or truth detectors, for that matter. One reason is that our social interactions usually occur in familiar situations, where we pay little attention to nonverbal clues. Moreover, idiosyncratic differences between individuals make it difficult to detect deception. The key to deception detection lies in perceiving *patterns* of the potential deceiver's behavior and facial expression over time. Without the chance to observe a person over time or in different situations, you are unlikely to be able to judge his or her honesty (Marsh, 1988).

Some lies involve false information; in those cases, the effort to hide the truth costs the liar some *cognitive effort*, resulting in heightened attention (evident in pupillary dilation), longer pauses in speech (to choose words carefully), and more constrained movement and gesturing (in an attempt to avoid "giving away" the truth). In contrast, when lies deceive an audience about the speaker's feelings, the liar becomes physically and behaviorally more *aroused*, revealing the deception in postural shifts, speech errors, and "adaptor" behaviors like nervous gestures and preening (touching one's hair or face), and "shrugging" as if to dismiss the lie.

The face is easier to control than the body, so a deceiver may work on keeping a poker face but forget to restrain bodily clues about his real intentions. A smart deception detective might therefore concentrate on a speaker's bodily movements: are they rhythmic? calculated? do the hands move freely or nervously? Further, although a practiced liar can look you straight in the eye while relating complete fiction, most people's amateurish efforts to deceive you will show up in averted gaze, reduced blinking (indicating concentration of attention elsewhere), and less smiling. There are no "dead giveaways" to lying, but there are some guidelines (from Kleinke, 1975; Marsh, 1988; Zuckerman et al., 1981).

Some clues to deception:

- Among your friends, you can probably detect emotional deception better than factual deception.
- Spontaneous, unplanned deceptions are easier to detect than well-rehearsed routines.
- Deception is fairly hard work for most people, so look for signs of cognitive effort such as nervousness and wooden gestures or expressions.

- If someone makes less eye contact with you than usual, he or she may be trying to hide dishonesty.
- Because an "acceptable" reason for lying might be to "save face," a person who is being less than honest may touch or cover his or her face more often than usual.

Managing Difficult Emotions Another challenge to managing emotional experience is deciding whether and how to express negative or threatening emotions. Showing your anger can get you in trouble; revealing your grief over a loss can leave you vulnerable. As a result, many societies discourage people from expressing unpleasant feelings unless they do so according to prescribed or ritualized rules. Throughout history, anger has been "channeled" into boxing matches, duels, and declarations of war. Bereavement and loss are often hidden except for rigidly formal mourning and funeral activities. It is hardly healthy to deny or suppress genuine emotion, but most societies recognize there are risks and dangers associated with uncontrolled expression of intense, negative feelings.

As discussed in Focus on Application: Managing Anger and Grief, scientific research and theory can supplement psychotherapeutic techniques in helping people to deal with and safely express difficult negative emotions.

Check Your Recall

Emotions serve several functions for both human and nonhuman species, promoting survival by arousing the organism both to fight or escape threats and to form helpful bonds with others. Emotional experiences blend mental activity with physiological arousal, as several theories have tried to explain. The James-Lange theory makes feedback of bodily arousal the central component in emotion. According to the largely discredited Cannon-Bard theory, brain processing causes simultaneous arousal and emotional feeling. The Lazarus-Schachter model argues that, when aroused, the organism searches for a cognitive label or interpretation. Cross-cultural research supports evolutionary theories that emotion promotes survival and is therefore universal, even to the point of generating facial expressions of emotion that are universally recognizable. Because individuals vary so much in emotional expression, there are no certain clues to deception. Negative emotions such as anger and grief may have to be masked or ritualized in order to be accepted or dealt with.

Understanding Motivation

Motivation *is the general term for all the processes involved in starting, directing, and maintaining physical and psychological activities.* Motivation includes the internal mechanisms involved in *preferring* one activity over another; the *strength* of responses; and the *persistence* of actions toward relevant goals. The highly motivated person seeks out certain activities over others; practices behaviors and perfects skills required to attain the objective; and focuses energy on reaching the goal despite frustrations.

While psychologists use the term "motivation" very precisely, in everyday language people use the term to refer to a variety of complex concepts involving intentions, energy, effort, or agendas. Professors wonder whether students who do poorly on exams are "not motivated enough." Sports commentators speculate that winning teams "were 'hungrier' and more motivated" than their opponents. Detectives seek to establish means, opportunity, and motive in

Managing Anger and Grief

While Marilyn Lovell waited for word about the fate of her husband and the other two crew members of Apollo 13, she kept her anguish and fear hidden. Such effort would be important to protect her children from suffering over events they could not possibly control. But part of her emotional reserve was also learned as part of the role of "astronaut's wife" in the U.S. space program, a role that was a necessary source of strength, privacy, and the coping skills that might be required should she ever have to face tragic news. People always find ways to control and even hide some emotions, especially if these would prove embarrassing or costly if exhibited in public. But exactly *how* can we learn both to exercise reasonable control and to respect feelings that need to be expressed and dealt with?

Anger

"Anger has long been a problem for me," writes Melvyn Fein. "Over the years it has cost me a great deal of pain and denied me much happiness" (1993, p. ix). Failing at various efforts to control and constructively express his anger, Fein himself became a clinician and developed an approach to anger disorders. Fein's program, Integrated Anger Management (I.A.M.), involves five stages:

■ Assuring that anger will be expressed *safely* and not spin out of control;

■ Developing *tolerance* by accepting feelings of anger without becoming enraged;

■ Identifying the underlying *goals* of one's anger, such as frustration with injustice or the inability to achieve a valued goal;

■ *Letting go* of unrealistic goals that feed the anger, such as the naïve belief that expressing anger will motivate others to "do the right thing"; and,

■ *Using anger* constructively to reach more realistic, achievable goals (Tavris, 1995).

This analysis of anger into action-oriented emotions that are sometimes confused and self-defeating represents an effort to correct the dangers created by popular myths about anger. On many television "talk shows" you can see people attacking and humiliating others as if the relief they get from "going public" to vent their feelings justifies cruelty and aggression. In fact, retaliation for a real or imagined wrong is likely not to end the feud but to fuel it—a reality obvious in the cyclic nature of religious and territorial wars. Ample evidence indicates that, when you are angry with someone, "getting it off your chest" by confronting or hurting that individual will not neutralize your bad feelings but intensify them. A saner and safer strategy is to keep your feelings to yourself, at least until the passion of your anger has subsided and you can be more rational about the nature of your real complaint and what might really be done to solve the problem (Tavris, 1983).

Grief

Anger has long been thought to be a major component of grief, and perhaps this is why so many cultures historically have urged the bereaved to "hide" their sorrow at the loss of a loved one. As reviewed in Chapter 4, death researcher Elisabeth Kübler-Ross argued that in dealing with one's own imminent death, the dying person experiences denial, anger, bargaining, and depression before reaching a sense of acceptance (Kübler-Ross, 1969; 1975). More recently, psychologists have examined the role of grief in the lives of those who lose important others. According to therapists, grief is not a single emotion but a complex process involving feelings and motives to complete several *tasks:*

■ *Facing* the reality of the loss;

■ Experiencing the *pain* and expressing the sadness caused by that loss;

■ *Engaging* with both work and people in the process of healing;

■ Reentering one's *new life*—without the lost other—in a changed world, with a changed sense of self (Davidsen-Nielsen & Leick, 1991; Rando, 1988).

One way to begin to construct one's new, post-loss identity is by relating your *account,* the story of how your relationship with the lost other began and developed, what it meant to you, and how it ended (Harvey et al.,1990). The account-making and -relating experience may seem automatic, so that a bereaved person spontaneously and eagerly tells her or his story to others, who may or may not be willing to listen. But account-distribution can also be more deliberately arranged, as when survivors of a painful breakup inform their respective friends and families of their split, its reasons and likely consequences (Duck, 1982). Ultimately, grief over a personal loss is private and impossible for others to understand completely—a common complaint among the bereaved is of the empty platitude, "I know just how you feel," coming from well-intentioned acquaintances who clearly cannot comprehend their suffering.

Perhaps because grief is so subjective, most cultures have developed customs and rituals for mourners and those who wish to help them: funeral practices, memorial services, appropriate gestures and gifts such as flowers and casseroles. What should you do when a close friend suffers a relationship loss? While a homemade pie might indeed be welcome, the best advice from psychologists is to offer to *listen* to your friend's account, complaints, and thinking out loud. By "being there," you can make the private and inexpressible emotions of loss feel less lonely and less isolating for someone you care about. Offering a shoulder to cry on and a sympathetic ear can help that person to heal and reenter a world that is changed, but still full of promise and possibility.

order to identify who committed a crime. Millions of soap opera fans watch their favorite melodramas to watch how the characters' motives—greed, envy, lust, or revenge—will affect the story line.

Motivation cannot be seen directly. Behavior, on the other hand, is observable. To explain the observable, behavioral changes we must make

Soap operas focus on basic human motivation, which accounts for their popularity.

inferences—or educated speculations—about the underlying psychological and physiological variables that influenced those changes. These inferences about an individual's goals, needs, wants, intentions, and purposes are formalized in the concept of motivation. Two terms that researchers frequently use are *drive* and *motive*. **Drive** *refers to motivation that is assumed to be primarily biological, such as hunger.* **Motive** *refers to psychological and social needs that are assumed to be learned through personal experience.* Motives can be either *conscious* or *unconscious*, but it is not always easy to distinguish them. Was astronaut Jim Lovell able to withstand the ordeal of the nearly stranded Apollo 13 mission because he was consciously motivated to succeed—or were his thoughts focused more on basic survival in a bizarre, high-tech situation?

The Concept of Motivation

Psychologists don't always agree on how motivational terms should be used. For example, some psychologists use the term *need* only in connection with biological demands (the body's need for water or oxygen). But others think *need* is equally appropriate in discussing psychological requirements (as in needs for achievement or power).

Another distinction psychologists make is whether motivation comes from the *person*—an individual's inner qualities—or is the response to outside *situations*—cultural expectations and social pressures. As assumptions vary, so do theorists' explanations of what makes people tick.

Psychologists have used the concept of motivation for five basic purposes in the study of behavior. Consider the central objective or idea in each of the following:

1. *Accounting for behavioral variability:* We use motivational explanations when the variations in people's performances are not obviously due to personal differences such as skill or rehearsal. Motivation explains why you might perform a particular task well on one day but poorly on another; it also explains why some people do better than others of comparable skill in competitive situations.

2. *Relating biology to behavior:* We are biological organisms with internal mechanisms that automatically regulate bodily functions to promote survival. States of deprivation (such as needing food) automatically trigger these mechanisms, which then influence bodily functioning (such as feeling hungry), creating motivational states.

3. *Inferring private states from public acts:* There are two ways to respond to another person's behavior: take it at face value, or see it as a symptom of an underlying motive. For example, if the one you love forgets to call you on your birthday, you may attribute this failure to circumstantial problems (such as a busy week), or blame a personal flaw (such as not really loving you, and thus not being motivated to remember the occasion).

4. *Assigning responsibility for actions:* The concept of personal responsibility, so basic in law and religion, presumes inner motivation and the ability to control one's own actions. The concept of personal responsibility dissolves without the assumption of consciously directed motivation. Motivated behavior is considered to be willful and deliberate; such actions deserve praise when they are good, but blame and punishment when they are bad.

5. *Explaining perseverance despite adversity:* Motivation helps us to understand why organisms can continue to perform reliably even under difficult or variable conditions. Motivation gets you to work on time even when you are tired some mornings or when the weather is very bad. When motivated, you persist to the best of your ability, even if you realize you cannot possibly succeed.

The fact that some people do better in competition than others can be explained in part by varying degrees of motivation. These men are participating in the international Games for the Disabled.

Conducting Motivational Research

In this classic text, *Purposive Behavior in Animals and Men* (1932), learning theorist **Edward C. Tolman** described motivation as a process that intervenes between stimulus input and response outcome in an organism. Instead of trying to link each separate aspect of some behavior to particular stimulus input, motivational psychologists postulate an overall *intervening variable*—a condition such as hunger, sex, or achievement that develops *between* the stimulus and the response—that connects the causes and the consequences. Figure 8.6 outlines how motivation as an intervening variable links stimulus input and response output. For example, if the stimulus input is deprivation of food, the intervening variable will be hunger motivation, and the response output will involve searching for food, eating, and bypassing other attractions in favor of a meal.

The Indicators of Motivation Think for a moment, before going on, about some of the motives in your life. We sometimes use vivid language to talk about motivation—events or circumstances can "turn you on" or "turn you off," "push your buttons" or "pull your strings," "roll right off your back" or "make you snap." What *stimuli* have caused these experiences? What *responses* did you make in these circumstances? Similarly, psychologists have tried to focus on the stimuli (including conditions and situations) that lead to motivation, and the responses (observable behaviors) that are produced by motivational states. Decades of observation have provided researchers with clues to inner motivational states. The following are some of the measurable qualities and events that indicate motivation underlying behavior:

- The more motivated an organism is, the higher its level of *activity* will be (up to an optimal point).
- Strong motivation increases an individual's *rate of learning*.
- Motivation enables one to attain a higher *level of performance*.
- Once learned, a motivated response will be more *resistant to extinction*.
- Being motivated in one task can *disrupt efforts in other activities*.

FIGURE 8.6 Motivation as an Intervening Variable ■ Any particular motivation, such as hunger, is assumed to be the result of a number of physiological and/or psychological variables. Motivation may lead to one or more of the kinds of response output shown. The intervening variable links the input to the output consequences that are observable, manipulable, or measurable.

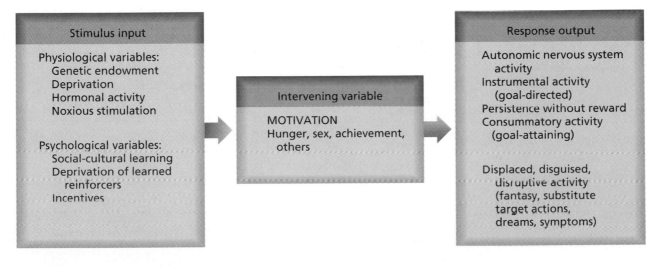

- Motivation leads an organism to *make certain choices* among goals, tasks, and rewards.
- Finally, behavior that *consummates or satisfies a motive* will be stronger than less motivated behavior.

Research Methods   Having a "checklist" of observable signs of motivation has enabled psychologists to devise several methods for studying motivation. Here we briefly review four strategies for conducting motivation research: experimentally manipulating drives; providing incentives; overcoming obstacles; and assessing self-descriptions.

Manipulating Drives   One way to study motivation is to identify different groups of individuals and compare their behavior—such as a group of people who have been deprived of a needed commodity and another group who have not. Such a correlational study evaluates the outcomes of existing differences. Correlational designs can indicate whether a relationship exists between individual differences and motivational states. But researchers often want to learn whether changes in motivation *cause* changes in behavior. To do this they must conduct experimental research. In a motivation experiment, a researcher manipulates conditions to induce the motivational state, or to make it stronger or weaker. Three procedures for experimental studies are *lesioning, deprivation,* and *stimulation*—all methods for manipulating drives states that cannot be observed directly.

Lesioning, discussed in Chapter 2, is a surgical procedure that destroys the specific brain tissue assumed to be vital to motivated behavior. If the operation destroys an area of the brain that triggers or controls motivated action, the subject will exhibit observable changes in behavior. For example, lesioning the part of the brain that triggers eating behavior results in an animal's refusal to eat even when it is deprived of food.

Deprivation involves denying a subject food, water, sexual contact, or specific substances (for example, calcium or salt). For humans, deprivation might involve withholding psychological conditions, such as social contact. For example, people may be motivated to seek out others when they are deprived of social contact (Schachter, 1959).

Finally, *stimulation* involves giving stimuli to an organism to create response tendencies. Aversive stimuli like pain or heat will prompt an animal to escape or flee; pleasant stimulation may arouse certain drives like desire for sexual contact. Researchers have used stimulation such as barriers, unsolvable tasks, and competition to study human motivation.

Incentive Motivation   Whether or not we are internally motivated, some external stimuli can independently move us to action. A beverage ad on TV, an attractive person, the illustrations on a menu, or the aroma of some foods can rouse us to act even when we are not impelled from within by thirst, sex, or hunger. *External stimuli that promise rewards are called* incentives.

Incentive motivation *is motivation that is aroused by external stimuli.* Although in animal research incentives always involve external stimuli, for humans incentive motivation may be self-induced by mental imagery. Being able to picture your goal, or seeing that it is closer than before, provides incentive motivation. Incentive motivation can also be induced by *negative incentives,* such as fear of developing an addiction to drugs, or feeling ashamed of dropping out of the marathon—or of staggering through its last lap. One example of an incentive in modern life is fame, celebrity, and the benefits of others' admiration. Jim Lovell knew that, as an Apollo astronaut, he would be considered famous—but that he and his family would miss the pleasures of privacy and anonymity.

Overcoming Obstacles The more motivated you are, the more you will strive to overcome obstacles between you and your goals. **C. J. Warden** first applied this principle experimentally in studying animal motivation in the 1920s at Columbia University. In these studies, Warden assessed the relative strengths of various drives by means of an *obstruction box*. This apparatus used an electrified grid to separate a deprived rat from incentives it could see on the other side of the grid. The incentives included food, water, a sexually responsive mate, and the rat's offspring. Behaviorally, drive strength was measured as the number of times the animal would cross the hot grid in a given period. Figure 8.7 shows the typical data obtained with this method.

The motivating effects of thirst and hunger were greatest after a short period of deprivation, and declined when water or food deprivation became extreme and the animals weakened. This declining response was not found in two cases, however. With sexual contact as a reward, sex-deprived rats kept running at a constant rate (after the first few hours). Mother rats separated from their newborn pups endured the most suffering, running most frequently across the hot grid even with a minimal period of social deprivation. This was interpreted at the time as evidence for the existence of a powerful maternal drive.

When a person does something that entails great cost or sacrifice, we infer a very high level of motivation. It is not easy to attend school while you also earn a living and care for personal relationships—you must be highly motivated to study in order to overcome the many difficulties of juggling so many roles. People who choose to become parents will have to sacrifice many selfish goals in order to provide for the well-being of their children.

Self-descriptions Only verbal self-descriptions provide the researcher with the behaver's view of her or his motivation. Human motivation can be assessed with self-reports and responses to projective tests (for example, interpretations offered of ambiguous patterns). Researchers may ask participants to fill out questionnaires that require them to evaluate their own needs, desires, and anxieties. The researchers use the scores as indicators of strength of motivation. These scores can then be correlated with behavioral measures. In other research, subjects create stories about ambiguous pictures, and researchers analyze the content of these themes to reveal different types of needs. The advantages of self-descriptions include their convenience and accessibility— many people are quite willing to explain their actions in great detail. A major disadvantage is the impossibility of verifying many self-reports; it is possible for respondents to exaggerate, err, or even lie in explaining their behavior.

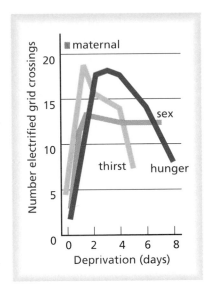

FIGURE 8.7 **Relative Strengths of Primary Drives** ■ In reaction to various incentives on the other side, rats crossed an electrified grid in the Columbia obstruction box. Their deprivation level was manipulated by time separated from the goal object. Thirst and hunger performance reached a peak and then declined as the animals became debilitated. Sexual motivation peaked soon and remained steady throughout the study. Mothers separated from their offspring showed the highest level of motivation by enduring the most electric shocks to get to their offspring after only a brief period of deprivation.

Check Your Recall

Motivation explains the processes involved in starting, directing, sustaining, and stopping behavior. Motivational mechanisms affect one's preferences for goals and activities, the strength of one's responses, and the persistence of one's actions. The concept of motivation serves several psychological purposes, including accounting for behavioral variability, relating biology to behavior, and assigning responsibility to actions.

Researchers infer motivation as an intervening variable between stimulus conditions and an organism's responses. The strength of motivation can be measured in such variables as activity level, rate of learning, and resistance to extinction. In experimental research, motivation has been manipulated through lesioning, stimulation, and deprivation. Among humans, self-reports and projective tests are convenient, but the information provided may be impossible to verify.

Theories of Motivation

For centuries, philosophers distinguished between human action (presumably guided by reason and free will) and nonhuman action (determined by "brute appetites"). Darwin's theory of evolution challenged this distinction, paving the way for a theory that both human and animal behaviors are driven by instinct. In this section, we examine five theoretical perspectives on motivation: instinct theory; drive theory; arousal theory; humanistic theory; and social-cognitive theories. As they developed, these theories influenced each other as well as the psychologists who conducted research and applied motivational discoveries in everyday life.

Instinct Theory

According to instinct theory, organisms are born with certain built-in tendencies that are essential for the species' survival. The instinct concept explains the behavior of many nonhumans. Animals engage in regular cycles of activity that enable their species to survive. Salmon swim thousands of miles back to the exact stream where they were spawned, leaping up waterfalls until they come to the right spot, where the surviving males and females engage in ritualized courtship and mating. Fertilized eggs are deposited, the parents die, and in time their young swim downstream to live in the ocean, until years later when they return to complete their part in the continuing drama. Bees communicate the location of food to other bees, army ants embark on synchronized hunting expeditions, birds build nests, and spiders spin complex webs—exactly as their parents and ancestors did.

Originally, instinct theorists merely described instincts in terms of mysterious inner forces that impelled certain activities. Today, instincts in animals are usually studied as **fixed-action patterns,** *unlearned patterns of action triggered by identifiable stimuli.* Ethologists study animal behavior and species' natural habitats in detail, over time. Experimental researchers focus on identifying the brain mechanisms that work with environmental cues in producing instinctive behavior.

William James, writing in 1890, stated his belief that humans rely on even more instincts than lower animals do to guide their behavior. In addition to the biological instincts they share with animals, a host of human social instincts—for example, sympathy, modesty, sociability, and love—come into play. For James, both human and animal instincts were *purposive,* serving important purposes in the organism's adaptation to its environment.

Sigmund Freud (1915) had a somewhat different view of instinct, though one that was hardly more flattering to humanity. Freud thought instincts—life instincts (such as sexuality) and death instincts (such as aggression)—had neither conscious purpose nor predetermined direction, and that organisms could learn many different means of satisfying them. He believed that instinctive urges exist to satisfy bodily needs, and that these urges create *psychic energy.* This tension drives us toward activities or objects that will reduce the tension. Freud assumed that most instincts operate unconsciously, but that they affect our conscious thoughts and feelings as well as our actions, sometimes putting us in conflict with society's demands. An angry driver may fantasize about driving aggressively on the highway, but curbs the impulse because of stringent laws against reckless driving.

By the 1920s, researchers' interests in the concept had led to a theoretical "catalogue" of thousands of human instincts (Bernard, 1924). But these "instincts" were merely labels for common patterns of behavior, not explanations for their origins. Further, anthropologists began to report enormous variations in human behavior from one culture to another (Benedict, 1959; Mead,

1939), thus contradicting any assumption about universal motivations. Finally, learning theorists demonstrated that much seemingly "inborn" behavior is really learned. These influences led to the demise of instinct theories as general approaches to human motivation.

Drive Theory

The concept of motivation as an inner *drive* that determines behavior was introduced by Robert Woodworth (1918), who had studied with William James. Woodworth defined drive in biological terms as energy released from an organism's store. Drive was the fuel of action, called forth by triggering stimuli and available to be channeled into various goal-directed activities. Other mechanisms, such as perceptual and learning processes, guided action in appropriate directions.

As later developed by theorist Clark Hull (1943, 1952), drive-reduction theory is *homeostatic* because it assumes that an organism is driven to maintain homeostasis, a balance among the systems and processes of the body. But in the mid-1950s, new data showed that humans and animals often do things in the *absence* of any apparent deprivation, drives, or drive reduction—in order to *increase* stimulation. Both humans and animals play and exhibit exploratory and manipulatory behaviors. Recall the rats in the Columbia obstruction box. Without deprivation of any kind, the animals still crossed the hot grid a few times. They crossed the painful barrier even when there was nothing on the other side—except a novel environment. Even rats deprived of food and water, when placed in a novel environment with plenty of opportunities everywhere to eat or drink, chose to explore instead. Apparently, for both people and animals, exploring and taking an interest in the world is a rewarding experience in itself. Only after they had first satisfied their curiosity did they begin to satisfy their hunger and thirst (Berlyne, 1960; Fowler, 1965; Zimbardo & Montgomery, 1957).

Arousal Theory

Arousal is a measure of the general responsiveness of an organism to activation of the brain stem's reticular system. One source of arousal theory was the concept of emergency reactions to stress situations. Early research confirmed that certain emotions, such as fear and rage, prepare or motivate us for action when we are faced with danger; these arousal reactions are accompanied by measurable bodily changes. Other research, taking EEG measures of the activity of brain structures, encouraged psychologists to focus on the ways arousal of the brain prepares individuals to respond to stimuli. Finally, a series of studies related performance to motivation level. These lines of research converged to indicate a particular relationship between arousal and performance. What exactly is that relationship?

How Arousal Affects Performance   For the hungry and thirsty rats in the Columbia obstruction box, as motivation increased, the curve of performance first rose and then later declined over time. This pattern, an *inverted U-shaped function,* suggests that either too little *or* too much motivation can impair performance. For example, consider the effects of motivation arousal on your ability to study for an important test. If you are not at all worried or aroused—for example, if the test seems far off and the course is not important to you—you will not study very hard or perform very well. As your arousal increases, you become more directed and attentive in your studying. However, above a certain level of arousal, you may be *too* worried to concentrate; last minute panic may scatter your efforts to study, and cause you to "freeze up" during the test.

Humans and animals often participate in activities to increase stimulation, rather than just to reduce drives.

The discovery of the inverted-U relationship between arousal and performance implies that an individual has a "best level" of arousal for performing a particular task. Such **optimal arousal level** *is the level of arousal at which one best performs tasks of varying levels of difficulty.* The concept of optimal arousal has been used in several ways: to identify the link between motivation, performance, and task difficulty; and to explain why some organisms will work to *increase* their arousal, by seeking rather than reducing stimulation.

The Yerkes-Dodson Law   On some tasks, performance is best when motivation is relatively low. How much arousal is too much? The key to the appropriate level of motivation is *task difficulty.* With difficult or complex tasks, even mild arousal quickly approaches the optimal level for the performer. As arousal increases beyond that optimum, performance of difficult tasks quickly deteriorates. In contrast, for simple or easy tasks, the optimal level of motivation is greater. One's performance gets better and better as arousal increases, up to a later point when it tapers off.

The **Yerkes-Dodson law** formalizes the relationship between arousal and performance. According to this law, as arousal increases, performance of difficult tasks *decreases* and performance of easy tasks *increases* (Yerkes & Dodson, 1908). See Figure 8.8 for an illustration of this principle. Note that, although the timing of the optimal level is different for simple versus difficult tasks, extreme arousal (low or high) always causes relatively poor performance.

Humanistic Theory

Humanistic psychologist **Abraham Maslow's** (1970) theory of human motivation explains both tension-reducing and tension-increasing actions. Maslow contrasted **deficiency motivation,** *in which individuals seek to restore physical or psychological equilibrium,* and **growth motivation,** *in which individuals do more than reduce deficits as they seek to realize their fullest potential.* Deficiency-motivated people dedicate their efforts to obtaining what they *need* in order to survive or be comfortable. Growth-motivated people may welcome uncertainty, tension, and even pain in order to *fulfill their potential* and achieve their goals.

FIGURE 8.8   The Yerkes-Dodson Law ■ Performance varies with motivation level and task difficulty. For easy or simple tasks, a higher level of motivation increases performance effectiveness. However, for difficult or complex tasks, a lower level of motivation is optimal. A moderate level of motivation is generally best for tasks of moderate difficulty. These inverted U-shaped functions show that performance is worst at both low and high extremes of motivation.

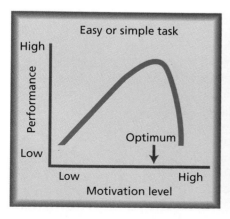
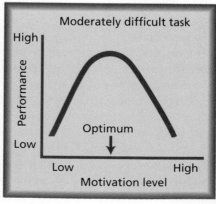
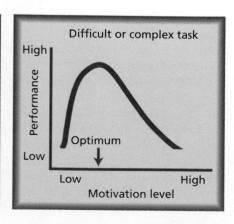

Maslow's Hierarchy of Needs Maslow's theory holds that our basic needs form a **needs hierarchy,** as illustrated in Figure 8.9. Our inborn needs are arranged in a sequence of stages, a hierarchy, from primitive to advanced goals:

1. The basic *biological needs*, such as hunger and thirst, are at the bottom of that hierarchy. They must be satisfied before other needs can begin to operate. When biological needs are pressing, other needs are put on hold and are unlikely to influence our actions.
2. When biological needs are reasonably well satisfied, the needs at the next level—*safety needs*—motivate us.
3. When we are no longer concerned about danger, we become motivated by *attachment needs*—needs to belong, to affiliate with others, to love, and to be loved.
4. If we are well fed and safe and if we feel a sense of social belonging, we move up to *esteem needs*. These include the needs to like oneself, to see oneself as competent and effective, and to do what is necessary to earn the esteem of others.
5. Humans are thinking beings, with complex brains that demand the stimulation of thought. We are motivated by strong *cognitive needs* to know our past, to comprehend the puzzles of our current existence, and to predict the future. The force of these needs enables scholars and scientists to spend their lives in the quest for new knowledge.
6. At the next level of Maslow's hierarchy, comes the human desire for beauty and order, in the form of *aesthetic needs* that give rise to the creative aspect of humanity.
7. At the top of the hierarchy are people who are nourished, safe, loved and loving, secure, thinking, and creative. These people have moved beyond basic human needs in the quest for the fullest development of their potential, or *self-actualization*. A self-actualizing person is self-aware, self-accepting, socially responsive, creative, spontaneous, and open to novelty and challenge—among other positive attributes.
8. Maslow's hierarchy includes a step beyond the total fulfillment of individual potential. The need for *transcendence* may lead to higher states of consciousness and a cosmic vision of one's part in the universe. Very few people develop the desire to move beyond the self to achieve union with spiritual forces.

There are varying lines of research support for the ideas promoted in Maslow's hierarchy. A great body of work has now been assembled on people's needs for relationships with others, a need originally postulated in Maslow's hierarchy (see Brehm, 1992; Hatfield & Rapson, 1993; Kelley et al., 1983; Weber & Harvey, 1994). The attachments people form and their reasons for seeking them can be as varied as the individuals themselves: best friendships, playmates, coworker connections, lovers, teammates, spouses, or members of the same club. Most psychologists specializing in relationships now agree that all these different liaisons and attachments provide for our fundamental human motivation to "belong" (Baumeister & Leary, 1995).

Another concept in Maslow's theory that might seem to defy scientific study is the power of "transcendence" as a behavioral goal. But work on happiness—what it is like to feel happy, who feels happy, and how they achieve happiness—indicates that a key factor in achieving joy is a striving toward something higher. This endeavor is not satisfied merely by "belonging" to a church or joining activist efforts, but must involve *meaningful faith* that is based on community support, purpose, and hope (Myers, 1992). In one study, a psychologist asked over 200 students to list the initials of people they knew and to rate each one, first for happiness-unhappiness and then for selfishness-unselfishness. Results showed that 70 percent of those judged to be unselfish

FIGURE 8.9 Maslow's Hierarchy of Needs ■ According to Maslow, needs at the lower level of the hierarchy dominate an individual's motivation as long as they are unsatisfied. Once these are adequately satisfied, the higher needs occupy an individual's attention.

An example of the kinds of ambiguous figures used by Murray and McClelland in their TAT technique.

seemed happy, but 95 percent of those deemed selfish seemed *unhappy* (Rimland, 1982). As much as materialistic and consumeristic cultures encourage individuals to promote their *own* happiness by acquiring things and seeking pleasure, some research indicates that giving to and caring for *others* is a surer road to personal happiness—as well as social good. Why would unselfishness—sacrificing or depriving oneself of comfort or safety for others' sake—promote real happiness? Myers (1992) suggests that through altruism people can create a meaning in their lives that will survive death, thus ironically promoting long-term self-preservation.

These are interesting and heartening findings. But overall, Maslow's theory is valued more for influencing therapy and education than for stimulating psychological research. For Maslow, the central motivational force for humans is the innate need to grow and actualize one's highest potentials. Such an upbeat approach was welcomed by many psychologists who had wearied of the earlier diet of negative motivational views. This emphasis on positive rather than negative concepts of motivation seemed to fit better with a new orientation in psychology—a focus on helping normal people achieve their potential, rather than satisfying the basic needs of disturbed or deficient individuals and families.

Motivation and Projection   Harvard psychologists Henry Murray and David McClelland used a special *projective technique called the* **Thematic Apperception Test (TAT)** *to identify a limited number of human motives that are central in people's lives* (McClelland et al., 1976). In the TAT, subjects are shown a series of ambiguous pictures and asked to generate a story about each one. A picture might show a lone individual in a particular place, or two persons near each other. To tell a story about the picture, the subject must interpret what appears to be going on in the picture, adding details and making decisions about missing information. These added interpretations are *apperceptions* (from the Latin *ad* ["toward"] + *perceptus* ["seen completely"]) based on the respondent's own experiences and biases.

In their research, Murray and McClelland found that their subjects' TAT stories reflected their personal needs and concerns. The researchers theorized that this occurs because needy subjects project their needs onto ambiguous stimuli and weave need-related themes into their interpretations. For example, if you are hungry, a picture of two people sitting at a table might seem to be "about" mealtime; but if you are currently worried about a personal relationship, the two people might appear to you to be arguing or discussing their future.

Using the TAT, Murray and McClelland uncovered many positive human motives similar to the ones Maslow described. Mingled with positive needs were needs that could demean human nature, such as abasement, self-blame, and humiliation. Many of the story themes centered on needs for power, dominance, and aggression—hardly the stuff of Maslow's higher levels of human potential. Thus, researchers felt challenged to develop more comprehensive theories of human motivation that included the "dark side" of human nature as well as its brighter lights.

Social-Cognitive Theories

To understand social-cognitive theories of motivation, consider a particular need state: loneliness. You tend to feel lonely when you think your social contacts are inadequate. But how do we define "inadequate"? Some people seem quite content in their own company, living alone, having contact with only a very few close friends. Others need to be where the action is, in the middle of a happy, close group, in order to feel adequately loved. And still others might forsake all their "friends" for just one intimate, romantic relationship. Just as there are many forms of companionship, there seem to be many definitions of loneliness.

Subjective Motivation   Social-cognitive theories of motivation share the concept that human motivation comes not from objective realities but from our *subjective interpretation* of them. What we do is controlled by what we *think* is or was responsible for causing our actions, what we *believe* we can do, and what we *anticipate* will be the outcome of our efforts. In the cognitive approach, it is these higher mental processes that control motivation, rather than physiological arousal or biological mechanisms. This explains why human beings are often more motivated by imagined, future events than by genuine, immediate circumstances.

Locus of Control   The importance of expectations in motivating behavior was developed by **Julian Rotter** in his *social-learning theory* (1954). For Rotter, the probability that someone will engage in a given behavior (for example, studying for an exam instead of partying) is determined by two factors: one's expectation of attaining a goal (getting a good grade) following that activity; and the personal value of that goal. Expectation of a future occurrence is based on our past reinforcement history, which in turn has helped us develop a personal sense of **locus of control,** *or the origin of one's life influences.* A **locus of control orientation** *is a belief that the outcomes of our actions are contingent on either what one does (internal control) or on events outside one's personal control (external control).* For example, if you believe that studying hard will lead to good grades (internal control), you will behave differently from someone who believes the tests are rigged, or that the teacher is biased against you (external control).

We have discussed general theories of motivation. In the next section, we will take a closer look at three very different motives and the behaviors they direct: hunger and eating, sexual motivation and sex, and achievement and work.

Check Your Recall

No single psychological theory of motivation has proven entirely satisfactory, but together the various theories have contributed valuable principles and insights to motivation research. Early instinct theories, based on observations of fixed-action patterns in nonhuman species, labeled behaviors rather than explaining them. Drive theories were based on the assumption that need-based tensions led to responses aimed at reducing those needs. However, drive theory could not account for stimulation-seeking motives the way arousal theory could. Arousal theory proposes that organisms have an optimal level of arousal for performance on a given task. The Yerkes-Dodson law states that performance is a function of both arousal and whether a task is simple or complex.

According to humanistic theories, behavior is motivated by growth as well as by deficiency. In Abraham Maslow's hierarchy of needs, once the more basic, survival-oriented needs are satisfied, an individual's behavior is influenced by higher-level motives. Researchers have used projective techniques such as the TAT to identify human motives. Social and cognitive psychologists have emphasized the power of individual perceptions and beliefs in influencing motivation.

Motivated Behaviors

Now that we have reviewed some essential motivational concepts and theories, we will examine how psychologists have begun to understand three motives that have been studied in great detail: eating, sexuality, and work. Obviously these motives and the behaviors they generate are rather important to all of us.

Eating

Primary drives such as hunger and thirst are part of the body's own maintenance mechanisms. If eating were a behavior that had to be learned, many people might starve to death before they mastered its complexities. But eating seems to come naturally once we experience hunger and know what to do about it. Being "natural" does not make eating a "simple" motivated behavior, however. Of the body's many homeostatic (balance-regulating) systems, those involved in hunger motivation are among the most complex. Biological regulation (including brain, biochemistry, and organ functions) must work with mental, behavioral, and social processes to control eating behavior.

To regulate food intake effectively, organisms must be able to accomplish four tasks:

1. Organisms must *detect* the need for food.
2. They must *initiate* eating behavior.
3. They must monitor the *quantity and nutritional value* of what they eat.
4. They must be able to tell when *enough food* has been consumed—and stop.

Researchers have related these tasks to both central brain mechanisms and peripheral mechanisms involving other parts of the body.

Does this photograph stimulate your appetite for pizza? Ads for food are effective because eating is a complex behavior, motivated not only by hunger but also by learned preferences and environmental stimuli.

Peripheral Cues to Hunger   Early work by Walter Cannon (1934), of the Cannon-Bard emotion theory, concentrated on linking hunger to the "pangs" produced by an empty stomach. This *peripheral cues hypothesis* argued that a person does not realize he or she is hungry until such distant signals of pain or discomfort are apparent (Cannon & Washburn, 1912). Later research soon showed, however, that not only is it possible to be and feel hungry without feeling hunger pains, but not all "pangs" are a signal of hunger. Surgical patients whose stomachs have been removed experience hunger when their nutrient levels are low, even though they have no stomachs in which to experience emptiness (Janowitz & Grossman, 1950). Rats without stomachs still perform learning tasks for food rewards, thus exhibiting motivation that does not originate in a peripheral cue (Pennick et al., 1963). Hunger pangs appear to be a familiar, but nonessential, accompaniment to the bodily experience of needing food and being motivated to eat.

A Multiple-System Approach   For many years, researchers used models of central regulation, presuming that the brain had "hunger centers" even if the stomach did not. These centers would start and stop hungry sensations and eating behavior. But the quest for these centers proved too limited, and the current view is that a more complex interaction of biological and psychological systems is involved in eating.

The *multiple-system approach* begins by specifying that the brain works with many other systems, biological and psychological, to gather information about energy requirements, nutritional state, acquired hungers, and food preferences, and also social and cultural demands. For example, your readiness to

actresses (with many hours of rehearsal) manage to engage in the
Advertisements, MTV, and gossip with acquaintances also contrib
young people's sexual scripts. As you can see, these scripts are neit
nor instructive; they merely suggest images and goals, and seld
realistic information (Gagnon, 1977). Different aspects of these
assembled through social interaction over one's lifetime. The attitu
values embodied in one's sexual script define one's general or
sexuality.

When people have *different* scripts for what they expect to l
interaction, adjustment problems can arise between partners. Fo
there is evidence that touch has different meanings for men and wo
researchers questioned male and female undergraduates about t
they attach to being touched on different parts of their anatomy
quite different meanings were found between the sexes. For femal
a touch was associated with sexual desire, the less it was consider
warmth, pleasantness, or friendliness. When a close male frienc
woman in an area of her body that communicates sexual desire
that is its *only* meaning to her. For males, the same touch is in
having a cluster of meanings: pleasantness, warmth, love, and se
Misunderstandings can arise when one person's "friendly touch"
by the other as a "sexual advance" (Nguyen et al., 1975). This stu
that, from the female perspective, male touch without the rituals
and the preliminaries of respect and commitment is interpreted
advance—for "easy," short-term mating. For males, female tou
preted as pleasant in most situations since it is assumed to sugge
ness to mate.

Date Rape As a society's ideas about individual rights and res
change, sexual scripts can become dangerously confused. *Dat*
trauma that illustrates devastating conflict between male and fe
scripts. In one sample of college women, 57 percent reported ha
enced what they thought of as rape (Koss, 1985). The accuracy of
ing figure is confirmed by surveys of male students. One in every
men said he would rape a woman if he were sure he would no
(Malamuth, 1984). When questioned about their actual experienc
the men in another survey admitted to forcing a date to perform
act, and 25 percent admitted to forcing intercourse (Koss & C
Researchers suggest that date rape may be a *result* of confusion
scripts. The female script may lead a woman to give in if a man's
coercive and insistent; the male script may consider some hum
woman acceptable, and may justify rape in light of peer pressure c
sexually aggressive (Muehlenhard & Cook, 1988 Murnen et al., 1
brutal realities of date rape are exposed, it is more likely that s
communities will develop strategies to counter the confused an
sexual scripts that make possible such abuse of intimate relations.

Sexual Orientation How would you describe your sexual
Many—but not all—readers of this book would answer "he
Consider your sexual orientation for a moment—what it means t
tity; your future plans; your chances for finding a partner and fri
ing in secure and meaningful work, having a family.

Now ASK YOURSELF:

- When did you first *know* what your sexual orientation was?
- Did you ever consider any alternatives?
- Is it possible you are mistaken, or that you should have give
  sexual orientation a "chance" in your life?

and even abnormal were actually quite widespread—or at least report
However, it was **William Masters** and **Virginia Johnson** (1966, 197
who really broke down the traditional sexual taboo. They legitim
study of human sexuality by directly observing and recording unde
tory conditions the physiological patterns involved in ongoing huma
performance. By doing so, they studied not what people said about se
carries obvious problems of response bias) but how they actually r
during intercourse and masturbation.

Since Masters and Johnson blazed the way to modern, scientific
on human sexual behavior, the topic has become less taboo and more
ble to social scientists. Wide-scale surveys are regularly conduc
updated by reputable and qualified researchers, and examine the patt
trends of sexual behavior in many populations and dimensions (see M
al., 1995). However, from the perspective of individual motivatic
broad-based polls offer less insight than the painstaking, controversia
ioral research of Masters and Johnson.

It is important to note that Masters and Johnson studied aro
response only. They did *not* study the psychologically significant init
of sexual responding—that of *sexual desire,* the motivation to se
sexual partner or to make oneself available for sexual experience. Fr
observations of subjects' sexual behavior, Masters and Johnson d
significant conclusions:

- Men and women have similar patterns of sexual responding, rega
  the source of arousal.
- Although the sequence of phases of the sexual response cycle is s
  the two sexes, women are more variable, tending to respond mo
  but often remaining aroused longer.
- Many women can have multiple orgasms, while men rarely do in a
  rable time period.
- Penis size is generally unrelated to any aspect of sexual perf
  (except in the male's *attitude* about the size of his penis).

Masters and Johnson found four phases in the human sexual
cycle: excitement, plateau, orgasm, and resolution (see Figure 8.11).

- In the *excitement phase*, there are blood vessel changes in th
  region. The penis becomes erect, the clitoris swells, and blood a
  fluids become congested in the testicles and vagina.

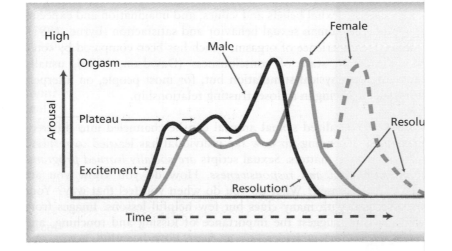

eat a slice of pizza depends on many factors, including how long it's been since
you last ate, whether you like pizza, and what time of day it is (breakfast?),
and whether your friends are encouraging you to have a slice. Assembling all
these data, the brain sends signals to neural, hormonal, organ, and muscle
systems to start or stop food-seeking and eating.

The brain region primarily involved in starting and controlling eating is the
lateral hypothalamus (LH). A separate region of brain cells nearby, the *ventromedial hypothalamus (VMH),* inhibits (stops) eating (Nisbett, 1972). Thus
eating behavior is regulated by the dual mechanisms of a "start center" and a
"stop center." Figure 8.10 summarizes many of the factors involved in detecting hunger, eating, and knowing when to stop.

In general, the biological systems respond to an organism's energy needs
and nutritional state. The psychological systems include acquired food preferences and responsiveness to social, emotional, and environmental cues about

FIGURE 8.10 Multiple-System Model of Hunger and Eating ■

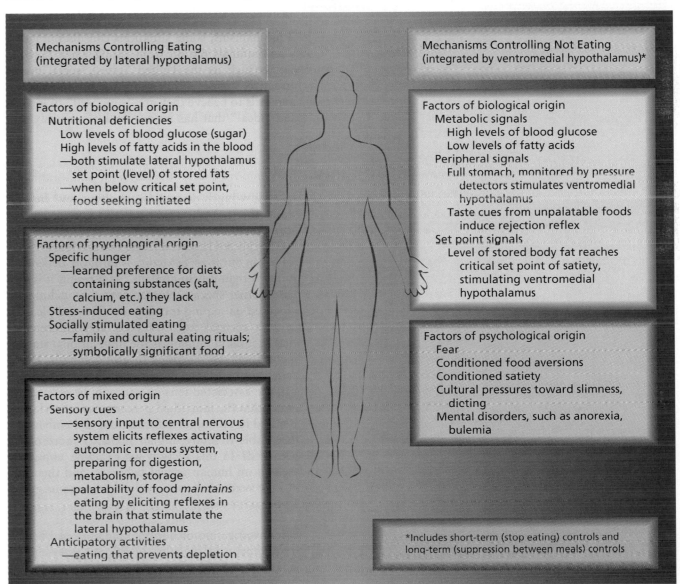

what to eat, when, where
factor:

- Glucose (blood sugar) a
  olism. Receptors monit
  to the LH to begin the e
  you are low on nutrien

- Most organisms mainta
  expenditure. An interr
  informs the central nerv
  specialized fat cells fall
  signals are sent to "ea
  work with mice sugge
  protein that signals tha
  tinue to eat even when

- High glucose levels and
  cators that the set poi
  processes this nutrition
  eater to *stop eating*. Pr
  food is bad, unpleasant

In addition to biologica
reduce eating. Both human
fearful. Also, in many soc
promote thinness as most a
especially influence women
if they do not eat—a distor
destructive eating disorders.

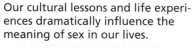

Our cultural lessons and life experiences dramatically influence the meaning of sex in our lives.

Sexual Motivation

How interested are you in s
and knowledge are not the
cause serious problems. Info
it does not "come naturally.
ically influence the meaning
on psychological factors in
more variable in humans th
evolved core of motivations
from sexual behavior, alon
toward sexual activities. Sex
excitement and tension bro
stimuli give rise to sexual e
ual experiences sexual arou
direct or indirect sexual acti

Discussion of sex can b
ment. How have scientists
tively, and what have they
survey and observational r
this evidence with theories c
tors and how it motivates o

Scientific Evidence Scien
ior was given the first impor
colleagues beginning in th
17,000 Americans about th
these researchers revealed t

- During the *plateau*
  increases occur in h
  tions, and muscle te

- During the *orgasm*
  pleasurable sense of
  characterized by rh
  of sperm in men, a
  women.

- During the *resoluti*
  preexcitement state
  down. After one or
  further orgasm for n
  are capable of multi

Sexual Cues The reas
is that human sexual bel
limited to responses invo
is what *you* find sexuall
that you have uniquely i
that may culminate in o
but involve an endless v
ditioned stimulus is tact
touch is a universal co
Virtually any stimuli th
can become conditione
only in memory or fant

Research suggests
provide the primal setti
able arousal (Storms, 1
images, odors—any tan
arousal through this co
us learn culturally acce
deviations. For better o
conditioned stimuli, suc
even pain (Rachman, 1

In humans, sexuali
need than with satisfy
sexual activity is "the at
of sexual satisfaction. T
originating in the expe
(Davidson, 1981, p. 2
specific sexual events, se
tion all play a part in h
Even the subjective expe
to a profound altered
depends not only on pl
sonal factors, such as be

Sexual Scripts Gener
specific behaviors, depe
and think about sexual
of sexual interpretatio
"supposed" to feel arou
culture provides you w
movies and television s
how to engage in the

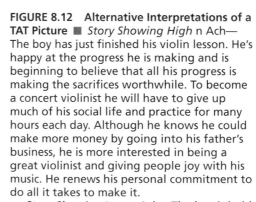

Tactile stimulation, touch, is an unconditioned stimulus which plays a universal part in sexual behavior.

---

self-worth. However, in some cases, achievement motives can become so extreme that they lead to limitless aspirations—the desire for perfection, being the best and being "number one" at everything.

Another feature of achievement motives is their *future orientation*. The future-oriented person uses cognitive strategies that rely on long-term instrumental steps toward near and distant goals rather than focusing on the potential pleasure of more readily available but less valuable present stimuli (DeCharms & Muir, 1978; Nuttin, 1985). For example, a future-oriented child, given five dollars by a visiting aunt, will save it as part of her plan to buy an expensive game she wants, while her present-oriented sister spends her dollars immediately on an inexpensive toy or treat.

The Need for Achievement As early as 1938, Harvard psychologist **Henry Murray** had postulated a "need to achieve" that varied in strength in different people and influenced their tendency to approach success and evaluate their own performances. As discussed earlier in the chapter, Murray and his colleague **David McClelland** used a special technique called the Thematic Apperception Test (TAT) to identify several important human motives. They asked subjects to tell stories in response to a series of ambiguous pictures. These stories, the psychologists believed, would represent "projections" of the respondent's needs, but it is more correct to regard the stories as simply reflecting themes that are important to the storyteller and that come readily to mind.

From subject responses to a series of these TAT pictures, McClelland worked out measures of several human needs. The **need for achievement** (**n Ach**), *reflected individual differences in the drive to meet a variety of goals.*

FIGURE 8.12 Alternative Interpretations of a TAT Picture ■ *Story Showing High* n Ach—The boy has just finished his violin lesson. He's happy at the progress he is making and is beginning to believe that all his progress is making the sacrifices worthwhile. To become a concert violinist he will have to give up much of his social life and practice for many hours each day. Although he knows he could make more money by going into his father's business, he is more interested in being a great violinist and giving people joy with his music. He renews his personal commitment to do all it takes to make it.

Story Showing Low n Ach—The boy is holding his brother's violin and wishes he could play it. But he knows it isn't worth the time, energy, and money for lessons. He feels sorry for his brother, who has given up all the fun things in life to practice, practice, practice. It would be great to wake up one day and be a top-notch musician but it doesn't happen that way. The reality is boring practice, no fun, and the likelihood that he'll become just another guy playing a musical instrument in a small-town band.

The variable of *n Ach* (pronounced *en-ATCH*) reflected individuals' different concerns about improving their performance, getting concrete feedback on how well they were doing, and taking personal responsibility for a performance so that they could get satisfaction from doing it well.

A great many studies in both laboratory and real-life settings have validated the usefulness of this measure. For example, persistence in working on an impossible task was greater for those with high *n Ach* when the task was announced as difficult rather than easy. Low *n Ach* subjects gave up sooner when they were led to believe the task was difficult, but they persisted for the supposedly easy (actually impossible) task. In other research, high-scoring *n Ach* people were found to be more upwardly mobile than those with low scores; and sons who had high *n Ach* scores were more likely than sons with low *n Ach* measures to advance above their fathers' occupational status (McClelland et al., 1976). Figure 8.12 shows an example of how a high *n Ach* individual and low *n Ach* individual might interpret a TAT picture.

The need to achieve clearly energizes and directs behavior. It also influences perceptions of many situations and interpretations of our own and others' behavior. Even the economic growth of a society can be related to its encouragement of achievement motivation (McClelland, 1961, 1985).

Intrinsic and Extrinsic Motivation   *Motivation to engage in an activity for its own sake, in the absence of external reward, is called* **intrinsic** *motivation.* Things that we do because we simply enjoy doing them—such as playing video games, singing in the shower, doing crossword puzzles, or keeping a secret diary—are intrinsically motivated. Work, too, can be intrinsically motivated when an individual is deeply interested in the job to be done.

Extrinsic motivation *is motivation to engage in an activity for some external consequence.* In extrinsic motivation, behavior is instrumental (useful) for obtaining something else. In intrinsic motivation, behavior is carried out without a purpose beyond the immediate rewards of doing it. Taking vitamins is extrinsically motivated; eating cream puffs is intrinsically motivated.

Overjustification   Consider what might happen when children are given extrinsic rewards for behavior that they were already motivated intrinsically to produce. Play becomes work when fun activities are given superfluous rewards, as shown in a series of classroom experiments by **Mark Lepper** and his colleagues (Lepper et al., 1973). When an extrinsic reward is given, the behavior is *overjustified*—the individual realizes there is too much justification for engaging in the activity. As a result, motivation to perform the task becomes extrinsic and the task itself is enjoyed less. When the extrinsic rewards are withdrawn, the activity loses its material value (Deci, 1975; Lepper, 1981; Lepper & Greene, 1978). The moral is that "A reward a day makes work out of play."

Extrinsic constraints on people, such as evaluation pressure or close surveillance during an activity, seem to have effects on motivation similar to those of rewards. Typically, students in courses where grades are heavily emphasized might find that their motivation, even for their favorite subjects, dwindles after the final exam—they were working only for the grade. Gold stars, grades, and penalties for failure or misbehavior are testament to the (false) belief that schoolchildren are extrinsically motivated and must be given threats or promises of external consequences to learn.

Flow   Intrinsically motivating activities have been described as producing a special state of mind called **flow,** *a near-ecstatic state achieved by total focus on the present activity with an increase in creative ability* (Csikszentmihalyi,

1990). Flow experiences are characterized by a pleasurable loss of self-awareness and of any sense of the passage of time, along with a deep concentration on the task rather than its outcome. Flow is inherent in the creative process, and is produced by the motivation of ultimate involvement in the activity and not by its possible outcomes. "Going with the flow" is the reward for intrinsic motivation. Although some people turn to drugs or alcohol to experience the flow feeling, researchers have found that work produces more of these optimal flow experiences than do leisure-time activities. In fact, one type of flow experience identified by Csikszentmihalyi (1990) is very similar to the goal of *n Ach* as identified by McClelland (1985), namely the intrinsic pleasure obtained from mastering a challenging task or doing something well. Thus McClelland (1985) has argued that the main social motives are developed through learning grounded in a few biologically given, intrinsically satisfying flow experiences.

Check Your Recall

A multiple-system approach characterizes hunger and eating as influenced by biological, psychological, social, and environmental factors. Regions of the hypothalamus are responsible for initiating eating and sending "stop eating" signals. Food intake and body weight are regulated according to a set point. Situations and social norms can also influence whether and how much one eats.

Human sexual motivation is unique because it is biologically influenced but not driven or necessary to individual survival. Human sexuality is more variable and less programmed than nonhuman sexual behavior. Scientific work on human sexual behavior began with Alfred Kinsey's surveys and was advanced with Masters and Johnson's investigation of human sexual response. Through various sources, people learn sexual scripts, which normally function adequately but can also conflict with others' scripts and expectations. No single theory of the origins of homosexuality is conclusive, but it has been found to be important for gay males and lesbians to recognize and cope with their sexual orientation.

Early research by Murray and McClelland identified the influence of the need for achievement in thought and planning. Work is motivated by both intrinsic and extrinsic influences, with intrinsic motives more likely to produce a state of flow.

CHAPTER REVIEW

Summary

Motivation and emotion share a common focus on what "moves" behavior. Emotions are complex patterns of bodily arousal, brain activity, subjective feelings, and cognitive interpretations. Emotions are expressed in facial and bodily cues as well as emotional action. Early evolutionary theory credits emotions in both humans and animals with promoting survival. Two models argue that a few basic emotions, present at birth, are later diversified and blended to make possible a wide range of feelings. Emotions serve several basic functions, including arousing action, organizing experience, and regulating social interaction. Historically, psychological theories have sought to explain emotions in terms of some combination of bodily

arousal, action, and cognitive interpretation. Emotional expressions vary among individuals, making it difficult to interpret facial cues or detect deception reliably, but cross-cultural researchers have identified seven expressions that seem to be universally recognizable.

Motivation is a dynamic concept used to describe the processes that direct behavior. Methods of study examine the strength and form of motivated behavior, as well as whether an organism will seek to overcome obstacles in pursuit of a goal. Theories of motivation have explained motivated action in terms of instincts, drives, arousal, humanistic concepts such as a hierarchy of needs, and social-cognitive factors such as perception and context.

Hunger is the most studied of all drives, and eating appears to be a function of a complicated set of influences, including brain processes, peripheral cues, and social influences. Sexual behavior in nonhumans is motivated by a drive to reproduce, but in humans its causes and forms are as variable as individual people. Early research by Alfred Kinsey and later research by Masters and Johnson have helped to document the realities of human sexual response. Much of sexual behavior may rely on how well people learn or conform to sexual "scripts," with errors and infractions resulting in violence such as rape. While political and cultural controversy abound over the origins of homosexuality, research to date on sexual orientation fails to support conclusively that gay men and lesbians are making a lifestyle choice, following a genetic predisposition, or responding to early psychological conflicts and disorders. Achievement and enjoyment of work can be driven by future-oriented motivations. Different individuals and societies promote different agendas for achievement. In the absence of external reward, one's activities are motivated by an intrinsic level of motivation; too much extrinsic reinforcement, however, can undermine intrinsic motivation.

Section Reviews

Understanding Emotion

Be sure to *Check Your Recall* by reviewing the summary of this section on page 293.

Key Terms
emotion (p. 287)
lateralization of emotion (p. 289)
emotion wheel (p. 292)

Names to Know
Robert Plutchik (p. 292)
Carroll Izard (p. 292)

Exploring Emotion

Be sure to *Check Your Recall* by reviewing the summary of this section on page 304

Key Terms
biocultural model of emotion (p. 297)
James-Lange theory of emotion (p. 299)
Cannon-Bard theory of emotion (p. 300)
two-factor theory of emotion (p. 300)
Lazarus-Schachter theory of emotion (p. 300)

Names to Know
Robert Levenson (p. 297)
William James (p. 298)
Walter Cannon (p. 299)
Richard Lazarus (p. 300)
Stanley Schachter (p. 300)
Paul Ekman (p. 301)

Understanding Motivation

Be sure to *Check Your Recall* by reviewing the summary of this section on page 309.

Key Terms
motivation (p. 304)
drive (p. 306)
motive (p. 306)
incentives (p. 308)
incentive motivation (p. 308)

Names to Know
Edward C. Tolman (p. 307)
C. J. Warden (p. 309)

Theories of Motivation

Be sure to *Check Your Recall* by reviewing the summary of this section on page 315.

Key Terms
fixed-action patterns (p. 310)
optimal arousal level (p. 312)
Yerkes-Dodson law (p. 312)
deficiency motivation (p. 312)
growth motivation (p. 312)
needs hierarchy (p. 313)
Thematic Apperception Test (TAT) (p. 314)

locus of control (p. 315)
locus-of-control orientation (p. 315)

Names to Know
William James (p. 310)
Sigmund Freud (p. 310)
Abraham Maslow (p. 312)
Julian Rotter (p. 315)

Motivated Behaviors

Be sure to *Check Your Recall* by reviewing the summary of this section on page 326.

Key Terms
critical set point (p. 318)
sexual scripts (p. 320)
need for achievement (*n Ach*) (p. 324)
intrinsic motivation (p. 325)
extrinsic motivation (p. 325)
flow (p. 325)

Names to Know
Alfred Kinsey (p. 318)
William Masters (p. 319)
Virginia Johnson (p. 319)
Simon LeVay (p. 323)
Henry Murray (p. 324)
David McClelland (p. 324)
Mark Lepper (p. 325)

REVIEW TEST

Chapter 8: Motivation and Emotion

For each of the following items, choose the single correct or best answer. The correct answers, explanations, and page references appear in Appendix B.

1. Research on the neural mechanisms affecting emotions indicates that emotional experiences and expressions are activated and controlled by the _____.
   a. limbic system
   b. reticular activating system
   c. autonomic nervous system
   d. all of the above.

2. According to the _____ theory of emotion, an emotional stimulus simultaneously produces two reactions in the individual: physical arousal and the subjective experience of emotion.
   a. Darwinian evolutionary adaptation
   b. James-Lange bodily reaction
   c. Cannon-Bard central neural processing
   d. Lazarus-Schachter cognitive arousal

3. Which of the following is *not* a good guideline for someone who wishes to determine whether another person is lying?
   a. If the other person looks you in the eye, he or she is probably telling the truth.
   b. People who are lying about their emotions, rather than about information, will show signs of greater arousal, perhaps by fidgeting nervously.
   c. People who are lying about facts, rather than their feelings, may pause longer in their speech in an effort to make their stories seem honest.
   d. It is easier for you to tell whether a friend is lying to you than a stranger.

4. Psychologists have used the concept of motivation for five basic purposes. Which of the following is *not* one of them?
   a. to identify the instincts causing human social behavior
   b. to infer private states from public acts
   c. to explain perseverance despite adversity
   d. to assign responsibility for actions

5. Very different theorists such as William James and Sigmund Freud all shared a common conviction that human motivation is best explained by the concept of _____, although they differed in their interpretations of this concept.
   a. drive
   b. arousal
   c. control
   d. instinct

6. In Abraham Maslow's needs hierarchy, your desire to have friends and express your love for others is considered part of your _____ needs.
   a. safety
   b. attachment
   c. biological
   d. esteem

7. Which of the following statements about hunger and eating does *not* accurately represent current thinking among psychological researchers?
   a. Hunger is primarily influenced and initiated by peripheral bodily cues.
   b. The central neural mechanisms involved in eating are located in the hypothalamus.
   c. While everyone has a set point that determines a sense of satiety, individuals differ in where that set point is "set."
   d. Despite the biological link between eating and hunger, many social and environmental cues can trigger or discourage eating.

8. The sexual behavior of humans is distinct from that of nonhuman animals because, for humans, sex is _____.
   a. more predictable and less variable
   b. essential to survival
   c. not influenced by other motivations
   d. far more dependent on psychological factors

9. Which of the following describes what a subject is asked to do to complete the TAT?
   a. Tell or write a story about each of a series of pictures.
   b. Examine an ambiguous stimulus and list the objects and ideas you associate with it.
   c. Draw in the missing lines in a series of incomplete sketches.
   d. Fill in the blanks among a set of self-descriptive written statements.

10. People who are high in the need for achievement have been found to be more likely to _____.
    a. be upwardly mobile
    b. persist in impossible tasks
    c. work independently
    d. all of the above.

IF YOU'RE INTERESTED . . .

Ackerman, D. (1994). *A natural history of love*. New York: Random House.

Fascinating reading about a basic emotional experience by poet Ackerman. *A Natural History* looks at the history of love, ancient and modern ideas about how it influences behavior, its evolution and biochemistry, the intertwining of sex and love, courtship, and varieties of love—including love of children, strangers, and pets.

Bear, The. (1989) Directed by Jean Jacques Annaud; starring Douce, Bart, Tcheky Karyo, Jack Wallace, Andre Lacombe.

An orphaned grizzly cub and the adult male Kodiak bear who becomes his protector must survive and elude hunters in late 19th-century British Columbia. An award-winning film, based on the American novel *The Grizzly King* by James Oliver Curwood. A stunning and moving film, probably the best-ever cinematic presentation of wild animals' motivations and emotions—and humans' difficulty in understanding them.

Everything You Always Wanted to Know About Sex (But Were Afraid to Ask). (Video: 1972, color, 87 min.). Directed by Woody Allen; starring Woody Allen, Lou Jacobi, Louise Lasser, Tony Randall, Lynn Redgrave, Burt Reynolds, Gene Wilder.

A very silly, but in places very funny, film spoofing the overly serious tone of the book of the same name by Dr. David Reuben (but resembling the book *only* in occasional question-and-answer format), and on a larger scale spoofing Americans' hypocritical and moralizing attitudes about sex—even as we are admittedly so fascinated by it.

Goleman, D. (1995). *Emotional intelligence*. New York: Bantam Books.

Daniel Goleman, award-winning behavioral science reporter for the *New York Times* and former editor of *Psychology Today*, carefully documents the many forms, factors, and expressions of human emotion, including appropriate emotions and self-control, temperament, family and relationships, and whether (and how) emotional intelligence can be taught.

Hirschmann, J. R., & Munter, C. H. (1995). *When women stop hating their bodies*. New York: Fawcett Columbine.

Subtitled "Freeing Yourself from Food and Weight Obsession," this book explores how the origins of many women's (and girls') addictions to diets and weight loss lie in their learned contempt for their own bodies and their desire to achieve an impossible "perfect" body. The solutions, the authors argue, are found in abandoning mindless acceptance of fashions or attitudes that suggest real bodies are somehow flawed and ugly, and instead cultivating a solid sense of self-esteem based on realism, self-acceptance, and self-love.

Masson, J. M., & McCarthy, S. (1995). *When elephants weep: The emotional lives of animals*. New York: Delacorte Press.

A manifesto and casebook by former psychoanalyst Masson and biologist McCarthy, detailing the persuasive evidence of feelings—from fear and greed to love and altruism—among nonhuman species. Both scholarly and personal, a touching and affecting work that will forever change the way you view your world, your diet, and what it means to be both human and humane.

Stacey, M. (1994). *Consumed*. New York: Simon & Schuster.

A fascinating tour of the meanings of food to modern Americans: a chronology of cuisines; "healthy" obsessions and catchwords ("fiber," "low fat"); food fads (oat bran, junk food); and stories of "food designers," obsessive dieters, and scientists who feed pastry to rats. A thought-provoking essay on Americans' view of food not as sustenance or sensuality, but demon or angel.

Tannahill, R. (1992). *Sex in history*. New York: Scarborough House.

An illustrated "treasure trove" (according to the *Sunday Times* [London]) of historical information, history, cultural influences, customs, and rituals developed around sex worldwide. Fascinating reading not only about sex but about the origins of ideas and ideals of romantic love.

Thomas, E. M. (1993). *The hidden life of dogs*. New York: Simon & Schuster.

Thomas, E. M. (1994). *The tribe of tiger: Cats and their culture*. New York: Simon & Schuster.

Elizabeth Marshall Thomas's two best selling works on our favorite companion animals, exploring the similarities and contrasts between domestic species and wild animals, as well as debunking many myths about the personalities, motives, and emotions of dogs and cats.

Weinrich, J. D. (1987). *Sexual landscapes: Why we are what we are, why we love whom we love*. New York: Charles Scribner's Sons.

Provocative and sensible review of historical and scientific research on topics including sexual orientation and bisexuality, sexual taboos, pornography, sissies and tomboys, and the power of sexual arousal in everyday life and identity.

CHAPTER 9

Stress, Health, and Well-Being

Lucy went to the hospital to visit a neighbor who had suffered a broken hip. Instead of a sterile white-walled corridor, the first thing Lucy saw when the elevator doors opened at the third floor was a clown in full costume, sporting an enormous orange nose, dancing down the hall pushing a colorfully decorated cart. In a hospital? The clown stopped in front of Lucy, bowed, and then somersaulted to the nurses' station. A cluster of patients, most of them in wheelchairs or on crutches, cheered at the clown's antics. When she asked for directions, Lucy was told that her friend was presently in the "Humor Room," where the comic film Blazing Saddles was just about to start.

Today humor is recognized as playing a respectable—and perhaps vital—role in hospital treatment, especially since the writer **Norman Cousins** explained how he had used humor in his own recovery from a debilitating and usually incurable disease of the connective tissue. A long-time literary magazine editor, Cousins decided to supplement his regular medical therapy with a steady diet of Marx brothers movies from the 1930s and 1940s, and with clips of the Candid Camera television program of the 1950s and 1960s. Though he never claimed that laughter alone effected his cure, Cousins is best remembered for his passionate support of the notion that, if negative emotions can cause distress, then positive emotions can enhance the healing process (Cousins, 1979, 1983, 1989).

The idea that humor can help in the recovery process caught on even before it had much empirical support. Today, hospitals in Houston, Los Angeles, and Honolulu provide patients with videotapes of comedy films. "Laugh wagons" carrying humorous books and tapes roll through the halls of health centers across the country. At a Catholic hospital in Texas, the nuns are expected to tell at least one joke a day (Cousins, 1989). Allen Funt, creator of Candid Camera, has set up a foundation to distribute his funny videos free to researchers, hospitals, and individual patients, so that humor therapy will be used to treat distress and illness and the effects of such therapy can be studied.

What are the medical benefits of humor? Cousins's doctor found that, according to one measure, his tissue inflammation decreased after only a few moments of robust laughter. This decrease in inflammation was also reflected in Cousins's ability to enjoy two hours of pain-free sleep after 10 minutes of hearty laughing (Cousins, 1989). Stanford psychiatric researcher William Fry, Jr., compares laughter to "stationary jogging," noting that laughing brings oxygen to the *blood very quickly by increasing respiration, heart rate, and blood circulation (Fry, 1986). Some biochemical changes, including reductions in the stress hormone cortisol, have also been detected (Berk, 1989). Salivary immunoglobulin A, thought to protect the body against certain viruses, increased significantly in people who viewed humorous videotapes for 30 minutes. In one study, people who said they used humor to deal with difficult situations in everyday life had the highest baseline levels of this protective substance (Dillon & Totten, 1989).*

People who must cope with devastating illness or trauma may find humor—a recognition of some of life's absurdities—a natural way to respond to their difficult circumstances. Former Saturday Night Live comedienne Julia Sweeney reported that she relied on "black humor" to get through first the illness and death of her brother from lymphatic cancer, and then her own diagnosis and successful treatment for cervical cancer: "We'd answer the phone, 'House of cancer,'" she told one interviewer (TV Guide, 1995). Such tactics may seem insensitive or shocking, but they acknowledge the reality of the challenges facing us—and can provide the positive energy, sense of control, and perspective necessary to cope (Lefcourt et al., 1995).

Introduction

The writings of Norman Cousins significantly enhanced the public's awareness of the relatively new field of **psychoneuroimmunology (PNI),** *the study of healing interactions between brain, body, emotions, and the immune system.* Researchers hope that advances in PNI will explain the physiological underpinnings of laughter's health-enhancing effect. Feelings, stress, illness, and health are all intertwined in the approach that uses humor to treat physical ailments. As we examined in the last chapter, emotions are the touchstones of human experience, engaging our attention and involving us in the surprises and challenges of life. But many of our emotions are negative, such as fear, anxiety, guilt, grief, and sadness. So while some emotions uplift the human spirit, others depress it—perhaps necessarily slow it down, control it, or rechannel it—as we deal with the harsher realities of living.

If the demands on our biological and psychological functioning are excessive, we may become overwhelmed and unable to deal with the stressors in our daily lives. This chapter begins with an examination of the stressors that challenge us physically and psychologically, and goes on to review the key elements of a coping strategy. Finally, we will accentuate the positive with a look at health, happiness, and well-being.

Stress

Our modern industrialized society sets a rapid, hectic, treadmill pace for our lives. We often live and try to work in crowded conditions, have too many demands placed on our time, worry about our uncertain futures, hold frustrating jobs (or no jobs at all), and have little time for family or fun. These are some of the circumstances that create stress in modern living. Wouldn't we be better off without stress? Surprisingly, the answer is no: A stress-free life would offer no challenge—no difficulties to surmount, no new fields to master, and since there would be no changes to adapt to, no reason to sharpen our wits or improve our abilities. In simplest terms, an unstressed organism is an unmotivated organism, taking no action and reaping no benefits of living.

The problem is not stress, but *excessive* stress. Basic stress is an unavoidable part of living. Every organism faces challenges from its external environment and from its personal needs; these challenges are life's problems that the organism must solve to survive and thrive. Psychologists define **stress** *as the pattern of specific and general responses made by an organism to stimulus events that disturb the organism's equilibrium and tax or exceed its ability to cope.* The stress response is triggered by a **stressor,** *an internal or external stimulus event that places a demand on an organism for some kind of adaptive response.*

Have you ever wondered why some people who experience stressful events seem to suffer few or no negative effects, while others are seriously upset by even minor hassles? For example, while stuck in an endless traffic jam, you may notice that some drivers calmly daydream or listen to their radios, while others frantically hit their horns or crane their necks for a better view of the obstruction. This difference can be found in people's responses to stress because the effects of a stressor depend both on what it is and what it *means.* Stress is a personal matter. How much stress we experience is determined by the quality and intensity of the stressor, how it is interpreted, the resources available to deal with the stressor, and the consequent difficulty of meeting the demands placed on us.

An individual's response to stress is a diverse combination of reactions—physiological, behavioral, emotional, and cognitive. How do psychologists study such a complex stress response? To better understand the concept of stress, researchers have tried to identify its specific components and their interactions. Figure 9.1 diagrams the elements of the stress process—stressors, stress, cognitive appraisal (mental evaluation of the situation), resources, and stress responses.

Modern society creates a stressful environment whether we are working of playing.

FIGURE 9.1   A Model of Stress ■ Cognitive appraisal of the stress situation interacts with the stressor and the physical, social, and personal resources available for dealing with the stressor. Individuals respond to threats on various levels—physical, behavioral, emotional, and cognitive. Some responses are adaptive and others are maladaptive or even lethal.

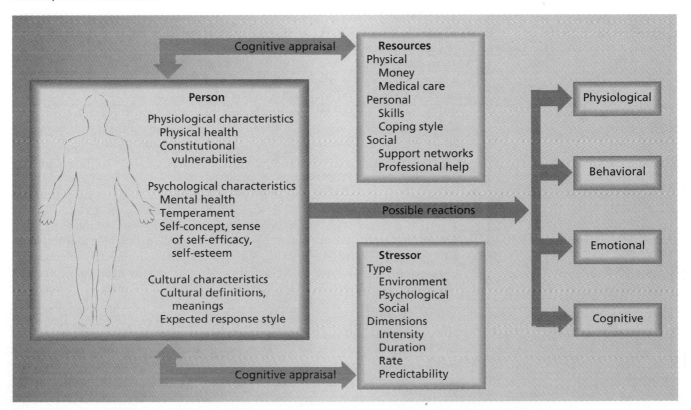

Sources of Stress

Everyone faces stress. Our patterns of responding to stress are a part of our evolutionary heritage, the legacy of those early humans who survived mortal dangers by responding quickly and well. Modern life is complex but much safer than it used to be for our species. Millennia ago, life was simpler in some ways for our primitive ancestors, but the threats to their survival were more likely to be lethal. Our ancestors needed to be able to make quick decisions and take effective action on three mortal threats in particular: starvation, exposure to the elements, and victimization by attack (whether by human or nonhuman predators). These *primitive stressors* required prompt and appropriate action: finding and storing food; seeking or constructing safe shelter; fleeing one's attacker—or making an effective counterattack. Many aspects of the human stress response reflect the body's inherited tendency to become quickly aroused to take certain physical actions that have some impact on the environment.

But the recurrent stressors most of us face today are seldom as clear-cut as our ancestors' fears of starving, freezing in the cold, or being eaten by a beast. The modern counterparts of primitive stressors might include losing your job or not getting a raise; failing to pay your power bill on time; or being insulted by a competitor—all unpleasant and arousing, but not immediately life threatening. In fact, modern stressors are many and complex, though they may trigger many of the same responses our ancestors made. When the power company threatens to cut off your power or your boss criticizes your work, you may feel an urge to flee or fight—but the "old remedies" don't work with the new problems. Today's stressors are more likely to challenge our sense of self-esteem than our physical survival. In this section we will review five categories of modern stressors: life changes; catastrophe; societal stressors; burnout; and hassles. After that, we will examine just how our bodies and minds react to stress in any form.

Life Changes   Sudden changes in our life situations are at the root of stress for many of us. Although change puts spice in our lives, all change demands some adjustment, and too much change can ruin our health. Even events that we welcome may require major changes in our routines and adaptation to new requirements. Recent studies reveal that one of the most desired changes in a married couple's life, the birth of their first child, is also a source of major stress, contributing to reduced marital satisfaction for many couples (Cowan & Cowan, 1988). On the other hand, stress may result more from anticipating decisions than from making and living with them. For example, a review of research on the psychological responses to abortion reveals that distress is generally greatest *before* the abortion. Severe distress is low for women following the abortion of an unwanted pregnancy, especially if they have had social support for their decision (Adler et al., 1990).

Some researchers have viewed stress as resulting from exposure to major *life changes* or *life events* (Dohrenwend & Dohrenwend, 1974; Dohrenwend & Shrout, 1985; Holmes & Rahe, 1967). Sometimes people can absorb stress and keep on functioning. Their reactions depend on their resources and the contexts in which stress occurs. If you have the money, time, and friends to help you pick up and go on after a disruption, you will certainly fare better than someone for whom more bad news is the last straw in a series of progressive setbacks they have faced alone.

The influence of major life changes on subsequent mental and physical health has been a source of considerable research. It started with the development of the *Social Readjustment Rating Scale* (SRRS), a simple scale for rating the degree of adjustment required by the various life changes that many people experience. To develop the scale, adults from all walks of life identified those life changes that applied to them, and rated the amount of readjustment each one required (Holmes & Rahe, 1967). *The degree of stress associated with different kinds of change experienced in a given period was measured in* **life-change units (LCU).** To measure your current stress level (and risk for stress-related problems) on the SRRS, you would merely total the LCU ratings accumulated in recent life experiences. Assess Yourself: The Student Stress Scale shows a modification of this scale for college students. What is your latest LCU rating? Compare it with classmates' ratings and consider whether among you and your classmates there seem to be relationships between life changes and well-being.

Early studies of life changes found support for a relationship between medical problems and the amount of readjustment required in life. Patients with heart disease, for example, had higher LCU scores than healthy subjects. Other studies reported that life stress increases a person's overall susceptibility to illness (Holmes & Masuda, 1974), and LCU values are also high for some time after an illness (Rahe & Arthur, 1978).

Assess Yourself

The Student Stress Scale

The Student Stress Scale on page 336 represents an adaptation of Holmes and Rahe's Social Readjustment Rating Scale. Each event is given a score that represents the amount of readjustment a person has to make in life as a result of that change. People with scores of 300 and higher have a high health risk. People scoring between 150 and 300 points have about a 50–50 chance of serious health change within two years. People scoring below 150 have a 1 in 3 chance of serious health change. Calculate your total Life Change Score (in LCU) for the past month, and then repeat the process every month. Keep track of *stress-related illnesses and setbacks,* such as physical problems (flu, colds, headaches), emotional changes (increased irritability, worrying), and behavioral difficulties (insomnia, relationship problems). Do you notice any connection between your LCU score and stress-related problems in that or subsequent periods of time?

MY 1ST TOTAL _____ DATE: _____
Notes on subsequent stress-related problems:

_____

MY 2ND TOTAL _____ DATE: _____
Notes on subsequent stress-related problems:

_____

MY 3RD TOTAL _____ DATE: _____
Notes on subsequent stress-related problems:

_____

MY 4TH TOTAL _____ DATE: _____
Notes on subsequent stress-related problems:

_____

Event	Life Change Units
Death of a close family member	100
Death of a close friend	73
Divorce between parents	65
Jail term	63
Major personal injury or illness	63
Marriage	58
Being fired from job	50
Failing an important course	47
Change in health of family member	45
Pregnancy	45
Sex problems	44
Serious argument with close friend	40
Change in financial status	39
Change of major	39
Trouble with parents	39
New boyfriend or girlfriend	38
Increased workload at school	37
Outstanding personal achievement	36
First quarter/semester in college	35
Change in living conditions	31
Serious argument with instructor	30
Lower grades than expected	29
Change in sleeping habits	29
Change in social activities	29
Change in eating habits	28
Chronic car trouble	26
Change in number of family get-togethers	26
Too many missed classes	25
Change of college	24
Dropping of more than one class	23
Minor traffic violations	20

The Stress of Loss What do most of the top ten stressful life events listed in the Student Stress Scale have in common? Most represent different kinds of loss—of loved ones, family stability, freedom, income, and even hope. It could even be argued that loss is the ultimate and basic stressor, limiting options, ending dreams, making the future unimaginable. Cultural anthropologists have found that rituals for dealing with loss, such as funeral ceremonies, are universal expressions of the need to cope. But some losses, while life-changing, may be too minor or personal to merit a public ritual, such as losing your car keys—or your virginity. Societies vary in the types of losses they recognize with public ceremonies. Although divorces require public legal action, announcements, and arrangements for property division and custody, nonmarital breakups have no such script or structure.

If you suffer through the termination of a romantic relationship, your loss will not be public knowledge unless you or your ex-partner disclose it to others. No lawyer appears to assist you in dividing up your books or CDs, no judge rules on which of you gets "custody" of your friends. Friends may even feel they must choose sides, or avoid acknowledging your loss altogether. Relationships scholars have found patterns in some nonmarital breakups (Hatfield & Rapson, 1993; Hill et al., 1976):

- Among heterosexual couples, women are more likely than men to terminate an unsatisfactory relationship.

- Among college students, breakups often coincide with planned breaks in the academic schedule: the beginning and end of summer break, and the winter holiday break. (*Note:* Forewarned is forearmed! Be aware that such seasonal changes can predict a breakup. Prepare yourself for such a possibility and consider how you might respond to it.)
- Regardless of who "really" initiated the breakup, when asked whose idea it was to part ways, *both* partners claim to have made the decision (perhaps in an effort to save face or self-esteem).

Although nonmarital breakups are difficult to study because they do not normally become part of an accessible record (unlike marriages, which are recorded in public documents), researchers now know that a breakup is not so much a life "event" as a *process*. Researcher **Steve Duck** (1982) suggests that the termination of a relationship progresses through part or all of four phases:

1. An *intrapsychic phase* (from Latin *intra*, "within," and Greek *psyche*, "mind"), in which one partner feels dissatisfied within his or her own mind and privately considers whether to end or exit the relationship.
2. The *dyadic phase*, begun when the unhappy partner makes his or her dissatisfaction known to the other member of the dyad (couple), and they discuss whether to reconcile or part.
3. The *social phase*, when partners make separation arrangements and inform their friends and families about the breakup and its causes and likely effects.
4. Finally, the *grave-dressing phase*, in which the now ended relationship is mourned, and both ex-partners reconstruct their ideas and memories of the relationship's history and demise.

As we will review further in a later section on coping in healthy ways with stressors and problems, it helps to make sense of your loss and to discuss your "breakup story" with those you confide in. Until you reach a new sense of life

Catastrophic events, like the Oklahoma City bombing, are particularly stressful because they are life-threatening, out of our control, unpredictable, and difficult to explain.

without your former partner, however, the loss and disruption you experience will be significant sources of stress in your life.

Catastrophe   When an event is negative, uncontrollable, unpredictable, or ambiguous, the experience is more stressful (Glass, 1977). These conditions hold especially true in the case of *catastrophic events.*

The 1989 World Series was about to begin at San Francisco's Candlestick Park. As people settled into their seats, the band began to play. Suddenly, the entire stadium started to shake violently, the lights went out, and the scoreboard turned black. Sixty-thousand fans fell silent. They had just experienced a major earthquake. Elsewhere in the city, fires erupted, a bridge collapsed, highways were crushed—and people were dying.

Shortly after the quake, a team of research psychologists began to study how people coped with the catastrophe. Nearly 800 people were chosen randomly from the San Francisco area and from several comparison cities some distance away. These subjects were interviewed at either 1, 2, 3, 6, 8, 16, 28, or 50 weeks after the quake. Subjects completed a ten-minute phone survey about their thoughts, social behavior, and health. Three distinct phases of stress reactions were found among the San Francisco residents. In the *emergency phase* (first 3 to 4 weeks), people's social contacts, anxiety, and obsessive thoughts about the quake increased. The *inhibition phase* (next 3 to 8 weeks) was characterized by a sudden decline in talking and thinking about the quake, but indirect, stress-related reactions increased, such as arguments and earthquake dreams. In the *adaptation phase* (from two months on), the psychological effects of the catastrophe were over for most people. However, as many as 20 percent of San Francisco area residents remained distressed about the quake a year later (Pennebaker & Harber, 1991).

A great deal of research on the physical and psychological effects of catastrophic events has been conducted (Baum, 1990). Researchers have found that response to disasters tends to occur in five stages (see Cohen & Ahearn, 1980):

- First, there is typically a period of shock, confusion, and even *psychic numbness,* during which people cannot fully comprehend what has happened.
- In the next phase, people engage in *automatic action,* trying to respond to the disaster. They may behave adaptively but have little awareness of their actions and later show poor recall of these experiences. Depending on the nature of the crisis, numbness may quickly give way to automatic action, or it may linger and paralyze victims into dangerous inaction. For example, when an earthquake shattered the city of Kobe, Japan, in January 1995, the citizens' shock and lack of preparedness prevented timely rescues. This delay in automatic action was later blamed for many of the almost 6000 related deaths.
- In the third stage, people often feel great accomplishment and even a positive sense of communal *effort* toward a shared purpose. Also in this phase, people feel weary and are aware that they are using up their reserves of energy. This phase builds on automatic action, but requires conscious planning and collaboration to prevent people from losing hope and giving up.
- During the next phase, people experience a *letdown;* their energy is depleted and the impact of the tragedy is finally comprehended and felt emotionally. For example, in recent years victims of hurricane damage have felt abandoned when, weeks after the natural disasters occurred, the rest of the country has turned their attention to other news events and seemingly forgotten about the continuing state of emergency in the stricken communities.

■ An extended final period of *recovery* follows, as people adapt to the changes brought about by the disaster. A flood may leave a small town so changed that some businesses are permanently shut down, while others move in and change the appearance and social activity of the post-flood community.

Knowledge of how people typically respond to catastrophe can provide a model to help predict what will happen the next time disaster strikes. This model enables rescue workers to anticipate and help victims deal with the problems that arise. Responses to events such as floods, tornadoes, airplane crashes, and factory explosions have all been shown to follow this model of disaster reactions.

Societal Stressors   How do overpopulation, crime, economic recession, pollution, AIDS, and the threat of nuclear war affect our mental well-being? Surveys of the attitudes of students throughout the United States have uncovered a general disquiet and uneasiness about the future (Beardslee & Mack, 1983). Studies in the last decade have shown a significant increase in junior high and senior high school students' expressions of fear, helplessness, and anger toward the adult generation. Adults are also worried about the state of the world, but they are also affected by the more immediate concerns of employment and economic security. According to research on the effects of the American economic recession in the early 1970s, many stress-related problems increase when the economy is in a downswing: admissions to mental hospitals, infant mortality, suicide, and deaths from alcohol-related diseases and cardiovascular problems all increase (Brenner, 1976).

Unemployed men have been found to report more symptoms, such as depression, anxiety, and worries about health, than do those men who are employed—but these symptoms disappear when the men are subsequently reemployed (Liem & Rayman, 1982). According to a recent investigation, high blood pressure among African Americans (long thought to be primarily genetic) appears to be a consequence of chronic stress caused by low status jobs, limited education, fruitless job seeking, and low socioeconomic status (Klag et al., 1991). Hypertension results from frustrations in efforts to achieve basic life goals; there is no current evidence that links it to genetic factors.

The times and circumstances into which we are born may deal us particularly difficult cards to play. Imagine for a moment the stress experienced by most people in Central Europe after the fall of Communism and the end of the Soviet Union's control of their lives. Despite the suppression of individual initiative and the constant looming presence of police surveillance, most citizens enjoyed at least a predictable, stable status quo. With the transition to democratic government and capitalism have come personal freedom and new responsibilities—but also unemployment, loss of security, increased crime and violence (Myers, 1996). Will a child born into this post-Communist generation experience more or less challenge from societal stressors than did her parents? Societal stressors are so large, and individual resources so comparatively puny, that you may wonder if it is worthwhile even to try to deal with the problems of government, public health, or the environment. But the more you learn about stress management, the better you can anticipate and respond to the challenges of your own lifetime.

Burnout   What will your life's work be? What kinds of tasks will you be engaged in? More Americans today have jobs connected with providing *services* than with making *products*. This creates a unique modern stress risk, because services require working with and for people—something most of us already do in our "private time." And unlike a worker who grows apples or builds CD players, the service professional cannot always point to concrete evidence of his or her productivity. The daily routine of nurses, teachers, law enforcement officers, emergency room staff, and other human services professionals includes dealing with struggle, pain, illness, poverty, and death. The feedback they get may be invisible or consistently negative. The complexity of clients' and patients' lives means that such workers may never get a sense of closure or "finishedness," much less success.

The special type of emotional stress experienced by these professional health and welfare practitioners has been termed *burnout* by **Christina Maslach**, a leading researcher on this widespread problem. **Burnout** *is a syndrome of emotional exhaustion, depersonalization, and reduced personal accomplishment often experienced by workers in professions that demand high-intensity interpersonal contact with patients, clients, or the public.* With job burnout, health practitioners begin to lose their caring and concern for patients and may come to treat them in detached and even dehumanized ways. These practitioners begin to feel bad about themselves and worry that they are failures. Burnout is correlated with greater absenteeism and job turnover, impaired job performance, poor relations with coworkers, family problems, and poor personal health (Leiter & Maslach, 1988; Maslach, 1982; Schaufeli, et al., 1993).

One's personal life and relationships can also create great risk for burnout, so that one's friends, spouse, and children are seen as unreasonably demanding and draining of one's dwindling energy. For example, women who work outside the home now make up a majority of mothers of young children—yet few reliable changes have taken place *inside* the home to accommodate the needs of working mothers. Most household labor, especially connected with meals and child care, is still regarded as the "responsibility" of wives. Consequently women with jobs as well as families may find their time divided

between a hostile work environment where they are regarded as less valuable than male workers and an unsupportive home where they labor hard for no pay or appreciation (Long & Kahn, 1993). Burned-out spouses find their marriages unsatisfactory, and burned-out parents find less—perhaps no—joy in their children. Are traditional power structures and divisions of labor so valuable that partners, parents, and children must suffer to keep such unrealistic arrangements in place?

Several social and situational factors affect the occurrence and level of burnout and, by implication, suggest ways of preventing or minimizing it. For example, among health care professionals, the quality of the patient-practitioner interaction is greatly affected by the *number* of patients for whom a practitioner is providing care: the greater the number, the greater the cognitive, sensory, and emotional overload. Another factor is the amount of *direct contact* with patients. Longer work hours with continuous direct contact with patients or clients are correlated with greater burnout, especially when the nature of the contact is difficult and upsetting, such as in interactions with patients who are dying or who are verbally abusive. The emotional strain of such prolonged contact can be eased by a work schedule that provides chances for a practitioner to withdraw temporarily from such high-stress situations. For example, team contact could replace individual contact, relieving team members of overload in intense cases. Additionally, team members and other coworkers can develop a program for giving positive feedback to colleagues for their efforts.

Similarly, the spouses, friends, and family of burned-out parents might collaborate in creating a team approach to providing child care services, regularly or in emergencies. Parents should collaborate on setting priorities for essential household chores, and reassign important chores on the basis of time availability and ability to contribute rather than according to status or income-related power. For example, if a husband earns more money than his wife but never works in the evenings, he can take charge of those chores that must be done later in the day, when his wife is more likely to be called to work late. As we shall explore in more detail later, few individuals can cope with modern stressors like burnout alone; most of us must rely on the support and fairness of those we are close to in order to make our lives better. It is essential to recognize that our individual lives work best when embedded in a meaningful social context—interactions and relationships with others whom we can count on.

Hassles To what extent do minor irritations pile up and become stressors that affect your health? One view of stress holds that an accumulation of small frustrations more often leads to stress than do big, infrequent jolts of change (Weinberger et al., 1987). If you interpret these *hassles* as salient, harmful, or threatening to your well-being, they affect you more than you might imagine (Lazarus, 1984b). Some people may be prone to see the world as hassle filled. One study showed that college students with a more pessimistic outlook reported experiencing both more hassles and poorer health (Dykema et al., 1995).

In a diary study, a group of white, middle-class, middle-aged men and women kept track of their daily hassles over a one-year period. They also recorded major life changes and physical symptoms. A clear relationship emerged between hassles and health problems: the more frequent and intense the hassles people reported, the poorer was their health, both physical and mental (Lazarus, 1981; 1984b). As daily hassles go down, well-being goes up (Chamberlain & Zika, 1990).

Although daily stressors have been shown to affect one's mood immediately, people habituate to them so that the negative effects do not carry over to the next day. The exception is in the case of interpersonal conflicts (Bolger et al., 1989). As you probably know, a problem in a close relationship—a dispute with a friend or a misunderstanding with a romantic partner—is harder to resolve than frustrations with objects or strangers. These relational stressors threaten to recur until they are dealt with effectively.

Some scholars (such as Gilligan, 1982) feel that problems with close relationships are more stressful for females than for males. Since females place a greater value on "concern for others," they become stressed when their concerns are misunderstood in problematic relationships. ASK YOURSELF the following questions:

- Does this gender analysis fit your own personal experiences?
- How severe are the hassles in your life? Compare your assessment with the rankings (1 = high, 4 = low) of the four groups outlined in Table 9.1 (students, mothers, general community members, and the elderly).

Some life choices lead to prolonged periods of adjustment and dealing with hassles. One example is relocation to an environment where the physical and social settings are entirely new to you. As reviewed in Cultural Context: Culture Shock, traveling and living abroad can provide great excitement and education, but also prove very demanding in terms of day-to-day adaptation.

The Physical Consequences of Stress

When you are stressed, you know it: you *feel* different physically—agitated or energized, ready to act, worried that you will not be able to deal with whatever is threatening your safety or peace of mind. The body's efforts to deal with threats and adapt to change involve physical responses that are sometimes costly to health, or to one's readiness to respond quickly to the next stressor. In this section we review the major physical effects of the stress response: arousal; the fight-or-flight response; the body's generalized adaptation to stress; and the impact of stress on immune function.

Arousal   The physical effects of stress begin with conditions that *arouse* bodily responses and efforts to adapt. This arousal may be sudden and brief, as when a loud noise causes you to gasp but you are relieved to recognize it

TABLE 9.1	SEVERITY OF HASSLES AS PERCEIVED AND RANKED BY FOUR GROUPS			
In these New Zealand samples, each hassle type differed significantly in severity among the four groups. The ranked perceived severity was almost reversed for student and elderly groups, with time pressures most important and neighborhood and health pressures least important for students, while the latter were the most important sources of hassles and time pressures the least for the elderly. Note the hassle priorities for these mothers, who had one or more young children at home and no household help.				
Hassle Type	Students (n = 61)	Mothers (n = 94)	Community (n = 20)	Elderly (n = 50)
Time pressure	1	2	3	4
Future security	2	4	1	3
Finances	3	1	2	4
Household	3	1	2	4
Neighborhood	4	3	2	1
Health	4	3	2	1

CULTURAL CONTEXT

Culture Shock

For people who have strong emotional ties to home, a move from their familiar surroundings can cause stress. Consider a time in your own life when you were away from home and felt discomfort because of your move—whether you were accompanying your family in a relocation, or went away to college. What were your feelings? Did you feel lonely, disconnected from others, frustrated at your inability to satisfy everyday needs, or clumsy and "out-of-place"? Consider the following situations:

1. An 18-year-old Navajo woman from rural Arizona, who had won awards as a high-school basketball player, begins studies at one of the large state universities on an athletic scholarship.
2. An African-American businessman accepts a vice-presidential position in a large company where almost all upper-level executives are male Caucasians.
3. An American college student joins a study-abroad program in Europe.
4. An American businesswoman travels to Japan to establish joint trade agreements for her computer company's marketing division.

All these individuals moved on their own, without others who had long shared their respective support groups. Faced with the everyday need to find food, secure housing, and travel locally, they had only their own resources to help them cope. Often such individuals feel overwhelmed in their new surroundings and experience high levels of stress (Barna, 1991). **Culture shock** *is the term commonly used to describe the stress experienced by people who move to unfamiliar surroundings.*

The term "culture shock" was originally coined to explain the intense experi-

Despite the fact that some aspects of our business and popular culture are shared around the world, you may find that a familiar situation in a foreign country is still quite different from what you are accustomed to at home.

ences of people who found themselves on overseas assignments in roles such as diplomats, international students, technical assistance advisers, or businesspeople (Oberg, 1960). The term has been expanded to include other types of experiences people have when they move across cultural boundaries *within any one country.* Occasionally, culture shock is used to explain reactions to the new and the unfamiliar. Examples include going away to college, getting married, or being forced to go on welfare after years of productive employment.

Irrespective of their circumstances, culture-shocked individuals experience a sense of frustration and helplessness at their inability to meet their everyday needs. They feel lonely and find it hard to meet people and to develop good interpersonal relationships. Victims of culture shock often become suspicious of others

and come to believe that others are "out to get them." People also report a predictable set of physical symptoms. They complain of stomach aches, inability to sleep, diarrhea, headaches, lack of sex drive, general feelings of tiredness, mild depression, and a lack of enthusiasm for life (Furnham & Bochner, 1986).

Many organizations now sponsor "cross-cultural training" programs to help prepare people for life's transitions (Brislin, 1993). One goal is to introduce people to the various experiences they are likely to encounter. Participants in the programs are commonly told that the experiences associated with "culture shock" are normal and are to be expected. Knowledge of what culture shock is, how frequently it is experienced, and effective coping strategies can aid in reducing people's stress.

was just a door slamming. Or arousal may be slow-growing and increasing, as when a developing problem first bothers you, then worries you, and finally disrupts your life with fear and threat. The first example of being briefly frightened illustrates **acute stress,** *a temporary pattern of arousal with a clear onset and offset.* The second case, of lasting and accumulating strain, is an example of **chronic stress,** *a continuous state of arousal persisting over time, in which demands are perceived to be greater than one's resources for dealing with them.* Whether chronic or acute, these states of arousal are expressed on and gathering information to empower ourselves, we become equipped to cope rather than merely defend.

Coping Styles

Researchers have found it helpful to distinguish between two coping strategies: *problem-solving focus,* in which the goal is to confront the problem directly, and *emotion-regulation focus,* in which the goal is to lessen the discomfort associated with the stress (Billings & Moos, 1982; Lazarus & Folkman, 1984). Table 9.2 shows several subcategories of these two basic approaches.

Problem-Focused Coping   Facing up to a problem includes all strategies designed to deal *directly* with the stressor, whether through overt action or through realistic problem-solving activities. We confront a difficult person or run away. We try to win a challenger over with treats or threats. If continually challenged by this person—say, a bully—we might take self-defense training, or notify the "proper authorities." In all these strategies, our focus is on the problem to be dealt with and on the agent that has induced the stress. Such problem-solving efforts are useful for managing *controllable* stressors. Focusing on the problem may lead nowhere, however, if a threat is too big or complex for an individual to control. For example, a single parent stressed by the demands of child care cannot use a "fight-or-flight" strategy to reduce the stress at its source. Instead, she might find ways of caring for and supporting her own health and ability to cope—a shift to *emotion-focused* coping.

Emotion-Focused Coping   The alternative to a problem-focused coping style is useful for managing the impact of the more *uncontrollable* stressors in one's life. If you cannot afford to quit your job or qualify for a different position, for example, you cannot directly control the problem of a critical and unfair boss. But you can take actions that relieve some of your frustration and pressure, so that the impact of the stressful boss is lessened.

TABLE 9.2	TAXONOMY OF COPING STRATEGIES	
Problem-Focused Coping		
Change stressor or one's relationship to it through direct actions and/or problem-solving activities	Fight (destroy, remove, or weaken the threat)	
	Flight (distance oneself from the threat)	
	Seek options to fight or flight (negotiating, bargaining, compromising)	
	Prevent future stress (act to increase one's resistance or decrease strength of anticipated stress)	
Emotion-Focused Coping		
Change self through activities that make one feel better but do not change the stressor	Somatically focused activities (use of drugs, relaxation, biofeedback)	
	Cognitively focused activities (planned distractions, fantasies, thoughts about oneself)	
	Unconscious processes that distort reality and may result in intrapsychic stress	

In emotion-focused coping, the individual does not look for ways to change the external stressful situation; instead, one tries to change one's feelings and thoughts about it. For example, suppose the "bully" in your life is an unidentified neighbor who blasts his stereo loudly through your dormitory or apartment complex. In response to this stressor, instead of becoming futility angry or obsessed, you might shrug your shoulders and remind yourself that intrusive noise is a fact of life for renters, and there's nothing you can do to permanently solve the problem at its source (although wearing ear plugs might provide occasional help). This strategy that regulates emotions is a *remedial coping strategy*. It does not eliminate stress at the source, but seeks to remedy your upset feelings by justifying or accepting the status quo. Notice that even though emotion-focused coping does not directly eliminate a stressor, it deals with problems stress can cause; for this reason it is still considered coping rather than defending.

Ego Defense Mechanisms Included in emotion-focused coping are **ego defense mechanisms,** *mental strategies to reduce conflict or anxiety.* Examples of ego defense mechanisms include denial of reality, rationalization, and repression. You might use *denial* by acknowledging a stressor but minimizing its seriousness. *Rationalization* involves manufacturing reasons for not focusing on the problem. *Repression* "hides" the problem in the unconscious; we react to inner conflicts and fantasies.

For example, suppose your roommate is failing an important class, but could successfully pass by putting in a lot of intense effort in the final weeks of the course. Instead of constructively coping, however, he or she might engage in conscious or unconscious defensive thinking, reducing the anxiety without facing the problem:

Denial

Conscious: "I'm not really 'failing,' not yet, at least. Some of my classmates are doing a lot worse than I am. The teacher seems to like me, maybe she'll pass me if she's in a good mood when she grades the final."

Rationalization

Conscious: "It will be really hard, probably impossible, to pull my grades up now. Why should I put in the effort? After all, this isn't even a required course in my major. There will be plenty of other courses I can do well in to make up for this one bad grade."

Repression

Unconscious: "My parents are paying for my tuition, not me. They don't love me, they just want to control my life. This will show them. They can't make me pass this course if I don't want to. I'll make them sorry, and I'll take control of my own life."

Ego defense mechanisms "defend" the ego (your sense of self) by changing your thoughts or emotional reactions to stressors rather than solving problems at the source. Obviously, long-term reliance on defense mechanisms can backfire, guaranteeing that unsolved problems will recur. But in the short term, ego defense mechanisms can reduce anxiety by enabling the individual to see stressful situations as less threatening—if only temporarily.

Moderator Variables The impact of a stressor can vary depending on the circumstances. A minor life event such as getting a parking ticket can ruin your day or barely ruffle you, depending on the state of your mind, health, and finances. *Such variables that change the impact of a stressor on a given type of stress reaction are called* **stress moderator variables.** Moderator variables filter or modify the usual effects of stressors on the individual's reactions. For example, your level of fatigue and general health are moderator variables: if you are unusually tired or just getting over an illness, a normally mild stressor like a misunderstanding with a friend might upset you or lead you to overreact. But if you are in good shape and are getting enough (not too much!) sleep, you should find you can respond to difficulties in a more clearheaded, efficient way.

Cognitive Assessment

Some moderator variables—such as whether or not you catch a cold that is going around—cannot be controlled. But others can, such as your mood, knowledge, and determination to solve your problems. We turn now to the role of cognitions, and how they can be modified in order to deal with stress.

Cognitive Appraisal   To cope with stress, you must first define the stressor, evaluate its severity, and determine the best ways to respond. A major moderator variable in this process is **cognitive appraisal,** *the process of recognizing a stressor, assessing the demands it makes, and identifying resources available to deal with it.* Some stressors—such as being personally harmed or suffering a major loss—would be experienced as threats by almost everyone. However, many other stressors can be defined in various ways, depending on the circumstances. A situation that causes acute distress for one person may be all in a day's work for another.

Your appraisal of a stressor and of your resources for meeting it can be as important as the stressor itself. For example, you could define a stressor as an interesting new challenge to test yourself against instead of as a threat; you could get psyched up for it instead of feeling anxious. Examinations are stressors for many students, but they can be stimulating challenges for those who are prepared and confident. Your appraisal of a stressor determines your conscious experience of it and your success in meeting its demands.

Richard Lazarus, a pioneer in stress research and emotion research, has distinguished two stages in our cognitive appraisal of demands. He uses the term **primary appraisal** *for the initial evaluation of the seriousness of a demand:* What is it? How big? How bad? How enduring? If the demand is considered *stressful,* an individual appraises the potential impact of the stressor by determining whether harm has occurred or is likely to and whether action is required (see Table 9.3). In **secondary appraisal,** *the individual evaluates the available personal and social resources for dealing with the stressful circumstance and considers what action to take* (Lazarus, 1976).

You continue cognitive appraisal as you try various coping responses. If your first efforts don't work and the stress persists, you initiate new responses and evaluate their effectiveness (Lazarus, 1991). For example, if you were counting on using a friend's computer this weekend to complete a paper due on Monday, you will be stressed to learn that the computer isn't available. During primary appraisal, you realize you must change your immediate plans and make time to find another computer so you can finish your work. During secondary appraisal, you try to think of whom you could contact about getting access to another computer, and also think of other time-saving strategies that will help you make the deadline.

Some early research on gender differences in coping had suggested that women and men favored different coping styles: men were found to favor problem-focused, instrumental strategies; women were thought to favor emotion-focused techniques. However, a recent study by Porter and Stone (1995) suggests that the gender difference lies not in coping styles but in the

TABLE 9.3	STAGES IN STABLE DECISION MAKING/COGNITIVE APPRAISAL

Stage	Key Questions
1. Appraising the challenge	Are the risks serious if I don't change?
2. Surveying alternatives	Is this alternative an acceptable means for dealing with the challenge?
	Have I sufficiently surveyed the available alternatives?
3. Weighing alternatives	Which alternative is best?
	Could the best alternative meet the essential requirements?
4. Deliberating about commitment	Shall I implement the best alternative and allow others to know?
5. Persevering despite negative feedback	Are the risks serious if I don't change?
	Are the risks serious if I do change?

types of stress individuals encounter. Specifically, the researchers asked individuals to categorize the hassles—mildly stressful daily events, they most often encountered, and asked them to describe what action they took "to try to feel better or handle the problem" (that is, emotional-focused versus problem-focused strategies) (Porter & Stone, 1995, p. 190). They found that women saw as most chronic problems they traced to themselves and close relationships (e.g., marriage, parenting). In contrast, the men reported more work-related problems, but did *not* report using different coping strategies from women. Gender differences—being raised and living in one's culture as a man or a woman—clearly lead to different contexts of experience and *perceptions* of the sources of stress in one's life. But it may be a popular myth, rather than a scientifically validated conclusion, that when they are stressed, men "take action" whereas women "wallow in their feelings." Porter & Stone's findings suggest "that it is the content of the problem rather than the gender of the individual that determines the selection of coping strategies" (p. 198).

Modifying Cognitions   A powerful way to handle stress more adaptively is to change our evaluations of stressors and our self-defeating cognitions about the way to deal with them. Two ways to cope mentally with stress are reappraising the nature of the stressors and restructuring our ideas about our stress reactions.

Reappraising Stressors   Learning to think differently about certain stressors can help. Relabeling them and imagining them in a less-threatening (perhaps even funny) context are forms of cognitive reappraisal that can reduce stress. If you are worried about giving a speech to a large, forbidding audience, imagine your potential critics sitting there in the nude—a less intimidating, perhaps more self-conscious than critical group. If you are anxious about being shy at a social function you must attend, think about finding someone who is more shy than you and reducing her social anxiety by starting a conversation. You can learn to reappraise stressors by engaging the creative skills you already possess, and by imagining and planning your life in more positive, constructive ways.

Giving the elderly an opportunity to continue to make a difference in the lives of those around them greatly improves their health and mood.

Restructuring Cognitions Two important factors in determining how stress is perceived are one's *uncertainty* about impending events and one's *sense of control* over them (Swets & Bjork, 1990). Consequently, two ways to reduce stress are to reduce uncertainty about stressful events, and increase your sense of control. You can accomplish both these tasks by engaging in *cognitive restructuring,* rethinking the situation and reacting less automatically, more rationally.

For example, depressed or insecure people often tell themselves that they are no good, that they'll do poorly; or, if something goes well, that it was a fluke or just random luck. In Focus on Application: Reassessing Stress, we explore two factors in cognitive restructuring: changing cognitions and perceiving control. In a very real sense, stress is ultimately in the mind of the beholder.

Personality Factors

Is there such a thing as a stress-prone personality? We have evidence that negative emotional states such as depression, anxiety, and hostility can affect physical conditions such as coronary disease, asthma, headache, gastric ulcers, and arthritis (Friedman & Booth-Kewley, 1988). Chronic negative emotional states tend to produce pathogenic (disease-causing) changes in the body, unhealthy behavior patterns, and poor personal relationships (Matthews, 1988). Fortunately, there is also evidence that some personalities are "coping oriented," especially effective in dealing with stress and resisting illness. In this section we briefly review evidence for three personality patterns that influence responses to stress: Type A; Type T; and Hardiness.

The Type A Pattern Much research has focused on a behavioral style found to be somewhat at risk for certain health problems. The **Type A syndrome** *is a complex pattern of angry, competitive, and perfectionistic behavior in response to stress.* Type A's tend to feel hostile, impatient, and anxious about time; their behavior tends to be competitive, aggressive, and future-oriented (rather than focused on the present). For example, a Type A person might engage in *polyphasic* behavior, doing several things simultaneously, such as eating, "watching" television, and writing a report at the same time.

Type A's tend to be ambitious, dissatisfied with some aspect of their lives, and are often loners. Many Type A characteristics are valued in our mobile, competitive society: speed, perfectionism, and time-urgency may help one to succeed in the workplace and in the interpersonal "marketplace," where people are admired for being strong and self-promoting. But in general the Type A style is very dysfunctional. For example, Type A businessmen are stricken with coronary heart disease more than twice as often as men in the general population (Friedman & Rosenman, 1974; Jenkins, 1976). Other studies show that Type A's are at greater risk for all forms of cardiovascular disease (Dembrowski et al., 1978, 1987; Haynes & Feinleib, 1980).

Type A patterns have been observed among high school and college students, and even among grade school children (Thoresen & Eagleston, 1983). In addition to cardiovascular risks, recent research links Type A habits to other illnesses: allergies, head colds, headaches, stomach disorders, and mononucleosis (Suls & Sanders, 1988; Suls & Marco, 1990). Currently researchers are focusing on identifying which specific dimensions of the Type A syndrome are its deadly components. Hostility is particularly suspect. When a slow-moving vehicle blocks you in traffic, it is reasonable to become momentarily angry, but it is Type A—and potentially dangerous—to become enraged.

Reassessing Stress

By telling yourself you will fail in some endeavor or that your success was a lucky accident, you may only doom yourself to disappointment and discouragement. Fortunately, it may be possible to intentionally change this self-defeating cycle. Cognitive-behavior therapist Donald Meichenbaum (1977) has proposed a three-phase process to overcome self-defeating thinking.

In Phase 1, people work to develop a greater awareness of their actual behavior, what instigates it, and what its results are. One of the best ways to do this is to keep daily logs or journals. By helping people redefine their problems in terms of their causes and results, logs can increase their feelings of control. In Phase 2, individuals begin to identify new behaviors that negate the maladaptive, self-defeating behaviors—perhaps smiling at someone, offering a compliment, or acting assertively. In Phase 3, after adaptive behaviors are being generated, individuals appraise their consequences, avoiding the former internal dialogue of put-downs. Instead of telling themselves, "I was lucky the professor called on me when I happened to have read the text," they say, "I'm glad I was prepared for the professor's question. It feels great to be able to respond intelligently in class."

This three-phase approach requires initiating responses and self-statements that are incompatible with previous defeatist cognitions. Once they start on this path, formerly self-defeating people realize that they are changing, and they take full credit for those changes, which in turn promotes further successes. The table in this box gives examples of coping self-statements that help in dealing with stressful situations.

Coping Self-statements

Preparation

I can develop a plan to deal with it.

Just think about what I can do about it. That's better than getting anxious.

No negative self-statements, just think rationally.

Confrontation

One step at a time; I can handle this situation.

This anxiety is what the doctor said I would feel; it's a reminder to use my coping exercises.

Relax; I'm in control. Take a slow deep breath.

Coping

When fear comes, just pause.

Keep focus on the present; what is it I have to do?

Don't try to eliminate fear totally; just keep it manageable.

It's not the worst thing that can happen.

Just think about something else.

Self-reinforcement

It worked, I was able to do it.

It wasn't as bad as I expected.

I'm really pleased with the progress I'm making.

One of the major variables that promotes positive adjustments is *perceived control* over the stressor, a belief that you have the ability to make a difference in the course or the consequences of some event or experience. If you believe that you can affect the course of the illness or the daily symptoms of the disease, you are probably adjusting well to the disorder (Affleck et al., 1987). However, if you believe the source of the stress is another person whose behavior you cannot influence or a situation that you cannot change, chances increase for a poor psychological adjustment to your chronic condition (Bulman & Wortman, 1977).

Classic research by **Ellen Langer** and **Judith Rodin** has shown that assigning simple responsibilities and choices to elderly nursing home residents—such as caring for houseplants or selecting movies to watch—caused measurable improvements in patients' moods and health (Langer & Rodin, 1976; Rodin & Langer, 1977; Rodin, 1983, 1986). Other research confirms that elderly residents in long-term care facilities are happier and may live longer when they are able to make personal choices about when to get up, what to eat, and which pastimes to pursue (Deci & Ryan, 1987; Timko & Moos, 1989). Jail inmates also respond positively—and make better progress toward rehabilitation in an otherwise inhuman institutional setting—when given moderate amounts of control and personal responsibility, such as caring for small pets or choosing how to spend "free" time (Ruback et al., 1986; Wener et al., 1987).

Apply these lessons to your own life by (1) reframing your interpretation of a difficult situation in terms of what you *can control;* and (2) taking *action,* even in small steps, to give yourself the experience of coping successfully. Be reasonable in what you aim for initially, but be sure that even the "easy" goals you choose are meaningful. As you try and increasingly succeed in coping, finally, be sure you are (3) *reassessing yourself* as a person who is increasingly competent and moving in a more healthy direction.

Another risky Type A quality is perfectionism, which has been linked to anxiety (about reaching impossible goals) and depression (from failing to reach them) (Joiner & Schmidt, 1995). As we shall see in Chapter 10, one theory of personality patterns is that they are largely learned and shaped by experience. If certain patterns, such as the Type A syndrome, are found to be unhealthy, it is at least possible to learn new ways of thinking, feeling, and behaving, in order to live healthier, less driven lives.

People who engage in risky behavior, such as mountain climbing, tend to have Type T personalities.

The Type T Pattern   Recall that in Chapter 4 we introduced the concept of temperament, an inherited tendency to respond to life conditions in particular ways, such as fearfully, aggressively, or boldly. Consider the implications of temperament for coping style: a fearful child might habitually flee from stressors; an aggressive child might go through life trying to fight whoever and whatever poses a threat; and a bold child might neither run nor fight, but rather engage with the situation to find a solution.

An extreme form of boldness leads an individual to engage in risk-taking behavior as a route to stimulation and excitement. Do you know someone—perhaps yourself—who would enjoy such activities as mountain climbing, hang gliding, skydiving, or even bungee-jumping? Such a description fits what psychologist **Frank Farley** (1990) has termed the **Type T personality**: *a behavior pattern that centers on taking risks, seeking stimulation and excitement.* The T stands for "thrills," one's subjective experience that the risk and stress of an experience make it emotionally rewarding. Farley distinguishes between two distinct extremes or shades of Type T's: the *creative* type, who is motivated to act constructively; and the *destructive* type, who engages in delinquent behaviors and crime, such as vandalism or substance abuse. The value and consequences of thrill-seeking will depend on how the Type T person expresses his or her boldness.

If you don't happen to be a Type T, you are not necessarily a coward! Most people fall along a continuum between the high-risk Type T extreme and those at the other end who seek to avoid risk at almost all costs. The Type T pattern is not a "strategy" for stress management, but rather represents a set of moderator variables affecting how an individual approaches and copes with stressors. If Type T is not your type, you still have lots of other options!

Hardiness   A personality pattern that has received much attention as a stress moderator is **hardiness**, *a resilient quality based on distinctive attitudes towards stress and how to manage it.* Psychologist **Suzanne Kobasa** (1984) has concluded that the hardy personality is especially effective in diffusing stress. She identified two groups of subjects from a pool of managers working for a big public utility in a large city. The members of one group experienced high levels of stress but were seldom ill, while the members of the second group had high stress and frequently experienced illness (Kobasa et al., 1979). The stress survivors possessed the characteristics of hardiness.

Hardy personalities respond to stressful situations with three distinctive attitudes or perspectives, called the "three C's of hardiness":

- *Challenge:* Hardy people welcome change as a challenge, not necessarily a threat;
- *Commitment:* Hardy individuals make a focused commitment to engaging in purposeful activity, solving problems and meeting the challenges they face;
- *Control:* A healthy approach to coping involves having an internal sense of control over one's actions and experiences, as hardy people show.

For example, suppose that on the day you must prepare for a major test, a friend confides in you about a terrible problem and begs for your help. These two stressors—an important test and a needy friend—could be overwhelming, especially if you feel you are already stretching some of your resources to the limit. But a hardy individual would employ the "three C's" to reduce the stress of the situation: *challenge* ("I want to be fully prepared for this test; how can I reassure my friend that I'll help as well?"); *commitment* ("My friend is important to me, and so is this test; I'll find a way to meet my obligations in both areas"); and *control* ("I can't take time out from studying, but I can plan to spend the evening discussing the problem; once the test is over I can give my friend my undivided attention").

The key to hardiness is not luck or an inherited ability to face stress with a smile. Rather hardiness is a learned approach to stress, based on *interpreting* stressful events in an adaptive way (Kobasa, 1984). When you choose to see life circumstances as manageable rather than overwhelming, you enable yourself to face and solve most problems.

Social Support

It is especially difficult—and not usually necessary—to cope with stress all alone. You should and usually can rely on your social and physical environment for support in dealing with the circumstances that threaten your survival and happiness. It appears to be especially important to form alliances with others. Research consistently shows that being part of a social support network and living and working in a healthy environment lead to an improvement in coping.

Social support *refers to the resources others provide to help an individual cope with stress.* Social support gives you the message that you do not have to face a threat alone. Social support can take many forms. *Socioemotional support* gives you the message that you are loved, cared for, esteemed, and connected to other people in a network of communication and mutual obligation (Cobb, 1976; Cohen & Syme, 1985). Other people can also provide *tangible support* (money, transportation, housing) and *informational support* (advice, personal feedback, information). Anyone with whom you have a significant social relationship can be part of your social support network in time of need.

Much research points to the power of social support in moderating vulnerability to stress (Cohen & McKay, 1983). When people have other people they can turn to, they are better able to handle job stressors, unemployment, marital disruption, serious illness, and other catastrophes, as well as the everyday problems of living (Gottlieb, 1981; Pilisuk & Parks, 1986). Lack of a social support system clearly increases one's vulnerability to disease and death (Berkman & Syme, 1979). Decreases in social support in family and work environments are related to increases in psychological maladjustment.

Social support is helpful in preventing and coping with stress.

Who is supportive?   Health psychologist **Shelley Taylor** and her colleagues at UCLA studied the effectiveness of different types of social support given to cancer patients. They found that helpfulness depended on who the helper was: patients appreciated information and advice from physicians but not from family members, and they valued a spouse's "just being there" but not a doctor's or nurse's mere presence (Taylor, 1986; Dakof & Taylor, 1990). Researchers are also trying to determine when sources of support might backfire and actually *increase* the recipient's anxiety. For example, if you prefer to attend a doctor's appointment or college interview alone, your mother's insistence on accompanying you might cause you to feel anxious, not relaxed (Coyne et al., 1988). Too much social support may become intrusive and not helpful in the long run; having one close friend may be as beneficial as having many. A close other who is not supportive may leave you in greater stress than if you were alone. For example, the symptoms of depression are more likely to increase for a married person who cannot communicate well with his or her spouse than for a control subject without a spouse (Weissman, 1987).

When you need help, you are most likely to seek (and receive) it from your close others: family members and friends who care about you and want to help. But you can also gain great benefit from the support offered by people you are not already close to. "Support groups," for example, are made up of people who share the same concerns or suffer from the same problems, such as the parents of terminally ill children, or victims of spouse abuse. Although when they begin meeting they may be strangers to each other, over time they form bonds of community. Support groups have a realistic focus, seeking not to solve individuals' problems but to *improve* coping by supplementing the work of individuals and their allies. Does it really help to spend time interacting with others who face the same stressors or illnesses? Research indicates that yes, far from being a depressing or time-wasting experience, participation in a support group gives individuals peers who understand their problems, and with whom they can compare their own concerns and progress (Gottlieb, 1987).

One's larger community can also be thought of as a potential support system. Families are often organized into tribes, clans, neighborhoods, or church congregations in order to identify those who require support and channel resources to them. In times of crisis, when natural disaster or technological catastrophe strikes a community, both individual and collective efforts are necessary to save lives (Ursano et al., 1994). As the human brain has evolved, we have inherited the capacity to connect with others as a way to promote our survival. Taking care of those who need help is an extension of self-protection motives: our social relationships increase the support we all have available, both to give and receive (Shaffer & Anundsen, 1993).

Relationship Qualities   Much work on social support has examined not only the benefits of providing it but the deficits produced when no such help is offered. Which would hurt more if you needed help: not having qualified professionals to provide treatment or services, or not having friends at your side as you face trouble? Interesting research suggests that companionship is a central part of social support (Rook, 1987). Efficient support provided by well-intentioned strangers has become important in coping with trauma, but knowing there is a well-staffed hospital down the road does not help you deal with the minor stressors and loneliness of daily life. The best physician in the world cannot provide the emotional comfort of a friend who will keep you company or listen to your worries.

The quality and quantity of social relationships visibly affects physical and mental health (House et al., 1988). Loneliness, social alienation, and loss all leave an individual vulnerable to stress without the buffering effects of friendship and love.

Supporting the Supporters.   In recent years, research has focused on the problems caregivers experience as they attempt to *provide* social support. These problems involve giving support that is intense, long-term, unappreciated, or rejected (Coyne et al., 1988; Kiecolt-Glaser et al., 1987; Schulz et al., 1987). In coming years, more people may be pressed into service as caregivers among their family and friends as a result of societal stressors like rising health care costs and a depressed economy. Middle-aged adults, for example, may find they must make room for grown children who cannot yet afford to live on their own at the same time they are caring for their own elderly parents. Caught between the demands of two sets of family members, this "sandwich generation" will increasingly need help and advice about how to cope.

Matching Strategies to Stressors   For coping to be successful, resources must match the perceived demand. Successful coping depends on a match between coping strategies and specific features of the stressful event. Thus, the availability of multiple coping strategies would be most adaptive because we are more likely to achieve a match and manage the stressful event. When we know we possess a large repertoire of coping strategies, we feel greater confidence—and enjoy a stronger sense of self-efficacy—about meeting environmental demands (Bandura, 1986).

Check Your Recall

Individuals respond to stress either by defending (reducing the symptoms) or coping (addressing or eliminating the problem or stressor). In problem-focused coping, one deals directly with a controllable stressor. In emotion-focused coping, less controllable stressors are dealt with indirectly by supporting resources necessary to deal with them. Ego defense mechanisms focus on emotions by reducing one's conflict or anxiety in dealing with stress. Stress moderator variables are changing conditions or assets that affect one's ability to deal with specific stressors.

Cognitions can operate as stressor variables because an individual engages in cognitive appraisal to assess the impact of a stressor and determine the best response. By reappraising stressors and restructuring cognitions, we can learn to reassess stress and experience less difficulty with previously stressful stimuli. Some personal factors moderate the impact of stress: Type A's may experience more stress and anger because of their competitiveness and perfectionism; Type T's may have the temperament to tolerate and even enjoy risk; and the hardy personality copes by interpreting stress as manageable. Social support is essential in coping with many stressors, including both the benefits of skilled personnel and the companionship offered by friends. Successful coping requires one to match resources and skills most appropriate to the nature of the stressor.

Health and Well-Being

Research on stress and on coping has piqued psychologists' interest in how behavior and mental processes affect health. Much of our health is influenced by or dependent on our behaviors and our choices: the food we eat, our drug use, whether we drive safely, how well we follow doctors' orders, even our willingness to get involved in "unhealthy" personal relationships. A new field has grown from this acknowledgment that social and psychological factors influence health. **Health psychology** *is the field devoted to understanding how people stay healthy, why they become ill, and how they respond when ill* (Taylor, 1990, 1992). Among the many areas of concern for health psychologists are health promotion and maintenance; prevention and treatment of illness; causes and correlates of health, illness, and dysfunction; and improvement of the health care system and health policy information (Matarazzo, 1980).

The Biopsychosocial Model of Health

For all of recorded time, psychological principles have been applied in the treatment of illness and the pursuit of health. Many ancient cultures understood the importance of communal health and relaxation rituals in enhancing the quality of life. Among the Navajo, for example, disease, illness, and well-being have been attributed to social harmony and mind-body interactions. Illness is seen as the outcome of any *disharmony,* and as caused by evil introduced through the violation of taboos, witchcraft, overindulgence, or bad dreams. The illness of any member of a tribe is seen not as his or her individual responsibility (and fault) but rather as a sign of broader disharmony that must be repaired by communal healing ceremonies. This cultural orientation guarantees a powerful social support network that automatically comes to the aid of the sufferer.

Traditional Western scientific thinking has relied exclusively on a *biomedical model* that distinguishes between body and mind. According to this model, medicine treats the physical body (*soma*) as separate from the mind (*psyche*); the mind is important only for emotions and beliefs and it has little to do with the reality of the soma. However, researchers are now employing a new view of health—new to the Western tradition, that is. This **biopsychosocial model** *of health examines health as a function of linkages among factors in the nervous system, immune system, personal behavior, cognition, and social and environmental factors.* In combination, these factors can either put us at risk for illness or increase our resistance to stress, trauma, and disease (Engle, 1976). Likewise, the biopsychosocial model sees all these systems as having the potential to benefit health and promote well-being.

Health *is the condition in which both body and mind are sound and vigorous as well as free from illness or injury.* Health is not simply the absence of illness or injury but is more a matter of how well all the body's component parts are working. "To be healthy is to have the ability, despite an occasional bout of illness, to live with full use of your faculties and to be vigorous, alert, and happy to be alive, even in old age" (Insel & Roth, 1985, p. xvii).

Your physical health is linked to your state of mind and the world around you. Health psychologists view health as a complex, dynamic experience. **Wellness** *is optimal health, including full, active functioning in the physical, intellectual, emotional, social, environmental, and spiritual domains.* When you undertake any activity for the purpose of preventing disease or detecting it in the asymptomatic stage (before the appearance of any symptoms), you are exhibiting *health behavior* (Kasl & Cobb, 1966). A healthy habit or behavior pattern is one that operates automatically without extrinsic reinforcement or incentives and contributes directly to your overall health (Hunt et al., 1979).

Is there a difference between illness and illness behavior? *Illness behavior* is exhibited when an individual acts sick. For example, if you don't feel like going to class, you may exhibit illness behavior: staying in bed, groaning, complaining of not feeling well, or changing your usual diet and activities. But

The Navajo believe illness comes from disharmony, and they seek to repair it through communal healing ceremonies, like this dance.

saying "ouch," visiting the doctor, or taking medicine is not "proof" of illness (Taylor, 1990). **Illness** *is disease or damage to the structure or function of bodily systems.* A diagnosis of illness is validated by documented evidence of pathology, such as biological or physiological damage, cell deterioration, or chemical imbalance. Health psychology researchers seek to learn more about illness behavior—what triggers it, how it is learned, how it affects feelings and other behaviors—as well as medical reasons for the illness itself.

Healthy Behavior

Healthy behavior is essential to health management. Health psychologists have identified four elements that determine the likelihood of someone engaging in a healthy habit or in changing a faulty one (Bandura, 1986; Janz & Becker, 1984; Rogers, 1984). Consider how each might affect whether a heavy smoker quits the nicotine habit:

1. *The person must believe the threat to health is severe.* For example, a heavy smoker must believe she is at risk for a stroke, not just a bad cough.
2. *The person must believe her perceived personal vulnerability and/or the likelihood of developing the disorder is high.* The heavy smoker must be convinced that she is already in a high-risk group for stroke, perhaps because of her age or her family's medical history.
3. *The person must believe she is able to perform the response that will reduce the threat (self-efficacy).* Once convinced she must quit smoking, the patient must believe she can learn to overcome her smoking habit if she tries.
4. *The response must be capable of effectively overcoming the threat.* Finally, the smoker must believe that it is not too late to reduce her risk for stroke, and that quitting her smoking habit can still save her life.

Modifying health behaviors is not a simple matter. Even when health habits change for the better, there is always the threat of **relapse,** *or recidivism, reverting to former, unhealthy behavior patterns that have been changed.* It is easy to fall back into bad habits; new health habits must be practiced regularly to become automatic. Many people have difficulty putting new resolve and new actions into a standard regimen when they remain in the same *behavior setting* that reinforced the unhealthy behavior patterns in the first place. Without changing their environment, ex-convicts, recovered drug addicts, and weight clinic clients often relapse into former ways of behaving even when they have learned new, healthy behaviors—ones that work in other environments.

Health Promotion   Why are people resistant to making behavior changes that can clearly prolong life and enhance health? Part of this recalcitrance may arise from refusing to believe that one's habits or addictions are really unhealthy. Another part of such attitudes may be fatalism or pessimism about the final outcome—believing that "we will all die of something," after all, and that some unhealthy habits provide satisfaction or relief in the short-run.

Psychologists find it can be less difficult for people to change unhealthy behaviors if they anticipate rewards. Healthier lifestyles not only reduce the risk of death or debilitation from disease, they also enhance the quality (the enjoyability) of living. A 30-year study examined the lifestyle changes and disease histories of more than 15,000 men. The researchers found that men who began moderate exercise programs and quit smoking not only reduced their risk of heart attack and lived longer than men who made no changes, they also worked better, looked better, and claimed to feel better (*San

Francisco Chronicle, February 25, 1993). Health is not only an absence of disease; it reflects the presence of wellness.

The promotion of health and wellness requires national and international efforts that go beyond a focus on the psychology of individuals to systemwide involvement. A general model for health promotion developed by the Canadian government outlines basic health challenges, mechanisms to promote health, and strategies for implementing changes designed to achieve health for all. In 1979, the U.S. Department of Health, Education, and Welfare (with a mission that is today part of Health and Human Services) published *Healthy People*, a report identifying 15 areas of priority for Americans' health that could be addressed with specific plans for health promotion, health protection, or clinical prevention by the goal year of 1990. In 1990, Health and Human Services continued goal-setting with *Healthy People 2000*, identifying 22 areas of priority, including physical fitness, tobacco and alcohol use, violent behavior, workplace safety, maternal and infant care, and infectious diseases (Winett, 1995). Implementing strategies to meet these goals requires considering which is the best *level* to target for prevention (individual behavior? the community? institutions?) and what *timing* to aim for (e.g., short-term laws against minors using tobacco? long-term education about healthier eating habits?). Legislators and policy makers all have the power to influence citizens' health in important ways—but only as individuals can people make the choice to live healthier lives.

Psychological Treatments   Many investigators believe that psychological strategies can improve the emotional well-being of individuals. The availability of a biopsychosocial model of health has resulted in increased scientific evidence supporting benefits of *psychological treatments* for diagnosed illness, both physical and mental. A recent study conducted by **David Spiegel,** a research psychiatrist at Stanford University School of Medicine, demonstrates the impact of psychosocial treatment on the course of disease. Breast cancer patients who participated in weekly group support and therapy were found to cope better and survive longer than control subjects who did not participate in such psychotherapy. The patients discussed their personal experiences in dealing with cancer; they could reveal their fears and other strong emotions in an understanding environment. Spiegel's finding indicates that psychological treatments can affect the course of disease, the length of one's life, and the quality of life (Spiegel et al., 1989).

The power of psychological treatments is beginning to affect the recommendations of health professionals. Many health psychologists want medical treatments to be more flexible. For example, many oncologists (cancer specialists) believe the treatment of metastatic cancer should include psychological practices in addition to traditional radiation and chemotherapy. Theirs is a call for flexibility—a medical arsenal augmented by psychological methods—not, as some traditionalists fear, a cry to abandon proven therapies in favor of untried methods.

Illness prevention *includes general and specific strategies to eliminate or reduce the risk that people will get sick.* The prevention of illness poses a much different challenge in the 1990s than it did at the turn of the century, according to pioneering health psychologist **Joseph Matarazzo** (1984). He notes that, in 1900, the primary cause of death was infectious disease. Health practitioners at that time launched the first revolution in American public health. Through the use of research, public education, the development of vaccines, and changes in public health standards (such as waste control and sewage), they were able to reduce substantially the deaths associated with such diseases

	TABLE 9.4	LEADING CAUSES OF DEATH, UNITED STATES, 1989	
Rank	% of Deaths	Cause of Death	Contributors to Cause of Death (D–diet; S–smoking; A–alcohol)
1	34.1	Heart disease	DS
2	23.1	Cancers	DS
3	6.8	Strokes	DS
4	2.3	Accidents; motor vehicles	A
	2.1	Accidents; all others	
5	3.9	Chronic obstructive lung diseases	S
6	3.5	Pneumonia and influenza	S
7	1.8	Diabetes	D
8	1.4	Suicide	A
9	1.2	Chronic liver disease	A
10	1.1	Homicide	A
11	1.0	AIDS, HIV disease	

as influenza, tuberculosis, polio, measles, and smallpox. Clearly, just as groups can accomplish what lone individuals cannot, so communities and governments can achieve remarkable success in saving lives by making information available and making prevention and treatment affordable.

The War on Lifestyle

To continue advancing the quality of life into the twenty-first century, health practitioners must seek to decrease those deaths associated with lifestyle factors (see Table 9.4). Smoking, weight problems, high intake of fat and cholesterol, drug and alcohol abuse, driving without seat belts, and stress contribute to heart disease, cancer, strokes, cirrhosis, accidents, and suicide.

Changing the behaviors associated with these *diseases of civilization* will prevent much illness and unnecessary premature deaths. Figure 9.4 shows the estimated percentage of deaths that could be prevented by changes in behavior, early detection, and prevention strategies.

What are prevention strategies in the "war on lifestyle"? One approach is to modify lifestyle to change or eliminate poor health habits. Familiar examples of this strategy are programs to help people become healthy or stay that way; to quit smoking; to stop using and abusing drugs; to exercise; to lose excess weight; and to be aware of sexually transmitted diseases and how to prevent them. People are more likely to stay well if they practice good health habits such as those listed in Table 9.5.

Heart Disease A major study to prevent heart disease was conducted in three towns in California. The goals of the study were to persuade people to reduce their cardiovascular risk via changes in smoking, diet, and exercise, and to determine which method of persuasion was more effective. In one town, a two-year advertising campaign was conducted through the mass media. A second town received the same two-year media campaign plus a personal instruction program on modifying health habits for high-risk individuals. The third town served as a control group and received no persuasive campaign.

FIGURE 9.4　Preventable Deaths ■ Changes in behavior, early detection of problems, and intervention could prevent death in many cases.

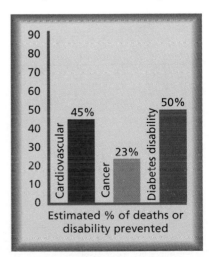

Estimated % of deaths or disability prevented

TABLE 9.5	TEN STEPS TO PERSONAL WELLNESS

1. Exercise regularly
2. Eat nutritious, balanced meals (high in vegetables, fruits, and grains, low in fat and cholesterol)
3. Maintain proper weight
4. Sleep 7–8 hours nightly, rest/relax daily
5. Wear seat belts and bike helmets
6. Do not smoke or use drugs
7. Use alcohol in moderation, if at all
8. Engage only in protected, safe sex
9. Get regular medical/dental checkups, adhere to medical regimens
10. Develop an optimistic perspective and supportive friendships

Results showed that the townspeople who had gotten only the mass-media campaign were more knowledgeable about the links between lifestyle and heart disease, but, as seen in Figure 9.5, they showed only modest changes in their own behaviors and health status. Personal instruction showed more substantial and long-lasting effects in changing health habits, particularly in reducing smoking (Farquhar et al., 1984; Maccoby et al., 1977).

Conclusions about this research are mixed. The good news is that lifestyle factors can be modified; the bad news is that it is difficult and expensive to do so. Passive mass-media campaigns are not very effective in changing certain health behaviors. But such campaigns can pervade the culture and contribute to long-term changes in social attitudes supporting individual lifestyle changes.

Smoking   Annual U.S. deaths related to smoking have climbed to roughly half a million (U.S. Department of Health & Human Services, 1991). Despite the steady trend toward reduced smoking in recent years, 29 percent of Americans continue to smoke. Among the estimated 50 million American pack-a-day smokers, male smokers are 22 times more likely than male nonsmokers to die of lung cancer, and the risk of death from lung cancer is 12 times higher for women smokers than for women nonsmokers. Despite protests by tobacco companies that they officially discourage smoking by minors, most adult smokers (90 percent) began the deadly habit before age 21.

ASK YOURSELF the following questions:

- What might be some of the immediate as well as long-term gains to society—in health as well as other indexes—if the 3000 children who start smoking each and every day of the year could be prevented from lighting that first cigarette?
- Would the health benefits to society outweigh the economic losses to those who now rely on employment in the tobacco industry—or on the advertising, jobs, and sponsored sports events that industry now supports?

The health benefits of becoming a nonsmoker are immediate and substantial for both genders and all ages. Even heavy smokers who kick the nicotine habit will improve their chances of avoiding disease and premature death due to smoking. Because tobacco is not only a highly addictive drug, but a legal, heavily promoted drug, most tobacco users find it difficult to quit once they have started. The best health policy appears to be either never to start smoking or to join the ranks of the estimated 35 million other Americans who have quit. Since the smoking habit usually begins in adolescence, some psychologists tackle the problem by studying ways to keep teenagers from smoking in the first place. The programs that seem to be most successful have several distinctive characteristics (Evans et al., 1978):

- They provide antismoking information in *formats that appeal* to adolescents;
- They portray a *positive image of the nonsmoker* as independent and self-reliant; and,
- Successful antismoking campaigns use *peer group techniques,* with popular peers serving as nonsmoking role models instructing others about how to resist peer pressure.

Fitness   Regular exercise has been established as an important factor in promoting and maintaining health. Major improvements in health are gained from *aerobic* exercises—such as bicycling, swimming, running, or fast walking—which are characterized by high intensity, long duration, and high endurance. Aerobic exercises lead to increased fitness of the heart and respiratory systems, improvement of muscle tone and strength, and other health benefits. In contrast, most sports involve *anaerobic* exercise, bursts of activity interrupted by pauses or breathers. Anaerobic activity is certainly better than no exercise at all, but it cannot produce the whole-body physical benefits that aerobic exercise yields.

FIGURE 9.5   Promoting Healthy Change ■ Knowledge of cardiovascular disease risk factors was greater among residents of Town B, who were exposed to a 2-year mass-media health campaign, than among residents of Town A, who were not exposed to the campaign. Knowledge gain was greater still when residents of Town C participated in intense workshops and instruction sessions for several months during the media blitz. As knowledge increased, bad health habits (risk behaviors) and signs (indicators) decreased, with Town C leading the way, followed by Town B.

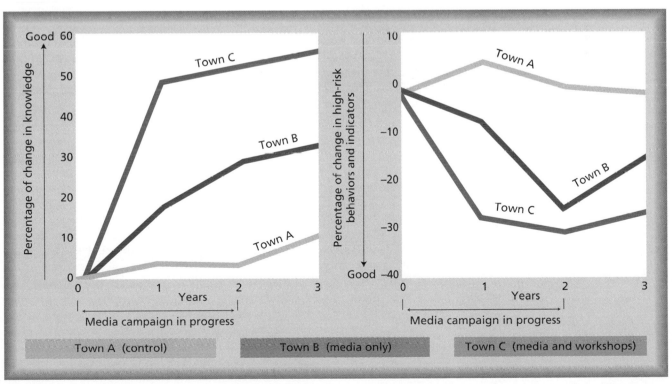

To promote wellness, it is important for health professionals and patients alike to be aware of lifestyle threats to health.

"BY GOLLY, YOU'RE RIGHT — THERE IS SOME SORT OF WARNING ON THE SIDE OF THE PACK."

Unfortunately, although the time commitments are only modest (a few half-hour sessions per week for the average individual), most people do not engage in aerobic exercise consistently. Researchers exploring questions of who exercises regularly and why they exercise have found that people are more likely to exercise regularly if it is easy and convenient to do so. This is one reason that many companies now provide exercise equipment, aerobics classes, or jogging tracks for their employees to use during work breaks.

Acquired Immune Deficiency Syndrome   It may be ironic that sex—which keeps our species alive—can be hazardous to our health. Sexually transmitted diseases (STDs) include ancient scourges like syphilis and gonorrhea, as well as more recently identified afflictions such as chlamydia, genital herpes, and AIDS. The physical intimacy necessary for most transmissions makes it difficult for societies to admit such diseases exist; STDs are not something people acknowledge or discuss casually. It is even more difficult, then, to maintain the objectivity and focus necessary to discuss how to prevent and treat STDs.

A deadly virus is the cause of AIDS, probably the most frightening disease we know today. AIDS is an acronym for *acquired immune deficiency syndrome*. Hundreds of thousands are dying from this virulent disease—but many more people are *living with* HIV infection, which almost always leads to AIDS. HIV (*human immunodeficiency virus*) is a virus that attacks the white blood cells in human blood, damaging the immune system and weakening the body's ability to fight other diseases. The infected individual then becomes vulnerable to infection by a host of other viruses and bacteria that can cause such life-threatening illnesses as cancer, meningitis, and pneumonia. HIV requires direct access to the bloodstream to produce an infection, and the incubation period can be as long as five years.

To diagnose AIDS (as opposed to mere HIV infection) requires documenting a severe deterioration of the immune system and an episode of a life-threatening infection. Although most of the estimated millions of those infected with HIV do not have AIDS, they must live with the continual stress that this life-threatening disease will eventually, perhaps suddenly, emerge. HIV is generally passed from one person to another either by the exchange of semen or blood during sexual contact, or by the sharing of intravenous needles and syringes used for injecting drugs. The virus has also been passed through blood transfusions and medical procedures in which infected blood or organs are unwittingly given to healthy people.

Who is at risk? Potentially everyone, since so many experiences and behaviors can introduce the HIV virus to the body: sex, injury, intravenous fluid exchange, and blood transfusions are not rare events in modern life. Although the initial discovery of AIDS in the United States was in the male homosexual community, the disease has spread widely, and AIDS is now found among heterosexuals and homosexuals of both sexes. According to a report by the National Centers for Disease Control (1990), as many as 35,000 college students, or one in 500, are estimated to be HIV positive. By 1993, AIDS had become "the No. 1 killer of people ages 25 to 44" (Associated Press, November 1995).

How can the worldwide spread of AIDS be limited? Behavioral intervention programs to modify sexual behavior and drug use have proven difficult and challenging for psychological and public agencies to implement. Four problems seem to make AIDS particularly resistant to intervention:

1. *Misinformation:* Many people still do not understand who is at risk or how their current behaviors can raise or lower that risk.
2. *Illusion of invulnerability:* Individuals at risk may incorrectly believe they cannot be harmed. Many teenagers often believe it is "safe" to have unprotected sex with young or inexperienced partners. Individuals at risk may engage in activities that endanger themselves and others in a vain effort to deny their vulnerability.
3. *Pleasure:* The short-term pleasures people associate with sexual behavior and habitual drug use may inhibit their efforts to make long-term changes in behavior. For example, a desire for spontaneity in sexual interaction may inhibit an individual from insisting on using a condom.
4. *Value conflicts:* People's beliefs, cultural mythology, and goals may conflict with scientific evidence about risk factors. Religious scruples may prevent individuals from using condoms but *not* from engaging in sexual activity—leading to the dangerous "compromise" of unprotected sex.

The only way to protect oneself from being infected with HIV is to change those lifestyle factors that put one at risk. This means making permanent changes in patterns of sexual behavior and in use of drug paraphernalia. The safest approach is to *abstain from risky behavior*—including unprotected or nonmonogamous sex, and intravenous drug use. The only way to prevent infection by HIV is to practice *safe* sex (use condoms during sexual contact and withdraw prior to ejaculation), use sterile needles, and know your HIV status. There is great potential for the media to show young people how to practice AIDS prevention behaviors while developing new healthful social norms and correcting inaccurate perceptions of social norms (Flora, 1991).

At present, there is neither a cure for AIDS nor a vaccine to prevent its spread. However, there are treatments that improve the quality and length of life of those afflicted with the disease. The drug AZT slows the progression of HIV, and there are new treatments that can more effectively manage the opportunistic infections, especially pneumonia. Aerobic exercise and other behavioral interventions at an early stage can slow the progression of HIV by improving immune functioning (Antoni et al., 1990). More and more people are living with HIV and AIDS because of advances in the treatment of the various components of the disease and the adoption of healthier lifestyles.

Educating young people about the risk of AIDS is an important step in eliminating the spread of this fatal disease.

Returning to Health

Medical treatment focuses on helping people adjust to their illnesses and recover from them. Knowledge about one's treatment is a critical factor in recovery; it is better to know what to expect than to leave it to the doctor. Researchers have found that patients who show the best recovery from surgery are those who received complete information before their operations (Janis, 1958; Johnson, 1983). However, other types of communication between doctor and patient often do not occur as planned.

Following Doctors' Orders   Patients are often given a *treatment regimen*, which might include medications, dietary changes, prescribed periods of bed rest and exercise, and follow-up procedures such as return checkups, rehabilitation training, and chemotherapy. One of the most serious problems in health care is **patient nonadherence**, *a patient's failure to follow medical guidelines or physicians' recommendations for treatment* (Rodin & Janis, 1982). The rate of patient nonadherence is estimated to be as high as 50 percent. The culprit seems to be the communication process between doctor and patient. For example, the reason a man fails to follow his doctor's recommendations for diet and medication may not be that he deliberately disregards her advice, but rather that he misunderstood her instructions or could not get clear reassurance from her about his fears.

When patients believe the cost of treatment is outweighed by its effectiveness, and when their practitioners communicate clearly, act courteously, and convey caring and support, patients are more satisfied with their health care. Some physicians critical of their profession argue that doctors must be taught to *care* in order to *cure* (Siegel, 1988). Social psychologists have developed strategies to help individuals gain others' compliance with their orders, and these are now being used to overcome the lack of cooperation between patients and practitioners (Zimbardo & Leippe, 1991). For example, research shows that people are more likely to comply with requests when they feel they have freedom of choice. Therefore, instead of demanding that a patient strictly adhere to one course of treatment, a physician could be more effective by offering the patient several different options, and asking him or her to choose one. Finally, patients are most likely to adhere to physicians' requests when they are informed and get active social support from friends and family (Gottlieb, 1987; Patterson, 1985). When someone close to you is receiving medical treatment, ask questions, stay informed, and offer encouragement to the patient to increase his or her compliance with doctors' orders.

Confiding in Others   While good communication between a doctor and a patient is necessary for good health, communication between an individual and his or her peers is also important. Have you ever had a secret too shameful to tell anyone? If so, tell someone you trust—now! That is the conclusion of a large body of research by health psychologist **James Pennebaker** (1990), who has shown that suppressing thoughts and feelings associated with personal traumas, failures, and guilty or shameful experiences takes a devastating toll on mental and physical health. Such inhibition is psychologically hard work and, over time, it undermines the body's defenses against illness. Confiding in others neutralizes the negative effects of inhibition; there are immediate changes in brain wave patterns and skin conductance levels, drops in blood pressure, and improvements in immune functions. This experience of *letting go* often is followed by improved physical and psychological health weeks and months later.

Research indicates that, in the wake of traumatic experiences such as relationship loss, crime, or injury, people formulate **accounts**, *stories that charac-*

Confiding in others is beneficial for health and happiness.

terize themselves and others and explain what happened and what it means. The accounts we keep and relate about our losses and traumas have been found to be an important part of efforts to interact with and explain ourselves to each other. Forming and transmitting such accounts may even reflect a more general human need to tell our stories and be understood by those close to us (Harvey, 1996; Harvey et al., 1990). While we formulate accounts and personal narratives about many life events, we seem especially likely to analyze and explain surprising and/or unpleasant experiences, such as trauma and loss (Holtzworth-Munroe & Jacobson, 1985). An important part of working through the pain of loss is formulating your account, and if possible, confiding it to one or more others (Weber & Harvey, 1994).

A remarkable work by psychologist Carolyn Ellis demonstrates both the account-making process "in action" and its therapeutic potential. Early in her academic career, Ellis had dealt with the tragic death of her brother in a plane crash. Years later, she watched her life partner of nine years die of emphysema—and then spent about as many years producing a book documenting her memories, grief, and struggles for meaning. In *Final Negotiations: A Story of Love, Loss, and Chronic Illness* (1995), Ellis candidly describes intimacy, withdrawal, agony, and relief. For Ellis, writing the book commemorated her love, structured her grieving, and gradually returned some control and hope to her life. "Opening up," therefore, is not a haphazard, indiscriminate act of disclosing to anyone who will listen or read; it is alternately private and public, a deliberate effort to sort through loss and reforge a sense of self.

The Power of Optimism   While health habits clearly contribute to physical well-being or illness, it is also clear that personality and thinking styles can play a causal role in health (Friedman, 1990). Positive thoughts and images promote other criteria of mental health, such as the ability to care about others, feel happy and content, and engage in creative work. A long-term research program by **Martin Seligman** (1991) and his associates at the University of Pennsylvania indicates that there are healthy benefits to an *optimistic style of thinking*. An optimistic style has three general characteristics:

- Attributing illness to *specific causes* rather than global problems: "I feel fine except for this headache."
- Blaming the problem on an *external* rather than an internal condition: "I probably got the headache from reading too long without a break; next study session, I'll remember to stop and stretch every half hour."

■ Assuming that the causes of pain or illness are *unstable* or temporary; for example, "I don't usually have headaches for very long, so I'm sure I'll feel better soon."

In contrast with the optimistic style, pessimistic thinking tends to see negative conditions like pain or illness as global, internal, and lasting: "This headache is terrible, it will ruin my whole day! I hate being prone to headaches. It's so depressing to think I'll probably never get better." Seligman and other researchers attest to the power of positive thinking in health. When you believe your problems are manageable and controllable, you are more likely to recover and effectively deal with them. Optimistic people have fewer physical symptoms of illness, are faster at recovering from certain disorders, are generally healthier, and live longer than pessimists do (Peterson et al., 1988). Thus, although it is important (as long as we are in the real world) to think realistically, the healthiest attitude appears to be one that is somewhat optimistic about your life and outlook—even if this requires a slight distortion of the facts.

Resolving to Be Healthy   You are probably aware of making many choices that contribute to your distress and lack of optimal health—choices to eat poorly, not to exercise regularly, to commute long distances, to be overly competitive, to work too much, to relax too little, or not to take time to cultivate friendships. What choices are you making, and how do they affect your well-being? Instead of waiting for stress or illness to strike and then reacting to it, set goals and structure your life in ways that forge a healthy foundation. The following guidelines are presented to encourage you to take a more active role in your own life and to create a more positive psychological environment for yourself and others.

1. *Understand the context of your behavior.* How does the current situation relate to your past experience? How can this help you to make healthy change?

2. *Give only constructive criticism.* This applies to yourself as well as to your evaluation of others. Instead of pinpointing complaints, identify what can be done differently in order to be more effective next time.

3. *Maintain realistic standards and ideals.* You will improve by aspiring to be better, but will suffer if your hopes are not realistic or achievable. To be fair and successful, do a reality check and compare your expectations and goals with those of others like yourself.

4. *Maintain and nourish your social support network.* Develop new friendships, invest in your close friendships, and communicate with others about feelings and values.

5. *Reach beyond your situation when necessary.* If you need help, ask for it. If you feel you are losing control, distance yourself from the situation until you gain perspective on the problem.

6. *Cultivate healthy, genuine pleasures!* Give yourself permission to take time out, relax, meditate, run, fly a kite, laugh, help someone who needs it, do something you really enjoy by yourself. Use freedom and happiness to learn about and appreciate yourself.

Happiness and Well-Being

Following the suggestions on the list above can clearly lead not only to wellness but *happiness,* a state that researchers call **subjective well-being (SWB):** *individuals' evaluative responses to their lives, including cognitive and emotional reactions* (Diener, 1984; 1995). Earlier in this chapter, in our discussion of the emotional consequences of stress, we defined hedonic capacity as one's ability to feel pleasure and joy. When hedonic capacity is fulfilled, an individual *feels* happy and is aware of reacting positively to life. This feeling makes up the "subjective" aspect of subjective well-being. Unlike "happiness," which can be defined many ways, SWB can be specified and measured, and linked with probable causes and outcomes. Most studies of SWB ask respondents to rate experiences in their lives, or answer questions about factors that affect satisfaction, well-being, mood, or success. In an important review of decades of study, researchers **David Myers** and **Ed Diener** (1995) conclude that, despite many and important individual differences in the causes and expressions of SWB, it is defined by three central components:

- *Satisfaction with present life:* People who are high in SWB like their work and are satisfied with their current personal relationships.
- *Relative presence of positive affect:* High SWB's more frequently feel pleasant emotions, mainly because they tend to evaluate the world around them in a generally positive way.
- *Relative absence of negative affect:* Individuals with a strong sense of subjective well-being experience fewer and less severe episodes of negative emotions such as anxiety, depression, and anger.

Myers and Diener point out that positive and negative emotions are not correlated: people may feel happy yet still feel angry or sad, and it is possible for individuals to be *neither* happy nor sad. The presence of one type of mood does not guarantee the absence of the other—because they are not "opposites." Thus subjective well-being depends on a complex of experiences and perspectives, not a single dimension of mood.

Who is happy? What is the secret to happiness? From their review of the SWB literature, Myers and Diener (1995) surmised that many of the "secrets of happiness" celebrated in song and story are actually based on myth or misunderstanding. Instead, consider the following conclusions:

- *There is no "happiest age" of life.* SWB cannot be predicted from someone's age. Most age groups studied exhibit similar levels of life satisfaction, for example, although the causes of their happiness do change with age (Inglehart, 1990).
- *Unlike misery, happiness has no "gender gap."* While women are more likely than men to suffer from anxiety and depression, and men are more at risk for alcoholism and certain personality disorders, approximately equal numbers of men and women report being fairly satisfied with life (Fujita et al., 1991; Haring et al., 1984; Inglehart, 1990).
- *There are few racial differences in happiness.* African Americans and European Americans report nearly the same levels of happiness, and African Americans are even slightly less vulnerable to depression (Diener et al., 1993). Despite racism and discrimination, disadvantaged minority groups seem to "think optimistically" by making realistic self-comparisons and attributing problems less to themselves than to unfair circumstances (Crocker & Major, 1989).
- *Money does not buy happiness.* At the level of nations, wealthier societies report greater well-being. But within countries—except for very poor, desperate nations such as Bangladesh and India—once the necessities of food, shelter, and safety are provided, there is only a very weak correlation between income and happiness. Having *no* money is a cause of misery, but wealth itself cannot guarantee happiness (Diener & Diener, 1995; Diener et al., 1993). The secret here is that happy people are not those who get what they want—but rather those who want what they have (Myers & Diener, 1995).

People who are high in SWB more frequently feel pleasant emotions because they evaluate the world in a positive way.

If life circumstances—one's age, sex, race, nationality, or income—do not predict happiness, then what *is* it that makes some of us happier than others? Not surprisingly, considering this is a psychology text, the key factors in subjective well-being appear to be psychological traits and processes: Happy people *like themselves,* and enjoy good health and high self-esteem (Janoff-Bulman, 1989, 1992). They have an *optimistic outlook,* and expect success in what they undertake (Seligman, 1991). They are *sociable,* outgoing, and willing to open up to others (Pavot et al., 1990). They *like what they do,* have a good sense of control in life events, and are able to enjoy the "flow" of engaging work (Crohan et al., 1989; Csikszentmihalyi, 1990; Larson, 1989). Finally, happy people are people who have and *express faith,* describing themselves as spiritual, hopeful, or committed to a religious identity (Brown, 1993; Gartner et al., 1991; Poloma & Pendleton, 1990; Solomon et al., 1991). In sum, happy people are happy *not* because of what they have but *how they live* (Myers & Diener, 1995).

People are enormously adaptive. Recall that in Chapter 2 we discussed how the evolution of the human brain and behavior have enabled members of our species to cope with new environments, learn from mistakes, and profit from experience. In fact, studies of subjective well-being have confirmed that people have an amazing ability to deal with the stressors and traumas life deals them. Perhaps this helps to explain why life circumstances alone—wealth or nationality, for example—do not predict happiness. Such circumstances change, and people's evaluations of their situations change accordingly. It is sometimes startling to discover how people are able to adapt. One study found that while the moods of victims of spinal cord injuries were extremely negative shortly after their accidents, several weeks later they reported feeling much happier than they had been *before* sustaining their injuries (Silver, 1980).

Life events can alter our moods, change and almost seem to destroy our lives. Not all life events can be forgotten; many people will find it daunting or impossible to recover from tragedies such as losing a loved one to war, violent crime, or diseases such as Alzheimer's (Bard & Sangrey, 1979; Janoff-Bulman, 1992; Silver et al., 1983; Silver & Wortman, 1980; Vitaliano et al., 1991). Even more common losses such as the death of a spouse are likely to be deeply painful and require *years* for bereavement and healing. But for most people, after an initially strong, emotional response and intense efforts to cope, it is possible to adapt, returning to a mood and level of well-being similar to that prior to the traumatic event (Headley & Wearing, 1992). Ultimately, a complete view of health and well-being requires us to accept that, while illness is part of the human condition, wellness is our natural goal. The ability to cope and adapt is apparently grounded in our ability—and determination—to be happy.

Check Your Recall

Health psychology examines the psychological factors involved in health and illness. The biopsychosocial model of health links physical well-being with psychological and social functioning. Health is not merely the absence of illness but a dynamic process of promoting well-being. Illness is distinguished from illness behavior, which does not necessarily indicate pathology. Behavior change can prevent illness, just as lifestyle change can reduce the diseases of civilization. Research has focused on ways to reduce heart disease, help people quit smoking, improve fitness, and reduce the risk of sexually transmitted diseases and AIDS.

Returning to health can be assisted through several strategies: finding support for one's efforts to adhere to a treatment regimen, opening up to others, thinking optimistically, and resolving to be and remain healthy. Research on happiness suggests that subjective well-being is based on life satisfaction, absence of negative affect, and presence of positive affect. Several myths about who is happy have been debunked by recent decades of research. Happiness has been related to psychological processes, perspectives on life, and effective behaviors. People's ability to cope and adapt is grounded in a broader potential for satisfaction and happiness. ☑

CHAPTER REVIEW

Chapter Summary

At the root of most stress is change and the need to adapt to environmental, physical, psychological, and social demands. Primitive stressors included mortal threats such as starvation, exposure to the elements, and attack. Modern stressors include life events, catastrophe, societal stressors, and hassles. The physical consequences of stress include arousal, fight-or-flight readiness, the general adaptation syndrome, and effects on the immune system. Psychological consequences include behavioral responses to mild, moderate, and severe stress; emotional patterns such as posttraumatic stress and reduced hedonic capacity; and cognitive effects such as errors in attention and memory.

Humans are physically and psychologically equipped to respond to most stressors. We engage in cognitive appraisal to identify the nature of the stressor and the resources required to cope. Coping strategies include problem-focused and emotion-focused coping and defense mechanisms. Stressors can be cognitively reassessed and thought patterns restructured to provide a greater sense of control and competence in responding to threat. Social support provides material resources and companionship to individuals dealing with stress, illness, and trauma. Effective stress management seeks to match resources appropriately with the nature of the stressors.

Health psychologists focus their work on the links between illness and people's thoughts and actions. The biopsychosocial model of health emphasizes linkages among mind and body systems in both illness and health. Unhealthy behavior can be changed under certain conditions, and illness can be prevented by combining efforts at the national and societal level. Patients can return to health by adhering to strategies that emphasize their responsibility and control in determining their own well-being. People are extremely adaptive in the wake of stress and illness, and appear to be capable of achieving not only wellness but happiness.

Section Reviews

Stress

Be sure to *Check Your Recall* by reviewing the summary of this section on page 350.

Key Terms
psychoneuroimmunology (PNI) (p. 332)
stress (p. 333)
stressor (p. 333)
life-change units (LCU) (p. 335)
burnout (p. 340)
culture shock (p. 343)
acute stress (p. 343)
chronic stress (p. 343)
fight-or-flight syndrome (p. 344)
general adaptation syndrome (GAS) (p. 345)
posttraumatic stress disorder (PTSD) (p. 348)
residual stress pattern (p. 349)
Stockholm syndrome (p. 349)
hedonic capacity (p. 349)

Names to Know
Norman Cousins (p. 331)
Steve Duck (p. 337)
Christina Maslach (p. 340)
Walter Cannon (p. 344)
Hans Selye (p. 345)

Responding to Stress

Be sure to *Check Your Recall* by reviewing the summary of this section on page 361.

Key Terms
coping (p. 351)
anticipatory coping (p. 351)
ego defense mechanisms (p. 353)
stress moderator variables (p. 354)
cognitive appraisal (p. 354)
primary appraisal (p. 354)
secondary appraisal (p. 354)
Type A syndrome (p. 356)
Type T personality (p. 358)
hardiness (p. 358)
social support (p. 359)

Names to Know
Richard Lazarus (p. 354)
Ellen Langer (p. 357)
Judith Rodin (p. 357)
Frank Farley (p. 358)
Suzanne Kobasa (p. 358)
Shelley Taylor (p. 360)

Health and Well-Being

Be sure to *Check Your Recall* by reviewing the summary of this section on page 374.

Key Terms
health psychology (p. 362)
biopsychosocial model (p. 362)
health (p. 362)
wellness (p. 362)
illness (p. 363)
relapse (p. 363)
illness prevention (p. 364)
patient nonadherence (p. 370)
accounts (p. 370)
subjective well-being (SWB) (p. 372)

Names to Know
David Spiegel (p. 364)
Joseph Matarazzo (p. 364)
James Pennebaker (p. 370)
Martin Seligman (p. 371)
David Myers (p. 373)
Ed Diener (p. 373)

REVIEW TEST

Chapter 9: Stress, Health, and Well-Being

For each of the following items, choose the single correct or best answer. The correct answers, explanations, and page references appear in Appendix B.

1. Which of the following life events is most likely to cause stress that would put a student's health at risk?
   a. getting married
   b. chronic car trouble
   c. having a serious argument with an instructor
   d. changing his or her major

2. Which of the following experiences would be considered a chronic societal stress?
   a. an earthquake
   b. a jail term
   c. being stuck in traffic
   d. widespread unemployment

3. You are just getting over a bad cold when your steady partner announces a desire to break up and see other people. Your present state of health is an example of a _____, because it affects how well you can deal with the stress of the breakup.
   a. defense mechanism
   b. moderator variable
   c. cognitive appraisal
   d. life change

4. Malcolm does not get upset when he encounters problems, seeing them as challenges to be overcome rather than threats to his well-being. Which of the following terms best describes Malcolm's approach to possible stressors?
   a. hardiness
   b. learned helplessness
   c. the Type A personality
   d. the Type T personality

5. The fight-or-flight syndrome is governed by the _____.
   a. PTSD
   b. PNI
   c. ANS
   d. GAS

6. Which of the following is *not* a stage in the general adaptation syndrome described by Hans Selye?
   a. alarm
   b. withdrawal
   c. resistance
   d. exhaustion

7. Nursing home patients had more positive moods, better health, and longer survival compared to others when they were provided with _____.
   a. round-the-clock medical care
   b. busy work and entertaining activities
   c. responsibilities that gave them perceived control
   d. service that relieved them of all aspects of self-care

8. Improving health by reducing incidences of heart disease and smoking, increasing exercise, and preventing sexually transmitted diseases is based on a strategy of waging a "war on _____."
   a. selfishness
   b. ignorance
   c. lifestyle
   d. human nature

9. A good friend of yours has recently suffered the loss of a close family member. To help your friend cope with this trauma, you should encourage her to _____.
   a. accept others' help with the demands of daily living
   b. talk about her loss, even if it is sad to do so
   c. keep busy with work and other distractions
   d. none of the above

10. Research on subjective well-being indicates that _____ are significantly happier than _____.
    a. women; men
    b. wealthy Americans; middle-class Americans
    c. young people; older adults
    d. none of the above

IF YOU'RE INTERESTED . . .

After the Shock. (Video: 1990 [made for cable], color, 100 min.). Directed by Gary Sherman; starring Jack Scalia, Yaphet Kotto, Scott Valentine, Rue McClanahan.

Moving depictions of ordinary citizens taking heroic action in rescue efforts following the 1989 San Francisco earthquake. Mixes reenacted scenes with actual footage of the quake and its aftermath.

Cousins, N. (1979). *The anatomy of an illness as perceived by a patient: Reflections on healing and rejuvenation.* New York: Norton.

The original, groundbreaking work by the late Norman Cousins, presenting his discoveries about the interconnections between physical well-being and psychology, and the responsibilities and opportunities the patient has to promote his or her own recovery.

Doctor, The. (Video: 1991, color, 123 min.). Directed by Randa Haines; starring William Hurt, Elizabeth Perkins, Christine Lahti, Mandy Patinkin.

Before television's *Chicago Hope* and *ER*, one of the few recent film presentations of the roles played by physician and patient was this intriguing portrayal of a doctor who finds the tables turned on him. A successful but insensitive surgeon is diagnosed with throat cancer and forced to experience life from the patient's perspective. Based on the true story, *A Taste of My Own Medicine*, by Ed Rosenbaum, M.D.

Falling Down. (Video: 1993, color, 115 min.). Directed by Joel Schumacher; starring Michael Douglas, Robert Duvall, Barbara Hershey, Rachel Ticotin, Tuesday Weld.

A stressed, repressed Californian abandons his car in a traffic jam and wanders Los Angeles in a frenzied, violent outburst. At one level, a movie about a man who has an incredibly bad day. But at another level, a review of how two men—the criminal and the police officer pursuing him—have responded so differently to the stressors and traumas of their lives. Well acted and realistic, it is also bleak and depressing.

Fearless. (Video: 1993, color, 122 min.). Directed by Peter Weir; starring Jeff Bridges, Isabella Rossellini, Rosie Perez, Tom Hulce, John Turturro, John DeLancie.

After he and a few others survive a devastating plane crash, a man loses perspective on the meaning of his life, work, and family. Suspecting that he has become indestructible, he engages in increasingly risky and careless—*fearless*—behavior, alienating everyone except fellow survivors who are similarly disoriented, traumatized, and guilt-ridden. Great writing and acting, and an intriguing look at what comes *after* surviving trauma.

Hannah and Her Sisters. (Video: 1986, color, 106 min.). Directed by Woody Allen; starring Woody Allen, Michael Caine, Mia Farrow, Barbara Hershey, Max von Sydow, Dianne Wiest.

Funny, urbane story about three New York sisters and their convoluted relationships with men and with each other. Key subplot involves the character of Mickey (played by Allen), an unhappy hypochondriac whose quest for the meaning in life leads him to "shop" for religion and ultimately find what he needs in humor, self-acceptance, and love.

Heartsounds. (Video: 1984, color, 135 min.). Directed by Glenn Jordan; starring Mary Tyler Moore, James Garner, Sam Wanamaker, Wendy Crewson.

Touching and wrenching film based on Martha Weinman Lear's novel about a woman whose husband, a physician, suffers a series of debilitating heart attacks. Outstanding presentation of the stresses and traumas that afflict not only the patient but family and friends who must meet and perhaps survive the challenges of illness and recovery.

Klein, A. (1989). *The healing power of humor.* Los Angeles: Jeremy P. Tarcher.

The subtitle is "Techniques for Getting through Loss, Setbacks, Upsets, Disappointments, Difficulties, Trials, Tribulations, and All That Not-So-Funny Stuff." It delivers on the promised techniques by reviewing what humor can (and cannot) be expected to accomplish; simple (if sometimes goofy) gimmicks for lightening things up; and explaining what research has shown about the connections between humor and well-being.

Neeld, E. H. (1990). *Seven choices: Taking the steps to new life after losing someone you love.* New York: Delta.

After her husband, a healthy and fit man, died suddenly while on an evening run, Elizabeth Neeld spent months observing and understanding her own and others' reactions to loss and grief, concluding that life after loss is conducted as a series of choices. Her story is also a guidebook for survivors of loss and those who wish to help bereaved loved ones.

Plotkin, M. J. (1993). *Tales of a shaman's apprentice: An ethnobotanist searches for new medicines in the Amazon rain forest.* New York: Viking.

"I had followed the old shaman through the jungle for three days and . . . we had developed an enigmatic relationship." Thus Mark Plotkin begins the story of his work with South American natives and their therapeutic uses of medicinal plants. This is a story not only of perspectives on healing, but also the changes and losses incurred when traditional cultures yield to "progress" and "development" by modern economic interests.

Siegel, Bernie S. (1986). *Love, medicine, & miracles.* New York: Harper & Row.

Stories of people who have made remarkable recoveries and their enlightening perspectives on survival, the characteristics survivors have in common, and suggestions for how patients can take control and develop courage in healing themselves

CHAPTER 10

Personality

On a sweltering day in July of 1912, nurse Margaret Sanger was called to a slum in New York City's Lower East Side, to the cramped apartment of Jake Sachs and his family. Jake, a truck driver, had found his wife, Sadie, mother of their three small children, unconscious and bleeding on the kitchen floor after attempting a self-induced abortion. Days later, after Sanger and the doctor had successfully fought the infection that threatened Sadie Sachs's life, her immediate plea was, "Doctor, what can I do to stop having babies?" The doctor, kind, but no doubt frustrated at hearing this question asked too often, gruffly replied, "Better tell Jake to sleep on the roof" (Sanger, 1971).

In 1912, medical advice was forbidden; condoms and diaphragms were virtually impossible to obtain. Reflecting the prevailing morality, legal codes outlawed any form of artificial birth control and condemned abortion. Nevertheless, up to 100,000 illegal abortions a year were performed in New York alone. People with education or money had always been able to prevent unwanted pregnancies. But among the poor and uneducated, those least able to bear the costliness of many children, little was known about sex, much less reproduction and family planning (Asbell, 1995). Furthermore, pregnancy was life-threatening. Between 1910 and 1925, more than 200,000 American women died in childbirth.

Margaret Sanger was to see Sadie Sachs one last time: three months later, pregnant once again, Sadie died of a back-alley abortion. After watching yet another needless death, Sanger resolved to find an answer to her patients' pleas for safe contraception, "no matter what it might cost" (Sanger, 1938, in Conway, 1992, p. 567).

The cost was high. Herself the mother of three children and happily married to an architect, Sanger left nursing and put her family in the background in order to research and promote contraception full-time. Margaret chose the term "birth control" for her movement in order to shift the focus from sexuality and morality and place it firmly on humanity, choice, and population. When in 1914 she was threatened with a prison term for "indecency," Sanger fled to England until charges were dropped a year later. In 1916 she opened a public birth control clinic and began to serve a series of jail sentences for illegally distributing information about contraception. For 40 years, Sanger persistently challenged laws making contraception a criminal act and insisted that women take control of—and responsibility for—their bodies, sexuality, and childbearing (Kennedy, 1970; Sanger, 1971). Finally in 1952, Sanger, now in her 70s, joined forces with philanthropist Katharine McCormick to commission the

379

development of an oral contraceptive, something that could be taken "like an aspirin. " Without government backing or funding, Sanger and McCormick supported the work of biological researcher Gregory Pincus and his staff. Pincus succeeded brilliantly— the first birth control pills were approved for prescription in 1960—and he is credited as the "Father of the Pill. " In view of its history, however, the Pill more accurately had two mothers: passionate, persistent Margaret Sanger and philanthropist Katharine McCormick.

What drove Sanger to begin her crusade, and what personal qualities empowered her to endure punishment and sacrifice? Let's look more closely at some of the details of her life and work.

■ *Born in 1879, Margaret Higgins Sanger was the sixth of eleven children. She was 19 when her mother died of tuberculosis. Although she remembered her father as generous and free-thinking (and may well have acquired her habit of independent thought from him), she blamed him for exhausting her mother with children and household labor.*

■ *Sanger's exile in England damaged her marriage irreparably. She had only just returned when her young daughter Peggy died of pneumonia. Stricken by guilt and grief, Sanger suffered a "nervous breakdown,"*

recovering in time to face a trial on new charges of obscenity (Asbell, 1995).

■ *Divorced after 22 years of marriage, Margaret, unembittered, married a wealthy businessman who adored her and supported her work. Never as fanatically exclusive as her early political allies had been, Sanger managed to become flexible and took her message to the powerful, affluent, and educated.*

As we have seen, strong emotions such as guilt and grief can motivate behavior throughout a long life. Sanger's intelligent frustration with a conventional patriarchy that supported unnecessary deaths may well have led her to wrestle meaning from despair—to honor those lost lives by changing what had brought their deaths. Such drive may account for Sanger's continuing to fight when others would have surrendered to loss and persecution.

While historians have criticized Sanger for seeking singular credit for the successes of the birth control movement, one biographer notes that "her ambitions would be considered normal in a male reformer" (Conway, 1992, p. 550). Perhaps Sanger experienced significant influences and made important choices because of her gender. Ultimately, however, it was her personal regard for humanity that drove her beyond gender to benefit all humankind.

Introduction

Margaret Sanger "got things moving" so effectively that the Pill she cosponsored was approved by the U.S. Food and Drug Administration in 1960, six years before her death. Thus within her own lifetime, Sanger saw her life's guiding mission begin, grow, and come to fruition. Why did she do it? Why sacrifice a comfortable, anonymous life for notoriety, punishment, and disruption? Why, when she watched young Sadie Sachs die from a botched illegal abortion, could she not walk away and forget about it? Like many health care professionals, who must deal with disease and death on a daily basis, Sanger could have disconnected herself from the Sachs tragedy. She could have rationalized the death, blaming Sadie herself, or her husband, or the impersonal cruelties of ignorance and poverty. Margaret Sanger could then have gone back to her relatively comfortable and safe life. But something about her *personality* made it impossible for her to forgive and forget, or to accept as inevitable so many unwanted births, miserable parents, and doomed children.

Where do such qualities—commitment to purpose, willingness to sacrifice, stubbornness, obsessiveness, creativity—come from? How do people's traits and life experiences produce the choices they make? In this chapter we examine these questions of nature and nurture, and their consequences for who we are and what we do.

The personality you develop, the sense of "self" you form, is certainly affected by both nature (inherited tendencies) and nurture (unique experiences and education). But your personality is more than a list of traits and traumas: it is a puzzle with mysterious origins and influences, and yet it helps to explain your choices, actions, and outcomes. In this chapter we focus on the puzzle of personality, its origins and applications.

The Psychology of the Person

If psychologists studied *you*, what portrait of your personality would they draw? What differentiates you from other individuals who function in many of the same situations as you?

Psychologists define personality in many different ways, but common to all of them are two basic concepts: *uniqueness* and *characteristic patterns* of behavior. **Personality** *is the complex set of unique psychological qualities that influence an individual's characteristic patterns of behavior across different situations and over time.* Investigators in the field of personality psychology seek to discover how individuals differ. They also study the extent to which personality traits and behavior patterns are consistent from one situation or occasion to another.

The field of *personality psychology* attempts to integrate all aspects of an individual's functioning. This integration requires the psychologist to build on the accumulated knowledge of all the areas of psychology we have already discussed, along with social psychology, which studies interpersonal and group processes. Personality psychology goes beyond an interest in the normally functioning individual. It provides the foundation for understanding personal problems and pathologies as well as a basis for therapeutic approaches to change personality. We begin with a review of how personality is assessed, and then examine how both personal and scientific theories of personality are formed and used.

Personality Assessment

Psychologists have long wondered how to measure the attributes that characterize an individual, set one person apart from others, or distinguish people in one group from those in another. Two assumptions are basic to these attempts

A counselor and her client review the results of a psychological test together. Information from these tests is used not only in research and therapy, but also in career counseling and personnel training.

to understand and describe human personality: first, the personal characteristics of individuals give coherence to behavior, and second, those characteristics can be assessed or measured. Psychologists use special tests designed to reveal important personal traits and the way those characteristics fit together in particular individuals. Such information is applied in psychological research, individual therapy, career counseling, or personnel selection and training. The many different types of personality tests can be classified as either objective or projective.

Objective Tests   The administration and scoring of objective tests of personality are relatively simple procedures that follow standardized, objective rules. The final score is usually a number along a single dimension (such as "adjustment versus maladjustment") or a set of scores on different traits (such as masculinity, dependency, or extroversion) reported relative to some comparison group.

A self-report inventory is an objective test in which individuals answer a series of questions about their thoughts, feelings, and actions. A **personality inventory** *is a self-report questionnaire used for personality assessment.* Typically a respondent reads a series of true-false statements and indicates whether each one is true for herself or himself. On some inventories the person is asked to assess how frequently each statement is true or how well each describes her own typical behavior, thoughts, or feelings.

The MMPI   The most famous personality inventory is the *Minnesota Multiphasic Personality Inventory* or MMPI (Dahlstrom et al., 1975). It is used by clinical psychologists as an aid in the diagnosis of patients and as a guide for their treatment. The MMPI was developed at the University of Minnesota during the 1930s by psychologist Starke Hathaway and psychiatrist J. R. McKinley. It was first published in the 1940s (Hathaway & McKinley, 1940, 1943). Its basic purpose is to diagnose individuals according to a set of psychiatric labels. The first test consisted of 550 items, to each of which the subject responded "true," "false," or "cannot say." From that item pool, scales were developed that related to the kinds of problems patients showed in psychiatric settings. Standards for response patterns were established for both psychiatric patients and normal subjects.

The MMPI has 10 *clinical scales,* each constructed to differentiate a special clinical group (such as schizophrenics or paranoids) from a normal control group. The test is scored by adding up the number of items on a particular scale that a person answered in the same way as the clinical group; the higher the score, the more the person is like the clinical group and unlike the normal group. This type of scale development is called *empirical* because items are chosen not because they are theoretically related or relevant to some category, but because they are answered in a particular way by a given clinical group. The test also includes scales that detect suspicious response patterns, such as blatant dishonesty, carelessness, defensiveness, and evasiveness. A respondent's score on these scales is considered by the tester before the clinical scale answers are interpreted. The pattern of the scores—which ones are highest, how they differ—forms the "MMPI profile," which can be depicted as a graph of changes in value from one scale to the next.

Recently the MMPI has undergone a major revision—changing items and rewriting language to remove sexist or culturally irrelevant themes—and is now called the *MMPI–2* (Boone, 1994; Butcher & Williams, 1992; Dahlstrom et al., 1975; Helmes & Reddon, 1993; Svanum et al., 1994). The most dramatic change is the addition of 15 new content scales. For each of 15 clinically relevant topics (such as anxiety or family problems), items were selected on two bases: if they seemed theoretically related to the topic area and if each scale measured a single, unified concept. The MMPI–2's clinical and content scales are given in Table 10.1. Notice that most of the clinical scales measure several related concepts and that the names of the content scales are simple and self-explanatory.

The benefits of the MMPI include its established strengths as a test, its ease and economy of administration, and its usefulness for research. However, the MMPI is not without its faults. Its clinical scales have been criticized because they measure several things at once, and because the scale names are confusing and do not correspond to what they measure. Another shortcoming of the MMPI is that it has little to do with normal personality; the items were originally developed to measure clinical problems, so the inventory is not well-suited to measure personality in nonpatient populations.

The CPI In 1957, **Harrison Gough** (1957) created the California Psychological Inventory (CPI) to measure individual differences in personality among people who are more or less normal and well adjusted. Its personality scales measure "folk concepts"—behavioral qualities that lay persons can easily understand, such as Dominance, Self-Control, Tolerance, and Intellectual Efficiency. All the scales are presented on a profile sheet that shows how a person scored on each scale relative to same-sex norms.

TABLE 10.1	MMPI-2 CLINICAL AND CONTENT SCALES, 1989

Clinical Scales and Descriptions	Content Scales
Hypochondriasis (Hs): Abnormal concern with bodily functions	Anxiety
Depression (D): Pessimism; hopelessness; slowing of action and thought	Fears Obsessiveness
Conversion hysteria (Hy): Unconscious use of mental problems to avoid conflicts or responsibility	Depression
Psychopathic deviate (Pd): Disregard for social custom; shallow emotions; inability to profit from experience	Health concerns Bizarre mentation
Masculinity-femininity (Mf): differences between men and women	Anger Cynicism
Paranoia (Pa): Suspiciousness; delusions of grandeur or persecution	Antisocial practices Type A (workaholic)
Psychasthenia (Pt): Obsessions; compulsions; fears; guilt; indecisiveness	Low self-esteem
Schizophrenia (Sc): Bizarre, unusual thoughts or behavior; withdrawal; hallucinations; delusions	Social discomfort Family problems
Hypomania (Ma): Emotional excitement; flight of ideas; overactivity	Work interference
Social introversion (Si): Shyness; disinterest in others; insecurity	Negative treatment indicators (negative attitudes about doctors and treatment)

The new version of the CPI (1996) contains 20 folk scales and 13 special-purpose scales with norms on 6000 men and women. It has been administered to thousands of people all over the world and has been the subject of many research studies, generating valuable archives of data (Weiser & Meyers, 1993; Zebb & Meyers, 1993). The CPI has been used to study personality structure in healthy adults and to evaluate characteristic personality structures of various groups, such as people in different occupations. Studies employing the CPI have helped psychologists understand how personality develops and how personality traits in young adulthood are related to life events. In addition, many newly created scales have been found to be valid for applied purposes such as selecting police officers for special training programs and predicting job performance for student teachers, dentists, and other professional groups (Gough, 1989, 1995; Gynther & Gynther, 1996).

Like the MMPI, the CPI has been criticized because many of its scales measure several different things at once, and because certain scales seem to measure overlapping concepts. However, unlike the MMPI, the CPI scales are easy to understand, because the names have been changed to reflect what the scales measure. In addition, the revised CPI's profiles include scores for three special scales that are nonoverlapping and uncorrelated with each other (they measure independent qualities). These scales measure broad dimensions having to do with the respondent's overall interpersonal style, acceptance of rules or social norms, and psychological adjustment (Gough, 1996).

The MBTI The Myers-Briggs Type Indicator (MBTI) was based on the typology theory of **Carl Jung** (1971), a theorist who was originally a colleague of Sigmund Freud (see Focus on Science: Post-Freudian Theories on page 407). The MBTI assigns people to one of sixteen categories or types. Developed by Peter Myers and Isabel Briggs, the test attempts to find "an orderly reason for personality differences" or the ways people perceive their world and make judgments about it (Myers, 1962, 1976, 1980).

The MBTI assumes that differences in individuals' behavior correspond to basic differences in perception and judgment. Thus to understand and predict individual behavior, the instrument asks a respondent questions about how he or she views the world and prefers to approach life situations. The two primary processes of Perception (P) and Judgment (J) are subdivided into (a) dual ways of perceiving—by direct sensing (S) and unconscious intuition (N)—and (b) dual ways of judging—by thinking (T) and feeling (F). The added factor in the Myers-Briggs test is the individual's preference for Extroversion (E) or Introversion (I). This factor is based on Jung's idea that people focus on either their outer (E) or inner (I) worlds. The notation of the MBTI summarizes the extremes of the four dimensions with initials in a consistent order: Extroverted or Introverted; Sensing or Intuiting; Thinking or Feeling; and Judging or Perceiving. The possible combinations of these four dimensions result in sixteen distinct types, such as *e*xtroverts who *j*udge their own *t*hinking with i*n*tuition (ENTJ's), or *i*ntroverts who *p*erceive by *s*ensing with *f*eeling (IPSF).

Given what you know about Margaret Sanger from having read the opening case, ASK YOURSELF the following questions:

- How do you think she saw the world?
- What might be her MBTI profile?

A major use of the MBTI is relating type to occupation—showing that certain preferences for perceiving, thinking, and extroversion or introversion influence occupational choice and job satisfaction (McCaulley, 1978). Its appeal lies in its ability to categorize people into a small number of types that simplify the enormous complexity of personality differences between individuals. However, critics complain about the absence of rigorous, controlled studies of the validity of the MBTI (Pittenger, 1993).

Projective Tests   Have you ever looked at a cloud and seen a face or the shape of an animal? If you shared your interpretations with friends, you probably found that they saw different images, because the visible shape of the cloud is *ambiguous*—not defined and therefore open to several interpretations (Piotrowski et al., 1985, 1993). Psychologists rely on the human tendency to interpret stimuli in using a particular assessment strategy in which a respondent *projects* inner concerns onto a stimulus that has no single meaning. A **projective test** *is an assessment technique in which a respondent is asked to interpret ambiguous stimuli.* Typically, a person is given a series of stimuli that are purposely ambiguous, such as abstract patterns, incomplete pictures, and drawings that can be interpreted in many ways. The respondent may be asked to describe the patterns, finish the pictures, or tell stories about the drawings. Because the stimuli are vague, responses are determined by what the person brings to the situation—namely, inner feelings, motives, and conflicts that are *projected* onto the situations. Two of the most common projective techniques in use today are the Rorschach test and the TAT.

The Rorschach   In the Rorschach test (pronounced *ROAR-shock*), developed by Swiss psychiatrist **Hermann Rorschach** in 1921, the ambiguous stimuli are symmetrical inkblots (Rorschach, 1942). Some are black and white and some are colored (see Figure 10.1). A respondent is first shown an inkblot and asked, "Tell me what you see, what it might be to you. There are no right or wrong answers." The tester first records verbatim what the subject says, how much time she takes to respond, the total time she takes per inkblot, and the way she handles the inkblot card. In a second phase called an *inquiry,* the respondent is reminded of the previous responses and asked to elaborate on them.

Assembling a person's scores into a coherent portrait of personality dynamics is a complex, highly subjective process that relies on clinical expertise and skilled intuition. The Rorschach's soundness as a testing instrument has been questioned because it is based on theoretical concepts (such as unconscious motives) that are impossible to "prove." However, many clinicians have championed the use of the Rorschach, arguing that it can be systematically applied to provide unique insights as part of a broader personality assessment (Exner, 1974, 1978; Exner & Weiner, 1982).

The TAT   Developed by U.S. psychologist **Henry Murray** in 1938, the *Thematic Apperception Test,* or TAT, involves showing a respondent a series of ambiguous scenes and having him or her generate a story about each one (see Figure 10.2). The story should describe what the characters in the scenes are doing and thinking, what led up to each event, and how each situation will end. In theory, the respondent perceives the elements in the actual picture and further *apperceives* (fills in) personal interpretations and explanations, based on his or her own thoughts, feelings, and needs. In describing a single TAT scene, no two people would tell the same story in the same way. (Recall that, in Chapter 8, we reviewed the use of the TAT in revealing people's need for achievement in work and life.)

The psychologist administering the TAT evaluates the structure and content of the stories, as well as the behavior of the individual telling them, in an attempt to discover some of the respondent's major concerns, motivations, and personality characteristics. For example, an examiner might evaluate a person as "conscientious" if his stories concerned people who lived up to their obligations and if he told them in a serious, orderly way. The test can be used

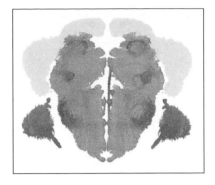

FIGURE 10.1   Rorschach Inkblot ■ What do you see? Does your interpretation of this inkblot reveal any thing about your personality?

FIGURE 10.2   Sample Card from the TAT ■

with clinical patients to reveal emotional problems, or with normal individuals to reveal dominant needs, such as needs for power, affiliation, and achievement (McClelland, 1961).

How Useful is Personality Assessment?   Strictly speaking, we cannot "test" personality in the way that we test for a person's knowledge of subject matter like mathematics. Unlike the kinds of tests you take in school, personality tests do not measure how *much* personality you have, but rather assess the measurable *qualities* of that personality. In essence, the goal of personality instruments is description, not evaluation. For this reason, many scholars prefer to call personality tests "techniques" or personality "assessment" instruments.

The most effective and useful personality assessments are based on one or more major personality theories. Recall that a theory is a collection of explanatory principles, concepts that help to understand and predict natural events. Using specific personality theories for guidance, personality psychologists are able to collect information that might not be readily available to casual observers. More importantly, psychologists are able to interpret and apply that information more precisely and fairly than if they had to rely only on impressions, hunches, and "intuitions" about people. We now consider the nature of both informal and scientific personality theories.

Personality Theories

Our language is rich in terms that describe and explain people and behavior: aggressive, boring, charming, diligent, extroverted, friendly . . . and on through the alphabet. However, a list of adjectives describing people is unwieldy to keep in mind, and not really helpful in understanding specific individuals. To simplify our task, most of us organize our observations and interpretations of personality into theories. To some extent we theorize automatically, applying opinions and beliefs quickly and without careful review. To correct the biases of such implicit theorizing, psychologists rely on scientific observations and data in an effort to form more reliable explicit personality theories.

Implicit Personality Theories   Think of someone you really trust. Now think of someone you know personally who is a role model for you. Imagine the qualities of a person with whom you would like to spend the rest of your life—and then of someone you can't stand to be around. In each case, what springs to mind immediately are personal attributes, such as honesty, reliability, sense of humor, generosity, outgoing attitude, aggressiveness, moodiness, or pessimism. Even as a child, you probably developed and used your own system for appraising personality. You tried to determine which new acquaintances would be friend or foe; you worked out ways of dealing with your parents or teachers based on how you read their personalities. You have probably spent a great deal of time trying to get a handle on who *you* are—on what qualities distinguish you from others, which ones to develop, and which to discard.

In each case, your judgments were, in fact, naive personality assessments reflecting your *implicit personality theory,* your personal explanation of how people's qualities and experiences influence their response patterns. Such judgments are based largely on intuition and limited observations. Such naive judgments can often be accurate, but they are also open to many sources of error. For example, your personal experiences and motives can influence your judgment of others; if you have had your heart broken by someone who was attractive but unwilling to make a commitment, you may quickly judge other attractive persons to be "insincere" or "untrustworthy." In addition, even if

THE FAR SIDE   By GARY LARSON

The four basic personality types

you try to be unbiased, you may have only limited opportunities to observe others' behavior. Most of us encounter others only within a narrow range of situations—in our classes, in the workplace, or in familiar social situations, for example. A person's behavior may be influenced by situational features you are not aware of, so that your impressions of him or her will be biased by what you don't know. For example, if someone has just received disappointing news—such as a poor grade on a test—when you first meet him or her, you may unfairly judge that person as sullen, or depressive, based on this single, superficial impression. Unless we learn to grant others the benefit of the doubt—and expect the same open-mindedness in return—it is risky to rely exclusively on implicit, unscientific theories of personality. Others may make the same errors in judging *your* personality as well. For that matter, as we find in Assess Yourself: Know Thyself, we are as fascinated and baffled by our own personalities as by those of other people.

Assess Yourself

"Know Thyself"

In ancient Greece, suppliants who wished to know the future would visit the temple of Apollo in the city of Delphi to consult the oracle, a woman who acted as a medium to channel messages from gods and spirits. Tellingly, a stone inscription at the entrance counsels visitors to "Know thyself." Good advice, now as then, before seeking the services of a seeress, prophet—or personality psychologist. But exactly what is the self? And what do we know about the self? Consider how you might apply classic and contemporary research in "knowing thyself" a little better.

From the early days of scientific psychology, **William James** advocated the study of self theory (1890). James identified three components of self-experience: the *material me* (one's body and personal possessions); the *social me* (one's awareness of his or her social reputation); and the *spiritual me* (which monitors private thoughts and feelings). For James, everything associated with one's identity became a part of self. For example, when our friends or family members are insulted, we react as though we have been attacked, because a part of ourselves has been threatened. We likewise take pride in possessions like cars and special collections, which are really extensions of our "selves" (Belk, 1988). You can begin to apply James' insights by listing some of the components of each of your three "me's":

■ Which of your possessions are most important, or say the most about you?

■ How do you believe others view you?

■ In what circumstances are you most likely to reflect on how you feel and what has been on your mind?

Examine your own experience of your *material, social,* and *spiritual me's* to detect patterns and gain insights you might otherwise overlook.

Now shift your gaze slightly and form an impression of yourself overall—not as the sum of three different "me's." What do you think of yourself? Your **self-concept** *is your awareness as an individual of your continuing identity as a person.* It includes all the conscious and potentially conscious thoughts, ideas, and evaluations you have of yourself. The self-concept is a dynamic structure, an ever-growing and changing mental structure that motivates, organizes, and regulates your behavior. Your self-concept influences you *intrapersonally,* within yourself, by affecting the way you process information about yourself (Cantor & Kihlstrom, 1987; Markus & Smith, 1981). For example, if you think of yourself as athletic, you will seek out certain activities and friends that enable you to express this aspect of your "self." The self-concept also affects you *interpersonally,* among others, by shaping your expectations of and interactions with others. Sometimes you may find yourself engaging in *impression management,* deliberately manipulating your public self to create a particular impact or image in others' minds. A similar type of influence can happen unconsciously, as when you are feeling anxious or depressed and your strong feelings become "contagious," bringing out anxiety or depression in those around you (Fong & Markus, 1982; Riggs & Cantor, 1981; Strack & Coyne, 1983).

To apply knowledge of the self-concept in your own life, start by making a list of your qualities, abilities, and weaknesses. Now ASK YOURSELF these questions:

■ Is my self-concept realistic? Do those who know me describe me in the same ways I describe myself? If not, why are there discrepancies? Could I be wrong about myself?

■ Is my self-concept bringing out my potential? Is it bringing out the best in me? Or instead, am I holding myself back or dooming myself by expecting mediocrity or failure?

There may be limits to your ability to know yourself *by* yourself, without input from others: many theorists argue that the self is ultimately directed not by a unique, pure inner will but by the social context in which one lives (Cross & Markus, 1991; Markus & Cross, 1990; Rosenberg, 1988). In this view, the self has meaning only in interpersonal experiences: without others, there can *be* no self. There is no clear distinction to you between what you think of yourself and what *you think* others think of you. All our interpersonal behavior—our hopes, regrets, actions, and evaluations—becomes incorporated into the self. Thus in order to know yourself it is essential that you "reach out and touch someone"—and get touched back. Through honest intimacy, contact, and communication you will have your best chance to see yourself as others—as the world—must see and know you.

You can begin to better understand your interpersonal self by writing down or relating your *account,* the story of your relationship experiences, interpreting your own and others' motives and the events involved. By engaging in *narrative thinking*—thinking in terms of the story that explains your experience—you get a sense of closure, completion, and meaning. By keeping a journal or relating parts of your account to close friends, you may more effectively cope with disappointment and get over a broken heart (Harvey, 1996; Harvey et al., 1982; Harvey et al., 1986; Weber et al., 1987). According to accounts researchers, the end result of account making is a change in *identity*—a new sense of self (Harvey et al., 1990). By generating and reviewing your story of your relationship experiences, you will integrate the lessons of even painful losses, and progress toward the self you can become.

Scientific Personality Theories   Because people's impressions of each other are critical in their choices and experiences, the field of personality psychology is devoted to studying personality with explicitly scientific methods. Personality researchers' data come from subjects' self-reports as well as observers' reports of subjects' behavior. Observers and interviewers can record specific instances of people's behavior, as well as biographical details and life events. By consulting several sources of information instead of relying on one person's perspective, personality research can reduce or even eliminate much bias. Finally, special instruments make it possible to record physiological data about subjects' bodily processes, including heart rate, hormone levels, and brain chemistry. Once the data are in, researchers make informed decisions about how to interpret what the data mean.

Uniqueness versus Common Themes   Personality researchers interpret the data they collect using either of two approaches: the *idiographic approach* or the *nomothetic approach.*

The **idiographic approach** *is a person-centered method of studying personality, emphasizing the ways in which each individual is unique and unlike anyone else.* This approach focuses on how distinctive aspects of an individual's personality form an integrated whole. The idiographic approach (from *idio,* "personal" + *graph,* "write") seeks to "write down" or document the peculiarities that distinguish people. This perspective assumes that the same personal qualities and events take on different meanings in different people's lives.

In contrast, the **nomothetic approach** *is theme-centered, identifying universal traits and patterns among all individuals' personalities.* Even if all personalities are organized around the same basic themes or variables, they remain distinctive because no two individuals possess the same degree of a quality or characteristic. For example, every person has some degree of sociability, but your "score" on a sociability test would be different from those of other people. Nomothetic research (from *nomo*, "law" + *thetos*, "put in place") seeks to identify the basic common factors or categories of personality qualities, and to put specific cases in the appropriate categories. This perspective looks for relationships between different personality traits in the general population.

Researchers and practitioners who focus on individuality favor the idiographic approach, emphasizing what makes a given person similar to, yet different from, others. In contrast, researchers interested in particular qualities—such as aggressiveness, or stress-management styles—prefer the nomothetic approach, learning all they can about the qualities that seem to describe most people, or the "average" person.

Both the idiographic and nomothetic approaches have a common goal: to formulate useful scientific theories of personality. Theories of personality are hypothetical statements about the structure and functioning of individual personalities. They help us achieve two of the major goals of psychology: *understanding* the structure and development of personality, and *predicting* behavior and life events based on what we know about personality.

Description versus Development   Different theories make different predictions about the way people will respond and adapt to certain conditions. Theoretical approaches to understanding personality can be grouped into five categories: *type, trait, psychodynamic, humanistic,* and *social-learning and cognitive* theories. Table 10.2 lists the six categories, their major concepts, and examples (approaches) of each theory. One way to summarize these six approaches is to make a distinction between theories that *describe* personality and those that seek to explain how personality *develops*. Type and trait theories are primarily descriptive.

In applying descriptive theories to the case of Margaret Sanger, for example, type and trait theories would focus on the terms, qualities, and categories that best describe the kinds of behaviors Margaret Sanger engaged in— "commitment" to her sense of mission, for example, and "extroversion" in her desire to influence public opinion. In contrast, the other major types of personality theories—psychodynamic, humanistic, and social-learning and cognitive theories—would all try to explain *how* Margaret Sanger became the person she was, perhaps how childhood influences or important life events had shaped her eventual choices and actions.

Why are there so many different—often competing—theories of personality? Theorists differ in their approaches to personality by varying their starting points and sources of data and by trying to explain different processes. Some are interested in the structure of individual personality and others in how that personality develops in one's life. Some are interested in what people do, while others study how people feel and think about their lives. Finally, some theories try to understand the nature of psychological problems, while others focus on healthy individuals. In the next section we examine the most important and influential personality theories. Each theory can teach us something about personality, but together they can teach us even more about human nature.

We will return to the example of Margaret Sanger throughout this chapter, to illustrate the contributions these theories make and how they complement teach other. Try as well to ASK YOURSELF:

- What "kind" of person are *you?* (Answering such a question leads you to use a trait or type theory).
- How did you get to *become* the person you are now—and what events and experiences are likely to have an impact on the rest of your life? (These are questions about personality development).

By seeing your own life and the lives of those you know through the eyes of the various personality theories, you will better appreciate both the complexity of personality and the value of a science-based approach to understanding who we are and what we do.

TABLE 10.2	SUMMARY OF PERSONALITY THEORIES	
Category	**Major Concept**	**Specific Approaches and Key Ideas**
Type theories	Personalities can be classified into a limited number of groups or types.	Hippocrates' Four-Humors Theory: blood, phlegm, black bile, and yellow bile
		Sheldon's Somatotyes: endomorph, mesomorph, and ectomorph
		Myers-Briggs Type Indicator: introversion-extroversion, sensing-intuiting, thinking-feeling, and judgment-perception
Trait theories	Human behavior can be organized by labeling and classifying observable personality characteristics.	Allport's Trait Approach: cardinal traits, central traits, and secondary traits
		Eysenck's Type-Trait Hierarchy: extroversion-introversion, neuroticism (stability-instability), and psychoticism
		The Big Five Personality Dimensions: extroversion, agreeableness, conscientiousness, emotional stability, openness to experience
Psychodynamic theories	Personality is shaped and behavior is motivated by inner forces.	Sigmund Freud: psychoanalysis: psychic determinism; early development; drives and instincts; unconscious processes
		Freudian Personality Theory: personality structure; ego defense mechanisms
		Alfred Adler: Lifestyle Adequacy: search for adequacy and competence; overcompensation for feelings of inferiority
		Carl Jung: Analytic Psychology: collective unconscious; archetypes
Humanistic theories	Personality is driven by self-actualization.	Carl Rogers's Person-Centered Approach: need for self-actualization vs. need for approval from self and others; unconditional positive regard
Social-learning and cognitive theories	Personality is shaped by environment and/or styles of thinking.	George Kelly's Personal Construct Theory: personal constructs influence behavior; new situations demand new constructs
		Cognitive Social-Learning Theories:
		Mischel: situational influence
		Bandura: reciprocal determinism

✓ **Check Your Recall** ✓✓✓✓✓✓✓✓✓✓✓

Personality consists of an individual's unique qualities and distinctive patterns of behavior. Personality can be assessed with either objective or projective techniques. Objective tests such as the MMPI–2 and the CPI are very reliable and valid for specific clinical or applied purposes. The MBTI, which identifies 16 different types of personality, has been used in vocational and career counseling. Projective techniques such as the Rorschach and the TAT depend heavily on the clinician's subjective judgment and are not as reliable or valid for revealing personality characteristics.

The implicit theories we use to understand and predict people's behavior may be biased because they are based on only limited observations and contexts. We also theorize about ourselves, and engage in patterns of thought and action designed to protect and enhance self-esteem and impression management. Personality psychologists build their scientific theories from systematic observations of individuals across many situations. They interpret data according to either an idiographic (person-centered) or nomothetic (variable-centered) approach. The five categories of personality theories to be examined in this chapter can be categorized as primarily either descriptive or developmental. An appreciation of various perspectives is vital to understanding personality. ✓

Descriptive Theories of Personality

The oldest approaches to personality sought to categorize or summarize people. These *descriptive theories of personality* are still popular because they offer the promise of simplifying a complex reality. You are taking a descriptive approach when you ask a friend about someone you want to meet, or characterize an acquaintance as being this or that "type" of person. In contrast, you are taking a *developmental approach* when you wonder "What's his problem?" about someone who has just insulted you. Instead of merely labeling the offender as "a jerk," you may speculate on the influences that would cause a person to behave in a mean or antisocial way. Because much popular thinking is influenced by the descriptive approach, we will examine that perspective first, and then review the better-known developmental theories of personality in the next section.

Two distinct lines of inquiry in descriptive personality theories are *type theories* and *trait theories*. Each theoretical approach has an intriguing history and offers helpful insights to understanding the people we are.

Type Theories

One of the oldest approaches to describing personality involves classifying people into a limited number of distinct types. In our everyday lives, we continually group people into a small number of categories according to some distinguishing features. These features may include college class, major, sex, race, and qualities such as honesty or shyness. Some personality theorists also group people according to their **personality types**—*distinct patterns of personality characteristics used to assign people to categories*. These categories do not overlap; if a person is assigned to one category, he or she is not in any other category within that system. When you remark that a new acquaintance seems to be "the shy type," you are expressing the assumption that all people either do or don't belong in this category—that everyone must be either shy or not shy.

Silent film comedians Stan Laurel and Olvier Hardy represent two somatotypes and some associated personality traits: the ectomorphic, sensitive personality versus the endomorphic, pleasure-loving personality. In most of their routines, however, Laurel was not especially bright and Hardy expressed anger more than jollity—in seeming contradiction to Sheldon's ideas.

Hippocrates theorized that the body contained four essential fluids, or humors, each associated with a particular temperament. Clockwise: melancholy patient suffers from an excess of black bile; blood impassions a sanguine lutist to play; a maiden, dominated by phlegm, is slow to respond to her lover; choler, too much yellow bile, makes an angry master.

Early personality typologies (classification systems) were designed to specify a connection between a simple, highly visible characteristic and behavior that can be expected from people of that type. If fat, then jolly; if an engineer, then conservative; if female, then sympathetic. Such systems have traditionally had much popular appeal and still do in the mass media; they oversimplify a very complicated process of understanding the nature of personality.

Four-Humors Theory   One of the earliest type theories was proposed in the fifth century B.C. by **Hippocrates,** the Greek physician who gave medicine the Hippocratic oath. He theorized that the body contained four basic fluids or *humors,* each associated with a particular *temperament.* An individual's personality depended on which humor was predominant in his or her body. Hippocrates paired body humors with personality temperaments according to the following scheme:

- Blood – *sanguine* temperament: cheerful and active
- Phlegm = *phlegmatic* temperament: apathetic and sluggish
- Black bile = *melancholy* temperament: sad and brooding
- Yellow bile = *choleric* temperament: irritable and excitable

Hippocrates' four-humors system was popular for centuries, although today we know it is baseless: personality and moods are not driven by bodily fluids. Nonetheless we still see references to it in our language—such as when we say someone is "hot-blooded." For example, *bilious* means both "bile-filled" and "ill-tempered." Our culture retains hints of four-humors theory in ideas and words that imply a biological origin to problematic moods and personalities. However, not since the Middle Ages have barber-surgeons or other professionals treated mood-afflicted patients with surgical bloodletting and leeches to remove the "bad blood."

Somatotypes   Another interesting type theory of personality was advanced by **William Sheldon** (1942), a U.S. physician who related physique to temperament. He assigned each individual to one of three categories based on the person's **somatotype,** *a body build presumed to correspond to particular personality patterns.* Sheldon identified three somatotypes: *endomorphic* (fat, soft, round), *mesomorphic* (muscular, rectangular, strong), or *ectomorphic* (thin, long, fragile). The typology specified relationships between each physique and particular personality traits, activities, and preferences.

According to Sheldon, endomorphs are relaxed, fond of eating, and sociable. Mesomorphs are physical people, filled with energy, courage, and assertive tendencies. Ectomorphs are brainy, artistic, and introverted; they would rather think about life than consume it or act upon it. Sheldon's theory is intriguing, but not substantiated. It has proven to be of little value in predicting an individual's behavior (Tyler, 1965). In addition, people come in many different shapes—certainly more than three—and not all can be assigned readily to one of Sheldon's three somatotypes.

Trait Theories

The practice of identifying personality traits is about as ancient as the type approach to personality. Labeling and classifying the many personality characteristics we observe may help us organize human behavior, but it is no simple task. In fact, a dictionary search by psychologists Gordon Allport and H. S. Odbert (1936) found over 18,000 adjectives in the English language to describe individual characteristics!

Type theories presume that there are separate, *discontinuous categories* into which people fit: you are *either* an introvert *or* and extrovert, for example. In contrast, trait theories propose *continuous dimensions*, such as intelligence or warmth, that vary in quality and degree. A **trait** *is a stable characteristic of individuals that determines their patterns of thought, feelings, and behavior.* People are assumed to possess traits in varying degrees. Traits describe what is consistent about a person's behavior in different situations and times. For example, if you possess the trait of "honesty," you may demonstrate it one day by returning a lost wallet and demonstrate it another day by not cheating on a test. Some trait theorists think that traits cause behavior, but more conservative theorists argue that traits merely describe or predict patterns of behavior.

FIGURE 10.3   Shyness as a Trait ■ Traits may act as intervening variables, relating sets of stimuli and responses that might seem, at first glance, to have little to do with each other.

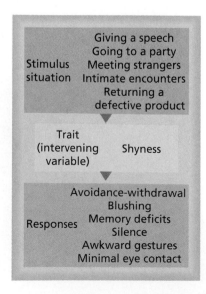

Allport's Trait Approach   Gordon Allport (1937, 1961, 1966) was one of the most influential personality theorists. He is the best known of the idiographic trait theorists, who believe that each person has some unique characteristics, as well as some common ones, that together form a unique combination of traits. Allport viewed traits as the building blocks of personality and the source of individuality. Traits connect and unify a person's reactions to a variety of stimuli, as shown in Figure 10.3. Allport identified three kinds of traits:

- A **cardinal trait** *is a trait around which a person organizes his or her life.* Not all people develop cardinal traits, but those who do may well have more than one. Margaret Sanger appears to have organized her life around a trait of social conscientiousness, seeking to educate others about how they could improve their lives and health.
- A **central trait** *is a trait that represents a major characteristic of a person,* such as honesty or optimism. Surely one of Margaret Sanger's central traits was her outspokenness, a willingness to overcome her discomfort with speaking before large audiences in order to broadcast her message about birth control.
- A **secondary trait** *is a trait that indicates enduring personal qualities, but is not assumed to explain general behavior patterns.* Personal styles and preferences are examples of secondary traits. Margaret Sanger was described by acquaintances and biographers as "artistic" and "passionate," but so are many people who do not share the same values or express

them in the same way. Thus these secondary traits are informative but not as predictive of a person's behavior as the more basic cardinal and central traits.

According to Allport, secondary, central, and sometimes cardinal traits form the structure of the personality—which, in turn, determines an individual's behavior. Even if you and your friends are exposed to similar circumstances, your different traits would lead you to react differently, sometimes in opposite ways. Allport remarked that "the same fire that melts the butter hardens the egg," to emphasize that identical environments have different results depending on the constitution of the individuals or substances involved. For example, if a mean-spirited instructor insulted the work your class had done, your own tendency to rise to a challenge might lead you to work that much harder on the next assignment, while the same provocation might depress a timid classmate into withdrawing from the class with a reduced sense of self-esteem.

Eysenck's Type-Trait Hierarchy   Hans Eysenck (pronounced *I-zenk*), a leading British trait theorist, proposed a model that links types, traits, and behavior into a single system that arranges different levels of behavior into a hierarchy (1947, 1990). At the lowest level of Eysenck's hierarchy are a person's *responses* such as actions or thoughts. Regularly occurring responses form *habits*, and related habits form *traits*. Based on his observations of behavior patterns, Eysenck concluded that there are three basic, broad dimensions underlying all personalities: Extroversion (outgoingness), Neuroticism (stability or instability), and Psychoticism (realistic or unrealistic thinking).

Personality differences on Eysenck's three basic dimensions are theorized to be caused by genetic and biological differences between people. Eysenck has proposed that his hierarchy be used in combination with other trait models to provide new insights into personality. For example, he relates extroversion-introversion and neuroticism (emotional stability or instability) to the physiological personality types of Hippocrates, as shown in Figure 10.4.

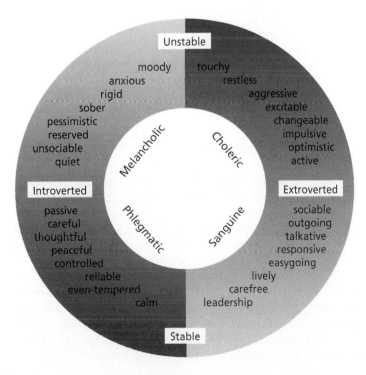

FIGURE 10.4   Eysenck's Personality Circle ■ For Eysenck, the many traits that describe personality can be categorized by degrees of four types: the extremes of the stable-unstable dimension, and the extremes of the introverted-extroverted dimension.

Eysenck's theory is not a strict typology (sorting system). Rather, people can fall anywhere in the quadrangle, ranging from very introverted to very extroverted and from very unstable (neurotic) to very stable. The traits listed around Eysenck's Personality Circle describe people with each combination of scores. For example, a person who scores high on the trait of extroversion and moderate on the trait of instability is likely to exhibit impulsive behavior.

The Big Five   One hazard of trait psychology is that different researchers study many different traits, design many different ways to measure them, and sometimes create their own idiosyncratic names for the dimensions they measure. This "free enterprise" system creates a difficult climate for scientific progress. The confusion over terminology can make it hard to know whether the empirical results of different studies even agree—or if they can be compared. This emerging confusion led to a search for common dimensions of meaning, efforts to develop a common language that all personality psychologists could use. The search began by examining trait terms found in natural language. The hope was that, over time, people would have developed words to describe the important dimensions they perceived in themselves and others.

Several research efforts started with a list of all the traits in the English language that Allport and Odbert (1936) had extracted from the dictionary. The traits were then reduced to about 200 synonym clusters that were used to form bipolar (two-ended) trait dimensions, such as "responsible-irresponsible." People rated themselves and others on these dimensions, and their ratings were analyzed to identify relationships among clusters of synonyms. The startling conclusion of researchers using this method was that there are only *five basic dimensions* underlying all the traits people use to describe themselves and others (Norman, 1967; Tupes & Christal, 1961).

These *five basic dimensions, theorized to underlie the many traits used to describe human behavior, are known as the* **Big Five.** In the following list of the Big Five, you'll notice that each dimension is *bipolar* although it has a one-word label; the name of the dimension describes the "high" pole, while an opposite term describes the "low" pole.

Study hint: Big Five researcher Oliver John (1990) suggests that the initials of the dimensions form an acronym whose letters can be arranged to symbolize the OCEAN of personality dimensions.

1. *Openness to Experience:* creative, intellectual, and open-minded *versus* simple, shallow, and unintelligent.
2. *Conscientiousness:* organized, responsible, and cautious *versus* careless, frivolous, and irresponsible;
3. *Extroversion:* talkative, energetic, and assertive *versus* quiet, reserved, and shy;
4. *Agreeableness:* sympathetic, kind, and affectionate *versus* cold, quarrelsome, and cruel;
5. *Neuroticism:* emotionally stable, calm, and contented *versus* anxious, unstable, and temperamental;

The Big Five dimensions are very broad, because each category includes many traits that have unique connotations but a common theme. They are not meant to replace the many specific trait terms that carry their own nuances and shades of meaning. Rather, these five dimensions outline a taxonomy (an organizing system) demonstrating how an individual's traits, theories, and actual behaviors are related (Costa & McCrae, 1992b; Eysenck, 1992).

The Big Five theory is a comprehensive descriptive system. Almost any trait imaginable can be related to one or a few of the dimensions. The dimensions accommodate many scientific approaches to personality, yet they are easy to understand because they are derived from natural language. Most importantly, the same five dimensions have been rediscovered with many different subject samples, with many different types of data, and have been translated to several languages. Finally, the five factors have been translated into a personality assessment instrument, the NEO-PI or "Big Five Inventory" (Caprara et al., 1993; Costa & McCrae, 1992a, 1992b). The Big Five Inventory has been used to study personality stability across the life span, the relationship of personality characteristics to physical health and various life events, and may also be useful in career counseling (Costa & McCrae, 1992).

Are Traits Inherited?   Perhaps when you apply descriptive labels to people—judge someone to be "the pushy type" or infer that someone has "leadership qualities"—you are accurately perceiving a biologically based predisposition to act a certain way. If an individual's biological functioning influences behavior patterns, this would explain how some aspects of personality seem to be inherited. Have you ever been told you have a quality, such as a short temper or a stubborn streak, that runs in your family or resembles a relative's? Indeed, certain behavioral tendencies may be passed from parents to offspring and expressed in patterns of observable responses (Loehlin, 1992).

Studies of identical twins reared apart have long seemed to indicate that one's preferences, habits, and idiosyncrasies can be influenced by heredity. Amy and Beth were identical twin girls born in the 1960s and raised in separate adoptive homes. Although they experienced very different parenting styles, sibling relations, and economic circumstances, they later were found to have exhibited the same nervous habits, emotional disorders, and adjustment problems since infancy. Another set of twins, males raised apart, were reunited in their late thirties, only to discover that both had been named Jim; both had had childhood dogs named "Toy"; both had first married women named Linda and after divorcing, remarried women named Betty; and both preferred the same vacation site, and the same brand of cigarettes and beer (Wright, 1955a).

The Genetic Basis of Personality.   It is hard to imagine how such seeming coincidences could be genetically "blueprinted" or inherited. Yet stories such as Amy and Beth's and the two Jims' emphasize that much of what we call personality may be composed not of unique life experiences but of biologically based influences on temperament, tempo, and mannerisms (Wright, 1996). Almost all personality traits appear to be influenced by genetic factors (Loehlin, 1992). Experts do not agree on what degree inherited tendencies determine your characteristics, but it is clear that the person you become is strongly influenced by the genetic mix you get from your biological parents (Plomin et al., 1990).

A genetic component to personality would explain the enduring power of temperament throughout an individual's life. A fascinating study conducted by Walter Mischel at Stanford University in the 1960s demonstrates that traits observable among young children continue to influence their behavior patterns for years (Shoda et al., 1990). Four-year-olds were given a simple choice: You can have a marshmallow now as a treat—or, if you can wait until the experimenter returns from running an errand, you can have *two* marshmallows. The choice made depends on the child's ability to resist giving in to impulse—a fundamental skill underlying much social behavior, and arguably a quality at the root of all emotional self-control (Goleman, 1995). About one-third of the subjects would not wait for their single treat and consumed it immediately. But the other children were able to delay gratification for about 20 minutes, enduring the interval by using various self-distraction tactics. Most interesting, when these same children were tracked down 12 or more years later, those who had been able to delay gratification at the age of four were now found to be more socially competent, less troubled by stress or

Sometimes your personality traits lead you to select certain situations over others. For example, a competitive person, like this swimmer, would seek out and participate in competitive events.

pressure, more self-confident and trustworthy than their impulsive, impatient peers. This simple childhood choice—waiting or not waiting for a desired goal—was found to be correlated with a wide range of adolescent tendencies, an indication that many characteristics may be explained by a smaller number of basic, enduring traits.

Exciting new research in the field of behavior genetics has identified a clear connection between a single human gene and a particular personality trait (Benjamin et al., 1996; Cloninger et al., 1996; Ebstein et al., 1996). The trait in question is one's tendency to seek novelty and explore—part of the Big Five "O" (Openness) factor. The gene may function by triggering the brain's receptivity to dopamine, a key neurotransmitter in motivation and emotion. While most people are somewhat novelty seeking, interested in new information and willing to move in new directions, a few people would score at either the high or the low extreme of this trait. High scorers would be not only open-minded, but also excitable, extravagant, or thrill seeking (such as the Type T personality introduced in Chapter 9). Low scorers would be more conservative, cautious, and conscientious in their personal habits and decision making. The gene does not account for a dramatic range of variability in the novelty-seeking trait: individuals with the long form of the "novelty-seeking gene" would score perhaps 10 percent higher than otherwise, while those with the short form would score only 10 percent lower than average. Thus this particular trait does not widely vary among people, and individuals are more alike than different with respect to these qualities (National Public Radio, 1996a).

Remember that behavior is genetically complex, influenced by many interactions among genes *plus* countless variations in individual experience and history. No single gene can "dictate" the richness of behavior, emotion, and thought summarized by a personality trait. If, as some researchers believe, there are perhaps 100 human genes that underlie basic personality traits, that deceptively small number still permits a staggering range of interactions among the genes involved (Cloninger et al., 1996). In other words, even if you possessed the gene for an extremely high level of the novelty-seeking trait, your other genetic and environmental traits would *interact* with its effects to produce a unique final product. However, the study of behavior genetics and the possibility of "gene mapping" human personality offers hopeful possibilities for treating *abnormal* personality. As we shall discuss in Chapters 13 and 14, a better understanding of the biological basis of personality can help us to develop therapeutic treatments for those who suffer from behavioral disorders.

Shyness One of the most interesting and methodologically sound research programs on temperament is that focusing on the inherited basis of shyness, being studied by **Jerome Kagan** of Harvard University (Kagan et al., 1994). This research clearly demonstrates that on the very day of life, some newborns already differ in the degree to which they are "inhibited" or "uninhibited"—that is, shy versus bold. About 10 to 15 percent of all children appear to be born shy or introverted, while a similar percentage appear to be born bold or extroverted, as assessed by a variety of measures. These initial differences in temperamental type are preserved over time, with the majority of children being classified within the same type at measurements taken over an 11-year interval. However, we also know that the percentage of shy college age students is much higher, about 40 percent or more (Zimbardo, 1991). It is thus reasonable to assume that some shyness is inherited, and more of it is learned through negative experiences in one's personal and social life. It is also the case that if a child is withdrawn, startles easily, is unlikely to smile, and is fearful of both strangers and novelty, then that child will *create* an environment that is not friendly, playful, or supportive. In this way, heredity and environment interact, with initially inherited characteristics becoming ampli-

Some shyness is inherited and some is learned through experience.

fied—or perhaps muted—over time, because they produce social signals telling others to either approach or stay away.

So is biology destiny? Of course not! An inherited *trait* may set the range of your responses to some life situations, but this legacy does not include a predetermined set of the life experiences that would "trigger" programmed responses. Even among your biological relatives, your unique family position, experiences, and sense of self guarantee that your personality pattern is a work in progress unlike that of anyone else (Bouchard & McGue, 1990).

Evaluating Type and Trait Theories

It is satisfying to find just the right word to describe a person or experience, and it would certainly be convenient if a single label or category, such as an individual's basic temperament, could predict his or her behavior. In ancient times, people's temperaments were sorted into types in order to predict their behavior or plan how best to treat an illness. Even at the end of the twentieth century, when most of us know better, many people rely on horoscopes and ask new friends what their astrological sun signs are, in hopes that such labels will summarize useful information. Toward these goals—information, communication and simplified prediction—personality psychologists have long worked to establish consistent and accurate terms for personal qualities and the relationships between them. But when we rely on such descriptive schemes, we run the risk of coming up with an oversimplified view of reality. As evolution scholar Stephen Jay Gould has remarked, "The world does not come to us in neat little packages" (1981, p. 158). If we impose simpler thought structures on a complex reality, we risk missing or misinterpreting vital information about people. This risk of oversimplification is a target for much criticism of descriptive theories of personality.

For example, suppose you were to judge Margaret Sanger as the "passionate type." Or imagine that you had assessed her as scoring very high on traits such as outgoingness and dominance but low on agreeableness or conventional thinking. Such judgments would validate others' observations of her, and even her own self-descriptions. But brief labels and concise categories also leave out important detail. Although many women may have been similar types or possessed similar traits, no one else did what Margaret Sanger did when she did it. A simpler picture of personality cannot provide the predictive power of a complex portrait.

Type and trait theories have also been criticized as inadequate because they do not explain the causes or development of personality. Instead, they merely identify and describe characteristics that are correlated with behavior. Trait theories typically portray a *static*, or at least stabilized, view of personality structure as it currently exists. In contrast, *dynamic* theories of personality emphasize conflicting forces within the individual and fast-paced environmental challenges. Together, these forces lead to continuous change and development within the individual. In the next section, we'll examine how developmental personality theories differ from descriptive theories, beginning with a review of the psychodynamic theories originated by Sigmund Freud.

Check Your Recall

Type theories and trait theories are descriptive theories of personality that seek to identify and interrelate the qualities and dimensions of personality. Type theories use personal characteristics to sort people into discrete groups or types, and attempt to predict behavior on the basis of a person's type. Trait

energy that drives individuals to experience sensual pleasure. ("Libido" comes from a Latin word meaning "lust").

But self-preservation and sexual desire did not explain such pervasive, devastating human acts as aggression and combat. Freud found that many patients who were veterans of the First World War continued to relive their wartime traumas in nightmares and hallucinations. He could not explain such continued misery, much less the hostility that had created war, in the context of Eros or libido. These clinical observations led Freud to add a third drive to his theory, one which underlay destruction rather than life or sexuality. He referred to this as the "death instinct," naming it **Thanatos,** *a negative force that drove people toward aggressive and destructive behaviors* (from the ancient Greek for "death"). He suggested that Thanatos was part of the tendency for all living things ultimately to die, disintegrate, and return to an inorganic state—just like any other material entity.

Psychic Determinism   Freud believed that physical and behavioral symptoms were related in a meaningful way to significant life events. For example, consistently forgetting a certain person's name or being late for appointments with that individual are not coincidental but, at an unconscious level, intentional signs of inner motives and conflicts. **Psychic determinism** *is the assumption that all mental and behavioral reactions are caused by earlier life experiences.* These experiences need not be consciously recalled in order to influence later behavior. Freud's work with patients suffering from *hysteria* convinced him that long-forgotten experiences *caused* many later life preferences and problems. In the late 1800s, physicians recorded many cases of hysteria, physical ailments for which no adequate physical explanations could be found. The afflicted (who were mostly women) would experience impaired bodily functioning—paralysis or blindness, for example—and yet they had intact nervous systems and no obvious organic damage to their muscles or eyes. As a young physician, Freud became interested in treating the bizarre symptoms of this disorder. His experiences with hysteria influenced his later theories.

Freud observed that the particular physical symptom often seemed related to an earlier forgotten event in a patient's life. For instance, under hypnosis, a "blind" patient might recall seeing her parents having intercourse when she was a small child. As she becomes an adult, she may anticipate her first sexual encounter, which might arouse powerful feelings associated with that upsetting memory. The young woman's blindness might represent an unconscious attempt to undo her vision of the original event—and to deny her own sexual feelings. Blindness would also bring her attention, comfort, and sympathy from others. Her inner psychic motives thus determine her condition.

Early Childhood Experiences   Freud assumed that personality develops continuously throughout life. He believed that experiences in infancy and early childhood had the most profound impact on personality formation and adult behavior patterns. Freud described a progression of **psychosexual stages,** *successive, instinctive patterns of associating pleasure with stimulation of specific bodily areas at different times of life:*

1. The *oral stage* is the first phase of psychosexual development, in which the mouth is the region associated with greatest gratification. During the first year of life, a baby not only takes in nourishment orally, but also connects with the environment by mouthing and sucking on objects.
2. The *anal stage* is the second psychosexual stage, in which the child experiences pleasure associated with retaining or eliminating feces. At about age

two, most children become toilet trained, learning to control and suppress anal stimulation. They also learn that society has strong rules about bodily self-control, order, and personal hygiene.

3. During the *phallic stage,* the child associates greatest gratification with stimulation of the genitals. Also during this stage, from about ages 3 to 6, a child develops unconscious feelings of possessive love toward the opposite-sex parent—a boy wants his mother "to himself" and a female becomes "Daddy's girl" and views her mother as a rival. Freud termed this conflict the *Oedipus conflict* in boys and the *Electra conflict* in girls, references to Greek mythological figures who were tragically fated to act out taboo fantasies of possession and revenge with their own parents. The child's phallic anxiety is reduced through closer identification with the same-sex parent, relying on him or her as a role model and example of appropriate gender role development.

4. By about age 6, a child's increased time with peers and in school shifts attention away from parents and family members. During this *latency stage,* bodily gratification is less important than the acquisition of skills and peer relationships. Unconscious associations of pleasure with bodily stimulation become "latent" (less overt or influential) while the child concentrates on acquiring knowledge and skills.

5. With the onset of puberty (about age 12 or 13), the child enters the *genital stage,* a process of associating greatest gratification with sexual relations with a partner. In this adolescent stage, one's sex organs are genitals that are understood to be used for sexually connecting to others. In contrast, in the earlier phallic stage, they were sensitive bodily organs that served primarily as the focus of self-stimulation or possessive fantasies.

During the phallic stage, a child must resolve feelings of conflict and anxiety by identifying more closely with the same-sex parent.

According to Freud, certain problems or difficulties early in life can lead to **fixation:** *arrested development caused by excessive stimulation or frustration in an earlier psychosexual stage.* Fixation prevents an individual from progressing normally through later stages of development. Themes or anxieties associated with the fixated stage may recur in conflicts and habits in later life. For example, psychoanalysts suggest that oral fixation leads to dependency on others, overeating, drug addiction, and even tendencies toward verbal fluency and sarcasm. Among these very different problems is a common theme: using the mouth as the way to connect with what one needs. Fixation in the anal stage is presumed to result in a stubborn, compulsive, stingy, excessively neat pattern of behavior—all related to common themes of "holding on" and not losing control of one's body or life.

Personality Structure   Freud assembled his basic concepts into specific theories about the structure of personality, and he described how its parts and processes work together to produce the behavior patterns of personality. In Freudian theory, personality differences arise from the different ways in which people deal with their fundamental drives. To explain these differences, Freud pictured a continuing battle between two antagonistic parts of the personality, the *id* and the *superego,* that is moderated by a third aspect of the self, the *ego.*

The **id** *is the primitive, unconscious part of the personality that stores the fundamental drives.* The id acts on impulse and pushes for immediate gratification—especially sexual, physical, and emotional pleasures—to be experienced here and now without concern for consequences.

The **superego** *is the storehouse of an individual's values, including moral attitudes learned from society.* The superego corresponds roughly to our common notion of *conscience.* It develops as a child develops values based on the prohibitions of parents and other adults against socially undesirable actions. It is the inner voice of "oughts" and "should nots." The superego also includes the *ego ideal,* an individual's view of the kind of person he or she should strive to become.

Understandably, the superego is often in conflict with the id. The id wants to do what feels good, while the superego insists on doing what is right. The third major part of the self develops to resolve the conflict between id and superego. The **ego** *represents an individual's personal view of physical and social reality.* Part of the ego's job is to choose actions that will gratify id impulses without undesirable consequences. For example, the ego would block an impulse to cheat on an exam because of concerns about getting caught, and it would substitute the resolution to study harder the next time or ask the teacher for help. When the id and superego are in conflict, the ego arranges a compromise that at least partially satisfies both. However, as id and superego pressures intensify, it becomes more difficult for the ego to work out optimal compromises.

Defending Against Anxiety Sometimes this compromise between id and superego involves "putting a lid on the id." Extreme desires are pushed out of conscious awareness into the privacy of the unconscious. **Repression** *is an unconscious process that excludes unacceptable thoughts and feelings from awareness and memory.* Repression protects an individual from experiencing extreme anxiety or guilt about unacceptable or dangerous impulses, ideas, or memories. The ego remains unaware of both the mental content that is censored and the process by which repression works. For example, a student who suspects she failed an important test may "forget" to attend class the day the graded tests are returned. This unconscious "memory lapse" protects her from feeling upset or anxious—at least temporarily.

Repression is the most basic of the **ego defense mechanisms,** *mental strategies employed to reduce the experience of conflict or anxiety.* The ego uses these defenses in the daily conflict between the id's impulses to express primitive urges and the superego's demand to deny them. (We introduced these mechanisms in Chapter 9, as part of an individual's approach to dealing with stressors.) By using ego defense mechanisms, a person can maintain a favorable self-image and sustain an acceptable social image. For example, if a child has strong feelings of hatred toward her father—which, if acted out, would be dangerous—repression may take over. The hostile impulse is then no longer consciously pressing for satisfaction or even recognized as existing. Although the impulse is not seen or heard, it is not gone; these feelings continue to play a role in personality functioning. Repressed childhood memories can have effects on the lives of adults. For a summary of some of the major ego defenses, see Table 10.3.

In Freudian theory, **anxiety** *is an intense emotional response triggered when a repressed conflict is about to emerge into consciousness.* Anxiety is a danger signal: "Repression is not working. Red alert: More defenses needed!" Anxiety signals the need for a second line of defense: one or more additional ego defense mechanisms that will relieve the anxiety and send the distressing impulses back into the unconscious. For example, a mother who did not really love her child—but feels terrible anxiety or guilt when she imagines losing him—might use *reaction formation,* which transforms her unacceptable impulse into its opposite: "I don't want my child" becomes "I love my child! See how I smother him with love?"

Though at times they can be useful, ego defense mechanisms are ultimately self-deceptive. When overused, they create more problems than they solve—steeping a person in denial, for example, and preventing her from going on with life after a painful experience or memory. Some forms of mental illness may result from excessive reliance on defense mechanisms to cope with anxiety, as we shall see when we examine mental disorders in Chapter 13.

TABLE 10.3	**MAJOR EGO DEFENSE MECHANISMS**
Denial	Protecting self from unpleasant reality by refusing to perceive its meaning
Displacement	Discharging pent-up feelings, usually of hostility, on objects less dangerous than those that initially aroused the emotion
Fantasy	Gratifying frustrated desires in imaginary achievements ("daydreaming" is a common form)
Identification	Increasing feelings of worth by identifying self with another person or institution, often of illustrious standing
Isolation	Cutting off emotional charge from hurtful situations or separating incompatible attitudes into logic-tight compartments (holding conflicting attitudes that are never thought of simultaneously or in relation to each other); also called *compartmentalization*
Projection	Placing blame for one's difficulties upon others or attributing one's own "forbidden" desires to others
Rationalization	Attempting to prove that one's behavior is "rational" and justifiable and thus worthy of the approval of self and others
Reaction Formation	Preventing dangerous desires from being expressed by endorsing opposing attitudes and types of behavior and using them as "barriers"
Regression	Retreating to earlier developmental levels involving more childish responses and usually a lower level of aspiration
Repression	Pushing painful or dangerous thoughts out of consciousness, keeping them unconscious; this is considered to be *the most basic of the defense mechanisms*
Sublimation	Gratifying or working off frustrated sexual desires in substitutive nonsexual activities socially accepted by one's culture.

Evaluating Freudian Theory   A psychoanalytic interpretation of Margaret Sanger's drive and sense of mission requires us to scrutinize her early life, and infer powerful conflicts about sexual feelings and experience. We might focus on her mother's death when Margaret was 19, and her later claim that she blamed her father for exhausting her mother with so many births. Unresolved anger toward her mother, a vestige of the phallic stage of psychosexual development, would be transformed into guilt over her mother's death, projecting blame instead onto her father—and ultimately onto all fathers, and men in general. Perhaps Margaret took up the banner of birth control in order to resolve her own unconscious guilt and anxiety about her unhappy family experiences. Or perhaps she identified with her mother's sacrifice, and sought to punish her father and other would-be fathers by depriving them of their exclusive control of women's reproductive fate. As usual with psychoanalysis, these guesses are guided by hindsight—and cannot be either proven or disproven.

Freud's ideas have had an enormous impact on the way many psychologists think about normal and abnormal aspects of personality. A recent critical review has validated many of his theories about how both normal and abnormal personality may develop in an individual's life (Fisher & Greenberg, 1985). However, more psychologists today would probably criticize Freudian concepts than support them. As we have seen, one problem is that psychoanalytic concepts are theoretically vague. Because they lack clear operational definitions, much of the theory is difficult to evaluate scientifically. How can the concepts of libido, the anal stage, or repression be studied in any direct fashion? How is it possible to predict whether an anxious person will use projection, denial, or reaction formation to defend a threatened ego?

A second, related criticism is that Freudian theory is good history but bad science. It does not reliably *predict* what will occur; it is applied *retrospectively*—after events have occurred. By overemphasizing historical origins of current behavior, the theory directs attention away from current events that may be inducing and maintaining the behavior.

Freud's theory was developed from speculation about clinical patients in therapy, almost all of them women with similar symptoms. Thus, another criticism is that the theory has little to say about healthy lifestyles, which are not primarily defensive or defective. Instead, it offers the pessimistic view that human nature develops out of conflicts, traumas, and anxieties. It does not fully acknowledge the positive side of our existence nor offer any information about healthy personalities striving for happiness and realization of their full potential.

From the beginning, critics of Freudian theory have offered alternative explanations of personality structure and function. As you can see in Focus on Science: Post-Freudian Theories, some of Freud's early colleagues ultimately proposed theories very different from his, although they based them on psychoanalytic concepts and assumptions.

The enduring power and appeal of Freudian concepts may be partially explained by their accessibility to *non*-psychologists. Freudian images and symbols abound in the art and literature of the twentieth century, and have influenced advertising and marketing as well. For example, one "theory" behind some manufacturers' promotion of new products is to first arouse consumers' fears that they are inadequate or unsuccessful, and then promise that the solution can be purchased. Television commercials for everything from mouthwash and cake mix to laxatives and life insurance work by first reminding you of threats to your happiness (social rejection, irregularity, untimely death) and then offering products and services to reduce your anxiety and restore hope. Among scientists—especially within psychology—Freudian ideas have long been regarded as suspect, primarily because of questions about his reliance on case studies rather than controlled observations for developing his theories. Yet, as one journalist remarks, Freud's "rich panoply of metaphors for the mental life has become, across wide swaths of the globe, something very close to common knowledge" (Gray, 1993, p. 47). This may be an artifact of how personality theory itself is marketed: Freudian theories, hard as they are to study, much less to validate, somehow feel familiar and insightful to people, more recognizable and warmer than behavioristic or cognitive approaches to personality.

Popular enchantment with Freudian theories may wane, however, as some ideas are increasingly, publicly questioned and even ridiculed. A vivid example is the question of whether "repressed memories" of childhood sexual abuse, recovered in adulthood, can be trusted and believed by science and the law. Tabloid talk shows, panicked parents, and angry patients insist that relatives and day care workers have indeed abused innocent children, and that the children's failure to report or confirm these accusations is due to "repression." But memory experts, notably cognitive psychologist **Elizabeth Loftus,** point out that human memory is *not* videotape, is extremely fragile, and can be error-prone, especially under interrogation (Neimark, 1996). Loftus warns that, by blithely accepting unscientific notions of repression and "recovery" of memories, society risks dangerous levels of paranoia, persecution of the innocent,

FOCUS *on* Science

Post-Freudian Theories

Sigmund Freud's revolutionary ideas inspired many early adherents to the psychoanalytic movement—some of whom eventually broke away to develop their own ideas in different directions. These post-Freudian theorists accepted essential psychodynamic ideas, such as psychic determinism and the power of the unconscious, but did not always agree with Freud about the sex or death instincts, for example, or the indelible nature of early life experiences. In general, the post-Freudians made several changes in psychodynamic theories:

■ They put greater emphasis on *ego* functions, including ego defenses, development of the self, and conscious thought.

■ They view social variables (culture, family, and peers) as playing a greater role in shaping personality.

■ They put less emphasis on the importance of general sexual urges, or libidinal energy.

■ Post-Freudians extended personality development beyond childhood to include the entire life span.

Two of Freud's most important followers, Alfred Adler and Carl Jung, also became his most severe critics. **Alfred Adler** (1929) accepted the notion that personality was directed by unrecognized wishes: "Man knows more than he understands"—that is, we know many things at a nonrational, intuitive level, even though we cannot "prove" them or argue them rationally. However, he rejected the significance of Eros, or pleasure, as the guiding force in action. Adler believed that as helpless, dependent, small children we all experience feelings of inferior-

Jungian archetypes can be found in ancient art and literature, such as in this depiction from classical Greece. Here Heracles, clad in the cured hide of the Nemean lion he had previously defeated, battles the serpent Hydra, the many-headed reptilian embodiment of evil.

ity. He argued that we dedicate our lives to trying to overcome those feelings. We compensate to achieve feelings of adequacy, or more often, *over*compensate for feeling inferior, by attempting to become superior. Personality is structured around this underlying striving to be competent and powerful. Conflict arises not when urges within the individual compete, but when environmental pressures clash with internal efforts for adequacy.

Carl Jung (pronounced *young*) had been considered Freud's "crown prince," the scholar most likely to carry on his original theoretical tradition. But Jung's creative and influential work greatly expanded the concept of the unconscious (Jung, 1936/1959). For him, the unconscious was not limited to an individual's unique life experiences but was filled with fundamental psychological truths shared by the whole human race. Jung developed the concept of a **collective unconscious,** *an inherited storehouse of unconscious ideas and forces common to all members of the human race.* Because all humans share these ideas, we are predisposed to react to certain stimuli in the same way, and to intuitively understand primitive myths, art forms, and symbols. *Such recognizable symbols, which reside in all humans' collective unconscious, are termed* **archetypes.** Each archetype is associated with an instinctive tendency to feel and think about it or experience it in a special way. Jung postulated many archetypes from history and mythology: the sun god, the hero, the earth mother, and the trickster—images and characters that can be found in cultures as diverse as ancient Egypt, classical Greece and Rome, Native American tribal traditions, and modern Christianity. To the basic urges of sex and aggression Jung added two equally powerful unconscious instincts: the need to *create* and the need to *self-actualize.* Jung's views became central to the emergence of humanistic psychology in America (Jung, 1965, 1973).

and self-inflicted misery (Loftus & Ketcham, 1991, 1994). Some Freudian ideas—such as the notion that memory is unquestionably accurate and can be repressed and later recovered, intact—seemed to "skip" scientific scrutiny, becoming revised by the media and absorbed by popular culture, whether scientifically sound or not. Now some of these semi-Freudian ideas, like the individuals accused of committing repressed crimes, must be put on trial, reevaluated not only by psychology but in the public arena—where laws are actually made and changed.

Central to all psychodynamic theories is the assumption that most of one's personality is governed by unconscious forces. We turn now to examine a very different approach, one that credits conscious thought and a deliberate quest for selfhood as the source of personality development.

created by one's culture? Experimental psychologists contend that too many of the concepts in humanistic psychology are so unclear that they defy testing in controlled research settings. Other psychologists note that humanistic psychologists neglect the influence of important environmental variables by emphasizing the role of the self in behavior. Last but not least, psychoanalytic theorists criticize the humanistic emphasis on present conscious experience. They argue that this approach does not recognize the power of the unconscious.

The last set of developmental personality theories we consider are those most influenced by behavioral and cognitive psychology, and by research on learning and memory. Before going on, we should pause and consider how unlikely it is, after all, that a single theory of personality will satisfy psychologists' many different concerns. Perhaps psychologists should embrace an *eclectic* point of view, collecting and appreciating the parts of each approach that seem to work best and make the most sense.

Social-Learning and Cognitive Theories

All of the theories we have reviewed so far emphasize hypothetical inner mechanisms—traits, instincts, impulses, self-actualizing tendencies—that propel behavior and establish a functioning personality. Psychologists with a *learning theory* orientation have a different focus. They look for environmental contingencies (reinforcing circumstances) that control behavior. From this perspective, behavior and personality are shaped primarily by the outside environment.

This somewhat restrictive, behaviorist conception of personality was first developed by a team of Yale University psychologists headed by John Dollard and Neal Miller (1950). This theory was considerably expanded by Albert Bandura and Walter Mischel into a meaningful integration of core ideas from the learning-behavioral tradition and newly emerging ideas from social and cognitive psychology. Dollard and Miller showed that one could learn by *social imitation*—by observing the behavior of others without actually performing the response first. This idea broadened psychologists' perceptions of the ways that both effective and destructive habits are learned. Personality emerges as the sum of these learned habits.

Bandura and Mischel emphasized the importance of learned behavioral patterns based on social learning, including observation of others and social reinforcement from others. They went one critical step further to emphasize the importance of cognitive processes as well as behavioral ones, returning a thinking mind to the acting brain.

Cognitive theories of personality point out that there are important individual differences in the way people think about and define situations. Cognitive theories stress the mental processes through which people turn their sensations and perceptions into organized impressions of reality. They emphasize that people actively *choose* their own environments to a great extent. Thus, even in influential environments, people are not merely passive reactors. Individuals weigh alternatives and select the settings in which they act and are acted upon. People choose to enter those situations that they expect to be reinforcing and to avoid those that are unsatisfying and uncertain.

One way we "choose" situations is by selecting features and interactions in our social experience. In a dining hall or restaurant, you sit with people you know—not with strangers or people you judge to be too different from yourself. Such judgments are likely to be superficial, based on the way others look or dress. College administrators and student development counselors actively urge students to cross racial and ethnic lines, break down the "barriers" between them, and get to know each other—all good strategies for reducing prejudice, misunderstanding, and discrimination in educational institutions.

Yet members of minority and ethnic groups persist in "sticking together" for their nonclass socializing for the simple reason that they are generally uncertain about being accepted by other groups. No one enjoys rejection. Why risk bad feelings if you can find instead a more comfortable, familiar social niche? Next time you look for someone to sit with as you grab lunch or coffee between classes, consider that in this very process you are *choosing your environment,* a choice that will admit certain social and personal possibilities—and rule out others.

The relationship between situational variables and cognitive variables in regulating behavior is found in several personality theories. In this section, we will review the *cognitive social-learning* theories of Walter Mischel and Albert Bandura and the *personal construct theory* of George Kelly.

Persons in Situations   Walter Mischel (pronounced *me-SHELL*) questioned the utility of describing personality according to traits. As an alternative, he proposed a cognitive theory of personality that also draws on principles from social-learning theory. In his view, much of what we do and many of our beliefs and values are not best thought of as emerging properties of the self. He sees them instead as *responses* developed, maintained, or changed by experiences—such as observing role models, or reinforcing specific stimulus-response connections. For example, your interpersonal "style"—shyness or boldness, a tendency to be manipulative or victimized—is a complex set of lessons and scripts you learned by watching your parents, friends, and even celebrities, as well as from first-hand experience of reward and punishment.

According to Mischel, your response to a specific environmental input depends on several factors: your abilities; your information processing style; your expectancies; your values; and your rules and plans. Each of these factors is distinctive for you, as a result of your particular experiences and influences. The combination of these distinct factors makes your response pattern unique. This pattern filters your experiences so that you see the world differently from anyone else. People respond differently to the same environmental input because of differences in these person-based variables (Mischel, 1973; Shoda et al., 1993a, 1993b).

Mischel argued that, because people are so sensitive to situational cues, features of situations are as important as features of people in our attempts to understand human behaviors. Person variables, he suggested, will have their greatest impact on behavior when cues in the situation are *weak* or *ambiguous.* When situations are strong and clear, there will be less individual variation in response. For example, suppose that one day when you are in class, a student collapses, apparently unconscious, onto the floor. After a stunned silence, the instructor asks the class to keep their seats and then points *at you,* demanding loudly, "Go to the office, call 911, and get an ambulance here!" What do you do? Well, this is a "strong" situation: someone is in control, an instructor you already see as an authority figure; that person has told you unambiguously what to do. You will most likely quickly comply—as would most people in that situation. In Mischel's characterization of person-situation interactions, there would be very little variation in how individuals respond to these circumstances.

But now suppose instead that you are not in a classroom but are walking through a crowded public space at a busy time of day in an unfamiliar part of town. Suddenly you see a stranger collapsing onto the ground. Passersby hurry along, no one stops to help or even seems to notice what has happened. Glancing quickly around, you do not recognize anyone and see no one taking charge of the situation. This is a "weak" situation: What do you do? Your feelings and actions will depend on your personality, rather than on situational forces. You may take quick action to help, especially if you identify with the victim for some reason, or feel competent to provide first aid. But if you are in a hurry, fear "getting involved," assume that other bystanders have good reasons *not* to stop and help, or simply hesitate too long while deciding what to do, you will not take the action that might save a person's life (Darley & Batson, 1973; Moriarty, 1975; Piliavin & Piliavin, 1972; Piliavin et al., 1969; Schroeder, 1995). Thus the qualities of the situation—whether it is weak or strong, how it influences and informs you—interact with personality variables such as conformity, empathy, or impatience in determining specific behaviors.

Social Learning   Through his theoretical writing and extensive research with children and adults, **Albert Bandura** (1986) has become an eloquent champion of a social-learning approach to personality. In Bandura's view, human beings are driven by neither inner forces nor environmental influences but rather by mentally monitoring the impact of their behavior on other people, the environment, and themselves.

Human beings are distinctively able to foresee the possible consequences of our actions without having to actually experience them. In addition to learning from our own experience, we learn vicariously by observing other people. Perhaps the most important contribution of Bandura's theory is this focus on **observational learning,** *the process of learning new responses by watching others' behavior.* Through observational learning, children and adults acquire an enormous range of information about their social environment—what gets rewarded and what gets punished or ignored. Skills, attitudes, and beliefs may be acquired simply by watching what others do and the consequences that follow. Even personality traits like altruism can be learned by observing models, whether they are live and immediate or viewed indirectly through books, movies, and television (Straub, 1974).

In addition to learning by copying (or rejecting the example of) models, we can also evaluate our own behavior according to personal standards and provide ourselves with reinforcements, such as self-approval or self-reproach. We are capable of *self-regulation,* but we often gauge our own behavior according to imposed standards. Someone who accepts an external standard as a behavioral guide will react differently than someone who has developed his or her own personal standard. For example, if your personal standards for neatness exceed those required by most of your instructors, you will work harder than you "have to" in preparing class papers. In contrast, if your personal standards are lower than your teachers', you will constantly struggle to produce acceptable work and earn satisfactory grades—and you will soon revert to your old, sloppy ways once the course is over.

Bandura's theory points to a complex interaction of individual factors, behavior, and environmental stimuli. Each factor can influence or change the others, and the direction of change is rarely one-way; it is *reciprocal* or bidirectional. Bandura calls this social-learning process **reciprocal determinism,** *a process in which the person, situation, and environment mutually influence each other* (Bandura, 1981). The simple but powerful relationship of these variables is summarized in Figure 10.5. How does it work? For example, if you would rather read literature than attend sports events, you may frequent local bookstores instead of attending or watching games on weekend afternoons. If you are also extroverted, you will engage in conversations with the store's staff and with fellow customers, rather than reading silently or keeping to yourself. The outcome of such interactions makes the bookstore a socially attractive environment for future visits. This, then, is one instance of the reciprocal determinism between person (extroverted book-lover), place (bookstore), and behavior (browsing instead of watching sports).

Finally, Bandura has elaborated on the concept of **self-efficacy,** *one's tendency to believe that one can perform adequately in a particular situation*

Children develop a clearer sense of identity by observing how men and women behave in their culture.

(Bandura, 1986; Schwarzer, 1992; Zimmerman et al., 1992). Your sense of self-efficacy influences your perceptions, motivation, and performance in many ways. You probably don't even try to do things or take chances when you expect to be ineffectual. You avoid situations where you don't feel adequate. Even when you do, in fact, have the ability, you may not take or maintain the required action if you think you lack what it takes. For example, if you have not played ball since you were a child, you may decline an invitation to participate in a friendly ball game, despite the fact that you are probably more coordinated and self-confident today than you were years ago. While it is no tragedy to pass up the chance to play ball, your poor sense of self-efficacy in this situation leads you to miss the opportunity to interact with friends, perhaps meet new people, learn new skills, and simply have fun.

Expectations of failure—and a corresponding decision to stop trying—may, of course, be based on the perception that a situation is unresponsive, punishing, or unsupportive instead of on a perception of one's own inadequacy. Such situational assumptions are called *outcome expectations;* perceptions of one's own inadequacy lead to *efficacy expectations* (see Figure 10.6). The person who believes that responding is useless because of low self-efficacy must develop competencies that will boost self-perception of efficacy. On the other hand, when a person believes that responding is useless because of outcome expectancies, then the environment, and not the person, may need to change so that reinforcements will follow competent responding. If you are having trouble using a friend's computer, is it because *you* are "doing it wrong" or because there is something wrong with the computer itself? If you believe the former, you must develop your skill and your efficacy. If you believe the latter, perhaps someone should fix the computer! In a sense, self-efficacy theory should remind us of the moral of the story of the children's book, *The Little Engine That Could:* Believing that you *can* do something is a powerful factor in actually succeeding.

Personal Construct Theory George Kelly (1955) argued that no one is ever a victim of either past history or the present environment. Kelly developed a theory of personality that places primary emphasis on each person's active, cognitive construction of his or her world. All events are open to alternative interpretations; people can always reconstruct their past or define their present difficulties in different ways.

In Kelly's view, all individuals function as amateur scientists. People want to be able to explain and predict the world around them, especially their interpersonal world. They build theories about the world from units called **personal constructs,** *individually unique systems for interpreting reality.* In its most basic sense, a personal construct is an individual's belief about what two objects or events have in common and what sets them apart from a third object or event. For example, if you have been hurt by broken relationships in the past, the qualities of loyalty and fidelity might be particularly relevant to you at this point in your life. Perhaps you can even "sort" the people you know according to whether or not they can be trusted to make and keep commitments. Thus your personal construct—this concept of the importance of faithfulness in friendship—is important in how you see and judge others and form relationships with them. You have many different personal constructs that you can apply to understanding any person or situation. All of your constructs are combined into a belief system that influences the way you respond to each situation you encounter. Personal constructs influence the way you evaluate information and form impressions of others.

Adapting to new situations requires that an individual's construct system be open to change. When someone has trouble understanding or predicting the course of events, it is helpful to find new ways to interpret them. Kelly believed

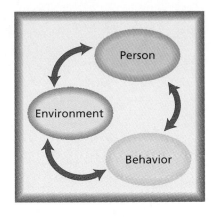

FIGURE 10.5 Reciprocal Determinism ■ In reciprocal determinism, the individual, the individual's behavior, and the environment all interact.

FIGURE 10.6 Bandura's Self-Efficacy Model ■ The model positions efficacy expectations between the person and his or her behavior; outcome expectations are positioned between behavior and its anticipated outcomes.

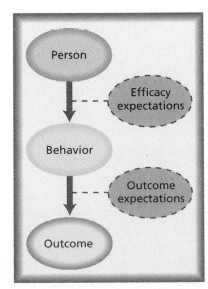

that people differ in their readiness to change their constructs. He also felt that they can run into trouble either by rigidly refusing to change their old, ineffective constructs or by nervously changing their constructs every time the wind turns in a new direction.

Evaluating Social-Learning and Cognitive Theories   A social-learning interpretation of Margaret Sanger's work and personality would focus on the contingencies in her life, the reinforcements and punishments she experienced and how these consequences shaped her behavior. Each time she gave a public lecture about birth control methods or printed and distributed an "outlawed" pamphlet with medical information, Sanger's actions brought about both punitive and rewarding consequences. As demonstrated by Mahatma Gandhi in India in the 1940s and by Martin Luther King, Jr., in the United States in the 1960s, peaceful protest and civil disobedience may result in penalties—jail terms and physical abuse—but they can also be rewarded with public attention, press coverage, and ultimately the revocation of unjust laws. Margaret Sanger learned that by enduring the hardships she invited by violating "obscenity" laws, she raised public awareness and changed the social climate. These compromises and successes in turn shaped her, making her less a private citizen with a private life, and more a public figure with a respected mission.

Cognitive personality theories would shift the focus to the lessons learned by Margaret Sanger in her social experience. As she became a celebrity—someone whom others saw as a symbol of a movement rather than a mere individual—she acquired a sense of self-efficacy that had eluded her in her early efforts to speak about health education. There is evidence that she held a high opinion of herself and engaged in competitive struggles with those she considered rivals. She broke with political organizations that had promoted her early work when she saw those alliances as less to her advantage. And she maintained a lifelong rivalry with her own sister Ethel Byrne, whom she resented for her prettiness and her status as their mother's favorite. Despite her progressive attitudes, Sanger was a product of her culture, one that even today values women especially for fertility and youth, and perhaps she hoped to project a romantic, even glamorous image of herself. In her 1938 autobiography, she styled herself as a heroine and martyr, interweaving inaccurate stories of her life with valid information and detail.

Critics of social-learning theories point to the limits of the behaviorist view of personality. Is personality all about stimulus variables—or living, mentally lively people? If personality is built on the learned repetition of previously reinforced responses, what is the origin of new behavior—such as creative achievements, innovative ideas, inventions, and works of art? Critics argue that much of the learning that behaviorists study is reinforced because an organism is in a state of tension due to some deficiency, and because other actions and reinforcements are not available. In contrast, your own experience may tell you that you don't have to be in a state of need or desperation to try something new or explore different forms of self-expression.

Critics of the cognitive-learning approach argue that such theories generally overlook *emotion* as an important component of personality. These theories emphasize rational information processing rather than emotions, which are viewed as mere by-products of thoughts and behavior. For those who feel that emotions are central to the functioning of human personality, this cognitive perspective has a serious flaw. Feelings may themselves be important determinants of cognitive content and structure. Other critics focus on the vague explanations given for how personal constructs and competencies are created. Cognitive theorists have little to say about the developmental origins of adult personality. Their focus on the individual's perception of the current behavior setting obscures the individual's history.

Despite these criticisms, social-learning and cognitive personality theories have made significant contributions to modern thought. Mischel's awareness of situational variables has brought about a better understanding of the interaction between what the person brings to a behavior setting and what that setting draws out of the person. Kelly's theory has influenced many cognitive therapists. Bandura's ideas have improved the way we educate children and help them to achieve.

Check Your Recall

In his psychodynamic theory of personality, Sigmund Freud asserted that unconscious motives and conflicts act as determinants of behavior. He proposed that personality develops through psychosexual stages, with excessive gratification or frustration leading to fixation at one or more stages. Personality conflicts occur between the id, superego, and ego. Ego defense mechanisms can reduce anxiety but are not a valid long-term conflict resolution strategy. Post-Freudian psychodynamic theories put greater emphasis on ego functions and social variables, and less emphasis on sexual urges. For Adler, personality is driven by a need to compensate for feelings of inferiority. Jung emphasized the ideas of the collective unconscious and archetypes, and the basic need to create.

Humanistic theories emphasize self-actualization and the importance of experiencing unconditional positive regard. These theories serve to explain the whole personality, including innate qualities, subjective feelings, and the challenges of existence. Humanistic theories apply best to normal personalities seeking growth and betterment, and are generally more optimistic about human nature than psychodynamic theories.

Social-learning theories view behavior as caused by combined environmental stimuli and reinforcements. Dollard and Miller applied the ideas of learning theory to personality theory, adding learned drives and habits to Freudian concepts. Mischel has combined social-learning theory with a cognitive approach, emphasizing that people's personality patterns are explained by interactions between personal and situational variables. Bandura emphasized that social and cognitive factors—especially observational learning, reciprocal determinism, and self-efficacy—influence behavior. Kelly suggested that personal constructs influence information processing.

CHAPTER REVIEW

Summary

Personality psychology seeks to explain patterns in individuals' thoughts, feelings, and behavior. Personality can be assessed by means of objective measures such as the MMPI, CPI, and MBTI. Projective techniques for personality assessment include the Rorschach and the TAT series. Assessment findings can be applied in clinical evaluations, educational placement, and career counseling. Personality theories explain the origins of and relationships among personality characteristics. Implicit personality theories are personal systems for judging our own and others' personality. Research on self-concept and impression management can be applied in self-improvement strategies. Scientific personality theories are either idiographic (focused on individuality) or nomothetic (focused on common patterns or themes). They can also be either descriptive or developmental in nature.

Type theories and trait theories are both descriptive approaches to personality. Early type theories, categorizing personality into specific extremes, include the ancient four-humors theory and Sheldon's theory of somatotypes. Trait theories such as Allport's approach, Eysenck's hierarchy, and the Big Five seek to identify basic dimensions underlying all personalities. Research suggests that traits may have a genetic basis, accounting for inherited tendencies and family resemblances in personality.

Developmental personality theories seek to explain the origins and influences that shape personality, however it is described. Psychodynamic theories assume that personality is driven by unconscious forces and shaped by early childhood experience. Humanistic theories argue that human action aims for self-actualization, and can be improved by unconditional positive regard. According to social-learning and cognitive theories of personality, one's

CHAPTER 11

Individual Differences

At the age of 37, newspaper and magazine columnist Bob Greene started to suspect that he "was dumber than [he] had been in high school" (Greene, 1985). At 17 he had been able to add, subtract, and multiply without using a calculator. Twenty years later, those skills seemed to have disappeared completely. To see if he could still make the grade, Greene decided to retake the Scholastic Aptitude Test (SAT), the three-hour examination of verbal and mathematical abilities that many colleges use to select students for admission. Greene sent in his fee, and on the designated Saturday morning, he showed up at his local high school with six sharpened No. 2 pencils in his pocket. After one hour, "all of us looked dazed, unhappy, and disoriented, although I believe that I was the only student to go to the water fountain and take an Inderal for his blood pressure" (Greene, 1985).

The SAT was designed as a standardized measure of high school students' academic aptitudes. Admissions officers had had difficulty interpreting grade-point averages from thousands of high schools with different standards and grading policies. Although the tests were intended to be objective evaluations, they have been accused of bias, and despite many revisions over the years, it has been difficult to quell those accusations. Across all ethnic groups, average SAT scores increase as family income goes up. Whites and Asian Americans consistently outperform Mexican Americans, Puerto Ricans, and African Americans (Hacker, 1986). Men on the average score higher than women (Gordon, 1990).

However, the SAT is changing. Consider the commonplace use of calculators, for example. When the SAT was introduced in 1941, pocket calculators did not even exist. In the mid-1980s, when Greene took the test for the second time, the proctor instructed that "Calculators or wristwatches with calculator functions may not be used." Later, in 1994, students were permitted to use calculators for the first time, and 20 percent of the math questions were constructed to require students to produce their own responses rather than merely select from a set of multiple-choice alternatives. Test-takers would have to come up with their own answers for questions such as "If the population of a certain country is increasing at the rate of one person every 12 seconds, by how many persons does it increase every half hour?" (Educational Testing Service, 1990a).

When Greene's test results finally arrived in the mail, his hands were shaking. He felt ridiculous. After all, he already had a college degree and a successful *career. Nevertheless, he nervously ripped open the envelope. Greene's verbal score had gone up 56 points, not surprising for a writer. But in math, over the two decades since Greene first took the test, his score had nose-dived by 200 points!*

Just as it is difficult to know why some groups perform better than others on the SAT, it is impossible to know with certainty why Bob Greene's math score plummeted. Wasn't the test supposed to measure his basic *aptitude for math—what he understood, and not just what he had learned? Perhaps his math aptitude had decreased because, in his work as a writer, he no longer used the math he had once practiced regularly in high school. Or perhaps the test itself didn't measure Bob Greene's aptitude or potential to learn*

and use math. Instead, perhaps the test actually measured his recent accomplishments and practice in the subjects covered on the test—accomplishments made possible because his adult life experience as a professional writer had enhanced his verbal ability, but seldom required use of his early math skills.

Greene (1985) wrote about his experiences with the SAT to document some problems that exist with this system of testing. Standardized group tests— paper-and-pencil instruments, uniformly administered to vast numbers of people—are heavily relied upon, for better or worse, by most college and university admissions offices. Consequently, tests such as the SAT are centrally important to the academic lives of millions of students.

Introduction

The use of psychological tests to assess differences between individuals' mental abilities is considered by some to be "one of psychology's unquestioned success stories" (Tyler, 1988). That "success" is determined in several ways. Psychological tests compare people on various dimensions according to objective standards that are not open to the biases of subjective interpreters. They are supposed to be fair comparisons of the mental capacities of all individuals taking the same test under the same conditions. These tests have been perceived as "tools of democracy," allowing selection of individuals for education and employment to be based on what those individuals know and can show, rather than on *whom* they know and what their family can show (Sokol, 1987).

Any test can be said to "work" well if it accurately predicts performance in future situations. Test results, such as those from the SAT, are generally good predictors of later academic grades, just as tests used in personnel selection predict some types of job performance. When a person's aptitudes, interests, attitudes, and personality are all taken into account, the chances of improving the fit between person and school or person and job greatly increase—to the benefit of all concerned. In the case of Bob Greene, however, it is not clear whether the "A" in SAT stands for "aptitude" or "achievement"—an important distinction for people such as high school graduates whose scores will determine their access to future opportunities.

Psychological testing is big business. Many psychologists spend a great deal of time on the construction, evaluation, administration, and interpretation of psychological tests. Testing is a multimillion-dollar industry; thousands of children and adults regularly take some form of the many tests distributed by more than 40 major U.S. test publishers. Virtually everyone in our society who has attended school, gone to work, joined the military services, or registered in a mental health clinic has undergone some kind of psychological testing.

Writer Bob Greene's SAT scores show that people's performance improves in the tasks they practice and worsens in the tasks they neglect. Similarly, practicing test-taking actually can improve performance. The Educational Testing Service, which designs and distributes the SAT, markets courses for high schools and how-to-succeed testing books for the general public. Because scores can be improved with practice, schools have been accused of "teaching the test" rather than enabling students to master the material on which they will be tested. Some students also pursue private "prep courses" that they hope will improve their performance on specific tests. Such practices underscore the significance of tests not only in planning life decisions, but as goals in themselves.

In this chapter we will examine the foundations and applications of psychological assessment. We will review the contributions psychologists have made to our understanding of individual differences in intelligence and vocational ability. Our focus will be on what makes any test useful, how tests work, and why such tests may not always do the job they were intended to do. We will conclude by considering the role of psychological assessment in our personal and professional lives.

Assessing Individual Differences

Psychological assessment *is the use of specified testing procedures to evaluate the abilities, performances, and personal qualities of people.* Assessment contributes to an individual's understanding of herself so that she can make better-informed decisions about current problems or future choices (Maloney & Ward, 1976). Psychological assessment is often referred to as the measurement of *individual differences,* since the majority of assessments specify how an individual is different from or similar to other people on a given dimension. To undertake any assessment, psychologists first assume that some of the differences between individuals are more important than the many ways in which human functioning is similar. This assumption, known as the *individual differences perspective,* contrasts with an assumption that people are more alike than they are different.

The Individual Differences Perspective

Psychological assessment brings into focus a basic tension in psychology: *individual differences* versus *situational influence.* The two perspectives are interwoven, and an appreciation of this tension is necessary to assess individual differences.

Everyone Is Different   It is easy to be fascinated by what seem to be pervasive differences among people's abilities, temperaments, and values. This fascination underlies our tendency to look for what is distinctive or unique among those we meet, or to assert our opinions as different from others'. Personality psychologists specialize in studying the basic ways that people really differ. The **individual differences perspective** *focuses on identifying the differentiations among people, the characteristics and patterns that distinguish one person from others.* For example, personality psychology favors an individual differences approach, whether it is *idiographic* (person-centered) or *nomothetic* (trait-centered) in emphasis.

People unfamiliar with professional psychology often assume that our entire discipline is focused on individual differences. For example, newspapers and magazines feature articles on how to classify yourself or those you know. You may have seen titles such as "Are You Commitment-Phobic?" and "How

Talk show hosts, like Sally Jessy Raphael, explore different behavior patterns (pathological liars, adulterous couples) as if they represented an unchangeable "type" of person. Such pseudoscience promotes a simplistic view of human nature.

to Tell If Your Friends Are Loyal." Talk shows and "pop psychologists" (people who may or may not be professionally trained in psychology) explore different behavior patterns as if they were completely different from others, or unchangeable. Such programs feature a line-up of alleged procrastinators, pathological liars, vain teenagers, or adulterous couples. A barrage of such pseudoscience can leave you with the impression that, to know yourself and others, you must first figure out what *kind* of person acts in certain ways. This notion is tempting because it is so simple; the problem is that it may also be simplistic.

Individual differences are fascinating and get lots of attention from researchers, who often try to correlate certain personal characteristics with behavior patterns. For example, what traits predict who is most likely to help a stranger in need? Perhaps measures of traits such as generosity, altruism, or religiousness could be taken; high scorers should be more likely than low scorers to respond in a helpful way when they get the chance. Such measures are a common model for research on individual differences.

However, researchers often find that the differences in people's characteristics do not adequately explain the differences in their behavior. Indeed, because the relationship between personality and behavior is so complex, researchers do not expect people's test scores or traits to be predictive of all the variance in their corresponding behavior patterns. In fact, the highest correlation researchers typically find between a given trait and related behavior is only 0.30 (Ross & Nisbett, 1991). Since 0.30 is a relatively low correlation, you can see that this statistic suggests many other factors besides a particular trait account for an individual's pattern of behavior. Although it seems desirable to be able to predict people's behavior from their distinctive qualities, human behavior is far more complex than the simpler models we might wish for.

Everyone Is the Same   Why do we think in terms of individual differences if such differences don't predict behavior very well? For one thing, as we shall consider in the next chapter, when we watch others, we notice *them*—not their circumstances. This biased perspective causes us to overlook a powerful source of influence: the *situation*. Individual differences in important qualities—such as intelligence, extroversion, and emotional stability—will have an influence and show up as general behavioral differences. But specific situations also influence how people behave. *Where* you are (your behavior setting) may matter as much as *who* you are (your personality dynamics).

Go back to the question we posed earlier: When is a person likely to stop to help a stranger in distress? Suppose you were that bystander. If you are especially friendly or "good," perhaps these qualities will motivate you to stop. But as we will see in the next chapter, all those helpful qualities may not be enough to overcome the situation if the circumstances do not cooperate. For instance, if it would be dangerous for you to interfere, or if you are in too much of a hurry to assist or even notice a person in need, or if you see many other bystanders also in a position to help, you probably will *not* intervene—regardless of your personal level of altruism (Darley & Batson, 1973; Ross & Nisbett, 1991). The conclusion is that situations have power, and this shows up in our behavior.

Situationism *is the principle that situations and circumstances outside oneself have the power to influence behavior* (Ross & Nisbett, 1991). Some situations are so powerful, in fact, that almost anyone—regardless of unique qualities and personality traits—will respond to them in the same ways. For example, you may think of yourself as a free spirit, more independent than most of your classmates, but if your instructor were to suddenly order the class to "Raise your right hands," you would most likely comply quickly, along with everyone else. Quickly obeying a direct order from a respected authority figure does not prove you are a weak-minded conformist—does it? It does show that some situations are compelling and leveling, affecting people similarly despite their differences.

The individual differences approach does not deny situational forces, but it minimizes the importance of situations and concentrates on the ways in which people differ and how these differences show up in our actions. In contrast, the situationist perspective sees behavior as influenced by external stimuli in the current behavioral situation.

In additional to the individual differences perspective and situationism, there is a third position that proposes a compromise between these extremes. This **interactionist perspective** *argues that behavior is the product of both personality variables and situational variables, which interact with each other in influencing the individual's behavior.* For example, some shy students who normally never speak up in the classroom might feel comfortable "talking" on the internet or using e-mail because it offers anonymity and a sort of "protection." Likewise, some of their normally vocal classmates might find that the intimacy of a one-on-one situation, even a telephone conversation, leads them to clam up. By observing any individual in only one type of situation, we miss the big picture of how that person's predispositions are influenced by different surroundings and circumstances.

The History of Assessment

When psychologists try to understand the causes of a given behavior, they search for variables in one of two places: inside the person, or outside, in the situation. In the last chapter we reviewed how our fascination with personality has led to assessment techniques and theories about the traits and patterns that distinguish individuals. In this chapter, we review how psychologists have investigated individuals' abilities, especially differences in talent, intelligence, and performance. How and why do people *differ* from each other—in the same situation or on the same task? Let's review some milestones in the history of assessment and examine how individual differences have been identified and evaluated.

The use of *objective* assessment procedures to evaluate a person's abilities and skills eliminates the need for the subjective and sometimes biased evaluations made by people in positions of power or authority. As we saw in Chapter 10, assessment is especially valuable in helping clinical psychologists detect problems that may require special counseling or treatment. Keep in mind that assessment in general makes assumptions about whether and how to compare individuals and scrutinize differences between them.

The development of formal tests and procedures for assessment is a relatively new enterprise in psychology, coming into wide use only in the early 1900s. Long before Western psychology began to devise tests to evaluate people, assessment techniques were commonplace in ancient China. In fact, China employed a sophisticated program of civil service testing over 4000 years ago. Officials were required to demonstrate their competence every third year at an oral examination. Two thousand years later, during the Han dynasty, written civil service tests were used to assess competence in the areas of law, the military, agriculture, and geography. During the Ming dynasty (1368–1644), public officials were chosen on the basis of their performance at three stages of an objective selection procedure, involving several days of examinations and written work. China's selection procedures were observed and described by British diplomats and missionaries in the early 1800s. Modified versions of China's system were soon adopted by the British and later by the Americans for the selection of civil service personnel (Wiggins, 1973).

Genius and "Morality"   The key figure bridging prescientific ideas to modern views of intelligence testing was an upper-class Englishman, **Sir Francis Galton** (1822–1911). Galton's book *Hereditary Genius,* published in 1869, greatly influenced subsequent thinking on the methods, theories, and practices of testing. Galton (who was a half-cousin to Charles Darwin) attempted to apply Darwinian evolutionary theory to the study of human abilities. He was interested in how and why people differ in their abilities. He wondered why some people were gifted and successful while many others were not.

Galton was the first to postulate that differences in intelligence were *quantifiable* in terms of degrees of intelligence that people possessed. He argued that these differences were *normally distributed* in the population, meaning that few people possessed extremely high or low intelligence and most people clustered in the middle of the range, around an average score. Galton also believed that intelligence could be measured by objective tests, and that the precise extent to which two sets of test scores were related could be determined by a statistical procedure he called *co-relation,* now known as *correlation.* These ideas all proved to be of lasting value. However, some of Galton's other notions have been quite controversial, as we shall see.

Galton believed that genius was inherited. He argued that talent (or eminence) passed through generations of families; nurture had only a minimal effect on intelligence. Then he went one big step further in his assumption: Galton believed that intelligence was somehow related to "moral worth" (Galton, 1884). That is, people deemed less intelligent were assumed to be more likely to engage in immoral or criminal behavior. Galton attempted to base public policy on the concept of genetically superior and inferior people. Galton coined the term **eugenics** *for his movement, which advocated improving the human species by applying evolutionary theory to family planning* (from the Greek *eugenes,* "well-born"). Supporters of the eugenics movement encouraged biologically superior people to interbreed and sought to discourage biologically inferior people from having offspring. Today such an assumption that one's moral worthiness is determined by inherited factors rather than one's own responsible actions seems preposterous. But in Galton's day the policies of eugenics won many adherents among policy-makers and wealthy social leaders. Protesting the short-sightedness of his critics, Galton wrote, "There exists a sentiment, for the most part quite unreasonable, against the gradual extinction of an inferior race" (Galton, 1907 p. 200).

These controversial ideas were endorsed and later expanded on by many who argued forcefully that the intellectually superior race should propagate at the expense of those with inferior minds. Among the proponents of these ideas were American psychologists Henry Goddard and Lewis Terman and, of course, Nazi dictator Adolf Hitler. The horrors of the Nazi Holocaust of the 1930s and 1940s, in which millions of people were exterminated for being "inferior" to the ideals of the Aryan race, made racist notions of "natural" superiority even more gruesome. Even today, groups of "white supremacists" argue that the best qualities of an individual are those inherited from his or her racial background, rather than the skills and accomplishments achieved in one's lifetime. Arguments for "racial purity" and "ethnic cleansing" lack both logic and any scientific support, but may be appealing to those people who feel this is the only resource they have about which to feel proud.

Modern Assessment   Most people do not use their interest in individual differences to justify racism. The assessment of individual differences has practical, everyday goals. The goals of formal assessment resemble your own concerns when you size up another person. You may want to know how smart, trustworthy, creative, responsible, or dangerous a new acquaintance is; you may attempt to evaluate these qualities with whatever evidence you can gather informally. You certainly want to understand and predict another person's behavior before making a lasting commitment to him or her.

Scientific psychology attempts to formalize the procedures by which accurate predictions about individual behavior can be made. Assessment begins with the measurement of a limited number of individual attributes and samples of behavior. This narrow body of personal information in a testing situation forms the basis of predictions about the individual's reactions at another time in a real-life situation that is not identical to the test situation. Psychologists use assessment techniques to understand individuals and how they differ from one another. The science of assessment is also used to test psychological theories and concepts, such as the nature of personality structure or of intelligence.

While a clinical psychologist uses testing to make predictions about a *particular* client, a researcher in personality psychology tries to discover the regularities in personality in the *general* population that relate to certain behavior patterns. For example, a research psychologist might test to see if there are differences in traits, such as sensation-seeking, that predict risk for abusing alcohol or drugs.

When certain questions arise about an individual's behavioral or mental functioning, the individual is referred to a psychologist who is trained to make an assessment that might provide some answers. A judge may want to know if a confessed murderer is capable of understanding the consequences of his or her actions, or a teacher may want to know why a child has difficulty learning. A mental health worker may want to know the extent to which a patient's problems result from psychological disorders or from physical, organic disorders. When a psychologist's judgment will have a profound impact on a person's life, a *complete* assessment must involve more than just psychological testing. Tests may be very helpful, but results should be interpreted in light of *all* available information about a person, including medical history, family life, previous difficulties, or noteworthy achievements (Matarazzo, 1990). When that complete profile is collected, then personal assessment can be a valuable tool in helping to make valid predictions about individual behavior.

Collecting Information

In the last chapter, we made an important distinction between informal, *implicit* personality theories in everyday social interaction and formal, scientific theories of the description and development of personality. Similarly, there are important differences in the ways individuals' abilities are assessed: *informal*, amateur assessments of self and others should not be equated with *formal* assessment techniques developed by scientists. Formal psychological assessments are developed more systematically, applied in a more organized way, and used for carefully specified purposes. You may informally size up a classmate as someone who would take good class notes, should you ever need to borrow them. But this is different from a careful evaluation of that same person's attention, comprehension of course material, note-taking practices, and conscientiousness.

While some assessment techniques are derived from particular *theoretical* perspectives, others are based on purely *empirical* grounds. Empirically constructed techniques are guided only by data; they are built to make specific predictions and, therefore, utilize the items or questions that do the job regardless of whether or not they make theoretical sense. For example, students might be asked to indicate their views on the importance of sexual intimacy in maintaining a personal relationship. If males consistently differ from females in their scores on this measure—for example, by expressing more permissive attitudes and a greater emphasis on the importance of sex—then these data

As part of psychological counseling, a client may be given a battery of tests to determine her level and quality of functioning in different areas.

could be used as one *test* of gender differences, even without offering any *theory* about why the two groups differ. Recall from the last chapter that one of the most useful personality tests, the MMPI, was developed empirically, not theoretically (see page 382).

Psychologists commonly rely on four types of resources for assessment data: *interviews; life history or archival data; psychological tests;* and *situational behavior observations*. To be especially effective and thorough, an assessor relies on more than one source and uses information from one technique to fill in the gaps left by others.

Interviews   An **interview** *is a face-to-face conversation conducted to gather information about the respondent*. An interview is a very direct approach to learning about someone. The interview content and style may be casual and unstructured, and tailored to fit the person being interviewed. On the other hand, interviews can be highly structured or standardized, asking very specific questions in a very specific way. Counselors find unstructured interviews useful in planning individualized treatment programs. Structured interviews are preferred for job interviews and psychological research, when it is important that many people be assessed accurately, completely, consistently, and without bias.

Interviewing may seem simple but is in fact hard to do well. A well-trained interviewer must be able to accomplish five goals: put the respondent at *ease;* elicit the desired *information;* maintain *control* of the direction and pace of the interview; establish and maintain *rapport* (a sense of comfortable relating) with the respondent; and finally, bring the interview to a satisfactory *conclusion*.

Life Histories   Interview data may be supplemented with **life history** *information, information about a person's life taken from different types of available records,* especially data from different ages and from other significant people, as well as the target individual. Life histories are often constructed from *archival data,* including public documents such as school or military records, the person's own written work (stories and drawings), personal journals, medical data, photographs, and videotapes.

Psychological Tests   A **psychological test** *is an instrument used to measure an individual's standing on some mental or behavioral characteristic relative to others*. A psychological test can measure virtually all aspects of human functioning, including intelligence, personality, and creativity. Unlike interviews, tests provide *quantitative* characterizations of an individual by using normative comparisons with others. In other words, tests can convert your performance to a number or set of numbers that can be directly compared to a standard, or *norm*.

For example, if an instructor tells you that your score on a test was at the "75th percentile" for the class, this means that 25 percent of your classmates $(100 - 75 = 25)$ earned higher scores than you—regardless of how many items were on the test. Thus a percentile score is a convenient single-number summary of test performance and relative class standing.

Observations of Behavior   Tests are economical, easy to use, and provide important normative data in quantitative form, but they are not always useful for finding out what a person actually *does,* especially when a person cannot objectively judge or report his or her own behavior. To assess behavior objectively in laboratory or real-life settings, psychologists use **situational behavior observations:** *first-hand study of an individual's actions and performance in one or more specific settings*. In this procedure, an observer watches an individual's behavioral patterns in one or more situations, such as at home, at work, or in school. The goal here is to discover the determinants and consequences of the various responses and habits of the individual.

Direct situational observations are useful to those therapists who hope to find the conditions in which patients' problem behaviors occur. Such observations are also useful for observing job applicants' behavior in a job-like situation, and for determining whether what people say corresponds to what they actually do. Behavioral observations ultimately serve to confirm data yielded by test and interview techniques.

Reporting the Data

Who provides the information being sought? This is determined by which reporting method an assessor chooses. For most psychologists, the two basic choices are *self-report* and *observer-report* methods. Each method has its advantages and liabilities.

Self-Reports   The easiest, if not the most accurate, way to get information is to get it "straight from the horse's mouth": If you want to know what someone thinks or does, ask him or her. This is the simple principle of **self-report methods,** *research techniques in which respondents are assessed by their answers to a series of questions.* You have probably provided many self-reports to investigators, surveyors, and teachers in your life. A self-report respondent may respond to questions on a survey or test form, in an interview, or by making entries in a personal journal. One popular and easily administered self-report is the *inventory,* a standardized written test composed in a multiple-choice, true-false, or rating format. The MMPI discussed in Chapter 10 is an example of a true-false inventory.

Self-report measures are valuable because they tap into an individual's personal experiences and feelings. They are convenient because they do not require trained interviewers, can be administered in groups, and are generally easy to score. The greatest shortcoming of self-report measures is that sometimes people are not in touch with their feelings or cannot objectively report their own behavior. Thus, psychologists often use methods that rely on observers' reports in addition to, or in place of, self-reports.

Observers' Reports   In **observer-report methods,** *another person evaluates some aspect of the behavior of the individual being studied.* Observer reports involve a systematic evaluation of some aspect of a person's behavior by another person, called a rater or judge. Observer reports may consist of very specific situational behavior observations or more generalized ratings. For example, teachers' aides may observe a preschool class and record the number of times each child performs particular behaviors—such as talking, shoving, hitting, or sharing a toy—during a particular period.

The observers who provide these reports are usually summarizing their observations at some point later than the time of the actual observation. To do this, observers provide a **rating,** *a quantified judgment of the observed behavior or behavior pattern.* In contrast with such retrospective ratings, psychologists who conduct situational behavior observations usually provide their ratings and scores "on-line," at the time the behavior is performed, or from videotaped recordings of the behavior. Observers who rate others are sometimes asked to first record and describe specific behaviors and later assign overall ratings based on those records.

Depending on how the information will be used, observers may be given either general guidelines or very precise instructions for how to define the values they assign to what they observe. For example, suppose you have been hired to rate the "competitiveness" of game players on a scale from 1 to 10.

Judges observe a wrestling match at the Olympic Games. To avoid charges that their decisions are biased, judges must first establish clear definitions and similar criteria.

You are instructed to rate as "1" any player with a pattern of failing to engage in either defensive or offensive play; a "10" would be awarded to a player you observe consistently playing offensively, attacking and preventing the opponent's moves. You would assign intermediate scores, between 1 and 10, according to your judgment of the player's overall degree of displayed "competitiveness." Initially your task will be somewhat slow and difficult, but as you gain familiarity with the players' actions, your confidence and efficiency as a rater will increase.

To avoid charges that ratings are biased, it is important to establish clear definitions and similar criteria. For example, when judges at the Olympic Games display their individual point assignments, spectators look for biases that might unfairly penalize some athletes and reward others. If a judge representing a particular country consistently displays ratings that downgrade the performance of athletes other than those from his or her own nation, it may seem obvious that the judge's ratings are biased and unfair.

What are the drawbacks to relying on observer ratings? One drawback is that ratings may tell more about the *judge*, or about the judge's relationship with the person being rated, than about the true characteristics of that person. If you already like the person you are rating, you may tend to judge him favorably on nearly every dimension. For example, if you think one of your professors is an enjoyable lecturer, then when you complete a course evaluation form, you might also tend to rate other aspects of the class very high, such as the quality of class discussions or the required text. *This type of rating bias—in which an overall positive or negative feeling about the person is extended to the specific dimensions being evaluated—is referred to as a* **halo effect.** You may have used the halo effect to your own advantage if you ever had a teacher whose high opinion of you in one subject led her to evaluate you well in other areas as well. You may also have been victimized by the negative halo effect if a boss or authority figure judged you to be generally incompetent simply because he rated your skills in a single specific ability to be very poor. Some halos are golden, but others are tarnished.

A different type of bias occurs when a rater believes that most people in a certain category (for example, Republicans, Serbians, "welfare mothers") share certain qualities. The rater may "see" those qualities in any individual who happens to be in that category. The **stereotype effect** *occurs when a judge's rating of an individual is biased by beliefs about that person's social category.* For example, if a student thinks that all professors who are middle-aged or older must be boring instructors, she may immediately experience disappointment when she finds that her new instructor appears to be an older adult.

Interjudge Reliability   Rating biases can be reduced by phrasing rating items in terms of specific, observed behaviors—not the rater's inferences. For example, "spends most time to oneself" is a less biased description than "withdrawn." Specific rules can also be established for each rating level judges are to apply, such as, "If the person does X, give a rating of 10." Finally, several raters can be employed so that the bias introduced by each judge's unique point of view is averaged with the combined ratings of all the judges.

Whenever you use more than one observer, you can calculate the **interjudge reliability,** *the degree to which the different observers make similar ratings or agree about a particular individual or case.* Typically, interjudge reliability will be highest when judges record the specific behaviors observed in a specific situation rather than general impressions of behavior. For example, suppose you are being evaluated by two judges to determine your suitability for employment as a day care worker. If they each have independent conversations with you, they may form different impressions of your qualifications, so interjudge reliability of the ratings based on these general impressions could be low. In contrast, if they each spent time observing and rating your interaction with a child in the same setting, their ratings are more likely to agree with each other, and their interjudge reliability will be higher.

Test Composition

What qualities make a test a "good" test? You have probably taken some "bad" tests in your school career, and recognize that a test is not good if it is unfair, unrelated to the material it was intended to cover, or difficult to understand. To effectively classify individuals or select those people with particular qualities, an assessment procedure should meet three requirements. The assessment instrument should be *reliable, valid,* and *standardized.* If it fails to meet these requirements, researchers cannot be sure whether the conclusions of the assessment can be trusted, nor can practitioners be confident about applying the test results.

Reliability   Reliability *is a test's consistency, the extent to which an assessment instrument yields the same score each time the same individual is measured.* A reliable test is "trustworthy" and can be counted on to provide consistent scores, either on retests or when different raters judge the same performance. If your bathroom scale gives you a different reading each time you step on it (even though you haven't eaten or changed your clothing and little time has passed between testings), the scale is not doing its job. You would call the instrument *unreliable* and throw it out, because you could not count on it to give consistent results. Reliability is often specified in terms of how it has been measured: through comparing results of *testing and retesting;* by comparing *parallel forms* of a test's coverage; and by evaluating a test's *internal consistency.*

Test-Retest Reliability   One straightforward way to determine whether a test is reliable is to calculate its *test-retest reliability,* a measure that indicates the correlation between the scores of the same subjects on the same test given at two different times. If subjects achieve the same or a score similar to one they earned previously, we can conclude that the test is reliably measuring the same thing—behavior, ability, or any other element. One caution in this measure of reliability is to consider the cost of testing each individual twice, and another is to be sure the test sessions occur close to each other in time. If the retest is significantly delayed, other information or changing experience may affect the second set of results.

Parallel Forms   Instead of giving exactly the same test twice, a second way to assess reliability is to administer parallel forms of a test: alternate versions of the same material that measure the same abilities or knowledge by using different words or examples. By presenting parallel forms, the researcher reduces the effects of direct practice of the test questions, and memorization of the test questions. Parallel tests also remove any test-taker's efforts to appear consistent from one version of a test to the next. Reliable tests yield comparable scores on parallel forms of the test. For example, what is the answer to the following multiple-choice question?

Ego defense mechanisms are explained by _____ theories of personality.
a. humanistic
b. social learning
c. trait
d. psychodynamic

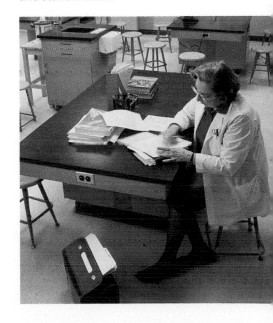

An instructor grades a test. To be sure a test measures what is intended, it should be reliable, valid, and standardized.

If you understand what ego defense mechanisms are and how they are theorized to work (see Chapter 10), you should be able to answer the above question correctly. You should also be able to answer the following question correctly:

True or false? Ego defense mechanisms are explained by psychodynamic theories of personality.

These two parallel items test for the same knowledge in a similar way. If you answer "d" to the first question, you will probably answer "true" to the second one.

Internal Consistency   The third measure of reliability is *internal consistency,* the degree to which different components within the same test yield similar scores. For example, we could compare a person's score on the odd-numbered items of a test to the score on the even-numbered items. A reliable test yields the same score for each of its halves. The test is then said to have high internal consistency on *split-half reliability*—which is obtained by splitting the test's items and assessing reliability between the two halves. If the test is indeed reliable, these two halves should be the same or very similar.

Although a reliable test tends to give the same test scores when it is repeated, obtaining different test scores does not necessarily mean that a test is unreliable. Sometimes the variable being measured actually changes from one testing to the next. For example, if you took the same test on theories of personality before and after reading Chapter 10, you would do better the second time—because you would know more. In addition, besides the quality or skill being tested, many other variables may affect test scores. You may have different scores on different occasions because of changes in your mood, amount of fatigue, and level of effort you put out. These extraneous variables will alter the desired test performance, giving a false picture of your ability. Similarly, a teacher may grade an essay differently if he or she is tired after reading many student essays. In such a case, the test itself would not be unreliable, but the scoring procedure would be. Assume now that we have a reliable test; what more must it be before it can be of value in assessment?

Validity   The **validity** *of a test is the degree to which it measures what an assessor intends it to measure.* A valid test of intelligence measures a person's intelligence and predicts performance in situations where intelligence is important. Scores on a valid measure of creativity reflect actual creativity, not drawing ability or moods. In general, then, validity is not a property of the test itself, but a feature of the test's ability to make accurate predictions about outcomes. Validity answers the basic question, "What is the test good for?" A good test can be evaluated in terms of two types of validity: *criterion validity* and *construct validity.*

Criterion Validity   The criterion validity of a test is the degree to which the test results match another standard of the tested quality. To assess criterion validity, performance is measured on both the test and on some other standard, and the two sets of results are compared. For example, we would compare someone's score on a typing *test* to how well (for example, how quickly and accurately) the subject actually *types* on the job. Typing performance is the *criterion* or standard that the test is intended to predict. Ideally, scores on the criterion directly reflect a personal characteristic or behavior that is related to, but not the same as, that assessed by the test. For example, if an aptitude test is designed to predict success in college, then college grades would be an appropriate criterion. If the test scores correlate highly with college grades, then the test has criterion validity. A major task of test developers is finding appropriate, measurable criteria to determine the validity of their tests.

Construct Validity For many personal qualities that interest psychologists, there is no single ideal criterion. For example, no single behavior or objective measure of performance can tell us how anxious, depressed, or aggressive a person is. Psychologists have theories or *constructs* about these abstract qualities. A construct is a set of ideas about the components of some trait or personal quality. For example, "height" is *not* a construct, because an individual's height is readily understood by others, and can be objectively measured. In contrast, "intelligence" *is* a construct, because that term includes many different ideas about an individual's abilities and about processes that cannot be directly observed but are still assumed to exist and influence behavior.

A particular construct can usually be measured in more than one way. For example, a construct like "anger" could be measured by observing a person's angry behaviors or by having him complete a self-report questionnaire on frequency of angry feelings. The *construct validity* of a particular test is the degree to which test scores of a specific characteristic correlate with other measures of the construct (Loevinger, 1957). For example, in addition to taking a psychological test for a quality such as "shyness," an individual might take other tests related to social anxiety and distress, and then have her social behavior on various tasks rated by judges. If the test score is positively correlated with her assessment on these other measures of the same construct—shyness—then the test is said to have construct validity.

Once we have determined that a construct is a good working model that explains a large body of data, we can examine separately each of the measures of the construct. The conditions under which a test is valid may be very specific, so it is always important to ask about a test, "For what purpose is it valid?"

For example, suppose you design a test to measure the ability of medical students to cope with stress, and you find that scores on it correlate well with students' ability to cope with classroom stress. You presume your test will also correlate with students' ability to deal with stressful hospital emergencies, but you discover it does not. Since you have demonstrated that it possesses some validity, the important question is not *whether* the test is valid, but *when* it is valid, and *for what purpose*.

Validity has something in common with reliability. While reliability is measured by the degree to which a test correlates with itself (administered at different times or using different items), validity is measured by the degree to which the test correlates with something external to it (another test, a behavioral criterion, or judges' ratings). If a test is *not* reliable, it is probably not valid either—because a test that cannot predict *itself* will be unable to predict anything else.

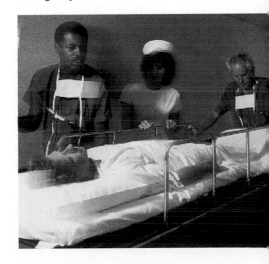

A test that measures the ability of medical students to handle classroom stress may not indicate whether the same students can someday handle the stress of an emergency room.

Standardization Suppose your instructor returns scored tests in class, and you discover you have a score of 18. What exactly does "18" mean? Did you do well, badly—or about the same as others? You cannot answer that question until you know who else took the test and how well (or poorly) *they* did. *The value of a test based on measurements of a large group of people, such as an entire class, is a* **norm.** If you learn that 30 students took the test, and for most of these the typical or "normal" score was 15, you should feel relatively proud of your performance—after all, you performed above the norm. The norms for your class might be different from those of other classes with different instructors and different classroom conditions. To make sense of your score, you must begin by comparing yourself with the appropriate group and setting.

You probably consult normative data informally when, after receiving test scores, you ask classmates "How did *you* do?" and use their responses to gauge the meaning of your particular score. You can do this more formally if you are given information about the entire group's performance, including the number of people who took the test, the average score, and the range of scores from lowest to highest achieved. (Actually, a better measure is the *standard deviation* of all the scores from the mean of the distribution; see the statistical review in Appendix A at the end of this text for a review of that concept.)

For norms to be meaningful, everyone in the group must take the same test under the same standardized circumstances. **Standardization** *is the administration of a test to all persons in the same way under the same conditions.* For example, all students should show up at the same time and place for the testing session. If you were to appear in class for a scheduled test only to find that most of your classmates had arranged to take the test individually at other times, how would you feel? Would you still be confident that it would be fair to compare your test score with all of theirs? When testing procedures are not *standardized,* it is impossible to compute group *norms,* and perhaps impossible to determine the meaning of any individual's score. You have probably encountered test norms when you received your scores on aptitude tests such as the SAT. The norms told you how your scores compared to those of other students and helped you interpret how well you had done relative to that *normative population.*

Group norms are most useful when the standardization group shares important qualities with the individuals tested (such as age, social class, ethnicity, and experience). The group norms are a useful measure against which an individual's score can be interpreted. So whenever you are given your results on any psychological test, the first question you should ask is, "Compared to what?" What norms were used to interpret *relative* performance? For example, a student who receives a score of 46 on a psychology test may be worried about her performance until she learns that the highest score possible was 50, that her classmates' scores ranged from 21 to 47, and that the average score was 36. In a sense, any particular score is meaningless *until* comparative information is provided.

✓ Check Your Recall ✓✓✓✓✓✓✓✓✓✓✓✓✓

Assessment, the controlled measurement of individual differences, is used to understand and predict the behavior of individuals. Assessment assumes an individual differences perspective on behavior. The tradition of assessment for applied purposes can be traced to civil service exams in ancient China. In the nineteenth century, British scientist Sir Francis Galton proposed important ideas about measuring human genius, but extended his theory to recommend moralistic social policies. Modern assessments are used to measure attributes, abilities, and skills for a variety of research and applied purposes. The goal of modern assessment is to use samples of behavior to predict future behavior.

The information used in assessments can come from many sources, including interviews, life histories, situational behavior observations, and psychological tests. Reporting methods can rely on the target of an assessment to provide information about himself or herself, or can ask judges to observe and rate others' behavior.

To be useful, an assessment technique must be reliable, valid, and standardized. Reliability is consistency of results. Validity indicates how well a technique measures what it is supposed to measure. A standardized test is administered and scored in the same way for all test-takers, so that a person's score may be compared to the appropriate group norms. ✓

Assessing Intelligence

What is intelligence? Scientists continue to consider and debate how to define intelligence. They have yet to agree on a single definition, but most would include in their measure of intelligence at least three types of skills:

1. adapting to new situations and changing task demands
2. learning or profiting from experience or training
3. thinking abstractly, using symbols and concepts (Phares, 1984)

More specific approaches to defining intelligence are linked to theories of human adaptation and intellectual functioning. These theories have emerged from all walks of psychology, including neurology-biology, learning theory, and human development. As an individual functioning in a complex, demanding world, you probably have your own informal theories about what it takes to be smart and capable—and how to recognize whether someone possesses such qualities. After reviewing the concept of intelligence and the history of intelligence testing, we will examine more formal theories of the origins and forms of intelligence.

We will define **intelligence** *as the complex mental capacity to profit from experience—to go beyond what is perceived, and to imagine symbolic possibilities and use them to act effectively.* Intelligence is a hypothetical construct: not directly observable, intelligence is verified only by the operations (tests) used to measure it and by how it functions in criterion situations that are developed to validate it. In everyday language, we usually equate "intelligence" with higher-level, abstract thought processes. Human intelligence provides us with a distinct advantage for survival in our world. Intelligence

enables us to respond flexibly and imaginatively to environmental challenges; it is the reason our species has survived and prospered so well in so many different environments around the planet.

The way we think about intelligence and mental functioning influences the way we try to assess it. Some psychologists believe intelligence can be quantified as one score, while others argue that assessment should reflect the complexities and many components of intelligence (Hunt, 1984; Sternberg, 1985). Is intelligence a *unitary attribute*—a single, measurable dimension, like height or weight—so that people can be assessed in terms of how much "intelligence" they have? Or is intelligence instead a *collection* of several mental competencies, involving different "intelligences" for different kinds of tasks?

Some people believe that assessment of intellectual abilities is one of psychology's most significant contributions to society. Others maintain that it is a fraud, at best a simplistic view of human nature, and at worst a systematic attempt by elitists to weed out undesirables (Gould, 1981). Before we examine some evidence for these conflicting claims, we first need a bit more history to set the stage. The movement to measure intelligence began in France as an attempt to identify children who were unable to learn in school. Soon, however, intelligence testing crossed the Atlantic to become an American enterprise.

Measuring Mental Age

The year 1911 marked the first published account of a workable intelligence test. French psychologist **Alfred Binet** had responded to the call of the French Minister of Public Instruction to develop a way to more effectively teach developmentally disabled children in the public schools (Binet, 1911). Binet and his colleague, Théodore Simon, believed that it was necessary to measure a child's intellectual ability in order to plan an instructional program. Their radical proposal argued that education should fit the child's level of competence and not that the child be fit into a fixed curriculum.

Binet tried to devise an objective test of intellectual performance that could be used to classify and separate developmentally disabled from normal schoolchildren. He hoped that such a test would reduce the school's reliance on the more subjective, and perhaps biased, evaluations of teachers. It could also result in selecting the children who might benefit from specialized instruction.

Four important features distinguish Binet's approach to testing intellectual ability:

1. He interpreted scores on his test as an estimate of *current performance* and not as a measure of innate intelligence.
2. Binet wanted the test scores to be used to identify children who *needed special help* and not to stigmatize them.
3. He emphasized that *training and opportunity* could affect intelligence, and he wanted to identify areas of performance in which special education could help these children.
4. Finally, he constructed his test *empirically*—based on how children were observed to perform—rather than tying it to a particular theory of intelligence.

Quantifying Intelligence   To *quantify* intellectual performance, Binet designed age-appropriate problems or test items on which many children's responses could be compared. The problems on the test were chosen so that they could be scored objectively, could vary in content, were not heavily influenced by differences in children's environments, and tested judgment and reasoning rather than rote memory (Binet, 1911).

Children of various ages were tested, and the average score for normal children at each age was computed. Then, each individual child's performance was compared to the average for other children of that age. Test results were expressed in terms of the average age at which normal children achieved a particular score. This measure was called the **mental age (MA):** *the average age at which normal (average) individuals achieve a particular intelligence score.* For example, when a child's scores on various items of the test added up to the average score of a group of 5-year-olds, the child was said to have a *mental age* of 5, regardless of his or her actual **chronological age (CA),** *the number of years since the individual's birth.* Binet then operationally defined *retardation* as being two MA years behind CA.

As he conducted longitudinal tests of the children (testing them repeatedly at various intervals), Binet found that those assessed as developmentally disabled at one age fell further behind the mental age of their birth cohorts (other children their age) as they grew older. A child of 5 who performed at the level of 3 year olds might, at the age of 10, perform at the level of 6-year-olds. Although the *ratio* of mental age to chronological age would be constant (3/5 = 6/10), the total number of MA years of retardation would have increased from 2 to 4.

American Intelligence Testing   Due to a unique combination of historical events and social and political forces, Binet's successful development of an intelligence test had great impact in the United States. At the beginning of the twentieth century, the United States was a nation in turmoil. Global economic, social, and political conditions resulted in millions of immigrants entering the country. New universal education laws flooded schools with students. When World War I began, millions of volunteers marched into recruiting stations. These events—world conditions, new education laws, and World War I—all resulted in large numbers of people needing to be identified, documented, and classified. Some form of assessment was needed to facilitate these tasks (Chapman, 1988). At the time, "intelligence test results were used not only to differentiate [among] children experiencing academic problems, but also as a measuring stick to organize an entire society" (Hale, 1983, p. 373). Assessment was seen as a way to inject order into a chaotic society and as an inexpensive, democratic way to separate those who could benefit from education or military leadership training from those who could not.

In 1917, when the United States declared war on Germany and joined the massive military campaign of World War I, it was necessary to establish quickly a military force led by competent leaders. Recruiters needed to determine which of the many draftees could learn quickly and benefit from special leadership training to become officers. New nonverbal, group-administered tests of mental ability were used to evaluate over 1.7 million recruits. Incidentally, a group of famous psychologists, including Lewis Terman, Edward Thorndike, and Robert Yerkes, designed these new tests in only one month's time (Lennon, 1985).

One consequence of this large-scale group testing program was that the American public came to accept the idea that intelligence tests could differentiate people in terms of leadership ability, intelligence and other socially important characteristics. This acceptance led to the widespread use of tests in schools and industry. Another, more unfortunate, consequence was that the tests reinforced prevailing prejudices, because the army reports indicated that differences in test scores were linked to race and country of origin (Yerkes, 1921). Of course, the same statistics *could* have been used to demonstrate that environmental disadvantages limit the full development of people's intellectual abilities. Instead, these statistics fueled racist ideology. Immigrants to America, with limited facility in English or even little understanding of how to take such tests, were found to be "morons," "imbeciles," and worse. Immigrants from Northern Europe did much better than those from Southern Europe. Consider whether that surprises you, given the differences in their educational levels and familiarity with English, after being in the United States for only a short time.

IQ Testing

Despite the risks of unfairness, the assessment of intelligence clearly had many practical applications, and this spurred further research and test development. After Binet began the standardized assessment of intellectual ability, statistics-minded U.S. psychologists took the ball from him and ran. Pychologists in the United States modified Binet's scoring procedure, improved the reliability of the tests, and studied the scores of enormous normative samples of people who took the new tests. They also developed the **intelligence quotient (IQ):** *a standardized, numerical measure of intelligence, obtained from an individual's score on an intelligence test.* Two sorts of individually administered IQ tests are used widely today: the Stanford-Binet scales and the Wechsler scales.

The Stanford-Binet Intelligence Scale Stanford University's **Lewis Terman,** a former public school administrator, adapted Binet's test questions for U.S. schoolchildren, standardizing its administration and its age-level norms. In 1916 he published the Stanford Revision of the Binet Tests, commonly referred to as the *Stanford-Binet Intelligence Scale* (Terman, 1916).

With his new test, Terman provided a base for the original concept of the *intelligence quotient,* a term originally coined by German psychologist William Stern in 1914. As originally conceived, the IQ was the ratio of mental age to chronological age (multiplied by 100 to eliminate decimals):

$$IQ = MA/CA \times 100$$

Follow the IQ equation through this example: A child with a CA of 8 whose test scores revealed an MA of 10 would have an IQ of 125 ($10/8 \times 100 = 125$). A child of that same chronological age who performed at the level of 6-year-olds had an IQ of 75 ($6/8 \times 100 = 75$). Individuals who performed at the mental age equivalent to their chronological age had IQs of 100, considered to be the average or normal IQ.

The new Stanford-Binet test soon became a standard instrument in clinical psychology, psychiatry, and educational counseling. Unlike Binet, Terman believed that intelligence was an inner quality, that it was largely hereditary, and that IQ tests could measure this inner quality throughout the range of abilities that make up intelligence. His implicit message was that IQ reflected something essential and unchanging about human intelligence.

IQ scores are no longer derived by dividing mental age by chronological age, although the concept of a "ratio" expressed as a multiple of 100 (a percentage-like number that is easy to understand) is retained. If you took an IQ test today, your score would be totaled and the sum not divided by your chronological age but rather directly *compared* to the scores of other people your age. An IQ of 100 (average) indicates that 50 percent of those your age earned lower scores. Scores between 90 and 110 are now labeled normal, above 120 are superior, and below 70 are evidence of developmental disability (see Figure 11.1).

The Stanford-Binet scales were criticized because the subtests used to measure IQ at different ages focused on different types of skills. For example, 2- to 4-year-olds were tested on their ability to manipulate objects, whereas adults were tested almost exclusively on verbal items. As the scientific under-

A psychologist administers an intelligence test to a 4-year-old child. The performance part of this test includes a block design task, an object completion task, and a shape identification task.

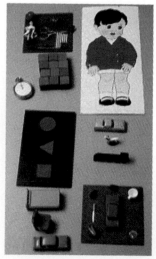

standing of intelligence increased, psychologists found it increasingly important to measure *several* intellectual abilities at *all* age levels. A recent revision of the Stanford-Binet now provides different scores for several mental skills, but it has not been widely accepted (Vernon, 1987).

The Wechsler Intelligence Scales   David Wechsler of Bellevue Hospital in New York set out to correct the dependence on verbal items in the assessment of adult intelligence. In 1939, he published the Wechsler-Bellevue Intelligence Scale, which combined *verbal* subtests with *nonverbal or performance* subtests. Thus, in addition to an overall IQ score, subjects were given separate estimates of verbal IQ and nonverbal IQ. After a few changes, the test was retitled the Wechsler Adult Intelligence Scale—the WAIS in 1955, and the revised WAIS-R today (Wechsler, 1981).

There are six *verbal* subtests of the WAIS-R (pronounced *wayce-AHR*): Information, Vocabulary, Comprehension, Arithmetic, Similarities (stating how two things are alike), and Digit Span (repeating a series of digits after the examiner). These verbal tests are both written and oral.

The WAIS-R's five *performance* subtests involve manipulation of materials and have little or no verbal content. In the Block Design test, for example, a subject tries to reproduce designs shown on cards by fitting together blocks with colored sides. The Digit Symbol test provides a key that matches 9 symbols to 9 numeric digits, and the task is to write the appropriate digits under the symbols on another page. Other performance tests involve Picture Arrangement, Picture Completion, and Object Assembly. If you were to take the WAIS-R, you would perform all 11 subtests, and receive 3 scores: a verbal IQ, a performance IQ, and an overall or full-scale IQ.

The WAIS-R is designed for people 18 years or older, but similar tests have been developed for children. The Wechsler Intelligence Scale for Children—Revised (WISC-R [1974], pronounced *wisk-AHR* or *whisker*) is suited to children ages 6 to 17, and the Wechsler Preschool and Primary Scale of Intelligence (WPPSI, pronounced *WHIP-see*) for children ages 4 to 6 years. Some subtests were specially created for use with children, but most have a direct counterpart in the WAIS-R.

The WAIS-R, the WISC-R, and the WPPSI form a family of intelligence tests that yield a verbal IQ, a performance IQ, and a full-scale IQ at all age levels. In addition, they provide comparable subtest scores that allow researchers to track the development of even more specific intellectual abilities. For this reason, the Wechsler scales are particularly valuable when the same individual is to be tested over time, at different ages.

FIGURE 11.1   Distribution of IQ Scores Among a Large Sample ■

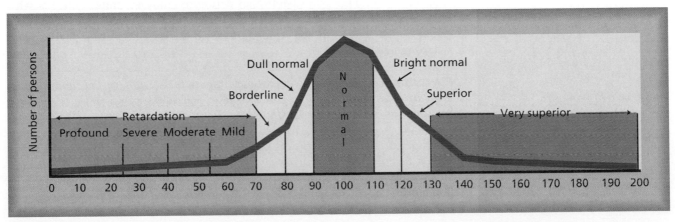

Group Tests of Intelligence   In addition to the individually administered Stanford-Binet and Wechsler scales, there are many other tests that are given to groups. If you went through a U.S. school system, chances are you took several of these; some students take as many as 20 standardized group tests before graduating from high school (Seligman, 1988). Because these tests are restricted to written items that can be scored easily, they measure a narrowly defined type of intellectual functioning, often called *school ability* or *scholastic aptitude*.

Two of the most popular group tests of intelligence are the Cognitive Abilities Test (CAT; Thorndike and Hagen, 1978) and the School and College Ability Tests (SCAT, Series III; Educational Testing Service, 1990b). They provide separate verbal and quantitative (math) scores, and the CAT also provides a nonverbal score. The developers of these tests maintain that they are valid predictors of school achievement, and are as reliable as the Stanford-Binet and the Wechsler tests. The primary benefits of group tests are that they require no special training to administer, they can be administered to a large group in relatively little time, and they are quickly and accurately scored by computer. These tests are ideal when a large number of people must be tested in an economical way.

Of all forms of intelligence testing, you are probably most familiar and experienced with group tests such as the SAT. Unlike the one-on-one administration of the Stanford-Binet or Wechsler tests, group tests canvass huge numbers of people at one time, and summarize each test-taker's performance in a single score with very few subscores. Careful standardization makes group tests useful for limited applications, such as selecting among large numbers of college applicants. But the lack of individual detail makes such application limited. Individualized tests provide detail that group tests cannot assess, such as firsthand observation of how a person tackles a problem, or which tasks someone most enjoys (Lennon, 1985). You know that *you* are more complex than your performance on a single test, and uniquely unlike anyone else who may happen to earn the same score—but where does that uniqueness show up in your test score?

Theories of Intelligence

By themselves, IQ scores do not tell how much children know or what they can do. A high school student with an IQ of 100 has knowledge and skills that a fourth-grader with a higher IQ of 120 does not have. In addition, people labeled "developmentally disabled" on the basis of their IQ scores vary considerably in what they can do and how much they can learn. Similarly, elderly subjects may perform more poorly than the young on test items where speed is important, but they still have greater measurable *wisdom* in many domains (Baltes, 1990). Thus, an operational definition such as "intelligence *is* what intelligence tests *measure*," does not cover all that we mean by the concept of human intelligence. We will examine several theories that attempt to explain what intelligence is.

Psychometric Theories   Psychometrics *is the field of psychology that specializes in all areas of mental testing,* including personality assessment, intelligence evaluation, and aptitude measurement. Psychometric approaches to intelligence study the *statistical relationships* between different measures—that is, how one set of scores is related to another set. One common approach uses a technique called *factor analysis*—a statistical procedure that locates a smaller number of dimensions, clusters, or factors from a larger set of independent variables or items on a test. (Reducing many thousands of trait terms into the Big Five personality factors, as reviewed in the last chapter, is one example of what factor analysis can do.) The goal of factor analysis is to identify a small number of factors that represent the basic psychological dimensions being investigated.

Spearman's g Factor An early, influential psychometric theory of intelligence was that proposed by **Charles Spearman** of England, the leading assessment theorist of the 1920s. Spearman strongly influenced the beliefs of Lewis Terman, developer of the Stanford-Binet Intelligence Scale. Using factor analysis, Spearman concluded that individuals' performances on all available mental tests were highly correlated—all pointing to sharing a single, common factor of *general intelligence*. Spearman called this common intellectual ability the **g factor**, *a general intelligence factor assumed to be the individual's inherited, basic, intellectual ability*. Spearman noted that individuals further differed in their possession of specific kinds of intelligence, which he terms *s factors* (Spearman, 1927). "It was almost universally assumed by psychologists and by the general public in these early years that individual differences in intelligence were innately determined. One's intellectual level was a characteristic one must accept rather than try to change" (Tyler, 1988, p. 128).

Crystallized Versus Fluid Intelligence Using advanced factor analytic techniques, **Raymond Cattell** (1963) determined that general intelligence can be broken down into two relatively independent components he called *crystallized* and *fluid* intelligence. **Crystallized intelligence** is *the knowledge a person has already acquired and the ability to access that knowledge.* Crystallized intelligence is measured by tests of vocabulary, arithmetic, and general information. It is "crystallized" because it is a type of "hardened" experience, with content set in place by past experience and effort. In contrast, **fluid intelligence** is *the ability to see complex relationships and solve problems.* Fluid intelligence is measured by tests of block designs and spatial visualization in which the background information needed to solve a problem is included or readily apparent. For Cattell, both types of intelligence are essential to adaptive living. You rely on crystallized intelligence to help you cope with recurring, concrete challenges in life; fluid intelligence helps you deal with novel, abstract problems.

Cognitive Science Approaches   Many psychologists have broadened their conceptions of intelligence to include much more than performance on traditional IQ tests. Cognitive scientists focus on the different *cognitive processes* or mental activities we use when we learn new things or find a novel solution to a problem. We will examine four contemporary attempts to broaden and enrich the construct of intelligence, its features, and alternative means of assessing it.

Hunt's Problem-Solving Intelligence **Earl Hunt** (1983), one proponent of the cognitive processes view, believes that the interesting individual differences in people's intelligence are not to be found in test scores but in the way different individuals go about solving a problem. He identifies three ways cognitive processes may differ in individuals: choice about the way to internally (mentally) *represent* a problem; strategies for *manipulating* mental representations; and the abilities necessary to *execute* whatever basic information-processing steps a strategy requires.

Using Hunt's model, scientists can design special tasks to observe individual differences in the way people represent problems. For example, a subject may mentally picture a calendar in order to remember an upcoming

the core of *The Bell Curve*. Herrnstein and Murray have argued that group differences in IQ should lead to more humane social policies. But it is easier to see the racist applications than the humane possibilities in their assumptions that the roots of intelligence are genetic, that races are genetically distinct, and that intelligence as measured by IQ tests is a society's greatest resource.

Critics of *The Bell Curve* (see Fraser, 1995) argue that Herrnstein and Murray's assumptions do not hold up to even casual scrutiny. For example, our review of intelligence theories (above) indicates that few psychologists support the idea of "intelligence" as a single, unitary quality that is best measured by IQ tests. Additionally, Herrnstein and Murray make an unwarranted assumption that intelligence, even if it could be summarized in a single score, is the most important virtue in a democratic society—more important than fairness, respect, or hard work. Finally, there is no demonstrated correlation between IQ test scores and life success, whether measured as college performance, job success, or achieved income level (Wolfe, 1995). Why then does *The Bell Curve* suggest that group differences and declines in IQ signal social decline and doom?

You too should weigh the evidence, and consider what the connection is, isn't, or should be between the origins of intelligence and the social policies that can affect individuals' lives.

Despite its pseudoscience and flawed logic, *The Bell Curve* may have struck a chord with many Americans not only because it seems to justify existing prejudices, but also because it is a part of our American culture to look for genetic "causes" for behavior rather than more complex explanations. For example, Chinese and Japanese schoolchildren, on average, vastly outperform their American peers in measures of mathematics achievement. When researchers asked both Asians and Americans to account for such differences in performance, American respondents emphasized "innate ability," whereas Asian respondents emphasized the importance of "studying hard" (Stevenson et al., 1993). Perhaps by blaming genetic forces, we excuse ourselves for failure ("It's not my fault, I just didn't inherit the same ability as other people") and exonerate ourselves from guilt ("It's too bad that others aren't doing as well as my group, but there's nothing I can do to help them"). However, scientific evidence supports the view that intelligence is like other human qualities and is the product of both inherited and experienced factors. Instead of rationalizing injustice and prejudice, we might find ways to develop individual potential while respecting diversity, whatever its influences and origins.

Social Class and IQ   The environmental position interprets IQ scores as a measure of current functioning and alleges that low scores often reflect social factors. Group differences in IQ scores are believed to be a symptom of larger social problems. In the United States the minority groups with the lowest average IQ scores are those for whom poverty, illiteracy, and hopelessness are most widespread. Supporters of the environmental position claim that racism and discrimination initially landed many minorities in the impoverished inner cities, and these same factors continue to keep them there today.

Why does social class affect IQ? Poverty creates circumstances that limit individual potential in many ways, particularly in terms of health and education. Poor health during pregnancy, low birth weight, susceptibility to childhood illness, and poor nutrition will all hurt children's ability to function both within and outside the classroom. Poor families cannot offer their children the books, computers, or even personal interaction necessary for mental stimulation, because poor parents are likely to concentrate on surviving rather than excelling. Finally, being poor in a materialistic society—where money counts—creates a stigma that hurts self-esteem and hinders individuals' efforts to anticipate a promising future.

The Racial Politics of IQ

Bad seed. Racial inferiority. Racial purity. Ethnic cleansing. These terms are charged with emotion, and steeped in prejudice. Is there any truth underlying beliefs that individual moral worth and value is genetically determined? Or are such ideas merely attempts to rationalize the repression and even destruction of groups of people considered to be "different" from the majority?

The belief that a family can be doomed by inheriting a "bad seed" or that national character can be "polluted" by "inferior races" seems difficult for educated people to comprehend, much less take seriously. Begin by taking a critical-thinking approach to the ideas promoted by Henry Goddard and others at the beginning of the twentieth century. Ask yourself these questions:

■ In the nineteenth and early twentieth centuries, *where* would educated people get the idea that racial and ethnic differences were important?

■ Which racial and ethnic groups would most *want or need* to believe in the concept of racial superiority or inferiority? Which would least want to believe it? Why?

■ What are some examples of modern individuals or groups who appear to believe in racial superiority? What factors might make such beliefs popular or appealing to those persons or groups?

■ How is racial "pride" different from the pride you take in your work or your achievements? How can emotions and beliefs bias our efforts to study human psychology?

Now question some of the assumptions on which Herrnstein and Murray base their arguments in *The Bell Curve* (1994):

■ Can intelligence be summed up by a single number? Is a score on an IQ test the best way to rate and rank a person's potential and value to society?

■ Is intelligence completely determined by genetic factors? Are racial groups so different from *each other* that individual group members cannot expect to perform outside their group's range of potential?

■ Is intelligence a stable quality that cannot be changed—either for better or worse—by environment and education?

Ample evidence shows that environmental interventions—such as Head Start and other early learning programs—can modify individuals' performance and demonstrated intelligence (Kassebaum, 1994). The conclusions we draw about the nature of intelligence will determine what we, as a society, decide to do for each other and for ourselves.

In most parts of the United States, public schools are funded by revenue from local property taxes. Thus wealthy neighborhoods can provide bigger and better school facilities and amenities, while poorer districts may suffer from crowding, physically deteriorating structures, threats to personal safety, and few "extras" such as media centers or computers. In such environments, even children with the aptitude to learn may find it difficult to rise above their mean circumstances. Proponents of the environmental view that environment is a strong influence on intelligence support equal opportunity legislation, better schools, and intervention programs, such as Head Start, which help disadvantaged children build self-confidence and learn the skills necessary to succeed in school (Zigler & Muenchow, 1992; Zigler & Styfco, 1994).

It now appears that previous attempts to boost IQ by special environmental interventions did not start early enough in the babies' lives. Recent experiments with rats, monkeys, and human babies all provide compelling evidence that the nurturing power of early life stimulation and a challenging environment can powerfully enhance mental ability. At a meeting of the American Association for the Advancement of Science (AAAS) in early 1996, researchers from the diverse fields of psychology, biology, anatomy, and pediatrics presented studies indicating that early educational intervention, starting in the first months of life, can raise infants' scores in intelligence tests by 15 to 30 percent compared to control groups (Perlman, 1996).

Similarly, being raised in a stimulus-enriched habitat from early on has been shown to result in a more complex, complete development of brain cells and cortical regions in rats. Their superior performance on a range of tasks persists until late in life. Young monkeys who are trained to solve problems and are offered the companionship of other monkeys display more active curiosity and livelier intelligence than those reared without this environmental stimulation. The practical message is clear: to effectively boost the intellectual functioning of the next generation, parents (and society) must start as early as possible, during an infant's first months of life, and continue during the phase when the mind is most ready to take in new information—when a child is learning language in his or her earliest years.

Bias and Fairness   Proponents of a third view are also interested in protecting the civil rights of minority group members. They believe that group differences in IQ scores are caused by systematic bias in the test questions. There are significant dialect differences between whites and blacks, for example, that could affect an African American's verbal scores on a standardized test with a bias toward standard English. Proponents of this view also believe that remedial classes do more harm than good for those minority children who are incorrectly assigned to them on the basis of unfair IQ tests. These classes stigmatize the students and encourage their distaste for the school experience. Minority students, however, have shown great progress when taught in non-biased classes and labs.

Should the courts restrict the use of IQ tests so that they can no longer be used to assign minority children to special classes? (This suggestion has been carried out in some states.) When test bias is seen as the sole cause for group differences, however, legislators may pretend that racial injustice in the larger society is not a serious problem, and thereby work to reduce incentives for remedial action programs.

Along with affirmative action legislation, the movement to ensure fair testing practices seeks to remove discriminatory practices in our society. Unfortunately, sometimes when standardized tests are forbidden, educators and employers must revert to more expensive, less valid, and perhaps *more* discriminatory assessment procedures—such as interviews that rely on the subjective impressions of teachers or supervisors. The rights and interests of many people must be considered, otherwise poor decisions may be made, with negative consequences for both the institution (the school or business) and the individual (the student or job applicant). The decision to use a test should always be based on the validity and fairness of the test as compared to other selection methods.

Check Your Recall

Because some racial and cultural groups score lower on IQ tests on the average than other groups, some critics believe that IQ is an unreliable or unfair basis for evaluating individuals' potential in society. Early work by Henry Goddard argued that intellectual ability was inherited, and that inferior genetic factors hurt the potential of families and societies. More recently, a book written by Herrnstein and Murray has drawn attention to and criticism for linking IQ with race.

Although IQ differences between groups are sometimes blamed on genetic differences between groups, the evidence suggests that group differences reflect environmental disadvantages that affect the health of the brain and stimulation of the mind. Some argue that group differences in IQ can be reduced, and in time probably eliminated, by improving public education for minority groups and through special early intervention programs to give disadvantaged children an enriched intellectual foundation.

Applications and Issues

As a college student, you may be struggling with decisions about the kind of job you would like to have when you finish school. In our final section, we will first discuss the role of assessment in vocational counseling. Then we will address some of the political and ethical issues posed by the widespread use of formal assessment procedures in our society today.

Career Planning

Have you already decided on a career path? Are you still undecided, or thinking of changing a present job? Many assessment instruments can help people learn which vocations best fit their personalities, values, interests, and skills—or, in some cases, can show them that the career they have chosen may not be the wisest choice.

Assessing Interests　Even if you do not yet know what careers you might like best, you would probably want a job that suits your interests and serves goals that you consider worthwhile. However, you may be unsure about what your major interests and abilities are. Furthermore, you may have little idea of what people in many occupations actually *do*, and you may not really know how their job activities relate to your personal values and goals. A number of tests have been designed to help people identify major interests, abilities, and appropriate career directions.

The most widely used test for measuring vocational interests is the Strong-Campbell Interest Inventory, which was constructed in 1927 by psychologist **Edward Strong**. The test is based on an empirical approach similar to that used later for the MMPI. In developing this test, Strong studied groups of men in different occupations who answered items about activities they liked or disliked. The answers of those who were successful in particular occupations were then compared with the answers of men in general to create a scale. Subsequent versions of the test have added scales relevant to women and to newer occupations. If you took this test, a vocational counselor could tell you what types of jobs are typically held by people with interests such as yours, since these are the jobs that are likely to appeal to you.

Assessing Abilities　Even if a job appeals to you and it suits your personality and fits your values and interests, you are unlikely to be satisfied with it unless you can do it well. Your employer will certainly not be satisfied with you if you are unable to do the job for which you were hired.

To recommend a career path for you, therefore, a vocational counselor will want to assess your abilities as well as your interests. Ability has two components: aptitude and achievement. An **aptitude test** *measures your potential for acquiring various skills—not necessarily how well you can perform tasks now, but how well you will be able to in the future*, with adequate training. On the other hand, an **achievement test** *measures your current level of competence*. A test of how well you can speak a foreign language or program a computer would be an example of an achievement test.

With knowledge of not only what you like to do but also what you can do well, a counselor is in a good position to predict your suitability for different jobs (Anastasi, 1982; Sundberg & Matarazzo, 1979; Tyler, 1974). Tests of ability are also used by companies seeking new employees. If you apply for a specific job, you may be asked to take tests involving the abilities and skills required for that job. If a job involves using a computer, you may be given a test of your familiarity with various software or word processing programs. If it involves hard physical labor like lifting and stacking heavy but fragile stock, you may be given a test of strength. If managing and directing salespeople will be an important part of the job, your ability to assert yourself or resolve conflicts may be assessed. The goal of such tests is to match people with the jobs for which they are best suited, thereby increasing the satisfaction of both employees and their employers.

Although this American student may have a high aptitude (natural ability) for learning foreign languages, her competence (achievement level) is a different matter, as shown by her dependence on her French/English dictionary.

Assessing Jobs   Organizations often invest substantial time and money in personnel selection. They rely not only on an assessment of an applicant's characteristics but also on a careful identification and analysis of the requirements of the job. A **job analysis** *is a study of a specific job, focusing on the skills required, effort demanded, the worker's responsibilities, and any job-related stressors* (Tenopyr & Oeltjen, 1982). The results of job analyses are used not only in selecting personnel, but also in determining the pay scale for different jobs.

Job assessment is performed in many ways. Workers, supervisors, and specially trained job analysts are asked to provide information about the abilities required for particular jobs. Subject-matter experts rate the relevance of knowledge, skills, and abilities. An inventory of appropriate requirements, tasks, and duties can then be prepared for each occupation. One such inventory that has been developed—the Occupational Analysis Inventory—provides information about a wide spectrum of occupations and can be very helpful to a job seeker (Pass & Cunningham, 1978).

Some companies supplement other assessment methods with *realistic job previews*. They show applicants what will be expected of them on the job through films, tapes, employee checklists of most- and least-liked aspects of a job, and simulations of critical incidents likely to arise (Wanous, 1980). These previews give applicants a clearer picture of what will be expected of them if they take the job, and help them decide how well the job fits their abilities and interests.

How well one person does in a job often depends on more than knowledge and hard work. Among the other variables affecting job performance might be assertiveness, social skills, appearance, and general congruence or fit with a company's picture of its ideal supervisor, manager, or executive. When these types of characteristics are important, personality tests such as the CPI can be used in employee selection—but *only* for those jobs for which a test has been specifically validated.

The Ethics of Assessment

The primary goal of psychological assessment is to reduce errors of judgment that bias accurate assessments of people. This goal is achieved by replacing subjective judgments of teachers, physicians, employers, and other evaluators with more objective measures that have been carefully constructed and are open to critical evaluation. This is the goal that motivated Alfred Binet in his pioneering work. Binet and others hoped that testing would help democratize society and minimize decisions based on arbitrary criteria of sex, race, nationality, or physical appearance.

Despite the lofty goals of the original developers of psychological tests, there is no area of psychology more controversial than assessment. Three unresolved issues central to the controversy are the *fairness* of test-based decisions, the utility of tests for *evaluating education*, and the implications of using test scores as *permanent labels*.

Fairness   Critics concerned with the fairness of testing practices argue that the costs or negative consequences may be higher for some test-takers than for others. The costs are quite high, for example, when low scores on certain tests are used to keep people from minority groups out of certain jobs. For example, in some cities, applicants for civil service janitor jobs must pass a verbal test, rather than a more appropriate test of janitorial manual skills.

Even when tests are valid predictors of job performance, they should not be used as an excuse to ignore the special needs of some specific groups in society. For example, some allegedly valid employment tests predict performance in training sessions but *not* performance on the job. People with less education or experience who have difficulty in training might, with a few extra training sessions, learn to perform a job as proficiently as people who already had the necessary skills when they were hired (Haney, 1982). Though still in school, for example, a college student could learn a mental hospital's jargon and policies well enough to work as a psychiatric aide before she completes work on her college degree. In addition, reliance on testing may all too often make personnel selection an automatic attempt to fit people into available jobs. Sometimes we might benefit more by changing the job duties and descriptions to fit the needs and abilities of people.

Evaluating Education　　Testing not only helps evaluate students; it also plays an indirect role in education. The quality of school systems and the effectiveness of teachers are frequently judged on the basis of how well their students score on standardized achievement tests. Local support of the schools through tax levies and even individual teacher salaries may ride on test scores.

These test scores, however, may not accurately reflect what students really know. Since the same tests are used for several years between revisions, teachers come to know what is on the test and prepare their students for those items. Scores improve, but the norms are not immediately updated, so students in each district *appear* to be doing better and better each year until a revision comes out that makes them look inept in comparison to the previous year's students with their inflated scores. Students may be made to feel overly anxious about their performance by teachers who spend more time teaching them to be "test-wise" than to think for themselves (Leslie & Wingert, 1990).

Tests as Labels　　We are a nation of test-takers and we sometimes forget that our test scores are, at best, statistical measures of our current functioning. Instead, we imbue the scores with an absolute significance that is not limited to appropriate normative comparisons. People too often think of themselves as *being* "an IQ of 110" or "a B student," as if the scores were labels stamped on their foreheads. Such labels may become barriers to advancement as people come to believe that their mental and personal qualities are fixed and unchangeable—that they cannot improve their lot in life.

This tendency to give test scores a sacred status has societal as well as personal implications. When test scores become labels that identify qualities *within* an individual, people begin to think about the "abnormality" of individual children rather than about educational systems that need to modify programs to accommodate all learners. Labels put the spotlight on deviant personalities rather than on problems in the environment. Human assessors need to recognize that what people are now is a product of where they've been, where they think they are headed, and what situation is currently influencing their behavior. Such a view can help to unite different assessment approaches and theoretical camps as well as lead to more humane treatment of those who do not fit the norm.

Assessing Your Life

We conclude on a personal note, one that may have some inspirational value to students who do not do well on objective tests. Although we, your text authors, have gone on to have successful careers as professional psychologists, relevant tests and assessments earlier in our schooling might have predicted otherwise. When he was in college, your first author, Phil Zimbardo, despite being an Honors undergraduate student, got his only C grade in Introductory Psychology, a course in which grades were based solely on multiple-choice exams. He was initially rejected for graduate training at Yale University, then

In the movie *Rain Man,* a young man (Tom Cruise) learns that the autistic label applied to his institutionalized brother (Dustin Hoffman) belies that man's many unique abilities.

became an alternate, and finally was accepted—reluctantly, in part because his GRE math scores were below the Psychology Department's cut-off level.

Your second author, Ann Weber, had taken psychology in high school and "tested out" of Introductory Psychology in her first year of college, going directly to second-year courses. Later she got her only relatively poor college grade in a course on psychological statistics. In graduate school, she was "assessed" as being perhaps in the wrong field, and sent by her advisor for career counseling. Despite such discouragement, she found support among classmates and other faculty and successfully completed her doctoral work right on schedule.

The moral of our two stories is that isolated assessments—a surprisingly low test score, condemning judgment, or a poor rating—cannot possibly tell an individual's story fairly or completely. We made it in our careers and lives, despite some dire predictions about our being "misfits."

As we now know, successful performance in a career and in life requires something more than the abilities recognized by standardized tests, or the impressions sought by scrutinizing interviewers. While the best tests can predict how well people will do on average, there is always room for error when their ambition, imagination, self-esteem, or personal pride come to the fore, for better or worse. Learn to know when and how to believe more in yourself than in the results of any one evaluation. Further, when you yourself are in a position to evaluate others' potential for work or school, keep your human limitations in mind, and let your humility remind you how complex human abilities really are.

Check Your Recall

Assessment instruments have been developed to identify people's vocational interests. In measuring work-related abilities, aptitude tests identify learning potential, while achievement tests reflect current competency levels. In job analysis, the skill, effort, responsibilities, and stresses associated with a particular job are assessed.

Political and ethical issues associated with applied assessment include developing fair tests and using tests to evaluate the effectiveness of educational programs. Test-takers as well as administrators often mistakenly see test results as unchangeable labels indicating individuals' worth. Because isolated test scores and assessment experiences cannot tell one's whole story, it is important to have faith in oneself and others beyond the results of any single evaluation.

CHAPTER REVIEW

Summary

We assess individual differences in order to predict behavior and performance. Skills assessment has an ancient human history, but was not based on scientific practice until the last century. Sir Francis Galton's conviction that genius was inherited inspired important developments in testing—as well as some racist applications of the eugenics movement. Modern assessment focuses on discovering people's abilities and applying these findings in professional, educational, and clinical settings. To conduct assessments, information is collected from interviews, personal records, behavioral observations, and psychological tests. Reports are provided by respondents themselves or by observers. Effective testing instruments must demonstrate that they are reliable, valid, and standardized.

Intelligence tests were originally developed to assess children's mental age for appropriate school placement. Later refinements included not only verbal and analytic tasks but also performance scales. Psychometric theories, including Spearman's concept of *g* and Cattell's distinction between fluid and crystallized intelligence, identify statistical relationships among mental abilities. Cognitive science approaches define intelligence more broadly, in terms of the tasks and problems they seek to deal with. This view has concluded that there are several components making up intelligence, or that there are several different kinds of intelligence to be demonstrated in human functioning. Ideas of intelligence are also influenced by cultural values and traditions.

Group differences in IQ have been accounted for by genetic, environmental, and test bias explanations. Genetic arguments maintain that intelligence is inherited and cannot be altered by experience. Environmental approaches argue that intelligence is influenced by an inherited factor but can be dramatically shaped by influences such as health, economics, and education. Critics have pointed out that intelligence testing itself may be biased in favor of those with particular language and cultural experiences. Group differences may be minimized by fairer testing practices and social programs that support early life education to overcome social and economic disadvantages.

Vocational assessment is used to ascertain an individual's interests, aptitudes, and achievement. By assessing both abilities and work requirements, testing can help match the right person with the appropriate job. Assessment is prevalent in many areas of our lives but it has also become highly controversial. Test results are often useful for indicating current performance or predicting potential, but should not be applied to limit individuals' opportunities for development. When assessment results touch your life, be sure the assessment is fair and thorough, and that you understand what the results mean and how best to apply them.

Section Reviews

Assessing Individual Differences

Be sure to *Check Your Recall* by reviewing the summary of this section on page 432.

Key Terms
psychological assessment (p. 421)
individual differences perspective (p. 421)
situationism (p. 422)
interactionist perspective (p. 423)
eugenics (p. 424)
interview (p. 426)
life history (p. 426)
psychological test (p. 426)
situational behavior observations (p. 426)
self-report methods (p. 427)
observer-report methods (p. 427)
rating (p. 427)
halo effect (p. 428)
stereotype effect (p. 428)
interjudge reliability (p. 428)
reliability (p. 429)
validity (p. 430)
norm (p. 431)
standardization (p. 432)

Names to Know
Sir Francis Galton (p. 424)

Assessing Intelligence

Be sure to *Check Your Recall* by reviewing the summary of this section on page 443.

Key Terms
intelligence (p. 433)
mental age (MA) (p. 435)
chronological age (CA) (p. 435)
intelligence quotient (IQ) (p. 436)
psychometrics (p. 438)
g-factor (p. 439)
crystallized intelligence (p. 439)
fluid intelligence (p. 439)
emotional intelligence (p. 442)

Names to Know
Alfred Binet (p. 434)
Lewis Terman (p. 436)
David Wechsler (p. 437)
Charles Spearman (p. 439)
Raymond Cattell (p. 439)
Earl Hunt (p. 439)
Robert Sternberg (p. 440)
Howard Gardner (p. 441)
Daniel Goleman (p. 441)

The Politics of Assessment

Be sure to *Check Your Recall* by reviewing the summary of this section on page 450.

Key Terms
heritability factor p. 445)

Names to Know
Henry Goddard (p. 444)
Stephen Jay Gould (p. 446)
Richard Herrnstein (p. 447)
Charles Murray (p. 447)

Applications and Issues

Be sure to *Check Your Recall* by reviewing the summary of this section on page 454.

Key Terms
aptitude test (p. 451)
achievement test (p. 451)
job analysis (p. 452)

Names to Know
Edward Strong (p. 451)

REVIEW TEST

Chapter 11: Individual Differences

For each of the following items, choose the single correct or best answer. The correct answers, explanations, and page references appear in Appendix B.

1. Any test can be said to "work" well if it _____.
   a. accurately predicts performance in future situations
   b. reflects what an individual has learned since prior testing
   c. distinguishes between different groups' inherited abilities or intelligence
   d. enables the person giving the test to assign values to individual test-takers

2. Which of the following best expresses the opinions of early supporters of the eugenics movement?
   a. A supportive and stimulating environment can overcome most genetic disadvantages.
   b. It is immoral for superior races to attempt to extinguish inferior races.
   c. Only the fittest and brightest individuals should be encouraged to reproduce.
   d. Individual accomplishments depend more on circumstance than on genetic inheritance.

3. A testing entrepreneur has invented the Big Toe Intelligence Test. To predict your intellectual ability, he measures the big toe of your left foot in centimeters, multiples that figure by 10, and adds your age. He says this yields your IQ. Given your knowledge of what it takes to make a "good test," you know that the Big Toe Test is _____.
   a. neither reliable nor valid
   b. reliable but not valid
   c. valid but not reliable
   d. both reliable and valid

4. By establishing _____, we are able to standardize the use and administration of a given test.
   a. internal consistency
   b. criterion validity
   c. construct validity
   d. norms

5. The major advantage of using _____ to collect information rather than other data-collection strategies is that it provides quantitative judgments of the individual being studied.
   a. an interview
   b. a life history
   c. a psychological test
   d. situational behavior observations

6. Psychologists formally define intelligence as _____.
   a. the sum of an individual's acquired knowledge, including episodic, semantic, and procedural information
   b. all cognitive abilities, including memory, problem solving, logical functions, and perception
   c. an individual's aptitude for acquiring new knowledge, regardless of past patterns of function
   d. the ability to profit from experience by going beyond perceptions to imagined possibilities

7. A child with a chronological age of 12 takes an intelligence test that shows a mental age of 15. According to Lewis Terman's mathematical formula, this child's IQ is _____.
   a. 103
   b. 120
   c. 125
   d. 150

8. One of Robert Sternberg's three types of intelligence is _____ intelligence, also known as business sense or street smarts.
   a. contextual
   b. componential
   c. performance
   d. interpersonal

9. According to Howard Gardner, there are actually seven "intelligences" instead of just one. Which of the following is not one of the abilities listed by Gardner?
   a. musical
   b. experiential
   c. linguistic
   d. intrapersonal

10. A(n) _____ measures a person's potential for acquiring some skill, not necessarily how well that person presently performs related tasks.
    a. achievement test
    b. aptitude test
    c. job analysis
    d. observer's report

IF YOU'RE INTERESTED . . .

Broadcast News. (Video: 1987, color, 131 min.). Directed by James L. Brooks; starring William Hurt, Holly Hunter, Albert Brooks, Joan Cusack, Jack Nicholson.

Three network news coworkers—an intense producer, a smart reporter, and a pretty-boy anchor—form the triangle at the center of this story of how abilities and ethics affect work and relationships. Albert Brooks is outstanding as a brilliant journalist and writer who utterly lacks the social skills and "camera presence" to be an anchor, and William Hurt seems disturbingly familiar as the affable "talking head" who has presence and social skills, but little substance and few scruples.

Charly. (Video: 1968, color, 103 min.). Directed by Ralph Nelson; starring Cliff Robertson, Claire Bloom, Lilia Skala, Leon Janney.

Powerful, provocative fantasy based on Daniel Keyes's short story, "Flowers for Algernon," about a retarded man who volunteers for experimental surgery that transforms him rapidly into a genius.

Examines the stigma of labels and the complex relationship of intelligence to other human abilities—and to one's overall sense of self.

Fraser, S. (Ed.). (1995). *The bell curve wars: Race, intelligence, and the future of America.* New York: Basic Books.

A fascinating collection of critical reviews prompted by the controversial publication in 1994 of *The Bell Curve: Intelligence and Class Structure in American Life* by Richard J. Herrnstein and Charles J. Murray. Among other authors featured, evolutionist Stephen Jay Gould critiques the questionable methodology of *The Bell Curve*, psychologist Howard Gardner points out that social class is not genetically determined, Jacqueline Jones questions any effort to generically "justify" racism, and Orlando Patterson exposes a series of assumptions—not all warranted—that Herrnstein and Murray have accepted about intelligence, IQ, and the nature of racial differences.

Gould, S. J. (1981). *The mismeasure of man.* New York: Norton.

Fascinating review of people's efforts to assess themselves and especially others, whether for noble or nefarious purposes. Stephen Jay Gould is a popular author, evolutionary theorist, and critical reviewer of intelligence tests and other assessments.

Higher Learning. (Video: 1995, color, 127 min.). Directed by John Singleton; starring Omar Epps, Kristy Swanson, Laurence Fishburne, Jennifer Connelly, Ice Cube.

An African-American college athlete suffers from confusion and rage about how to respond to racism and to social injustice. A black political science professor tries to guide him toward a more realistic view of the world—and his abilities to live in it. Except for simplistic subplot about evil skinheads, an involving and well-done film about how racism corrupts our promise and possibilities.

Little Man Tate. (Video: 1991, color, 99 min.). Directed by Jodie Foster; starring Jodie Foster, Dianne Wiest, Adam Hann-Byrd, David Hyde Pierce, Harry Connick, Jr.

A working-class single mother must determine how best to bring up her son, a child genius whose abilities challenge the good intentions and resources of the adults who care about him. Moving, involving, and not simplistic, this exploration of what "intelligence" means in a complete life is also well produced and boasts a great jazz score.

Rain Man. (Video: 1988, color, 140 min.). Directed by Barry Levinson; starring Dustin Hoffman, Tom Cruise, Valeria Golino, Jerry Molden, Jack Murdock, Michael D. Roberts.

After his wealthy father's death, a selfish, high-living young man discovers he has an older brother, institutionalized most of his life, who is an *autistic savant:* he cannot function well in the outside world, but is capable of remarkable feats of memory and calculation. The relationship they develop—as men, brothers, and persons with very different individual abilities—highlights important questions about the intelligence, personal qualities, and personal relationships essential to a happy life.

Roxanne. (Video: 1987, color, 107 min.). Directed by Fred Schepisi; starring Steve Martin, Daryl Hannah, Rick Rossovich, Shelley Duvall, Damon Wayans, Kevin Nealon.

A modern, comic retelling of Rostand's *Cyrano de Bergerac,* with Martin as C.D., a funny, smart fire chief afflicted with a big nose and a big crush on a beautiful astronomer visiting his small resort town. When she shows interest in a cute but dumb friend, C.D. agrees to write the letters and speak the words that will win her heart. A light, funny story of the ironies of seeking beauty while respecting intelligence. What if you can't get everything in one package?

Searching for Bobby Fischer. (Video: 1993, color, 110 min.). Directed by Steven Zaillian; starring Joe Mantegna, Max Pomeranc, Joan Allen, Ben Kingsley, Laurence Fishburne.

Based on a true story; a father promotes his young son's genius for chess, entering him in competitions and soon eroding the boy's spirit and original enjoyment of the game. Touching, brilliantly acted, well done. Consider the implications of talent and competition for a person's peace of mind and love of life.

Tavris, C. (1992). *The mismeasure of woman.* New York: Simon & Schuster.

Psychologist Carol Tavris reviews how, when "man is the measure" of human pursuits, woman is left forever trying (and failing) to measure up. Examines why women are neither inferior nor superior to men; tend to be misdiagnosed as sick or handicapped; and disadvantaged not by genetic endowment but by social myths and unevenly distributed power and resources.

CHAPTER 12

Social Psychology

O n a summer Sunday in California, a siren shattered the serenity of college student Tommy Whitlow's morning. A police car screeched to a halt in front of his home. Within minutes, Tommy was charged with a felony, informed of his constitutional rights, frisked, and handcuffed. After he was booked and fingerprinted, Tommy was blindfolded and transported to the Stanford County Prison, where he was stripped, sprayed with disinfectant, and issued a smock-type uniform with an I. D. number on the front and back. Tommy became Prisoner 647. Eight other college students were also arrested and assigned numbers.

The prison guards were not identified by name, and their anonymity was enhanced by khaki uniforms and reflector sunglasses—Prisoner 647 never saw their eyes. He referred to each of his jailers as "Mr. Correctional Officer, Sir"; to them, he was only number 647.

The guards insisted that prisoners obey all rules without question or hesitation. Failure to do so led to the loss of a privilege. At first, privileges included opportunities to read, write, or talk to other inmates. Later on, the slightest protest resulted in the loss of the "privileges" of eating, sleeping, and washing. Failure to obey rules also resulted in the assignment of menial, unpleasant work such as cleaning toilets with bare hands, doing push-ups while a guard stepped on the prisoner's back, and spending hours in solitary confinement. The guards were always devising new strategies to make the prisoners feel worthless. Every guard Prisoner 647 encountered engaged in abusive, authoritarian behavior at some point during his incarceration; the only difference was in the frequency and regularity of their hostility toward the prisoners.

Less than 36 hours after the mass arrest, prisoner 8412, one of the ringleaders of an aborted prisoner rebellion that morning, began to cry uncontrollably. He experienced fits of rage, disorganized thinking, and severe depression. On successive days, three more prisoners developed similar stress-related symptoms. A fifth prisoner developed a psychosomatic rash all over his body when the parole board rejected his appeal.

At night, Prisoner 647 tried to remember what Tommy Whitlow had been like before he became a prisoner. He also tried to imagine his tormentors before they became guards. He reminded himself that he was a college student who had answered a newspaper ad and agreed to be a subject in a two-week experiment on prison life. He had thought it would be fun to do something unusual, and he could always use some extra money.

Everyone in the prison, guard and prisoner alike, had been selected from a large pool of student volunteers. On the basis of extensive psychological tests and interviews, the volunteers had been judged as law-abiding, emotionally stable, physically healthy, and "normal-average" on all psychological measures. In this mock prison experiment, assignment of participants to "guard" or "prisoner" roles had been randomly determined by the flip of a coin. The prisoners lived in the jail around the clock and the guards worked standard eight-hour shifts.

As guards, students who had been pacifists and "nice guys" in their usual life settings behaved aggressively—sometimes even sadistically. As prisoners, psychologically stable students soon behaved pathologically, passively resigning themselves to their unexpected fate of learned helplessness. The power of the simulated prison situation had created a new social reality—a real prison—in the minds of the jailers and their captives.

Because of the dramatic and unexpected emotional and behavioral effects the researchers observed, those prisoners with extreme stress reactions were released early from their "pretrial detention" in this unusual prison, and the psychologists decided to terminate the two-week study after only six days. Although Tommy Whitlow said he wouldn't want to go through it again, he valued the personal experience because he learned so much about himself and about human nature. Fortunately, he and the other students were basically healthy, and they readily bounced back from that highly charged situation. Follow-ups over many years revealed no lasting negative effects. The participants had all learned an important lesson: Never underestimate the power of a bad situation to overwhelm the personalities and good upbringing of even the best and brightest among us (Haney et al., 1973; Zimbardo, 1973; Zimbardo, 1975; Zimbardo et al., 1974; replicated in Australia by Lovibond et al., 1979).

Introduction

Suppose *you* had been a subject in the Stanford Prison Experiment. Would you have been a "nice guy" guard—or a sadist? A model prisoner—or a rebel? Could you have resisted the powerful pressures and stresses of your bizarre circumstances? We'd all like to believe we would be good guards and heroic prisoners, but the best predictor for the way you might react in such a setting is the way some typical students, like yourself, actually behaved. The results of this study indicate that, despite our optimistic beliefs, most of us would fall on the negative side of the good-bad, hero-victim dichotomy. The results do not offer an upbeat, positive message. However, it is a message that social psychologists feel obliged to pass along in the hope that such knowledge may deter mindless submission to the powerful situational forces that can subtly and pervasively shape human behavior.

Welcome to the study of *social psychology*, which investigates how individuals affect each other. **Social psychology** *is the study of how individuals' thoughts, feelings, perceptions, motives, and behavior are influenced by interactions and transactions between people.* Social psychologists try to understand behavior within its *social context*. Defined broadly, the "social context" includes the real, imagined, or symbolic *presence* of other people; the *activities and interactions* that take place between people; the *settings* in which behavior occurs; and the *expectations and norms* governing behavior in a given setting (Sherif, 1981).

The Stanford Prison Experiment conducted by **Philip Zimbardo** underscores the *power of social situations* to control human behavior—a major theme to emerge from innovative research social psychologists have conducted over the past 50 years. In the first part of this chapter, we will consider a large body of research that shows how minor features of social settings can have a significant impact on what we think and how we feel and act.

A second theme of social psychology is that situations matter not so much in their objective features as in their *subjective* nature—in the way that people perceive, interpret, and find meaning in them. We will study this second theme, the *construction of social reality,* by investigating how people create social realities for themselves and others.

Finally, we will look at a third theme of social psychology: the determination to solve *social problems* by applying information about social processes. Social psychologists are at the forefront of work in such applied fields as health psychology, relationship studies, criminology, and peace psychology. On this dimension of *social relevance,* abstract theory meets the stern test of practicality: Does the theory make a difference in the lives of people and society?

The Power of the Situation

Social psychologists believe that the primary determinant of individual behavior is the nature of the social situation in which that behavior occurs. They argue that social situations exert significant control over individual behavior, often dominating one's personality and past history of learning, values, and beliefs. Situational aspects that appear trivial to most observers—labels, rules, social roles, the mere presence of others—can powerfully influence how we behave. Often, subtle situational variables affect us without our awareness. In this section, we will review some classic research and recent experiments that explore **situationism,** *the assumption that situational variables can have both subtle and powerful effects on people's thoughts, feelings, and behaviors.*

Rules, Roles, and Norms

An obvious example of a situational effect on your behavior would be the presence of someone who is influencing or putting pressure on you. For example, you might use different language when talking just with close friends than you would if your boss or a professor were also present. We learn to size up our social circumstances, assess who else is present and how they affect us, before engaging in certain actions. But although you might move from one situation to another in the course of your day, you probably remain within the same general cultural or social environment. Consequently, that social environment continually influences what you are thinking, feeling, and doing. An explicit form of situational influence is the application of **rules,** *formal guidelines for behavior in certain social settings.*

Some rules are explicitly stated in signs ("Don't Smoke," "No Eating in Class") or in socialization practices ("Respect the elderly," "Never take candy from a stranger"). Other rules are implicit; they are learned through transactions with others in particular settings. How loud you can play your stereo, how close you can stand to another person, when you can call your teacher or boss by a first name, and how you should react to a compliment or a gift all depend on the situation. For example, the Japanese do not open a gift in the presence of the gift-giver for fear of not showing sufficient appreciation; foreigners not aware of this unwritten rule will misinterpret the behavior as rude instead of sensitive.

Social Roles The situations in which you live and function also determine the *roles* available to you. Being a college student diminishes the likelihood that you will become a warrior, drug pusher, shaman, or prisoner, for example. Because you have college experience, numerous other roles (such as manager, teacher, and politician) are available to you. Situations help define the social meaning that each role will have for the people who have assumed it. A single

Commands
Insults
Deindividuating reference
Aggression
Threats
Questions
Use of instruments
Information
Individuating reference
Helping
Resistance

Guards
Prisoners

0 10 20 30 40 50 60 70   110
Frequency

FIGURE 12.1   Guard and Prisoner Behavior ■ During the Stanford Prison Experiment, their assigned roles drastically affected the behavior of "prisoners" and "guards." Results of 25 observation periods over 6 days show that the prisoners increasingly engaged in passive forms of resistance, while the guards became more dominating, controlling, and hostile.

action can be interpreted in many different ways, depending on the meaning different people assign to it. For example, defying authority can be interpreted as admirable and heroic, foolish and troublemaking, or dangerous and deviant. A **social role** *is a socially defined pattern of behavior that is expected of a person functioning in a given setting or group.* People play many different social roles in the various situations in which they usually operate.

For example, at the conclusion of the Stanford Prison Experiment, guards and prisoners differed from one another in virtually every observable way; yet, just a week before, their role identities (college students) had been interchangeable. Chance, in the form of random assignment, had decided their roles, and these roles created status and power differences that were validated in the prison situation. The social context induced a host of differences in the way those in each group thought, felt, and acted (see Figure 12.1).

No one taught the participants to play their roles. Each student had the capacity to become either a prisoner or a guard by calling upon stored structures of knowledge about those roles. In our schemas and scripts, a "guard type" is someone who uses *coercive rules* to limit the freedom of "prisoner types." Prisoners can only *react* to the social structure of a prisonlike setting created by those with power. Rebellion or compliance are the primary options of the prisoners. Some prisoners resign themselves to helplessness; they passively wait until the situation changes.

The student participants had already experienced such power differences in many of their previous social interactions: parent-child; teacher-student; doctor-patient; boss-worker; male-female. The participants merely refined and intensified their improvised scripts for this particular setting. Many students in the guard role were surprised at how easy it was for them to enjoy controlling other people, and how just putting on the uniform transformed them from college-student research subjects into "prison guards" ready to manage "inmates."

Social Norms   In addition to developing expectations about role behaviors, groups develop many expectations for the ways their members should act. *Expectations for socially appropriate attitudes and behaviors that are embodied in the stated or implicit rules of a group are called* **social norms.** Social norms can be broad guidelines, such as ideas about which political or religious attitudes are considered acceptable. Social norms can also embody specific standards of conduct, such as allowable actions or duties. Norms can guide conversation, as when they restrict discussion of sensitive or taboo subjects in certain company. Finally, norms can define habits, such as dress codes for group members, whether requiring uniforms or "fashionable" attire, or prohibiting inappropriate or outmoded clothing.

Adjustment to a group typically involves discovering the set of social norms that regulates desired behavior in the group setting. Individuals experience this adjustment in two ways: by noticing the *uniformities* in certain behaviors of all or most members and by observing the *negative consequences* when someone behaves in a non-normative way, violating a social norm. For example, a child whose parents move her from a public school to a private academy sees that her new classmates all wear the same outfits and behave in very similar ways during class or when talking with the teacher. If a child dresses "wrong" one day, the others laugh at her, and misbehavior (for example, talking out of turn) is quickly penalized.

Norms serve several important functions. Awareness of the norms operating in a group orients members and regulates their social interaction. Each participant can anticipate the way others will enter the situation—the way they will dress, what they are likely to say and do, as well as what type of behavior will be expected of them and will gain approval. Adhering to the norms of a group is the first step in establishing *identification* with the group. Such identification allows an individual to have the feeling of sharing in whatever prestige and power the group possesses. For example, a young man visits his best friend's church and notes that others his age are dressed more formally than his own jeans and T-shirt, that they claim not to drink, and that their taste in music is different from his own. When invited to visit again, he dresses more conservatively, does not mention having attended a drinking party, and listens politely to music he would normally reject as bland. To his pleasure, he finds his new friends are more interesting than he thought and treat him as if he "belongs."

Social Deviance In exchange for adhering to group norms, one finds some *tolerance for deviating* from the standard is also part of the norm. The degree of deviation tolerated can be wide in some cases, narrow in others. Members are usually able to estimate how far they can go before experiencing the coercive power of the group in the form of the three painful R's: *ridicule, reeducation,* and *rejection.* The young man visiting his friend's church, for example, finds that as he spends time with his new friends, he is better able to relax—as long as he does not break any important rules. Good-natured joking keeps him in line when he says or does something that offends others (ridicule). Some church members take him aside to explain religious doctrine and urge him to join (reeducation). He knows that if he "goes too far"— disagrees too much with accepted beliefs or customs—his new friends will no longer welcome him (rejection).

Social norms can define rigid dress codes for group members.

Reference Groups Norms emerge in a new group through two processes: *diffusion* and *crystallization.* When people first enter a group, they bring with them their own expectations, previously acquired through other group memberships and life experiences. These various expectations are diffused and spread throughout the group as the members communicate with each other. As people talk and carry out activities together, their expectations begin to converge or crystallize into a common perspective. For example, as members of a new landscaping crew work together, they learn to understand and speak each other's language, soon referring to plants and tools by the same set of terms and using these to agree on their goals and tasks.

Once norms are established in a group, they tend to perpetuate themselves. Current group members exert social pressure on incoming members to adhere to the norms, and they in turn put direct or indirect pressure to conform on successive newcomers. Norms can be transmitted from one generation of group members to the next and can continue to influence people's behavior long after the original group that created the norm no longer exists (Insko et al., 1980). In natural groups like families, group *rituals* often serve the purpose of transmitting symbols, history, and values important to the group from old to new members. Social clubs conduct initiation ceremonies for new members, just as initiates in a church undergo baptism and military recruits must survive basic training. Such experiences are often personally poignant and memorable, and can strengthen one's loyalty to the group.

Group norms have a strong impact on an individual's behavior as long as the individual values the group. If the person comes to value and identify with a new group, then he or she will change to follow the norms of the new group. A **reference group** *is a formal or informal group from which an individual derives attitudes and standards of acceptable and appropriate behavior.* One who belongs or hopes to belong to the group *refers* to its standards and patterns for information, direction, and support for a given lifestyle. For example, when you started college, you probably left behind many or most members of your high school reference group, but eventually came to identify with a new reference group of college campus acquaintances.

Newcomb's Bennington Studies The power of a reference group in shaping personal norms was illustrated in classic research conducted by **Theodore Newcomb,** a social psychologist who studied the endurance of norms acquired by college women in the 1930s. Twenty years later, Newcomb followed up the observed effects of their college reference group on the women's enduring attitudes. When in the late 1930s the women first attended Bennington College in Vermont, its prevailing norm was political and economic liberalism, encouraged by a young, dynamic, and liberal faculty. But most of the young women attending Bennington had come from privileged, conservative homes—and had brought decidedly nonliberal values with them. Which forces would prevail in the students' eventual adult attitudes? Newcomb found that the women's initial conservatism steadily declined as they progressed through their college years, so that by their senior year they had clearly converted to liberal thinking and causes.

Newcomb attributed the conservative-to-liberal attitude shift among Bennington students to the power of reference group norms. While living on campus, the women belonged to a close-knit, self-sufficient social community. Their interactions were often focused on social activism and liberal causes. Those who recognized and embraced the emerging group norms were rewarded with popularity and student leadership positions. Those who resisted risked exclusion and rejection by the majority. Over time, pressures and incentives to conform became *internalized* (personally accepted), not merely role played. A few students continued to resist the norm, retaining their conservatism as part of their own isolated group, and conforming to their families' standards rather than the school's (Newcomb, 1943).

Twenty years later, the marks of the Bennington experience were still evident. Women who had graduated as liberals were still liberals, those who resisted the prevailing norm were conservatives. Most had married husbands with values similar to their own and created supportive new home environments. In the 1960 presidential election, the liberal Bennington allegiance was evident when 60 percent of the class Newcomb had studied voted for John F. Kennedy (rather than Richard M. Nixon)—in contrast to less than 30 percent support for Kennedy among graduates of comparable colleges at that time (Newcomb et al., 1967).

Campus culture is not the only source of norms and reference-group pressure, of course. One's workplace, neighborhood, church, and family relationships can all communicate standards for behavior to the individual—and threaten sanctions (such as firing, ostracism, or excommunication) for violating the norms of that particular community. But a college or university environment warrants study because of the impact it can have on young people who have not previously encountered certain attitudes or acquired certain experiences. For example, a new student may find it difficult to resist classmates' encouragement or expectations not only about political opinions, as in the Bennington study, but also about risky personal decisions, such as sexual experience and alcohol use (Prentice & Miller, 1993; Schroeder & Prentice, 1995).

Sometimes the reference group that most influences an individual is not a real social group but an imaginary set of wished-for friends and associates—the reference group one *aspires to* belong to. Aspirational reference groups are often groups you hope one day to join, but in which you don't currently qualify for membership. These may be either formal organizations or general social categories you find appealing—"beautiful people," "smart people," people you consider successful. You may know some of these people personally, or you may only encounter images of attractive celebrities who represent an appealing social category. Either way, your sense of how different you are from such people can present you with a dilemma: How can you "get in"?

We invite you to consider which groups you aspire to belong to—and how much influence they may be having on your life choices now. ASK YOURSELF the following questions.

- Who are your *aspirational reference groups?*
- Think of one category or group you'd like to belong to. Do you ever find yourself considering these group members' values and opinions before you make your own decisions? Do you wonder, "What would *they* do in my situation?"

The more you aspire to belong to a group, the more influenced you may be—not by the group itself, which may not even be aware of your situation, but by your own efforts to be like the people you hope will accept you. For example, a television commercial may suggest that you can be "just like" the attractive or high-status individuals depicted merely by making certain choices in what you buy, wear, drink, or drive—that is, by aping the actions and preferences of your aspirational reference group. If you hope to "buy" your way into "belonging" to a group, you may make costly or useless choices for all the wrong reasons. Instead, base your choices on your personal goals and the real people in your life—while still aspiring to improve yourself.

The Total Situation The force of social norms depends on the extent to which group members are in a *total situation.* A **total situation** *is one in which group members have no access to contrary points of view and in which sources of information, social rewards, and punishments are all highly controlled by group leaders.* The more people rely on social rewards from a group for their primary sense of self-worth, the greater will be the social influence that the group can bring to bear on them. Group leaders usually recognize their potential for retaining members' loyalty and cooperation. The social influence of the total situation is one source of cults' influence on their followers, and of military institutions' on those in their ranks.

Social situations also include the operation of roles, rules, and norms, which can be powerful agents of change. They can affect people in socially prescribed ways or inhibit and restrain them from changing in socially inappropriate or situationally unacceptable ways. In this way, people take on different roles in different contexts: They may become liberals or conservatives in American politics, supporters of apartheid in South Africa, revolutionary nationalists in a former communist-bloc country, or pro-life extremists willing to bomb abortion clinics.

Smile—You're on Candid Camera! As exemplified at the beginning of this chapter, social psychologists have attempted to demonstrate the power of situational forces by devising experiments that reveal the ease with which smart, independent, rational, good people can be led into behaving in ways that are dumb, compliant, irrational, and even evil. Although social psychologists have shown the *serious* consequences of situational power, it is equally possible to demonstrate this principle with *humor.* Indeed, *Candid Camera* scenarios, created by the television program's producer and intuitive social psychologist Allen Funt, have been demonstrating the power of situational forces for over 40 years. Funt showed how human nature seems to follow a situational script. Millions in his TV audiences laughed when a diner stopped eating a hamburger whenever a "Don't Eat" counter light flashed; when pedestrians stopped and waited at a red traffic light above the *sidewalk* on which they were walking; when highway drivers turned back upon seeing a road sign that read "Delaware is Closed"; and when customers jumped from one white tile to another in response to a store sign that instructed them not to walk on black tiles, for no reason. One of the best *Candid Camera* illustrations of the subtle power of implicit situational rules is the "elevator caper." A person riding a rigged elevator first obeyed the usual silent rule to face the front, but when a group of other passengers all faced the rear, the hapless victim followed the new *emerging group norm* and faced the rear as well.

In these slice-of-life episodes, we see the minimal situational conditions needed to elicit unusual behaviors in ordinary people. We laugh when people similar to ourselves behave foolishly and act irrationally in odd situations, and we distance ourselves from them by assuming we would not act that way. The lesson of social psychological research is that (more than likely) we would behave exactly as others if we were placed in the same situation.

How would you behave if you found yourself in a situation that pressured people to act in evil, foolish, or irrational ways? The wise reply appears to be, "I don't know; it depends on how powerful the situation is." Researchers can predict your behavior by knowing the rate or extent of compliance of others in that situation and making the conservative assumption that you would probably behave as the majority did. It is the heroes among us who are able to behave otherwise—to resist and overcome situational forces—and there are fewer heroes than followers in everyday life.

Conformity

In Newcomb's Bennington study, conformity to the group norm had clear adaptive significance for the students; they were more likely to be accepted, approved of, and recognized for various social rewards if they adopted the liberal norm. However, in the *Candid Camera* vignettes, the subjects were not part of a reference group that controlled vital social reinforcements and punishments. Their conformity to the norm of a transient group was not based on *normative pressures* but rather on other needs, such as the need for cognitive clarity about one's world. When uncertain, we typically turn to others in the situation to satisfy *information needs* that will help us understand what is happening (Deutsch & Gerard, 1955). Two processes explain why people conform to group pressures and comply with pressures from individuals: **Normative influence** *is based on wanting to be liked, accepted, and approved of by others.* **Informational influence** *is motivated by wanting to be correct and to understand how best to act in a given situation* (Insko et al., 1985).

The Asch Effect   Even if you were caught in the act of "being yourself" in a *Candid Camera* scene, you could rationalize your compliance by insisting that these are only habits of action, not matters of life and death or right and wrong. But what if your dilemma really were a matter of fact, not merely opinion? In other words, what if you were part of a group asked to judge some aspect of physical reality, and you found that the rest of the group saw the world differently from you—*wrongly*, in fact? This situation was created by one of the most important social psychologists, **Solomon Asch** (1940; 1956). Asch wondered whether the constraints of physical reality on perception would be stronger than the power of the social context to distort individual judgments. His studies led to a significant psychological finding. The **Asch effect** *describes the influence of a unanimous group majority on the judgments of individuals even under unambiguous conditions.* The Asch effect has become the classic illustration of **conformity**—*the tendency for people to adopt the behavior and opinions presented by other group members.*

FIGURE 12.2 Conformity in the Asch Experiments ■ In this photo from Asch's study, the naive subject, number 6, displays obvious concern about the majority's erroneous judgment. At top right, you see a typical stimulus array. At top left, the graph illustrates conformity across 12 critical trials, when subjects were grouped with a unanimous majority, or had the support of a single dissenting partner. (A lower percentage of correct estimates indicates a greater degree of conformity with the group's false judgment.)

In Asch's study, groups of seven to nine male college students were told they would be participating in a study of simple visual perception. They were shown cards with three lines of differing lengths and asked to indicate which of the three lines was the same length as a separate, standard line (see Figure 12.2). The lines were different enough so that mistakes were rare, and their relative sizes changed on each series of trials.

On the first three trials, everyone agreed on the correct comparison. However, the first person to respond on the fourth trial reported an obviously wrong answer, seeing as equal two lines that were clearly different. So did the next person and so on, until all members of the group but the remaining one unanimously agreed on a judgment that conflicted with the perception of that final student. That student had to decide whether he should go along with everyone else's view of the situation and conform, or remain independent, standing by what he clearly saw. That dilemma was repeated on 12 of the 18 trials. Unbeknownst to this last subject, all of the others were experimental confederates who were following a prearranged script. Their script allowed for no communication other than calling out the perceptual judgment. The genuine subject showed signs of disbelief and discomfort when faced with a majority who saw the world so differently from the way he did. What did he and others in his position finally do?

In Asch's complete series of trials, 75 percent of these real subjects conformed to the false judgment of the group one or more times, while one-fourth remained completely independent. In various related studies, between 50 and 80 percent of the subjects conformed with the majority's false estimate at least once, while a third of the subjects yielded to the majority's wrong judgments on half or more of the critical trials. In other words, the fact that subjects were judging matters of fact—not merely personal opinions—did not make most of them immune to conformity pressures. On the other hand, it is important to note that conformity researchers regularly find "independents," individuals who are bothered and even dismayed to find themselves in disagreement with the majority, but who nonetheless stand their ground and "call 'em as they see 'em" (Friend et al., 1990). Pressure to conform may be greater than we like to admit in our lives—but the fact is that some of us, at least, can withstand the penalties of deviance and act in ways we perceive as honest and true.

Group Influence In other studies, Asch varied three factors: the size of the unanimous *majority,* the presence of a *partner* who dissented from the majority, and the size of the *discrepancy* between the correct answer and the majority's position. He found that strong conformity effects were elicited with a unanimous majority of only three or four people, but no conformity effect was obtained with only one confederate. Giving the naive subject one ally who dissented from the majority opinion sharply reduced conformity (as shown in Figure 12.2). With such a "partner," the subject was usually able to resist the pressures to conform to the majority. Remarkably, a certain proportion of individuals continued to yield to the group even with a partner present. All who yielded underestimated the influence of the social pressure and the frequency of their conformity; some even claimed that they really had *seen* the lines as the majority had claimed (Asch, 1955, 1956).

Numerous studies of conformity have confirmed these results. The power of the group majority depends on its unanimity. Once that is broken in any way, the rate of conformity drops dramatically (Allen & Levine, 1969; Morris & Miller, 1975). A person is also more likely to conform when a judgment task is difficult or ambiguous, the group is cohesive, the members are perceived as competent, and the person's responses are made public (Deutsch & Gerard, 1955; Lott & Lott, 1961; Saltzstein & Sandberg, 1979). For example, when you vote in a group election, you are more likely to go along with the majority if the issue being decided is complex (difficult) or confusing (ambiguous); if most others present are friends of yours (cohesive group); if they seem to know what they are talking about (are perceived as competent); and if you must vote by raising your hand instead of casting an anonymous ballot (public response). In many cases, people conform without awareness that they have been affected, maintaining an *illusion* of freedom and independence that is unwarranted by their actions.

Societal Conformity In society, the majority tends to be the defender of the *status quo* (the existing state of affairs), while the force for innovation and change comes from the minority members or individuals either dissatisfied with the current system or able to visualize new options and creative alterna-

"GOSH, ACKERMAN, DIDN'T ANY- ONE IN PERSONNEL TELL YOU ABOUT OUR CORPORATE CULTURE?"

tives for dealing with current problems. For example, issues of protecting the natural environment are still viewed as "special interests" in many regions of North America. However, through persistence and flexibility, environmentalists in many communities have succeeded in winning broad-based support for such innovations as recycling, waste control, and wildlife conservation. The conflict between the entrenched majority view and the dissident minority perspective is an essential precondition of innovations that can lead to positive social change.

An individual is constantly engaged in a two-way exchange with society—adapting to its norms, roles, and status prescriptions but also acting *upon* society to reshape those norms (Moscovici, 1985). Perhaps the greatest challenges for social psychologists to understand are the dynamics of group forces that influence individual behavioral and mental processes, and those individual factors that maintain or change group functioning.

Obedience

So far, we've seen how groups influence individuals, but certain individuals—such as leaders and authorities—influence groups by exerting considerable power on group behavior. The ultimate demonstration of this effect was seen in the 1930s with the emergence of Adolf Hitler in Germany and Benito Mussolini in Italy. These dictators were able to transform rational citizens into mindless masses with unquestioning loyalty to a fascist ideology bent on world conquest. Their authoritarian regimes threatened democracies and freedom everywhere. Curiously, modern social psychology developed out of this crucible of fear, war, and prejudice. The early concerns of social psychology focused on the nature of the authoritarian personality behind the fascist mentality (Adorno et al., 1950), the effects of propaganda and persuasive communications (Hovland et al., 1949), and the impact of the group on its members. Later research by **Stanley Milgram** extended these studies to focus on how individuals become so blindly obedient to the commands of authorities.

The Paradox of Obedience What made "good" German citizens as well as fanatical Nazis willing to send millions of Jews to the gas chambers? Did a character defect lead them to carry out orders blindly, even if the orders violated their own values and moral principles? How can we explain the 1978 mass suicide-murders of the members of the Peoples Temple? Over 900 American citizens belonging to the cult, who had relocated from the United States to a jungle settlement in Guyana, willingly administered cyanide poison to their children and to themselves because their leader, Reverend Jim Jones, told them to commit "revolutionary suicide." More recently, why did nearly 100 members of the Branch Davidian religious sect join their leader, David Koresh, in defying federal agents who charged their compound in Waco, Texas? After a standoff of several weeks during the spring of 1993, cult members apparently set fire to their quarters rather than surrender to authorities; scores of men, women, and children perished in the resulting blaze.

Let's get personal: How about *you*? Would *you* electrocute a stranger if a respected authority figure asked you to? Are there any conditions under which you would blindly obey an order from a religious leader to poison others and then commit suicide? Could you imagine participating in the American military massacre of hundreds of innocent civilians in the Vietnamese village of My Lai (pronounced *me-LYE*)—merely on the orders of the young commanding officer (Hersh, 1971; Opton, 1970, 1973)?

Your answer is most likely, "No! What kind of person do you think I am?"—as if your actions are determined by the "kind" of person you happen to be. After reading this next section, you may be more willing to answer,

"Maybe I would obey orders to harm others. I don't know for sure." Depending on the power of the social forces operating on your moral judgment and weakening your will to resist, you might do what others have done in those situations, however horrible and alien their actions may seem outside that setting. The study of obedience brings into critical focus the tension between the power of individual differences and that of situations.

 The most convincing demonstration of situational power was created by Stanley Milgram, a student of Solomon Asch. Milgram's research (1965, 1974) showed that the blind obedience of Nazis was less a product of dispositional characteristics (their unusual personality or German national character) than it was the outcome of situational forces that could engulf anyone—even you and us. How did he demonstrate this "banality of evil," that evil deeds could be engaged in by decent people who were merely (and mindlessly) doing their jobs (Hannah Arendt, 1963, 1971)? Milgram's obedience research is one of the most controversial in psychology both because of the ethical issues it raises and its significant implications for real world phenomena (Miller, 1986; Ross & Nisbett, 1991).

Milgram's Experiment   To separate the variables of personality and situation, which are always entangled in natural settings, Milgram used a series of controlled laboratory experiments involving more than 1000 subjects. Milgram's first experiments were conducted at Yale University with Yale college students and then with male residents of New Haven who received payment for their participation. In later variations, Milgram set up a storefront research unit in Bridgeport, Connecticut, recruiting through newspaper ads a broad cross section of the population. Subjects eventually included both sexes and varied widely in age, occupation, and education. Volunteers were told they were participating in a scientific study of memory and learning.

In the basic experimental paradigm, individual subjects delivered a series of what they thought were extremely painful electric shocks to another person. Subjects were led to believe that the purpose of the study was to discover how *punishment* affects memory so that learning and memory could be improved through the proper balance of reward and punishment. In their *social roles* as *teachers*, the subjects were to punish each error made by someone playing the role of *learner* (unbeknownst to the subjects, this was always the same actor). The major *rule* they were to follow was to increase the level of shock by a fixed amount each time the learner made an error until the learning was errorless. The white-coated experimenter acted as the *legitimate authority* figure; he presented the rules, arranged for the assignment of roles (by a rigged drawing of lots), and ordered the *teachers* to do their jobs whenever they hesitated or dissented.

The *dependent variable* was the final level of shock a subject delivered. Shocks were measured on a "shock generator" that went from 15 to 450 volts in 15-volt steps. The initial study was simply a demonstration of the phenomenon of obedience; there was no manipulation of an independent variable. Later versions varied many situational factors, such as the physical distances between the *teacher* and the *authority* and the *learner*. Milgram did not use a formal control or comparison group that received no treatment. As with the Stanford prison simulation, the comparison group was implicit—typical readers of the research who had beliefs about the way they themselves (you and other ordinary people) *would have behaved* under such circumstances.

Each *teacher* had been given a sample shock of about 75 volts to feel the amount of pain it caused. Thus Milgram's study was staged to make a subject think that he or she was causing pain and suffering and perhaps even killing an innocent person by following orders. The part of the *learner* was played by a pleasant, mild-mannered man, about 50 years old, who mentioned having a "heart condition" but was willing to go along with the procedure. He was strapped into an "electric chair" in the next room and communicated with the teacher via an intercom. His task was to memorize pairs of words, then choose the correct response for each stimulus word from a multiple-choice listing. The learner soon began making errors, and the teacher began shocking the learner. The protests of the victim rose with the shock level. At 75 volts, he began to moan and grunt; at 150 volts he demanded to be released from the experiment; at 180 volts he cried out that he could not stand the pain any longer. At 300 volts he insisted that he would no longer take part in the experiment and must be freed. He cried out about his heart condition and refused to reply any further. What would the teacher do?

If a teacher hesitated or protested about delivering the next shock, the experimenter objected, stating that the experiment "must continue" and asking the teacher to "please continue." As you might imagine, this situation was stressful for the subjects. Most teachers complained and argued, insisting they would not go on with their task. To the unwavering experimenter, they complained, "He can't stand it! I'm not going to kill that man in there! You hear him hollering? He's hollering . . . I mean, who is going to take the responsibility if anything happens to that gentleman?" Protesting all the way, the teachers spoke as though the experimenter were extracting each shock from them: "Aw, no. You mean I've got to keep going up with that scale? No sir, I'm not going to kill that man! I'm not going to give him 450 volts!" (1965, p. 67).

When the learner simply stopped responding to the teacher's questions, some subjects called out to him, urging him to get the answer right so they would not have to continue shocking him. All the while they protested loudly to the experimenter, but the experimenter *insisted* that the teacher continue: "Rules are rules!" Even when there was only silence from the learner's room, the teacher was ordered to keep shocking him more and more strongly, all the way up to the button that was marked "Danger: Severe Shock XXX (450 volts)."

Results and Reasons Did they obey? How far do you think the average subject in Milgram's experiment actually went in administering the shocks? What percentage do you estimate went all the way up to the end of the shock scale in blindly obeying authority? Suppose for a moment that *you* were the subject-teacher, and ASK YOURSELF the following questions:

- How far up the scale would you go?
- At which level of shock would you absolutely refuse to continue?

Psychiatrists asked to predict the performance of Milgram's subjects estimated that most would not go beyond 150 volts. In their professional opinions, fewer than 4 percent of the subjects would still be obedient at 300 volts and only 0.1 percent would continue to 450 volts. The psychiatrists presumed that only those few individuals who were "abnormal" in some way—the sadists—would blindly obey orders to harm another person in an experiment. Do you agree with these experts?

If so, you are both wrong! The psychiatrists based their evaluations on presumed *dispositional* qualities of people who would engage in such abnormal behavior; they overlooked the power of this special *situation* to influence the thinking and actions of most people caught up in its social context. The *majority of subjects obeyed the authority fully!* Nearly two-thirds delivered the maximum 450 volts to the learner. The average subject did not quit until about 300 volts. No subject who got within five switches of the end ever refused to go all the way. By then their resistance was broken; they had resolved their own conflicts and just tried to get it over with as quickly as possible. It is important to note that most people *dissented* verbally, but the

Milgram's obedience experiment from top to bottom: the "teacher" instructed by the authority, the shock generator, and the "learner" being strapped into his electrified chair. Experts incorrectly predicted the behavior of Milgram's subjects because they failed to consider the influence of the special situation created in the experiment. Although many of the subjects in Milgram's study dissented verbally, the majority obeyed behaviorally.

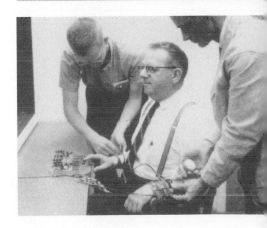

majority did not *disobey* behaviorally. From the point of view of the victim, that's a critical difference.

Remember that no actual shocks were ever delivered to the learner. The victim of the "shocks" was an accomplished actor who congenially chatted with his "tormentor" after the experiment, and assured him he was fine and had never felt any shocks at all. The ethical controversy about Milgram's research has focused on whether it was acceptable to torture the teachers, by allowing them to *believe* they were inflicting actual pain on the learner, before they were debriefed. Consider this ethical dilemma: Is it important to know the potential we might have for obediently harming others—even if, to gain that knowledge, we must subject people to psychological pain and discomfort, and perhaps unpleasant realizations about themselves?

Why Do We Obey Authority?   From the many variations Milgram conducted on his original study, we can conclude that the obedience effect is strongest under the following conditions (Milgram, 1965, 1974; Rosenhan, 1969), also shown in Figure 12.3:

■ When a peer *models* obedience by dutifully complying with the authority figure's commands;

■ When the *victim is remote* from the subject, and cannot be seen or heard;

■ When, instead of acting privately, the teacher is under *direct surveillance* of the authority figure giving the commands;

■ When a subject acts as an *intermediary bystander*—merely "assisting" the one who is actually delivering the shock;

■ When the authority figure has *higher relative status* than the subject.

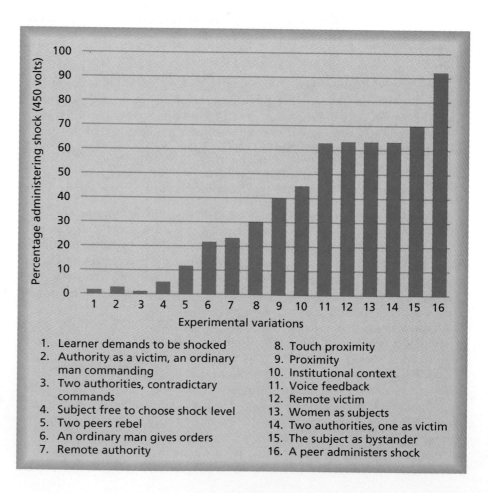

FIGURE 12.3   Obedience in Milgram's Experiments ■ The graph shows a profile of weak to strong obedience effects across situational variations of Milgram's study of obedience to authority.

1. Learner demands to be shocked
2. Authority as a victim, an ordinary man commanding
3. Two authorities, contradictary commands
4. Subject free to choose shock level
5. Two peers rebel
6. An ordinary man gives orders
7. Remote authority
8. Touch proximity
9. Proximity
10. Institutional context
11. Voice feedback
12. Remote victim
13. Women as subjects
14. Two authorities, one as victim
15. The subject as bystander
16. A peer administers shock

If you carefully review these conditions, you can see that the obedience effect is due to situational variables and not personality variables. In fact, personality tests administered to the subjects did *not* reveal any traits that differentiated those who obeyed from those who refused, nor did they identify any psychological disturbance or abnormality in the obedient punishers. These findings enable us to rule out the role of personality in obedient behavior.

Situations versus Rationalizations So why did they do it? One possibility is that the subjects did not really believe the "cover story" of the experiment, and knew that the victim was not really getting hurt. This guess was ruled out by an independent replication (replay of Milgram's scenario) that made the effects of being obedient even more vivid and direct for the subjects.

In this replication of a Milgram-type scenario, college students were asked to train a puppy on a discrimination task by punishing it with increasing levels of shock whenever it made an error. They could see it jumping around on an electrified grid when they pressed a switch. Actually, the puppy received only a low level of shock—just enough to make it squeal, but not to hurt it. The students dissented, complained, and became upset—some even cried. Then, at a given point, an odorless, colorless anesthetic was secretly released into the puppy's enclosed chamber. The dog wobbled and finally fell asleep, but the subjects thought they had killed the puppy. Then the experimenter reminded them of the *situational rule:* Failure to respond is a punishable error; they must continue to give shocks.

Three-fourths of all students delivered the maximum shock possible. Every one of the female subjects proved to be totally obedient despite her dissent (Sheridan & King, 1972). In this case, subjects could have no doubt that their compliance with orders had harmful and distressing consequences. In light of these findings, it is unlikely that the obedience of Milgram's subjects was fostered by a rationalization that they were not really causing anyone harm.

Demand Characteristics Another explanation for subjects' behavior is that the effect is limited to the **demand characteristics:** *cues in the experimental setting that influence subjects' perceptions and behavior.* For example, the experimenter's words or tone of voice might give subjects cues as to how exactly they are expected to behave. Was subjects' blind obedience to authority in Milgram's study merely a response to the demands of the unusual experimental setting?

Consider the results of a field experiment that tested the obedience of nurses in a hospital setting. In this study, a nurse received a telephone call from a staff doctor she had never met, who told her to administer medication to a particular patient in the doctor's absence. The dose he ordered was twice the maximum dosage indicated on the drug container, as the nurse could plainly see. Would the nurse violate standard medical practices by following a stranger's orders without authorization? In fact, almost every nurse obeyed: 20 of the 22 subjects began to administer the "drug" (actually a harmless substance) before being stopped by a researcher (Hofling et al., 1966). Thus even when there are good reasons to hesitate or defy authority, some aspects of the situation are so scripted and well learned that they are hard to resist. Doctors give orders, and nurses obey—usually with little room for error or question.

When researchers recently surveyed nurses about whether they had ever complied with an order they felt might have "harmful consequences" for a patient, one major difference was found between nurses who reported they complied and those who were noncompliant: those who reported disobeying the order felt they were almost equally responsible for the patient's welfare, whereas those who complied with questionable orders held the physician significantly more responsible than themselves (Krackow & Blass, 1995). In other words, one's willingness to obey an authority is increased if the authority figure can be "blamed" for any wrongdoing. If you feel personally responsible for the victim, or that you share responsibility with the person giving the order, you are more likely to resist an order you fear might cause harm. (The practical advice for all of us when we are the patients and clients of health care services is to make each health care *provider* feel personally responsible for our well-being.)

The Rules of Influence Two reasons people obey authority in compelling situations can be traced to the effects of *normative* and *informational* sources of influence, which we discussed earlier. People want to be liked and they want to be right. They tend to do what others are doing or requesting (normative influence) in order to be socially acceptable and approved. When in an ambiguous, novel situation, people rely on others for cues as to the appropriate and correct way to behave (informational influence). They are more likely to do as they are told when experts or credible communicators tell them what to do.

A third factor in the Milgram paradigm is that subjects were probably confused about *how to disobey;* nothing they said in dissent satisfied the authority. They did not know how to exit without suffering the "exit costs" of confronting the authority figure. Had they known a simple, direct way out of the situation—for example, by pressing a "quit" button—it is likely more people would have disobeyed (Ross, 1988).

Finally, obedience to authority in this experimental situation is part of an *ingrained habit* that is learned by children in many different settings: Obey authority without question (Brown, 1986). This heuristic (rule of thumb) can serve us well when authorities are legitimate and deserving of our obedience. The problem is that the rule gets overapplied, just as when children first learn the grammatical rules for past tense and add "ed" to all verbs, even when it is wrong to do so. Blind obedience to authority means obeying any and all authority figures simply because of their status, regardless of whether they are unjust or just in their requests and commands.

What does obedience research signify to you personally? Recall the image of a lone man standing defiantly before tanks in Beijing's Tiananmen Square during the rebellion of Chinese students in June 1989. Would you have done the same? What choices will you make when faced with moral dilemmas throughout your life? Many of the scandals exposed at the highest levels of government, the military, and business involve authorities who expect their subordinates to behave in unethical and illegal ways. Even people who should "know better" because they enjoy positions of favor and status will find it hard to "rock the boat" by questioning the very authorities who have exalted them. When the president of a company invites his advisors to speak candidly about what he is doing wrong, for example, few will believe he wants to hear criticism. No one likes to be the bearer of bad news—especially to the boss. People prefer, perhaps, to keep silent and hope things will work out, or at least that they will not get too much worse.

When and How to Disobey You are subject to the same kinds of circumstantial pressures as Milgram's research subjects. Resisting situational forces requires first being aware of and accepting the fact that they can be powerful enough to affect almost anyone, even you. Second, you need to analyze the situation mindfully and critically for the details that don't fit, the flaws in the "cover story," or the rationales that don't make sense upon careful analysis. For example, imagine that someone you work for—a teacher, artist, or politician whom you respect and admire—asks you for help. Suppose this person has done something wrong or made a mistake, confides in you, and requests your assistance in dealing with the problem. Initially you might be flattered to be singled out as a trusted advisor. But what if you were asked to do something incriminating or unethical? Ask yourself why the authority figure needs *you* to do the dirty work. Perhaps you are really being set up to take the fall— pay the consequences—in case something goes wrong and a scapegoat is needed. In that case, is it still desirable—is it your *duty*—to follow orders without qualm or question? At what point must you refuse to comply and instead think for yourself?

Disobeying authority is seldom easy, because our socialization emphasizes the value of respecting role models and doing as we are told. Remember these important strategies for resisting all compliance-gaining situations (see Zimbardo & Anderson, 1993, for a fuller presentation):

- Be mindful: pay attention.
- Leave the situation.
- Take a "time out" to think things over.
- Never sign on the dotted line the first time.
- Be willing to admit you have made a mistake, or that you are willing to deviate from the crowd.
- Be ready to give up early and cut your losses: you may have to stop what you are doing and suffer the short-term loss of time, money, or effort rather than try to justify your "investment" by continuing with a negative process.

Like the Stanford prison study, obedience research challenges the myth that evil lurks in the minds of evil people—that the bad "they" are different dispositionally from the good "us" who would never do such things. The purpose in recounting these findings is not to debase human nature or to excuse evil deeds, but to make clear that even normal, well-meaning individuals are subject to the human potential for giving in to strong situational and social influences to do wrong. As TV's kindly neighbor, Mr. Rogers, tells his little viewers, "Sometimes even nice people do bad things." What he doesn't add, but you now know, is that *It all depends on the power of the situation*.

Helping

Consider a different perspective on Milgram's obedience situation: If you were a *bystander* to the teacher-learner transaction, would you intervene to help one of the distressed subjects disobey the authority and exit from the situation? When would you be more likely to intervene: if you were the only bystander on the scene, or if you were one of several observers? Before answering, you might want to reflect on what social psychologists have discovered about the nature of *bystander intervention* and the way it reflects another aspect of situational forces.

Consider a news event that stunned the nation and triggered years of research into the apparent problem of bystander apathy:

> For more than half an hour, 38 respectable, law-abiding citizens in Queens, New York, watched a killer stalk and stab a woman in three separate attacks. Two times the sound of the bystanders' voices and the sudden glow of their bedroom lights interrupted the assailant and frightened him. Each time, however, he returned and stabbed her again. Not a single person telephoned the police during the assault; only one witness called the police—after the woman was dead (*New York Times*, March 13, 1964, cited in Darley & Latané, 1968).

At a September 1995 antiviolence rally in Detroit, protesters hold a photo of Deletha Word, who days earlier had jumped to her death from the Belle Isle Bridge while fleeing a man who was beating her.

This newspaper account of the murder of Kitty Genovese shocked a nation that could not accept the idea of such apathy on the part of its responsible citizenry. The outrage of the Kitty Genovese murder drew unprecedented attention to the problem of bystander "apathy," an apparent lack of concern on the part of witnesses who might have intervened and helped victims in need.

Despite decades of social outrage and media attention, however, bystander apathy has proved difficult to alter. In August 1995 in Detroit, Michigan, a young woman named Deletha Word was pursued and attacked by a man whose vehicle had been dented in a minor fender-bender by her car. With friends in his car, the man, Martell Welch, followed Word as she drove onto a bridge to downtown Detroit. Welch cornered Word, pulled her from her car, ripped her clothes, and pushed her onto her car to beat her. Word broke free and ran to the bridge railing, threatening to kill herself, while Welch's friends urged her to "Jump!" A crowd had gathered and watched Deletha Word fall into the Detroit River 32 feet below. Two young men, Orlando Brown and Lawrence Walker, happened by at this point, noting that the onlookers were "standing around like people taking an interest in sports" (Stokes & Zeman, 1995, p. 26). When the two men saw Word struggling in the current below, they quickly took off their shoes and shirts and dove in after her. But she swam away, perhaps fearing they were her attackers, and soon sank from sight.

Would you have called the police to help Kitty Genovese? Or would you have risked your life, like Lawrence Walker and Orlando Brown, to try to save Deletha Word? The temptation is to say, "Yes, of course." However, we must be careful to resist overconfidence about the way we would react in an unfamiliar situation. Why *don't* bystanders help in cases such as these? What would make them more likely to do so?

Abandoned in the Laboratory   Social psychologists **Bibb Latané** and **John Darley** conducted a classic series of studies of the bystander intervention problem soon after the Kitty Genovese murder. The psychologists ingeniously created in the laboratory an experimental analogue of the bystander-intervention situation. A college student, placed in a room by himself with an intercom, was led to believe that he was communicating with one or more students in adjacent rooms. During the course of a discussion about personal problems, the subject heard what sounded like one of the other students having an epileptic seizure and gasping for help. During the "seizure" it was impossible for the subject to talk to the other students or to find out what, if anything, they were doing about the emergency. The dependent variable was the speed with which he reported the emergency to the experimenter. The major independent variable was the number of people he believed were in the discussion group with him. It turned out that the likelihood of intervention depended on the number of bystanders he thought were present. The more there were, the slower he was in reporting the seizure, if he did so at all. As you can see in Figure 12.4, all subjects in a two-person situation intervened within 160 seconds, but nearly 40 percent of those who believed they were part of a larger group never bothered to inform the experimenter that another student was seriously ill (Latané & Darley, 1968).

Personality tests showed no significant relationship between particular personality characteristics and speed or likelihood of intervening. The best predictor of bystander intervention is the situational variable of *size of the group* present. The likelihood of intervention *decreases* as the group *increases* in size, probably because each person makes the assumption that others will help, so he or she does not have to make that commitment. Individuals who perceive themselves as part of a large group of potential interveners experience a **diffusion of responsibility:** *a dilution or weakening of each group member's* *obligation to help as total responsibility is shared with all group members.* You may have experienced moments of diffused responsibility if you have driven past a disabled car beside a busy highway because "surely someone else" would stop and help. In contrast, if you believe you are the only bystander to know of a victim's plight, you will feel a greater degree of responsibility—and opportunity—for providing assistance.

Rescued in the Real World When similar studies of bystander intervention are carried out in *field situations* rather than in the laboratory, a victim's chances of getting help increase significantly. Consider what researchers learned from the following staged series of events: A man on a moving New York subway train suddenly collapsed and fell to the floor. A number of bystanders witnessed this event. The experimenters manipulated the situation by varying the characteristics of the "victim"—an invalid with a cane, a drunk smelling of liquor, or, in a companion study, a disabled person apparently bleeding (or not bleeding) from the mouth. The researchers unobtrusively recorded the bystanders' responses to these emergency situations. One or more persons responded directly in most cases (81 out of 103) with little hesitation. Help was slower when the apparent *cost* of intervening was higher (that is, slower for a bloody victim who might require a greater degree of involvement than for a victim who simply collapsed), but it still usually came (Piliavin & Piliavin, 1972; Piliavin et al., 1969).

Why don't students help as much in a laboratory situation as citizens do in a natural setting? Intervention in the laboratory setting may be inhibited

FIGURE 12.4 Bystander Intervention in an Emergency ■ The more people present in a crisis, the less likely it is that any one bystander will intervene. As this summary of research findings shows, bystanders act most quickly in two-person groupings.

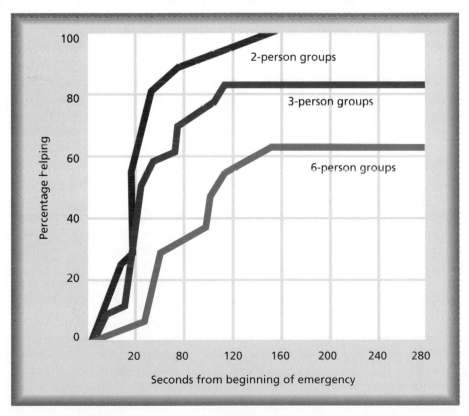

because the college students have already adopted the *passive* role of "subject," and they assume that the experimenter is responsible and "in charge." Laboratory subjects often do not actually see the victim-in-distress, and even when they do, they are severely restricted by their obedience to an unstated rule of the laboratory setting: Remain in your seat; stay put and follow instructions until you are told you can get up. In unstructured, informal settings, none of these conditions holds, and the decision to intervene is based more on an observer's weighing the personal costs of intervening against the consequences of not doing so. Further, as reviewed in Focus on Science, this cost-benefit analysis may be more difficult and time consuming than effective help can allow.

Even if you would do the right thing eventually, a genuine victim in distress likely needs the help sooner rather than later, and cannot afford the delay caused by a would-be helper's crisis of conscience. It is all the more important, therefore, to identify the circumstances that prompt or inhibit helping responses, so that we can give help when others need it, and get it when we do.

Need Help? Ask for It!   To demonstrate the positive effects of situational power, social psychologist **Tom Moriarity** (1975) arranged two fascinating experiments. In the first study, New Yorkers watched as a thief snatched a woman's suitcase in a restaurant when she left her table. In the second, they watched as a thief snatched a portable radio from a beach blanket when the owner left it for a few minutes. What did these onlookers do? Some did nothing, letting the thief go on his merry way. But others did intervene. What were the conditions under which some helped and others did not?

In each experiment, the would-be theft victim (the experimenter's accomplice) had first asked the soon-to-be observer of the crime either "Do you have the time?" or "Will you please keep an eye on my bag (radio) while I'm gone?" The first interaction elicited no personal responsibility, and the bystander stood by idly as the theft unfolded. However, of those who had agreed to watch the victim's property, almost every bystander intervened. They called for help, and some even tackled the runaway thief on the beach.

The encouraging message is that we can convert apathy to action and transform callousness to kindness just by asking for it. The act of requesting a favor forges a special human bond that involves other people in ways that materially change the situation. It makes them responsible to you, and thereby responsible for what happens in your shared social context. There are several ways you can increase your chances of getting aid from would-be helpers (Schroeder et al., 1995):

- *Ask for help;* let others know you need it rather than assuming they realize your need or know what is required.
- *Reduce the ambiguity* of the situation by clearly explaining the problem and what should be done: "She's fainted! Call an ambulance right away and help me keep her warm" or "Someone broke into my house—call the police and give them this address!"
- *Identify specific individuals* so they do not diffuse responsibility with others present: "You, in the red shirt: call 911!" or "Will the person in the blue Toyota please call for a tow truck right away?"

Will people help? Recall that while Deletha Word drowned in the Detroit River, two strangers pushed past a crowd of unhelpful onlookers in an effort to save her life. The positive message is that even an apathetic crowd cannot smother the impulse of some citizens to offer help to a fellow human in distress.

FOCUS on Science

The Good Samaritan—If There's Time

The presence or absence of other people is one situational factor that apparently affects bystander intervention. In addition, if a bystander is in a hurry to do something else, he or she is less likely to offer help. In the biblical tale of the Good Samaritan (see Luke 10:30–37), several important people are too busy to help a stranger in distress. He is finally assisted by an outsider, a Samaritan who takes the time to offer aid. Could the failure of the "important" people to help really be due to time pressures rather than their personal dispositions? A research team recreated the story of the Good Samaritan.

Students at the Princeton Theological Seminary were the subjects of an experiment that they thought involved evaluation of their sermons, one of which was to be about the parable of the Good Samaritan. Before they left the briefing room to have their sermons recorded in a nearby building, they were each told something about the time they had available to get to the studio. Some were randomly assigned to a *late condition,* in which they had to hurry to make the next session; others to an *on-time condition,* in which they would make the next session just on time; and a third group to an *early condition,* in which they had a few spare minutes before they would be recorded.

When each seminarian walked down an alley between the two buildings, he came upon a man slumped in a doorway, in obvious need of help. On their way to deliver a sermon about the Good Samaritan, these seminary students now had the chance to practice what they were about to preach. Did they? Of those who were in a hurry, only 10 percent helped. Ninety percent failed to act as Good Samaritans! If they were on time, 45 percent helped the stranger. The greatest bystander intervention came from those who were not in any time bind—63 percent of these seminarians acted as Good Samaritans (Darley & Batson, 1973).

The situational manipulation of time had a marked effect on the altruism of these young men, increasing it sixfold between the late and early conditions, when all else was held constant. We can hardly attribute the lack of intervention of those in the late condition to their callousness or other dispositions since they were randomly assigned to that condition and had chosen a career based on helping others. It is likely that, while fulfilling their obligation to the researcher to hurry and not be late for their appointment, their single-minded purpose blinded them to "irrelevant events" that might interfere with that obligation. Some of those who did not help may not have noticed the man in distress, others might have misinterpreted what they saw as a man merely resting.

In applying these results to your own life, consider that helping is more a matter of taking the right actions than of thinking the right thoughts. Carrying scriptural aphorisms in your head will not enable you to do good if the stresses of daily life—feeling hurried, harried, or worried—crowd out your awareness of what is really important in life. It is possible that we will overlook our own values because we are caught up in the demands or inertia of our situations.

If you wish to break free of these numbing, dulling constraints, change your habits and stay alert—be mind*ful,* not mind*less*—and look for ways to be helpful *in spite of* pressures that inhibit helping (see Kohn, 1991).

Check Your Recall

We have explored the basic theme of social psychology—the power of situational variables to influence individual behavior. Controlled laboratory experiments and field studies both strongly support the generalization that human thought and action are affected by situational influences to a far greater extent than we realize.

Social norms function within groups to direct and shape members' behavior. Informational influence leads to conformity and compliance when the situation is ambiguous and the person wants to be right and act correctly. The Bennington studies pointed to the power of social norms to affect students' basic attitudes and values, sometimes for a lifetime. Even in highly structured situations, perceptions can be influenced by conformity pressures, as demonstrated in the Asch experiment.

One of the most powerful and controversial demonstrations of situational power was Milgram's series of studies on obedience to authority, in which many ordinary people typically behaved in antisocial ways with the best of situationally provided motives. The final proof of the significance of situational forces came from studies in which bystander intervention in crises decreased as the number of observing bystanders increased and as bystanders' sense of time urgency increased. The positive effects of situational power showed up in research that indicates we can induce altruism in others by specifically and clearly asking for help. ✔️

Constructing Social Reality

Even if you accept the logical conclusions of the research reviewed in the last section, you may experience discomfort with the idea that situations can so easily overwhelm you. You have values, after all, and you do your best to act on them. How, then, could you yield to situational pressure and still be an honorable or healthy human being? The answer lies in understanding how situations come to wield so much influence in so many human endeavors.

To understand how situation is so significant, we need to discover how the behavioral setting is perceived and interpreted by those people in it and what meanings they attribute to its various components. This second lesson of social psychology thus emphasizes the nature of *the subjective reality* that individuals construct from a situation's objective features. An actor's view of the circumstances sets in motion certain psychological processes. These processes change the situation itself, so that it fits the actor's other perceptions, values, and attitudes. It is not so much the physical, objective features of a situation that control individual and group behavior; it is the *mental representations of the person in the situation* that matter most.

For the social psychologist, an adequate account of any behavior includes three basic components: the *features* of the current situation, the specific *content* and *context* of the observed behavior, and the actor's subjective *interpretations* of the important elements in the behavioral setting. This type of behavior analysis is complicated when we realize that different people often interpret shared events in different ways. When members of a group reach a common interpretation of an event, activity, or person, their shared perspective is known as *social reality*. **Social reality** *is the consensus of perceptions and beliefs about a situation generated by group members' social comparisons.*

In this section, we will see the power of situations in a slightly different light, as it is filtered through a person's mind. After reviewing studies that illustrate how our subjective constructions of reality operate, we will outline several theoretical approaches that social psychologists have taken to help them make sense of the ways people think about and perceive their social world. It will become apparent that a strong cognitive orientation is at the core of much of social psychology.

Beliefs and Expectations

Have you ever disagreed with a friend about what *really* took place at some event you both experienced? People's beliefs can lead them to view the same situation from different vantage points and to make contrary conclusions about what "really happened." One example of these contrary conclusions comes from a study of a famous football game that took place some years ago between two Ivy League teams. The undefeated Princeton team played Dartmouth in the final game of the season. Ultimately won by Dartmouth, the game was rough, filled with penalties and serious injuries to both sides. After the game, the newspapers of the two schools offered very different accounts of what had happened. A team of social psychologists surveyed students at both schools, showed them a film of the game, and recorded their judgments.

Nearly all Princeton students interviewed judged the game as "rough and dirty," none saw it as "clean and fair," and most believed that Dartmouth players started the dirty play. In contrast, the majority of Dartmouth students

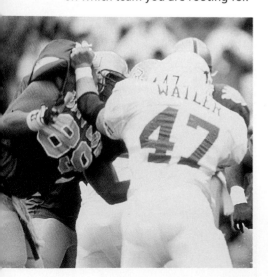

The thrill of victory or the agony of defeat? According to a classic study, what you see when you watch a competitive event depends on which team you are rooting for.

surveyed thought both sides were equally to blame for the rough game, and many thought it was "rough, clean, and fair." When viewing the same film, Dartmouth students "saw" both sides commit the same number of penalties (Hastorf & Cantril, 1954). Clearly, a complex social occurrence, such as a football game, cannot be observed in an objective fashion. In this case, people *looked* at the same activity, but they *saw* two different games—based on what they believed, felt, and wished.

Self-Fulfilling Prophecies   Can beliefs and expectations actually shape social reality? Much research suggests that the very nature of some situations can be modified significantly by the beliefs and expectations people have about them. Such *social expectancy effects* are similar to placebo effects—belief that a medical treatment will work can *make* it work for many people. For example, ordinary students or underachievers can be transformed into high achievers if their teachers believe they are "special," or if the students are led to think so.

In Greek mythology, the sculptor Pygmalion created—and then fell in love with—a statue of his ideal woman, naming her Galatea. With the intervention of the goddess of love, Pygmalion's creation came to life, fulfilling the wish from which he had first sculpted her. In honor of this classic tale of wishes that come true, the influence of social expectancy has been dubbed the *Pygmalion effect*. This effect was re-created in an experiment by psychologist **Robert Rosenthal,** in conjunction with school principal Lenore Jacobson (Rosenthal & Jacobson, 1968a, 1968b).

Several elementary school teachers in Boston were led to believe that particular students of theirs were "intellectual bloomers" who would show unusual gains during the coming year. In fact, there was no objective basis for that prediction; the names of these rapid bloomers had been chosen *randomly*. By the end of that school year, 30 percent of the arbitrarily labeled "spurters" had gained an average of 22 IQ points. Almost all of them had gained at least 10 IQ points. Their gain in intellectual performance was significantly greater than that of their control group classmates. In absolute terms, their improvement is remarkably significant for any known kind of enriched education program over such a short time, and these were students in ordinary classes.

How did the false expectations of the teachers come to produce such positive student performance? In some way the teachers must have used influence strategies that motivated the targeted students to work harder and more efficiently. These strategies were probably communicated in many nonverbal ways, perhaps even unconsciously, through the teachers' facial expressions and body language. Rosenthal points to several processes that were activated by the teachers' expectations:

- They acted with greater warmth and friendliness to the chosen students, even while they were putting greater demands on their performance.
- They gave more immediate feedback about the selected students' performance.
- They created more opportunities for the special students to respond, "show their stuff," and be reinforced in class.

In one sense, this research put some students on the fast track. The opposite happens when students are assigned to slow learner or learning disability tracks; their performance often deteriorates further when they have been identified in this way. Negative teacher expectations may be responsible for poorer performance by females and some minority students in science and mathematics courses even at the college level.

Self-fulfilling prophecies *are predictions about some future behavior or event that modify its outcome so as to produce what is expected* (Merton,

1957). Social reality can be changed in several ways by such "prophecies." A shy student has the expectation that he won't have a good time at an upcoming dance. An extroverted student predicts the same dance will be fun and enjoyable. Whatever the dance is "really" like, both students are likely to experience what they expected, because they help create situations that fit their expectations, negative for the shy guy, positive for the extroverted one.

The Power of Positive Thinking   An optimistic outlook can generate positive outcomes. In earlier chapters, we noted the positive effects on health and well-being of an optimistic outlook on life (Seligman, 1991). Optimism is a general system of beliefs that gets translated into actions that affect one's health and well-being. Research has shown that our wishes and hopes for how life will turn out can actually have some influence on what does happen. Motivated reasoning can determine the kind of evidence we focus on in making our self-predictions, the methods we use to make those predictions, the confidence we invest in our predictions, and our insensitivity to contrary evidence that might disconfirm our predictions (Kunda, 1990).

Optimists assume setbacks are temporary, and they persevere in the face of adversity until they reach their goals. For example, you can probably think of something you do well today, such as an athletic activity, playing a musical instrument, painting, typing, or cooking that you once did far less competently. Think how different your life would be now if, when you experienced early discouragement, you had not persisted in thinking—perhaps optimistically, or even unrealistically—that you could do better.

Confirming Expectations   Mark Snyder (1984) uses the term **behavioral confirmation** *for the process by which an observer's expectations about another person influence that person to behave in ways that confirm the observer's hypothesis.* In a series of studies, students were led to expect that they would interact with another person who was described in particular terms (not necessarily true) such as *introvert, extrovert, depressed,* or *intelligent.* After interacting with the target person, the subject rated the person on a variety of dimensions. Typically, the target person was more likely to act in whatever way the subject expected him or her to behave. The subjects, as well as the observers (who did not know what the expectation was), agreed that those hypothesized to be outgoing were indeed very sociable, that the introverted target people behaved unsociably, and so forth (Kulik, 1983; Snyder & Swann, 1978).

How were these impressions confirmed? The extroverted target person was likely to be asked how she would liven up a party, while the shy target person was asked why it's hard to open up to others. Different questions elicited different responses that, in turn, guided the evaluation. The evaluator was not aware that the question had a strong role in creating and distorting social reality.

People who have strong self-concepts are particularly resistant to the effects of behavioral confirmation (Swann & Ely, 1984). For example, if you know you are a good student, even a professor who seems to expect the worst from you will not shake your faith in your ability to perform well over all.

A disturbing news report from the late 1980s shows how expectations can lead to false conclusions and regrettable actions. Two California police officers used their batons to beat a blind man who was standing at a bus stop. Why? They mistakenly thought that the folding cane in his pocket was an illegal martial arts weapon and they "demanded that he hand over the contents of his pockets." The man believed he was being robbed because the police officers did not identify themselves; they assumed he could see their uniforms. When the blind man reached for his cane to defend himself from being mugged, the police felt his behavior confirmed their suspicions and they began to hit him (*New York Times*, May 17, 1989).

Like other errors in social thinking, self-fulfilling prophecies are exaggerations of cognitive processes that normally serve us well (Myers, 1996). Living in a social world, we must regularly form impressions and make predictions about what others are like and how they will perform. Sometimes our eagerness to make such predictions exceeds our ability to do so accurately, as when our information or observations are limited. As long as we understand the difference between correctly predicting someone's behavior and setting up a situation to create the actions we expect, we can reduce our tendency to make "prophesies" and elicit "confirming" behaviors.

Constructing Social Perceptions

How do people construct their views of others and understand their transactions within a shared social context? They do so by observing the ways that they and others behave in various settings and over time. *The general process by which we come to perceive and know our own personal attributes and those of others is called* **social perception.** Social psychology is understood as *cognitively oriented.* Social psychology conceives of the individual as an active agent in the social world—a person who is always collecting information about people and events, thinking about what is happening and what to do, and organizing these thoughts into lessons imparting knowledge and meaning.

A major task of everyday social perception involves figuring out what behavior *means,* forming accurate impressions, and making sound predictions about what we and others are likely to do. We constantly try to make sense of our world by applying already acquired knowledge and beliefs to new events and assimilating the new to the familiar. For example, if a new friend suddenly acts distressed and upset, we may try to remember what caused old friends to act in similar ways, and how we may have helped them. If these rehearsed tactics succeed, we will learn how to help our new friend; if they fail, we must experiment with other strategies and add them to our interpersonal skills.

Our quest to construct a meaningful view of the social world is illuminated by research on three processes: prejudice, self-justification, and explaining or attributing causes to life events. Patterns in these processes lay the foundation of our relationships with others and for our ability to solve social problems.

The Development of Prejudice   Few human weaknesses are more destructive to the dignity of the individual and the social bonds of humanity than prejudice. The Supreme Court's 1954 decision to outlaw segregated public education was, in part, based on research, presented in federal court by social psychologist **Kenneth Clark,** that showed the negative impact on black children of their separate and unequal education (Clark & Clark, 1947).

Prejudice is a prime example of social reality gone awry—a situation created in people's minds that can demean and destroy the lives of others. **Prejudice** *is defined as a learned negative attitude toward a person based on that person's membership in a particular group.* Prejudice involves negative affect (dislike or fear), negative beliefs (stereotypes) that justify the attitude, and a behavioral intention to avoid, control, dominate, or eliminate those in the target group. Prejudiced attitudes serve as biasing filters that influence the way individuals are perceived and treated once they are categorized as members of a target group. Once formed, prejudice exerts a powerful force for selectively processing, organizing, and remembering pertinent information.

Although prejudice has many origins and serves a variety of needs (Allport, 1954; Pettigrew, 1985; Sarnoff & Katz; 1954), one of its most basic

purposes is to simplify a complex environment and increase other individuals' predictability by categorizing them in certain ways. The simplest and most pervasive form of categorizing involves individuals determining whether other people are like themselves. This categorization results in an *in-group bias,* an evaluation of one's own group as better than others (Brewer, 1979).

Social categorization *is the process by which people organize their social environment by sorting themselves and others into groups* (Wilder, 1986). This categorization has been shown to have the following consequences: perception of similarity of those within one's group (the in-group) and dissimilarity of those who are not members (the out-group); failure to distinguish among individuals in the out-group; reduced influence of out-group members on the in-group; and hostile attitudes toward and beliefs in the inferiority of the out-group (Tajfel, 1982; Tajfel & Billig, 1974). These consequences developed regardless of limited exposure to the out-groups and despite the contradictory experience of their individual members with any other out-group category (Park & Rothbart, 1982; Quattrone, 1986). For example, if your softball team were matched with a new team for a single game, despite your lack of familiarity with the other team and its individual members, you could readily think of them as "the opponents" and assure yourself that your team and teammates were superior.

Does there need to be a kernel of truth in the basis for categorization that leads to prejudiced attitudes and discriminatory actions? The answer is no; all that is necessary is any salient cue on which individuals can be sorted into exclusive categories. A third-grade teacher, **Jane Elliott,** wanted her pupils from an all-white, rural Iowa farm community to experience how prejudice and discrimination felt to those in minority groups. She devised an activity to provide her students with that experience. One day she arbitrarily designated brown-eyed children as "superior" to the "inferior" blue-eyed children. The superior, allegedly more intelligent, brown-eyes were given special privileges, while the inferior blue-eyes had to obey rules that enforced their second-class status. Within a day, the blue-eyed children began to do more poorly in their schoolwork and became depressed, sullen, and angry. The brown-eyed superiors mistreated their former friends, called them "blue-eyes," refused to play with them, got into fights with them, and worried that school officials should be notified that the blue-eyes might steal things.

The second day of the activity, Elliott told the class that she had been wrong. It was really the blue-eyed children who were superior and the brown-eyed ones who were inferior. The brown-eyes now switched from their previously positive self-labels to derogatory labels similar to those used the day before by the blue-eyes. Their academic performance deteriorated, while that of the new ruling class improved. Old friendship patterns between children temporarily dissolved and were replaced with hostility—until the experiment was ended at the end of the second day (Elliott, 1977).

Sadly, in many schoolrooms throughout the country, students are made to feel inferior through their negative interactions with other pupils or their teachers. These students often begin to act in ways to confirm this prejudiced belief and come to internalize their sense of academic inadequacy. In the competition for the scarce resource of teacher attention and affection, the more verbal, advantaged students take charge; the others back off, fearing failure and further rejection. In many schools, teachers respond more to "take-charge" students. Often these dominant students tend to be the Caucasian males in the class. Females and members of minority groups consequently receive less attention and less constructive support from teachers. This system fosters a situation for out-group members that is characterized by envy, competitiveness, suspicion, self-derogation, and eventually an inability to identify with school and academics.

Jane Elliott's experiment measured overt changes in prejudicial behavior among children and changes in their schoolwork. She obtained measures of their feelings toward each other by asking the children to draw pictures of the way they felt. The picture on the top was drawn by a child who felt "on top," confident, and capable because he had the superior eye color. Nonetheless, the children were generally delighted when the experiment—and discrimination—ended.

Self-Justification   People prefer consistency in their social perceptions and cognitions. That is, we like new information to agree with or fit into old beliefs and assumptions. Several theories have been proposed to explain why and how people seek to maintain consistency in their thoughts and experiences. The most influential of these approaches is theorist **Leon Festinger's** notion of *cognitive dissonance* (1957). Festinger defined **cognitive dissonance** *as the state of conflict someone experiences after making a decision, taking an action, or being exposed to information that is contrary to prior beliefs, feelings, or values.* We assume that when cognitions about one's behavior and relevant attitudes are dissonant—when they clash and contradict each other—an unpleasant tension arises that the individual is motivated to reduce. Dissonance-reducing activities modify this unpleasant state and achieve consonance among one's cognitions.

For example, suppose the two dissonant cognitions are a fact about yourself ("I smoke") and a belief you hold ("Smoking causes lung cancer"). To reduce the dissonance involved, you could take one of several different actions. For example, you could change your belief ("The evidence that smoking causes lung cancer is not very convincing"); change your behavior (stop smoking); reevaluate the behavior ("I don't smoke very much"); or add new cognitions that make the inconsistency less serious ("I smoke low-tar cigarettes").

Cognitive dissonance motivates people to make discrepant behaviors—contradictory actions or statements—seem more rational, as if they followed naturally from personal beliefs and attitudes. If you can't deny that you took a certain action, you might change your attitudes to make them fit that action. You then internalize your attitude change to make acceptable what otherwise appears to be "irrational behavior." Hundreds of experiments and field studies have shown the power of cognitive dissonance to change attitudes and behavior (Wicklund & Brehm, 1976).

According to dissonance theory, under conditions of high dissonance (for example, when one has just done something that completely contradicts a previously stated attitude), an individual acts to justify his or her behavior after-the-fact, engages in self-persuasion, and often becomes a most convincing communicator and convinced target audience. The principle of cognitive dissonance can be deftly applied by those who wish to influence your actions and beliefs. For example, a young woman smoking a cigarette is asked by a friend why she doesn't quit. The smoker believes that smoking does cause cancer, emphysema, heart disease, and other life-threatening conditions. She knows that her family has a history of circulatory ailments and that she may put herself at risk if she continues to smoke. She experiences cognitive dissonance because she must consciously confront two conflicting self-cognitions: "I keep smoking" but "I know smoking is bad for my health." Unfortunately (for reducing dissonance), tobacco advertisements have taught the smoker many rationalizations for her behavior. Why doesn't she quit? The smoker insists, "I know it's probably not good for me, but smoking makes me feel good, and it calms me down when I feel nervous. I just enjoy smoking too much to quit right now." By convincing herself that she thoroughly enjoys smoking now and can always quit later, the smoker temporarily ignores health worries, justifies her behavior, and reduces cognitive dissonance—but not, alas, her risk of developing a smoking-related illness!

Making Attributions   One of the most important inferential tasks for social perceivers is determining the causes for events. We want to know the "whys" of life. Why did my girlfriend break off the relationship? Why did he get the job and not I? Why did my parents divorce after so many years of marriage? All such why's lead to an analysis of possible causal determinants for some action, event, or outcome.

Attribution theory *is a general approach to describing the ways the social perceiver uses information to generate causal explanations for events.* We engage in attributional thinking when we ask "why" questions—"Why did I get such a poor grade on my psychology test?" or "Why hasn't my date called about this weekend?"—and subsequently attempt to identify causes. Attribution theory has come to play an important role not only in social psychological thinking but in many other areas of psychology, because it focuses on a basic aspect of human functioning: the way individuals make *causal attributions* (explanations about causes) for achievement (Weiner, 1986), depression (Abramson et al., 1978), and other life domains.

Although you might wonder about the exact causes of any kind of behavior, you are especially likely to engage in causal analysis about events that are either *surprising* or *negative* (Holtzworth-Munroe & Jacobson, 1985). For example, you may not wonder why someone says hello or compliments you, but you are very likely to wonder why someone gives you an extravagant present—or seems very angry with you.

The Intuitive Psychologist   Attribution theory originated with the writings of Gestalt psychologist **Fritz Heider** (1958). Heider argued that people continually make causal analyses as part of their attempts to comprehend the social world. Such causal understanding helps predict and control future events. If you know what makes your roommate upset, then you may be able to reduce or induce that reaction by manipulating those causal conditions.

Heider believed that most attributional analyses focus on two questions: Is the cause for the behavior found in the *person* (internal causality) or in the *situation* (external causality)? Who is responsible for the outcomes? For example, suppose a woman is charged with killing her husband and her defense is that he had battered her for years. She feared for her life and her children's whenever he drank too much, and this was a more and more frequent problem. The legal resolution of this case will rest largely on determining what *caused* the woman's admitted crime, given the mitigating circumstances. The defense will argue that she was the victim, driven to act in self-defense—her circumstances left her no other choice. The prosecution will insist that she did have choices, but committed murder willfully, and must now pay for her crime. To decide the case, the jurors must decide which attributional analysis they agree with.

Heider suggested that instead of developing theories about how people are supposed to think and act, psychologists should discover the personal theories (belief systems) that ordinary people themselves use to make sense of the causes and effects of behavior. After all, he argued, aren't all people **intuitive psychologists,** *trying to figure out what people are like and what causes their behavior,* just as professional psychologists do for a living? Heider used a simple film to demonstrate the tendency for people to leap from observing actions to making causal inferences and attributing motives to what they see. The film involved three geometric figures that moved around an object without any prearranged plan. Research subjects, however, always made up scripts that animated the action, turning the figures into actors and attributing personality traits and motives to their causal actions (see Figure 12.5).

Attributional Analyses   Attribution theory was given a boost by the contributions of **Harold Kelley** (1967), who focused on the fact that we often make causal attributions for events under conditions of uncertainty. We may not have sufficient or precise information, our self-confidence may be low, or our attention or perspective may be limited. We seek out additional information and are susceptible to social influence from peers and experts.

FIGURE 12.5   Heider's Demonstration of the Natural Tendency to Make Causal Attributions ■ When Fritz Heider showed subjects a short film of geometric figures moving in a two-dimensional field, the observers inferred that the shapes had "motives," indicated by their movements. For example, they often saw the triangles as two male "characters" fighting over a female circle. The larger triangle was seen as "aggressive" and the smaller as "heroic." In the sequence here, observers "saw" T chase t and c into the "house" and close the door.

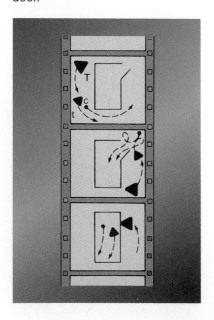

Thousands of studies have been conducted to refine and extend attribution theory (Fiske & Taylor, 1991). These studies reveal the conditions under which the search for causal explanations proceeds rationally—and also when the social thinker is more rationalizing than rational. When a desired outcome is *not* realized, who or what is to blame? When things do turn out well, what or who should get the credit? These patterns in *attributional analysis* are critical influences on our behavior. For example, you would probably persist in working on a difficult task if you perceived it as "challenging," but not if it were merely "tedious" or "stressful" (see Chapter 9 for a review of how the hardy personality views demanding circumstances). Conversely, you can probably sustain interest in a subject if you attribute a poor performance so far to a temporary problem, even if it is an internal one, such as being exhausted from studying for exams or suffering from an attack of the flu. But you might feel discouraged and give up if you blamed initial failure to a chronic, broad, personal problem: "I'm just not smart enough to do well in this class." Thus your attributional analyses affect not only your expectations about tasks and relationships, but also your view of yourself.

Attributional Biases One challenge to attributional analyses is that people are often biased in their efforts to explain important experiences. Two patterns of bias have received particular attention from researchers: the *fundamental attribution error* and *self-serving biases*.

The **fundamental attribution error** (**FAE**) *is a biased pattern of explanation in which an observer overestimates the power of dispositional forces and underestimates situational influences on others' behavior* (Harvey et al., 1981; Jones & Harris, 1967; Ross, 1977). For example, if you overhear a classmate raising her voice in an argument with someone, you commit the FAE if you "blame" her behavior on an angry mood or having a terrible temper. If you could see things from her perspective, you might be able to see how her situation provoked her—perhaps the other person insulted her, or perhaps they are practicing roles for a play. Although, when we don't know otherwise, there is an equal chance the causes are situational, people have a tendency to ascribe behavior, especially negative behavior, to the actor's disposition.

The FAE is not always an "error," of course; if the causes really are dispositional, the observer's guess is correct. So the FAE is best thought of as a *bias* rather than a mistake. However, the FAE can be detrimental to forming accurate impressions, because the observer then overlooks legitimate, situational explanations for another's actions. For example, if the car in front of you brakes suddenly so that you almost collide, your first impression may that the driver is at fault, a dispositional judgment. But what if the driver slowed down in order to avoid hitting a dog that ran into the road? Then the explanation for the near-accident would be situational, not dispositional. By reminding ourselves that there may be circumstances that account for seemingly inexplicable actions, we are less likely to commit the FAE.

Another class of attributional biases, complementary to the FAE, affects the way we sometimes distort explanations for our *own* behavior. For example, when you do something good—succeed in a task, or earn a high grade on a test—you would like to give yourself credit. In contrast, if you do something bad—fail on a test, or hurt someone's feelings—you seek to blame your actions on your situation, not your disposition. *This pattern of thinking in which one credits internal factors for one's own success but blames external factors for personal failure is the* **self-serving bias.** Self-serving biases are quite robust, occurring in many situations for most people and even across cultures (Fletcher & Ward, 1988). In our efforts to serve our needs for self-esteem, we tend to make dispositional attributions for success and situational attributions for failure: "I *earned* a B in Economics because I worked hard, but my Political Science instructor dislikes me and *gave* me a D." This example illustrates the motivated tactician at work to protect the self-esteem of the social thinker.

Self-serving biases are probably rooted in the need for self-esteem, a preference for interpretations that save face and cast our actions in the best possible light (Epstein & Feist, 1988; Ickes & Layden, 1978; Schlenker et al., 1990). Self-serving biases also result from errors in judgment and confidence: we are overconfident, so we persist in chancy—even risky—behaviors, and we come to believe things that just aren't so (Gilovich, 1983, 1991). The FAE, on the other hand, may result from genuine differences in perspective—the inability of an observer to see, and thus take into account, situational factors that might explain the actor's behavior (Jones, 1976; Jones & Nisbett, 1971; Storms, 1973). The FAE may also be part of a general Western (Euro-American) bias to see people as "agents" or powerful causes of their own experiences, rather than to take a more balanced view and admit that many unfortunate outcomes are no one's fault and cannot be blamed on individuals' behavior (Miller, 1984). Such research findings show us that our quest to know "why" some unexpected or awful event occurred can be clouded by mixed motivations, self-esteem needs, and distorted perspectives.

Rather than viewing attribution as a single cognitive exercise triggered by an event, it makes more sense to see causal analysis as a collection of cognitions aroused by the human need to understand. While attributional analysis is vulnerable to some distortion, learning about biases can makes us less likely to commit them. Our experiences—and our mistakes—can teach us to make more reasonable and accurate attributions. Causal analysis is the very basis of *narrative thinking*—the storytelling and reflection that help us to make sense of our experiences (Gerrig, 1993). By explaining to ourselves what has happened and why, we can comprehend and construct meaning in our lives and lay the foundation for our choices and plans.

Relating to Others

Social perceptions, prejudices, and attribution are certainly interesting in themselves (especially to social psychologists), but they may be all the more relevant to you because they help to explain relationships with other people. An important quality of social psychology is its assumption that people live in a social world, not a vacuum, and that we are motivated to seek out others, interact with them, and understand them. We reach outside ourselves, affiliate with others, become particularly attracted to a few of those we meet, and work to establish and maintain intimacy. Closeness is desirable but certainly not automatic; it does not "come naturally."

This irony—that close relationships are important but difficult to sustain—is apparent to anyone who has suffered the loss of a loved one, whether family or friend, through death or breakup. To become close to anyone is to risk the complex pains of loss—grief and bereavement, loneliness and depression, the anger and humiliation of being rejected. To judge from themes in popular literature, music, and films, most of us are hungry for information about how to find love, resolve conflicts, and make up after breakups. If intimacy is so important to well-being and happiness, why is it so hard to find? And if we are not the first to ask these questions, why are there so few answers, beyond the questionable opinions of columnists, cartoonists, and television characters?

From Attraction to Intimacy   One social psychologist has wryly observed that his discipline has been the last to arrive at the "party" of those interested in liking and loving—long after poets, journalists, and the lovers themselves

(Rubin, 1973). However, for over four decades social psychologists have been slowly but steadily assembling the data necessary to draw some conclusions about how people might best form and strengthen intimate bonds. The earliest work on relationships focused on interpersonal attraction, and identified key factors that determine whom we like: similar attitudes, physical attractiveness, shared values and history, compatibility of needs, and fair exchange of resources (for example, see Hendrick & Hendrick [1992] for a summary). Laboratory studies of these processes—for example, whether receiving a compliment would increase a subject's liking for someone—were usually restricted to short-term interactions between strangers. How well might their results predict the course of long-term relationships among intimates?

Although the study of existing relationships—real people interacting with their friends and lovers—is a messier, less precise business than manipulating encounters in the lab, it is essential for an understanding of genuine intimacy. Social psychologists **Ellen Berscheid** and **Elaine Hatfield** published the first text on interpersonal attraction in 1969 (see Berscheid & Hatfield, 1969; 1978). Among other topics they explored, Berscheid and Hatfield tackled a basic mystery—the nature of love. Why is it that people in so many cultures expect a special emotional experience (romantic or passionate love) to signal that they have found their life partner? And further, if love is the key to a successful intimate relationship, why do so many relationships end in breakup or divorce? The questions Berscheid and Hatfield asked three decades ago may seem reasonable and worthwhile to us today, but when they first proposed their work, the two social psychologists had to defy both popular derision and political pressure in order to conduct their research. Despite the difficulties of this endeavor, Berscheid, Hatfield, and other investigators persisted in exploring the psychology of the human heart, identifying patterns not only in how people become attracted and fall in love, but also in how relationships develop, are maintained, and often break down (Hatfield & Rapson, 1993).

From early work on **affiliation**, *the motivation to seek the presence or interaction of others,* social psychologists further focused on which factors seemed most powerful in predicting *interpersonal attraction,* the preference for the company of specific individuals. Here are some of their consistent findings about why people go beyond mere acquaintanceship to form liking, friendship, and even love for specific others:

For decades social psychologists have been exploring the psychology of the human heart, collecting and interpreting data about how people fall in love and strengthen their bonds of intimacy.

- We form greater liking for those we more frequently *interact* with, through geographical proximity or common interests (Simpson & Harris, 1994).
- We like people who agree with us, and who have backgrounds, goals, and attitudes *similar* to our own (Hatfield & Rapson, 1993; Hendrick & Hendrick, 1992; Kelley et al., 1983; Simpson & Harris, 1994).
- We are attracted to people who have *desirable qualities,* such as being physically attractive, generally competent, and rewarding to be with (Brehm, 1992; Simpson & Harris, 1994).
- While definitions of love vary with different individuals, within a culture there are *common themes defining love*—such as sexual arousal, attachment, concern for the other's welfare, and a willingness to make a commitment—that we look for in determining whether what we feel for others is "love" (Aron & Aron, 1994; Beall & Sternberg, 1995; Berscheid, 1988; Fehr, 1988; Hatfield, 1988; Sprecher & McKinney, 1994).

By the early 1970s, social psychologists were more frequently sharing their interests and findings with relationship researchers in other disciplines—communication, sociology, counseling, and anthropology. Since then scholars have occasionally left the lab to study meeting, mating, and dating in the "field," including singles bars and personal ads (Harrison & Saeed, 1977;

Pennebaker et al., 1979). Their scrutiny of people's relationships has been intensified by what has been referred to as the "divorce epidemic" (Brehm, 1992). In a nutshell, if current rates hold, approximately half of all today's first marriages—and up to 60 percent of second marriages—will end in divorce. Research into the nature of relationship conflict and breakdown has provided many insights into the ideas and feelings people bring with them into interactions and intimacy:

- When relationships end, families (the functional units of society) are *disrupted,* especially the children of divorcing parents (for example, Hetherington, 1987, 1988; Wallerstein & Blakeslee, 1989; Wallerstein & Kelly, 1980).
- The process of breaking up or divorcing typically causes individuals to experience extreme financial, physical, and emotional *stress* (for example, Bloom, et al., 1978; Somers, 1981; Weber & Harvey, 1994a; Weiss, 1975; Weitzman, 1985)
- At the very least, the ending of an intimate relationship represents *loss of access to the social support, care, and happiness* a partner may provide (for example, Campbell, 1981; Weingarten, 1985; Weiss, 1975).

Relationship Maintenance   In the last decade, researchers' interest has shifted to the processes by which people actually maintain and develop their relationships *beyond* initial attraction. As a result of efforts by scholars in many different disciplines, we can identify what some of those processes are (for a review, see Brehm [1992], Duck [1992], and Hatfield & Rapson [1993]). For example, we know that the *social exchange* of resources between partners must be rewarding and equitable. *Communication* between partners must be open, ongoing, and mutually validating (Gottman & Silver, 1994). *Conflicts* must be faced early and resolved fairly and effectively. Ultimately, each partner must take *responsibility* for his or her own identity, self-esteem, and commitment to the relationship—rather than expect the partner to engage in mind reading or self-sacrifice.

Though young compared to its parent disciplines, the study of close relationships has already yielded some benefits in addressing social concerns. Teachers familiar with research findings can now inform their students about the basic principles of healthy relationships with friends and partners. Therapists apply these principles in advising clients on how to communicate with partners, negotiate the terms of their relationships, and resolve inevitable conflicts. More immediately, as you yourself learn about the factors that influence how you perceive and relate to others, you should gain a greater sense of control and well-being in your own connections with others (Harvey, 1996; Harvey et al., 1990).

Recap: The Two Lessons of Social Psychology

To recapitulate: The two main lessons that emerge from the social psychological tradition are the *power of the situation* and the *construction of social reality.* Taken together, these two principles lead to a significant conclusion with important implications for action: People are basically similar in their biological and psychological processes. Whenever this principle is violated—(as when someone seems or acts different from us)—we should base our subsequent actions on the awareness of two possibilities—first, that their *situation is different* from ours or has changed in some way we don't notice, and second, that their *perception of the situation* differs from our perception in an important way that we may not recognize.

The source of much human misunderstanding and social conflict between groups and nations is the belief that "we," as a group of reasonable people, perceive the world or some vital part of it accurately—the only rational way it could be seen. "They," the other side who sees it differently, are wrong. Obviously, however, *we* are *they* to them. Each group or nation attributes negative dispositions to other groups and nations and positive ones to itself, all the while ignoring the situational determinants of the differences that, if changed, could reverse its perceptions and actions. By learning to recognize how situations shape us—for example, by imagining ourselves in others' circumstances, growing up in their cultures and surroundings—we can take a step toward eliminating the prejudice that threatens to destroy our society. In our quest for meaning, we may impose a framework or label on the world we encounter that is not only inaccurate, but dangerously distorted or unfair to others. We would do well to remember that just as wishing does not make it so, judging does not make us right.

Check Your Recall

The construction of social reality is the second major lesson of social psychology. People use predictions as self-fulfilling prophecies that lead to desirable outcomes, such as improved student achievement; these predictions change the way the relevant behavioral actors view the situation, and can elicit behaviors that confirm those predictions.

Cognitive frameworks are developed and applied to understand social phenomena. People construct mental representations of their social world. Our cognitive tendency to simplify information by categorizing individuals can contribute to prejudice and discrimination. Dissonance theory accounts for the self-justification that people engage in when they have behaved in ways that are discrepant with their internal states. Tension between one's beliefs and one's actions creates cognitive dissonance, which can be reduced by changing some aspect of the situation or of oneself.

Attribution theory describes how people seek the causes for the behavior they observe in themselves and others. Though we are subject to the fundamental attribution error and self-serving biases, our causal analyses of unexpected or negative events can help us to understand and predict our social world better.

Early work on interpersonal attraction enabled social psychologists to identify some factors influencing social interactions and personal relationships. Later work has examined the nature of intimacy, including social exchange, communication skills, and conflict resolution between partners. A greater understanding of what draws people together can enable us to strengthen relationships during times of difficulty, both for ourselves and others.

The two lessons of social psychology emphasize the power of the situation and the construction of social reality. By learning these lessons we are less likely to isolate ourselves from others and more able to see that "we" and "they" are very much alike in our life experiences, goals, and social influences.

Solving Social Problems

Many social psychologists are motivated by psychology's ultimate goal: to improve the human condition. This concern is expressed in two major ways. First, studies by social psychologists are often carried out in natural field settings—in housing projects, at dances, in nursing homes, or in factories, for example—as well as in laboratory recreations of those natural settings (Rodin,

1985). Efforts are made to include elements of real-world settings. Second, the knowledge obtained from basic research and theories is used to explain social phenomena, and systematic attempts are made to apply that knowledge to remedy a range of social problems (Deutsch & Hornstein, 1975). The Society for the Psychological Study of Social Issues (SPSSI), a major organization of social psychologists and also a division (Division 9) of the American Psychological Association, is dedicated to just that principle.

Reducing Prejudice and Aggression

The focus on solving social problems moves us a long way from the traditional view of psychology as the scientific study of individual actions and mental processes. The person is only one level in a complex system that includes social groups, institutions, cultural values, historical circumstances, political and economic realities, and specific situational forces. Modern social psychologists expand the domain of their inquiry to include this broader network of interactive elements. Many new areas of application have opened up to both the curious investigator and the psychologist as agents of social change (Fisher, 1982). Over time, shifting norms and social perceptions cause us to reexamine practices that once may have gone unquestioned.

For example, one social debate that has received much media attention has been whether traditionally all-male institutions, such as The Citadel in South Carolina, should either open their doors to female cadets or risk losing state funding for refusing to admit women. In 1993 a young South Carolina woman named Shannon Faulkner was accepted for admission to The Citadel because she met school standards and admissions officers mistakenly assumed she was male. When school officials discovered their error they blocked her admission to the corps of cadets, and thus began a two-year legal battle over whether a state-supported institution could be permitted to exclude qualified applicants strictly on the basis of a one-sex tradition (Faludi, 1995). Ultimately the courts insisted Faulkner be accepted, so most Citadel officials and students grudgingly prepared for her arrival. But during "Hell Week," an initiation period in which new cadets are harassed and threatened by upperclassmen, Faulkner became ill and decided to withdraw from The Citadel. In response to Faulkner's decision, her classmates cheered and whooped, celebrating their "victory" at keeping their military school at least temporarily free from the presence of female peers (Peyser, 1995).

Why was it so important to these young men to live in an all-male institution? How did this "men only" policy—nonexistent outside of tightly controlled institutional settings such as religious cloisters or military encampments—become so essential to these boys' and men's sense of pride and identity?

At the heart of all such discrimination is injustice: people are denied their rights or treated unfairly because the people with power are prejudiced. Prejudices such as sexism (prejudice against others based on their gender), like racism (prejudice based on race) and homophobia (antihomosexual prejudice), become persistent and powerful when they are *institutionalized* by tradition, law, and social policy. A "tradition" is a historical pattern of norms, which we have already seen are the products of social perceptions. By understanding the normal social processes underlying social problems, we can decipher these complex challenges and break them down into simpler, perhaps more solvable problems. Thus an understanding of social psychology is vital in order to move toward a future where diversity is recognized and even honored, and away from practices that discriminate against others solely on the basis of their belonging to certain "undesirable" social categories.

Social psychology's relevance to life problems provides great opportunities and challenges to psychologists just beginning their professional careers. A

Male cadets at The Citadel whoop with joy that their military school will remain free of female cadets—but only for a short time.

number of exciting liaisons between social psychology and other disciplines and issues can be found in the fields of law, education, health care, counseling, interpersonal relations, politics (including international relations, terrorism, conflict, and public policy), consumerism, business, the environment, and the promotion of world peace (see Oskamp [1984] and Rodin [1985] for more applications of social psychology to everyday life). We dealt at length with health psychology in Chapter 9. Here we will briefly review social psychological perspectives on two related social issues: how to reduce crime and violence; and how to promote world peace.

Crime and Violence

We live in a violent society. In the United States, more than one million assaults are reported annually (Myers, 1996). Locally and nationally, the nightly news regales us with the latest instances of assassination, gang war, drive-by shootings, car jacking, and terrorism. Impressions formed from the media—whether fictional or factual—are that law-abiding citizens are increasingly outnumbered and surrounded by criminals who respect no authority and feel no mercy. In fact, however, about 70 percent of those currently incarcerated in American prisons have been jailed for *non*-violent crimes. Once inside, they share space and culture with more violent offenders and may well learn a more aggressive style by the time they are released.

Why do people "break the rules"? Indeed, why do so many criminals seem never to have learned or lived by any rules in the first place? Politicians are quick to blame the breakdown of the family or the erosion of "traditional family values" for the rise in violent crime. Yet social psychologists must assume that each violent offender begins life with at least some goals and concerns in common with more law-abiding citizens: the urge to survive and protect oneself; a longing for security, love, and comfort; a hope for a meaningful and happy life. If most of us begin with such similar goals, why do we seem to end up taking such different paths? Considering the two main lessons of social psychology, we might consider that, compared with law-abiding citizens, violent offenders experience different *situational forces* and construct a different *social reality*.

In terms of situational forces, consider that while criminals deviate from law-abiding society, they clearly abide by some social norms. They form relationships, often have families, join groups and gangs, and live by sometimes rigid codes. If imprisoned, they contribute to institutional "culture" in order to survive as prisoners. But an outsider may not be willing or able to understand the "culture of the street" that landed a criminal in jail, or the prison "society" to which he has adapted (National Public Radio, 1996b). For example, members of mainstream society generally maintain a *rational choice perspective,* presuming that criminals rationally consider their choices and likely consequences before committing a crime (Cornish & Clarke, 1986). But there is no evidence that stiffer sentences, such as the mandatory death penalty for "capital crimes," have a deterrent effect. Instead, there is evidence that states instituting and enacting the death penalty experience an attendant *increase* in capital crime (Akers, 1990; Paternoster et al., 1983).

One explanation for the link between harsh sentences and a rise in crime can be found in the "social reality" lesson of social psychology. Most Americans favor the death penalty, regardless of whether it has a deterrent effect. This could be based on a common desire for revenge that leads citizens to demand violent punishment. The consequence is that, every time a harsh sentence is carried out, aggression (whether or not it is just) is modeled to all members of the culture. Punishment and vengeance are viewed as normal and acceptable, so criminals who can obtain weapons have few qualms about

Media violence may both model aggression and reduce inhibitions against aggressive behavior. In 1995, this subway token booth was fire-bombed after the perpetrators watched a similar bombing in the violent movie the *Money Train*.

using them. Finally, weapons are extremely easy to obtain, especially in the United States, where the right to bear arms is protected by the Constitution. Some research suggests that merely seeing or possessing a weapon produces a **weapons effect,** *a greater likelihood of behaving aggressively as a result of stimulation by the presence of a weapon* (see Berkowitz, 1993).

To reduce crime and violence, therefore, we must first understand the *situations*—such as poverty, discrimination, and desperation—that lead people to break the law. Second, we must change the *messages* sent by the media, politics, and even through casual conversation about the acceptability of lying, cheating, stealing, and hurting others. We can begin this work with the most impressionable members of our culture, our children. We can teach children to reject aggression, to practice nonviolent conflict resolution, to enjoy the rewards of collaboration and compromise, and to be strong and informed instead of ignorant and afraid. Schools can assist in much of this work, but it must begin in homes and families, where children are most greatly impressed and influenced.

There is no simple solution. To reduce crime and violence, each member of society is responsible and has an opportunity to make a difference. We must rethink myths about human nature and realize that punishment must be done correctly if it is to be effective in changing behavior. Finally, as individuals, we should recognize our own aggressive impulses, including our desire for revenge against those who we believe have harmed us or our loved ones. Vengeance may be a "natural" response, and victims' rights must be considered in any system of justice, but vengeful punishment is no substitute for effective crime prevention and rehabilitative intervention. Individuals may be unable to relinquish the desire for counterattack, but as a society we have the power and the responsibility to take the long-term view, and to consider what is best and most effective for everyone, now and in the future.

Promoting Peace

Just as social psychology can focus light on interpersonal relationships, it can also illuminate the complexities and conflicts of international relations. Psychologists for Social Responsibility is an organization of psychologists who not only study various aspects of the complex issues involved in war and peace but conduct educational programs on these topics for professionals, schoolchildren, and the lay public. In addition, they try to have input in relevant political decision-making policies at the state and national levels. This organization is just one example of the dual roles that many psychologists have chosen to play as dedicated, objective scientists and, at other times, as committed, impassioned advocates of social-political action.

Attempting to help resolve the dilemmas of superpower competition, or, for that matter, many of the domestic and international problems that we now face, poses challenges that psychology is uniquely equipped to study. **Peace psychology** *represents an interdisciplinary approach to the prevention of nuclear war and maintenance of peace* (Plous, 1985). Psychologists committed to contributing their talents and energies to this vital element of our future draw on the work of investigators in many areas. Among them are political scientists, economists, physicists, mathematicians, computer scientists, anthropologists, climatologists, and physicians.

Dehumanizing the Enemy Some peace psychologists are conducting research that examines the basis for false beliefs, misperceptions, and erroneous attributions on issues germane to nuclear arms, military strength, risk, national security, and even language. They study the fears of children and the anxieties of adults about nuclear war. To explore the individual and cultural forces that create war, peace psychologists study propaganda and media images that glorify war and violence and demonize the enemy.

Although most cultures oppose individual aggression as a crime, nations train millions of soldiers to kill. Part of this mass social influence involves dehumanizing the soldiers of the other side into "the enemy"—nonhuman objects to be hated and destroyed. This dehumanization is accomplished through political rhetoric and through media (for example, movies and cartoons) and popular culture (for example, anti-enemy "jokes"). A dehumanized enemy—a subhuman or even a nonhuman—can be killed without guilt. The problem of military psychology is to convert the act of murder into patriotism (Keen, 1986), and this is most effectively accomplished by giving every soldier not a gun but an exaggerated, internalized view of the hated enemy (see Figure 12.6). In recent years Americans have been urged by politicians, journalists, cartoonists, and entertainers to loathe and ridicule the people of Iran, Grenada, Panama, Iraq, Cuba, as well as others. A major challenge to peace psychology is that humans can readily and vividly imagine many different kinds of people as "enemies."

FIGURE 12.6 Faces of the Enemy ■
Notice how the propagandists have created images of the enemy that are fearsome, monstrous, or dehumanized.

Peace psychologists have taken several different directions in their work. For quite some time, social scientists have been investigating arms negotiations, international crisis management, and conflict resolution strategies. They have developed experimental gaming studies to test the utility of different models of the nuclear arms race, using the players' responses as clues to the motivations and political decisions of national leaders. Arms negotiations or international crises are simulated to resemble historical situations. Participants communicate and make decisions in teams with different power structures (Guetzkow et al., 1963). By varying factors such as arrangements of the problem or the participants, researchers can observe which structures and strategies work best. Such simulations also generate new negotiating strategies and techniques for crisis management (Bazerman, 1990).

Power and Policy Making   Some psychologists believe that to affect policy making toward nuclear war, it is necessary to study the way those in authority have handled past nuclear crises. By learning how decision makers have made sense of events that could have led to nuclear war, psychologists can offer more fully formed decision rules that minimize the cognitive and motivational biases of policymakers. This work may prevent future crises through an understanding of past and current crisis management (Blight, 1987).

From a psychodynamic perspective, the nuclear arms race is driven by the quest for personal power among national leaders (Frank, 1987). Superpower leaders may possess a constellation of personality traits—including, persuasiveness, suspiciousness, optimism, and competitiveness—that can lead to errors in judgment. For example, only a strong, independent person is likely to reach a high level of power, but strength and independence may isolate such a leader from sensible advice just when he or she needs it most. Psychologists realize how difficult it is to change the very traits that have made leaders successful in many aspects of their jobs. Consequently, they urge leaders to become aware of superordinate goals on which they can agree. Alternatives to violence as the ultimate expression of power must also be identified.

The New (Psychological) World Order?   Psychologists have a new role in the revolution that is sweeping away entire political systems and economic orders throughout the world. The transition of hundreds of millions of people from a totalitarian to a democratic mentality and from a central collectivist society to a free-market economy is a change of unprecedented proportions. Generations of formerly Communist citizens have never experienced the free-

In times of violent conflict, successful leaders may need to modify their strong independence in order to find alternatives to violence.

doms and responsibilities of democratic ideas and practices. Democracy is more than a political system; it is a unique way of thinking about the significance of the individual and about one's role in shaping shared societal goals. Those who have lived with some sense of security in a government-controlled economy and state-run industries, such as in the former Soviet Union, must learn to cope with the risks and uncertainties of competitive market economies. Additionally, individuals and whole communities need help in dealing with the aftermath of decades of abuses by totalitarian regimes—exiles, imprisonments, forced labor, displacement, and ecological catastrophes. This psychological help involves education, research, therapy, and social policy–planning. The Center for the Psychology of Democracy is a newly formed organization of psychologists committed to assisting people and societies in reshaping their lives and country within the framework of democratic principles and practices (Balakrishnan, 1991).

Promoting world peace requires knowledge—and perhaps reeducation—about psychology. According to *The Seville Statement on Violence,* a report on ending war and promoting peace disseminated by UNESCO (Adams, 1991), world peace is possible only if we accept five propositions about the nature of human aggression:

1. War is not natural to animals or humans. Animals do not make war, and human culture can be changed to be less warlike.
2. Aggression is not inevitable in "human nature," because we are influenced by—and can reshape—our culture from one generation to the next.
3. War does not promote survival; people and animals do best when they learn how to collaborate and work together.
4. Aggressive behavior is not driven by brain mechanisms. The brain has the capacity to be influenced by learning. Thus the brain can provide the basis for cooperation as well as for violence.
5. There is no scientific basis for blaming war on a human aggressive "instinct." People wage war only when they learn to do so. To change learned warfare, we must question the people and policies that teach war and violence in the first place.

Our brief discussion of peace psychology barely touches on the many new directions that researchers and social change agents are taking to reduce the threat of war and increase the prospects for peace. For example, what can the world community do about the deep-seated hatreds and fears that have so long held sway in Northern Ireland? Or consider Bosnia, the battle-torn province in the former Yugoslavia. What can be done for nations that are emerging from decades of Communist oppression only to take up arms against each other and renew long-buried grudges and feuds with their neighbors? The umbrella of peace psychology must grow larger to accommodate this latest challenge to the world community. The basic research and theories we have been discussing can be applied to solve the urgent problems facing us. Our goal in this is to improve the quality of life for individuals, societies, and the planet.

Check Your Recall

Social psychologists seek ways to improve the human condition. Much social psychological research has focused on coping with the conditions that foster crime and violence, and the most effective ways for society to respond. By understanding the situations that foster criminal behavior and the influences on how criminals view reality, social psychologists can suggest strategies for solving these chronic social problems. Stiff sentences and wide availability of weapons may encourage a cultural norm that accepts violence and aggression. We can begin to reduce aggression on an individual level by understanding and controlling our own anger, and rechanneling aggressive impulses into alternative and constructive activities.

Peace psychology endeavors to understand the nature of international competition and conflict so that problems can be defused before they pose a nuclear threat. Peace psychologists have found that hostilities are based in prejudices, misperceptions, and dehumanizing images of "the enemy." By reframing our view of human nature as not necessarily aggressive, and by avoiding errors in social thinking, we can transform our energies into constructive commitments between peoples and nations. ✔

CHAPTER REVIEW

Summary

The two major themes of social psychology are that situations influence individual thoughts, feelings, and behavior, and that individuals construct their understanding of social reality. A major source of situational influence is norms, which shape the behavior of groups as well as members of society in general. Reference groups influence members who wish to avoid penalties such as rejection, ridicule, or reeducation. The Asch effect demonstrates that even in informal groups members often endeavor to agree with obviously incorrect group decisions. The most memorable demonstration of situational power was Stanley Milgram's series of experiments on obedience to authority. Research on factors that influence whether bystanders will offer help in crises has shown that individuals are inhibited by situational factors such as the number of bystanders, the ambiguity of the situation, and their resultant perception of their social role and responsibility.

In an effort to construct perceptions and interpretations of social reality, individuals rely on cognitive frameworks to categorize people and events. Overreliance on social categorization leads to prejudice, an unjustified negative attitude about a group and its members. Another cognitive experience is dissonance, the perception that one's attitudes and behaviors are inconsistent with each other. The need for self-justification motivates individuals to change dissonant thoughts or actions. The need to understand social events and relationships leads us to search for explanations for our own and others' behaviors. When making attributions about others' behaviors, individuals are often biased by the fundamental attribution error—overestimating dispositional factors and underestimating situational factors. When explaining their own behavior, individuals may rely on self-serving biases to maintain self-esteem by taking personal credit for success but blaming failures on external forces. Social perceptions and attributions influence our choices about

those we interact with and relate to. Research has shown that liking is a function of proximity, similarity, and perceived attractiveness. Relationship maintenance is a function of effective communication and conflict resolution between partners. The costs of failed relationships are severe both for society and individuals' lives.

Social psychology seeks to address serious social problems such as reducing violent crime and promoting world peace. To reduce aggression, individuals must first eliminate the culture of violence and offer positive rewards and rehabilitation. World peace can be promoted by first neutralizing images of the enemy. By avoiding misperceptions of those who are different, we can begin to rethink our views of human nature and build better relations among nations.

Section Reviews

The Power of the Situation

Be sure to *Check Your Recall* by reviewing the summary of this section on page 479.

Key Terms
social psychology (p. 460)
situationism (p. 461)
rules (p. 461)
social role (p. 462)
social norms (p. 462)
reference group (p. 463)
total situation (p. 465)
normative influence (p. 466)
informational influence (p. 466)
Asch effect (p. 466)
conformity (p. 466)

demand characteristics (p. 473)
diffusion of responsibility (p. 476)

Names to Know
Philip Zimbardo (p. 460)
Theodore Newcomb (p. 464)
Solomon Asch (p. 466)
Stanley Milgram (p. 469)
Bibb Latané (p. 476)
John Darley (p. 476)
Tom Moriarity (p. 478)

Constructing Social Reality

Be sure to *Check Your Recall* by reviewing the summary of this section on page 491.

Key Terms

social reality (p. 480)
self-fulfilling prophecies (p. 481)
behavioral confirmation (p. 482)
social perception (p. 483)
prejudice (p. 483)
social categorization (p. 484)
cognitive dissonance (p. 485)
attribution theory (p. 486)
intuitive psychologists (p. 486)

fundamental attribution error (FAE) (p. 487)
self-serving bias (p. 487)
affiliation (p. 489)

Names to Know

Robert Rosenthal (p. 481)
Mark Snyder (p. 482)
Kenneth Clark (p. 483)
Jane Elliott (p. 484)
Leon Festinger (p. 485)
Fritz Heider (p. 486)
Harold Kelley (p. 486)
Ellen Berscheid (p. 489)
Elaine Hatfield (p. 489)

Solving Social Problems

Be sure to *Check Your Recall* by reviewing the summary of this section on page 497.

Key Terms

weapons effect (p. 494)
peace psychology (p. 494)

REVIEW TEST

Chapter 12: Social Psychology

For each of the following items, choose the single correct or best answer. The correct answers, explanations, and page references appear in Appendix B.

1. Which of the following is the social psychological principle illustrated by the Stanford Prison Experiment and its findings about participants' behavior?
   a. Social situations have powerful influences on human behavior.
   b. An experience is only socially real when the group is unanimous about interpreting it.
   c. Because everyone is basically different, no two people will respond to the same circumstances in the same way.
   d. Even in healthy circumstances, disturbed people will behave in unhealthy ways.

2. According to your text, *ridicule, reeducation,* and *rejection* are the most common examples of _____.
   a. behavior by deviants or nonconformists
   b. causes of cognitive dissonance
   c. how Asch's subjects behaved in his classic research
   d. coercive tactics to encourage group conformity

3. Theodore Newcomb's study of the attitudes of Bennington College students showed that, 20 years after they were first studied, _____.
   a. all the women had gradually shifted to more conservative attitudes
   b. all the women had gradually shifted to more liberal attitudes
   c. the liberals were still liberal, and the conservatives still conservative
   d. none of the above

4. According to research on the Asch effect, which of the following is *not* a condition that breeds greater conformity?
   a. the task being judged is difficult or ambiguous
   b. each group member votes privately and anonymously
   c. the group is extremely cohesive
   d. the group members perceive each other to be highly competent

5. Which of the following statements about Milgram's obedience experiments is true?
   a. All subjects were unable to resist the authority figure's orders, no matter how high the level of shock they believed they were administering.
   b. The majority of subjects delivered increasingly intense shocks until the learner complained of a heart condition, at which point most subjects refused to go on.
   c. Although most subjects verbally dissented and complained, most did not disobey.
   d. Despite predictions by human nature experts that no one would comply, subjects enjoyed the experiment and had no trouble obeying the authority figure's commands.

6. Research on the factors that influence helping behavior suggest that the best predictor of bystander intervention is _____.
   a. each individual's measurable level of personal altruism
   b. the appearance or attractiveness of the victim
   c. an individual's degree of religiousness or agreement with conventional religious values
   d. the size of the group of bystanders to the emergency

7. Which of the following situations would likely create a feeling of cognitive dissonance in the mind of the individual described?
   a. A woman who claims to be on a diet orders a second helping of dessert.
   b. A young man who says he loves his girlfriend spends a great deal of time choosing just the right valentine card to send her.
   c. When a man finds out the car he wants costs more than he can afford, he decides not to buy it and looks instead for a less expensive vehicle.
   d. You hesitate to attend the party of a new friend, but hope for the best and agree to go. Once there, you have a surprisingly good time and are glad you decided to come.

8. Which of the following illustrates the effects of the fundamental attribution error?
   a. Explaining why he is turning his paper in late, a student tells the professor that he had car trouble on the way to campus.
   b. Watching an acquaintance hurry from the dining hall, a woman remarks, "Amy's in such a hurry—she must be a pretty impatient person."
   c. After waiting an unusually long time to be waited on in a restaurant, a customer thinks there must be something wrong in the kitchen that is interfering with the waitress' ability to work as quickly as usual.

d. All of the above illustrate the fundamental attribution error.

9. According to research on interpersonal attraction and close relationships, which of the following is *false?*

a. The more you interact with someone, the more likely you are to like him or her.

b. We form friendships on the basis of our similarity of backgrounds and attitudes.

c. Despite some disruption, divorce usually creates feelings of relief and, eventually, satisfaction on the part of both ex-partners and children.

d. Despite the universal human need for closeness to others, relationships skills must be learned and do not "come naturally."

10. The "weapons effect" is a research finding that the mere presence of a weapon _____.

a. can prompt calm, cooperative individuals to feel anger and hostility

b. can trigger aggressive behavior among individuals who are in conflict or competition

c. has no impact on human behavior unless participants are experiencing severe conflict

d. leads individuals gradually to accept and ultimately to like and want to use it

IF YOU'RE INTERESTED . . .

Birdman of Alcatraz, The. (Video: 1962, B&W, 143 min.). Directed by John Frankenheimer; starring Burt Lancaster, Karl Malden, Thelma Ritter, Betty Field, Telly Savalas.

Absorbing true story of convicted murderer Robert Stroud, who devoted his sentence of life in prison to the study of diseases afflicting birds and how to treat them. Not a whitewash of Stroud's original character or crimes, but an affecting reflection on society's choice between punishment and rehabilitation, and the consequences of that choice for individual and society alike.

Canada, G. (1995). *Fist stick knife gun: A personal history of violence in America.* Boston: Beacon Press.

Reflecting on his own life and upbringing in the inner city's culture of violence, Geoffrey Canada presents powerful arguments about what causes aggressive criminal behavior, how aggression must be rechanneled, how at-risk children must be cared for, and what specific changes can and must be made in society's laws, attitudes, and norms.

Guyana Tragedy: The Story of Jim Jones. (Video: 1980 [made for TV], color, 192 min.). Directed by William A Graham; starring Powers Boothe, Ned Beatty, Veronica Cartwright, Brad Dourif, LeVar Burton, Randy Quaid, Diana Scarwid, James Earl Jones.

Powerful, detailed recreation of the 1979 mass suicide of over 900 members of Rev. Jim Jones Peoples Temple in Jonestown, Guyana, and the events in Jones's life and ministry that led the cult to form, leave the United States, and follow Jones to their deaths. Vivid reminders of how easily individuals seek meaning and comfort in groups—and the subsequent pressure they feel to conform to group norms, even to disastrous extremes.

Kohn, A. (1990). *The brighter side of human nature: Altruism and empathy in everyday life.* New York: Basic Books.

Uplifting review of the many ways in which people help and cooperate with each other, and the challenges this poses for more cynical views of human nature as essentially aggressive and competitive. The appendix includes *The Seville Statement on Violence,* UNESCO's manifesto of the incorrectness of brutish or defeatist views of human nature. Rich with examples and case histories as well as practical suggestions for living more helpful, collaborative lives.

Ox-Bow Incident, The. (Video: 1943, B&W, 75 min.). Directed by William A. Wellman; starring Henry Fonda, Dana Andrews, Anthony Quinn, Harry Morgan, Harry Davenport.

A group of frontier citizens, outraged by rumors of a murder, takes the law into their own hands and threatens to become a lynch mob. Upsetting and familiar story of how emotion overrules reason when individuals lose their sense of personal responsibility and yield to the brutality of the group mind.

Six Degrees of Separation. (Video: 1993, color, 111 min.). Directed by Fred Schepisi; starring Stockard Channing, Donald Sutherland, Will Smith, Ian McKellen, Mary Beth Hurt, Bruce Davison, Richard Masur, Anthony Michael Hall.

Years ago, social psychologists gave subjects envelopes addressed to strangers in all parts of the world—with names only, no addresses—and asked them to use their social networks to have the letters hand-delivered, from friend to friend, in order to reach the addressee. It took the senders on average only five "connector" people between sender and recipient—thus each sender was separated from any randomly identified stranger in the world by only six degrees. Similarly, this film explores the possible connections among those who seem socially unconnected. Based on a true incident, the plot deals with how an affluent New York couple are conned by a young man who claims to be a celebrity's son. Like it or not, the world is perhaps much smaller than we thought.

Stepford Wives, The. (Video: 1975, color, 115 min.). Directed by Bryan Forbes; starring Katharine Ross, Paula Prentiss, Peter Masterson, Patrick O'Neal.

What happens when your aspirational reference group's norms require you to sacrifice your identity? After moving to a suburban community, two housewives are pressured to yield to community standards of traditional gender roles, mindlessness, and subservience to their husbands. An eerie story of "suburban body snatchers," in which the invaders are not aliens or communists, but social pressures to conform.

12 Angry Men. (Video: 1957, B&W, 95 min.). Directed by Sidney Lumet; starring Henry Fonda, Lee J. Cobb, E. G. Marshall, Ed Begley, Jack Klugman, Jack Warden, Robert Webber.

Absorbing drama about jurors' deliberation over the outcome of a murder trial, in which one outnumbered man argues for acquittal. Though all the action takes place in the jury room without flashbacks, the jurors' recollections of the evidence and eyewitnesses' accounts creates a vivid impression of the trial. Elegant portrayal of many social psychological processes: person perception, prejudice, norms, group pressure, and reconstructive memory.

CHAPTER 13

Psychopathology

Dear Dr. Zimbardo,

"I want to let you know what it is like to be a functional scitzophrenic in these days and times and what someone with my mental illness faces.

"I live by myself and am 30. I live on SSI and work part-time as I go through college. Im not allowed to go into Nursing despite past patient care experience and college classes, because of my illness. Im majoring in Human Services to help others with problems, because when I first was sick, I suffered bad and can relate with the suffering.

"I live pretty normal and no one can tell Im mentally ill unless I tell them. . . . My sister (not a twin) has this illness too, for 12 years, and wont take her medicine because she refused to understand she has this illness. Ive had mine for 5 years. I became convinced the 1st year through my suffering by reading the book, 'I Never Promised You a Rose Garden.' So I improved, thanks to the antipsychotic medicine availible. The patient and public, in my opnion needs to be educated about mental illness, because people ridicule and mistreat, even misunderstand us at crucial times. Like how family, husband, friends, or social services react to what they don't know about us. The medicine works good on some of us.

"I can tell the difference between a noise of my illness and a real noise, because Ive studied myself reading about it. There is a common sense rule I use. I just try hard to remember what the world and people are really like. The illness picks such silly nonsense to bother the mind with. The medicine is strong with me and my body chemistry so I don't have too many illness symptoms bothering me.

"The delusions before I got my medicine picked any storyline it chose, and changed it at will. As time went by before help, I felt it was taking over my whole brain, and I'd cry wanting my mind and life back. . . .

"Every person that comes down with an illness is going to be different in handling it. The things that are consistant are the usual symptoms that come along with the illness.

"I hope my letter fits in with some pattern that you see in other scitzophrenics. If they can master it with medicine, medical help, and recognize the illness in themselves, they can live pretty normal lives if given the opportunity, which isn't easy to be lucky enough to have.

"Everyone that wants to succeed in life needs opportunities for them to prove themself. Im a person besides just a person with an illness. . . .

"I hope this letter does some good, it was nagging my mind to write a letter about this illness to you, Dr. Zimbardo.

"Much Respect and Thanks,
        'Cherish'" (fictitious name)

Introduction

What are your reactions as you read this young woman's letter? You might feel a mixture of sadness at her plight, delight in her willingness to do all she can to cope with the many problems her mental illness creates, anger toward those who stigmatize her because she may act differently at times, and hope that, with medication and therapy, her condition may improve. These are but a few of the emotions that clinical psychologists and psychiatrists feel as they try to understand and treat mental disorders. Clinical psychologists—both practitioners working with patients and researchers learning about them—are on the front lines, working directly with individuals suffering from the many forms that mental illness can take. Additionally, an army of clinical, counseling, and personality psychologists conducting research in university laboratories, clinics, hospitals, and government-sponsored research centers investigates the causes, correlates, and consequences of mental disorders.

This chapter focuses on the nature and causes of psychological disorders: what they are, what they look like, why and how they develop. The next, and final, chapter builds on this knowledge to describe strategies for treating and preventing mental illness.

The Nature of Psychopathology

A common bias in social thinking is the belief that people who are in trouble or unhappy must have caused their own problems and deserve it. This faith in a just world helps us to feel "safe," because we tell ourselves we are good, and bad things don't happen to good people (Lerner, 1980). So before going on—and before assuming that people with problems are "others" who are not at all like you—ASK YOURSELF: Have you ever:

- worried excessively?
- felt depressed or anxious without really knowing why?
- felt afraid of a thing or situation that you rationally knew could not harm you?
- believed you were not living up to your potential?
- had thoughts about suicide?
- used alcohol or drugs to escape a problem?

Almost everyone will answer "yes" to at least one of these questions. Occasional periods of worry, self-doubt, sadness, and escapism are all part of normal life. But taken to excess, such experiences endanger healthy functioning and are considered abnormal. This chapter looks at the range of psychological functioning that is considered unhealthy or abnormal, often referred to as *psychopathology* or *psychological disorder*. **Psychopathology** *refers to any pattern or event involving disrupted emotions, behaviors, or thoughts leading to personal distress or inability to achieve important goals.* The field of abnormal psychology is the area of psychological investigation most directly concerned with understanding individual pathologies of mind, mood, and behavior.

Psychopathology touches the daily lives of millions of us, directly and indirectly. It can be insidious, working its way into many situations and diminishing our emotional and physical well-being. It can be devastating, destroying the effective functioning of individuals and their families. It can create an enormous financial burden through lost productivity and the high costs of prolonged treatment. A major study conducted by the National Institutes of

Advertisements, like the one shown here, have gone a long way toward correcting our views of mental illness and creating sympathy for its sufferers.

Mental Health of five U.S. metropolitan areas found that as many as 32 percent of Americans have suffered from some type of identified psychological disorder, and that in any given month, about 15.4 percent of the population suffer from diagnosable mental health problems (Regier et al., 1988). A recent update to that study indicates that during the coming year, the behavior of over 56 million Americans will meet the criteria for a diagnosable mental disorder or substance abuse problem (Carson et al., 1996; Regier et al., 1993).

Statistics on the most dreaded mental disorder, *schizophrenia*, are frightening. More than 1 of every 100 Americans—approximately 2 million over the age of 18—is likely to become affected (Holmes, 1994; Regier et al., 1993). Schizophrenia has been the main diagnosis for about 40 percent of all patient admissions to public mental hospitals—far out of proportion to all other possible categories of mental illness (Manderscheid et al., 1985). Because schizophrenic patients require prolonged or recurrent treatment, they can be expected to occupy about half of all mental hospital beds in the nation (Carson et al., 1996). Most sobering, about one-third of all schizophrenics will never fully recover, even with therapy.

Throughout this chapter, as we present more statistics, discuss categories of psychological disorders, and consider theoretical models that help us understand these problems, try to envision the real people who live with a psychological disorder every day. Remember Cherish: Her words convey the personal distress and struggles that accompany psychopathology.

What Is Abnormal?

Experts in the field of abnormal psychology do not agree completely about what behaviors constitute psychological disorders. The judgment that someone has a mental disorder is typically based on the evaluation of the individual's *behavioral* functioning by people who have special authority or power. The terms used to describe these phenomena—*mental disorder, mental illness,* or *abnormality*—depend on the particular perspective, training, and cultural background of the evaluator; on the situation; and on the status of the person being judged. In some cases, judgments of abnormality are confused with evaluations of an individual's character and social desirability. For example, our culture frowns upon hallucinations, because they are taken as signs of mental disturbance; other cultures value hallucinations, because they are interpreted as mystical visions from spirit forces.

The first step in classifying someone as having a psychological disorder is making a judgment that some aspect of the person's functioning is *abnormal*. A **psychological diagnosis** *is a descriptive label that identifies and explains mental disorders according to information collected by observation, testing, and analysis.*

Diagnosing Abnormality   The evidence on which a diagnosis is based comes from interpretations of a person's actions. Consider what it means to say someone is "abnormal" or "suffers from a psychological disorder." How do psychologists decide what is abnormal? Is the point at which behavior moves from the normal to the abnormal category always clear? Judgments about abnormality are far from being clear cut; mental disorder is best thought of as a *continuum,* as shown in Figure 13.1. The definition of *abnormality* is not very precise; there are no fail-safe rules for identifying abnormality.

No single definition can summarize a widely accepted meaning of "abnormality." Instead, most clinicians judge a possible abnormality according to the presence of six indicators (Rosenhan & Seligman, 1995).

1. *Distress.* The individual suffers from personal distress or intense anxiety. For example, almost anyone will get nervous before an important test, but some people may feel so overwhelmed with unpleasant emotions that they are unable to concentrate or even show up.
2. *Maladaptiveness.* The person acts in ways that interfere with goals, his or her own well-being, and the goals and needs of society. Someone who drinks so heavily that he cannot hold down a job or drive a car without endangering others is engaging in maladaptive behavior—behavior that fails to adapt well to the normal demands of life.
3. *Irrationality.* One acts or talks in ways that are irrational or incomprehensible to others. A woman who converses with her long-dead sister, whose voice she hears in her head, is behaving irrationally.
4. *Unpredictability.* The individual behaves unpredictably or erratically from one situation to another, as if experiencing a loss of control. A child who suddenly smashes a fragile toy with his fist for no apparent reason is behaving unpredictably.
5. *Unconventionality and Statistical Rarity.* The person behaves in ways that are statistically rare and violate social standards of what is morally acceptable or desirable. However, merely being "unusual" in the population is not a sign of psychological "abnormality." For example, possessing genius-level intelligence may be statistically rare, but it is also considered highly desirable. At the other extreme, extremely low intelligence is both rare and undesirable, so it is often interpreted as "abnormal."
6. *Observer Discomfort.* The person creates discomfort in others by making them feel threatened or distressed in some way. A total stranger who sits down

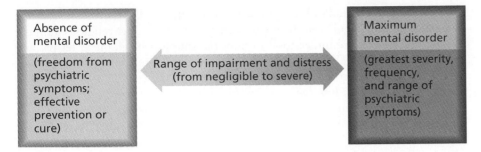

FIGURE 13.1   Mental Disorder Continuum ∎

beside you in a restaurant and begins to question you loudly may make you so uncomfortable that you seek to escape the situation entirely.

Most of these indicators of abnormality are not immediately apparent to all observers; in other words, they involve a large degree of *judgment*. At the end of this chapter we will consider the negative consequences and dangers associated with such judgments.

Is the presence of just one indicator "enough" to demonstrate abnormality? In fact, psychologists are more confident in labeling behavior as "abnormal" when two or more of the six indicators are present and valid. The more extreme and prevalent the indicators are, the more confident psychologists can be about identifying an abnormal condition.

None of these six criteria is a *necessary* condition shared by all cases of abnormality; many diagnoses of abnormality include some but not all of the above list. And not one of these criteria, by itself, is a *sufficient* condition that distinguishes all cases of abnormal behavior from normal variations in behavior. The distinction between normal and abnormal is not so much a difference between two independent types of behaviors as it is a matter of the *degree* to which a person's actions resemble a set of agreed-upon criteria of abnormality. When making judgments of normality, it is important to operate from a *mental health* perspective as well as from a mental illness perspective. As shown in Figure 13.2, one's mental health is not simply either good or bad, but rather can be described as some point on a continuum between optimal (best possible) mental health and minimal (worst) mental health. To be healthy, one must be more than just illness-free—one must be functioning in a way that secures and maintains healthiness beyond present conditions.

Before we consider specific examples of abnormality that are classified as psychological disorders, we will look at some historical views of psychological problems. We will then illustrate how these perspectives have contributed to our current understanding of psychological disorders.

Perspectives on Psychopathology

Throughout history, humans have feared psychological disorders, often associating them with evil. Because of their fear, people have reacted aggressively and decisively to any behaviors they perceive as bizarre or abnormal. Not until very recently have people begun to accept the notion that psychological disorders are a form of illness that is very often treatable.

Evolving Attitudes Toward Mental Illness   Attitudes about the link between mental illness and evil may be as old as human history. Archaeologists have found prehistoric skulls with surgical holes drilled in them. These discoveries might indicate that our ancestors believed such holes would allow the escape of demons that had possessed a loved one.

FIGURE 13.2   Mental Health Continuum ∎

Optimal mental health

Individual, group, and environmental factors work together effectively, ensuring:

- subjective well-being
- optimal development and use of mental abilities
- achievement of goals consistent with justice
- conditions of fundamental equality

Minimal mental health

Individual, group, and environmental factors conflict, producing:

- subjective distress
- impairment or under-development of mental ability
- failure to achieve goals
- destructive behaviors
- entrenchment of inequities

Through the Middle Ages, concepts of mental and physical illness were intertwined and primitively blended with superstition and religious fantasy. Bodily functions were understood in only the simplest mechanical terms, and the complexities of the nervous system were completely undeciphered. For example, the modern term **conversion disorder** *refers to a loss of sensory or motor function (e.g., blindness or paralysis) without a corresponding organic cause.* But *the ancient term for this affliction was* **hysteria** (from the Greek *hustera,* "womb"), because it was thought to afflict only women in whom the uterus—under the devil's control—interfered with healthy body functions (Veith, 1965).

During the Renaissance (about A.D. 1350–1630), intellectual and artistic enlightenment flourished. But before the Enlightenment, a period of greater understanding of science and natural phenomena, people still relied on superstitions and religious images to "explain" mental illness. In early 1692 in the Massachusetts town of Salem Village, several girls and young women began experiencing convulsions, nausea, and weakness. They reported sensations of being pinched, pricked, or bitten. Many became temporarily blind or deaf; others reported visions and sensations of flying through the air. These strange symptoms sparked a frantic search for an explanation. Many people theorized that the symptoms were the work of the devil, who, through the efforts of earthbound witches, had taken over the minds and bodies of the young women. These theories led to a witchcraft panic and to the execution of over 20 men and women believed to be witches. A recent analysis strongly suggests that the "bewitched" Salem women may have been suffering from *ergot* poisoning; ergot, a fungus that grows on rye, is a source of LSD (Caporeal, 1976; Matossian, 1982, 1989).

Until the end of the eighteenth century, the mentally ill in Western societies were perceived as mindless beasts who could be controlled only with chains and physical discipline. They were not cared for in hospitals but were incarcerated with criminals. A society cannot deal with what it cannot understand; people tend to fear what they cannot explain. For this reason the treatment of the mentally ill has always depended on the state of the science of psychology. Modern approaches are a vast improvement over the demonic nightmares and persecutions of past centuries, but we are still a long way from knowing all we need to know.

A painting of the Salem witchcraft trials, Salem, Massachusetts, 1692. Twenty people were executed before the hysteria subsided.

The Medical Model   In the latter part of the eighteenth century, a new perspective about the origins of abnormal behavior emerged. People began to perceive those with psychological problems as *sick* (suffering from illness), rather than as possessed or immoral. A number of reforms were gradually implemented in the facilities for the insane. **Philippe Pinel** (1745–1826) was one of the first clinicians to attempt to develop a classification system for psychological difficulties based on the idea that disorders of thought, mood, and behavior are similar in many ways to the physical, organic symptoms of illness. In Pinel's system, each disorder is seen as having a group of characteristic symptoms that distinguishes it from other disorders and from healthy functioning. Disorders are classified according to the patterns of symptoms, the circumstances of onset, their usual course of development, and their response to treatment. Classification systems, such as Pinel's, are created to help clinicians identify common disorders more easily, and are modeled after the biological classification systems naturalists use.

In 1896, **Emil Kraepelin** (1855–1926), a German psychiatrist, was responsible for creating the first truly comprehensive *classification system* of psychological disorders. Psychiatrists continue to draw from his terminology and perspective when they speak of *mental illness* and *treating* mental *patients* in the hope of *curing* their *diseased* brains. This medical model is based on the perspective that mental illness is caused by deficits in structure or neurobiological functioning. By using a medical model based on physical illness as the model for understanding "mental illness," physicians developed treatments that were greatly improved over earlier approaches. But as we will see in the next chapter, "Psychotherapy," such overreliance on a specific model can lead psychiatrists to a conception of the causes and treatments of mental disorders that is narrowly defined in terms of organic and biological processes and that fails to consider psychological, social, and environmental factors in psychopathology.

Psychological Models   An alternative perspective to the medical approach focuses on the psychological causes and treatment of abnormal behavior. This perspective began to emerge most clearly at the end of the eighteenth century, helped along by the dramatic work of **Franz Anton Mesmer** (1734–1815). Mesmer believed that many disorders, including hysteria, were caused by disruptions in the flow of a mysterious force that he called *animal magnetism*. He unveiled several new techniques to study animal magnetism, including one originally called *mesmerism* that was later termed *hypnotism* because of its use of hypnosis (Darnton, 1968; Pattie, 1994).

Mesmer's animal magnetism theory was discredited by scientists, but his hypnotic techniques were adopted by many researchers, including a prominent French neurologist, **Jean-Martin Charcot** (1825–1893). Charcot found that some of the symptoms of hysteria, such as paralysis of a limb, could be eliminated when a patient was under hypnosis. Hypnosis even had the power to *induce* the symptoms of hysteria in healthy individuals, dramatically illustrating the potential of *psychological factors* to cause problems that were once thought to have an exclusively physical basis.

One of Charcot's students was the young Sigmund Freud, who continued to experiment with hypnosis. Freud used his experiments to elaborate on his own theories of personality and abnormality that influence current theories of the nature and causes of psychopathology today. Eventually Freud developed psychoanalysis as a more effective system for explaining and treating psychological disorders, and abandoned the use of hypnosis to reveal unconscious conflicts.

All psychological models are based on the perspective that there is no known *organic* disorder responsible for the symptoms of mental illness. These

A nineteenth-century painting of neurologist Jean-Martin Charcot (1825–93) demonstrating his use of hypnosis to treat symptoms of hysteria.

models identify learning, reinforcement, motivation, cognitions, cultural factors, family systems, and other psychological processes as contributing to mental disorders.

Psychopathology Today

Understanding why a particular disorder occurs, what its origins are, and how it affects thought and emotional and behavioral processes may lead scientists to new ways of treatment and, ideally, prevention. Approaches to understanding the causal factors in psychopathology can be grouped into two major categories: biological and psychological.

Biological Approaches   Building on the medical model, modern biological approaches assume that psychological disturbances are directly attributable to underlying biological factors, most often linked to the brain or nervous system.

The brain is a complex organ whose interrelated elements are held in delicate balance. Subtle alterations in the brain's tissue or in its chemical messengers—the neurotransmitters—can have significant effects. Genetic factors, brain injury, and infection are a few of the causes of these alterations. Technological advances in brain scanning techniques, such as PET scans, have enabled biologically oriented researchers to discover links between psychological disorders and specific brain abnormalities (Gur & Pearlson, 1993). For example, extreme violence has been linked to brain tumors located in an area of the brain (in the limbic system) associated with aggressive behavior. Biochemical approaches to psychopathology include studies showing how drugs can alter the normal reality of the mind and how drug therapies can alleviate certain symptoms of psychological disorders (Elkin et al., 1989; Kane & Marder, 1993; Papolos & Papolos, 1987; Schatzberg, 1991).

Advances in the field of behavioral genetics have improved researchers' abilities to identify the links between specific genes and the presence of psychological disorders (Joyce, 1989; Kelsoe et al., 1993; Kendler & Diehl, 1993; Rutter et al., 1990). However, despite the promise of these approaches, there are still many unknowns about the connections between biology, genes, and psychopathology.

Psychological Approaches   Psychological approaches focus on the causal role of psychological or social factors in the development of psychopathology. These approaches perceive personal experiences, traumas, conflicts, and environmental factors as the roots of psychological disorders. The three dominant psychological approaches to abnormality are the *psychodynamic, behaviorist,* and *cognitive* models.

Psychodynamic Approaches   The psychodynamic model holds that the causes of psychopathology are forces inside the person. According to Sigmund Freud, who developed this model, these internal causal factors are psychological rather than biological. Freud developed psychoanalytic theory as a rational explanation for apparently irrational and senseless behavior. He believed that many psychological disorders developed when "normal" processes of psychological conflict and defensiveness were taken to abnormal extremes. In the psychodynamic model, early childhood experiences and personal development shape both normal and abnormal behavior in life. (Refer back to our discussion of psychodynamic theories of personality in Chapter 10 for a review of Freudian and post-Freudian concepts.)

According to the psychodynamic perspective, symptoms of psychopathology have their roots in *unconscious conflict* and thoughts. If the unconscious is in conflict and tension-filled, a person will be plagued by anxiety and other disorders. Individuals attempt to avoid the pain caused by conflicting motives and anxiety with *ego defense mechanisms,* such as repression or denial (review Table 10.2 on p. 391). For example, a woman who has been through a humiliating breakup may defend against her grief and anxiety by avoiding the people and places she associates with the lost relationship. However, defenses can become overused, distorting reality or leading to self-defeating behaviors. The woman who spends so much energy avoiding unpleasant associations may find she has fewer and fewer "safe" havens and relationships. When psychic energy is bound up in attempts to defend against the emergence of repression-bound anxiety, little is left for a productive and satisfying life.

A therapist relying on the psychodynamic perspective will pay attention to patterns in the client's past actions and relationships, and will try to identify the unconscious conflicts that lie at the heart of present difficulties. For example, if a woman enters therapy because she is grieving over a lost relationship, a psychoanalyst will encourage her to talk about past relationships and losses in order to unearth insights into unconscious wishes and fears about intimacy. The psychodynamic perspective assumes that insight into the origins of one's problems is essential to making successful adjustments.

Behavioral Approaches   Freudian notions gained ready acceptance among clinical psychologists and psychiatrists. However, you will recall that American research psychology from the 1930s to the early 1970s was dominated by a behavioristic orientation. Those who insisted that only observable responses could be acceptable psychological data had no use for hypothetical psychodynamic processes.

Behavioral theorists argue that abnormal behaviors are acquired in the same fashion as healthy behaviors—through learning and reinforcement. They focus not on internal psychological phenomena or early childhood experiences, but rather on one's *current* behavior and the *current* conditions or reinforcements that sustain it—whether it is adaptive or not. Symptoms of psychological disorders arise because an individual has learned self-defeating or ineffective ways of behaving. By discovering the environmental contingencies that maintain any undesirable, abnormal behavior, an investigator or clinician can then recommend treatment to change those contingencies and extinguish the unwanted behavior (Emmelkamp, 1986). Behaviorists rely on both classical and operant conditioning models to understand the processes that can result in maladaptive behavior.

For example, a behavioral therapist treating a woman grief-stricken over a broken relationship will focus primarily on the immediate problems associated with the woman's bereavement and pain. Is she unable to work because she is depressed or unable to concentrate? Does she dread being alone at night because she expects to feel lonely and abandoned? Behavioral therapy will emphasize identifying problem behaviors, analyzing the contingencies (conditions) that keep those in place, and identifying ways to encourage and reinforce changed behavior. Instead of investigating the past origins of the client's disorder, the behavioral perspective examines the lessons and associations that presently determine her experience.

Cognitive Approaches The cognitive perspective on human nature that has evolved over the last several decades is often used to supplement behavioristic views. The cognitive perspective suggests that we should not expect to discover the origins of psychological disorders in the *objective reality* of stimulus environments, reinforcers, and overt responses. Rather, we must look at how we *perceive* or *think* about ourselves and our relations with other people and our environment. Some of the cognitive variables that can guide (or misguide) adaptive responses are our perceived control over important reinforcers, belief in our own ability to cope with threat, and patterns of attributing causes of behavior to either situational or personal factors (Bandura, 1986).

For example, a cognitive therapist whose client has suffered a painful relationship loss will question the client's assumptions about the experience. Did her partner really "reject" her or were there signs that the relationship was not likely to last? Was the breakup a genuine "catastrophe" or merely a hurtful disappointment that she will ultimately survive? Was he truly "the only one" for her, or is she likely to have other chances for satisfying personal relationships? The woman must examine her own thoughts and perceptions, and question how rational or realistic they are. According to the cognitive perspective, her grief and disorientation will be magnified if she sustains irrational ideas about the breakup. By correcting these beliefs, she can develop more constructive, positive feelings and behaviors.

The cognitive approach views psychological problems as the result of distortions in the reality of a situation or of ourselves, faulty reasoning, or poor problem solving. Whether they help us or harm us, our personal cognitions are our own way of dealing with the complexities and uncertainties of everyday life (Ellis & Grieger, 1986). For example, a woman may be fooling herself by believing that she initiated a recent breakup, but this may be preferable (and easier for her to live with) than the "truth" that it was her partner who rejected her.

Toward an Interactionist View Today researchers increasingly view psychopathology as the product of a complex *interaction* between a number of biological and psychological factors (Cowan, 1988). For example, genetic predispositions may make a person vulnerable to a psychological disorder by affecting neurotransmitter levels or hormone levels, but psychological or social stresses or certain learned behaviors may be required for the disorder to develop fully. Why does one person seem to get over a relationship breakup fairly quickly, while another suffers prolonged grief and distraction? The first survivor may have recovered quickly because the relationship had lasted only a brief time, so both partners had few expectations from the start. Additionally, the first survivor may be genetically equipped to deal better with stress, while the latter may be predisposed to depression no matter what

Within a year of their wedding, actress Julia Roberts and singer Lyle Lovett had separated. Why do some people rebound easily from a relationship breakup, while others suffer prolonged grief?

circumstances trigger its onset. If no single factor or set of factors (such as the environment or one's inherited constitution) "causes" disordered behavior, therapists must develop various combinations of treatments to address the different factors involved.

Classification Systems

Whichever theoretical approach we find most useful, it is essential for a clinician's diagnostic system to be based on observed patterns of disordered behavior, a record that can be consulted in identifying and treating new cases. However, a number of challenges confront the clinician who wishes to catalogue observations in this way. A number of distinctly different approaches exist for explaining psychological disorders. Thus, the diagnosis of a disturbed person often has as much to do with the theoretical orientation of the clinician as it does with the actual symptoms presented (Franklin, 1987). To create greater consistency among clinicians and greater coherence in their diagnostic evaluations, psychologists have developed a system of diagnosis and classification that provides precise descriptions of symptoms to help clinicians decide whether a person's behavior is evidence of a particular disorder.

The Goals of Classification   To be most useful, a diagnostic system should meet three goals: to provide common, concise *language;* to *explain* the probable causes and development of the observed disorder; and to recommend a course of *treatment.* Our discussion will consider how difficult each is to achieve, and the advantages of each.

1. *Common Shorthand Language.* To facilitate understanding among clinicians or researchers working in psychopathology, it is helpful to have a common set of terms with agreed-upon meanings. A single diagnostic category such as *depression* summarizes a large and complex collection of information, including characteristic symptoms and the typical course of a disorder. Clinical practitioners can use such a diagnostic system to communicate more effectively about the people they are helping, and researchers devising new approaches to treatment can build on the work of other researchers using the same language and labels.

2. *Understanding Origins.* Ideally, diagnosis of a specific disorder should suggest the causes of the symptoms. A thoroughly researched classification system permits a clinician to look up diagnoses appropriate for certain symptoms and case histories, and then goes on to suggest typical *etiology* (origins and development) as well as commonly recommended treatments. Unfortunately, because there is substantial disagreement or lack of knowledge about the causes of many psychological disorders, this goal is difficult to meet. The key to providing information about origins and development in a classification system is first to collect ample data from experienced professionals.

3. *Treatment Plans.* A diagnosis should also suggest what types of treatment to consider for particular disorders. Researchers and clinicians have found that certain treatments or therapies work most effectively for specific kinds of psychological disorders. For example, drugs that are quite effective in treating schizophrenia do not help and may even hurt people with depression.

Cataloguing Disorders   In the United States, the most widely accepted classification scheme is one originally developed by the American Psychiatric Association. It is called the *Diagnostic and Statistical Manual of Mental Disorders. The latest revision, the fourth edition of the manual, was published in 1994, and is known by clinicians and researchers as* **DSM-IV** *(*"DSM-four"*).* It classifies, defines, and describes over 200 mental disorders. The

DSM relies on clinicians' and researchers' reports of their observations of patients' self-reports, tests, analyses, and observations of symptoms and syndromes (patterns or collections of symptoms that tend to co-occur). In turn, the classifications are statistically evaluated, checked and rechecked, and published as both a diagnostic tool and catalog for use by psychologists, psychiatrists, and other mental health professionals.

In DSM, each category of mental disorders is described in terms of a behavioral or psychological syndrome that occurs *within the person* and that is associated with either *present distress* (a painful symptom); the risk of *future distress; impairment* in one or more important areas of functioning; or an important *loss of freedom* (American Psychiatric Association, 1994). DSM emphasizes the description of patterns of symptoms and courses of disorders rather than theories about what causes them or strategies for treatment. These purely descriptive terms allow clinicians and researchers from different backgrounds to describe psychiatric problems in a common language, even though there is still much disagreement about how best to explain particular problems.

How DSM Changes   The first version of DSM (DSM-I), which appeared in 1952, listed several dozen mental illnesses. Introduced in 1968, DSM-II revised the diagnostic system to make it more compatible with another popular system, the World Health Organization's International Classification of Diseases (ICD). The fourth edition, DSM-IV, was introduced in the summer of 1994, scheduled for about the same time as the tenth version of the ICD (American Psychiatric Association, 1994).

The diagnostic categories and the methods used to present them have shifted with each edition of DSM, reflecting changing opinions among mental health experts about identifying and distinguishing among different disorders. Changes in DSM also reflect changing perspectives among the public about what constitutes *abnormality*. The revisions for the latest edition reflect the contributions and reports of hundreds of mental health experts, working as advisory panels in specific areas of psychopathology. In each revision, some diagnostic categories are dropped and others are added, reflecting the passing of old ideas and the introduction of validated new perspectives. For example, with the introduction of DSM-III in 1980, the traditional distinctions between *neurotic* and *psychotic* disorders were eliminated. A **neurotic disorder** or **neurosis** *was originally conceived of as a relatively common pattern of subjective distress or self-defeating behavior which did not show signs of brain abnormalities, grossly irrational thinking, or the violation of basic norms.* In short, a "neurotic" was someone who might be unhappy or dissatisfied and in need of coping skills, but he or she was not considered dangerously ill or out of touch with reality. In contrast, a **psychotic disorder** or **psychosis** was thought to differ from neurosis in both the quality and severity of symptoms. A disorder was designated as psychotic if it *deviated significantly from social norms and was accompanied by profound disturbances in rational thinking, general affect, and thought processes.* More recent DSM committees judged the terms "neurotic" and "psychotic" to have become too general in their meaning to be useful, so the official distinction in terminology was dropped. Now the word "neurosis" has largely been supplanted by the term "disorder," although the term "psychotic" is still used to connote a pervasive loss of contact with reality and is applied particularly to descriptions of *schizophrenic* disorders, as we shall discuss below (Carson et al., 1996; Holmes, 1994).

The committee that produced the fourth edition of DSM considered how to make the document more politically sensitive as well as more useful in clinical diagnosis. For example, DSM-IV listings for some disorders now describe how culture or ethnicity can influence the expression of symptoms. The committee received several hundred suggestions for new diagnostic categories, based on patterns clinicians have encountered and tried to diagnose. Some new diagnostic categories reflect the distinct stresses and modes of modern culture ("Revising Psychiatric Diagnoses," 1993):

- Caffeine withdrawal
- Mild cognitive disorder (found among HIV-positive patients)
- Binge eating disorder (overeating without purging)
- Telephone scatalogia (making obscene phone calls)

Is DSM Effective? In order for a diagnostic system to become a shorthand language for communicating, its users must be able to agree reliably on what the criteria and symptoms are for each disorder and what the diagnoses would be in specific cases. Reliability improved substantially with the introduction of the more descriptive and precise DSM-III-R (Klerman, 1986), although it was still far from complete, especially for certain categories of disorders. Improved reliability helps facilitate research efforts to better understand psychopathology and its treatment.

Some practitioners have raised concerns about the *validity* of the DSM. Validity in descriptions and diagnoses of mental disorders is a complex concept. It involves, in part, fulfilling the second and third goals of classification systems: whether this catalog does more than merely list and describe, but also identifies causes and recommends treatments. For example, is it valid to consider disorders with some common features as different *versions* of the *same* disorder—or should they be viewed as completely different disorders? This issue has plagued those who study and treat schizophrenic disorders: Is it "one" mental disease with many different forms, or rather many different disorders (Heinrichs, 1993)? Because of these ongoing questions, DSM is still a "work in progress" rather than "the last word" in psychopathology. Even though it has its critics, DSM has been the most widely used classification system in clinical practice and is typically used in training new clinicians. With its increased emphasis on requiring scientific evidence for diagnoses, the more streamlined, "user-friendly" DSM-IV continues in that tradition.

Check Your Recall

Psychologists classify behavior as abnormal by making a judgment based on observations and analysis. Psychopathology is judged by the degree to which a person's actions resemble a set of indicators including distress, maladaptiveness, irrationality, unpredictability, unconventionality, and observer discomfort. Throughout history, people have tried to explain the origins of psychopathology. Early attitudes and superstitions regarded psychopathology as the product of evil spirits or weak character. By the late eighteenth century, emerging modern perspectives viewed mental illness in terms of medical problems, and ultimately as the result of psychological or bodily disturbances.

Modern biological approaches to mental illness concentrate on structural abnormalities in the brain, biochemical processes, and genetic influences. Among psychological approaches, the psychodynamic model focuses on early childhood experiences, unconscious conflicts, and defenses. The behavioral perspective focuses on overt behavioral reactions and environmental conditions that create and maintain them. In the cognitive model, distortions in an individual's beliefs and perceptions of self and the world are at the heart of psychological disorders. Interactionist approaches combine these psychological and biological views.

A useful system for diagnosing and classifying psychological disorders should meet the goals of providing a common shorthand language, explaining probable causes, and suggesting appropriate treatment plans. The most widely accepted diagnostic and classification system used by psychologists and psychiatrists is DSM-IV. This system emphasizes the description of symptom patterns rather than identifying causes or treatments. Changes in each new edition of DSM reflect the evolving views of experts and nonexperts alike about the nature and meaning of mental illness. While recent editions have improved the reliability of diagnosing psychological disorders, some critics caution that DSM has limited usefulness in making treatment decisions or explaining the causes of psychological disorders.

Major Psychological Disorders

We now turn to a more detailed analysis of several prominent categories of psychological disorders. For each category, we will begin by describing what sufferers experience and how they appear to observers. Then we will consider how the biological and psychological approaches explain the development of these disorders.

We will look closely at six categories of disorders: personality disorders, dissociative disorders, anxiety disorders, depressive disorders, eating disorders, and schizophrenia. It is beyond the scope of this text to examine in detail all the major DSM categories; before we go on, here is a very brief list of some other important types of disorders (see Carson et al., 1996; Holmes, 1994):

- *Sexual disorders* involve problems with sexual inhibition or dysfunction and deviant sexual practices.
- *Substance-use disorders* include both dependence on and abuse of alcohol and drugs, whether technically legal (such as caffeine and nicotine) or illegal (such as cocaine or heroin). (Refer back to Chapter 3 for a discussion of the major categories of psychoactive drugs, their effects, and consequences of their abuse).
- *Somatoform disorders* involve physical (from Greek *soma,* "body") symptoms, such as paralysis or pains in a limb, that arise without a physical cause. (This category includes the symptoms of *conversion disorder,* which used to be called *hysteria*).
- *Disorders usually first diagnosed in infancy, childhood, or adolescence* include mental retardation, communication disorders such as stuttering, and *autism* (a developmental disorder involving a wide range of deficits in perception, language, motor development, reality testing, and social functioning).
- *Dementia and disorders of cognitive function* include **Alzheimer's disease,** *a chronic brain disorder that affects thinking, memory, and personality.* Alzheimer's disease (pronounced *AWLT-symers*) afflicts about 5 percent of Americans over 65 and 20 percent of those over 80 years of age. The causes are not yet understood and there is no known cure. In the advanced stages, Alzheimer's patients may become completely mute and inattentive, forgetting the names of their spouses and children. In the final stages, Alzheimer patients can become incapable of caring for themselves, lose all memory of their identities, and eventually die. Experiencing such cognitive losses and isolation, elderly Alzheimer's patients are, not surprisingly, also at great risk for depression (Devanand et al., 1996).

As you read about the symptoms and experiences that are typical of the various psychological disturbances, you may begin to feel that some of the characteristics apply to you—at least part of the time—or to someone you know. Some of the disorders that we have considered here are not uncommon, so it would be surprising if they sounded completely alien. Many of us have some human frailties that appear on the list of criteria for a particular psycho-

One year after his 83rd birthday in 1994, former president Ronald Reagan announced that he had Alzheimer's disease, a disorder affecting the cognitive functions of thinking, memory, and personality.

logical disorder. Recognizing this familiarity can be a useful way of furthering your understanding of abnormal psychology, but remember that a diagnosis for any disorder depends on a number of criteria and requires the judgment of a trained mental health professional. Please *resist the temptation* to use this new knowledge to diagnose friends and family members as pathological! On the other hand, being sensitive to others' needs for counsel and social support in times of personal trouble is always appropriate.

Personality Disorders

A **personality disorder** *is a long-standing (chronic), inflexible, maladaptive pattern of perceiving, thinking, or behaving.* These patterns can seriously impair an individual's ability to function in social or work settings and can cause significant distress. They are usually recognizable by the time a person reaches adolescence or early adulthood. There are many types of personality disorders (ten types are recognized in DSM-IV). We will discuss two of the better known forms: *narcissistic personality disorder* and *antisocial personality disorder.*

People with a **narcissistic personality disorder** *have a grandiose sense of self-importance, a preoccupation with fantasies of success or power, and a need for constant attention or admiration.* These people often respond inappropriately to criticism or minor defeat, either by acting indifferent to criticism or by overreacting. They have problems in interpersonal relationships; they tend to feel entitled to favors without obligations, exploit others selfishly, and have difficulty recognizing how others feel. For example, an individual with narcissistic personality disorder might express annoyance—but not empathy—when a friend has to cancel a date because of a death in the family.

Antisocial personality disorder *is marked by a long-standing pattern of irresponsible behavior that indicates a lack of conscience and no sense of responsibility to others.* Lying, stealing, and fighting are common behaviors of this disorder. People with antisocial personality disorder often do not experience shame or intense emotion of any kind; they can "keep cool" in situations that would arouse and upset normal people. Violations of social norms begin early in their lives—disrupting class, getting into fights, and running away from home. Their actions are marked by indifference to the rights of others. Individuals who show the most severe criminal patterns of antisocial personality disorder may commit serial murders and other crimes, and are popularly (though not professionally) referred to as "psychopaths" or "sociopaths."

Although sufferers of the antisocial type of personality disorder can be found among street criminals and con artists, they are also well represented among successful politicians and businesspeople who put career, money, and power above everything and everyone. Two to three percent of the population in the United States is believed to have antisocial personality disorder. Men are four times more likely to be so diagnosed than women (Regier et al., 1988, 1993).

Personality disorders as a group are among the least reliably judged of all the psychological disorders and are the most controversial. Psychologists even disagree about whether personality disorders can truly be said to exist, and whether it is possible to diagnose a personality disorder independently of the contexts—the social and cultural factors—in which an individual's behavior is seen to develop.

Dissociative Disorders

A **dissociative disorder** *is a disturbance in the integration of identity, memory, or consciousness.* To be healthy and adaptive, it is important for us to see ourselves as *whole* selves, in control of our own behavior. Psychologists believe that, in dissociated states, individuals escape from their conflicts by giving up

When found in a Florida park in 1980, this woman (dubbed "Jane Doe" by authorities) was emaciated, incoherent, and near death. She was suffering from a rare form of psychogenic amnesia in which she had lost the memory of her name, her past, and even the ability to read and write.

this precious consistency and continuity—in a sense, disowning part of themselves. Not being able to recall details of a traumatic event—amnesia without the presence of neurological damage—is one example of dissociation.

Psychologists have only recently begun to appreciate the degree to which such memory dissociation accompanies instances of sexual and physical childhood abuse (Spiegel & Cardeña, 1991). *The forgetting of important personal experiences caused by psychological factors in the absence of any organic dysfunction is termed* **psychogenic amnesia**. One pattern of psychogenic amnesia is the *fugue* state (pronounced *fyoog*, derived from the French word for "flight"), in which an individual has departed from his or her original home, but has no memory of that home or original identity, or how and why he or she came to be lost. Such was the case of "Jane Doe," a woman who in 1980 was found to be incoherent, suffering the effects of exposure, and near death in a Florida park. She had no memory of her identity, nor any ability to read or write. Drug therapy revealed general information about the kind of past she must have had, but no good clues to her origins. After a nationwide television appeal, Jane Doe and her doctors were flooded with calls from possible relatives, the most promising of which was an Illinois couple, certain she was their daughter. They had not heard from her for over four years, since she had moved from Illinois to Florida. Despite their confidence they had found her, she was never able to remember her past or what really happened to her (Carson et al., 1996).

Dissociative identity disorder (DID), formerly known as multiple personality disorder (MPD), *is a rare dissociative disorder in which two or more distinct personalities exist within the same individual.* At any particular time, one of these personalities—the "host"—is dominant in directing the individual's behavior. Dissociative identity disorder has become a familiar category of disorder because of its portrayal in fact-based books and movies, such as *The Three Faces of Eve* (Thigpen & Cleckley, 1957), *Sybil* (Schreiber, 1973), and *The Flock* (Casey & Wilson, 1991). Nonprofessionals sometimes casually refer to DID as "split personality," and mistakenly confuse it with *schizophrenia*, a disorder in which, as we shall see, personality often is impaired but is not "split" into multiple versions.

In DID, although the original personality is unaware of the others, the others are aware of the host and often of each other. Each of the emerging personalities contrasts in some significant way with the original self; they might be outgoing if the person is shy, tough if the original personality is weak, and sexually assertive if the other is fearful and sexually naive. Each personality has a unique identity, name, behavior pattern, and even characteristic brain-wave activity. In some cases, dozens of different characters emerge to help the person deal with a difficult life situation. The emergence of these alternate personalities, each with its own consciousness, is sudden and typically precipitated by stress.

For better or worse, DID has become a popular plot device in television soap operas and melodramas, in which a character's bizarre behavior changes are "explained" with the DID label. In reality, however, a diagnosis of DID is extremely rare and not easy to validate. Changes in society and social thinking may account for the "popularity" of DID: up to about 25 years ago, only 100 cases were documented worldwide; since then the numbers have gone up dramatically, possibly because more patients are being misdiagnosed with DID or more are feigning the symptoms—or because the trauma and abuse associated with creating the syndrome have increased along with a variety of other societal "sicknesses" (Carson et al., 1996).

Typically, DID victims are women who were severely abused mentally or physically by family members or close others during their childhood. Victims of DID may have been beaten, locked up, or abandoned by those who were

TABLE 13.1	RESPONSES TO INQUIRIES REGARDING ABUSE: COMPARING DISSOCIATIVE IDENTITY DISORDER AND DEPRESSION	
Questionnaire Item	**DID (percent)**	**Major Depression (percent)**
Abuse incidence	98	54
Type(s)		
Physical	82	24
Sexual	86	25
Psychological	86	42
Neglect	54	21
All of above	47	6
Physical and sexual	74	14
	(N = 355)	(N – 235)

supposed to love them—those on whom they were so dependent that they could not fight them, leave them, or even hate them. Instead, they have fled their terror symbolically through dissociation. One questionnaire survey of several hundred clinicians who had treated DID cases (see Table 13.1) found an almost universal incidence among female patients of abuse at a very early age, starting around 3 years old and continuing for more than a decade (Schultz et al., 1989).

Psychologists believe that multiple personalities develop to serve a vital survival function. Individuals in horrifying situations may protect their egos by creating stronger internal characters to help them cope with the ongoing traumatic situation and also to relieve their pain by numbing the dominant personality to the abuse. As a leading researcher in the study of multiple personality disorder, F. W. Putnam (1989) has found that in the typical case there are many different alter egos of different ages and even of both sexes within the mind of the troubled person.

These two paintings by Sybil, a dissociative identity disorder (DID) victim, illustrate the differences between the personalities. The painting on the left was done by Peggy, Sybil's angry, fearful personality. The painting above was done by Mary, a home-loving personality.

Until recently, information on DID had come from single cases treated by one therapist over an extended period. However, newer research being conducted with the collaboration of the National Institute of Mental Health (NIMH) and other institutions is enabling clinicians to get a more complete picture of this remarkable disorder that puts too many actors on stage for any one director to manage (Putnam, 1984). The wise scientist must be skeptical about the validity of any one diagnosis of DID, but even normal functioning and everyday social behavior requires us to wear several masks and play several parts. It is therefore highly likely that, for at least some traumatized individuals, the masks themselves may take control, and one may lose flexibility and awareness of making the transition between roles (Carson et al., 1996; Horevitz, 1994; Spanos et al., 1985).

We might add a note of caution here about what is and is not yet understood about dissociative disorders. There is an ongoing debate in psychology, psychiatry, and the public arena about the validity of the recent increase in cases of DID that are based on adult women's claims to have been abused as children. Some of these women may be led by the suggestive questioning of their therapists, who seek to uncover what they suspect are repressed memories of trauma and molestation. However, such incidents may never have happened—and the therapists' encouragement can become pressure on the client to fabricate memories, as we explored in the opening case to Chapter 7. In some cases, clients are reinforced for generating not only repressed memories but also multiple personalities. The "pop psych" portrayals of such cases—unverified, anecdotal television and print media reports—additionally reinforce new patients' beliefs that such "explanations" are real and socially acceptable. After all, having multiple personalities would explain why the memories, once "recovered," are sometimes imprecise and inconsistent. As horrible as it is for an innocent family member to be accused on the basis of fabricated recollections and identities, the courtroom demands that remembered testimony must stand a tough test of validity and evidence before judge or jury will rule against a defendant. Thus the public shame and ordeal of a trial may actually be the innocent individual's main hope for vindication (Loftus, 1993; Loftus & Ketcham, 1991, 1994; Ofshe & Watters, 1994). Although like any other category of disorders, DID is subject to misdiagnosis, such tragic errors and witch-hunts do not invalidate genuine cases of dissociative identity disorder.

Anxiety Disorders

Everyone experiences anxiety or fear in certain life situations. The feelings of uneasiness that characterize anxiety and fear are often accompanied by physical reactions, such as a sweaty brow or clammy palms, and may include a sense of impending harm. For some people, anxiety interferes with their ability to function effectively or enjoy everyday life. It has been estimated that 15 percent of the general population has, at some time, experienced the symptoms that are characteristic of various anxiety disorders recognized in DSM (Regier et al., 1988). While anxiety plays a key role in each category, the disorders differ in the extent to which anxiety is experienced, the severity of the anxiety, and the situations that trigger the anxiety.

We will review four major categories of anxiety: generalized anxiety disorder, panic disorder, phobic disorder, and obsessive-compulsive disorder. (In Chapter 9 we briefly discussed a fifth kind of anxiety disorder listed in DSM-IV, *posttraumatic stress disorder*).

Generalized Anxiety Disorder   A generalized anxiety disorder *is diagnosed when for at least a six-month period, a person feels anxious or worried most* *of the time, but not specifically threatened.* The anxiety might focus on specific life circumstances, such as unrealistic concerns about finances or the well-being of a loved one, or it just might be a general apprehensiveness about impending harm. The specific symptoms vary from person to person, but the common symptoms include *body tension, physical arousal,* and *vigilance* (hyperattentiveness to events and one's reactions to them). If you ever found yourself unable to relax or get to sleep at night because of worries, you will recognize the form and effects of anxiety.

Pathological anxiety is far more severe than the normal anxiety associated with life's tensions and fears. A pathologically anxious person may continue to function with only a mild impairment of work or social life—controlling where she goes and what she plans, for example, to minimize upsetting experiences. But for the chronically anxious individual, the constant physical and psychological drain takes a toll that may show up as lowered resistance to other normal stressors, and thus a greater susceptibility to common ailments like colds, headaches, and infections.

Panic Disorder   *Sufferers of* **panic disorder** *experience unexpected but severe attacks of anxiety that may last only minutes.* These attacks occur at least several times a month and typically begin with a feeling of intense apprehension, fear, or terror. Accompanying these feelings are physical symptoms of anxiety such as rapid heart rate, dizziness, faintness, or sensations of choking or smothering. As one sufferer described the experience of a panic attack, "It feels, I just get all, like hot through me, and shaky, and my heart just feels like it's pounding and breathing really quick. . . . It feels like I'm going to die or something" (Muskin & Fyer, 1981, p. 81).

Because of the unexpected nature of these "hit and run" attacks, *anticipatory anxiety* often develops as an added complication in panic disorders. The dread of the next attack and of being helpless and suddenly out of control can lead a person to avoid public places yet fear being left alone.

One type of panic disorder that has been much publicized in recent years was once thought to be a type of *phobia* or irrational fear, a notion still reflected in its name. **Agoraphobia** *is an extreme fear of being in public places or open spaces from which escape may be difficult or embarrassing.* The term "agoraphobia" is a literal translation from the ancient Greek for "fear of the marketplace," generalized to include public places and interactions. Individuals with agoraphobia experience anxiety in such places as crowded rooms, malls, buses, and freeways (Magee et al., 1996). They often fear that, if they experience some kind of difficulty outside the home, help might not be available or the situation will be embarrassing to them. These fears deprive individuals of their freedom, and, in extreme cases, agoraphobics become prisoners in their own homes. They cannot hold a job or carry on normal daily activities because their anxieties restrict contact with the outside world.

Phobic Disorders   Fear is a rational reaction to an objectively identified external danger (such as a fire in one's home or being mugged) that may induce a person to flee or to fight back in self-defense. In contrast, *a person with a* **phobic disorder,** *or* **phobia,** *suffers from a persistent and irrational fear of a specific object, activity, or situation that creates a compelling desire to avoid it.* Phobic disorders, like panic disorders, are based in the experience of anxiety, not fear.

Many of us have irrational fears of spiders or snakes—or perhaps multiple-choice tests! We may avoid wildlife settings or seek out reassurance prior to test sessions in an effort to deal with such minor anxieties. Targeted anxieties become full-fledged phobic disorders only when they interfere with our adjustment, cause significant distress, or inhibit necessary action toward goals.

Consider the following example. Calla is afraid of writing her name in public. When placed in a situation where she might be asked to sign her name, Calla is terrified, and she experiences muscle tension, rapid heart rate, and apprehension—the common symptoms of anxiety. Calla's phobia has far-reaching effects on her life. She can't use checks or credit cards to shop or to eat in a restaurant. She can no longer visit the gym she belongs to because she can't register at the fitness center. She can't go to the bank unless all transactions are prepared ahead of time in her home. She can't sign any papers that require approval of a notary public, and she can't vote because she can't sign the voting register.

Phobias are a relatively common psychological problem. Recent studies suggest that 12.5 percent of Americans suffer from some form of phobia at some point in their lives (Regier et al., 1988). Some phobias are oddly specific, such as an irrational fear of a certain type of insect; others are so common, such as fear of public speaking, that they seem almost normal (Stein et al., 1996). Almost any stimulus can come to generate a phobic avoidance reaction (see Table 13.2), although some phobias are much more common than others. The most common phobic disorders are *social phobias,* irrational fears of

TABLE 13.2	THE COMMON PHOBIAS		
	Approximate Percentage of All Phobias	Sex Difference	Typical Age of First Occurrence
Agoraphobias (fear of places of assembly, crowds, open spaces)	10–50	Large majority are women	Early adulthood
Social Phobias (fear of being observed doing something humiliating)	10	Majority are women	Adolescence
The Specific Phobias	5–15	Vast majority are women	Childhood
Animals Cats (allurophobia) Dogs (cynophobia) Insects (insectophobia) Spiders (arachnophobia) Birds (avisophobia) Horses (equinophobia) Snakes (ophidiophobia) Rodents (rodentophobia)			
Inanimate Objects or Situations Dirt (mysophobia) Storms (brontophobia) Heights (acrophobia) Darkness (nyctophobia) Closed spaces (claustrophobia)	20	None	Any age
Illness-Injury (nosophobia) Death (thanatophobia) Cancer (cancerophobia) Venereal disease (venerophobia)	15–25	None	Middle age

normal social situations such as speaking in public or interacting with others (Magee et al., 1996).

A **social phobia** *is a persistent, irrational fear that arises in anticipation of a public situation in which one can be observed by others.* Like Calla, who is afraid of writing her name in public, a person with a social phobia fears that he or she will act in ways that could be embarrassing. The person recognizes that the fear is excessive and unreasonable, yet he is compelled by the fear to avoid situations in which public scrutiny is possible. The fear of choking on food when eating in front of others and the fear of trembling embarrassingly when speaking in public are examples of social phobias. Sometimes the phobia is more general and may include fears about acting foolishly in social situations. It is a much more extreme and debilitating disorder than what is sometimes referred to as *chronic shyness.*

Obsessive-Compulsive Disorders   Because fear and anxiety are similar, it seems obvious that phobias are a form of anxiety disorder. Less obvious are anxiety-based patterns of thought and behavior that seem driven but not fearful—in fact, driven by anxiety. For example, just last year, 17-year-old Jim seemed to be a normal adolescent with many talents and interests. Then, almost overnight, he was transformed into a lonely outsider, excluded from social life by his psychological disabilities. Specifically, he developed an obsession with washing. Haunted by the notion that he was dirty—in spite of what his senses told him—Jim began to spend more and more of his time cleansing himself of imaginary dirt. At first his ritual ablutions were confined to weekends and evenings, but soon they began to consume all his time, forcing him to drop out of school (Rapoport, 1989).

Jim is suffering from a condition known as **obsessive-compulsive disorder,** *a mental disorder characterized by patterns of obsessive thoughts and compulsive behaviors.* Obsessive-compulsive disorder is estimated to affect 2.5 percent of Americans at some point during their lives (Regier et al., 1988). *Obsessions* are thoughts, images, or impulses that recur or persist despite a person's efforts to suppress them. Obsessions are experienced as an unwanted invasion of consciousness, seem to be senseless or repugnant, and are unacceptable to the person experiencing them. Frequently, the individual avoids the situations that relate to the content of the obsessions. For example, a person with an obsessive fear of germs may avoid using bathrooms outside his or her home or refuse to shake hands with strangers. As is the case with Jim, behavior driven by obsessive thinking can increasingly interfere with other aspects of one's life.

You probably have had some sort of mild obsessional experience, such as petty worries ("Did I remember to lock the door?" or "Did I forget to turn off the oven?") or the persistence of a haunting melody that kept running through your mind. The thoughts of obsessive-compulsive people are much more compelling, cause much more distress, and may interfere with the social or role functioning of the affected individuals.

Compulsions are repetitive, purposeful acts performed according to certain rules or in a ritualized manner in response to an obsession. Compulsive behavior is intended to reduce or prevent the discomfort associated with some dreaded situation, but it is either unreasonable or clearly excessive. Typical compulsions include irresistible urges to clean, to check that lights or appliances have been turned off, and to count objects or possessions. People with obsessive-compulsive disorder initially resist carrying out their compulsions. When they are calm, they view the compulsion as senseless. When their anxiety rises, however, the power of the compulsive behavior ritual to relieve tension seems irresistible—and the action must be performed. Part of the pain experienced by people with this problem is that they are frustrated by the irrationality of their obsessions but cannot eliminate them.

Causes of Anxiety Disorders   Each of the four approaches that we have outlined—psychodynamic, behavioral, cognitive, and biological—emphasizes different factors. Let's analyze how each adds something unique to our understanding of anxiety disorders.

Psychodynamic Explanations   The psychodynamic model begins with the assumption that the symptoms of anxiety disorders and obsessions and compulsions come from underlying psychic conflicts or fears. The symptoms are attempts to protect the individual from psychological pain. In anxiety disorders, intense pain attacks and phobias are the result of unconscious conflicts bursting into consciousness. The unconscious conflicts are seen as having their roots in early childhood experiences.

For example, perhaps a child is punished by being isolated in a small room or closet until she agrees to behave. In her later life, enclosed spaces remind her of her early shame and guilt, and she avoids closets and phone booths to escape this anxiety. Instead of developing healthy self-esteem and overcoming her discomfort over her childhood experiences, she takes the unconscious "short cut" of avoiding all cramped spaces. Unfortunately, this *claustrophobic* behavior—attaching an irrational fear to enclosed spaces—increasingly intrudes on her ability to lead a normal life. Ironically, her phobic efforts to avoid remembering childhood anxiety seem to guarantee that she will be haunted by reminders.

In obsessive-compulsive disorders, the obsessive pattern is an attempt to displace anxiety created by a related but far more feared desire or conflict. By substituting an obsession that symbolically captures the forbidden impulse, a person gains some relief. For example, obsessive fears of dirt may have their roots in conflict about having "dirty" (sexual) thoughts. Compulsive performance of a minor ritualistic task also allows the individual to avoid the issue that creates unconscious conflict, or the task may seem intended to undo feelings of guilt over real or imagined sins.

Behavioral Explanations   Behavioral explanations of anxiety focus on how symptoms of anxiety disorders are reinforced or conditioned. A previously neutral object or situation becomes a stimulus for a phobia by being paired with a frightening experience. For example, a woman calls home while away on her first overnight camping trip only to receive the painful news that a loved one has suddenly died. Now she may develop a phobia of camping or visiting wilderness sites. After this experience, whenever she approaches a campground or even discusses going on wilderness excursions with friends she may experience a wave of fear and dread that cannot be relieved. By avoiding the phobic situation—deciding she does not like camping, or parks or scenic routes—the individual reinforces the phobia with the reward of feeling relief.

The essence of the behavioral approach is that many abnormal patterns are *learned*. But why and how would an individual "learn" to experience something as crippling as a social phobia, for example? What could possibly be rewarding about such behavior, or worth imitating? One answer might lie in considering how social phobias are extreme and disordered versions of more familiar *normal* patterns in personality, such as shyness. There are good reasons why many people might *learn* social phobias. Is society making us shy? Let us examine how pervasive social forces might actually "teach" individuals to develop unhappy and unhealthy patterns of behavior.

Shyness *is not a disorder but rather a normal, if often distressing, pattern of avoiding or withdrawing from social contact.* Shy behavior often resembles some types of social phobias, as afflicted individuals seek to limit or escape from social interactions; yet they suffer the consequences of missing out on

In the Alfred Hitchcock film, *Vertigo,* actor James Stewart clings to the side of a building as he struggles to combat his sensation of rotating in space. His vertigo is caused by his anxiety disorder, a phobia of heights.

opportunities for companionship, shared activity, and intimacy. Where does such a costly habit begin?

As we reviewed in Chapter 4, a shy pattern reflects one of three basic temperaments that have been observed among infants and traced through adult life (Kagan et al., 1994; Kagan et al., 1988). But there is also evidence that shyness and other forms of social anxiety are *learned* responses, so that even those who are not "born shy" can acquire shy behavior patterns. Several social forces and societal changes in recent decades have reduced people's experience of daily, casual, face-to-face interaction. Adults are less likely to engage in such conversations, and children are less likely to learn interaction skills either first-hand or by observation. Consider five such social forces and their consequences for social contact (National Public Radio, 1995b; Zimbardo, 1995):

- *Computer technology and the "information superhighway"* make it possible for people to engage in faster and more numerous exchanges with people they never actually meet, see, or touch. Faxes and electronic mail enable us to focus on others' words without the experience of their facial expressions, tone of voice, or nonverbal gestures.
- *Automation* in the workplace and in human services replaces people with more efficient, but nonhuman, computer chips. We conduct transactions with ATMs (automatic teller machines) instead of human bank tellers, and we fill our gas tanks by sliding credit cards into automated gas pumps without having to speak to a clerk or mechanic.
- *The perception of widespread, uncontrolled crime* has frightened citizens into hiding indoors. Fearful for their children's safety, parents either restrict their outdoor play or supervise them closely. Turning to video games instead, children are lulled into passivity by television and may even come to regard their computers as their "best friends."
- *Changes in family structure* such as divorce, single parenting, and households where both parents work outside the home have led many children to become "prematurely mature." Because they see less interaction among their parents or other adults, they end up with no real-life models for their own social behavior, and may rely too much on stereotyped media imagery.
- *Perceptions of a culture-wide "time crunch"* lead individuals to feel busier and more pressured than ever—an irony since we have more time-saving options than any previous generation. When we make and take less time for hobbies, social groups, leisure, and household chores, we lose valuable opportunities for unique interactions with family and friends. We also develop a prejudice against such socializing as time-wasting and unproductive, so we continue to minimize its value in our lives.

This confluence of social forces leaves many people alienated and lonely—but unskilled in knowing how to correct anxiety about dealing with social situations. What was once, and still should be, natural—the ability to interact with others—instead feels artificial and inadequate. No longer a source of pleasure, the very prospect of conversing with someone can be a source of tension or distress.

More and more people seem to be responding to their social discomfort with shyness: In the last ten years, the number of Americans who describe themselves as shy has increased from 40 percent in earlier decades to almost 50 percent (Carducci & Zimbardo, 1995). The conveniences of high technology and the challenges of living in a complex society have *taught* people a particular type of social phobia: a learned fear of people. If you extend this analysis, you can easily see how difficult childhood experiences might teach a few individuals to develop irrational fears—phobias—about social interactions or other once-normal life challenges.

The numbers say that one or two people in five describe themselves as shy. ASK YOURSELF:

- Are you shy?
- If you find yourself withdrawing from social contact and hiding from opportunities to meet others, why might you have learned such a pattern?
- If it is basically unrewarding, how can you "retrain" yourself to take small steps toward better and more frequent interaction with other people?
- If it is your friend or partner who is shy and wants to change, what can you do to counteract the lessons that have shaped that behavior?

By taking some reasonable risks, we can learn to break out of our societal stupor, extend ourselves to others, and make our own lives that much richer.

Cognitive Explanations   Cognitive perspectives on anxiety concentrate on the perceptual processes or attitudes that may distort a person's estimation of the danger that he or she is facing. Faulty thinking processes, such as a tendency to *catastrophize* (to focus selectively on the worst possible outcomes in a situation) are at the heart of anxiety disorders. In the case of panic attacks, for example, a person may attribute undue significance to minor distress, such as shortness of breath after some physical exertion. A vicious cycle is initiated when a person mistakenly interprets the distress as a sign of impending disaster (like a heart attack), leading to increased anxiety and aggravated physical sensations (Beck & Emery, 1985).

Biological Explanations   Various investigators have suggested that anxiety disorders have biological origins. Certain phobias seem to be more common than others. For example, a fear of spiders or heights is more common than a fear of electricity, possibly because the former stimuli (spiders or heights) represent ancient threats from our evolutionary past. Perhaps humans are born with a predisposition to fear whatever is related to sources of serious danger in our distant past. This *preparedness hypothesis* suggests that we carry around an evolutionary tendency to respond quickly and "thoughtlessly" to stimuli our ancestors once feared (Seligman, 1971).

The fact that certain drugs can relieve and others can produce symptoms of anxiety offers evidence of a biological role in anxiety disorders. Studies also suggest that abnormalities in sites within the brain stem might be linked to panic attacks. Currently, work is under way to investigate how these abnormalities may influence obsessive-compulsive symptoms.

Each of the major approaches to anxiety disorders may explain part of the puzzle, but continued research on each approach is needed to further our understanding of the most important factors.

Affective Disorders

In an **affective disorder** *the primary symptoms involve disturbances of mood and emotion.* Everyone experiences occasional unpleasant or extreme emotional reactions—emotional reactions are a normal part of our ability to interpret and adapt to our world. However, when an individual's moods are not tied to experience, or when one cannot control the severity or shifting of his or her emotions, affect is no longer adaptive and may cause distress and maladjustment. The three best-known affective disorders are *manic episodes, bipolar disorders,* and *unipolar depression.*

Manic Episodes   A **manic episode** *is a period of mania, during which an individual feels and acts unusually elated and expansive.* Sometimes the individual's predominant mood is irritability rather than elation, especially if the person feels thwarted in some way. Other symptoms, such as inability to concentrate or impulsive behavior, often accompany these highly charged mood states, which typically last from a few days to months.

During a manic episode, a person often experiences an inflated sense of self-esteem or an unrealistic belief that he or she possesses special abilities or powers. The person may feel a dramatically decreased need to sleep and may engage excessively in work or in social or other pleasurable activities. The individual may speak faster, louder, or more often than usual and his or her mind may be racing with thoughts. Caught up in this manic mood, the person shows unwarranted optimism, takes unnecessary risks, promises anything, and may give away everything. Ironically, the manic episode may set in place circumstances that are increasingly difficult to rationalize or accept. To continue to live in the fantasy world he has constructed, the manic person must withdraw further and further from real events, real people, and personal responsibility.

Bipolar Disorder   It is not unusual for people in manic episodes to spend their life savings on extravagant purchases and to engage promiscuously in a number of sexual liaisons or other potentially high-risk actions. When the mania begins to diminish, they are left trying to deal with the damage and predicaments they have created during their frenetic period. Those who have manic episodes will almost always also experience periods of severe depression. This condition is called **bipolar disorder,** or *manic-depressive disorder, to signify the experience of both types of mood disturbance—the two "poles" or extremes of emotion.*

The duration and frequency of the mood disturbances in bipolar disorder vary from person to person. Some people experience long periods of normal functioning punctuated by occasional, brief manic or depressive episodes. A small percentage of unfortunate individuals go right from manic episodes to clinical depression and back again in continuous, unending cycles that are devastating to them, their families, their friends, and their coworkers.

Unipolar Depression   Depression has been characterized as the "common cold of psychopathology" because it occurs so frequently and almost everyone has experienced elements of the full-scale disorder at some time in life. We have all, at one time or another, experienced grief after the loss of a loved one or felt sad or upset when we failed to achieve a desired goal. Are you depressed? Before going on, consider how you would answer the questions in the Assess Yourself box.

Assess Yourself

Are You Depressed?

Most people think that "depression" is always and mainly marked by sadness and its usual emotional expressions: weeping, whining, and frowning. But depression affects other aspects of thought and behavior, as well. Answer yes or no to each of the following questions, adapted from DSM-IV:

1. Do you feel deeply depressed, sad, or hopeless most of the day?

2. Do you feel you have lost interest in most or all activities?

3. Have you experienced any major change in appetite or body weight, though not from dieting?

4. Have you experienced a significant change in your sleeping patterns?

5. Do you feel more restless than usual—or more sluggish than usual?

6. Do you feel more fatigued than you ought to?

7. Do you feel persistently hopeless or inappropriately guilty?

8. Have you been finding it increasingly difficult to think or concentrate?

9. Do you have recurrent thoughts of death or suicide?

Your answers to these items do not constitute any proof that you are or are not depressed. Recall that self-report is always subject to some bias—we prefer to think of and present ourselves as healthy and accomplished. An authentic diagnosis by a mental health professional would take into account not only your self-descriptions but also observable behaviors and performance. Further, there is no "magic number" of items you must answer "yes" to in order to qualify as depressed. It is the *pattern* of change, and the *quality* of your life, experience, and behavior that determine whether or not you are depressed.

Unipolar depression *is an affective disorder involving intense, extended depression without interruption by manic periods.* Sad feelings are only one symptom of unipolar depression, also referred to as *clinical depression* (see Table 13.3). In contrast with victims of bipolar depression, those who suffer from unipolar depression do not also experience manic highs. Novelist William Styron (1990) writes movingly about his own experience with severe depression. The pain he endured convinced him that clinical depression is much more than a bad mood—is better characterized as "a daily presence, blowing over me in cold gusts" and "a veritable howling tempest in the brain" that can begin with a "gray drizzle of horror" and result in death.

Individuals diagnosed with unipolar depression differ in terms of the severity and duration of their depressive symptoms. While many individuals struggle with clinical depression for only several weeks at one point in their lives, others experience depression episodically or chronically for many years.

TABLE 13.3	CHARACTERISTICS OF CLINICAL DEPRESSION
Characteristic	**Example**
Dysphoric mood	Sad, blue, hopeless; loss of interest or pleasure in almost all usual activities
Appetite	Poor appetite; significant weight loss
Sleep	Insomnia or hypersomnia (sleeping too much)
Motor activity	Markedly slowed down (motor retardation) or agitated
Guilt	Feelings of worthlessness, self-reproach
Concentration	Diminished ability to think or concentrate; forgetfulness
Suicide	Recurrent thoughts of death; suicidal ideas or attempts

The New Yorker by Bruce Eric Kaplan, August 14, 1995

"Wait! Come back! I was just kidding about wanting to be happy."

It is estimated that about 20 percent of females and 10 percent of males suffer a major unipolar depression at some time in their lives. Bipolar disorder is much rarer, occurring in about 1 percent of adults and distributed equally between males and females.

Unipolar and bipolar disorders take an enormous toll on those afflicted, their families, and society. In the United States, depression accounts for the majority of all mental hospital admissions, but it is still believed to be under-diagnosed and undertreated (Bielski & Friedel, 1977; Lichtenstein, 1980; Robins et al., 1991). For example, according to a 1983 NIMH survey, 80 percent of those suffering from clinical depression never receive treatment.

Causes of Affective Disorders   Because it is more prevalent, unipolar depression has been studied more extensively than bipolar depression. We will look at it from the cognitive, psychodynamic, behavioral, and biological approaches.

Psychodynamic Explanations   In the psychodynamic approach, uncon-scious conflicts and hostile feelings that originate in early childhood play key roles in the development of depression. Freud was struck by the degree of self-criticism and guilt that depressed people displayed. He believed that the source of this self-reproach was anger, originally directed at someone else, that had been turned inward against the self. Losses, real or symbolic, in adulthood trigger hostile feelings that were originally experienced in childhood. The anger that is reactivated by a later loss is now directed toward the person's own ego, creating the self-reproach and guilt that characterize depression.

Behavioral Explanations   Rather than searching for the roots of depres-sion in past relationships or for the unconscious meaning of a recent experi-ence of loss, one behavioral approach focuses on the effects of the amount of positive reinforcement and punishment a person receives (Lewinsohn, 1975). In this view, depressed feelings result from a lack of sufficient positive rein-forcement and from many punishments in the environment following a loss or other major life change. For example, after she and her husband separate, a young woman may spend less time in social activities because she feels awkward about running into friends who will be curious or perhaps accusatory about the breakup. By withdrawing from others, she also misses out on the pleasures of social life, so she begins to feel sad and sorry for herself, and isolates herself even further. Old friends who initially offered support and company grow tired of her self-pitying and make themselves less available to her—so that she becomes even lonelier and more depressed. She may feel that she has only two choices: an unhappy relationship, or unbearable loneliness—both the emotional loneliness of lacking an intimate partner and the social loneliness of being a misfit in a couple-oriented society (Weiss, 1975).

A similar cycle of reduced reinforcement can be set in motion because a mood-disordered person *lacks the skills* to obtain social reinforcements—as, for example, when a shy man who has not learned effective ways of making conversation with new acquaintances relocates to a *new environment* with a different, as-yet-unknown social network. Research confirms that depressed people give themselves fewer rewards and more punishment than others (Nelson & Craighead, 1977; Rehm, 1977).

Cognitive Explanations   Two theories are at the center of the cognitive approach to unipolar depression. One theory suggests that *negative cognitive sets* lead people to take a negative view of bad events in their lives for which they feel responsible. According to **Aaron Beck,** a leading researcher on depression, depressed people seem to have three types of negative cognitions. Beck calls these three the "cognitive triad" of depression: negative views of *themselves,* negative views of ongoing *experiences,* and negative views of the *future* (Beck, 1983; 1985; 1988). This pattern of negative thinking clouds all experiences and produces the other characteristic signs of depression. An individual who always anticipates a negative outcome is not likely to be motivated to pursue any goal, leading to the *paralysis of will* that is prominent in depression.

Though related, a somewhat different view of the power of explanatory style is supported by the *learned-helplessness model* of depression. In this view, depression arises from the belief that one has little or no personal control over significant life events. In the learned helplessness view, individuals learn that they cannot control future outcomes that are important to them. This conclusion creates feelings of helplessness that lead to depression (Abramson et al., 1978; Peterson & Seligman, 1984; Seligman, 1975). The learned helplessness theory suggests that individuals who attribute failure to causes that are *internal, stable* (unchangeable), and *global* are most vulnerable to depression. A study of college students supports the notion that depressed people have a negative type of attribution style. Depressed students attributed failure on an achievement test to an internal, stable factor—their lack of ability—while attributing successes to luck. In comparison, on an achievement test, nondepressed students took more credit for successes and less blame for failures than they were due, blaming failures on an external, unstable (changeable) factor—bad luck (Barthe & Hammen, 1981). Research further confirms that students who begin their college careers using internal-stable-global explanations for bad experiences such as poor test performance later earn lower grade point averages than their less negative-thinking classmates (Peterson & Barrett, 1987). The good news about the cognitive approach, however, is that thinking styles are learned and modifiable; if you work on changing the way you *think,* perhaps blaming yourself less and focusing more on constructive plans for doing better, you can ultimately change your feelings and your performance.

Biological Explanations   The ability of certain drugs such as lithium (a salt compound) to relieve the symptoms of depression supports a biological view of unipolar depression. Reduced levels of two chemical messengers in the brain, called serotonin and norepinephrine, have been linked with depression. Drugs that are known to increase the levels of these neurotransmitters are commonly used to treat depression. However, the exact biochemical mechanisms of depression have not yet been discovered.

While our overall understanding of the cause of bipolar disorder remains similarly limited, there is growing evidence that it is influenced by genetic factors. Because family members usually share the same environment, similarities among family members do not prove that the cause of a psychological disorder is hereditary. To separate the influence of heredity from environmental or learned components in psychopathology, researchers study twins and adopted children.

Studies of identical twins (twins who have the same genetic material) show that when one twin is afflicted by bipolar disorder, there is an 80 percent chance that the second twin also will have the disorder. Studies of adopted children with bipolar disorder show a higher incidence of the same disorder among the biological parents than among the adoptive parents. More direct evidence of this genetic role seemed to come from a 1987 study that linked bipolar disorder to a specific gene in a unique population. In this study, the pattern of transmission of bipolar disorder was traced among the Amish community in Pennsylvania (Egeland et al., 1987). Researchers isolated a piece of DNA that was present in all affected members of one extended Amish family who experienced bipolar disorder. Localized at the tip of chromosome 11, the defective gene was passed on to children half of the time, and of those who received it, 80 percent had experienced at least one manic episode in their lives.

This result was hailed as a real breakthrough—until the predictions made by extending this genetic analysis to other Amish relatives failed to be supported. When a team of independent researchers checked out the procedures, they were forced to declare there was no convincing proof (Kelsoe et al., 1989). Either the gene for manic depression is not on chromosome 11, or the Amish have two such genes, only one of which may be in that chromosome location (Barinaga, 1989). Here you have another demonstration of the importance of *independently replicating* research findings in scientific disciplines such as psychology. A single surprising result may seem newsworthy, but only with repeated studies can scientists be confident that they have identified not a "fluke" (an unusual, unrepresentative finding) but a genuine trend in the data.

The biological approach to understanding one type of psychological disorder has shed new light on an unusual form of depression. Some people regularly become depressed during the winter months; this is especially apparent for people living in the long Scandinavian winters (see Figure 13.3). This

FIGURE 13.3 Seasonal Affective Disorder ■ People who suffer from seasonal affective disorder experience symptoms of depression during seasons with shortened periods of sunlight. The figure displays a strong inverse relationship between the incidence of depression (part A) and the duration of sunlight (part B).

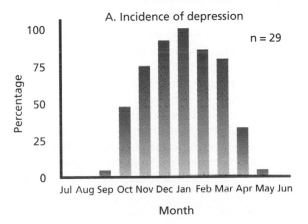
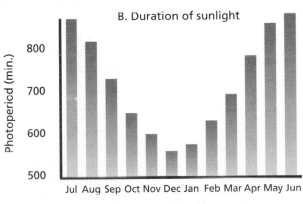

disturbance in mood has been appropriately named *seasonal affective disorder (SAD)*. An internal body rhythm involving the hormone melatonin, which is secreted by the pineal gland into the blood, has been linked to SAD. In most species, including humans, the level of melatonin rises after dusk and falls at or before dawn. Melatonin is implicated in sleep processes as well as circadian (24-hour) rhythms that set the body's biological clock. While it is not clear that disrupted melatonin cycles *cause* the depressive symptoms of SAD, it does appear that a biological intervention that "resets" the abnormal circadian rhythm is an effective treatment (Lewy et al., 1987).

Sex Differences in Depression   Psychologists have been challenged to explain the finding that women are twice as likely to experience unipolar depression as men (Boyd & Weissman, 1981). According to **Susan Nolen-Hoeksema** (1987, 1990), the response styles of men and women once they begin to experience negative moods may account for the difference. In this view, when women experience sadness, they tend to think about the possible causes and implications of their feelings. In contrast, men attempt to distract themselves from depressed feelings, either by focusing on something else or by engaging in a physical activity that will take their minds off their current mood state. This model suggests that the more *ruminative* response of women—characterized by a tendency to obsessively focus on problems—increases women's vulnerability to depression. From a cognitive approach, paying attention to one's negative moods can increase thoughts of negative events, which eventually increases the quantity and/or intensity of negative feelings.

The response styles of both men and women can be seen as a product of socialization, a lifelong process of learning what society expects of us (Nolen-Hoeksema & Girgus, 1994). In the United States and many other cultures, the female schema ("femininity") includes being passive, paying attention to feelings, and experiencing emotions fully as well as sharing them with others. In contrast, the male schema ("masculinity") is focused on being tough, physical, and nonemotional and on not displaying signs of weakness by talking about one's moods—bad or otherwise.

When a task force of the American Psychological Association reviewed research on the origins of sex differences in rates of unipolar depression (McGrath et al., 1990), they concluded that women's higher risk for depression can be understood as the product of an interaction among a number of psychological, social, economic, and biological factors. Many of these factors relate to the experience of being female in many cultures, such as a greater likelihood that women will experience physical or sexual abuse, that they will live in poverty, and that they will be the primary caregivers for children and elderly parents.

Another issue that women frequently face and that can contribute to depression is the difference between their personal goals and limited opportunities for women in society. Women may prepare themselves for important careers in the business world, for example, but they can become frustrated if they encounter the "glass ceiling"—invisible but insuperable prejudices and policies that keep them from rising to positions of greater power and authority. Finally, because the feminine gender role—the learned behavior pattern considered appropriate for women—emphasizes relationships with others rather than personal independence or achievement, women may be at greater risk than men for burnout. (Review our discussion of burnout in Chapter 9.) Thus the causes of depression may be a complex combination of factors; there are multiple paths that might lead from normal affective states to unipolar depression.

The Tragedy of Depression   Psychologists give great attention to depression not only because depression itself is a horribly painful experience, but also because it represents a risk of suicide. As we consider in Focus on Application: Understanding and Preventing Suicide, the connection between this mood disorder and the risk for suicide gives us a window into this otherwise inscrutable tragedy. The more we can learn about depression and all affective disorders, the better we will be able to help ourselves and those we love.

Eating Disorders

When you think of examples of abnormal behavior, it may be easiest to imagine self-defeating patterns that are somehow beyond the individual's control or awareness—overwhelming anxiety that terrifies a person and keeps her from going out, or paralyzing depression that cannot be explained. Surely no one would willingly take on such difficult or uncomfortable behavior if it could be helped. Less easy to understand are disorders that seem to involve deliberate acts of self-destruction. For example, since eating is necessary to survival, and good food provides satisfaction and pleasure, why do some people willingly starve themselves?

This is the riddle of **eating disorders,** *patterns of abnormal behavior in which a person starves herself, prevents her body from digesting food, or combines starvation with bingeing and purging.* The deadly result of such unnatural habits is dangerous weight loss and a severely disordered metabolism. Eating disorders are classified in DSM-IV as among those that develop and are diagnosed during childhood and adolescence rather than later adulthood. Like drug addiction, an eating disorder seems to "take over" the individual's body, so that she cannot resume normal eating behavior without great difficulty. For example, an eating-disordered individual may feel "full" after eating only a bite or two, or may spontaneously vomit after a meal, thus risking malnourishment and sickness. Eating disorders are most prevalent in cultures in which hunger is not a widespread problem. These disorders are especially likely to develop among middle-class and upper-middle-class young women (which is why we tend to use feminine pronouns to describe a typical case). Psychological research has brought to light new understanding of the causes, associations, and effective treatments of eating disorders. Here we examine the two best-known eating disorders: *anorexia nervosa* and *bulimia.* Both afflict many high school and college women—especially those who live together in residence halls.

Anorexia Nervosa   It is normal behavior to eat when hungry, as we reviewed in Chapter 8, but there are times when people refrain from eating even when they want to eat, such as when they are dieting or fasting for health or religious reasons. The general condition of *anorexia* (persistent lack of appetite) may develop as a consequence of certain physical diseases or conditions, such as shock, nausea, or allergic reactions. However, *when loss of appetite that endangers an individual's health stems from emotional or psychological reasons rather than from these organic causes, the syndrome is called* **anorexia nervosa** ("nervous anorexia"). A person suffering from anorexia nervosa may act as though she is unconcerned with her condition, although she is visibly undernourished and emaciated. In contrast, a familiar problem for normal dieters is their desire for food and their exaggerated awareness of their calorie intake.

What causes anorexia nervosa? Most anorexics are young white females from middle-class homes. They have backgrounds of good behavior and academic success, but they "starve" themselves to become acceptably thin and

On July 20, 1993, Vincent W. Foster, Jr.—White House deputy counsel and lifelong friend of President Bill Clinton—was found dead of a self-inflicted gunshot wound in a park outside Washington, D.C. Foster, 48, had seemed content and successful, and associates were unable to explain his suicide. Later a note was found in Foster's handwriting, confessing "mistakes," and expressing pain at being victimized by political attacks and media criticism. "I was not meant for the job or the spotlight of public life in Washington. Here, ruining people is considered sport."

FOCUS on Application

Understanding and Preventing Suicide

"The will to survive and succeed had been crushed and defeated. . . . There comes a time when all things cease to shine, when the rays of hope are lost" (Shneidman, 1987, p. 57). This sad statement by a young suicidal man reflects the most extreme consequence of any psychological disorder—taking one's own life. While most depressed people do not commit suicide, most suicides are attempted by those who are suffering from depression (Shneidman, 1985). Depressed people commit suicide at a rate 25 times higher than nondepressed people in comparison groups (Flood & Seager, 1968). In the general population, the number of suicidal deaths is estimated to run as high as 100,000 per year, with attempted suicides estimated to reach up to half a million yearly in the United States alone. Based on data compiled by the National Center for Health Statistics (1990), the following patterns hold for suicide:

■ More than 200 people will commit suicide today. Of these, most (almost 80 percent) will be male, white, and adult (25 to 65 years of age).

■ Suicide is the eighth leading cause of death in the United States, the third among the young, and the second among college students.

■ On average, a suicide is committed every 17 minutes.

■ Five million living Americans have attempted to kill themselves.

■ For every completed suicide, there are 8 to 20 suicide attempts.

The perceived quality of one's life figures importantly in the decision to take one's life. Suicide is most often committed by persons who are unemployed, living alone, in poor health, and divorced. Feeling hopeless about the future can also lead a depressed individual to choose suicide as "a way out." Women attempt suicide about three times more often than men do; attempts by men, however, are more successful. Men more often use guns, while women tend to use less lethal means, such as sleeping pills (Perlin, 1975; Rosenhan & Seligman, 1995).

A most alarming social problem in recent decades is the rise of youth suicide.

Every 9 minutes a teenager attempts suicide; and every 90 minutes a teenager succeeds. In one week, 1000 teenagers will try suicide, and 125 will succeed in killing themselves. In the last two decades, the suicide rate among American teenagers has jumped by 300 percent (Coleman, 1987).

With so much of life and so many options ahead of them, why would young people even consider suicide? Among young men, most suicides are by those who abuse drugs and are viewed as aggressive and unruly. Next most at risk are young men who are hard-driving perfectionists but who are socially inhibited and anxious about personal and school problems. Among females, depression ranks as the primary predictor of youth suicide (Berman & Jobes, 1991). A survey of students who reported past suicidal thoughts or intentions revealed that while some cited specific fears or issues (for example, grades, parents, or money), the majority blamed negative mood (hopelessness, depression) or interpersonal problems (loneliness) (Westerfeld & Fuhr, 1987). Because adolescence is a time of great pressure to express a social and sexual identity that conforms with the norms of one's peers, it is not surprising that young people with a gay or lesbian orientation are at some risk for despair and suicide (D'Augelli, 1993).

Suicide is an extreme reaction to acute stressors; it is especially likely when adolescents feel unable to cry out to others for help. Several precipitating factors can trigger suicidal actions, including, especially, experiences that trigger feelings of rejection, shame, or guilt: going through the breakup of a close relationship; being assaulted or raped; or being arrested for the first time. Youth suicide is not an impulsive act, but typically occurs as the final stage of a period of inner turmoil and outer distress.

The majority of young suicide victims have talked to others about their intentions or have written about them. Talk of suicide should therefore always be taken seriously (Shafii et al., 1985). Because girls are usually more involved in a social

support network than boys are, they can more readily confide in others about their distress (Holden, 1986).

Edwin Shneidman has studied and treated people with suicidal tendencies for almost 40 years. He concludes that "Suicide is the desperate act of a perturbed and constricted mind, in seemingly unbearable and unresolvable pain. . . . The fact is that we can relieve the pain, redress the thwarted needs, and reduce the constriction of suicidal thinking" (1987, p. 58). Being sensitive to signs of suicidal intentions and caring enough to intervene are essential to save the lives of both youthful and mature people who have come to see no exit for their troubles except total self-destruction.

You (yes, you!) should be aware of the clues to suicidal intentions. Clearly, suicidal despair may be indicated by depression: lethargy (persistently sluggish or sleepy behavior), expressing hopelessness, social withdrawal or isolation, or expressing the fear that one's problems cannot be solved. Some would-be suicides also make telltale, exaggerated gestures, such as giving away prized possessions, or impulsively acting in a dangerous or risky manner. Contrary to the myth that those who talk suicide don't actually do it, people who discuss committing suicide—whether they openly joke about it or privately confide in someone—are most at risk for going through with their plans (Shneidman, 1985).

If you recognize suicidal signs in someone you care about, what can you do? Equip yourself with names and numbers so you can get professional help. Here are some to get you started:

■ The American Association of Suicidology in Washington, D.C.: call (202) 237–2280 (operates Monday–Friday, 9:00 A.M.–5:00 P.M., Eastern time). *This organization keeps a directory of suicide and crisis centers and hotlines throughout the United States and Canada.*

■ Your campus counseling center and community mental health center will provide licensed, professional, confidential assistance.

■ Your local telephone directory or operator can provide crisis and suicide prevention numbers, and you can dial 911 for emergency assistance.

attractive (Brumberg, 1988; Gilbert and DeBlassie, 1984). While cultural ideals of feminine beauty change over time, in recent decades the mass media—including fashion magazines and MTV—have promoted images of unrealistically slim models and celebrities (Andersen & DiDomenico, 1992; Rolls et al., 1991). Especially during adolescence, people tend to evaluate themselves in terms of physical attractiveness, judging themselves harshly for failing to live up to cultural ideals (Conger & Petersen, 1984). A victim of anorexia typically holds a distorted body image, believing herself to be unattractively fat, and rejects others' reassurances that she is not overweight (Bruch, 1978; Fallon & Rozin, 1985). In an effort to lose imagined "excess" weight, the anorexic rigidly suppresses her appetite, feeling rewarded for such self-control when she does lose pounds and inches—but never feeling quite thin enough.

Despite the vivid cultural fantasy that thinness equals success and happiness, most adolescent girls do not develop eating disorders, regardless of their disappointment or social anxieties about their bodies. What is it that pushes a desperate few (about 1 percent of adolescents) over the edge into anorexia nervosa? Situational explanations for many cases of this eating disorder blame problems in family interactions. One hypothesis is that overdependence on their parents leads some girls to fear becoming sexually mature and independent. Extreme self-starvation interrupts sexual development, causes cessation of menstruation, and retains a childish, immature body shape—in this sense, then, a girl can "keep from growing up." Thus this life-threatening condition may develop for personal reasons stemming from combinations of family and social pressures (Polivy & Herman, 1985). Unfortunately, as most anorexics discover, being thin and unhealthy is not the same as remaining young.

Bulimia Somewhat more complex than anorexia nervosa is the behavior pattern involved in **bulimia**, *a "binge-and-purge" syndrome in which the sufferer indulges in episodes of overeating (binges) followed by efforts to lose weight (purging) by means of self-induced vomiting, laxative use, or fasting* (Rand & Kuldau, 1992). Those who suffer from bulimia (pronounced *boo-LEE-me-uh*) usually keep their disorder inconspicuous and may even be supported in their behavior patterns by peers and by competitive norms in their academic, social, and athletic lives (Polivy & Herman, 1993; Rodin et al., 1985; Squire, 1983; Striegel Moore et al., 1993).

To the normal population, a secret life of bingeing and purging to the point of being unable to resume normal eating behavior seems obviously unnatural and disordered. How could such a habit go undetected or unchallenged? One answer is suggested in the following anecdote by psychologist James Pennebaker (1990), explaining his early research on *active inhibition* (deliberate strategies for behavior change):

> In the late 1970s, I intended to begin to study inhibition by surveying people to get an idea of the ways they dieted and the relative effectiveness of their weight-loss techniques. Before the project started, however, my plans changed after some discussions with my students.
>
> It was 1979 and one of my students was complaining about her roommate, who was eating tremendous quantities of food each night and then vomiting what she had eaten. I told this story to a group of my researchers with the air of you'll-never-believe-this. Over the next week, at least half of my research team spoke privately with me and admitted that they, too, binged and purged food on a regular basis. Here was a phenomenon that I had never heard of that was apparently affecting a respectable number of college students. Who were these people and why were they doing it? (Pennebaker, 1990, pp. 24–25)

In subsequent research, Pennebaker and his colleagues surveyed more than 700 university women about their eating behavior and dieting experiences (see Pennebaker, 1990). Somewhat unexpectedly, the researchers found that, before they developed the disorder, bulimic women were no different from other women in terms of their backgrounds, body images, and food preferences. The major difference between normal and disordered women was that bulimic women had tried and failed with more different weight-loss programs. In other words, for these women, bulimia appeared to be "an extreme form of dieting" (Pennebaker, 1990, p. 25).

Other research indicates that bulimics rely on local norms—standards of behavior among their immediate circle of friends and classmates—with an emphasis on thinness and an acceptance of bingeing and purging to attain the ideal (see, for example, Johnson & Connors, 1987). Pennebaker found that bulimic women were not as worried about the threat to their health as they were stressed by the practical difficulties of concealing their "secret lives" from family and friends. Time spent with others interfered with their need to binge and purge, and they constantly ran the risk of being "discovered." For some women, the solution was to sever social ties with those who might disapprove of their bulimic behavior. By associating only with other bulimics, each woman could convince herself that her habit was relatively normal and acceptable—at least among her circle of bulimic friends. But this isolation led to loneliness and depression, which in turn led to more eating and overeating, so that the disorder took on a momentum of its own.

Eating disorders are often associated with other forms of psychopathology. For example, there may be common risk factors for both bulimia and major depression (Walters et al., 1992). Further, while hungry normal people look forward to eating and enjoying a good meal, eating-disordered individuals do not associate pleasure with food, and may even dread having to eat. In comparison with control subjects, bulimic patients in one study took longer to begin eating a scheduled meal, ate more slowly, and reported significantly more negative moods during eating (Hetherington et al., 1993). Although their original rationale might have been to lose weight, anorexics and bulimics apparently take little joy in their slimmer states. Ironically, the negative emotions these individuals exhibit may eventually help them, by attracting the attention of friends and family members who can urge them to seek professional treatment for their disorder.

Explaining Eating Disorders   Psychodynamic explanations to understanding eating disorders primarily examine family interactions and origins, as cited above. Disordered eating behavior may represent an unconscious wish to remain young, dependent, or vulnerable.

Behavioral approaches focus on the life-threatening habits that must be changed if the disordered individual is to recover. One strategy for behavior change is to remove the individual from the environment or social arrangement that may be tolerating or encouraging her habit. Anorexics have been found to resist cooperating with such programs more than bulimic patients (Van Strien et al., 1992). Perhaps self-starvation reflects a greater need for control than does the binge-and-purge habit of bulimics. Effective behavioral strategies must take into account the importance of control and self-determination in maintaining the pattern of disordered behavior.

Cognitive explanations for eating disorders analyze how the individual sees herself and thinks about food, eating, and weight. Anorexics may exhibit more mental rigidity (less flexibility in their thinking) than normal individuals (Korkina et al., 1992). Among bulimics, those who purge more often than others have been found to suffer interference in performing certain cognitive tasks (Cooper & Fairburn, 1993). Findings such as these suggest that eating-

Diana, Princess of Wales, publicly divulged her struggle with bulimia, an eating disorder in which the sufferer overeats (binges), and then purges, through self-induced vomiting, laxatives, or fasting.

disordered individuals have distorted ways of perceiving and thinking. Accordingly, many successful treatments of eating disorders are based on cognitive strategies that focus first on building up self-esteem and self-efficacy (Baell & Wertheim, 1992).

Treating Eating Disorders   Because as a college student you are likely to know someone affected by an eating disorder, we will briefly discuss their treatment here rather than postponing that discussion until the next chapter, where we examine psychotherapy in general.

Considering the personal, social, and cultural factors in their development, it's not surprising to find that eating disorders are difficult to treat. Both anorexia nervosa and bulimia have a high rate of relapse; those who have been successfully treated remain at some risk for redeveloping the same disorder (Kennedy & Garfinkel, 1992). Victims of anorexia nervosa may resist admitting that they have a problem in the first place. Those who suffer from bulimia may have become so secretive that they are reluctant to confide in a friend or therapist.

Confiding is important. Although therapists have difficulty agreeing on reliable treatments for eating disorders, those surveyed in one study overwhelmingly favored "talking therapy" for both anorexia and bulimia patients (Herzog et al., 1992). Support groups (especially in clinical settings) can help treat bulimia by bringing together sufferers who sympathize with and accept each other, and relieve each other of the need to go on "hiding" (Garfinkel & Garner, 1982; Pennebaker, 1990). Students surveyed about their preferences favor psychologically based treatment, such as counseling and behavior change, over medical approaches such as drugs (Sturmey, 1992). Does your school have such support services to help overcome eating disorders? Find out, so that you can recommend them to friends in need—including, perhaps, your best friend: you.

Researchers have sought to inform and reassure health care professionals about the importance of identifying and treating anorexia nervosa and bulimia (Herzog, 1992). Still, a major hurdle for psychologists is our diet-obsessed culture, whose imagery undercuts therapists' efforts to have their clients resume normal eating and regain lost weight. After all, how readily can you name an "attractive" media personality, celebrity, or heroic figure—other than a comic entertainer—who is also clearly overweight? As long as "fat" is a dirty word, self-conscious individuals will worry about their weight and risk their mental and physical well-being in the impossible quest to be "perfect."

Schizophrenic Disorders

Everyone knows what it is like to feel depressed or anxious, even though few of us experience these feelings severely enough to be disordered. *Schizophrenia* (pronounced *skits-a-FRENNY-a*), however, is a disorder that represents a qualitatively different experience from normal functioning (Bellak, 1979). The word *schizophrenia* comes from the Greek for "split or broken mind." A **schizophrenic disorder** *is a severe form of psychopathology in which personality seems to disintegrate, perception is distorted, emotions are blunted, thoughts are bizarre, and language is strange.* Schizophrenia is the disorder we usually mean when we refer to "madness," psychosis, or insanity.

Between two and three million living Americans have, at one time or another, suffered from this most mysterious and tragic mental disorder (Regier et al., 1988). Schizophrenic patients currently occupy half of the beds in this nation's mental institutions. For as yet unknown reasons, the first occurrence of schizophrenia typically occurs for men before they are 25 and for women between 25 and 45 years of age (Lewine et al., 1981).

To get just a brief sense of how schizophrenia can affect one's thoughts and feelings, consider the experience of a young woman called Sylvia Frumkin, as recorded by her biographer:

> Shortly after midnight on Friday, June 16, 1978, Sylvia Frumkin decided to take a bath. Miss Frumkin, a heavy, ungainly young woman who lived in a two-story yellow brick building in Queens Village, New York, walked from her bedroom on the second floor to the bathroom next door and filled the tub with warm water. . . . She washed her brown hair with shampoo and also with red mouthwash. . . . She imagined that the red mouthwash would somehow be absorbed into her scalp and make her hair red permanently.
>
> After a few minutes of contented frolicking [in the tub], Miss Frumkin stepped out of the tub. She slipped on the bathroom floor . . . and cut the back of her head as she fell. The cut began to bleed. She attempted to stop the bleeding by applying pressure to the cut, then wrapped her head in a large towel. . . . She poured the [some expensive perfume] on her cut, partly because she knew that the perfume contained alcohol, . . . and partly because she suddenly thought that she was Jesus Christ and that her bleeding cut was the beginning of a crown of thorns. She also thought that she was Mary Magdalene, who had poured ointment on Christ. . . .
>
> Miss Frumkin's head burned when the perfume came in contact with the open cut, and the bleeding subsided but didn't altogether stop. [By now it was after one o'clock, so Sylvia dressed and went to the building's night supervisor to request a ride to the local emergency room.]. . . The [car] radio was playing Paul McCartney's song "The Lovely Linda," . . . and Miss Frumkin thought that McCartney was singing the lyrics sarcastically, because he had fallen in love with her and was no longer in love with Linda, his wife. [After she was admitted to the hospital, she told the psychiatric resident] not only that Paul McCartney had sung to her but also that she was going to marry another former Beatle, Ringo Starr. . . . His impression of Miss Frumkin's condition was that it was an acute exacerbation of chronic schizophrenia—one of the most common forms of serious mental illness in the world (Sheehan, 1983, pp. 3–7).

Symptoms of Schizophrenia This brief glimpse into the world of a real woman suffering from chronic schizophrenia shows that its impairment of perception, judgment, and interaction essentially puts the schizophrenic individual into another world. In the world of schizophrenia, *thinking* becomes illogical; associations among ideas are remote or without apparent pattern. *Language* may become incoherent—a "word salad" of unrelated or made-up words—or an individual may become mute. *Emotions* may be flat, with no visible expression, or they may be inappropriate to the situation. *Psychomotor behavior* may be disorganized (grimaces, strange mannerisms), or posture may become rigid. Even when only some of these symptoms are present, deteriorated functioning in work, social relations, and self-care is likely. *Interpersonal relationships* are often difficult as individuals withdraw socially or become emotionally detached. These same symptoms of schizophrenia are found in many different cultures (Draguns, 1980, 1990). There appears to be more similarity among schizophrenics in all parts of the world than among people who suffer from other major psychological disorders.

Schizophrenics often experience **hallucinations,** *involving imagined sensory perceptions (sights, smells, sounds, usually voices) that are assumed to be* *real.* For example, a person may hear one voice that provides a running commentary on his or her behavior, or several voices in conversation.

Also common in schizophrenia are **delusions,** *false or irrational beliefs maintained in spite of clear evidence to the contrary.* Delusions are often patently absurd, such as Sylvia Frumkin's beliefs that red mouthwash would dye her hair permanently red, or that Paul McCartney was singing to her of his love. In other cases, delusions may not seem so outlandish, but they are still not realistic or true. For example, a man may experience delusions that his sexual partner is being unfaithful, or that he is being unfairly persecuted.

Psychologists divide schizophrenic symptoms into two categories, *positive* and *negative.* Positive symptoms involve the presence or appearance of abnormal psychological experiences such as hallucinations; negative symptoms involve a reduction or dulling in otherwise normal behavior, such as expressing emotions. During *acute phases* of schizophrenia, the positive symptoms—hallucinations, delusions, incoherence, and disorganized behavior—are prominent. At other times, the negative symptoms—social withdrawal and flattened emotions—become more apparent.

Some individuals diagnosed with schizophrenia experience only one or very few acute phases of schizophrenia, going on to recover and live normal lives. Others, like Sylvia Frumkin, often described as chronic sufferers, experience either repeated acute phases with short periods of negative symptoms or occasional acute phases with extended periods marked by the presence of negative symptoms. Even the most seriously disturbed are not acutely delusional all the time (Liberman, 1982).

Major Types of Schizophrenia Investigators consider schizophrenia a constellation of separate types of disorders. The five most commonly recognized subtypes are outlined in Table 13.4.

Disorganized Type In this subtype of schizophrenia, a person displays incoherent patterns of thinking and grossly bizarre and disorganized behavior. Emotions are flattened or inappropriate to the situation. Often, a person acts in a silly or childish manner, such as giggling for no apparent reason. Language can become so incoherent—full of unusual words and incomplete sentences—that communication with others breaks down. Delusions or hallucinations are common, but are not organized around a coherent theme.

TABLE 13.4	TYPES OF SCHIZOPHRENIC DISORDERS
Type of Schizophrenia	**Major Symptoms**
Disorganized	Inappropriate behavior and emotions, incoherent language
Catatonic	Frozen, rigid, or excitable motor behavior
Paranoid	Delusions of persecution or grandeur
Undifferentiated	Mixed set of symptoms, with thought disorders, and features from other types
Residual	Free from major symptoms but evidence from minor symptoms of continuation of the disorder

Catatonic Type The catatonic person seems frozen in a stupor. For long periods of time, the individual can remain motionless, often in a bizarre position, showing little or no reaction to anything in the environment. When the individual is moved, he or she freezes in a new position, assuming the waxy flexibility of a soft plastic toy.

Catatonic negativity sometimes involves motionless resistance to instructions, or doing the opposite of what is requested. For the catatonic person, stupor sometimes alternates with excitement. During the excited phase, motor activity is agitated, apparently without purpose, and not influenced by external stimuli.

Paranoid Type Individuals who suffer from this form of schizophrenia experience complex and systematized delusions focused around specific themes. Individuals suffering *delusions of persecution* feel that they are being constantly spied on and plotted against and that they are in mortal danger. Those with *delusions of grandeur* believe that they are important or exalted beings—millionaires, great inventors, or religious figures such as Jesus Christ. Delusions of persecution may accompany delusions of grandeur: an individual may believe he is a great person who is continually opposed by evil forces.

Individuals may suffer *delusional jealousy,* becoming convinced that their mates are unfaithful, and contriving data to "prove" the truth of the delusion. Finally, those suffering *delusions of reference* misconstrue chance happenings as being directed at them. A paranoid individual who sees two people in earnest conversation readily concludes that they are talking about him. Even lyrics in popular songs or words spoken by radio or television actors are perceived as having some special message for the individual, or exposing some personal secret.

The onset of symptoms in paranoid schizophrenic individuals tends to occur later in life than it does in other schizophrenic types. Paranoid schizophrenic individuals rarely display obviously disorganized behavior. Instead, it is more likely that their behavior will be intense and quite formal.

Undifferentiated Type This "grab bag" category of schizophrenia describes a person who exhibits prominent delusions, hallucinations, incoherent speech, or grossly disorganized behaviors that fit the criteria of more than one type, or of no clear type. The hodgepodge of symptoms experienced by these individuals does not clearly differentiate among various schizophrenic reactions.

Residual Type Individuals diagnosed with the residual type of schizophrenia have suffered from a major past episode but are currently free of positive symptoms such as hallucinations or delusional thinking. The disorder is indicated by minor positive symptoms, or by negative symptoms such as flat affect (expressing little or no emotion). The diagnosis of residual type may indicate that the disease is entering *remission,* or becoming dormant.

Causes of Schizophrenia Different models point to very different initial causes of schizophrenia, different developmental pathways, and different avenues for treatment. A review of several of these models can help us understand how a person may develop a schizophrenic disorder.

Psychodynamics and Family Interaction Sociologists, family therapists, and psychologists all study the influence of family role relationships and communication patterns in the development of schizophrenia. Researchers have provided some evidence to support theories that deviations in parental communication influence the development of schizophrenia (Liem, 1980). One such deviation is a family's inability to share a common focus of attention, such as when everyone talks at once but no one listens. Another is indicated when parents have difficulty taking other family members' perspectives or communicating clearly and accurately. Studies suggest that the speech patterns of families with a schizophrenic member show less responsiveness and less interpersonal sensitivity than those of normal families. It may be that *having* a schizophrenic member contributes to families' interaction problems. But research also supports the conclusion that schizophrenia is somewhat fostered by poor communication, confusion, and double messages (for example, a parent saying, "Come give Mommy a hug" and then pushing her child away because she is too tired or the child is too demanding).

Deviant communication in families may contribute to the child's distortion of reality by concealing or denying the true meaning of an event or by injecting a substitute meaning that is confusing (Wynne et al., 1979). Anthropologist **Gregory Bateson** used the term **double bind** to describe *a situation in which a child receives from a parent multiple messages that are contradictory and cannot all be met.* A mother may complain to her little boy that he is not affectionate enough toward her—and yet for some reason reject his attempts to touch or get close to her. Torn between these different verbal and nonverbal meanings (between demands and feelings), a child's grip on reality may begin to slip. The result may be that the child will see his or her feelings, perceptions, and self-knowledge as unreliable indicators of the way things really are (Bateson et al., 1956).

There is not sufficient evidence to rally confidence in the hypothesis that family factors play a causal role in the *development* of schizophrenia. However, there is reliable evidence that family factors do influence the functioning of an individual *after* the first symptoms appear. When parents reduce their criticism, hostility, and intrusiveness toward schizophrenic offspring, the recurrence of acute schizophrenic symptoms and the need for rehospitalization is also reduced (Doane et al., 1985).

Cognitive Processes The hallmarks of schizophrenia include abnormalities in attention, thought, memory, and language. Some cognitive psychologists argue that these abnormalities may play a role in causing schizophrenia instead of being consequences of the disorder. One view focuses on the role of attentional difficulties. *Attentional deficits* may involve ignoring important environmental or cultural cues that most people use to socially regulate or "normalize" their behavior. For example, in order to "fit in" and not disturb others if you arrive late to class, you glance quickly around the room to see what's going on and how your classmates are behaving. If you do not or cannot notice that the others are working very quietly, you draw reproving glances as you enter in your usual noisy manner. A pattern of such social errors makes it difficult for someone to win acceptance and social support.

The speech of some schizophrenic individuals seems to be under the control of immediate stimuli in the situation. The incoherence of schizophrenic speech is due, in part, to bizarre *intrusions* by thoughts that are not directly relevant to the statement being uttered—intrusions that the person cannot suppress. Normal speaking requires that a speaker remember what has just been said (past), monitor where he or she is (present), and direct the spoken sentence toward some final goal (future). This coherence between past, present, and future may be difficult for some schizophrenic individuals, accounting for their inability to maintain long strings of interconnected words. What comes out is the "word salad" we described earlier, a wildly tossed semantic confusion.

According to the cognitive approach taken by psychologist **Brendan Maher** (1968), the bizarre speech of schizophrenic individuals may be a result of deviant processing whenever a person comes to a "vulnerable" word—one that has multiple meanings to him or her. At that point, a personally relevant but semantically inappropriate word is used. For example, a patient may say, "Doctor, I have pains in my chest and hope and wonder if my box is broken and heart is beaten." *Chest* is a vulnerable word; it can mean a *respiratory cage* or a *container* such as a *hope* chest. *Wonder* could mean *Wonder Bread* that is kept in a bread *box*. Hearts *beat* and are *broken*.

Reality testing is also impaired in schizophrenia. While most of us evaluate the reality of our inner worlds against the external world, individuals with schizophrenic disorders typically *reverse* this usual procedure for testing reality. Their inner experiences are the criteria against which they test the validity of outer experience (Meyer & Ekstein, 1970). Theirs is a world in which thinking makes it so—as in the fantasy world of children or the dream world of adults. By carefully listening to schizophrenic speech, it is often possible for a clinician to decode the sense in what appears at first to be pure nonsense (Forest, 1976).

Genetic Factors It has long been known that schizophrenia tends to run in families (Bleuler, 1978; Kallmann, 1946). Persons related genetically to someone who has been schizophrenic are more likely to become affected than those who are not (Kessler, 1988). The risk is greater for first-degree relatives (siblings and children), greater in families with many affected relatives, and greater where schizophrenic reactions are severe (Hanson et al., 1977). In fact, for all close relatives of a diagnosed *index case* of schizophrenia, the risk factor may be as great as 46 times higher than for the general population (see Figure 13.4).

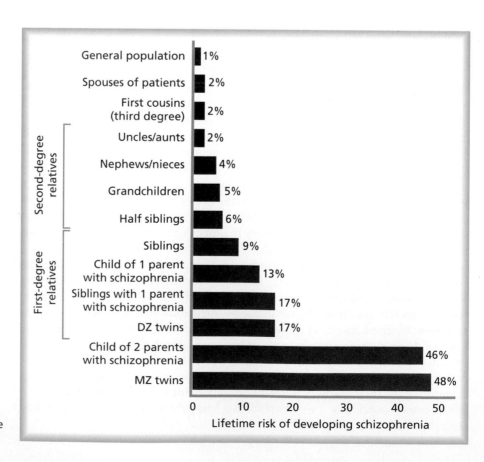

FIGURE 13.4 Genetic Risk of Developing Schizophrenia ■ The graph shows average risks for developing schizophrenia. Data were compiled from family and twin studies conducted in European populations between 1920 and 1987; the degree of risk correlates highly with the degree of genetic relatedness.

The most compelling evidence for the role of genetic factors in the etiology (origins and development) of schizophrenia comes from adoption studies. When the offspring of a schizophrenic parent are reared by a normal parent in a foster home, they are as likely to develop the disorder as if they had been brought up by the biological parent (Heston, 1970; Rosenthal et al., 1975). In addition, adoptees who are schizophrenic have significantly more biological than adoptive relatives with schizophrenic disorders (Kety et al., 1975).

While there is certainly a strong relationship between genetic similarity and the risk of schizophrenia, even in the groups with the greatest genetic similarity, the risk factor is less than 50 percent. This indicates that, although genes play some role, schizophrenia is a complex disorder that involves other contributing factors.

The genetics of schizophrenia is still undetermined. Critics of the genetic hypothesis of schizophrenia argue that the available evidence is weak for all types of schizophrenia except for *chronic* forms of the disorder. They point out that 90 percent of the relatives of schizophrenics do not have schizophrenia (Barnes, 1987). Taken as a whole, research suggests that genetic factors may contribute to schizophrenia but may not by themselves be sufficient for the development of schizophrenia (Nicol & Gottesman, 1983).

One widely accepted hypothesis for causes of schizophrenia is the **diathesis-stress hypothesis,** *the proposal that genetic factors place the individual at risk, but environmental stress factors trigger this potential into being manifested as an actual schizophrenic disorder.* (The word *diathesis* refers to a predisposition or physical condition that makes one susceptible to disease.) Thus, individuals who are genetically predisposed to develop schizophrenia may never do so if they do not experience certain damaging conditions or stressors that push them "over the edge."

Brain Structure and Biochemistry   Are the brains of individuals who are genetically at risk for schizophrenia unusual in some way? Particular neurotransmitters and processes in the brain have been associated with the production and reduction of schizophrenic reactions. The most promising line of biochemical research focuses on the influence of a specific neurotransmitter, dopamine, and its receptor sites in the brain.

The **dopamine hypothesis** *holds that schizophrenia is associated with a relative excess of the chemical dopamine at specific receptor sites in the central nervous system* (Carlsson, 1978; Snyder, 1986). Schizophrenic symptoms result from an increase in the activity of nerve cells that use dopamine as their neurotransmitter. Although impressive evidence has been accumulated for the dopamine hypothesis, we still must be cautious. It is possible that dopamine availability may be one factor in the sequence of development of schizophrenia, but not the original cause.

Another area of interest in the biology of schizophrenia is the association of schizophrenic symptoms with subtle brain abnormalities, such as reduced brain volume in specific areas of the brain or enlarged ventricles (fluid-filled chambers in the brain). Further research comparing structure and functions of the brains of twins who are *discordant* for schizophrenia (one has the disorder, the other does not) and normal control twins has been conducted by an interdisciplinary research team headed by Irving Gottesman and E. Fuller Torrey using brain scanning and other assessment techniques (Gottesman, 1991).

Support for a general brain-based theory of schizophrenia comes from research on how various "biological insults" to developing fetuses have been found to increase those individuals' probability of developing schizophrenic symptoms in later life. For example, for pregnant women who survived the Dutch Hunger Winter of 1944, when the Nazis blockaded Holland and no food could get in, the risk of schizophrenia for their children was twice the rate for those born before or after that time (Susser et al., 1996). Additional research shows a similar doubling of the risk for schizophrenia among fetuses whose mothers contracted influenza during the second trimester of pregnancy, and those whose Rh factor—a blood type—is incompatible with that of their mothers (Hollister et al., 1996). One conclusion of this three-pronged review—the effects of malnutrition, flu, and Rh incompatibility on developing fetuses—is that, in the words of researcher Edward Jones, "[t]he schizophrenic brain, when it's born, is just slightly miswired" (National Public Radio, 1996c). A recent review of this research suggests that early in pregnancy a developing fetus's brain cells must differentiate and migrate from the central core of the brain to positions dictated by a genetic blueprint (Wyatt, 1996). The biological insult inflicted by illness or other disruption at this critical point in prenatal development means that the fetus's brain never develops appropriately. However, not all children at "risk" for developing schizophrenia go on to develop symptoms, so further work must be done to determine the precise factors that turn a risk into a consequence.

Check Your Recall

Many categories of disorders are included in DSM-IV; only six of them are examined here. Personality disorders are long-standing, inflexible, maladaptive patterns of perceiving, thinking, or behaving that seriously impair an individual's functioning or cause significant distress. Two of the better known personality disorders are narcissistic personality disorder and antisocial personality disorder.

Dissociative disorders involve a basic disruption of the integrated functioning of memory, consciousness, or personal identity. Psychogenic amnesia and fugue states may represent a form of flight from traumatic experiences or memories. In cases of dissociative identity disorder, two or more separate identities emerge to cope with the trauma of childhood sexual and physical abuse.

Anxiety disorders all involve extreme efforts to avoid or reduce anxiety. The four major types of anxiety disorders include generalized anxiety disorder, panic disorder, phobic disorders, and obsessive-compulsive disorder.

Affective disorders involve disturbances of mood. One main type of affective disorder is unipolar depression, the "common cold of psychopathology," characterized by sad feelings as well as other symptoms. Bipolar disorder is much rarer and is marked by the alternating occurrence of depression and periods of mania. Least common are "pure" manic episodes, without the balancing pole of depression. Explanations for affective disturbances may lie in a complex combination of psychodynamic, behavior, and biochemical factors.

Eating disorders, categorized with a larger class of disorders that develop in childhood and adolescence, are characterized by deliberately refusing to eat or by preventing digestion. In anorexia nervosa, the individual starves herself, whereas a bulimic binges and then purges. Both disorders are related to unrealistic body images and are difficult to treat.

Schizophrenia is a severe form of psychopathology affecting about 1 percent of the population. Someone with a schizophrenic disorder experiences extreme distortions in perception, thinking, emotion, behavior, and language. Hallucinations and delusions are common, and there may be a disintegration of the coherent functioning of personality. Psychologists have identified five subtypes of schizophrenia: disorganized, catatonic, paranoid, undifferentiated, and residual. Explanations for the causes of schizophrenia include genetic influences, biological factors, and an interaction between predisposition and stress. There is little evidence that environmental traumas alone account for schizophrenia.

Judging Abnormality

The goal of clinical judgment is not to label or categorize *people*, but to understand and diagnose *disorders*, in order to offer the best and most appropriate kind of treatment. In the next chapter we will examine the range of treatments that have been developed for psychological disorders. In the last section of this chapter, we review how psychologists seek to understand causes based on observable symptoms. Finally, we consider the personal and social consequences of being judged abnormal.

Understanding Causes: A Case Study

Humorists in the 1990s have ridiculed society's eagerness to see problems as "disorders": a person in a bad mood is "temperamentally challenged"; an employee who is often late for work jokes about suffering from "chronic oversleeping syndrome." A fancy label can deflect criticism and shift the blame for one's troubles elsewhere. But every personal problem is not necessarily a "disorder." More importantly, the goal of classifying and labeling disorders is not to create new excuses but to prevent and treat genuine difficulties. In the beginning of this chapter we reviewed several key criteria for judging a behavior pattern to be abnormal. Patterns that meet these general criteria are studied in hopes of identifying causes. As complex as they may be, once the causes of a disorder are understood, more precise and effective treatment can be developed. Consider the following case of a disordered pattern that meets many of the criteria we listed in the outset of this chapter, such as personal distress, maladaptive behavior, and irrational thinking.

Recent research and theorizing points to several self-destructive behavior patterns that may be linked to a biological "common denominator" in the brain. Addictive, impulsive, and compulsive disorders—including alcoholism, drug abuse, binge eating, and attention deficit disorder—may be in part the consequence of an inborn chemical imbalance of the neurotransmitter dopamine. **Reward deficiency syndrome (RDS)** *is the term for this genetically caused biochemical imbalance that is manifested as one or more behavioral disorders of addiction, impulsivity, or compulsivity* (Blum et al., 1996). The collection is blamed on "reward deficiency" because the individual suffers from the inability to derive reward or satisfaction from everyday, ordinary pleasures that usually stimulate the brain. Instead of a feeling of well-being, negative emotions surface, such as anxiety, anger, or a craving for a mood-altering substance. Reward deficiency syndrome is not itself a DSM-IV category; rather, it is a pattern across disorders in several categories, such as substance-related disorders and anxiety disorders.

While researchers are confident that the syndrome is rooted in imbalanced transportation or reception of dopamine in the brain, the problem can express itself in a wide variety of problems. Additionally, each individual's problems are also supported by many personal experiences and social attitudes, making it unlikely that a drug therapy alone would "fix" the person's troubles. In the United States alone, there are 18 million alcoholics, 26 million children of alcoholics, 6 million cocaine addicts, nearly 15 million abusers of other drugs, 25 million nicotine addicts, 3.5 million people suffering from attention-deficit disorders, and about 500,000 compulsive gamblers. That adds up to a staggering number of people—and loved ones—who are suffering, and represents enormous costs to society. Reward deficiency syndrome might help to explain how such different problems might be related, at least by a biochemical "malfunction."

The search for causes usually results in a complex rather than a simple solution. Not everyone with a dopamine imbalance necessarily develops symptoms of disordered behavior. So what "triggers" the problem pattern? What personal factors might cause someone biologically predisposed for RDS to actually overuse or abuse a substance or develop a maladaptive habit in the first place? What social forces would keep such unhealthy patterns in place? For example, a perfectionistic person might express a predisposition for RDS by relying too heavily on stimulants so she can work harder and faster. Or a person with family problems might begin to use alcohol to excess in an effort to dull the pain of unhappy relationships. Once begun, such habits might be supported by media and advertising messages promising that a simple substance will make life better: a good cup of coffee will start your day right, a cigarette will be "smooth and satisfying," or having a beer with friends will make those friendships last.

Labels are deceptive in their simplicity because the causes of most disorders are somewhat complex, with biochemistry, personality, and social influences all interweaving in shaping a particular disorder. Keep in mind, therefore, that the goal of diagnosis is not simply to slap a label on a person and pronounce him or her "excused." Instead, the diagnosis is the *beginning* of a complex process of finding a general category to help understand the individual's problems, proceeding to understanding specific factors, and finally proposing the best options for changing behavior and experience. In light of the need for *understanding* before we can diagnose and treat a problem, it is probably not a bad idea to err on the side of labeling and "excusing" some problems rather than blaming and shaming those who suffer. By making disordered individuals feel bad, we might indeed force some to try to mend their ways, but people with real problems are more likely to seek help if they feel they can expect sympathy rather than condemnation. *Not* every problem is a "disorder," but all disorders are problems we might help to solve by being more understanding and forgiving of those—including ourselves—who have difficulty with the demands of everyday living.

The Problem of Objectivity

Although diagnosis and classification yield benefits for research and clinical purposes, these same processes can have negative consequences. The task of actually assigning a person the label "psychologically or mentally disordered" remains a matter of human judgment—thus open to bias and error. The labels of mental illness, insanity, or psychological disorder can be acquired in a number of ways other than by the diagnosis of a trained clinician. When psychologically untrained people are in a position to judge the mental health of others, their decisions are often vulnerable to biases based on expectations, status, gender, prejudice, and context. Too often those identified as psychologically disordered suffer from stigma, as we saw in the letter from Cherish at the beginning of the chapter.

Labeling Abnormal Behavior   The label "mentally ill" is typically assigned because the person is under some form of *care*. Influential members of the community or family agree that the person's behavior is *dangerously maladjusted*, the person's scores on psychological tests *deviate* from standards of normality, the person declares himself or herself to be "mentally sick," and/or the person's public behavior is *dangerous* to himself or herself or to others.

The criteria psychologists and psychiatrists use to make diagnostic decisions also influence judgments of the legal system and of the insurance and health care businesses. The *legal determination of* **insanity** *carries with it serious implications regarding a defendant's competence to stand trial and to be held responsible for criminal indictments.*

The decision to declare someone psychologically disordered or insane is always a *judgment* about behavior. It is a judgment made by one or more people about another individual who often has less political power or socioeconomic status than those making the judgment.

Research has shown that clinicians in the United States use a double standard to assess the maladjustment of men and women. In one study, both male and female clinicians ascribed more positive characteristics to males and less desirable characteristics to normal, healthy females (Broverman et al., 1972). Other research shows that clinicians tend to judge females as maladjusted when they show behaviors that are incongruent with their gender role. When women act "like men"—use foul language, drink excessively, or exhibit uncontrollable temper—they are seen as neurotic or self-destructive. Moreover, clinicians reflect the biases of their society when they regard masculinity as more important than femininity. In one study, male behavior that was incongruent with the male gender role was rated as a more serious violation than was female gender–role incongruity (Page, 1987).

The Context of Mental Illness We have seen throughout our study of psychology that the meaning of behavior is jointly determined by its *content* and by its *context*. The same act in different settings conveys very different meanings. A man kisses another man: it may signify a gay relationship in the United States, a ritual greeting in France, and a Mafia "kiss of death" in Sicily.

Unfortunately, the diagnosis of a behavior as abnormal can depend on where the behavior occurs—even professionals' judgments may be influenced by context. Is it possible to be judged as sane if you are "a patient" in an insane place? This question was addressed in a classic study by **David Rosenhan** (1973, 1975). Rosenhan and seven other sane people (colleagues and friends who collaborated with him) gained admission to different psychiatric hospitals

The same act in different settings conveys different meanings. In William Blake's nineteenth-century watercolor, Judas kisses Jesus not in friendship, but as an act of betrayal.

by pretending to have a single symptom: hallucinations. All eight of these *pseudopatients* were diagnosed on admission as either paranoid schizophrenic or manic-depressive. Once admitted, they behaved normally in every way. When a sane person is in an insane place, he or she is likely to be judged insane, and any behavior is likely to be reinterpreted to fit the context. When the pseudopatients discussed their situation in a rational way with the staff, they were reported to be using "intellectualization" defenses, while the notes they made of their observations were evidence of "writing behavior." The pseudopatients remained on the wards for almost three weeks, on the average, and not one was identified by the staff as sane. When they were finally released—only with the help of spouses or colleagues—their discharge diagnosis was still "schizophrenia" but "in remission"; that is, their symptoms were not active (Fleischman, 1973; Lieberman, 1973).

Rosenhan's research raised basic issues about the validity of judgments of abnormality in other people, about how dependent such judgments may be on factors other than behavior itself, and about how difficult psychological labels are to remove once they are "stuck" on a person. In the view of radical psychiatrist **Thomas Szasz**, mental illness does not even exist; it is a "myth" (1961, 1977). Szasz argues that the symptoms used as evidence of mental illness are merely medical labels that sanction professional intervention into what are social problems—deviant people violating social norms. Once labeled, these people can be treated for their "problem of being different," with no threat of disturbing the existing status quo.

Few clinicians would go this far today, but there is a movement of psychologists who advocate a *contextual* or *ecological model* in lieu of the classic medical model (Levine & Perkins, 1987). In an ecological model, abnormality is viewed as a product of an interaction between individuals and society. Abnormality is seen as a mismatch between a person's abilities and the needs and norms of society. For example, schools typically demand that children sit quietly for hours at desks and work independently in an orderly fashion. Some children who are not able to do this may be labeled "hyperactive." The abilities of these children do not conform to the needs of most school settings and they quickly come to the attention of school authorities. However, if these same children were placed in an alternative school setting where they were free to roam around the classroom and talk to others as part of their work, the mismatch would not exist, and these children would not be labeled in this negative, stigmatizing way.

The Problem of Stigma

Psychopathology is not statistically so abnormal: It has been estimated that 32 percent of Americans have struggled with some kind of psychopathology—making the experience at least relatively normal (Regier et al., 1988). In practice, being "deviant" connotes moral inferiority and brings social rejection. In addition, the term "deviant" implies that the whole person "is different in kind from ordinary people and that there are no areas of his personality that are not afflicted by his 'problems'" (Scott, 1972, p. 14). There is little doubt that in our society, to be mentally disordered is to be publicly degraded and personally devalued. Society extracts costly penalties from those who deviate from its norms (see Figure 13.5).

People who are psychologically disordered are stigmatized in ways that most physically ill people are not. A stigma is a mark or brand of disgrace. In the psychological context, *a* **stigma** *is a set of negative attitudes about a person that sets him or her apart as unacceptable* (Clausen, 1981). Negative attitudes toward the psychologically disturbed come from many sources. Prominent among these are strangers' jokes; media portrayals of psychiatric patients as

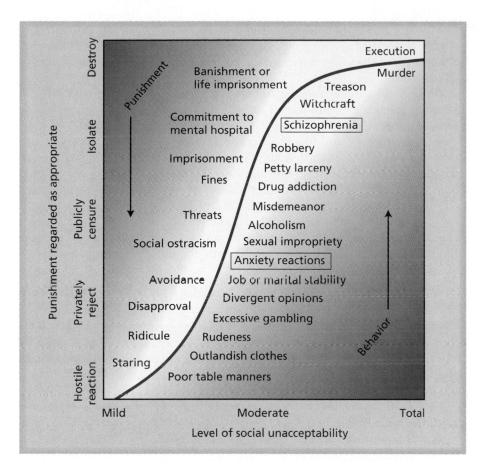

FIGURE 13.5 **"Let the Punishment Fit the Crime"** ■ This figure illustrates a continuum of behaviors that are deemed increasingly unacceptable and are responded to with increasing severity. In essence, each reaction is a punishment for deviance. Thus behavior toward those who suffer from psychopathology can be seen to resemble behavior toward criminals or other deviants.

dangerous; the family's denial that a member is mentally distressed; the individual's fear of losing employment or respect if others learn of the diagnosis; and legal procedures that punish mental incompetence (Rabkin et al., 1980). The stigmatizing process discredits a person as "flawed" (Jones et al., 1984).

Stigma can create discrimination and injustice in how mental illness is treated—and whether treatment and research are funded fairly. At a 1986 congressional hearing, the director of the National Institute of Mental Health reported on several aspects of the national neglect of schizophrenia. Although in 1986 one in every 100 Americans were diagnosed as sufferers of this insidious disease, only $17 in federal funds per year per schizophrenic victim were being spent on research. In comparison, $300 were being spent for each cancer victim. Nearly 60 percent of all schizophrenia sufferers received no treatment. At some level, budgetary decisions were clearly influenced by prejudices that favor caring for the victims of physical illness more than those of mental illness.

Our negative attitudes toward psychologically disturbed people bias our perceptions of and actions toward them and also influence their behavior toward us. A series of experiments conducted in laboratory and naturalistic settings demonstrates the unfavorable influences of the social situation on both the behavior of a person perceived to be a mental patient (even when not so) and the behavior of the person making that judgment. When one member of a pair of male college students was falsely led to believe the other had been a mental patient, he perceived the pseudo ex-patient to be inadequate, incompetent, and not likable. When one of a pair of interacting males falsely believed he was perceived by the other as stigmatized, he behaved in ways that actually caused the other, naive subject to reject him (Farina, 1980; Farina et al., 1971).

Our growing understanding of psychopathology does more than enable society to reclaim its "familiar strangers," such as the young woman whose personal account of schizophrenia opened this chapter. In making sense of psychopathology, we are forced to come to grips with basic conceptions of normality, reality, and social values. We must also broaden our horizons to include other cultural perceptions and interpretations of what is normal and abnormal. A mind "loosed from its stable moorings" does not just go on its solitary way; it bumps into other minds, sometimes challenging their stability. In discovering how to understand, treat, and ideally, to prevent psychological disorders, we not only help those who are suffering and losing out on the joys of living, we also expand the basic understanding of our own human nature.

Check Your Recall

Diagnosing and labeling mental disorders enable us to understand the causes of psychopathology, and ultimately to treat it. Labeling a person as mentally disordered is a process of human judgment. The criteria professionals use to make such judgments also have an influence on legal and social status. Research by David Rosenhan has shown that clinical labels bias the perceptions people form of patients, even perceptions formed by professional mental health staff members.

Behavior patterns may be labeled as psychopathological merely because they are mismatched with one's culture or with social expectations. Another problem with labeling abnormality is the stigma it attaches to labeled persons. Until education helps society to be both informed and fair, disordered individuals may suffer misunderstanding and prejudice.

CHAPTER REVIEW

Summary

Abnormality is judged by the degree to which a person's actions resemble a set of indicators that include distress, maladaptiveness, irrationality, unpredictability, unconventionality, and observer discomfort. In the past, psychopathology was considered to be the result of evil spirits or weak character. Today, psychologists use a number of approaches in studying the origins of psychopathology. The biological approach concentrates on abnormalities in the brain, biochemical processes, and genetic influences. The psychological approach includes the psychodynamic, behavioral, and cognitive models. The interactionist approach combines these views.

Classification systems for psychological disorders should provide a common shorthand for communicating about general types of psychopathology and specific cases. The most widely accepted diagnostic and classification system is DSM-IV. It emphasizes descriptions of symptom patterns and encourages mental health professionals to consider psychological, physical, and social factors that might be relevant to a specific disorder.

Personality disorders are patterns of perception, thinking, or behavior that are long-standing and inflexible and that impair an individual's functioning. Dissociative disorders involve a disruption of the integrated functioning of memory, consciousness, or personal identity. The four major types of anxiety disorders are generalized anxiety, panic, phobic, and obsessive-compulsive disorders.

Affective disorders involve disturbances of mood. Unipolar depression is the most common affective disorder, while bipolar disorder is much rarer. Suicides are most frequent among people suffering from depression. There are two common patterns of eating disorders: anorexia nervosa (self-starvation) and bulimia (bingeing and purging). Both are related to unrealistic, negative body images and are difficult to treat.

Schizophrenia is characterized by extreme distortions in perception, thinking, emotion, behavior, and language. The five subtypes of schizophrenia are: disorganized, catatonic, paranoid, undifferentiated, and residual. Evidence for the causes of schizophrenia has been found in a variety of factors including family environment and communication, faulty cognitive processes, genetic factors, and abnormal brain structure and biochemistry.

By understanding the causes of a disorder, such as in the case of reward deficiency syndrome, psychologists are able to develop better treatments. Labeling someone as psychologically or mentally disordered is ultimately a matter of human judgment. Therefore even professional judgments can be biased by prejudices. Those with psychological disorders are often stigmatized in ways that most physically ill people are not, so it is important not to abuse the knowledge that enables us to categorize and understand both normal and abnormal behavior.

Section Reviews

The Nature of Psychopathology

Be sure to *Check Your Recall* by reviewing the summary of this section on page 515.

Key Terms

psychopathology (p. 504)
psychological diagnosis (p. 506)
conversion disorder (p. 508)
hysteria (p. 508)
DSM-IV (p. 513)
neurotic disorder or neurosis (p. 514)

psychotic disorder or psychosis (p. 514)

Names to Know

Philippe Pinel (p. 509)
Emil Kraepelin (p. 509)
Franz Anton Mesmer (p. 509)
Jean-Martin Charcot (p. 509)

Major Psychological Disorders

Be sure to *Check Your Recall* by reviewing the summary of this section on page 544.

Key Terms

Alzheimer's disease (p. 516)
personality disorder (p. 517)
narcissistic personality disorder (p. 517)
antisocial personality disorder (p. 517)
dissociative disorder (p. 517)
psychogenic amnesia (p. 518)
dissociative identity disorder (DID) (p. 518)
generalized anxiety disorder (p. 520)
panic disorder (p. 521)
agoraphobia (p. 521)
phobic disorder or phobia (p. 521)
social phobia (p. 523)
obsessive-compulsive disorder (p. 523)
shyness (p. 524)
affective disorder (p. 526)
manic episode (p. 526)
bipolar disorder (p. 527)

unipolar depression (p. 528)
eating disorders (p. 533)
anorexia nervosa (p. 533)
bulimia (p. 535)
schizophrenic disorder (p. 537)
hallucinations (p. 538)
delusions (p. 539)
double bind (p. 541)
diathesis-stress hypothesis (p. 543)
dopamine hypothesis (p. 543)

Names to Know

F. W. Putnam (p. 519)
Aaron Beck (p. 530)
Susan Nolen-Hoeksema (p. 532)
Edwin Shneidman (p. 534)
Gregory Bateson (p. 541)
Brendan Maher (p. 542)

Judging Abnormality

Be sure to *Check Your Recall* by reviewing the summary of this section on page 550.

Key Terms

reward deficiency syndrome (RDS) (p. 545)
insanity (p. 546)
stigma (p. 548)

Names to Know

David Rosenhan (p. 547)
Thomas Szasz (p. 548)

REVIEW TEST

Chapter 13: Psychopathology

For each of the following items, choose the single correct or best answer. The correct answers, explanations, and page references appear in Appendix B.

1. Which of the following is *not* one of the six indicators of possible abnormality agreed upon by psychologists?
   a. chronic physical illness
   b. observer discomfort
   c. unconventionality
   d. irrationality

2. DSM-IV refers to _____.
   a. a personality inventory
   b. the most widely used diagnostic system
   c. the neurochemical implicated in anxiety disorders
   d. a class of psychoactive drugs effective in the treatment of schizophrenia

3. A long-standing pattern of irresponsible behavior that hurts others without causing feelings of guilt or remorse is typical of _____.
   a. an obsessive-compulsive disorder
   b. an antisocial personality disorder
   c. a narcissistic personality disorder
   d. paranoid schizophrenia

4. A young woman wanders into a hospital, claiming not to know who she is, where she came from, or how she got there. Her symptoms indicate that she might be suffering from a(n) _____ disorder.
   a. anxiety
   b. affective
   c. personality
   d. dissociative

5. Which of the following statements about phobic disorders is true?
   a. Any irrational fear, such as of spiders or multiple-choice tests, is considered a "phobia."
   b. The "preparedness hypothesis" is suggested by biological explanations for common human fears.
   c. Phobias represent one form of affective disorders.
   d. All of the above.

6. _____ has been called the "common cold of psychopathology" because it occurs so frequently, and almost everyone has experienced elements of the disorder at some time in life.
   a. Obsessive-compulsive disorder
   b. Bipolar disorder

c. Unipolar depression

d. Paranoid schizophrenia

7. A person who suffers from _____ cannot eat normally, but engages in a ritual of "bingeing"—overeating fattening foods—followed by "purging" with induced vomiting or use of laxatives.

a. anorexia

b. bulimia

c. inhibition

d. mania

8. The _____ type of schizophrenia is characterized by delusions of persecution, grandeur, jealousy, and reference.

a. disorganized

b. paranoid

c. catatonic

d. undifferentiated

9. Which of the following different types of disorders reflect the pattern known as reward deficiency syndrome (RDS)?

a. anxiety disorders and substance-abuse disorders

b. dissociative disorders and schizophrenic disorders

c. affective disorders and anxiety disorders

d. personality disorders and affective disorders

10. The common problem experienced by those diagnosed with mental illness is _____, one's sense of disgrace and deviance with which the rest of society has branded them.

a. hysteria

b. diathesis

c. stigma

d. delusional thinking

IF YOU'RE INTERESTED . . .

Alvarez, A. (1971). *The savage god: A study of suicide.* New York: W. W. Norton & Company.

Somewhat high level but a fascinating study of famous suicides plus a history of social, religious, literary, and "romantic" attitudes toward suicide, and theories of its causes and influences, from medieval to modern times.

Caine Mutiny, The. (Video: 1954, color, 125 min.). Directed by Edward Dmytryk; starring Humphrey Bogart, Jose Ferrer, Van Johnson, Fred MacMurray, E. G. Marshall.

Based on Herman Wouk's prizewinning novel, the story of a U.S. Navy court martial and the events that led to it. Humphrey Bogart is outstanding as the paranoid Captain Queeg, whose nervous habits and delusional thinking frighten his officers into taking mutinous action.

Invasion of the Body Snatchers. (Video: 1956, B&W 80 min.). Directed by Don Siegel; starring Kevin McCarthy, Dana Wynter, King Donovan, Carolyn Jones.

The first and best science fiction/paranoia story about the aliens who conquer the world, one individual at a time, in the form of plant "pods" that somehow take over the mind and bodies of their human hosts. Two themes to watch for are the loneliness of the one man who knows about the danger but cannot save his community in time, and the importance of being ever vigilant so that "they"—the nation's enemies, alien ideologies, and Big Brother—do not "possess" their unwitting and unprepared victims (an allusion to the Senate's anti-communist hearings in the late 1940s and early 1950s). Much better than the well-cast 1978 remake.

Jamison, K. R. (1995). *An unquiet mind: A memoir of moods and madness.* New York: Alfred A. Knopf.

Kay Redfield Jamison, a doctor and professor of psychiatry specializing in manic-depressive (bipolar) disorder, reflects with drama and clarity on her own struggle with that very illness. The book charts the development of her illness from her adolescence—through college and graduate school, passionate love and desperate loss, bouts of violence and even attempted suicide. She candidly explores how the energy of her "high highs" led her to resist medications that might reduce the intensity of both her highs and lows. Beautifully written and personal.

One Flew Over the Cuckoo's Nest. (Video: 1975, color, 133 min.). Directed by Milos Forman; starring Jack Nicholson, Louise Fletcher, Brad Dourif, Will Sampson, Danny DeVito, Christopher Lloyd, Scatman Crothers.

Captivating (and Oscar-capturing) film based on Ken Kesey's novel, about the confrontation created by a criminal's entry into a psychiatric hospital, his relationships with voluntary patients, and his doomed struggle against institutional authority. Gross inaccuracies about everything from nurses' power in psychiatric settings to the uses and abuses of psychosurgery, but with those cautions in mind, the viewer enjoys terrific insights into the nature of mental disorders, the complexity of deciding who is "normal," and what to do about individuals who are *not.*

Pipher, M. (1994). *Reviving Ophelia: Saving the selves of adolescent girls.* New York: Grosset/Putnam.

Involving account of the paradoxical challenges facing adolescent women today: with more opportunities and freedoms than women of any previous generation, they also struggle with vicious, ironic assaults on self-esteem, drops in intelligence, relationship conflicts and impasses, and risk for a variety of psychopathologies ranging from depression and obsession to life-threatening eating disorders.

Promise. (Video: 1986 [made for TV], color, 100 min.). Directed by Glenn Jordan; starring James Garner, James Woods, Piper Laurie, Peter Michael Goetz, Michael Alldredge, Alan Rosenberg.

When his mother dies, a middle-aged bachelor must honor a promise he made to her to care for his schizophrenic younger brother. Wonderfully written, the story does not gloss over the real problems of living with (and being) someone who is thought-disordered. Outstanding portrayals of personalities, feelings, and the delicate balance between freedom, love, and responsibility.

Sheehan, S. (1982). *Is there no place on earth for me?* New York: Vintage.

Originally published as a series of articles in *The New Yorker.* Susan Sheehan reports her impressions and the experiences of a young schizophrenic woman, "Sylvia Frumkin," with whom she lived and spent time in order to understand better the nature of thought disorders and the difficulties of treating them.

Styron, W. (1990). *Darkness visible: A memoir of madness.* New York: Random House.

In this brief, poetic essay, the author of *Sophie's Choice* documents his own plunge into clinical depression and his gradual progress back to the light.

Three Faces of Eve, The. (Video: 1957, B&W 91 min.). Directed by Nunnally Johnson; starring Joanne Woodward, Lee J. Cobb, David Wayne.

Based on fact, the story of a woman found to have at least three distinct personalities, and the efforts she and her therapists make to find the source— and the resolution—of her disorder.

CHAPTER 14

Psychotherapy

Sharon felt overwhelmed by a sense of impending doom. Nothing in her childhood or her current life explained her anxiety. Her therapist, Dr. José Stevens, suggested that Sharon focus her attention inward to discover what part of her body was most affected by these feelings. After Sharon identified the area just above her solar plexus, Dr. Stevens asked her to breathe deeply into that place, allowing her body to move spontaneously, expressing any images that came to her. This is how Dr. Stevens described Sharon's experience:

As she began to stir, I accompanied her movements with soft drumbeats. She began to curl up, then abruptly she straightened and circled the room in a gliding movement that ended with some low guttural sounds. The dance continued with many flying gestures, sounds, and much emotional intensity, coming to a resolution and completion after some time. She was quite out of breath, but her eyes were clear and bright; her face was flushed with excitement. . . .

She explained she had begun with an image of a dark cave deep in her body at the place where she had focused. This cave felt familiar but filled her with dread. She cried for help and a bird appeared who lifted her on his back and circled out above a strange landscape.

There she could look down and see a double of herself hurriedly leading a group of others toward the cave. Before the group could make it, they were overtaken by an avalanche, and all were buried except her double who lay dying, pinned under a tree. The bird swooped with her down to where the people lay; she climbed off and rushed to the side of her dying double. She was able to comfort her, explaining to her double that the avalanche was not her fault, but an act of nature, and that her life and the lives of the others had come to an end in the natural course of events. With this done, the bird swept her up and returned her to the cave which now felt bright and homelike, without the former feeling of dread. The bird then told her a number of things that were to be kept in absolute confidence until many days later. The dance ended there (Stevens, 1986, p. 48).

After this therapy session, Sharon's vague sense of dread disappeared. She felt more powerful and decisive, and she started using her leadership skills, taking responsibility without feeling guilty when plans didn't work out. "Her previous, limiting feelings were literally worked out of her system in the concentrated and intense healing dance with her guardian spirit" (Stevens, 1986).

When traditional Western "talk therapy" had not helped Sharon, Dr. Stevens turned to **shamanism,** an ancient spiritual tradition that combines healing with making contact with the spirit world. *Still used in contemporary Native American cultures, shamanism (pronounced SHAH-mun-izm) has been practiced for close to 30,000 years. Shamanism originally referred to the religion of the Ural-Altaic peoples of Siberia. It was characterized by belief in demons, gods, and ancestral spirits. According to Native American psychologist Leslie Gray, in the shamanistic tradition "all forms of suffering and disease are diagnosed as powerlessness. The remedy is to regain power for the patient by restoring a vital soul, retrieving a guardian spirit, or instructing in ceremonial practices that return power" (Gray, 1989). Drumming, chanting, and other rituals are used to inspire awe and induce altered states of consciousness that facilitate the quest for knowledge and empowerment (Walsh, 1990).*

Recently, the medical, psychiatric, and psychological professions have begun to work with shamans in an effort to integrate Western psychotherapies that involve self-analysis with the therapies of collectivist societies that view the individual within his or her current communal context. These attempts at integration will make therapies more culturally appropriate to a wider range of clients (Kraut, 1990). (For an excellent analysis of shamanism, consult Mircea Eliade's book Shamanism: Archaic Techniques of Ecstasy, *1964.)*

Introduction

Before you became a student of psychology, your most vivid images and expectations about the discipline probably had to do with its therapeutic role—the use of psychological knowledge in providing help and treatment to people suffering from problems and mental disorders. Sometimes our impressions of therapy are very judgmental: we might criticize a difficult acquaintance by saying "You need help." But certainly, if people *need* help and would benefit from therapy, we should support such treatment, not stigmatize it. Even when we accept psychotherapy as a good idea for others, however, we might resist the idea that we ourselves can benefit from it, as if this would be a recognition of a personal failure or flaw. Our confusion and cultural ambivalence about how best to treat mental disorders often takes the form of humor, ranging from comedians' jokes about going into "analysis" to cartoons depicting stereotypes of patients reclining on couches as they relate their stories to aloof, bearded "shrinks" (a shortened term for "headshrinkers," alluding to popular fears of psychotherapists as mysterious "medicine men").

In this last chapter of our journey through *Psychology,* we begin our review of psychotherapy with a series of questions: What is the truth about therapists and the people who seek their help? What processes and practices are employed in treatment, whether for personal problems or severe mental disorders? How are therapeutic practices influenced by history and culture? What can be done to influence irrational thinking, modify uncontrolled behavior, or alter unchecked emotions? Can therapy be applied to correct abnormalities of the brain and even genes themselves?

To find answers, we start by examining the context of therapy, the circumstances affecting why an individual seeks treatment, the nature of the relationship between therapist and client, and the ways that history and culture have shaped that relationship. We next consider the major types of treatments currently used by health care providers, and how these treatments work. Finally, we will also consider some basic questions—and evidence—regarding the effectiveness of therapy and its success in providing help and relief: Does it really work?

The Context of Therapy

Why seek therapy? There are many reasons why people seek help—and why others who need it do not. The purposes or goals of therapy, the settings in which therapy occurs, and the kinds of therapeutic helpers vary. Regardless of the differences between therapies, however, all are *interventions* into a person's life, designed to change that person's functioning in some way.

Treatment of physical illness and mental illness is determined by the severity of illness. Some illnesses, such as cancer or schizophrenia, are so serious that they require long-term, intensive treatment by highly trained professionals in special institutional settings. Relatively minor problems, whether occasional head colds or a phobia about riding escalators (one that is not impossible to deal with), do not usually require any formal treatment. A person with such a mild disorder might mention it to a physician, or ask advice from friends, and ultimately find effective solutions that do not involve entering therapy. Between these two extremes of severe versus mild disorders lie a variety of problems: illnesses may be short-term but intense; they may be mild but persistent and increasingly difficult to cope with; problems may be disturbingly repetitive; and they may vary in the degree to which they interfere with the daily life of the afflicted person. Because the experience of abnormality affects the individual uniquely and subjectively, people's willingness to consider therapy will vary widely even for similar problems. When appropriate for the problem and willingly chosen by the individual, therapy can be a great source of help and reassurance.

Entering Therapy

Why would *you* go into therapy? Why would anyone? Most often, people enter therapy when their everyday functioning violates societal criteria of normality or their own sense of adequate adjustment. They may seek therapy on their own initiative after trying ineffectively to cope with their problems, or they may be advised to do so by family, friends, doctors, or coworkers.

"*You are a very sick rabbit.*"

Psychotherapy can help with problems associated with long-term illnesses that drastically affect the person's life. Sudden life changes due to unemployment, death of a loved one, or divorce may trigger or worsen one's psychological problems. Students who seek therapy from college mental health facilities often do so because of difficulties in their interpersonal relationships and concerns about academic performance. Finally, those whose behavior is judged as dangerous to themselves or others can be involuntarily committed by a state court to a mental institution for a limited period of time for treatment, testing, or observation.

Why *don't* people seek therapy? Many people who might benefit from therapy do not seek it. Sometimes it is inconvenient for them to do so. People also often lack community mental health facilities, are ignorant of available resources, lack the money, fear stigmatization, or have prejudices against seeking help from a psychologist.

One's ability to get help can be affected even by the psychological problems themselves. The person with agoraphobia finds it hard, even impossible, to leave home to seek therapy; a paranoid person will not trust mental health professionals. Extremely shy people cannot call for an appointment or go to an initial diagnostic interview precisely because of the problem for which they desire help. In many communities, it is still much easier to get help from a medical doctor for physical health problems than it is to find a qualified mental health worker who has time to provide needed, affordable psychological help.

People who do enter therapy are usually referred to as either *patients* or *clients*. The term "patient" is used by professionals who take a biological or medical approach to the treatment of mental disorders, and for those who are hospitalized for their treatment. The term "client" is used by professionals who think of psychological disorders not as mental *illnesses* but rather as problems in living for which people seek the assistance of specially trained professionals (Rogers, 1951; Szasz, 1961). The distinction may not be important in how we view psychotherapies in general, but it does suggest some distinctions in the way different professionals relate to individuals seeking help, and what those individuals discover about the therapeutic experience.

The Therapeutic Relationship

A therapist is not merely a "paid friend," because friends have needs and agendas of their own that may not always coincide with those of the person seeking assistance. Sometimes you may only need to talk out a problem with a sympathetic friend, perhaps to "hear yourself think" or to receive reassurance that he or she still cares for you. But for other, more persistent or difficult problems, you might want expert help and an objective point of view. You might also wish to keep your problems and concerns confidential, which would not necessarily be possible if you sought advice from a friend. When friends and family can offer only limited help, it may be appropriate to seek the help of a professionally trained therapist, who must maintain the confidentiality of your relationship.

Despite the differences between therapy and friendship, however, the essence of therapy is still a *relationship* between the therapist and the patient/client seeking assistance. You must be able to trust your therapist, just as you would a reliable friend. You and your therapist must be able to work as *allies,* on the same side, joining forces to cope with and solve some of the problems that have brought you to therapy (Horvath & Luborsky, 1993). Finally, you must agree with your therapist about your concerns, values, and goals. An effective therapist first establishes whether he or she and the client can achieve this trusting, collaborative alliance—and then builds on this relationship to accomplish the more specific work of therapy. It also helps if you *believe* that therapy will be effective for your problem.

In addition to the relationship between therapist and client, the therapeutic process can involve the following four primary tasks or goals:

1. Reaching a *diagnosis* about what is wrong, possibly determining an appropriate psychiatric (DSM-IV) label for the presenting problem, and classifying the disorder.
2. Identifying the *etiology* of the disorder—its probable origins, its development, and the functions served by its symptoms.
3. Making a *prognosis,* or estimate, of the future course the problem will take, with and without any treatment.
4. Prescribing and carrying out some form of *treatment,* a therapy designed to minimize or eliminate the troublesome symptoms and, perhaps, also their sources.

Therapy is conducted in a variety of different settings: hospitals, clinics, schools, and private offices. Newer community-based therapies that aim to take the treatment to the client may operate out of local store fronts or church facilities. *Therapists who practice* **in vivo therapy** *work with clients in the life setting that is associated with their problem.* For example, they work in airports and airplanes with people who suffer from flying phobias, or in shopping malls and other busy, public places with people who have social phobias.

Professional Therapists   When psychological problems arise, most of us initially seek out informal counselors who operate in familiar settings. Many people turn to family members, close friends, physicians, lawyers, or favorite teachers for support, guidance, and counsel. Those with religious affiliations may seek help from a religious advisor. Others get advice and a chance to talk by "opening up" to neighborhood bartenders, beauticians, cab drivers, or other people willing to listen. In our society, these informal therapists carry the bulk of the daily burden of relieving people's pent-up frustration and conflict.

However, as college professors, we authors know from our personal experience that students often fail to come to the aid of dormitory mates or even friends who are in obvious psychological distress. They may fear getting too involved in an emotionally unpleasant, time-consuming process; or, not knowing exactly how to approach the individual, they may worry that they will only say the wrong thing and end up making matters worse. *What do you do* in such situations? We urge you to take action, even by making the simple gesture of showing that you are concerned, whether you have solutions or not. It is usually sufficient to tell the distressed person that you *are* concerned, and that while you have limited time or experience to be directly helpful, you can listen and offer social support.

Although more people seek out therapy now than in the past, people usually turn to trained mental health professionals only when their psychological problems become severe or persist for extended periods of time. When they do, they usually turn to one of six main types of therapists: counseling psychologists, clinical psychologists, psychiatrists, clinical social workers, pastoral counselors, or psychoanalysts. We'll consider briefly what distinguishes each type.

Counseling Psychologists The term **counseling psychologist** *describes a member of the general category of professional psychologists who provides guidance in dealing with the problems of normal living.* Even "normal" life presents challenges and stressors that can make it difficult to cope. A counseling psychologist might advise clients in a variety of areas, such as selecting a vocation, school problems, drug abuse, and marital conflict. Typically these

cathy®   **by Cathy Guisewite**

counselors work in community settings related to the problem areas—within a business, a school, a prison, the military service, or a neighborhood clinic—and use interviews, tests, guidance, and advice to help individuals solve specific problems and make decisions about future options.

Clinical Psychologists Specifically trained in psychology, a **clinical psychologist** *diagnoses and treats individuals with severe disorders, often in clinical settings such as a psychiatric hospital.* A typical clinical psychologist has concentrated his or her graduate school training in the assessment and treatment of psychological problems, completed a supervised internship in a clinical setting, and earned a Ph.D. (Doctor of Philosophy degree). These psychologists tend to have a broader background in psychology, assessment, and research than do psychiatrists; however, the day-to-day work of psychologists and psychiatrists may be similar.

Psychiatrists A **psychiatrist** *is not a psychologist but a physician, trained in medicine, and specializing in the treatment of mental and emotional disorders.* Psychiatrists' training lies more in the biomedical base of psychological problems, and they are the only therapists who can, at present, legally prescribe medications or physically based therapy.

Clinical Social Workers A **clinical social worker** *is a mental health professional with specialized training in social work that focuses on the social context of the problem.* Typically, training prepares a social worker to collaborate with psychiatrists and clinical psychologists. However, unlike psychiatrists and psychologists, these counselors are trained to consider the *social contexts* of people's problems, so they may involve other family members in the therapy or at least become acquainted with clients' home and work settings.

Pastoral Counselors A **pastoral counselor** *is a member of a religious order or ministry who has been trained and specializes in the treatment of psychological disorders.* Pastoral counselors often combine spiritual and practical problem-solving directions. In a sense, shamanistic healing ceremonies (as described in our opening case on Sharon) represent a "pastoral-religious" approach to healing mental disorders—even though they may not resemble mainstream American religious traditions.

Psychoanalysts A **psychoanalyst** *is a therapist specializing in applying Freudian principles in the treatment of mental disorders.* Whatever their original field or background, psychoanalysts must complete specialized postgraduate training in psychoanalytic theory and practice. We will discuss the details of psychoanalytic treatment in a later section when we describe the basic features of the major psychotherapies. Before that discussion, we will review the history of psychological treatment and examine some forms of treatment for mental problems that have been practiced for centuries in different cultures.

Therapy in Historical and Cultural Context

The treatment you might get if you seek therapy depends on at least two broad sets of factors: how you determine your personal *need* for therapy, and how your *culture* views this need. What kind of treatment might you have received in past centuries if you suffered from psychological problems? If you lived in Europe or the United States, chances are the treatment would not have helped and could even have been harmful. In other cultures, treatment of psychological disorders has usually been seen within a broader perspective that includes religious and social values. This point of view has resulted in kinder treatment of those with aberrant behavior.

Western Attitudes Toward Treating Mental Illness Population increases and migration to big cities in fourteenth-century western Europe created unemployment, poverty, and social alienation. These conditions led to crime and psychological problems. Special institutions were soon created to warehouse European society's three emerging categories of misfits: the poor, criminals, and the mentally disturbed.

In 1403, a London hospital—St. Mary of Bethlehem—admitted its first patient with psychological problems. For the next 300 years, mental patients of the hospital were chained, tortured, and exhibited to an admission-paying public. Over time, "Bedlam"—a mispronunciation of *Bethlehem*—came to

In this engraving from the 1730s, we see the chaos of a cell in the London hospital, St. Mary of Bethlehem. Here the upper classes have paid to see the horrors, the fiddler who entertains, and the mental patients chained, tortured, and dehumanized. The chaos of Bethlehem eventually became synonymous with the corruption of its name—Bedlam.

mean *chaos* because of the horrible confusion reigning in the hospital and the dehumanized treatment of patients there (Foucault, 1975).

In fifteenth-century Germany, the mad were assumed to be possessed by the devil, who had deprived them of reason. As the Inquisition's persecutory mania spread throughout Europe, mental disturbances were "cured" by painful death or prosecuted as evidence of witchcraft.

During the late eighteenth century the perception of psychological problems as *mental illness* emerged in Europe. The French physician **Philippe Pinel** wrote in 1801, "The mentally ill, far from being guilty people deserving of punishment, are sick people whose miserable state deserves all the consideration that is due to suffering humanity. One should try with the most simple methods to restore their reason" (cited in Zilboorg & Henry, 1941, pp. 323–324).

In the United States, psychologically disturbed citizens were confined for their own protection and for the safety of the community, but they were given no treatment. However, by the mid-1800s, when psychology as a field of study was gaining some credibility and respectability, "a cult of curability" emerged throughout the country. Eventually, madness came to be viewed as a social problem to be cured through mental hygiene, just as contagious physical diseases were being treated by physical hygiene. This was the perspective of the disease model.

One of the founders of modern psychiatry, German psychiatrist **J. C. Heinroth,** helped provide the conceptual and moral justification for the disease model of mental illness. In 1818, Heinroth wrote that madness was a complete loss of inner freedom or reason, depriving those afflicted of any ability to control their lives. Others who "knew best" what was good for the patient would have to be put in charge of care (Szasz, 1979). Initially the state had an interest in confining the mentally ill, to protect them as well as society. However, from Heinroth's time to the present, with the assistance of the mental health profession, this initial interest has been "transformed into a power . . . to treat . . . the mental disorder thought to be the basis of the problem" (White & White, 1981, p. 954).

Heinroth's work heralded a change. One of his former mental patients, **Clifford Beers,** carried on the work of a *mental hygiene movement* in the 1900s. Beers's 1908 book, *A Mind That Found Itself,* helped to make the welfare of the mentally ill a matter of public concern and social action. Eventually, the confinement of the mentally ill assumed a new *rehabilitative* goal. The *asylum* then became the central fixture of this social-political movement. The disturbed were confined to asylums in rural areas, far from the stress of the city, not only for protection but also for treatment (Rothman, 1971). Unfortunately, many of the asylums that were built became overcrowded. Then the original, humane goal of rehabilitation was replaced with the pragmatic goal of *containing*—and later "warehousing"—strange people in remote places.

Contemporary Approaches to Therapy   Modern approaches to therapy are applications of scientific theory. In many ways a theory about mental illness is a model, a simpler idea about a complex reality, that might help researchers and clinical practitioners to understand where problems come from and how best to treat them. Each model is based on its own assumptions and sets of observations, and may focus on one aspect of personality or healthy functioning while deemphasizing others. For example, using the computer as a model or metaphor for how the brain functions, we can say that mental problems may occur either in the brain's *hardware* (physical components) or its *software* (programs or patterns of operation). Following this model, contemporary approaches to therapy can be viewed as focusing on either the hardware or software. The first class of therapies, which we will examine at the end of this chapter, includes *biomedical techniques*. The second group of therapies are those that use techniques based on *psychological* theories and processes.

Biomedical therapy *focuses on changing the hardware—the mechanisms that run the individual's central nervous system, endocrine system, and metabolism.* Biomedical therapies try to alter brain functioning with chemical or physical interventions. Laws often specify which professions are licensed to provide biomedical therapy, but most mental health practitioners collaborate to meet both legal requirements and patients' needs. For example, therapists with the M.D. degree (Doctor of Medicine) can prescribe drugs while those with the Ph.D. (Doctor of Philosophy) cannot, but Ph.D. clinical psychologists are likely to work with physicians in making diagnoses and recommendations for the proper course of medication.

Psychological therapies, *which are collectively called psychotherapy, focus on changing disordered thoughts, feelings, and behavior using psychological techniques.* In the computer metaphor, these processes make up our "software"—the faulty behaviors we have learned, and the cognitive interpretations and social feedback that direct our daily strategies for living. Briefly, we will review (in the next section) four major types of psychotherapy: *psychodynamic, behavioral, cognitive,* and *existential-humanistic.*

The *psychodynamic approach* views adult neurotic suffering as the outer symptom of inner, unresolved childhood traumas and conflicts. The best-known psychodynamic treatment is *psychoanalysis,* the so-called talking cure in which a therapist helps a person develop insights about the relationship between the overt symptoms and the unresolved hidden conflicts that are presumably causing those symptoms.

Behavior therapy treats the behaviors themselves as disturbances that must be modified. Disorders are viewed as learned behavior patterns rather than as the symptoms of some underlying mental disease. Behavior therapists believe that changing the problem behavior corrects the disorder.

Cognitive therapy tries to restructure how a person thinks by altering the often distorted self-statements a person makes about the causes of a problem. Cognitions (thoughts, beliefs, and attitudes) are viewed as changeable behaviors.

Therapies emerging from the *existential-humanistic tradition* emphasize the *values* of patients. Existential-humanistic therapies are directed toward self-actualization, psychological growth, the development of more meaningful interpersonal relationships, and the enhancement of freedom of choice.

Healing in Cultural Context Modern Western views and practices regarding psychological disorders emphasize how natural processes in survival and evolution—such as competitiveness, independence, mastery of the environment, and experiences of success and failure—all influence whether one's behavior is considered adaptive and healthy. In one sense, the modern scientific view of psychopathology has something in common with both demonology and the disease model of abnormality: all these models regard mental disorders as something that happens *inside* a person, as an outcome of some type of "failure" to adapt or succeed in one's environment.

But many other cultures do not share this view (Triandis, 1990). For example, a common African view emphasizes not individual failure and fallibility, but "groupness," commonality, cooperation, interdependence, tribal survival, unity with nature, and collective responsibility (Nobles, 1976). Treatment of mentally ill individuals by *removing* them from society is *contrary* to the thinking of many non-European cultures. Among the Navajo

In Mozambique, a Femba tribe's medicine woman, one of their *curandeiros* or healers, "catches the bad spirit" of her patient.

CULTURAL CONTEXT

Universals in Therapy

Often, people will seek help from family members and close friends for their problems. At other times, though, they will seek help from individuals outside their families who have a reputation for skillfulness in helping people. In different cultures, these helpers can be clinical psychologists, psychiatrists, counselors, native healers, medicine men, herbalists, religious figures, shamans, or social workers. Do people who seek help share common experiences regardless of who provides that help? Various researchers have concluded that there are indeed common experiences, called "universals," that characterize the relationship between help-seeker and help-giver (Draguns, 1980, 1990; Ponterotto & Benesch, 1988; Torrey, 1986). We will discuss six universals here, and we'll use the general term "therapist" for the person with the reputation or role-expectation for offering help.

1. *Therapists apply a name to the problem people have.* When people learn that a problem has a name, they come to believe that others may have experienced the same difficulties and that there may be some solutions.

2. *The qualities of the therapist are important.* The therapist must be seen as caring, competent, sensitive, and able to find solutions to problems. While all therapies are solution oriented, people in some cultures *expect to be told what to do.* With this expectation, they are less comfortable examining many possibilities and developing *their own* solutions.

Members of some cultures may expect early relief, and consider long, "talk-oriented" therapies unhelpful. Therapists need to use their contact with clients to learn what they expect and to educate them about likely outcomes.

Cultural differences between therapist and client can be overcome if the therapist is culturally sensitive (Sue, 1988). For example, many African Americans believe that their cultural experiences include a history of rejection due to prejudice and discrimination. If therapists are Anglo Americans, they must demonstrate an understanding about and sensitivity toward this viewpoint (Locke, 1992).

3. *Therapists have to establish their credibility.* This can be done by using the symbols of status that are well known in a culture. In middle-class American culture, an attractive office and diplomas on the wall can establish the therapist's credibility. In other cultures, such impression management can include ceremonial robes that can be worn only by people who have served a long apprenticeship. In any culture, credibility is aided when therapists benefit from positive "word of mouth" references. If one person is helped and tells many others, the therapist's positive reputation will spread.

4. *Therapists place the help-seeker's problem and their interventions into a framework that will be familiar to the help-seeker.* If the help-seeker believes in spirits, the therapist may introduce an intervention to drive out or to appease the spirits. If the client believes adult problems usually stem from unresolved childhood conflicts, he or she will seek a

therapist—such as a psychoanalyst—who is sympathetic to that framework. If the client wishes to change a specific behavior without any deep analysis of motives or origins, a behavioral or cognitive therapy may provide the most comfortable therapeutic framework.

5. *Therapists apply a set of techniques that are meant to address the problem and to bring eventual relief.* Again, specific techniques will either be familiar to a help-seeker, or the therapist will educate the help-seeker about their importance. There are many specific techniques; mastery of even a limited number of such techniques demands years of study and (or) apprenticeship.

6. *The actual therapy occurs at a specific time and in a special location.* Setting aside a special time and place gives people a chance to deal with their problems in an intense, emotionally charged manner, away from their day-to-day lives. Examples of special places for therapy include well-furnished offices; hospitals; churches; and, in tribal villages, huts that are taboo except when used for healing ceremonies.

People seek help from therapists either because they feel overwhelmed by problems they perceive as beyond their control, or because they are so rebellious or deviant that others in their culture demand that they seek help. The goal of therapy, no matter where it occurs, is to bring relief to people and to contribute to harmonious relationships within a culture. When therapy is successful, there is typically a better "fit" between the person and his or her life setting and culture.

and African cultures, for example, healing always takes place in a social context, involving a distressed person's beliefs, family, work, and life environment. The African use of group support in therapy has been expanded into a procedure called "network therapy," where a patient's entire network of relatives, coworkers, and friends becomes involved in the treatment (Lambo, 1978). As you can see in the box on Cultural Context: Universals in Therapy, despite varied assumptions about health and spirituality, therapists around the world agree on the qualities that make therapy effective and promote healing.

In many cultures, the treatment of mental and physical disease is bound up with religion and witchcraft; certain persons are assumed to have special mystical powers to help in the transformation of their distressed fellow beings. Common to all folk healing ceremonies are the important roles of symbols, myths, and ritual (Levi-Strauss, 1963). **Ritual healing** *ceremonies infuse special emotional intensity and meaning into the healing process.* They heighten patients' suggestibility and sense of personal importance, and, combined with the use of symbols, they connect the individual sufferer, the shaman, and the society to supernatural forces to be won over in the battle against madness (Devereux, 1981; Wallace, 1959).

Some of these non-Western views have begun to work their way into Western practices. The influence of the social-interactive concept and the focus on *family context* and *supportive community* are evident in newer therapeutic approaches that emphasize social support networks and family therapy.

All over the world, people seek help from specially trained and talented members of their community. Regardless of the differences among cultures and the assumptions about the causes and specific treatments for various disorders, all therapies have one goal in common: they all seek to change the individual's behavior in the direction of health and well-being. When they work as planned, psychotherapies reduce suffering, and patients or clients are able to resume their healthy and productive roles in society.

Check Your Recall

People enter therapy for help with mental or emotional problems that are causing suffering, dysfunctional behavior, or social problems. The therapeutic process involves four tasks: diagnosing what is wrong; figuring out the source of the problem; making a prognosis about probable outcomes with or without treatment; and carrying out a specific kind of treatment. Various kinds of professionals provide therapy, including counseling psychologists, clinical social workers, pastoral counselors, clinical psychologists, psychiatrists, and psychoanalysts.

Historically, conceptions of disease and deviant behavior were influenced by religious, social, and political agendas of different cultures in different eras. Emerging conceptions of the afflicted person as mentally ill led to more humane treatment and hospitalization in mental institutions. Modern therapeutic techniques can be classified as either biomedical or psychological.

Western psychological views of mental disorder and therapy have been extended to reveal a broader social-religious context. Folk healing typically involves a blend of "magic," myth, and ritual practiced by a healer or shaman, who depends on the patient's total belief in that cultural system of cure. People seek and provide therapy everywhere in the world, and several universal criteria have been identified in therapy worldwide. All therapies have in common the goal of changing behavior according to cultural ideas of health and well-being.

Psychological Therapies

Psychological techniques of therapy emphasize the application of psychological processes—such as learning, development, and communication—to influence individual experience and well-being. Although some psychotherapists specialize in a particular theory or tradition, most adopt an *eclectic* approach, choosing and applying concepts and strategies from different perspectives. They use a mixture of ideas and techniques borrowed from several approaches, according to what a particular client seems to need. The four perspectives we will review here are the *psychodynamic, behavioral, cognitive,* and *existential-humanistic therapies.*

Psychodynamic Therapies

Psychodynamic therapies are based on psychodynamic theories of personality, originated by the work of **Sigmund Freud**. Classic Freudian theories assume that a patient's problems have been caused by the psychological tension between unconscious impulses toward certain actions and the constraints of the individual's life situation. **Psychoanalytic therapy** *involves intensive and prolonged exploration of patients' unconscious motivations and conflicts.* Psychoanalytic techniques were designed to help neurotic, anxiety-ridden individuals to change their disruptive, often self-defeating patterns of thinking and acting by understanding the true causes of their problems. The major goal of psychoanalysis is to reveal the unconscious.

Of central importance to the psychoanalyst is understanding how a patient uses the process of *repression* to handle conflicts. Symptoms are considered to be messages from the unconscious that something is wrong. A psychoanalyst's task is to help a patient bring repressed thoughts to consciousness and to gain *insight* into the relationship between the current symptoms and the repressed conflicts. In this psychodynamic view, therapy works and patients recover when they are "released" from repression established in early childhood (Munroe, 1955). *Because a central goal of a therapist is to guide a patient toward discovering insights between present symptoms and past origins, psychodynamic therapy is often called* **insight therapy.**

The goals of psychoanalysis are ambitious. They involve not just the elimination of the immediate symptoms of psychopathology but a total reorganization of personality. Because traditional psychoanalysis is an attempt to reconstruct long-standing repressed memories and then work through painful feelings to an effective resolution, it is a therapy that takes a long time. It thus requires patients who are highly motivated, introspective, verbally fluent, and able to bear the considerable expense in time and money. Classic psychoanalysis might involve three to five sessions of analysis per week, although contemporary psychoanalytic techniques usually involve fewer sessions.

Sigmund Freud's study, including the famous couch (right), is housed in London's Freud Museum. The 82-year-old Freud fled to London in 1938 upon the Nazi occupation of Austria. He died there the following year.

The Talking Cure   Psychoanalysts use several techniques to bring repressed conflicts to consciousness and to help a patient resolve them (Langs, 1981; Lewis, 1981). These techniques include *free association,* analysis of *resistance, dream analysis,* and analysis of *transference and countertransference.*

Free Association   The principal procedure used in psychoanalysis to probe the unconscious and release repressed material is called **free association,** *a process in which a patient gives a running account of thoughts, wishes, sensations, and mental images as they occur.* A patient, sitting comfortably in a chair or lying in a relaxed position on a couch, lets his or her mind wander freely and orally reports ideas, impressions, memories, and feelings to the attentive psychoanalyst. The patient is encouraged to reveal every thought or feeling, no matter how personal, painful, or seemingly unimportant.

For example, a patient might say, "It's nice to relax. I hope I don't fall asleep. I couldn't sleep well last night and I'm really tired. I kept tossing and turning. Remember that song about 'tossing and turning all night'? I hated that song. But I love music. I miss dancing. I wish I had someone to dance with. Sometimes I feel so lonely, it's like a pain inside." One statement may lead to another statement, or the patient's thoughts might seem to ramble, but these free associations are all important clues for the psychoanalyst's investigative work.

Although these reports seem rambling and unconnected to the free-associating patient, Freud maintained that free associations are not random but *predetermined.* An analyst must track the associations to their source and identify the significant patterns that lie beneath the surface of the words. The patient is encouraged to express strong feelings (usually toward authority figures) that have been repressed for fear of punishment or retaliation. Whatever processes produce it, *any such emotional release, termed* **catharsis,** *can promote beneficial emotional purging—and healing.* This treatment encourages a client to face up to and talk openly about these strong, repressed feelings and to examine them honestly and constructively.

Resistance   At some time during the process of free association, a patient will show **resistance,** *an inability or unwillingness to discuss certain ideas, desires, or experiences.* Resistance prevents repressed material from returning to consciousness. This material is often related to an individual's sexual and pleasurable feelings, or to hostile, resentful feelings toward parents. Sometimes a patient shows resistance by coming late to therapy or "forgetting" a session altogether. When the repressed material comes out in therapy, a patient may claim that it is unimportant, absurd, irrelevant, or too unpleasant to discuss. The therapist is alerted to the likelihood that the opposite is true because the patient "protests too much." Whenever a patient shows such resistance, the psychoanalyst pays particular attention to the issues that may have prompted it.

A psychoanalyst thus attaches particular importance to subjects that a patient does *not* wish to discuss. The aim of psychoanalysis is to break down resistance and enable the patient to face these painful ideas, desires, and experiences, but to do so in the safety of the therapeutic setting. Breaking down resistance is a long and difficult process that is essential if the underlying problem is to be brought to consciousness where it can be resolved.

Dream Analysis   Psychoanalysts believe that dreams are an important source of information about a patient's unconscious motivations. When a person is asleep, the superego is presumably less on guard against the unacceptable impulses originating in the id, so a motive that cannot be expressed in waking life may find expression in a dream. Some motives are so unacceptable to the conscious self that they cannot be revealed openly, even in dreams, but must be expressed in disguised or symbolic form.

In analysis, dreams are assumed to have two kinds of content: *manifest* (openly visible) content and *latent* (hidden) content. The manifest content is what we remember upon awakening. Latent content includes the actual motives that are seeking expression but are so painful or unacceptable to us that we do not want to recognize them. Therapists attempt to uncover these hidden motives by using **dream analysis,** *a therapeutic technique for interpreting dreams in order to achieve insight into the patient's unconscious motives or conflicts.* The analyst examines the content of a person's dreams to discover the underlying or disguised motivations and symbolic meanings of significant life experiences and desires.

For example, in one patient's dream an elaborate dinner attended by familiar guests may really symbolize a family funeral she has recently attended. The analyst assumes that the patient's dream images of food, faces, and feelings all symbolize her unconscious motives and fears about this event and about her family in particular.

Transference and Countertransference During the course of the intensive therapy of psychoanalysis, a patient usually experiences an emotional reaction toward the therapist. Often the therapist is identified with a person who has been at the center of an emotional conflict in the past—most often a parent or a lover. *This emotional reaction, attaching to the therapist's feelings that were originally focused on a significant other, is called* **transference.** *Positive transference* occurs when the feelings attached to the therapist are those of love or admiration, such as feeling the therapist is "like" one's beloved, now-deceased grandparent. *Negative transference* occurs when the patient's feelings consist of hostility or envy, such as might be felt about a rivalrous sibling or critical parent. Often a patient's attitude is *ambivalent,* including a mixture of positive and negative feelings.

An analyst's task in handling transference is a difficult and potentially dangerous one because of the patient's emotional vulnerability; however, it is a crucial part of treatment. A therapist helps a patient to interpret the present transferred feelings by understanding their original source in earlier experiences and attitudes about significant others (Langs, 1981).

Personal feelings are also at work in a therapist's reactions to a patient. **Countertransference** *refers to what happens when a therapist comes to like or dislike a patient who is perceived as similar to significant people in the therapist's life.* In working through countertransference, a therapist may discover some unconscious dynamics of his or her own. Because of the emotional intensity of this type of therapeutic relationship and the vulnerability of the patient, therapists must guard against crossing the boundary between professional caring and personal involvement with their patients. Professional ethics do not allow therapists to become involved with their patients—although, unfortunately, some therapists *have* violated the therapist-client relationship. When these transgressions are reported to authorities, the therapist may lose his or her license to practice.

Post-Freudian Therapies Some of Freud's followers have retained many of his basic ideas but modified certain of his principles and practices. Classical Freudian psychoanalysis emphasizes the importance of three factors: the unconscious in motivation and conflict; the power of early childhood development; and the dynamics within one's personality. In contrast, post-Freudian theories generally have different emphases, including:

- the importance of the individual's *current* social environment
- the *ongoing influence* of life experiences beyond childhood
- the role of social and interpersonal *relationships*
- the significance of one's conscious *self-concept*

To get the flavor of more contemporary psychodynamic approaches of the neo-Freudians, we will look at the work of two of them: Harry Stack Sullivan and Karen Horney. (For a look at the other members of the Freudian and post-Freudian circle, see Ruitenbeek's 1973 book, *The First Freudians*.)

Sullivan's Self-System **Harry Stack Sullivan** (1953) emphasized the social dimension of a patient's life and its role in creating mental problems. He felt that Freudian theory and therapy did not recognize the importance of social relationships or a patient's needs for acceptance, respect, and love. Mental disorders, he insisted, involve not only traumatic intrapsychic processes but troubled interpersonal relationships and even strong societal pressures. A young child needs to feel secure and to be treated by others with caring and tenderness. Anxiety and other mental ills arise out of insecurities in relationships with parents and significant others. In Sullivan's view, the individual creates a self-system to hold anxiety down to a tolerable level. This self-system is derived from a child's interpersonal experiences and is organized around conceptions of the self as "good," "bad," and unacceptably "other."

Therapy based on Sullivan's interpersonal view involves observing a *patient's feelings* about the *therapist's attitudes*. The therapeutic interview is seen as a social setting in which each party's feelings and attitudes are influenced by the other's. Above all, the therapeutic situation, for Sullivan, was one where the therapist learned and taught lovingly (Wallach & Wallach, 1983).

Horney's Relationship Patterns **Karen Horney** (pronounced *HORN-eye*) expanded the boundaries of Freudian theory in many ways (see Horney, 1937; 1945; 1950). She stressed the importance of environmental and cultural contexts in which neurotic behavior is expressed. Rather than viewing personality as determined solely by early childhood experiences and instincts, Horney took a more flexible view. She believed that personality involved rational coping and continual development to deal with current fears and impulses.

One of Horney's contributions to therapy was her emphasis on patterns of interpersonal relationships. Horney pointed out three *neurotic patterns* in close relationships: approaching others, attacking others, and avoiding others. Each neurotic pattern is based on a maladaptive view of the self and leads to repetitive and unsatisfying choices and behaviors. "Approachers" seek love from others to feel complete and secure; they may end up behaving passively and feeling victimized. "Attackers" earn power and respect by competing successfully against others, but risk being feared and ending up "lonely at the top." "Avoiders" withdraw from others to protect themselves from real or imagined hurt and rejection, but can end up closing themselves off from intimacy and support. By understanding these unhealthy patterns—and unraveling the neurotic self-concepts that underlie them—patients can achieve the insights necessary to forge new habits and constructive relationships.

Although psychoanalytic therapy and Freud's theories have been widely criticized (Fisher & Greenberg, 1985), there are still many enthusiastic supporters, especially in Western European countries and in large urban centers in the United States. But the obstacles of expense and limits on available time have led to more short-term psychodynamic therapies and pragmatic approaches that focus on changing symptoms, not the whole personality.

From top left clockwise, the photographs above illustrate Karen Horney's theory of patterns of interpersonal relationships that may become neurotic: attacking others, avoiding others, and approaching others.

Behavioral Therapies

While psychodynamic therapies focus on presumed inner causes, behavioral therapies focus on observable outer behaviors. Behavioral therapies apply the principles of conditioning and reinforcement to modify undesirable behavior patterns associated with mental disorders. Rejecting the medical model of disorders, with its assumptions about "patients" suffering from mental "illness" that must be *cured*, behavioral therapists instead focus on the problem behaviors, examining how they might have been learned and, more importantly, how they can be eliminated and replaced by more effective patterns.

Behavioral therapists argue that abnormal behaviors are acquired in the same way as normal behaviors—through a learning process that follows the basic principles of conditioning and learning. These therapists assert that all pathological behavior, except where there is established organic causation, can be best understood and modified by focusing on the behavior itself rather than by attempting to alter any underlying pathology.

Behavior modification *is the therapeutic approach that applies principles of operant and classical conditioning in changing a client's behavior.* Bootzin (1975) has defined behavior modification as "the attempt to apply learning and other experimentally derived psychological principles to problem behavior." The terms *behavioral therapy* and *behavior modification* are often used interchangeably. Both refer to the systematic use of principles of learning to increase the frequency of desired behaviors and/or decrease the frequency of problem behaviors. Behavioral therapy is used to treat an extensive range of deviant behaviors and personal problems, including fears, compulsions, depression, addictions, aggression, and delinquent behaviors. In general, behavioral therapy works best with specific behavior problems, such as anxiety, rather than general types of personal problems. For example, it is more effective in treating a phobia than a dissociative disorder.

Behavioral therapies are based on classical conditioning, operant conditioning, or a combination of the two. In the sections that follow, consider how the treatment developed is related to assumptions about the nature of the *response* or behavior that is to be changed. If the problem behavior was classically conditioned, then classical conditioning techniques can be applied to modify it. If the response pattern was operantly conditioned, then changes in its contingent consequences—reinforcement or punishment—are applied to effect the desired change.

Classical Conditioning Techniques   The development of irrational fears and other undesirable *emotional* reactions is assumed to follow the paradigm of classical conditioning—the association of a new stimulus to a familiar, powerful stimulus, resulting in the attachment of the same response to both. For example, a woman may experience anxiety (an emotional response) when she walks into an elevator (a conditioned stimulus) because she associates the confined space of the elevator with memories of being locked in a closet when she was a child (the frightening confinement operated as an unconditioned stimulus for fear and anxiety).

When a problem behavior is the result of classical conditioning, a favored treatment is **counterconditioning,** *a behavioral therapy technique in which a new response is substituted for the unwanted or inadequate one.* Counterconditioning is often applied when an individual suffers from an anxiety disorder such as a phobia, an irrational fear of a harmless object or situation. Why would someone become anxious when faced with a harmless stimulus, such as a fly, a nonpoisonous snake, an open space, or a social contact? Is the anxiety due to simple conditioning principles we reviewed earlier? From our discussion of classical conditioning, we know that *any* neutral stimulus may acquire the power to elicit strong conditioned reactions on the basis of prior association with an unconditioned stimulus.

However, not everyone who is exposed to situations that are alarming, dangerous, or traumatic develops long-lasting conditioned fears that become *phobias* that lead to avoidance of those situations. In fact, it is surprising that relatively few people do develop such fears. Strong emotional reactions that disrupt a person's life "for no good reason" are often conditioned responses that the person does not recognize as having been learned previously. To weaken the strength of negative learned associations, behavioral therapists use the counterconditioning techniques of *systematic desensitization, implosion, flooding,* and *aversion therapy.*

Systematic Desensitization   The nervous system cannot be relaxed and agitated or anxious at the same time because different, incompatible processes cannot be activated simultaneously. This simple notion was central to a *theory of reciprocal inhibition* developed by South African psychiatrist **Joseph Wolpe** (1958, 1973) who used it to treat fears and phobias. He taught his patients to *relax* their muscles, and then to *imagine* visually their feared situation. They did so in gradual steps that moved from initially remote associations to direct images of it. Psychologically confronting the feared stimulus while being relaxed and doing so in a *graduated* sequence is the therapeutic technique known as **systematic desensitization,** *a behavioral therapy technique in which the client learns to relax in order to prevent anxiety arousal.*

Desensitization therapy involves three major steps. The client identifies the stimuli that provoke anxiety and arranges them in a *hierarchy* ranked from weakest to strongest (Shapiro, 1995). For example, a student suffering from severe test anxiety constructed the hierarchy in Table 14.1. Note that she rated immediate anticipation of an examination as more stressful than taking the exam itself. Next, the client is trained in a system of progressive deep-muscle relaxation. Relaxation training requires several sessions in which the client learns to distinguish between sensations of tension and relaxation and to let go of tension to achieve a state of physical and mental relaxation. Finally, the actual process of desensitization begins: the relaxed client vividly imagines the *weakest* anxiety stimulus on the list. If the stimulus can be visualized without discomfort, the client goes on to the next stronger one. After a number of sessions, the client can imagine the most distressing situations on the list without anxiety—even situations that she could not face originally (Lang & Lazovik, 1963).

A number of evaluation studies have shown that this behavioral therapy works remarkably well with most phobic patients (Smith & Glass, 1977). Desensitization has also been successfully applied to a diversity of human problems, including such generalized fears as stage fright and anxiety about sexual performance (Kazdin, 1994; Kazdin & Wilcoxin, 1976).

Implosion Another behavior modification technique uses an approach that is the opposite of systematic desensitization. **Implosion therapy** *exposes the client to the stimuli that provoke the greatest anxiety, in order to extinguish anxiety associated with the entire class of stimuli.* At the start of implosion therapy, a client is exposed to the most frightening stimuli at the top of his or her anxiety hierarchy—but in a safe setting, one that will not cause the client to experience extreme or uncontrolled distress. The idea behind this procedure is that the client is not allowed to deny, avoid, or otherwise escape from the anxiety-arousing stimulus situations. He must discover that contact with the stimulus does not actually have the anticipated negative effects (Stampfl & Levis, 1967).

To expose the client to contact with the feared stimulus, the therapist *describes* an extremely frightening situation relating to the client's fear, such as snakes crawling all over his body. The therapist then urges the client to *imag-*

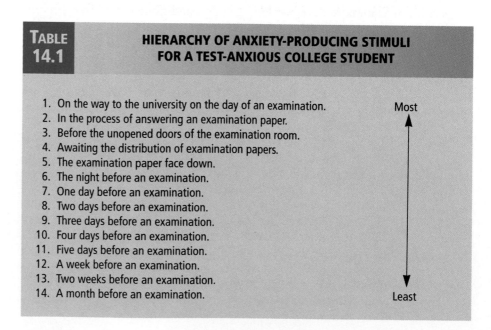

TABLE 14.1	HIERARCHY OF ANXIETY-PRODUCING STIMULI FOR A TEST-ANXIOUS COLLEGE STUDENT

1. On the way to the university on the day of an examination.   Most
2. In the process of answering an examination paper.
3. Before the unopened doors of the examination room.
4. Awaiting the distribution of examination papers.
5. The examination paper face down.
6. The night before an examination.
7. One day before an examination.
8. Two days before an examination.
9. Three days before an examination.
10. Four days before an examination.
11. Five days before an examination.
12. A week before an examination.
13. Two weeks before an examination.
14. A month before an examination.   Least

ine it fully, experiencing it through all the senses as intensely as possible. Such imagining is assumed to cause an explosion of panic. Because this explosion is an inner one, the process is called *implosion;* hence the term *implosion therapy.* As the situation happens again and again, the stimulus loses its power to elicit anxiety. When anxiety no longer occurs, the maladaptive behavior previously used to avoid it disappears.

Flooding The success of implosion therapy depends greatly on the client's imagination: the more vividly he or she can imagine each anxiety-provoking situation, the better he or she will be able to learn new behavior when confronted with the real situation. Instead of asking the client to exercise imaginative skills, another approach to this principle addresses the arousing reality directly. **Flooding** *is a therapy for phobias in which clients agree to be exposed to stimuli they consider most frightening, in order to force them to test reality.* Flooding is similar to implosion except that it places clients, with their permission, in the actual phobic situation. A claustrophobic client might sit in a dark closet, or a child with a fear of water be encouraged to get into a pool. A therapist might choose to "work up to" flooding by first stimulating the imagination. For example, the phobic client may be required to listen to a tape that describes the most terrifying version of her phobic fear in great detail for an hour or two. Once her terror subsides and she feels able to act, the client is then taken to the feared situation, which, of course, is not nearly as frightening as she just imagined. Flooding has been found to be more effective than systematic desensitization in the treatment of agoraphobia, and treatment gains are shown to be enduring for most clients (Emmelkamp & Kuipers, 1979).

A behavioral therapist uses flooding therapy to help a client overcome fear of flying.

Aversion Therapy The forms of "exposure therapy" just discussed help clients deal directly with stimuli that are not really harmful. After all, even though an individual may have a phobic reaction to insects, the mere presence of bugs cannot actually harm her, so therapy can be conducted without too much risk. But what can be done to help those who are *attracted* to stimuli that *are* harmful or illegal? For example, drug addiction, sexual perversions, and uncontrollable violence are human problems in which deviant behavior is elicited by tempting stimuli. **Aversion therapy** *uses counterconditioning procedures of aversive learning to pair attractive stimuli with strong noxious stimuli.* Noxious or aversive stimuli might include electric shocks or nausea-producing drugs, whose effects are unpleasant but not in themselves destructive or dangerous to the client. In time, through conditioning, the negative reactions associated with the aversive stimuli are elicited by the conditioned stimuli, formerly tempting stimuli like addictive drugs, and the person develops an aversion for them that replaces her former desire.

For example, the drug Antabuse is sometimes prescribed for alcoholics who wish to control their drinking. The drug has no side effects—unless the patient drinks even a small amount of alcohol; then he or she becomes severely nauseous. By anticipating such aversive consequences, the patient can significantly strengthen her resolve *not* to take a drink by making the single daily decision to take the prescribed Antabuse.

In the extreme, aversion therapy resembles torture, so why would anyone submit voluntarily to it? Usually people do so only because they realize that the long-term consequences of continuing their maladaptive behavior will destroy their health or ruin their careers or family lives. They may also be coerced to do so by institutional pressures, as in some prison treatment programs. Many critics are concerned that the painful procedures in aversion therapy give too much power to the therapist, can be more punitive than therapeutic, and are most likely to be used in situations where people have the least freedom of choice about what is done to them. The 1971 movie *A*

Clockwork Orange, based on Anthony Burgess's 1962 novel, depicted aversion therapy as an extreme form of mind control in a police state. In recent years, use of aversion therapy in institutional rehabilitation programs has become regulated by state laws and ethical guidelines for clinical treatment. The hope is that, under these restrictions, it will be a therapy of choice rather than coercion.

Operant Conditioning Techniques   When the problem behavior has been acquired as the result of reinforcement, behavior modification can be accomplished by *contingency management* or *social learning therapy.* Contingency management involves altering the rewards and punishers that shape the individual's behavior. Social learning therapy applies this principle to one's larger social environment, changing behavior by changing the behavior of others, such as one's role models.

Contingency Management   In **contingency management,** *behavior is changed by modifying its consequences, with reinforcers increasing and punishers decreasing the probability of the response being modified.* For example, friends and family of the smoking client agree they will refuse to cooperate with the smoker's request to smoke, approving of (rewarding) nonsmoking alternatives ("Here, have a stick of gum instead") and punishing relapses into smoking by breaking off conversation and leaving the room if the person insists on lighting a cigarette. Over time, the changing contingencies help keep the new habit—not smoking—in place, and retrain the individual who hopes to change his or her behavior.

The operant conditioning approach of **B. F. Skinner** to developing desirable behavior is simple: Find the reinforcer that will maintain a desired response, apply that reinforcer (contingent upon the appropriate response), and evaluate its effectiveness. If it works, continue using it; if it doesn't, search for other reinforcers and then apply those. One variation of contingency management involves *positive reinforcement strategies,* pairing preferred response patterns with rewards. In contrast, *extinction strategies* eliminate unwanted behavior by removing the reinforcers that have sustained it. Let's look at each of these procedures in more detail.

When a response is followed immediately by a reward, the response will tend to be repeated and will increase in frequency over time. This central principle of operant learning becomes a therapeutic strategy when used to modify the frequency of a desirable response in place of an undesirable one. The application of positive reinforcement procedures to the behavior problems of children with psychiatric disorders has met with dramatic success. For example, combative children can learn to cooperate with others when reinforced with privileges, and victims of abuse can be encouraged to talk about their experiences if they are rewarded with praise, sympathy, and acceptance.

Is there a behavior you would like to engage in more often than you do— studying, initiating conversations with others, exercising to keep fit? To increase your likelihood of engaging in the response, apply some positive reinforcement therapy. Choose an appropriate reward, identify the specific behavior that will "earn" it, and consistently reinforce your new behavior by rewarding yourself for those actions. In time, you may discover that the desired behavior carries its own rewards—better grades, or a more satisfying social life—and that these expectations will reinforce your new habits. Positive reinforcement strategies also have the advantage of building pleasant and rewarding experiences into your life, because you control and administer them yourself. When you know you are able to reward yourself for a job well done—by enjoying a pleasant mental image, relaxing for five minutes, or enjoying a beautiful sunset—you are more likely to do the job well in the first place (Kazdin, 1994). Positive reinforcement strategies can be highly effective in helping an individual to *increase the frequency* of a desirable behavior.

But what if you have the opposite problem: you regularly engage in a behavior that you wish to *reduce?* For example, maybe you overeat, smoke cigarettes, or say "the wrong thing" in awkward social situations. Why would people continue to do something that causes pain and distress when they are capable of doing otherwise? The answer is that many forms of behavior have multiple consequences—some negative and some positive. Often, subtle positive reinforcements keep a behavior going despite its obvious negative consequences. Just as positive reinforcement can increase the incidence of a behavior, *lack* of desirable consequences can decrease its incidence. By removing the rewards—or removing the individual from a rewarding situation when he or she manifests the unwanted behavior—the therapist can weaken and ultimately extinguish the problem behavior. For example, a child who no longer receives attention when he throws a tantrum, or who is placed in a "time-out" room when he misbehaves, will eventually cease his ineffective displays. The essence of *extinction strategies* is to correctly identify the reinforcers for the problem behavior and remove them quickly and consistently. Without any rewards or supports to maintain the response, it will eventually be extinguished.

Extinction is useful in therapy when dysfunctional behaviors have been maintained by unrecognized reinforcing circumstances. Those reinforcers can be identified through a careful situational analysis, and then a program can be arranged to withhold them in the presence of the undesirable response. When this approach is possible, and everyone who might inadvertently reinforce the person's behavior cooperates, extinction procedures work to diminish the frequency of the behavior and eventually to eliminate the behavior completely.

Social Learning Therapy Social learning theorists point out that humans learn—for better or worse—by observing the behavior of other people. **Social learning therapy** *is designed to modify problematic behavior patterns by establishing conditions in which the client will observe models being reinforced for the desired response.* Social learning therapies are based on the theory that behavior is influenced by observation and imitation of others. This vicarious learning process has been of special value in overcoming phobias and in building social skills.

When we discussed phobias in Chapter 13, we noted that one way such fears could be learned was through vicarious conditioning—through the transmission of fear displayed by others, such as from mother to child. An interesting series of studies with monkeys illustrates this imitation of modeled behavior. In one study, young monkeys were reared in the laboratory, where they never saw a snake. In the experimental situation, these monkeys observed their parents, who had been raised in the wild and who reacted fearfully to real snakes and toy snakes. The young monkeys promptly showed a strong fear of snakes. The more disturbed the parents were at the sight of the snakes, the greater the fear in their offspring (Mineka et al., 1984). In a follow-up study, young, laboratory-raised rhesus monkeys observed the fearful reactions of adult monkeys who were strangers to them. Figure 14.1 shows the young monkeys revealed little fear in the initial pretest; however, after observing models that reacted fearfully, they did also, both to the real and toy snakes. This fear persisted but was less strong and more variable than that of the other young monkeys who had observed their own parents' fearful reactions (Cook et al., 1985).

Many new responses, especially complex ones, can be acquired more readily if a person can observe and imitate another person performing the desired behavior and be reinforced for doing so. In **participant modeling,** *the therapist*

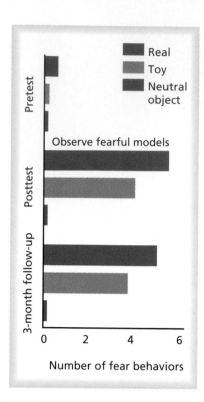

FIGURE 14.1 Fear Reactions in Monkeys ■ After young monkeys raised in laboratories observe unfamiliar adult monkeys showing a strong fear of snakes, they are vicariously conditioned to fear real snakes and toy snakes with an intensity that persists over time.

demonstrates the desired behavior, and encourages the client to imitate the modeling actions. For example, if a fear of snakes can be learned by observing others with fearful reactions, then it should be possible for people with snake phobias to unlearn them through imitation of models. In treating a phobia of snakes, a therapist will first demonstrate fearless behavior, such as approaching a caged snake, then touching the snake, and so on. The client is urged and helped to imitate each modeled behavior. At no time is the client forced to perform any behavior. Resistance at any level is overcome by having the client return to a previously successful, less threatening approach behavior.

The power of participant modeling has emerged in research that compared the participant modeling technique with symbolic modeling, desensitization, and a control condition (see Figure 14.2). In *symbolic modeling therapy,* subjects who had been trained in relaxation techniques watched a film in which several models fearlessly handled snakes; the subjects could stop the film and relax themselves whenever a scene made them feel anxious. In the control condition, no therapeutic intervention was used. Participant modeling was clearly the most successful of these techniques. Snake phobia was eliminated in 11 of the 12 subjects in the participant modeling group (Bandura, 1970).

Social learning therapy extends the lessons of the "life laboratory"—the influences that shape all our behaviors as we seek to reach our goals, please others, and deal well with the circumstances of our lives. In Focus on Application: Learning Social Skills, we note that such therapy can also correct mislearned lessons about how to interact successfully with other people.

Before turning to cognitive therapies, take a few minutes to review the major differences between the two dominant psychotherapies outlined thus far—the psychoanalytic and the behavioral—as summarized in Table 14.2.

FIGURE 14.2 Participant Modeling Therapy ■ The subject shown in the photo first watches a model make a graduated series of snake-approach responses and then repeats them herself. Eventually, she is able to pick up the snake and let it move about on her. The graph compares the number of approach responses subjects made before and after receiving participant modeling therapy (most effective) with the behavior of those exposed to two other therapeutic techniques and a control group.

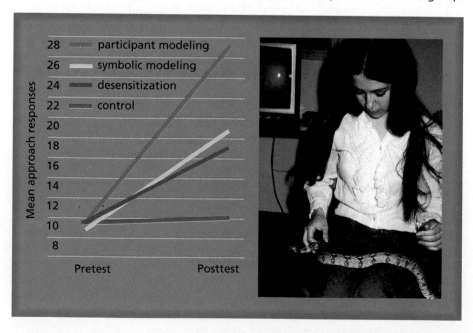

	COMPARISON OF PSYCHOANALYTIC AND BEHAVIORAL APPROACHES TO PSYCHOTHERAPY	

TABLE 14.2

Issue	Psychoanalysis	Behavior Therapy
Basic human nature	Biological instincts, primarily sexual and aggressive, press for immediate release, bringing people into conflict with social reality.	Similar to other animals, people are born with the capacity for learning, which follows similar principles in all species.
Normal human development	Growth occurs through resoluton of conflicts during successive stages. Through identification and internalization, mature ego controls and character structures emerge.	Adaptive behaviors are learned through reinforcement and imitation.
Name of psychopathology	Pathology reflects inadequate conflict resolution and fixations in earlier development, which leave overly strong impulses and/or weak controls. Symptoms are defensive responses to anxiety.	Problematic behavior derives from faulty learning of maladaptive behaviors. The *symptom* is the problem; there is no *underlying disease*
Goal of therapy	Psychosexual maturity, strengthened ego functions, and reduced control by unconscious and repressed impulses are attained.	Symptomatic behavior is eliminated and replaced with adaptive behaviors.
Psychological realm emphasized	Motives, feelings, fantasies, and cognitions are experienced.	Therapy involves behavior and observable feelings and actions.
Time orientation	Past conflicts and repressed feelings are uncovered and interpreted in light of the present.	There is little or no concern with early history or etiology. Present behavior is examined and treated.
Role of unconscious material	This is primary in classical psychoanalysis and somewhat less emphasized by neo-Freudians.	There is no concern with unconscious processes or with subjective experience, even in the conscious realm.
Role of insight	Insight is central; it emerges in "corrective emotional experiences."	Insight is irrelevant and/or unnecessary.
Role of therapist	The therapist functions as a *detective*, searching out basic root conflicts and resistances; detached and neutral, to facilitate transference reactions.	The therapist functions as a trainer, helping patients unlearn old behaviors and/or learn new ones. Control of reinforcement is important; interpersonal relationship is minor.

Cognitive Therapies

Behavioral therapies apply the principles of conditioning to change behavior. In contrast, cognitive theories assume that many behaviors are influenced or determined by thought processes. If so, then one's thoughts and beliefs must be changed in order to effect lasting behavior change.

Cognitive therapy *is a psychotherapeutic approach to changing problem feelings and behaviors by changing how clients perceive or think about significant experiences.* The underlying assumption of such therapy is that abnormal behavior patterns and emotional distress start with problems in *what* we think (cognitive content) and *how* we think (cognitive process). Cognitive therapies focus on different types of cognitive processes and different methods of cognitive restructuring. The two major forms of cognitive therapy involve cognitive behavior modification and alteration of false belief systems.

FOCUS on Application

Learning Social Skills

Many difficulties will arise for someone who lacks *social skills,* sets of responses that enable people to effectively achieve their social goals when approaching or interacting with others (Hersen & Bellack, 1976). Such skills include knowing *what* to say and do (content) in given situations in order to elicit a desired response (consequences), *how* to say and do it (style), and *when* to say and do it (timing). One of the most common social skill problems is lack of assertiveness—the inability to state one's own thoughts or wishes in a clear, direct, nonaggressive manner (Bower & Bower, 1991).

For those who have social skills, it is easy to assume that they "come naturally." But social skills are not inborn; like other complex human behaviors, they are learned in the course of experience, in the laboratory of everyday life. To overcome problems such as shyness or unassertiveness, many social learning therapists recommend **behavioral rehearsal**—*visualizing how one should behave in a given situation and the desired positive consequences.* Rehearsal can be used to establish and strengthen any basic skill, from personal hygiene to work habits to social interactions. Behavioral rehearsal procedures are being widely used in social skills training programs with many different populations (Yates, 1985). Adult pathology has often been preceded by deficits in social skills in childhood (Oden & Asher, 1977). A considerable amount of research and therapy is currently directed at building competence in shy and withdrawn disturbed children (Conger & Keane, 1981; Zimbardo & Radl, 1981).

One study demonstrated that preschool-age children diagnosed as *social isolates* could be helped to become sociable in a short training period (Furman et al., 1979). Twenty-four subjects were randomly assigned to one of three play conditions: with a same-age peer, with a peer 1 to 1½ years younger, or with no partner (control condition). The pairs were brought together for ten play sessions, each only 20 minutes long, over a period of about a month. Their classroom behavior before and after this treatment was recorded, and it revealed that the intervention had a strong effect. The opportunity to play with a *younger* playmate doubled the frequency with which the former social isolates interacted later on with other classmates—bringing them up to the average level of the other children. Playing with a *same-age* peer also increased children's sociability, but not nearly so much. The researchers concluded that the one-on-one play situation had offered the shy children safe opportunities to be socially assertive. They were allowed to practice leadership skills that were likely to be approved by the nonthreatening, younger playmates (Furman et al., 1979).

In another study (Matson et al., 1980), social skills training with a group of hospitalized emotionally disturbed children changed both verbal and nonverbal components of their behavior in social settings. The children were taught to give appropriate verbal responses in various social situations (giving help or compliments, making requests). They were also taught to display appropriate affect (for example, to smile while giving a compliment) and to make eye contact and use proper body posture (face the person being talked to). These improved social skills were generalized to "untreated" situations outside of training. The children also put them into practice on their own when on the ward. These positive effects continued even months later.

Even students of psychology can occasionally forget that social skills—and errors—are probably learned. Next time someone makes a "bad impression" on you, try to consider whether that bad impression might be due to the other's poor social skills. It might be worthwhile to take time to encourage and help an acquaintance to interact more successfully. Inside many awkward or hesitant manners we may still find good hearts and great virtues. Others' poor social skills should not stigmatize them or prevent us from sharing the benefits of friendship and cooperation. Learn to practice "attributional charity," giving others the benefit of the doubt when you make inferences about why they behave unpleasantly. Consider their situations, and imagine how and why you might react as they seem to be doing. A little psychological tolerance goes a long way toward self-help, too, because "what goes around, comes around," so others may be more charitable when they size you up!

Cognitive Behavior Modification   We are what we tell ourselves we can be, and we are guided by what we believe we ought to do. These assumptions initiate the process of **cognitive behavior modification,** *the therapeutic technique that combines an emphasis on thoughts and attitudes with strategies for changing behavior by altering reinforcement contingencies.* Prior to committing any maladaptive action, the individual is assumed to make a *self-statement* that is irrational or self-destructive. For example, an addicted smoker might automatically tell himself, "One more cigarette won't hurt me," "I'll go crazy if I don't have a smoke now," or even "I can quit any time I want—I just don't want to." Before unacceptable behavior patterns can be modified, the individual's negative self-statements must be changed or replaced with rational, constructive coping statements.

In this therapeutic approach, the therapist and client must discover the way the client thinks about and expresses the problem for which therapy is sought. Once both therapist and client understand the kind of thinking that is leading to unproductive behaviors, they can develop new self-statements that are constructive, and minimize the use of self-defeating ones (Meichenbaum, 1977). For example, they might substitute the negative self-statement "I was so boring at that party that I'll never get invited back" with constructive criticism: "Next time, to be more interesting, I will plan some effective opening lines, practice telling a good joke, and respond to other people's stories." Instead of dwelling on negatives in past situations that are unchangeable and part of past history, the client is taught to focus on positives in the future that can be realized.

Building *expectations of being effective* increases the likelihood of behaving effectively. It is through setting attainable goals, developing realistic strategies for attaining them, and evaluating feedback realistically that people develop a sense of mastery and *self-efficacy* (Bandura, 1986, 1992; Schwarzer, 1992).

Changing False Beliefs Some cognitive behavior therapists argue that many psychological problems arise because of the way we think about ourselves in relation to other people and the events we face. Faulty thinking can be based on three kinds of unhealthy cognitive elements.

1. *Unreasonable attitudes.* Problems are caused by irrational or extreme attitudes: "It's unacceptable for someone to make mistakes if the goal is to be a good student," or "To attract a romantic partner, I must be physically perfect and totally unselfish."
2. *False premises.* Some self-statements are based on false premises: "If I agree to do everything my friends ask me to do, then I'll be popular," "If I never complain and always do my job, my employers will surely reward me with a promotion," or "If I refuse to have sex with my boyfriend, he'll stop loving me—and I'll never find anyone else."
3. *Rigid rules.* These rules put behavior on "automatic pilot," so that prior patterns are repeated even when they have not worked. Examples of such statements include: "I must obey authorities" and "Being honest always hurts other people's feelings."

Do any of these examples seem familiar to you? Cognitive therapists believe that emotional distress is caused by misunderstandings and by the failure to distinguish between current reality and one's imagination (or expectations). A cognitive therapist induces a patient to correct faulty patterns of thinking by applying more effective problem-solving techniques. She might remind a client that giving in to a boyfriend's demands just so she can "keep him" is really dishonest and manipulative—and carries no guarantee that the relationship will last. When the client examines her own beliefs and assumptions, such thoughts become less automatic and powerful, and she can begin to reconstruct a more rational, effective view of the world.

Cognitive Therapy for Depression **Aaron Beck** has successfully pioneered the application of cognitive therapy to the problem of *depression*. Beck states the formula for treatment in simple form: "The therapist helps the patient to identify his warped thinking and to learn more realistic ways to formulate his experiences" (1976, p. 20). For example, depressed individuals may be instructed to write down negative thoughts about themselves, figure out why these self-criticisms are unjustified, and come up with more realistic (and less destructive) self-cognitions.

A student, depressed about a poor grade, may well stay depressed if he berates his own intelligence rather than reattributing the blame to the situation of a tough test.

Beck believes that depression is maintained because depressed patients are unaware of the negative automatic thoughts that they repeat to themselves, such as "I will never be as good as my brother"; "Nobody would like me if they really knew me"; and "I'm not smart enough to make it in this competitive school."

Given the insidious nature of these unhealthy thinking habits, a cognitive therapist relies on specific tactics to change the cognitive foundation that supports the depression. These tactics include the following suggestions from Beck et al. (1979):

- evaluating the *evidence* the patient has for and against these automatic thoughts;
- reattributing blame to *situational factors* rather than to the patient's incompetence;
- openly discussing *alternative solutions* to the problem;
- *challenging* the client's basic assumptions.

This therapy is similar to behavioral therapies in that it centers on the present state of the client. Regardless of how problem thinking got to be so firmly established, the cognitive behavior therapist focuses on the client's current thinking, and how best to realign it so that it is more realistic and healthy.

One of the worst side-effects of being depressed is having to live with all the negative feelings and lethargy associated with depression. Becoming obsessed with thoughts about one's negative mood cues memories of all the bad times in life, which further worsens the depressive feelings. By filtering all input through the dark lens of depression, depressed people see criticism where there is none and hear sarcasm when they listen to praise—further "reasons" for being depressed (Diamond, 1989). Therapy can direct the client so that he doesn't become further depressed about depression itself (Teasdale, 1985).

Rational-Emotive Therapy   One of the earliest forms of cognitive therapy was that developed by **Albert Ellis** (1962, 1977) to help clients replace ineffective thought patterns with ideas and beliefs that are reasonable and valid. Ellis dubbed this treatment **rational-emotive therapy** (**RET**), *a system of personality change based on changing irrational beliefs that cause problematic emotional reactions*. RET is intended to help clients to understand how flawed beliefs might lead them to experience undesirable feelings such as anxiety—and to question and eventually replace those flawed beliefs.

What are such flawed beliefs, and how do they lead to maladaptive feelings and actions? According to Ellis, individuals develop core values, *demanding* that they succeed and receive approval, *insisting* that they be treated fairly, and *dictating* that the universe be more pleasant. For example, in your own daily life, you may frequently tell yourself what you "should," "must," and "ought to" do; these self-corrections are seldom questioned, and come to control your actions or even prevent you from choosing the life you want. If you participated in RET, your therapist would teach you to recognize these self-statements, question how rational they are, and replace faulty ideas with more valid ones.

A rational-emotive therapist attempts to break through a client's close-mindedness by showing that an emotional reaction that follows some event is really the effect of unrecognized *beliefs* about the event. For example, behaving in a possessive and clingy way toward a romantic partner when that partner seems less interested or is distracted may be an emotional overreaction triggered by an irrational fear of abandonment. Signs that the other person is pulling away are unreasonably interpreted to mean, "My partner will leave me if I don't take emergency action." Experiencing a real breakup may prompt the irrational thought that "Without this person to love me, I'll have no one in my life at all!" In RET, these beliefs are openly disputed through rational confrontation and examination of alternative reasons for the event. For example, if your romantic partner seems distracted, it may be due to worries about school, work, or family concerns that have nothing to do with you or your relationship.

By learning to consider other perspectives and explanations, you can learn not to take things personally or to overreact, and to avoid creating problems where there may not be any. It is important to be sensitive and vigilant, but habitual scrutinizing and worrying may cause difficulties where there were none before. Thus a balance must be learned between paying attention and indulging in self-blame or anxiety. In RET, these lessons are followed by a variety of other cognitive techniques—those used in behavior modification, humor, and role-playing to replace dogmatic, irrational thinking with rational, situationally appropriate ideas.

By definition, cognitive therapies rely on individuals to use their own *mental processes* to effect a change in *behavior*. New research suggests that such treatments may enable the mind to "fix the brain" for severe problems such as obsessive-compulsive disorders. Patients who suffered from obsessions about whether they had turned off their stoves and compulsions to wash and rewash their hands to expunge imaginary germs were given cognitive behavior modification (Schwartz et al., 1996). When they felt an urge to run home and check the stove, or to repeatedly wash their hands, they were trained to *relabel* their experience as an obsession or compulsion—not a rational concern. They then focused on waiting out this "urge" rather than giving in to it, by distracting themselves with other activities for about 15 minutes (Begley & Biddle, 1996). Positron emission tomography (PET) scans of the brains of subjects who were trained in this relabeling-and-distracting technique indicated that, over time, the part of the brain responsible for that nagging fear or urge gradually became less active (Schwartz et al., 1996). Thus, "the mind can fix the brain."

Existential-Humanistic Therapies

The primary symptoms for which many college students seek therapy include general dissatisfaction, feelings of alienation, and failure to achieve all they feel they should. Problems in everyday living, the lack of meaningful human relationships, and the absence of significant goals to strive for are common *existential crises*. These critical life dilemmas focus on one's very existence, according to proponents of humanism and existentialism. Ways of dealing with these existential crises have been combined to form the core of a type of therapy addressing the basic problems of existence common to all human beings.

The *humanistic movement* has been called a "third force in psychology" because it grew out of a reaction to the two dominant forces that held a pessimistic view of human nature: first, early psychoanalytic theory, and later, the mechanistic view offered by early radical behaviorism. When the humanistic movement was forming in the United States, similar viewpoints had already gained acceptance in Europe; these viewpoints came to be known collectively as *existentialism*. One of the first American therapists to embrace existentialism was **Rollo May** (1969; 1975; 1977). May's popular books and therapy are designed to combat feelings of emptiness, cynicism, and anomie (social alienation) by emphasizing basic human values such as love, creativity, and free will.

At the core of both humanistic and existential therapies is the concept of a *whole person* who engages in the continual process of changing and of becoming. Despite the restrictions of environment and heredity, we always remain free to choose what we will become by creating our own values and committing ourselves to them through our decisions. Along with this *freedom to choose,* however, comes the *burden of responsibility.* Since we are never fully aware of all the implications of our actions, we experience anxiety and despair. We also suffer from guilt over lost opportunities to achieve our full potential.

Existential and humanistic psychotherapies attempt to help clients define their own freedom, value their experiencing selves and the richness of the present moment, cultivate their individuality, and discover ways of realizing their fullest potential (see Schneider & May, 1995).

Person-Centered Therapy   As we pointed out in Chapter 10, Freud's original theories of personality and therapy were based on his observations of patients with disorders. Later critics questioned how well such observations could possibly apply to normal behavior, which may be challenged and stressed but is not severely disordered. Other questions involved whether it was appropriate for the therapist or analyst to be consulted as the "expert" on the patient's condition—when in actuality the individual seeking treatment knew better than anyone else about his or her own problems and experiences. This line of inquiry led humanistic therapist **Carl Rogers** (1951, 1977) to develop a therapeutic approach based on the premise that the person seeking help, referred to as the client (not as the patient), must be understood and accepted in order for the therapist to provide the best help. Rogers's **person-centered therapy** *emphasizes individuals' natural tendency to seek ways to behave that are productive, healthy, and self-actualizing.* The primary goal of person-centered therapy is not to "cure" the person or "fix" a serious disorder, but rather to promote the person's healthy psychological growth.

Person-centered therapy (also called *Rogerian therapy*) begins with the assumption that all people share the basic tendency to self-actualize; that is, to realize one's potential. Healthy development is hindered by faulty learning patterns in which a person accepts the evaluation of others in place of those provided by his or her own mind and body. A conflict between one's naturally positive self-image and negative external criticisms creates anxiety and unhappiness. The task of Rogerian therapy is to create an environment that allows a client to learn how to behave in order to achieve self-enhancement and self-actualization. Three guiding principles of person-centered therapy are *unconditional positive regard, genuineness,* and *nondirective guidance* from the therapist.

People are assumed to be basically good. The therapist's task is mainly to help remove barriers that limit the expression of this natural positive tendency and help the client clarify and accept his or her own feelings. This is accomplished within an atmosphere of *unconditional positive regard*—nonjudgmental acceptance and respect for the client, with no strings attached and no performance evaluations. The therapist allows his or her own feelings and thoughts to be transparent to the client. In addition to maintaining this *genuineness,* the therapist tries to experience the client's feelings. Such total empathy requires that the therapist care for the client as a worthy, competent individual—not to be judged or evaluated but to be assisted in discovering his or her individuality (Meador & Rogers, 1979). Unlike practitioners of other therapies who interpret, give answers, or instruct, the client-centered therapist is a supportive listener who reflects and, at times, restates the client's evaluative statements and feelings. Person-centered therapy strives to be *nondirective* by having the therapist merely facilitate the patient's search for self-awareness and self-acceptance and never direct it.

Rogers believes that individuals have the potential to lead themselves back to psychological health once they are freed to relate to others openly and to accept themselves. This optimistic view and the humane relationship between therapist-as-caring-expert and client-as-person has influenced many practitioners (Smith, 1982).

Gestalt Therapy   Recall from Chapter 5 that one influential theory of perception was that promoted by Germany's Gestalt psychologists, who argued that humans seek wholeness and meaning in their sensory experiences. In a similar way, another approach to therapy promotes the importance of meaning and completeness in the healthy personality. **Gestalt therapy** *is a system of treatment that emphasizes the union of mind and body to make the person whole*. Its primary goal is self-awareness, which the client can reach (with the therapist's help) in several ways:

- by *expressing* pent-up feelings in group situations;
- by recognizing how *"unfinished business"* from past conflicts is carried into new relationships;
- by accepting that incomplete *life tasks must be finished* for growth to proceed.

Fritz Perls (1969), the originator of Gestalt therapy, asked participants to act out fantasies concerning conflicts and strong feelings and also to recreate their dreams, which were seen as repressed parts of one's personality.

In Gestalt therapy workshops, therapists borrow from Zen teachings a focus on immediate experience, so that the client is aware of emerging feelings, attitudes, and actions. As in some Eastern philosophies, Gestalt therapy uses *paradox* to instruct: "Change is possible only when we accept who we are at the moment, and awareness is itself the cure" (Thompson, 1988). Instead of interpreting present dissatisfaction as a "conflict" that makes you unhappy, perhaps you might consider it a form of tension that is essential to taking the first step to change.

Assess Yourself

What Do You Really Feel and Think?

An example of a Gestalt therapy technique that you might attempt on your own is the "empty chair" exercise:

1. Imagine that someone important to you—someone you need to interact with, whether available or not—is seated in a real chair positioned before you.

2. Imagine her or him in that chair and talk aloud to the chair, emphasizing the feelings you need to express and the ideas you may have kept to yourself.

3. Now imagine her or his response; listen to it in your imagination, and respond aloud honestly and fairly.

You may surprise yourself with the words you say and the feelings you admit. Although this is an imaginary role-playing exercise, it can help you clarify what you really feel and assume now—and how these personal experiences shape your life.

Group Therapies   All the treatment approaches we have discussed thus far are primarily designed as one-to-one relationships between a patient or client and therapist. However, there are many reasons that group therapy can have value and benefit for a variety of concerns. Existential and humanistic therapies have often made use of group contexts in order to provide clients with role models, social support, or evidence that they are not alone.

Some of the benefits of group therapy are feelings of belonging and acceptance; opportunities to observe, imitate, and be socially rewarded; the chance to experience the universality of human problems, weaknesses, and strengths; and the experience of recreating scenes from one's original family system, allowing people to relive and correct basic emotions and relationships (Klein, 1983).

Self-Help Groups   The most dramatic development in therapy has been the surge of interest and participation in *self-help groups*. It is estimated that there are 500,000 such groups, which are attended by 15 million Americans every week (Leerhsen, 1990). These group support sessions are typically free, especially when they are not directed by a health care professional, and they give people a chance to meet others with the same problems who are surviving and sometimes thriving (Christensen & Jacobson, 1994; Jacobs & Goodman, 1989).

Beginning in the mid–1930s, Alcoholics Anonymous (AA) pioneered the application of the self-help concept to community group settings. The feminist consciousness-raising movement of the 1960s helped to extend self-help beyond the arena of alcoholism. Today, support groups deal with four basic categories of problems:

- *addictive* behavior problems;
- physical and mental *disorders;*
- life transition or other *crises;*
- the stress and trauma experienced by *people close to* those who have specific types of problems.

Central to the original AA structure was the concept of "twelve steps" to recovery, based not on psychological theory but on the trial-and-error experience of early AA members. The first step begins with recognizing that one has become powerless over alcohol; the second affirms that faith in a "greater power" is necessary for recovery. Most of the remaining steps refer to this greater power, or explicitly to God, and set goals for making amends to those who have been hurt by the addicted or disordered person's actions. In most

In the United States, there are an estimated 500,000 self-help groups attended by 15 million people every week (Leerhessen, 1990).

twelve-step programs, members are urged and helped to accept as many of the steps as possible in order to maintain recovery, but this is in no way mandatory or required.

Virtually every community now has a self-help clearinghouse you can phone to find out where and when a local group that addresses a given problem meets. To get started, you can call the *National Self-Help Clearinghouse* at (212) 354–8525.

Group therapy techniques and traditions have made valuable contributions to the challenges confronting terminally ill patients. The goals of such therapy are to help patients and their families live their lives as fulfillingly as possible during their illnesses; to cope realistically with impending death; and to adjust to the terminal illness (Adams, 1979; Yalom & Greaves, 1977). One general focus of such support groups for the terminally ill is to help them learn "how to live fully until you say goodbye" (Nungesser, 1990).

Group therapies can provide social support or acceptance to individuals whose problems would otherwise isolate them and prevent them from reaching help. However, sometimes the problems for which we seek therapy *are* our relationships, or they *begin* with our group memberships. An otherwise skilled and confident worker, for example, may find herself tongue-tied and intimidated by supervisors or groups of colleagues who seem to be "ganging up" on her. Or a man may be weary of making poor choices in romantic partners, and suspect that he is incapable of attracting a loving, respectful partner. In such cases, we cannot solve our problems purely by seeking help for ourselves. We must involve our loved ones in the therapeutic process, and win their cooperation if we are to change our thoughts and behavior patterns. Perhaps the best example of this sort of "therapeutic intimacy" is the development of marital and family therapy.

Marital and Family Therapy Relationship therapies offer well-established strategies for resolving the tensions and conflicts that are a normal part of intimacy and interaction with others. Relationships are important to us, but unfortunately love and communication skills do not "come naturally." The fact is that loving and getting along with others—and their getting along with us—requires learning, commitment, and *work*. Fortunately, the fascinating challenges confronting couples and families have intrigued therapists, who have devised several approaches to helping more than one person at a time.

Couples counseling for marital and relationship problems seeks to clarify the typical communication patterns of the partners and then to improve the quality of their interaction. By seeing a couple together (and sometimes videotaping and playing back their interactions) a therapist can help both partners appreciate the verbal and nonverbal styles they use to dominate, control, or confuse each other. Each party is taught how to reinforce desired responses in the other and withdraw reinforcement for undesirable reactions; they are also taught nondirective listening skills to help the other person clarify and express feelings and ideas (Dattilio & Padesky, 1990; O'Leary, 1987). Therapy focuses not on the personalities involved but on the *processes* of their relationship, particularly their patterns of conflict and communication (Gottman, 1994; Greenberg & Johnson, 1988; Notarius & Markman, 1993). Although such patterns may be deeply ingrained, they are the product not of unchangeable instinct but of learning; therefore, ineffective patterns can be unlearned and new, more successful and satisfactory ones acquired. Both partners must be willing to make some changes in the ways they think and behave, and to take responsibility for their part in a dysfunctional relationship. However, relationship therapy can be much "easier" than efforts to change one's personality, because both partners work together and support each other in reaching mutually desired goals. Couples therapy is more effective in resolving marital problems than is individual therapy with only one partner, and it has been shown to reduce marital crises and keep marriages intact (Cookerly, 1980; Gottman, 1994; Gurman & Kniskern, 1978).

In *family therapy*, the "client" is an entire nuclear family, and each family member is treated as a member of a *system* of relationships (Fishman, 1993). A family therapist works with troubled family members to help them perceive the issues or patterns that are creating problems for one or more of them. The focus is on altering the psychological "spaces" between people and the interpersonal *dynamics* of people acting as a unit, rather than on changing processes within maladjusted individuals (Foley, 1979; Schwebel & Fine, 1994). This therapy considers the *synergy* or joined power of the group as its members interact and stimulate each other.

Family therapy can reduce tensions within a family and improve the functioning of individual members by helping clients recognize the positives as well as the negatives in their relationships. **Virginia Satir** (1967), an innovative developer of family therapy approaches, noted that the family therapist plays many roles, acting as an interpreter and clarifier of the interactions that are taking place in the therapy session and as influence agent, mediator, and referee. Family therapists focus on the *situational* rather than the *dispositional* aspects of a family's problem—for example, how one family member's unemployment affects everyone's feelings and relationships, rather than seeking to assign blame or label anyone as lazy or selfish. The goal of a family therapy meeting is not to have a "gripe session" free-for-all of complaints, but to develop constructive, cooperative problem solving together.

In a *structured family therapy* approach, the family is seen as the system that is creating disturbances in the individuals rather than the other way around (Fishman, 1993; Minuchin, 1974). The therapist focuses on the way the family interacts in the present in order to understand its organizational structure, power hierarchy, channels of communication, and who gives and gets blame for what goes wrong. Like a consultant to an organization, a family therapist tries to help the family reorganize so it can better meet the needs and demands of its members. Family therapists can also help forge harmony between conflicted generations, as in the case of grandparents who seek to visit grandchildren whose parents have divorced (see Nichols, 1984).

To understand how family or relationship therapy can work in your own life, consider how you behave when you return home for a holiday visit, or make a date to spend time with an old friend. In the time you have been away, you have grown and changed. But "going back" to earlier relationships—especially if you are also returning to familiar scenes—can trigger old patterns of behavior you thought were long outgrown. For example, you might become too easily angered by a sibling's silly teasing. Or you may feel guilty about refusing your mother's home cooking, despite your reasonable wish to eat sensibly and adhere to a healthier diet. And even though years have passed, a few minutes with a former romantic partner might "push your buttons" and revive old feelings of jealousy, inadequacy, or insecurity.

To change such patterns, or be less susceptible to the circumstances that seem to trigger them, you must "relearn" your assumptions and interactions *with* the other people involved. This may not be a practical solution, especially if you have moved away or do not expect many reunions. Most of us resign ourselves to never quite overcoming the quirks and ironies of old relationship patterns. If the patterns are not that old and the people are more accessible, the ideal solution is to endeavor to rework entire relationships along with our partners—not just to modify our one-sided, personal contributions to them.

Sigmund Freud's psychoanalytic therapy is the main form of psychodynamic therapy. One of Freud's main contributions was postulating the dynamic role of unconscious processes in normal and pathological reactions. The goal of psychoanalysis is to reconcile these conflicts into a stronger ego that mediates these drives. Neo-Freudians differ from classic Freudian psychoanalysts in their emphasis on the patient's current social situation, interpersonal relationships, and self-concept.

Behavioral therapy views abnormal behavior as a set of learned responses that can be modified with principles of reinforcement and conditioning. Counterconditioning includes systematic desensitization, implosion, flooding, and aversive learning. Contingency management uses operant conditioning to modify behavior. Social learning therapy uses imitation of models and social skills training to make individuals feel more confident about their abilities.

Cognitive therapy changes a person's behavior by altering negative or irrational thought patterns about oneself and social relationships. Cognitive behavior modification involves discovering how the client thinks about a problem, learning more constructive thought patterns, and applying these new techniques to other situations. Two popular types of cognitive therapy are Aaron Beck's treatment for depression and Albert Ellis's use of rational-emotive therapy (RET).

Existential-humanist therapies focus on the process of becoming more fully self-actualized. Carl Rogers's client-centered therapy emphasizes the therapist's unconditional positive regard for the client. The therapist strives to be genuine and nondirective in helping the client to establish congruence between a naturally positive self-image and external criticisms. Gestalt therapy, developed by Fritz Perls, attempts to combine body and mind to make a person more whole and able to experience the present moment.

Group therapy can be used as immediate social support, for example, with terminally ill patients. In marital and family therapy the unit of analysis is not the individual but a distressed couple or an entire nuclear family. These therapies focus on situations that the couple or group can change or minimize instead of treating the dispositional tendencies of the individuals involved.

Biomedical Therapies

The ecology of the mind is held in delicate balance. It can be upset by mishaps in the workings of our genes, hormones, enzymes, and metabolism. Behavior, thinking, and emotions are end products of brain mechanisms. When something goes wrong with the brain, we see the consequences in abnormal patterns of behavior and peculiar cognitive and emotional reactions. Environmental, social, or behavioral disturbances—such as certain kinds of pollution, drug abuse, and violence—can also alter brain chemistry. Just consider how your moods and outlook change when you have a cold or the flu, and then you are once more ready to appreciate how moods, thoughts, and actions are tied to our biology.

Biomedical therapies treat mental disorders as "hardware problems" in the brain and in the nervous and endocrine systems. These therapies emerge from a medical model of abnormal mental functioning that assumes an organic basis for mental illnesses and treats schizophrenia, for example, as a disease. One approach to correcting upset biology has been to change the functioning of the brains of disturbed people by either precise neurosurgery or electroshock stimulation of the brain's neural activity. However, the most dramatic and now most commonly used form of modern biomedical therapy is the administration of drugs to alter mood and mental states.

Psychosurgery

The headline in the *Los Angeles Times* read, "Bullet in the Brain Cures Man's Mental Problem" (February 23, 1988). The article revealed that a 19-year-old man suffering from severe obsessive-compulsive disorder had shot a .22 caliber bullet through the front of his brain in a suicide attempt. Remarkably, he survived, his pathological symptoms were cured, and his intellectual capacity was not affected—although some of the underlying causes of his problems remained.

This case illustrates the potential effects of one of the most direct biomedical therapies: intervention in the brain. Such intervention may involve lesioning connections between parts of the brain, removing small sections of the brain, or subjecting the whole brain to intensive electrical stimulation. These therapies are often considered methods of last resort to treat psychopathologies that have proven intractable with other, less extreme forms of therapy. There is an ongoing, heated controversy about their usefulness and their side effects, as well as the ethics of taking such drastic measures to change behavior.

Psychosurgery *is the general term for surgical procedures performed on brain tissue to alleviate psychological disorders.* In medieval times, psychosurgery involved "cutting the stone of folly" from the brains of those suffering from madness, as shown vividly in many engravings and paintings from that era (there is, of course, no such "stone"). Modern psychosurgical procedures include severing the fibers of the corpus callosum to reduce violent seizures of epilepsy (as we saw in Chapter 2), severing pathways through the limbic system, and performing *prefrontal lobotomy*. The best-known form of psychosurgery is the prefrontal lobotomy—an operation that severs certain nerve fibers connecting the frontal lobes of the brain with the diencephalon, especially the fibers of the thalamus and hypothalamus. The procedure was developed by neurologist **Egas Moniz,** who in 1949 won a Nobel Prize for this treatment, which seemed to transform the functioning of mental patients.

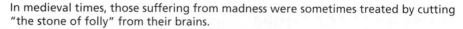

In medieval times, those suffering from madness were sometimes treated by cutting "the stone of folly" from their brains.

The original candidates for lobotomy were agitated schizophrenic patients and patients who were compulsive and anxiety ridden. The effects of this psychosurgery were dramatic; a new personality emerged, without intense emotional arousal and thus without overwhelming anxiety, guilt, or anger. In part, this positive effect occurred because the operation disconnected present functioning from memory for past traumas and conflicts and also from future concerns. However, the operation permanently destroyed basic aspects of human nature. Lobotomized patients lost something special—their unique personality. Specifically, the lobotomy resulted in inability to plan ahead, indifference to the opinions of others, childlike actions, and the intellectual and emotional flatness of a person without a coherent sense of self. (One of Moniz's own patients was so distressed by these unexpected consequences that she shot Moniz, partially paralyzing him.) Because the effects of psychosurgery are permanent, the negative effects are severe and common, and the positive results are less certain, the continued use of psychosurgery is limited to special cases (Valenstein, 1980).

Electroconvulsive Therapy

Electroconvulsive therapy (ECT) *is a type of medical therapy in which mild electric current is briefly applied to a patient's brain to influence central nervous system function.* ECT is not a panacea or cure-all, but it has been found to be more useful than other medical or psychological approaches in the treatment of certain psychiatric disorders, particularly severe depression, mania, and schizophrenia. The therapy consists of applying weak electric current (75–100 volts) to a patient's temples for a period of time from one-tenth to a full second, until a convulsion occurs. The convulsion usually runs its course in 45 to 60 seconds. Patients are prepared for this traumatic intervention by sedation with a short-acting barbiturate and a muscle relaxant, which renders the patient unconscious and minimizes violent, uncontrolled physical reactions (Abrams, 1992; Malitz & Sackheim, 1984).

Electroconvulsive therapy has proven extremely successful in alleviating the symptoms of serious depression—more successful, in fact, than some of the drug therapies we will review in the next section (Scovern & Kilmann, 1980). One benefit of ECT is that it works quickly: typically the symptoms of depression are reduced in a three- or four-day course of treatment, in contrast with the one- to two-week period required for drug therapy to be effective. Nonetheless, most therapists regard ECT as a treatment of last resort, reserving it for emergency treatment of suicidal or severely malnourished depressed patients for whom drug therapy is ineffective or inappropriate.

Contrary to the imagery provoked by the inappropriate term "shock therapy," the use and effects of ECT are not "shocking" or radical. Properly administered ECT does *not* cause painful electrical shocks or wrenching physical jolts to a conscious, anxious patient. In contrast, the ECT patient is comfortable, relaxed, and sedated, and is carefully prepared for the experience by informed and sympathetic medical professionals. One reason ECT has been demonized is that critics fear it might be abused—used to silence dissent or punish patients who are uncooperative (Holmes, 1994). Among scientists themselves, suspicion of ECT comes from the fact that its effects are not well understood. To date no definitive theory "explains" why inducing a mild convulsion should alleviate disordered symptoms.

Finally, ECT does produce some negative side effects, of course, including temporary disorientation and a variety of memory deficits (Breggin, 1979, 1991). However, research shows that patients generally recover their specific memories within months of the treatment (Calev et al., 1991), and that patients who had received over 100 ECT treatments showed no deficit in

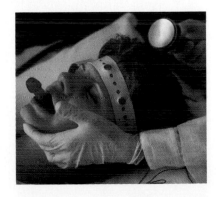

A sedated patient about to receive ECT. Electroconvulsive therapy applies a weak electrical current to a patient's temples, until a convulsion occurs. ECT has proven extremely successful in alleviating symptoms of severe depression, but remains a treatment of last resort for most therapists.

functioning compared with those who had never received ECT (Devanand et al., 1991). To minimize even short-term side effects, ECT is now often administered "unilaterally," to only the right temple, in order to reduce the possibility of speech impairment, and is still an effective antidepressant (Scovern & Kilmann, 1980).

Drug Therapy

In the history of the treatment of mental disorder, nothing has ever rivaled the revolution created by the discovery of drugs that could calm anxious patients, restore contact with reality in withdrawn patients, and suppress hallucinations in psychotic patients. This new therapeutic era began in 1953 with the introduction of tranquilizing drugs, notably *chlorpromazine* (Thorazine), into mental hospital treatment programs.

Drug therapy *is a general term for any form of therapy that treats disorders with drugs and chemicals.* You are probably familiar with references to "chemotherapy" in the treatment of cancer. The application of *chemotherapy* (chemical therapy) to psychological disorders was first developed by researchers in the field of psychopharmacology. It gained almost instant recognition and status as an effective therapy for transforming patient behavior. When they had received appropriate drug therapy, unruly, assaultive patients became cooperative, calm, and sociable. Thought-disordered patients who had been absorbed in their delusions and hallucinations began to be responsive to the real physical and social environment around them. No longer did mental hospital staff have to act as guards, putting patients in seclusion or straitjackets; staff morale improved as rehabilitation replaced mere custodial care of the mentally ill (Swazey, 1974).

Another profound effect of the drug therapy revolution was its impact on the nation's mental hospital population. Over half a million Americans were living in mental institutions in 1955, staying an average of several years. The introduction of chlorpromazine and other drugs reversed the steadily increasing numbers of patients. By the early 1970s, it was estimated that less than half the country's mental patients actually resided in mental hospitals; those who did were institutionalized for an average of only a few months.

Categories of Drugs   Three major categories of drugs are used today in drug therapy programs: *antipsychotic, antidepressant,* and *antianxiety* compounds. As their names suggest, these drugs chemically alter specific brain functions that are responsible for psychotic symptoms, depression, and extreme anxiety, respectively.

Antipsychotic Drugs   Antipsychotic drugs alter the psychotic symptoms of delusions, hallucinations, social withdrawal, and occasional agitation (Gitlin, 1990; Holmes, 1994; Kane & Marder, 1993). Antipsychotic drugs work by reducing the activity of the neurotransmitter dopamine in the brain. Drugs such as *chlorpromazine* (Thorazine, derived from the compound *phenothiazine,* and *haloperidol* [Haldol]) work by blocking or reducing the sensitivity of dopamine receptors in the brain. A new antipsychotic drug, *clozapine* (Clozaril), both decreases dopamine activity and increases the activity of another neurotransmitter, serotonin, which inhibits the dopamine system. Though these drugs reduce overall brain activity, they do not merely tranquilize the patient. They eliminate agitation, and may eliminate the positive symptoms of schizophrenia, including delusions and hallucinations.

Unfortunately, there are several negative side effects of long-term administration of antipsychotic drugs. *Tardive dyskinesia* is an unusual disturbance of motor control (especially of the facial muscles) caused by antipsychotic drugs. Although the newer drug, clozapine, has reduced motor side effects because of its more selective dopamine blocking, its use involves a 1 to 2 percent risk of causing *agranulocytosis,* a rare blood disease caused by bone marrow dysfunction. With the possibility of such side effects, are antipsychotic drugs worth the risk? While it is true that there is no *cure* for schizophrenia, appropriate drug treatments can promote great relief and symptom reduction. The chance of relapse for schizophrenics is highest when they cease taking medication (Gitlin, 1990).

Antidepressant Drugs Antidepressant drugs work by increasing the activity of the neurotransmitters norepinephrine and serotonin (Holmes, 1994). *Tricyclic* compounds such as *Tofranil* and *Elavil* work by reducing the body's reabsorption of neurotransmitters after they have been released in the synapse between brain cells. A *bicyclic* compound such as *Prozac* specifically reduces bodily reabsorption of serotonin—so more of that chemical remains available for brain activity. A third class of antidepressant drugs includes *monoamine oxidase (MAO) inhibitors,* which limit the activity of an enzyme that breaks down norepinephrine. When MAO is inhibited, more norepinephrine is available in the body.

Another remarkable chemical is *lithium salt,* the extract of a rock, which can influence the uniquely subtle property of mind that regulates mood. It has proven effective in the treatment of manic disorders. People who experience uncontrollable periods of hyperexcitement—when their energy seems limitless and their behavior extravagant and flamboyant—are brought down from their state of manic excess by doses of lithium. Regular maintenance doses of lithium can help break the cycle of recurring episodes of mania and/or depression. Lithium also allows a person to be alert and creative (Ehrlich & Diamond, 1980). Given that lithium is only a "salt of the earth," it qualifies as a miracle medicine for natural healing of severe mental mood disturbances.

Few recent drug developments have been as highly touted as Prozac, which can dramatically relieve depression (Kramer, 1993). But some critics warn it may also "relieve" patients of their personality and creativity (Breggin & Breggin, 1994). Bear in mind that no drug therapy is a cure, although many medications can relieve disruptive symptoms. Before "shopping" for psychoactive drugs, an individual seeking therapy should be realistic about the complexity of most mental problems and disorders, and open to the idea of using several different treatments in conjunction. Medications cannot solve life's problems, and overmedication can create new ones that are especially resistant to solutions.

Antianxiety Drugs To cope with everyday hassles, untold millions of Americans take pills to reduce tension and suppress anxiety. In general, these antianxiety drugs work by sedating the user (Holmes, 1994; Schatzberg, 1991). Their greatest value may be in getting patients through a difficult period—allowing them to get much-needed tension-relief, rest, and the time and perspective necessary before the particular problem can be tackled and solved. People who suffer frequent periods of anxiety or stress run some risk for overusing antianxiety agents, and may overlook the fact that while the drugs may make the problem seem less immediate, their anxiety is only a symptom of forces that must sooner or later be dealt with more directly.

Two commonly prescribed classes of antianxiety compounds are *barbiturates* and *benzodiazepines.* Barbiturates are central nervous system (CNS) depressants; they have a relaxing effect, but they can be dangerous if taken in excess or in combination with alcohol. Benzodiazepine drugs, such as Valium and Xanax, work by increasing the activity of the neurotransmitter GABA, thereby decreasing activity in brain regions involved in generalized anxiety disorder.

Antidepressant drugs can be used to reduce the symptoms not only of depression but also of certain anxiety disorders such as panic disorders and agoraphobia. Obsessive-compulsive disorders may arise from low levels of serotonin; such disorders may respond well to drugs like Prozac that specifically affect serotonin function.

The Context of Medication   Even when an effective drug is available, chemical medication only "works" when a clinician's careful diagnosis indicates the exact nature of the patient's disorder. The wrong diagnosis may result not only in prescribing an inappropriate drug, but in postponing the use of a drug that might have worked. Further, we in the United States may be a "medication happy" culture, a bit too prone to pop a pill instead of facing a problem. After reviewing a day's worth of television commercials for symptom relievers—antacids, pain relievers, and laxatives—do you get the idea that, in our culture, we are being urged to search only for quick symptom relief rather than to make major changes in diet, lifestyle, and stress management?

In this section we briefly review the factors important in making effective use of drug therapy, and the challenges and responsibilities that come with using psychoactive medications.

Cultural Factors in Diagnosis   In Chapter 13, we introduced the story of "Sylvia Frumkin," the pseudonym for a schizophrenic young woman who suffered from recurrent delusional episodes. Miss Frumkin's biographer, Susan Sheehan, notes that Sylvia's frequent hospital admissions sometimes resulted in errors in diagnosis—and in medication. For example, in one admissions screening, Sylvia was interviewed by a psychiatrist, a nurse, and a clinical social worker. The psychiatrist was a native of Taiwan, where he had received his medical degree, and had lived in the United States for only five years. As he skimmed Miss Frumkin's record, she began to pace, fidget, hum, and talk (Sheehan, 1982):

> "Everybody needs sex," she said. "I haven't had sex for five years. The clock is in this room because they want patients to learn how to tell time. I know Mary Poppins, and she lives in Massachusetts. I didn't like the movie *Mary Poppins*. They messed up the book so they could try to win the Oscar. Movies come from real life. This morning, when I was at Hillside [Hospital], I was making a movie. I was surrounded by movie stars. The X-ray technician was Peter Lawford. The security guard was Don Knotts. That Indian doctor in Building 40 was Lou Costello. I'm Mary Poppins. Is this room painted blue to get me upset? My grandmother died four weeks after my eighteenth birthday." Miss Frumkin laughed. (p. 25)

During her brief outburst, Sylvia's behavior shows many symptoms of schizophrenia, such as rapid "flight of ideas" (changing the subject) and inappropriate affect (laughing about her grandmother's death). However, the Asian-born psychiatrist reported that he had not elicited any delusional thinking—because he did not recognize the name "Mary Poppins" or the names of the actors Sylvia mentioned. Focusing instead on her motor activity, rapid speech, and flight of ideas, the doctor instead judged Miss Frumkin as suffering from a manic episode (Sheehan, 1982, 1995). The medication of choice for manic-depressive disorders, lithium, is ineffective in relieving the delusions and hallucinations of schizophrenia. Clearly, the lesson is that any therapy must first be based on accurate diagnosis, which takes into account a familiarity with the patient's culture and background.

Caution: Being on "Good" Drugs Because these tranquilizers work so well, it is easy to become psychologically dependent on them or physically addicted to them. Many people choose chemical treatments to cope with conflicts or emotional distress rather than confronting their problems, trying to solve them, or accepting pain and grief as part of the human experience.

In 1975, Valium was the most frequently prescribed drug in the United States. Since then its sales have fallen somewhat, but the 8 to 9 million Americans who still take doses of Valium every day make it the nation's most popular tranquilizer. Valium has a high *abuse potential* and is being overly relied upon to handle the emotional chores of modern life. Critics argue that it is self-defeating for people to believe that pills, rather than their own actions, control their stress. Unfortunately, drug therapy is often given in place of, and not as an adjunct to, the psychotherapy a person may need to learn how to cope effectively with life's recurring hassles.

Here are some *cautions* to bear in mind about tranquilizers—the drugs that students are most likely to take (Hecht, 1986):

- Benzodiazepines should not be taken to relieve anxieties that are part of the ordinary stresses of everyday life.
- When used for extreme anxiety, they should not be taken for more than four months at a time, and their dosage should be gradually reduced by a physician. Abrupt cessation can lead to *withdrawal symptoms,* such as convulsions, tremors, and abdominal and muscle cramps.
- Because these drugs depress the central nervous system, they can impair one's ability to drive, operate machinery, or perform other tasks that require alertness (such as studying or taking exams).
- In combination with alcohol (also a central nervous system depressant) or with sleeping pills, benzodiazepines can lead to unconsciousness and even death.

As a student of psychology, you are now in a better position to make informed decisions about how best to face life's problems, and to advise those you love as they deal with those decisions for themselves.

✓ Check Your Recall

Biomedical therapies try to change the physiological aspects of mental illness. These therapies now rely primarily on a range of psychoactive drugs to alleviate the pathological symptoms of behavioral and mental disorders. However, they do not cure the disorder. Psychosurgery, such as the prefrontal lobotomy (once a popular medical treatment), is used infrequently because of the irreversible nature of its negative side effects. Electroconvulsive therapy is undergoing a resurgence of use for severely depressed patients. Current techniques have neither the aversiveness nor the same negative consequences as earlier forms of ECT.

Drug therapy includes antipsychotic medication for schizophrenics. Antidepressants, such as tricyclics and MAO inhibitors, are used to provide chemical control of depression. Lithium is used to treat bipolar mental disorders. Antianxiety medication is used to reduce tension and sometimes to promote sleep. Antianxiety drugs include barbiturates and benzodiazepines. This type of medication is particularly susceptible to abuse because it is readily prescribed, is self-administered, and has calming, reinforcing effects for millions of normal people suffering from the ordinary stress of living. ✓

How Effective Is Therapy?

Does therapy work? Does it make a difference? The answer to such questions depends somewhat on the expectations of the client, and the kinds of problems that originally led him or her to seek treatment. Obviously, there are many kinds of therapies to choose from. How can you know which one will work best to relieve your distress? We now examine research into the effectiveness of the therapies themselves. Keep in mind that the general goals of all therapies include relieving distress and suffering, and changing behavior. Thus the simplest answer might be found in whether the individual client is satisfied that he or she has changed for the better. Now that you know something about psychopathology and about psychotherapy, you can ask yourself: Do you have problems that rob you of the satisfaction and success you feel should be possible in your life? Could some of these problems be better solved in collaboration with a therapist? Can you be realistic about what to expect from therapy, and are you ready to take responsibility for your part in that relationship? If you answer "yes" to most of these questions, then therapy with a qualified practitioner is a good investment of your time, resources, and hope. As in all such undertakings, be a cautious and informed consumer. Get referrals from trusted friends, physicians, or advisors about good therapists. You might "interview" a therapist by phone, or agree to a single appointment, before committing yourself to an alliance with any particular practitioner. Remember you are both on the same side, and you both need to discover whether and how you can work together. Therapy is not for everyone—but *if it is for you*, it can be extremely helpful, and thus definitely worth a try.

Evaluating Therapy

British psychologist **Hans Eysenck** (pronounced *I-zenk*) created a furor some years ago by declaring that psychotherapy does not work at all (Eysenck, 1952). He reviewed the effects of various therapies and found that patients who received no therapy had just as high a recovery rate as those receiving psychoanalysis or other forms of insight therapy. His claim was that roughly two-thirds of all people with neurotic problems will recover spontaneously within two years of the onset of the problem.

Does therapy *really* help—or do clients improve only because they hope and expect to receive special help? If the latter is true, then therapy is a kind of *placebo*, a behavioral sugar pill that only "works" because the individual wishes it to be effective. Many psychologists and psychiatrists believe that the key placebo ingredients in any therapy's success are a patient's *belief* that therapy will help and a therapist's social influence in conveying this suggestion (Fish, 1973). Psychiatrist **Jerome Frank** (1963; 1990; Frank & Frank, 1991) has compared the processes that take place in modern psychotherapy, religious revivalism, native healing ceremonies, and Communist thought-reform programs. He argues that "belief is really crucial to all of these processes because without the belief the person does not participate in any real way. . . . Nothing happens unless they really believe that this could help them" (Frank, 1990). As noted at the beginning of this chapter in the Cultural Context discussion on page 564 called "Universals in Therapy," a person's belief that he or she will be helped is central to all relationships between help-seekers and therapists worldwide.

Most psychotherapy researchers agree with Eysenck that it is important to show that psychotherapy is more effective than spontaneous recovery or client expectations. However, they criticize his findings because of many method-

Group therapy can be designed to accommodate a variety of goals and can provide much-needed support in difficult times.

ological problems in the studies he reviewed. A later evaluation of nearly a hundred therapy-outcome studies found that psychotherapy *did* lead to greater improvement than spontaneous recovery in 80 percent of the cases (Meltzoff & Kornreich, 1970). Thus, we begin to feel a little more confident that the therapeutic experience itself is a useful one for many people much of the time.

One well-controlled study compared patients who had undergone psychoanalytic or behavioral therapy with patients who had simply been on a waiting list for therapy. Both types of therapy turned out to be beneficial, with behavioral therapy leading to the greatest overall improvement. The researchers also concluded that the improvement of patients in therapy was "not entirely due either to spontaneous recovery or to the placebo effect of the nonspecific aspects of therapy, such as arousal of hope, expectation of help, and an initial cathartic interview" (Sloane et al., 1975, p. 224).

Recently, thousands of adults responded to a survey distributed to subscribers of *Consumer Reports* (1995) and reported on their personal experiences in therapy. They indicated how much their treatment helped, their overall satisfaction with the therapist's treatment of their problems, their change in "overall emotional state" following therapy, as well as details about the kind of therapy. Of the 7000 respondents, about 3000 just talked to friends, to relatives, or to clergy (as might be expected from our discussion earlier in this chapter), and 2900 saw a mental health professional; the rest saw family doctors or support groups. The main results can be summarized as follows: (a) therapy works—that is, treatment by mental health professionals helped clients to improve or reduced or eliminated their psychological problems; (b) long-term therapy was better than short-term therapy; (c) psychotherapy plus medication was not better than psychotherapy alone; (d) all forms of therapy were reported to be equally effective for improving clients' problems; and (e) those active in making the decision to enter therapy and shopping for a therapist did better in treatment than "passive shoppers" (see Seligman, 1995). We leave it to you—our now methodologically sophisticated reader—to outline the possible methodological artifacts that might confound interpretation of these results on the effectiveness of therapy and those of other studies on the efficacy of one kind of treatment versus another or versus a control condition (see Kasdin, 1986).

A general model of the way theory, clinical observation, and research all play a role in the development and evaluation of any form of treatment (for mental and physical disorders) is shown in the flowchart in Figure 14.3. It demonstrates that systematic research is needed to help clinicians discover if their therapies are having the impact that their theories predict. Theory, clinical observation, and research all play a role in developing and evaluating any form of treatment, for both mental and physical disorders. Clinicians and researchers may work on different tracks, but they work *in parallel*—starting with similar questions and working toward the same ultimate goals. The flowchart structure of the figure indicates that every discovery, including admissions that some treatments are not effective or certain important data still need to be collected, becomes a source of feedback to keep the process going and refine its findings.

Prevention Strategies

Two friends were walking on a riverbank. Suddenly, a child swept downstream in the current. One of the friends jumped in the river and rescued the child. Then the two friends resumed their stroll. Suddenly, another child

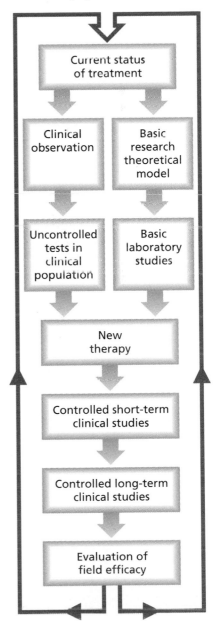

FIGURE 14.3   Building Better Therapies ■ Flow chart of stages in the development of treatments for mental/physical disorders.

Current status of treatment

Clinical observation

Basic research theoretical model

Uncontrolled tests in clinical population

Basic laboratory studies

New therapy

Controlled short-term clinical studies

Controlled long-term clinical studies

Evaluation of field efficacy

appeared in the water. The rescuer jumped in and again pulled the victim to safety. Soon, a third drowning child swept by. The still-dry friend began to trot up the riverbank. The rescuer yelled, "Hey, where are you going?" The dry one replied, "I'm going to get the bastard that's throwing them in." (Wolman, 1975, p. 3)

The moral of this story is clear: *Preventing* a problem is the best solution. All of the traditional therapies that we examined here focus on changing a person who is already distressed or disabled. They begin to do their work only *after* the problems show up and the suffering starts. By the time a person enters therapy, it is often too late to keep the psychological disorder from "settling in" and having disruptive effects on one's daily functioning, social life, or work.

The *prevention* of psychological problems is being practiced by a number of community mental health centers under the general direction of the National Association for Mental Health. To meet this goal, mental health workers use systematic methods for combatting psychological problems. These methods include reducing the *severity* of existing disorders (using traditional therapies); reducing the *duration* of disorders through new programs for early identification and prompt treatment; and reducing the *incidence* of new cases among the unaffected, normal population that is potentially at risk for a particular disorder (Klein & Goldston, 1977).

A Public Health Model   A medical approach to psychological health involves treating people who are afflicted. In contrast, a *public health model* includes identifying and eliminating the sources of disease and illness that exist in the environment. In this approach, an affected individual is seen as the host or carrier—the end product of an existing process of disease. Change the conditions that breed illness and there will be no need to change people later with expensive, extensive treatments. The dramatic reduction of many contagious and infectious diseases, such as tuberculosis, smallpox, and malaria, has come about through this approach. With psychopathology, too, many sources of environmental or organizational stress can be identified; plans can then be made to alleviate them, thus reducing the number of people who will be exposed to them. *The field of* **clinical ecology** *relates mental disorders to the presence of environmental irritants and pollutants.* Clinical ecology expands the boundaries of biomedical therapies by connecting behavioral health not only to drugs but also to such everyday environmental threats as chemical solvents, noise pollution, seasonal changes, and radiation (Bell, 1981). Some therapists have broadened the meaning of the term "environment" to include all factors and conditions that can interfere with normal adaptations in everyday life, such as nutrition, drugs, crime and terrorism, natural disasters, and the availability of personal and social support (Ghadirian & Lehmann, 1992).

These newer mental health approaches are directing attention toward the *precipitating* factors—origins and triggers—in a person's current environment and focusing on practical ways to change *what is* rather than reinterpreting *what was*. In recognizing that certain situations are likely to foster psychopathology—such as when people are made to feel anonymous, rejected, isolated, or abused—new approaches instruct people in ways to avoid or modify these noxious life situations individually or through community action. These newer approaches often target members of culturally diverse groups (such as African Americans and Hispanics) who have been denied access to society's opportunities because of prejudice and discrimination.

Understanding Social Pathology The prevention of mental disorders is a complex and difficult task. It involves not only understanding the relevant causal factors but also overcoming individual, institutional, and governmental resistance to change. Educational efforts directed at the public and government would serve to demonstrate the long-range utility of prevention and the community mental health approach to psychopathology—and justify the necessary expense of prevention.

As we write this final chapter, your authors take note of the fact that recent dramatic changes in the U.S. workplace and economy are taking a toll on the lives of millions of citizens. To be more competitive in a global marketplace, many corporations are seeking to increase profits by eliminating positions and reducing salaries. More than 43 million jobs have been eliminated since 1979, many of them replaced by lower paid, more temporary jobs for white-collar workers. Thus a 1996 *New York Times* poll revealed that "about 19 million people acknowledged that a lost job in their household had precipitated a major crisis in their lives" (Uchitelle & Kleinfeld, 1996, p. A–2). Successful corporations now regularly lay off loyal workers as part of their planned "downsizing"—a euphemism that, for individual employees, really means firing, demotion, and loss of fringe benefits such as health care. In Chapter 10, we discussed the psychoanalytic concept of ego defense mechanisms, psychological strategies to reduce anxiety. One such mechanism we have not already discussed is *intellectualization,* a pattern of using abstract thought and language to make a threat seem distant and less personal. Using the term "downsizing" instead of "firing" or "laying off" might be executives' intellectualizing defense against taking responsibility for profiting while their workers suffer.

Widespread anxiety stems from workers' insecurity about future options. It is important for such workers and their families to realize that the source of their anxiety is not some form of personal pathology, but rather a form of *social pathology*—a society-wide problem—created by changing economic conditions, a problem whose suffering is shared by many other workers. Prevention efforts must go beyond individual, psychological "fixes" to require broader economic, political, and social reform, in the workplace, in education, and in job retraining programs. Finally, workers and their families must learn to see and treat each other not as antagonists or stressors, but as allies in their mutual quest for security and well-being.

Check Your Recall

Critics have charged that psychotherapy may not be any more effective than the healing effects of the normal passage of time. Some critics have suggested that therapy's strongest influence may be merely a placebo effect, the result of the patient's awareness of and faith in the effectiveness of treatment. While belief is an important component to therapeutic cooperation, there is also evidence that therapy is objectively useful when applied expediently and appropriately—that it does work.

Prevention strategies may be more effective than treatment that begins only after a problem is established. Public health and clinical ecology models focus on controlling the factors that precipitate and develop mental disorders. Such factors can include social pathologies caused by societal stressors such as widespread unemployment and insecurity. Such complex and large-scale problems call for broad-based therapeutic changes rather than simplistic "quick fixes."

A Personal Endnote

We come to the end of our long journey through *Psychology*. When you reflect on the lessons of this course (and ideally, when you take your final examination), you will realize just how much you have learned on the way. Yet we have barely scratched the surface of the excitement and challenges that await students of psychology, those curious people-watchers who choose to continue on to the next phase of the journey into more advanced realms of this discipline.

We hope you will be among them, and that you may even go on to contribute to this dynamic enterprise as a scientific researcher or a clinical practitioner or by applying what is known in psychology to the solution of social and personal problems.

Playwright Tom Stoppard reminds us that "Every exit is an entry somewhere else." We would like to believe that the entry into the next phase of your life will be facilitated by what you have learned from *Psychology* and from your introductory psychology course. In that next journey, may you infuse new life into the study of human nature, while strengthening the human connections among all people you encounter. Till we meet again,

Phil Zimbardo

Ann Weber

CHAPTER REVIEW

Summary

Therapeutic tasks involve diagnosing the problem, finding the source of the problem, making a prognosis about probable outcomes with and without treatment, and carrying out treatment. A variety of professionals work under this model. In earlier times, treatments for those with mental problems were usually harsh and dehumanizing. Only recently in history have people with emotional problems been treated as individuals with illnesses to be cured. This view of mental illness has led to more humane treatment of patients. Many cultures have their own ways of understanding and treating mental disorders, although some "universals" hold true for all forms of therapy.

Psychodynamic therapies grew out of Sigmund Freud's psychoanalytic theory. Free association, repression, resistance, and dream analysis are all important components of this therapy. Neo-Freudians place more emphasis on the patient's current social situation, interpersonal relationships, and self-concept.

Behavioral therapy attempts to apply the principles of learning and reinforcement to problem behaviors. Counterconditioning and systematic desensitization are two categories of techniques commonly employed. Contingency management uses operant conditioning to modify behavior, primarily through positive reinforcement and extinction strategies. Social learning therapy involves the use of models and social skills training to help individuals gain confidence about their abilities.

Cognitive therapy concentrates on changing negative or irrational thought patterns about oneself and one's social relationships. The client must learn more constructive thought patterns in reference to a problem and apply the new technique to other situations. Rational-emotive therapy helps clients recognize that their irrational beliefs about themselves interfere with life and helps them learn how to change those thought patterns.

Existential-humanist therapies focus on individuals becoming more fully self-actualized. Therapists strive to be nondirective in helping their clients establish a positive self-image that can deal with external criticisms. Group therapy has many applications, including community self-help groups and support groups. Gestalt therapy focuses on the whole person—body, mind, and life setting. Family and marital therapy concentrate on situational difficulties and interpersonal dynamics as a total system in need of improvement.

Biomedical therapies concentrate on changing the physiological aspects of mental illness. Psychosurgery has lost popularity in recent years because of its radical, irreversible side effects. Electroconvulsive therapy is undergoing a resurgence of use with depressed patients, but it remains controversial. Drug therapy includes antipsychotic medicine for schizophrenics as well as antidepression and antianxiety drugs. Antianxiety medication is susceptible to abuse and should not be used to relieve the ordinary stress of daily living. Some researchers have argued that therapy for mental illness does not work any better than the passage of time or nonspecific placebo treatment. But recent research shows that psychotherapy is effective in treating mental health problems and that different forms of therapy are equally effective. Innovative evaluation projects are helping to answer the question of what makes therapy effective. Prevention strategies have become especially important in the new public health model, since some problems are widespread throughout society, and will require careful, broad-based plans for prevention and treatment.

Section Reviews

The Context of Therapy

Be sure to *Check Your Recall* by reviewing the summary of this section on page 565.

Key Terms

shamanism (p. 556)
in vivo therapy (p. 559)
counseling psychologist (p. 559)
clinical psychologist (p. 560)
psychiatrist (p. 560)
clinical social worker (p. 560)
pastoral counselor (p. 560)

psychoanalyst (p. 560)
biomedical therapy (p. 563)
psychological therapies (p. 563)
ritual healing (p. 565)

Names to Know

Philippe Pinel (p. 562)
J. C. Heinroth (p. 562)
Clifford Beers (p. 562)

Psychological Therapies

Be sure to *Check Your Recall* by reviewing the summary of this section on page 587.

Key Terms

psychoanalytic therapy (p. 566)
insight therapy (p. 566)
free association (p. 567)
catharsis (p. 567)
resistance (p. 567)
dream analysis (p. 568)
transference (p. 568)

countertransference (p. 568)
behavior modification (p. 570)
counterconditioning (p. 571)
systematic desensitization (p. 571)
implosion therapy (p. 572)

flooding (p. 573)
aversion therapy (p. 573)
contingency management (p. 574)
social learning therapy (p. 575)
participant modeling (p. 575)
cognitive therapy (p. 577)
behavioral rehearsal (p. 578)
cognitive behavior modification (p. 578)
rational-emotive therapy (RET) (p. 580)
person-centered therapy (p. 582)

Gestalt therapy (p. 583)

Names to Know

Sigmund Freud (p. 566)
Harry Stack Sullivan (p. 569)
Karen Horney (p. 569)
Joseph Wolpe (p. 571)
B. F. Skinner (p. 574)
Aaron Beck (p. 579)
Albert Ellis (p. 580)
Rollo May (p. 581)
Carl Rogers (p. 582)
Fritz Perls (p. 583)
Virginia Satir (p. 586)

Biomedical Therapies

Be sure to *Check Your Recall* by reviewing the summary of this section on page 593.

Key Terms

psychosurgery (p. 588)
electroconvulsive therapy (ECT) (p. 589)
drug therapy (p. 590)

Names to Know

Egas Moniz (p. 588)

How Effective Is Therapy?

Be sure to *Check Your Recall* by reviewing the summary of this section on page 597.

Key Terms

clinical ecology (p. 596)

Names to Know

Hans Eysenck (p. 594)
Jerome Frank (p. 594)

Chapter 14: Psychotherapy

For each of the following items, choose the single correct or best answer. The correct answers, explanations, and page references appear in Appendix B.

1. Despite the differences between various types of therapy, all therapeutic strategies are designed to _____.
   a. make the client feel better about herself
   b. help the individual fit better into her society
   c. change the individual's functioning in some way
   d. educate the person without interfering with his or her usual patterns of behavior

2. While professionals with somewhat different training and orientations can provide similar forms of therapy, only _____ are qualified to prescribe medications for the treatment of mental or behavioral disorders.
   a. psychiatrists
   b. psychiatric social workers
   c. psychoanalysts
   d. all of the above

3. Because a central goal of the therapist is to guide a patient toward understanding the connections between past origins and present symptoms, psychodynamic therapy is often called _____ therapy.
   a. insight
   b. cognitive
   c. existential
   d. rational-emotive

4. A psychoanalyst finds herself feeling personally fond of a young client who reminds her of her son when he was the client's age. If the therapist has difficulty separating her own feelings from the needs of her patient, this may be an example of the psychoanalytic process known as _____.
   a. resistance
   b. transference
   c. countertransference
   d. negative transference

5. Lola has an irrational fear of speaking in front of others. With the support of her instructor and her entire psychology class, Lola confronts her fear by standing alone in front of her classmates and talking about her phobia. This strategy of placing the individual in the dreaded situation is called _____.
   a. systematic desensitization
   b. catharsis
   c. implosion
   d. flooding

6. To teach his young daughter not to be afraid to swim, a man tells her to "Watch me!" as he wades into the surf, then rolls with the waves, and finally invites her to join him if she wants to try. In behavioral therapy, this technique is known as _____.
   a. clinical ecology
   b. counterconditioning
   c. behavioral rehearsal
   d. participant modeling

7. Which of the following problems might best be corrected through rational-emotive therapy (RET)?
   a. An addicted smoker wants to quit.
   b. A young man pursues a difficult, unenjoyable career because it is the only work his father approves of.
   c. An average-weight woman diets constantly, believing that she must be thin in order to have anyone love her.
   d. None of the above.

8. Which of the following statements about electroconvulsive therapy (ECT) is true?
   a. Proper ECT applies a very strong electric current to a patient's brain without the interference or insulation of sedatives or anesthetic medication.
   b. ECT has been found to be especially effective in the treatment of severe depression.
   c. It is known to work by increasing the stimulation of a particular neurotransmitter in the brain.
   d. It works best with manic patients.

9. Valium, a drug with a high "abuse potential," is classified as an _____ medication.
   a. antianxiety
   b. antidepressant
   c. antipsychotic
   d. antihistamine

10. Psychiatrist Jerome Frank argues that, like religious and political indoctrination programs, all healing processes rely on a common crucial element: _____.
    a. deception
    b. fear of authority
    c. rejection of culture
    d. belief in the experience

IF YOU'RE INTERESTED . . .

Amadeus. (Video: 1984, color, 158 min.). Directed by Milos Forman; starring Tom Hulce, F. Murray Abraham, Elizabeth Berridge, Jeffrey Jones.

Absorbing (and musically astounding) film based on Peter Shaffer's play about the psychological rivalry between eighteenth century composer Antonio Salieri and Wolfgang Amadeus Mozart, the young musical genius who seemed to be favored by God. Told in flashbacks, the story is framed by Salieri's retrospective confession from his asylum cell, surrounded by powerful scenes of the "therapies" of the day—the cages and restraints shackling the mentally ill, suicidal, and eccentric citizens of early modern Europe.

Berger, L., & Vuckovic, A. (1995). *Under observation: Life inside the McLean Psychiatric Hospital.* New York: Penguin Books.

A vivid picture of life at psychiatric institutions across the country, illustrated with the case histories and personal stories of diverse patients who emerge as real people, some disturbingly familiar. Dispells myths and challenges stereotypes about how the mentally ill are treated, leaving the reader both saddened and hopeful.

Kaysen, S. (1993). *Girl, interrupted*. New York: Turtle Bay Books.

Susanna Kaysen's frank and vivid account of her two years, beginning in 1967 when she was 18, in McLean Hospital, a psychiatric hospital with a ward for teenage girls. Dark, funny stories of herself, her jumbled thinking, and the other patients are interspersed with pages from her medical record.

Keyes, D. (1981). *The minds of Billy Milligan*. New York: Bantam.

A factual account of the life of William Stanley Milligan, the first person in the United States to be judged not guilty of major crimes by reason of insanity, because he possessed multiple personalities. Explores whether Milligan fractionated into at least ten personalities as a result of childhood abuse. By the author of the book *Flowers for Algernon*, the basis for the 1968 film *Charly* (see "If You're Interested," Chapter 11).

Kramer, P. D. (1993). *Listening to Prozac: A psychiatrist explores antidepressant drugs and the remaking of the self*. New York: Viking.

Probably no other mood-changing medication since Valium has so captivated the nation's attention and imagination as Prozac, an antidepressant that reputedly makes patients "better than well." Is it a wonder drug, releasing the real self from the pervasive burden of depression and disordered thinking? Or is it an artificial mask, an identity-change in tablet form, a popular but ultimately limited form of self-deception? Through before-and-after interviews with patients who have embraced or rejected Prozac, the author presents the case for and against Prozac, and speculates on the power and meaning of psychoactive medications.

The Madness of King George. (Video: 1994, color, 107 min.). Directed by Nicholas Hytner; starring Nigel Hawthorne, Helen Mirren, Ian Holm, Rupert Everett, John Wood, Amanda Donohoe.

In the late eighteenth century, England's happy and benevolent George III (the very "tyrant" denounced in the American Declaration of Independence) becomes suddenly ill and irrational, prompting his friends, enemies, and physicians to take drastic actions. Based on Alan Bennett's play, the film vividly portrays the well-intentioned but utterly useless efforts of "medical science" at that time to treat mental illness.

My Name is Bill W. (Video: 1989, color, 100 min.). Directed by Daniel Petrie; starring James Garner, James Woods, JoBeth Williams, Fritz Weaver, Gary Sinise.

Story of the founding of Alcoholics Anonymous, and the blueprint for many self-help programs and support groups. Set in the mid-1930s, the film shows how two alcoholics—stockbroker William Griffith Wilson ("Bill W.") and Dr. Robert Holbrook Smith ("Dr. Bob S.")—form a partnership to help each other quit drinking. With superb acting, the film explores the combination self-discipline, friendship, and support essential to therapeutic behavior change.

Ordinary People. (Video: 1980, color, 123 min.). Directed by Robert Redford; starring Donald Sutherland, Mary Tyler Moore, Judd Hirsch, Timothy Hutton.

Powerful film version of Judith Guest's novel about an upper-middle-class family's struggles to cope with the death of their older son, including the suicidal guilt of his surviving younger brother. Appealing portrayal of a psychotherapist as an important relationship in a troubled life.

Snake Pit, The. (Video: 1948, B&W, 108 min.). Directed by Anatole Litvak; starring Olivia de Havilland, Mark Stevens, Leo Genn.

Affecting film portrayal of a young woman's acute schizophrenia and gradual recovery through psychotherapy. Powerful images of what mental institutions were like in most of this country before the development of effective drug therapy for mental disorders.

Spellbound. (Video: 1945, B&W, 111 min.). Directed by Alfred Hitchcock; starring Gregory Peck, Ingrid Bergman, Leo G. Carroll.

Classic Hitchcock mystery, blending psychoanalytic jargon and techniques with old-fashioned detective skills in solving the dilemma of an amnesiac suffering from a guilt complex. Compelling dream sequences were appropriately designed by surrealist artist Salvador Dali.

Stuart Saves His Family. (Video: 1995, color, 95 min.). Directed by Harold Ramis; starring Al Franken, Laura San Giacomo, Vincent D'Onofrio, Shirley Knight, Harris Yulin, Julia Sweeney.

Based on satirist Al Franken's character, Stuart Smalley, the chronic "twelve-stepper" and support group member on TV's "Saturday Night Live." Pokes gentle fun at the New Age jargon and saccharine optimism of some self-improvement programs. Some uncanny, on-target depictions of difficult family dynamics make this film poignant and helpful as well as funny.

Appendix A: Understanding Statistics: Analyzing Data and Forming Conclusions

As we noted in Chapter 1, psychologists use statistics to make sense of the data they collect. They also use statistics to provide a quantitative basis for the conclusions they draw. Knowing something about statistics can, therefore, help you appreciate the process by which psychological knowledge is developed. On a more personal level, having a basic understanding of statistics will help you make better decisions.

Most students perceive statistics as a dry, uninteresting topic. However, statistics have many vital applications in your life. Consider the following items taken from the front pages of the newspaper. They show how statistics help answer some crucial questions about human behavior.

- Fred Cowan was described by relatives, by coworkers, and by acquaintances as a "nice, quiet man," a "gentle man who loved children," and a "real pussycat." The principal of the parochial school Cowan had attended as a child reported that his former student had received A grades in courtesy, cooperation, and religion. According to a coworker, Cowan "never talked to anybody and was someone you could push around." Cowan, however, surprised everyone who knew him when, one Valentine's Day, he strolled into work toting a semiautomatic rifle and shot and killed four coworkers, a police officer, and, finally, himself.
- To friends and neighbors, Patrolman Stephen Richard Smith seemed a polite, shy man with a taste for classical music and a habit of feeding stray cats. One day this 31-year-old police officer was shot to death by his best friend, who was his former patrol partner. Authorities alleged that Smith's former partner had been forced to shoot his friend in the line of duty—Smith was suspected of being a brutal vigilante who had beaten and murdered several people.

Stories such as these lead all of us—laypeople and research psychologists alike—to wonder about the meaning and causes of human behavior. How could people who were perceived by everyone who knew them as "gentle" and "shy" commit such atrocities? These stories also make us wonder how well we *really* know anyone.

Both stories have a common plot: a shy, quiet person suddenly becomes violent, shocking everyone who knows him. What do Fred Cowan and Stephen Smith have in common with other people who were suddenly transformed from gentle and caring into violent and ruthless? What personal attributes might distinguish them from us?

A team of researchers had a hunch that there might be a link between shyness and other personal characteristics and violent behavior (Lee et al., 1977). Therefore, they began to collect some data that might reveal such a connection. The researchers reasoned that seemingly nonviolent people who suddenly commit murders are probably typically shy, nonaggressive individuals who keep their passions in check and their impulses under tight control. For most of their lives, they suffer many silent injuries. Seldom, if ever, do they express anger, regardless of how angry they really feel. On the outside, they appear unbothered, but on the inside they may be fighting to control furious rages. They give the impression that they are quiet, passive, responsible people, both as children and as adults. Since they are shy, they probably do not let others get close to them, so no one knows how they really feel. Then, suddenly, something explodes. At the slightest provocation—one more small insult, one more little rejection, one more bit of social pressure—the fuse is lit and they release the suppressed violence that has been building up for so long. Because they did not learn to deal with interpersonal conflicts through discussion and verbal negotiation, these sudden murderers act out their anger physically.

The researchers' minitheory led them to the hypothesis that shyness would be more characteristic of people who had engaged in homicide—without any prior history of violence or antisocial behavior—than it would of those who had committed homicide but had had a previous record of violent criminal behavior. In addition, sudden murderers should have higher levels of control over their impulses than habitually violent people. Finally, their passivity and dependence would be manifested in more feminine and androgynous (both male and female) characteristics, as measured on a standard sex-role inventory, than those of habitual criminals.

To test these hypotheses, the researchers collected three kinds of data from two types of subjects: shyness scores, impulse control scores, and sex-role identification scores from people who had recently committed murder, with and without previous criminal records. This type of research, in which the behavior of interest—the dependent variable—has already occurred before the study begins, uses an *ex post facto experimental design*. The task of the researcher is to figure out what kinds of independent variables could have influenced the known outcomes.

A second form of ex post facto design is one in which subjects are matched *after* the independent variable has already been administered. Here the research task is to find out the consequences of this existing difference between subjects. Subjects are not randomly assigned to conditions; instead, they are categorized according to existing characteristics—specifically, something they did or some personal attribute. Because alternative explanations cannot be ruled out, this design does not permit causal conclusions from the data. However, it does allow for the discovery of variables that may help to explain some existing phenomenon that may then lead to controlled experiments assessing the causal connections.

To test their ideas about sudden murderers, the researchers obtained permission to administer psychological questionnaires to a group of inmates serving time for murder in California prisons. Nineteen inmates (all male) agreed to participate in the study. Prior to committing murder, some had committed a series of crimes, while the other part of the sample had had no previous criminal record. All participants filled out three different questionnaires. Each questionnaire required a different type of information from the subject.

The first was the Stanford Shyness Survey (Zimbardo, 1990). The most important item on this questionnaire asked if the subject was shy; the answer could be either yes or no. Other items on the scale tapped degree and kinds of shyness and a variety of dimensions related to origins and triggers of shyness.

The second questionnaire was the Bem Sex-Role Inventory (BSRI), which presented a list of adjectives, such as *aggressive* and *affectionate,* and asked how well each adjective described the subject (Bem, 1974, 1981). Some adjectives were typically associated with being "feminine," and the total score of these adjectives was a subject's femininity score. Other adjectives were considered "masculine," and the total score of those adjectives was a subject's masculinity score. The final sex-role score, which reflected the difference between a subject's femininity and masculinity, was calculated by subtracting the masculinity score from the femininity score. A combination of the masculinity and femininity scores shows up as a subject's androgyny score.

The third questionnaire was the Minnesota Multiphasic Personality Inventory (MMPI), which was designed to measure many different aspects of personality (see Chapter 10). The study used only the "ego-overcontrol" scale, which measures the degree to which a person acts out or controls impulses. The higher the subject's score on this scale, the more ego overcontrol the subject exhibits.

The researchers predicted that, compared with murderers with a prior criminal record, sudden murderers would (1) more often describe themselves as shy on the shyness survey; (2) select more feminine traits than masculine ones on the sex-role scale; and (3) score higher in ego overcontrol. What did they discover?

Before you find out, you need to understand some of the basic procedures that were used to analyze these data. The actual sets of data collected will be used as the source material to teach you about some of the different types of

statistical analyses and also about the kinds of conclusions they make possible.

Analyzing the Data

For most researchers in psychology, analyzing the data is an exciting step. They can find out if their results will contribute to a better understanding of a particular aspect of behavior or if they have to go back to the drawing board and redesign their research. In short, they can discover if their predictions were correct.

Data analysis can involve many different procedures, some of them surprisingly simple and straightforward. In this section, we will work step-by-step through an analysis of some of the data from the Sudden Murderers Study. If you have looked ahead and are turned off at the sight of numbers and equations, your feeling is understandable. However, you do not need to be good in math to be able to understand the concepts we will be discussing. You just need the courage to see mathematical symbols for what they are—a shorthand for presenting ideas and conceptual operations.

TABLE A.1	RAW DATA FROM THE SUDDEN MURDERERS STUDY		
Inmate	Shyness	BSRI Femininity-Masculinity	MMPI Ego Overcontrol
Group 1: Sudden murderers			
1	yes	+5	17
2	no	−1	17
3	yes	+4	13
4	yes	+61	17
5	yes	+19	13
6	yes	+41	19
7	no	−29	14
8	yes	+23	9
9	yes	−13	11
10	yes	+5	14
Group 2: Habitual criminal murderers			
11	no	−12	15
12	no	−14	11
13	yes	−33	14
14	no	−8	10
15	no	−7	16
16	no	+3	11
17	no	−17	6
18	no	+6	9
19	no	−10	12

NOTE: BSRI = Bem Sex-Role Inventory; MMPI = Minnesota Multiphasic Personality Inventory.

The raw data—the actual scores or other measures obtained—from the 19 inmates in the Sudden Murderers Study are listed in Table A.1. As you can see, there were ten inmates in the sudden murderers group and nine in the habitual criminal murderers group. When first glancing at these data, any researcher would feel what you probably feel: confusion. What do all these scores mean? Do the two groups of murderers differ from one another on these various personality measures? It is difficult to know just by examining this disorganized array of numbers.

Psychologists rely on a mathematical tool called *statistics* to help make sense of and draw meaningful conclusions from the data they collect. There are two types of statistics: descriptive and inferential. **Descriptive statistics** use mathematical procedures in an objective, uniform way to describe different aspects of numerical data. If you have ever computed your grade-point average, you already have used descriptive statistics. **Inferential statistics** use probability theory to make sound decisions about which results might have occurred simply through chance variation.

Descriptive Statistics

Descriptive statistics provide a summary picture of patterns in the data. They are used to describe sets of scores collected from one subject or, more often, from different groups of subjects. They are also used to describe relationships among variables. Thus, instead of trying to keep in mind all the scores obtained by each of the subjects, researchers get special indexes of the scores that are most *typical* for each group. They also get measures of the way those scores are typical—whether the scores are spread out or clustered closely together. Two types of descriptive statistics are frequency distributions and measures of central tendency. We will describe each of these, as well as show how they are displayed in graphs, in the following sections.

Frequency Distributions The shyness data are easy to summarize. Of the 19 scores, there are 9 *yes* and 10 *no* responses; almost all the *yes* responses are in Group 1 and almost all the *no* responses are in Group 2. On the overcontrol scale, the scores range from 6 to 19; it is harder to get a sense, from just looking at the scale, of how the groups compare. We'll need a way to reorganize those scores.

Now let's examine the sex-role scores. The highest score is 61 (most feminine) and the lowest is −33 (most masculine). Of the 19 scores, 9 are positive and 10 negative—this means that 9 of the murderers described themselves as relatively feminine and 10 as relatively masculine.

To get a clearer picture of how these scores are distributed, we can draw up a **frequency distribution**—a summary of how frequently each of the various scores occurs. The first step in preparing a frequency distribution for a set of numerical data is to *rank order* the scores from highest to lowest. The rank ordering for the sex-role scores is shown in Table A.2. The second step is to group these rank-ordered scores into a smaller number of categories called *intervals*. In this study, 10 categories were used, with each category covering 10 possible scores. The third step is to construct a frequency distribution table,

TABLE A.2	RANK ORDERING OF SEX-ROLE DIFFERENCE SCORES	
Highest +61		−1
+41		−7
+23		−8
+19		−10
+6		−12
+5		−13
+5		−14
+4		−17
+3		−29
		−33 Lowest

NOTE: + scores are more feminine; − scores are more masculine.

listing the intervals from highest to lowest and noting the *frequencies*—the number of scores within each interval. Our frequency distribution shows us that the sex-role scores are largely between −20 and +9 (see Table A.3). The majority of the inmates' scores did not deviate much from zero. That is, they were neither strongly positive nor strongly negative.

We can now make some preliminary conclusions about the data. By examining frequency distributions for our variables, we can already see that each of our three predictions is accurate. Forty percent of the American people describe themselves as shy. By comparison, eight out of ten of the sudden murderers (80 percent) described themselves as shy, while only one of nine of the habitual criminal murderers (11 percent) did so. On the sex-role scale, 70 percent of the sudden murderers chose adjectives that were more feminine than masculine, while only 22 percent of the habitual criminals said that the feminine adjectives described them more accurately than did the

Table A.3	FREQUENCY DISTRIBUTION OF SEX-ROLE DIFFERENCE SCORES
Category	**Frequency**
+60 to +69	1
+50 to +59	0
+40 to +49	1
+30 to +39	0
+20 to +29	1
+10 to +19	1
+0 to +9	5
−10 to −1	4
−20 to −11	4
−30 to −21	1
−40 to −31	1

masculine ones. Sudden murderers scored higher in over-controlling their impulses than did habitual criminal murderers (Lee et al., 1977). In addition, there was a noticeable difference in the circumstances that precipitated the murders committed by the shy men. In virtually every case, the precipitating incidents for the sudden murderers were minor, compared with the incidents that triggered the violence of the habitual criminal murderers.

Although summaries of data such as this are compelling, there are a number of other analyses we must look at before we can state our conclusions with any certainty. The researchers' next step was to arrange the distributions in graphic form.

Graphs   Distributions are often easier to understand when they are displayed in graphs. The simplest type of graph is a *bar graph*. We can use a bar graph to illustrate how many more sudden murderers than habitual criminal murderers described themselves as shy (see Figure A.1). Bar graphs allow one to see patterns in the data.

For more complex data, such as the sex-role scores, we can use a *histogram,* which is similar to a bar graph except that the histogram's bars touch each other and its categories are *intervals*—number categories instead of the name categories used in the bar graph. A histogram gives a visual picture of the number of scores in a distribution that are in each interval. It is easier to see from the sex-role scores shown in the histograms (in Figure A.2) that the distributions of scores are different for the two groups of murderers.

Measures of Central Tendency   So far, we have formed a general picture of how the scores are *distributed*. Tables and graphs increase our general understanding of research results, but we want to know more—for example, the one score that is most typical of the group as a whole. This score becomes particularly useful when we compare two or more groups; it is much easier to compare the typical scores of two groups than their entire distributions. A single, *representative* score that can be used as an index of the most typical score obtained by a group of subjects is called a **measure of central tendency.** (It is located in the center of the distribution, and other scores tend to cluster around it.) Typically, psychologists use three different measures of central tendency: the *mode,* the *median,* and the *mean.*

FIGURE A.1   Shyness for Two Groups of Murderers ■

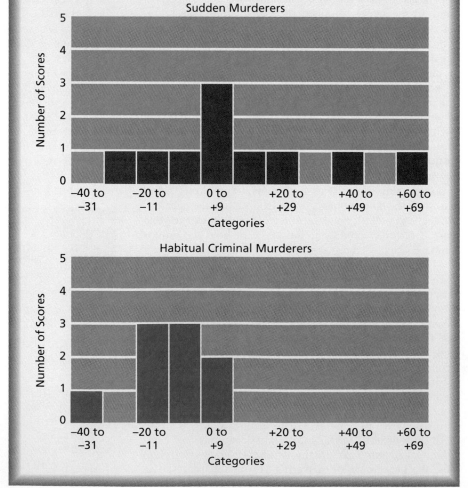

FIGURE A.2   Sex-Role Scores ■

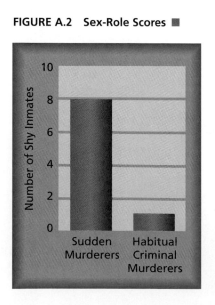

The **mode** is the score that occurs more often than any other. For the measure of shyness, the modal response of the sudden murderers was *yes*—eight out of ten said they were shy. Among habitual criminal murderers, the modal response was *no*. The sex-role scores for the sudden murderers had a mode of +5. Can you figure out what the mode of their ego-overcontrol scores is?

The mode is the easiest index of central tendency to determine, but it is often the least useful. You will see one reason for this relative lack of usefulness if you notice only one overcontrol score lies above the mode of 17, while six lie below it. Although 17 is the score obtained most often, it may not fit your idea of "typical" or "central."

The **median** is more clearly a central score; it separates the upper half of the scores in a distribution from the lower half. The number of scores larger than the median is the same as the number that are smaller. If you rank-order the sex-role scores of only the sudden murderers on a separate piece of paper, you will see that the median score is +5 (in this case, the same as the mode, although this is not always true). Four scores are higher than +5, and four scores are lower. Similarly, the median overcontrol score for these subjects is 15, with four scores below it and four above it. The median is quite simply the score in the middle of the distribution.

The median is not affected by extreme scores. For example, even if the highest sex-role score had been +129 instead of +61, the median value would still have been +5. That score would still separate the upper half of the data from the lower half.

The **mean** is what most people think of when they hear the word *average*. It is also the statistic most often used to describe a set of data. To calculate the mean, you add up all the scores in a distribution and divide by the total number of scores. The operation is summarized by the following formula:

$$M = \Sigma X \div N$$

In this formula, M is the mean, X is each individual score, Σ (the Greek letter *sigma*) is the summation of what immediately follows it, and N is the total number of scores. Since the summation of all the scores (ΣX) is 115 and the total number of scores (N) is 10, the mean (M) of the sex-role scores of the sudden murderers would be calculated as follows:

$$M = 115 \div 10 = 11.5$$

Try to calculate their mean overcontrol scores yourself. You should come up with a mean of 14.4.

Unlike the median, the mean *is* affected by the specific values of all scores in the distribution. Changing the value of an extreme score *does* change the value of the mean. For example, if the sex-role score of inmate 4 were +101 instead of +61, the mean for the whole group would increase from 11.5 to 15.5.

Variability In addition to knowing which score is most representative of the distribution as a whole, it is useful to know how representative that measure of central tendency really is. Are most of the other scores fairly close to it or widely spread out? **Measures of variability** are statistics that describe the distribution of scores around some measure of central tendency.

Can you see why measures of variability are important? An example may help. Suppose you are a grade school teacher. It is the beginning of the school year, and you will be teaching reading to a group of 30 second graders. Knowing that the average child in the class can now read a first-grade-level book will help you to plan your lessons. You could plan better, however, if you knew how *similar* or how *divergent* the reading abilities of the 30 children were. Are they all at about the same level (low variability)? If so, then you can plan a fairly standard second-grade lesson. What if several can read advanced material and others can barely read at all (high variability)? Now the mean level is not so representative of the entire class, and you will have to plan a variety of lessons to meet the children's varied needs.

The simplest measure of variability is the **range**, the difference between the highest and the lowest values in a frequency distribution. For the sudden murderers' sex-role scores, the range is 90: (+61) to (−29). The range of their overcontrol scores is 10: (+19) to (+9). To compute the range, you need to know only two of the scores: the highest and the lowest.

The range is simple to compute, but psychologists often prefer measures of variability that are more sensitive and that take into account all the scores in a distribution, not just the extremes. One widely used measure is the **standard deviation** (SD), a measure of variability that indicates the *average* difference between the scores and their mean. To figure out the standard deviation of a distribution, you need to know the mean of the distribution and the individual scores. Although the arithmetic involved in calculating the standard deviation is very easy, the formula is a bit more complicated than the one used to calculate the mean and, therefore, will not be presented here. The general procedure, however, involves subtracting the value of each individual score from the mean and then determining the average of those mean deviations.

The standard deviation tells us how variable a set of scores is. The larger the standard deviation, the more spread out the scores are. The standard deviation of the sex-role scores for the sudden murderers is 24.6, but the standard deviation for the habitual criminals is only 10.7. This shows that there was less variability in the habitual criminals group. Their scores clustered more closely about their mean than did those of the sudden murderers. When the standard deviation is small, the mean is a good representative index of the entire distribution. When the standard deviation is large, the mean is less typical of the whole group.

Correlation Another useful tool in interpreting psychological data is the **correlation coefficient,** a measure of the nature and strength of the relationship between two variables (such as height and weight or sex-role score and overcontrol score). It tells us the extent to which scores on one measure are associated with scores on the other. If people with high scores on one variable tend to have high scores on the other variable, the the correlation coefficient will be positive (greater than 0). If, however, people with high scores on one variable tend to have *low* scores on the other variable, then the correlation coefficient will be negative (less than 0). If there is *no* consistent relationship between the scores, the correlation will be close to 0 (see also Chapter 1).

Correlation coefficients range from +1.00 (perfect positive correlation) through 0 to −1.00 (perfect negative correlation). The further a coefficient is from 0 in *either* direction, the more closely related the two variables are, positively or negatively. Higher coefficients permit better predictions of one variable, given knowledge of the other.

In the Sudden Murderers Study, the correlation coefficient (symbolized as *r*) between the sex-role scores and the overcontrol scores turns out to be +0.35. The sex-role scores and the overcontrol scores are, thus, positively correlated—in general, subjects seeing themselves as more feminine also tend to be higher in overcontrol. However, the correlation is modest compared with the highest possible value, +1.00. So we know that there are many exceptions to this relationship. If we had also measured the self-esteem of these inmates and found a correlation of −0.68 between overcontrol scores and self-esteem, it would mean that there was a negative correlation. If this were the case, we could say that the subjects who had high overcontrol scores tended to be lower in self-esteem. It would be a stronger relationship than the relationship between the sex-role scores and the overcontrol scores because −0.68 is farther from 0, the point of no relationship, than is +0.35.

Inferential Statistics

We have used a number of descriptive statistics to characterize the data from the Sudden Murderers Study, and now we have an idea of the pattern of results. However, some basic questions remain unanswered. Recall that the research team hypothesized that sudden murderers would be shyer, more overcontrolled, and more feminine than habitual criminal murderers. After we have used descriptive statistics to compare average responses and variability in the two groups, it appears that there are some differences between the groups. But how do we know if the differences are large enough to be meaningful? Are they reliable? If we repeated this study, with other sudden murderers and other habitual criminal murderers, would we expect to find the same pattern of results, or could these results have been an outcome of chance? If we could somehow measure the entire population of sudden murderers and habitual criminal murderers, would the means and standard deviations be the same as those we found for these small samples?

Inferential statistics are used to answer these kinds of questions. They tell us which inferences we can make from our samples and which conclusions we can legitimately draw from our data. Inferential statistics use probability theory to determine the likelihood that a set of data occurred simply by chance variation.

The Normal Curve   In order to understand how inferential statistics work, we must look first at the special properties of a distribution called the *normal curve*. When data

on a variable (height, IQ, or overcontrol, for example) are collected from a large number of subjects, the numbers obtained often fit a curve roughly similar to that shown in Figure A.3. Notice that the curve is symmetrical (the left half is a mirror image of the right) and bell shaped—high in the middle, where most scores are, and lower the farther you get from the mean. This type of curve is called a **normal curve**, or *normal distribution*. (A *skewed* distribution is one in which scores cluster toward one end instead of around the middle.)

In a normal curve, the median, mode, and mean values are the same. A specific percentage of the scores can be predicted to fall under different sections of the curve. Figure A.3 shows IQ scores on the Stanford-Binet Intelligence Test. These scores have a mean of 100 and a standard deviation of 16. If you indicate standard deviations as distances from the mean along the baseline, you find that a little more than 68 percent of all the scores are between the mean of 100 and 1 standard deviation above and below—between IQs of 84 and 116. Roughly another 27 percent of the scores are found between the first and second standard deviations below the mean (IQ scores between 68 and 84) and above the mean (IQ scores between 116 and 132). Less than 5 percent of the scores fall in the third standard deviation above and below the mean, and *very* few scores fall beyond—only about one quarter of 1 percent.

Inferential statistics indicate the probability that the particular sample of scores obtained are actually related to whatever you are attempting to measure or whether they could have occurred by chance. For example, it is more likely that someone would have an IQ of 105 than an IQ of 140, but an IQ of 140 is more probable than one of 35.

A normal curve is also obtained by collecting a series of measurements whose differences are due only to chance. If you flip a coin 10 times in a row and record the number of heads and tails, you will probably get 5 of each—most of the time. If you keep flipping the coin for 100 sets of 10 tosses, you probably will get a few sets with all heads or no heads, more sets where the number is between these extremes, and, most typically, more sets where the number is about half each way. If you made a graph of your 1000 tosses, you would get one that closely fits a normal curve, such as the one in the figure.

Statistical Significance   A researcher who finds a difference between the mean scores for two samples must ask if it is a *real* difference or if it occurred simply because of chance. Because chance differences have a normal distribution, a researcher can use the normal curve to answer this question.

A simple example will help to illustrate the point. Suppose your psychology professor wants to see if the gender of a person proctoring a test makes a difference in the test scores obtained from male and female students. For this purpose, the professor randomly assigns half of the students to a male proctor and half to a female proctor. The professor then compares the mean score of each group. The two mean scores would probably be fairly similar; any slight difference would most likely be due to chance. Why? Because if only chance is operating and both

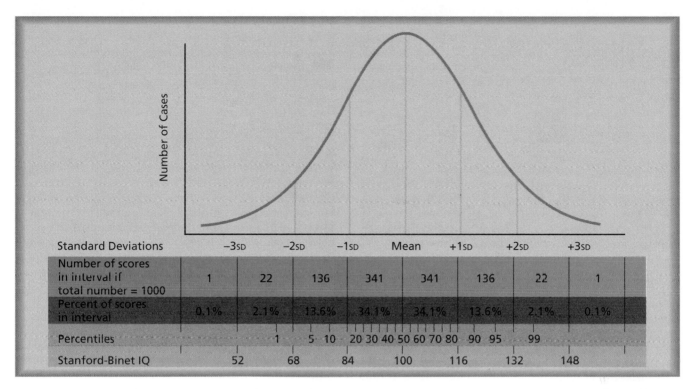

FIGURE A.3   A Normal Curve ■

Standard Deviations	−3SD	−2SD	−1SD	Mean	+1SD	+2SD	+3SD
Number of scores in interval if total number = 1000	1	22	136	341	341	136	22	1
Percent of scores in interval	0.1%	2.1%	13.6%	34.1%	34.1%	13.6%	2.1%	0.1%
Percentiles		1	5 10	20 30 40 50 60 70 80	90 95	99	
Stanford-Binet IQ	52	68	84	100	116	132	148

groups are from the same population (no difference), then the means of male proctor and female proctor samples should be fairly close most of the time. From the percentages of scores found in different parts of the normal distribution, you know that less than a third of the scores in the male proctor condition should be greater than one standard deviation above or below the female proctor mean. The chances of getting a male proctor mean score more than three standard deviations above or below most of your female proctor means would be very small. A professor who *did* get a difference that great would feel fairly confident that the difference is a real one and is somehow related to the gender of the test proctor. The next question would be *how* that variable influences test scores.

If male and female students were randomly assigned to each type of proctor, it would be possible to analyze whether an overall difference found between the proctors was consistent across both student groups or was limited to only one sex. Imagine the data show that male proctors grade female students higher than do female proctors, but both grade male students the same. Your professor could use a statistical inference procedure to estimate the probability that an observed difference could have occurred by chance. This computation is based on the size of the difference and the spread of the scores.

By common agreement, psychologists accept a difference as "real" when the probability that it might be due to chance is less than 5 in 100 (indicated by the notation $p < .05$). A **significant difference** is one that meets this criterion. However, in some cases, even stricter probability levels are used, such as $p < .01$ (less than 1 in 100) and $p < .001$ (less than 1 in 1000).

With a statistically significant difference, a researcher can draw a conclusion about the behavior that was under investigation. There are many different types of tests for estimating the statistical significance of sets of data. The type of test chosen for a particular case depends on the design of the study, the form of the data, and the size of the groups. We will mention only one of the most common tests, the *t-test*, which may be used when an investigator wants to know if the difference between the means of two groups is statistically significant.

We can use a *t*-test to see if the mean sex-role score of the sudden murderers is significantly different from that of the habitual criminal murderers. If we carry out the appropriate calculations, we find that there is a very slim chance, less than 5 in 100 ($p < .05$) of obtaining such a large *t* value if no true difference exists. The difference is, therefore, statistically significant, and we can feel more confident that there is a real difference between the two groups. The sudden murderers *did* rate themselves as more feminine than did the habitual criminal murderers. On the other hand, the difference between the two groups of murderers in overcontrol scores turns out *not* to be statistically significant ($p < .10$), so we must be more cautious in talking about this difference. There is a *trend* in the predicted direction—the difference is one that would occur by chance only 10 times in 100—but the difference is not within the standard 5-in-100 range. (The difference in shyness, analyzed using another statistical test for frequency of scores, *is* highly significant.) So, by using inferential statistics, we are able to answer some of the basic questions with which we began, and we are closer to understanding the psychology of people who suddenly change from mild-mannered, shy individuals into mass murderers. Any conclusion, however, is only a statement of the *probable* relationship between the events that were investigated; it is never one of certainty. Truth in science is provisional, always open to revision by later data from better studies, developed from better hypotheses.

How to Mislead with Statistics

Now that we have considered what statistics are, how they are used, and what they mean, we should talk about how they can be misused. Many people accept unsupported "facts" that are bolstered by the air of authority of a statistic. Others choose to believe or disbelieve what the statistics say without having any idea of how to question the numbers that are presented in support of a product, politician, or proposal.

There are many ways to give a misleading impression using statistics. The decisions made at all stages of research—from who the subjects are to how the study is designed, what statistics are selected, and how they are used—can have a profound effect on the conclusions that can be drawn from the data.

The group of subjects can make a large difference that can easily remain undetected when the results are reported. For example, a survey of views on abortion rights will yield very different results if conducted in a small fundamentalist community in the South rather than a university in New York City. Likewise, a pro-life group surveying the opinions of its membership will very likely arrive at conclusions that differ from those obtained by the same survey conducted by a pro-choice group.

Even if the subjects are randomly selected and not biased by the methodology, the statistics can produce misleading results if the assumptions of the statistics are violated. For example, suppose 20 people take an IQ test; 19 of them receive scores between 90 and 110, and 1 receives a score of 220. The mean of the group will be strongly elevated by that one outlying high score. With a data set like this one, it would be much more accurate to present the median or the mode, which would accurately report the group's generally average intelligence, rather than the mean, which would make it look as if the average member of this group had a high IQ. This sort of bias is especially powerful in a small sample. If, on the other hand, the number of people in this group was 2000 instead of 20, the one extreme outlier would make virtually no difference, and the mean would be a legitimate summary of the group's intelligence.

One good way to avoid falling for this sort of deception is to check on the size of the sample—large samples are less likely to be misleading than small ones. Another method of checking is to look at the median or the mode as well as the mean—the results can be interpreted with more confidence if they are similar than if they are different.

One way to guard against being misled by the misuse of statistics is to closely examine the methodology and results of the research reported. Check to see if the experimenters report their sample size, significance levels, and margins of error. Try to find out if the methods they used

accurately and consistently measure whatever they claim to be investigating.

No test is 100 percent accurate all the time, but it is possible to calculate a range within which the "true" score probably lies. Responsible statisticians report this range as the *margin of error*. For example, examine the data in Table A.4, which summarizes the results from a survey asking Americans about their beliefs in the supernatural. Nearly half of the respondents indicated that they believed that the devil could possess humans. Notice in the small print at the bottom of the chart that there is a margin of error of plus or minus 4 percent. In other words, 49 percent may not be a truly accurate representation of the population at large. However, it is highly probable that somewhere between 45 percent and 53 percent of the population really does believe in devil possession. Since the survey was conducted using representative sampling techniques with 1225 American adults, it is likely that the sample is fairly representative of the population as a whole.

Before drawing your own conclusions from the results presented, it is always a good idea to check such things as sample size and margin of error. Paying attention to the fine print and applying what you have learned in this book should make you less likely to be taken in by statistical misdirection and make you a much wiser consumer of psychological research.

Statistics are the backbone of psychological research. They are used to understand observations and to determine whether findings are, in fact, correct and significant. Through the methods we have described, psychologists can prepare a frequency distribution of data and find the central tendencies and variability of the scores. They can use the correlation coefficient to determine the strength and direction of the association between sets of scores. Finally, psychological investigators can then find out how representative the observations are and whether they are significantly different from what is observed among the general population. Statistics can also be used poorly or deceptively, misleading those who do not understand them. But when statistics are applied correctly and ethically, they allow researchers to expand the body of psychological knowledge.

TABLE A.4	BELIEF IN THE SUPERNATURAL: GALLUP POLL RESULTS, 1990	
Beliefs in	**People Who Believe**	**People Who Are Not Sure**
The devil	55%	8%
ESP	49%	22%
Devil possession	49%	16%
Psychic healing	46%	20%
Telepathy	36%	25%
Extraterrestrials	27%	32%
Astrology	25%	21%

N = 1225 U.S. adults; margin of error ± 4%.

Appendix B: Review Test Answer Key

In each Chapter Review you will find a 10-item Review Test to assist you in your understanding of the key points of that chapter. This appendix provides correct answers to each chapter's Review Test. For each Review Test item, this answer key provides the correct answer, a page reference, and a brief explanation about why each answer choice is correct or incorrect. In this answer key, the *key point for each correct answer* is printed in *italics* in the explanation. The page reference indicates the location of that key point.

To get the most out of these brief Review Tests, consult the Answer Key only *after* you have completed the entire test. Score yourself, calculating your approximate grade on the test. For example, if you answered 7 of the 10 items correctly, you earned a 7/10 or 70%—a low C. Is the grade you earned acceptable to you? If you hope to do better on class tests, go back and reread the chapter. Pay particular attention to sections discussing the concepts you answered *incorrectly*. Clinch your efforts by also reexamining the sections about which you answered *correctly*. This review process will strengthen your understanding of the material you are beginning to comprehend, as well as correct any misunderstandings or concepts that are still challenging you.

Don't forget the Mastery Tests! At the end of this volume is a perforated section of pages making up a Mastery Test collection. For each chapter, we provide a detachable page with a 25-item test, consisting of 20 multiple-choice items and 5 short-answer items. *Your instructor has the Answer Key to the Mastery Tests, included as part of the Instructor's Manual.* In order to score your Mastery Test to obtain one more preview of your likely course test performance, please see your instructor, who also has page references for the key concepts addressed in each Mastery Test item.

There is some overlap between the item coverage of each chapter's Review Test and its Mastery Test. However, we cannot promise that either of the tests in this volume will reflect your instructor's emphases on a particular course test. To prepare for a class test, always collaborate with your instructor. Ask for review sheets, review your class notes, and study *actively* by composing your own review questions, writing out your answers, and if possible taking turns "teaching" the material to study partners. In such a comprehensive program of preparation and self-testing, you will get the most out of your course and earn the evaluations you deserve.

If you have problems with or questions about the Review Tests or answers, please contact the second author of this text:

Dr. Ann L. Weber
Department of Psychology
University of North Carolina at Asheville
Asheville, NC 28804
(704) 251–6833
E-mail: weber@unca.edu

Chapter 1: Mind, Behavior, and Science

1. A (p. 5). Empirical investigations involve collecting *sensory or experiential data*. The scientific method relies on observation for data, rather than on speculation or traditional beliefs. Scientists also seek to be objective and to avoid subjective biases in recording their observations.

2. D (p. 8). Psychology has five goals: describing, explaining, predicting, controlling, and improving behavior. Prediction requires using past or current data in evaluating the likelihood of an *individual's future behavior*.

3. A (p. 11). Social psychology studies the individual in social context but does not deliver therapeutic services. Counseling, clinical, and community psychology are all *professional practices in which treatments and solutions* are offered for psychological problems.

4. B (p. 11). *Wilhelm Wundt established the first psychological laboratory* in 1879. Wundt's student Edward Titchener furthered the cause of structuralism. Sigmund Freud founded the psychodynamic perspective. John B. Watson pioneered the behavioristic approach in psychology.

5. B (p. 13). Functionalism emphasizes understanding the *function or adaptive purpose* of behavior. Structuralism focuses on the contents of the mind. Behaviorism advocates the study only of overt, observable behavior. Humanism proposes that human action is oriented toward growth and fulfillment of human potential.

6. C (p. 15). The psychodynamic approach proposes that psychological dynamics or *forces result from conflicts within the individual*. Biological approaches look for bodily processes to explain behavior. Cognitive approaches argue that all behaviors begin with thought processes. The sociocultural approach posits that the individual is influenced by the social and cultural context.

7. C (p. 19). Human evolution is theorized to occur when the genetically fittest individuals produce offspring with the best chance of *adaptation to the environment*. Conformity is a concept in the sociocultural perspective. Information processing is part of how cognitive perspectives characterize human functioning. Psychodynamic views suggest that individual behavior is influenced when personal goals are restricted by society.

8. D (p. 28). Debriefing involves providing information about the true purpose of a study to *human subjects who were deceived* in the course of the research investigation. Answers A, B, and C all describe human subjects in situations they do not completely understand, whereas D involves nonhuman subjects in a nondeceptive situation.

9. C (p. 25). A hypothesis is an *explanation proposed to answer a research question*. A model is an analogy between a familiar system and a process being studied. A theory is a set of principles to explain a psychological phenomenon. A correlation is a relationship between two variables or data sets.

10. B (p. 31). This study is an experiment in which the independent variable involves *two "story" conditions* (listening to stories versus making up stories) and the dependent variable includes the children's *performance* in other reading, writing, and art classes.

Chapter 2: Biopsychology

1. C (pp. 39–40). The opening case discusses Field's and Schanberg's discoveries, which indicate that *gentle massaging stimulates* the physical and sensory development of premature infants.

2. A (p. 42). Variation within a species refers to the *variety of phenotypes and genotypes* among the population's individuals. Variety does not cause competition, but when environmental forces are strong or resources are scarce, variety ensures that some individuals will survive while others will not.

3. C (p. 43). Encephalization—the greater growth of the cerebral cortex—permitted humans to *develop special language skills* not found in other species. Bipedalism is present among other species (e.g., birds) but neither caused nor was caused by language, encephalization, or culture.

4. A (p. 47). Descartes was first to insist that the *physical body was governed by physical laws* and thus could be studied like other physical objects and phenomena. Darwin proposed the natural selection of species, accounting for distinctive outcomes in human evolution. Broca did early studies of brain injuries, and Penfield used electrical stimulation to localize brain functions.

5. A (p. 48). Lesioning involves *inflicting controlled damage or injury* and observing the results. The EEG, CT scanning, and MRI are all noninvasive (nonsurgical) techniques for brain research.

6. C (p. 54). *The occipital lobe is one of four lobes in each cerebral hemisphere*. The hypothalamus is in the limbic system, not the brain stem. The medulla is part of the brain stem, not the limbic system.

7. C (p. 58). The autonomic nervous system controls the muscles and glands that *automatically maintain those processes vital to homeostasis and survival,* such as breathing, swallowing, and responding to emergencies. Voluntary movements are controlled by the somatic nervous system, and problem solving is part of the cortical activity of the central nervous system.

8. B (p. 61). When a *neuron's internal charge changes* relative to the outer environment, it becomes depolarized, a process known as "firing." Nerve cells never move or touch each other directly. A firing neuron releases neurotransmitter molecules into the synaptic gap, not into the bloodstream. The axon is the "transmitter" of a neuron, not the "receiver."

9. C (p. 66). The left hemisphere specializes in a sequential processing style common to *language, speech, logic, analysis, and mathematical reasoning*. The right hemisphere specializes in processing several experiences at once, as in appreciating music or art, and navigating spatial movement.

10. D (p. 70). The brain is seen as *"responding" to the environment*, so that it adapts to and changes with environmental stimulation. Brain "control centers" are not so specialized that they cannot adapt to different tasks. The brain is the organ by which bodily systems communicate with both internal and external stimulation. Even individual brain cells have varied functions and work in combination with various other cells and subsystems.

Chapter 3: States of Mind

1. B (p. 78). This question deals with theories of the *relationship between brain and mind*. Choices A, C, and D are all approaches that focus on the interpretation or meaning of dreams, not the brain-mind relationship. Emergent-interaction theory proposes that *mind emerges from brain processes*, after which *brain and mind interact* with each other.

2. C (p. 79). In the dichotic listening method, *different stimuli are presented to a subject's two ears* in an effort to learn how the subject divides attention and awareness. In contrast, both think-aloud protocols and experience-sampling methods are modern forms of introspection in which subjects report what they are thinking in various situations.

3. D (p. 80). *A, B, and C are all functions of consciousness*. D is a possible outcome of an altered state such as meditation, but it is not a basic function of normal waking consciousness.

4. A (p. 82). The unconscious retains *repressed memories and thoughts* that provoke anxiety. Preconscious memories are available but must be brought to consciousness. Subconscious processes deal with input that has not been actively attended to. Nonconscious processes such as regulating blood pressure are never available to conscious review.

5. B (p. 86). *Rapid eye movement (REM) sleep* is associated with the most clear and vivid reports of dreaming. REM typically occurs at the end of the sleep cycle, after

the sleeper has gone from light to deep sleep and then to a lighter level for REM.

6. A (p. 90). Apnea is a sleep disorder caused by *interrupted breathing*, in which the sleeper's halted breath causes brief awakening, then resumption of sleep. Insomnia refers to general inadequate sleep, daytime sleepiness results from sleep deprivation, and analgesia is a synonym for pain relief.

7. B (p. 95). Not everyone can be hypnotized, no matter what technique is used. Only subjects who can *respond to suggestion* are hypnotizable, irrespective of their intelligence, educational level, or other personal factors.

8. D (pp. 96–97). Meditation is most popular as a form of *relaxation* and stress management. Meditators also claim to be refreshed and to have greater peace of mind.

9. D (pp. 97–98). Hallucinations are induced by *either extreme overstimulation or understimulation*. Hallucinogenic drugs such as mescaline can induce hallucinations, as can withdrawal from alcohol. Social isolation can also induce hallucinations.

10. A (p. 102). Stimulants *increase the rate of bodily function,* heightening energy, alertness, and sense of well-being. Depressants lower the bodily rate, opiates reduce pain, and hallucinogens create hallucinatory effects.

Chapter 4: Psychological Development

1. A (p. 112). Most developmental psychology researchers investigate *behavior (the dependent variable) as a function of age (the independent variable).* Cross-sectional research does not study behavior over time (so B is wrong). Not all developmental research necessarily studies the behavior of children (so C is wrong) or the aging process (so D is wrong).

2. B (p. 112). British philosopher John Locke originally developed the *empiricists' view that the mind is a "tabula rasa"* or blank slate at birth. In contrast, Rousseau proposed the nativist view that men at birth are "noble savages" who are corrupted by contact with society. Erikson and Piaget are twentieth-century developmental theorists.

3. D (pp. 117–119). *A, B, and C are all true of neonatal abilities.* Newborn babies can orient and reach; they have preferences in taste and smell; and, though born "legally blind," they soon develop visual discrimination.

4. B (p. 113). *Longitudinal studies track the development of a single group of subjects over time.* Normative designs compare test subjects with established standards. Cross-sectional designs study different age groups at one time. Sequential designs study small groups of different ages for limited periods.

5. B (p. 124). *Overregularization occurs when a child learns and overapplies the rules of grammar.* "Foots" incorrectly pluralizes "foot" and "handses" overuses the s-plural. Answer A illustrates babbling; C and D both illustrate telegraphic speech.

6. C (p. 127). Judi has mistaken her *sensory impression of the volume* of ice cream in Tonio's as evidence that he

has more, though they began with the same amount. This is an error in recognizing how the *volume or mass of material is conserved* despite changes in form. The other answers are also aspects of cognitive development, but do not deal with understanding the conservation of mass. Centration involves a single perceptual focus—not a comparison like Judi is making with Tonio's ice cream. Egocentrism is a self-centered focus on the world, and object permanence is the concept that objects exist even when one cannot sense them.

7. B (p. 136). When Harlow gave baby monkeys a choice between milk-giving wire "dummies" of mother monkeys and milkless cloth-covered models, *they preferred and mainly clung to the soft dummies* when they were not feeding. This confirmed other findings that physical contact and touch are critical to healthy early development.

8. C (p. 138). The early school years are the time for Erikson's *psychosocial crisis of competence versus inferiority,* when relations with peers help children ascertain their skills and abilities. Trust versus mistrust characterizes the first year, autonomy versus doubt is the second psychosocial crisis, and the identity crisis is the crisis of adolescence.

9. D (pp. 142–143). It was Sigmund Freud who argued that love and work are critical to a healthy adult life. Specifically, the *crisis of early adulthood focuses on intimacy ("love"), and that of middle adulthood focuses on generativity (most commonly "work" and child rearing).* Not all quests for love focus on youth and beauty (so C is wrong), and not all generativity crises seek resolution in success or power (so A and B are wrong).

10. D (p. 146). Hearing loss may cause an older person to *imagine others are whispering about or excluding him or her* from interaction. Paranoia develops when isolation is blamed on the talkers' behavior rather than the listener's hearing loss.

Chapter 5: Sensation and Perception

1. C (p. 157). In transduction, *one form of energy is transduced* (literally "led across") to a different form of energy and processing. During sensory adaptation, a sense stops responding to an unchanging stimulus. Psychophysics is the field that studies transduction and sensory processing. Kinesthesis is the sense of bodily movement.

2. B (pp. 160–162). In signal detection theory, sensation is affected by both stimulus sensitivity and *the perceiver's judgment.* Luisa is judging other sounds to be the baby's cries. In classical absolute threshold theory, she would hear the cries if they were loud enough and would not hear them if they were below threshold. The law of Prägnanz, that the simplest meaningful interpretation prevails, does not apply to Luisa's sensory impressions. Weber's law says that sensations depend on background intensity, not on the sensing person's expectations.

3. C (pp. 171–172). *The basilar membrane is part of the inner ear;* the other structures listed are involved in visual, not auditory, processing.

4. D (p. 170). Place theory and frequency theory both seek to explain how one perceives *the pitch of sound.* Place refers to the site on the basilar membrane that is most activated by a particular sound. Frequency refers to the rate of neural activity in the inner ear. Olfactory stimuli are smelled, while hue and light are seen. Timbre refers to sound's complexity, not its pitch.

5. A (p. 174). *Smell or olfaction is processed in the rhinencephalon,* a structure in the oldest part of the brain. Some species communicate by means of pheromones, chemical signals that are relevant to motivation and survival.

6. A (p. 181). An illusion is a *perception of a pattern that is demonstrably false.* Closure is wholeness that one perceives even when the stimulus pattern is partial or incomplete. False alarms and correct rejections are possible response outcomes in signal detection.

7. B (p. 184). In the Gestalt view, *perception works by establishing a meaningful whole or pattern.* Signal matching (A) might be part of signal detection. Analyzing separate components (C) is a structuralist process (see Chapter 1), not a Gestalt explanation. Using concepts to explain percepts (D) is an example of top-down processing in general, not the Gestalt approach in particular.

8. B (p. 187). People selectively give *more attention to more demanding stimuli.* Louder sounds are more attention demanding than normal or whispered voices. A visual stimulus is not necessarily more attention getting than an auditory one.

9. A (p. 190). Seeing the larger dark spots as "belonging" together involves *grouping them according to similarity.* They are not described as closer to each other, so this does not show proximity. Common fate only applies to moving stimuli. Closure leads a perceiver to see incomplete figures as whole.

10. C (pp. 190–191). *Without context information, the detective has no hypothesis or concept* to "drive" her interpretation of the symbols. Therefore her interpretation must be data-driven or bottom-up rather than top-down processing.

Chapter 6: Learning and Remembering

1. D (p. 202). John B. Watson, founder of behaviorism, first argued that *only observable change and behavior* could be the focus of scientific psychology. This led to the development of behavior analysis, which carefully examines and explains how organisms learn. Wundt founded structuralism, James advocated functionalism, and Freud established the school of psychoanalysis.

2. B (p. 209). Rescorla's research has shown that a CS must seem to *reliably predict a UCS that is contingent on it.* Further work by Kamin indicates that the CS must provide information about the UCS in order for the stimulus-stimulus association to be learned.

3. A (p. 212). From his work with cats in puzzle boxes, Thorndike concluded that responses (like successfully escaping from the box) *increase in frequency if they have sat-* *isfying consequences,* and eventually become the dominant response when the organism is placed in that environment.

4. C (p. 214). A consistent relationship between a reinforcing consequence (such as a paycheck) and a response (such as a full week's work) indicates that *the outcome is contingent on the response.* Reinforcement contingencies determine organisms' behavior.

5. B (p. 215). If your friend's response succeeds in *removing the unwanted stimuli of stress and work,* vacation-taking is increased by negative reinforcement—increasing responses by removing noxious stimuli.

6. B (p. 218). To be effective, *punishment should* not *be too intense.* It should, however, be immediate, swift and brief, and focused on the response (rather than the responder).

7. D (p. 220). According to the Premack principle, a *more valued activity is a more probable response, and can be used to reinforce* a less preferred response, as when a child is permitted to practice her piano (something she prefers) only after first doing her homework.

8. C (p. 225). Tolman concluded that rats' *place-learning ability depended on cognitive maps* and expectancies about their maze-running responses. Cognitive maps are an example of cognitive learning, not classical conditioning (involving stimulus-response connections) or operant conditioning (involving reinforcement).

9. A (p. 234). Procedural memory involves *remembering how to do things.* Semantic memory retains meaning; sensory memory retains sensory impressions or images. In constructive memory, information is added to the original memory.

10. C (p. 243). In proactive interference, *old memories (such as where you used to store things) distort efforts to retain new knowledge* (such as where these items are currently stored). Retrieval cues are important for remembering information that was encoded in a particular context. Retroactive interference moves "backward" when new information prevents recall of old memories. Only traumatic memories are subject to repression.

Chapter 7: Cognitive Processes

1. A (p. 253). The information processing model of cognition proposes that cognitive processes operate at various points along a *hierarchical continuum of operations.* B, C, and D are not the names of cognitive models.

2. D (pp. 253–254). *Think-aloud protocols employ a modern version of introspection.* Other methods for studying cognitive processes include measuring reaction time to stimuli, analyzing errors, and objectively observing behavior.

3. A (p. 256). Thinking, the process of forming new representation by *transforming available information,* has three features: it cannot be directly observed but can be inferred from observable behavior; it manipulates knowledge in a person's cognitive system; and it is directed toward solving one's problems.

4. B (p. 257). *A concept is a category linking items with common features.* In contrast, a schema is a cluster of

ideas and preconceptions about related items. A heuristic is a rule of thumb that generally works to solve some problem. And a memory is the product of the process of encoding and storing a sensory and cognitive experience.

5. B (p. 262). *A script is an event schema, a cluster of knowledge about a sequence of activities.* Schemas in general may be about objects, persons, or roles. An algorithm is a problem-solving strategy that guarantees a solution. A mental map is an image that stores and organizes spatial and locational information.

6. B (p. 266). *The syllogism is a common form of deductive reasoning.* In contrast, inductive reasoning is typical of scientific research, in which particular findings are built upon to establish general theories or truths. An algorithm is a guaranteed but sometimes tedious problem-solving method, while a heuristic is a rule of thumb that may be easier though it cannot guarantee a solution.

7. D (p. 268). In information-processing terms, *a problem has three parts: an initial state, a goal state, and a set of operations.* A prototype is an ideal or most representative example of a concept. A concept is a category whose members share recognizable features. Assimilation is a process of incorporating new information into familiar ways of thinking.

8. B (p. 270). *An algorithm is a guaranteed strategy for solving a problem,* although a less-reliable heuristic may be faster or easier. A prototype is an ideal example of a concept. A syllogism is a common form of deductive reasoning. A mnemonic is a verbal strategy for memorizing complex material.

9. A (p. 272). *Judgments involve drawing conclusions by making inferences about evidence, based on prior beliefs.* Biased assimilation and functional fixedness are both sources of error in making judgments or solving problems. Autistic thinking involves fantasy, rather than reality-based cognition.

10. D (p. 278). *A frame is the structure or context of a problem's presentation.* By presenting the loan in a persuasive way, Susanne is framing her request to make a certain impression. Cognitive biases affect judgment but do not necessarily influence presentation. Prototypes are ideal concepts; and scripts are event schemas.

Chapter 8: Motivation and Emotion

1. D (pp. 288–289). *The limbic system, reticular activating system, and autonomic nervous system have all been found to be involved in emotional experience.* The RAS stimulates arousal, the ANS prepares the body for emotional responses, and the limbic system and hypothalamus are the two CNS structures that integrate emotional processes.

2. D (p. 300). *The Lazarus-Schachter theory is also known as the two-factor theory of emotion, requiring both physiological arousal and subjective interpretation of what has caused it.* Darwinian theory explores the survival value of certain emotions. The James-Lange theory says that emotion is caused by recognizing how emotional stimuli have aroused bodily responses. The Cannon-Bard theory says that both arousal and emotional experience are caused simultaneously.

3. A (pp. 303–304). The key to detecting deception is in perceiving patterns of behavior. If a person looks you in the eye, it may or may not have anything to do with truth-telling—*a single instance of eye contact is not a reliable source of information for deception detection.* Answers B, C, and D are all true and are all reliable guidelines about how to interpret patterns of behavior.

4. A (p. 306). *Identifying social "instincts" is not a basic purpose of motivation theory and research.* There is no evidence that instinct theories can explain complex human social behavior. Answers B, C, and D are all basic purposes of using the concept of motivation, along with "accounting for behavioral variability" and "relating biology to behavior."

5. D (p. 310). James and Freud *both offered instinct theories of motivation.* James saw instincts as purposive or goal-oriented. Freud thought instincts had neither conscious purpose nor predetermined direction, and that one might learn many ways to satisfy one's instincts.

6. B (p. 313). *Attachment needs are needs to belong, to affiliate with others, to love and to be loved.* Safety needs include shelter and security. Biological needs include hunger and thirst. Esteem needs include respect and achievement.

7. A (p. 316). Early theories blamed hunger on peripheral cues such as hunger pains, but *modern theories favor viewing hunger as influenced by both central nervous system function and environmental cues.* Answers B, C, and D are all accurate conclusions about modern research on hunger.

8. D (p. 318). *In humans, unlike in nonhuman species, sexuality is more dependent on psychological factors such as feelings and interpretations.* Human sexuality is less predictable than animals', is not essential to individual survival, and is often influenced by other motivations such as social acceptance and personal values.

9. A (p. 324). The TAT, or Thematic Apperception Test, invites subjects to "*apperceive*" or add to their perceptions *of pictures by telling a story, and then examines themes* in those stories.

10. D (p. 325). People who score *high in* n Ach *have been found to be more persistent, upwardly mobile, and independent* in their work habits than those who score low on need for achievement.

Chapter 9: Stress, Health, and Well-Being

1. A (p. 336). *Getting married is one of the top ten most stressful life changes,* according to the Student Stress Scale. The other stressors—car trouble, arguments, a change of major—rank lower and are associated with less likelihood of stress-related illness. A life change is stressful because it demands adaptation, whether it means something positive or negative in the long run.

2. D (p. 339). *Societal stressors include problems that are society-wide* like overpopulation, economic recession,

pollution, epidemics, and the threat of war. An earthquake is a catastrophic event. A jail term is considered a stressful life change. Being stuck in traffic is an example of a hassle.

3. B (pp. 353–354). A stress *moderator variable filters or modifies how stressors will affect one's reactions.* A defense mechanism is an automatic coping strategy that protects one's self or self-esteem. Cognitive appraisal is a process of evaluating stressors and one's abilities to respond. A life change is caused by an event that requires adaptation.

4. A (p. 358). *Hardiness is an ability to welcome change as a challenge* instead of as a threat. The Type A personality is highly prone to stress. The Type T profile involves risk-taking and thrill-seeking. Learned helplessness indicates a complete loss of perceived control.

5. C (p. 344). *The fight-or-flight response is governed by the autonomic nervous system.* PTSD stands for posttraumatic stress disorder. PNI refers to psychoneuroimmunology. The GAS is the general adaptation syndrome for responding to stress.

6. B (p. 345). *The three stages of the GAS are alarm, resistance, and exhaustion.* Withdrawal is a common part of fear or desire to escape a stressor, but it is not a stage in the adaptation to severe stress.

7. C (p. 357). Researchers Judith Rodin and Ellen Langer found that nursing home patients *thrived on perceived control when they had responsibilities* such as caring for houseplants and choosing entertainment. In contrast, having others care for them and take complete responsibility for their well-being left them helpless and less healthy.

8. C (p. 365). The *"war on lifestyle" refers to preventing diseases of civilization* by encouraging people to change unhealthy habits and replace them with healthier actions.

9. B (p. 370). Research by James Pennebaker confirms the value of *"opening up" and talking about loss.* Keeping one's pain to oneself or seeking distractions can prolong stress and postpone recovery. Accepting too much help can create learned helplessness.

10. D (p. 373). Research on subjective well-being shows that *there is no age range, gender effect, or financial status that guarantees happiness.*

Chapter 10: Personality

1. D (p. 385). The *TAT is the only projective technique listed;* the other three acronyms describe objective personality inventories.

2. D (p. 386). Implicit personality theories are informal models of what people are like, *based on individuals' impressions and interactions with others.* Scientific personality theories are based on case studies, inventories, and systematic research.

3. B (p. 388). *Your self-concept is your awareness of your continuing identity.* Self-report is a research method of collecting information from respondents. Self-efficacy is Bandura's concept of feeling effective in reaching personal goals. Self-actualization is Maslow's concept of fulfilling one's potential.

4. B (p. 389). The *nomothetic approach is variable-centered, meaning that the same traits or dimensions are used to describe everyone,* as in the assertion that all students can be described as having "a certain degree of laziness." The idiographic approach is person centered, so traits mean different things to different people. Humanistic and psychodynamic theories focus on personality development, not personality traits.

5. A (p. 392). *Sorting people into categories that share common features and traits (such as thinking that thin people are always nervous)* favors a type theory rather than a trait theory. There is no connection between such sorting and the personality-development theories of social-learning or personal construct theory.

6. B (p. 396). The Big Five include Extroversion, Agreeableness, Conscientiousness, Neuroticism, and Openness to Experience—*not Intelligence.*

7. D (p. 403). *The superego includes two components: the conscience (what not to do) and the ego ideal (the right way to be).* The id is the primitive, selfish personality; the ego is the executive that balances the demands of the id and superego. The libido is psychic energy that drives one to seek sensual pleasure.

8. B (p. 407). Alfred Adler theorized that instead of being driven to achieve sexual gratification, *individuals seek power and competence in their lives.* Self-actualization is Maslow's humanistic concept, and self-efficacy is theorized as important by Albert Bandura.

9. C (p. 408). In contrast with the driven, instinctive, and unconscious motivations asserted by psychodynamic theories, *humanistic theories assert that human action and growth are free,* healthy, and self-actualizing.

10. D (p. 412). *Albert Bandura's theory of personality combines principles of learning with an emphasis on social interactions.* Kelly's theory focuses on personal constructs. Eysenck combined type and trait theories in his model. Adler was a post-Freudian psychodynamic theorist.

Chapter 11: Individual Differences

1. A (p. 420). *The "job" of a test is to predict future performance.* Not every test assesses learning or achievement, so B is wrong. Human abilities are too complex to be determined solely by inherited potential, so C is not a reasonable goal for any test. Values and labels can be assigned on any basis, whether an individual is "tested" or not, so D is not correct.

2. C (p. 424). *The eugenics movement encouraged selective breeding to promote reproducing only the best, brightest, and fittest human characteristics.* Eugenicists believed some races were superior to others and would eventually overwhelm and replace inferior ones. They rejected the notion of environmental influence on human potential.

3. B (pp. 429–430). Your left big toe *will not vary* in length over several test sessions, so any measure of its length is *reliable, but it is not a valid indicator* of your intelligence, because big toe length is clearly unrelated to any definition of intelligence.

4. D (pp. 431–432). *Norms are statistical standards* for how to administer a test, who takes it, and how that group scores. To be useful, a test must not only be standardized, but must also show reliability (e.g., internal consistency) and validity (construct validity or criterion validity).

5. C (p. 426). Psychological tests provide *quantitative information such as numerical scores* that can be compared to indicators of others' performance. Life histories, interviews, and behavior observations all involve subjective judgment that is impossible to quantify.

6. D (p. 433). Intelligence is defined as *the capacity to profit from experience,* to go beyond what is perceived and to imagine symbolic possibilities.

7. C (p. 436). Terman's equation is MA/CA × 100 = IQ. Using this formula, *15/12 × 100 = 125.*

8. A (p. 440). For Sternberg, *contextual intelligence represents the practical management of day-to-day living and adaptability.* Componential intelligence is made up of the cognitive processes underlying all thinking and problem-solving. Experiential intelligence is reflected in how people deal with novel versus familiar experiences.

9. B (p. 441). Gardner's seven intelligences include linguistic, logical-mathematical, spatial, musical, bodily-kinesthetic, interpersonal, and intrapersonal abilities. The answer that does not belong is *experiential intelligence, which is one of Sternberg's three types of intelligence.*

10. B (p. 451). One's *aptitude for a task is one's potential ability, not a learned or achieved skill.* Achievement tests measure what one has already learned. A job analysis assesses what is required by certain work and tasks. An observer's report deals with observable behavior in a specific setting.

Chapter 12: Social Psychology

1. A (p. 460). The Stanford Prison Experiment demonstrated that *even artificial situations like a mock prison can powerfully influence participants' behavior.* The simulation focused on normal (not disturbed) individuals, whose responses were very similar depending on the roles they played.

2. D (p. 463). The so-called *three R's are examples of how groups coerce members into conforming.* These are consequences or penalties for deviating or failing to adhere to group norms.

3. C (p. 464). While most Bennington students had become more liberal in their college years, *they retained the general attitudes they had formed* by the time they left college. Twenty years later, the liberals were still liberal, and the conservatives were still conservative.

4. B (p. 468). Conformity is greater when the task is ambiguous, when the group is cohesive, and when the members consider each other to be competent. *Conformity is reduced when members' votes are private* rather than public.

5. C (p. 471). *Most subjects obeyed the authority fully,* though they protested and expressed discomfort. Some refused to go on, but most complied, even when the victim complained of having a heart condition.

6. D (pp. 476–477). According to research on *the bystander effect, the larger the group of witnesses to an emergency, the less responsible for helping each bystander will feel.* No personality variable or value—such as altruism—has been found to consistently predict greater likelihood of helping.

7. A (p. 485). Claiming to be on a diet *conflicts with* the public behavior of having extra dessert, and *such conflict creates cognitive dissonance.* Answers B, C, and D all illustrate how individuals act in agreement with their original values or attitudes and so do not experience dissonance.

8. B (p. 487). The FAE involves blaming internal factors for unexpected or negative behavior rather than considering external explanations. *Saying that Amy "must be . . . impatient" demonstrates the fundamental attribution error.* Answer A demonstrates a self-serving explanation for one's own behavior, not blaming another. Answer C involves blaming the situation rather than the waitress for the delay.

9. C (p. 490). Even when divorcing partners expect "relief," *loss of a close relationship involves severe disruption and long-term feelings of dissatisfaction* for both individuals. Answers A, B, and D are all true.

10. B (p. 494). The *mere presence of a weapon can stimulate a person to experience aggressive impulses,* increasing the likelihood of conflict and violence.

Chapter 13: Psychopathology

1. A (p. 506). The six indicators of possible abnormality are distress, maladaptiveness, irrationality, unpredictability, unconventionality and statistical rarity, and observer discomfort. *Chronic physical illness is not one of them.*

2. B (p. 513). DSM-IV stands for *Diagnostic and Statistical Manual, Fourth Edition, Revised.* Developed by the American Psychiatric Association, it classifies, defines, and describes over 200 mental disorders.

3. B (p. 517). Personality disorders involve a long-standing, inflexible, maladaptive behavior pattern. The *antisocial type shows a lack of conscience and no sense of responsibility towards others.* The narcissistic type shows grandiose self-importance. Obsessive-compulsive disorder is a type of anxiety disorder. Paranoid schizophrenia is a type of the most severe form of mental illness, involving paranoid delusions and loss of contact with reality.

4. D (p. 518). *Dissociative disorders include disturbances in the integration of identity, memory, or consciousness,* such as amnesia about one's identity or origins. Anxiety disorders involve anxiety, not memory loss. Affective disorders affect mood and emotion. Personality disorders are chronic, inflexible patterns of maladaptive behavior.

5. B (p. 520). Irrational fears are not phobias unless they interfere with adjustment and goal-attainment, so A is wrong. Phobias are anxiety disorders, not affective disorders, so C is wrong. If A and C are wrong, so is D. *The "preparedness hypothesis" suggests that phobias have their origins in inherited tendencies to avoid dangerous stimuli.*

6. C (pp. 521–523). *Almost everyone has experienced mild versions of symptoms of unipolar (one-sided) depression after a painful loss.* Those diagnosed with unipolar depression suffer from longer-lasting and more severe symptoms than those who have only mild depression.

7. B (pp. 535–536). *Bulimia is a pattern of binge-eating followed by purging.* Anorexia is self-starvation. Inhibition merely means withholding a response. Mania is an extreme form of affect, the opposite or complement to depression.

8. B (p. 540). *Paranoid schizophrenia involves complex delusions focused around specific themes.* The most common delusions involve grandeur (believing oneself to be very important), persecution (thinking that others are out to hurt you), delusional jealousy (believing one's spouse is unfaithful), and delusions of reference (misconstruing chance happenings as directed at oneself).

9. A (p. 545). *Reward deficiency syndrome is a genetically based biochemical imbalance that causes disorders of addiction, impulsivity, and compulsivity.* Impulsive and compulsive behaviors are driven by anxiety.

10. C (p. 548). A stigma is a set of negative attitudes about a person that sets him or her apart as unacceptable. *Stigma is a major problem experienced by those who have been labeled mentally ill.* Hysteria is the old term for conversion disorder. Diathesis is a predisposition or vulnerability for experiencing certain symptoms. Delusional thinking is a common symptom of schizophrenia.

Chapter 14: Psychotherapy

1. C (p. 557). All therapies are interventions into a person's life, *designed to change that person's functioning in some way.* Not all forms of therapy will make one feel good about oneself at a given moment, or shape the individual to fit better into his or her society.

2. A (p. 560). *Psychiatrists are trained in medicine,* and are the only therapists licensed by governments to prescribe medication.

3. A (p. 566). *Psychoanalysis is called insight therapy because it seeks to help a patient gain insights into the unconscious conflicts that underlie his or her symptoms.* Cognitive therapies—including rational-emotive therapy—regard thought processes as behaviors that can be changed by applying learning principles. Existential thera-

pies emphasize the here-and-now more than the client's past.

4. C (p. 568). Transference refers to a patient's emotional identification of the therapist with another person significantly related to the patient. *In countertransference, the therapist feels this involvement with the patient.* Negative transference is transference of emotions like hate or envy. Resistance involves denying or avoiding feelings and ideas the therapy is revealing.

5. D (p. 573). *In flooding, the client is put into the phobic situation.* Systematic desensitization pairs phobic imaginings gradually with relaxation exercises. Implosion therapy involves imagining the worst phobic situation first instead of building up to it. Catharsis is a psychoanalytic concept of intense emotional release.

6. D (pp. 575–576). *Participant modeling treats phobias by first demonstrating (modeling) the feared behavior, and then inviting the client to imitate the model.* Counterconditioning refers to behavior modification to undo or reverse maladaptive lessons. Behavioral rehearsal involves visualizing acting in desirable ways. Clinical ecology is a specialty relating behavioral disorders to environmental stressors.

7. C (p. 580). *The goal of RET is to increase a person's self-worth by getting rid of faulty beliefs like "I must be thin before anyone will love me."* Behavior therapies work well with changing problem behaviors like smoking. Person-centered therapy focuses on self-actualization by providing acceptance and unconditional positive regard for persons who fear harsh judgments, such as parental disapproval.

8. B (p. 589). *ECT is effective in treating severe depression,* although the reasons for its effectiveness are unknown. In properly applied ECT, the patient is always prepared with sedatives and muscle relaxants to minimize violent physical reactions.

9. A (pp. 591–592). *Like other antianxiety drugs, Valium reduces tension by sedating the user.* Antidepressant drugs include Elavil and the antimanic extract lithium. Antipsychotic drugs like Thorazine reduce schizophrenic symptoms. An antihistamine drug reduces allergic symptoms.

10. D (p. 594). *Frank has argued that "belief is really crucial to all the healing processes. . . . Nothing happens unless they really believe that this could help them."* If a client believes in therapy, he or she will be more willing to cooperate in making the desired changes.

Glossary

absolute threshold (p. 158) Minimum amount of physical energy needed to stimulate a sensory system.

accommodation (p. 126) A process that restructures or modifies the child's existing schemes so that new information is better understood.

account (p. 370) The story of one's experience, especially of a trauma or loss, including attributions of blame, social perceptions, beliefs, memories, and emotions.

achievement test (p. 451) Standardized test designed to measure an individual's current level of competence in a given area.

acquisition (p. 206) Stage of classical conditioning when conditioned response is first elicited by the conditioned stimulus.

activation-synthesis theory (p. 92) Theory that all dreams begin with random electrical discharges from deep within the brain.

acute stress (p. 343) Temporary pattern of arousal, with clear onset and termination.

addiction (p. 100) Physical state in which withdrawal occurs if a certain drug is not present in the body.

adolescence (p. 139) The stage of life that begins at the onset of puberty and continues until adulthood.

affective disorders (p. 526) Class of disorders in which primary symptoms are associated with disturbances of mood and emotion.

afferent systems (p. 157) Sensory systems that process information coming into the brain.

affiliation (p. 489) Motivation to seek the presence of or interaction with others.

ageism (p. 147) Prejudice against older people.

agoraphobia (p. 521) Extreme fear of being in public places or distant from familiar surroundings.

algorithm (p. 270) Problem-solving procedure that guarantees reaching a correct outcome by reviewing every possible strategy.

Alzheimer's disease (p. 516) Chronic, organic brain disorder, characterized by gradual loss of cognitive abilities and memory, and deterioration of personality.

amygdala (p. 53) Limbic system structure involved in emotion (especially aggression), memory, and basic motivations such as hunger, thirst, and sexuality.

animistic thinking (p. 127) Thought pattern, common to young children, in which inanimate objects are imagined to have life and mental processes.

anorexia nervosa (p. 533) Pattern of self-starvation with psychological rather than physical causes.

anticipatory coping (p. 351) Efforts made in advance of a potential stressor to balance perceived demands with available resources.

antisocial personality disorder (p. 517) Personality disorder in which symptoms include absence of conscience and lack of a sense of responsibility to others.

anxiety (p. 404) Intense, negative emotional reaction to the threat of becoming conscious of a repressed conflict.

aptitude test (p. 451) Test designed to measure an individual's potential for acquiring various skills.

archetype (p. 407) Jungian concept of universal symbol of human experience, part of collective unconscious.

Asch effect (p. 466) Pattern of conformity in which, even when conditions are ambiguous, a unanimous group majority influences individuals' judgments.

assimilation (p. 126) A process that modifies new environmental information to fit into what is already known.

association cortex (p. 56) Part of the cortex where processes such as planning and decision making occur.

attachment (p. 133) The intense, enduring, social-emotional relationship between a child and a parent or other regular caregiver.

attention (p. 185) Complex mental process, combining a focusing of awareness of stimuli with a readiness to respond.

attribution theory (p. 486) System of explanations for individual and social causes of behavior.

auditory cortex (pp. 55, 171) Part of the cortex that processes auditory information. Area of temporal lobes in brain that receives and processes sound information.

auditory nerve (p. 171) Bundle of axons from inner-ear cells carrying sound information to the brain.

autistic thinking (p. 265) Distinctive, personal cognition involving fantasy, daydreaming, unconscious processes, and untestable ideas; contrasted with *realistic thinking*.

autonomic nervous system (p. 58) Subdivision of the PNS which sustains basic life processes.

availability heuristic (p. 277) Cognitive strategy that estimates probabilities based on personal experience.

aversion therapy (p. 573) Behavioral therapy technique in which individuals are presented with a pairing of the attractive stimuli with unpleasant stimuli in order to condition a negative reaction.

aversive conditioning (p. 206) Type of classical conditioning in which the conditioned stimulus (CS) predicts the presentation of an aversive or unpleasant unconditioned stimulus (UCS).

axon (p. 60) A single, extended fiber that conducts information about stimulation along its length, usually from neuron cell body to terminal buttons.

bait shyness (p. 211) Aversion to novel foods or to familiar foods in novel environments or conditions.

base rate (p. 9) A statistic that identifies the most common frequency or probability of a given event.

basic level (p. 260) Optimal level in a hierarchy of concepts, where a stored item can best be remembered and thought about.

basilar membrane (p. 171) Thin membrane (tissue) that runs through the cochlea; hair cells on the basilar membrane are activated by sound (vibration) energy.

behavior (p. 5) Observable action; the means by which organisms adjust to their environment.

behavior genetics (p. 45) New field that unites geneticists and psychologists interested in determining the genetic basis of behavioral traits and functioning, such as intelligence, mental disorders, and altruism.

behavior modification (p. 570) In behavioral psychotherapy, approach that applies operant conditioning and classical conditioning to change client's behavior.

behavioral confirmation (p. 482) Process of acting in ways that another person expects, thus validating those expectations.

behavioral data (p. 7) Reports of observations about the behavior of organisms and the conditions under which the behavior occurs or changes.

behavioral measures (p. 30) Techniques used to study overt, observable, and recordable actions.

behavioral rehearsal (p. 578) Procedures used to establish and strengthen basic skills by requiring client to mentally practice a desirable sequence of actions.

behaviorism (p. 16) Assertion that only the overt behavior of organisms is the proper subject of scientific study.

behavioristic approach (p. 16) Approach that focuses on overt behaviors that can be objectively recorded and manipulated.

biased assimilation (p. 274) Collecting data without careful attention because the information supports one's preexisting beliefs.

Big Five (p. 396) Five basic dimensions underlying the traits used to describe people's behavior: Extroversion; Agreeableness; Consciousness; Emotional Stability; and Openness to Experience.

biocultural model of emotion (p. 297) Robert Levenson's theory that personal and social stimuli are appraised, responses are channeled, and expressions of feeling are guided by learned cultural rules and traditions.

biological approach (p. 14) Approach that searches for the causes of behavior in the functioning of genes, the brain, the nervous system, and the endocrine system.

biological constraints on learning (p. 221) Limitations on an organism's capacity to learn that is caused by inherited capabilities of the species.

biomedical therapy (p. 563) Any of several treatments of psychological disorders that change biological or physical mechanisms.

biopsychosocial model (p. 362) New view of body-mind interaction which examines the health consequences of links among factors in the nervous system, immune system, behavior, cognition, and environment.

bipedalism (p. 43) The ability to walk upright.

bipolar disorder (p. 527) Type of affective disorder in which individual's behavior alternates between periods of mania and depression.

blind (p. 29) Uninformed about the purpose of a research study.

body image (p. 140) The way one views one's appearance.

bottom-up processing (p. 180) Processing in which incoming stimulus information is perceived as coming from sensory data and is sent upward to the brain for analysis and interpretation.

brain scans (p. 49) Mechanical and electronic measures of biochemical and electric activity at specific brain sites.

brain stem (p. 51) A brain region common to all vertebrates, containing five structures that collectively regulate the internal state of the body: the medulla, pons, reticular formation, thalamus, and cerebellum.

bulimia (p. 535) Disorder characterized by pattern of binging (overeating) and purging (vomiting or using laxatives to prevent digestion).

burnout (p. 340) Pattern of symptoms—including emotional exhaustion, depersonalizing others, and sense of failure—that especially afflicts human services professionals.

cannabis (p. 100) Drug, derived from hemp plant, whose psychoactive effects include altered perception, sedation, pain relief, and mild euphoria.

Cannon-Bard theory of emotion (p. 300) Theory, developed independently by Walter Cannon and Philip Bard, that arousal and emotional experience do not cause each other but are both produced by an emotional stimulus.

cardinal trait (p. 394) Trait around which people organize their lives.

catharsis (p. 567) Process and outcome of expressing strongly felt emotions that are usually inhibited.

central nervous system (p. 56) Subsystem of the nervous system composed of all the neurons in the brain and spinal cord.

central trait (p. 394) Major trait assumed to explain an individual's pattern of behavior.

centration (p. 127) Thought pattern characterized by inability to take into account more than one factor at a time.

cerebellum (p. 52) Structure of the brain at the base of the skull, which organizes bodily motion, posture, and equilibrium.

cerebral cortex (p. 53) Area of the brain that regulates the brain's higher cognitive and emotional functions.

cerebral dominance (p. 66) Tendency of each hemisphere of the brain to dominate the control of different functions.

cerebral hemispheres (p. 53) Two nearly symmetrical halves of the cerebral cortex.

cerebrum (p. 53) Brain structure that regulates higher levels of cognitive and mental functioning.

chromosomes (p. 44) Structures along which genes are assembled.

chronic stress (p. 343) Continuous state of arousal in which demands are perceived to be greater than resources available to deal with them.

chronological age (CA) (p. 435) Number of months or years since an individual's birth.

chunk (p. 233) Meaningful unit of information.

chunking (p. 233) Recording information into a single meaningful unit.

circadian rhythms (p. 85) Physiological patterns that repeat approximately every 24 hours.

classical conditioning (p. 204) Form of learning in which two stimuli become associated so that one acquires the power to elicit the same behavioral response as the other.

clinical ecology (p. 596) Field that relates disorders to environmental irritants and sources of trauma.

clinical psychologist (p. 560) Professional psychologist (with training and degree in psychology) specializing in assessing and treating psychological disorders.

clinical social worker (p. 560) Mental health professional trained in social work with emphasis on the social context of individuals' problems.

closure (p. 189) Organization process leading to perception of incomplete figures as complete.

cognition (pp. 223, 251) Processes of knowing, including attending, remembering, and reasoning; contents of cognitive processes, including concepts and memories.

cognitive appraisal (p. 354) Recognition and evaluation of stressor to assess the threat, demand, resources available to deal with it, and appropriate strategies.

cognitive approach (p. 18) View that emphasizes human thought and all the processes of knowing as central to the study of psychology.

cognitive behavior modification (p. 578) Therapeutic technique that combines emphasis on thoughts and attitudes with strategies for changing performance by altering reinforcement contingencies.

cognitive bias (p. 275) A systematic error in the sequence of inference, judgment, and decision.

cognitive development (p. 125) The study of the processes and products of the mind as they emerge and change over time.

cognitive dissonance (p. 485) According to theory developed by Leon Festinger, motivating state of tension produced by inconsistency or contradiction between an individual's feelings, beliefs, or actions.

cognitive economy (p. 257) Minimizing time and effort required to process information.

cognitive map (pp. 225, 263) Mental representation of physical space.

cognitive model (p. 252) An explanatory metaphor that describes how information is detected, stored, and used by people and machines.

cognitive psychology (p. 252) The scientific study of mental processes and mental structures.

cognitive science (p. 252) An interdisciplinary field that studies the variety of systems and processes that manipulate information.

cognitive therapy (p. 577) Psychotherapeutic approach to changing problem feelings and behaviors by changing how clients perceive or think about significant experiences.

collective unconscious (p. 407) Jungian concept of inherited, unconscious ideas and forces common to all members of a species.

comparative psychology (p. 224) Field of psychology that studies similarities in behavior and mental processes of humans and nonhumans.

concepts (p. 257) Mental representations of categories of items or ideas, based on experience.

conditioned reinforcers (p. 219) In operant conditioning, a formerly neutral stimulus that has become a reinforcer.

conditioned response (CR) (p. 206) In classical conditioning, response elicited by previously neutral stimulus that has become associated with the unconditioned stimulus.

conditioned stimulus (CS) (p. 206) In classical conditioning, previously neutral stimulus that comes to elicit the conditioned response.

conformity (p. 466) Tendency for people to adopt the behaviors, attitudes, and values of other members of a reference group.

confounding variables (p. 29) Factors that could be confused with the independent variable in a research study and thus distort the results.

consciousness (p. 77) Awareness of the general condition of one's mind, awareness of particular mental contents, or self-awareness.

conservation (p. 127) The understanding that physical properties of an object do not change when nothing is added or taken away, even though its appearance changes.

contact comfort (p. 136) Reassurance derived from physical touch and access of caregiver.

context of discovery (p. 24) Initial phase of research during which an investigator comes up with a new idea or a different way of thinking about phenomena.

context of justification methods (p. 27) Second phase of research, in which results are tested and prepared for useful communication with the scientific community.

contingency management (p. 574) General treatment strategy for changing behavior by changing its consequences.

controlled experiment (p. 31) Observations of specific behavior made under systematically varied conditions, in which subjects have been randomly assigned to experimental and control (nontreatment) conditions.

conversion disorder (p. 508) Type of psychological disorder in which there is loss of motor or sensory function without corresponding organic cause.

coping (p. 351) Means of dealing with a situation perceived to be threatening.

corpus callosum (p. 53) Thick mass of nerve fibers that connects the two hemispheres of the cerebral cortex.

correlation coefficient (p. 31) A statistical measure used to determine the precise degree of correlation between two variables; symbolized as r.

correlational measures (p. 30) Measures used to determine the extent to which two variables, traits, or attributes are related.

counseling psychologist (p. 559) Professional psychologist specializing in providing guidance in solving problems of normal adjustment.

counterconditioning (p. 571) Therapeutic technique which uses conditioning to substitute a new response for an inadequate one.

countertransference (p. 568) In psychoanalysis, process in which a therapist comes to like or dislike a patient because the patient is perceived as similar to significant people in the therapist's life.

critical feature (p. 257) Quality that is a necessary and sufficient condition for including a concept in a category.

critical periods (p. 111) A sensitive time in an organism's development when it will acquire a particular behavior if certain stimuli and experiences occur.

critical set point (p. 318) The certain level of fats stored in specialized fat cells below which signals are sent to "eat" once again.

cross-sectional design (p. 114) A type of investigation in which groups of subjects of different chronological ages are observed and compared at a given time.

crystallized intelligence (p. 439) Knowledge a person has already acquired and the ability to use that knowledge.

culture (p. 20) A set of concepts, values, and assumptions about life developed to increase survival and satisfaction, and communicated or shared with others in the same environment.

culture shock (p. 343) Stress experienced by people who move to unfamiliar surroundings.

cycles per second (cps) (p. 169) Unit in which frequency is usually expressed.

daydreaming (p. 84) Mild form of consciousness alteration, in which attention shifts away from the immediate situation.

daytime sleepiness (p. 90) A sleep disorder, not remedied simply by getting more sleep, in which an individual has difficulty remaining awake during normal waking hours.

debriefing (p. 28) Procedure conducted with subjects at the end of an experiment, in which researcher explains hypothesis, reveals deception, and provides emotional support.

decision making (p. 272) Choosing between alternatives; selecting or rejecting available options.

declarative memory (p. 234) Memory for explicit information; also known as *fact memory*.

deductive reasoning (p. 266) Drawing a conclusion intended to follow logically from two or more statements (premises).

deficiency motivation (p. 312) Motivation to restore physical or psychological equilibrium (balance).

delusion (p. 539) False belief maintained despite contrary evidence and lack of social support.

demand characteristics (p. 473) Cue in an experimental setting that influences subjects' perception of how they are expected to behave.

dendrites (p. 59) Branched fibers that extend outward from the cell body and take information into the neuron.

dependent variable (p. 9) Any behavioral variable whose values result from or depend upon changes in one or more independent variables.

depressants (p. 101) Drugs that slow down the mental and physical activity of the body by inhibiting transmission of nerve impulses in the central nervous system.

determinism (p. 12) Doctrine that physical, behavioral, and mental events are not random but rather are determined by specific causal factors.

developmental psychology (p. 110) The branch of psychology that is concerned with the changes in physical and psychological functioning that occur from conception across the entire life span.

developmental stages (p. 111) Periods during which physical or psychological functioning differs from earlier or later functioning.

diathesis-stress hypothesis (p. 543) Proposal that genetic factors place some individuals at risk for schizophrenia, but environmental stressors trigger this potential into taking the form of schizophrenic symptoms.

dichotic listening task (p. 79) Experiment where a subject listens through stereo earphones to two different channels of input while being instructed to attend to just one channel.

difference threshold (p. 159) Smallest recognizable difference between two stimuli, also known as the *just noticeable difference (JND)*.

diffusion of responsibility (p. 476) Dilution or weakening of each group member's obligation to act when responsibility is shared with all group members.

dishabituation (p. 114) Recovery from habituation; occurs when novel stimuli are presented.

dissociative disorder (p. 517) Psychological reaction in which an individual experiences sudden, temporary alteration of consciousness through severe loss of memory or identity.

dissociative identity disorder (DID) (p. 518) Dissociative disorder in which different aspects of a personality function independently, creating the appearance of two or more distinct personalities within the same individual.

distal stimulus (p. 179) Object in environment that is source of external stimulation; contrasted with *proximal stimulus*.

distraction (p. 186) Inability to perceptually process available stimuli due to interference.

dopamine hypothesis (p. 543) Explanation proposing relationship between many schizophrenic symptoms and relative excess of the neurotransmitter dopamine at specific brain receptor sites.

double blind (pp. 29, 541) A control strategy that employs both uninformed experimenters and uninformed subjects; conflict situation in which individual receives multiple, contradictory messages from a significant other.

dream analysis (p. 568) Psychoanalytic interpretation of dreams, used to achieve insight into one's unconscious motives or conflicts.

drive (p. 306) Biologically instigated motivation.

drug therapy (p. 590) Any use of drugs to treat mental, behavioral, or physical disorders.

DSM-IV (p. 513) *Diagnostic and Statistical Manual of Mental Disorders, Fourth Edition*; American Psychiatric Association catalogue that classifies, defines, and describes over 200 mental disorders.

dual-code model (of memory) (p. 237) Memory coding theory that proposes that both visual and verbal codes are used to store information.

eating disorders (p. 533) Loss of appetite behaviors in which one deprives oneself of food or prevents food from being digested.

efferent systems (p. 157) Motor systems or systems that process information from the brain to muscles and glands.

ego (p. 404) Freudian concept of self; the personality structure focused on self-preservation and appropriate channeling of instinctual drives.

ego defense mechanisms (pp. 353, 404) Freudian concept of mental strategies used to reduce conflict or anxiety.

egocentrism (p. 127) Self-centered focus; the inability to distinguish mental from physical worlds.

elaboration (p. 229) Relating new input to previously acquired information or to relevant goals or purposes.

electroconvulsive therapy (ECT) (p. 589) Medical therapy in which mild electric current is briefly applied to patient's brain to influence central nervous system function.

emergent-interaction theory (p. 78) Theory that brain activities give rise to mental states, but these mental states are not the same as and not reducible to brain states.

emotion (p. 287) Complex pattern of changes in response to a situation perceived as personally significant, including physiological arousal, feelings, thoughts, and behaviors.

emotion wheel (p. 292) Theorist Robert Plutchik's model of innate emotions, involving eight basic emotions made up of four pairs of opposites: joy-sadness, fear-anger, surprise-anticipation, and acceptance-disgust.

emotional intelligence (p. 442) Self-awareness and motivation necessary to excel in work, society, and personal life; independent of IQ.

empathy (p. 131) The condition of feeling someone else's emotion.

empirical investigation (p. 23) Research that relies on sensory experience and observation as research data.

encephalization (pp. 43, 229) Increases in brain size.

encoding specificity principle (p. 236) Assumption that information retrieval is enhanced if cues received at time of recall are consistent with those present at time of encoding.

endocrine system (p. 56) A network of glands that manufacture and secrete chemical messengers called hormones into the bloodstream.

Eros (p. 401) Freudian concept of life instinct that energizes growth and survival.

eugenics (p. 424) Movement that advocated improving the human species by encouraging biologically superior people to interbreed while discouraging biologically inferior types from having offspring.

evolution (p. 41) The theory that over time organisms originate and adapt to their unique environments.

evolutionary approach (p. 19) Approach that assumes that human mental abilities, like physical abilities, evolved over millions of years to serve particular adaptive purposes.

experience-sampling method (p. 79) Research technique where subjects wear electronic pagers and record what they are feeling and thinking whenever the pager signals.

extinction (p. 207) In learning, the weakening of a conditioned association in the absence of unconditioned stimulus or reinforcer.

extrinsic motivation (p. 325) Desire to engage in activity to achieve external consequences.

false memory syndrome (p. 241) A pattern of thoughts, feelings, and actions based on mistaken or distorted recollection of experiences the rememberer claims to have previously repressed; not a qualified DSM category.

fight-or-flight syndrome (p. 344) Sequence of internal activities preparing organism for struggle or escape, triggered when a threat is confronted.

figure (p. 188) Object-like region in forefront of visual field, distinguished from *ground*.

fixation (p. 403) Arrested development caused by excessive stimulation or frustration in an earlier psychosexual stage.

fixed-action pattern (p. 310) Unlearned set of responses triggered within a given species by a specific stimulus.

flooding (p. 573) Therapy for phobias in which clients agree to be exposed to stimuli they consider most frightening, in order to force them to test reality.

flow (p. 325) Near-ecstatic state achieved by total, present focus on activity, increasing creative ability.

fluid intelligence (p. 439) Ability to perceive complex relationships and solve problems.

frame (p. 278) The structure or context of a problem's presentation.

free association (p. 567) Principal procedure in psychoanalysis, in which patient provides a running account of thoughts, wishes, physical sensations, and mental images as they occur.

functional fixedness (p. 269) Inability to perceive a new use for an object associated with a different purpose; limits problem solving and creativity.

functionalism (p. 13) School that gave primary importance to learned habits that enabled organisms to adapt to their environment and to function effectively.

fundamental attribution error (FAE) (p. 487) Biased pattern of explaining behavior, in which the observer overestimates the power of disposition forces and underestimates the influence of the situation in the actor's behavior.

g-factor (p. 439) General intelligence factor, assumed to be the individual's inherited basic intelligence.

general adaptation syndrome (GAS) (p. 345) Pattern of nonspecific bodily mechanisms activated in response to a continuing threat by almost any serious stressor.

generalized anxiety disorder (p. 520) Disorder in which an individual experiences anxiety that persists for at least one month and is not focused on a specific object or situation.

generativity (p. 144) In Erikson's theory of psychosocial crises, a process of making a commitment beyond oneself to family, work, society, or future generations.

genes (p. 44) Functional units of the chromosomes; genes influence heredity by directing protein synthesis.

genetics (p. 44) The study of heredity—the inheritance of physical and psychological traits from ancestors.

genotype (p. 42) Genetic structure inherited from one's parents.

Gestalt psychology (p. 184) School of psychology that maintains that psychological phenomena can only be understood when viewed as organized, structured wholes, not when broken down into component elements.

Gestalt therapy (p. 583) Psychological treatment emphasizing the union of mind and body to make the person whole.

glia (p. 60) Cells that bind neurons to each other.

glossolalia (p. 99) Fabricated speech occurring chiefly in states of religious ecstasy and altered states of consciousness.

grammar (p. 123) Set of rules within a language about how to use words, word units, and order in producing understandable sentences.

ground (p. 188) Background areas of visual field against which figures stand out.

growth motivation (p. 312) Motivation to help oneself beyond what one has been and done in the past; central to humanistic theories.

gustation (p. 174) Sense of taste.

habituation (p. 114) Decrease in response to any repeatedly presented event.

hallucinations (pp. 97, 538) Vivid perceptions that occur in the absence of objective stimulation.

hallucinogens (p. 100) Drugs that alter perceptions of the external environment and inner awareness.

halo effect (p. 428) Bias in which an observer's judgment of a single characteristic affects judgments of most or all other qualities.

hardiness (p. 358) Quality resulting from the three C's of health: challenge (welcoming change), commitment (focused involvement in purposeful activity), and control (internal guide for actions).

health (p. 362) Condition in which body and mind are sound and vigorous as well as free from illness or injury.

health psychology (p. 362) Field of psychology devoted to understanding how people stay healthy, why they become ill, and how they respond when ill.

hedonic capacity (p. 349) An individual's ability to experience pleasure and joy.

heritability factor (p. 445) Degree to which an individual's IQ is determined by genetic background.

hertz (Hz) (p. 169) Unit of sound frequency, also expressed as cycles per second (cps).

heuristic (p. 271) Cognitive strategy or "rule of thumb," used as a shortcut to solve a complex mental task.

hierarchy of needs See *needs hierarchy.*

hippocampus (p. 52) Limbic system structure that is involved in memory.

homeostasis (p. 53) The body's internal balance or equilibrium.

hormones (p. 56) Chemical substances secreted into the bloodstream.

humanistic approach (p. 18) View that the main task for human beings is to strive for growth and development of their potential.

hypnosis (p. 94) An induced alternate state of awareness, characterized by deep relaxation and heightened suggestibility.

hypnotizability (p. 94) The degree to which an individual is responsive to standardized hypnotic suggestions.

hypothalamus (p. 53) Limbic system structure that regulates the physiological processes involved in emotional and motivated behavior, including eating, drinking, temperature regulation, and sexual arousal.

hypothesis (p. 25) A tentative and testable explanation of the relationship between two or more events or variables.

hysteria (p. 508) Archaic term for mental illness characterized by clusters of painful or paralyzing symptoms without clear physical cause.

id (p. 403) Freudian concept of primitive, unconscious personality structure that operates irrationally, impulsively, and selfishly.

identification and recognition (p. 178) Two processes in which meaning is assigned to percepts.

idiographic approach (p. 389) Method of studying personality that emphasizes individual uniqueness rather than common dimensions.

illness (p. 363) Pathology or damage to the structure or function of bodily systems.

illness prevention (p. 364) General and specific strategies to reduce or eliminate the risk that one will become sick.

illusion (p. 181) Demonstrably incorrect experience of a stimulus pattern, shared by others in the same perceptual environment.

implosion therapy (p. 572) Behavioral therapy technique in which a client is exposed to the most anxiety-provoking stimuli in order to extinguish anxiety associated with the class of stimuli.

imprinting (p. 133) Primitive learning in which some infant animals follow and form an attachment to the first moving object they see and hear.

in vivo therapy (p. 559) Therapeutic approach in which professionals treat clients in settings associated with clients' disorders.

incentive motivation (p. 308) Motivation aroused by external stimuli.

incentives (p. 308) External stimuli that promise rewards.

independent variable (p. 9) The stimulus condition that can vary independently of other variables in the situation; presumed to predict or influence behavior.

individual differences perspective (p. 421) Distinctions and variations among people's characteristics and behavior patterns.

inductive reasoning (p. 266) Drawing a conclusion about the probability of an event or condition based on available evidence.

inference (p. 272) Logical assumption or conclusion based, not on direct observation, but on samples of evidence or prior beliefs and theories.

informational influence (p. 466) Effect of a group on an individual who desires to be correct and understand how best to act in a given situation.

information-processing approach (p. 128) Perspective on cognitive development that likens the child's mental processes to those of computers and artificial intelligence.

information-processing model (p. 253) Cognitive perspective that proposes that thinking and all other forms of cognition can be understood by analyzing them into parts.

initiation rites (p. 139) Rituals (or rites of passage) that usually take place around puberty and serve as a public acknowledgment of the transition from childhood to adulthood.

innateness theories of language (p. 121) Theories of speech production that argue that children acquire language by following an inborn program of steps for acquiring vocabulary and grammar.

insanity (p. 546) Legal designation for the state of an individual judged to be irresponsible or incompetent.

insight therapy (p. 566) Treatment in which therapist guides patient (or client) toward perceiving relationships between present symptoms and past origins.

insomnia (p. 90) Chronic failure to get adequate sleep, characterized by an inability to fall asleep quickly, frequent arousals during sleep, and/or early morning awakening.

instinctual drift (p. 222) Tendency over time for learned behavior to relapse and resemble instinctual behavior.

intelligence (p. 433) Global capacity to profit from experience and go beyond given information.

intelligence quotient (IQ) (p. 436) Index derived from standardized tests of intelligence.

interactionist perspective (p. 423) Argument that both person variables and situational variables interact with each other to produce and influence an individual's behavior.

interjudge reliability (p. 428) Degree to which different observers agree about a particular individual or case.

interneurons (p. 60) Neurons that relay messages from sensory neurons to other interneurons or to motor neurons.

intervening variable (pp. 8, 426) Hypothetical condition that is assumed to function as the link between observable stimulus input and measurable response output.

intimacy (p. 142) The capacity to make a full commitment—sexual, emotional, and moral—to another person.

intrinsic motivation (p. 325) Desire to engage in activity for its own sake.

intuitive psychologists (p. 486) Laypersons who rely on their personal theories about personality, behavior, and motivation.

James-Lange theory of emotion (p. 299) Theory, developed independently by William James and Carl Lange, that emotional stimulus triggers behavioral response that sends sensory and motor feedback to the brain and creates feeling of a specific emotion.

job analysis (p. 452) Study of a specific job, focusing on skills required, effort demanded, worker's responsibilities, and job-related stressors.

judgment (p. 271) Process of forming opinions, reaching conclusions, and making evaluations based on available material; the product of the judgment process.

just noticeable difference (JND) (p. 159) Difference threshold.

kinesthetic sense (p. 173) Sense of body position and movement of body parts relative to each other (also called *kinesthesis*).

language acquisition device (LAD) (p. 121) Biologically predetermined mental structure that facilitates the comprehension and production of speech.

lateralization of emotion (p. 289) Different influences of the two brain hemispheres on various emotions, with the left hemisphere assumed to influence positive emotions (for example, happiness) and the right hemisphere to influence negative emotions (for example, anger).

law of effect (p. 213) Basic law of learning that states that the power of a stimulus to evoke a response is strengthened when the response is followed by a reward, and weakened when it is not followed by a reward.

law of Prägnanz (p. 190) Gestalt principle of meaningfulness, which asserts that the simplest organization requiring the least cognitive effort will emerge.

Lazarus-Schachter theory of emotion (p. 300) Theory, developed independently by Richard Lazarus and Stanley Schachter, that emotional experience is the joint effect of physiological arousal and cognitive appraisal, which determines how an ambiguous inner state will be interpreted; also called the *two-factor theory of emotion*.

learned helplessness (p. 219) Pattern of not responding to noxious stimuli after an organism learns its behavior has no effect.

learning (p. 201) Process based on experience that results in a relatively permanent change in behavior or behavior potential.

lesions (p. 48) Carefully inflicted injuries or alterations of tissue applied to specific brain areas.

libido (p. 401) Freudian concept of psychic energy that drives individuals to experience sensual pleasure.

life-change units (p. 335) Measures of stress caused by different kinds of change experienced during a specific time period.

life history (p. 426) Information about an individual's experiences based on school or military records, personal accounts, and medical data.

life-span developmental psychology (p. 139) Study of personality, mental functioning, and behavior as they develop and change throughout the entire life cycle.

limbic system (p. 52) Brain system that processes motivated behaviors, emotional states, and certain kinds of memory.

locus of control (p. 315) An individual's sense of where his or her life influences originate.

locus-of-control orientation (p. 315) General belief about whether one's actions are controlled by internal or external factors.

longitudinal design (p. 113) A type of investigation in which researchers repeatedly observe and test the same individuals over time.

long-term memory (LTM) (p. 233) Memory processes associated with preserving information for retrieval at any later time; theorized to have unlimited capacity.

loudness (p. 170) Perceived intensity or amplitude of sound energy.

manic episode (p. 526) A period of mania, during which an individual generally acts and feels unusually elated and expansive.

maturation (p. 116) Systematic changes occurring over time in bodily functioning and behavior, influenced by physical factors that are the same for all members of a species.

meditation (p. 96) A form of consciousness change designed to enhance self-knowledge and well-being by reducing self-awareness.

medulla (p. 51) The brain center for breathing, waking, and the beating of the heart; nerve fibers connecting the brain and the body cross over at the medulla.

menarche (p. 140) The onset of menstruation in women.

mental age (MA) (p. 435) Average age at which normal individuals achieve a particular score on a measure of intelligence.

mental set (p. 269) Tendency to respond to a new problem in the manner used for a previous problem.

morality (p. 129) A system of beliefs, values, and underlying judgments about the rightness or wrongness of human acts.

morphemes (p. 124) The meaningful units that make up words.

motherese (p. 122) An exaggerated, high-pitched intonation adults use when speaking to young children.

motivation (p. 304) Process that starts, directs, and maintains physical and psychological activity, including activity preference, strength, and persistence.

motive (p. 306) Psychologically and socially instigated motivation, assumed to be at least partially learned.

motor cortex (p. 54) Part of the cortex that controls the actions of the body's voluntary muscles.

motor neurons (p. 60) Also called *efferent neurons,* nerve cells that carry messages away from the central nervous system toward the muscles and glands.

mnemonics (p. 236) Short, verbal devices that encode a long series of facts by associating them with familiar and previously encoded information.

myelin sheath (p. 60) Fatty insulation coating some types of neural axons, which biochemically speeds the conduction of internal impulses.

narcissistic personality disorder (p. 517) Personality disorder marked by exaggerated sense of self-importance, preoccupation with success or power fantasies, and need for constant attention or admiration.

natural selection (p. 41) The theory that the forces of nature select the organisms—and the features of those organisms—that will survive, reproduce, and pass their advantageous traits to the next generation.

nature-nurture controversy (p. 111) A long-standing debate among scholars over the relative importance of heredity and learning.

**need for achievement (*n Ach)* ** (p. 324) Concept developed by Henry Murray and David McClelland of basic human drive to meet a wide variety of goals.

needs hierarchy (p. 313) Abraham Maslow's theoretical sequence of needs motivating human behavior, from the most primitive level to higher needs only satisfied after lower ones are achieved; also *hierarchy of needs.*

negative reinforcer (p. 215) Stimulus that increases the probability of a response when it is terminated or avoided after that response.

nervous system (p. 56) A massive network of nerve cells that relays messages to and from the brain.

neuron (p. 56) Nerve cell specialized to receive, process, and/or transmit information to other cells within the body.

neurosis See *neurotic disorder.*

neurotic disorder or neurosis (p. 514) Mental disorder characterized not by irrational thinking or violation of norms but by personal distress, especially anxiety.

neurotransmitters (pp. 56, 61) Chemical messengers that relay messages to and from the brain. Biochemical substances that stimulate other neurons and the endocrine system.

nodes of Ranvier (p. 60) Indentations in the myelin sheath coating some neural axons, facilitating faster internal impulse conduction.

nomothetic approach (p. 389) Method of studying personality that emphasizes identifying universal traits and patterns.

nonconscious processes (p. 81) Information that is not represented in consciousness or memory but still influences fundamental bodily or mental activities.

non-REM (NREM) sleep (p. 86) The time when a sleeper is not showing REM.

norm (p. 431) Standard or value based on measurements of a large group of people; in social psychology, the group standard for approved behavior.

normative influence (p. 466) Effect of a group on an individual who strives to be liked, accepted, and approved of by others.

normative investigations (p. 113) A type of investigation in which researchers describe a characteristic of a specific age or developmental stage.

object permanence (p. 126) The perception that objects exist independently of one's own actions or awareness.

observational learning (pp. 226, 412) Process of learning new responses by watching others' behavior.

observer-report methods (p. 427) Evaluation of some aspect of an individual's behavior by another person.

obsessive-compulsive disorder (p. 523) Mental disorder characterized by patterns of obsessions (persistent, unwanted thoughts) and compulsions (undesired, repetitive actions).

olfaction (p. 174) Sense of smell.

olfactory bulb (p. 174) Brain site of olfactory processing, below frontal lobes, where odor-sensitive receptors send their signals.

operant (p. 213) Behavior that can be characterized in terms of its effects on the environment.

operant extinction (p. 216) Withholding a positive reinforcer to extinguish an operant behavior.

operational definition (p. 28) Definition of a concept in terms of how the concept is measured or what operations produce it.

opiates (p. 101) Class of drugs, derived from opium, that suppresses physical sensation and response to stimulation.

optic nerve (p. 165) Bundled axons of ganglion cells carrying information from the eyes to the brain.

optimal arousal level (p. 312) Level of arousal at which people best perform tasks of different levels of difficulty.

overregularization (p. 124) Applying a grammatical rule too widely and creating incorrect forms.

pain (p. 176) Bodily sensation of noxious stimuli intense enough to threaten or cause tissue damage.

panic disorder (p. 521) Anxiety disorder characterized by recurrent episodes of intense anxiety, feelings of unpredictability, and symptoms of arousal usually lasting several minutes.

parasympathetic division (p. 58) Division of the autonomic nervous system that monitors the routine operation of the body's internal functions and returns it to calmer functioning after sympathetic arousal.

participant modeling (p. 575) Therapeutic technique in which a therapist demonstrates, and encourages client to imitate, desired behavior.

pastoral counselor (p. 560) Member of a religious order who specializes in treating psychological disorders, often combining spiritual guidance with practical problem solving.

patient nonadherence (p. 370) Patient's failure to abide by medical guidelines or follow physicians' recommendations for treatment.

peace psychology (p. 494) Interdisciplinary approach to the prevention of nuclear war and the promotion and maintenance of peace.

percept (p. 177) The experienced outcome of the process of perception.

perception (p. 157) Processes that organize sensory information and interpret it in terms of its environmental origins.

perceptual grouping (p. 189) Process of perception in which sets of stimuli are judged to belong together; focus of several Gestalt principles of perception.

perceptual organization (p. 188) Putting sensory information together to create coherence.

perceptual set (p. 192) Readiness to detect a particular stimulus within a given context.

peripheral nervous system (p. 56) Subsystem of the nervous system composed of all the neurons forming the nerve fibers that connect the central nervous system to the rest of the body.

personal construct (p. 413) George Kelly's theoretical concept of an individual's unique system for interpreting reality.

personality (p. 381) Unique qualities and distinctive behavior patterns of an individual across time and situations.

person-centered therapy (p. 582) Humanistic approach to treatment developed by Carl Rogers, emphasizing individual's tendency for healthy psychological growth through self-actualization.

personality disorder (p. 517) Chronic, inflexible, maladaptive pattern of perception, thought, and behavior that seriously impairs an individual's ability to function personally or socially.

personality inventory (p. 382) Self-report questionnaire used for personality assessment.

personality types (p. 392) Patterns of behavior and characteristics used to assign people to categories.

phenotype (p. 42) Observable features by which individuals are recognized.

pheromones (p. 174) Chemical signals released by organisms to communicate with other members of their species; often a sexual attractor.

phobia See *phobic disorder.*

phobic disorder or phobia (p. 521) Maladaptive pattern of behavior in which anxiety is associated with a specific external object or situation that the individual seeks to avoid.

photoreceptors (p. 164) Light-sensitive cells in the retina that convert light energy to neural responses.

physiological dependence (p. 100) A process by which the body adjusts to and becomes dependent on a particular drug.

physiological measures (p. 30) Data based on subjects' biological responses to stimuli.

pitch (p. 170) Perceived frequency of sound.

pituitary gland (p. 64) Gland that secretes hormones that influence the secretions of all other endocrine glands, as well as a hormone that influences growth.

pons (p. 52) Brain structure involved in dreaming and waking from sleep.

positive reinforcer (p. 215) Stimulus, received after a response, that increases the probability of that response.

postformal thought (p. 144) A more dynamic, less abstract way of thinking that can accept inconsistencies and contradictions.

posttraumatic stress disorder (PTSD) (p. 348) Reaction in which individual involuntarily reexperiences emotional, cognitive, and behavioral aspects of past trauma.

Prägnanz See *law of Prägnanz.*

preattentive processing (p. 186) Processing that operates on sensory inputs from receptors before they are attended to.

preconscious memories (p. 81) Memories accessible to consciousness only after something calls attention to them.

prejudice (p. 483) Negative attitude and feelings about a group and its members.

Premack principle (p. 220) Principle developed by David Premack that a more preferred activity can be used to reinforce a less preferred activity.

primary appraisal (p. 354) First stage of cognitive appraisal of stress, in which one evaluates a stressful situation and how serious it is.

proactive interference (p. 243) Memory process in which stored information prevents learning similar new information.

problem solving (p. 267) Moving from an initial state (the problem) to a goal state (the solution) by means of a set of mental operations.

procedural memory (p. 234) Long-term memory (LTM) component that stores memory for how things are done.

projective test (p. 385) Personality assessment technique in which respondent is asked to interpret ambiguous stimuli.

proposition (p. 237) Expression of relationship between concepts, objects, or events.

prototype (p. 257) Ideal or most representative example of a category.

proximal stimulus (p. 179) Sensory system's impression of external stimulation, for example, image on the retina; contrasted with *distal stimulus*.

pseudomemory (p. 259) Form of memory in which one confidently believes a new stimulus was experienced previously because several of its features have been remembered.

psychiatrist (p. 560) Physician (with training and degree in medicine) specializing in treatment of mental and emotional disorders.

psychic determinism (p. 402) Assumption that mental and behavioral reactions are caused by earlier experience.

psychoactive drugs (p. 98) Chemicals that affect mental processes and behavior by temporarily changing conscious awareness.

psychoanalyst (p. 560) Individual (physician, psychologist, or layperson) who is trained and qualified in practicing Freudian approach to assessing and treating mental disorders.

psychoanalytic therapy (p. 566) Psychodynamic therapy developed by Sigmund Freud, involving intensive, prolonged exploration of patients' unconscious motivations and conflicts.

psychedelics (p. 100) Drugs that produce the most dramatic changes in consciousness.

psychodynamic approach (p. 15) Approach that views behavior as driven or motivated by powerful mental forces and conflicts.

psychodynamic personality theory (p. 400) Any models that share assumptions that inner forces shape personality and motivate behavior.

psychogenic amnesia (p. 518) Memory loss involving inability to recall important personal information, caused not by physical damage but by psychological distress.

psychological assessment (p. 421) Use of specified procedures to evaluate people's abilities, behaviors, and personal qualities.

psychological dependence (p. 100) Pervasive desire to obtain or use a drug; not based on physical addiction.

psychological diagnosis (p. 506) Identifying and explaining mental disorders according to clinical interview and observation, testing, and analysis of mental and behavioral development.

psychological test (p. 426) Instrument used to measure an individual's standing relative to others on some mental or behavioral characteristic.

psychological therapies (p. 563) Treatments for psychological disorders that work by changing behaviors, thoughts, perceptions, and emotions; also *psychotherapies*.

psychology (p. 5) The scientific study of the behavior of individuals and their mental processes.

psychometrics (p. 438) Field of psychology that specializes in mental testing.

psychoneuroimmunology (PNI) (p. 332) Research specialty that investigates the healing interactions among brain, body, emotions, and the immune system.

psychopathology (p. 504) Abnormality or disorder in patterns of thought, emotion, or behavior.

psychophysics (p. 158) Study of correspondence between physical stimulation and psychological experience.

psychosexual stages (p. 402) Freudian concept of successive phases—oral, anal, phallic, latency, and genital—of development in which a child associates pleasure with different bodily regions.

psychosis See *psychotic disorder*.

psychosocial crisis (p. 136) According to Erikson, one of several successive choice-points that occur in an individual's development, focusing on one's orientation to self and others.

psychosurgery (p. 588) Surgical procedures that alter brain tissue in order to alleviate psychological disorders.

psychotherapies See *psychological therapies*.

psychotic disorder or psychosis (p. 514) Severe mental disorder characterized by impaired reality testing due to difficulties in thought, emotional, or perceptual processes.

puberty (p. 140) Attainment of sexual maturity (ability to reproduce).

punisher (p. 214) Aversive stimulus that decreases the probability of the preceding response.

randomization (p. 32) Assignment of subjects so that every subject has an equal chance of ending up in any of the conditions, experimental or control.

rapid eye-movement (REM) sleep (p. 86) Eye movements that occur at periodic intervals during sleep.

rating (p. 427) Quantitative judgment of the degree to which some characteristic is present or influential.

rational-emotive therapy (RET) (p. 580) System of personality change developed by Albert Ellis, based on changing irrational beliefs that cause problematic emotional reactions such as anxiety.

reaction time (p. 254) Time elapsed between stimulus presentation and organism's response; used to measure time required by mental processes.

realistic thinking (p. 266) Fitting one's ideas to situational demands, time limits, rules of operation, and accurate evaluation of one's personal resources; contrasted with *autistic thinking*.

reasoning (p. 266) Realistic thinking process that draws a conclusion from a set of facts; goal-directed thinking.

recall (p. 229) Retrieval method in which one must reproduce previously presented information.

reciprocal determinism (p. 412) Albert Bandura's social-learning theory concept of the mutual influence between person, behavior, and environment.

recognition (p. 229) Retrieval method in which one must identify present stimuli as having been previously presented.

reference group (p. 463) Formal or informal group from which an individual derives norms and seeks information, direction, and lifestyle support.

reflex (p. 204) Unlearned response elicited by specific stimuli that are biologically relevant to the organism.

reinforcement contingency (p. 214) Consistent relationship between a response and the changes it produces in the environment.

reinforcers (p. 214) Significant event that strengthens an organism's responses when it is only delivered in connection with those responses.

relapse (p. 363) Reversion to former behavior patterns that had been changed.

reliability (p. 429) Degree to which an assessment method yields the same score each time an individual is measured; consistency.

representative heuristic (p. 277) Cognitive strategy that assigns items to categories based on whether items possess some characteristics representative of the category.

repression (pp. 244, 404) In Freudian theory, basic defense mechanism that excludes painful or unacceptable thoughts, feelings, or memories from consciousness.

residual stress pattern (p. 349) Chronic pattern in which symptoms of posttraumatic stress disorder persist over time.

resistance (p. 567) Inability or unwillingness of psychoanalytic patient to discuss certain ideas, desires, or experiences.

reticular formation (p. 52) Dense network of nerve cells situated between the medulla and pons that arouses the cerebral cortex to attend to new stimulation and keeps the brain alert.

retina (p. 164) Layer of cells at the back of the eye containing photoreceptors.

retrieval (p. 229) Recovery of stored information from memory.

retrieval cues (p. 237) Available internal or external stimuli that help in recovering information from memory.

retroactive interference (p. 243) Memory process in which newly learned information prevents retrieval of previously stored, similar material.

reward deficiency syndrome (RDS) (p. 545) Genetically caused biochemical imbalance that is manifested in one or more disorders of addictive, impulsive, or compulsive behavior.

ritual healing (p. 565) Ceremonial process of infusing emotional intensity and meaning into treating illness by heightening patients' suggestibility and sense of importance.

rules (p. 461) Behavioral guidelines for how to act in certain situations.

schema (p. 238) Mental collection of knowledge and expectations about a topic or event.

schemes (p. 125, 260) In Piaget's theory, mental structures or programs that guide a developing child's sequences of thought.

schizophrenic disorder (p. 537) Severe disorder characterized by the breakdown of personality functioning, withdrawal from reality, distorted emotions, and disturbed thought.

scientific method (p. 5) A set of orderly steps used to analyze and solve problems by relying on objective research data; also, an open-minded yet skeptical attitude toward evidence and conclusions.

script (p. 262) A cluster of knowledge about sequences of interrelated, specific events and actions expected to occur in a certain way in particular settings.

secondary appraisal (p. 354) Second stage of cognitive appraisal of stress, in which individual evaluates personal and social resources needed to respond and determines action to take.

secondary trait (p. 394) Trait that indicates enduring personal qualities but is not assumed to explain general behavior patterns.

selective social interaction (p. 148) Maintaining only the most rewarding contacts for the investment of precious physical and emotional energy.

self-actualization (p. 409) Humanistic concept of an individual's lifelong process of striving to realize his or her potential.

self-awareness (p. 81) Cognizance that personally experienced events have an autobiographical character.

self-concept (p. 388) Individual's awareness of his or her continuing identity as a person.

self-efficacy (p. 412) Albert Bandura's concept of beliefs an individual has that he or she can perform adequately in a particular situation.

self-fulfilling prophecies (p. 481) One's private expectations of how others will act that influence them to behave in the predicted manner.

self-report measures (p. 30) Verbal answers to researchers' questions.

self-report methods (p. 427) Popular research techniques in which respondents are assessed by their answers to a series of questions.

self-serving bias (p. 487) Attributional pattern in which one takes credit for success but denies responsibility for failure.

sensation (p. 157) Process of converting physical energy into stimulation of receptor cells (for example, converting light energy into visual stimulation).

sensory adaptation (p. 162) Loss of responsiveness in receptor cells after stimulation has remained unchanged.

sensory memory (p. 231) Initial process that preserves brief impressions of stimuli; also *sensory register*.

sensory neurons (p. 60) Also called *afferent neurons*, nerve cells that carry messages from sense receptor cells toward the central nervous system.

sensuality (p. 156) State or quality of appreciating sensory pleasures.

separation distress (p. 135) Pattern of negative emotions, mental disruption, and anxiety experienced when an attachment figure is not available.

sequential design (p. 114) A type of investigation in which subjects who span a certain, small age range are grouped according to their birth years and observed repeatedly over several years.

set (p. 192) Temporary readiness to perceive or react to stimulus in a particular way.

sexual scripts (p. 320) Socially learned programs of sexual interpretation and responsiveness.

shamanism (p. 556) Ancient spiritual tradition, still practiced in Native American cultures, combining healing with making contact with the spirit world.

shaping (p. 221) Operant learning technique in which a new behavior is produced by reinforcing responses that approach the desired performance; also called *learning by successive approximations*.

shyness (p. 524) A normal but distressing pattern of avoiding or withdrawing from social contact.

signal detection theory (SDT) (p. 160) Theory that a perceptual judgment combines sensation and decision-making processes.

situational behavior observations (p. 426) First-hand study of an individual's actions and performance in one or more settings.

situationism (pp. 422, 461) Argument that conditions and forces in behavior settings determine individuals' behavior as much as or more than personal qualities do.

skin senses (p. 175) Sensory systems for processing reception and experience of pressure, warmth, and cold.

sleep apnea (p. 90) Upper respiratory disorder in which the person intermittently stops breathing while asleep.

social categorization (p. 484) Process by which people organize their social environment by classifying themselves and others into groups.

social learning therapy (p. 575) Treatment system based on theory that behavior is influenced by observation and imitation of others.

social norms (p. 462) Group's expectations regarding what is appropriate and acceptable for its members' attitudes and behaviors.

social perception (p. 483) Process of recognizing the personal attributes of oneself and others.

social phobia (p. 523) Category of phobic disorders in which an individual irrationally fears engaging in public action or display; extreme form of shyness.

social psychology (p. 460) Branch of psychology that studies the effects of social variables on individual behavior, cognitions, and motives, as well as group and intergroup processes.

social reality (p. 480) The consensus of perceptions and beliefs about a situation that is derived from social comparisons among group members.

social role (p. 462) Socially defined pattern of behavior expected of a person when functioning in a given setting or group.

social support (p. 359) Resources, materials, sympathy, or information provided by others to help a person cope with stress.

socialization (p. 133) The life-long process of shaping an individual's behavior patterns, values, standards, skills, attitudes, and motives to conform to those regarded as desirable in a particular society.

sociocultural approach (p. 20) Psychological perspective arguing that, to predict individual behavior, it is necessary to take into account very broad influences, including the individual's environment, social organization, community, cultural values, and family.

soma (p. 59) The cell body containing the nucleus of the cell and the cytoplasm that sustains its life.

somatic nervous system (p. 58) Subdivision of the PNS that regulates the actions of the body's skeletal muscles.

somatosensory cortex (p. 54) Part of the cortex that processes information about temperature, touch, body position, and pain.

somatotype (p. 393) Descriptive category that classifies personality pattern according to physical characteristics.

spontaneous recovery (p. 207) Reappearance of an extinguished conditioned response after a rest period.

standardization (pp. 27, 432) Second phase of research, in which results are tested and prepared for useful communication with the scientific community; uniformity of procedures in applying treatments or recording data; in test construction, specifying population and conditions for establishing norms.

stereotype effect (p. 428) Bias in which judge's beliefs about most people in a social category influence how a particular individual in the category is perceived.

stigma (p. 548) A mark or brand of disgrace; in the psychological context, a set of negative attitudes about a person that sets him or her apart as unacceptable.

stimulants (p. 102) Drugs that increase central nervous system activity, speeding up both mental and physical activity.

stimulus discrimination (p. 208) In conditioning, responding differently to stimuli that differ from the conditioned stimulus.

stimulus generalization (p. 208) Making conditioned responses to similar stimuli that have never been paired with the unconditioned stimulus.

Stockholm syndrome (p. 349) Pattern of behavior displayed when hostages and prisoners identify and sympathize with their captors.

storage (p. 229) Retaining encoded information over time.

stress (p. 333) The pattern of specific and general responses made by an organism to stimulus events that disturb the organism's equilibrium and tax or exceed its ability to cope.

stress moderator variables (p. 354) Variables that change the impact of a stressor on a particular reaction.

stressor (p. 333) Internal or external stimulus event that induces stress.

structuralism (p. 13) The study of the structure of mind and behavior, including elements and components.

subconscious awareness (p. 82) The processing of information not currently in consciousness but retrievable from memory by special recall or attention-getting procedures.

subjective contours (p. 189) Edges or boundaries perceived in proximal stimulus that do not exist in distal stimulus.

subjective well-being (SWB) (p. 372) An individual's evaluative response to his or her life, including cognitive and emotional reactions.

superego (p. 403) Freudian concept of personality structure that embodies society's values, standards, and morals.

syllogism (p. 266) Form of deductive reasoning with a major premise, a minor premise, and a logical conclusion.

sympathetic division (p. 58) Division of the ANS that governs responses to stress in emergencies.

synapse (p. 61) Space between neurons that provides a junction for information transfer.

synaptic transmission (p. 61) Process in which information is relayed from one neuron to another across the synaptic gap.

systematic desensitization (p. 571) Behavioral therapy technique in which client learns to relax in order to prevent anxiety arousal.

taste buds (p. 174) Receptors for taste, located primarily on upper side of the tongue.

taste-aversion learning (p. 210) Biological constraint on learning in which an organism learns after a single experience to avoid a food if eating it is followed by illness.

temperament (p. 131) Individual's specific manner of behaving or reacting.

terminal buttons (p. 60) Swollen, bulb-like structures, located at the far end of the axon, through which stimulation passes to nearby glands, muscles, or other neurons.

thalamus (p. 52) Relay station that channels incoming sensory information to the appropriate area of the cerebral cortex, where that information is then processed.

Thanatos (p. 402) Freudian concept of death instinct, theorized to energize destructive and aggressive behavior.

Thematic Apperception Test (TAT) (p. 314) Projective test in which an individual tells stories about each of a series of ambiguous pictures.

theory (p. 25) A body of interrelated principles used to explain or predict some psychological phenomenon.

think-aloud protocols (pp. 79, 254) Reports used to document the mental strategies of subjects and analyze their awareness of using them; reports of mental processes subjects make while working on tasks.

thinking (p. 256) Mental process that transforms available information to form a new mental representation.

timbre (p. 171) Perceived complexity of sound wave.

tolerance (p. 100) The reduced effectiveness a drug has as a result of repeated use.

top-down processing (p. 180) Processing in which perceiver's past experience, knowledge, expectations, motivation, and background influence analysis and interpretation of perceived stimuli.

total situation (p. 465) Environmental conditions in which people are isolated from contrary points of view, and in which group leaders control distribution of information, rewards, and punishments.

trait (p. 394) Relatively stable personality tendency.

transduction (p. 157) Transformation of one form of energy into another (for example, transformation of vibration energy into neural impulses later interpreted as sound).

transference (p. 568) In psychoanalysis, process in which patient attaches to therapist feelings formerly held toward another significant person associated with emotional conflict.

two-factor theory of emotion (p. 300) See *Lazarus-Schachter theory of emotion.*

Type A syndrome (p. 356) Pattern of angry, competitive, and perfectionistic behavior in response to stress; assumed to increase risk of coronary heart disease.

Type T personality (p. 358) Personality pattern of taking risks, and seeking thrills, stimulation, and excitement.

unconditional positive regard (p. 409) Acceptance and approval given to an individual that is not contingent on that individual's behavior.

unconditioned response (UCR) (p. 206) In classical conditioning, the response elicited by an unconditioned stimulus without prior learning.

unconditioned stimulus (UCS) (p. 205) In classical conditioning, the stimulus that elicits an unconditioned response.

unconscious (pp. 82, 401) Mental processes that keep out of conscious awareness any information that would cause extreme anxiety; psychoanalytic concept of psychic domain that stores repressed and primitive impulses; unconscious processes repress impulses that motivate thoughts, feelings, and actions.

unipolar depression (p. 528) Category of affective disorder involving intense, extended depression without interruption by manic periods; also called *clinical depression.*

validity (p. 130) Extent to which a test measures what it is intended to measure.

variable (p. 9) Any condition, process, or event that changes or varies.

variation (p. 42) Differences in biological and psychological traits among individuals within a given population.

vestibular sense (p. 173) Sense of body orientation with respect to gravity.

visual cortex (pp. 55, 165) Region of occipital lobes in back of brain where visual information is processed.

volume transmission (p. 63) Process of neural communication in which remote cells are influenced by neurons that release chemical signals into the extracellular spaces in the brain.

weapons effect (p. 494) Increased likelihood of behaving aggressively when one is stimulated by the presence of a weapon.

Weber's law (p. 159) Assertion that the size of the difference threshold is proportional to the intensity of the standard (background) stimulus.

wellness (p. 362) Optimal health, including full, active functioning in the physical, intellectual, emotional, spiritual, and social domains.

withdrawal (p. 100) Pattern of painful physical symptoms experienced when, after addiction, level of drug is decreased or drug is eliminated.

working memory or short-term memory (STM) (p. 232) Memory processes that preserve recently perceived events or experiences; also *short-term memory.*

Yerkes-Dodson law (p. 312) Correlation between task difficulty and optimal level of arousal; as arousal increases, performance of difficult tasks decreases, while performance of simple tasks increases, to form an inverted-U function.

References

ABC News. (1995). "My Family, Forgive Me." *20/20*, Transcript #1526, June 30, pp. 6–10. New York: American Broadcasting Companies, Inc.

Abelson, R. P. (1981). Psychological status of the script concept. *American Psychologist, 36,* 715–729.

Abrams, A. R. (1992). *Electroconvulsive therapy.* New York: Oxford University Press.

Abramson, L. Y., Garber, J., Edwards, N., & Seligman, M. E. P. (1978). Expectancy changes in depression and schizophrenia. *Journal of Abnormal Psychology, 87,* 102–109.

Abramson, L. Y., Seligman, M. E. P., & Teasdale, J. (1978). Learned helplessness in humans: Critique and reformulation. *Journal of Abnormal Psychology, 87,* 32–48.

Achenbach, T.M. (1982). *Developmental psychopathology,* 2nd ed. New York: Wiley.

Ackerman, D. (1990). *A natural history of the senses.* New York: Vintage.

Adams, J. (1979). Mutual-help groups: Enhancing the coping ability of oncology clients. *Cancer Nursing, 2,* 95–98.

Adams, D. (Ed.). (1991). *The Seville statement on violence.* Washington, DC: Psychologists for Social Responsibility.

Ader, R., & Cohen, N. (1993). Psychoneuroimmunology: Conditioning and stress. *Annual Review of Psychology, 44,* 53–85.

Ader, R., & Cohen, N. (1975). Behaviorally conditioned immunosuppression. *Psychosomatic Medicine, 37,* 333–340.

Adler, A. (1929). *The practice and theory of individual psychology.* New York: Harcourt, Brace & World.

Adler, J., & Salzhauer, A. (1995). Escaping the diet trap. *Newsweek, 126* (6), 54.

Adler, N. E., David, H. P., Major, B. N., Roth, S. H., Russo, N. F., & Wyatt, G. E. (1990). Psychological responses after abortion. *Science, 248,* 41–44.

Adorno, T. W., Frenkel-Brunswick, E., Levinson, D. J., & Sanford, R. N. (1950). *The authoritarian personality.* New York: Harper.

Affleck, G., Tennen, H., Pfeiffer, C., & Fifield, J. (1987). Appraisals of control and predictability in adapting to a chronic disease. *Journal of Personality and Social Psychology, 53,* 273–279.

Agnati, L. F., Bjelke, B., & Fuxe, K. (1992). Volume transmission in the brain. *American Scientist, 80,* 362–373.

Ahern, G. L., & Schwartz, G. E. (1985). Differential lateralization for positive and negative emotion in the human brain: EEG spectral analysis. *Neuropsychologia, 23,* 744–755.

Ainsworth, M.D.S., Blehar, M., Water, E., & Wall, S. (1978). *Patterns of attachment.* Hillsdale, NJ: Erlbaum.

Ainsworth, M. D. S. (1989). Attachments beyond infancy. *American Psychologist, 44,* 709–716.

Ainsworth, M.D.S., & Wittig, B.A. (1969). Attachment and exploratory behavior of one-year-olds in a strange situation. In B.M. Foss (Ed.), *Determinants of infant behavior,* (Vol. 4). London: Methuen.

Akers, R. (1990). Rational choice, deterrence, and social learning theory: The path not taken. *Journal of Criminal Law and Criminology, 81,* 653–676.

Allen, V. S., & Levine, J. M. (1969). Consensus and conformity. *Journal of Experimental Social Psychology, 5,* 389–399.

Allison, T., & Cicchetti, D. (1976). Sleep in mammals: Ecological and constitutional correlates. *Science, 194,* 732–734.

Allport, G. W. (1961). *Pattern and growth in personality.* New York: Holt, Rinehart & Winston.

Allport, G. W. (1954), *The nature of prejudice.* Cambridge, MA: Addison-Wesley.

Allport, G. W. (1966). Traits revisited. *American Psychologist, 21,* 1–10.

Allport, G. W. (1937). *Personality: A psychological interpretation.* New York: Holt, Rinehart & Winston.

Allport, G. W., & Odbert, H. S. (1936). Trait-names, a psycholexical study. *Psychological Monographs, 47* (1, Whole No. 211).

Alper, J. (1993). Echo-planar MRI: Learning to read minds. *Science, 261,* 556.

Alter, J. (1995). "Will it be publish—or perish?" *Newsweek, Vol. CXXVI,* No. 2 (July 10), 40–43.

American Psychological Association. (1982). *Guidelines and ethical standards for researchers.* Washington, DC: American Psychological Association.

American Psychiatric Association. (1994). *Diagnostic and statistical manual of mental disorders,* 4th edition, Washington, DC: American Psychiatric Association.

Anastasi, A. (1982). *Psychological testing* (5th ed.). New York: Macmillan.

Anderson, A. E., & DiDomenico, L. (1992). Diet vs. shape content of popular male and female magazines: A dose-response relationship to the incidence of eating disorders? *International Journal of Eating Disorders, 11,* 283–287.

Anderson, J. R. (1982). Acquisition of cognitive skill. *Psychological Review, 89,* 369–406.

Anderson, J. R., & Bower, G. H. (1973). *Human associative memory.* Washington, DC: Winston & Sons.

Anderson, J. R. (Ed.). (1981). *Cognitive skills and their acquisition.* Hillsdale, NJ: Erlbaum.

Anderson, J. R. (1976). *Language, memory, and thought.* Hillsdale, NJ: Erlbaum.

Antelman, S. M., Rowland, N. E., & Fisher, A. E. (1976). Stimulation bound ingestive behavior: A view from the tail. *Physiology and Behavior, 17,* 743–748.

Antelman, S. M., & Caggiula, A. R. (1980). Stress-induced behavior: Chemotherapy without drugs. In J. M. Davidson & R. J. Davidson (Eds.), *The psychobiology of consciousness* (pp. 65–104). New York: Plenum.

Antoni, M. H., Schniederman, N., Fletcher, M. A., Goldstein, D. A., Ironson, G., & Laperriere, A. (1990). Psychoneuroimmunology and HIV-1. *Journal of Consulting and Clinical Psychology, 58,* 38–49.

Antrobus, J. (1991). Dreaming: Cognitive processes during cortical activation and high afferent thresholds. *Psychological Review, 98,* 96–121.

Arendt, H. (1963). *Eichmann in Jerusalem: A report on the banality of evil.* New York: Viking Press.

Arendt, H. (1971). Organized guilt and universal responsibility. In R. W. Smith (Ed.), *Guilt: Man and society.* Garden City, NY: Doubleday Anchor Books.

Aron, A., & Aron, E. (1994). Love. In A. L. Weber & J. H. Harvey (Eds.), *Perspectives on close relationships,* (Chapter 7), pp. 131–152. Boston: Allyn & Bacon.

Aronson, E., & Mills, J. (1959). The effect of severity of initiation on liking for a group. *Journal of Abnormal and Social Psychology, 59,* 177–181.

Asbell, B. (1995). *The Pill: A biography of the drug that changed the world.* New York: Random House.

Asch, S. E. (1956). Studies of independence and conformity: A minority of one against a unanimous majority. *Psychological Monographs, 70* (9, Whole No. 416).

Asch, S. E. (1940). Studies in the principles of judgments and attitudes: 11. Determination of judgments by group and by ego standards. *Journal of Social Psychology, 12,* 433–465.

Asch, S. E. (1955). Opinions and social pressure. *Scientific American, 193*(5), 31–35.

Aserinsky, E., & Kleitman, N. (1953). Regularly occurring periods of eye mobility and concomitant phenomena during sleep. *Science, 118,* 273–274.

Associated Press. (1995, November 24). "AIDS threatens more young adults." Cited in *The Asheville Citizen-Times,* p. A-1.

Auerbach, S. M., Kiesler, D. J., Strentz, T., & Schmidt, J. A. (1994). Interpersonal impacts and adjustment to the stress of simulated captivity: An empirical test of the Stockholm syndrome. *Journal of Social and Clinical Psychology, 13,* 207–221.

Averill, J. R. (1976). Emotion and anxiety: Sociocultural, biological, and psychological determinants. In M. Zuckerman & C. O. Spielberger (Eds.), *Emotion and anxiety: New concepts, methods and applications* (pp. 87–130). Hillsdale, NJ: Erlbaum.

Ayllon, T., & Azrin, N. H. (1965). The measurement and reinforcement of behavior of psychotics. *Journal of Experimental Analysis of Behavior, 8,* 357–383.

Baars, B. J., & McGovern, K. (1994). Consciousness. *Encyclopedia of Human Behavior, 1,* 687–699.

Baars, B. J. (1988). *A cognitive theory of consciousness.* Cambridge: Cambridge University Press.

Baddeley, A. D. (1986). *Working memory.* New York: Oxford University Press.

Baell, W. K., & Wertheim, E. H. (1992). Predictors of outcome in the treatment of bulimia nervosa. *British Journal of Clinical Psychology, 31(3),* 330–332.

Baillargeon, R. (1986). Representing the existence and the location of hidden objects: Object permanence in 6- and 8-month-old infants. *Cognition, 23,* 21–42.

Balakrishnan, S. (1991). Psychology of democracy. *The California Psychologist, 24,* pp. 16, 21.

Balsam, P. D., & Tomie, A. (Eds.). (1985). *Context and learning.* Hillsdale, NJ: Erlbaum.

Baltes, P. B., & Kliegl, R. (1992). Further testing of limits of cognitive plasticity: Negative age differences in a mnemonic skill are robust. *Developmental Psychology, 28,* 121–125.

Baltes, P. B. (1987). Theoretical propositions on life-span developmental psychology: On the dynamics between growth and decline. *Developmental Psychology, 23,* 611–626.

Baltes, P. B. (1993). The aging mind: Potential and limits. *The Gerontologist, 33,* 580–594.

Baltes, P. B. (1990, November). *Toward a psychology of wisdom.* Invited address presented at the annual convention of the Gerontological Society of America, Boston, MA.

Bandura, A. (1970). Modeling therapy. In W. S. Sahakian (Ed.), *Psychopathology today: Experimentation, theory and research.* Itasca, IL: Peacock.

Bandura, A. (1981). In search of pure unidirectional determinants. *Behavior Therapy, 12,* 30–40.

Bandura, A. (1986). *Social foundations of thought and action: A social cognitive theory.* Englewood Cliffs, NJ: Prentice-Hall.

Bandura, A. (1992). Exercise of personal agency through the self-efficacy mechanism. In R. Schwarzer (Ed.), *Self-efficacy: Thought control of action* (pp. 3–38). Washington: Hemisphere.

Bandura, A., Ross, D., & Ross, S. A. (1963). Imitation of film-mediated aggressive models. *Journal of Abnormal and Social Psychology, 66,* 3–11.

Banks, M. S., & Bennet, P. J. (1988). Optical and photoreceptor immaturities limit the spatial and chromatic vision of human neonates. *Journal of the Optical Society of America, 5,* 2059–2079.

Barber, T. X. (1986). Realities of stage hypnosis. In B. Zilbergeld, M. G. Edelstein, & D. L. Araoz (Eds.), *Hypnosis: Questions and answers.* New York: Norton.

Barber, T. X. (1979). Suggested ("hypnotic") behavior: The trance paradigm versus an alternative paradigm. In E. Fromm & R. E. Shor (Eds.), *Hypnosis: Developments in research and new perspectives.* New York: Aldine.

Barber, T. X. (1976). *Hypnosis: A scientific approach.* New York: Psychological Dimensions.

Bard, M., & Sangrey, D. (1979). *The crime victim's book.* New York: Basic Books.

Barinaga, M. (1989). Manic depression gene put in limbo. *Science, 246,* 886–887.

Barinaga, M. (1993). Carbon monoxide: Killer to brain messenger in one step. *Science, 259,* 309.

Barker, L. M., Best, M. R., & Domjan, M. (Eds.). (1978). *Learning mechanisms in food selection.* Houston: Baylor University Press.

Barna, L. (1991). Stumbling blocks in intercultural communication. In L. Samovar & R. Porter (Eds.), *Intercultural communication: A reader* (6th ed., pp. 345–352). Belmont, CA: Wadsworth.

Barnes, D. M. (1987). Biological issues in schizophrenia. *Science, 235,* 430–433.

Baron, L., & Straus, M. A. (1985). *Four theories of rape in American society: A state-level analysis.* New Haven, CT: Yale University Press.

Barthe, D. G., & Hammen, C. L. (1981). The attributional model of depression: A naturalistic extension. *Personality & Social Psychology Bulletin, 7(1),* 53–58.

Bartlett, F. C. (1932). *Remembering: A study in experimental and social psychology.* Cambridge: Cambridge University Press.

Bartoshuk, L. M. (1990, August-September). Psychophysiological insights on taste. *Science Agenda,* 12–13.

Bartoshuk, L. M. (1993). The biological basis of food perception and acceptance. *Food Quality and Preference, 4,* 21–32.

Bartoshuk, L. M., Duffy, V. B., & Miller, I. J. (1992). PTC/PROP tasting: Anatomy, psychophysics and sex effects. *Physiology and Behavior, 51.*

Basseches, M. (1984). *Dialectical thinking and adult development.* Norwood, NJ: Ablex.

Bateson, G., Jackson, D. D., Haley, J., & Weakland, J. H. (1956). Toward a theory of schizophrenia. *Behavioral Science, 1,* 251–264.

Baum, W. M. (1994). *Understanding behaviorism: Science, behavior, and culture.* New York: HarperCollins.

Baum, A. (1990). Stress, intrusive imagery, and chronic distress. *Health Psychology, 9,* 653–675

Baumeister, R. F., & Leary, M. R. (1995). The need to belong: Desire for interpersonal attachments as a fundamental human motivation. *Psychological Bulletin, 117,* 427–529.

Baumeister, R. F., Stillwell, A. M., & Hetherington, T. F. (1994). Guilt: An interpersonal approach. *Psychological Bulletin, 115 (2),* 243–267.

Bazerman, M. H. (1990). *Judgment in managerial decision making* (2nd ed.). New York: Wiley.

Beall, A. E., & Sternberg, R. J. (1995). The social construction of love. *Journal of Social and Personal Relationships, 12 (3),* 417–438.

Beardslee, W. R., & Mack, J. E. (1983). Adolescents and the threat of nuclear war: The evolution of a perspective. *Yale Journal of Biological Medicine, 56(2),* 79–91.

Beck, A. T. (1976). *Cognitive therapy and emotional disorders.* New York: International Universities Press.

Beck, A. T. (1983). Cognitive theory of depression: New perspectives. In P. J. Clayton, & J. E. Barrett (Eds.), *Treatment of depression: Old controversies and new approaches* (pp. 265–290). New York: Raven Press.

Beck, A. T. (1985). Cognitive therapy. In H. I. Kaplan & J. Sandock (Eds.), *Comprehensive textbook of psychiatry* (4th ed.). Baltimore: Williams & Wilkins.

Beck, A. T. (1988). Cognitive approaches to panic disorders: Theory and therapy. In S. Rachman & J. D. Maser (Eds.), *Panic: Psychological perspectives.* New York: Guilford Press.

Beck, A. T., & Emery, G. (1985). *Anxiety disorders and phobias: A cognitive perspective.* New York: Basic Books.

Beck, A. T., Rush, A. J., Shaw, B. F., & Emery, G. (1979). *Cognitive therapy of depression.* New York: Guilford Press.

Beck, J. (Ed.). (1982). *Organization and representation in perception.* Hillsdale, NJ: Erlbaum.

Beck, M. (1995). Flummoxing the Feds. *Newsweek, Vol. CXXVI, No. 2* (July 10), 44–45.

Bee, H. (1994). *Lifespan development.* New York: HarperCollins.

Begg, I., & Paivio, A. V. (1969). Concreteness and imagery in sentence meaning. *Journal of Verbal Learning and Behavior, 8,* 821–827.

Begley, S. (1995). Lights of madness. *Newsweek, CXXVI (21),* November 20, pp. 76–77.

Begley, S., & Biddle, N. (1996). For the obsessed, the mind can fix the brain. *Newsweek, Vol. CXXVII (9),* p. 60.

Belk, R. W. (1988). Possessions and the extended self. *Journal of Consumer Research, 15,* 139–168.

Bell, A. P., Weinberg, M. S., & Hammersmith, S. K. (1981). *Sexual preference.* Bloomington: Indiana University Press.

Bell, I. R. (1982). *Clinical ecology.* Bolinas, CA: Common Knowledge Press.

Bellak, L. (Ed.). (1979). *Disorders of the schizophrenic syndrome.* New York: Basic Books.

Bem, D. J., & Allen, A. (1974). On predicting some of the people some of the time: The search for cross-situational consistencies in behavior. *Psychological Review, 81(6),* 506–520.

Benedict, R. (1959). *Patterns of culture.* Boston: Houghton Mifflin.

Benjamin, J., Li, L., Patterson, C., Greenberg, B. D., Murphy, D. L., & Hamer, D. H. (1996). Population and familial association between the D4 dopamine receptor and measures of novelty seeking. *Nature Genetics, 12* (1) (January 1996), pp. 81–84.

Benson, H. (1975). *The relaxation response.* New York: Morrow.

Berenbaum, H., & Connelly, J. (1993). The effect of stress on hedonic capacity. *Journal of Abnormal Psychology, 102,* 474–481.

Berk, L. S., Ian, S. A., Fry, W. F., Napier, B. J., Lee, J. W., Hubbard, R. W., Lewis, J. E., & Eby, W. C. (1989). Neuroendocrine and stress hormone changes during mirthful laughter. *American Journal of Medicine Science, 298,* 390–396.

Berkowitz, L. (1993) *Aggression: Its causes, consequences, and control.* New York: McGraw-Hill.

Berkman, L. F., & Syme, S. L. (1979). Social networks, host resistance, and mortality: A nine-year follow-up study of Alameda County residents. *American Journal of Epidemiology, 109,* 186–204.

Berlyne, D. E. (1960). *Conflict, arousal, and curiosity.* New York: McGraw-Hill.

Berman, A. L., & Jobes, D. A. (1991). *Adolescent suicide.* Washington, DC: American Psychological Association.

Bernard, L. L. (1924). *Instinct.* New York: Holt, Rinehart & Winston.

Berndt, T. J. (1979). Developmental changes in conformity to peers and parents. *Developmental Psychology, 15,* 608–616.

Berndt, T. J. (1992). Friendship and friends' influence in adolescence. *Current Directions in Psychological Science, 1,* 156–159.

Bernstein, I. L. (1988). What does learning have to do with weight loss and cancer? *Proceedings of the Science and Public Policy Seminar of the Federation of Behavioral, Psychological and Cognitive Sciences.* Washington, DC.

Bernstein, I. L. (1991). Aversion conditioning in response to cancer and cancer treatment. *Clinical Psychology Review, 11,* 185–191.

Bernstein, I. L. (1990). Salt preference and development. *Developmental Psychology, 26,* 552–554.

Berry, J. (1992). Cree conceptions of cognitive competence. *International Journal of Psychology, 27,* 73–88.

Berscheid, E., & Hatfield, E. (1969). *Interpersonal attraction.* Reading, MA: Addison-Wesley.

Berscheid, E., & Hatfield, E. (1978). *Interpersonal attraction,* 2nd edition. Reading, MA: Addison-Wesley.

Berscheid, E. (1988). Some comments on love's anatomy: or, Whatever happened to old-fashioned lust? In R. J. Sternberg & M. L. Barnes (Eds.), *The psychology of love.* New Haven, CT: Yale University Press.

Bianchi, A. (1992, September–October). Dream chemistry. *Harvard Magazine,* 21–22.

Biederman, I. (1989). Higher-level vision. In D. N. Osherson, H. Sasnik, S. Kosslyn, K. Hollerbach, E. Smith, & N. Block (Eds.), *An invitation to cognitive science.* Cambridge, MA: MIT Press.

Bielski, R. J., & Friedel, R. O. (1977). Subtypes of depression, diagnosis and medical management. *Western Journal of Medicine, 126,* 347–352.

Billings, A. G., & Moos, R. H. (1982). Family environments and adaptation: A clinically applicable typology. *American Journal of Family Therapy, 10,* 26–38.

Binet, A. (1911). *Les idées modernes sur les enfants.* Paris: Flammarion.

Blacher, R. S. (1987). General surgery and anesthesia: The emotional experience. In R. S. Blacher (Ed.), *The psychological experience of surgery* (pp. 9–14). New York: Wiley.

Blakeslee, S. (1994). New ideas on mystery of how anesthetics work. *The New York Times,* August 30, pp. B5, B9.

Blanchard-Fields, F. (1986). Reasoning on social dilemmas varying in emotional saliency: An adult developmental perspective. *Psychology and Aging, 1,* 325–333.

Blass, E. M. (1990). Suckling: Determinants, changes, mechanisms, and lasting impressions. *Developmental Psychology, 26,* 520–533.

Blass, E. M., & Teicher, M. H. (1980). Suckling. *Science, 210,* 15–22.

Bleuler, M. (1978). The long-term course of schizophrenic psychoses. In L. C. Wynne, R.

L. Cromwell, & S. Mattysse (Eds.), *The nature of schizophrenia: New approaches to research and treatment* (pp. 631–636). New York: Wiley.

Blight, J. G. (1987). Toward a policy-relevant psychology of avoiding nuclear war: Lessons for psychologists from the Cuban missile crisis. *American Psychologist, 42,* 12–19.

Block, R. I., Ghoneim, M. M., Sum Ping, S. T., & Ali, M. A. (1991). Efficacy of therapeutic suggestions for improved postoperative recovery presented during general anesthesia. *Anesthesiology, 75,* 746–755.

Bloom, B., Asher, S. J., & White, S. W. (1978). Marital disruption as a stressor: A review and analysis. *Psychological Bulletin, 85,* 867–894.

Blum, K., Cull, J. C., Braverman, E. R., & Comings, D. E. (1996). Reward deficiency syndrome. *American Scientist, 84,* (March–April, 1996), 132–145.

Boldizar, J.P., Deemer, D.K., and Wilson, K.L. (1989). Gender, life experiences, and moral judgement development: A process-oriented approach. *Journal of Personality and Social Psychology, 57,* 229–238.

Bolger, N., DeLongis, A., Kessler, R. C., & Schilling, E. A. (1989). Effects of daily stress on negative mood. *Journal of Personality and Social Psychology, 57,* 808–818.

Bond, C. F., & Brockett, D. R. (1987). A social context-personality index theory of memory for acquaintances. *Journal of Personality and Social Psychology, 52,* 1110–1121.

Bongiovanni, A. (1977). A review of research on the effects of punishment in the schools. *Conference on Child Abuse,* Children's Hospital National Medical Center, Washington, DC.

Boone, D. E. (1994). Validity of the MMPI–2 depression content scale with psychiatric inpatients. *Psychological Reports, 74,* 159–162.

Booth, L. (1991). *When God becomes a drug: Breaking the chains of religious addiction and abuse.* Los Angeles: Jeremy P. Tarcher.

Bootzin, R. R. (1975). *Behavior modification and therapy: An introduction.* Cambridge, MA: Winthrop.

Bootzin, R. R., & Nicasio, P. M. (1978). Behavioral treatments for insomnia. In M. Hersen, R. Eisler, & P. Miller (Eds.), *Progress in behavior modifica-*

tion. New York: Academic Press.

Borkovec, T. D. (1982). Insomnia. *Journal of Consulting and Clinical Psychology, 50,* 880–985.

Bornstein, P.A., & Quinna, K. (Eds.). (1988). *Teaching a psychology of people: Resources for gender and sociocultural awareness.* Washington, DC: American Psychological Association.

Borod, C., Koff, E., Lorch, M. P., Nicholas, M., & Welkowitz, J. (1988). Emotional and non-emotional facial behavior in patients with unilateral brain damage. *Journal of Neurological and Neurosurgical Psychiatry, 5,* 826–832.

Bouchard, T. J., Jr., & McGue, M. (1990). Genetic and environmental influences on adult personality: An analysis of adopted twins reared apart. *Journal of Personality, 58,* 263–295.

Bower, G. H. (1981). Mood and memory. *American Psychologist, 36,* 129–148.

Bower, S. A., & Bower, G. H. (1991). *Asserting yourself: A practical guide for positive change.* Reading, MA: Addison-Wesley. (Original work published 1976).

Bowers, K. S. (1983). *Hypnosis for the seriously curious,* 2nd edition. New York: Norton.

Bowlby, J. (1973). *Attachment and loss: Vol. 2. Separation, anxiety and anger.* London: Hogarth.

Boyd, J. H., & Weissman, M. M. (1981). Epidemiology of affective disorders: A reexamination and future directions. *Archives of General Psychiatry, 38,* 1039–1046.

Bradshaw, J. L. (1989). *Hemispheric specialization and psychological function.* New York: Wiley.

Braine, M. D. S. (1976). Children's first word combinations. *Monographs of the Society for Research in Child Development, 41* (Serial No. 164).

Bransford, J. D., & Franks, J. J. (1971). The abstraction of linguistic ideas. *Cognitive Psychology, 2,* 331–350.

Breggin, P. R. (1979). *Electroshock: Its brain disabling effects.* New York: Springer.

Breggin, P. R. (1991). *Toxic psychiatry.* New York: St. Martin's Press.

Breggin, P. R., & Breggin, G. R. (1994). *Talking back to Prozac.* New York: St. Martin's Press.

Brehm, S. S. (1992). *Intimate relationships*, 2nd edition. Boston, MA: McGraw-Hill.

Breland, K., & Breland, M. (1961). A misbehavior of organisms. *American Psychologist, 16*, 681–684.

Breland, K., & Breland, M. (1951). A field of applied animal psychology. *American Psychologist, 6*, 202–204.

Brenner, M. H. (1976). *Estimating the social costs of national economic policy: Implications for mental and physical health and criminal violence.* Report prepared for the Joint Economic Committee of Congress, Washington, DC: U.S. Government Printing Office.

Brewer, M.B., Dull, V., and Lui, L. (1981). Perceptions of the elderly: Sterotypes and prototypes. *Journal of Personality and Social Psychology, 41*, 656–670.

Brewer, M. B. (1979). In-group bias in the minimal intergroup situation: A cognitive-motivational analysis. *Psychological Bulletin, 86*, 307–324.

Brim, O. G., & Kagan, J. (1980). *Constancy and change in human development.* Cambridge: Harvard University Press.

Brislin, R. (1993). *Understanding culture's influence on behavior.* Fort Worth, TX: Harcourt Brace Jovanovich.

Brislin, R. (1974). The Ponzo illusion: Additional cues, age, orientation, and culture. *Journal of Cross-Cultural Psychology, 5*, 139–161.

Broadbent, D. E. (1954). The role of auditory localization in attention and memory span. *Journal of Experimental Psychology, 47*, 191–196.

Broadbent, D. E. (1958). *Perception and communication.* London: Pergamon Press.

Brody, R. V. (1986). Pain management in terminal disease. *Focus: A Review of AIDS Research, 1*, 1–2.

Brody, J. (1994). Personal health: Feeling sleepy in the middle of the day? You're probably not getting enough rest at night. *The New York Times*, January 26.

Broman, S. H., Nichols, P. I., & Kennedy, W. A. (1975). *Preschool IQ: Prenatal and early developmental correlates.* Hillsdale, NJ: Erlbaum.

Bronfenbrenner, U., & Ceci, S. J. (1994). Nature-nurture reconceptualized in developmental perspective: A bioecological model. *Psychological Review, 101*, 568–586.

Broverman, I. K., Vogel, S. R., Broverman, D. M., Clarkson, F. E., & Rosenkrantz, P. S. (1972). Sex-role stereotypes: A current appraisal. *Journal of Social Issues, 28*(2), 59–78.

Brown, A. M. (1990). *Human universals.* Unpublished manuscript, University of California, Santa Barbara.

Brown, C. C. (Ed.), (1984). *The many facets of touch.* Skillman, NJ: Johnson & Johnson.

Brown, L. B. (Ed.), (1993). *Religion, personality, and mental health.* New York: Springer Verlag.

Brown, R. (1986). *Social psychology: The second edition.* New York: The Free Press.

Bruch, H. (1978). *The golden cage: The enigma of anorexia nervosa.* Cambridge, MA: Harvard University Press.

Brumberg, J. J. (1988). *Fasting girls: The history of anorexia nervosa.* New York: Plume.

Bruner, J. S., Olver, R. R., & Greenfield, P. M. (1966). *Studies in cognitive growth.* New York: Wiley.

Bruner, J. S. (1973). *Beyond the information given.* New York: Norton.

Brunner, H. G., Nelen, M., Breakefield, X. O., Ropers, H. H., & van Oost, B. A. (1993). Abnormal behavior associated with a point mutation in the structural gene for monoamine oxidase A. *Science, 262*, 578.

Bryan, C. D. B. (1995). *Close encounters of the fourth kind: Alien abduction, UFOs, and the conference at MIT.* New York: Alfred A. Knopf.

Bryden, M. P. (1982). *Laterality: Functional asymmetry in the intact brain.* New York: Academic Press.

Buck, L., & Axel, R. (1991). A novel multigene family may encode odorant receptors: A molecular basis for odor recognition. *Cell, 65*, 175–187.

Buck, R. (1984). *The communication of emotion.* New York: Guilford.

Bullock, M. (1995). What's so special about a longitudinal study? *Psychological Science Agenda, 8*, 9–10.

Bulman, J. R., & Wortman, C. B. (1977). Attribution of blame and coping in the "real world": Severe accident victims react to their lot. *Journal of Personality and Social Psychology, 35*, 351–363.

Butcher, J. N., & Williams, C. L. (1992). *Essentials of MMPI-2 and MMPI-A interpretation.* Minneapolis: University of Minnesota Press.

Butler, R. N., & Lewis, M. I. (1982). *Aging and mental health: Positive psychosocial and biomedical approaches* (3rd ed.). St. Louis: Mosby.

Byne, W. (1995). The biological evidence challenged. *Scientific American, 270* (5), 50–55.

Byrne, D. (1981, August). Predicting human sexual behavior. G. Stanley Hall Lecture, meeting of American Psychological Association, Los Angeles, CA.

Cairns, R. B., & Valsinger, J. (1984). Child psychology. *Annual Review of Psychology, 35*, 553–577.

Calev, A., Nigal, D., Shapira, B., Tubi, N., Chazan, S., Ben-Yehuda, Y., Kugelmass, S., & Lerer, B. (1991). Early and long-term effects of electroconvulsive therapy and depression on memory and other cognitive functions. *Journal of Nervous and Mental Disorders, 179*, 526–533.

Campbell, A. (1981). *The sense of well being in America: Patterns and trends.* New York: McGraw Hill.

Campos, J. J., Barrett, K. C., Lamb, M. E., Goldsmith, H. H., & Stenberg, C. (1983). *Socioemotional development* (Vol. 2). New York: Wiley.

Candland, D. K. (1993). *Feral children and clever animals: Reflections on human nature.* New York: Oxford University Press.

Cann, A., Calhoun, L. G., Selby, J. W., & Kin, H. E. (Eds.). (1981). Rape. *Journal of Social Issues, 37* (Whole No. 4).

Cannon, W. B. (1927). The James-Lange theory of emotion: A critical examination and an alternative theory. *American Journal of Psychology, 39*, 106–124.

Cannon, W. B. (1929). *Bodily changes in pain, hunger, fear and rage* (2nd ed.). New York: Appleton-Century-Crofts.

Cannon, W. B. (1934). Hunger and thirst. In C. Murchison (Ed.), *A handbook of general experimental psychology.* Worcester, MA: Clark University Press.

Cannon, W. B., & Washburn, A. L. (1912). An explanation of hunger. *American Journal of Physiology, 29*, 441–454.

Cantor, N., & Kihlstrom, J. F. (1987). Social intelligence: The cognitive basis of personality. In P. Shaver (Ed.), *Review of personality and social psychology, Vol. 6* (pp. 15–34). Beverly Hills, CA: Sage.

Cantor, N., & Mischel, W. (1979). Traits as prototypes: Effects on recognition memory. *Journal of Personality and Social Psychology, 35*, 38–48.

Caplow, T. (1982). *Middletown families: Fifty years of change and continuity.* Minneapolis: University of Minnesota Press.

Caporeal, L. R. (1976). Ergotism: The Satan loosed in Salem? *Science, 192*, 21–26.

Caprara, G. V., Barbaranelli, C., Borgoni, L., & Perugini, M. (1993). The Big Five Questionnaire: A new questionnaire for the measurement of the five-factor model. *Personality and Individual Differences, 15*, 281–288.

Carducci, B. J., & Zimbardo, P. G. (1995). Are you shy? *Psychology Today, 28*, 34–40ff.

Carey, S. (1978). The child as word learner. In M. Halle, J. Bresnan, & G. A. Miller (Eds.), *Linguistic theory and psychological reality* (pp. 265–293). Cambridge, MA: MIT Press.

Carlsmith, J. M., & Gross, A. (1969). Some effects of guilt on compliance. *Journal of Personality and Social Psychology, 11*, 232–240.

Carlsson, A. (1978). Antipsychotic drugs, neurotransmitters, and schizophrenia. *American Journal of Psychiatry, 135*, 164–173.

Carmichael, L. (1970). The onset and early development of behavior. In P. H. Mussen (Ed.), *Carmichael's manual of child psychology* (3rd ed., Vol. 1). New York: Wiley.

Carpenter, G. C. (1973). Differential response to mother and stranger within the first month of life. *Bulletin of the British Psychological Society, 16*, 138.

Carson, R. C., Butcher, J. N., & Mineka, S. (1996). *Abnormal psychology and modern life*, 10th ed. New York: HarperCollins.

Carstensen, L. L. (1987). Age-related changes in social activity. In L. L. Carstensen & B. A. Edelstein (Eds.), *Handbook of clinical gerontology* (pp. 222–237). New York: Pergamon Press.

Carstensen, L. L. (1991). Selectivity theory: Social activity in life-span context. In K. W. Schaie (Ed.), *Annual Review of Geriatrics and Gerontology* (Vol. 11). New York: Springer.

Carstensen, L.L., and Freund, A.M. (1994). Commentary: The resilience of the aging self. *Developmental Review, 14*, 81–92.

Cartwright, R. D. (1984). Broken dreams: A study of the effects of divorce and depression on dream content. *Psychiatry, 47,* 251–259.

Cartwright, R. D. (1982). The shape of dreams. In *1983 Yearbook of Science and the Future.* Chicago: Encyclopaedia Britannica.

Cartwright, R. D. (1978). *A primer on sleep and dreaming.* Reading, MA: Addison-Wesley.

Carver, C. S., & Scheier, M. P. (1981). *Attention and self-regulation: A control theory approach to human behavior.* New York: Springer-Verlag.

Carver, C. S., Scheier, M. P., & Weintraub, J. K. (1989). Assessing coping strategies: A theoretically based approach. *Journal of Personality and Social Psychology, 56,* 267–283.

Casey, J. F., & Wilson, L. (1991). *The flock.* New York: Fawcett Columbine.

Castaneda, C. (1968). *The teachings of don Juan: A Yaqui way of knowledge.* New York: Washington Square Press.

Cattell, R. B. (1963). Theory of fluid and crystallized intelligence: A critical experiment. *Journal of Educational Psychology, 54,* 1–22.

Ceci, S. J., & Liker, J. K. (1986). A day at the races: A study of IQ, expertise, and cognitive complexity. *Journal of Experimental Psychology: General, 115,* 255–266.

Chamberlain, K., & Zika, S. (1990). The minor events approach to stress: Support for the use of daily hassles. *British Journal of Psychology, 81,* 469–481.

Chapman, P. D. (1988). *Schools as sorters: Lewis M. Terman, applied psychology, and the intelligence testing movement, 1890–1930.* New York: New York University Press.

Cherry, E. C. (1953). Some experiments on the recognition of speech, with one and with two ears. *Journal of the Acoustical Society of America, 25,* 975–979.

Chilman, C. S. (1983). *Adolescent sexuality in a changing American society* (2nd ed.). New York: Wiley.

Chomsky, N. (1957). *Syntactic structures.* The Hague: Mouton.

Chomsky, N. (1965). *Aspects of a theory of syntax.* Cambridge, MA: MIT Press.

Chomsky, N. (1975). *Reflections on language.* New York: Pantheon Books.

Christensen, A., & Jacobson, N. S. (1994). Who (or what) can do psychotherapy: The status and challenge of nonprofessional therapies. *Psychological Science, 5,* 8–14.

Churchland, P. M. (1995). *The engine of reason, the seat of the soul: A philosophical journey into the brain.* Cambridge, MA: MIT Press.

Chwalisz, K., Diener, E., & Gallagher, D. (1988). Autonomic arousal feedback and emotional experience: Evidence from the spinal cord injured. *Journal of Personality and Social Psychology, 54,* 820–828.

Clark, H. H., & Clark, E. V. (1977). *Psychology and language: An introduction to psycholinguistics.* New York: Harcourt Brace Jovanovich.

Clark, E.V. (1983). Meanings and concepts. In J.H. Flavell & E.M. Markman (Eds.), *Handbook of child psychology: Cognitive development* (Vol. 3) (pp. 787–840). New York: Wiley.

Clark, E.V. (1987). The principal of contrast: A constraint on language acquisition. In B. MacWhinney (Ed.), *Mechanisms of language acquisition* (pp. 1–34). Hillsdale, NJ: Erlbaum.

Clark, K., & Clark, M. (1947). Racial identification and preference in Negro children. In T. M. Newcomb & E. L. Hartley (Eds.), *Readings in social psychology.* New York: Holt.

Clausen, J. A. (1981). Stigma and mental disorder: Phenomena and mental terminology. *Psychiatry, 44,* 287–296.

Cleek, M. B., & Pearson, T. A. (1985). Perceived causes of divorce: An analysis of interrelationships. *Journal of Marriage and the Family, 47,* 179–191.

Cloninger, C. R., Adolfsson, R., & Svrakic, N. M. (1996). Mapping genes for human personality. *Nature Genetics, 12* (1) (January 1996), pp. 3–4.

Clopton, N.A., and Sorell, G.T. (1993). Gender differences in moral reasoning: Stable or situational? *Psychology of Women Quarterly, 17,* 85–101.

Cobb, S. (1976). Social support as a moderator of stress. *Psychosomatic Medicine, 35,* 375–389.

Cohen, R. E., & Ahearn, F. L., Jr. (1980). *Handbook for mental health care of disaster victims.* Baltimore: Johns Hopkins University Press.

Cohen, S., & McKay, G. (1983). Social support, stress, and the buffering hypotheses: A theoretical analysis. In A. Baum, S. E. Taylor, & J. Singer (Eds.), *Handbook of psychology and health* (Vol. 4). Hillsdale, NJ: Erlbaum.

Cohen, S., & Syme, S. L. (Eds.). (1985). *Social support and health.* Orlando, FL: Academic Press.

Coleman, L. (1987). *Suicide clusters.* Winchester, MA: Faber & Faber.

Collins, N. L., & Read, S. J. (1990). Adult attachment, working models, and relationship quality in dating couples. *Journal of Personality and Social Psychology, 58,* 644–663.

Colman, A. M. (1987). *Facts, fallacies, and frauds in psychology.* London: Hutchinson.

Conger, J. C., & Keane, S. P. (1981). Social skills intervention in the treatment of isolated or withdrawn children. *Psychological Bulletin, 90,* 478–495.

Conger, J. J., & Peterson, A. C. (1984). *Adolescence and youth,* 3rd edition. New York: Harper & Row.

Conrad, R. (1964). Acoustic confusions in immediate memory. *British Journal of Psychology, 55,* 75–84.

Consumer Reports. (1995, November). Mental health: Does therapy help? 734–739.

Conway, J. K. (1992). *Written by herself: Autobiographies of American women: An anthology.* New York: Vintage.

Cook, M., Mineka, S., Wolkenstein, B., & Laitsch, K. (1985). Observational conditioning of snake fear in unrelated rhesus monkeys. *Journal of Abnormal Psychology, 94,* 591–610.

Cookerly, J. R. (1980). Does marital therapy do any lasting good? *Journal of Marital and Family Therapy, 6,* 393–397.

Cooper, M. J., & Fairburn, C. G. (1993). Demographic and clinical correlates of selective information processing in patients with bulimia nervosa. *International Journal of Eating Disorders, 13*(1), 109–116.

Cornish, D. B., & Clarke, R. V. (Eds.). (1986). *The reasoning criminal: Rational choice perspective on offending.* New York: Springer.

Corr, C.A. (1993). Coping with dying: Lessons that we should and should not learn from the work of Elisabeth Kübler-Ross. *Death Studies, 17,* 69–83.

Costa, P. T., Jr., & McCrae, R. R. (1985). *The NEO personality inventory manual.* Odessa, FL: Psychological Assessment Resources.

Costa, P. T., Jr., & McCrae, R. R. (1992a). Four ways five factors are basic. *Personality and Individual Differences, 13,* 653–665.

Costa, P. T., Jr., & McCrae, R. R. (1992b). Revised NEO Personality Inventory (NEO-PI-R) and NEO Five-Factor Inventory (NEO-FFI) professional manual. Odessa, FL: Psychological Assessment Resources.

Cousins, N. (1979). *The anatomy of an illness as perceived by a patient: Reflections on healing and rejuvenation.* New York: Norton.

Cousins, N. (1983). *The healing heart.* New York: Norton.

Cousins, N. (1989). *Head first: The biology of hope.* New York: Dutton.

Covington, D. (1995). *Salvation on Sand Mountain: Snake handling and redemption in Southern Appalachia.* Reading, MA: Addison-Wesley.

Cowan, C.P., Cowan, P.A., Heming, G., Garrett, E., Coysh, W.S., Curtis-Boles, H., and Boles, A.J. (1985). Transitions to parenthood: His, hers and theirs. *Journal of Family Issues, 6,* 451–481.

Cowan, N. (1993). Activation, attention, and short-term memory. *Memory and Cognition, 21,* 162–167.

Cowan, P. A. (1988). Developmental psychopathology: A nine-cell map of the territory. In E. Nannis & P. A. Cowan (Eds.), *Developmental psychopathology and its treatment: New directions for child development* (No. 39, pp. 5–29). San Francisco: Jossey Bass.

Cowan, P., & Cowan, P. A. (1988). Changes in marriage during the transition to parenthood. In G. Y. Michaels & W. A. Goldberg (Eds.), *The transition to parenthood: Current theory and research.* Cambridge: Cambridge University Press.

Cowan, W. M. (1979). The development of the brain. In *The brain* (pp. 56–69). San Francisco: Freeman.

Cowles, J. T. (1937). Food tokens as incentives for learning by chimpanzees. *Comparative Psychology Monographs, 74,* 1–96.

Coyne, J. C., Wortman, C. B., & Lehman, D. R. (1988). The other side of support: Emotional overinvolvement and miscarried helping. In B. Gottlieb (Ed.), *Marshalling social support* (pp. 305–330). Newbury Park, CA: Sage.

Craik, K. (1943). *The nature of explanation.* Cambridge: Cambridge University Press.

Cranston, M. (1991). *The noble savage: Jean-Jacques Rousseau, 1754–1762.* Chicago: University of Chicago Press.

Crapo, L. (1985). *Hormones: The messengers of life.* Stanford, CA: Stanford Alumni Association Press.

Crick, F. (1994). *The astonishing hypothesis: The scientific search for the soul.* New York: Charles Scribner's Sons.

Crick, F., & Mitchison, G. (1983). The function of dream sleep. *Nature, 304,* 111–114.

Crocker, J., & Major, B. (1989). Social stigma and self-esteem: The self-protective properties of stigma. *Psychological Review, 96,* 608–630.

Crohan, S. E., Antonucci, T. C., Adelmann, P. K., & Coleman, L. M. (1989). Job characteristics and well-being at mid-life. *Psychology of Women Quarterly, 13,* 223–235.

Cross, S., & Markus, H. (1991). Possible selves across the life span. *Human Development, 34,* 230–255.

Crowder, R. G. (1976). *Principles of learning and memory.* Hillsdale, NJ: Erlbaum Associates.

Csikszentmihalyi, M. (1990). *Flow: The psychology of optimal experience.* New York: Harper & Row.

Csikszentmihalyi, M., Larson, R., & Prescott, S. (1977). The ecology of adolescent activity and experience. *Journal of Youth and Adolescence, 6,* 281–294.

Cumming, E., & Henry, W. F. (1961). *Growing old: The process of disengagement.* New York: Basic Books.

Dackman, L. (1986). Everyday illusions. *Exploratorium Quarterly, 10,* 5–7.

Dahlstrom, W. G., Welsh, H. G., & Dahlstrom, L. E. (1975). *An MMPI handbook, Vol. 1: Clinical interpretation.* Minnesota: University of Minnesota Press.

Daily Californian, The. (1995, July 7). "Unabomber letter targets Berkeley professor." Pp. 1, 6.

Dakof, G. A., & Taylor, S. E. (1990). Victims' perceptions of social support: What is helpful from whom? *Journal of Personality and Social Psychology, 58,* 80–89.

Daly, M., & Wilson, M. (1983). *Sex, evolution and behavior.* Boston: Willard Grant Press.

Damasio, H., Grabowski, T., Frank, R., Balaburda, A. M., & Damasio, A. R. (1994). The return of Phineas Gage: Clues about the brain from the skull of a famous patient. *Science, 264,* 1102–1105.

Dannefer, D., and Perlmutter, M. (1990). Development as a multidimensional process: Individual and social constituents. *Human Development, 33,* 108–137.

Darley, J. M., & Batson, C. D. (1973). From Jerusalem to Jericho: A study of situational and dispositional variables in helping behavior. *Journal of Personality and Social Psychology, 27,* 100–108.

Darley, J. M., & Latané, B. (1968) Bystander intervention in emergencies: Diffusion of responsibility. *Journal of Personality and Social Psychology, 8,* 377–383.

Darnton, R. (1968). *Mesmerism and the end of the Enlightenment in France.* Cambridge, MA: Harvard University Press.

Darwin, C. J., Turvey, M. T., & Crowder, R. G. (1972). The auditory analogue of the Sperling partial report procedure: Evidence for brief auditory stage. *Cognitive Psychology, 3,* 255–267.

Darwin, C. (1963). *On the origin of species.* London: Oxford University Press. (Original work published in 1859.)

Dattilio, F. M., & Padesky, C. A. (1990). *Cognitive therapy with couples.* Sarasota, FL: Professional Resource Exchange.

D'Augelli, A. R. (1993). Preventing mental health problems among lesbian and gay college students. *The Journal of Primary Prevention, 13,* 245–261.

Davidsen-Nielsen, M., & Leick, N. (1991). *Healing pain: Attachment, loss and grief therapy.* New York: Routledge.

Davidson, J. M. (1981). The psychobiology of sexual experience. In J. M. Davidson & R. J. Davidson (Eds.), *The psychobiology of consciousness* (pp. 271–331). New York: Plenum.

Davidson, R. J. (1984). Hemispheric asymmetry and emotion. In K. Scherer & P. Ekman (Eds.), *Approaches to emotion.* Hillsdale, NJ: Erlbaum.

Davidson, R. J. (1992). Anterior cerebral asymmetry and the nature of emotion. *Brain and Cognition, 20,* 125–151.

Davis, I. P. (1985). *Adolescents: Theoretical and helping perspec-*

tives. Boston: Kluwer-Nijhoff Publishing.

DeBoer, R. (1994). *Losing Jessica.* New York: Doubleday.

DeCasper, A. J., & Fifer, W. P. (1980). Of human bonding: Newborns prefer their mothers' voices. *Science, 208,* 1174–1176.

DeCasper, A.J., and Spence, M.J. (1986). Prenatal maternal speech influences newborns' perception of speech sounds. *Infant Behavior and Development, 9,* 133–150.

DeCharms, R. C., & Muir, M. S. (1978). Motivation: Social approaches. *Annual Review of Psychology, 29,* 91–113.

Deci, E. L., & Ryan, R. M. (1987). The support of autonomy and the control of behavior. *Journal of Personality and Social Psychology, 53,* 1024–1037.

Deci, E. L. (1975). *Intrinsic motivation.* New York: Plenum.

Delgado, J. M. R. (1969). *Physical control of the mind: Toward a psychocivilized society.* New York: Harper & Row.

Delisi, C. (1988). The human genome project. *American Scientist, 76,* 488–493.

DeLoache, J. (1987). Rapid change in the symbolic functioning of very young children. *Science, 238,* 1556–1557.

Delprato, D. J., & Midgley, B. D. (1992). Some fundamentals of B. F. Skinner's behaviorism. *American Psychologist, 47,* 1507–1520.

Dembrowski, T. M., & Costa, P. T., Jr. (1987). Coronary prone behavior: Components of the Type A pattern and hostility. *Journal of Personality, 55,* 211–235.

Dembrowski, T. M., Weiss, S. M., Shields, J. L. et al. (1978). *Coronary-prone behavior.* New York: Springer-Verlag.

Dement, W. C. (1976). *Some watch while some must sleep.* San Francisco: San Francisco Book Co.

Dement, W. C., & Kleitman, N. (1957). Cyclic variations in EEG during sleep and their relations to eye movement, body mobility and dreaming. *Electroencephalography and Clinical Neurophysiology, 9,* 673–690.

Deregowski, J. B. (1980). *Illusions, patterns and pictures: A cross-cultural perspective* (pp. 966–977). London: Academic Press.

DeRivera, J. (1984). Development and the full range of emotional experience. In C. Malatesta & C. Izard (Eds.),

Emotion in adult development (pp. 45–63). Beverly Hills: Sage.

DeToffol, B., Autret, A., Gaymard, B., & Degiovanni, E. (1992). Influence of lateral gaze on electroencephalographic spectral power. *Electroencephalography and Clinical Neurophysiology, 82,* 432–437.

Deutsch, J. A., & Deutsch, D. (1963). Attention: Some theoretical considerations. *Psychological Review, 70,* 80–90.

Deutsch, M., & Hornstein, H. A. (1975). *Applying social psychology.* Hillsdale, NJ: Erlbaum.

Deutsch, M., & Gerard, H. B. (1955). A study of normative and informational social influence upon individual judgment. *Journal of Abnormal and Social Psychology, 51,* 629–636.

Devanand, D. P., Verma, A. K., Tirumalasetti, F., & Sackheim, H. A. (1991). Absence of cognitive impairment after more than 100 lifetime ECT treatments. *American Journal of Psychiatry, 148,* 929–932.

Devanand, D. P., Sano, M., Tang, M.-X., Taylor, S., Gurland, B. J., Wilder, D., Stern, Y., & Mayeux, R. (1996). Depressed mood and the incidence of Alzheimer's disease in the elderly living in the community. *Archives of General Psychiatry, 53,* 175–182.

Devereux, G. (1981). Mohave ethnopsychiatry and suicide: The psychiatric knowledge and psychic disturbances of an Indian tribe. *Bureau of American Ethology* (Bulletin 175). Washington, DC: Smithsonian Institution.

DeWaal, F. (1982). *Chimpanzee politics: Power and sex among apes.* New York: Harper & Row.

Diamond, J. (1990). The great leap forward. *Discover* (Special Issue), pp. 66–77.

Diamond, D. (1989, Fall). The unbearable darkness of being. *Stanford Medicine,* pp. 13–16.

Dickman, H., & Zeiss, R. A. (1982). *Incidents and correlates of post-traumatic stress disorder among ex-Prisoners of War of World War II.* Manuscript in progress. Palo Alto, CA.: Veterans Administration.

Diener, E. (1984). Subjective well-being. *Psychological Bulletin, 95,* 542–575.

Diener, E. (in press, 1996). Traits are great, but not enough: Lessons from subjective well-being. *Journal of Research in Personality.*

Diener, E., & Diener, M. (1995). Cross-cultural correlates of life satisfaction and self-esteem. *Journal of Personality and Social Psychology, 68,* 653–663.

Diener, E., Sandvik, E., Seidlitz, L., & Diener, M. (1993). The relationship between income and subjective well-being: Relative or absolute? *Social Indicators Research, 28,* 195–223.

Dillbeck, M. C., & Orme-Johnson, D. W. (1987). Physiological differences between transcendental meditation and rest. *American Psychologist, 42* (9), 879–881.

Dillon, K. M., & Totten, M. C. (1989). Psychological factors affecting immunocompetence and health of breastfeeding mothers and their infants. *Journal of Genetic Psychology, 150,* 155–162.

Discovering Psychology. (1990). PBS Video Series. Washington, D.C.: Annenberg/CPB Project.

Dixon, R. A., Kramer, D. A., & Baltes, P. B. (1985). Intelligence: A life-span developmental perspective. In B. B. Wolman (Ed.), *Handbook of intelligence* (pp. 301–352). New York: Wiley.

Doane, J. A., Falloon, I. R. H., Goldstein, M. J., & Mintz, J. (1985). Parental affective style and the treatment of schizophrenia. *Archives of general psychiatry, 42,* 34–42.

Dohrenwend, B. P., & Shrout, P. E. (1985). "Hassles" in the conceptualization and measurement of life stress variables. *American Psychologist, 40,* 780–785.

Dohrenwend, B. S., & Dohrenwend, B. P. (1974). *Stressful life events: Their nature and effects.* New York: Wiley.

Dollard, J., & Miller, N. E. (1950). *Personality and psychotherapy.* New York: McGraw-Hill.

Dowling, J. E. (1992). *Neurons and networks: An introduction to neuroscience.* Cambridge, MA: Harvard University Press.

Draguns, J. (1980). Psychological disorders of clinical severity. In H. Triandis & J. Draguns (Eds.), *Handbook of cross-cultural psychology, Vol. 6: Psychopathology* (pp. 99–174). Boston: Allyn & Bacon.

Draguns, J. (1990). Applications of cross-cultural psychology in the field of mental health. In R. Brislin (Ed.), *Applied cross-cultural psychology* (pp. 302–324). Newbury Park, CA: Sage.

Drake, R. A. (1985). Lateral asymmetry of risky recommendations. *Personality and Social Psychology Bulletin, 11,* 409–417.

Drake, R. A., & Seligman, M. E. P. (1989). Self-serving biases in causal attributions as a function of altered activation asymmetry. *International Journal of Neuroscience, 45,* 199–204.

Driver, J., & Tipper, S. (1989). On the nonselectivity of "selective" seeing: Contrasts between interference and priming in selective attention. *Journal of Experimental Psychology: Human Perception and Performance, 15,* 304–314.

Duck S. (1982). A topography of relationship disengagement and dissolution. In S. Duck (Ed.), *Personal relationships 4: Dissolving personal relationships.* London: Academic Press.

Duck, S. (1992). *Human relationships,* 2nd edition. Newbury Park, CA: Sage.

Duncker, K. (1945). On problem solving. *Psychological Monographs, 58* (No. 270).

Dutton, D. G., & Aron, A. P. (1974). Some evidence for heightened sexual attraction under conditions of high anxiety. *Journal of Personality and Social Psychology, 30,* 510–517.

Dykema, J., Bergbower, K., & Peterson, C. (1995). Pessimistic explanatory style, stress, and illness. *Journal of Social and Clinical Psychology, 14,* 357–371.

Ebbinghaus, H. (1973). *Psychology: An elementary textbook.* New York: Arno Press. (Original work published 1908).

Ebstein, R. P., Novick, O., Umansky, R., Priel, B., Osher, Y., Blaine, D., Bennett, E. R., Nemanov, L., Katz, M., & Belmaker, R. H. (1996). Dopamine D4 receptor (D4DR) exon III polymorphism associated with the human personality trait of Novelty Seeking. *Nature Genetics, 12* (1) (January 1996), pp. 78–80.

Educational Testing Service. (1990a, October 31). Background on the new SAT-I and SAT-II. Announcement at the College Board National Forum.

Educational Testing Service. (1990b). *Manual and technical report for the School and College Ability Tests, Series III.* Menlo Park, CA: Addison-Wesley.

Edwards, A. E., & Acker, L. E. (1962). A demonstration of the long-term retention of a conditioned galvanic skin response. *Psychosomatic Medicine, 24,* 459–463.

Egeland, J. A., Gerhard, D. S., Pauls, D. L., Sussex, J. N., Kidd, K. K., Allen, C. R., Hostetter, A. M., & Housman, D. E. (1987). Bipolar disorders linked to DNA markers on chromosome 11. *Nature, 325,* 783–787.

Ehrlich, B. E., & Diamond, J. M. (1980). Lithium, membranes, and manic-depressive illness. *Journal of Membrane Biology, 52,* 187–200.

Eich, E., Reeves, J. L., & Katz, R. L. (1985). Anesthesia, amnesia, and the memory/awareness distinction. *Anesthesiology and Analgesia, 64,* 1143–1148.

Eisenberg, N., & Miller, , P. A. (1987). Empathy, sympathy, and altruism: Empirical and conceptual links. In N. Eisenberg & J. Strayer (Eds.), *Empathy and its development* (pp. 292–316). Cambridge, England: Cambridge University Press.

Ekman, P. (1984). Expression and the nature of emotion. In K. R. Scherer & P. Ekman (Eds.), *Approaches to emotion.* Hillsdale, NJ: Erlbaum.

Ekman, P., & Friesen, W. V. (1975). *Unmasking the face: A guide to recognizing emotions from facial clues.* Englewood Cliffs, NJ: Prentice-Hall.

Ekman, P., & Friesen, W. V. (1986). A new pan-cultural facial expression of emotion. *Motivation and Emotion, 10,* 159–168.

Elkin, I., Shea, M. T., Watkins, J. T., Imber, S. D., Sotsky, S. M., Collins, J. F., Glass, D. R., Pilkonis, P. A., Leber, W. R., Kocherty, J. P., Fiester, S. J. & Parloff, M. B. (1989). National Institutes of Mental Health treatment of depression collaborative research program: General effectiveness of treatments. *Archives of General Psychiatry, 46,* 971–982.

Elliott, J. (1977). The power and pathology of prejudice. In P. G. Zimbardo & F. L. Ruch, *Psychology and life* (9th ed., Diamond Printing). Glenview, IL: Scott, Foresman.

Ellis, A. (1962). *Reason and emotion in psychotherapy.* New York: Lyle Stuart.

Ellis, A., & Grieger, R. (1986). *Handbook of rational emotive therapy* (Vol. 2). New York: Springer.

Ellis, C. (1995). *Final negotiations: A story of love, loss, and chronic illness.* Philadelphia: Temple University Press.

Eme, R., Maisiak, R., & Goodale, W. (1979). Seriousness of adolescent problems. *Adolescence, 14,* 93–99.

Emmelkamp, P. M. G. (1986). Behavior therapy with adults. In S. L. Garfield & A. E. Bergin (Eds.), *Handbook of psychotherapy and behavior change* (pp. 385–442). New York: Wiley.

Emmelkamp, P. M. G., & Kuipers, A. (1979). Agoraphobia: A follow-up study four years after treatment. *British Journal of Psychology, 134,* 352–355.

Emmons, R. A. (1986). Personal strivings: An approach to personality and its subjective well being. *Journal of Personality and Social Psychology, 51,* 1058–1068.

Engle, G. L. (1976). The need for a new medical model: A challenge for biomedicine. *Science, 196,* 129–136.

English, H. B., & English, A. C. (1958). *A comprehensive dictionary of psychological and psychoanalytical terms: A guide to usage.* New York: David McKay.

Epstein, S., & Feist, G. J. (1988). Relation between self- and other-acceptance and its moderation by identification. *Journal of Personality and Social Psychology, 54,* 309–315.

Erikson, E. H. (1963). *Childhood and society* (2nd. ed.). New York: Norton.

Erikson, E. H. (1968). *Youth: Identity and crisis.* New York: Norton.

Estes, D., and Wellman, H.M. (1986). Early understanding of mental entities: A reexamination of childhood realism. *Child Development, 57,* 910–923.

Evans, C., & Richardson, P. H. (1988). Improved recovery and reduced post-operative stay after therapeutic suggestions during general anesthesia. *The Lancet, 2,* 491–493.

Evans, R. I., Rozelle, R. M., Mittelmark, M. B., Hansen, W. B., Bane, A. L., & Havis, J. (1978). Deterring the onset of smoking in children: Knowledge of immediate physiological effects and coping with peer pressure, media pressure, and parent modeling. *Journal of Applied Social Psychology, 8,* 126–135.

Exner, J. E., Jr. (1974). *The Rorschach: A comprehensive system: Vol. 1.* New York: Wiley.

Exner, J. E., Jr. (1978). *The Rorschach: A comprehensive system: Vol. 2: Current research and interpretation.* New York: Wiley.

Exner, J. E., Jr., & Weiner, I. B. (1982). *The Rorschach: A comprehensive system: Vol. 3: Assessment of children and adolescents.* New York: Wiley.

Eysenck, H. J. (1947). *Dimensions of personality.* London: Routledge and Kegan Paul.

Eysenck, H. J. (1952). The effects of psychotherapy: An evaluation. *Journal of Consulting Psychology, 16,* 319–324.

Eysenck, H. (1990). Biological dimensions of personality. In L. A. Pervin (Ed.), *Handbook of personality theory and research* (pp. 244–276). New York: Guilford Press.

Eysenck, H. J. (1992). Four ways five factors are not basic. *Personality and Individual Differences, 13,* 667–673.

Fallon, A., & Rozin, P. (1985). Sex differences in perceptions of desirable body states. *Journal of Abnormal Psychology, 84,* 102–105.

Faludi, S. (1995, September 5). The naked Citadel. *The New Yorker, Vol. LXX,* No. 27, pp. 62–81.

Fanslow, C. A. (1984). Touch and the elderly. In C. Caldwell Brown (Ed.), *The many facets of touch* (pp. 183–189). Skillman, NJ: Johnson & Johnson.

Fantz, R. L. (1963). Pattern vision in newborn infants. *Science, 140,* 296–297.

Farah, M. J. (1984). The neurological basis of mental imagery: A componential analysis. *Cognition, 18,* 245–272.

Farina, A. (1980). Social attitudes and beliefs and their role in mental disorders. In J. G. Rabkin, L. Gelb, & J. B. Lazar (Eds.), *Attitudes toward the mentally ill: Research perspectives* (pp. 35–37). Rockville, MD: National Institute of Mental Health.

Farina, A., Gliha, D., Boudreau, L. A., Allen, J. G., & Sherman, M. (1971). Mental illness and the impact of believing others know about it. *Journal of Abnormal Psychology, 77,* 1–5.

Farley, F. (1990, May). The Type T personality, with some implications for practice. *The California Psychologist, 23,* 29.

Farquhar, J. W., Maccoby, N., & Solomon, D. S. (1984). Community applications of behavioral medicine. In W. D. Gentry (Ed.), *Handbook of behavioral medicine* (pp. 437–478). New York: Guilford Press.

Featherman, D.L. (1980). Schooling and occupational careers: Constancy and change in worldly success. In O.G. Brim, Jr. and J. Kagan (Eds.), *Constancy and change in human development.* Cambridge, MA: Harvard University Press.

Fechner, G. T. (1860). *Elemente der Psychophysik.* Germany: Breitkopf und Hartel.

Fehr, B. (1988). How do I love thee? Let me consult my prototype. *Journal of Personality and Social Psychology, 55* (4), 557–579.

Fein, M. L. (1993). *I.A.M.: A common sense guide to coping with anger.* Westport, CT: Praeger/Greenwood.

Fernald, A., Taeschner, T., Dunn, J., Papousek, M., De Boysson-Bardies, B., & Fukui, I. (1989). A cross-cultural study of prosodic modification in mothers' and fathers' speech to preverbal infants. *Journal of Child Language, 16,* 477–501.

Festinger, L. (1957). *A theory of cognitive dissonance.* Stanford, CA: Stanford University Press.

Field, T. (1990). In *Discovering Psychology,* Program 4 [PBS video series]. Washington, DC: Annenberg/CPB Project.

Field, T. F., & Schanberg, S. M. (1990). Massage alters growth and catecholamine production in preterm newborns. In N. Gunzenhauser (Ed.), *Advances in touch* (pp. 96–104). Skillman, NJ: Johnson & Johnson Co.

Fields, H. L., & Levine, J. D. (1984). Placebo analgesia: A role for endorphins. *Trends in Neuroscience, 7,* 271–273.

Fiorito, G., & Scotto, P. (1992). Observational learning in *Octopus vulgaris. Science, 256,* 545–547.

Fish, J. M. (1973). *Placebo therapy.* San Francisco: Jossey-Bass.

Fisher, H. E. (1992). *Anatomy of love: The natural history of monogamy, adultery, and divorce.* New York: W. W. Norton and Company.

Fisher, R. J. (1982). *Social psychology: An applied approach.* New York: St. Martin's Press.

Fisher, S., & Greenberg, R. P. (1985). *The scientific credibility of Freud's theories and therapy.* New York: Columbia University Press.

Fishman, H. C. (1993). *Intensive structural therapy: Treating families in their social context.* New York: Basic Books.

Fiske, S. T., & Pavelchak, M. A. (1986). Category-based versus piecemeal-based affective response: Developments in schema-triggered affects. In R. M. Sorrentino & E. T. Higgins (Eds.), *The handbook of motivation and cognition: Foundations of social behavior* (pp. 167–203). New York: Guilford Press.

Fiske, S. T., & Taylor, S. E. (1991). *Social cognition.* New York: McGraw-Hill.

Flavell, J. H. (1985). *Cognitive development* (2nd ed.). Englewood Cliffs, NJ: Prentice-Hall.

Fleischman, P. R. (1973). [Letter to the editor concerning "On being sane in insane places"]. *Science, 180,* 356.

Fletcher, G. J. O., & Ward, C. (1988). Attribution theory and processes: A cross-cultural perspective. In M. H. Bond (Ed.), *The cross-cultural challenge to social psychology* (pp. 230–244). Newbury Park, CA: Sage.

Flood, R. A., & Seager, C. P. (1968). A retrospective examination of psychiatric case records of patients who subsequently committed suicide. *British Journal of Psychiatry, 114,* 433–450.

Flora, J. A. (1991, May). AIDS prevention among young people. *California Psychologist,* pp. 14, 18.

Fodor, J. (1983). *The modularity of mind.* Cambridge, MA: MIT Press.

Fogel, A. (1991). Movement and communication in human infancy: The social dynamics of development. *Journal of Human Movement Studies.*

Foley, V. D. (1979). Family therapy. In R. J. Corsini (Ed.), *Current psychotherapies* (2nd ed., pp. 460–469). Itasca, IL: Peacock.

Folkman, S. (1984). Personal control and stress and coping processes: A theoretical analysis. *Journal of Personality and Social Psychology, 46,* 839–852.

Folkman, S., Lazarus, R. S., Dunkel-Schetter, C., DeLongis, A., & Gruen, R. J. (1986). Dynamics of a stressful encounter: Cognitive appraisal, coping, and encounter outcomes. *Journal of Personality and Social Psychology, 50,* 992–1003.

Fong, G. T., & Markus, H. (1982). Self-schemas and judgments about others. *Social Cognition, 1,* 191–204.

Ford, C. S., & Beach, F. A. (1951). *Patterns of sexual behavior.* New York: Harper & Row.

Forest, D. V. (1976). Nonsense and sense in schizophrenic language. *Schizophrenia Bulletin, 2,* 286–381.

Foucault, M. (1975). *The birth of the clinic.* New York: Vintage Books.

Fowler, H. (1965). *Curiosity and exploratory behavior.* New York: Macmillan.

Frank, J. (1987). The drive for power and the nuclear arms race. *American Psychologist, 42,* 337–344.

Frank, J. (1990). In *Discovering Psychology,* Program 2 [PBS video series]. Washington, DC: Annenberg/CPB Project.

Frank, J. D., & Frank, J. B. (1991). *Persuasion and healing: A comparative study of psychotherapy,* 3rd edition. Baltimore: Johns Hopkins University Press.

Franklin, D. (1987, January). The politics of masochism. *Psychology Today,* pp. 52–57.

Fraser, S. (Ed.). (1995). *The bell curve wars: Race, intelligence, and the future of America.* New York: Basic Books.

Freeman, F. R. (1972). *Sleep research: A critical review.* Springfield, IL: Charles C Thomas.

Freud, S. (1914). *The psychopathology of everyday life.* New York: Macmillan. (Original work published 1904).

Freud, S. (1915). Instincts and their vicissitudes. In S. Freud, *The collected papers.* New York: Collier.

Freud, S. (1923). *Introductory lectures on psycho-analysis* (J. Riviera, Trans.). London: Allen & Unwin.

Freud, S. (1925). The unconscious. In S. Freud, *The collected papers* (Vol. 4). London: Hogarth.

Freud, S. (1953). *The interpretation of dreams.* New York: Basic Books. (Original edition published in 1900).

Frey, W. H., & Langseth, M. (1986). *Crying: The mystery of tears.* New York: Winston Press.

Frey, W. H., II, Hoffman-Ahern, C., Johnson, R. A., Lydden, D. T., & Tuason, V. B. (1983). Crying behavior in the human adult. *Integrative Psychiatry, 1,* 94–98.

Fridlund, A. J. (1990). Evolution and facial action in reflex, social motive, and paralanguage. In P. K. Ackles, J. R. Jennings, & M. G. H. Coles (Eds.), *Advances in psychophysiology.* Greenwich, CT: JAI Press.

Friedman, H. S. (Ed.). (1990). *Personality and disease.* New York: Wiley.

Friedman, H. S., & Booth-Kewley, S. (1988). Validity of the Type A construct: A reprise.

Psychological Bulletin, 104, 381–384.

Friedman, M., & Rosenman, R. F. (1974). *Type A behavior and your heart.* New York: Knopf.

Friend, R., Rafferty, Y., & Bramel, D. (1990). A puzzling misinterpretation of the Asch "conformity" study. *European Journal of Social Psychology, 20,* 29–44.

Frijda, N. (1986). *The emotions.* London: Cambridge University Press.

Frijda, N., Kuipers, P., & Peter Schure, E. (1986). Relations among emotion, appraisal, and emotional action readiness. *Journal of Personality and Social Psychology, 57,* 212–228.

Fromm, E., & Shor, R. E. (Eds.). (1979). *Hypnosis: Developments in research and new perspectives* (2nd ed.). Hawthorne, NY: Aldine.

Fry, W. F., Jr. (1986). Humor, physiology, and the aging process. In L. Nahemow, K. A. McCluskey-Fawcett, & P. E. McGhee (Eds.), *Humor and aging* (pp. 81–98). Orlando, FL: Academic Press.

Fujita, F., Diener, E., & Sandvik, E. (1991). Gender differences in dysphoria and well-being: The case for emotional intensity. *Journal of Personality and Social Psychology, 61,* 427–434.

Fuller, J. L. (1982). Psychology and genetics: A happy marriage? *Canadian Psychology, 23,* 11–21.

Furman, W., Rahe, D., & Hartup, W. W. (1979). Rehabilitation of socially withdrawn preschool children through mixed-aged and same-sex socialization. *Child Development, 50,* 915–922.

Furnham, A., & Bochner, S. (1986) *Culture shock: Psychological reactions to unfamiliar environments.* London: Methuen.

Gagnon, J. H. (1977). *Human sexualities.* Glenview, IL: Scott, Foresman.

Gallagher, J. M., & Reid, D. K. (1981). *The learning theory of Piaget and Inhelder.* Monterey, CA: Brooks/Cole.

Gallagher, W. (1994). How we become what we are. *The Atlantic Monthly,* 39–55.

Galluscio, E. H. (1990). *Biological psychology.* New York: Macmillan.

Galton, F. (1869). *Hereditary genius.* London: Macmillan.

Galton, F. (1884). Measurement of character. *Fortnightly Review, 42,* 179–185.

Galton, F. (1907). *Inquiries into human faculty and its development.* London: Dent Publishers. (Original work published 1883).

Garcia, J. (1993). Misrepresentations of my criticisms of Skinner. *American Psychologist, 48,* 1158.

Garcia, J., & Garcia y Robertson, R. (1985). Evolution of learning mechanisms. In B. L. Hammonds (Ed.), *Psychology and learning: 1984 Master Lecturers* (pp. 187–243). Washington, DC: American Psychological Association.

Garcia, J. (1990). Learning without memory. *Journal of Cognitive Neuroscience, 2,* 287–305.

Garcia, J., & Koelling, R. A. (1966). The relation of cue to consequence in avoidance learning. *Psychonomic Science, 4,* 123–124.

Gardner, H. (1985). *The mind's new science: A history of the cognitive revolution.* New York: Basic Books.

Gardner, H. (1983). *Frames of mind.* New York: Basic Books.

Garfinkel, P. E., & Garner, D. M. (1982). *Anorexia nervosa: A multi-dimensional perspective.* New York: Brunner/Mazel.

Garland, A., & Zigler, E. (1993). Adolescent suicide prevention: Current research and social policy implications. *American Psychologist, 48,* 169–182.

Garnets, L. D., & Kimmel, D. C. (Eds.). (1993). *Psychological perspectives on lesbian and gay male experiences.* New York: Columbia University Press.

Garnsey, S. M. (1993). Event-related brain potentials in the study of language: An introduction. *Language and Cognitive Processes, 8,* 337–356.

Gartner, J., Larson, D. B., Allen, G. D., & Gartner, A. F. (1991). Religious commitment and mental health: A review of the empirical literature. *Journal of Psychology and Theology, 19,* 6–25.

Gazzaniga, M. (1970). *The bisected brain.* New York: Appleton-Century-Crofts.

Gelman, S.A., & Wellman, H.M. (1991). Insides and essences: Early understandings of the non-obvious. *Cognition, 38,* 213–244.

Gerrig, R. J. (1993). *Experiencing narrative worlds.* New Haven, CT: Yale University Press.

Ghadirian, A. M., & Lehmann, H. E. (1992). *Environment and psychopathology.* New York: Springer.

Ghoneim, M. M., & Block, R. I. (1992). Learning and consciousness during general anesthesia. *Anesthesiology, 76,* 279–305.

Gibbs, N. (1993, August 16). In whose best interest? *Time, 142,* 44–50.

Gilbert, E. H., & DeBlassie, R. R. (1984). Anorexia nervosa: Adolescent starvation by choice. *Adolescence, 19,* 839–853.

Gilligan, C. (1982). *In a different voice: Psychological theory and women's development.* Cambridge, MA: Harvard University Press.

Gilovich, T. (1983). Biased evaluation and persistence in gambling. *Journal of Personality and Social Psychology, 44,* 1110–1126.

Gilovich, T. (1991). *How we know what isn't so: The fallibility of human reason in everyday life.* New York: The Free Press.

Gitlin, M. J. (1990). *The psychotherapist's guide to psychopharmacology.* New York: The Free Press.

Givens, D. B. (1983). *Love signals: How to attract a mate.* New York: Crown.

Glass, A. L., Holyoak, K. J., & Santa, J. L. (1979). *Cognition.* Reading, MA: Addison-Wesley.

Glass, D. C. (1977). *Behavior patterns, stress, and coronary disease.* Hillsdale, NJ: Erlbaum.

Goddard, C. R., & Stanley, J. R. (1995). Viewing the abusive parent and the abused child as captor and hostage: The application of hostage theory to the effects of child abuse. *Journal of Interpersonal Violence, 9,* 258–269.

Goddard, H. H. (1914). *The Kallikak family. A study of the heredity of feeble-mindedness.* New York: Macmillan.

Goddard, H. H. (1917). Mental tests and immigrants. *Journal of Delinquency, 2,* 243–277.

Goldfried, M. R., Greenberg, L., & Marmar, C. (1990). Individual psychotherapy: Process and outcome. *Annual Review of Psychology, 41,* 659–688.

Goldin-Meadow, S., & Mylander, C. (1990). Beyond the input given: The child's role in the acquisition of language. *Language, 66,* 323–355.

Goleman, D. (1995). *Emotional intelligence.* New York: Bantam Books.

Goodall, J. (1972). *In the shadow of man.* London: Collins.

Goodkind, M. (1989, Spring). The cigarette habit. *Stanford Medicine,* 10–14.

Goodman, F. D. (1971). Glossolalia and single-limb trances: Some parallels. *Psychotherapy and Psychosomatics, 19,* 92–103.

Goodman, F. D. (1969). Phonetic analysis of glossolalia in four cultural settings. *Journal for the Scientific Study of Religion, 8,* 227–239.

Gordon, L. (1990, September 2). Proposal to overhaul SAT to consider relevance, bias. *The Seattle Times/Post-Intelligencer.*

Gottesman, I. I. (1991). *Schizophrenia genesis: The origins of madness.* New York: Freeman.

Gottlieb, B. H. (Ed.). (1981). *Social networks and social support.* Beverly Hills, CA: Sage.

Gottlieb, B. H. (1987). Marshalling social support for medical patients and their families. *Canadian Psychology, 28,* 201–217.

Gottman, J., & Silver, N. (1994). *Why marriages succeed or fail.* New York: Simon and Schuster.

Gottman, J. M. (1994). *What predicts divorce?* Hillsdale, NJ: Erlbaum.

Gough, H. G. (1957). *California psychological inventory manual.* Palo Alto, CA: Consulting Psychology Press.

Gough, H. G. (1989). The California Psychological Inventory. In C. S. Newmark (Ed.), *Major psychological assessment inventories (Vol. 2).* Boston: Allyn & Bacon.

Gough, H. G. (1996). *California Psychological Inventory,* 3rd ed. Palo Alto, CA: Consulting Psychologists Press.

Gough, H. G. (1996). *CPI Manual.* Palo Alto, CA: Consulting Psychologists Press.

Gould, S. J. (1981). *The mismeasure of man.* New York: Norton.

Graf, P., Squire, L. R., & Mandler, G. (1984). The information that amnesic patients do not forget. *Journal of Experimental Psychology: Learning, Memory, and Cognition, 10* (1), 164–178.

Gray, C. R., & Gummerman, K. (1975). The enigmatic eidetic image: A critical examination of methods, data, and theories. *Psychological Bulletin, 82,* 383–407.

Gray, L. (1989, June). Quoted in M. Knaster, Paths to power. *East West,* pp. 42–50.

Gray, P. (1993, November 29). The assault on Freud. *Time, 142* (23), 46–51.

Greenberg, L. S., & Johnson, S. (1988). *Emotionally focused therapy for couples.* New York: Guilford.

Greene, B. (1985). A testing time. In B. Greene, *Cheeseburgers* (pp. 56–61). New York: Ballantine.

Greenfield, P.M., & Smith, J. H. (1976). *The structure of communication in early language development*. New York: Academic Press.

Greenwald, A. G. (1992). New Look 3: Unconscious cognition reclaimed. *American Psychologist, 47* (6), 766–779.

Guetzkow, H., Alger, C. F., Brody, R. A., Noel, R. C., & Snyder, R. C. (1963). *Simulation in international relations*. Englewood Cliffs, NJ: Prentice-Hall.

Guilleminault, C., Dement, W. C., & Passonant, P. (Eds.). (1976). *Narcolepsy*. New York: Spectrum.

Guilleminault, C. (1989). Clinical features and evaluation of obstructive sleep apnea. In M. Kryser, T. Roth, & W. C. Dement (Eds.), *Principles and practice of sleep medicine* (pp. 552–558). New York: Saunders Press.

Gummerman, K., Gray, C. R., & Wilson, J. M. (1972). An attempt to assess eidetic imagery objectively. *Psychonomic Science, 28,* 115–118.

Gunzenhauser, N. (Ed.). (1990). *Advances in touch. New implications in human development*. Skillman, NJ: Johnson & Johnson Co.

Gur, R. E., & Pearlson, G. D. (1993). Neuroimaging in schizophrenia research. *Schizophrenia Bulletin, 19, 337–353*.

Gurman, A. S., & Kniskern, D. P. (1978). Research on marital and family therapy: Progress, perspective, and prospect. In S. L. Garfield & A. E. Bergin (Eds.), *Handbook of psychotherapy and behavior change: An empirical analysis* (2nd ed.). New York: Wiley.

Gustafson, S.B., and Magnusson, D. (1991). *Female life careers: A pattern approach*. Hillsdale, NJ: Erlbaum.

Gynther, M. D., & Gynther, R. A. (1976). Personality inventories. In I. B. Weiner (Ed.), *Clinical methods in psychology*. New York: Wiley-Interscience.

Hacker, A. (1986, February 13). The decline of higher learning. *The New York Review*.

Hale, R. L. (1983). Intellectual assessment. In M. Hersen, A. E. Kazdin, & A. S. Bellack (Eds.), *The clinical psychology handbook* (pp. 345–376). New York: Pergamon.

Hall, C. (1953/1966). *The meaning of dreams*. New York: Harper & Row/McGraw-Hill.

Hall, C., (1951). What people dream about. *Scientific American, 184,* 60–63.

Hall, C., & Van de Castle, R. L. (1966). *The content analysis of dreams*. New York: Appleton-Century-Crofts.

Haney, C. (1982). Employment tests and employment discrimination: A dissenting psychological opinion. *Industrial Relations Law Journal, 5,* 1–86.

Haney, C., Banks, W. C., & Zimbardo, P. G. (1973). Interpersonal dynamics in a simulated prison. *International Journal of Criminology and Penology, 1,* 69–97.

Haney, C., & Zimbardo, P. G. (1977). The socialization into criminality: On becoming a prisoner and a guard. In J. L. Tapp & F. L. Levine (Eds.), *Law, justice and the individual in society: Psychological and legal issues* (pp. 198–223). New York: Holt, Rinehart & Winston.

Hanson, D., Gottesman, I., & Meehl, P. (1977). Genetic theories and the validation of psychiatric diagnosis: Implications for the study of children of schizophrenics. *Journal of Abnormal Psychology, 86,* 575–588.

Haring, M. J., Stock, W. A., & Okun, M. A. (1984). A research synthesis of gender and social class as correlates of subjective well-being. *Human Relations, 37,* 645–657.

Harlow, H. F. (1965). Sexual behavior in the rhesus monkey. In F. Beach (Ed.), *Sex and behavior*. New York: Wiley.

Harlow, H. F., & Harlow, M. K. (1966). Learning to love. *American Scientist, 54,* 244–272.

Harris, B. (1979). Whatever happened to Little Albert? *American Psychologist, 34,* 151–160.

Harris, G., Thomas, A., & Booth, D. A. (1990). Development of salt taste in infancy. *Developmental Psychology, 26,* 534–538.

Harrison, A. & Saeed, L. (1977). Let's make a deal: An analysis of revelations and stipulations in lonely hearts advertisements. *Journal of Personality and Social Psychology, 35,* 257–264.

Hart, R. A., & Moore, G. I. (1973). The development of spatial cognition: A review. In R. M. Downs & D. Stea (Eds.), *Image and environment*. Chicago: Aldine.

Hartmann, E. L. (1973). *The functions of sleep*. New Haven, CT: Yale University Press.

Harvey, J. H. (1996). *Embracing their memory: Loss and the social psychology of storytelling*. Boston: Allyn & Bacon.

Harvey, J. H., Town, J. P., & Yarkin, K. L. (1981). How fundamental is the fundamental attribution error? *Journal of Personality and Social Psychology, 40,* 346–349.

Harvey, J. H., Weber, A. L., Galvin, K. S., Huszti, H. C. and Garnick, N. N. (1986). Attribution in the termination of close relationships: A special focus on the account. In R. Gilmour and S. Duck (Eds.), *The emerging field of personal relationships* (Chapter 12: pp. 189–201). Hillsdale, NJ: Erlbaum.

Harvey, J. H., Weber, A. L., & Orbuch, T. L. (1990). *Interpersonal accounts: A social psychological perspective*. Cambridge, MA: Basil Blackwell.

Harvey, J. H., Weber, A. L., Yarkin, K. L. and Stewart, B. E. (1982). An attributional approach to relationship breakdown. In S. W. Duck (Ed.), *Personal relationships 4: Dissolving personal relationships* (Chapter 5, pp. 107–126). London: Academic Press.

Harvey, P. H., & Krebs, J. R. (1990). Comparing brains. *Science, 249,* 140–146.

Hass, A. (1979). *Teenage sexuality: A survey of teenage sexual behavior*. New York. Macmillan.

Hastorf, A. H., & Cantril, H. (1954). They saw a game: A case study. *Journal of Abnormal and Social Psychology, 49,* 129–134.

Hatfield, E. (1988). Passionate and compassionate love. In R. J. Sternberg & M. L. Barnes (Eds.), *The psychology of love*. New Haven, CT: Yale University Press.

Hatfield, E. & Rapson, R. (1993). *Love, sex, and intimacy: Their psychology, biology, and history*. New York: HarperCollins.

Hatfield, E., & Sprecher, S. (1986). *Mirror, mirror: The importance of looks in everyday life*. New York: State University of New York Press.

Hathaway, S. R., & McKinley, J. C. (1940). A multiphasic personality schedule (Minnesota): I. Construction of the schedule. *Journal of Psychology, 10,* 249–254.

Hathaway, S. R., & McKinley, J. C. (1943). *The Minnesota Multiphasic Personality Inventory*. Minneapolis: University of Minnesota Press.

Hayes-Roth, B., & Hayes-Roth, F. (1979). A cognitive model of planning. *Cognitive Science, 3,* 275–310.

Haygood, R. C., & Bourne, L. E., Jr. (1965). Attribute and rule-learned aspects of conceptual behavior. *Psychological Review, 72,* 175–195.

Haynes, S. G., & Feinleib, M. (1980). Women, work, and coronary heart disease: Prospective findings from the Framingham Heart Study. *American Journal of Public Health, 70,* 133–141.

Hazan, C., & Shaver, P. R. (1990). Love and work: An attachment-theoretical perspective. *Journal of Personality and Social Psychology, 59,* 270–280.

Hazan, C., & Shaver, P. R. (1992). Broken attachments: Relationship loss from the perspective of attachment theory. In T. L. Orbuch (Ed.), *Close relationship loss: Theoretical approaches*, (pp. 90–108). New York: Springer Verlag.

Hearst, E. (1988). Fundamentals of learning and cognition. In R. C. Atkinson, R. J. Herrnstein, G. Lindzey, & R. D. Luce (Eds.), *Stevens' handbook of experimental psychology: Vol. 2. Learning and cognition* (2nd ed., pp. 3–109). New York: Wiley.

Headey, B. & Wearing, A. (1992). *Understanding happiness: A theory of well-being*. Melbourne: Longman Cheshire.

Hebb, D. O. (1980). *Essay on mind*. Hillsdale, NJ: Erlbaum.

Hecht, A. (1986, April). A guide to the proper use of tranquilizers. *Healthline Newsletter,* pp. 5–6.

Heider, F. (1958). *The psychology of interpersonal relationships*. New York: Wiley.

Heinrichs, R. W. (1993). Schizophrenia and the brain: Conditions for a neuropsychology of madness. *American Psychologist, 48,* 221–233.

Helmes, E., & Reddon, J. R. (1993). A perspective on developments in assessing psychopathology: A critical review of the MMPI and MMPI-2. *Psychological Bulletin, 113,* 453–471.

Henderson, N. D. (1980). Effects of early experience upon the behavior of animals: The second twenty-five years of research. In E. C. Simmel (Ed.), *Early experiences and early behavior: Implications for social develop-*

ment (pp. 39–77). New York: Academic Press.

Hendrick, S. S., & Hendrick, C. (1992). *Liking, loving, and relating*, 2nd edition. Pacific Grove, CA: Brooks/Cole.

Henley, N. (1977). *Sexual politics: Power, sex, and nonverbal communication*. Englewood Cliffs, NJ: Prentice-Hall.

Herrnstein, R. J., & Murray, C. (1994). *The bell curve*. New York: Free Press.

Hersen, M., & Bellack, A. J. (1976). Assessment of social skills. In A. R. Ciminero, K. R. Calhoun, & H. E. Adams (Eds.), *Handbook of behavioral assessment* (pp. 509–554). New York: Wiley.

Hersh, S. M. (1971). *My Lai 4: A report on the massacre and its aftermath*. New York: Random House.

Herzog, D. B. (1992). Eating disorders: New threats to health. *Psychosomatics, 33*(1), 10–15.

Herzog, D. B., Keller, M. B., Strober, M., & Yeh, C. (1992). The current status of treatment for anorexia nervosa and bulimia nervosa. *International Journal of Eating Disorders, 12*(2), 215–220.

Heston, L. L. (1970). The genetics of schizophrenia and schizoid disease. *Science, 112*, 249–256.

Hetherington, E. M. (1987). Family relations six years after divorce. In K. Pasley & M. Ihinger-Tallman (Eds.), *Remarriage and stepparenting* (pp. 185–205). New York: Guilford.

Hetherington, E. M. (1988). Parents, children, and siblings: Six years after divorce. In R. A. Hinde & J. Stevenson-Hinde (Eds.), *Relationships within families* (pp. 311–331). Oxford: Clarendon Press.

Hetherington, E. M., & Parke, R. D. (1975). *Child psychology: A contemporary viewpoint*. New York: McGraw-Hill.

Hetherington, M. M., Spalter, A. R., Bernat, A. S., Nelson, M. L. et al. (1993). Eating pathology in bulimia nervosa. *International Journal of Eating Disorders, 13*(1), 13–24.

Hilgard, E. R. (1968). *The experience of hypnosis*. New York: Harcourt Brace Jovanovich.

Hilgard, E. R. (1973). The domain of hypnosis with some comments on alternative paradigms. *American Psychologist, 28*, 972–982.

Hilgard, E. R. (1980). Consciousness in contemporary psychology. *Annual Review of Psychology, 31*, 1–26.

Hilgard, E. R. (1987). *Psychology in America: A historical survey*. New York: Harcourt Brace Jovanovich.

Hill, C. T., Rubin, Z., & Peplau, L. A. (1976). Breakups before marriage: The end of 103 affairs. *Journal of Social Issues, 32*, 147–168.

Hilts, P. J. (1995). *Memory's ghost: The strange tale of Mr. M. and the nature of memory*. New York: Simon & Schuster.

Hinton, G. F., & Anderson, J. A. (1981). *Parallel models of associative memory*. Hillsdale, NJ: Erlbaum.

Hiroto, D. S. (1974). Locus of control and learned helplessness. *Journal of Experimental Psychology, 102*, 187–193.

Hirsch, J., Harrington, G., & Mehler, B. (1990). An irresponsible farewell gloss. *Educational Theory, 40*, 501–508.

Hobson, J. A. (1988). *The dreaming brain*. New York: Basic Books.

Hobson, J. A. (1992). A new model of brain-mind state: Activation level, input source, and mode of processing (AIM). In J. S. Antrobus & M. Bertini (Eds.), *The neuropsychology of sleep and dreaming*. Hillsdale, NJ: Erlbaum.

Hobson, J. A., & McCarley, R. W. (1977). The brain as a dream state generator: An activation-synthesis hypothesis of the dream process. *American Journal of Psychiatry, 134*, 1335–1348.

Hoffman, M. L. (1982). Development of prosocial motivation: Empathy and guilt. In N. Eisenberg (Ed.), *The development of prosocial behavior* (pp. 281–313). San Diego, CA: Academic Press.

Hoffman, M. L. (1987). The contribution of empathy to justice and moral judgment. In N. Eisenberg & J. Strayer (Eds.), *Empathy and its development* (pp. 47–80). New York: Cambridge University Press.

Hoffman, M. (1986). Affect, cognition, and motivation. In R. Sorrentino & E. Higgins (Eds.), *Handbook of motivation and cognition: Foundations of social behavior* (pp. 244–280). New York: Guilford.

Hofling, C. K., Brotzman, E., Dalrymple, S., Graves, N., & Pierce, C. M. (1966). An experimental study in nurse-physician relationships. *Journal of Nervous and Mental Disease*.

Hofstede, G. (1986). Cultural differences in teaching and learning. *International Journal of Intercultural Relations, 10*, 301–320.

Hofstede, G. (1991). *Cultures and organizations: Software of the mind*. London and New York: McGraw-Hill.

Holahan, C. J., & Moos, R. H. (1987). Personal and contextual determinants of coping strategies. *Journal of Personality and Social Psychology, 52*, 946–955.

Holden, C. (1978). Patuxent: Controversial prison clings to belief in rehabilitation. *Science, 199*, 665–668.

Holden, C. (1986). Depression research advances, treatment lags. *Science, 233*, 723–725.

Hollister, J. M., Laing, P., & Mednick, S. A. (1996). Rhesus incompatibility as a risk factor for schizophrenia in male adults. *Archives of General Psychiatry, 53*, 19–24.

Holmes, D. S. (1984). Meditation and somatic arousal: A review of the experimental evidence. *American Psychologist, 39*, 1–10.

Holmes, D. S. (1994). *Abnormal psychology*. New York: HarperCollins.

Holmes, T. H., & Masuda, M. (1974). Life change and stress susceptibility. In B. S. Dohrenwend & B. P. Dohrenwend, (Eds.), *Stressful life events: Their nature and effects* (pp. 45–72). New York: Wiley.

Holmes, T. H., & Rahe, R. H. (1967). The social readjustment rating scale. *Journal of Psychosomatic Research, 11*(2), 213–218.

Holtzworth-Munroe, A., & Jacobson, N. S. (1985). Causal attributions of marital couples: When do they search for causes? What do they conclude when they do? *Journal of Personality and Social Psychology, 48*, 1398–1412.

Homme, L. E., de Baca, P. C., Devine, J. V., Steinhorst, R., & Rickert, E. J. (1963). Use of the Premack principle in controlling the behavior of nursery school children. *Journal of the Experimental Analysis of Behavior, 6*, 544.

Hopkins, B., Jacobs, D., & Westrum, R. (1992). The UFO abduction syndrome. In The Roper Organization, *Unusual personal experiences: An analysis of the data from three national surveys*. Las Vegas, NV: Bigelow Holding Corporation.

Hopson, J. L. (1988, July-August). A pleasurable chemistry. *Psychology Today*, pp. 29–33.

Horevitz, R. (1994). Dissociation and multiple personality: Conflicts and controversies. In S. J. Lynn & J. W. Rhue (Eds.), *Dissociation: Clinical and theoretical perspectives* (pp. 434–462). New York: Guilford.

Horne, J. A. (1988). *Why we sleep: The functions of sleep in humans and other mammals*. Oxford: Oxford University Press.

Horney, K. (1937). *The neurotic personality of our time*. New York: Norton.

Horney, K. (1945). *Our inner conflicts: A constructive theory of neurosis*. New York: Norton.

Horney, K. (1950). *Neurosis and human growth*. New York: Norton.

Horvath, A. O., & Luborsky, L. (1993). The role of the therapeutic alliance in psychotherapy. *Journal of Consulting and Clinical Psychology, 61*, 561–573.

Houle, M. C. (1991). *Wings for my flight: The peregrine falcons of Chimney Rock*. Reading, MA: Addison-Wesley.

House, J. S., Landis, K. R., & Umberson, D. (1988). Social relationships and health. *Science, 241*, 540–545.

Hovland, C. I., Lumsdaine, A. A., & Sheffield, F. D. (1949). *Studies in social psychology in World War II—Vol. 3, Experiments in mass communication*. Princeton, NJ: Princeton University Press.

Hull, C. L. (1943). *Principles of behavior: An introduction to behavior theory*. New York: Appleton-Century-Crofts.

Hull, C. L. (1952). *A behavior system: An introduction to behavior theory concerning the individual organism*. New Haven, CT: Yale University Press.

Humphrey, T. (1970). The development of human fetal activity and its relation to postnatal behavior. In H. W. Reese & L. P. Lipsitt (Eds.), *Advance in child development and behavior* (Vol. 5). New York: Academic Press.

Hunt, E. (1983). On the nature of intelligence. *Science, 219*, 141–146.

Hunt, E. (1984). Intelligence and mental competence. *Naval Research Reviews, 36*, 37–42.

Hunt, J. M. (1982). Toward equalizing the developmental opportunities of infants and preschool children. *Journal of Social Issues, 38*(4), 163–191.

Hunt, W. A., Matarazzo, J. D., Weiss, S. M., & Gentry, W. D. (1979). Associative learning, habit, and health behavior.

Journal of Behavioral Medicine, 2, 111–123.

Hurlburt, R. T. (1979). Random sampling of cognitions and behavior. *Journal of Research in Personality, 13,* 103–111.

Huston, A. C., Donnerstein, E., Fairchild, H., Feshbach, N. D., Katz, P. A., & Murray, J. P. (1992). *Big world, small screen: The role of television in American society.* Lincoln, NE: University of Nebraska Press.

Hyman, I. A., McDowell, E., & Raines, B. (1977). Corporal punishment and alternatives in the schools: An overview of theoretical and practical issues. In J. H. Wise (Ed.), *Proceedings: Conference on corporal punishment in the schools* (pp. 1–18). Washington, DC: National Institute of Education.

Ickes, W., & Layden, M. A. (1978). Attributional styles. In J. H. Harvey, W. Ickes, & R. F. Kidd (Eds.), *New directions in attributional research (Vol. 2).* Hillsdale, NJ: Erlbaum.

Inglehart, R. (1990). *Culture shift in advanced industrial society.* Princeton, NJ: Princeton University Press.

Insel, P. L., & Roth, W. T. (1985). *Core concepts in health.* Palo Alto, CA: Mayfield.

Insko, C. A., Smith, R. A., Alicke, M. D., Wade, J., & Taylor, S. (1985). Conformity and group size: The concern with being right and the concern with being liked. *Personality and Social Psychology Bulletin, 11,* 41–50.

Insko, C. A., Thibaut, J. W., Moehle, D., Wilson, M., Diamond, W. D., Gilmore, R., Solomon, M. R., & Lipsitz, A. (1980). Social evolution and the emergence of leadership. *Journal of Personality and Social Psychology, 39,* 431–448.

Irwin, M., Daniels, M., Smith, T. L., Bloom, E., & Weiner, H. (1987). Impaired natural killer cell activity during bereavement. *Brain Behavior Immunology, 1,* 98–104.

Isen, A. (1984). Toward understanding the role of affect in cognition. In R. Wyer & T. Srull (Eds.), *Handbook of social cognition* (pp. 174–236). Hillsdale, NJ: Erlbaum.

Itard, J. M. G. (1962). *The wild boy of Aveyron* (G. & M. Humphrey, Trans.). New York: Appleton-Century-Crofts.

Izard, C. E. (1977). *Human emotions.* New York: Plenum.

Izard, C. E. (Ed.). (1982). *Measuring emotions in infants and children.* New York: Cambridge University Press.

Jacobs, B. L. (1987). How hallucinogenic drugs work. *American Scientist, 75,* 386–392.

Jacobs, M. K., & Goodman, G. (1989). Psychology and self-help groups: Predictions on a partnership. *American Psychologist, 44,* 536–545.

Jacoby, L. L., Baker, J. G., & Brooks, L. R. (1989). Episodic effects of picture identification: Implications for theories of learning and theories of memory. *Journal of Experimental Psychology: Learning, Memory & Cognition, 15,* 275–281.

Jacoby, L. L., Woloshyn, V., & Kelley, C. (1989). Becoming famous without being recognized: Unconscious influences of memory produced by divided attention. *Journal of Experimental Psychology: General, 118 (2),* 115–125.

James, W. (1950). *The principles of psychology* (2 vols.). New York: Holt, Rinehart & Winston. (Original work published 1890).

Janis, I. L. (1958). *Psychological stress.* New York: Wiley.

Janis, I. L. (1982). Decisionmaking under stress. In L. Goldberger & S. Breznitz (Eds.), *Handbook of stress* (pp. 69–87). New York: Free Press.

Janis, I. L., & Frick, F. (1943). The relationship between attitudes toward conclusions and errors in judging logical validity of syllogisms. *Journal of Experimental Psychology, 33,* 73–77.

Janoff-Bulman, R. (1989). The benefits of illusions, the threat of disillusionment, and the limitations of inaccuracy. *Journal of Social and Clinical Psychology, 8,* 158–175.

Janoff-Bulman, R. (1992). *Shattered assumptions: Towards a new psychology of trauma.* New York: The Free Press.

Janowitz, H. D., & Grossman, M. I. (1950). Hunger and appetite: Some definitions and concepts. *Journal of the Mount Sinai Hospital, 16,* 231–240.

Janz, N. K., & Becker, M. H. (1984). The health belief model: A decade later. *Health Education Quarterly, 11,* 1–47.

Jenkins, C. D. (1976). Recent evidence supporting psychologic and social risk factors for coronary disease. *New England Journal of Medicine, 294,* 987–994, 1033–1038.

Jenkins, J. G., & Dallenbach, K. M. (1924). Oblivescence during sleep and waking. *The American Journal of Psychology, 35,* 605–612.

John, O. P. (1990). The "Big Five" factor taxonomy: Dimensions of personality in the natural language and in questionnaires. In L. A. Pervin (Ed.), *Handbook of personality: Theory and research,* (Chapter 3, pp. 66–100). New York: Guilford Press.

Johnson, C., & Connors, M. (1987). *The etiology and treatment of bulimia nervosa.* New York: Basic Books.

Johnson, E. I., & Tversky, A. (1983). Affect, generalization, and the perception of risk. *Journal of Personality and Social Psychology, 45,* 20–31.

Johnson, J. E. (1983). Psychological interventions and coping with surgery. In A. Baum, S. E. Taylor, & J. E. Singer (Eds.), *Handbook of psychology and health* (Vol. 4). Hillsdale, NJ: Erlbaum.

Johnson-Laird, P. (1983). *Mental models.* Cambridge, England: Cambridge University Press.

Johnson-Laird, P. N., & Byrne, R. M. J. (1989). Only reasoning. *Journal of Memory and Language, 28,* 313–330.

Johnston, L. D., O'Malley, P. M., & Bachman, J. G. (1989). *Drug use, drinking, and smoking: National survey results from high school, college, and young adult populations, 1975–1988.* Rockville, MD: U.S. Department of Health and Human Services.

Joiner, T. E., Jr., & Schmidt, N. B. (1995). Dimensions of perfectionism, life stress, and depressed and anxious symptoms: Prospective support for diathesis-stress but not specific vulnerability among male undergraduates. *Journal of Social and Clinical Psychology, 14,* 165–183.

Jones, E. E. (1976). How do people perceive the causes of behavior? *American Scientist, 64,* 300–305.

Jones, E. E., Farina, A., Hastod, A. H., Markus, H., Miller, D. T., & Scott, R. A. (1984). *Social stigma: The psychology of marked relationships.* New York: Freeman.

Jones, E. E., & Harris, V. A. (1967). The attribution of attitudes. *Journal of Experimental Social Psychology, 3,* 2–24.

Jones, E. E., & Nisbett, R. E. (1971). *The actor and the observer: Divergent perceptions of the causes of behavior.* Morristown, NJ: General Learning Press.

Joyce, L. (1989, Fall). Good genes, bad genes. *Stanford Medicine,* pp. 18–23.

Julesz, B. (1982). Textons, the elements of texture perception and their interaction. *Nature, 290,* 91–97.

Jung, C. G. (1959). The concept of the collective unconscious. In *The archetypes and the collective unconscious, collected works* (Vol. 9, Part 1, pp. 54–74). Princeton, NJ: Princeton University Press. (Original work published 1936).

Jung, C. G. (1965). *Memories, dreams, reflections.* New York: Random House.

Jung, C. G. (1971). Psychological types [Bollingen Series XX]. *The collected works of C. G. Jung* (Vol. 6). Princeton: Princeton University Press. (Original work published 1923).

Jung, C. G. (1973). *Memories, dreams, reflections* (Rev. ed., A. Jaffe, Ed.). New York: Pantheon Books.

Kagan, J., Reznick, J. S., & Snidman, N. (1986). Temperamental inhibition in early childhood. In R. Plomin & J. Dunn (Eds.), *The study of temperament: Changes, continuities, and challenges.* Hillsdale, NJ: Erlbaum.

Kagan, J., Reznick, J. S., & Snidman, N. (1988). Biological basis of childhood shyness. *Science, 20,* 167–171.

Kagan, J., & Snidman, N. (1991). Infant predictors of inhibited and uninhibited profiles. *Psychological Science, 2,* 40–44.

Kagan, J., Snidman, N., Arcus, D., and Reznick, J.S. (1994). *Galen's prophecy: Temperament in human nature.* New York: BasicBooks.

Kahneman, D. (1973). *Attention and effort.* Englewood Cliffs, NJ: Prentice-Hall.

Kahneman, D. (1991). Judgment and decision making: A personal view. *Psychological Science, 2,* 142–145.

Kahneman, D., & Snell, J. (1990). Predicting utility. In R. Hogarth (Ed.), *Insights in decision making.* Chicago: University of Chicago Press.

Kahneman, D., Slovic, P., & Tversky, A. (Eds.). (1982). *Judgment under uncertainty: Heuristics and biases.* Cambridge, MA: Cambridge University Press.

Kahneman, K. (1992). Reference points, anchors, norms, and mixed feelings. *Organizational Behavior and Human Decision Processes, 51,* 296–312.

Kalat, J. W. (1984). *Biological*

psychology. (2nd ed.). Belmont, CA: Wadsworth.

Kalish, R. A. (1985). The social context of death and dying. In R. H. Binstock & E. Shanas (Eds.), *Handbook of aging and the social sciences* (pp. 149–172). New York: Van Nostrand Reinhold.

Kallmann, F. J. (1946). The genetic theory of schizophrenia: An analysis of 691 schizophrenic index families. *American Journal of Psychiatry, 103,* 309–322.

Kamil, A. C., Krebs, J., & Pulliam, H. R. (1987). *Foraging behavior.* New York: Plenum.

Kamin, L. J. (1974). *The science and politics of IQ.* Potomac, MD: Erlbaum.

Kamin, L. J. (1969). Predictability, surprise, attention, and condi-tioning. In B. A. Campbell & R. M. Church (Eds.), *Classical conditioning: A symposium.* New York: Appleton-Century-Crofts.

Kane, J. M., & Marder, S. R. (1993). Psychopharmacologic treatment of schizophrenia. *Schizophrenia Bulletin, 19,* 287–302.

Karlsen, C. F. (1987). *The devil in shape of a woman: Witchcraft in Colonial New England.* New York: W. W. Norton & Company.

Kasl, S. V., & Cobb, S. (1966). Health behavior and illness behavior: I. Health and illness behavior. *Archives of Environmental Health, 12,* 246–266.

Kassebaum, N. L. (1994). Head Start: Only the best for America's children. *American Psychologist, 49,* 1323–1326.

Kastenbaum, R. (1986). *Death, society, and the human experience.* Columbus, OH: Merrill.

Kazdin, A. E. (1986). Comparative outcome studies of psychotherapy: Methodological issues and strategies. *Journal of Consulting and Clinical Psychology, 54,* 95–105.

Kazdin, A. E. (1994). *Behavior modification in applied settings,* 5th edition. Pacific Grove: Brooks/Cole.

Keen, S. (1986). *Faces of the enemy: Reflections of the hostile imagination.* New York: Harper & Row.

Keesey, R. E., & Powley, T. L. (1975). Hypothalamic regulation of body weight. *American Scientist, 63,* 558–565.

Kelley, H. H. (1967). Attribution theory in social psychology. In D. Levine (Ed.), *Nebraska Symposium on Motivation* (Vol.

15). Lincoln, NE: University of Nebraska Press.

Kelley, H. H., Berscheid, E., Christensen, A., Harvey, J., Huston, T., Levinger, G., McClintock, E., Peplau, A., & Peterson, D. (1983). *Close relationships.* San Francisco: Freeman.

Kelly, G. A. (1955). *A theory of personality: The psychology of personal constructs* (2 vols.). New York: Norton.

Kelsoe, J. R., Ginns, E. I., Egeland, J. A., Gerhard, D. S., Goldstein, A. M., Bale, S. J., Pauls, D. L., Long, R. T., Kidd, K. K., Conte, G., Housman, D. E., & Paul, S. M. (1989). Reevaluation of the linkage relationship between chromosome 11p loci and the gene for bipolar affective disorder in the Old Order Amish. *Nature, 342,* 238–243.

Kelsoe, J. R., Kristbjanarson, H., Bergesch, P., Shilling, P., Hirsch, S., Mirow, A., Moises, H. W., Helgason, T., Gillin, J. C., & Egeland, J. A. (1993). A genetic linkage study of bipolar disorder and 13 markers on chromosome 11 including the D2 dopamine receptor. *Neuropsychopharmacology, 9,* 293–301.

Kendler, K. S., & Diehl, S. R. (1993). The genetics of schizophrenia: A current, genetic-epidemiologic perspective. *Schizophrenia Bulletin, 19,* 261–285.

Kennedy, S. H., & Garfinkel, P. E. (1992). Advances in diagnosis and treatment of anorexia nervosa and bulimia nervosa. *Canadian Journal of Psychiatry, 37*(5), 309–315.

Kessler, S. (1980). The genetics of schizophrenia: A review. In S. J. Keith & L. R. Mosher (Eds.), *Special report: Schizophrenia, 1980* (pp. 14–26). Washington, DC: U.S. Government Printing Office.

Kennedy, D. M. (1970). *Birth control in America: The career of Margaret Sanger.* New Haven, CT: Yale University Press.

Kessler, J. W. (1988). *Psychopathology of childhood* (2nd edition). Englewood Cliffs, NJ: Prentice Hall.

Kesner, R., & Olton, D. S. (1990). *The neurobiology of comparative cognition.* Hillsdale, NJ: Erlbaum Associates.

Kety, S. S., Rosenthal, D., Wender, P. H., Schulsinger, F., & Jacobsen, B. (1975). Mental illness in the biological and adoptive families of adopted

individuals who have become schizophrenic: A preliminary report based on psychiatric interviews. In R. R. Fieve, D. Rosenthal, & H. Brill (Eds.), *Genetic research in psychiatry* (pp. 147–165). Baltimore: Johns Hopkins University Press.

Kiecolt-Glaser, J. K., & Glaser, R. (1987). Psychosocial moderators of immune function. *Annals of Behavioral Medicine, 9,* 16–20.

Kiecolt-Glaser, J. K., Glaser, R., Shuttleworth, E. C., Dyer, C. S., Ogrocki, P., & Speicher, C. E. (1987). Chronic stress and immunity in family caregivers of Alzheimer's disease victims. *Psychosomatic Medicine, 49,* 523–535.

Kihlstrom, J. F. (1987). The cognitive unconscious. *Science, 237,* 1445–1452.

Kihlstrom, J. F. (1990). The psychological unconscious. In L. Pervin (Ed.), *Handbook of personality: Theory and research* (pp., 445–464. New York: Guilford Press.

Kihlstrom, J. F., Barnhardt, T. M., & Tartaryn, D. J. (1992). The psychological unconscious: Found, lost, and regained. *American Psychologist, 47,* 788–791.

Kihlstrom, J. F., Schacter, D. L., Cork, R. C., Hurt, C. A., & Behr, S. E. (1990). Implicit and explicit memory following surgical anesthesia. *Psychological Science, 1,* 303–306.

Kihlstrom, J. F., & Harackiewicz, J. M. (1982). The earliest recollection: A new survey. *Journal of Personality, 50,* 134–148.

Kimura, D. (1987). Are men's and women's brains really different? *Canadian Psychology, 28* (2), 133–147.

Kinsey, A. C., Pomeroy, W. B., & Martin, C. E. (1948). *Sexual behavior in the human male.* Philadelphia: Saunders.

Kinsey, A. C., Pomeroy, W. B., Martin, C. E., & Gebhard, P. H. (1953). *Sexual behavior in the human female.* Philadelphia: Saunders.

Kintsch, W. (1981). Semantic memory: A tutorial. In R. S. Nickerson (Ed.), *Attention and performance* (Vol. 8). Hillsdale, NJ: Erlbaum.

Kirkpatrick, L. A., & Shaver, P. R. (1992). An attachment-theoretical approach to romantic love and religious belief. *Personality and Social Psychology Bulletin, 18,* 266–275.

Klag, M. J., Whelton, P. K., Grim, C. E., & Kuller, L. H. (1991). The association of skin

color with blood pressure in U.S. blacks with low socioeconomic status. *Journal of the American Medical Association, 265,* 599–602.

Klagsbrun, F. (1985). *Married people: Staying together in the age of divorce.* New York: Bantam Books.

Klein, D. C., & Goldston, S. E. (Eds.). (1977). *Primary prevention: An idea whose time has come.* Washington, DC: U.S. Government Printing Office.

Klein, R. H. (1983). Group treatment approaches. In M. Hersen, A. E. Kazdin, & A. S. Bellack (Eds.), *The clinical psychology handbook.* New York: Pergamon Press.

Klein, K. E., & Wegmann, H. M. (1974). The resynchronization of human circadian rhythms after transmeridian flights as a result of flight direction and mode of activity. In L. E. Scheving, F. Halberg, & J. E. Pauly (Eds.), *Chronobiology* (pp. 564–570). Tokyo: Igaku.

Kleinke, C. (1975). *First impressions: The psychology of encountering others.* Englewood Cliffs, NJ: Prentice Hall.

Klerman, G. L. (1986). Historical perspectives on contemporary schools of psychopathology. In T. Millon & G. L. Klerman (Eds.), *Contemporary directions in psychopathology: Toward the DSM-IV* (pp. 3–28). New York: Guilford Press.

Klinger, E. (1987, May). The power of daydreams. *Psychology Today,* pp. 37–44.

Kobasa, S. O., Hilker, R. R., & Maddi, S. R. (1979). Who stays healthy under stress? *Journal of Occupational Medicine, 21,* 595–598.

Kobasa, S. O. (1984). How much stress can you survive? *American Health, 3,* 64–77.

Kochman, T. (1981). *Black and white styles in conflict and communication.* Chicago: University of Chicago Press.

Kohlberg, L. (1964). Development of moral character and moral ideology. In M. L. Hoffman & L. W. Hoffman (Eds.), *Review of child development research* (Vol. 1). New York: Russell Sage Foundation.

Kohlberg, L. (1981). *The philosophy of moral development.* New York: Harper & Row.

Köhler, W. (1925). *The mentality of apes.* New York: Harcourt Brace Jovanovich.

Kohn, A. (1991). *The brighter side of human nature: Altruism and empathy in everyday life.* New York: Basic Books.

Kolb, B. (1989). Development, plasticity, and behavior. *American Psychologist, 44,* 1203–1212.

Kolb, L. C. (1973). *Modern clinical psychiatry.* Philadelphia: Saunders.

Konner, M. J. (1977). Report in J. Greenberg, The brain and emotions. *Science News, 112,* 74–75.

Korkina, M. V., Tsivil'ko, M. A., Kareva, M. A., & Zhigalova, N. D. et al. (1992). Clinico-psychological correlates of mental rigidity in anorexia nervosa. *Journal of Russian and East European Psychiatry, 25(2),* 21–28.

Koss, M. P. (1985). The hidden rape victim: Personality, attitudinal, and situational characteristics. *Psychology of Women Quarterly, 9,* 193–212.

Koss, M. P., & Oros, C. J. (1982). Sexual experiences survey: A research instrument in vestigating sexual aggression and victimization. *Journal of Consulting and Clinical Psychology, 50,* 455–457.

Kosslyn, S. M. (1983). *Ghosts in the mind's machine: Creating and using images in the brain.* New York: Norton.

Kounios, J., & Holcomb, P. J. (1994). Concreteness effects in semantic processing: ERP evidence supporting dual-coding theory. *Journal of Experimental Psychology: Learning, Memory, and Cognition, 20,* 804–823.

Krackhow, A., & Blass, T. (1995). When nurses obey or defy inappropriate physician orders: Attributional differences. *Journal of Social Behavior and Personality, 10 (3),* 585–594.

Kramer, P. D. (1993). *Listening to Prozac: A psychiatrist explores antidepressant drugs and the remaking of the self.* New York: Viking.

Krasner, L. (1985). Applications of learning theory in the environment. In B. L. Hammonds (Ed.), *Psychology and learning: 1984 master lecturers* (pp. 51–93). Washington, DC: American Psychological Association.

Kraut, A. M. (1990). Healers and strangers: Immigrant attitudes toward the physician in America—A relationship in historical perspective. *Journal of the American Medical Association, 263,* 1807–1811.

Kübler-Ross, E. (1969). *On death and dying.* Toronto: Macmillan.

Kübler-Ross, E. (1975). *Death: The final stage of growth.* Englewood Cliffs, NJ: Prentice-Hall.

Kulik, J. A. (1983). Confirmatory attribution and the perpetuation of social beliefs. *Journal of Personality and Social Psychology, 44,* 1171–1181.

Kunda, Z. (1990). The case for motivated reasoning. *Psychological Bulletin, 108,* 480–498.

Kurtines, W., & Greif, E. B. (1974). The development of moral thought: Review and evaluation of Kohlberg's approach. *Psychological Bulletin, 8,* 453–470.

Labouvie-Vief, G. (1985). Intelligence and cognition. In J. E. Birren & K. W. Schaie (Eds.), *Handbook of the psychology of aging* (2nd ed., pp. 500–530). New York: Van Nostrand Reingold.

Lachman, R., Lachman, J. L., & Butterfield, E. C. (1979). *Cognitive psychology and information processing: An introduction.* Hillsdale, NJ: Erlbaum.

Lackner, J. R., & Garrett, M. (1973). Resolving ambiguity: Effects of biasing context in the unattended ear. *Cognition, 1,* 359–372.

Lambo, T. A. (1978). Psychotherapy in Africa. *Human Nature, 1(3),* 32–39.

Lampl, M., Veldhuis, J. D., & Johnson, M. L. (1992). Saltation and stasis: A model of human growth. *Science, 258,* 801–803.

Lang, F.R., & Carstensen, L.L. (1994). Close emotional relationships in late life: Further support for proactive aging in the social domain. *Psychology and Aging, 9,* 315–324.

Lang, P. J. (1995). The emotion probe. *American Psychologist, 50 (5),* 372–385.

Lang, P. J., & Lazovik, D. A. (1963). The experimental desensitization of a phobia. *Journal of Abnormal and Social Psychology, 66,* 519–525.

Langer, E. J., & Rodin, J. (1976). The effects of choice and enhanced personal responsibility for the aged: A field experiment in an institutional setting. *Journal of Personality and Social Psychology, 34,* 191–198.

Langs, R. (Ed.). (1981). *Classics in psychoanalytic technique.* New York: Jason Aronson.

Larson, R. (1989). Is feeling "in control" related to happiness in daily life? *Psychological Reports, 64,* 775–784.

Latané, B., & Darley, J. M. (1968). Group inhibition of bystander intervention in emergencies. *Journal of Personality and Social Psychology, 10,* 215–221.

Lazarus, R. S. (1976). *Patterns of adjustment* (3rd ed.). New York: McGraw-Hill.

Lazarus, R. S. (1981, July). Little hassles can be hazardous to your health. *Psychology Today,* pp. 58–62.

Lazarus, R. S. (1982). Thoughts on the relations between emotion and cognition. *American Psychologist, 37,* 1019–1024.

Lazarus, R. S. (1984). On the primacy of cognition. *American Psychologist, 39,* 124–129.

Lazarus, R. S. (1991a). Cognition and motivation in emotion. *American Psychologist, 46,* 352–367.

Lazarus, R. S. (1991b). Progress on a cognitive-motivational-relational theory of emotion. *American Psychologist, 46,* 819–834.

Lazarus, R. S., & Folkman, S. (1984). *Stress, appraisal, and coping.* New York: Springer.

Leask, J., Haber, R. N., & Haber, R. B. (1969). Eidetic imagery in children: II. Longitudinal and experimental results. *Psychonomic Monograph Supplements, 3 (3,* Whole No. 35).

Lee, M., Zimbardo, P. G., & Bertholf, M. (1977, November). Shy murderers. *Psychology Today,* pp. 68ff.

Leerhsen, C. (1990, February 5). Unite and conquer: America's crazy for support groups. *Newsweek,* pp. 50–55.

Lefcourt, H. M., Davidson, K., Shepherd, R., Phillips, M., Prkachin, K., & Mills, D. (1995). Perspective-taking humor: Accounting for stress moderation. *Journal of Social and Clinical Psychology, 14,* 373–391.

Leff, H. (1984). *Playful perception: Choosing how to experience your world.* Burlington, VT: Wakefront Books.

Leiter, M. P., & Maslach, C. (1988). The impact of interpersonal environment on burnout and organizational commitment. *Journal of Organizational Behavior, 9,* 297–308.

Lempert, H., & Kinsbourne, M. (1982). Effect of laterality of orientation on verbal memory. *Neuropsychologia, 20,* 211–214.

Lennon, R. T. (1985). Group tests of intelligence. In B. B. Wolman (Ed.), *Handbook of intelligence* (pp. 825–847). New York: Wiley.

Lepper, M. R. (1981). Intrinsic and extrinsic motivation in children: Detrimental effects of superfluous social controls. In U. A. Collins (Ed.), *Aspects of the development of competence: The Minnesota Symposium on Child Psychology* (Vol. 14, pp. 155–214). Hillsdale, NJ: Erlbaum.

Lepper, M. R., & Greene, D. (Eds.). (1978). *The hidden costs of reward.* Hillsdale, NJ: Erlbaum.

Lepper, M. R., Greene, D., & Nisbett, R. E. (1973). Undermining children's intrinsic interest with extrinsic reward: A test of the over-justification hypothesis. *Journal of Personality and Social Psychology, 28(1),* 129–137.

Lerner, M. J. (1980). *The belief in a just world: A fundamental delusion.* New York: Plenum.

Lerner, R. M., Orlos, J. R., & Knapp, J. (1976). Physical attractiveness, physical effectiveness and self-concept in adolescents. *Adolescence, 11,* 313–326.

Leslie, C., & Wingert, P. (1990, January 8). Not as easy as A, B, or C. *Newsweek,* pp. 56–58.

LeVay, S. (1991). A difference in hypothalamic structure between heterosexual and homosexual men. *Science, 253,* 1034–1037.

LeVay, S., & Hamer, D. (1995). Evidence for a biological influence in male homosexuality. *Scientific American, 270 (5),* 44–49.

Leventhal, H. (1980). Toward a comprehensive theory of emotion. In L. Berkowitz (Ed.), *Advances in experimental social psychology* (Vol. 13, pp. 139–207). New York: Academic Press.

Leventhal, H., & Tomarken, A. J. (1986). Emotion: Today's problems. *Annual Review of Psychology, 37,* 565–610.

Levi-Strauss, C. (1963). The effectiveness of symbols. In C. Levi-Strauss (Ed.), *Structural anthropology.* New York: Basic Books.

Levine, M. (1987, April). *Effective problem solving.* Englewood Cliffs, NJ: Prentice-Hall.

Levine, M., & Perkins, D. V. (1987). *Principles of community psychology: Perspectives and applications.* New York: Oxford University.

Levinson, B. W. (1967). States of awareness during general anesthesia. In J. Lassner (Ed.), *Hypnosis and psychosomatic medicine* (pp. 200–207). New York: Springer-Verlag.

Levy, S. (1996). Tangled up in Deep Blue. *Newsweek, Vol. CXXVII (9),* February 26, 1996; p. 51.

Lewin, R. (1987). The origin of the modern human mind. *Science, 236,* 668–670.

Lewine, R. R., Strauss, J. S., & Gift, T. E. (1981). Sex differences in age at first hospital admission for schizophrenia: Fact or artifact? *American Journal of Psychiatry, 138,* 440–444.

Lewinsohn, P. M. (1975). The behavioral study and treatment of depression. In M. Hersen, R. M. Eisler, & P. M. Miller (Eds.), *Progress in behavior modification* (pp. 19–64). New York: Academic Press.

Lewis, C. (1981). The effects of parental firm control: A reinterpretation of findings. *Psychological Bulletin, 90,* 547–563.

Lewy, A. J., Sack, R. L., Miller, S., & Hoban, T. M. (1987). Antidepressant and circadian phase-shifting effect of light. *Science, 235,* 352–354.

Liberman, R. P. (1982). What is schizophrenia? *Schizophrenia Bulletin, 8,* 435–437.

Lichtenstein, E. (1980). *Psychotherapy: Approaches and applications.* Pacific Grove, CA: Brooks/Cole.

Lieberman, L. R. (1973, April 3). [Letter to *Science* concerning "On being sane in insane places"]. *Science, 179.*

Liem, J. H. (1980). Family studies of schizophrenia: An update and commentary. In S. J. Keith & L. R. Mosher (Eds.), *Special report: Schizophrenia, 1980* (pp. 82–108). Washington, DC: U.S. Government Printing Office.

Liem, R., & Rayman, P. (1982). Health and social costs of unemployment: Research and policy considerations. *American Psychologist, 37,* 1116–1123.

Lindsay, D. S. (1990). Misleading suggestions can impair eyewitnesses' ability to remember event details. *Journal of Experimental Psychology: Learning, Memory, and Cognition, 16* (6), 1077– 1083.

Lindsay, D. S. (1993). Eyewitness suggestibility. *Current Directions in Psychological Science, 2,* 86–89.

Lindsley, D. B. (1951). Emotion. In S. S. Stevens (Ed.), *Handbook of experimental psychology.* New York: Wiley.

Linton, M. (1975). Memory for real-world events. In D. A. Norman & D. E. Rumelhart (Eds.), *Explorations in cognition* (Chapter 14). San Francisco: Freeman.

Lipsitt, L. P., Reilly, B., Butcher, M. G., & Greenwood, M. M. (1976). The stability and interrelationships of newborn sucking and heart rate. *Developmental Psychobiology, 9,* 305–310.

Locke, D. (1992). *Increasing multicultural understanding: A comprehensive model.* Newbury Park, CA: Sage.

Locke, J. L. (1994). Phases in the child's development of language. *American Scientist, 82,* 436–445.

Loehlin, J. C. (1992). *Genes and environment in personality development.* Newbury Park, CA: Sage.

Loehlin, J. C., Lindzey, G., & Spuhler, J. N. (1975). *Race differences in intelligence.* San Francisco: Freeman.

Loevinger, J. (1957). Objective tests as instruments of psychological theory. *Psychological Reports, 3,* 635–694.

Loftus, E. F. (1979). *Eyewitness testimony.* Cambridge, MA: Harvard University Press.

Loftus, E. F. (1980). *Memory.* Reading, MA: Addison-Wesley.

Loftus, E. F. (1984). The eyewitness on trial. In B. D. Sales & A. Alwork (Eds.), *With liberty and justice for all.* Englewood Cliffs, NJ: Prentice Hall.

Loftus, E. F. (1992). When a lie becomes memory's truth: Memory distortion after exposure to misinformation. *Current Directions in Psychological Science, 1,* 121–123.

Loftus, E. F. (1993). The reality of repressed memories. *American Psychologist, 48,* 518–537.

Loftus, E. F., & Ketcham, K. (1991). *Witness for the defense: The accused, the eyewitness, and the expert who puts memory on trial.* New York: St. Martin's Press.

Loftus, E. F., & Ketcham, K. (1994). *The myth of repressed memory: False memories and allegations of sexual abuse.* New York: St. Martin's Griffin.

Loftus, G. R., Duncan, J., & Gehrig, P. (1992). On the time course of perceptual information that results from a brief visual presentation. *Journal of Experimental Psychology: Human Perception and Performance, 18* (2), 530–549.

Logan, G. (1980). Attention and automaticity in Stroop and priming task: Theory and data. *Cognitive Psychology, 12,* 523–553.

London, K. A., Mosher, W. D., Pratt, W. F., & Williams, L. B. (1989, March). Preliminary findings from the National Survey of Family Growth, Cycle IV. Paper presented at the annual meeting of the Population Association of America, Baltimore, MD.

Long, B. C., & Kahn, S. E. (Eds.). (1993). *Women, work, and coping: A multidisciplinary approach to workplace stress.* Ottawa, Canada: McGill-Queen's.

Loomis, A. L., Harvey, E. N., & Hobart, G. A. (1937). Cerebral states during sleep as studied by human brain potentials. *Journal of Experimental Psychology, 21,* 127–144.

Los Angeles Times. (1988, February 23). Bullet in the brain cures man's mental problem.

Lott, A. J., & Lott, B. E. (1961). Group cohesiveness, communication level, and conformity. *Journal of Abnormal and Social Psychology, 62,* 408–412.

Lovell, J., & Kluger, J. (1994). *Lost moon (Apollo 13).* New York: Pocket Books.

Lovibond, S. H., Adams, M., & Adams, W. G. (1979). The effects of three experimental prison environments on the behavior of nonconflict volunteer subjects. *Australian Psychologist, 14,* 273–285.

Lynch, J. J. (1979). *The broken heart: The medical consequences of loneliness.* New York: Basic Books.

Maccoby, N., Farquhar, J. W., Wood, P. D., & Alexander, J. K. (1977). Reducing the risk of cardiovascular disease: Effects of a community-based campaign on knowledge and behavior. *Journal of Community Health, 3,* 100–114.

MacLean, H. N. (1993). *Once upon a time: A true story of memory, murder, and the law.* New York: HarperCollins.

Magee, W. J., Eaton, W. W., Wittchen, H.-U., McGonagle, K. A., Kessler, R. C. (1996). Agoraphobia, simple phobia, and social phobia in the national comorbidity survey. *Archives of General Psychiatry, 53,* 159–168.

Maher, B. A., & Ross, J. S. (1984). Delusions. In H. E. Adams & P. B. Sutker (Eds.), *Comprehensive handbook of psychopathology* (pp. 383–987). New York: Plenum.

Maher, B. A. (1968, November). The shattered language of schizophrenia. *Psychology Today,* pp. 30ff.

Maier, N. R. F. (1931). Reasoning in humans: II. The solution of a problem and its appearance in consciousness. *Journal of Comparative Psychology, 12,* 181–194.

Maier, S. F., & Seligman, M. E. P. (1976). Learned helplessness: Theory and evidence. *Journal of Experimental Psychology: General, 105,* 3–46.

Maier, S. F., Watkins, L. R., & Fleshner, M. (1994). Psychoneuroimmunology: The interface between behavior, brain, and immunity. *American Psychologist, 49,* 1004–1017.

Majewska, M. D., Harrison, N. L., Schwartz, R. D., Barker, J. L., & Paul, S. M. (1986). Steroid hormone metabolites are barbiturate-like modulators of the GABA receptor. *Science, 232,* 1004–1007.

Malamed, E., & Larsen, B. (1977). Regional cerebral blood flow during voluntary conjugate eye movements in man. *Acta Neurological Scandinavia, 56* (Suppl. 64), 530–531.

Malamuth, N. M. (1984). Aggression against women: Cultural and individual causes. In N. M. Malamuth & E. Donnerstein (Eds.), *Pornography and sexual aggression* (pp. 19–52). Orlando, FL: Academic Press.

Malitz, S., & Sackheim, H. A. (1984). Low dosage ECT: Electrode placement and acute physiological and cognitive effects. *American Journal of Social Psychiatry, 4,* 47–53.

Maloney, M. P., & Ward, M. P. (1976). *Psychological assessment: A conceptual approach.* New York: Academic Press.

Malony, H. N., & Lovekin, A. A. (1985). *Glossolalia: Behavioral science perspectives on speaking in tongues.* New York: Oxford University Press.

Manderscheid, R. W., Witkin, M. J., Rosenstein, M. J., Milazzo-Sayre, L. J., Bethel, H. E., & MacAskill, R. L. (1985). In C. A. Taube & S. A. Barrett (Eds.), *Mental Health, United States, 1985.* Washington, DC: National Institute of Mental Health.

Mandler, G. (1972). Helplessness: Theory and research in anxiety. In C. Spielberger (Ed.), *Anxiety: Current trends in theory and research* (pp. 359–374). New York: Academic Press.

Mandler, G. (1984). *Mind and body: The psychology of emotion and stress.* New York: Norton.

Manfredi, M., Bini, G., Cruccu, G., Accornero, N., Beradelli, A., & Medolago, L. (1981). Congenital absence of pain. *Archives of Neurology, 38,* 507–511.

Manschreck, T. C. (1989). Delusional (paranoid) disorders. In H. I. Kaplan & B. J. Sadock (Eds.), *Comprehensive textbook of psychiatry* (pp. 816–829). Baltimore: William & Wilkins.

Markus, H., & Cross, S. (1990). The interpersonal self. In L. A. Pervin (Ed.), *Handbook of personality theory and research* (pp. 576–608). New York: Guilford Press.

Markus, H., & Kitayama, S. (1991). Culture and self: Implications for cognition, emotion and motivation. *Psychological Review, 98,* 224–253.

Markus, H., & Smith, J. (1981). The influence of self-schemas on the perception of others. In N. Cantor & J. F. Kihlstrom (Eds.), *Personality, cognition, and social interaction* (pp. 233–262). Hillsdale, NJ: Erlbaum.

Marsh, P. (1988). Detecting insincerity. In Marsh, P. (Ed.), *Eye to eye: How people interact.* (Ch. 14, pp. 116–119). Oxford, England: Oxford Andromeda Ltd.

Marshall, G. D., & Zimbardo, P. G. (1979). Affective consequences of inadequately explained physiological arousal. *Journal of Personality and Social Psychology, 37,* 970–988.

Martin, J. A. (1981). A longitudinal study of the consequences of early mother-infant interaction: A microanalytic approach. *Monographs of the Society for Research in Child Development, 46* (203, Serial No. 190).

Marty, M. E. (1984). *Pilgrims in their own land: 500 years of religion in America.* Boston: Little, Brown and Company.

Maslach, C. (1979). Negative emotional biasing of unexplained arousal. *Journal of Personality and Social Psychology, 37,* 953–969.

Maslach, C. (1982). *Burnout: The cost of caring.* Englewood Cliffs, NJ: Prentice-Hall.

Maslow, A. H. (1970). *Motivation and personality* (Rev. ed.). New York: Harper & Row.

Mason, J. W. (1975). An historical view of the stress field: Parts 1 & 2. *Journal of Human Stress, 1,* 6–12, 22–36.

Masson, J. M., & McCarthy, S. (1995). *When elephants weep: The emotional lives of animals.* New York: Delacorte Press.

Masters, W. H., & Johnson, V. E. (1966). *Human sexual response.* Boston: Little, Brown.

Masters, W. H., & Johnson, V. E. (1970). *Human sexual inadequacy.* Boston: Little, Brown.

Masters, W. H., & Johnson, V. E. (1979). *Homosexuality in perspective.* Boston: Little, Brown.

Matarazzo, J. D. (1980). Behavioral health and behavioral medicine: Frontiers for a new health psychology. *American Psychologist, 35,* 807–817.

Matarazzo, J. D. (1984). Behavioral immunogens and pathogens in health and illness. In B. L. Hammonds & C. J. Scheirer (Eds.), *Psychology and health: The Master Lecture Series, Vol. 3* (pp. 9–43). Washington, DC: American Psychological Association.

Matarazzo, J. D. (1990). Psychological assessment versus psychological testing: Validation from Binet to the school, clinic, and courtroom. *American Psychologist, 45,* 999–1017.

Matossian, M. K. (1982). Ergot and the Salem witchcraft affair. *American Scientist, 70,* 355–357.

Matossian, M. K. (1989). *Poisons of the past: Molds, epidemics, and history.* New Haven: Yale University Press.

Matson, J. L., Esveldt-Dawson, K., Andrasik, F., Ollendick, T. H., Petti, T., & Hersen, M. (1980). Direct, observational, and generalization effects of social skills training with emotionally disturbed children. *Behavior Therapy, 11,* 522–531.

Matthews, K. A. (1988). Coronary heart disease and Type A behavior: Update on an alternative to the Booth-Kewley and Friedman (1987) quantitative review. *Psychological Bulletin, 104,* 373–380.

May, R. (1969). *Love and will.* New York: Norton.

May, R. (1972). *Power and innocence: A search for the sources of violence.* New York: Delta.

May, R. (1975). *The courage to create.* New York: Norton.

May, R. (1977). *The meaning of anxiety* (revised edition). New York: Norton. (Original work published in 1950).

Mayer, J. D., & Salovey, P. (1995). Emotional intelligence and the construction and regulation of feelings. *Applied and Preventive Psychology, 4,* 197–208.

Mayer, J. D., & Salovey, P. (In press). What is emotional intelligence? In P. Salovey & D. Sluyter (Eds.), *Emotional development, emotional literacy, and emotional intelligence.* New York: BasicBooks.

Mayer, R. E. (1981). *The promise of cognitive psychology.* San Francisco: Freeman.

McAdams, D.P., de St. Aubin, E., and Logan, R.L. (1993). Generativity among young, midlife, and older adults. *Psychology and Aging, 8,* 221–230.

McCaulley, M. H. (1978). *Application of the Myers-Briggs Type Indicator to medicine and health professions* [Monograph 1]. Gainesville, FL: Center for Applications of Psychological Type.

McClelland, D. C. (1961). *The achieving society.* Princeton, NJ: Van Nostrand.

McClelland, D.C. (1985). *Human motivation.* New York: Cambridge University Press.

McClelland, D. C., Atkinson, J. W., Clark, R. A., & Lowell, E. L. (1976). *The achievement motive* (2nd ed.). New York: Irvington.

McCoy, E. (1988). Childhood through the ages. In K. Finsterbusch (Ed.), *Sociology 88/89* (pp. 44–47). Guilford, CT: Dushkin.

McFarland, R. A., & Kennison, R. (1986). Sex, handedness, and hemispheric asymmetry in the emotional and skin temperature responses to music [Abstract]. *Psychophysiology, 23,* 451.

McGaugh, J. L., Weinberger, N. M., Lynch, G., & Granger, R. H. (1985). Neural mechanisms of learning and memory: Cells, systems and computations. *Naval Research Reviews, 37,* 15–29.

McGrath, E., Keita, G. P., Strickland, B. R., & Russo, N. F. (1990). *Women and depression: Risk factors and treatment issues.* Hyattsville, MD: American Psychological Association.

McLintock, T. T. C., Aitken, H., Dowie, C. F. A., & Kenny, G. N. C. (1990). Post-operative analgesic requirements in patients exposed to positive intraoperative suggestions. *British Journal of Medicine, 301,* 788–790.

McNeil, B. J., Pauker, S. G., Sox, H. C., Jr., & Tversky, A. (1982). On the elicitation of preferences for alternative therapies. *New England Journal of Medicine, 306,* 1259–1262.

McPherson, K. S. (1985). On intelligence testing and immigration legislation. *American Psychologist, 40,* 242–243.

Mead, M. (1939). *From the South Seas: Studies of adolescence and sex in primitive societies.* New York: Morrow.

Meador, B. D., & Rogers, C. R. (1979). Person-centered therapy. In R. J. Corsini (Ed.), *Current psychotherapies* (2nd ed., pp. 131–184). Itasca, IL: Peacock.

Mehrabian, A. (1971). *Silent messages.* Belmont, CA: Wadsworth.

Meichenbaum, D. (1977). *Cognitive-behavior modification: An integrative approach.* New York: Plenum.

Meier, R. P. (1991). Language acquisition by deaf children. *American Scientist, 79,* 60–70.

Meltzoff, J., & Kornreich, M. (1970). *Research in psychotherapy.* New York: Atherton.

Menzel, E. M. (1978). Cognitive mapping in chimpanzees. In S. H. Hulse, H. Fowler, & W. K. Honzig (Eds.), *Cognitive processes in animal behavior* (pp. 375–422). Hillsdale, NJ: Erlbaum.

Merckelbach, H., & van Oppen, P. (1989). Effects of gaze manipulation on subjective evaluation of neutral and phobia-relevant stimuli. *Acta Psychologica, 70,* 147–151.

Merton, R. K. (1957). *Social theory and social structures.* New York: Free Press.

Mervis, C. B., & Rosch, E. (1981). Categorization of natural objects. *Annual Review of Psychology, 32,* 89–115.

Meyer, M. M., & Ekstein, R. (1970). The psychotic pursuit of reality. *Journal of Contemporary Psychotherapy, 3,* 3–12.

Michael, R. T., Gagnon, J. H., Laumann, E. O., & Kolata, G. (1994). *Sex in America: A definitive survey.* New York: Little Brown.

Milgram, S. (1965). Some conditions of obedience and disobedience to authority. *Human Relations, 18,* 56–76.

Milgram, S. (1974). *Obedience to authority.* New York: Harper & Row.

Miller, A. G. (1986). *The obedience paradigm: A case study in controversy in social science.* New York: Praeger.

Miller, G. A. (1956). The magic number seven plus or minus two: Some limits on our capacity for processing information. *Psychological Review, 63,* 81–97.

Miller, J. (1984). Culture and the development of everyday social explanation. *Journal of Personality and Social Psychology, 46,* 961–978.

Miller, J., Bersoff, D., & Harwood, R. (1990). Perceptions of social responsibilities in India and the United States: Moral imperatives or personal decisions? *Journal of Personality and Social Psychology, 58,* 33–47.

Miller, L., & Milner, B. (1985). Cognitive risk-taking after frontal or temporal lobectomy—II. The synthesis of phonemic and semantic information. *Neuropsychologia, 23,* 371–379.

Miller, M. E., & Bowers, K. S. (1993). Hypnotic analgesia: Dissociated experience of dissociated control? *Journal of Abnormal Psychology, 102,* 29–38.

Miller, P. Y., & Simon, W. (1980). The development of sexuality in adolescence. In J. Adelson (Ed.), *Handbook of adolescent psychology.* New York: Wiley.

Mineka, S., Davidson, M., Cook, M., & Keir, R. (1984). Observational conditioning of snake fear in rhesus monkeys. *Journal of Abnormal Psychology, 93,* 355–372.

Minuchin, S. (1974). *Families and family therapy.* Cambridge, MA: Harvard University Press.

Mischel, W. (1973). Toward a cognitive social learning reconceptualizalion of personality. *Psychological Review, 80,* 252–283.

Mizukami, K., Kobayashi, N., Ishii, T., and Iwata, H. (1990). First selective attachment begins in early infancy: A study using telethermography. *Infant Behavior and Developmemt, 13,* 257–271.

Moar, I. (1980). The nature and acquisition of cognitive maps. In D. Cantor & T. Lee (Eds.), *Proceedings of the international conference on environmental psychology.* London: Architectural Press.

Moffitt, A., Kramer, M., & Hoffman, R. (Eds.). (1993). *The functions of dreaming.* Albany, NY: State University of New York Press.

Mogilner, A., *et al.* (1993). Somatosensory cortical plasticity in adult humans revealed by magnetoencephalography. *Proceedings of the National Academy of Sciences, 90* (8), 3593–3597.

Moncrieff, R. W. (1951). *The chemical senses.* London: Leonard Hill.

Montague, A. (1986). *Touching: The human significance of the skin.* New York: Harper & Row.

Moore, P. (1990). In *Discovering Psychology,* Program 18 [PBS video series]. Washington, DC: Annenberg/CPB Program.

Moore-Ede, M. (1993). *The twenty-four-hour society: Understanding human limits in a world that never stops.* Reading, MA: Addison-Wesley.

Morgan, A. H., Hilgard, E. R., & Davert, E. C. (1970). The heritability of hypnotic susceptibility of twins: A preliminary report. *Behavior Genetics, 1,* 213–224.

Morgenthau, T. (1995, July 10). Chasing the Unabomer. *Newsweek,* Vol. CXXVI, No. 2, 46.

Moriarity, T. (1975). Crime, commitment and the responsive bystander: Two field experiments. *Journal of Personality and Social Psychology, 31,* 370–376.

Morrell, E. M. (1986). Meditation and somatic arousal. *American Psychologist, 41* (6), 712–713.

Morris, D. (1967). *The naked ape.* New York: McGraw-Hill.

Morris, W. N., & Miller, R. S. (1975). The effects of consensus-breaking and consensus-preempting partners on reduction of conformity. *Journal of Experimental Social Psychology, 11,* 215–223.

Moscovici, S. (1985). Social influence and conformity. In G. Lindzey & E. Aronson (Eds.), *Handbook of social psychology* (3rd ed.). (pp. 347–412). New York: Random House.

Moskowitz, H. (1985). Marihuana and driving. *Accident Analysis & Prevention, 17, 323–345.*

Mowrer, O. (1960). *Learning theory and symbolic processes.* New York: Wiley.

Muehlenhard, C. L., & Cook, S. W. (1988). Men's self-reports of unwanted sexual activity. *The Journal of Sex Research, 24,* 58–72.

Mullin, P. A., & Egeth, H. E. (1989). Capacity limitations in visual word processing. *Journal of Experimental Psychology: Human Perception and Performance, 15,* 111–123.

Munroe, R. L. (1955). *Schools of psychoanalytic thought.* New York: Dryden.

Murnen, S. K., Perolt, A., & Byrne, D. (1989). Coping with unwanted sexual activity: Normative responses, situational determinants, and individual differences. *The Journal of Sex Research, 26,* 85–106.

Murray, J. P., & Kippax, S. (1979). Children's social behavior in three towns with differing television experience. *Journal of Communication, 28,* 19–29.

Muskin, P. R., & Fyer, A. J. (1981). Treatment of panic disorder. *Journal of Clinical Psychopharmacology, 1,* 81–90.

Myers, I. B. (1962). *The Myers-Briggs type indicator.* Palo Alto, CA: Consulting Psychologists Press.

Myers, I. B. (1976). *Introduction to type* (2nd ed.). Gainesville, FL: Center for Applications of Psychological Type.

Myers, I. B. (1985). *Gifts differing.* Palo Alto, CA: Consulting Psychologists Press.

Myers, D. G. (1992). *The pursuit of happiness: Who is happy—and why.* New York: William Morrow and Company.

Myers, D. G., & Diener, E. (1995). Who is happy? *Psychological Science, 6,* 10–19.

Myers, L. (1996). Europe's new criminal class: Under capitalism a violent crime wave is sweeping Central nations. *San Francisco Examiner,* January 7, p. A–8.

Naigles, L.G., & Kako, E.T. (1993). First contact in verb acquisition: Defining a role for syntax. *Child Development, 64,* 1665–1687.

Naigles, L. (1990). Children use syntax to learn verb meanings. *Child language, 17,* 357–374.

National Center for Health Statistics. (1990). Vital and health statistics. *Data from the national study of family growth.* Hyattsville, MD: U.S. Department of HEW, Public Health Service, Office of Health Research, Statistics, and Technology.

National Centers for Disease Control. (November, 1990). *Report on HIV and AIDS.* Atlanta: U.S. Department of Health and Human Services.

National Public Radio. (1995a, June 25). The Stockholm syndrome: Empathy with captors discussed. *Weekend Edition.* Washington, DC: National Public Radio.

National Public Radio. (1995b, August 30). Americans are generally shy, and getting shyer. *Morning Edition.* Washington, DC: National Public Radio.

National Public Radio. (1996a, January 1). Gene for personality trait discovered. *All Things Considered.* Washington, DC: National Public Radio.

National Public Radio. (1996b, January 30). The rational criminal and crime prevention. *Morning Edition.* Washington, DC: National Public Radio.

National Public Radio. (1996c, February 5). Schizophrenia. *Morning Edition.* Washington, DC: National Public Radio.

Natsoulas, T. (1981). Basic problems of consciousness. *Journal of Personality and Social Psychology, 41,* 132–178.

Natsoulas, T. (1988). Gibson, James, and the temporal continuity of experience. *Imagination, Cognition, and Personality, 7,* 351–376.

Nauta, W. J. H., & Feirtag, M. (1979). The organization of the brain. *Scientific American, 241* (9), 88–111.

Needleman, H., Schell, A., Belinger, D., Leviton, A., & Allred, E. (1990). The long-term effects of exposure to low doses of lead in childhood: An 11-year follow-up report. *New England Journal of Medicine, 322,* 83–88.

Neese, R. M. (1990). Evolutionary explanations of emotions. *Human Nature, 1,* 261–289.

Neimark, J. (1996, January/February). The diva of disclosure. *Psychology Today, 29* (1), pp. 48ff.

Neisser, U. (1967). *Cognitive psychology.* New York: Appleton-Century-Crofts.

Nelson, R. E., & Craighead, W. E. (1977). Selective recall of positive and negative feedback, self-control behaviors and depression. *Journal of Abnormal Psychology, 86,* 379–388.

Newcomb, M. D. & Bentler, P. M. (1988). *Consequences of adolescent drug use: Impact on the lives of young adults.* Newbury Park, CA: Sage.

Newcomb, T. M. (1943). *Personality and social change.* New York: Holt.

Newcomb, T. M., Koenig, D. E., Flacks, R., & Warwick, D. P. (1967). *Persistence and change: Bennington College and its students after twenty-five years.* New York: Wiley.

Newell, A., Shaw, J. C., & Simon, H. A. (1958). Elements of a theory of human problem solving. *Psychological Review, 65,* 152–166.

Newell, A., & Simon, H. A. (1972). *Human problem solving.* Englewood Cliffs, NJ: Prentice-Hall.

New York Times. (1989, May 17). Police officers beat blind man. (p. 17).

Nguyen, T., Heslin, R., & Nguyen, M. L. (1975). The meanings of touch: Sex differences. *Journal of Communication, 25,* 92–103.

Nhat Hanh, T. (1991). *Peace is every step: The path of mindfulness in everyday life.* New York: Bantam.

Nichols, M. P. (1984). *Family therapy: Concepts and methods.* New York: Gardner Press.

Nicol, S. E., & Gottesman, I. I. (1983). Clues to the genetics and neurobiology of schizophrenia. *American Scientist, 71,* 398–404.

Nisbett, R. E. (1972). Hunger, obesity, and the ventromedial hypothalamus. *Psychological Review, 79,* 433–453.

Nissen, M. J., & Bullimer, P. (1987). Attentional requirements of learning: Evidence from performance measures. *Cognitive Psychology, 19,* 1–32.

Nobles, W. W. (1972). African psychology: Foundations for black psychology. In R. L. Jones (Ed.), *Black psychology.* New York: Harper & Row.

Nobles, W. W. (1976). Black people in white insanity: An issue for black community mental health. *Journal of Afro-American Issues, 4,* 21–27.

Nolen-Hoeksema, S. (1987). Sex differences in unipolar depression: Evidence and theory. *Psychological Bulletin, 101,* 259–282.

Nolen-Hoeksema, S. (1990). *Sex differences in depression.* Stanford, CA: Stanford University Press.

Nolen-Hoeksema, S., & Girgus, J. S. (1994). The emergence of gender differences in depression during adolescence. *Psychological Bulletin, 115,* 424–443.

Norman, D. A., & Rumelhart, D. E. (1975). *Explorations in cognition.* San Francisco: Freeman.

Norman, W. T. (1967). *2,800 personality trait descriptors: Normative operating characteristics for a university population* (Research Rep. No. 08310-1-T). Ann Arbor: University of Michigan Press.

Notarius, C.I. (1996). Marriage: Will I be happy or sad? In N. Vanzetti and S. Duck's *A lifetime of relationships.* New York: Brooks/Cole Publishing Company.

Notarius, C. I., & Johnson, J. S. (1982). Emotional expression in husbands and wives. *Journal of Marriage and the Family, 44,* 483–489.

Notarius, C., & Markman, H. (1993). *We can work it out: Making sense of marital conflict.* New York: G. P. Putnam's Sons.

Nungesser, L. G. (1986). *Epidemic of courage: Facing AIDS in America.* New York: St. Martin's Press.

Nungesser, L. G. (1990). *Axioms for survivors: How to live until you say goodbye.* Santa Monica, CA: IBS Press.

Nurmi, J.E. (1991). How do adolescents see their future? A review of the development of future orientation and planning.

Developmental Review, 11, 1–59.

Nuttin, J. (1985). *Future time perspective and motivation: Theory and research method.* Hillsdale, NJ: Erlbaum.

O'Leary, K. D. (1988). Physical aggression between spouses: A social learning theory perspective. In V. B. Van Hasselt, R. L. Morrison, A. S. Bellack, & M. Hersen (Eds.), *Handbook of family violence* (pp. 31–55). New York: Plenum.

O'Leary, K. D. (Ed.). (1987). *Assessment of marital discord: An integration for research and clinical practice.* Hillsdale, NJ: Erlbaum.

Oberg, K. (1960). Cultural shock: Adjustments to new cultural environments. *Practical Anthropology, 7,* 177–182.

Oden, S., & Asher, S. R. (1977). Coaching children in social skills for friendship making. *Child Development, 48,* 495–506.

Offer, D., Ostrov, E., & Howard, K. I. (1981). *The adolescent: A psychological self-portrait.* New York: Basic Books.

Ofshe, R., & Watters, E. (1994). *Making monsters: False memories, psychotherapy, and sexual hysteria.* New York: Charles Scribner's Sons.

Olson, J. M., & Zanna, M. P. (1981). *Promoting physical activity: A social psychological perspective. Report prepared for the Ministry of Culture and Recreation,* Sports and Fitness Branch, 77 Bloor Street West, 8th Floor, Toronto, Ontario M7A.2R9, Canada (November).

Olton, D. S. (1992). Tolman's cognitive analyses: Predecessors of current approaches in psychology. *Journal of Experimental Psychology: General, 121,* 427–428.

Olton, D. S. (1979). Mazes, maxes, and memory. *American Psychologist, 34,* 583–596.

Oppel, J. J. (1854–55). Ueber geometrisch-optische Tauschungen. *Jahresbericht des physikalischen Vereins zu Frankfurt a. M.,* 34–47.

Opton, E. M., Jr. (1973). "It never happened and besides they deserved it." In W. E. Henry & N. Sanford (Eds.), *Sanctions for evil* (pp. 49–70). San Francisco: Jossey-Bass.

Opton, E. M. (1970). Lessons of My Lai. In N. Sanford & C. Comstock (Eds.), *Sanctions for evil.* San Francisco: Jossey-Bass.

Orne, M. T. (1980). Hypnotic control of pain: Toward a clarification of the different psy-

chological processes involved. In J. J. Bonica (Ed.), *Pain* (pp. 155–172). New York: Raven Press.

Ornstein, R., & Sobel, D. (1989). *Healthy pleasures.* Reading, MA: Addison-Wesley.

Ornstein, R. E. (1986a). *Multimind: A new way of looking at human behavior.* Boston: Houghton-Mifflin.

Ornstein, R. E. (1986b). *The psychology of consciousness* (Rev. ed.). New York: Penguin Books.

Oskamp, S. (1984). *Applied social psychology.* Englewood Cliffs, NJ: Prentice-Hall.

Osterhout, L. & Holcomb, P. J. (1992). Event-related brain potentials elicited by syntactic anomaly. *Journal of Memory and Language, 31,* 785–806.

Page, S. (1987). On gender roles and perception of maladjustment. *Canadian Psychology, 28,* 53–59.

Page, T. L. (1994). Time is the essence: Molecular analysis of the biological clock. *Science, 263,* 1570–1572.

Paivio, A. (1983). The empirical case for dual coding. In J. C. Yuille (Ed.), *Imagery, memory and cognition* (pp. 307–332). Hillsdale, NJ: Erlbaum.

Paivio, A. (1986). *Mental representations: A dual coding approach.* New York: Oxford University Press.

Papolos, D. F., & Papolos, J. (1987). *Overcoming depression.* New York: Harper & Row.

Pappas, A. M. (1983). Introduction. In A. M. Pappas (Ed.), *Law and the status of the child* (pp. xxvii–lv). United Nations Institute for Training and Research.

Park, B., & Rothbart, M. (1982). Perception of out-group homogeneity and levels of social categorization: Memory for the subordinate attributes of in group and out-group members. *Journal of Personality and Social Psychology, 42,* 1051–1068.

Parr, W. V., and Siegert, R. (1993). Adults' conceptions of everyday memory failures in others: Factors that mediate the effects of target age. *Psychology and Aging, 8,* 599–605.

Pass, J. J., & Cunningham, J. W. (1978). Occupational clusters based on systematically derived work dimensions: Final report. *Journal of Supplemental Abstract Service: Catalogue of Selected Documents: Psychology, 8,* 22–23.

Paternoster, R., Saltzman, L. E., Waldo, G. P., & Chiricos, T. G.

(1983). Perceived risk and social control: Do sanctions really deter? *Law and Society Review, 17,* 457–480.

Patterson, J. M. (1985). Critical factors affecting family compliance with home treatment for children with cystic fibrosis. *Family Relations, 34,* 74–89.

Pattie, F. A. (1994). *Mesmer and animal magnetism: A chapter in the history of medicine.* New York: Edmonston.

Paul, S. M., Crawley, J. N., & Skolnick, P. (1986). The neurobiology of anxiety: The role of the GABA/benzodiazepine complex. In P. A. Berger & H. K. H. Brodie (Eds.), *American handbook on psychiatry: Biological psychology* (2nd ed.). New York: Basic Books.

Pavlov, I. P. (1928). *Lectures on conditioned reflexes: Twenty-five years of objective study of higher nervous activity (behavior of animals)* (Vol. 1, W. H. Gantt, Trans.). New York: International Publishers.

Pavot, W., Diener, E., & Fujita, F. (1990). Extraversion and happiness. *Personality and Individual Differences, 1,* 1299–1306.

Paykel, E. S. (1973). Life events and acute depression. In J. P. Scott & E. C. Senay (Eds.), *Separation and depression* (pp. 215–236). Washington, DC: American Association for the Advancement of Science.

Penfield, W., & Baldwin, M. (1952). Temporal lobe seizures and the technique of subtotal lobectomy. *Annals of Surgery, 136,* 625–634.

Pennebaker, J. W. (1990). *Opening up: The healing power of confiding in others.* New York: Avon Books.

Pennebaker, J. W., & Harber, K. D. (1991, April). *Coping after the Loma Prieta earthquake: A preliminary report.* Paper presented at the Western Psychological Association Convention, San Francisco, CA.

Pennebaker, J. W., Dyer, M. A., Caulkins, R. J., Litowitz, D. L., Ackerman, P. L., Anderson, D. B., & McGraw, K. M. (1979). Don't the girls get prettier at closing time: A country and western application to psychology. *Personality and Social Psychology Bulletin, 5,* 122–125.

Pennick, S., Smith, G., Wienske, K., & Hinkle, L. (1963). An experimental evaluation of the relationship between hunger and gastric motility. *American Journal of Physiology, 205,* 421–426.

Perlin, S. (Ed.). (1975). *A handbook for the study of suicide.* New York: Oxford University Press.

Perls, F. S. (1969). *Gestalt therapy verbatim.* Lafayette, CA: Real People Press.

Pert, C. B., & Snyder, S. H. (1973). Opiate receptor: Demonstration in the nervous tissue. *Science, 179,* 1011–1014.

Peterson, C., & Barrett, L. C. (1987). Explanatory style and academic performance among university freshmen. *Journal of Personality and Social Psychology, 53,* 603–607.

Peterson, C., & Seligman, M. E. P. (1984). Explanatory style and depression: Theory and evidence. *Psychological Review, 91,* 341–374.

Peterson, C., Seligman, M. E. P., & Vaillant, G. E. (1988). Pessimistic explanatory style is a risk factor for physical illness: A thirty-five year longitudinal study. *Journal of Personality and Social Psychology, 55,* 23–27.

Pettigrew, T. F. (1985). New patterns of racism: The different worlds of 1984 and 1964. *Rutgers Law Review, 37,* 673–706.

Peyser, M. (1995). Sounding retreat. *Newsweek, Vol. CXXVI,* No. 9, August 28, pp. 38–40.

Phares, E. J. (1984). *Clinical psychology: Concepts, methods, and professionals* (Rev. ed.). Homewood, IL: Dorsey.

Piaget, J. (1977). *The development of thought: Equilibrium of cognitive structures.* New York: Viking Press.

Piaget, J. (1954). *The construction of reality in the child.* New York: Basic Books.

Pifer, A., & Bronte L. (Eds.). (1986). *Our aging society: Paradox and promise.* New York: Norton.

Piliavin, J. A., & Piliavin, I. M. (1972). Effect of blood on reactions to a victim. *Journal of Personality and Social Psychology, 23,* 353–361.

Piliavin, I. M., Rodin, J., & Piliavin, J. A. (1969). Good Samaritanism: An underground phenomenon? *Journal of Personality and Social Psychology, 13,* 289–300.

Pilisuk, M., & Parks, S. H. (1986). *The healing web: Social networks and human survival.* Hanover, NH: University Press of New England.

Pimentel, B. (1995, August 4). Bay boy first in U.S. to get new transplant. *San Francisco Chronicle,* pp. A1, A19.

Piotrowski, C., Keller, J. W., & Ogawa, T. (1993). Projective techniques: An international perspective. *Psychological Reports, 72,* 179–182.

Piotrowski, C., Sherry, D., & Keller, J. W. (1985). Psychodiagnostic test usage: A survey of the Society for Personality Assessment. *Journal of Personality Assessment, 49,* 115–119.

Pittenger, D. J. (1993). The utility of the Myers-Briggs Type Indicator. *Review of Educational Research, 63,* 467–488.

Plomin, R. (1989). Environment and genes: Determinants of behavior. *American Psychologist, 44,* 105–111.

Plomin, R, Chipuer, H. M., & Loehin, J. C. (1990). Behavioral genetics and personality. In L. A. Pervin (Ed.), *Handbook of personality: Theory and research* (pp. 225–243). New York: Guilford Press.

Plomin, R., & McClearn, G. E. (Eds.). (1993). *Nature, nurture, and psychology.* Washington, DC: American Psychological Association.

Plomin, R., Owen, M. J., & McGuffin, P. (1994). The genetic basis of complex human behaviors. *Science, 264,* 1733–1739.

Plomin, R., & Rende, R. (1991). Human behavioral genetics. *Annual Review of Psychology, 42,* 161–190.

Plous, S. (1985). Perceptual illusions and military realities: A social-psychological analyses of the nuclear arms race. *Journal of Conflict Resolution, 29,* 363–389.

Plutchik, R. (1980). *Emotion: A psychoevolutionary synthesis.* New York: Harper & Row.

Plutchik, R. (1984). Emotions: A general psychoevolutionary theory. In K. Scherer & P. Ekman (Eds.), *Approaches to emotion.* Hillsdale, NJ: Erlbaum.

Polivy, J., & Herman, P. (1985). Dieting and bingeing: A causal analysis. *American Psychologist, 40,* 193–201.

Polivy, J., & Herman, C. P. (1993). Etiology of binge eating: Psychological mechanisms. In C. G. Fairburn & G. T. Wilson (Eds.), *Binge eating: Nature, assessment, and treatment* (pp. 173–205). New York: Guilford Press.

Poloma, M. M., & Pendleton, B. F. (1990). Religious domains and general well-being. *Social Indicators Research, 22,* 255–276.

Ponterrotto, J., & Benesch, K. (1988). An organizational frame-work for understanding the role of culture in counseling. *Journal of Counseling and Development, 66,* 237–241.

Poon, L. W. (1985). Differences in human memory with aging: Nature, causes, and clinical implications. In J. E. Birren & W. K. Schaie (Eds.), *Handbook of the psychology of aging* (pp. 427–462). New York: Van Nostrand Reinhold.

Porter, L. S., & Stone, A. A. (1995). Are there really gender differences in coping?: A reconsideration of previous data and results from a daily study. *Journal of Social and Clinical Psychology, 14,* 184–202.

Posner, M. I. (1990). In *Discovering Psychology,* Program 10 [PBS video series]. Washington, DC: Annenberg/CPB Project.

Posner, M. I. (1982). Cumulative development of attentional theory. *American Psychologist, 37,* 168–179.

Posner, M. I. (1988). Structures and functions of selective attention. In T. Boll & B. Bryant (Eds.), *Master lectures in clinical neuropsychology* (pp. 173–202). Washington, DC: American Psychological Association.

Posner, M. I. (1993). Seeing the mind. *Science, 262,* 673–674.

Premack, D. (1965). Reinforcement theory. In D. Levine (Ed.), *Nebraska Symposium on Motivation* (pp. 128–180). Lincoln, NE: University of Nebraska Press.

Prentice, D. A., & Miller, D. T. (1993). Pluralistic ignorance and alcohol use on campus: Some consequences on misperceiving the social norm. *Journal of Personality and Social Psychology, 64,* 243–256.

Pryor, K. (1975). *Lads before the wind.* New York: Harper & Row.

Putnam, F. W. (1989). *Diagnosis and treatment of multiple personality disorder.* New York: Guilford.

Quadrel, M. J., & Fischoff, B. (1993). Adolescent (in)vulnerability. *American Psychologist, 48,* 102–116.

Quattrone, G. (1986). On the perception of a group's variability. In S. Worchell & W. Austin (Eds.), *The psychology of intergroup relations* (Vol. 2, pp. 25–48). New York: Nelson-Hall.

Rabkin, J. G., Gelb, L., & Lazar, J. B. (Eds.). (1980). *Attitudes toward the mentally ill: Research perspectives* [Report of an NIMH workshop]. Rockville, MD: National Institutes of Mental Health.

Rachman, S. (1966). Sexual fetishism: An experimental analogue. *Psychological Record, 6,* 293–296.

Rahe, R. H., & Arthur, R. J. (1978, March). Life change and illness studies: Past history and future directions. *Journal of Human Stress,* pp. 3–15.

Raichle, M. E. (1994). Visualizing the mind. *Scientific American, 270* (4), 58–64.

Rakic, P. (1985). Limits of neurogenesis in primates. *Science, 227,* 1054–1057.

Rand, C. S., & Kuldau, J. M. (1992). Epidemiology of bulimia and symptoms in a general population: Sex, age, race, and socioeconomic status. *International Journal of Eating Disorders, 11,* 37–44.

Rando, T. A. (1988). *Grieving: How to go on living when someone you love dies.* Lexington, MA: Lexington Books.

Rapoport, J. L. (1989, March). The biology of obsessions and compulsions. *Scientific American, 263,* pp. 83–89.

Regier, D. A., Boyd, J. H, Burke, J. D., Rae, D. S., Myers, J. K., Kramer, M., Robins, L. N., George, L. K., Karno, M., & Locke, B. Z. (1988). One-month prevalence of mental disorders in the United States. *Archives of General Psychiatry, 45,* 977–986.

Regier, D. A., Narrow, W. E., Rae, D. S., Manderscheid, R. W., Locke, B. Z., & Goodwin, F. K. (1993). The de facto US mental and addictive disorders service system: Epidemiologic Catchment Area prospective 1-year-prevalence rates of disorders and services. *Archives of General Psychiatry, 50,* 85–94.

Rehm, L. P. (1977). A self-control model of depression. *Behavior Therapy, 8,* 787–804.

Reisenzein, R. (1983). The Schachter theory of emotion: Two decades later. *Psychological Bulletin, 94,* 239–264.

Reiser, B. J., Black, J. B., & Abelson, R. P. (1985). Knowledge structures in the organization and retrieval of autobiographical memories. *Cognitive Psychology, 17,* 89–137.

Rescorla, R. A. (1966). Predictability and number of pairings in Pavlovian fear conditioning. *Psychonomic Science, 4,* 383–384.

Rescorla, R. A. (1972). Information variables in Pavlovian conditioning. In G. Bower (Ed.), *The psychology of learning and motivation* (Vol. 6). New York: Academic Press.

Rescorla, R. A., & Wagner, A. R. (1972). A theory of Pavlovian conditioning: Variations in the effectiveness of reinforcement and nonreinforcement. In A. H. Black & W. F. Prokasy (Eds.), *Classical conditioning, II: Current research and theory* (pp. 64–94). New York: Appleton-Century-Crofts.

Rest, J. R., & Thoma, S. J. (1976). Relation of moral judgment development to formal education. *Developmental Psychology, 21,* 709–714.

Revised Standard Version, The Layman's Parallel New Testament. (1970). Grand Rapids, MI: Zondervan Publishing House.

"Revising Psychiatric Diagnoses." (1993, 11 June). *Science, 260,* 1586–1587.

Richardson-Klavern, A., & Bjork, R. A. (1988). Primary versus secondary rehearsal in an imaginary voice: Differential effects recognition memory and perceptual identification. *Bulletin of Psychonomic Society, 26,* 187–190.

Riddle, D., & Morin, S. (1977). Removing the stigma from individuals. *American Psychological Association Monitor, 16,* 28.

Riger, S. (1992). Epistemological debates, feminist voices: Science, social values, and the study of women. *American Psychologist, 47,* 738–740.

Riggs, J. M., & Cantor, N. (1981). *Information exchange in social interaction: Anchoring effects of self-concepts and expectancies.* Unpublished manuscript, Gettysburg College.

Rimland, B. (1982). The altruism paradox. *The Southern psychologist, 2* (1), 8–9.

Rips, L. (1988). Deduction. In R. J. Sternberg & E. E. Smith (Eds.), *The psychology of human thought* (pp. 118–152). Cambridge: Cambridge University Press.

Roberts, A. H., Kewman, D. G., Mercier, L., & Hovell, M. (1993). The power of nonspecific effects in healing: Implications for psychosocial and biological treatments. *Clinical Psychology Review, 13,* 373–391.

Robins, L. N., Locke, B. Z., & Regier, D. A. (1991). An overview of psychiatric disorders in America. In L. N. Robins & D. A. Regier (Eds.), *Psychiatric disorders in America: The epidemiologic catchment area study.* New York: Free Press.

Rodin, J. (1983, April). Behavioral medicine: Beneficial effects of self control training in aging. *International Review of Applied Psychology, 32,* 153–181.

Rodin, J. (1985). The application of social psychology. In G. Lindzey & E. Aronson (Eds.), *Handbook of social psychology* (3rd ed., Vol. 2, pp. 805–882). New York: Random House.

Rodin, J. (1986). Aging and health: Effects of the sense of control. *Science, 233,* 1271–1276.

Rodin, J., & Janis, I. J. (1982). The social influence of physicians and other health care practitioners as agents of change. In H. S. Freidman & M. R. DiMatteo, *Interpersonal issues in health care* (pp. 33–49). New York: Academic Press.

Rodin, J., & Langer, E. (1977). Long-term effects of a control-relevant intervention among the institutionalized aged. *Journal of Personality and Social Psychology, 35,* 897–902.

Rodin, J., Striegel-Moore, R. H., & Silberstein, L. R. (1985, July). *A prospective study of bulimia among college students on three U. S. campuses.* Unpublished manuscript. New Haven: Yale University.

Rogers, C. R. (1947). Some observations on the organization of personality. *American Psychologist, 2,* 358–368.

Rogers, C. R. (1951). *Client-centered therapy: Its current practice, implications and theory.* Boston: Houghton-Mifflin.

Rogers, C. R. (1977). *On personal power: Inner strength and its revolutionary impact.* New York: Delacorte.

Rogers, R. W. (1984). Changing health-related attitudes and behavior: The role of preventive health psychology. In J. H. Harvey, J. E. Maddux, R. P. McGlynn, & C. D. Stoltenberg (Eds.), *Social perception in clinical and consulting psychology* (Vol. 2, pp. 91–112). Lubbock, TX: Texas Tech University Press.

Rogoff, B. (1990). *Apprenticeship in thinking: Cognitive de-velopment in social context.* New York: Oxford University Press.

Rolls, B. J., Federoff, I. C., & Guthrie, J. F. (1991). Gender differences in eating behavior and body weight regulation. *Health Psychology, 10,* 133–142.

Rook, K. S. (1987). Social support versus companionship: Effects on life stress, loneliness, and evaluations by others. *Journal of Personality and Social Psychology, 52* (6), 1132–1147.

Roper Organization, The. (1992). *Unusual personal experiences: An analysis of the data from three national surveys.* Las Vegas, NV: Bigelow Holding Corporation.

Rorschach, H. (1942). *Psychodiagnostics: A diagnostic test based on perception.* New York: Grune & Stratton.

Rosch, E. H. (1973). Natural categories. *Cognitive Psychology, 4,* 328–350.

Rosch, E. H., Mervis, C. B., Gray, W. D., Johnson, D. M., & Boyes-Braem, P. (1976). Basic objects in natural categories. *Cognitive Psychology, 8,* 382–439.

Roseman, I. J. (1984). Cognitive determinants of emotions: A structural theory. In P. Shaver (Ed.), *Review of personality and social psychology: Vol. 5, Emotions, relationships, and health* (pp. 11–36). Beverly Hills, CA: Sage.

Rosenberg, S. (1988). Self and others: Studies in social personality and autobiography. In L. Berkowitz (Ed.), *Advances in experimental social psychology* (Vol. 21, pp. 57–95). New York: Academic Press.

Rosenhan, D. L. (1969). Some origins of concern for others. In P. Mussen, J. Langer, & M. Covington (Eds.), *Trends and issues in developmental psychology.* New York: Holt, Rinehart & Winston.

Rosenhan, D. L. (1973). On being sane in insane places. *Science, 179,* 250–258.

Rosenhan, D. L. (1975). The contextual nature of psychiatric diagnoses. *Journal of Abnormal Psychology, 84,* 462–474.

Rosenhan, D. L., & Seligman, M. E. P. (1995). *Abnormal psychology,* 3rd edition. New York: Norton.

Rosenthal, R., & Jacobson, L. F. (1968a). *Pygmalion in the classroom.* New York: Holt.

Rosenthal, R., & Jacobson, L. F. (1968b). Teacher expectations for the disadvantaged. *Scientific American, 218*(4), 19–23.

Rosenthal, D., Wender, P. H., Kety, S. S., Schulsinger, F., Weiner, J., & Rieder, R. (1975). Parent-child relationships and psychopathological disorder in the child. *Archives of General Psychiatry, 32,* 466–476.

Rosenzweig, M. R. (1984b). Experience, memory, and the brain. *American Psychologist, 39,* 365–376.

Ross, L., & Lepper, M. R. (1980). The perseverance of beliefs: Empirical and normative considerations. In R. A. Shweder & D. Fiske (Eds.), *New directions for methodology of behavioral science: Fallible judgments in behavioral research* (pp. 17–36). San Francisco: Jossey-Bass.

Ross, L. (1977). The intuitive psychologist and his shortcomings: Distortions in the attribution process. In L. Berkowitz (Ed.), *Advances in experimental social psychology (Vol. 10).* New York: Academic Press.

Ross, L. (1988). Situational perspectives on the obedience experiments. [Review of The obedience experiments: A case study of controversy in social science]. *Contemporary Psychology, 33,* 101–104.

Ross, L., & Nisbett, R. E. (1991). *The person and the situation: Perspectives of social psychology.* New York: McGraw-Hill.

Roth, T., Roehrs, T., Carskadon, M. A., & Dement, W. C. (1989). Daytime sleepiness and alertness. In M. Kryser, T. Roth, & W. C. Dement (Eds.), Principles and practice of sleep medicine (pp. 14–23). New York: Saunders.

Rothman, D. J. (1971). *The discovery of the asylum: Social order and disorder in the new republic.* Boston: Little, Brown.

Rotter, J. B. (1954). *Social learning and clinical psychology.* Englewood Cliffs, NJ: Prentice-Hall.

Rozin, P. (1976). The evolution of intelligence and access to the cognitive unconscious. In J. M. Sprague & A. A. Epstein (Eds.), *Progress in psychobiology and physiological psychology* (pp. 245–280). New York: Academic Press.

Ruback, R. B., Carr, T. S., & Hopper, C. H. (1986). Perceived control in prison: Its relation to reported crowding, stress, and symptoms. *Journal of Applied Social Psychology, 16,* 375–386.

Rubin, J. Z., Provenzano, F. J., & Luria, Z. (1974). The eye of the beholder: Parents' views on sex of newborns. *American Journal of Orthopsychiatry, 44,* 512–519.

Rubin, Z. (1973). *Liking and loving.* New York: Holt, Rinehart & Winston.

Ruitenbeek, H. M. (1973). *The first Freudians.* New York: Jason Aronson.

Rutter, M., Macdonald, H., Le Courteur, A., Harrington, R., Bolton, P., & Bailey, A. (1990). Genetic factors in child psychiatric disorders—II. Empirical findings. *Journal of Child Psychology and Psychiatry, 31,* 39–83.

Ryff, C.D. (1989). In the eye of the beholder: Views of psychological well-being among middle-aged and older adults. *Psychology and Aging, 4,* 195–210.

Rymer, R. (1993). *Genie: A scientific tragedy.* New York: Harper Perennial.

Saarinen, T. F. (1987). Centering of mental maps of the world: Discussion paper. Tucson: University of Arizona, Department of Geography and Regional Development.

Sacks, O. (1995). *An anthropologist on Mars.* New York: Random House.

Salter, S. (1993). "Buried Memories/Broken Families," *San Francisco Examiner,* April 4, pp. A1,ff.

Saltzstein, H. D., & Sandberg, L. (1979). Indirect social influence: Change in judgmental processor anticipatory conformity. *Journal of Experimental Social Psychology, 15,* 209–216.

Samarin, W. J. (1969). Glossolalia as a learned behavior. *Canadian Journal of Theology, 15,* 60–64.

Samarin, W. J. (1971). Evolution in glossolalic private language. *Anthropological Linguistics, 13* (2), 55–67.

Samarin, W. J. (1973). Glossolalia as regressive speech. *Language and Speech, 16* (1), 177–189.

San Francisco Chronicle (1993, February 23). "Bad habits, violence raise health costs."

San Francisco Chronicle (1993, February 25). "Exercise slashes risk of heart disease," p. A20.

San Francisco Chronicle. (1995, May 1). "Bombings linked to social malaise," p. A1.

Sanger, M. (1971). *Margaret Sanger: An autobiography.* New York: W. W. Norton/Dover Publications, Inc. (Original work published in 1938).

Sapolsky, R. M. (1990). Adrenocortical function, social rank, and personality among wild baboons. *Biological Psychiatry, 28,* pp. 1–17.

Sapolsky, R. M. (1992). *Stress: The aging brain and the mechanisms of neuron death.* Cambridge, MA: MIT Press.

Sarbin, T. R., & Coe, W. C. (1972). Hypnosis: A social psychological analysis of influence communication. New York: Holt, Rinehart & Winston.

Sarnoff, I., & Katz, D. (1954). The motivational basis of attitude change. *Journal of Abnormal and Social Psychology, 49,* 115–124.

Satir, V. (1967). *Conjoint family therapy* (Rev. ed.). Palo Alto, CA: Science and Behavior Books.

Scarr, S. (1988). Race and gender as psychological variables: Social and ethical issues. *American Psychologist, 43,* 56–59.

Schachter, S. (1959). *The psychology of affiliation.* Stanford, CA: Stanford University Press.

Schachter, S. (1971). *Emotion, obesity and crime.* New York: Academic Press.

Schachter, S., & Gross, L. (1968). Manipulated time and eating behavior. *Journal of Personality and Social Psychology, 10,* 98–106.

Schachter, S., & Singer, J. (1962). Cognitive, social and physiological determinants of emotional state. *Psychological Review, 69,* 379–399.

Schacter, D. L. (1989). Modality specificity of implicit memory for new associations. *Journal of Experimental Psychology: Learning, Memory, and Cognition, 15,* 3–12.

Schaie, K.W. (1980). Intelligence and problem solving. In J. E. Birren & R. B. Sloan (Eds.), *Handbook of mental health and aging* (pp. 262–284). Englewood Cliffs, NJ: Prentice-hall.

Schanberg, S. M. (1990). In *Discovering Psychology,* Program 4 [PBS video series]. Washington, DC: Annenberg/CPB Project.

Schank, R. C., & Abelson, R. (1977). *Scripts, plans, goals and understanding: An inquiry into human knowledge and structures.* Hillsdale, NJ: Erlbaum.

Schatzberg, A. F. (1991). Overview of anxiety disorders: Prevalence, biology, course, and treatment. *Journal of Clinical Psychiatry, 42,* 5–9.

Schaufeli, W. B., Maslach, C., & Marek, T. (Eds.) (1993). Professional burnout: Recent developments in theory and research. Washington, DC: Taylor & Francis.

Scherer, K. R. (1984). On the nature and function of emotion: A component process approach. In K. R. Scherer & P. Ekman (Eds.), *Approaches to emotion* (pp. 293–317). Hillsdale, NJ: Erlbaum.

Schleifer, S. J., Keller, S. E., Camerino, M., Thornton, J. C., & Stein, M. (1983). Suppression of lymphocyte stimulation following bereavement. *Journal of the American Medical Association, 250,* 374–377.

Schlenker, B. R., Weingold, M. F., Hallam, J. R. (1990). Self-serving attributions in social context: Effects of self-esteem and social pressure. *Journal of Personality and Social Psychology, 58,* 855–863.

Schmidt, W. E. (1987, June 7). Paddling in school: A tradition is under fire. *The New York Times,* pp. A1, A22.

Schneider, K., & May, R. (1995). *The psychology of existence: An integrative, clinical perspective.* New York: McGraw-Hill.

Schreiber, F. R. (1973). *Sybil.* New York: Warner Books.

Schroeder, D. A., Penner, L. A., Dovidio, J. F., & Piliavin, J. A. (1995). *The psychology of helping and altruism.* New York: McGraw-Hill.

Schroeder, D. A., & Prentice, D. A. (1995). *Pluralistic ignorance and alcohol use on campus II: Correcting misperceptions of the social norm.* Unpublished manuscript, Princeton University.

Schrof, J.M. (1994). Brain power. *U.S. News and World Report,* 89–97.

Schultz, R., Braun, R. G., & Kluft, R. P. (1989). Multiple personality disorder: Phenomenology of selected variables in comparison to major depression. *Dissociation, 2,* 45–51.

Schultz, R., Tompkins, C., Wood, D., & Decker, S. (1987). The social psychology of caregiving: The physical and psychological costs of providing support to the disabled. *Journal of Applied Social Psychology, 17,* 401–428.

Schwartz, P. (1994). *Peer marriage: How love between equals really works.* New York: The Free Press.

Schwartz, S. (1990). Individualism-collectivism: Critique and proposed refinements. *Journal of Cross-Cultural Psychology, 21,* 139–157.

Schwartz, G. E. (1975). Biofeedback, self-regulation, and the patterning of physiological processes. *The American Scientist, 63,* 314–324.

Schwartz, J. M., Stoessel, P. W., Baxter, L. R., Martin, K. M., & Phelps, M. E. (1996). Systematic changes in cerebral glucose metabolic rate after successful behavior modification treatment of obsessive-compulsive disorder. *Archives of General Psychiatry, 53,* 109–116.

Schwarzer, R. (Ed.). (1992). *Self-efficacy: Thought control of action.* Washington: Hemisphere.

Schwebel, A. I., & Fine, M. A. (1994). *Understanding and helping families: A cognitive behavioral approach.* Hillsdale, NJ: Erlbaum.

Scott, J. P. (1963). The process of primary socialization in canine and human infants. *Monographs of the Society for Research in Child Development, 28,* 1–47.

Scott, R. A. (1972). A proposed framework for analyzing deviance as a property of social order. In R. A. Scott & J. D. Douglas (Eds.), *Theoretical perspectives on deviance.* New York: Basic Books.

Scovern, A. W., & Kilmann, P. R. (1980). Status of electro-convulsive therapy: Review of outcome literature. *Psychological Bulletin, 87,* 260–303.

Segall, M., Campbell, D., & Herskovits, M. (1966). *The influence of culture on visual perception.* Indianapolis: Bobbs-Merrill.

Seger, C. A. (1994). Implicit learning. *Psychological Bulletin, 115* (2), 163–196.

Selfridge, O. G. (1955). Pattern recognition and modern computers. *Proceedings of the Western Joint Computer Conference.* New York: Institute of Electrical and Electronics Engineers.

Seligman, K. (1988, October 9). Educators are alarmed over testing frenzy. *San Francisco Examiner,* pp. B–1, B–5.

Seligman, M. E. P. (1971). Preparedness and phobias. *Behavior Therapy, 2,* 307–320.

Seligman, M. E. P. (1975). *Helplessness: On depression, development, and death.* San Francisco: Freeman.

Seligman, M. E. P. (1991). *Learned optimism.* New York: Norton.

Seligman, M. E. P. (1995). The effectiveness of psychotherapy: The *Consumer Reports* study. *American Psychologist, 50,* 965–974.

Seligman, M. E. P., & Maier, S. F. (1967). Failure to escape traumatic shock. *Journal of Experimental Psychology, 74,* 1–9.

Selye, H. (1956). The stress of life. New York: McGraw-Hill.

Shaffer, C. R., & Anundsen, K. (1995, September-October). The healing powers of community. *Utne Reader*, No. 71, pp. 64–65.

Shafii, M., Carrigan, S., Whittinghill, J. R., & Derrick, A. (1985). Psychological autopsy of completed suicide in children and adolescents. *American Journal of Psychiatry 142*, 1061–1064.

Shapiro, D. H. (1985). Clinical use of meditation as a self-regulation strategy: Comments on Holmes's conclusions and implications. *American Psychologist, 40*, 719–722.

Shapiro, F. (1995). *Desensitization and reprocessing: Basic principles, protocols, and procedures.* New York: Guilford.

Shattuck, R. (1981). The forbidden experiment: The story of the wild boy of Aveyron. New York: Farrar, Straus & Giroux.

Shatz, M., Wellman, H. M., & Silber, S. (1983). The acquisition of mental verbs: A systematic investigation of the first reference to mental state. *Cognition, 14,* 301–321.

Shaver, P. R., & Hazan, C. (1993). Adult attachment: Theory and research. In W. Jones & D. Perlman (Eds.), *Advances in personal relationships*, Vol. 4, 29–70. London, England: Jessica Kingsley.

Shaver, P. R., & Hazan, C. (1994). Attachment. In A. L. Weber & J. H. Harvey (Eds.), *Perspectives on close relationships* (Chapter 6, 110–130). Boston: Allyn & Bacon.

Sheehan, S. (1983). *Is there no place on earth for me?* Boston: Houghton Mifflin.

Sheehan, S. (1995). Postscript: The last days of Sylvia Frumkin. *The New Yorker*, February 20 & 27, 1995.

Sheingold, K., & Tenney, Y. J. (1982). Memory for a salient childhood event. In U. Neisser (Ed.), *Memory observed.* San Francisco: Freeman.

Sheldon, W. (1942). *The varieties of temperament: A psychology of constitutional differences.* New York: Harper.

Sheridan, C. L., & King, R. G. (1972). Obedience to authority with an authentic victim. *Proceedings of the 80th Annual Convention, American Psychological Association, Part 1, 7,* 165–166.

Sherif, C. W. (1981, August). *Social and psychological bases of social psychology.* The G. Stanley Hall Lecture on social

psychology, presented at the annual convention of the American Psychological Association, Los Angeles, CA.

Shettleworth, S. J. (1993). Where is the comparison in comparative cognition? Alternative research programs. *Psychological Science, 4* (3), 179–184.

Shiffrin, R. M. (1993). Short-term memory: A brief commentary. *Memory and Cognition, 21* (2), 193–197.

Shneidman, E. (1985). *At the point of no return.* New York: Wiley.

Shneidman, E. (1987, March). At the point of no return. *Psychology Today*, pp. 54–59.

Shoda, Y., Mischel, W., & Peake, P. K. (1990). Predicting adolescent cognitive and self-regulatory competencies from preschool delay of gratification. *Developmental Psychology, 26* (6), 978–986.

Shoda, Y., Mischel, W., & Wright, J. C. (1993a). Links between personality judgments and contextualized behavior patterns: Situation-behavior profiles of personality prototypes. *Social Cognition, 11,* 399–429.

Shoda, Y., Mischel, W., & Wright, J. C. (1993b). The role of situational demands and cognitive competencies in behavior organization and personality coherence. *Journal of Personality and Social Psychology, 65,* 1023–1035.

Siegel, B. (1988). *Love, medicine & miracles.* New York: Harper & Row.

Siegel, J. M. (1990). Stressful life events and use of physician services among the elderly: The moderating role of pet ownership. *Journal of Personality and Social Psychology, 58,* 1081–1086.

Siegel, R. K. (1992). *Fire in the brain.* New York: Dutton.

Siegler, R. S. (1983). Information processing approaches to cognitive development. In W. Kessen (Ed.), *Handbook of child psychology: History, theory, and methods* (Vol. 1). New York: Wiley.

Silbersweig, D. A., Stern, E., Frith, C., Cahill, C., Holmes, A., Grootoonk, S., Seaward, J., McKenna, P., Chua, S. E., Schnorr, L., Jones, T., & Frackowiak, R. S. J. (1995). A functional neuroanatomy of hallucinations in schizophrenia. *Nature, 378* (November 9), 176–179.

Silver, R. L., Boon, C., & Stones, M. L. (1983). Searching for meaning in misfortune: Making

sense of incest. *Journal of Social Issues, 39, 81–101.*

Silver, R. L., & Wortman, C. B. (1980). Coping with undesirable life events. In J. Garber & M. E. P. Seligman (Eds.), *Human helplessness: Theory and application.* New York: Academic Press.

Simmel, E. C. (1980). *Early experiences and early behavior: Implications for social development.* New York: Academic Press.

Simpson, J. A. (1990). The influence of attachment styles on romantic relationships. *Journal of Personality and Social Psychology, 59,* 971–980.

Simpson, J. A., & Harris, B. A. (1994). Interpersonal attraction. In A. L. Weber & J. H. Harvey (Eds.), *Perspectives on close relationships* (pp. 45–66). Boston: Allyn & Bacon.

Sinclair, J. D. (1983, December). The hardware of the brain. *Psychology Today*, pp. 8, 11, 12.

Singer, J. L. (1966). *Daydreaming: An introduction to the experimental study of inner experience.* New York: Random House.

Singer, J. L. (1975). Navigating the stream of consciousness: Research in daydreaming and related inner experience. *American Psychologist, 30,* 727–739.

Singer, J. L., & McCraven, V. J. (1961). Some characteristics of adult daydreaming. *Journal of Psychology, 51,* 151–164.

Singer, J. L. (1990). *Seeing through the visible world: Jung, Gnosis, and chaos.* New York: Harper & Row.

Skinner, B. F. (1981). Selection by consequences. *Science, 213,* 501–504.

Skinner, B. F. (1990). Can psychology be a science of mind? *American Psychologist, 45,* 1206–1210.

Skoog, I., Nilsson, L., Palmertz, B., Andreasson, L. A., Svanborg, A. (1993). A population-based study of dementia in 85-year-olds. *New England Journal of Medicine, 328,* 153.

Sloane, R. B., Staples, F. R., Cristol, A. H., Yorkston, N. J., & Whipple, K. (1975). *Psychotherapy versus behavior therapy.* Cambridge, MA: Harvard University Press.

Slobin, D. I. (1979). *Psycholinguistics* (2nd ed.). Glenview, IL: Scott, Foresman.

Slobin, D. I. (1985a). Introduction: Why study acquisition crosslinguistically? In D.I. Slobin (Ed.), *The crosslinguistic study of language acquisition.*

Vol. 1: The data (pp.3–24). Hillsdale, NJ: Erlbaum.

Slobin, D. I. (1985b). Cross-linguistic evidence of the language making capacity. In D.I. Slobin (Ed.). *The crosslinguistic study of language acquisition.* Vol. 2: Theoretical issues (pp. 1157–1256). Hillsdale, NJ: Erlbaum.

Slovic, P. (1984). Facts vs. fears: Understanding perceived risk. Presentation at a Science and Public Policy Seminar. Federation of Behavioral, Psychological, and Cognitive Sciences, Washington, DC.

Smith, C. A. (1989). Dimensions of appraisal and physiological response in emotion. *Journal of Personality and Social Psychology, 56,* 339–353.

Smith, C. A., & Ellsworth, P. C. (1985). Patterns and cognitive appraisal in emotion. *Journal of Personality and Social Psychology, 48,* 813–838.

Smith, D. (1982). Trends in counseling and psychotherapy. *American Psychologist, 37,* 802–809.

Smith, E. E., & Medin, D. L. (1981). *Cognitive Science Series: 4. Categories and concepts.* Cambridge, MA: Harvard University Press.

Smith, M. L., & Glass, G. V. (1977). Meta-analysis of psychotherapy outcome studies. *American Psychologist, 32,* 752–760.

Snarey, J. (1985). Cross-cultural universality of social-moral development: A critical review of Kohlbergian research. *Psychological Bulletin, 97,* 202–232.

Snyder, M. (1984). When beliefs create reality. In L. Berkowitz (Ed.), *Advances in experimental social psychology, Vol. 18* (pp. 247–305). New York: Academic Press.

Snyder, M., & Swann, W. B., Jr. (1978). Hypothesis-testing processes in social interaction. *Journal of Personality and Social Psychology, 36,* 1202–1212.

Snyder, S. H. (1986). *Drugs and the brain.* New York: Scientific American Books.

Sokol, M. M. (Ed.). (1987). *Psychological testing and American society, 1890–1930.* New Brunswick, NJ: Rutgers University Press.

Solomon, R., Gerrity, E. T., & Muff, A. M. (1992). Efficacy of treatments of posttraumatic stress disorder. *Journal of the American Medical Association, 268,* 633–638.

Solso, R. L. (1991). *Cognitive psychology* (3rd ed.). Boston: Allyn and Bacon.

Solso, R. L., & McCarthy, J. E. (1981). Prototype formation of faces: A case study of pseudomemory. *British Journal of Psychology, 72,* 499–503.

Solvason, H. B., Ghanta, V. K., & Hiramoto, R. N. (1988). Conditioned augmentation of natural killer cell activity: Independence from nociceptive effects and dependence on interferon-beta. *Journal of Immunology, 140,* 661–665.

Somers, A. R. (1981). Marital status, health, and the use of health services: An old relationship revisited. In P. J. Stein (Ed.), *Single life: Unmarried adults in social context* (pp. 178–190). New York: St. Martin's Press.

Sorenson, R. C. (1973). *Adolescent sexuality in contemporary America.* Cleveland, OH: World.

Spanos, N. P., Weekes, J. R., & Bertrand, L. D. (1985). Multiple personality: A social psychological perspective. *Journal of Abnormal Psychology, 94,* 362–376.

Spearman, C. E. (1927). *The abilities of man.* London: Macmillan.

Spelke, E.S., and Owsley, C.J. (1979). Intermodal exploration and knowledge in infancy. *Infant Behavior and Development, 2,* 13–27.

Sperling, G. (1960). The information available in brief visual presentations. *Psychological Monographs, 74,* 1–29.

Sperling, G. (1963). A model for visual memory tasks. *Human Factors, 5,* 19–31.

Sperry, R. W. (1968). Mental unity following surgical disconnection of the cerebral hemispheres. *The Harvey Lectures,* Series 62. New York: Academic Press.

Sperry, R. W. (1976). Changing concepts of consciousness and free will. *Perspectives in Biology and Medicine, 20,* 9–19.

Sperry, R. W. (1982). Some effects of disconnecting the cerebral hemispheres. *Science, 217,* 1223–1226.

Sperry, R. W. (1987). Consciousness and causality. In R. L. Gregory (Ed.), *The Oxford companion to the mind* (pp. 164–166). New York: Oxford University Press.

Spiegel, D., Bloom, J. R., Kraemer, H. C., & Gottheil, E. (1989, October 14). Effect of psychosocial treatment on sur-

vival of patients with metastatic breast cancer. *The Lancet,* pp. 888–891.

Spiegel, D., & Cardeña, E. (1991). Disintegrated experience: The dissociate disorders revisited. *Psychological Bulletin, 100,* 366–378.

Sprecher, S., & McKinney, K. (1994). Sexuality in close relationships. In A. L. Weber & J. H. Harvey (Eds.), *Perspectives on close relationships* (pp. 193–216). Boston: Allyn & Bacon.

Springer, S. P., & Deutsch, G. (1993). *Left brain, right brain,* 4th edition. New York: W. H. Freeman.

Squire, L. R. (1992). Memory and the hippocampus: A synthesis from findings with rats, monkeys, and humans. *Psychological Review, 99,* 195–231.

Squire, S. (1983). *The slender balance: Causes and cures for bulimia, anorexia, and the weight loss/weight gain seesaw.* New York: Putnam.

Stacy, A. W., Newcomb, M. D., & Bentler, P. M. (1991). Cognitive motivation and drug abuse: A 9-year longitudinal study. *Journal of Abnormal Psychology, 100,* 502–515.

Stampfl, T. G., & Levis, D. J. (1967). Essentials of implosive therapy: A learning theory-based psychodynamic behavioral therapy. *Journal of Abnormal Psychology, 72,* 496–503.

Stein, M. B.,. Walker, J. R., & Forde, D. R. (1996). Public-speaking fears in a community sample: Prevalence, impact on functioning, and diagnostic classification. *Archives of General Psychiatry, 53,* 169–174.

Stern, W. (1914). The psychological methods of testing intelligence. *Educational Psychology Monographs* (No. 13).

Stern, W. C., & Morgane, P. S. (1974). Theoretical view of REM sleep function: Maintenance of catecholomine systems in the central nervous system. *Behavioral Biology, 11,* 1–32.

Sternberg, R. (1985). *Beyond IQ.* Cambridge, MA: Cambridge University Press.

Sternberg, R. (1986). Inside intelligence. *American Scientist, 74,* 137–143.

Sternberg, S. (1966). High-speed scanning in human memory. *Science, 153,* 652–654.

Sternberg, S. (1969). Memory-scanning: Mental processes revealed by reaction time

experiments. *American Scientist, 57,* 421–457.

Stevens, J. (1986, Fall). The dance of the tonal. *Shaman's Drum* (pp. 47–52).

Stevenson, H. W., Chen, C., & Lee, S-Y. (1993). Mathematics achievement of Chinese, Japanese, and American children: Ten years later. *Science, 259,* 53–58.

Stevenson, J., Graham, P., Fredman, G., & McLoughlin, V. A. (1987). Twin study of genetic influences on reading and spelling ability and disability. *Journal of Child Psychiatry, 28,* 229–247.

Stokes, M., & Zeman, D. (1995). The shame of the city. *Newsweek,* Vol. CXXVI, No. 10 (September 4), p. 26.

Storms, M. D. (1973). Videotape and the attribution process: Reversing actors' and observers' points of view. *Journal of Personality and Social Psychology, 27,* 165–175.

Storms, M. D. (1980). Theories of sexual orientation. *Journal of Personality and Social Psychology, 38,* 783–792.

Storms, M. D. (1981). A theory of erotic orientation development. *Psychological Review, 88,* 340–353.

Strack, S., & Coyne, J. C. (1983). Social confirmation of dysphoria: Shared and private reactions to depression. *Journal of Personality and Social Psychology, 50,* 149–167.

Straub, E. (1974). Helping a distressed person: Social, personality, and stimulus determinants. In L. Berkowitz (Ed.), *Advances in experimental and social psychology* (Vol. 7). New York: Academic Press.

Striegel-Moore, R. H., Silberstein, L. R., & Rodin, J. (1993). The social self in bulimia nervosa: Public self-consciousness, social anxiety, and perceived fraudulence. *Journal of Abnormal Psychology, 102,* 297–303.

Stroebe, W., Stroebe, M. S., Gergen, K. J., & Gergen, M. (1982). The effects of bereavement on mortality: A social psychological analysis. In J. R. Eiser (Ed.), *Social psychology and behavioral medicine* (pp. 527–560). New York: Wiley.

Strong, E. K. (1927). Differentiation of certified public accountants from other occupational groups. *Journal of Educational Psychology, 18,* 227–238.

Sturmey, P. (1992). Treatment acceptability for anorexia nervosa:

Effects of treatment type, problem severity and treatment outcome. *Behavioural Psychotherapy, 20* (1), 91–93.

Styron, W. (1990). *Darkness visible: A memoir of madness.* New York: Random House.

Suchman, A. L., & Ader, R. (1989). Placebo response in humans can be shaped by prior pharmacologic experience. *Psychosomatic Medicine, 51,* 251.

Sue, S. (1988). Psychotherapeutic services for ethnic minorities: Two decades of research findings. *American Psychologist, 43,* 301–308.

Suedfeld, P. (1980). *Restricted environmental stimulation: Research and clinical applications.* New York: Wiley.

Sullivan, H. S. (1953). *The interpersonal theory of psychiatry.* New York: Norton.

Suls, J., & Marco, C. A. (1990). Relationship between JAS- and FTAS-Type A behavior and non-CHD illness: A prospective study controlling for negative affectivity. *Health Psychology, 9,* 479–492.

Suls, J., & Sanders, G. S. (1988). Type A behavior as a general risk factor for physical disorder. *Journal of Behavioral Medicine, 11,* 201–226.

Sundberg, N. D., & Matarazzo, J. D. (1979). Psychological assessment of individuals. In M. E. Meyer (Ed.), *Foundations of contemporary psychology* (pp. 580–617). New York: Oxford University Press.

Susser, E., Neugebauer, R., Hoek, H. W., Brown, A. S., Lin, S., Labovitz, D., & Gorman, J. M. (1996). Schizophrenia after prenatal famine: Further evidence. *Archives of General Psychiatry, 53,* 25–31.

Svanum, S., McGrew, J., & Ehrman, L. (1994). Validity of the substance abuse scales of the MMPI–2 in a college student sample. *Journal of Personality Assessment, 62,* 427–439.

Swann, W. B., Jr., & Ely, R. J. (1984). A battle of will: Self-verification versus behavioral confirmation. *Journal of Personality and Social Psychology, 46,* 1287–1302.

Swazey, J. P. (1974). *Chlorpromazine in psychiatry: A study of therapeutic innovation.* Cambridge, MA: MIT Press.

Swets, J. A., & Bjork, R. A. (1990). Enhancing human performance: An evaluation of "new age" techniques considered by the U.S. Army. *Psychological Science, 1,* 85–96.

Szasz, T. S. (1961). *The myth of mental illness.* New York: Harper & Row.

Szasz, T. S. (1977). *The manufacture of models.* New York: Dell.

Szasz, T. S. (1979). *The myth of psychotherapy.* Garden City, NY: Doubleday.

Tajfel, H., & Billig, M. (1974). Familiarity and categorization in inter-group behavior. *Journal of Experimental Social Psychology, 10,* 159–170.

Tajfel, H. (Ed.). (1982). *Social identity and intergroup relations.* New York: Cambridge University Press.

Targ, R., & Harary, K. (1984). *The mind race: Understanding and using psychic abilities.* New York: Villard Books.

Tavris, C. (1983). *Anger: The misunderstood emotion.* New York: Simon & Schuster.

Tavris, C. (1995). From excessive rage to useful anger. *Contemporary Psychology, 40* (11), 1101–1102.

Taylor, S. E. (1986). *Health psychology.* New York: Random House.

Taylor, S. E. (1990). Health psychology: The science and the field. *American Psychologist, 45,* 40–50.

Taylor, S. E. (1992). *Health psychology* (3rd. ed.). New York: Random House.

Taylor, S. E., & Brown, J. D. (1988). Illusion and well-being: A social psychological perspective on mental health. *Psychological Bulletin, 103,* 193–210.

Teasdale, J. D. (1985). Psychological treatments for depression: How do they work? *Behavior Research and Therapy, 23,* 157–165.

Tellegen, A., Lykken, D. T., Bouchard, T. J., Wilcox, K. J., Segal, N. L., & Rich, S. (1988). Personality similarity in twins reared apart and together. *Journal of Personality and Social Psychology, 54,* 1031–1039.

Templin, M. (1957). Certain language skills in children: Their development and interrelationships. *Institute of Child Welfare Monograph,* Series No. 26. Minneapolis: University of Minnesota Press.

Tennen, H., & Herzberger, S. (1987). Depression, self-esteem, and the absence of self-protective attributional biases. *Journal of Personality and Social Psychology, 52,* 72–80.

Tenopyr, M. L., & Oeltjen, P. D. (1982). Personnel selection and

classification. *Annual Review of Psychology, 33,* 581–618.

Terman, L. M. (1916). *The measurement of intelligence.* Boston: Houghton-Mifflin.

Thigpen, C. H., & Cleckley, H. A. (1957). *Three faces of Eve.* New York: McGraw-Hill.

Thomas, E. M. (1993). *The hidden life of dogs.* New York: Houghton Mifflin.

Thomas, E. M. (1994). *The tribe of tiger: Cats and their culture.* New York: Simon & Schuster.

Thompson, K. (1988, October 2). Fritz Perls. *San Francisco Examiner-Chronicle,* This World Section, pp. 14–16.

Thompson, R. F. (1986). The neurobiology of learning and memory. *Science, 233,* 941–944.

Thoresen, C. E., & Eagleston, J. R. (1983). Chronic stress in children and adolescents [Special edition: Coping with stress]. *Theory into Practice, 22,* 48–56.

Thorndike, E. L. (1898). Animal intelligence. *Psychological Review Monograph Supplement, 2* (4, Whole No. 8).

Thorndike, R. L., & Hagen, E. (1978). *The cognitive abilities test.* Lombard, IL: Riverside.

Thorndyke, P. W., & Hayes-Roth, B. (1979). *Spatial knowledge acquisition from maps and navigation.* Paper presented at the Psychonomic Society Meeting, San Antonio, TX.

Timko, C., & Moos, R. H. (1989). Choice, control, and adaptation among elderly residents of sheltered care settings. *Journal of Applied Social Psychology, 19,* 636–655.

Tipper, S. P., & Driver, J. (1988). Negative priming between pictures and words in a selective attention task: Evidence for semantic processing of ignored stimuli. *Memory and Cognition, 16,* 64–70.

Titchener, E. B. (1898). The postulates of structural psychology. *Philosophical Review, 7,* 449–453.

Todd, J. T., & Morris, E. K. (1992). Case histories in great power of steady misrepresentation. *American Psychologist, 47,* 1441–1453.

Todd, J. T., & Morris, E. K. (1993). Change and be ready to change again. *American Psychologist, 48,* 1158–1159.

Tolman, E. C. (1932). *Purposive behavior in animals and men.* New York: Appleton-Century-Crofts.

Tolman, E. C. (1948). Cognitive maps in rats and men. *Psychological Review, 55,* 189–208.

Tolman, E. C., & Honzik, C. H. (1930). "Insight" in rats. *University of California Publications in Psychology, 4,* 215–232.

Tolman, E. C., Ritchie, B. G., & Kalish, D. (1946). Studies in spatial learning: I. Orientation and the short-cut. *Journal of Experimental Psychology, 36,* 13–24.

Tomkins, S. (1981). The quest for primary motives: Biography and autobiography of an idea. *Journal of Personality and Social Psychology, 41,* 306–329.

Torrey, E. F. (1986). *Witchdoctors and psychiatrists: The common roots of psychotherapy and its future.* New York: Harper & Row.

Treisman, A. M. (1964). Verbal cues, language and meaning in selective attention. *American Journal of Psychology, 77,* 206–219.

Treisman, A. M. (1988). Features and objects: The fourteenth Bartlett Memorial Lecture. The *Quarterly Journal of Experimental Psychology, 40,* 201–237.

Treisman, A. M. (1990). Conjunction search revisited. *Journal of Experimental Psychology: Human Perception and Performance, 16,* 459–478.

Treisman, A. M. (1992). Perceiving and re-perceiving objects. *American Psychologist, 47,* 862–875.

Triandis, H. (1989). The self and social behavior in differing cultural contexts. *Psychological Review, 96,* 506–520.

Triandis, H. (1990). Cross-cultural studies of individualism and collectivism. In J. Berman (Ed.), *Nebraska Symposium on Motivation, 1989* (pp. 42–133). Lincoln, NE: University of Nebraska Press.

Triandis, H. C. (1994). *Culture and social behavior.* New York: McGraw-Hill.

Trinder, J. (1988). Subjective insomnia without objective findings: A pseudodiagnostic classification. *Psychological Bulletin, 103,* 87–94.

Trivers, R. L. (1972). Parental investment and sexual selection. In B. Campbell (Ed.), *Sexual selection and the descent of man* (pp. 139–179). Chicago: Aldine.

Troiden, R. R. (1989). The formation of homosexual identities. *Journal of Homosexuality, 17,* 43–73.

Tronick, E., Als, H., & Brazelton, T. B. (1980). Moradic phases: A structural description analysis of infant mother face to face interaction.

Merrill-Palmer Quarterly, 26, 3–24.

Trope, I., Rozin, P., Nelson, D. K., & Gur, R. C. (1992). Information processing in separated hemispheres of the callosotomy patients: Does the analytic-holistic dichotomy hold? *Brain and Cognition, 19,* 123–147.

Tulving, E. (1983). *Elements of episodic memory.* Oxford: Clarendon Press.

Tulving, E. (1985). Memory and consciousness. *Canadian Psychology, 26,* 1–12.

Tulving, E., & Pearlstone, Z. (1966). Availability versus accessibility of information in memory for words. *Journal of Verbal Learning and Verbal Behavior, 5,* 381–391.

Tulving, E., & Thomson, D. M. (1973). Encoding specificity and retrieval processes in episodic memory. *Psychological Review, 80,* 352–373.

Tupes, E. G., & Christal, R. C. (1961). *Recurrent personality factors based on trait ratings* (Tech. Rep. No. ASD-TR–61–97). Lackland Air Force Base, TX: U.S. Air Force.

Turk, D. C. (1995). Chronic pain and depression: Role of perceived impact and perceived control in different age cohorts. *Pain, 61,* 93–101.

TV Guide. (1995). "From black humor to monkeyshines." *Vol. 43,* (45), Issue #2224, p. 3.

Tversky, B. (1981). Distortions in memory for maps. *Cognitive Psychology, 13,* 407–433.

Tyler, L. (1988). Mental testing. In E. R. Hilgard (Ed.), *Fifty years of psychology* (pp. 127–138). Glenview, IL: Scott, Foresman.

Tyler, L. E. (1965). *The psychology of human differences* (3rd ed.). New York: Appleton-Century-Crofts.

Tyler, L. E. (1974). *Individual differences.* Englewood Cliffs, NJ: Prentice-Hall.

Tyler, T. (1995). Personal communication to Philip G. Zimbardo, November 1. Department of Psychology, Stanford University.

Uchitelle, L., & Kleinfield, N. R. (1996, March 3). Downsizing humbles white-collar workers. *San Francisco Examiner* (from *New York Times* news service), p. A–2.

Uleman, J. S., & Bargh, J. A. (1989). *Unintended thought.* New York: Guilford Press.

UPI. (1986, December 22). Athlete's run ends in tragedy. *United Press International.*

Ursano, R. J., Boydstun, J. A., & Wheatley, R. D. (1981). Psychiatric illness in U.S. Air Force Vietnam prisoners of war: A five-year follow-up. *American Journal of Psychiatry, 138,* 310–314.

U.S. Department of Health and Human Services. (1991). *The health benefits of smoking cessation: A report of the Surgeon General.* (DHHS Publication No. CDC 90–8416). Washington, D.C.: U.S. Government Printing Office.

Valenstein, E. S. (Ed.). (1980). *The psychosurgery debate.* New York: Freeman.

Van de Castle, R. L. (1983). Animal figures in fantasy and dreams. In A. Katcher & A. Beck (Eds.), New perspectives on our lives with companion animals. Philadelphia: University of Pennsylvania Press.

Van de Castle, R. L. (1994). *Our dreaming mind.* New York: Ballantine Books.

van Goozen, S. H. M., van de Poll, N. E., & Sergeant, J. A. (Eds.). (1994). *Emotions: Essays on emotion theory.* Hillsdale, NJ: Erlbaum.

Van Wagener, W., & Herren, R. (1940). Surgical division of commissural pathways in the corpus callosum. *Archives of Neurology and Psychiatry, 44,* 740–759.

Van Strien, D. C., Van der Ham, T., & Van Engeland, H. (1992). Dropout characteristics in a follow-up study of 90 eating-disordered patients. *International Journal of Eating Disorders, 12* (3), 341–343.

Vangelisti, A. L., Daly, J. A., & Rudnick, J. R. (1991). Making people feel guilty in conversations: Techniques and correlates. *Human Communication Research, 18,* 3–39.

Veith, I. (1965). *Hysteria: The history of the disease.* Chicago: University of Chicago Press.

Vernon, P. E. (1969). *Intelligence and cultural environment.* London: Methuen.

Vernon, P. E. (1987). The demise of the Stanford-Binet Scale. *Canadian Psychology, 28,* 251–258.

Vitaliano, P. P., Russo, J., Young, H. M., Becker, J., & Maiuro, R. D. (1991). The screen for caregiver burden. *The Gerontologist, 31,* 76–83.

von Hofsten, C., & Lindhagen, K. (1979). Observations on the development of reaching for moving objects. *Journal of Child Psychology, 28,* 158–173.

Wade, T.J. (1991). Race and sex differences in adolescent self-perceptions of physical attractiveness and level of self-esteem during early and late adolescence. *Journal of Personality and Individual Differences, 12,* 1319–1324.

Waldvogel, S. (1948). The frequency and affective character of childhood memories. *Psychological Monographs, 62* (Whole No. 291).

Walker, E., Wade, S., & Waldman, I. (1982). The effect of lateral visual fixation on response latency to verbal and spatial questions. *Brain and Cognition, 1,* 399–404.

Wallace, A. F. C. (1959). Cultural determinants of response to hallucinatory experience. *Archives of General Psychiatry, 1,* 58–69.

Wallach, M. A., & Wallach, L. (1983). *Psychology's sanction for selfishness.* San Francisco: Freeman.

Wallerstein, J. S., & Kelly, J. B. (1980). *Surviving the breakup: How children and parents cope with divorce.* New York: Basic Books.

Wallerstein, J. S., & Blakeslee, S. (1989). *Second chances: Men, women, and children a decade after divorce.* New York: Tickner & Fields.

Wallis, C. (1984, June 11). Unlocking pain's secrets. *Time,* pp. 58–66.

Walsh, R. N. (1990). *The spirit of Shamanism.* Los Angeles: J. P. Tarcher.

Walters, C. C., & Grusec, J. E. (1977). *Punishment.* San Francisco: Freeman.

Walters, E. E., Neale, M. C., Eaves, L. J., Heath, A. C. et al. (1992). Bulimia nervosa and major depression: A study of common genetic and environmental factors. *Psychological Medicine, 22* (3), 617–622.

Wanous, J. P. (1980). *Organizational entry: Recruitment, selection, and socialization of newcomers.* Reading, MA: Addison-Wesley.

Washington Post. (1994, June 6). Heat kills trapped infant. From Associated Press Reports, p. A9.

Wasserman, E. A. (1993). Comparative cognition: Beginning the second century of the study of animal intelligence. *Psychological Bulletin, 113* (2), 211–228.

Watkins, L. R., & Mayer, D. J. (1982). Organization of the endogenous opiate and nonopiate pain control systems. *Science, 216,* 1185–1193.

Watson, J. B. (1919). *Psychology from the standpoint of a behaviorist.* Philadelphia: Lippincott.

Watson, J. B., & Rayner, R. (1920). Conditioned emotional reactions. *Journal of Experimental Psychology, 3,* 1–14.

Webb, W. B. (1974). Sleep as an adaptive response. *Perceptual and Motor Skills, 38,* 1023–1027.

Weber, A. L., & Harvey, J. H. (Eds.) (1994a). *Perspectives on close relationships.* Boston, MA: Allyn & Bacon.

Weber, A. L., & Harvey, J. H. (1994b). Accounts in coping with relationship loss. In A. L. Weber & J. H. Harvey (Eds.), *Perspectives on close relationships,* pp. 285–306. Boston: Allyn & Bacon.

Weber, A. L., Harvey, J. H., & Stanley, M. A. (1987). The nature and motivations of accounts for failed relationships. In R. Burnett, P. McGhee and D. D. Clarke (Eds.), *Accounting for relationships: Explanation, representation and knowledge* (pp. 114–133). London: Methuen.

Weber, B. (1996, February 18). Computer's ability against chess champion has surprised and intrigued. *The New York Times,* National Edition, p. 17.

Wechsler, D. (1981). *Manual for the Wechsler Adult Intelligence Scale—Revised.* New York: Psychological Corporation.

Wechsler, D. (1989). *WPPSI-R manual.* New York: Psychological Corporation.

Wechsler, D. (1991). *WISC-III manual.* New York: Psychological Corporation.

Wegner, D. M. (1989). *White bears and other unwanted thoughts.* New York: Guilford.

Wegner, D. M., Schneider, D. J., Carter, S., III, & White, T. (1987). Paradoxical effects of thought suppression. *Journal of Personality and Social Psychology, 53,* 5–13.

Weil, A. T. (1977). The marriage of the sun and the moon. In N. E. Zinberg (Ed.), *Alternate states of consciousness* (pp. 37–52). New York: Free Press.

Weinberger, M., Hiner, S. L, & Tierney, W. M. (1987). In support of hassles as a measure of stress in predicting health outcomes. *Journal of Behavioral Medicine, 10,* 19–31.

Weiner, B. (1986). *An attributional theory of motivation and emotion.* New York: Springer-Verlag.

Weingardt, K. R., Loftus, E. F., & Lindsay, D. S. (1995). Misinformation revisited: New evidence on the suggestibility of memory. *Memory and Cognition, 23,* 72–82.

Weingarten, H. R. (1985). Marital status and well-being: A national study comparing first-married, currently divorced, and remarried adults. *Journal of Marriage and the Family, 47,* 653–662.

Weinstein, N. D. (1980). Unrealistic optimism about future life events. *Journal of Personality and Social Psychology, 39,* 806–820.

Weisenberg, M. (1977). Cultural and racial reactions to pain. In M. Weisenberg (Ed.), *The control of pain.* New York: Psychological Dimensions.

Weiser, N. C., & Meyers, L. S. (1993). Validity and reliability of the revised California Psychological Inventory's Vector 3 Scale. *Educational and Psychological Measurement, 53,* 1045–1054.

Weiss, R. S. (1975). *Marital separation.* New York: Basic Books.

Weissman, W. W. (1987). Advances in psychiatric epidemiology: Rates and risks for depression. *American Journal of Public Health, 77,* 445–451.

Weitzman, L. J. (1985). *The divorce revolution: The unexpected social and economic consequences for women and children in America.* New York: The Free Press.

Wellman, H.M., & Estes, D. (1986). Early understanding of mental entities: A reexamination of childhood realism. *Child Development, 57,* 910–923.

Wener, R., Frazier, W., & Farbstein, J. (1987, June). Building better jails. *Psychology Today,* 40–49.

Wertheimer, M. (1923). Untersuchungen zur Lehre von der Gestalt, II. *Psychologische Forschung, 4,* 301–350.

Westerfeld, J. S., & Fuhr, S. R. (1987). Suicide and depression among college students. *Professional Psychology: Research and Practice, 18,* 119–123.

Whitbourne, S. K., & Hulicka, I. M. (1990). Ageism in undergraduate psychology texts. *American Psychologist, 45,* 1127–1136.

White, M. D., & White, C. A. (1981). Involuntarily committed patients' constitutional right to refuse treatment. *American Psychologist, 36,* 953–962.

Wicklund, R. A., & Brehm, J. W. (1976). *Perspectives on cognitive dissonance.* Hillsdale, NJ: Erlbaum.

Wiggins, J. S. (1973). *Personality and prediction: Principles of personality assessment.* Reading, MA: Addison-Wesley.

Wilder, D. A. (1986). Social categorization: Implications for creation and reduction of intergroup bias. *Advances in Experimental Social Psychology, 19,* 291–355.

Williams, T. M. (Ed.). (1986). *The impact of television: A natural experiment in three communities.* Orlando, FL: Academic Press.

Wills, T. A. (1986). Stress and coping in early adolescence: Relationships to substance use in urban school samples. *Health Psychology, 5,* 503–529.

Wilson, E. D., Reeves, A., & Culver, C. (1977). Cerebral commissurotomy for control of intractable seizures. *Neurology, 27,* 708–715.

Wilson, M. (1959). *Communal rituals among the Nyakusa.* London: Oxford University Press.

Winett, R. A. (1995). A framework for health promotion and disease prevention programs. *American Psychologist, 50,* 341–350.

Wingerson, L. (1990). *Mapping our genes.* New York: Dutton.

Wolcott, J. (1995). I lost it in the saucer. *The New Yorker, Vol. LXXI,* No. 22 (July 31), pp. 75–78.

Wolfe, A. (1995). Has there been a cognitive revolution in America? The flawed sociology of *The Bell Curve.* In S. Fraser (Ed.), *The bell curve wars: Race, intelligence, and the future of America.* New York: BasicBooks.

Wolfe, T. (1979). *The right stuff.* New York: Doubleday.

Wolman, C. (1975). Therapy and capitalism. *Issues in Radical Therapy, 3* (1).

Wolpe, J. (1958). *Psychotherapy by reciprocal inhibition.* Stanford, CA: Stanford University Press.

Wolpe, J. (1973). *The practice of behavior therapy* (2nd ed.). New York: Pergamon.

Woodworth, R. S. (1918). *Dynamic psychology.* New York: Columbia University Press.

Workman, B. (1990, December 1). Father guilty of killing daughter's friend in '69. *San Francisco Examiner-Chronicle,* pp. 1, 4.

Wright, L. (1995a). Double mystery. *The New Yorker, Vol. LXXI,* No. 23 (August 7), pp. 45–62.

Wright, R. (1995b, July 9). It's all in our heads: Review of Churchland, *The engine of reason, the seat of the soul. The New York Times Book Review,* pp. 1, 16.

Wright, R. (1996). *The moral animal.* New York: Pantheon.

Wundt, W. (1907). *Outlines of psychology* (7th ed., C. H. Judd, Trans.). Leipzig: Englemann. (Original work published 1896).

Wyatt, G. E., Peters, S. D., & Guthrie, D. (1988). Kinsey revisited, Part I: Comparisons of the sexual socialization and sexual behavior of white women over 33 years. *Archives of Sexual Behavior, 17,* 201–239.

Wyatt, R. J. (1996). Neurodevelopmental abnormalities and schizophrenia: A family affair. *Archives of General Psychiatry, 53,* 11–18.

Wynne, L. C., Roohey, M. L., & Doane, J. (1979). Family studies. In L. Bellak (Ed.), *The schizophrenic syndrome.* New York: Basic Books.

Yalom, I. D., & Greaves, C. (1977). Group therapy with the terminally ill. *American Journal of Psychiatry, 134,* 396–400.

Yam, P. (1995). A skeptically inquiring mind. *Scientific American, 273* (1), 34–35.

Yates, B. (1985). *Self-management.* Belmont, CA: Wadsworth.

Yerkes, R. M. (1921). Psychological examining in the United States Army. In R. M. Yerkes (Ed.), *Memoirs of the National Academy of Sciences: Vol. 15.* Washington, DC: U.S. Government Printing Office.

Yerkes, R. M., & Dodson, J. D. (1908). The relation of strength of stimulus to rapidity of habit formation. *Journal of Comparative Neurology and Psychology, 18,* 459–482.

Zadeh, L. A. (1965). Fuzzy sets. *Information Control, 8,* 338–353.

Zahn-Waxler, C., & Radke-Yarrow, M. (1982). The development of altruism: Alternative research strategies. In N. Eisenberg-Berg (Ed.), *The development of prosocial behavior* (pp. 109–138). New York: Academic Press.

Zajonc, R. B. (1980). Feeling and thinking: Preferences need no inferences. *American Psychologist, 35,* 151–175.

Zanchetti, A. (1967). Subcortical and cortical mechanisms in arousal and emotional behavior. In G. C. Quarton, T. Melnechuk, & F. O. Schmitt (Eds.), *The neurosciences: A study program.* New York: Rockefeller University Press.

Zebb, B. J., & Meyers, L. S. (1993). Reliability and validity of the revised California Psychological Inventory's Vector 1 Scale. *Educational and Psychological Measurement, 53,* 271–280.

Zigler, E., & Muenchow, S. (1992). *Head Start: The inside story of America's most successful educational experiment.* New York: Basic Books.

Zigler, E. & Styfco, S. J. (1994). Head Start: Criticisms in a constructive context. *American Psychologist, 49,* 127–132.

Zilboorg, G., & Henry, G. W. (1941). *A history of medical psychology.* New York: Norton.

Zimbardo, P. G. (1973). On the ethics of investigation in human psychological research: With special reference to the Stanford Prison Experiment. *Cognition, 2,* 243–256.

Zimbardo, P. G. (1975). On transforming experimental research into advocacy for social change. In M. Deutsch & H. Hornstein (Eds.), *Applying social psychology: Implications for research, practice, and training* (pp. 33–66). Hillsdale, NJ: Erlbaum.

Zimbardo, P. G. (1990). *Shyness: What it is, what to do about it* (Rev. ed.). Reading, MA: Addison-Wesley. (Original work published 1977).

Zimbardo, P. G., & Andersen, S. A. (1993). Understanding mind control: Exotic and mundane mental manipulations. In M. Langone (Ed.), *Recovery from cults* (pp. 104–125). New York: Norton.

Zimbardo, P. G., Andersen, S. M., & Kabat, L. (1981). Induced hearing deficit generates experimental paranoia. *Science, 212,* 1529–1531.

Zimbardo, P. G., Haney, C., Banks, W. C., & Jaffe, D. (1973, April 8). The mind is a formidable jailer: A Pirandellian prison. *The New York Times Magazine,* pp. 36ff.

Zimbardo, P. G., & Montgomery, K. D. (1957). The relative strengths of consummatory responses in hunger, thirst, and exploratory drive. *Journal of Comparative and Physiological Psychology, 50,* 504–508.

Zimbardo, P. G., & Radl, S. (1981). *The shy child.* New York: McGraw-Hill.

Zimmerman, B. J., Bandura, A., Martinez-Pons, M. (1992). Self-motivation for academic attainment: The role of self-efficacy beliefs and goal setting. *American Educational Research Journal, 29,* 663–676.

Zubeck, J. P., Pushkar, D., Sansom, W., & Gowing, J. (1961). Perceptual changes after prolonged sensory isolation (darkness and silence). *Canadian Journal of Psychology, 15,* 83–100.

Zuckerman, M. (1990). Some dubious premises in research and theory on racial differences: Scientific, social, and ethical issues. *American Psychologist, 45,* 1297–1303.

Zuckerman, M., & DePaulo, B. M. (1981). Verbal and nonverbal communication and deception. In L. Berkowitz (Ed.), *Advances in experimental social psychology.* New York: Academic Press.

Zuckerman, M., & Koestner, R. (1984). Anchoring in the detection of deception and leakage. *Journal of Personality and Social Psychology, 47,* 301–311.

Acknowledgments

Photo Credits

Unless otherwise acknowledged, all photographs are the property of Scott, Foresman and Company. Page abbreviations are as follows: (T)top, (C)center, (B)bottom, (L)left, (R)right.

Chapter 1: Page 2, Tony Demin/International Stock; page 6, R. Lord/Image Works; page 7, Superstock, Inc.; page 12, archives of the History of American Psychology, University of Akron; page 13, Corbis-Bettman Archive; page 14, Pete Turner/Image Bank; page 15, Corbis-Bettmann Archive; page 17, Mark Richards/PhotoEdit; page 19, from "Puck's Almanac for 1882"; page 24(T), Bob Daemmrich/Stock Boston; page 24, (B), Janet Century/PhotoEdit; page 25, Sidney Harris; page 26, drawing by D. Reilly © 1993 The New Yorker Magazine, Inc.; page 29, Sidney Harris; page 30, Superstock, Inc.; page 32(T), Carol Palmer/Picture Cube, Inc.; page 32(B), from "The Cartoon Guide to Statistics," by Larry Gonick & Wollcott Smith

Chapter 2: Page 38, Superstock, Inc.; page 41, by permission of the *Darwin Museum, Down House,* courtesy of Mr. G. P. Darwin.; page 45, Nick Downes/reprinted with permission from *Science* Vol. 238, 1989 © 1989 American Association for the Advancement of Science; page 47, John W. Verano, National Museum of Natural History/Smithsonian Institution; page 48 Warren Anatomical Museum, Harvard Medical School; page 49(T), courtesy Monte S. Buchsbaum, M.D.; page 49(TC), Dan McCoy/Rainbow; page 49(C), Howard Sochurek; page 49(CB), Dan McCoy/Rainbow; page 49(B), courtesy of Monte S. Buchsbaum, M.D.; page 50, courtesy of Professor Rodolfo Llinas; page 58, Loren/Fisher/Gamma Liaison; page 68, Christopher Brown/Stock Boston

Chapter 3: Page 74, Stacy Pick/Stock Boston; page 77, Globe Photos, Inc.; page 79, David Young-Wolff/PhotoEdit; page 80 Greco/Image Works; page 85, Rhoda Sidney/Image Works; page 90, Ogust/Image Works; page 92, Network Pro/Image Works; page 96, Michael Newman/PhotoEdit; page 99, Mike Maple/Woodfin Camp & Associates; page 100(T), David Young-Wolff/Tony Stone Images; page 100(B), Mark M. Lawrence/Stock Market; page 102(T), Superstock, Inc.; page 102(B), Michael Newman/PhotoEdit

Chapter 4: Page 108, Myrleen Fergunson/PhotoEdit; page 112, Springer/Bettmann Film Archive; page 115, Reuters/Rebecca Cook/Archive Photos; page 116, from *A Child Is Born,* Lennart Nilsson/Bonnier-Fakta; page 120, Amy C. Etra/PhotoEdit; page 122, Rangefinders; page 123, D. Grecco/Image Works; page 125(T), Peter Menzel/Stock Boston; page 125(C), George Goodwin/Monkmeyer; page 125(B), Sue Ann Miller/Tony Stone Images; page 126(all), Lew Merrim/Monkmeyer Press Photo Service, Inc.; page 127(all), Marcia Weinstein; page 129, Paul Conklin/PhotoEdit; page 130(L), Michael Newman/PhotoEdit; page 130(R), Robert Nese/Globe Photos, Inc.; page 132(L), Michael Newman/PhotoEdit; page 132(R), Kindra Clineff/Picture Cube, Inc.; page 133, 1996 Thomas Hoepker/Magnum Photos ; page 134, Nina Leen/Life Magazine/Time Warner, Inc.; page 136, Martin Roger/Tony Stone Images; page 139(T), Miro Vintonio/Picture Cube, Inc.; page 139(C), James Chimbidis/Tony Stone Images; page 139(B), Christopher Langridge/Sygma; page 141, Grantpix/Stock Boston; page 143, Genaro Moline from *A Day in California*; page 144, Bob Daemmrich/Image Works; page 146(T), Bob Daemmrich/Image Works; page 146(B), Bob Daemmrich/Uniphoto; page 147(all), Annenberg/CDB Program 18/WGBH; page 149, Scott Thode/International Stock

Chapter 5: Page 154, *Kandinsky, Vasily, Picture with an Archer* (1909), oil on canvas, 69 X 57 (175.2 X 144.7 cm), Museum of Modern Art, New York, fractional gift of Mrs. Bertram Smith, photograph ©1966 Museum of Modern Art, New York.; page 157, Stephen Dalton/Animals Animals; page 166, Comstock Inc.; page 167(T), Fitz Goro, Life Magazine, Time Warner, Inc.; page 168 MacMillan Science Company, Inc.; page 174, Superstock, Inc.; page 176(all), Superstock, Inc.; page 183(TL), by Victor Vasarel, courtesy of artist; page 183(TR), Cordon Art-Bam-Holland, M. C. Esher Heirs, collection of C. V. S. Roosevelt Washington, DC; page 183(B), "Slave Market with the Disappearing Bust of Voltair" (1940), oil on canvas 18 1/4 x 25 3/8, collection of The Salvador Dali Museum, St. Petersburg, Florida, copyright 1996 Salvador Dali Museum, Inc.; page 184(all), DeKeerle Sygma; page 190 Tom Wurt/Stock Boston; page 191, "The Moment Before Death," Russell Sorgi, from *Life: The First Fifty Years,* 1936–1986 (Little Brown);

Chapter 6: Page 198, Tom Wurt/PhotoEdit; page 202, *The Far Side,* by Gary Larson, © 1986 Universal Press Syndicate; page 204, Bettmann Archive; page 208, archives of the History of American Psychology, University of Akron; page 213, Joe McNally; page 216, Jacob H. Bauchman; page 217, *Calvin & Hobbes* by Bill Watterson/Universal Press Syndicate; page 221, Randy Taylor/Sygma; page 222, Animal Behavior Enterprises; page 223, drawing by S. Gross, © 1994 The New Yorker Magazine, Inc.; page 226(all), from A. Bandura and R. Walters/Photo courtesy of Dr. Albert Bandura; page 234, Globe Photos, Inc.; page 237, David Sipress; page 239, Rick Browne/Stock Boston; page 240 John Greeen/San Mateo Times

Chapter 7: Page 248, Archive Photos/Reuters/Blake Sell; page 250, Globe Photos, Inc.; page 254, Superstock, Inc.; page 256, © 1985 *Bloom County,* Washington Post Writers Group, reprint with permission.; page 258, Spencer Grant/Stock Boston; page 260, Frozen Images/Image Works; page 261, L. Kolvoord/Image Works; page 266, Sidney Harris; page 271, Superstock, Inc.; page 272, Uniphoto; page 274, NBC/Globe Photos, Inc.; page 277, Superstock, Inc.; page 278(T), Elena Rooraid/PhotoEdit; page 278(B), Charles Feil/Stock Boston; page 278(C), Superstock, Inc.

Chapter 8: Page 284, Globe Photos, Inc.; page 291, Barbara Brown/Adventure Photo; page 295, Superstock, Inc.; page 295(T), H. Armstrong Roberts; page 300(all), Dr. Paul Ekman/Human Interaction Laboratory; page 302(TL), Barry Lewis/Network/Matrix; page 302(TC), Erika Stone; page 302(TR), Ted Kerasote/Photo Researchers; page 302(BL), Francie Manning/Picture Cube; page 302(BC), John Giordano/SABA; page 302(BR), [MISSING]; page 306(B), Bob Daemmrich/Stock Boston; page 306(T), Dana Feinman/Fotos International; page 311(B), J. Nettis/H. Armstrong Roberts, Inc.; page 311(T), Joyce Wilson/Animals Animals; page 316, Superstock, Inc.; page 318(B), Joel Gordon; page 318(C), Sullivan/TexaStock; page 318(T), Olive R. Pierce/Stock Boston; page 320 Bachmann/PhotoEdit

Chapter 9: Page 330, Globe Photos, Inc.; page 333(B), Paul Souders/Allstock, Inc./Tony Stone Images; page 333(T), Willaim Traufic/Image Bank; page 337, J. Pat Carter/Gamma Liaison; page 340, Chronicle Features Syndicate; page 343, Cary S. Wolinsky/Stock Boston; page 348, Reuters/Win McNamee/Archive Photos; page 349, Andrew Lictenstein/JB Pictures; page 356, Superstock, Inc.; page 358, Joe Bensen/Stock Boston; page 359, B. Bachmann/Image Works; page 362, Wilson North/International Stock; page 368, Nick Downs; page 369, Robert McElroy/Woodfin Camp & Associates; page 371, Sidney/Image Works; page 374, Chuck Savage/Uniphoto.

Chapter 10: Page 378, Archive Photos; page 381, Lawrence Migdale/Stock Boston; page 385(B), reprinted by permission of the publishers from Thematic Apprecption Test, by Henry A. Murray, Cambridge, MA: Harvard University Press, copyright ©1943 by the President and Fellows of Harvard College: ©1971, by Henry A. Murray; page 387, *The Far Sice* by Gary Larson/Universal Press Syndicate; page 392, Globe Photos, Inc.; page 393, Zentralbibliothek, Zurich; page 397, Focus on Sports, Inc.; page 398, David Young-Wolff/PhotoEdit; page 401, Punch/Rothco; page 403, 1970 Leonard Freed/Magnum Photos ; page 407, Scala/Art Resource; page 408, Myrleen Fergunson/PhotoEdit; page 412, Bob Daemmrich/Stock Boston

Chapter 11: Page 418, Bob Daemmrich/Image Works; page 422, photo by John Barrett/Globe Photos, Inc.; page 425, Merrim/Monkmeyer; page 428 Bob Daemmrich/Stock Boston; page 429, Bob Daemmrich/Stock Boston; page 431, Pete Saloutos/Tony Stone Images; page 433, Chronicle Features Syndicate; page 440 Iikka Uimonen/Sygma; page 441, Patrick Ward/Stock Boston; page 447(T)(B), Edward Clark, Life Magazines, © Time, Inc. & Joan Clifford/Picture Cube, Inc.; page 451, K. Preuss/Image Works; page 454, Globe Photos, Inc.

Chapter 12: Page 458 Globe Photos, Inc.; page 463(B), Ted Horowitz/Stock Market; page 463(T), Bob Daemmrich/Stock Boston Bob; page 467, William Vandivert; page 468 Ted Goff; page 471(all), from the film *Obedience*, copyright 1965 by Stanley Milgram, and distributed; page 476, Jeff Kowalsky/AP/Wide World; page 480, Bob Daemmrich/Stock Boston; page 483, © 1993 Tribune Media Services, Inc., all rights reserved; page 484(all), courtesy, Mrs. Jane Elliott and ABC Television, photos by Charlotte Button; page 489, David Stewart/Tony Stone Images; page 492, Mic Smith/The Post & Courier/Sygma; page 494(T), courtesy of The New York Post; page 494(B), Alex Tehrani/Gamma Liaison; page 495(TL)(TR)(B), from: Keen, S., *Faces of the Enemy: Reflections of the Hostile Imagination,* copyright © 1986 Sam Keen. all right reserved. Reprinted by permis-

sion of Harper, Collins Publisher, Inc; page 496, Reuters/Corbis-Bettmann

Chapter13: Page 502, Christy's, London/Superstock, Inc.; page 505, National Mental Health Association; page 508, Peabody Essex Museum; page 510, Mary Evans Picture Library; page 512, Reuters/Corbis-Bettmann; page 516, Gamma Liaison; page 518 Susan Greenwood/Gamma Liaison; page 519(R), Courtesy Dr. Corneila Wilbur; page 519, Courtesy Dr. Corneila Wilbur; page 524, Archive Photos; page 529, drawing by Eric Kaplan; page ©1995, The New Yorker Magazine, Inc.; page 533, AP/Wide World; page 536, Archive Photos; page 547, Tate Gallery, London/Art Resource

Chapter14: Page 554, Zigy Kaluzny/Tony Stone Images; page 557, Drawing by Mick Stevens © 1995, The New Yorker Magazine, Inc.; page 560, *Cathy* by Cathy Guisewite/Universal Press Syndicate; page 561, Sir John Soane's Museum; page 563, Gamma Liaison; page 566, Freud Museum, London ; page 570(B), Tony Stone Images; page 570(TR), Superstock, Inc.; page 570(TL), Superstock, Inc.; page 573, Rick Freidman/Black Star; page 576, Dr. Philip G. Zimbardo; page 579, David Young-Wolff/PhotoEdit; page 584, Robert Nebecker/ Leerhessen 1990; page 588, Hieronymus Bosch: Extraction of The Stone of Folly. Prado Madrid, Giraudon/Art Resource, NY; page 589, Will McIntyre/Photo Researchers; page 594, Joel Gordon

Literary Credits

Chapter 2: Figure 2.2, page 44, "Approximate Time Line for the Major Events in Human Evolution" from *Human Evolution: An Illustrated Introduction,* by Robert Lewin. copyright © 1992 by Scientific American Library, used with permission of W. H. Freeman and Company; **Figure 2.5,** page 51, from *Psychology and Life,* 14th Edition by Philip G. Zimbardo and Richard J. Gerrig. copyright © 1996 Philip G. Zimbardo, Inc., and Richard J. Gerrig, Addison-Wesley Educational Publishers Inc.; **Figure 2.19,** page 69, from *The Harvey Lectures.* Series 62, by R. W. Sperry, copyright © 1968 by Academic Press, reprinted by

permission of the author and the publisher.

Chapter 3: Figure 3.4, page 89, from "Ontogenic Development of the Human Sleep-Dream Cycle," by H. P. Roffwarz et al., in *Science,* April 1996, Vol. 152, No. 9, pp. 604–19. copyright 1966 by AAAS, reprinted by permission of the American Association for the Advancement of Science.

Chapter 4: Figure 4.1, page 117, "The Development of the Human Brain" adapted from figure on p. 59, *The Brain,* by Thompson. copyright © 1985 by W. H Freeman and Company, used with permission; **Figure 4.2,** page 118, from *The First Two Years,* by Mary M. Shirley, reprinted by permission of the University of Minnesota Press; **Marginal Note,** page 119, entry for Tuesday, May 5, 1991, from *The Dave Barry Calendar 1922;* **Figure 4.3,** page 123, adapted from "The Acquisition of Language," by Breyne Arlene Moskowitz, *Scientific American,* November 1978, p. 94D, copyright © 1978 by Scientific American, Inc, all rights reserved, reprinted by permission; **Table 4.2,** page 129, from "A Conception of Adult Development, " by D. J. Levinson, in *American Psychologist,* Vol. 41, pp. 3–13, copyright © 1986 by the American Psychological Association, adapted by permission; **Table 4.3,** page 137, from p. 18 of *Child Development* by L. P. Lipsitt and H. W. Reese, copyright © 1979 by HarperCollins Publishers, reprinted by permission of the publisher.

Chapter 5: Table 5.1, page 158, adapted by permission from "Sensation," p. 254 of *The Encyclopedic Dictionary of Psychology,* 3rd ed, copyright © 1986 by the Dushkin Publishing Group, Inc. Reprinted by permission of the author; **Table 5.2,** page 159, from *New Directions in Psychology,* by Roger Brown, Eugene Galanter, and Eckhard H. Hess, copyright © 1962 by Holt, Rinehard and Winston, Inc, reprinted by permission of Dr. Eugene Galanter; **Figure 5.5,** page 166, adapted from *Seeing: Illusion, Brain and Mind,* by John P. Frisby, copyright © 1979 by John P. Frisby, reprinted by permission of Oxford University Press; **Figure 5.10,** page 171, from *The Science of Musical*

Sounds, by D. C. Miller, Figure 145, page 315, Macmillan Company, 1926, reprinted by permission of Case Western Reserve University; **Box Illustration,** page 173, "New Help for the Hearing Impaired," by Steve Kearsly, appearing in the article "Sounds of Success" by Benjamin Pimentel, *San Francisco Chronicle,* August 4, 1995, p. A19, copyright © 1995 San Francisco Chronicle, reprinted by permission; **Figure 5.17,** page 181, figure from *Fundamentals of Sensation and Perception,* by M. W. Levine and J. Shefner, reprinted by permission of Michael W. Levine; **Figure 5.19,** page 186, from "Features and Objects in Visual Processing," by Ann Triesman, in *Scientific American,* November 1986, copyright © 1986 by Scientific American, Inc., all rights reserved, reprinted by permission.

Chapter 6: Figure 6.2, page 207, from *Psychology,* by William Buskist, copyright © 1991 by HarperCollins Publishers, Inc., reprinted by permission; **Figure 6.5,** page 225, from "Degrees of Hunger, Reward and Nonreward, and Maze Learning in Rats," by E. C. Tolman and C. H. Honzik, in *University of California Publication in Psychology,* Vol. 4, No 16, December 1930, reprinted by permission of the University of California Press; **Figure 6.7,** page 231, from *Human Memory: Structures and Processes,* 2nd ed., by Roberta Klatsky, copyright © 1975, 1980 by W. H. Freeman and Company, used with permission.

Chapter 7: Figure 7.1, page 251, from *Cognitive Psychology,* 3rd ed., by Robert L. Solso, copyright © 1991 by Allyn and Bacon, reprinted with permission; **Figure 7.3,** page 259, "Prototype formatin of faces: A case study of pseudo-memory," by Robert L. Solso and Judith E. McCarthy, *British Journal of Psychology,* 72, pp. 499–503, reprinted by permission of The British Psychological Society; **Figure 7.4,** page 260, from "Retrieval Time from Semantic Memory," by Collins and Quillan, *Journal of Verbal Learning and Verbal Behavior,* Vol. 8, pp. 240–47, copyright © 1969 by Academic Press, Inc., reprinted by permission; **Figures 7.5and 7.6,** page 264, from *Cognitive Psychology,* 3rd ed., by Robert L. Solso, copyright © 1991 by Allyn and Bacon, reprinted by permission;

Figures 7.7 and 7.8, pages 267–68, from *How to Solve Problems: Elements of a Theory of Problems and Problem Solving,* by Wayne A. Wickelgren, copyright © 1974 by W. H. Freeman and Company, reprinted by permission.

Chapter 8: Figure 8.1, page 290, reprinted by permission of the author and the publisher from "Crying Behavior in the Human Adult," by William H. Frey, II, Ph.D., et al., in *Integrative Psychiatry,* September/October 1983, copyright © 1983 by Elsevier Science Publishing Company, Inc.; **Figure 8.2,** page 292, from "A Language for the Emotions," by Robert Plutchik, *Psychology Today,* February 1980, reprinted with permission from Psychology Today Magazine, copyright © 1980 Sussex Publishers, Inc.; **Figure 8.4,** page 299, figure from *Psychology,* Third Edition, by Spencer A. Rathus, copyright © 1987 by Holt, Rinehart and Winston, Inc., reproduced by permission of the publisher; **Figure 8.7,** page 309, from *Animal Motivation: Experimental Studies on the Albino Rat,* by Carl John Warden, copyright 1931 by Columbia University Press, reprinted with permission of the publisher; **Figure 8.8,** page 312, from Psychology, 3rd ed., by Rathus, copyright © 1987 by Holt, Rinehart and Winston, Inc, reprinted by permission; **Figure 8.11,** page 319, from p. 207 of *Human Sexualities,* by J. H. Gagnon. copyright © 1977 by HarperCollins Publishers, Inc., reprinted by permission.

Chapter 9: Table 9.1, page 342, adapted from Table 3, p. 475, of "The Minor Events Approach to Stress: Support for the Use of Daily Hassles," by Kerry Chamberlain and Sheryl Zika, in *British Journal of Psychology,* 1990, Vol. 81, reprinted by permission; **Figure 9.3,** page 346, from Figure 7.10 of *Psychology,* by Michael S. Gazzaniga, copyright © 1980 by Michael S. Gazzaniga, reprinted by permission of HarperCollins Publishers, Inc., table from Table 6.1, p. 147, of *Health Psychology,* by Feuerstein. New York: Plenum Publishing Corporation, 1986, reprinted by permission; **Table 9.3,** page 355, reprinted with the permission of The Free Press, a division of Simon & Schuster from *Decision Making: A Psychological Analysis of Conflict, Choice and Commitment,* by Irving L. Janis and Leon Mann, copyright © 1977 by The Free Press; **Table 9.4,** page 365, adapted from *Monthly Vital Statistics* Report, January 1991, published by the Center for Disease Control; **Figure 9.5,** page 367, from *Health and Human Services,* Office of Disease Prevention and Health Promotion.

Chapter 10: Figure 10.4, page 395, adapted from *The Inequality of Man,* by H. J. Eysenck, copyright © 1973 by Hans J. Eysenck, reprinted by permission of the author.

Chapter 11: Figure 11.1, page 437, from *Wechsler's Measurement and Appraisal of Adult Intelligence,* 5th ed., by J. D. Matarazzo, copyright © 1972 by Oxford University Press, Inc, reprinted by permission; **Table 11.1,** page 445, "Familia Studies of Intelligence: A Review, " by Bouchard and McGue from *Science,* 1981, Vol. 212, pp. 1055–59, copyright © 1981 American Association for the Advancement of Science, reprinted with permission from the American Association for the Adancement of Science and the author; **Figure 11.2,** page 446, from "Achievement and Social Mobility: Relationships Among IQ Score, Education and Occupation in Two Generations," by Jerome H. Waller, in *Social Biology,* September 1971, Vol. 18, No. 3. Copyright © 1971 by The American Eugenics Society, Inc.

Chapter 12: Figure 12.1, page 462, from *The Obedience Experiments: A Case Study of Controversy in the Social Sicences,* by A. G. Miller, copyright © 1986 by Praeger Publishers, reprinted by permission of Greenwood Publishing Group, Inc. Westport, Conn.; **Figure 12.4,** page 477, adapted from "Bystander Intervention in Emergencies: Diffusion of Responsibilities," by Darley and Latané, in *Journal of Personality and Social Psychology,* 1968, Vol. 8, No. 4, pp. 377–84, copyright © 1968 by the American Psychological Association, adapted by permission of the author; **Figure 12.5,** page 486, "Heider's Demonstration of the Natural Tendency to Make Causal Attributions," from "An Experimental Study of Apparent Behavior," by F. Heider and M. Simmel in *American Journal of Psychology,* 1944, Vol. 57, pp. 243–59, copyright 1944 by the Board of Trustees of the University of Illinois, used with permission of the University of Illinois Press.

Chapter 13: Figures 13.1 and 13.2, page 507, from p. 9 of *Mental Health for Canadians: Striking a Balance. Minister of National Health and Welfare,* 1988; **Table 13.1,** page 519, from "Multiple Personality Disorder: Phenomenology of Selected Variables in Comparison to Major Depression," by R. Schults, B. G. Braun, and R. P. Kluft, in *Dissociation,* 1989, Vol. 2, p. 45; **Table 13.2,** page 522, from *Abnormal Psychology,* Third Edition, by David L. Rosenhan and Martin E. P. Seligman, copyright © 1994, 1989, 1984 by W. W. Norton & Company, Inc., reprinted by permission of W. W. Norton & Company, Inc.; **Figure 13.3,** page 531, "Seasonal Affective Disorder" by Rosenthal et al. from *Archives of General Psychiatry,* Vol. 41, 1984, pp. 72–80, copyright © 1984, American Medical Association, reprinted by permission; **Table 13.4,** page 539, from *Diagnostic and Statistical Manual of Mental Disorders,* 34d ed., Revised. Copyright © 1987 by the American Psychiatric Association. Reprinted with permission; **Figure 13.4,** page 542, from Schizophrenia Genesis by Gottesman. Copyright © 1991 by Irving I. Gottesman. Used with permission of W. H. Freeman and Company.

Chapter 14: Table 14.1, page 572, from *The Practice of Behavior Therapy,* 2nd ed., by J. Wolpe, copyright © 1973 by Pergamon Books Ltd, reprinted with permission; **Figure 14.1,** page 576, from p. 603 of *Journal of Abnormal Psycology,* Vol. 94, by Cook et al., copyright © 1985 by the American Psychological Association, adapted by permission; **Figure 14.2,** page 552, from "Modeling Therapy," by Albert Bandura, reprinted by permission of the author; **Table 14.2,** page 577, adapted from *Modern Clinical Psychology: Principles of Intervention* in the Clinic and Community, by Sheldon J. Korchin, copyright © 1976 by Sheldon J. Korchin, reprinted by permission of Basic Books, Inc., Publishers; **Figure 14.4,** page 569, from pp. 555–58 of American Journal of Psychiatry, 1979, Vol. 136, by Wrissman et al., reprinted with permission.

Subject Index

Mastery Tests

In this section of *Psychology, Second Edition*, Mastery Tests are provided to permit assessment of students' mastery of text material beyond that provided in each chapter's Review Test. For each chapter, the Mastery Test consists of two parts: 20 multiple-choice items, and five short-answer items. These items are designed to be a bit more challenging to answer than the 10-item Review Test that concludes each chapter. Completing a Mastery Test will give you additional practice in using each chapter's terms and concepts to answer questions and solve problems. Because the Mastery Tests are collected in a special perforated section, they can be torn out one at a time for individual student use and submission.

Answers to the Mastery Test items are provided in a special section of the Instructor's Manual, in your instructor's possession. *Students do not have a copy of the Mastery Test Answer Key; the answer key cannot be found either in this text or in the supplemental Study Guide and Workbook that accompanies this text.* Thus the only way students can check the accuracy of their Mastery Test answers is to consult with their instructors. We deliberately arranged the answer keys in this fashion, so that students and teachers would collaborate in using the Mastery Tests. We urge you, the student reading this section, to rely on your instructor as *your best resource* in getting the most out of this text, and this course!

How should the Mastery Tests be used? Instructors may choose to administer Mastery Tests as reviews of chapter and lecture comprehension, or as either graded or nongraded "rehearsals" for formal examinations. Alternatively, students may be asked to complete Mastery Tests as homework assignments, or they may choose to complete specific Mastery Tests on their own and request scoring by the instructor.

How should Mastery Tests be graded? Because only instructors have access to answer keys, performance on Mastery Tests can be assessed only through student-teacher collaboration. In the answer key, page references are provided for every answer, and guidelines are provided for the best answers to short-answer items.

We have included these Mastery Tests in a special section of this text so that every student gets the most from using *Psychology, Second Edition*, and every instructor has ample opportunity to assess students' mastery of the material. Let us know how you use the Mastery Tests, and what *we* can do—in future editions of this text—to correct errors, improve the material and its organization, and make more creative recommendations. Please send your comments, complaints, and constructive criticism to:

Ann L. Weber, Ph.D.
Department of Psychology
University of North Carolina at Asheville
Asheville, NC 28804

You are also welcome to make contact via electronic mail: **weber@unca.edu.** We look forward to hearing from you! Thanks for your input, and best wishes in getting the most out of *Psychology, Second Edition*.

Mastery Test

Chapter 1: Mind, Behavior, and Science

Name _____ Date _____

Multiple-Choice Items

1. Which of the following concepts is *not* part of the formal definition of psychology?
   a. scientific
   b. normality
   c. behavior
   d. mental processes

2. Because psychology analyzes the causes and consequences of people's actions, it is considered a _____ science.
   a. social
   b. cognitive
   c. biological
   d. behavioral

3. The psychologist conducting basic research has four goals. Which of the following is a goal of applied psychology, *not* of basic psychological research?
   a. to explain behavior
   b. to improve the quality of life
   c. to control behavior
   d. to predict how individuals will behave

4. The first task in psychology is to carefully observe and to objectively describe _____.
   a. animals
   b. behavior
   c. social institutions
   d. symptoms of abnormality

5. Which of the following would be an example of what psychologists call an "intervening variable"?
   a. hunger
   b. a public speech
   c. a large crowd
   d. short reaction time

6. A person's mood, quality of performance, and body temperature are all examples of _____, because each process changes with different times and conditions.
   a. biases
   b. stimulus events
   c. hypotheses
   d. variables

7. An experimenter gives different sets of instructions to students solving problems to see whether some strategies work better than others. In this research, the students' problem-solving performance is the _____ variable.
   a. intervening
   b. external
   c. dependent
   d. independent

8. Psychologist Hermann Ebbinghaus once observed that psychology has a long _____ but a short _____.
   a. history; memory
   b. history; past
   c. past; history
   d. future; past

9. Many early psychologists advocated _____, the doctrine that physical, behavioral, and mental events result from specific causes.
   a. determinism
   b. functionalism
   c. behaviorism
   d. humanism

10. Both Edward Titchener and Wilhelm Wundt favored the approach known as _____, which presumed that mental experience is composed of combinations of simpler elements.
    a. functionalism
    b. determinism
    c. empiricism
    d. structuralism

11. The _____ approach to psychology is associated with the work of the early twentieth-century theorist Sigmund Freud.
    a. biological
    b. behavioristic
    c. psychodynamic
    d. cognitive

12. If you wanted to study "anger" by using the approach supported by John B. Watson and B. F. Skinner, your research should concentrate on _____.
    a. angry behaviors such as shouting or hitting
    b. the unconscious origins of anger
    c. the physiological changes that accompany angry emotions
    d. the cultural context of anger

13. From the cognitive perspective, people act a certain way because of _____.
    a. inner forces and motivations
    b. environmental conditions
    c. inherited tendencies and traits
    d. thought processes

14. Bonita thinks of herself as overweight, and believes that this makes her unattractive to others. In trying to understand Bonita, a humanistic psychologist would focus on _____.
    a. her observable behaviors, not her thoughts and feelings
    b. Bonita's personal view of what is real in her life
    c. identifying Bonita's most adaptive behaviors
    d. helping her to lose weight so she will be more attractive

15. According to the sociocultural approach in psychology, which of the following sequences outlines the order of influence of various conditions on the individual?
    a. ecology, culture, socialization, personality, behavior
    b. culture, behavior, personality, society, the environment
    c. individual action, family values, social attitudes, government policies
    d. behavior, personality, socialization, culture, ecology

16. A psychologist is working in the context of _____ when her research is in the initial phase and her data, beliefs, and knowledge lead her to think about an idea or event in a new way.
    a. investigation
    b. discovery
    c. justification
    d. measurement

17. In a 1959 experiment by Aronson and Mills, women who wished to join a group discussion about sex were first required to read aloud either a hard list (with embarrassing, obscene words) or an easy list (with inoffensive words). Although the discussion afterwards was scripted to be boring, women who _____ thought it was very interesting.
    a. read the easy list
    b. read the hard list
    c. were permitted to join the group
    d. who were not allowed to join the group

18. To be useful in conducting research, a _____ must be testable, so that researchers can learn whether or not the data they collect support it.
    a. theory
    b. hypothesis
    c. correlation
    d. behavioral measure

19. A psychologist administers a self-report scale of shyness to a college class. After scoring the forms, he decides to define everyone who scored above the mean as "high" in shyness, and those below it as "low." This illustrates the procedure known as _____.
    a. operational definition
    b. reliability
    c. random assignment
    d. placebo control

20. Citizens' groups complain that television violence is related to children's aggressive behavior. Television executives argue that aggressive children watch aggressive programs. The only way to determine whether television violence is causing aggressive behavior is to _____.
    a. do a correlational study
    b. conduct an experiment
    c. complete self-report measures
    d. collect physiological measures

Short-Answer Items

Briefly define or explain each term.

21. base rate

22. independent variable

23. functionalism

24. behaviorism

25. double-blind control

Multiple-Choice Items

1. According to research by psychologist Tiffany Field and biologist Saul Schanberg, compared to a control group, premature infants who _____ gained more weight, were more active and alert, and later showed greater cognitive, emotional, and motor development.
   a. were fed a high-sugar formula
   b. received periodic massages
   c. were housed in a colorful environment
   d. listened to tapes of their biological mothers' voices

2. According to Charles Darwin's theory of evolution, organisms that inherit biological characteristics that are not adaptive to their environment will _____.
   a. develop new, more adaptive traits
   b. compensate by procreating at a greater rate
   c. behave in frustrated and aggressive ways
   d. eventually become extinct

3. Sasha's mother has blue eyes, but Sasha has brown eyes like her father. The color of Sasha's eyes is an example of _____.
   a. her genotype
   b. her phenotype
   c. encephalization
   d. a maladaptive trait

4. Human beings live in more geographical locations and greater environmental extremes of the world than most other species. This extensive migration and relocation is a result of the evolutionary adaptation known as _____.
   a. bipedalism
   b. encephalization
   c. variation
   d. competition

5. A hunger researcher carefully applies electrical current to a minute portion of a rat's brain in order to destroy the cells thought to be responsible for eating behavior. Which brain research technique does this illustrate?
   a. mapping
   b. MRI
   c. lesioning
   d. CT scanning

6. The structures in the _____ are involved with processes that regulate the body's internal state.
   a. frontal lobe
   b. cerebral cortex
   c. limbic system
   d. brain stem

7. Marcel feels thirsty and looks for something to drink. The structure in Marcel's brain triggering these feelings and actions is the _____.
   a. hippocampus
   b. hypothalamus
   c. cerebellum
   d. corpus callosum

8. Your nose itches, so you scratch it. The sensations of itching are processed by the _____ lobe of your brain, whereas scratching movements are controlled by your _____ lobe.
   a. frontal; parietal
   b. frontal; temporal
   c. parietal; frontal
   d. temporal; occipital

9. Processes such as planning and decision making take place in the _____ cortex, which is not located in any single lobe.
   a. association
   b. auditory
   c. motor
   d. somatosensory

10. The _____ nervous system consists of the brain and spinal cord, while the _____ nervous system is made up of all the nerve fibers connecting to the rest of the body.
    a. autonomic; peripheral
    b. autonomic; somatic
    c. central; somatic
    d. central; peripheral

11. After the stress of dealing with a family emergency, Sonya is tired, out of energy, and sleepy. Her body and actions are presently most influenced by the _____ division of her nervous system.
    a. somatic
    b. sympathetic
    c. parasympathetic
    d. peripheral

12. Which of the following is not a structure in a typical neuron?
    a. terminal button
    b. nucleus
    c. axon
    d. glia

13. According to the law of forward conduction, neurons only transmit information from _____.
    a. the dendrites to the axon
    b. the axon to the dendrites
    c. the soma to the dendrites
    d. the axon to the soma

14. As you take notes in class, neurons send messages from your brain to the muscles in your arm and hand to guide your handwriting. These neurons are classified as _____.
    a. sensory neurons
    b. afferent neurons
    c. efferent neurons
    d. interneurons

15. Which of the following is *not* one of the neurotransmitters identified in your text?
    a. serotonin
    b. dopamine
    c. GABA
    d. CNS

16. Hormones are manufactured and secreted by the _____.
    a. medulla
    b. endocrine glands
    c. transmitting neuron
    d. somatic nervous system

17. The _____ is the part of the brain responsible for the experience of consciousness.
    a. cerebral cortex
    b. limbic system
    c. central core
    d. cerebellum

18. Which of the following statements best summarizes the findings of research on cerebral dominance?
    a. The two hemispheres have completely different functions.
    b. The hemispheres' functions oppose each other.
    c. Hemispheric differences are not very obvious; the hemispheres usually work together.
    d. Hemispheric differences are caused by gender differences.

19. Research on cerebral hemispheric differences suggests that relying more on your left hemisphere in decision making will lead you to _____.
    a. feel worse about whatever you decide
    b. be more creative and innovative
    c. become more cautious
    d. take more risks

20. Scientists say the brain is _____ because it is changed by the behavior it generates and by environmental stimulation.
    a. responsive
    b. behaving
    c. controlling
    d. static

Short-Answer Items

Briefly define or explain each term.

21. natural selection

22. reticular formation

23. visual cortex

24. volume transmission

25. split-brain surgery

Name _____   Date _____

Multiple-Choice Items

1. A subject in a study of consciousness talks into a tape recorder to describe his thoughts while he solves various problems. This illustrates the _____ method of research.
   a. think-aloud protocol
   b. experience-sampling
   c. emergent-interaction
   d. dichotic listening

2. The "astonishing hypothesis" proposed by theorist Francis Crick is that the mind is _____.
   a. a function of the physical brain
   b. a fictional concept created by self-awareness
   c. the product of processes that are impossible to observe or measure
   d. a collection of psychological processes unrelated to the physical body

3. From an evolutionary perspective, consciousness probably evolved because it helped individuals to _____.
   a. understand and adapt to their environment
   b. communicate clearly with each other
   c. focus attention on one important task at a time
   d. experience sensory pleasure

4. When you talk about things you have personally experienced, you realize that these events have an autobiographical character. This demonstrates the level of consciousness known as _____.
   a. self-awareness
   b. nonconsciousness
   c. preconsciousness
   d. the unconscious

5. Although she was startled awake by a late-night telephone call, Hannah is soon able to relax and go back to sleep. Her body's automatic adjustments reflect the operation of _____.
   a. preconscious processes
   b. nonconscious processes
   c. subconscious processes
   d. unconscious processes

6. Which of the following illustrates the functioning of a circadian rhythm?
   a. A college student feels out of shape if she doesn't go for a run every other day.
   b. At least once a week, a salesman gets a craving for sweets.
   c. A manager finds that he does his best work if he schedules it for the early morning every day.
   d. All of the above illustrate circadian rhythms.

7. Which of the following statements about sleep is *false*?
   a. If sleepers are awakened during REM, they report having dreams.
   b. In stage 1 sleep, the sleeper's EEG pattern is very similar to that of the waking state.
   c. Personal problems and worries have been found to shorten the duration of individuals' sleep.
   d. According to research, the more one dreams, the more waking fantasies and obsessive thoughts one will have.

8. According to _____ theory, the content of our dreams is the result of random stimulation in our brains, with meaning added as an afterthought.
   a. Freudian
   b. activation-synthesis
   c. content-analysis
   d. mindful-awareness

9. One of the most common and undisputed values of hypnosis is that it _____.
   a. increases intelligence
   b. improves memory
   c. helps to control pain
   d. enhances creativity

10. Buddhist traditions view meditation as a life-long practice of thinking imaginatively, while Western science views meditation as _____.
    a. a loss of consciousness
    b. an altered state of consciousness
    c. equivalent to a light sleep
    d. an addictive practice that can limit mental function

11. Sam sees a terrifying visual image of something that isn't really there. Sam is experiencing _____.
    a. a hallucination
    b. an illusion
    c. a nightmare
    d. REM sleep

12. Which of the following can cause hallucinations?
    a. migraine headaches
    b. psychoactive drugs
    c. sensory isolation
    d. all of the above

13. A person who has developed _____ to a drug will suffer painful withdrawal symptoms—such as shakes, sweats, or nausea—if he or she is deprived of the substance.
    a. addiction
    b. tolerance
    c. psychological dependence
    d. physiological dependence

14. Which of the following is *not* technically classified as a hallucinogenic drug?
    a. mescaline
    b. morphine
    c. PCP
    d. LSD

15. Drugs such as heroin and codeine that reduce physical sensation and responsiveness to stimulation are known as _____.
    a. barbiturates
    b. depressants
    c. stimulants
    d. opiates

16. Oliver is suffering from anxiety, so his physician has prescribed _____, which can help Oliver to feel calm without sedating him or making him sleepy.
    a. cannabis
    b. depressants
    c. benzodiazepines
    d. barbiturates

17. A diagnosis of alcoholism is appropriate when _____.
    a. a person drinks every day
    b. each drink a person takes contains at least 15 percent alcohol
    c. the drinker exhibits slurred speech or muscle incoordination
    d. drinking impairs one's job, health, and relationships

18. Heavy users of _____ develop paranoid delusions, such as believing that others intend to harm them.
    a. stimulants
    b. depressants
    c. cannabis
    d. opiates

19. In terms of mortality and medical costs, the total negative impact of _____ on health is greater than that of all other psychoactive drugs combined.
    a. nicotine
    b. caffeine
    c. marijuana
    d. cocaine

20. Human intelligence and consciousness evolved as a result of competition with the most hostile force in the environment: _____.
    a. natural elements such as weather and terrain
    b. the scarcity of food
    c. predatory animals
    d. other humans

Short-Answer Items

Briefly define or explain each term.

21. dichotic listening task

22. the unconscious

23. hypnotizability

24. tolerance

25. conscious mind

Multiple-Choice Items

1. In research on psychological development, the usual independent variable is_____.
   a. intelligence
   b. education
   c. gender
   d. age

2. Which of the following questions illustrates the nature-nurture controversy?
   a. Who usually mature faster, boys or girls?
   b. Is intelligence influenced more by education or inherited ability?
   c. What mental skills must a child acquire before developing language?
   d. On the average, at what age do children begin to walk?

3. Which of the following is *not* an example of what developmental researchers call constitutional factors?
   a. Five-year-old Carly has a shy temperament.
   b. Four-year-old Matt copies his father's facial expressions.
   c. Marta has always had a thin, fragile body shape.
   d. Devon is very susceptible to digestive illnesses.

4. A female infant monkey is raised by human caretakers and has no contact with other monkeys. When she is an adult, she is placed in a refuge with other monkeys. Which of the following is true, according to research?
   a. She will not mate or rear children normally.
   b. Mating will come naturally, but child rearing will not.
   c. Mating and child rearing will develop more slowly, but both will be normal and effective.
   d. Both mating and child rearing will develop instinctively in the same time and manner as for other monkeys.

5. In studying how children develop a sense of humor, a researcher tells the same jokes to children who are 5, 7, and 9 years old, and observes the reactions of each age group. This illustrates the use of _____ in developmental research.
   a. a longitudinal investigation
   b. a cross-sectional design
   c. a sequential investigation
   d. internal processes

6. Developmental psychologists believe that, without infants' basic interest in _____, there would be no motivation for children to learn language.
   a. comfort
   b. colors
   c. social interaction
   d. self-control

7. Which of the following is an example of telegraphic speech?
   a. "I can dress myself."
   b. "Mikey hitted me!"
   c. "Want drink milk."
   d. "Mamama."

8. The mental programs that guide basic sensorimotor sequences such as sucking, grasping, and pulling are called _____.
   a. schemes
   b. scaffolds
   c. morphemes
   d. imprints

9. According to Piaget's theory of cognitive development, by the time a child enters the _____ stage, he or she has usually acquired the concept of conservation.
   a. sensorimotor
   b. preoperational
   c. concrete operational
   d. formal operational

10. In stage 1 of Kohlberg's theory of moral development, a child's "moral" behavior is motivated by a desire to _____.
    a. gain acceptance and avoid disapproval
    b. promote the welfare of society
    c. avoid painful punishment
    d. obey the rules

11. Two-year-old Jessica cannot tie her own shoes, but she complains that she wants to do it herself and does not want others' help. According to Erikson's theory, which psychosocial stage of development does Jessica's behavior demonstrate?
    a. competence versus inferiority
    b. autonomy versus self-doubt
    c. initiative versus guilt
    d. trust versus mistrust

12. Harry Harlow studied the behavior of infant monkeys who had been separated from their mothers and provided with artificial mother models. What conclusion did the baby monkeys' behavior support?
    a. that attachment is based on contact comfort
    b. that attachment is based on imprinting
    c. the cupboard theory of attachment
    d. Erikson's theory of psychosocial development

13. Which of the following is *not* one of the three basic attachment patterns identified by Mary Ainsworth and colleagues?
    a. secure
    b. avoidant
    c. socialized
    d. anxious-ambivalent

14. Which of the following is considered to be the central task of adolescence?
    a. achieving competence in one's chosen field
    b. forming an intimate relationship
    c. separating from parents and family
    d. establishing an integrated identity

15. Which of the following statements about adolescence is *not* true?
    a. Shyness reaches its highest level during the early teenage years.
    b. Females are less likely than males to give in to social pressure to behave antisocially.
    c. Adolescents talk to their peers four times as much as adults talk to theirs.
    d. Teenagers rely on their friends for structure and support, and no longer look to their families for these resources.

16. Which of the following is an example of the psychosocial crisis of *generativity versus stagnation?*
    a. An adolescent boy is depressed about breaking up with his girlfriend.
    b. Now that her children are older and less dependent on her, a woman in her forties wants to do something more meaningful with her life.
    c. A young woman believes that, once she and her fiance get married, they will live happily ever after.
    d. A successful executive loves his work, but wishes he had someone special in his life.

17. In a "peer marriage," spouses see each other as _____.
    a. opponents in a power struggle
    b. lovers rather than friends
    c. obligated to fulfill their traditional roles as "wife" and "husband"
    d. partners

18. According to Erikson's theory of psychosocial development, the greatest danger of old age is that, instead of achieving ego-integrity, the individual will experience _____.
    a. despair
    b. inferiority
    c. stagnation
    d. isolation

19. Which of the following is a psychological change common among older adults?
    a. loss of memory for knowledge and past events
    b. loss of hearing, especially high-frequency sounds
    c. decline in general intelligence and cognitive abilities
    d. loss of sexual interest and ability to perform sexually

20. Which of the following is *not* one of the emotional stages in Kübler-Ross's theory of coping with death?
    a. anger
    b. denial
    c. dementia
    d. depression

Short-Answer Items

Briefly define or explain each term.

21. maturation

22. habituation

23. temperament

24. initiation rites

25. postformal thought

Name _____   Date _____

Multiple-Choice Items

1. _____ is the process by which a stimulated receptor cell creates neural impulses that result in an awareness of conditions in or outside the body.
   a. Sensation
   b. Sensuality
   c. Perception
   d. Kinesthesis

2. Which of the following is *not* a subject of importance in psychophysics?
   a. the just noticeable difference
   b. the AI approach
   c. signal detection theory
   d. absolute thresholds

3. After your roommate agrees to turn the television down, you notice the volume has not been turned down "enough." You and your roommate disagree about a sensory judgment abbreviated as _____.
   a. dB
   b. Hz
   c. SDT
   d. JND

4. Leaving a darkened theater after seeing a movie, Yolanda walks outdoors and is briefly blinded by the bright sunlight. Soon, however, because of the process known as _____, she can see clearly enough to resume walking into the parking lot.
   a. sensory adaptation
   b. saturation
   c. transduction
   d. automaticity

5. In vision, the _____ is the structure that carries information from the eye to the brain.
   a. bipolar cell
   b. retina
   c. fovea
   d. optic nerve

6. Brian squints from the glare of sunlight on the car in front of his as he tries to blink away the sunlike flashes that seem imprinted on his eyes. What is interfering with Brian's vision?
   a. afterimages
   b. color blindness
   c. the blind spot
   d. perceptual instability

7. Hertz or cycles-per-second is a measurement of _____.
   a. color intensity
   b. loudness of sound
   c. frequency of sound
   d. chemical concentration

8. Where in the ear is sound energy transformed into neural activity?
   a. the eardrum
   b. the hammer, anvil, and stirrup
   c. the basilar membrane
   d. the pinna

9. Pheromones are stimuli that are best detected by which sensory process?
   a. the vestibular sense
   b. the kinesthetic sense
   c. olfaction
   d. gustation

10. Which of the following statements about human sensitivity to pain is *false*?
    a. Pain is a purely physical process that is unaffected by psychological factors.
    b. Research shows that pain can be influenced by one's gender role.
    c. People born with an insensitivity to pain are at greater risk for illness, injury, and early death.
    d. About one-third of Americans are estimated to suffer from persistent or recurring pain.

11. The process of perception is actually made up of three sequential processes: _____.
    a. hits, misses, and false alarms
    b. stimulation, cognition, and motion
    c. detection, attention, and automaticity
    d. sensation, perception, and identification/recognition

12. Alonso sits at his desk by the window, looking outside at his little boy who is playing in the yard. In this example, the distal stimulus is _____.
    a. the window
    b. the little boy
    c. the yard and other outdoor scenery
    d. the image of the little boy on Alonso's retina

13. A woman visiting an art gallery gazes at the abstract painting on the wall and remarks to her companion, "This is very ambiguous." She means that the painting _____.
    a. could be interpreted in more than one way
    b. distorts her visual perception
    c. is easy to analyze
    d. has no meaning

14. "People see and remember whole experiences, rather than breaking them down into separate parts." This statement agrees with which approach to explaining perception?
    a. Helmholtz's theory of experience-based inference
    b. Gibson's theory of environmental adaptation
    c. the Gestalt approach
    d. the AI approach

15. Sorting his laundry, Jamal separates white socks from light blue socks. Because the socks differ in this single simple feature—their color—the difference will "pop out," a sign of _____ processing.
    a. selective
    b. bottom-up
    c. preattentive
    d. figure-ground

16. Nilda's friend whispers some gossip to her during a lecture. As a result, Nilda misses hearing what the professor was saying at the same time. Nilda's experience illustrates the _____ function of attention.
    a. sensory filter
    b. response selection
    c. perceptual grouping
    d. gateway-to-consciousness

17. Because she worked several years as a secretary, Anna can type up to 90 words a minute, sometimes while doing other tasks like watching television or talking on the phone. For Anna, typing meets the conditions of _____.
    a. automaticity
    b. perceptual set
    c. limited capacity
    d. region segregation

18. In the passing zone of a highway, the yellow center line is dotted rather than solid, but a driver still sees it as a dotted "line" rather than a series of separate short dashes. This perceptual experience is caused by the organizational process known as _____.
    a. figure-ground distinction
    b. subjective contours
    c. region segregation
    d. closure

19. A children's map of a zoo is illustrated with small symbols for buildings and trees along the pathway. Even though the symbols are all the same size, a child reading the map sees the trees as "belonging with" the other trees. Which principle of perceptual grouping does this illustrate?
    a. Weber's law
    b. the law of similarity
    c. the law of proximity
    d. the law of common fate

20. Aaron recently got a speeding ticket. Now, even though his driving does not exceed the speed limit, he notices every police car and state trooper on the road. Aaron's readiness to detect the presence of traffic police is an example of _____.
    a. perceptual set
    b. sensory adaptation
    c. selective attention
    d. the law of common fate

Short-Answer Items

Briefly define or explain each term.

21. transduction

22. false alarm

23. timbre

24. illusion

25. Prägnanz

Multiple-Choice Items

1. Allan's pet lizard sees his reflection in a mirror and immediately behaves as if confronted by another lizard, striking a pose that is normally part of mating or defending territory. Such a built-in, unlearned set of responses is an example of _____.
   a. spontaneous recovery
   b. a conditioned reflex
   c. instinctual drift
   d. a fixed-action pattern

2. When your cat is hungry, she walks to her food dish, sits, and waits. She has learned that when you see her, you will put food in the dish. This illustrates operant conditioning, because through experience, the cat's behavior has become affected by _____.
   a. the stimuli that provoked the behavior
   b. the consequences of her behavior
   c. the purpose of her behavior
   d. the sight of the food dish

3. Based on how learning is defined, which of the following is *not* an example of a learned behavior?
   a. After weeks of practice, a gymnast is able to perform a series of leaps and turns without making an error.
   b. When she poses for a photograph, a child facing bright sunlight reflexively squints and smirks.
   c. Now that he has memorized the presidents' names as lyrics to a familiar song, Marcus can recite them in order.
   d. Although Tamara now drives a car with an automatic transmission, she can still drive a vehicle with a standard transmission when she has to.

4. A learning researcher deprives a rat of food and then trains it to press a lever by delivering a food pellet every time the rat does so. According to a behaviorist, which of the following is *not* one explanation for the rat's actions?
   a. hunger
   b. food deprivation
   c. delivery of food pellets
   d. environmental consequences

5. During classical conditioning, an organism learns a new association between _____.
   a. two stimuli
   b. two responses
   c. an old stimulus and a new response
   d. an old environment and a new reflex

6. In his original research on classical conditioning, Pavlov studied _____ behavior.
   a. maternal
   b. emotional
   c. reflexive
   d. aggressive

7. When 5-year-old Jesse's father acts angry, Jesse feels afraid. Jesse's father usually slams the door if he is in an angry mood when he returns home. Now Jesse starts to feel afraid any time he hears a door slam. In this example of classical conditioning, the conditioned response is _____.
   a. acting angry
   b. feeling frightened
   c. slamming a door
   d. returning home

8. Vanessa took a cherry-flavored medicine while she was sick, and found that anything that tastes like cherries makes her feel ill. Still later she associated sickness with other fruit flavors besides cherry. Vanessa's experience is an example of _____.
   a. extinction
   b. spontaneous recovery
   c. stimulus generalization
   d. stimulus discrimination

9. According to Leon Kamin's research on why CS-CR connections are formed, of the many stimuli we encounter in our experiences, we pay particular attention to those that provide _____.
   a. sensory pleasure
   b. comfortable levels of arousal
   c. distraction from unpleasant tasks
   d. important information about the environment

10. Rae got sick after a seafood dinner while on vacation in an ocean resort. Now she feels nauseous when she eats or smells any type of seafood. Rae's experience shows the effects of _____.
    a. observational learning
    b. instinctual drift
    c. taste aversion
    d. bait shyness

11. E. L. Thorndike's research with cats escaping from puzzle boxes led him to conclude that learning is a process of acquiring habits or _____ connections through trial and error.
   a. S-R
   b. UCS-CS
   c. reflexive
   d. positive-negative

12. Literally, an "operant" is any behavior that _____.
   a. is elicited by an environmental stimulus
   b. affects the environment
   c. elicits a response
   d. is reflexive

13. Which of the following is *not* one of the recommendations researchers make for using punishment effectively?
   a. Administer punishment immediately after the unwanted response occurs.
   b. Punishment should be limited in intensity.
   c. Punish the person, not just the person's behavior.
   d. Penalties are a more effective punishment than pain.

14. Learned helplessness results when an individual _____ after receiving prolonged, noncontingent, inescapable punishment.
   a. stops responding
   b. increases responding
   c. behaves aggressively
   d. finally makes the desired response

15. Talia would rather study for her psychology class than for her history class. She promises herself she can work on her psychology only *after* she reads her history assignment. Talia's plan is an example of _____.
   a. shaping
   b. instinctual drift
   c. conditioned reinforcement
   d. the Premack principle

16. "Children should not see violence on television, because it teaches them to copy aggressive models." This statement draws conclusions from research on the power of _____.
   a. learned helplessness
   b. appetitive conditioning
   c. continuous reinforcement
   d. observational learning

17. An inner representation of the learning situation as a whole is _____.
   a. an operant
   b. a fixed action pattern
   c. a reinforcement contingency
   d. a cognitive map

18. While studying for a test, Adrienne tries to think up associations among new information and older, familiar knowledge. This encoding strategy is known as _____.
   a. elaboration
   b. recognition
   c. pseudomemory
   d. biased assimilation

19. You would most likely use "chunking" as a strategy for retaining information in _____ memory.
   a. sensory
   b. working
   c. episodic
   d. declarative

20. According to the _____ theory of forgetting, trying to remember one set of information can prevent you from retaining other lessons.
   a. decay
   b. repression
   c. interference
   d. retrieval-failure

Short-Answer Items

Briefly define or explain each term.

21. acquisition

22. stimulus generalization

23. law of effect

24. bait shyness

25. false memory syndrome

Chapter 7: Cognitive Processes

Name _____ Date _____

Multiple-Choice Items

1. The first person to link human thought processes with the digital operations of computers was _____.
   a. John von Neumann
   b. Hermann Ebbinghaus
   c. Allen Newell
   d. Herbert Simon

2. As a subject in a cognition experiment, Julie solves problems and talks aloud about how she uses trial-and-error to find each solution. This research is using _____ to study thought processes.
   a. introspection
   b. reaction time
   c. error analysis
   d. behavioral observation

3. "I believe the best way to understand cognitive processes is to organize them into their component parts." This statement indicates support for the _____ model.
   a. information-processing
   b. language-acquisition
   c. functional-fixedness
   d. cognitive-economy

4. The human brain is more flexible and complex than computer programs, because the brain can conduct _____ processing of several messages, while computers rely on _____ processing.
   a. long-term; short-term
   b. sensory; semantic
   c. deductive; inductive
   d. parallel; serial

5. An *event-related potential* is a change in mental activity that can be measured by _____.
   a. error patterns in reasoning
   b. intelligence test scores
   c. behavioral observation
   d. brain scanning

6. From the perspective of cognitive psychology, thinking has three general features. Which of the following is *not* one of them?
   a. Thinking is directed toward solving an individual's problems.
   b. Thinking is limited by an individual's experience and cannot by itself overcome biased information.
   c. Thinking manipulates knowledge within one's cognitive system.
   d. Thinking occurs in the mind but can be inferred from observable behavior.

7. When Marla finds a kitten to adopt at the animal shelter, she picks it up and holds it the way she has learned with other cats. In other words, though she has never seen this particular kitten before, her behavior toward it is guided by her _____.
   a. concept of cats
   b. sensory register
   c. inductive reasoning
   d. cognitive map

8. When hurrying to pack for a beach vacation, Leon forgets his sunglasses. "I was in a hurry to pack things I usually wear," he explains, "but I only thought of clothes like shirts and pants, and forgot things I wear on my face." In other words, _____.
   a. sunglasses lack the critical features of "things to wear"
   b. sunglasses resemble the prototype of "things to wear"
   c. Leon's cognitive economy has no room for "sunglasses"
   d. none of the above.

9. As she works on a grade school homework assignment, Tom's daughter asks her father, "Is a bat a mammal?" Tom pauses before answering yes, because he normally pictures cats and dogs as mammals, but not bats. This shows that Tom's concept of "mammals" is influenced by _____.
   a. framing
   b. pseudomemory
   c. critical features
   d. the prototype approach

10. When asked to name a color, Ronnie quickly responds "red." This suggests that the color red _____.
    a. is a "fuzzy concept" for Ronnie
    b. was arrived at by use of an algorithm
    c. was arrived at through the use of inductive reasoning
    d. is at the basic level of Ronnie's hierarchy of color concepts

11. A "script" is defined as a schema for a particular _____.
    a. event
    b. language
    c. age-group
    d. relationship

12. Of the following questions, identify the one that probably requires forming a mental image in order to come up with the answer:
    a. How many quarts are in a gallon?
    b. What are the colors of your state flag?
    c. How long does it take you to get home after school?
    d. Is the gas tank of your car located on the driver's side or the passenger's side?

13. Which of the following is an example of autistic thinking?
    a. calculating the steps necessary to solve a math problem
    b. imagining a landscape you would like to paint
    c. planning to assemble ingredients to bake a cake
    d. using available data to draw a conclusion about something

14. In information-processing terms, which of the following is *not* one of the three parts of a problem?
    a. a goal state
    b. a set of operations
    c. an initial state
    d. a conflict or crisis

15. Corbett can't find his recipe for pancakes and is not sure how many eggs it requires. Corbett experiments with the ingredients, methodically making pancakes with one egg, two eggs, and three eggs, until he gets it right. Corbett has solved his problem by using _____.
    a. a heuristic
    b. inductive reasoning
    c. an algorithm
    d. inference

16. Inductive reasoning uses available evidence to generate a conclusion about _____.
    a. how to behave in a new set of circumstances
    b. whether an example belongs to a concept category
    c. whether the tools available can help solve a problem
    d. the likelihood that a particular solution is correct

17. Engaged to a man from another country, Lisa is surprised to find that her fiancé's parents are very strict about codes of behavior and seem nervous when they encounter unpredictable people and situations. Lisa's future in-laws live in a country that is high in _____.
    a. assimilation bias
    b. uncertainty avoidance
    c. critical features
    d. cognitive biases

18. _____ is the process of choosing between alternatives, selecting and rejecting available options.
    a. Realistic thinking
    b. Chunking
    c. Deciding
    d. Judging

19. Before inviting a new friend to attend a basketball game with you, you wonder whether or not she is a sports fan. To decide, you consider whether her behavior resembles that of other sports fans you know. In other words, you are relying on _____.
    a. the representativeness heuristic
    b. the availability heuristic
    c. pseudomemory
    d. mental set

20. A television commercial for a pain reliever claims that "nothing works faster!" But a consumer magazine reporting on the same product concludes that "all products tested were equally fast." The same information is presented in both statements, but it is _____ differently.
    a. set
    b. biased
    c. framed
    d. reasoned

Short-Answer Items

Briefly define or explain each term.

21. cognitive economy

22. schema

23. realistic thinking

24. functional fixedness

25. availability heuristic

Name _____ Date _____

Multiple-Choice Items

1. Which of the following is *not* one of the brain structures involved in the physiology of emotion?
   a. reticular activating system
   b. hypothalamus
   c. thalamus
   d. limbic system

2. The emotion wheel developed by _____ proposes an innate set of eight emotions, made up of four pairs of opposites.
   a. W. B. Cannon
   b. Robert Plutchik
   c. Carroll Izard
   d. Stanley Schachter

3. One day your professor behaves out of the ordinary by arriving just in time for class, abruptly beginning to lecture, not smiling, and answering only a few questions. You decide your professor is probably angry, so you plan to wait until later to ask for an extension on a project. This example illustrates the _____ function of emotions.
   a. arousing
   b. amplifying
   c. communication
   d. socially regulating

4. "The emotion you express is produced after you process stimuli and then determine which learned responses are appropriate." This statement best reflects _____ theory of emotion.
   a. Izard's developmental
   b. Darwin's adaptive
   c. Lazarus and Schachter's arousal-label
   d. Levinson's biocultural

5. _____ plays a role in determining how emotions are displayed, when it is appropriate to express them, to whom, and how.
   a. Evolution
   b. Biology
   c. Instinct
   d. Culture

6. Which of the following statements about deception is *false*?
   a. The face is easier to control than the body.
   b. Liars may try to "save face" by touching or covering their faces more frequently than usual.

   c. Most people are very good at lie-detection even without any special training.
   d. It is easier to detect spontaneous, unplanned lies than calculated deceptions.

7. _____ refers to needs that are primarily biological, while _____ refers to learned psychological and social needs.
   a. Goal; incentive
   b. Motivation; emotion
   c. Drive; motive
   d. Instinct; goal

8. Researcher C. J. Warden studied the relative strength of various drives influencing rats' behavior by means of _____.
   a. an obstruction box
   b. a Skinner box
   c. an operant chamber
   d. a puzzle box

9. Alden's grades are suffering because he is taking so many classes during his last semester of college. He would rather take a lighter load now and finish up in the summer, but his parents want to attend the graduation ceremony this spring, and he doesn't want to disappoint them. Alden's behavior is affected by a negative form of _____.
   a. intrinsic motivation
   b. incentive motivation
   c. achievement motivation
   d. optimal arousal

10. Today, what used to be called instincts in animals are usually studied as _____, unlearned patterns of behavior triggered by identifiable stimuli.
    a. primary drives
    b. scripts
    c. deficiency motives
    d. fixed-action patterns

11. Which of the following motivation theorists did *not* support the concept of instinct as an explanation for human behavior?
    a. Abraham Maslow
    b. Sigmund Freud
    c. William James
    d. William McDougall

12. When Jade is doing something simple, like writing a letter home, she seems to do a better job when she has the additional stimulation of conversation or listening to the radio. But when Jade is doing something difficult like writing a paper for school, such stimuli distract her and hurt her efforts. Jade's behavior is explained by _____.
   a. the hierarchy of needs
   b. the concept of flow
   c. the Yerkes-Dodson law
   d. the two-factor theory

13. According to the theory of Maslow's hierarchy of needs, of the following, the highest level of needs are the _____ needs.
   a. aesthetic
   b. attachment
   c. esteem
   d. safety

14. If a hungry person is asked to complete the Thematic Apperception Test, she will probably _____.
   a. not be able to do so until she has something to eat
   b. compose stories with themes related to eating and food
   c. compose stories about everything *except* eating and food
   d. compose stories similar to those of people who are not hungry

15. According to Julian Rotter's social learning theory, the probability that you will engage in a given behavior—such as studying for an exam tomorrow—depends on _____.
   a. who else will be engaging in the same behavior
   b. how strongly you want to succeed in school
   c. whether you have met more basic needs in the hierarchy
   d. whether you expect to achieve a valued goal by doing so

16. Which of the following statements about hunger and eating is true?
   a. Modern research has concluded that all eating behavior originates in a brain region that acts as a "hunger center."
   b. The *critical set point* is the minimum number of calories needed in a given meal.
   c. Only social customs—such as mealtimes—prevent humans from eating all the time, whatever the circumstances or emotions.
   d. People who are born with more fat cells than others may be biologically "programmed" to be obese.

17. Sex is considered a unique source of human motivation because it _____.
   a. is essential to both the species and the individual
   b. can be aroused by almost any type of stimulus
   c. motivates only a narrow range of behaviors
   d. all of the above

18. According to Masters and Johnson's research on human sexual response, during the _____ phase, a maximum level of arousal is reached, with rapid increases in bodily responses.
   a. resolution
   b. excitement
   c. plateau
   d. orgasm

19. Crimes such as date rape may be the result of confusion over _____.
   a. sexual orientation
   b. sexual scripts
   c. evolutionary rules
   d. sex roles

20. _____ activities can produce a special state of mind called "flow."
   a. Extrinsically motivating
   b. Intrinsically motivating
   c. Emotionally disrupting
   d. Achievement-oriented

Short-Answer Items

Briefly define or explain each term.

21. lateralization of emotion

22. James-Lange theory

23. deficiency motivation

24. lateral hypothalamus (LH)

25. *n Ach*

Name _____ Date _____

Multiple-Choice Items

1. Psychoneuroimmunology examines the healing interactions between the _____.
   a. brain, body, emotions, and immune system
   b. patient, patient's family, and physician
   c. individual, health care system, and society
   d. nervous, cardiovascular, and respiratory systems

2. Holmes and Rahe have developed the Social Readjustment Rating Scale for evaluating the degree of adjustment required by various _____ that many people experience.
   a. hassles
   b. illnesses
   c. life changes
   d. catastrophic events

3. Researchers have found that people's responses to disasters typically progress through five stages. Which of the following summarizes them correctly?
   a. shock; effort; letdown; numbness; resignation
   b. confusion; action; focus; completion; recovery
   c. shock; automatic action; effort; letdown; recovery
   d. effort; automatic action; shock; recovery; letdown

4. A teacher who used to love her work now feels exhausted, unappreciated, and often angry at her students. Her symptoms suggest she may be suffering from _____.
   a. relapse
   b. burnout
   c. nonadherence
   d. immunosuppression

5. _____ is a state of enduring arousal, continuing over time, in which demands are perceived as greater than one's resources for coping with them.
   a. Societal stress
   b. Residual stress
   c. Chronic stress
   d. Relapse

6. At the center of the fight-or-flight response is the _____, referred to as the "stress center" because it controls the autonomic nervous system and activates the pituitary gland.
   a. reticular formation
   b. limbic system
   c. hypothalamus
   d. medulla

7. Grief-stricken at the sudden death of his wife, an elderly man becomes physically less able to fight illness and risks his own premature death. This is an example of _____.
   a. residual stress
   b. immunosuppression
   c. anticipatory coping
   d. secondary appraisal

8. Which of the following acronyms refers to Hans Selye's discovery that all stressors trigger the same, nonspecific set of physical responses?
   a. GAS
   b. PNI
   c. SWB
   d. PTSD

9. In a coping strategy with a(n) _____ focus, one's goal is not to confront the problem directly, but rather to lessen the discomfort associated with experiencing stress.
   a. problem-solving
   b. primary-appraisal
   c. emotion-regulation
   d. residual-stress

10. Arvid's humanities grades have been so low he may fail. Though he is worried, Arvid puts off confronting the problem or talking to his professor. He tells himself it would do no good to complain—it might only make things worse. Arvid is using the ego defense mechanism known as _____.
    a. denial
    b. projection
    c. repression
    d. rationalization

11. For a person in a stressful setting, thinking differently and more constructively about the situation is a way of achieving _____ control.
    a. information
    b. behavioral
    c. cognitive
    d. decision

12. Which types of social support are most helpful for specific events? Research by Shelley Taylor and her colleagues indicates that the answer depends on _____.
   a. the victim's relationship with the person providing it
   b. the victim's anxiety level
   c. the victim's physical health
   d. whether the provider has professional training

13. According to health psychologists, a _____ is a behavior pattern that operates automatically—without extrinsic reinforcement or incentives—and that contributes directly to your overall well-being.
   a. general adaptation syndrome
   b. healthy habit
   c. Type A syndrome
   d. Type T personality

14. The personality quality known as hardiness is characterized by which of the following attitudes and abilities?
   a. cognition, competition, and creativity
   b. coping, competence, and companionship
   c. challenge, commitment, and control
   d. calm, concern, and community

15. Which of the following would *not* describe an individual who fit the Type-A profile?
   a. impatient
   b. depressed
   c. aggressive
   d. hostile

16. Health psychologists have identified four elements that determine whether someone can change from unhealthy to healthy behavior. Which of the following is *not* one of them?
   a. believing one's health is severely threatened
   b. feeling one's likelihood of developing the disorder is high
   c. feeling unable to perform the threat-reducing response
   d. believing it is not too late to change to healthy habits

17. Which of the following would not be considered a "disease of civilization"?
   a. heart disease
   b. automobile accidents
   c. cirrhosis
   d. smallpox

18. _____ represents a problem that makes AIDS resistant to intervention because individuals at risk incorrectly believe they cannot be harmed.
   a. Relapse
   b. Anticipatory coping
   c. Patient nonadherence
   d. The illusion of invulnerability

19. _____ results from maintaining positive illusions about one's well-being.
   a. Adaptive, health-maintaining behavior
   b. Taking unnecessary risks with one's health
   c. A feeling of learned helplessness
   d. A higher risk of stress-related disorders

20. Which of the following collections of experiences best defines subjective well-being?
   a. life satisfaction, absence of bad feelings, presence of good feelings
   b. physical health, absence of mental illness, strong social support system
   c. high level of physical energy, relative wealth, social status
   d. optimism, competence, productivity

Short-Answer Items

Briefly define or explain each term.

21. intrapsychic phase of a breakup

22. cognitive appraisal

23. biopsychosocial model

24. accounts

25. patient nonadherence

Multiple-Choice Items

1. Psychologists define personality in many different ways, but common to all of them are two basic concepts: _____.
   a. positive and negative influences
   b. genetic heritage and experiential or educational factors
   c. the push of the past and the pull of the future
   d. uniqueness and characteristic patterns of behavior

2. As part of a personality assessment, a client examines a series of drawn stimuli and makes up stories about them. Which of the following techniques is being used?
   a. the Rorschach
   b. TAT
   c. MMPI
   d. CPI

3. The most effective and useful personality assessments are based on _____.
   a. close observations of an individual over several months
   b. interviews with family and friends of the subject
   c. data about the groups to which the subject belongs
   d. one or more major personality theories

4. Which of the following is an example of relying on an implicit personality theory?
   a. Gina's new roommate is quietly reading a book when they first meet, so Gina assumes she is a studious, introverted person.
   b. A personnel officer assesses job candidates by assigning trait names to them based on how they answer various test questions.
   c. After several therapy sessions, a clinical psychologist decides her client's problems stem from unresolved unconscious conflicts.
   d. A personality inventory indicates that a man is more shy and lacking in confidence than he would ideally like to be.

5. The nomothetic approach to personality is said to be _____-centered, because it assumes that the same personality traits apply to everyone in the same way.
   a. situation
   b. variable
   c. theory
   d. person

6. "I just took the Myers-Briggs personality test at the Career Center," your roommate announces, "and it turns out I'm an ENTJ. This explains so much about my personality!" Your roommate apparently favors _____ theories of personality.
   a. type
   b. trait
   c. psychodynamic
   d. social-learning

7. According to Gordon Allport, a _____ trait is one around which a person organizes his or her life, the way Margaret Sanger worked to develop legal, safe contraception.
   a. maximal
   b. cardinal
   c. central
   d. primary

8. _____ is the assumption that all mental and behavioral reactions are determined by one's earlier personal experiences.
   a. Radical behaviorism
   b. Reciprocal determinism
   c. Psychic determinism
   d. Social-learning theory

9. According to Freudian theory, during the _____ stage of psychosexual development, a child explores his or her own body, and discovers the pleasure associated with self-stimulation.
   a. oral
   b. latency
   c. genital
   d. phallic

10. Though Julio knows he ought to spend the evening studying for tomorrow's test, he wants to attend a party tonight. According to Freudian theory, if Julio gives in to the urging of his _____, he will attend the party instead of studying.
    a. id
    b. ego
    c. libido
    d. superego

11. In humanistic theory, _____ is a constant striving to realize one's inherent potential, to fully develop one's potential and talents.
    a. psychic determinism
    b. self-actualization
    c. self-efficacy
    d. the ego ideal

12. The post-Freudian theorist _____ proposed that people's lives are dominated by the search for ways to overcome feelings of inferiority and inadequacy.
    a. Carl Jung
    b. Carl Rogers
    c. Alfred Adler
    d. Albert Bandura

13. An important person-centered concept is that child rearing should emphasize _____ so that children will feel loved and accepted regardless of their mistakes.
    a. conditional positive reinforcement
    b. unconditional positive regard
    c. self-actualization
    d. self-efficacy

14. In their social-learning theory of personality, John Dollard and Neal Miller argued that one can learn a behavior pattern through a process of _____.
    a. classical conditioning
    b. trial-and-error
    c. social imitation
    d. ego defense

15. According to theorist Walter Mischel, "person variables" will have their greatest impact on behavior when _____.
    a. the individual is high in Extroversion
    b. fixation has occurred early in psychosexual development
    c. situational forces are equally powerful
    d. cues in the situation are weak or ambiguous

16. Which of the following illustrates the concept of self-efficacy?
    a. After her husband leaves her, a young woman believes she herself will be able to fill the household roles he once filled.
    b. A man who likes pornographic materials publicly announces his support for censorship and laws to ban such materials.
    c. A child who has lived in a series of foster homes sees most families as unstable and unreliable.
    d. A battered wife has given up trying to change her husband's behavior and no longer seeks to escape her circumstances.

17. Marnie likes to run for fitness, so she meets other people who run on the same route. Because she spends more time with these people, she spends more time talking and thinking about being fit. This circular relationship of traits and forces illustrates the process Bandura calls _____.
    a. self-efficacy
    b. reciprocal determinism
    c. observational learning
    d. reaction formation

18. Critics of cognitive theories of personality have argued that such theories generally overlook _____ as an important aspect of personality.
    a. thoughts
    b. beliefs
    c. emotions
    d. expectations

19. A person's _____ is a generalized self-evaluation of the self, which can strongly influence our thoughts, moods, and behavior.
    a. self-concept
    b. self-enhancement
    c. self-handicap
    d. self-esteem

20. Of the following categories of personality theories, which places the *least* emphasis on past causes or influences in determining individuals' behavior?
    a. psychodynamic
    b. learning
    c. trait
    d. humanistic

Short-Answer Items

Briefly define or explain each term.

21. projective technique

22. idiographic approach

23. the Big Five

24. anxiety

25. personal construct

Multiple-Choice Items

1. Psychological assessment is often referred to as the measurement of _____, since the majority of assessments specify how a person compares or contrasts with others.
   a. situationism
   b. psychometrics
   c. fluid intelligence
   d. individual differences

2. Which of the following is *not* one of the arguments put forth by Sir Francis Galton?
   a. Evolutionary theory should be applied to family planning.
   b. Differences in intelligence can be quantified and measured.
   c. Differences in intelligence are randomly distributed in the population.
   d. Biologically inferior people should not produce offspring.

3. Why does a clinical psychologist typically use testing?
   a. to make predictions about a population
   b. to make predictions about a particular client
   c. as a substitute for direct observation of an individual
   d. to discover regularities in personality that indicate patterns of behavior or life events

4. If a test yields the same results consistently but does not measure what its users intend it to measure, it is _____.
   a. neither reliable nor valid
   b. both reliable and valid
   c. reliable but not valid
   d. valid but not reliable

5. When a psychologist identifies several attitudes and behaviors that measure a personal quality she calls "fussiness," she develops a test of individual fussiness, finding that test scores correlate positively with people's fussy ideas and actions. This means her test is high in _____ validity.
   a. construct
   b. criterion
   c. test-retest
   d. split-half

6. The process of standardization is necessary to establish _____, test performance standards to which individual scores can be compared.
   a. constructs
   b. *g* factors
   c. aptitudes
   d. norms

7. Which of the following is the most direct approach to learning about a given individual?
   a. a personality inventory
   b. a psychological test
   c. archival data
   d. an interview

8. Stephanie, positively impressed with the good looks and self-assured manner of the young man she interviews for her company's position, interprets all his traits in a positive way. This illustrates a type of bias called the _____ effect.
   a. halo
   b. stereotype
   c. inter-judge
   d. heritability

9. Human intelligence provides us with a distinct advantage for survival in our world because it enables us to _____.
   a. outsmart our enemies, whatever they might be
   b. repeatedly use the same effective problem-solving strategies
   c. calculate the limits and possibilities for our personal achievement
   d. respond to environmental challenges with flexibility and imagination

10. Which of the following is *not* one of the four features that distinguished Alfred Binet's approach to testing mental age?
    a. He interpreted test scores as a measure of innate intelligence.
    b. He believed training and opportunity could affect intelligence.
    c. He based the test on how children were observed to perform.
    d. He meant the test to identify children who needed help.

11. Which of the following conditions made it most necessary for American psychologists to quickly develop nonverbal, group-administered tests of mental ability?
    a. America's entry into World War I
    b. passage of new universal education laws
    c. a wave of immigrants entering the United States
    d. the discovery that intelligence is largely inherited

12. The Stanford-Binet Intelligence Scale was developed by _____.
    a. Alfred Binet
    b. Leland Stanford
    c. Lewis Terman
    d. Raymond Cattell

13. According to the formula for calculating IQ, a person with a chronological age of 20 and a mental age of 25 has an IQ of _____.
    a. 80
    b. 105
    c. 120
    d. 125

14. David Wechsler developed intelligence tests with both _____ subtests.
    a. verbal and spatial
    b. verbal and performance
    c. performance and insight
    d. internal and external

15. Group tests of intelligence measure a narrowly defined type of intellectual functioning often called school ability or _____.
    a. mental age
    b. crystallized intelligence
    c. scholastic aptitude
    d. factor analysis

16. Young Jeremy is better than most children his age at seeing complex relationships and solving problems. He would probably score high in what researcher Raymond Cattell calls _____ intelligence.
    a. fluid
    b. semantic
    c. componential
    d. crystallized

17. According to the model developed by Earl Hunt, the basic application of intelligence is in _____.
    a. learning
    b. deciding
    c. remembering
    d. problem-solving

18. Which of the following reflects what psychologist Robert Sternberg calls "contextual intelligence"?
    a. manipulating mental representations to solve problems
    b. practical skills and adaptability to daily living
    c. artistic or creative endeavors
    d. IQ scores and college grades

19. Psychologists' studies of the Juke and Kallikak families were original undertaken to demonstrate that extremes of intelligence were powerfully determined by _____.
    a. educational opportunity
    b. socioeconomic status
    c. gender differences
    d. heredity

20. Lawrence is taking a test of his current level of competency in the German language. This would be an example of a(n) _____ test.
    a. aptitude
    b. achievement
    c. vocational
    d. job analysis

Short-Answer Items

Briefly define or explain each term.

21. aptitude test

22. eugenics

23. parallel forms

24. stereotype effect

25. experiential intelligence

Mastery Test

Chapter 12: Social Psychology

Name _____ Date _____

Multiple-Choice Items

1. The best social psychological explanation for the behavior of the participants in Zimbardo's prison simulation is that a new "social reality" was created by _____.
   a. the presence of so many personalities susceptible to violence
   b. individuals with behavior disorders
   c. the power of the prison situation
   d. none of the above

2. Months ago Jordan joined a religious congregation that discouraged its members from having contact with anyone outside the church. The church leaders have unquestioned control over members' status, and Jordan never hears anyone contradict those in charge. In short, Jordan's experience is an example of _____.
   a. a typical reference group
   b. demand characteristics
   c. a total situation
   d. the Asch effect

3. Members of a group are usually able to estimate how much they may deviate before they experience coercion through the three "painful R's." Which of the following is *not* one of them?
   a. ridicule
   b. rejection
   c. reeducation
   d. reinforcement

4. According to research by Theodore Newcomb, students at Bennington College in the late 1930s were most influenced in their later social attitudes by _____.
   a. world events
   b. their parents
   c. their reference groups
   d. their romantic partners

5. The Asch effect describes the influence of _____ on an individual's judgments, even when conditions are unambiguous.
   a. a lone opponent
   b. one's reference group
   c. unpopular social opinions
   d. a unanimous group majority

6. Stanley Milgram's research showed that blind obedience to authority is more a matter of _____ than of _____.
   a. situational forces; personality
   b. situational forces; powerful circumstances
   c. dispositional characteristics; personality
   d. dispositional characteristics; situational influence

7. Which of the following best summarizes the results of Milgram's study of obedience, in which teachers were ordered to administer "shocks" to a learner?
   a. Most subjects obeyed to the highest level of shock.
   b. None of the subjects obeyed to the highest shock level.
   c. None of the subjects obeyed to the midpoint level of shock.
   d. Most subjects refused to go on after the learner first complained about pain.

8. According to the "rules of influence," people give in to normative influence when they want to be _____, and to informational influence when they want to be _____.
   a. liked; appreciated
   b. right; informed
   c. right; liked
   d. liked; right

9. Latané and Darley created a laboratory version of bystander intervention, in which individual subjects overheard another student having a "seizure." The more witnesses the subject believed could overhear the crisis, _____.
   a. the slower the subject was to respond to the emergency
   b. the faster the subject was to respond to the emergency
   c. the more likely the subject was to ask them for help
   d. none of the above

10. In Darley and Batson's "Good Samaritan" experiment, seminarians on their way to keep an appointment were most likely to offer help to a needy stranger if they _____.
    a. were in a hurry
    b. were not in a hurry
    c. were on time for the appointment
    d. had just evaluated a sermon about helping others

11. According to research by Tom Moriarity, if you find yourself in need of assistance, the best way to get help from the strangers around you is to _____.
    a. demand it
    b. ask for it
    c. promise a reward for it
    d. pretend you do not need it

12. _____ is the consensus of perceptions and beliefs about a situation created by group members' social comparisons.
    a. A norm
    b. Covariation
    c. Social reality
    d. Cognitive dissonance

13. The Pygmalion effect refers to the influence of _____.
    a. self-serving bias
    b. social expectancies
    c. group pressure to conform
    d. diffusion of responsibility

14. Carlos has been told that Carmen is very shy. Meeting her at a party, he talks about school instead of asking her about herself, and invites her to sit at a quiet table instead of asking her to dance. As a result of _____, Carmen acts as shyly as Carlos expects her to.
    a. attribution
    b. self-serving bias
    c. social facilitation
    d. behavioral confirmation

15. _____ is a learned attitude toward a target, involving negative feelings, negative beliefs, and negative intentions toward the target.
    a. Prejudice
    b. Covariation
    c. Social categorization
    d. Informational influence

16. Third-grade teacher Jane Elliott was able to generate hostility toward minority-group members in her classroom simply as a result of _____.
    a. cognitive dissonance
    b. the bystander effect
    c. social categorization
    d. demand characteristics

17. Attribution theory is a general approach to the way individuals ask and answer questions about _____.
    a. "who" they are
    b. "what" they should do
    c. "how" to solve social problems
    d. "why" people act and talk as they do

18. According to Fritz Heider, we are all "intuitive psychologists" because each one of us tries to _____.
    a. analyze others so we can control what they do
    b. understand other people and their actions
    c. develop close relationships with others
    d. help people when they are suffering

19. When her team wins a game, the coach brags, "We worked hard and it paid off!" When the team loses, she rationalizes, "Because we've had to sideline our best players due to injuries, we could not overcome our opponents' tactics." This pattern of explanations reflects the operation of _____.
    a. social perception
    b. the self-serving bias
    c. demand characteristics
    d. the covariation principle

20. Although most cultures frown on individual aggression, nations encourage military aggression against their opponents by a process of _____.
    a. bystander intervention
    b. social categorization
    c. dehumanization
    d. situationism

Short-Answer Items

Briefly define or explain each term.

21. demand characteristics

22. normative influence

23. self-fulfilling prophecies

24. cognitive dissonance

25. weapons effect

Multiple-Choice Items

1. Which of the following descriptions would *not* be considered an indicator of abnormality, as outlined in the text?
   a. acting in ways that interfere with one's well-being, personal goals, and society's goals
   b. experiencing periods of worry, self-doubt, anxiety, and escapism
   c. acting or talking in ways that are irrational or incomprehensible to others
   d. making others feel uncomfortable by causing them to feel threatened or distressed

2. Which of the following is true of the "medical model" of abnormal behavior?
   a. Mental disorders are considered to be caused by processes such as learning, cognitions, and cultural factors.
   b. It adopts the perspective that no known organic disorder is known to be responsible for causing mental illness.
   c. Afflicted individuals are considered to be sick and are treated as patients who must be cured.
   d. None of the above.

3. According to the psychodynamic model of mental illness, the symptoms of psychopathology have their roots in _____.
   a. unconscious conflict
   b. maladaptive reinforcement patterns
   c. irrational or unrealistic thinking
   d. structural or functional problems in the nervous system

4. To be most useful, a good system of classifying forms of psychopathology should meet several goals. Which of the following is *not* one of them?
   a. to suggest how best to treat certain types of problems
   b. to demonstrate that there is no such thing as abnormality, since everyone fits in at least one of the categories
   c. to establish an agreed-upon language for clinicians and researchers to use in discussing mental illness
   d. to suggest the causes of the symptoms of any particular case

5. Jake, an inmate in a federal prison, has a history of breaking laws and hurting people since childhood, and seems indifferent to the feelings or rights of others. Jake's symptoms suggest that he might be diagnosed with _____.
   a. a social phobia
   b. paranoid schizophrenia
   c. a dissociative disorder
   d. antisocial personality disorder

6. Which of the following is *not* an example of an anxiety disorder?
   a. obsessive-compulsive disorder
   b. psychogenic amnesia
   c. panic disorder
   d. agoraphobia

7. Lorena is abnormally worried about cleanliness and hygiene, and sometimes feels she has to wash her hands dozens of times before they feel clean enough. This repetitive handwashing behavior is an example of a(n) _____.
   a. social phobia
   b. manic episode
   c. compulsion
   d. obsession

8. According to the Assess Yourself box, which of the following is a current social influence that could be creating greater levels of shyness in modern society?
   a. increased levels of interaction between family members
   b. automation in the workplace
   c. computer technology in commerce
   d. fear of widespread crime

9. The two "poles" in bipolar disorder are different extremes in _____.
   a. cognitive processing
   b. behavioral control
   c. affect or emotion
   d. social conformity

10. According to Aaron Beck, depressed people seem to have a "cognitive triad" of negative views, focused on three aspects of their lives. Which of the following is *not* one of the three?
    a. themselves
    b. other people
    c. their own future
    d. ongoing experiences

11. The biological view of unipolar depression is supported by the ability of _____ to relieve depressive symptoms.
    a. lithium
    b. psychoanalysis
    c. cognitive therapy
    d. environmental change

12. Which of the following statements about suicide is *not* true?
    a. Most suicides are attempted by those suffering from anxiety disorders.
    b. Suicide is most often committed by unemployed, older, white males.
    c. Women attempt suicide about three times more often than men.
    d. The leading traumatic incident that triggers suicide for both sexes is the breakup of a close relationship.

13. Which of the following statements about individuals suffering from anorexia nervosa is true?
    a. The typical victim maintains a distorted body image, believing herself to be unattractively fat.
    b. Anorexics alternate between episodes of overeating and efforts to lose weight by vomiting, fasting, or using laxatives.
    c. Anorexic symptoms can usually be quickly and thoroughly treated with drug therapy.
    d. None of the above.

14. Which of the following is *not* one of the symptoms of schizophrenia?
    a. hallucinations
    b. flat or inappropriate emotions
    c. unexpected, severe anxiety attacks
    d. disorganized or rigid psychomotor behavior

15. A schizophrenic patient claims she knows about secret plans by the CIA to support an invasion from Mars, and that because of this she is being persecuted both by space aliens and government officials. This patient is probably suffering from _____ schizophrenia.
    a. undifferentiated
    b. disorganized
    c. catatonic
    d. paranoid

16. According to the _____ hypothesis of schizophrenia, genetic factors place a particular individual at risk for the disorder, but environmental factors provide the pressure that causes the individual to manifest the symptoms of schizophrenia.
    a. diathesis-stress
    b. double-bind
    c. dopamine
    d. GAS

17. According to psychologist Brendan Maher, the "word salad" typical of some schizophrenics' speech is caused by processing difficulties whenever the speaker utters a(n) _____ word.
    a. abstract
    b. vulnerable
    c. antisocial
    d. stigmatized

18. Reward deficiency syndrome is a label for a collection of problems that primarily include _____ disorders.
    a. thought and affective
    b. affective and anxiety
    c. anxiety and substance-abuse
    d. substance-abuse and eating

19. Although many people suffer from psychopathological symptoms, the label "mentally ill" is usually applied to an individual only if that person _____.
    a. is under some form of care
    b. violates civil or criminal law
    c. has attempted to harm himself or others
    d. is diagnosed with a problem of organic origin

20. Which of the following is true of Rosenhan's study in which pseudopatients falsely gained admission to psychiatric hospitals?
    a. Though all were admitted to the hospitals, none was able to be diagnosed.
    b. Though some fellow patients were fooled, all of the hospital staff members recognized that the pseudopatients were not disordered at all.
    c. Though healthy when they were admitted, the pseudopatients soon developed symptoms very similar to those they had described to gain admission.
    d. None of the above.

Short-Answer Items

Briefly define or explain each term.

21. conversion disorder

22. DID

23. catastrophizing

24. bulimia

25. delusion

Name _____ Date _____

Multiple-Choice Items

1. The therapeutic tradition of _____ combines healing practices with belief in spirits.
   a. rational-emotive therapy
   b. Gestalt therapy
   c. psychoanalysis
   d. shamanism

2. _____ therapy views disordered behavior as the result of _____.
   a. Behavior; faulty self-statements
   b. Biomedical; malfunctioning body systems or metabolism
   c. Psychodynamic; learned patterns
   d. Behavior; unresolved traumas and conflicts

3. The therapeutic process can involve four primary tasks or goals: diagnosis, etiology, _____, and treatment.
   a. participant modeling
   b. prescription
   c. prognosis
   d. prediction

4. In the late eighteenth century, the French physician Philippe Pinel advocated the position that the mentally ill _____.
   a. were afflicted by moral corruption
   b. were sick and should be treated
   c. had lost their reason and must be cared for by others
   d. should be rehabilitated by their social communities

5. One universal feature of therapy is the fact that therapists must establish _____. This can be done by using the status symbols that are already well known in a culture.
   a. how long a disorder has been developing
   b. the organic bases of the disorder
   c. the incompetency of the patient
   d. their own credibility

6. _____ is also known as "the talking cure."
   a. Psychoanalysis
   b. Behavior modification
   c. Participant modeling
   d. Person-centered therapy

7. To avoid discussing what's really bothering him, even though he needs help, David has been canceling appointments with his psychoanalyst, or arriving late and leaving early. This is an example of _____.
   a. catharsis
   b. resistance
   c. transference
   d. aversion therapy

8. Marina had a dream in which she had to open a series of drapes and curtains to find her mother. Marina thinks this dream was really about her difficulty in talking to her mother. In dream analysis, the story of the curtains represents the _____ content while the story of Marina's relationship with her mother represents the _____ content.
   a. hidden; visible
   b. latent; open
   c. manifest; latent
   d. realistic; symbolic

9. Dion's therapist reminds Dion of his father, with whom he does not get along. Sometimes Dion expresses anger toward his therapist that is really meant for Dion's father. This is an example of the Freudian concept of _____.
   a. transference
   b. countertransference
   c. counterconditioning
   d. flooding

10. Post-Freudian theorist Karen Horney identified three types of neurotic patterns in interpersonal relationships. Which of the following is *not* one of them?
    a. approaching
    b. ambivalent
    c. avoiding
    d. attacking

11. In the behavioral technique known as _____, behavior is changed by modifying its consequences.
    a. contingency management
    b. participant modeling
    c. counterconditioning
    d. implosion

12. Toni is afraid of flying. With her permission, Toni's therapist accompanies her on a short airplane trip, helping her to cope directly with her most dreaded fear. Toni's experience is an example of the treatment strategy known as _____.
    a. systematic desensitization
    b. social-learning therapy
    c. aversion therapy
    d. flooding

13. "My coworker Jake always whistles at me when he walks by my desk. It makes me so mad, and I know he does it just to irritate me," complains Carla. Her friend Alice suggests, "Don't act irritated—just ignore him! If you stop paying attention, he'll quit bothering you." Alice is recommending that Carla use _____ to change Jake's behavior.
    a. symbolic modeling
    b. negative transference
    c. an extinction strategy
    d. cognitive behavior modification

14. In a study of social learning, researchers showed live snakes to young monkeys and observed that those who showed the greatest fear were the monkeys who _____.
    a. had not seen how their own parents reacted to a snake
    b. had seen their own parents display fear of snakes
    c. had previously acted fearless with toy snakes
    d. had never seen a real snake before

15. In cognitive behavior therapy, clients develop a sense of _____ by setting attainable goals, developing realistic strategies to attain them, and evaluating feedback realistically.
    a. catharsis
    b. self-efficacy
    c. self-actualization
    d. unconditional positive regard

16. Rational-emotive therapy is a comprehensive system of personality change based on transforming _____.
    a. free association
    b. irrational beliefs
    c. negative transference
    d. unconscious conflicts

17. At the core of _____ is the concept of a whole person who engages in the continual process of changing and becoming.
    a. humanistic and existential therapies
    b. insight therapies
    c. family therapies
    d. in vivo therapy

18. As part of her therapy, Eve sometimes imagines her brother, who died when she was young, seated in an empty chair. She finds it helpful to talk to the chair as if she were talking to her brother, and to imagine how he might respond. Eve's technique is a common part of _____ therapy.
    a. Gestalt
    b. aversion
    c. person-centered
    d. cognitive behavior

19. Couples-counseling generally focuses on clarifying and improving _____ in the partners' relationship.
    a. individual self-esteem
    b. rational thinking
    c. communication
    d. synergy

20. Much controversy and research was stimulated by the assertion by _____ that psychotherapy does not really work.
    a. Egas Moniz
    b. Jerome Frank
    c. Hans Eysenck
    d. Albert Ellis

Short-Answer Items

Briefly define or explain each term.

21. in vivo therapy

22. insight therapy

23. participant modeling

24. person-centered therapy

25. clinical ecology